HUMANS AS
SELF-CONSTRUCTING LIVING SYSTEMS
A Developmental Perspective
on Behavior and Personality

HUMANS AS
SELF-CONSTRUCTING LIVING SYSTEMS
A Developmental Perspective
on Behavior and Personality

DONALD H. FORD
The Pennsylvania State University

LEA LAWRENCE ERLBAUM ASSOCIATES, PUBLISHERS
Hillsdale, New Jersey   Hove and London

This printing has been sold out. A second
edition is published by IDEALS, INC.
P.O. Box 391 State College, Pa. 16804
ISBN 0-932990-06-1
SAN # 221-0770

Lawrence Erlbaum Associates, Inc., Publishers
365 Broadway
Hillsdale, New Jersey 07642

Library of Congress Cataloging-in-Publication Data

Ford, Donald Herbert, 1926–
   Humans as self-constructing living systems.

   Includes index.
   1. Psychology—Philosophy.   2. Personality.
3. Human behavior.   I. Title.   [DNLM: 1. Behavior.
2. Personality. BF 698 F699h]
BF38.F66   1987   150   86-32901
ISBN 0-89859-666-1
ISBN 0-8058-0017-4 (pbk.)

Printed in the United States of America
10   9   8   7   6   5   4   3   2   1

To Carol, Russell, Douglas, Martin,
and Cameron who make it all worthwhile

Contents

Preface

The purpose of this effort is to develop a conceptual framework for understanding individual humans as complex, functional entities. A sound developmental theory of human personality and behavior would help synthesize existing scientific and clinical information into a coherent representation of a person as a functional unit, guide future research, and facilitate the work of the health and human services professions.

HISTORY OF THE EFFORT

For over 3 decades, my personal life and professional work in psychotherapy, counseling, and administration have deeply impressed me with the stable, yet ever-evolving, elaborately organized nature of individuals. It has been with interest, caring, and sometimes awe, anxiety, and frustration that I have observed, studied, participated with, and sought to help people with their hopes and aspirations—their willingness to, or their inability or refusal to, meet their obligations and responsibilities—the elaborate tapestry of their thoughts and emotions—the consequences of their accomplishments and failures—the nature of, and the joys, sorrows, and hurts of, their human relationships, or lack of them—the impact of their physical illnesses, injuries, and handicaps on their activities, their relationships, their dreams for the future, or their view of themselves—their patterns of awareness and unawareness, of self-direction, self-control, and self-deception—and their implicit and explicit struggle about the values by which to understand, guide, and evaluate their lives.

I have been continually impressed with the extent to which all aspects of a person's life are linked in a dynamic flow of reciprocal influences. Increasingly, I sought a way of understanding how and why the pieces of a person's life fit together so that they function as a coherent whole. Sound professional intervention must be based on an accurate understanding of the content and dynamics of people's behavior. I found existing personality and psychotherapy theories and methods excitingly human, but seriously limited in scope and/or empirical validation, and minimally connected (if at all) to the basic scientific literature in the human sciences. Dogma and tradition significantly influence professional efforts.

I sought a more firmly established understanding of human behavior in the human sciences, particularly psychology. But, that was also a discouraging experience. Analytical science has taken apart humans to try to figure out what "makes them tick," but has provided no way for putting the pieces back together again to reveal our personhood. Scientific study of humans seemed to have led to a kind of dehumanization, appropriate to a mechanistic world view. But, such views inadequately represent the richness of our humanness. People not only react to events; they also appear to initiate and direct their behavior toward objectives and ideals. Frequently, they sacrifice their own welfare for that of others. Phenomena such as consciousness, values, and emotions are fundamental in our humanity. There seemed as much over simplification and concern with minutia in the human sciences as overgeneralization in the professions.

I concluded that we must somehow combine the integrative qualities of personality theories and information derived from professional work with humans and the study of persons with the rigorous qualities of evidence and theories that are derived from careful empirical study of particular response processes to construct a clear and useful understanding of human development. Bases for such a synthesis exist because scholars and professionals often study similar phenomena under different concept labels. For example, organizing cognitive functions have been referred to with labels such as *fictions* (Adler), *cognitive maps* (Tolman), *ego* and *super ego* (Freud), *images* and *plans* (Miller, Galanter, & Pribram), *executive* and *monitor* (Hilgard), *metacognition* (Flavell), and *referential processes* (Sullivan).

Believing that such concepts were built by careful observers and creative thinkers, my objective has been to try to identify similarities and differences among seemingly disparate views as a basis for synthesis of an understanding of humans as integrated, functional units. Hugh Urban and I spent 4 years analyzing influential points of view in psychotherapy that were published as *Systems of Psychotherapy: A Comparative Study* (Ford & Urban, 1963). We began to visualize the vague outlines of a more integrative framework.

For 10 years, I served as an academic Dean responsible for the creation of a new multidisciplinary-multiprofessional college (The College of Human Development at The Pennsylvania State University). Creating and institutionalizing such an environment is exceedingly difficult. The principle of "specialization" is well entrenched. Seeking synthesis and collaboration across specialities is resisted by many other factors (e.g., guild interests and methods, personal histories, job and institutional structures and processes, laws and funding streams, implicit world views, and existing conceptual models). Specialization produces increased efficiency and effectiveness in the production of that speciality's product, but may contribute to increased inefficiency and ineffectiveness with regard to other objectives, unless properly related to other specialties. This academic administrative experience strengthened my conviction that renewed efforts are needed to create a synthesis of knowledge about humans.

As an undergraduate, I studied engineering and majored in mathematics. I appreciate Cattell's (1980) plea for a " . . . disciplined, experimental, mathematical, conceptually-precise and imaginative . . . " approach to studying humans. However, presenting a theoretical model, rigorously formulated in mathematical terms, is impossible at this time. Mathematics only have utility if their form is isomorphic with that of the phenomena of interest. Therefore, the first task is to formulate the apparent form of the phenomena themselves. That is the focus of this effort. What follows is a conceptual framework designed to be heuristically useful to both scholars and professionals. It is not yet sufficiently precise to be considered a formal theory.

A diversity of colleagues have influenced my thinking. Hugh Urban helped formulate the foundation of ideas upon which this framework is built. John Nesselroade stimulated my thinking about the study of development. Martin Ford has tested the framework's heuristic utility in his graduate students' research as well as in his own. Arnold Goldstein, a clinical psychologist; Robert Burgess, an operant sociologist; Richard Lerner, a developmental psychologist; Adam Anthony, an endocrinologist-physiologist; and Ray Studer, an architect-planner-environmental designer have stimulated my thinking with their creative ideas and critiques. My thinking has also benefited from association with the excellent multidisciplinary faculty in the College of Human Development and Department of Individual and Family Studies at Pennsylvania State University.

I am also in debted to many graduate students who have helped to shape these ideas through their research and participation in my graduate seminars. Kathie Hooven and Joy Barger have my gratitude for their extensive help in producing this manuscript.

OVERVIEW

The central objective of this book is to assemble diverse, specialized pieces of knowledge in such a way as to tell a "coherent story" about the nature of individual human development and functioning, and to provide a framework for integrating professionally and scientifically derived knowledge. The goal is to develop a conceptual framework that has two types of utility (Manicas & Secord, 1983): (a) a framework for understanding persons in general (nomothetic knowledge), and (b) to serve as a tool for understanding a particular person, as many professionals seek to do (idiographic knowledge). The material is divided into two parts, each of which is divided into several chapters. Part I develops the general conceptual framework. Part II organizes and synthesizes existing evidence and theory about humans within that conceptual framework.

Part I has five chapters. Chapter 1 summarizes assumptions about the nature of humans that represent design criteria that must be met by an adequate conceptual framework. Chapter 2 addresses the concepts of organization and complexity and considers systems models as one type of organization. Chapter 3 transforms a mechanistic control system into a living system by adding self-organizing and self-constructing capabilities. An analogy is then drawn between its components and the different kinds of response processes studied in various disciplines (e.g., cognition, emotions, actions). But, humans develop and continually change. Therefore, chapter 4 summarizes ideas about change processes developed in several fields, and chapter 5 derives a set of developmental principles for understanding living systems from that information base.

Part II contains 11 chapters. Chapter 6 focuses on the biological bases of self-organization and self-construction. Chapter 7 examines the role of attention and consciousness in those processes. Chapter 8 focuses on information collection and perceptual processes, whereas chapter 9 considers how humans use their information-processing capabilities to construct and reconstruct or remember schemata, concepts, and propositions from information. Chapters 10 through 12 consider how humans use their goal-setting, evaluative, and problem-solving thought processes to organize and govern complex behavior patterns. Chapter 13 examines the nature and role of activity and emotions in organizing and energizing behavior patterns. Chapter 14 addresses the ways in which humans organize and execute actions. Chapter 15 considers communication as another influential method of environmental transactions. Finally, chapter 16 briefly sketches some implications of these ideas for understanding complex personality and behavior patterns. A companion volume, *Humans as Self-Constructing Living Systems: Putting the Framework to Work* (Ford & Ford, 1987) presents additional information for research methods, for understanding dysfunctions in development, and for counseling and psychotherapy, as well as illustrative research reports.

The references cited are considered illustrative rather than representing a thorough review of the enormous relevant literature. The objective is to make this presentation sufficiently plausible to encourage its use in exploring other relevant information. The ideas presented are extensively shaped both by the knowledge generated by formal research and by a quarter of a century of observations and attempts to help promote the development of thousands of individuals and families in my clinical, counseling, administrative, and teaching roles.

The framework is seen as a rough beginning, not a completed product. If it helps stimulate efforts to revise and improve it, or to create more adequate frameworks, I will consider my objectives met. Each of us builds upon the shoulders of those who have built before us. Where possible, I have tried to credit sources of ideas brought together here. I have intentionally cited a variety of older sources to illustrate how the same basic ideas periodically re-emerge in different forms as human knowledge advances and dominant philosophical and theoretical assumptions change. However, I recognize the impossibility of remembering where all of my ideas have their roots. Therefore, I apologize in advance for any oversights in citations that may occur. I suspect there are no basically new ideas here. The way in which the ideas are organized may provide some new perspectives.

This volume is aimed at a multidisciplinary-multiprofessional audience. Although specialized, technical "jargon" is useful for people within each field, it has the unfortunate consequence of making it harder for people with different backgrounds to understand one another. Although I have tried to be technically sound, I have also tried to write so that the ideas are not obscured by the jargon, and so that educated people of many backgrounds might be able to understand and evaluate the ideas. Specialists in each field may consider the discussion of their domain oversimplified and incomplete, while simultaneously considering the presentation of other domains too elaborate and complex. It is easier to write for a narrow audience than for a broader one. Trying to straddle several fences simultaneously can lead to awkward and sometimes painful positions.

This volume has been used as a base for teaching in several different ways over the past 6 years. Because it provides the only available conceptualization of development intentionally designed to be relevant to adults as well as children, and because it combines examination of development of response processes with development of persons, this book provides a solid base of information for a course in life-span development or developmental theory. Because it provides a thorough examination of the structural-functional content, the organization, and the development of individual behavior patterns, it has been useful as a base for seminars on personality development. It has also proven useful to anchor the study of particular topics in this larger framework. Examples include a seminar on motivation, another on cognition, and another on emotional development and functioning. It could also be useful for seminars examining communication or motor behavior as influenced by other aspects of human functioning. Finally, I have found it useful as a framework for helping students with professional interests (e.g., counseling and psychotherapy) compare intervention strategies in terms of the part(s) of the system on which they focus and the assumptions about change underlying them.

I present what follows with deep confidence in the importance of the objectives, and discomforting awareness of my own shortcomings for an effort that requires a range of knowledge and competence that few if any of us possess in this highly specialized society. Nevertheless, I hope this effort may contribute some small steps toward the goal of "putting Humpty Dumpty back together again," and that it may encourage others to make similar efforts. I subscribe to the view, attributed to Sir Francis Bacon, that truth emerges more readily from error than from confusion.

I

THE CONCEPTUAL FRAMEWORK

SEE PAGE 26   SYSTEMS THEORY

1

The Nature of Humans

INTRODUCTION

How can we understand people—what they are, how they function, how they may develop or change? Some way of thinking about a person as an entity, as a unitary being, is needed (Royce, 1961). The purpose of this chapter is to establish and to place in some historical perspective the need for, the basic characteristics of, and the evolution of a view that can serve that purpose.[1] These ideas are used in later chapters to outline a framework for understanding the organization, functioning, and development of persons.

---

[1]I could at this point discuss the philosophy of science, the mind-body problem, the principles of theory construction, or the influence of one's "world view" on the way one chooses to represent things. A scholar's initial assumptions have a basic influence on how he or she studies and construes the phenomena they choose to study. While recognizing the importance of these issues I have chosen to refrain from discussing them because it could be a major diversion from my primary purpose. There are many good discussions of these issues elsewhere (e.g., Bhaskar, 1978; Hayek, 1952; Kuhn, 1978; Manicas & Secord, 1983, 1984; McMullen, 1983; Popper, 1963). The effort to formulate a philosophical position appropriate to understanding humans in their contexts may be facilitated by monitoring efforts of other disciplines to elaborate or transform their philosophical assumptions to fit their expanding data and knowledge. Comparison of the epistemological and ontological assumptions of classical determinism and quantum mechanics is an example (Rohrlich, 1983). Prigogine and Stengers (1984) have summarized basic conceptual shifts important in the history of natural sciences (e.g., from mechanics to thermo-dynamics).

One key scholarly strategy involves the use of analogies from one domain of knowledge to try to understand phenomena in a different one. Historically, attempts to study and understand humans have been significantly influenced by models borrowed from the natural sciences (e.g., the mechanistic model of Newtonian physics). What follows is an attempt to profit from new ideas developing in the larger scientific context. Capra (1977), Jantsch (1980), and Zukav (1979) provide relatively nontechnical discussions of many aspects of such emerging perspectives.

This chapter begins with the identification of basic human attributes, and an examination of the issues of units of analysis, parts, and wholes as they relate to the concept of organization. Then a brief historical perspective is provided to illustrate how different kinds of units and models of organization have influenced attempts to understand the natural world in general, and humans in particular. The utility and limitations of a mechanistic model of organization are briefly considered and compared with alternate models of organization that have been evolving in other efforts to understand humans. The concept of a *system* is then selected as a promising alternate model for understanding self-regulating organizations. Organisms, as a special kind of system, are referred to in this book as *living systems.* The methodological implications of conceiving of humans as living systems are briefly considered.

BASIC ATTRIBUTES OF INDIVIDUAL HUMANS

The first step in constructing any conceptual framework should be to clearly identify the domains of phenomena which that framework will be expected to encompass. Therefore, this section addresses the question, "What are the fundamental attributes of individual development and functioning that must be encompassed in a conceptual framework designed to represent individuals as functional units?" Eight categories of attributes are identified that may be considered "design criteria" for the creation of such a framework.

Biological Structure Makes Possible Functional or Behavioral Capabilities

Behavioral capabilities are made possible by the physical structure of each organism. For example, the structure of a bird makes flying a behavioral possibility, while a hippopotamus must plod through life on land or in water. The biological structure provides only the *potential* for different kinds of behavior. The extent to which behavioral potentials become effective *actualities* is a function of individual organisms' interactions with their environments.

The physical structure and organization of the human body both define and limit its potential functional capabilities. For instance, the human ear and eye are designed to respond to certain sound frequencies or wavelengths of light, and not to others. Individuals may differ in their biological structure and therefore in their behavioral potentials as a result of both their genetic inheritance and their life experiences. One of the distinguishing features of humans is their capability for inventing supplementary structures to expand their functional capabilities (e.g., airplanes enable humans to fly; X-ray machines make it possible to "see" things they cannot detect with the "natural" senses; prostheses compensate for structural deficiencies).

Different Kinds of Functions and the Concept of Behavior

Life is often defined as a state that is characterized by metabolism and growth, reproduction, and internally initiated adaptations to the environment. Entities that display such properties may be called living systems (J. Miller, 1978). All life processes or functions are included under the term *behavior* in this book. For example, the action of a hormone on selected brain cells, a happy thought, and jogging all represent different kinds of behavior. Not everyone uses the term this broadly. Some prefer to limit it to overt actions, so that speech but not thinking would be considered behavior. But, since all human responses are functions made possible by the biological structure, the use of one term to encompass all functional capabilities seems both logical and useful.

Behavior is a many-splendored thing, and its diversity provides the constituents of the stream of life. Skinner (1966) emphasized that to identify the occurrence of an operant (or response) requires specifying some "defining property" so that responses of different kinds could be distinguished from one another. To a considerable extent, the science of psychology has been organized around different kinds of behavior or response classes, as, for example, sensation and perception, memory and cognition, and motivation and emotion.

Structural-Behavioral Organization Produces Unitary Functioning

Although a person's functioning may be thought of as composed of many different kinds of behavior, specific responses do not occur in random relationship to one another. A person is a complexly organized array of substances, events, and processes occurring together in integrated arrangements as a functioning unit. Analytical science divides humans into pieces and parts to see "what makes them tick." However, understanding the parts will no more reveal the nature of a person than would components of steel, lumber, stone, cement, wire, glass, and the like reveal whether they composed a school, prison, hospital, church, factory, or home. It is the way the components are organized in relationship to one another and to their larger contexts that reveals the nature of the entity of which they are a part. Therefore, understanding people requires understanding the nature both of their structural and functional parts and of their organization.

It is a property of living systems that they function to maintain and to elaborate upon their structural and functional organization. Attempts to account for this property of organization have taken several forms throughout the history of psychology (e.g., as manifested in associationism, holism, and organismic and field theories). The two most commonly used terms in psychology, *stimulus* and *response*, denote not the *content* of phenomena but *types of relationships* among phenomena, that is, their organization.

Contextual and Temporal Consistency and Variability

Two seemingly contradictory properties of human behavior are consistency (e.g., habits) and variability (e.g., change). Each person develops a physical appearance, a pattern of abilities, a personality, a manner of dress and grooming, a manner of speech, a typical occupation, a consistent pattern of personal relationships, and a characteristic biological balance. It is such structural-functional consistency across diverse situations and times that gives people their individuality and identity.

On the other hand, people seem to need and seek variability in their experience (Fiske & Maddi, 1961); human "plasticity" is a pervasive phenomenon (Lerner, 1984). Variability-seeking is represented in both everyday and scientific language by the term *curiosity* (e.g., Berlyne, 1960). Variability or change appears in long term behavior patterns as well. For example, an accountant who always bought black Fords with no chrome and seldom drove over 55 miles an hour retired and bought himself a race car. A woman began an active artistic career after her husband retired.

Consistency in behavior is valuable and efficient when individuals must deal with repetitive situations. Variability is valuable because it opens up new behavioral options. Consistency and change live side by side as essential interacting parts of an integrated whole (Brim & Kagan,

1980). Moreover, phenomena may appear variable at one level of analysis, and stable at another (Block, 1977; Epstein & O'Brien, 1985; Mischel, 1983). Consistency and variability are evident not only in kinds of behavior, but in other behavioral attributes such as the rate and intensity of activity, the level of alertness, and the intensity of emotions (e.g., Buss & Plomin, 1984; Cofer & Appley, 1964; Duffy, 1962). Consistency and variability are functions of environmental conditions. For example, the behavior of a child is more similar to that of other children in the same context (e.g., playground) than to his or her own behavior in different settings (e.g., playground vs. classroom) (Barker, 1968). Therefore, interindividual and intraindividual consistency and variability in behavior cannot be understood separately from their context, and are often subject to contextually embedded social evaluation (e.g., may be labeled *deviant* or *creative*) (Bronfenbrenner, 1979).

People Change Both Structurally and Functionally

It is important to distinguish between cyclical variations in functioning within limits (e.g., heart rate, hormonal secretions, rate of walking) and progressive, cumulative, relatively permanent changes in structural-functional capabilities (e.g., increases in height, learning to talk). Being (functioning) is different from becoming (development), although each influences the other. Changes in structural organization may alter functions (e.g., brain damage may produce paralysis), and functional organization may alter structure (e.g., smoking may produce cancer). Four kinds of terms—*growth, maturation, learning,* and *development*—have been used to refer to the more permanent kinds of progressive changes. Careful distinctions among such terms are essential for clarity and scientific advances, and those made by Weiss (1939) are still sound.

The term *growth* refers to a permanent increase in the total mass of the body via tissue accretion. *Maturation* typically refers to the differentiation and the elaboration of biological structures and functional capabilities resulting from the interaction of genetic and experiential factors. All humans follow essentially the same pattern and sequence of biological growth and maturation, but there are marked individual differences in the presence of some biological attributes and in the rate at which various maturational changes occur. Many "stage" theories of psychological development have their roots, at least by analogy, in the concept of maturation.

In contrast, *learning* is change that is also relatively enduring (in contrast to temporary performance changes such as those produced by fatigue or drugs); but it results primarily from a person's experiential history rather than being heavily influenced by genetic or biological makeup. It is a far more flexible and variable method of development than biological maturation. Hilgard and Bower (1966, 1975) identify six sets of issues considered important in the learning process, as follows:

1. What are the limits of learning? Our culture clearly believes that people differ in their learning capabilities. It is not clear to what extent these capacities are fixed at birth or can be modified through factors of living such as diet, experience, or genetic manipulation (e.g., Barnes, 1967; Brozek, 1978; Coursin, 1967; Witkop, 1967). Nor is it clear to what extent such capacities change with age (e.g., Baltes, et al., 1978; Plemons, Willis, & Baltes, 1978; Schaie, 1979).

2. What is the role of practice in learning? Football coaches, music teachers, and theatrical directors exemplify professionals who obviously believe practice makes "better" if not "perfect."

3. How important are drives and incentives, rewards and punishments? Every parent who criticizes, praises or spanks a child clearly believes in the value of rewards and punishments.

4. What is the place of understanding and insight in learning? Public education is obviously designed on the assumption that cognitive learning is fundamental.

5. Does learning one thing in one setting help you learn something else in another setting? This has been a particularly vexing problem to educators, psychotherapists, and behavior modifiers (Goldstein & Kanfer, 1979).

6. What happens when we remember and when we forget? Those dealing with emotionally troubled persons have developed other terms to signify memory difficulties (e.g., repression; suppression; amnesia).

Development is a fourth term referring to individual change. Until recent years, this term was usually applied to approximately the first two decades of life (Harris, 1957) and involved specific progression-related changes represented as unidirectional, sequential, qualitative, irreversible, normative, and oriented toward maturity. It was assumed that behavioral capabilities matured in a sense similar to physiological capabilities. However, the concept of life-span development recognizes that people can and do change throughout their lives. Moreover, developmental changes are now viewed as multidimensional, multidirectional, and often individualistic in timing, rate, and substance (Baltes, Reese, & Lipsitt, 1980; Baltes & Willis, 1978; Lerner, 1976). In its evolving usage, development has become a superordinate concept whose meaning encompasses growth, maturation, and learning. Terms such as *to impair* or *to disable* also refer to a kind of permanent change.

Such a reduction of structural or functional capabilities (e.g., with age) is increasingly also being encompassed by the term development.

The broad issues of what changes (e.g., the content or organization of behavior, or of behavior-environment interactions), when, under what circumstances, and whether such changes are continuous, emergent, or reversible, are issues fundamental to most developmental theories and technologies (e.g., Brim & Kagan, 1980; Kitchener, 1978; Lerner, 1980; Rothenberg, 1978, 1979).

Human Behavior Both Shapes and is Shaped by the Environment

It is through transactions with the environment that a person stays alive, grows, and develops behavioral capabilities. The environment provides people with different kinds of material and information necessary for living and behaving.

Formal learning theories give major emphasis to the environment in shaping behavior, with concepts such as *discriminative stimulus, reinforcer,* and *cue* (e.g., Hilgard & Bower, 1966). The primary focus and power of Skinner's (1953) operant conditioning approach, for example, lies in its emphasis on the notion that behavior development and functioning are under the control of environmental contingencies and consequences.

Psychotherapy theorists vary in their emphasis on situational events, from those who make them primary (e.g., Sullivan and the behavior therapists) to others who focus primarily on subjective kinds of behaviors, such as thoughts and feelings (e.g., Rogers and Rank). However, all of them use the manipulation of situational events as their primary means of therapeutic intervention, whether it is some attribute of the therapist's behavior (e.g., Freud's "interpretations") or some other type of event such as a token economy (Ford & Urban, 1963, 1967). Formal education is primarily a process of exposing people to a planned and systematic array of situational events (e.g., lectures, books, pictures, sounds), and having them interact with those events.

In fact, the meaning of a person's behavior cannot be accurately understood without knowledge of the contexts in which it occurs. For example, a graceful leap into the air may be a part of a basketball game, a ballet, or sitting on a bee. Recognition of which interpretation is correct depends upon contextual characteristics (Rank, 1961). The person-environment relation is interactive or transactional. People both seek to shape and are shaped by their environments (Altman & Wohlwill, 1978; Studer, 1970; Studer & Barton, 1974). Moreover, environments must be understood as a nested set of contingencies ranging from immediate stimuli to larger cultural patterns (Bronfenbrenner, 1979).

The Influence of Potential Futures on Current Behavior

The apparent capability of humans to intentionally direct their behavior towards preselected consequences has been a source of alternate views of humans for centuries. Terms such as *teleology, vitalism, purpose,* and *self-direction* have been associated with notions of final cause, often of supernatural or superhuman origin.

Two general views appear to be at least implicitly present in many theories about the nature of humans (Urban & Ford, 1962). Sometimes people are seen as "pilots" of their lives—choosing the destinations toward which they will sail; choosing the means of getting there with some knowledge of the characteristics of their ship and the factors that influence it such as the force of the winds, the currents of life, and the availability of essential supplies; and taking account of interesting new circumstances discovered along the way. This perspective assumes that people seek to exercise control over their behavior, and to shape or use their environments to serve their purposes. They may be seen as responsible for their own courses of action.

Another view sees people as machines or "robots" responding automatically to events which impinge upon them. In this view, the winds and currents of the sea of life carry a person's ship wherever they may go. The nature of the design of the ship, the power of the currents, winds, and other forces to which it is subjected, determine its direction and movement. People may seem to be directing their behavior toward goals, but cannot in fundamental ways control the direction of their lives. Behavior is regarded as a function of the environment in which it occurs and determined and controlled by the situations in which people develop and live. Therefore, they cannot be considered basically responsible for their actions, any more than can any other type of machine.

Various forms and combinations of these two perspectives have dominated human thinking on this matter with first one and then another being the prevailing theme. But each theory leaves critical questions unattended, giving rise to consideration of alternate ones (von Bertalanffy, 1975). A significant problem with the reductionistic and mechanistic world view is that it cannot account for some of the most important properties of living systems. J. Miller (1978) points out that the dominant metaphors of the 19th and early 20th century concerned linear effects rather than field forces, but that currently dominant metaphors tend to be much more heavily influenced by Einstein's relativistic field theory. The fundamental perspectives which guide the scientific endeavor are not independent of the broader culture of the times (e.g., Meadows, 1957).

The scientific study of human behavior, gaining major impetus in the late 1800s, was heavily influenced by a scientific Zeitgeist which assumed that all complex phenomena could best be understood by reducing them to their basic elements (e.g., their "atoms"). Complex entities could be understood, then, as various kinds of combinations of the basic elements, linked or "associated" in various ways. *Associationistic psychology* grew from this perspective.

Initially, the kinds of behavior given primary focus were "mental" events or "states of consciousness" (James, 1890; Titchner, 1913). Later, psychology moved from the study of mental events to the study of behavior. Consciousness was considered just as unprovable and unobservable as the old concept of soul, and "intangibles" and "unapproachable" phenomena were rejected as an appropriate basis for a natural science of behavior (e.g., Watson, 1924). This led Cyril Burt (1962) to comment that psychology having first bargained away its soul and then gone out of its mind, finally seemed to have lost all consciousness.

As a result, distinctions between voluntary and involuntary behavior were considered unnecessary and it became possible to "...dismiss all inner agents of whatever sort" (Skinner, 1953). A person's sense of purpose or self-knowledge is, according to this view, "...at best a by-product of contingencies." A thought or felt intention as a "...current surrogate for future events" is "not a cause of behavior" but a by-product of contingencies represented by discriminative and reinforcing stimuli (Skinner, 1966). This strategy led to a major explosion of productive research and theorizing during the first half of the 20th century. It also led to a variety of practical applications (e.g., Bijou & Ruiz, 1981; Ullman & Krasner, 1965).

The aspects of human existence and other methodological perspectives that this strategy chose to deemphasize or ignore did not disappear and continued to demand attention (Mackenzie, 1977). Modern operant psychologists recognize that responses, such as thoughts, can also serve as discriminative and reinforcing stimuli; Skinner had also recognized this (Brigham, 1980). A new synthesis of mentalism and behaviorism is emerging.

Modern neurophysiology and designers of modern automata support a much more dynamic perspective closer to the personal sense of self-initiated, directed and controlled activity. As Ralph Gerard (1968) put it, we have moved from a "telephone exchange model," which can "explain repetitive, invariable behavior," to "a dynamic, spontaneous, modifiable model," more able "to explain variable creative and integrative behavior." The old concept of a conscious entity intending its goals is beginning to take on a new form and new credibility (Hawkins, 1968; Hilgard, 1980). Humans establish goals and seek to reach them "through decisive action and deliberate effort." Without "consciousness of plans and purposes," and of means of achieving them, nothing that is "inventive and self-originated" would happen (Hilgard, 1977).

Behavior Serves Multiple Purposes and is Multiply Influenced

One of the complications in understanding people is that their behavior is not a set of discrete events linked together through time. It is more like a flowing stream, constantly moving and changing in its components, its current direction, its rate, and its interaction within its contexts (Atkinson & Birch, 1970). Depending on an observer's purposes, the stream of behavior may be examined or understood at different levels of complexity using different units of analysis. For example, a biologist might try to understand a person's physical symptoms at a cellular level, while a psychologist might interpret them from a more molar level. People often misinterpret, or are led to misinterpret, one another's behaviors because they interpret the behavior they observe in terms of one set of purposes when it is primarily relevant to a different set.

Therefore, an adequate conceptual framework must encompass behavioral episodes that manifest multiple influences and are directed simultaneously toward multiple consequences. It must recognize that there is some hierarchical "order of relative importance" among the interacting components or "subepisodes" of each behavioral episode. Moreover, it must accommodate different levels of analysis and units of analysis to deal with the hierarchical nature of person-environment functioning, recognizing that no level or unit is better than another, but that each may yield different information about what is occurring.

UNITS OF ANALYSIS

People are capable of a great variety of responses. For example, they see and hear; they think and talk; they walk and smile; they breathe and they digest food; they feel frightened or happy; they socialize, share, compete and exploit; they create and destroy. As long as people are alive they are behaving. Whether they are at work or at play, awake or asleep, healthy or ill, their behavior occurs in a constantly flowing stream with many sources and currents. What kinds of behaviors are occurring, at what rate and intensity, and in what patterns of organization will vary from moment to moment and context to context. One can take a sample out of the stream at any moment in any context and describe its attributes. However, if the purpose is to understand the stream itself, then multiple samples must be examined in the context of the flow of the stream and its environments.

The metaphor of a flowing stream is useful because it symbolizes the interacting variabilities and consistencies both of the attributes of individuals and of their contexts. While the behavior-environment stream of an individual can be divided into pieces for the purposes of study, the divisions used are arbitrary since it is possible to divide the stream in many ways. However, the choice of units of analysis is not capricious. It is an act of theoretical choice: the choices made depend upon the purposes to be served. Meehl (1978) refers to the task of "...slicing up the raw behavioral flux into meaningful intervals" as the *response class* problem, and the "...adequate classification and sampling of environments and situations..." as the *situation taxonomy* problem. Moreover, people's behaviors and their environments are so inextricably intertwined so that classes of behavior-environment interactions and their organization might be treated as units, e.g., as behavior settings (Barker, 1963).

Changes in units of analysis have occurred periodically in the natural sciences and have marked scientific advances. Classical Newtonian physics assumed that the universe is composed of permanent material objects that could be "hooked up" together in causal relationships in both 3-dimensional space and linear time. The search was for the basic material building blocks and the laws representing their associations or relationships. Associationistic psychology represents an application of that fundamental view to psychological phenomena. That classical view is now recognized as a special case of a more general case. In both nuclear physics and cosmology, objects are now understood as "temporarily" organized patterns of energy within larger "fields." Moreover, understanding of their properties is relative to the vantage point of observation. Space and time are intertwined into 4-dimensional space-time conditions. At the nuclear level, material objects dissolve into patterns of probable relationships of dynamic energy patterns. The universe is understood not in terms of a collection of material objects, but as "a complicated web" of interrelationships between "the various parts of a unified whole" (Capra, 1977). The old basic units (e.g., molecules; atoms) are still useful for certain purposes, but understanding of them has been influenced by new units of analysis that are interrelated patterns of energy ebb and flow. There are no absolute units of analysis, but only units both *relative* to and *relevant* to one's observational frames, methods, and purposes. The human sciences are struggling to break free from their outdated conceptual roots and to "catch up" with this more dynamic view now emerging in the natural sciences. To do so requires significant revision of habits of thought and theoretical formulations implicitly anchored in Newtonian-like associationistic traditions to a more dynamic organizational perspective.

It follows from this perspective that a part can never be fully understood separate from the entity of which it is a part. It is the way the parts are organized, in addition to the properties of each, that reveals the nature of the complete entity. In modern mathematical terms, von Foerster (1962) demonstrates that interactive components in a system are represented by a superadditive rule. New properties become apparent as a result of the combined organization of the components so that "...we do not (fully) know the part until we know the whole" (Cattell, 1980). There appears to be little utility in trying to specify which units are "best" in any absolute sense. Presently, the human sciences use a plethora of conceptual units which vary in content, size, and complexity, which help standardize a way of thinking about and observing some phenomena of interest. However, inadequate ways of translating one set of concepts into another is a primary source both of poor communication among specialized disciplines and professions, and of slow progress towards a more integrated view of humans.

Parts and Wholes

The terms *part* and *whole* refer to units of different size and to particular kinds of relationships among those units; for example, larger units (wholes) may be understood as a particular organization of smaller units of various kinds (parts). In some entities, the interactions between the parts are negligible (e.g., the molecules of a gas enclosed in a container), while the forces operating within the parts (e.g., forces holding a molecule of gas together) are very powerful. In such an entity, the parts can be treated as if they are independent of one another. Other entities are composed of parts among which the interactions are not negligible (e.g., the living cells composing an organism). In such a "nearly decomposable" whole, some aspects of the parts can be examined while ignoring their interactions with other parts, but other aspects can be understood only in the context of the interactions of the parts (Simon, 1969).

Reductionism in science is built on the assumption that wholes can be understood by decomposing them into their parts. Simon identifies two main theoretical findings with regard to hierarchical systems that can be treated as nearly decomposable systems: (a) The "short-run behavior" of each part is "approximately independent" of that of the other parts; and (b) the "long-run behavior" of any part depends in "an aggregate way" on the behavior of the other components. For example, at any moment the internal functioning of each cell in a person's body functions relatively independently of all the others. However, over a period of hours or days each cell is greatly influenced by the extent to which all the other cells carry out their functions effectively. Koestler (1967) used the term "holon" for a part, and "holarchy" for the whole of which it is a part, to convey the fact that parts are themselves a kind of whole. Thus, while thinking in terms of parts and wholes is a powerful tool, the relationship between the two ideas is not at all simple. Murphy (1949) stated that the issue of wholes and parts was the most acute of all contemporary psychological issues.

Therefore, one of the basic decisions in any effort (i.e., scientific, professional, or personal) is the selection of the units by which the phenomena or events of interest will be represented. Parts and wholes are both units, but they differ in the amount of phenomena included, their complexity, and their continuity (i.e., their duration in time). Thus a person may be considered a unit, but so may the cells of his or her body, or individual habits of thought. To understand a person requires understanding both intraperson and person-context interactions. One value of the framework presented in this book is its flexibility in making possible the identification and use of multiple types of units, and the interrelationships among them within and between nested levels of organization (e.g., cells, organs, and organisms).

Since the person is our central focus, the person is our "whole" for purposes of this effort; his or her component structures and processes are our "parts." The objective is to understand a person as a coherently organized, structural-functional unit. However, specific studies cannot focus on all aspects of an individual simultaneously. Therefore, research aimed at understanding humans characteristically addresses a selected subset of "parts." Information collected through the study of such subsets can contribute to an understanding of persons only if it can be integrated into a larger conceptual framework representing a person as a functional unit. It is usually easier to fit the parts of a jigsaw puzzle together if one has a general idea of what the finished picture should look like. Facilitating such integration is the objective of the following chapters.

Wholes as Organizations of Parts

There are two basic ways of looking at the organization of persons. One way is to examine their physical *structures*, identifying the parts and their organization (e.g., the leg bone's connected to the knee bone). A second way is to identify the different kinds of *functions* performed and to specify their interrelationships.[2] These are interrelated but different perspectives. The functional organization of the person is made possible by, and simultaneously bounded or limited by, the structural organization, but the structural organization does not fully determine the functional one. Changes in one may alter the other. Therefore, understanding the nature and relationships of both is important (Gottlieb, 1976).

What is needed then is a framework that makes it possible to think in terms of different *kinds* of structural and functional parts, and also in terms of the ways they are *interrelated* into that intricately organized entity called a person. Such a framework might apply to other organisms as well (J. Miller, 1978), but our concern here is with understanding humans.

Conceptual units quite molar in nature will be used. Some may feel a legitimate concern that the strategy of presenting a very broad and simplified framework may omit too much that is important. However, faced with an extensive mass of detailed information (and that is certainly characteristic of the scientific information available about humans), it is often impossible to see the order or organization within it. Simplification is an essential tactic for understanding the basic order as well as its particulars. In his Nobel Prize acceptance, Anderson (1978) observed that model-building involves "the exclusion of real but irrelevant parts of the problem," which involves hazards for both the builder and the user. The builder may omit important parts. The user, armed with overly sophisticated measures or computations, may take literally a model "whose main aim is to be a demonstration of possibility." Simplified models often throw more light on "the real workings of nature" than large numbers of *ab initio* calculations of individual situations, which often contain so much detail "as to conceal rather than reveal reality." It is expected that the broad concepts used here will provide a framework for specifying, relating, and understanding units

---

[2]In the human sciences, the term *structure* is frequently used in at least two different ways, and that is often confusing. It is used to refer to organizations of physical components (e.g., *skeletal* structures) and also to organized patterns of functioning (e.g., *cognitive* structures). In this book, the term will be used only to refer to organizations of physical components. Other terms (e.g., organization, pattern) will be used to refer to organizations of functions.

of other sizes and scope at a later time. Before further considering the concept of organization, some historical perspective on the influence of different kinds of guiding assumptions will be useful.

HISTORICAL CONCEPTUAL CONTEXT

Certain assumptions about the nature of humans, life, and the world are so deeply embedded in our thought patterns and culture that they shape how we are willing to think and what we are prepared to believe, often without our realizing it, both in daily life and in science (e.g., Lerner, 1983). Some brief recognition of certain intellectual traditions is desirable as a context for considering alternatives.

Material and Non-Material Phenomena

In their book *The Architecture of Matter*, Toulmin and Goodfield (1962) discuss developments in human thinking about material things, both inanimate and animate. Throughout most of human history, natural philosophy and daily experience have recognized a fundamental difference between uniform, inanimate substances and complex, highly differentiated living organisms. Until the 17th century, the differences were generally attributed to a "Divine Craftsman." For example, Plato asserted that initially the material elements were in disorder until God conferred on them "...every possible kind of measure and harmonious proportion." Thus, living systems were complex organizations of divine creation. The assumption that all natural phenomena must be either *animate* or *inanimate* dominated human thinking. Inanimate matter was incapable of thinking or feeling. Therefore, these properties of nature must come from some other, nonmaterial factor, such as a God.

This view constrained advances in understanding living organisms for centuries. Eventually an alternate view began to emerge which had profound impact. In 1747, *Man, a Machine* was published by de la Mettrie. He built upon, but went significantly beyond, the ideas of Albrecht von Haller who taught that the behavior of muscles and organs represented natural properties of those material entities, which Glisson in 1677 had termed "irritability." De la Mettrie extended this principle to *all* functioning of organisms, including mental functioning. He rejected the powerful historically assumed dichotomies of matter and nonmatter, and their derivatives: organic and inorganic, animate and inanimate, mental and physical. Instead he proposed that these basic differences in the states of material things resulted not from their intrinsic nature, but from the different ways in which these materials were *organized*. Toulmin and Goodfield (1962) quote him as saying:

> Let it only be granted to me that organized Matter is endowed with a motive principle, which alone marks it off from unorganized (matter)— and can one deny that most indisputable of observations?—and that in Animals everything depends on the diversity of this Organization, as I have shown: that is enough to solve the Riddle of the Substances (Mind and Matter) and that of Man. Only one (substance) is to be seen in the World, and Man is the most perfect (form) of it. (p. 315)

This revolutionary idea was slow to gain acceptance, but it merged with other conceptual streams and came to have a profound impact. However, shifting the focus to organization raised other basic questions such as, "What is organized, and how?" "How is such organization maintained and elaborated?" "How is it transmitted from generation to generation?" For the last three centuries the basic distinctions between matter and nonmatter have been eroding. Particle physics has demonstrated that the "bricks" from which matter is constructed are *patterns* of energy and activity, rather than material objects in the classical sense (Capra, 1977). Thus, nature exists as a hierarchy of active, organized forms—a hierarchy which appears to be open at both ends (e.g., Jantsch, 1980; Koestler, 1967). Einstein believed firmly in an ordered and organized universe full of definite shapes and patterns (Weisskopf, 1980).

The Machine as a Model for Understanding Organization of Phenomena

Culturally linked to this new view that the properties of living organisms were emergents from increasingly complex organizations of physical materials was the use of a machine model to represent the nature of that organization. Simple machines (e.g., levers) came into existence early in human history, but machines of some complexity such as clocks and pumps became widespread during the later Middle Ages. New machines were invented, old ones improved and elaborated, and the power of humans to control and manipulate their world was greatly multiplied. The power of machines gave credibility to the idea that all aspects of the universe—from the natural sciences through theories of government—could be understood as mechanisms, albeit complicated ones. Surely, even humans could be understood as machines, and so de la Mettrie entitled his book *Man, a Machine*.

Deutsch (1950) has characterized the classical mechanistic model and its implications and limitations:

Classical mechanism implied the notion of a whole which was completely equal to the sum of its parts; which could be run in reverse; and which would behave in exactly identical fashion no matter how often those parts were disassembled and put together again, and irrespective of the sequence in which the disassembling or re-assembling would take place. It thus implied the notion that the parts were never significantly modified by each other, nor by their own past, and that each part once placed into its appropriate position, with its appropriate momentum, would stay exactly there and continue to fulfill its completely and uniquely determined function. (p. 187)

By specifying the parts of a machine and the determinate causal relations among them, one can fully describe a machine and its functions. Mechanistic processes follow fixed pathways. Therefore, the final state is fully determined by the initial conditions and the process pathway. Such a mechanism "behaves" in response to the forces impinging upon it according to the nature of its parts and their causal connections. Machines are reactive entities.

Certain methods for studying mechanisms fit the model's assumptions. For example, analytic thinking and research methods appropriate to mechanistic assumptions were developed to examine the manner in which one part was causally connected to another (e.g., independent and dependent variables), and to reflect the assumption of temporal linear causal chains, such as mathematical assumptions of linearity and additivity (Rapoport & Horvath, 1959). This approach produced major advances in knowledge and technologies, encouraging the belief that any complex entity, including organisms, could be understood by using that model. Thus, in 1847 in Berlin, Ludwig Von Helmholtz and DuBois-Reymond asserted that all living processes, including consciousness, could be explained in terms of physics and chemistry. That "reductionistic manifesto" has influenced thinking about and investigation of living systems ever since.

In summary, the mechanistic model assumed that any complexity could be understood by identifying a set of simple, unchanging parts connected by simple, unchanging laws (e.g., atoms in physics, molecules in chemistry, or economic man in society), reacting in predictable and controllable ways to external events imposed or impinging upon them. Within such a view, it made sense to think of humans as automatically shaped by environmental processes.

The application of such assumptions and methods was instrumental in producing the explosion of knowledge and technology which occurred in the 17th, 18th, and 19th centuries. However, attempts to understand other phenomena, such as heat exchange processes and living organisms, required the invention of concepts different from those of the classical mechanistic model (Prigogine & Stengers, 1984).[3]

An alternate "organismic" perspective began to emerge that represented living entities as wholes that could not be fully understood by disassembling them into their parts, and that recognized that trying to do so would destroy them; wholes which elaborated and maintained themselves according to organic laws within them that governed their birth, maturity, and death and that could be influenced, but not fundamentally altered, by environmental events; wholes whose history could affect their present and future functioning; wholes that could not be analyzed and represented solely in terms of clearly identifiable mechanical causes; wholes not assembled from parts but from which specialized parts were progressively differentiated (e.g., Deutsch, 1951). Analytic methods were, therefore, insufficient for studying and understanding them.

Assumptions Influencing the Development of Psychology as a Discipline

As part of the great scientific and technological momentum of the 19th century, scientific psychology began emerging as a distinct field. It adopted the dualistic view separating phenomena into two kinds of realities—matter and nonmatter, mind and body (Boring, 1960). Psychology first opted for units representing the nonmatter side of the duality and was described as the science of the mind and mental activity (Kirsch, 1977). The basic notion of parts assembled to create wholes took the mechanistic/organizational form of associationism, the basic empirical principle by which the mind was thought to be organized through experience (Boring, 1960). The parts that became organized were sensations (attributes of mind) that were produced by stimuli (attributes of matter). Psychology also adopted the prevailing analytic methods for disassembling complexity into its basic parts and seeking to identify the fundamental laws through which the parts were associated. Pioneering American psychologists like James, Hall, and Cattell retained the general mechanistic orientation but began to broaden the domain of phenomena to be studied to include nonmentalistic behaviors.

---

[3]It could be (and has been) argued that the classical mechanism represents a limited type of machine, and that a more complex concept of machine is possible. However, that simply trades one set of questions for another. Instead of identifying an alternate type of organizational model, it becomes necessary to identify alternate types of machines to accommodate the properties of organisms. Either way the issue is addressed, questioning some basic assumptions about the classical machine model and finding alternatives will be required.

John Watson (1924) also retained the mechanistic view, but chose to emphasize the material side of the material—nonmaterial duality. He did not deny the existence of mental events. He simply argued that the only way animals or humans could ever exhibit the phenomena of their mind to one another was through their behavior. Therefore, by studying behavior—the material events manifested by the organism that could be observed by others—everything important about animal or human functioning could come to be understood (Boring, 1960). Proponents of the behavioristic tradition used the concept of *responses* as their general unit and assumed every response (regardless of kind) in all mammals, including man "...occurs according to the same set of primary laws" (Hull, 1943). Armed with that assumption, it made no difference what kinds of responses (e.g., walking, salivating, blinking, thinking) were studied in what kinds of mammals (e.g., rats, pigeons, monkeys, or men); the laws discovered would be the same and could be generalized to any kind of response in any kind of mammal.

Thus, two early basic perspectives in psychology (i.e., mentalism and behaviorism) differed as to which units or categories of phenomena—matter or nonmatter, behavior or mind—represented the best avenue for understanding animals and men; but both shared the machine model of organization implicit in associationistic theory and research methods. However, the mentalistic tradition accepts the experiencing organism (or subjective observer) as the primary source of observational data (e.g., the mind may be studied directly through introspection); while the materialistic or behavioristic tradition follows the dictum of the natural science tradition that observations should be independent of the experiencing organisms (i.e., made by "objective" observers) (Kirsch, 1977).

This is not ancient history, but something of current relevance. Both mentalistic and behavioristic psychological traditions shared the same basic premises: (a) the distinction between mind and matter; (b) a machine model, composed of reversible processes, that could be under-stood by disassembling it using analytical methods; (c) an associationistic concept of functional organization; and (d) the belief in experience through the senses as the sole source of knowledge and behavior. Therfore, current psychological concepts and methods which emerged from those traditions are suffused with these (usually implicit) assumptions. For example, our dualistic tradition is reflected in the continued distinctions between phenomenological and behavioristic terminology (*experience*, psychological *field*, *perceived meaning*; versus *environment*, *responses*, *behavior*, *operants*). The machine model manifests itself in terminology such as *conditioned responses, reinforcement, stimuli,* and *behavior shaping*. Associationism as a model of organization and the related notion of linear temporal causality are pervasively present in most *S(timulus)* → *O*(rganism) → *R*(esponse) formulations; as well as the independent-dependent variable research designs, and statistical models which require assumptions of linearity and additivity, dealing with variables two by two (Stacey, 1975). Another manifestation of psychology's mechanistic history is the classical partitioning of psychological knowledge into basic categories such as sensation, perception, cognition, and motivation (mentalistic parts); and speech, motor skills, physiological responses, and social behaviors (behavioristic parts). Scientific journals tend to focus on knowledge about one or another part, leading Miller (1956a) to characterize them as "...catalogues of spare parts for a machine they never build." Many scholars now recognize that these ideas and methods inherited from psychology's early traditions are adequate for dealing with relatively simple static events but not for the complex, dynamic, self-organizing processes found in humans (Meehl, 1978; Petronovich, 1979; Rorer & Widiger, 1983). Unfortunately, traditions and language continue to maintain those outdated views through their implicit meanings.

The purpose of this very brief historical sketch is not to imply that those early assumptions should be rejected as false or without value. Major advances in human knowledge and technology have grown from their use, and they even appear acceptable for representing some kinds of phenomena. Rather, the intent is to explicitly recognize certain basic assumptions implicit in many influential present-day concepts and activities, and to recognize that they exert a limiting influence on current efforts to understand humans.

The fundamental theoretical images and paradigms of science are often represented as products of inductive reasoning based upon observations and formal research. Boulding (1980) asserts that science is more accurately viewed as "...the product of organized fantasy about the real world," continually tested "...by an internal logic of necessity and an external public record of expectations" sometimes realized and sometimes disappointed.

Being sure that we understand the foundations on which our "organized fantasies" are built is an important part of the testing process. The question of *what kind of being* humans are is probably not ultimately answerable based solely upon empirical observations or "facts" (e.g., Murphy, 1949), but rests also upon some initial philosophical assumptions about their "nature" or "essence" (Royce, 1961). Different assumptions will lead one in different directions, so being clear about them is important. For example, misunderstandings between physical and life scientists often result from their different assumptions about the living and inanimate worlds (Lewin, 1982; Mayr, 1982).

AN EMERGING NEW PERSPECTIVE

A change in fundamental perspective is struggling to be born as we approach the end of the 20th century. It is a change in which the complex *organization* of phenomena, in addition to the components of the phenomena themselves, is becoming the center of attention; and in which the concept of energy, that underlies so much of the natural sciences, is being supplemented by the concept of *information* that also seems of fundamental importance, particularly for understanding humans. It is a change growing from the recognition that people can continue to develop throughout their lives, and that they are active organisms shaping events as well as being shaped by them.

It is also a change growing out of dissatisfaction with the way the human sciences have ignored or seemed to distort some of the most significant aspects of being alive and being human; and a change in protest against what seems to be the dehumanization of people in modern, mass, mechanistic, production-oriented societies. It is a change that appears, in part, to be a new search for meaning in life at a time when old assumptions and values have for many people lost considerable credibility. For example, Stacey (1975) argues that the scholarship of "the mechanistic reductionists" is "shot through with ideological influences" growing from "notions of power, authority, control, precision, manipulation, orderliness, efficiency and such" that are influential in modern technological societies.

In his essay "On Not Flogging Dead Horses," Koestler (1967) (who saw dehumanization in the extreme in Nazi Germany) observes that although many scholars assure us that "...the crudely mechanistic 19th century conceptions" in biology, medicine, and psychology are "dead," those basic ideas continue to be manifested in textbooks, technical journals, and lecture rooms. Human languages and cultures have become suffused with them. He expresses agreement with von Bertalanffy's view that a large part of modern psychology "is a sterile and pompous scholasticism" blinded by "preconceived notions or superstitions," and which hides the "triviality" of its data and ideas "with a preposterous language bearing no resemblance to normal English or sound theory." He argues that psychological ideologies and technologies have contributed to "reducing man to the lower aspects of his animal nature," and into "a feeble-minded automaton of consumption or a marionette of political power," which dehumanizes him ever farther.

It is not our purpose here to explore such larger socio-political-philosophical issues. Our purpose is to remind ourselves that humans are in a sense shaping their own future by what they choose to believe and how they choose to act. Science is one of the key tools for trying to shape our own destiny, and science is not and cannot be value-free (McMullen, 1983). If there are alternative futures possible depending on what we choose to believe and do (and evolutionary theory indicates that alternative destinies are possible for every type of organism), then it behooves us to keep in mind the broader and deeper potential significance of the ways we choose to construe the world and ourselves, and the facets on which we choose to focus, as they bear upon our common humanity. While there is undoubtedly disagreement about the sentiments expressed by Stacey and Koestler, surely all can agree that the models of humans that we use to guide our thinking and activities hold the potential of becoming self-fulfilling prophecies. We may turn ourselves into what we believe ourselves to be. All thinking and acting (at least in adults) starts with prior assumptions that need to be periodically reexamined to be sure they are not misguiding us.

Illustrative Efforts

Some alternate conceptual frameworks are being built. Examples exist in the natural sciences (Jantsch, 1980; Prigogine & Stengers, 1984). The following examples are intended to convey the flavor but not the full scope of relevant efforts in the human sciences.

"Third Force" Psychology. From the beginning of psychological study the seeds of alternatives to a mechanistic model have been present and sometimes cultivated. For example, Brentano, a contemporary of Wundt's, sought to develop a holistic point of view that he contrasted to the associationism and elementism of Wundt's view. Stumpf and Husserl were students of Brentano's. Wertheimer, one of the founders of Gestalt psychology, was a student of Stumpf's (Heidbreder, 1933). Koffka (1924), Kohler (1929), and Lewin (1935) were students of Stumpf's and Wertheimer's, so their gestalt and field theory approaches were intellectually descended from Brentano. Goldstein (1939) sought to combine organismic and gestalt perspectives to help understand the functioning of brain-injured men in World War I. Maslow (1954), a student of Wertheimer's and Koffka's at the New School for Social Research in the early 1930s, was also influenced by Goldstein's views. Snygg and Combs (1949) sought to combine phenomenological and gestalt emphases, and Rogers' (1951) personality and therapy theory was influenced by the views of Goldstein, Maslow, and Snygg and Combs. Thus, today's "third force" psychology is one of the manifestations of a continuous stream of effort to develop an alternate view of humans (Dagenais, 1972).

Lewin also influenced some of the work in psychiatry (Frank, 1978) and in general psychology as illustrated by the dissonance theory and research of another of his students, Leon Festinger (Eng, 1978). Bronfenbrenner (1977) felt the impact of Lewin's ideas while a colleague of his in the U.S. Office of Strategic Services during World War II, and his ecological focus reflects that influence. It is worth noting that this stream of effort has been most influential in fields that by their very nature have to deal with individuals as functional units in their natural environments (e.g., personality and social psychology, psychiatry and psychotherapy).

Developmental, Personality, and Social Psychology. Another stream of effort focuses primarily on how people change over time and on understanding person-environment interactions in relationship to the phenomena of change (Pepper, 1942). It is found mainly in the literature of developmental, personality, and social psychology and their professional applications. Werner (1957) built upon the organismic theoretical tradition and sought to represent development in terms of an "orthogenetic" principle, which states that development proceeds from relative globality towards a condition of "...increasing differentiation, articulation, and hierarchic integration." Schneirla (1957a, 1957b) also emphasized that development progressed through levels of organization as a product of the interaction between biological and experiential variables. Floyd Allport (1934, 1937) developed the concept of a *telic continuum* as a label for the extent to which "...a certain purposive, meaningful, prescribed act is carried out in practice." Later (1954) he attempted to formulate a comprehensive theory of human behavior utilizing dynamic patterning of behavioral events occurring in "cycles of operation" which are "self-closing." He argued that a somewhat different view of causality was necessary because patterns of behavior seem to evolve "...from patterns already existing" rather than from "...linear trains of causes and effects."

Kagan (1967) called for a shift to a "relativistic view" of psychological phenomena similar to that occurring in physics and biology. Endler and Magnusson (1976) have formulated an interactional psychology of personality in which behavior is conceived to evolve and occur by "...a continuous and multidirectional interaction between person variables and situation variables." Riegel (1976) argued for the study of "...the temporal order of concrete events brought about by conflicts and contradictions" as they produce change in both the short term and longer term, to which the label of *dialectical psychology* has been given. Lerner (1978) combines Riegel's dialectical perspective with organismic and probabilistic epigenetic viewpoints to characterize development as arising from "...a dynamic interaction between qualitatively different, yet totally interdependent nature and nurture variables." Brent (1978a; 1978b) describes a model of individual development which combines homeostatic steady-state postulates with structural levels-and-stages postulates utilizing new developments in systems theory. Bronfenbrenner (1977) is utilizing ecological, developmental, and systems concepts to create a new approach which focuses on the progressive accommodation, throughout the life span, between developing persons and the changing environments in which they actually live and grow. Baltes and Willis (1977), after reviewing theories of aging, recommended development and utilization of paradigms that explicitly center on "biology-behavior-environment interactions" and "...convergence of ontogenetic and evolutionary approaches..." to produce more adequate theories of the aging process. At the other end of the age spectrum, Sroufe (1979) views the task of infant research as "...understanding the total organization of development." Baltes, Reese, and Lipsitt (1980) have reviewed the burgeoning work in life-span developmental psychology and see that perspective as providing a potentially "integrative framework." Views similar to these developmental psychology perspectives also appear in some other fields, such as ethology and anthropology.

Angyal (1965) developed an approach to the treatment of neurosis that views personality as a dynamic whole, its processes resulting from an interplay of organismic and environmental forces, with the parts having meaning only in the context of the whole. Santostefano (1980) combines ideas from developmental ego psychology, cognitive-developmental and organismic-developmental theory, leavened with a bit of systems theory in a framework for clinical child psychology. Hilgard (1977b) has brought the concepts of consciousness and volition back to center stage in attempting to understand humans. Luria (1976) concludes that memory processes are an integral part of cognitive processes that are "...active and selective forms of reflection of reality," which are influenced by personal motives "...and based on hierarchical systems of self-regulatory acts."

Systems Theory. A third stream of influence is modern systems theory, which has been evolving from a multidisciplinary base. While systems theory emerged into prominence after 1940, it has earlier roots. For example, Whitehead (1925) expressed a philosophy of the nature of organisms and viewed life as composed of systems. Much as did Floyd Allport thirty years later, Whitehead used the concepts of event and dynamic processes, relating events as tools in trying to represent his view of "...nature (as) a structure-evolving process." The first general statement of systems theory was published by von Bertalanffy (1940), and the development of system-design methods and concepts to solve wartime problems laid a practical cornerstone on which future efforts could be built. Von Bertalanffy's General Systems Theory (1968) brought together the ideas he had been developing during the previous three decades. Cannon (1939) introduced the concept of homeostasis to account for processes by which biological steady states were maintained. His work anticipated the more extensive and general exposition of the attributes of self-regulating systems, such as servomechanisms, described by Weiner (1948) in his book *Cybernetics,* and elaborated upon by Ashby (1956).

Information theory was developing in this same time frame (e.g., Shannon & Weaver, 1949; Weaver, 1948), adding the concept of *information* (and methods of quantifying and manipulating it) to the concept of *energy* as two essentials for describing systems. The advent of computer technology facilitated exploration of information and systems concepts. These advances provided a conceptual and methodological framework for bringing the concept of purposive behavior back under scientific scrutiny (e.g., Churchman & Ackoff, 1950; Rosenbluth & Weiner, 1950).

By the 1950s, information and systems theory attracted the interest of a broad range of professionals. For example, Menninger (1954) used the concepts of homeostasis and *open systems* to try to account for the functioning of individuals under stress. A multidisciplinary group of scientists and professionals sought some unifying conception of human behavior and converged on the emerging systems framework (Grinker, 1956). G. Allport (1967) considered personality theory in an open system context. Miller, Galanter, and Pribram (1960) used the emerging concepts of feedback and control to propose a unit for understanding behavior called the TOTE unit (i.e., *Test-Operate-Test-Exit).* Yamamoto and Brobeck (1965) brought the same kinds of principles to bear on efforts to better understand physiological controls and regulation.

Attempts to more fully explore and explicate basic aspects and applications of systems theory continue to appear, such as, for example, *purposiveness* (Ackoff & Emery, 1972; von Foerster et al., 1968); *hierarchy theory* (Whyte et al., 1969); *self-organization* (von Foerster & Zopf, 1962); *personality and individual development* (Koestler, 1967; Royce & Buss, 1976; Urban, 1978); *families* (Hoffman, 1981); *sociology* (Buckley, 1967); and *social issues and systems* (Churchman, 1979; DeGreene, 1978). Periodic summaries of systems perspectives have been published (e.g., Laszlo, 1972). Simon (1969) outlined a science of the "artificial" for understanding products synthesized to function and to attain goals. Prigogine (1978) demonstrated that nonequilibrium may become a source of order and lead to new dynamic states. J. Miller (1978) has made a massive attempt to develop and apply one type of system framework to several levels of living systems. Systems perspectives are having an impact in Europe, Russia, and many other countries (e.g., Kossakowski, 1980; Rose, 1978; Rose & Bilciu, 1977).

Attributes of the Emerging View

These efforts to formulate a science of "organized complexity" may be contrasted to the classical physics perspective characterized by Weaver (1948) as a successful effort to develop the theory of "unorganized complexity." Notions like wholeness, differentiation of parts from a whole, elaborating organizations, unpredictable emergents, developing hierarchies, or self-regulation, all of which have no place in conventional physics, represent phenomena of fundamental importance for a theory of organized complexity.

The three streams of effort identified in the previous section share six basic themes.

1. The first, and perhaps the most fundamental, is a focus on the *organized complexity* of person-environment functioning. For nearly two centuries scholars "conceived of the world as chaos" involving "the blind play of atoms," and with life "as an accidental product of physical processes, and mind as an epiphenomenon." By conceiving now of "the world as organization," both "basic scientific thought" and "practical attitudes" will be "profoundly" influenced (von Bertalanffy, 1968). De la Mettrie's premise, first stated in 1747, is flowering anew.

2. They also share in the rejection of linear S(timulus) → R(esponse) representations of humans, inherited from classical mechanistic thinking, and in the search for a model of organization that can deal with patterns of mutually influential variables. For example, Pribram (1971) asserts that "reflex organization is not an S → R arc, but a servosystem." This means that the "usual Newtonian and Sherringtonian chaining of agent and reaction" becomes transformed by "the introduction of feedback and feedforward operations," but that "most behaviorists have ignored the new complexity." Concepts involving hierarchical organization are common to all three streams, although clear specification of what that means is not always provided.

3. A person is viewed as an active organism, not just a reactive mechanism. People display properties of self-construction, self-direction, self-control, and self-regulation, properties which give the appearance of purposive or goal-directed behavior. People's functioning appears to be directed towards maintaining and elaborating the effectiveness and complexity of their behavioral organization and the organization of their relationships with environments. To a considerable

extent, they are producers of their own development (Lerner & Busch-Rossnagel, 1981).

4. A person develops from simple to increasingly complex organized patterns and the course of that development is not necessarily smooth. Structural-functional patterns may evolve in a relatively continuous way for awhile; then stabilize (e.g., at a stage) for awhile; then for some reason or reasons begin to change again. Behavioral organization at any point in time is seen as a product of mutually influential interactions among innate and acquired properties of the person and salient factors in his or her environment. Disrupting conditions appear to be one prerequisite for change (Jantsch, 1980; Prigogine, 1976); this pattern may even typify human functioning. Blissful equilibrium appears not to be the "best" state, or even a possible state, for a person. Growth, progress, enjoyment, and misery all are products of the continual necessity for dealing with some kind of "discombobulation" of life.

5. The selection, organization, and use of information are viewed as important in human development. All living organisms exchange energy and material with their environments. It is the *elaborateness* of their information exchange and utilization processes that gives humans their distinctive characteristics. One special aspect of information use is people's capability for monitoring internal as well as external events, and focusing that information to organize, direct, and control their functioning.

6. Finally, all three perspectives recognize that new properties may emerge at increasingly complex levels of organization, and may not be predictable from the properties of the components that combined into the more elaborate organization. Understanding living (biological) systems may require different units of analysis and different principles at different organizational or interpretive levels (Novikoff, 1945).

Methodological Implications. One's assumptions guide one's choice of methods for studying phenomena of interest. In turn, methods shape the information collected and affect its interpretation. For example, if different species of mammals represent evolutionary "shifts" or "jumps" in patterns of organization, and if different types or levels of complex organization may involve different functional principles, then the common assumption that findings concerning behavioral organization and functioning in one species are generalizable to other species may not always be valid. There may be some species-specific patterns (e.g., Seligman, 1970; Seligman & Hager, 1972).

The human sciences have generally proceeded with the basic strategy of looking at one thing at a time (a dependent variable) and noting its response when exposed to one other thing (the independent variable).

Most multivariable research designs and data analytic models (e.g., complex ANOVAs; factor analysis) are simply elaborations of this basic strategy. Another variation is the consideration of several factors as "chains" of elements, each acting on the next in sequence (consequently, shaping of behavior through conditioning procedures has sometimes been referred to as the "chaining" of responses). While this tactic has revealed much, it cannot tell us how attributes simultaneously act together when exposed to a pattern of multiple influences, and how the products of those interactions influence the interactions themselves (e.g., autocatalytic processes). This is an important shortcoming, because such mutually and simultaneously influential processes appear to be pervasively characteristic of human life, and life in general (Prigogine & Stengers, 1984). The methods so successful in the study of nonliving organization "work" reasonably well there because the phenomena have properties of constancy of both state and change that can be reasonably well represented by a linear, additive model of causality; because of the linear model's success, "it has a terrible seductive power over the human mind" (Rapoport & Horvath, 1959). Methods constructed to serve mechanistic assumptions are inadequate for the study of living systems whose dynamics of organization and change are characterized by multivariate mutual causal processes (Nesselroade & Ford, 1985, 1987). The development and verification of nonmechanistic models of humans will be severely constrained until other appropriate research methods are created.

Efforts are growing to develop methods and mathematics appropriate to the emerging "organized complexity" perspective. This is a far more difficult methodological and mathematical problem than representing linear, additive, sequential patterns. Statistics as a whole is, in a sense, an emergent mathematical form that tries to deal with the sort of complexity that is resistant to explicit mechanistic, linear, cause-effect analysis. Where the perturbing influences are large and unknown, the classical statistical assumption of *randomness* is adopted and its offspring, probability theory, is applied. While the effort to develop multivariate approaches appropriate to this alternative view has only begun (in an historical sense), a variety of possibilities have been or are being developed, such as, for example, *factor analysis* (Cattell, 1980) and *configural frequency analysis* (von Eye, 1984).

Information theory has introduced the notion that information is a basic quantifiable entity analogous to energy. This analogy was reinforced by the discovery that a mathematical representation of information turned out to be the opposite of the energy-related concept of entropy in physics, leading to the invention of the term *negentropy*. Information theory, combined with cybernetics principles of control and regulation, involving feedback and feedforward or reciprocal causal processes, has stimulated further search for new quantitative methods. Topology, graph theory, network theory, fuzzy sets, catastrophe theory and group theory all illustrate relational mathematics of potential usefulness. In his important work on stability and change in dissipative or nonequilibrium structures, Prigogine (1976) developed a new class of nonlinear stochastic equations because traditional methods, when applied to nonlinear processes far from equilibrium, are not adequate for modeling some dynamic systems. The development of more and more complicated computers, and their use in simulation and modeling, provide a tool which makes feasible the exploration of quantitative methods for handling multivariate problems that were impossibly complex without them.

Systems Theory: An Alternative Model

I have concluded that of the alternative traditions illustrated earlier, information and systems theory appear to provide the most promising approach. Systems theories have contributed to the evolution of more sophisticated attempts to develop or find relevant empirical methods and mathematical tools; they have a history of utility in a number of different disciplines and professions (e.g., engineering and computer sciences), and have demonstrated their practical utility by providing the framework for a number of important technological innovations. I believe some type of systems framework can encompass (and perhaps even shed new light on) the most important ideas in the other two streams of effort, thereby accomplishing a synthesis of the three.

Some students and colleagues have asked from time to time why systems theory has had relatively little impact on psychology as of now if it has so much potential. I believe that there are several reasons. The first, and perhaps the most important, has been demonstrated by Powers (1978) and described by him as the "machine analogy" blunder. (As Koestler said, that centuries-old model of man is not a "dead horse.") Often the cybernetics servomechanism model described by Weiner and elaborated upon by others has been taken as the general case. Human functioning, as a special instance of that general case, should, according to such thinking, fit the general model. That is just a new version of the old view of man as a machine.

Powers argues that the reverse is true, that is, that humans represent the general case and machines are the special case. Servomechanisms are only narrow imitations of some limited aspects of a complex living system. Humans design servomechanisms to do something *for them.* Therefore, the designer's primary interest is in how the machine can serve humans (the function called output in cybernetics jargon). The machine is only provided with the materials, energy, and information (called input) necessary for producing the result humans want. Thus, from the human designer's point of view, *output is the end* to be achieved, and *input is the means* to that end. This is expressed in the cybernetics generalization "input controls output"; or in the Skinnerian version as behavior (i.e., output) is controlled by its consequences (i.e., input). But such cybernetics machines function that way because *that is the way they are designed.* Humans want their machines to do what they are designed to do, every time and all of the time. To accomplish this, they have to omit from the design of the machine the broader properties of living systems which make them less predictable and less controllable, or else their machines might tell them to "go to hell" and do something else. (And who among us hasn't sometimes felt that a balky car or other machine was deliberately thwarting us?)

Humans are not organized primarily to achieve objective effects in an external world to serve the "wants" of some "great designer" (though despots throughout history have tried to make them so). Rather they are designed to produce effects from the external world on themselves. In fact, that is a central premise underlying evolutionary theory: organisms survive only if they are able to get what they need from their environment. An individual's behavior is not the end but the means. How we behave is determined by whether we are achieving the results *we need and want.* Ordinary people will tell you that is the case for them. Stated in cybernetics jargon, *output controls input* rather than the reverse, that is, behavior serves to produce and control the impact of its consequences, rather than the reverse.[4]

This is what some personality, psychotherapy, and developmental psychology theorists have been saying all along, but sciences dominated by a machine analogy and by methods designed to serve that premise couldn't hear or see the truth in such a drastically different view. It is possible to make people "act like" machines to some extent (e.g., to influence what they do by what you tell them), as every successful propagandist knows, but that is simply "designing" them to be servomechanisms rather than permitting them to function fully as

---

[4]The recognition that the reverse of the Skinnerian principles is the accurate way to represent human behavior does not entail "throwing out" all of the important work and technology that has grown out of those ideas. In fact, close analysis of the operant method reveals that the more accurate view has been hidden there all along in the procedures for selecting reinforcers for a particular "behavior-shaping" enterprise. For example, in one study an elderly woman was observed during the base rate period, not only to get a picture of the behavior to be modified, but also to determine the kinds of things *she likd.* In this case, she liked certain kinds of music and candy, so they were used as the "reinforcers." Thus, they gave her the "input" *she* wanted when she provided the "output" (i.e., behavior) *they* wanted. So her output controlled their input, and vice versa.

natural living systems. When systems (e.g., people) can transform carefully calibrated inputs, then the scientist does not have full control over the behavior outputs (Mancuso & Ceely, 1980). Therefore, cybernetics or systems type theories have not yet had a major impact on psychology (except in some technological applications where the machine analogy can be made to work), partly because they have been encapsulated by a mechanistic model.

There are probably at least two other reasons. Cybernetics and systems models are complex. Their jargon is catchy and has become a part of our technological society. Too many people have adopted the jargon and used it in a superficial way, and this may have helped discredit the potential of systems models in the minds of many serious scholars. In addition, new scientific (and professional) perspectives advance, in part, through the development of relevant instruments and methods, and through demonstration that the perspective and methods have utility. In psychology, computer simulation of aspects of human behavior (e.g., cognitive functioning) has been a new tool useful in systems perspectives. But systems-oriented people have made more progress in some domains of science and technology than has occurred in psychology, where methodological problems are much greater. However, by utilizing the insight expressed and illustrated by Powers, a new synthesis of previous theoretical and empirical findings could (in my judgment) produce the momentum and eventual impact earlier anticipated for a systems approach.

Therefore, I outline in the following pages the general properties of a conceptual framework that transforms a mechanistic control system model into a living system (J. Miller, 1978). I hope, however, the focus of the reader will be upon the goal and not the label. As Selye (1976) illustrates autobiographically, scientists and professionals not infrequently get into useless arguments because they interpret concept labels in different ways. In later chapters I attempt to organize multiple aspects of humans within the living systems framework to see if the analogy will enable us to fit some of the general pieces of humans back together again. Therefore, the outline which follows is presented in a relatively abstract form without extensive attempts to relate it to the aspects of a person. The first objective is to outline a general framework as simply as possible, and then later to relate it to the organization and functioning of a person. The framework to be presented has much in common with that proposed by Anokhin (1969), a Russian physiological psychologist. To paraphrase him, the objective is a framework which can deal with the fundamental questions involved in all behavioral acts, that is, what to do, how to do it, when to do it, and how to know when it is done (or cannot be done).

I reemphasize that I am not suggesting that the mechanistic, associationistic, simple deterministic models of human organization are completely wrong or worthless. That is not the case. It is my view, however, that such models represent a special case within a more general case. Paul Weiss (1971) observes that the "mechanists" and "holists" alike have "...become entrenched behind mutually exclusive doctrinal claims." He concludes that they are both right and their claims are "mutually compatible." Organisms include both "linear cause-effect sequences" and "self-adjusting operations." Characteristics such as cell behavior, biological development and nervous functions are "partly chains, partly networks." Eventually a larger view will have to emerge that can encompass both.[5] I believe that there is unity or patterns of consistency in the way the universe is organized, and that advances in human knowledge represent successive approximations towards identifying and representing it. As the biochemist Paul Althouse, an old Pennsylvania Dutch friend of mine, used to put it, "We proceed steady by jerks." Hopefully, what follows is another small step in the right direction.

---

[5]Note that this is different from the reductionist manifesto that eventually all phenomena will be reducible to the principles of chemistry and physics. While I believe it is true that understanding the "parts" contributes to understanding the "whole," I believe it is also true that understanding the organization of the "whole" contributes to an understanding of the "parts." Therefore, the larger view which I believe will eventually emerge must encompass both within it.

2

Organized Complexity and the Concept of System

INTRODUCTION

The purpose of this chapter is to briefly consider basic concepts that are used in later chapters to construct a living systems framework. The first question for consideration is what it means to say something is "organized." There may be different kinds of organization. The concept of *system* is used to represent one kind of organization, and its properties are summarized. Finally, one type of system has special properties symbolized by the term *living;* this chapter concludes with consideration of the properties of such living systems.

ORGANIZATION

An entity is not just a collection of parts. It is a combination of related parts, and it is the *specific pattern* of relatedness that gives the entity its individual identity. For example, a collection of pieces of slate and wood, blocks of stone, pieces of metal, wire, and colored glass would be a pile of junk, an accidental grouping of materials in space and time with no connections between them. Relate such parts in one way and a nightclub could be constructed. Relate them in another way and a gothic cathedral could evolve. The key properties of being a nightclub or a cathedral do not lie in the nature of the parts but in the way that they are assembled, and the possibilities thereby created. It is this pattern of relatedness to which the term *organization* refers. In organizations with a material identity, physical relatedness is often an important clue to organization. In nonmaterial organizations (e.g., mathematics) the organization must be represented by other kinds of relatedness, such as symbols representing logical rules.

Constraining and Facilitating Conditionalities

Because the concept of organization is fundamental to a living systems framework, it is desirable to probe more deeply into it. Let us start with a familiar example. An automobile is a physical structure. One of its parts is a tire. A tire by itself, as a kind of whole in its own right, has a variety of potentials. It can be rolled or bounced, floated in water, used to cushion boats anchored to a dock, filled with soil and used as a flower bed, or hung up and used as a swing. But if combined with other parts to create an organized entity called an automobile, its potentials become limited to a few actualities, i.e., rolling, bouncing on a rough road, and occasionally going flat. *It is in this limiting of all the potentialities of something to a few actualities that we find one key to the idea of organization.*

In more formal terms, the core of the concept of organization is *conditionality* (Ashby, 1962). When several components exist, each with multiple possibilities, and when they are related in such a way that the actualities of each are restricted to some subset of the possibilities for each part, then organization exists. Such limiting relationships among components Ashby termed *constraining conditionalities.* He observed that viewed this way, the theory of organization is related to the theory of functions of more than one variable. The statistical concept of degrees of freedom is an example of this general idea. Organization implies constraints on the subunits. If X and Y are coupled in a particular way, it implies there must be some kind of "communication" between them. If for a given state of X all possible states of Y may occur and their probability of occurrence is not affected by the state of X, then there is no coupling, no relationship, no communication, no constraint and, therefore, no organization.

There is a second kind of conditionality which Ashby did not describe. Parts may be related in such a way that an attribute or capability may emerge which is not a part of the potentialities of any part separately. For example, neither Na or Cl taste "salty," but when combined into NaCl the new compound does taste salty. Stated simply, *if parts are related in such a way that together they produce a property that none may manifest by itself, then organization exists.* Such property-producing relationships among components might be termed *facilitating conditionalities.* Facilitating conditionalities are particularly characteristic of living systems, and probably underlie the phenomena of discontinuities in development with which developmental psychology theorists have struggled (Lerner, 1976).

In fact the reason for, or value of, different or increasingly complex organizations is to produce possibilities the parts do not have separately. If different organizations of parts created no new possibilities there would be no reason for new organizations to occur or continue. That is a central premise underlying evolutionary theory. New organismic organizations evolved because they provided characteristics of greater survival and reproductive value in a particular environmental niche than did other organismic organizations. Much human effort is focused on trying to create new material (e.g., spaceships) and social organizations (e.g., oil cartels) with new potentialities. However, as an old adage says, one usually gives up something to get something else. Organizations that create new possibilities (manifesting facilitating conditionalities) do so, in part, by limiting other possibilities (manifesting constraining conditionalities). Therefore, the two kinds of conditionalities are coupled properties of organizations. Organizations may be of different size and scope; that is, they may differ in the number and diversity of the parts of which they are composed. The selection of units of analysis therefore involves the selection of the level(s) and type(s) of organization appropriate to the observer's interests.

Boundaries as a Property of Organization

Weiss (1971) proposes that an organization is "something that tends to stay together and to retain its pattern when shifted in space," and that tends to "retain identity over a time span outlasting the fortuitous constellations of the moment." In short, organization is identified by coherence and conservation of pattern. The relevant period of time in which identity must be retained to be considered an organization or unit depends upon the interests and objectives of the observer. For example, physicists study units whose identity may exist for a millionth of a millisecond; psychologists study behaviors whose time span may be represented in seconds, minutes, hours, or days; biologists study organisms whose existence may be measured in years or decades; astronomers study planets whose continuity of existence is represented in billions of years. Stated in another way, units are organizations of phenomena which show relatively greater consistency and interdependence in space and time within themselves than in relationship to other phenomena or events in their context, like the beans in bean soup.

This difference between units and their contexts is apparent in a set of *boundary conditions* that set off the internally organized phenomena from their relationships to their larger context. There are two types of boundary conditions. The classification of the world into spatially identified organizations or objects is based on *physical boundaries*. The classification of societal phenomena into organizational or institutional units is based primarily on *interaction* boundaries defined by the consistency, frequency, or intensity of interactions among participants. The consistency, frequency, or intensity of interactions *within* a unit are greater than those *between* that unit and its surroundings. Simon (1969) notes that in most biological or physical units "...relative intense interaction implies relative spatial propinquity," and in such units the physical and interaction boundaries may coincide. However, physical spatial connection becomes less important in identifying units when the information interactions within the unit are more important than the physical ones, and are accomplished through specialized communication and transportation systems (e.g., corporate interactions through computers and telephones).

In summary, organization is a coupling of subunits so that an exchange of information and/or energy or material occurs among them, producing both constraining and facilitating conditionalities on the functioning of the subunits and of the total organization in the interest of maintaining both of them. The conditionalities are mutually beneficial. For example, the functioning of an automobile engine operates an electricity generator which provides electricity which the engine needs to operate. Deficiencies or defects in the structure or organization will alter in some way its activity boundaries and possibilities. For example, if the automobile engine is not provided with electricity it will not work, and if the engine does not work there will be no electricity generated.

A SYSTEM

The term *system* has become a popular way to refer to all kinds of complexly organized entities, such as *organ* system, *communication* system, *production* system, *political* system, or *conceptual* system. However, not all forms of organization are appropriately termed systems, although definitions of systems start by defining basic organizational properties (Hall & Fagan, 1956; A. Rapoport, 1970).

A System as a Special Type of Organization

Weiss (1971) has proposed that not all organized clusters of phenomena should be considered as systems. He distinguishes among types of units on the basis of the kinds of processes by which subunits relate "...to establish and preserve the rather definite pattern of the compound unit." Some units, such as crystals, show organizational consistency in terms of symmetry, polarity, or periodicity. Others, such as the letters in a word, may be a uniquely irregular array of parts. The organization of such units is quite firmly determinate or mechanistic in nature, and are not systems according to Weiss's criteria. In organizations such as crystals, the functioning of the unit can be predicted unequivocally from the information about its parts or subunits and their relationships. However, Weiss describes a different type of organization in which the functioning of the components is in part controlled "...by their collective state," or by the organization of the larger unit of which they are a part. Weiss (1971) calls that type of organization a system, and defines it as "...a complex unit in space and time so constituted that its component subunits, by 'systematic' cooperation, preserve its integral configuration of structure and behavior and tend to restore it after non-destructive disturbances." (p. 14)

He points to the spider's web as a simple monotonic system (i.e., involving a single mode of dynamics). The web maintains its geometric pattern as a function of the distribution of mechanical pressures and tensions. Sever a strand of such a web and it will maintain itself by redistributing the pattern of mechanical pressures and tensions; this is reflected in the changes in the angles among the strands. To make an analogy which anticipates later discussion, visualize the points of intersection in the web as organs in a person and the strands as functional connections among organs. Disrupt one of those functional connections, and the remaining patterns of organ interactions will modify themselves to try to maintain the integrity of the whole. Other organs will compensate as best they can for the disruption. However, the processes involved are far more complicated in living systems because they involve not only mechanical dynamics, but mutually and simultaneously influential chemical, electrical, informational, and (in humans) psychological dynamics as well.

Control Systems

Spider webs are still mechanical organizations in which the method of response to disruptions is either completely specified in its organization, or is composed of both "fixed rules" and "fixed strategies." What is needed is a model of organization which can "recognize" and "interpret" disruptions, and "select"—from among multiple potential courses of action—one action which seems best suited to protecting the integrity of the organization against current disruptions. A model of organization is needed which utilizes both fixed and flexible *rules* and fixed and flexible *strategies*.

Control systems provide a basic model of organization with such properties. The term *cybernetics* was coined to identify the body of knowledge and technology which related information theory to control system theory as a means of understanding and designing organizations with such self-regulating properties. Servomechanisms, such as "automatic pilots" in airplanes and spaceships, illustrate control systems. The term "automation" in modern industrial processes reflects the widespread use of such control systems in technologically oriented societies. They go beyond simple machines in that they have the capacity for specifying a desired status of important events or variables, for monitoring those relevant variables, and for controlling and regulating the system's functioning to influence the relevant variable(s) in the specified ways. Such regulation and control are accomplished by using information about the current status of relevant variable(s), called *feedback*, to "make decisions" about how to change the system's functioning to produce more desirable results and then to "instruct" the system's action components, called *feedforward*, to alter their functioning in specific ways. Such systems are discussed in detail in chapter 3. Readers who would like more detail now could examine Fig. 3.1 and 3.2 in that chapter, and read the section headed "A Simple Engineering Control System."

Once a particular system becomes the focus of interest, its parts are typically called *subsystems* or *components*, and its context the *suprasystem* or *environment*. Several control systems can be combined to form a larger control system, sometimes called a nested system, as described by Miller, Galanter, and Pribram (1960). Thus, the designation of a particular unit as a *system* rather than a subsystem or suprasystem is an arbitrary choice, but it is not capricious because it must be appropriate to the purpose. Lomov (1980) emphasizes that the choice of units does not mean that people are "...simply looking at phenomena from different viewpoints." Rather, the phenomena themselves are manifest in "...different levels of organization." For example, he asserts that one level that evolves and functions "...by its own laws" (e.g., neurophysiological processes) may give rise "...to a specific organization of another level" which evolves and functions by somewhat different laws (e.g., cognitive processes). The choice of unit, then, depends on the organizational level of interest. However, a comprehensive view will always keep in mind that functioning at any organizational level is influenced both by subsystem and suprasystem organizational factors.

Autopoietic Living Systems

Living systems, such as humans, have and maintain an organizational integrity that gives them an important degree of autonomy from their environment. This is accomplished in systems that have an organization of components and processes that can continuously and recursively produce the same kinds of components that produced the network of processes in the first place. To this self-constructing capability Maturana (1975) gave the Greek name of *autopoieses*, which literally means "to make self." In autopoietic systems, of which humans are the most complex example, all functioning is subordinated to the self-organizing and self-constructing properties of the system, or disintegration (disorganization) will occur (Zeleny, 1981).

Certain properties must be added to a mechanical control system to transform it so as to represent organisms such as humans. These include openness, nonequilibrium steady states, irreversible processes, and self-organizing and self-constructive functioning.

Open Systems. Systems are differentiated in terms of whether or not they exchange material, energy, and/or information with their environments. They are called *open* if they do and *closed* if they do not.

One fundamental law of physics, the second law of thermodynamics, was developed to account for the functioning of processes in *closed systems*—that is, systems "isolated" so they exchange no material, energy or information with their environments. Only intrasystem interactions can occur. Therefore, such systems do not gain or lose anything to their environments; only their internal organization may change. Completely closed systems are impossible in the natural world, but some systems approximate such a hypothetical state. The second law of thermodynamics can be described in several ways, all of which refer to the organizational properties of phenomena; the concept of *entropy* is used to refer to those properties (von Bertalanffy, 1968). For example, entropy may be considered a measure of probability. A closed system tends towards a state of most probable distribution of its components, which is the *complete absence of organization*. For example, in a closed container of gas, the conditions of all fast molecules (e.g., a high temperature) being on one side while all slow ones (e.g., a low temperature) were on the other side would be a highly improbable state of affairs. So change toward maximum entropy or the most probable distribution is change toward maximum disorganization. A typical dictionary definition characterizes entropy as the degree to which the total energy of a thermodynamic system is uniformly distributed and thus unavailable for conversion into work, called a state of equilibrium. In closed systems, the final equilibrium or state is determined by the initial conditions. For example, the initial concentrations of reactants determine the final concentrations in a chemical equilibrium. If the initial conditions or process is changed, the final result will be changed. Analogies to this principle appear in some views of human behavior. For example, the concept of *drive reduction* involves the notion that behavior tends towards a state of equilibrium. The biblical "ashes to ashes and dust to dust" could be considered an early version of this law.

But living systems such as humans do not function as closed systems and do not conform to the second law of thermodynamics as long as they are alive. They have a continuous exchange of energy, material, and information with their environments, and are therefore referred to as open systems. As a result of these exchanges, humans tend toward increasingly improbable structures, that is, toward states of increasingly complex organization. Just think of the difference between the fertilized ovum and the newborn baby. The opposite of entropy has occurred.

Living systems are never in simple equilibrium, like a clock that has run down. They are more like a clock that is wound up, with potential energy available to power all its processes. In fact, a unique thing about living systems is that *they* keep *themselves* "wound up." In an equilibrium there is no dissipation of total energy whereas in steady states there is constant dissipation. An equilibrium has only potential energy, but steady states have both potential and kinetic energy (Wilder, 1967). This capacity of open systems for fabricating new patterns of physical and behavioral organization (Herrick 1956), for creating complex patterns out of shapelessness, order out of randomness, has whimsically been termed by physical scientists negative entropy (negentropy).

Nonequilibrium and Steady States.   Recent work by 1977 Nobel Prize winner Ilya Prigogine (1978) and colleagues (Nicolis & Prigogine, 1978) demonstrate that nonequilibrium (which characterizes living systems) may become a source of order, and that irreversible processes may lead to a new type of dynamic state. Prigogine called this *dissipative structure* (or organization) because he wanted to bring together two fundamental ideas: (a) structure, which usually refers to static or stable organization; and (b) dissipation, which refers to the continual import and export of energy. Together, the two terms identify a dynamic unit whose organization can be modified and elaborated through its energy exchange and utilization capabilities. Jantsch (1980) has taken these and some other principles and combined them to represent all levels of organization from cells to galaxies.[1] A less technical summary of these ideas and their

---

[1]It is not yet clear whether the universe as a whole is slowly running down as the second law of thermodynamics suggests, or whether entropy is only a special case of some broader principles which govern the universe. It is clear that systems that do not exchange energy with their hierarchies tend to "run down." However, the fact that the universe, everywhere we look, seems to be complexly organized seems to suggest that the maintenance of complex organization may involve laws at least as fundamental as the

implications for psychological theory may be found in Brent (1978b) and Prigogine and Stengers (1984). One key idea is that any open system can increase in complexity as long as it "imports" more energy and material than it "exports," thereby providing an internal surplus which can be used for "new construction," for "repair work," and to fuel the various functions of the system. The same principle could probably be applied to "imports" and "exports" of information, through which a person learns or "constructs" new behavior patterns by the acquisition, transformation, and use of new information; but that idea has not been addressed in Prigogine's work.

These exchange processes produce two seemingly contradictory but interrelated properties: stability and nonequilibrium. The same exchange processes that maintain organizational stability also continuously disturb the system's current state. Thus, there is stability in the midst of variability. Rather than the stability of a closed system's equilibrium, there is the opposite—the stability of a high degree of organization (complexity) with a continual and varying flow of energy, material, and information through the system. Subunits and processes change while the larger structure of which they are a part retains a stable organization. For example, you will still look the same tomorrow as you do today, despite the death and birth of cells in your body during the night. This kind of stability is called a *steady state*, or sometimes a *dynamic equilibrium*; these terms define the maintenance of a stable identity in a state of some degree of nonequilibrium. It is some distance from the true equilibrium, and therefore has free energy and information available for "work," such as initiating further growth or behavior. Therefore, Prigogine recognized that nonequilibrium was actually a source of organization and order. Such steady states are more susceptible to changes in their organization and functioning the further they are from equilibrium.

Irreversible Processes. Classical science sought to transcend time, to see it simply as a parameter. The universe was viewed as composed of fundamental, unchanging substances (such as atoms) whose organization was governed by universal, unchanging, time-independent laws. The related concept of classical mechanism incorporated the idea of reversible processes (Deutsch, 1950): Machines could be disassembled and reassembled in any sequence, but would always behave in identical fashion when reassembled. Irreversible processes were recognized (e.g., energy loss from friction in a machine) but were not of primary theoretical interest. In contrast, Prigogine considered irreversibility a

---

second law of thermodynamics. Energy is conserved; its organization and distribution varies in an apparently unending space-time matrix (Capra, 1977).

key concept. According to this view, many phenomena change into forms from which it is impossible to return to their previous state. Organisms are dramatic examples of irreversible change. For example, an adult can never return to being a child again. Irreversible processes contribute to the evolution of more complicated systems (Prigogine and Stengers, 1984), of which humans are a prime example. Thus, organization and change are embedded in time, but the road is not just downhill to oblivion (entropy); it is also upward towards more complex levels of organization and functioning (negentropy).

Self-Organizing and Self-Constructive Functioning. Prigogine's work has excited people with its broad implications because he demonstrated that material entities can be self-organizing. For example, as the heating of a liquid from below grows more intense, the liquid can suddenly self-organize into a new material state in which cell-like patterns of brilliant stained-glass colors appear (called the Bernard Instability). Such self-organization or reorganization can vary in stable patterns, as for example, in Zhabotinsky reactions certain chemical compounds will change in color from red to blue and back again with clocklike precision. This sudden appearance of new states of matter at critical points of disequilibrium was termed *bifurcation* by Prigogine. The further a system is from equilibrium, the more unstable its organization becomes (that is, the more susceptible it is to change as a function of its exchange processes). Disorganization leads to reorganization, which is a function of the system's own properties, and the reorganization will be more complex than the previous state (Prigogine & Stengers, 1984).

Historically, the apparent self-governing capabilities of organisms were considered an epiphenomenon since all systems were believed to be externally controlled (e.g., by gods or by laws of nature). Emerging scientific evidence now demonstrates the self-organizing capabilities of systems that are "dissipative structures," which includes all living systems. Moreover, the self-reorganization that occurs is not completely predictable. Unexpected new forms may appear.

Humans have these special capabilities. They can transform and recombine the material, energy and information they exchange with their environment into different forms that can be used to maintain, repair, or elaborate their structural and functional organization (e.g., cell division, creative thought). Machines are structural-functional organizations in which many properties that are variable in living systems are either nonvariable or nonexistent. The most important difference is the machine's lack of self-organizing, self-constructing capabilities.

In open, self-organizing, self-constructing systems, a resultant organization is not strictly determined by the initial conditions but is also influenced by the system parameters themselves. Such systems reach their final states "by means of processes which may vary according to the initial conditions" (von Bertalanffy, 1975). This means that *the same outcome may occur from different combinations of system parameters*—that starting from different places, and traveling different routes, such systems may reach the same end point. This property is called *equifinality*. For example, an organism reaches its final size irrespective of its initial size and growth pattern; an animal can reach the same goal by different movements. Folk wisdom recognizes the principle of equifinality with sayings such as, "More than one road leads to Rome." Tyler (1978) formulated a theory of individuality that starts with the assumption that each person has innumerable possibilities for development, and makes daily personal choices about which possibilities to actualize. One's choices are only bounded by one's biological and environmental limitations. Such choices cumulate to form developmental trajectories. Two persons may start from different states and converge on similar trajectories, or start from similar states and construct divergent trajectories.

Thus, unlike a machine, the course of human development is not fixed entirely by its initial properties or by the fortuitous events of life. Growth and development not predictable from the original conditions are possible *because people are living systems*. If only the second law of thermodynamics could be applied to human life, then all that could be expected would be that from its beginning life could run only in one direction: downhill to oblivion. But the fact that there are other principles opens other vistas. As a living system exhibiting equifinality, a person can start from the lowliest of origins and experience the worst of the world early in life, and still arrive at the highest of accomplishments. As active, not merely reactive organisms, people can continue to grow, develop, and create throughout life—not just decline. This perspective provides solid underpinnings for current explorations of phenomena of aging and for a life-span development view (Baltes, Reese, & Lipsitt, 1980). Entropy leads to death, but negative entropy or "dissipative structure" leads to life and development.

Hierarchical Organization

Every entity may be considered to be composed of parts related to one another in some way that constrains some possibilities for the subunits, but facilitates new possibilities for the larger entity. The term *hierarchy* refers to an organizational attribute of these relationships. The whole, in our instance a person, is a multilevel organization of semiautonomous subunits.

The notion of hierarchy has a long history tracing at least from Plato and Aristotle (Whyte, 1969) and from ancient Chinese and Egyptian biology to modern medical science (Leake, 1969). It has many aspects (Whyte et al., 1969), but Gerard (1968) points out that the essence of the concept of hierarchy is in subsumption. One can subordinate, subdivide, or deal with subspecies, subroutines, subheadings, or subadjacent elements. In some way, each subunit is constrained by its relationship to, and at the same time is an important contributor to, the larger whole of which it is a part. Because the flow of influence is both up, down, and within organizational levels, the term *heterarchy* is sometimes used.

Koestler (1967) likened this duality to the Roman god Janus with two faces looking in opposite directions. As a subunit, a component shows the face of a servant serving the whole of which it is a part. As a unit in its own right, it shows the face of the master as its own subunits serve it. Thus, each subunit is functionally partly independent of and partly subordinated to its larger context. All of the natural world reveals such hierarchical characteristics. For example, the atom, a word derived from the Greek for indivisible, was once considered to be the basic unit from which all material objects were constructed. But we now know it is only one level of nature's hierarchical design ranging from energy patterns through atoms to galaxies. Wherever orderly, stable systems exist in nature, they are hierarchically organized because "without such structuring of complex systems into sub-assemblies, there could be no order and stability" except that of "a dead universe filled with a uniformly distributed gas" (Koestler, 1967).

The living cell is an excellent example (Leake, 1969). Cells are vastly complex and highly organized structures with many coordinated subcellular components manifesting rule-governed interactions. Simultaneously, cells are components of larger units (organs) which are components of still larger units (organisms). This kind of organization is sometimes called an *embedded hierarchy* or *nested system*. Each level is constrained and facilitated in its *possibilities* by its relationship to the other levels, but its specific internal *functioning* as a subsystem in its own right is not fully determined by its hierarchical relationships. Each level in an organizational hierarchy may function, in part, according to principles of its own. And this great hierarchy of the universe appears to be open at both ends. The search for the smallest elements of nature has led ever downward in the hierarchy through atoms, electrons, protons, neutrons, quarks, and glueons. The bedrock of existence is yet to be found. Similarly, as the reach of astronomers has extended, so has our knowledge of the larger hierarchy of the universe; and yet its limits still appear to be infinite.

Hierarchical organization resolves the dilemma that a reductionist view can lead to an infinite regress, and to the fallacy of linear, mechanistic thinking which suggests that because the nature of any event is a function of its interaction history, ultimately everything must be related to everything else (DeLong, 1972). For example, classical mechanics proposed that thermal energy in an atomic system should be divided among all the models of motion (e.g., the electrons and protons of an atom should move faster; their parts should move faster, etc.). This would lead to an infinite "sink" of heat energy, and immense amounts of energy would be required to heat the smallest element of matter. An hierarchical view termed the *quantum ladder* resolved this dilemma: At each level of material organization, only those types of motion whose energies can be excited at the prevailing temperatures (i.e., whose threshold of quantum excitation has been exceeded) will participate in the heat exchange (Weisskopf, 1961). This illustrates the general principle that hierarchical organization *limits the influence* of one event upon another, in effect by establishing limits to the relatedness of events.

Each component or subsystem of an entity is partially dependent on and partially independent of the entity of which it is a part. It is important, therefore, to distinguish between the interactions *within* components of a system on the one hand and the interactions *among* components on the other. For example, organ differentiation in fetal development is influenced by the fetus's general biological state which is a function of its uterine environment; but once organs have differentiated (e.g., kidneys, lungs) they will follow different developmental trajectories appropriate to their specialization. Simon (1969) asserts that intracomponent linkages are generally stronger than intercomponent linkages. This has the effect of separating the intracomponent "high-frequency dynamics of a hierarchy" from the intercomponent, "low-frequency dynamics" resulting in what he termed hierarchical organizations "with the property of near decomposability." Nearly decomposable systems are quite common. Simon says that far less typical are systems in which each variable is linked "with almost equal strength" with most other parts of the system.

For example, interactions *within cells* are much more intense and elaborate than *between cells*; intrapersonal processes are more complex than interpersonal processes. Boundaries function to both separate and link intra- and intercomponent processes. This means that any system can be decomposed (dissected) into its subsystems to some degree, and each subsystem can be examined as a semiautonomous unit in its own right (e.g., cells may be studied in vitro or in vivo). It is this organizational property which makes the reductionistic strategy of analytical science sensible. However, studying a component in isolation from its system eliminates information about the system and component-system interactions, and the component may manifest different properties within and without the system (Wilder, 1967). Moreover, for any system there may be alternate possible decompositions, and these may differ radically. For example, organizations may be divided by subproblems or products, subfunctions or processes, and so forth. These structural and functional subdivisions may be relatively unrelated, but still valid according to some set of criteria. Thus, there may be several different useful ways to "decompose" or subdivide human behavior for purposes of study.

This kind of hierarchical organization greatly simplifies coordination of the functioning of complex systems. A relatively simple signal (low frequency interaction) from the larger system can trigger a complex pattern of activity (high frequency interaction) within a component. For example, an executive can instruct a department to produce a certain product. She or he does not need to specify what each member of the department should do, when or where, or how each will relate to the others. The department is organized and trained to make those decisions and carry out those activities on its own. Similarly, when a person wants to throw a ball to someone else, the brain doesn't have to send specific instructions to each participating muscle fiber and sensory system. "Throwing a ball" appears to operate as a functional subunit of a total activity system, and a relatively simple signal (e.g., thought) appears sufficient to trigger a complicated unit of activity which, once triggered, is executed in a self-regulating pattern.

Thus, in such a hierarchical organization, nature utilizes the principles of division of labor, specialization, delegation of authority, and coordination to produce stable and efficient functioning of complex organizations (Koestler, 1967). Each subdivision should operate "as an autonomous, self-reliant unit" which, though subject to influence from other parts of the organization, must "take routine contingencies in its stride, without asking higher authority for instructions." Otherwise "communication channels would become overloaded," the whole organization "clogged up," the higher levels "kept occupied with petty detail" and apt to neglect more important factors. The partial solutions provided, as each subunit solves a subproblem effectively, combine to produce the solution of the overall task if all the units on different levels function properly (Mesarovic & Macke, 1969). The units higher in the hierarchy do not need detailed knowledge of the activities on the lower levels, and vice versa. They need only information about some relevant feature(s) of the subordinate unit's functioning. Complex operations can be regulated with simple feedforward and feedback signals.

Coordination and Integration. Differentiation and coordination of a "whole" into subordinate partial systems, while still retaining the "wholeness," imply an increase in the complexity of the system. This increased complexity requires a corresponding increase in the effectiveness of the coordination of the parts. Some "integral guidance" produces "coordination of the collective behavior of its parts" (Weiss, 1971). Thus *specialization* and *coordination* are coupled requirements in a complex system. Since increasing complexity requires increased coordination, it leads to an organizational property that von Bertalanffy (1968) labels *centralization*. Increasing complexity also involves increasingly specialized parts. However, the more specialized the parts are the more irreplaceable they become, and "loss of parts may lead to the breakdown of the total system." Therefore, with greater complexity and integration within the system, "the forces going vertically from the larger system to the smaller units" become more influential relative to "the increase in the forces going from the lower to the higher elements" (Gerard, 1969). Both the welfare of the whole and each of its parts depend upon careful integration of many specialized components. Thus, "the principle of progressive *centralization* also constitutes *progressive individualization*." A person may be thought of as "a centered system," which produces a "more unified and indivisible individual." Smith (1969) reaches a similar conclusion after analyzing inorganic systems. The process of *cephalization* in human embryonic development is a neurophysiological manifestation of the evolution of centralized coordination in complex systems.

Centralized coordination is a necessary antidote to the decrease in flexibility that results from the increased subsystem specialization. If each subsystem simply "did its own thing," anarchy and chaos would exist. Through centralized coordination, the functioning of the specialized components can be combined in a variety of ways to produce a diversity of results, simultaneously producing both efficiency and flexibility.

For example, early in embryonic development, embryonic tissue has a multipotential capacity to develop in a variety of directions depending upon the characteristics of its context. However, with each step in progressive specialization of cells, only a set of more limited options for future development remain and are rigidly prescribed. For example, if potential eye tissue from an amphibian embryo is later transplanted to an older embryo after it has become fully "determined"; it will become an eye whether it is transplanted to a host's back, belly, or thigh.

It follows that the functioning and developmental trajectory of every component or subsystem must be understood in relationship to its contexts, that is, to the larger hierarchies of which it is a part. From among multiple developmental possibilities of a component, the particular ones that blossom into realities will be the result of the interactions of the characteristics of that component in its current developmental state with the hierarchies to which it belongs, so that causality and hierarchical organization are interrelated (Ando et al., 1963). Hierarchical restructuring (e.g., Platt, 1970b) is probably an important facet of developmental processes (e.g., Piaget & Inhelder, 1973). Figure 2.1 illustrates the concept of an embedded hierarchy involving humans, and makes it clear that the selection of units of analysis for any problem should be a function of the hierarchical level(s) being studied.

ENVIRONMENT

System concepts such as *boundary, open and closed systems,* and *hierarchical organization* imply the importance of the idea of environment. An open system can be understood only in relationship to its necessary and actual environments. Trying to understand people's functioning separate from their contexts would be the same as treating them as closed systems.

The definition of environment requires identification of a specific system as the reference point; or, in gestalt terms, distinctions between figure

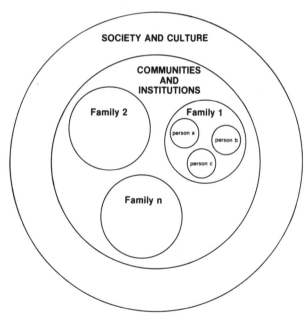

Fig. 2.1 An illustration of the concept of embedded hierarchies applied to living systems, indicating that different kinds of information are available at different levels of organization. For example, information about cell biology cannot be obtained by studying families, and information about communities cannot be obtained solely by studying individuals. Therefore, different disciplines have evolved as a result of focusing on different levels of living systems organization.

and ground can only be made relative to one another. Once a system is specified, its environment may be considered "the set of all objects a change in whose attributes affect the system" and "all objects whose attributes are changed" by the functioning of the system (Hall & Fagan, 1956). Specifying such an environment is not a trivial problem.

The typical scientific tactic is to try to identify those environmental characteristics that are most important for the scientist's purposes. Sorting out essential from nonessential environmental factors when studying living systems is particularly difficult. There are a diversity of ways of subdividing environments (Bronfenbrenner, 1977), and here again the choice in a particular instance is arbitrary but not capricious. It depends on which will best serve the purpose at hand. Since the existence of an open system depends on environmental transactions, some environmental aspects are always involved as components in an open system's functioning. Environmental components are also hierarchically organized, and the term *embeddedness* is sometimes used to refer to a unit's relationship to its contexts.

This view of environment-organism relationships has methodological as well as theoretical implications. For example, in the typical research design, environmental variables are usually considered the independent variables, and response variables the dependent variables. The reverse is equally legitimate. Behavior influences its environments (e.g., children influence parents and vice versa). However, what is needed is research designs which make it possible to treat both as interacting and simultaneously mutually influential variables. As subsystems within a common system (i.e., an individual-environment system) they exert both facilitating and constraining conditionalities on one another. Auger's (1980) attempt to mathematically represent a way of conceptualizing the functioning of each level in an N level system, and the coupling of the levels, may provide a starting point for a more formal theoretical representation of hierarchical systems.

SUMMARY

A living system has been identified as the model of organization most useful for understanding humans. Several of its characteristics have been considered. It has a material structure composed of an organization of physical components delineated by a recognizable boundary that distinguishes it from its context. It maintains and elaborates the stability and complexity of its physical organization through a continuous exchange of materials and energy with its environment.

The structural organization makes possible certain functions and functional organizations or activities, bounding but not strictly determining what the system may do in any set of circumstances. Among its most important distinguishing characteristics are its self-organizing, self-constructing capabilities. This type of functional system can be permanently affected by its informational transactions with its environments. Its functional organization is maintained, elaborated, and changed as a product of its transformation, recombination, and use of the information acquired through its processes of living. Its relevant environments are those things which it can or does affect or which can or do affect it. Its structural-functional organization is hierarchical, involving both facilitating and constraining conditionalities, such that subsystems function autonomously in some respects and as "team members" in others. The rigidity that can come with the specialization of components that accompanies increased complexity is compensated for by the increased flexibility that comes from the greater diversity of possible component combinations which result from increasing degrees of centralized coordination.

Rapoport (1970) describes three fundamental properties of all organismlike systems as follows: First, each has a physical structure composed of interrelated parts. Second, it maintains a "short term steady state" by reacting to changes in the environment in whatever way is required to maintain its identity—that is, it functions. Third, it undergoes slow, long-term changes; it grows, develops, or evolves—or else it degenerates, disintegrates, dies. All living systems have these three attributes: structure, function, and history; or, if you prefer, being, acting and becoming.[2] The next two chapters outline a way of understanding individual humans within this general framework. Chapter 3 describes a framework for understanding the structural and functional organization of individuals, that is, "being" and "acting." Chapters 4 and 5 describe an approach to understanding development or change, that is, "becoming."

---

[2]The similarity of these terms to those used in existential philosophy and psychotherapy, such as being, being-in-the-world, and becoming, is interesting. Psychotherapists, perhaps more than any others, have sought to observe, understand, and intervene in some aspects of a person as a functioning unit, and thus have struggled to develop conceptual frameworks to encompass that complexity. To paraphrase the question which guided Carl Rogers' theorizing, if people truly are as they appear in psychotherapy, then what kind of theory would best represent them? Rapoport's view hints at the potential bridge between these two streams of thought. The word "development" is a synonym for the word "becoming" in this sense.

3

The Person as a Self-Constructing Living System

INTRODUCTION

The purpose of this chapter is to apply a control system model of organization to understanding humans. The characteristics of control systems have been extensively studied and are well understood in the engineering sciences and technologies. Their utility has been demonstrated by their many technological uses (e.g., servomechanisms). However, to be applicable to humans, engineering control system models must be transformed by adding self-organizing and self-constructing properties, producing a model that distinguishes living systems from machines. Stated simply, humans may be understood as self-organizing, self-constructing, open, hierarchically organized control systems. The term *living system* is used as a short label for a system having all of those properties.

The conceptual framework presented here has some similarities to a view that is influential in Europe and Russia; it is called *action theory*, or the study of goal-directed action (GDA). It emphasizes "means-end structures" that emerge through the interaction of "goal-setting and rule-selection" processes, temporal and hierarchical organization, and regulation by feedback cycles (Kuhl & Beckman, 1985; von Cronach & Harrè 1982).

The notion of humans as self-constructing living systems is developed here in three stages. First, a *simple control system* model is described. Then a slightly more complex version, an *adaptive control system*, is illustrated. Next, it is proposed that the components of an adaptive control system are analogous to several types of human behavioral functions. But, to transform a control system into a living system, it is necessary to add the additional biological and behavioral self-organizing, self-constructing capabilities, that do not exist in engineering control systems. The result will be a framework within which a person can be understood as a structural-functional unit, that is, a living system. It will encompass all of the structures and response processes traditionally studied in biology and psychology, and will provide a framework for representing human personality and behavior from a developmental perspective.

THE CONTROL SYSTEMS MODEL

An engineering control system may be viewed as a special, limited case of a living system. The difference between it and a living system is that certain attributes that are permitted to vary in a living system are omitted or held constant in an engineering control system. As Simon (1969) put it, man-made systems may imitate living systems in their appearance and/or functioning "... while lacking the reality of the latter in one or many respects." Since living systems are the most versatile and adaptive of all known patterns of organization, however, the ability to imitate aspects of them has great practical value. Much is known about engineering control systems—how to design them for different purposes, how the different functions must interact, and how they work. This means that to some extent hypotheses about human functioning can be studied by simulating them in a control system model. Conversely, knowledge about how humans function may make it possible to build more complex and effective engineering control systems.

Simple Control Systems

Figure 3.1 is a generalized representation of a negative feedback control system, and provides the starting point for our discussion. It includes two additional characteristics (i.e., structure and energizing function) that are always implied but often omitted from such representations.

Structure-Being[1]. Some kind of physical structure is necessary to make possible the various functions of the system. Fundamentally, the

---

[1]The hyphenated captions—Structure-Being, Functions-Behaving, Change-Becoming— are used to relate the more general and abstract concept label to a concept label with more

structure must make possible some kind of activity and the collection and transmission of information to organize and coordinate that activity. A wall thermostat for a home heating system illustrates a control system component. One type is a case containing a coil of metal that is sensitive to temperature. The case has openings so that air in the room can circulate past the metal coil. If the air cools, the metal will contract; if the air grows warmer, it will expand. Through the metal's contraction and expansion, it opens and closes an electrical circuit sending patterns of electrical current to the heating unit "telling it" to turn on or off.

There are various kinds of structures that can be built to perform the same control function, but the functional design must be fundamentally the same; for example, any type of thermostat must be able to designate a desired room temperature, compare the existing with the desired temperature, and send signals to an action component that can act to influence the temperature. Such arrangements designed to exert control over some variable have existed for at least 300 years (Rubin, 1968), but it was the development of electronic theory and circuitry that made more elaborate and flexible control systems possible. Modern computers triggered an explosion of control system theory and technology after World War II, symbolized by the term *cybernetics*. The organizational principles of the functional design are the same in all control systems, although the supporting structural design can be quite different. Therefore, control system diagrams often omit a representation of structure. The border on Fig. 3.1 specifies but does not describe a necessary structure. If the structural organization is inappropriate (e.g., the metal in the thermostat is relatively insensitive to temperature changes), or breaks down (e.g., a wire in the electrical circuit becomes disconnected), the functions cannot be performed. The structure is sometimes called the "hardware" and the programs of information organizing the functional activity the "software."

The structure of an engineering control system is unchanging, except through deterioration or "wear and tear." The parts cannot get bigger or smaller, cannot repair or replace themselves, and cannot elaborate themselves by producing more or different parts. The interrelationships among the structural and functional components are fixed and cannot change. In other words, all components of the structure and their relationships are essentially "constants," as in any type of machine. Thus, living systems are distinguished from machines by the kinds of

---

human implications. People's existing bodily structures are their current state of being; their current functional capabilities represent their potential for behaving; their susceptibility to change represents their potential for becoming structurally or functionally different than they are at present.

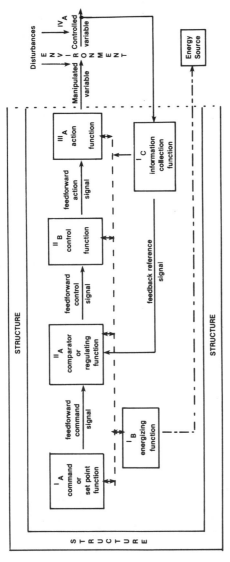

Fig. 3.1 A representation of a simple control system. Through some physical structure, a set of interrelated functions is made possible, organized to control some variable(s) in an appropriate environment. A desired consequence is specified (command or set point function, I_A), which organizes (control function II_B) action on a relevant environment (action functions III_A) to control the occurrence and/or value of some variable(s) reflecting the desired consequences (controlled variables IV_A). The status of the controlled variable(s) (or some correlate) is monitored (information collection function, I_C), and that information (feedback reference signal) is compared with (comparator or regulating function, II_A), the command signal. If the two are discrepant, an altered control signal initiates an adjustment in the rest of the system functioning to reduce the discrepancy between the command and feedback signals. Energy must be provided to fuel all of the other functions (energizing source, I_B). All of these functions are continuous and continuously interacting as long as the control system is in operation, so it functions as a coordinated unit. Components I_A, I_B, and I_C are frequently referred to as *input* functions. Components II_A and II_B are referred to as *throughput* functions. Components III_A and IV_A are termed *output* functions.

variability or changes that are possible in the organization and functioning of the entity.

Functions-Behaving. All control systems must have six interrelated functional capabilities which, through their interaction, can control some variable(s). Four of these functions, I_A, I_C, II_A, and II_B, have to do with information collection and use. Two of them, I_B and III_A, are involved with material and energy exchange processes.[2] It will be useful to consider each of these functions and their interrelationships, beginning with I_A on the left side of Fig. 3.1.

The *command function* (I_A) specifies some consequence that the functioning of the system is to produce. For example, if you set your wall thermostat at 70 degrees, that specifies an intended air temperature. That information is fed forward into a *comparator function* (II_A) where the intended consequence can be compared with the current status of the relevant variable(s) (e.g., the current room temperature is compared to the intended temperature). If they are different, information about the difference is fed forward to a *controlling function* (II_B) which can "select" a course of action that will reduce the difference (e.g., turning the heating plant on or off). Once a course of action is selected, a signal is sent to the *action function* (III_A) to trigger the appropriate course of action. The action occurs, operating on the *relevant environmental variable* (IV_A) (i.e., the air in the room being heated). There are always many things occurring in that environment. The *information collection function* (I_C) concentrates only on information that reflects the consequence or variable(s) to be controlled (i.e., the room temperature). There may be a variety of things happening to influence the controlled variable. For example, body heat dissipation, the warmth of electric lights, or cold air filtering in through window cracks or open doors may all be influencing the room temperature. But the control system need not monitor each of those influences, because their relevant effects will all be reflected in the variable being monitored (IV_A), (e.g., the air temperature in the room). Information concerning the current status of the monitored variable(s) is fed back (I_C) to the comparator function (II_A), where another comparison can be made leading to further control function adjustment. This cycle is a continuous process, doing what is necessary to maintain the status of the controlled variable(s) as close as possible to the intended status.

---

[2]It is possible to have a control system physically structured so that all functions are carried out directly and completely as a result of physical (e.g., biochemical) interactions. However, since our purpose is to illustrate some of the properties of a living system with a mechanical control system, those functions which can be information-based will be interpreted that way.

Every activity expends energy. Therefore, an *energy source* (I_B) must be available to fuel the functions (e.g., electricity). The role of an energy source in fueling system functions is indicated by connecting the energy source (I_B) with a dotted line to I_A, I_C, II_A, II_B, and III_A.

Classical machines differ from control systems in that they cannot vary their functioning as conditions within and around them vary. For a classical machine to "work," its designer must anticipate all potential conditions that might disrupt the machine's functioning, and build into the machine specific mechanisms to deal with, or protect the machine from, each potential disruption. By eliminating the functions labeled I_C, II_A, and IV_A, Fig. 3.1 can be converted into a representation of a classical machine. The addition of the information collection, feedback, and comparator functions elaborate the capabilities of a classical machine to those of a self-regulating system.

Beer (1964) has described the benefits of such a control system. It is always on duty, ever watchful, never distracted or sleeping. The basic principle is that some attribute of the output (i.e., the action and its consequences) is used as a part of the input controlling the functioning of the system (i.e., the feedback reference signal). This makes it possible for the activity of the system to influence its own future activity. It is self-controlling in that sense. This is very different from externally imposed types of control. Visualize, for example, a prison warden trying to keep a prisoner confined in the prison. Despite all the Warden's efforts to control him, the prisoner may escape (e.g., by bribing a guard). The "controller" and the "controllee" are interacting, but are not unalterably linked. In contrast, as Beer pointed out, in control systems the "controllee" cannot escape because any move towards freedom from constraint itself operates the controller. They are "inexorably coupled," and so the feedback controller cannot fail unless the structure itself breaks down. In humans, conflict between mechanisms of self-control and external (societal) control is a frequent source of personal and social difficulties (Rogers, 1951).

A related point is vital. As illustrated in the room temperature example, many factors may be influencing the variable being controlled. The control system will control against all extraneous influences, including random and unknown disturbances, so long as it can monitor and influence the variable(s) of concern. This simplifies matters greatly. Since in most complex situations all possible influences on the variable(s) to be controlled cannot be identified and monitored, a system that can control against complex patterns of many (often unknown) influences is the only practical solution.

A simple experiment by Powers (1978) is illustrative. He placed a person in front of a television screen onto which was projected an abstract figure whose form could be changed in many ways. The person was given a "controller," much like those that come with TV games. It could be manipulated to affect the shape of the figure on the screen. The person was asked to select a particular shape he or she liked and to maneuver the controller to maintain that shape—while unaware that Powers was inserting different kinds of electrical signals into the system to alter the shape of the figure, including random signals. Despite that, the person was able to manipulate the controller to maintain the selected shape. Directly controlling the states of the variable(s) of concern rather than trying to control all the influences on it is a simple, efficient solution to a complex, potentially insoluble problem! It is not necessary to know about all (or any) of the influences on the variable(s) of interest. It is only necessary to have an effective method for producing the desired consequences no matter what disrupting influences may be at work.

Kinds of Feedback Signals. One of the key ways in which the system's functioning can be varied is through the use of different kinds of feedback signals. In general, a signal must be selected that can be compared with the "command signal" of the system to detect discrepancies between the existing and intended states. This is sometimes referred to as the "error signal" criterion.

Many different kinds of feedback signals are possible, and different kinds provide different regulatory capabilities. The most obvious kind is a direct *measure* of the results sought, such as a measure of the existing room temperature that can be compared with the intended temperature. Sometimes a *correlate* of the result sought may be used, such as a measure of the consistency of some material which changes with temperature. A system may also be controlled on the basis of trajectories of change in the controlled variable. One way to do this is to monitor the *amount of change* of the relevant variable or some correlate thereof, instead of the actual amount of the variable. For example, a person could keep a bank account balanced, without actually knowing how much money was in the account, by regularly putting in as much money as he or she took out. A second way is to monitor the *rate of change* of the controlled variable. For instance, the rate of change of air temperature could be monitored and the heating system turned on before the air temperature dropped below a critical point, *in anticipation of the need* for more heat. A rate-of-change index has a special value because it enables one to *anticipate* a deficit (or surplus) before it occurs, and to take steps to avoid the development of an imbalance.

Kinds of Regulatory Interactions. Since it is the comparison between the command signal and the feedback signal that regulates the system's functioning, different kinds of relationships between the command and feedback signals can produce different consequences. There are two basic types, with variations possible within types. If the command signal and feedback signal differ, there will be a *discrepancy* of some kind between the two. One basic type of regulatory interaction results in the reduction of the discrepancy. The term *negative feedback* is used when a *discrepancy-reducing* comparison is regulating a system. A second basic type of consequence of regulatory interaction increases the deviation from steady states. The term *positive feedback* is used when *deviation amplification* is a consequence of the regulatory process.

Because there is often misunderstanding about the meaning of the terms *positive* and *negative feedback,* it is necessary to emphasize that it is not the *nature* of the feedback reference signal itself that is positive or negative. The terms only designate the nature of the comparison process. This misunderstanding is illustrated in the different uses of the terms in common language. For example, a person may say "My boss is giving me a lot of positive feedback," or "I'm getting a lot of negative feedback about the proposals I made." That usage refers to an attribute of the feedback reference signal rather than to the nature of the regulatory comparison. In a sense, it reverses the meanings; that is, positive appraisal from the boss is what is wanted (deviation-reducing) and negative appraisal is what is not wanted (deviation-amplifying). As will be discussed in more detail later, negative feedback (deviation-reducing) arrangements contribute to the stability of systems (sometimes termed *morphostasis)* while positive feedback (deviation-amplifying) arrangements contribute to variability and change in systems (sometimes termed *morphogenesis)* (Buckley, 1967; Maruyama, 1963).

Most discussions of control systems concentrate on negative (stability producing) feedback arrangements. Cannon's (1939) influential concept of homeostasis is an application of a negative feedback model. Since the maintenance of stability is critical for the continued existence of living systems, many attempts to apply a control system model to living systems concentrate solely on negative feedback arrangements. However, without the concept of positive feedback, a control system model cannot adequately account for the growth and development that are fundamental to living systems (R. Lerner, 1984).

Many kinds of *negative feedback* (deviation-reducing) comparisons are possible, just as a diversity of types of feedback reference signals are possible. The most obvious possibility is a comparison aimed at reducing the deviation to zero. Examples of other possibilities include the following: (a) producing an average of zero deviation; (b) keeping the deviation within some range of an average; (c) regulating the deviation around some *floating* average (e.g., an average derived from activity of the most recent three days). Different types and combinations of feedback signals and regulatory comparisons will produce different control possibilities.

The element of time must be considered in the operation of negative feedback arrangements. A deviation-correcting action takes time to affect the monitored variable; time is needed for information concerning that change to be fed back for comparison. The deviation-reducing activity continues until it is signaled to stop. As a result it may "overshoot" by some amount the intended value of the controlled variable. Similarly, "undershooting" may occur because a discrepancy may continue to increase during the time it takes for the system's actions to produce the intended effects.

In addition, many other conditions that may affect the monitored variable (e.g., room or body temperature) are continually varying. As a result, other factors in addition to the action of the system continue to disrupt the system's attempt to reduce the discrepancy. For these and other reasons, negative feedback systems in the natural world are always oscillating back and forth around some "set point"; that is, they are always some distance from actual equilibrium. Yet there is a stability to those oscillations. There are boundaries beyond which they do not fluctuate because a negative feedback arrangement will dampen the fluctuations as they approach the boundaries, reducing the discrepancy that has developed. A pendulum illustrates how there may be oscillations that, despite their movement, provide a stable pattern. When a system displays stability, while still displaying fluctuating variability within boundary conditions, it is said to be in a *steady state* or in a *dynamic equilibrium*. This kind of "nonequilibrium" stability (an arrangement Prigogine, 1978, has termed *order through fluctuation)* may be found in many kinds of systems, but is especially characteristic of living systems. They are a little unbalanced, but still stable (like me and most of my friends). That is why Cannon (1939) used the term *homeostasis* rather than equilibrium: Equilibrium means balanced, at rest. Homeostasis refers to a condition "... which may vary, but which is relatively constant."

Positive feedback (deviation-amplifying) comparison processes are also pervasive throughout nature, but they have received less attention. Maruyama (1963) suggests that this is because cybernetics, the anchoring point for the post-World War II development of control systems, focused on stability-producing, deviation-counteracting feedback arrangements. As a result, the misunderstanding sometimes exists that control systems can and do function with only negative feedback arrangements.

In general, in positive feedback some consequence of the system's activity is fed back into the system in a way that increases rather than decreases the deviation from a specified condition or steady state. For example, imagine you are driving a car in which you do not know that the brake pedal is hooked to the accelerator. You see a police car with a radar scope parked ahead. You step on the brake pedal to slow down so you won't get a ticket. However, since your brake pedal is attached to the accelerator, stepping on the brake causes the car to speed up. So you step on the brake harder, the car goes even faster, which leads you to press harder on the brake, which increases your speed even further. Your actions are increasing the deviation of your actual speed from your desired speed. What will happen? There are three possibilities. First, unchecked positive feedback (deviation amplifying) regulatory consequences will lead to disruption and perhaps destruction of the system (e.g., you will wreck the car and perhaps kill yourself). Second, a negative feedback regulation may be coupled to the positive one to control the extent or rate of deviation amplification. Third, at some critical level of deviation (some "boundary condition") the system may reorganize itself into a somewhat different system to accommodate the effects of the disruptive positive deviation (e.g., as in a James Bond movie, after the car reaches 100 miles an hour it may sprout wings, turn into an airplane, and fly away). Ashby (1956) describes an amplifier as a device that "... if given a little of something will emit a lot." Technological amplifiers are commonplace (e.g., sound amplifiers). Amplifying as well as attenuating functions appear in many neural and biochemical physiological processes. DeGreene (1970) points out that the release of epinephrine by the adrenal glands helps enhance the action of the sympathetic nervous system by a positive feedback mechanism. Tomkins (1962) has suggested that emotions perform amplifying and attenuating functions through positive and negative feedback arrangements. Since the function of negative feedback is to maintain stability, change or development in humans must involve deviation producing or positive feedback arrangements. Something must disrupt existing stabilities if new capabilities are to develop.

Several examples will illustrate the concept of positive feedback (see also Milsum, 1968). Consequences may feed upon themselves even in entities that are not control systems. For example, visualize a boulder with a small crack on its surface. The crack collects water; the water freezes and expands, enlarging the crack. The larger crack collects and retains water, small organisms live in the water, and organic matter begins to collect in the crack. Plants take root in the organic matter, the growth of their roots applying further pressure to the expansion of the crack. This deviation-amplifying process will continue until the boulder breaks into pieces. The activity that is made possible by the crack (the collection of water and organic material) exerts an effect (enlarging the crack) that increases the activity which produced the effect in the first place. When a process and its consequences are continually amplified by the effects of their own activity, the essence of the concept of positive feedback is present. Profound later effects can result from small initial ones (Tomkins, 1963).

A person's thought processes can display this property. For example, some persons may fear that others evaluate them as incompetent in a particular role. As a result they become more likely to selectively notice other instances which imply appraisals of incompetence. That results in an accumulation of evidence to elaborate the idea that they are considered incompetent in other roles as well. As that idea becomes strengthened, it exerts further selective influence on what events will be paid attention to and how these events are interpreted. Thus, through a positive feedback process the selective activity influenced by a person's hypothesis of incompetence functions to elaborate the scope and influence of that self-appraisal. It becomes a self-fulfilling prophecy.

Deviation amplifying processes have been a part of economic theory for a long time. For example, there is the principle that the larger the amount of capital, the more rapid the ratio of its increase; that is, the rich get richer. In chemistry, autocatalytic and cross-catalytic processes may function as positive feedback mechanisms. Evolutionary theory also involves deviation-amplifying processes. An organism develops with characteristics somewhat different than others of its species, characteristics that give it a survival and reproductive advantage. Its advantaged offspring pass along that advantage to their offspring, and so on until a large population of that kind of organism results.

Embryonic development involves rapid cell division and elaboration which probably occurs, at least in part, as a result of positive feedback processes. A cancerous growth is a biological process manifesting positive feedback. Normal cell growth and differentiation in adults is limited by boundary conditions built into the genetic history and current structural-functional organization of the individual. One hypothesis about cancer is that something (e.g., a virus) affects cell processes in such a way that cell division mechanisms essential for embryonic development are reactivated to function in some distorted way, "snowballing" into an out-of-control growth process.

Combinations of Negative and Positive Feedback. The simple control system represented in Fig. 3.1 is the kind of unit Miller, Galanter, and Pribram (1960) suggested as a replacement for the reflex arc as the basic unit of behavioral analysis, that is, a TOTE unit. The simplest kind of control system is designed to specify only one option in each component: one command signal, one regulatory comparison, one control capability (e.g., on-off), one action capability, and one feedback reference signal. However, a great diversity of control possibilities could be devised by combining different options in each component. Miller et al. (1960) proposed that more complex behavior is created by combining different kinds of simple control (or TOTE) units in various ways. For example, a positive feedback unit might be combined with a negative feedback unit to produce variability (deviation) from some steady state, while limiting the deviation to keep the organism from destroying itself. For example, a person may actively seek stimulation, excitement, or "thrills." However, if such activity were to continue uninterrupted, that person could become exhausted and die. In humans, stimulation and activity-seeking "needs" appear to be coupled to rest and sleep "needs" so that each serves to limit the functioning of the other. Maruyama (1963) has illustrated the coupling of variables in positive and negative feedback arrangements in a mutual causal process as they may influence the growth of a community.

Simple control systems are designed to function in one way, and they will always function that way. However, it is possible to design a control system whose functioning is more flexible and can be modified by its own performance experience. Such adaptive control systems will be described next.

Adaptive Control Systems

Figure 3.2 summarizes the characteristics of an adaptive control system that can differ from a simple control system in two important ways. First, more than one option may be built into each of its component functions. This produces a more elaborate and flexible functional capability. Second, it may have an information-processing capability which enables it to use information resulting from its present functioning to permanently alter its future behavior capabilities.

Adaptation Through Multiple Options. The first difference between adaptive and simple control systems can be illustrated by imagining the functioning of a complex guided missile. Such a missile has a physical structure that enables it to fly through the air efficiently. It has a power plant that can provide variable amounts of energy to power its flight and energize its other functions. It has structural components that can be adjusted to alter its flight pattern. It has structures that can collect and/or use information.

Consider first the *command function.* It may emit several command signals simultaneously. One command may be to "hit the hot spot," for example, the exhaust of the engine of the target plane. A second

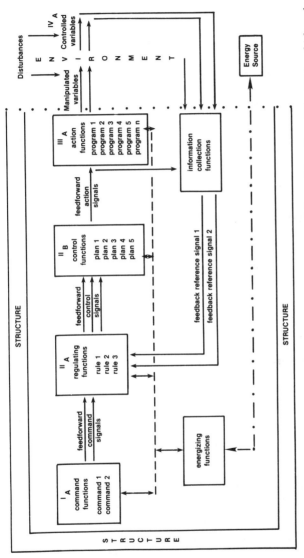

FIG. 3.2. A representation of a simple, adaptive control system. It is an elaboration of Fig. 3.1 in which each component function has more than one option built into it. The system is more adaptive because it can produce more combinations of different functions as a result of the multiple options built into each component. That enables it to simultaneously pursue more than one consequence and to effectively cope with more environmental variables while doing so. A system operating under multiple simultaneous commands must also have multiple regulatory and feedback reference signals simultaneously operating.

command might be to avoid being hit by a defensive missile aimed at it. Multiple commands require a more complex *regulatory function.* Both commands may be regulated by negative feedback comparison rules. However, the rules may be in competition with each other. If the missile takes evasive action it will deviate from its target. If it heads directly for its target, it may get shot down. Therefore, another comparison rule dealing with the relationship between the two may be necessary; for example, there might be a rule to give priority to evasive action while keeping the deviation from the target as small as possible. The *control function* needs a variety of flight plan alternatives from which it can select depending upon the conditions of flight. It may have to vary its speed, flight angle, direction, or altitude to accommodate changing flight conditions, changes in the flight pattern of the target, or changes in the flight pattern of a defensive missile. The *action function* must be able to perform various combinations of maneuvers, or programs of behavior, in different sequences depending upon the flight plans implemented. It must be possible to quickly vary the *energizing function* or the engine thrust to change speed. The *information collection function* must monitor variables relevant to both commands and provide two or more *feedback reference signals* to serve the multiple comparisons necessary in the regulatory function. In other words, to implement more than one command simultaneously, or to have multiple alternatives for implementing a command, the system requires a more complex and flexible behavioral repertoire in each of its functions and in relationships among functions. As Miller, Galanter and Pribram (1960) proposed, it may be an organization of component TOTE units. In that sense, it is more adaptive than a simple control system.

Such adaptive control systems are increasingly present in the "automation" revolution. Examples include the guidance and environmental control systems on spacecrafts, many different types of control systems for industrial processes, chess-playing computer programs, and a mechanical turtle that explores its environment and periodically returns to its "nest" to recharge its batteries.

However, such control systems are still only complicated versions of classical machines. They can only do what their designers designed them to do in the contexts for which they are designed. They cannot change themselves in any way. If they meet circumstances that their designer did not anticipate, and therefore did not program them for, they cannot adapt. Obviously, the more elaborately the "designer" can design functional patterns of information and rules to guide such a control system, the more complex will be the functions the system can perform. Computer equipment (hardware) is increasingly capable of handling more and more complicated programs. Most experts agree that the major bottleneck to elaborating the use of computers to perform more complex control system functions is the difficulty of developing the programs of information and instruction to guide them (*Science*, 1982).

Adaptation Through Self-Programming. Obviously, a multiply programmed control system would be even more adaptive if, as a result of its interaction with the environments in which it operates, it could write its own informational programs to guide its functioning. Rather than the designer having to try to anticipate all of the possible circumstances under which the control system might operate, it would only be necessary to start it off with rules for writing its own programs. Then it could become adaptive in any range of environments suited to its structural and functional potentials (i.e., its environmental niche).

Efforts to do exactly that are under way. For example, a mechanical rat was designed so that it could find its way through a maze from a starting point to some end point or goal box. The first time through the "rat" used trial and error procedures; that is, it was programmed to keep trying until it got there. However, after it successfully completed the maze once from starting point to goal box using trial and error procedures, it could traverse the maze correctly and quickly thereafter. It had "learned" how to run that maze. Or, one might say, it had "written its own program" for coping effectively with that particular environment. Researchers in artificial intelligence are making progress towards designing computer software that makes feasible some degree of self-programming of computers through experience. Robotics is a new engineering science that is likely to produce advances of this kind.

Feedforward

When people think of control systems, *feedback* is the term most likely to come to mind. However, it has a serious limitation. Feedback reflects only the present moment. The information in the feedback reference signal only "tells" the control system what has just happened or is happening. It enables a system to react to circumstances *after* they occur. It does not tell it what is likely to happen next. That is not a great problem if the control system does not have to deal with a variable environment. If the circumstances of the future are likely to be nearly identical with those of the present, then knowing about the present is sufficient for organizing and guiding the system's functioning. However, if the future is likely to be different in some relevant way from the present, then acting solely on the basis of information about the present may well be nonadaptive, or even maladaptive. Since there is always some time lag between feedback and the action that follows from it, by the time the action occurs it may already be out of date. Because of that, action based on feedback alone would be action guided solely by the past. In a highly variable environment, "current news" quickly becomes "old news."

For a control system to be adaptive in a variable environment, it must be able to combine "current news" with "old news" to predict "future news." That ability would enable it to act not only in terms of what *has* happened, but in terms of what *is likely* to happen. It could behave in terms of future possibilities, as well as current and past realities. It could anticipate as well as react. If the future is a simple linear function of the past, then prediction is easy. However, it is often more complicated than that, particularly if the control system is pursuing multiple objectives simultaneously. The most adaptive control systems, then, would be those with the greatest capacity to efficiently and effectively combine information about the past and present to accurately predict the future, and therefore to most effectively produce the results towards which its functioning is directed. Feedforward makes that possible. It is a method of control in which disturbances influencing the output and input variables are *anticipated*, and that information is used to generate compensating activity. Knowledge of the dynamics of the system's processes is necessary to achieve the correct anticipatory compensation (Meethan, 1969).

The control system models represented in Figs. 3.1 and 3.2 have this potential in their design. It is represented by the arrows leading from II_A to II_A to II_B to III_A.

Stated in everyday language, the command function says, "OK fellows, this is the result I want. Get organized so that you can produce it." The regulatory function says "This is how we will decide when the result has been achieved. This is where we seem to be now in relationship to the desired result. You people in control get busy and figure out what can be done and how to do it to produce the results the commander wants. However, not all possible courses of action are acceptable. Only those that meet the following design criteria will be OK. We'll be monitoring the results and will let you know how things are going." The control function says "What have we done in the past that has produced those kinds of results? What are the present circumstances under which we're going to have to achieve those results? Which of the actions that worked in the past are likely to work under the present circumstances? Which of those actions adequately fit the limiting design criteria specified by the people in the regulating division? Let's pick action program seven. OK, you guys in the power plant get iready to give us the energy we're going to need. You guys over in nformation collection watch for the following kinds of information that we'll need to guide and monitor this effort. You guys in the action function get yourselves prepared to move!"

Notice that all of the activities characterized in this fictitious dialogue are future oriented. They are informed by past and present circumstances to enable them to carry out their functions against probable future conditions to produce desired future results. This kind of activity—involving preparation for action against expected contingencies in order to produce specified results—is, in control systems jargon, represented by the term *feedforward*. Feedback says "This is what *has just* happened or *is* happening now." Feedforward says "This is what *may* happen, and what we *want to* happen, and this is what we will do to try to produce the results we want under these expected circumstances." When feedback and feedforward are combined, a dynamic control system potential emerges that *can combine information about past, present, and projected future events to guide the flow of its current* activity *in a variable environment to either maintain or alter its current steady states.*

Such arrangements produce an advance in adaptive capabilities that is of dramatic importance. Feedback arrangements make it possible to react to events after they have occurred. However, that may be too late. For example, after one is hit and killed by a car, feedback is of no use. The capability for organizing behavior in anticipation of probable events produces a proactive as well as a reactive system. Stated in human terms, feedforward processes are a cornerstone of purposive behavior.

Closed and Open Loops. The kind of arrangement summarized in Fig. 1 is sometimes referred to as a *closed loop*, in that information flows in a "circle," or functioning is organized in repetitive cycles of activity. However, systems people also talk about *open loop* arrangements which can be explained by referring to Fig. 3.1. If the information collection function (I_C) and the feedback reference signal were omitted, then only the feedforward-action components of the system would remain. That is an open loop. It represents a component in which, once the implementation of a program of action begins, the entire program of action runs off as designed without regard to, or benefit of, any correcting or adjusting feedback. Some behavioral components appear to function as open loops, as is illustrated later when motor behavior is discussed. Classical machines are open loop arrangements.

It is curious that the concepts of feedforward and positive feedback have received so little attention in attempts to use a control system model to understand human functioning. The functions are there in all control systems, as illustrated in Figs. 3.1 and 3.2. In some machines, feedforward may be overlooked because it is a constant rather than a variable; that is, the instructions and preparations for action are always the same. A classical machine differs from a control system in that all of the components and their "connections" are fixed (i.e., are constants rather than variables). Such a machine will always do the same things in the same ways regardless of varying conditions. A classical machine takes on the properties of a simple control system when it can vary some of what it does as a function of varying conditions within and around it, and yet accomplish the same result. The more it can vary the pattern of its functioning, vis-a-vis its contexts, the more adaptive a control system it becomes. Therefore, a classical machine may be thought of as a special or limited case of a control system.

Linear Causality and Dynamic Systems. There may be a more fundamental reason why feedforward aspects of control systems have been underemphasized. The basic assumptions that have dominated scientific thinking for several centuries have rejected the possibility that the "future" could influence the "present." The dominant concept of time that humans use is linear, it goes in only one direction. Classical determinism requires that all action be understood as a consequence of previous or antecedent events. All units are considered reactive. Teleological thinking is unacceptable. Even Man is a machine.

Rapoport (1968) summarizes the logic of classical determinism for inferring causality. Given two kinds of events, A and B, A may "cause" B or B may "cause" A but they cannot "cause" one another because that would mean that an event was a "cause" of itself. This follows from the transivity of causality which implies that if A causes B and B causes C, then A is also a cause of C. Therefore, if A causes B and B causes A, then A is a cause of A which "... contradicts the denial of self-causality."

Recognizing this logical construction to be "man-made" rather than a "natural law" permits consideration of other alternatives. Rapoport (1968) asserts that the development of the concept of *continuum* in mathematics is such an alternative. Viewing the world as "... a collection of mutually exclusive classes" is adequate for a static theory, describing something "as it is." However, it is inadequate for describing the "flux of interdependent events"; that is, for understanding dynamics. That requires being able to describe the flow of events and their interrelationships with reference to time. The invention of analytical geometry and calculus in the 17th century, utilizing the notion of mathematical functions of time, made that possible.

Time itself is not a cause. The values of some variables change over time because the values of other variables change. Variables are interrelated in a process, that is, a pattern of interactions that may be indexed by time. As Rapoport puts it, "... all of the variables are interrelated in 'mutual causality.' " For example, thought processes influence brainbiochemistry and brain biochemistry influences thought processes. If one "slices into" the process at some point, the "slice" can be designed to reveal whether A (e.g., thought processes) "causes" a change in B (e.g., brain biochemistry). A different "slice" of the same process could reveal whether B "causes" A to change. Living systems must be understood as an organization of interdependent variables interacting in mutually influential processes. It is not a "one-way street"; traffic flows in both directions. The classical mechanistic formulation of linear cause-effect relationships, S(timulus) → R(esponse), would be more accurately represented as patterns of mutually influential events flowing through a space-time continuum.

To study or to change a living system it is not necessary to ask what is the "real" cause, but only what variables are accessible to manipulation and how their manipulation might influence the network of causal relationships among the variables that compose the relevant pattern of functioning. The importance of positive feedback arrangements is that they function to alter the parameters and patterns of relationships among a set of variables rather than to maintain the status quo. A small deviation from the status quo may become amplified into a major change through positive feedback processes. Only events that are contiguous in a space-time (SP-T) continuum can influence one another. The past does not influence the present nor the present the future. Only the present influences the present. However, if events are viewed as patterns of organization, dynamically varying in a space-time continuum, the the pattern at SP-T_2 must have evolved from its antecedent pattern at SP-T_1. Since space-time is a continuum, adjacent states of a pattern are contiguous and therefore related. One very important implication of this more dynamic view is that the human sciences must emphasize, far more than they have in the past, research designs and forms of mathematical analysis which can capture the patterned flow of mutually influential events in a space-time continuum. The natural sciences have been moving towards this broader view of determinism or causality, as have some behavioral scientists (Brand, 1976; Cook & Campbell, 1979; Meehl, 1977). Yet old assumptions die hard. They are embedded so deeply in a culture's language and habits of thought (including those of scientific cultures) that they often affect theorizing and action even in ways of which the individuals involved are unaware. Thus, the concept of negative feedback as the significant process in control systems was acceptable because it fit certain historically dominant assumptions that humans function as reactive machines. It is probable that less attention has been given to the future-oriented function of feedforward, and the change-oriented function of positive feedback, because they do not easily fit a machine metaphor and a classical deterministic model. We tend to see what we look for, and not to see other things, even when they are there.

But the mechanistic strategy has not worked completely. There *are* other phenomena there—they have always been there. They have simply been ignored or "controlled" out of existence as scientists studied humans. It is impossible to have a control system which does not utilize both feedback and feedforward processes. It is impossible to have a self-changing system unless positive (deviation amplifying—variability producing) and negative (deviation reducing—stability producing) feedback regulation are coupled. As we will try to demonstrate later in this book, it is the enhancement of feedforward and positive feedback processes that provide the key to making a human the most complex, adaptive control system that has yet emerged from evolutionary processes.

A CONTROL SYSTEM TRANSFORMED INTO A LIVING SYSTEM

We have not yet fully described a living system. Something fundamentally important is missing. A living system, specifically a human being, is self-organizing (Jantsch, 1980) and autopoietic or self-constructing (Zeleny, 1981). Yates and Iberall (1973) provide a succinct definition: "Living systems are autonomous, nonlinear, dissipative, active, open, thermodynamic systems that persist, adapt, evolve, reproduce, and construct themselves. In a number of complex ways, they are hierarchical in both structure and function" (p. 17). These authors characterize structure as organization in space, and function as organization in time, and emphasize their interdependence. Structure makes possible and preserves processes or functions, which in turn make possible and preserve structure.

These qualities manifest themselves in both the biological and behavioral processes of living systems. Therefore, to transform an adaptive control system to a living system, capabilities must be added for constructing, elaborating, and repairing the biological structures composing the system (i.e., its "hardware"); and for constructing, elaborating, and revising its behavioral repertoire (i.e., its "software"). It must become self-organizing and self-constructing in both a biological and behavioral sense in a space-time continuum. Other attempts to apply cybernetics models to represent human functioning have been appropriately criticized (e.g., Bandura, 1982b) because they are still machine-like in their functioning. Using his own terms, Bandura also emphasizes humans' self-organizing and self-regulatory characteristics. His conceptualization of humans is becoming increasingly similar to a living systems model (see Bandura, 1986).

Biological Self-Construction and Self-Organization

Biological processes are a function of material and energy exchanges between the individual and the environment and between biological components within the individual. Primarily through eating, drinking, and breathing, materials that are essential for all other functions are ingested into the body. Through self-constructing, self-organizing biological processes, those materials are decomposed, reorganized into new combinations, and used to build, maintain, and repair biological structures and to produce energy to fuel activity. For example, a single human cell is a complex production system. It produces and synthesizes various types of macromolecules such as proteins, lipids, and enzymes. It consists of about 10^5 macromolecules that are renewed about 10^4 times during a cell's lifetime. Yet despite this staggering change in its physical makeup, a cell retains a stable existence. Not only does it produce specific material components, but in so doing it also produces itself.

Living systems create their biological existence by differentiating increasingly complex components and organization from an initial simple structure, and maintain and repair those components that already have been constructed. This massive process continues throughout life. Through a process of cellular proliferation and division, trillions of cells of about 100 different types are constructed and replaced to form the adult organism. Every 24 hours approximately one percent of a person's cells are discarded and renewed, with different tissues renewing at different rates (Timiras, 1972). All of this is orchestrated primarily by internal "rules of the game" built into us genetically through evolutionary processes, as long as the process takes place in an appropriate environmental niche. In addition, biological processes generate energy in varying amounts to fuel all the functions of the system. They also excrete waste products that result from the biological functions and that could poison or destroy the system (i.e., in a sense, they excrete entropy).

Thus, biologically, humans are dissipative structures (Prigogine & Stengers, 1984). Instead of slowly disintegrating until they reach a stable equilibrium ("ashes to ashes, dust to dust"), they are able to do the opposite until they die. They become physically bigger, more elaborate, more complex. A single individual (or cell), selectively taking materials from the rest of the universe, converting them to its use, and selectively discarding the unwanted by-products, constructs a complex metropolis. This highly organized "city" of cells is composed of trillions of "individuals," and innumerable complexes of "factories" and "warehouses," networks of "transportation" and "communication," and systems of "waste disposal." Every person is such a metropolis, composed of diverse yet cooperative and mutually interdependent cells. In turn, the by-products of each person are used by other parts of the universe. It might be said that what is entropy to one organism is negentropy to another. One organism's "junk" is another's "treasure."

Moreover, such living systems generate their own energy rather than having to rely on an external energy source such as an electric power generator. Metabolic processes convert material into energy analogous to a power plant burning coal or oil to produce electricity. Such internal energy-generating capabilities give living systems far greater functional flexibility and autonomy.

Behavioral Self-Construction and Self-Organization

The elaboration and organization of behavior patterns result from information exchange and processing functions analogous to biological self-construction through material-energy exchange processes. The infant enters this world with a very limited set of "built-in" behavior patterns (e.g., sucking; sensory-motor reflexes). This primitive behavioral repertoire elaborates into the complex cognitive-emotional-sensory-motor repertoire of the adult. Observers come to know and create their environment through interactions with it (Uribe, 1981).

Information is a concept as fundamental as material and energy (see Chapter 8 for further discussion of the concept of information). It is always conveyed on some medium of material or energy, but it is not the medium itself. A simple example will illustrate this point. A person says to you, "I love you." The speech sets up a pattern of air pressure between that person's mouth and your ears (material medium one). That pressure causes your eardrums to vibrate (material medium two). Those vibrations jiggle some little bones in your ear (material medium three). That jiggling sets up some wave motions in the liquid of your inner ear (material medium four). The wave motion wiggles some little hairlike projections in your inner ear (material medium five). The wiggling triggers reactions in neurons connected to those hairlike projections (material medium six). An electro-chemical exchange takes place across a synapse connecting those neurons to others (material medium seven). That electro-checmical exchange is repeated many times within your brain until you "hear" the words "I love you."

How can that something go from air pressure waves to vibrations to jiggles to wave motions to wiggles to electro-chemical flows and still remain the same? Despite seven (or more) material transformations, the information remains invariant. That is because the information is contained in the *pattern of organization of the material medium* on which it is carried. It can be transformed from one medium to another and yet the pattern of organization can remain invariant, regardless of the medium. It is this fact that makes modern communication technology possible. Of course, information and meaning are not the same concepts. The words "I love you" are information. What they mean to you when spoken by another person depends on the context in which they occur, and the thoughts and reactions they elicit in you (see Chapters 8 and 9).

A person's sensory mechanisms and nervous system provide the material-energy mediums for information collection, organization and transformation, storage, and use. The human brain is the material-energy *structure* that makes possible the information processing *function*, although the structure and the function are not the same thing. Neither can be reduced to the other, but they are mutually interdependent. Without continual information flow (or *stimulus nutriment*, to use a term analogous to the continuous flow of material-energy nutriments necessary for the biological functions), the physical structure of the nervous system will atrophy. If the physical structure is damaged, information processing will be blocked or distorted. "Mind" (information transformation and use) and "body" (material-energy transformation and use) are basically different—but mutually interdependent—phenomena which are linked by invariant forms of organized functioning. The historic mind-body problem can be seen in a new light with this formulation, which is similar to the views recently presented by Pribram (1986).

Just as with biological functions, each human enters this world with some inborn potentials for processing information that are the result of our evolutionary history, and which will become functional if the fetus and infant develop in appropriate environmental conditions. By applying these capabilities, people gradually build informational representations that can be used to organize and guide their other functions. Thus, just as we construct, elaborate, maintain, and repair our physical bodies through material and energy transactions with our environment and through biological processes, so too do we construct, elaborate, maintain, and revise our repertoire of behavioral patterns through information transactions with our environment and through using information-processing capabilities. To make an analogy in computer jargon, humans construct, maintain, repair, and operate their own "hardware," and design, revise, store, and selectively use their own "software"; but this occurs within structural-functional boundaries that have emerged from evolutionary processes in typical terrestrial environments, and to some extent from individual developmental processes.

It doesn't take very many different kinds of processing rules to create a huge number of options. Koestler (1967) encompasses this idea with the simple terms "fixed rules" and "flexible strategies." By that he means that a set of developmental or behavioral boundaries or influences (e.g., genetic organization; rules of reasoning or problem solving) can lead to a diversity of biological or behavioral outcomes. Sociobiologists (e.g., Wilson, 1975) provide illustrations of such interactions in various organisms. For example, a bird called the Chaffinch develops a characteristic courtship song when it grows up with other Chaffinches. However, if raised in isolation and exposed to recordings of a "wrong" courtship song, they will develop a "wrong" song. However, their "wrong" song will have the same general structure or pattern as the "correct" courting song. There appears to be a predisposition (i.e., "fixed rules") that guides their song development, but they may actually develop a diversity of versions of the song, each of which manifests the predisposition in a somewhat different way (i.e., "flexible strategies"), depending on the courtship songs they hear while they are growing up. Analogously, Skinnerians refer to "rule-governed" behavior, in which the action elements may vary but the pattern manifests organizing "rules."

It is possible to construct many variations of behavior patterns starting with inborn information-processing capabilities (e.g., perceptual and remembering processes). Moreover, it is probable that these initial capabilities are elaborated through experience. Living systems, then, have special functional capabilities through which they continuously renew themselves, and regulate this process in such a way that their structural-functional integrity is maintained (Jantsch, 1980). Machines are designed to "output" products. Their input controls their output. Living systems are primarily concerned with renewing and elaborating themselves in their contexts. Their "output" controls their "input."

Living systems require a kind of organization or structure quite different from stable equilibrium structures that involve no energy or informational flow. Jantsch (1980) proposes that "dissipative structures" (as described in Chapter 2), through their ability to construct and maintain their own characteristics through exchanges with their environments, make possible self-organization and self-production. They provide a "self-organizing dynamic order" which can maintain itself "through continuous exchange of energy with the environment," that is, "through maintaining a metabolism." They arise under conditions that are far from equilibrium. Unlike equilibrium structures (e.g., crystals), they find and maintain their "optimal size" and establish a "certain autonomy from the environment." Jantsch asserts that "only a cyclical organization of processes" can maintain nonequilibrium indefinitely; and autopoiesis, or self-construction, requires such nonequilibrium. Similarly, Yates and Iberall (1973) conclude that life must be characterized by periodic processes and that the basic element of temporal organization is the limit cycle.

Thus, by combining the properties of adaptive control systems with material and information processing capabilities to maintain and elaborate themselves and to fuel and organize action, living systems such as humans can be characterized as dynamic, self-organizing and self-constructing, structural-functional entities.

HUMAN'S STRUCTURAL-FUNCTIONAL
ORGANIZATION

We have described the essential characteristics of control systems. They are (a) an appropriate structure and (b) a variable energy source, which make possible functions that can (c) direct, regulate, and control the (d) action and (e) information-collection capabilities of the system, using (f) feedback and feedforward processes, to (g) selectively produce relevant consequences from an appropriate but variable environment. By adding self-constructing, self-organizing biological and behavioral processes, based on capabilities for selecting, transforming, and using material and information, we transform an engineering control system into a living system. Such a living system doesn't just react to "inputs" to produce "outputs" (though it can and sometimes does do that). It also selects specific kinds of material, energy, and information ("inputs"); transforms and utilizes them to construct, elaborate, maintain, and operate itself ("throughputs"); and initiates selective transactions with its environments ("outputs") to produce the specific kinds of information, material, and energy that it needs and wants ("inputs"). Machines react. In them, input controls output, or behavior is controlled by its consequences. People act as well as react. In them, output functions to control input. Behavior functions to control its consequences.

The basic assumption being proposed is that an adaptive control system, supplemented by the biological and behavioral self-constructing, self-organizing functions, provides a general structural-functional model through which the general categories of human characteristics and behaviors that have been the focus of study in the human sciences can be interpreted in terms of their functional roles and relationships. Fig. 3.3 summarizes that transition. It contains a great deal of information for the reader to study while reading the explanation that follows.

The *structure* of the control system corresponds to the biological

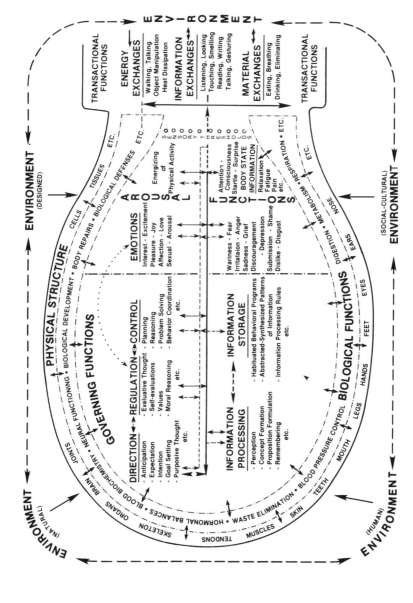

FIG. 3.3 A representation of a person an an open, living control system which exists, functions, and develops through a varying flow of transactions within a variable environment.

structure of the *human body*. The *information-processing, directive, regulatory,* and *control governing functions* along with the various *feedback* and *feedforward* signals correspond to the *cognitive functions* of humans. The *action* and *information-collection transactional* functions correspond to the diversity of *sensory-perceptual-motor functions* that have been the primary focus of classical behaviorism in psychology. The *energizing functions* correspond to the *arousal functions* of *emotions, attention,* and *consciousness* in humans. The *material- and energy-based self-constructing functions* correspond to *biological functions* in humans. The information-based *self-constructing functions* correspond to information-processing and learning functions in humans.

To illustrate the plausibility of this model for representing a human being, the interpretation of each control system component in Fig. 3.3 will be briefly summarized without citing supporting evidence. The purpose is to provide an overview. Later chapters examine each component and related evidence in considerable detail.

Being - Structure

The Human Body. Individuals are units with physical continuity of existence in time and space. The basic structure of the human body is the same for all individuals, because it is the derivative of their shared evolutionary history as members of the same species; but variations on that basic pattern occur because of individual differences in genetic and environmental factors.

Humans evolved in environments with certain constant properties, such as a general level of gravitational force, a gaseous rather than liquid environment, three-dimensional space, limited temperature ranges, and patterns of light and darkness. Therefore, certain properties of the structure of humans evolved to function within those conditions. If those "standard" conditions are altered, as in exposure to atomic radiation, space travel, or deep sea diving, some natural capabilities will be disrupted unless the person is protected.

Similarly, body structures evolved to serve physical activity. The skeletal-muscular structures will deteriorate if they are inactive for significant periods. That is why hospitalized patients are now required to get out of bed and move about as soon as possible to help prevent deterioration through inactivity. Visual and manipulative capabilities have upper limits on the rate at which they can function, and if the speed or motion of events exceeds those rates, such transactional systems cannot accurately perform their functions. Through evolutionary processes, human structures have developed that nicely fit the "standard" environmental conditions of humans' earthly terrestrial environment (see Chapter 6 and the initial sections of Chapters 7–15 for more extensive discussion).

However, there are structural differences among individuals and groups in some attributes (e.g., hair texture, sexual organs, body build or conformation) because different populations of the species evolved in somewhat different environmental niches. There is renewed interest in exploring the potential base in hereditary differences of important behavioral differences. For example, there is evidence accumulating that some individuals may be genetically more vulnerable to alcoholism than others (McClearn, 1981; Wilson et al., 1982).

The physical structure of the body is composed of an interrelated set of components. The nature of the structural components (illustrated in the outer boundary of Fig. 3.3), and the way they are organized, makes possible certain functions but not others. For example, the structure of the human eye makes it possible to see certain kinds of electromagnetic radiation but not others. The structure does not completely determine the functions that will be performed, but it places limits on the functional possibilities. The number of structural components is quite limited, but functional diversity results from using the structures in many ways and in many combinations. For example, a mouth can be used for eating, breathing, talking, expressing disgust, smiling, kissing, singing, playing a horn, and so forth.

Structural damage may alter functional capabilities. Restoration of damaged functional capabilities may be possible in two ways. First, the nonfunctional structure may be replaced with artificial or man made substitutes, such as artificial organs or limbs. Second, some other structure may be used to perform the function. For example, some people whose arms are paralyzed have learned to write or to skillfully paint pictures while holding the tools in their mouths or between their toes. People who have lost speech capability through cancer of the throat may learn to speak by taking in and belching air from their stomachs. To some extent, different structures can perform similar functions, and each structure has the potential to participate in multiple functions. Humans have learned to expand their functional capabilities beyond those made possible by their biological structure by learning new ways of using existing structures and by inventing additional structures that supplement their own (Lewontin, 1981). That is the fundamental significance of the multitude of tools and machines that humans have created.

The primary knowledge base for understanding the physical organization or structure of the human body is the discipline of biology, and subdisciplines such as cell biology, anatomy and physiology, neurology, sensory physiology, and embryology. In the evolution of all organisms,

"Mother Nature" used components earlier evolved to efficiently construct more elaborate components (e.g., Frederick, 1981). Therefore, comparative study of the structure of other organisms can also contribute useful knowledge about humans. Other fields such as physical anthropology, orthopedic medicine, and physical education also produce relevant information. Recognition that body structures can to some degree be imitated by humanly constructed mechanical devices (e.g., the heart—a pump; the kidney—a filter; the arm or leg—a lever) has led to cooperative efforts between biologists and engineers to design such artificial body parts.

Behaving - Functions

Structures make possible and preserve functions, while functioning helps construct and preserve structures in living systems.

Biological Functions. The structure of a living system, in contrast to that of an inanimate machine, is maintained, elaborated, and repaired through functions made possible by the structure itself. A variety of processes, functions, or behaviors of the biological structure combine, transform, and transport materials and energy to accomplish the maintenance, growth, operation, and repair of the biological structure. In addition, this category of functions produces energy to fuel all functions (see Chapter 6 for further discussion).

Biological functions are inborn arrangements that have resulted from humans' evolutionary history and that develop in individuals through interaction with their contexts in order to maintain an essential degree of biological stability in a variable environment; while at the same time providing some range of flexibility to increase the ability to adapt to environmental variability. These functions are usually carried out relatively automatically, that is, without awareness or intentional action, thereby freeing the individual's attention for other functions. Because of their machinelike automaticity, these functions can sometimes be approximated by servomechanisms or cybernetic-type feedback control and regulation arrangements (Toates, 1975).

These functions (e.g., cell metabolism, blood circulation, body temperature control, tissue elaboration and repair) are represented adjacent to the structural components in Fig. 3.3. They are separated from the structure and other functions by dotted line boundaries to connote their role in developing and maintaining the structural components, and in making possible and fueling all other functions. The arrows from the biological functions to the structure and to the other functions indicate the continual process of interaction necessary between these biological functions and other human attributes for the person to develop and function effectively. The arrows are two-headed to indicate that the interactions are bidirectional; that is, the many variables represented in the organization of a person are mutually influential. For example, other functions such as attention, thinking, or emotions will affect and be affected by biological functioning. Physical activity influences and is influenced by biological functions (e.g., fatigue, muscle cramps, respiratory and circulatory changes). The arrows are dotted rather than solid to connote that the biological functions typically go on outside of a person's awareness. A few manifestations of them can sometimes be observed if people direct their attention to them (e.g., pulse rate; smooth muscle contractions), or hook up some tool that will measure and display some attribute of them (e.g., a blood pressure measuring device). That fact is a cornerstone of biofeedback training procedures (N. Miller, 1978).

Because these biological functions are responsible for the self-construction and self-organization of the physical structure and underlie all other functions, any disruption of biological functions may alter the person's structural and functional development. The effects on the fetus of the mother's habits and diet (e.g., taking drugs, eating nutritionally deficient meals) provide dramatic and sad examples of this fact (e.g., mentally retarded or physically deformed babies). Because biological functions keep the general "equipment" of the body in good operating condition and provide the energy to fuel all other functions, their serious disruption at any age will have important effects on the structure and other functions. Death is defined by the termination of these essential biological functions. The heartbeat is a convenient index of whether the material and energy exchange processes essential to life are still going on. Therefore, if the heart stops beating, the person is considered dead. Termination of electrical activity in the brain is a second standard indicator of death. That is a convenient indicator that the information exchange processes essential for life are no longer occurring. Medical treatments exert their effects by enhancing the body's own self-constructing properties in one of two ways: (a) by facilitating or amplifying such processes (e.g., through diet, exercise, rest, or drugs); and (b) by attenuating or removing influences that are interfering with those self-constructing properties (e.g., through surgery or antibiotics).

The primary knowledge base for understanding biological functions is provided by various fields of biology and medical science, such as genetics, biochemistry, endocrinology, nutrition, gastroentorology, reproductive biology, cardiology, urology, immunology, neurology, and cell biology. Physiological psychology and professions such as medicine, nursing, pharmacology, exercise physiology, and dietetics, in part focus upon and provide relevant information about biological functioning and how to influence it.

Transactional Functions. To maintain and elaborate the complexity of their structural and functional organization, people must function as "dissipative structures." They must be able to interact with their environment to exchange essential materials, energy, and information; to discharge waste products to avoid self-pollution; to avoid damage or destruction; and to reproduce. Living systems are open systems. Some behaviors make it possible for people to move around in or to manipulate their environments. Some make it possible for them to collect and ingest or to get rid of different kinds of materials. Some make it possible to collect or emit information. The right-hand side of Fig. 3.3 summarizes such transactional functions. The vertical line of circles in the open end of Fig. 3.3, separating transactional from other functions, is intended to indicate that while transactional functions occur at the interface of the body surface and its environment, they interact with other functions that occur within the body. The body's boundaries must be permeable to both information, material, and energy to function as an open system.

Some of these transactional capabilities are focused primarily on the exchange of *material* essential for biological construction, organization, operation, and energy production. Eating, drinking, breathing, sweating, defecating, and urinating illustrate such transactions. Others are focused primarily on the exchange of *energy*. Actions through which a person manipulates the environment and moves around in it are accomplished essentially through energy transactions (i.e., an object moves when some force is applied to it). Examples include body heat dissipation, walking, manipulating (e.g., lifting, striking, or throwing) objects, jumping, swimming, and pushing (see Chapter 13 for further discussion).

Other transactional capabilities are focused primarily on the exchange of *information*. These, too, are accomplished through some medium of energy exchange. However, that simply provides the material medium (sometimes called the "marker") for carrying information[3] (see Chapter 8 for further discussion).

---

[3]One of the conceptual difficulties with ESP theory and research is that it implies information exchange not carried on through any known material or energy medium. "Psychic energy" is yet to be demonstrated to exist. Until some carrier medium for such postulated information transactions is demonstrated, alternate explanations for ESP-like phenomena appear more plausible.

There are two interrelated types of information transactions. One type is focused on the *collection of information*. Action on and movement through the environment, and social interactions, must be guided by information. A variety of sensory mechanisms collect information about the environment and the person's relationship to it. Not only does such information serve as an antecedent to the initiation of motor behavior, but it also provides the necessary feedback to maintain the coordination and direction of motor activity. For example, feedback through the ears tells you when you strike a "sour note" while playing the piano. Feedback through the eyes guides the hand to pick up a desired object. Feedback through the kinesthetic and vestibular senses maintains body balance and coordinated movement. Functionally, such feedback can represent what some learning theorists have called *reinforcement* (Glaser, 1971).

Various actions are necessary to bring sensory structures into contact with relevant stimuli, so action and information transactions must function cooperatively. The eyes must be exposed to light to see; hands must contact some substance to feel; the ears must be exposed to variations in air pressure waves to hear. Therefore, the orientation of sensory structures provides an objective observer with clues about the information to which people are attending. If their eyes are closed, they cannot see. If their hands cover their ears, they cannot hear.

A second type involves *emitting or communicating information* as a means of testing and influencing the environment. Humans have many ways of doing this. They may send out "signals" or information through various body postures or hand and arm gestures, from a threatening or insulting gesture to a gentle caress. The muscles of the face make possible a great variety of communicative gestures or expressions, particularly about emotional states (and the implied actions that may accompany them) (Darwin, 1872; Ekman & Oster, 1979). Some human facial gestures were probably originally components of action-related display gestures evolved from other animals (Guthrie, 1970).

Their capacity for communicating information to others through vocalizations and speech particularly distinguishes humans from other animals. Speech is the major transactional capability through which people convey to one another what is going on in their "private world." For example, the most frequent diagnostic tool used by physicians is still some version of the old question "Where does it hurt," to obtain information that only patients can observe. Speech is the primary tool through which humans seek to influence one another, by way of such things as instructions, commands, and persuasion (see Chapter 15).

Through experience, a relatively limited array of transactional capabilities can become organized into a great diversity of complex sensory-motor patterns. Children first construct several basic action capabilities as a foundation for more complex patterns. They must learn to position themselves in relationship to space through balance and posture before they can walk. They must be able to move objects through propulsion and receipt, to move themselves through space, overcoming obstacles, bending, twisting, and turning as necessary, and changing pace through locomotion. By reaching, grasping, and releasing they must acquire the capability for relating to other objects through contact and manipulation (Singer, 1968). Only after such "rudimentary" patterns or *behavioral components* are formed can they be combined and elaborated to diversify and refine a person's transactional capabilities, until he or she can finally become a virtuoso of the violin, perform with the grace of a ballerina, or display the manual skill of an excellent mechanic.

The helplessness of persons without transactional capabilities is poignantly apparent in those who have suffered some cerebral accident that has destroyed the neural basis for transactional functioning. It is evident that such persons know what is going on around them, but cannot respond or communicate their wants or ideas to others. They survive only if other people provide substitutes for their lost transactional competence.

Transactional behaviors are the only functions that it is possible for one person to directly observe in another (without the aid of special instruments such as a thermometer), and from which people can make inferences about other aspects of one another's functioning (e.g., thoughts or emotional states). The objectively observable functions were the only ones called behavior by classical behaviorists, except perhaps for a few biological functions.

The primary knowledge base for understanding the transactional functions lies in some aspects of psychology and sociology, such as developmental psychology, sensory psychology, motor behavior or performance skills, social interactions and communication; in the disciplines focused on information exchange functions such as speech and hearing; in some aspects of physiology, such as kinesiology; and in some professional fields such as physical education, sports medicine, orthopedic medicine, prosthetic engineering, physical rehabilitation, speech pathology and audiology, and education of the blind and deaf.

Arousal Functions. People must be able to selectively vary the amount, rate and amplitude or intensity of their behavior if they are to effectively cope with the variable and frequently unpredictable environment around them.

The arousal functions perform this role as seen in Fig.3.3. The broken vertical line separating arousal from governing functions is intended to convey that the two functions influence one another but are qualitatively different kinds of functions. The two horizontal lines through the middle of Fig. 3.3 indicate that all functions are interacting and mutually influential. The solid horizontal line indicates that some of the interactions can enter consciousness, while the broken line indicates that many of the interactions occur outside of consciousness. The broken arrows connecting arousal and biological functions symbolizes their mutually influential interactions. *Energizing physical activity, emotional arousal,* and *consciousness - attention* represent three types of arousal functions.

The energy requirements and their utilization of the system vary. Life is generally not like the steady pace of the skilled jogger, in which the rate of energy consumption is closely balanced with the rate of energy availability. It is more like the activity of a football player, with periods of relative stillness, interspersed with spurts of major exertion, sudden accelerations and slowdowns, episodic accomplishments, failures, or pain, and all accompanied by periods of joy, anger or discouragement, fatigue and rest.

It is not just variations in the *kinds* of transactions required but also variations in their *rate, amplitude,* or *intensity* that are important. The search for food, an attack upon another organism, fleeing from danger, the processes of mating, playing, sleeping, the searchlight of intense alertness and the diffuse light of undirected attention—all represent circumstances that reveal the need for variability in the level of system activity. Duffy (1962) described the individual as an "energy system," collecting, storing, and releasing energy in various ways. (The term *dissipative structure* now has a similar meaning.) She suggested that a person's behavior is a function of both variations in the amount of energy release or "activation," and the distribution of that activation among parts of the body.

In variable and unpredictable environments, the level of system activity needed will also be variable and unpredictable. For example, an automobile driving at a steady rate of 55 miles an hour consumes a predictable amount of fuel for energy, enabling the driver to replenish the fuel-energy supply at regular, predictable intervals. However, an ambulance driver trying to move rapidly through heavy traffic to get a critically ill patient to the hospital will have to speed up and slow down in unpredictable fashion, at times jamming the accelerator to the floor and at other times hitting the brakes to avoid a collision. In such circumstances fuel-energy usage is unpredictable and the driver will try to restore his fuel-energy storage between runs to insure having sufficient supplies, since he cannot take time to stop for gas in an emergency, and a gas station may not be available when he needs it.

Moreover, the ambulance engine has considerable surplus power potential, beyond that needed for ordinary driving, which can be used at an instant's notice to meet any unusual circumstances that might occur. However, if the driver places extreme power demands on his engine too often, or for too long a period, he will damage it, and could ruin it. As energy systems, humans are designed to function in a similar manner.

Patterns of activity and emotional arousal enable a human to function in an even more variable environment than an ambulance. Humans must also be able to store potential energy beyond that needed for the ordinary routine activity of their systems. They must be able to draw upon that stored energy in controlled fashion to meet the variable demands of their behavior-environment transactions (energizing behavioral activity), and have quick access to supplementary amounts of energy to meet the different kinds of contingencies that might arise during those transactions (emotional arousal).

Effective action in a variable environment requires capabilities for quickly shifting the rate, amplitude, or intensity of activities. Such shifts require changes in energy availability and expenditure. For example, a pedestrian leisurely crossing a street may have to suddenly bolt for the other side to avoid being struck by a careless driver's car. Individuals may have to shift the rate or intensity of their effort to achieve a desired result, such as succeeding at a valued task, seducing a desired lovemate, or abandoning a fruitless effort. There is great adaptive value in this ability to rapidly shift the energy-activity "tuning" of behavioral functioning to match changing environmental pressures in order to progress towards personal objectives. Excessive, chronic arousal can produce biological damage, however (e.g., stress symptoms).

The energizing of physical activity is the basic kind of arousal function for all of behavior. Emotional arousal of different types represents specialized arousal functions which produce variations in the basic activity arousal patterns when necessary. Therefore, the emotions have evolved to perform a regulatory function (i.e., evaluation of personal relevance → selective activation). This primitive evaluative-regulatory function of emotion is associated with subjectively experienced positive or aversive qualities, as well as differentially altering biological processes related to variations in activity levels. There are a limited number of basic emotional arousal patterns which represent evolutionarily based, inborn patterns (Schellenbach, 1987). The patterns appear early in infancy, and are triggered into operation by different types of events. Thus, an infant when physically constrained will display anger; when exposed to a novel object will display interest; and when exposed to a noxious odor will display disgust.

Emotions have three other significant attributes. First, they function to prepare for different kinds of action-environment contingencies and potential consequences; that is, they are *anticipatory* in nature. For example, fear is an adaptive emotion in part because it helps keep an individual out of damaging circumstances, as illustrated by fear-avoidance behavior patterns. Because emotional arousal involves preparation for a shift in action, many biological functions may change in preparation for action when emotions occur.

Second, emotional arousal patterns are *highly learnable*. There are initially only a few kinds of events that will trigger emotions. However, under appropriate learning arrangements almost any kind of event can come to elicit almost any kind of emotional arousal pattern. This makes possible "self-programming" through experience. Evolutionary processes could not "anticipate" and "design into" mobile organisms the appropriate behavior patterns for all possible circumstances they might confront in a highly variable environment. The alternative of "building in" basic types of arousal patterns that can get "hooked up" with any kind of conditions confronted in the process of living is far more flexible and adaptive. Unfortunately, some of the "hook-ups" may turn out to be maladaptive as illustrated by symptoms such as phobias. Emotions are also learnable in the sense that different patterns may come to occur in combined or merged forms.

Finally, emotional arousal patterns *provide information* which facilitates the regulatory function of the system. It is probable that emotional arousal is a more primitive regulatory mechanism than is thought. However, in humans, thoughts and emotional patterns are related in both preparation for action and regulation of the system, as symbolized by the two headed arrow connecting regulation with emotional arousal in Figure 3.3 (see Chapter 13 for further discussion).

Complex systems must also meet *variable energy-information processing* demands in addition to energy-activity demands (Amosov, 1968). The use of energy in information processing is illustrated by the complex electronic circuitry in a television or stereophonic music system. In such electronic systems, the "signal" is the information important to the system at the time; all other information, including random events, which tend to confuse or obscure the relevant information are considered distortion or "noise." To facilitate clear transmission and reception of the signal, power sources and processes are applied to amplify the signal's intensity or clarity and to reduce the level of distortion and noise, by using filters and attenuators sensitive to these attributes (Raisbeck, 1964). The strength and clarity of the "signal" in relationship to the noise is important both in terms of reception and reproduction of the information and the clarity with which it can be permanently recorded (e.g., tape recording music).

Humans must have analogous capabilities for collecting, organizing, storing, and using information by selecting currently relevant "signals" and eliminating "noise." At times people "tune out" information inputs, when it is disrupting or boring, or when they sleep. Sometimes people casually collect and inspect information in a relatively unorganized manner, as in lazily watching clouds float through the sky. They may specifically attend to or search for currently relevant kinds of information in their environment or memory, as in trying to locate a misplaced object or in concentrating on completing a task. In dangerous situations they may become extremely alert, searching for subtle information that may be useful, as in listening for unusual sounds in a dark house late at night. Differences in focus and intensity of awareness, attention, consciousness, or concentration serve to selectively amplify, attenuate, filter, and exclude information available to people from within and without their bodies.

Such information selectivity might be compared with tuning a radio or television receiver. You can tune in to different stations or signals, thereby selecting the information that interests you. Once a station is selected, all other stations are filtered out so that you only get one program. Other electronic circuits filter out extraneous information that may distort reception, such as the static you may hear on your car radio from the operation of the car's engine. You may also selectively amplify or attenuate aspects of the selected signal by adjusting the volume and the high, low, or middle range sound frequencies or adjusting the color, contrast, and brightness of the TV picture. Note in this electronic analogy that selection, filtering, amplifying or attentuating the information can be applied to any station, that is, to *any kind* of information (e.g., visual or auditory). To put this point in human terms, *the phenomena of attention and consciousness are different from, but related to, the content of consciousness.* Too often the two are treated as one. For example, when people talk about consciousness they often talk about *what* a person is thinking or perceiving rather than the *process* of information selection, filtering, and amplification.

In Fig. 3.3, this distinction is made clear in the lines and arrows running horizontally through the middle of the diagram. The solid line indicates that people can monitor information both from their environments and from within their bodies (e.g., pain). Monitored information will become the content of consciousness (analogous to tuning in to one TV station or another). The focus and intensity of their attending behavior influences the substance and clarity of their consciousness. From the continual flow of information attended to, individuals abstract consistencies or redundancies concerning the nature and relationships of things and events. Those generalized abstractions become cognitive information components. Once a cognitive pattern becomes a habit, it can function relatively automatically when triggered into action; it then requires no attention. Thus, people can carry out complex patterns of activity, including thinking, without being aware of many aspects of what they are doing (e.g., as in driving a car), while they reserve their attention for the variable or unexpected circumstances with which they may have to cope (such as a child running into the street in front of the car). Thus, people can do more than one thing at a time—although not many more.

At any point in time, an individual is carrying out much habitual behavior that is not represented in current consciousness, as symbolized by the dotted line running horizontally through the middle of Fig. 3.3. Most habitual behavior is "unconscious" in that sense. Often, if need be, people can make unconscious behavior conscious by focusing their attention on it, and they may do that, particularly if they want to change a "habit." Unconscious cognitions may indirectly influence conscious content (e.g., through influencing perceptual processes).

Thus, attention and consciousness are key functions in the capability of individuals to create new "software" to guide their behavioral programs. When learning a skill, one has to concentrate on the specifics and practice them extensively to make them automatic. However, after the behavioral program is "written" (i.e., becomes a habit), it can be carried out most efficiently if it is not interfered with by focusing attention on its details. When highly skilled people perform, the flow of their finely tuned behavior is guided primarily by their exquisitely formed, habitual behavioral programs, called "open loops" in systems language. As an Olympic gymnastic champion put it, "Once I start my routine, I let my body take over." (See Chapter 7 for a more extensive discussion of attention and consciousness.)

The primary knowledge base for understanding arousal functions is found in aspects of psychology and sociology such as physiological psychology, attention and consciousness, motivation and emotion, social interactions, and psychopathology; in some aspects of biology such as endocrine functioning; in comparative studies of other animals; in some aspects of anthropology; and in professions such as psychiatry, clinical or counseling psychology, psychiatric social work, organizational, industrial, and advertising psychology, and teaching.

Governing Functions. A complex system requires coordination of its components if they are to function as a unit. The activity of the system is fueled by energy, but the coordination and control of the system is made possible by information.

The functions that organize, transform, store, and use information to produce coordination and control of human behavior are labeled *governing functions* in Fig. 3.3. In psychology, terms like perception, information processing, and cognition represent these functions. The term *governing* is chosen because it connotes more of an interactive process than similar terms sometimes used, such as commander, executive, director, ruler, or decider. It implies a conditional superordinate authority appropriate to the concept of hierarchy, in contrast to the absolute authority of a dictator. Governments administer programs in the public interest, and construct, organize, utilize, and make available to other parts of the system vast amounts of information. Thus, the term governing appears to best symbolize the multiple facets of this major set of functions.

Fig. 3.3 separates governing functions from biological and arousal functions by broken lines, to indicate that they are different but mutually influential functions. Note that all cognitive functions are connected to one another by their mutual connections to the two horizontal lines in the center of Fig. 3.3. That signifies that their operation and interaction may be both conscious and unconscious. The exception is information storage. It is connected directly only to information processing and the broken horizontal line. The information processing connection signifies that information storage results from information processing in which consciousness is involved, and remembering is a function of current information processing activities. The broken line connection symbolizes the influence of arousal functions in amplifying or attenuating information storage. Although regulative thought and emotions are connected by the two midfigure horizontal lines, they are also connected by a curved dotted line to emphasize their special relationship. Emotional arousal is a more primitive form of regulation than human thought. Regulative thought triggers emotional arousal and emotional arousal influences regulative thought. Finally, the two horizontal midfigure lines connected to all governing functions indicate the mutual influence of governing and transactional functions on one another.

The governing functions provide the centralized coordination that is necessary to maintain the flexibility and adaptability of complex systems. Just as the biological functions use material and energy to be self-constructing, so too the governing functions use information to be self-constructing. They transform information into new forms and use it to organize and operate complex behavior patterns, as well as to repair and revise existing information components and complex behavior patterns. To renew the computer analogy, they are continually writing, revising, storing, and using "software" packages which represent behavioral programs that can be flexibly combined to serve varying objectives and contingencies.

The information from which such "programs" are built comes simultaneously and continually both from within the body and from the environment. It is impossible to simultaneously interact with, or change interactions with, such a continuing, changing stream of events. The governing functions make it possible for people to select, from the flow of information in which they are continually immersed, those aspects that are specifically relevant and useful for their current concerns.

In humans the directive, regulatory, and control functions found in all control systems are represented by different kinds of cognition. The *directive function* of thought is characterized by terms such as intention, goal setting, purpose, wants, and desires. The *regulatory function* of thought is characterized by terms such as evaluative thought, self-evaluation, values, and moral reasoning. The *control function* of thought is characterized by terms such as reasoning, planning, problem solving, analyzing, decision making, predicting, attribution of causality, and behavior coordination. Terms such as anticipation, expectation, or coordination refer to *feedforward processes* from the directive, regulatory, or control processes. Terms such as monitoring refer to information *feedback processes.*

The elaborate capacity to build new informational-behavioral forms, to store them, and to selectively use them particularly distinguishes humans from other living systems. Humans are always collecting information about current circumstances, because it is needed to guide current activity in the present environment and to evaluate the consequences of current efforts. No news is bad news when it comes to maintaining effectively organized behavior patterns in variable environments. But new information is of little current utility if it is truly new. An experience completely unlike any that one has had before may elicit confusion, curiosity, or fear, but will be of little help in guiding current behavior. New information becomes useful when related to old, so that predictions about the future can be made on the basis of the comparison of present events with similar past circumstances. By mechanisms and processes yet to be understood, a person is able to retain organized informational abstracts of past experiences and to selectively reactivate information relevant to present concerns and activities.

The process of conscious recall, like the process of perception or recognition, seems to involve both a search for information and a rule, guide, template, or clue that guides the search. Recall, in its conscious form, may well be the perceptual process turned inward to a person's retained information, rather than outward to the "hard news" coming from his or her environment (Tomkins, 1962). Apparently, much of the moment-to-moment matching of current perceptions with conceptions that is involved in the control of behavior occurs outside of awareness, as is typical of well-established habits in all behavioral realms (Held, 1965). It also appears that "current news" just arriving at the "information center" is held in temporary storage (short-term memory) for immediate use in guiding behavior. Some of the temporary storage is transformed to permanent retention (long-term memory), while some of it may be discarded, but it is not yet clear how or why that occurs.

The governing functions are active, not just reactive. The capability making that possible is represented in Fig. 3.3 by the term *information processing*. A computer can be programmed to store much information. Mechanical control systems can perform directive, regulatory, and control functions. But *they cannot program themselves*. As a product of their evolutionary history, humans have a capability, made possible by the design of the human brain and nervous system, for processing information to "write" their own behavioral programs. There are probably certain basic "processing rules" built into the human brain. As they operate on the flow of information through the infant's nervous system, these "rules" function to abstract, organize, combine, transform, and store information in behaviorally relevant patterns appropriate to the different kinds of contexts and "behavioral problems" from which the information was initially derived. Through this information processing capability, individuals progressively construct and revise their goals, the means they may use to pursue their goals, the criteria and values by which they regulate their activity, and the informational context in which those are embedded and given meaning. However, because information collection and processing is selective through the functioning of attention and directive, regulatory, and control functioning, and because there may be genetically based differences in the operation of the inborn "processing rules," two individuals in the same or similar situations will not necessarily form the same abstracts or informational-behavioral-situational programs.

As a person's self-constructed repertoire of information-behavior-situation programs grows, those functional components exert influence on the way new information is processed. Information which fits existing cognitions is readily assimilated, but information that is discrepant creates a conflict between conceptions and perceptions. As with any dynamic organization, such conflict or disruption must be dealt with if the organization is to retain its internal coherence. Discrepant information can be handled either by rejecting it, reinterpreting it to "make it fit," or reorganizing the existing patterns to accommodate it. Therefore, the disrupting influence of discrepant information is the basic source of cognitive and behavioral change. Many of the "defense mechanisms" identified by psychoanalysis represent ways of handling discrepant information (e.g., repression, projection, rationalization).

Some information-processing rules must be inborn and only the products of their operation are acquired. It is also probable that the inborn processing rules can themselves become elaborated through experience. The rules for mathematical reasoning might be such an example. Information-processing rules can be applied to new information inputs, or existing "stored" information (e.g., theory construction).

The concept of human rationality has been very influential, particularly in Western cultures. Is this living system perspective a view that requires humans to be "rational"? This question refers to both the content of human thought and the processing rules used. There is nothing in this position that requires the content of human thought to be only verbal-symbolic. In fact, information is collected in many forms (e.g., visual, auditory, chemical) and it goes through several transformations from one material medium to another on its way to the brain (see Chapter 8). Words are not the only form in which information is coded, and it is probable that the rules of logical thought are not the only kinds of information processing rules that the human brain uses (see Chapters 9–12). For example, Freud's concept of "primary process" thought is different from "secondary process" (i.e., rational) thought (Ford & Urban, 1963). Current interest in studying and understanding differences in "right" and "left" brain functioning make a similar distinction between verbal and nonverbal thought. Piaget's (1954) proposal that sensorimotor functioning is the initial form from which thoughts are constructed suggests that governing functions are initially "nonverbal" in content. Different kinds of thought processes may serve different purposes.

The primary knowledge base for understanding governing functions is found in the disciplines of perceptual and cognitive psychology, sensory physiology and neurology, and linguistics; and in professional fields such as education, management science, psychotherapy, moral development, and planning. Information-processing technologies, such as computers and the design of software for them, provide a machine analogy for simulating some aspects of governing functions, as in artificial intelligence (AI) research.

Environment - Contexts

Organismic evolution is the product of interactions between properties of the evolving organism and its environmental niches. Individual development is a product of the interaction of genetic potentials with environmental factors. Human behavior is a function of the situations under which it occurs. We are what we eat. Such generalizations are examples of the basic significance of thinking of humans as open systems. An open system exists, develops, and functions only through continual exchanges of material, energy, and information with relevant contexts. Therefore, people can be fully understood only in relation to their contexts. Attempts to alter their functioning involve selective manipulation of aspects of their environments, from pills to persuasion.

People's understanding and interpretation of one another's behavior is context dependent. Their behavior can be accurately understood only in its relevant context. For example, Rank (1961) wrote descriptions of brief episodes of individuals' behavior from which she excluded almost all contextual referents. For example:

> She stood there, hands before her, tears streaming from her eyes. He leaped into the air, turning gracefully, arms stretched above his head.

People were then asked, "Why is she crying?" or "What is he doing?" Under these circumstances, people gave such diverse answers as the following: She hurt herself; she is sad or mad about something; she is peeling onions; or, he is a ballet dancer; he is playing basketball; he sat on a bee. There was little consensus in the answers. A different sample of people were given exactly the same descriptions, but with contextual referents added, and asked the same questions. For example:

> Dressed in black, she stood there before the casket, hands before her in prayerful pose, tears streaming from her eyes.
> He leaped into the air with the basketball, turning gracefully toward the basket, arms stretched above his head to make the shot.

With contextual referents added, observers were nearly unanimous about what was going on.

The natural sciences are not primarily interested in understanding or predicting a particular instance, as in the experiment just described. They are interested in formulating the general case (Henshel, 1971). However, in this conceptual framework the normative functioning of any type of system cannot be understood solely as a property of such systems. To formulate a general case requires specifying both the type of system and the type of context. Then it is possible to formulate useful normative statements. Stated simply, people behave differently in different contexts. Environmental factors are integral components of living systems' functioning. Behavior always occurs in a specific context and both must fit together to form a functional unit, as subject, verb, and object must fit together to form a sentence. This fact has been underemphasized in much research. All "habits" are linked to some kind of environment, whether narrowly or broadly defined. One of the weaknesses of "trait" psychology is that it tries to represent the consistencies in behavior independent of the kinds of contexts to which different consistencies were linked.

There are a variety of ways of classifying environmental variables, and different ways are useful for different purposes (e.g., proximity and behavior settings). However, most must include, in some way, distinctions as to *kinds* of environments and their attributes. The following illustrates one useful subdivision of kinds of environments.

Natural Environment. There are aspects of the environment that are considered products of "nature," such as rain, clouds, sun, plants, animals, land, gravity, air pressure, and oxygen. A variety of disciplines and professions—such as meteorology, botany, ecology, geology, agriculture, astronomy, mining, and weather forecasting—focus primarily on these phenomena.

Designed Environment. People shape their environments to serve human objectives. Human environments are increasingly dominated by environmental forms created by humans rather than by "Mother Nature." Examples are homes, electric lights, books, computers, cars, prepared foods, clothing, medicines, eyeglasses, music, and furniture. Environmental designers, such as the engineering professions, manufacturing enterprises, and the arts, are major components of the cultures and economic systems of modern societies.

Human Environment. Human evolution appears to have made the human being a "social animal"; we seem to need close association with others like ourselves to survive, reproduce, and be happy and effective. "Significant others" play a powerful role in the development and functioning of individuals. Examples include parents, siblings, spouses, relatives, friends, lovers, teammates, co-workers, teachers, plumbers, bridge partners, and drinking buddies. Some disciplines and professions that focus on human environments are family sociology and psychology, small group social psychology, the study of interpersonal relationships, and of social support networks, industrial psychology, family counseling, group therapy, and leadership training.

Socio-Cultural Environment. Throughout their history, humans have designed not only new physical objects and tools, but also social forms and processes necessary for effective living in social groups. These social forms and processes acquire a relatively permanent existence independent of the individuals participating in them (i.e., they become institutionalized), and therefore exert important influences on, and provide important living conditions for, successive generations. Examples include governments, schools, religions, languages, industries, labor unions, laws, health services, and social norms. Disciplines and professions focused on socio-cultural forms include history, sociology, cultural anthropology, political science, economics, philosophy, religion, mathematics, business administration, community development, social policy planning, government and human services administration, law, and language teaching.

Environmental Attributes. Many human beings' interactions with their environments are influenced by variable aspects of their environment such as size, weight, color, length, or shape; and some forms of change or action such as frequency, rate of occurrence, intensity of occurrence, direction or rate of motion, competition, conflict, cooperation, attack, retreat, and services provided by an institution. Human perceptual capabilities appear to have evolved particularly to track attribute changes and actions, since for an organism which itself is mobile, its environments are in a sense always moving. In Fig. 3.3, the environment is symbolized as completely surrounding the person as it does in life. However, the "open" end of the figure is oriented towards only one part of the environment to symbolize the selectiveness of a person's transactions with the environment.

Personality: Persistent Functional Patterns

A person functions as an entity—a coherently integrated structural-functional unit. That means that all functions in Fig. 3.3 are always occurring, in some form, in organized patterns of relationship with one another and with environmental conditions. One may choose to observe or study only one function but the others are always there too. Through experience and practice, people develop consistent or habitual patterns of functioning appropriate for different purposes and different kinds of environmental conditions. One way to identify and characterize a particular person, then, is to represent his or her in terms of such consistencies in patterns of functioning. People can be differentiated from one another in terms of interpersonal differences in such consistent patterns. *Personality* is the term often used to characterize such consistencies. Fields such as personality theory and assessment, psychopathology, developmental psychology, and clinical and counseling psychology focus on such personality-behavior consistencies (Ford & Urban, 1963; Loevinger & Knoll, 1983; Parke & Asher, 1983; Rorer & Widiger, 1983).

Concepts about personality differ in terms of the kinds of functions or behaviors included, the kinds and diversity of environmental conditions encompassed, and the way they are spatially and temporally organized. For example, some concepts represent patterns operative only in one specific type of situation (e.g., a snake phobia). Others focus only on consistencies within one function such as governing functions (e.g., moral reasoning and self-concept). Still others encompass a great diversity of patterns and environments by trying to identify broad, pervasive generalities in system function (e.g., life style, inferiority complex, introversion-extraversion, Oedipus complex, Parataxic mode, schizophrenia, being-in-the World). Personality theorists argue over how much of such consistencies resides within a person's behavioral repertoire, how much is a function of environmental consistencies, and how much is a function of their interactions (see Chapter 16).

Figure 3.3 provides a set of criteria for the form that personality constructs should take. Consistencies and differences in people's action patterns (transactional functions) are products of what they are trying to do and the values with which they are guiding their efforts (directive and regulatory functions); their existing physical capabilities and behavioral repertoire (biologicals structure and functions; control and information-processing functions); their attentional and emotional processes (arousal functions); and the environmental contingencies with which they must deal. It is useful to try to identify different types of patterns of consistency within each component and their hierarchical relationships (e.g., directive function-personal goals; regulatory function-moral values) as some personality theorists have done. However, if the objective is to try to understand a person as a functional unit and to help that person change and develop (as psychotherapists try to do), it is essential that the organizational patterns of all the functions represented in Fig. 3.3 be understood and dealt with. For example, in some circumstances a person may lack knowledge of how to do something, may perform inadequately, may evaluate themselves as incompetent to achieve certain goals, may feel discouraged and fearful of rejection, as well as tired and sick. In other circumstances, a different pattern may occur. The central task of personality theory and research should be to identify such patterns, the conditions under which different patterns occur, and learn how they develop and become generalized. The central task in much psychotherapy work is to modify such overgeneralized patterns. In later chapters, the concept of behavior episode schemata (BES) is introduced to provide a basis for functional consistency within behavioral variability.

Overview

With this brief overview of the ways in which the biological and behavioral characteristics of humans might be cast into the model of a self-organizing, self-constructing control system—a living system—we have sought to make such a model plausible. Later, a more detailed examination of the theoretical and empirical literature potentially relevant to each aspect of this conceptual framework explores its heuristic value for organizing existing knowledge. It is important to emphasize that Fig. 3.3 is *a model of functional organization that is "content free."* People's behavior patterns vary because of qualitative differences in the content of each function but the basic functional organization is *always* the same. For example, behavior patterns will differ depending on content of the personal goals performing the directive function; the content of the evaluative thoughts performing the regulatory function; the content of the emotions experienced; or the specific action patterns performed to carry out environmental transactions.

But there is one more basic issue to be addressed. Humans are not static entities. In their lives they manifest both stability and change. As living systems, humans must be understood as having not only stability but the capability for continued development throughout their lives. A way of thinking about this quality of *becoming* is examined in the next two chapters.

4

Processes of Change in Living Systems

INTRODUCTION

Living systems are never static. As described in Chapter 3, they are always in process. A human is a "being," but is also continually "becoming." The apparent stability of humans is a dynamic stability, a steady state, not an equilibrium. In a steady state, functions vary within boundary conditions (e.g., the oscillations of a pendulum). Moreover, as dissipative structures or open systems, humans are continually disrupting their steady states through the import, transformation, and export of information, material, and energy, and constructing new, more elaborate structures and states. Therefore, an integral part of any conceptual framework for understanding individuals must include a representation of how their structural and functional organization evolves, varies, and changes.

A person's behavior may vary but that does not necessarily mean he or she has changed in any permanent sense. It is useful to distinguish among three types of functional changes: (a) *variability*, or differences that occur as a manifestation of steady states (e.g., normal variations in blood sugar levels or the cyclical rhythms of walking behavior); (b) *temporary changes*, or differences resulting from reversible changes from one steady state to another (e.g., an unusually high blood sugar level resulting from overindulgence in desserts; walking with crutches until a sprained ankle heals); and (c) *permanent changes*, or persisting alterations of steady state functioning (e.g., developing diabetes; a child's shift from crawling to walking). Types (a) and (b) are sometimes referred to as *performance changes*.

How, when, and why permanent changes in structures and patterns of steady state functioning occur is the focus of research on development and on the effects of training, teaching, counseling, and psychotherapy. Several types of permanent change may occur. For example, steady state boundaries may change (as in people who develop high blood pressure). The kinds of variability possible within a steady state may change (e.g., in a child first learning to walk on an unobstructed surface, who then elaborates his walking competence to multiple terrains). New functional capabilities may develop (e.g., in a child learning to jump).

It is the purpose of Chapters 4 and 5 to evolve and summarize a way of understanding and explaining how the structural-functional organization of individuals proposed in Chapter 3 may change and develop. Discussions of development and personality often represent change processes primarily in terms of *what* happens rather than *why* it happens. This chapter attempts to construct the base for a formulation that does both.

Evolutionary, Biological, Learning, and Systems Theories

The amount of information available about humans in various fields is vast. It is difficult to discern a basic pattern in such an overwhelming mass of detail—one can't see the forest for the trees. Some method of simplifying the situation is essential. One method of simplification is to develop or adopt some general model of how the phenomena of interest are organized or how they work. Chapter 3 does that with regard to individual humans. Since that organizational model is dynamic and changeable, principles of change must be added to it.

Four large bodies of knowledge have generated principles of change. Evolutionary theory and biological disciplines such as genetics, embryology, and developmental biology provide two elaborate and empirically supported models concerning change and development of all kinds of living systems; and efforts to fuse embryology, genetics and evolutionary theory are underway (Raff & Kauffman, 1983). Learning or developmental theories in psychology provide a third potential source of useful principles. A fourth source is systems theory and related theoretical and empirical work focused on understanding the nature of steady state stability and the dynamics of transformations to new steady states.

Since these four domains of knowledge are all focused on understanding developmental or change processes in living systems, there should be some underlying commonalities in the general principles of change they have developed. If such commonalities can be identified, they should provide a credible starting point for a general explanation of developmental processes since they would represent emergent agreement from four relatively separate streams of theory and research.

This chapter attempts to summarize the principles of change developed in each of those domains. Chapter 5 attempts to derive a set of developmental or change principles based on similarities among them. The relevance of the proposed principles is tested in later chapters when evidence concerning different functions is examined in more detail.

Deutch (1951), in discussing the historic models of mechanism, organism, and process, anticipated the basic view of development that emerges in Chapters 4 and 5.

> It should have been possible to imagine a process of genuine growth or evolution, involving fundamental rearrangements of the elements, and even of the laws and probabilities of the ensemble, including changes in *kinds* of its interactions with its environment; so as to transform the original system into a new one, with long run properties not predictable from its previous states. Genuine evolution in this sense involves the possibility of sudden change and genuine novelty, including both internal change within the system and its interaction with the environment. It does not necessarily lead to one fixed goal, nor does it have to approximate any such goal ever more closely. Rather, it is an open ended process, containing the possibility of self-disruption or self-destruction as well as of a change of goals. Such a possibility seemed at least hinted in the words of the New Testament, 'Now we are the sons of God, and it does not yet appear what we shall be.' (p. 187)

An adequate theory of humans or living systems development must capture this idea of growth, change or elaboration that displays constrained organization and direction, but with no predetermined destination.

EVOLUTIONARY THEORY AND GENETICS

Modern evolutionary theory, as recently elaborated by various scholars (e.g., Gould, 1982; Mayr, 1982; Stebbins & Ayala, 1985), was constructed as a means of understanding change and development in living systems at the population and species levels. However, the primary unit through which evolutionary products are transmitted is through advantageous survival and reproductive rates of individual organisms. Evolution of populations and species is a function of changes in individuals.[1] Therefore, the principles and processes that govern evolutionary development and genetic influences cannot be independent from one another.

The many great voyages by 16th and 17th century European seamen to all parts of the world made European scholars aware of the diversity of plants, animals, and people in the world. Geologic and fossil evidence accumulated showing similarities and differences among organisms and suggesting apparent patterns in their historic emergence. In 1859, Charles Darwin published *Origin of the Species*, a theory utilizing and synthesizing ideas similar to some that had been previously suggested by others. Because his documentation was careful and convincing, evolutionary theory then became a powerful new influence on efforts to understand the development of living things (including humans) (Raup, 1981), despite opposition by historically dominant, religiously based beliefs.

Darwinian Theory

Knowledge of genetics did not yet exist in the mid-1850s, so Darwin simply proposed that some occasional random change would sometimes occur in individual organism(s) that gave them a survival and reproductive advantage over similar organisms in a particular kind of environmental niche. Another accidental but advantageous change might occur, and then another and another. Thus, over thousands of years, many such accidental changes could slowly and continuously accumulate within a particular kind of organism until a quite different organism emerged that proliferated because of its resultant survival and reproductive advantage. The less fortunate earlier versions were often progressively crowded into extinction. This natural selection process, sometimes termed "survival of the fittest," came to be termed the *gradualism doctrine* because it proposed that evolution and extinction occurred through a slow accumulation of many small changes selected by environmental pressures.

---

[1]Gould (1982) points out that evolution may be thought of in hierarchical terms, making it possible to think of a species as an evolutionary unit as well. I believe this is a sound view, but it, too, assumes that the mechanism of biological (as contrasted to cultural) evolution lies in individual genetic changes. One of the important differences between physical and life sciences lies in the phenomena of individual differences. The physical scientist can, for all practical purposes, assume that the components being studied are identical (e.g., all atoms of sodium are alike). That assumption cannot be made about complex living systems, such as humans. Therefore, a science of the living must accommodate individual differences (e.g., Lewin, 1982).

Variability. Darwin's theory was built from three basic ideas. The first is the idea of variability. Through natural processes both existing organisms and environments changed. Either kind of change would create a somewhat different set of potential options for organism-environment interrelationships. Thus, the evolutionary significance of organism or environmental variability lay not in the variability of each but in the change or disruption of the dynamics and possibilities of their interaction; that is, in the relationship between the organism and its environmental niche. Therefore, evolutionary pressures could also develop as a result of the transport or migration of some existing members of a species to a different environmental niche, resulting in a change of interaction potentials even though neither organismic nor environmental change occurred.

Adaptation and Natural Selection. Such changes in organism-environment interaction possibilities and pressures result in changes in actual interaction patterns, called *adaptation.* Several kinds of consequences could result from such changes. For example, some organisms might die because their changed interaction pattern no longer produced all the conditions necessary for their survival. Others might survive, but with greater difficulty than before the change, which might result in a decline in the efficiency of some living system function, such as reproduction. For some, the change might make no significant difference. For others it might produce significant new advantages, such as in obtaining food, in the competition for mates, or in the number or survival rates of their offspring. Such differential survival and reproductive consequences resulting from adaptation processes were termed by Darwin *natural selection,* his third basic idea.

Cast in living systems terms, Darwin's unit of analysis was an organism-environment interaction pattern. He saw such units as systems that achieved and maintained steady state functioning against minor perturbations of their adaptation pattern. However, any change that significantly disrupted the current steady state accommodation would require some adaptive reorganization of the organism-environment interaction pattern. Individuals would differ in the relative success of their efforts to create a new steady state pattern or in the adaptive value of the pattern resulting from the reorganization. Those individual differences would exert selective pressures on rates of survival and reproduction, so that some forms of living systems would increase in number and others would decrease. Through positive feedback, a snowball effect could occur leading to the eventual dominance of one form of living system or the extinction of another.

However, Darwin visualized *opportunity as well* as *disruption as an impetus for change.* For example, suppose the environmental niche for some type of organism remained stable, but some individuals within that population of organisms were born with some additional structural-functional capabilities. They could use the same adaptation possibilities as their parents, aunts, uncles, and siblings. However, their additional capabilities created new adaptive possibilities which, if discovered and used, would enable those individuals and their descendants to flourish in ways their ancestors could not.

It is clear that Darwin saw adaptation as a dynamic process impor-tantly influenced both by an active organism and by environmental factors. It is historically interesting that extensions of his views tended to emphasize environmental-selective pressures, perhaps because that fit a mechanistic model, while organism-initiated selection factors did not (Ghiselin, 1969). Darwin's theory also made it clear that evolutionary processes were a function of organisms' behavior patterns made possi-ble by structural changes. Finally, evolution is probabilistic with un-known future possibilities which themselves may change as organisms and environments change. Development is open-ended. Many trajecto-ries are possible and none are fully predetermined.

After Darwin's theory became well known, Mendel's work on genetics was discovered. Genetic theory provided a mechanism for understand-ing both the stability of existing species and the appearance and proliferation of new organismic characteristics as described in evolution-ary theory.

Neo-Darwinism—The Modern Synthesis

Waddington (1976) asserts that the idea that evolution consisted of nothing more than random mutation ("chance") and natural selection ("necessity") reached its peak around 1930. Then new ideas began to emerge that influenced some elaboration and reinterpretation of the original theory which came to be called neo-Darwinism or the modern synthesis (Stebbins & Ayala, 1985). It utilizes the concepts of genes, organisms, populations, species, and environments.

Genes are a part of the structure of the nucleus of each cell of which individual organisms are composed. They carry the information or "rules" that guide the biological development of each individual organ-ism. Different kinds and combinations of genes produce different kinds of *organisms* (e.g., hamsters and humans). Initially, it was assumed that all members of each species (i.e., organisms of the same kind capable of interbreeding and producing fertile offspring) had the same combina-tion of genes. Change could occur only if a new or modified gene appeared in a member of that species (e.g., through point mutation).

However, as genetic knowledge grew it became apparent that individuals within a species had different combinations of genes. For example, each human differs in some way from every other in his or her genetic characteristics.

This new information led to the concept of a *genetic pool*. The totality of all genes found within a species was considered the genetic pool for that species. Variations in individuals could occur, then, through different combinations of genes from the larger genetic pool (i.e., through mating), in addition to mutational change. Within each species, subgroups called *populations* can be identified which differ from others of the same species in some consistent ways (e.g., American Indians, Asians, Europeans, and Africans). If some population or subpopulation is isolated (i.e., protected) from the influences that affect the rest of their species (e.g., by being on an island to which there is no access), they will, over a period of many years, produce a population of organisms somewhat different from other members of their species because of their genetically based differences interacting with their special environmental niche.

Many variants of organisms are presumed to result from this process of gradual accumulation of such small genetic differences; but only those proliferate who manage to effectively adapt to their environments so as to produce a survival and reproductive advantage. Slow and continuous evolutionary change results from selection of different patterns of environmental influences (called an *environmental niche*) operating on genetic variations in individual organisms.

Biological attributes resulting from natural selection may continue even after changes in the organism's environmental niche eliminate the adaptive value of such attributes. For example, Afro-American blacks' genetic inheritance facilitates sickle cell production because it provided some protection against the most severe form of malaria in Africa. It is now maladaptive for American blacks, producing high mortality and disability rates, since malaria is no longer a problem for them (i.e., their environmental niche has changed) (Maugh, 1981).

Darwinian theory could be interpreted to support the view that humans are passive receivers of environmental influences and are automatically shaped by them, making the theory compatible with the dominant mechanistic zeitgeist in science.

Types of Genetic Change.   Genetic changes make possible the evolutionary process and are of two basic types (Stebbins & Ayala, 1981). First, gene mutations represent actual changes in *genetic content*. And second, chromosomal mutations affect the number of chromosomes, or the arrangement of genes in chromosomes (Dobzhansky et al., 1977).

They represent changes in the *organization* of genetic material. At least four ways of producing such changes have been identified (Stebbins & Ayala, 1981).

But the influence of genetic changes on the development of organisms is not always automatically the same. The same set of genes (genotypes) may produce somewhat different organisms (phenotypes) if they develop in different environments. Conversely, somewhat different genotypes may produce similar phenotypes depending on their environments. This lack of a one-to-one correspondence between genotype and phenotype led Waddington (1976) to conclude that the idea that natural selection can be reduced to the simple notion of "necessity" is completely untenable. In fact, much of the environment that will exert natural selection on a mobile animal (like a human) is a result of the animal's own behavior. By moving to or creating a different environment, an organism alters the influences upon it. Humans exert considerable control over the influences upon them not only by their mobility, but also as a result of their ability to design aspects of their environment to serve their purposes. Thus, genetic research reaffirmed Darwin's view that evolution was a consequence of dynamic, mutually influential interactions between organisms and their environments.

Neo-Neo-Darwinism: Punctuated Equilibrium

The gradualism doctrine, while coordinate with many observations, has been inadequate to account for others (e.g., Koestler, 1967, 1978). The principle problem is that fossil records suggest that many species remain relatively unchanged throughout their history (e.g., Stanley, 1979; Williamson, 1981a), despite considerable environmental change and stress on the species. Technically, this is called *morphological stasis* (a kind of evolutionary steady state). Fossil evidence reveals that long-term, gradual transformation of single lineages seldom occurs (Eldridge & Gould, 1972; Stanley, 1979), and that when it does occur it generally involves "...simple size increase or trivial phenotypic effects" (Williamson, 1981a). Stated in systems terms, all living systems achieve stability by creating and maintaining steady state conditions both within themselves and between themselves and the larger systems of which they are components (i.e., their environmental niche).

Because the theory of gradualism in evolution required it, there has been an assumption that the lack of evidence showing the gradual transition from one species to another was simply the result of "gaps" in fossil evidence, and that if scholars kept searching, the "gaps" could be filled. An example is the search for the "missing link" between apes and humans.

However, debate among scholars of evolutionary biology (Lewin, 1980, 1985) turned the issue around and suggested that the problem lies in an incomplete theory rather than inadequate data. An important reinterpretation and elaboration of evolutionary theory is emerging. It acknowledges that organisms do undergo some evolutionary modifications in line with the "gradualism" doctrine. However, the emerging view of *speciation* is that different types of organisms often remain relatively unchanged during long periods, and that these periods are sometimes punctuated by relatively abrupt events that result in the branching off of a somewhat different type of organism from the old one. This process has been termed *punctuated equilibria* by Eldridge and Gould (1972), and Stanley (1979) includes this idea in his representation of macroevolution.

This idea has been emerging for some time. For example, Goldschmidt (1940) argued that the first step in macroevolution "...requires another evolutionary method" besides "sheer accumulation of micromutations." Mayr (1963) proposed some form of "developmental homeostasis" to account for the extensive morphological stasis of most modern species. Speciation involves a disruption of such a homeostatic system. Williamson (1981a) presents convincing evidence supporting this view. His studies of speciation in the Turkana Basin mollusc sequence revealed that it was "... invariably accompanied by major developmental instability" (Williamson, 1981b). Ten years earlier, Levin (1970) pointed out the importance of developmental disruption and instability during speciation events. For several decades, Waddington (1976) has considered a notion like developmental homeostasis important, pointing out that cybernetic control is clearly evident in individual development. He noted that a normal adult will develop from a fertilized egg despite wide variation in environmental factors, and that environmental stresses have to be "quite severe" before they produce developmental changes. He argued that homeostatic or cybernetic controls produce "resistance to change."

Thus, there appear to be two qualitatively different evolutionary change processes, one gradual and one more abrupt. Carson (1975) proposed the idea of "open" and "closed" genetic systems. Open ones involve minor adaptive alterations within species populations. Closed ones involve more profound changes during speciation. Stebbins and Ayala (1981, 1985) assert that both gradualism and punctuated equilibrium processes are compatible with the theory of population genetics concerning microevolutionary processes and propose that the influence of natural (environmental) selection on the evolution of living systems is constrained by three types of influences: (a) the organism's existing structural and functional organization (which reflects and encompasses its history); (b) the genetic variation available to it within its current species boundaries; and (c) the specific circumstances of that organism's physical and biotic environment (i.e., its environmental niche). Mayr (1954) proposed certain conditions necessary for speciation, which Williamson's (1981a) evidence supports. In general, homeostatic mechanisms and gene flow prohibit significant evolutionary change in large populations. However, a small population that is geographically isolated from the rest of its species, and is subject to some kinds of internal and/or external stresses that disrupt existing homeostatic or "stability maintaining" mechanisms, may display rapid evolution. Developmental disruption and instability are important in the speciation process due to a breakdown in the canalization of individual development (ontogeny) (Levin, 1970). During this period of developmental instability, the population's phenotypic variance increases (Williamson, 1981a), which may produce a variety of new alternate directions for development. Through the kinds of constraints mentioned earlier, some of these variants become "selected out" (i.e., don't survive) and others become "selected in" (i.e., survive and multiply). Geographic isolation during the period of developmental instability protects the population from the competition and influence of other stable population forms until it has restabilized in a somewhat different form. Then the new, stable variant may be able to survive and multiply in competition with older, stable forms.

The combination of gradual and more abrupt processes in evolution just described appears to represent a pattern of *organization, elaboration* (through gradual change), *disorganization* (through disruption and instability), *reorganization,* and *elaboration.* The pattern involves both continuity and discontinuity in development. Major changes appear to require some period of protected disruption during which a new steady state adaptive pattern (i.e., reorganization) can be stabilized. The emerging new forms that survive must fit within the constraints of both organismic and environmental organization.

Gould (1980) asserts that the result is the need for a concept of hierarchy in the study of evolution. Evolution produces a world "...constructed not as a smooth and seamless continuum" but as a hierarchical series of levels, "each bound to the one below it in some ways and independent in others"; and "emergent features" not present in the operation of lower level processes, may control events at "higher levels."

Social Groups and Evolution

Genetic material is the means of retaining and transmitting the fruits of evolutionary processes to future generations (as libraries retain and transmit cultural knowledge), and individual organisms are the carriers of genes and the means of reproduction. Evolutionary theory has also emphasized the importance of environmental forces, but largely in terms of their influence on individuals. Therefore, there has been an historic tendency to interpret evolution as functioning solely in the selfish interest of individual organisms or their genes (M. Hoffman, 1981).

Evolutionary theory has recently added important new emphases on the relationships between social group living and evolutionary processes. Early humans lived in small, nomadic hunting and gathering social groups that produced survival and reproductive advantages. Evolutionary processes probably selected for both individuals and social groups through interacting processes (Gould, 1977). The most influential current model for these phenomena is called *kin selection*, which rests on the basic concept of "inclusive fitness," that is, individuals' genetic fitness results not only from their and their offsprings' capabilities for survival and reproduction, but also from the enhancement of kin who share the same genetic characteristics. While the individual is the mechanism of evolution, the evolution of species depends only upon the existence of *some* of all those individuals who share an advantageous genetic endowment. Mother Nature doesn't care which ones. Therefore, evolutionary processes probably selected for characteristics that facilitated both individual and kinship group survival and reproductive advantages. Hoffman (1981) argues that evolution probably did not select directly for altruistic social behavior, but for some mediating behavior mechanism(s) that would facilitate altruistic behavior. He suggests that empathic emotional responding may be such a mechanism. A somewhat similar view is presented in Chapter 13 where "social" emotions are discussed.

As with all characteristics, although mechanisms mediating social group living might have evolved to facilitate kin survival and reproduction, once such mechanisms existed they could come into play in facilitating non-kin social groups (e.g., patriotism to one's nation and the Christian belief in the "fellowship of man").

A concept like inclusive fitness is supported by a living systems model. Individuals function simultaneously as living systems and as components or subsystems of larger living systems. Both the individual and the larger living system facilitate and constrain the welfare and functioning of one another. Functional properties may emerge at more complex levels of organization (e.g., social groups) that may not be present at lower levels of organization (e.g., individuals). The concept of inclusive fitness is an example of those living system principles manifest in evolutionary theory.

Genetics and Evolution

Scientific advances have made possible much more sophisticated study of genetic processes through cell biology (Abelson, 1980). Watson and Crick reported in 1953 that DNA, the basic genetic material, is organized in a "double helix." It is like a zipper twisted about itself in a corkscrew shape. DNA is duplicated by "unzipping" it, creating two "half-zippers." (Actually, it is like a breaking zipper, splitting open here and there until completely separated.) Special enzymes within the cell enclosing the DNA then construct and match interlocking parts to each half-zipper, and through that process create two new complete DNA zippers or strands. The elements or segments of the DNA zipper are called genes. Once scientists learned how to purify and use enzymes to "unzip" and rebuild DNA strands, they became able to "cut" pieces out of one DNA zipper and to reinsert them into another. They could build somewhat different DNA strands by recombining components (i.e., the genetic elements), in different ways. This is what the term *recombinant DNA* means.

Using this procedure, human genes have been transplanted into bacterial DNA. Such bacteria then "read" the human gene along with their own and manufacture human proteins (e.g., insulin, interferon, growth hormone) which may be used to treat human deficiencies. In other words, through such "genetic engineering" it is becoming possible for humans to manipulate the genetic basis of an individual organism's development and functioning.

It is now apparent from this expanding work that *it is not just the nature of different genes, but the way they are organized* that influences the nature of the organism that will develop (Singer, 1980; Stebbins & Ayala, 1985). There are "transposable components," "on-off components," and "exon" and "intron components" mixed in varying patterns through "chromosome cross-talk." The same genes, if organized differently can produce a different morphology (Kolata, 1981; Lewin, 1981a, 1981c; Marx, 1981a). In his Nobel Prize address, Gilbert (1981) noted that some evidence suggests that as one moves up the evolutionary ladder the organization of genetic material appears to provide increasingly complex organization having more complex and flexible options. Research in molecular biology has revealed that DNA instability, mediated by mobile genetic elements, makes possible some genomic rearrangement in most biological systems (Shapiro, 1983). Brenner and Stent (as quoted in Lewin, 1984) emphasize that genetic influences on development do not appear to represent a linear sequential process, analogous to a computer program. Rather, at the cellular level, they appear to function "as a cascade of complex stochastic interactions." Rather than there being a controlling program, "the interaction between components shapes the system." This reminds one of the notion of mutual entrainment discussed in Chapter 7. What appears to be somewhat disorderly at one level of organization may appear to be quite orderly at another.

What has emerged is a recognition that evolution is the product of a hierarchy of processes. Genetic influences are filtered through a net of developmental constraints, producing a set of possible phenotypes on which processes of natural selection can then operate (Gould, 1982; Lewin, 1980): (a) Whether or not a genetic change can become manifest in organismic change is influenced and constrained by the existing kind and organization of genetic characteristics of that organism and the environment within which the genetic material operates; (b) Whether or not an organismic change can become a permanent characteristic of the organism is influenced and constrained by the existing structural and functional organization of the organism; (c) Whether or not the organism will survive with that change is influenced and constrained by characteristics of its relationship with its environment; (d) whether or not the change will proliferate through a population of such organisms depends upon whether the new characteristics (combined with the old) give the organism a survival and reproductive advantage over others (or are correlated with characteristics that yield such advantages). Fundamental constraints on morphological evolutionary possibilities result not only from environmental influences, but also from the basic properties of the materials and the "construction and operational" rules characteristic of different kinds of organisms. Evolutionary diversity is possible, but only within the constraints of the organism-environment system. Koestler (1967) anticipated these ideas by arguing that the concept of internal selection through a hierarchy of controls is necessary to link "the 'atoms' of heredity and the living stream of evolution."

To anticipate our later formulation about individual development, the fundamental rationale of neo-neo-Darwinism might be summarized as follows. Living systems are always organized, both within themselves and in relationship to their environments. Externally or internally precipitated disruptions or alterations may occur in some aspect of that organization. Four possible consequences of such disruptions exist: (a) the organism may die because it cannot accommodate the change; (b) it may reject or suppress the change and continue with its traditional steady state organization; (c) it may reorganize itself so that the change is compatible with other attributes of its organization; and (d) it may reorganize its relationships with its environments to accommodate the change. Thus, the concepts of organization (both intra- and extra-organism), and reorganization of steady states have become cornerstones of modern evolutionary theory. The streams of theorizing about evolution, genetics and living systems have converged on common properties, like three streams which unite to produce a larger and more powerful river.

Adaptive and Nonadaptive Changes

Evolutionary change in genetic content and/or organization results in a reorganization of the organism. For example. a baby born with a sixth finger on one hand has not only added an extra finger. Other attributes, such as circulatory and neural characteristics, had to be reorganized so that the sixth finger was appropriately integrated into the rest of the body. Any component in that pattern of changes could give that child a survival and reproductive advantage. Because it is an organization of changes, all the changes linked to the initially advantageous one would also be selected for. Such fortuitous correlates of a currently advantageous change in an organism provide it with additional, latent potentialities which might later prove advantageous (or disadvantageous) as its environmental niche changes.

Traditionally, these "nonadaptive" correlates of evolutionary change have typically been given little attention. Gould (1982) argues that this pool of "nonadaptations" is quite large, serving as "a higher-level analog of genetic variation" and as "a phenotypic source of raw material for further evolution" because they are available for cooptation. Thus, one cannot safely infer from the present utility of some human capability its evolutionary sources. Stated simply, structural and functional characteristics evolved because of *specific* advantages they provided, or something they were linked to provided, in the organism's environmental niche at the time. However, once the characteristic was there, many other uses for it and for its correlates that also resulted from reorganization of the organism could be found. And those "other" uses might turn out to be much more important to the organism in the long run, particularly if important changes occur in its environmental niche. Analogously, a person may develop a behavior pattern for a specific purpose in a specific setting, and later in life find some component of that pattern of new and special value (e.g., a child who learns to obtain attention and approval from other children by being a "clown," and later finds some of that latent skill useful in an acting career).

Evolutionary Design: Components and Hierarchies

Using a model based on thermodynamic considerations and assumptions of the modern synthesis, Jacobson (1955) arrived at estimates of the time required for evolution of all presently existing living systems estimates that were so large as to be highly improbable. Simon (1969) made similar estimates but added the concept of stable intermediate forms of organization or "subassemblies" (i.e., components). He demonstrated that if there exists a hierarchy of potential "stable subassemblies," a complex entity can evolve in a much shorter time by utilizing existing simpler components than if it were to start from "scratch." Simon illustrated this point by comparing two hypothetical methods of constructing watches. One watchmaker assembles one entire watch at a time. Whenever he is interrupted, he must lay down the watch on which he is working. If it is not completed, it will fall apart and when he returns he must start all over. In contrast, a second watchmaker designed his watch so that it was composed of several components or subassemblies. First he constructs many components of each type. Then he assembles sets of components into a complete watch. If he is interrupted, he does not need to start at the very beginning, but only with the last component with which he was working.

This componentized approach is typical of modern production methods. Componentization is used to produce functional efficiency as well. In economics, functional componentization is called *specialization*, or the division of labor. Simon concluded that the reason hierarchies predominate in the complex forms found in nature is that of all possible forms, "hierarchies are the ones that have had the time to evolve." He notes that there can be many kinds of hierarchies, but they all involve the notion of componentizing structures and functions, and organizing them in interdependent patterns. The nature of the conditionalities among the components (i.e., parts) defines the nature of the hierarchy (i.e., wholes).

Homologous Structures. The biological phenomena of homologous structures, (i.e., structures that have the same general design even though their exact form and function may vary) provide evidence of evolutionary componentization. Koestler (1967) points out that homologous design is apparent at every level from the subcellular levels through the level of brain structure. For example, the cells of mice and men have the same type of organelles; the same kind of contractile protein "serves the motion of amoeba and of the pianist's fingers." Such homologous structures are not created by the same specific gene but by "genetic micro-hierarchies" that permit considerable variation, but only in limited directions on a limited number of themes. For example, Fig. 4.1 illustrates that the skeletal structure of the forelimbs of a man, a dog, a bird, and a whale are fundamentally the same in organization, although the components differ somewhat in size and shape (i.e., they

FIG. 4.1 An example of the concept of homologous organs. The number and organization of bones in the forelimbs of these four vertebrates are the same, but their relative size and the functions they make possible are quite different. (From LIFE; AN INTRODUCTION TO BIOLOGY by George Gaylord Simpson, et al., copyright 1957 by Harcourt Brace Jovanovich, Inc.; renewed 1985 by Anne R. Simpson, Helen Vishniac, Joan Simpson Burns, Elizabeth Leonie S. Wurr, and Ralph Tiffany. Reproduced by permission of the publisher.)

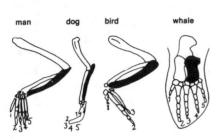

man   dog   bird   whale

Vertebrate forelimbs (after Life, An Introduction to Biology, by G.G. Simpson et al)

are homologous organs) (Simpson et al., 1957). But, although they are structurally homologous, they perform quite different functions: grasping or manipulating, walking or running, flying or swimming.

Thompson (1917) demonstrated that one type of organism might be transformed into another while preserving the same basic structural design by "evenly distorting" the whole structure so as to retain the same geometric relationships; an example is the skulls of the baboon, chimpanzee, and man. The point of this example is to make it clear that the transformation of a component from use in one species to use in another is one continuous and integral process, not a random shaping of elements; the jaws, brain case, and so on are all transformed in proportion to, and in relationship to, one another. It appears as if there are some basic "organizational rules" that restrict the pattern of changes that can occur.

Most living systems appear to have certain basic components in common. For example, genetic research has demonstrated that animal and bacterial genes are transposable (Science, 1980). The closer that species are in terms of their evolutionary origins, the more similar appear to be their component structures and their organization (O'Brien & Nash, 1982). For example, 18 of 23 pairs of human chromosomes are essentially identical with those of our "common hominoid ancestor," with the remaining pairs differing only slightly (Yunis & Prokash, 1982).

With increasing evolutionary complexity, the same fundamental components may become more diversified and specialized. Recent research on hormones is illustrative (e.g., Kolata, 1982). Hormones are produced by highly specialized glands. However, many different kinds of cells also produce different kinds of hormones (e.g., Olson et al., 1979). This has raised the question of how far back in evolutionary history the ability to make hormones goes. It now appears that hormones emerged in evolution before plants and animals diverged, and that cell hormones and neurotransmitters began as "tissue factors," or substances that stimulate cells to grow or to interact biochemically. As evolution proceeded, plants and animals continued to make similar hormonelike substances but in somewhat different forms. For example, plant alkaloids have molecular structures different from animal hormones, but they bind very well to animal hormone receptors. In a sense, every cell is also a "gland," a capability inherited from its primitive ancestors. Similarly, cellular diversification and specialization within individual organisms, which has required increasing levels of cellular synchronization, has reached "...a remarkable level of complexity in the nervous system" (Black, 1982).

Thus, living systems do not, and cannot, evolve in unlimited directions. More than chance is involved. Evolutionary development results from the shaping or transformation of an existing system and must conform to its basic continuing components, organizational rules, and attributes. Once Mother Nature evolved a useful component, she used it over and over again in many different organisms. Moreover, new uses for old components were found, and by combining them with other components useful functions could be improved or elaborated and new ones developed. And these principles apply to both structural (i.e., biological) and functional (i.e., behavioral) components. In this manner, evolution could proceed in a very efficient, cumulative manner. Through use of componentization, an increasing diversity and complexity of organisms (both structurally and functionally) could occur in an accelerating progression with more options.

Body Temperature Regulation: An Example of Componentized Evolution. . The organization of thermal regulation in mammals illustrates the notion of componentized evolution (Bennett & Ruben, 1979; Satinoff, 1978).

Within a control system model, body temperature is detected by heat-sensitive neurons that can trigger autonomic and behavioral activity to counteract deviations from an innate "set point" defining optimal body temperature (Yamamoto & Brobeck, 1965). The preoptic area of the hypothalamus appears to contain centrally regulating thermal homeostats. This was explored in Benzinger's (1961) study of hypothalamic control of sweating, one means of controlling body temperature. Sweating began at 98.4 °F or 36.9 °C. A temperature change of .01 °C measurably increased the dissipation of heat through sweating at that critical temperature. It was as if the subject's "thermostat" was set for that temperature. Above it, sweating sharply increased. Below it, sweating hardly occurred.

Further experimental evidence indicated that there are multiple autonomic and behavioral mechanisms for thermal regulation. It now appears that there is "...hierarchical organization of the parallel integrative systems...," with each component having its own broad set point, all of which through their hierarchical interaction "...give the illusion of a single integrator for a single narrow set point." The hypothalamic thermostat, then, serves to coordinate and organize "...the activity of thermoregulatory systems located at several lower levels of the neuraxis" (Satinoff, 1978). By combining several component processes into a larger functional component, temperature regulation sensitive to a variety of potentially disturbing variables is achieved.

How might such a temperature regulation arrangement have evolved? The evolution of endotherms' (e.g., humans) involved the development of a diversity of means of regulating body temperature, such as shivering, panting, sweating, chemical thermogenesis, peripheral circulation, and insulators such as fur, feathers, or fat. These did not all develop at the same time, and no animal has them all. As different methods of temperature control evolved within a single animal species, they had to become coordinated with one another so they would complement rather than contradict each other (Satinoff, 1978). Componentized hierarchical organization increases flexibility and adaptiveness. Having several different means of controlling body temperature, all of which can be implemented separately or in various combinations, makes adaptation to a greater diversity of conditions possible, and provides some "back-up" safeguards if a particular mechanism malfunctions.

In general, the evolutionary process takes existing components and transforms them to serve additional functions. For example, Cowles (1958) has proposed that the mechanisms for controlling blood flow at the body surface first served a respiratory function in amphibia. This later evolved into the function of heat collection and dispersion in reptiles (primarily controlling heat flow from the outside in). Still later, it became one of several temperature-regulating mechanisms in endotherms (regulating the flow of heat from the inside out). But why did endothermic temperature regulation evolve at all? Bennett and Ruben (1979) propose an answer that illustrates an even broader notion of hierarchical organization. An organism is a complexly organized, functional whole. A change in one set of components and functions is likely to directly or indirectly affect the entire organization (or organism) through mutual causal processes. Their evidence suggests that physiological thermoregulation evolved as a correlate of vertebrates' increased mobility and activity capabilities. Ectoderms, such as snakes and lizards, depend primarily on anaerobic metabolism to sustain high levels of activity (e.g., speedy movement); this works for only limited periods of time before exhaustion occurs, and recovery from exhaustion takes considerable time. Animals who evolved to sustain greater levels of pursuit, flight, or competition in gathering food or avoiding predators, in territorial defense or invasion, or in courtship and mating had an advantage (Bennett & Ruben, 1979). However, sustained activity levels require increased oxygen exchange processes, which necessitated development of aerobic metabolism as the primary energy production mechanism supplemented by anaerobic metabolism. However, maximal oxygen consumption and aerobic capabilities are temperature dependent. Therefore, the ability to maintain higher body temperatures, greater aerobic capabilities, and greater diversity in activity levels evolved as interdependent capabilities (Bennett & Ruben, 1979).

Hierarchically related structures require hierarchically related control and regulatory functions. In complex organisms, homeostasis is not a product of a single simple control system but of an organized hierarchy of such controls (Toates, 1975, 1979), which produces a much more flexibly adaptive system.

Implications from Evolution and Genetics for Developmental Principles

1. The current structural-functional organization of an organism and its environment represent a set of constraining and facilitating boundary conditions which limit and channel the kinds of changes that can occur.

2. An organism functions to maintain its existence as a unit within its contexts. Therefore, for any structural-functional change to become a permanent part of a surviving and reproducing organism, it must be integrated into the overall organization of the organism and its patterns of environmental transactions.

3. An organism is organized as a hierarchy of structural-functional components in an environment similarly organized. Individuals have some similar kinds and organizations of components as other individuals because of their shared evolutionary and genetic histories, and some different components because of unique aspects of their evolutionary and genetic history. Organismic change can result either from changes in *kind* (e.g., gene mutations) or *organization* (e.g., genetic sequencing) of components. Somewhat different conditions (genotypes) may produce similar results (phenotypes) and similar conditions may produce somewhat different results.

4. Change may be a gradual process resulting from progressive and cumulative selective elaboration, and minor changes of existing possibilities within the species as a function of differentially advantageous environmental consequences.

5. Change may occur relatively abruptly as a result of some reorganization of the organism to accommodate some influence(s) that have disrupted the existing dynamic stability of the organism. The continuation of such changes is also a function of differentially advantageous environmental conditions. This reorganization opens up new developmental options for future gradual evolution. Such changes are irreversible.

6. Significant change is most likely to emerge in a population of organisms if they are isolated, or sheltered from competition and interaction with similar organisms, while the transition or change process is occurring.

7. Adaptative potentials increase as the diversity of potential developmental options increase (e.g., a more diverse genetic pool). Characteristics evolve because of specific adaptive utility (i.e., survival and reproductive consequences), or as correlates of such characteristics. However, once available they represent a set of potentials for future adaptive use regardless of the reasons for their original development.

8. Individuals evolved as components within social groups. Therefore, some of the attributes of individuals that evolved did so to facilitate adaptive functioning of social groups as larger living systems.

EMBRYONIC AND ORGANISMIC DEVELOPMENT

From the moment of conception, the fertilized ovum functions as a self-constructing living system. The process by which a single cell evolves into a person is a dynamic changing pattern of differentiation, elaboration, specialization, and organization of cells and their basic properties. It is a process of componentization which requires an increasingly complex organization in order to maintain unity.

Genetic Organization and Individual Differences

The nucleus of the cell contains the genetic information that regulates the biological development and functioning of individual organisms. All new cells result from cell division by existing cells. Special germ cells in the human gonads divide through a process called *meiosis* that produces daughter cells (i.e., ova or sperm) with only half of the human chromosome complement.

The joining of a female and a male haploid germ cell, an ovum and a sperm, each containing information for only "half a human," is necessary to produce a cell from which a human can evolve; and this is a primary source of the variability of characteristics of individuals of the same species. Mathematically, there are an enormous number of different genetic combinations possible within the genetic pool of a species. Except for identical twins, no two organisms start with exactly the same genetic instructions. Moreover, the way the genetic instructions are implemented is influenced by the constraining, facilitating, and disrupting conditions of the embryo's environment. For example, a young embryo is undifferentiated in terms of its sexual or reproductive structures and functions. In normal fetal environments, genetic influences will determine whether the embryo differentiates into a female or a male. However, a fetus with mixed characteristics may develop if subject to an atypical embryonic environment (Levine, 1966). Thus, individual differences are an important fundamental evolutionary and biological fact to be understood, valued and preserved.

The new cell (a zygote) begins to elaborate itself through *mitosis*, first dividing into two cells, then four, and so on in geometric progression. Each cell is a reproduction of its parent cell and contains in its nucleus duplicate genetic instructions for an entire person.

However, as embryonic development continues, each cellular offspring specializes in only a few of the potentials inherited from the parent cell and inhibits the development of all other possibilities. Each cell's specialized skills serve the body in some important way. This collection of "specialists," working cooperatively together, create and maintain a harmonious, effective unit, the human body. Thus, the efficient principles of division of labor, componentization, and cooperation that are so fundamental to modern technological societies are also basic in organismic development.

Interpreting Genetic Instructions to Fit the Cell's Environment. Rather than providing rigid blueprints, genes provide a set of guidelines that constrain the developmental options, but that have to be interpreted and applied in relationship to the conditions of their environment during the "construction" process (Plomin, 1986). Koestler (1967) refers to this approach as "fixed rules and flexible strategies." The initial zygote is a complete, complexly organized living system. Through all its transformations during the developmental process, from a cell to a person, it must maintain organizational unity if the embryo is to survive.

The genetic guidelines are subject to an embedded hierarchy of environmental influences; the intracellular cytoplasm, the cell's intercellular fluid and neighboring cells, the mother's fallopian tubes and uterus, her body, and her physical and social environment (e.g., what she eats and inhales) (Peters et al., 1981). If each component of this hierarchy of interacting environments provides the prototypical environmental niche, then the genetic guidelines will manifest themselves in a "normal" developmental pattern. Significantly deviant environments will alter the expression of the genetic guidelines and the resulting developmental pattern.

Environmental factors exert influence continuously because organisms are open systems. The first point at which developmental deviations may begin is during germ cell production. If the male sperm or female ovum have anomalies, their union through fertilization is likely to initiate a deviant developmental pattern. For example, usage of marijuana (Margolis & Popkin, 1980) or the hallucinogenic drug LSD (Jacobson & Magyar, 1968), exposure to radiation and excessive consumption of alcohol (Thompson, 1979; Timiras, 1972) all can potentially produce deviations in germ cells.

Once the cell division process begins, any unusual environmental variations can produce developmental deviations in the embryo. For example, like many other drugs, thalidomide may have no harmful effects on adults but may have serious effects on embryos (e.g., babies born without arms or legs). The third to eighth week after conception appears to the be most critical time during which fetal malformation from thalidomide may occur (Timiras, 1972). Since a woman may not discover that she is pregnant until several weeks after fertilization actually occurs, fetal damage from substances she is ingesting may occur before she even realizes she is pregnant. Incidentally, this tragic human episode of thalidomide damaged infants illustrates the practical importance of understanding species differences; thalidomide produces major malformations in human babies, but not in other animals (Timiras, 1972).

Thus, each step in the biological developmental progression from a small, multipurpose unit to a complex, specialized living system is controlled by the interplay between the cell(s) and its surroundings through mutual causal processes rather than linear causality.

Functional Specialization and Organizational Complexity

The parent zygote is a kind of Jack and Jill of all trades with the potential for performing at least eight basic functions in addition to reproducing itself.[2] These are irritability, conductivity, contractibility, absorption and

---

[2]It is interesting to note that this level of understanding of cells emerged before advances in biochemistry, biophysics, and cell biology (and the related technologies) made it possible to look "inside" cells to try to understand what was behind their functional properties. In an analogous way, behavioristic psychology has been trying for the past half century to define broad, observable properties of human behavior. Now the focus of attention in psychology is shifting toward trying to understand what lies behind those broad, observable properties.

assimilation, secretion, excretion, respiration, growth, and reproduction.

As cells differentiate from the original "parent cell," they specialize in one or more of these eight functions, by activation and suppression of different organizations of genetic material. At least four kinds of factors appear to be involved: timers, cytoplasmic characteristics, biochemical environment, and neighboring cells. It is worth emphasizing that all of these are organizational properties.

Timers. Small developmental timing differences may generate large shifts in physical form (Lewin, 1981b). Small initial deviations can become amplified into large differences through positive (i.e., deviation-amplifying) feedback arrangements. This may be a basis for a mode of evolution called *heterochrony,* in which new species emerge because the timing of some developmental events is altered (Gould, 1977; Marx, 1984). The timing mechanisms orchestrating the beautiful complexity of embryonic development are yet to be established. Proposals all appear to lean upon organizational properties, such as local forces within and between cells, and position in a developmental field. There appear to be spatial and dynamic laws of organization that control such developmental processes (Malacinski & Bryant, 1984).

Soll (1979) concludes that there are a minimum of six timers in developing systems, each identified with at least one morphological stage, that appear to function in parallel. Edmunds and Adams (1981) suggest that there may exist a "...collection of timing loops of different lengths" that can be combined in various ways "...to form a flexible timer," which they term a *cytochron.* Developmental timers appear to be different from functional timers such as circadian clocks or rhythms (Aschoff, Daan, & Groos, 1982).

Cytoplasmic Characteristics. The biochemical activity of the cellular material surrounding the gene-containing nucleus is a second set of influences (Ham, 1969). The cytoplasm may be organized into distinguishable zones providing a polarity to which naturally generated electric currents may be related and which may also influence cell division and specialization (Marx, 1981c). Once some genes are activated and some repressed in the cell nucleus, the protein composition of the cytoplasm becomes specialized; this process of specialized protein synthesis provides a cytoplasmic composition that functions to keep the same genes activated and suppressed. Once a cell has specialized, all its daughter cells will have the same pattern of gene activation and suppression.

The Biochemical Environment. Cells are surrounded by a fluid that provides the medium from which each cell obtains nutrients and into which it discharges its manufactured products and waste. Variations in that medium may differentially affect the cytoplasm, as, for example, in producing messenger RNA (Ham, 1969). Moreover, in the earliest cell divisions the cytoplasmic material is not equally divided among the daughter cells. Therefore, differential cytoplasmic material may be interacting with a variable cellular fluid environment.

Neighboring Cells. Spatial proximity among cells is a fourth kind of influence. Embryonic induction involves the appearance of morphological changes in one type of cell as a result of its physical association with other types of cells. Bryant, French, and Bryant (1981) have proposed a polar coordinate model in which cells acquire information about their physical position in a developing cell population. For example, a frog's eye develops from the optic vesicle in the embryonic frog head. The head tissue over the optic vesicle develops into the lens of the eye. If the optic vesicle is transplanted to the wall of the frog's stomach at a certain embryonic stage, the stomach tissue over the vesicle will evolve into a lens. This will not occur during other developmental phases. In general, each cell's development is influenced by its "closest neighbors." With cell development as with individual human development, no person is an island.

In 1961, Jacob and Monod proposed a genetic mechanism called an *operon* to account for the differentiation process (Miller & Resnikoff, 1978), but its generality for living systems has not been demonstrated. It is more likely that in complex living systems such as humans, a variety of mechanisms regulating cellular differentiation and organization exist, probably functioning in some hierarchical fashion (J. Miller, 1978; Wright, 1966).

The Process of Embryonic Development

In general, then, the new embryo develops through cell replication by subdivision and irreversible specialization into a more complex entity through interactions within and among its genetic nucleus, its cytoplasm, and the cell's environment. The embryo develops "steady by jerks" through a sequence of phases, with each phase building upon the structures and functions evolved by the previous ones. Developmental transitions begin when one embryonic phase evolves to the point where the patterns of intra- and intercellular influence both disrupt the existing organization and provide somewhat different options for future development. Cellular specialization is irreversible. A cell cannot "change its mind." With this componentized "division of labor" comes interdependence of components. Thus, the development of a mature biological structure is shaped each step along the way by the mutual influence of (a) the previous evolutionary and ontogenetic developmental history and the limits resulting therefrom; (b) the properties of the structural-functional organization at that stage; and (c) the properties of its environments as they influence the embryo. Stated in system terms, each step in the development of a living system is controlled by the interplay of the properties of its own internal system and hierarchy, and the properties of the larger system hierarchies of which it is a part.

The first *blastula phase* of embryonic development extends from the first cell division of the zygote to its implantation in the uterus as a mulberry-looking clump of cells with a fluid-filled inner cavity, within which a plate of irregularly arranged cells provides the precursor of the first transition phase of fetal development. The highest human death rate occurs during the blastula phase, and the next highest during the first part of the next phase. In other words, the *period of transition* between being a fertilized ovum and being an implanted, progressively differentiating organism is an embryonic human's most vulnerable period. This may be an evolutionary safeguard. A primitive new living system that is grossly imperfect because of some genetic malfunction or some early physical or biochemical damage becomes destroyed because of its inability to successfully complete the first developmental phases.

The *gastrulation phase* produces the transition-reorganization of the blastula into a more complex unit composed of three primary germ cell layers: the endoderm, an interior cell layer; the ectoderm, an external layer; and the mesoderm, a middle layer. As a part of this process, a rod-shaped structure called the notochord appears which is a precursor to the vertebral column. The transition from a "three-layered" organism to a fully formed fetus involves a progression of successively more differentiated and specialized structural developments (e.g., organs). The three germ cell layers differentiate into four tissue types (i.e., epithelial, connective, muscular, and nervous) that specialize in different patterns of cellular functions. For example, nervous tissue specializes in the functions of irritability, conductivity, and secretory functions—the new endocrinology of the neuron (Guillemin, 1978).

Organs resulting from tissue differentiation begin to become apparent in the fourth week after fertilization. Approximately three months after fertilization, the basic organ systems of the fetus and their interrelationships are established and from there on biological development focuses primarily on their further growth, elaboration, and integration. These organs emerge in a sequential order, and they generally cannot be stimulated to differentiate "out of order," (e.g., to have the liver develop before the nervous system) (Timiras, 1972).

Each of the three specialized germ cell layers is the primary source from which organs specializing in three different classes of living systems functions are differentiated: a *selection* function; a *self-con structing* or *autopoietic* function; and an *adaptation* function (LeGare, 1980).

The *ectoderm* is the primary source of most of those structures supporting *transactional functions* that involve material and informational exchanges with the environment and the use of information to coordinate those transactions, that is, the selection functions. These structures include all of the external body surfaces (e.g., skin and hair); structures immediately under those surfaces such as the lining of glands opening onto the surface; the sense organs and almost all of the nervous system which collect, organize, and use information from the environment; the teeth and linings of the nose, sinuses, mouth and anal canal which are involved in the collection, ingestion, and rejection or expulsion of materials; and certain key glands closely related to such functions (e.g., the pituitary gland).

The *endoderm* is the primary source of most of those structures supporting *biological self-construction and energy producing functions*. This includes most of the alimentary canal lining; the lining of most glands that secrete into the alimentary canal (e.g., pancreas, liver); the epithelium lining of structures involved with gaseous material exchanges (e.g., the larynx, trachea, alveoli and air saccules and other smaller air passages); the epithelium linings of structures associated with the collection of liquid wastes (e.g., the urinary bladder, urethra and prostate); and the epithelium of certain glands that appear to be closely related to these processes (e.g., the thyroid and parathyroid).

The *mesoderm* is the primary source of most of those structures that make possible *motoric transactions* with the environment (i.e., energy exchanges) and circulatory processes that provide nutrients, carry away wastes, and defend against intruders. This includes the blood vascular system, lymphatic system, and the blood itself; the entire body musculature (except for the eye's iris); all connective and sclerous tissue; the lining of the pericardial, pleural, and peritoneal cavities; most of the urogenital system; and certain related glands (e.g., the adrenal cortex).

As each organ begins to emerge as an identifiable structure, it represents a transition-reorganization phase that involves not only the tissue which differentiates into the new organ, but also the development of the physical and functional coordinating arrangements that will ensure its integration as a cooperating component within the total system. Thus, a consolidation-elaboration phase must follow each transition-reorganization phase to establish a solid framework for further transitions. All organs do not differentiate at the same time or evolve at the same rate. As some organs begin to emerge, other parts of the embryo remain in a relatively steady state. The unity of the entire organism can be retained as long as the disruptions of transitions involving organ development do not simultaneously encompass toomuch of the organism. Integrative transition of a part occurs within a sufficient degree of stability of the whole.

The transition phases in which tissues and organs undergo accelerated differentiation and/or elaboration are sometimes referred to as critical periods because they are the times when influences of various types (e.g., biochemical, radiation) may be amplified so as to produce helpful or deleterious consequences for later development and functioning. *Times of transition are both times of opportunity and times of danger.* While the first three months of fetal development are characterized by many such critical transitional phases, such phases also occur at other times of life, such as, for example, the production of immunoglobulins in early infancy, or the differentiation of hypothalamic and other CNS cells under the influence of a flood of sex hormones in adolescence (Timiras, 1972).

Neoteny and Paedomorphism. The biological concepts of neoteny and paedomorphosis represent a way in which embryological development and evolutionary processes might interact to produce new evolutionary directions (Gould, 1977).

As an embryo develops towards its mature adult form which can then reproduce, it goes through successive stages of increasingly complex organization. These stages appear to involve a series of binary decisions which permanently shut off some possibilities for future development while retaining others. For example, once cells have specialized as connective tissue they cannot back up and become neural tissue, but they can further differentiate into blood, bone, and cartilage cells. Therefore, as the organism develops towards its biologically mature adult form, the number of alternate developmental directions potentially available to it are progressively reduced to one adult form. As in a game of "Twenty Questions," things narrow down until there is only one right answer. Mature organisms reproduce and their offspring mature into organisms like their parents following the same timing and sequence of development.

Sometimes evolutionary processes produce a change in the timing with which different organs or parts mature, called *heterochrony.* One form is called *neoteny,* which means that an organism reaches sexual maturity while some of its components are still in a juvenile stage of development. It would be like a human two-year-old having babies. The result is *paedomorphosis* which means the retention of juvenile characteristics in the adult organism. Because such juvenile or immature characteristics are less specialized, they retain more flexibility for future evolutionary directions. Offspring produced by a sexually mature organism still in such a "juvenile" stage of development may mature in a somewhat different way than their ancestors, and produce a somewhat different adult form. Koestler (1967) cites as an example of this mechanism for "undoing and redoing" a primitive echinoderm (prickly-skinned) organism like a sea cucumber. In its mature form, it lay on the sea bottom. However, its larvae (juveniles) were free-floating in the water and had bilateral symmetry like a fish. Evolutionary processes made it possible for this larval form to reproduce while still in that juvenile stage. Thus, a new developmental direction began which some theorists think was the starting point for the evolution of vertebrates such as humans. As one possible illustration of paedomorphosis, deBeer (1940) noted that the human adult more closely resembles the embryo of an ape than it resembles an adult ape. The basic idea is that the less specialized an organism or a structural-functional component, the greater the diversity of developmental directions potentially available to it.

Life-Span Biological Development

Biological development continues after birth (e.g., brain myelinization, pulmonary branching, increases in size and weight). However, the basic biological structures and functions have all been established, and nearly all that remains is further consolidation and elaboration of that existing organization.

There are wide individual differences in the timing, rate and final characteristics of developmental patterns in infancy and childhood. Some individuals may develop slowly at first and speed up later, while others may do the opposite. Some may suffer developmental disruptions from negative environmental factors (e.g., nutritional deficiencies or ingestion of some drugs by the mother) and yet recover from those disruptions later, whereas others may suffer some permanent distortion of their development. Some may differ from the normative picture because of their unique genetic makeup. However, deviations from the normative pattern are generally not in themselves "bad" or for that matter "good." These are evaluative judgments, not factual statements. For example, a child born without legs is unlikely to become a fine athlete, but may become a creative artist partly because her mobility restriction led her to concentrate on other developmental possibilities. Individual development occurs along pathways open to individuals as a result of attributes of themselves and their environments. Current efforts to enhance opportunities for handicapped and mentally retarded people are implicitly based on that idea.

When an organism reaches it mature size, cell reproduction shifts from a primary focus on elaboration to one of replacement and repair. Cancer, a disease involving uncontrolled proliferation of malformed cells, appears to represent an inappropriate return to embryonic-like cell reproduction and elaboration processes (Yunis, 1983).

While most research has focused on understanding biological development during the early years, recent interest in adult development and aging has lead to the study of biological changes in those years as well (e.g., Birren & Sloan, 1980; Finch & Hayflick, 1977; Kart, Metress, & Metress, 1978; Poon, 1980; Timiras, 1972; Weiss, 1966). In general, the earlier years of biological development carry the image of being the time for biological elaboration, growth, and integration, whereas the later years carry the image of biological maintenance and deterioration. Although the nature of the changes is different, they both may be viewed as processes of differentiation (Weiss, 1966). Timiras (1972) asserts that all biological changes "...reflect a prior state or foreshadow events to follow," and therefore applies a developmental perspective to the adult years as well as to childhood.

While genetic influences appear to affect biological development and functioning throughout life (Plomin, 1986; Plomin & Thompson, in press), there is not yet theoretical agreement about why many biological changes occur in the adult organism. Biological changes in the adult are both structural and functional. In general, the changes in adult biological functioning represent changes in efficiency or effectiveness. For example, some functions take more time to occur; material exchanges may be less complete (e.g., a smaller portion of total food value is absorbed in the gut); energy production and utilization decline in both quantity and efficiency; sensory acuity declines; regulatory functions (e.g., water balance and temperature control) become less effective; and the organization or coordination of various functions become less adequate. As in any system, changes in one component (e.g., biological) may be compensated for by changes in another component (e.g., cognitive).

Recognition and understanding of biological changes across the life span have important practical consequences. For example, most drug dosages are based on normative assumptions about how the typical body will process such drugs. However, a variety of age-related changes in biological functioning affect the body's absorption and utilization of drugs. Therefore, a drug dosage that may be quite appropriate for a young adult may be unsatisfactory (e.g., perhaps damaging or ineffective) for an older adult, and vice versa.

One other developmental attribute of basic importance should be noted. The biological organism is *always organized* so that all of the components function in a cooperative, mutually beneficial way. Therefore, change must interact with the existing biological organization. For example, there is evidence that neurons retain considerable plasticity throughout life (Lerner, 1984), but there is also evidence of further "withdrawal" or decline of synapses in senescence. Bondareff (1980) has suggested that such neural changes may result from "...sequential, age-related interactions between extracellular and intracellular factors." Changes in extracellular events may precipitate "...a cascading series of cellular events" which eventually appear as changes in neuronal structure and function.

What might produce such extracellular changes? One possibility is life-style patterns. The accumulating effects of poor diet and inadequate exercise, or changes in diet and exercise patterns with age, may alter biological processes which in turn may further alter life-style patterns (e.g., Wishell, 1980). The message is if you don't use it, or if you abuse it, you may lose it!

Everitt and Huang (1980) point out that the neuroendocrine system, along with the neural system, is basic to the control and regulation of biological functioning. With aging, there is a decline in the daily secretion of some hormones and a compensatory increase in others. High levels of hormones resulting from frequent sympathetic overstimulation and a hyperactive adrenal cortex appear to have damaging effects on the cardiovascular, digestive, immune, and nervous systems. They conclude that the very hormones that facilitate successful coping with stressful environments also may produce "...an early onset of the breakdown phenomena" loosely associated with aging (see also Selye, 1976).

The body functions to maintain a steady state, and the concept of *equifinality* says that the same consequence can be achieved in more than one way. Evolution has built that principle into much of the complex biological organization of humans. Within the boundaries built into its structural and functional organization, the human body will do its best to reorganize its functioning to compensate for any significant disruptions or component malfunctions.

This fact is one of the things that makes medical diagnosis difficult. The symptom pattern of an illness will include not only direct manifestations of a disruption or disease, but also manifestations of the body's efforts to reorganize its functioning to deal with that malfunction. The latter symptoms may obscure the former and lead to a misdiagnosis. In fact, the concept of *syndrome*, upon which medical diagnosis is built, assumes that the body functions as an organized system and that a disruption anywhere within it will have multiple interrelated manifestations. Any single symptom may be the consequence of a variety of antecedents, and so by itself is an inadequate basis for diagnostic appraisal. It is the *pattern* of symptoms (or the syndrome), including those symptoms both present and not present, that provides the basis for inferring the nature of the malfunction. Identification of the points at which structural-functional transitions begin is particularly valuable information for determining probable causes and potential consequences of changes. That is why medical diagnosticians typically ask "When did it start?"; "What else was occurring then?"; "What happened next?"

Thus, biological development and functioning during the mature years must also be understood as permanent structural-functional organizations and reorganizations which are a product of properties of the organism and properties of its ongoing transactions with its environments. That is the very nature of a complex living system like a human. It functions to conserve existing organization, to construct and to cope.

IMPLICATIONS FROM EMBRYOLOGY AND DEVELOPMENTAL BIOLOGY FOR DEVELOPMENTAL PRINCIPLES

1. The greater the diversity of developmental potentials for an organism the more flexably adaptive it can be in dealing with variable environmental circumstances.

2. The actual course of development of an embryo is the result of mutually influential interactions between the embryo's own properties and those of its environment. It is both self-directing and responsive to outside influences.

3. An embryo is organized to function as a unit throughout its development from zygote to neonate, and the resulting organism functions as a unit throughout adulthood. If disrupting influences occur, the embryo functions to contain the impact of the disruption within its genetically programmed basic developmental pattern, although some aspects may become distorted (as with thalidomide babies). Disruptions so severe that their impact cannot be adequately limited will result in destruction of the organism (e.g., through early abortion).

4. Embryonic development occurs in a sequence of phases. Within each phase, development focuses primarily upon progressive elaboration of the existing structural-functional organization. However, this elaboration process eventually creates imbalances within the existing steady state patterns sufficiently disruptive to trigger some transition processes leading to some revised organization (i.e., a new steady state), within which progressive development can then proceed. Thus, embryonic development combines both continuous and discontinuous change processes; it must occur in a certain basic sequence, and it is irreversible.

5. Both development within embryonic phases, and transition processes leading to new phases, occur through differentiation and/or

elaboration of some existing aspect of embryonic organization. There must be some starting point within the existing structural-functional organization from which further development can proceed. This method of building complex entities by differentiating parts from the existing whole has a great advantage. It insures that newly developing components will be effectively integrated with other aspects of the organism and that the organism will always be currently organized.

6. Genetic influences on development are modified by the constraining and facilitating conditionalities present in the environment. When the environmental conditions are representative of those that are typical for that species' evolutionary history, the embryonic development will follow the species' normative pattern. Significant deviations from the typical environment are likely to result in deviations in embryonic development. Environmental influences are likely to have greater deviation producing influence when embryonic development is in transition between stages.

7. Development proceeds from relatively simple organization of a limited number of components with little specialization, to increasingly complex organization of a growing diversity of components that are increasingly specialized. Specialization produces efficient functioning but at the expense of restricting future developmental options. Complex organization produces increased stability for an organism and may increase some developmental options for the organism as a whole, while restricting options for its specialized components.

LEARNING AND DEVELOPMENT: ELABORATION OF A BEHAVIORAL REPERTOIRE

All functions of an organism are its behavioral capabilities. Behavior always occurs in organized patterns composed of biological, arousal, governing, and transactional functions. When a particular behavior pattern becomes a part of a person's capabilities, it functions as a unit. It becomes a functional component. All such functional components of which a person is capable compose his or her *behavioral repertoire*.

Functional Componentization

Theories of *macroevolution* are essentially based on evidence about the evolution of biological structures, because the primary evidence comes from fossil remains preserved over millions of years in geological layers that can be labeled in terms of time sequences. The evolution of functional organization leaves no fossil remains through which it can be traced, although indirect evidence of functional organization may appear in archeological findings. However, it is the evolution of functional capabilities which give survival and reproductive advantages that is the cornerstone of evolutionary theory. Since structure makes function possible, structural evolution provides indirect evidence of functional evolution. *Microevolutionary* theory and research by population biologists, geneticists, naturalists, ethologists, and anthropologists, provide additional evidence for inferences concerning the evolution of functional organization. The principle of *inclusive fitness* illustrates propositions aimed at understanding why some functional components (e.g., basic social behaviors) might be genetically linked (Axelrod & Hamilton, 1981; Bickhard, 1979; Burgess & Garbarino, 1982; Gubernick & Klopfer, 1981; M. Hoffman, 1981; Lovejoy, 1981; Lumsden & Wilson, 1981). Since genetic material is the means of transmission of the fruits of evolution from one generation to the next, and the evolution of functional capabilities is what provides survival and reproductive advantages, it follows that genetic processes should influence both structural and functional development. That is the assumption underlying the field of developmental behavior genetics (Ehrman & Parsons, 1981; Henderson, 1982; Plomin, 1986; Plomin & Thompson, in press).

In general, it appears that functional organization also evolves in hierarchically componentized patterns. This makes theoretical, logical, and practical sense. If functions are made possible by structural organization, and if structural organization evolves in hierarchically componentized fashion in both evolutionary and embryonic terms, then functional organization should evolve in a similar way. If hierarchically organized, componentized evolution is the most rapid, efficient, and effective way to create new living systems, then it seems reasonable to expect that *hierarchical, componentized functional organization* would also be an efficient method of behavioral development. If componentized organization increases functional options, then it should increase behavioral variability and effectiveness.

Inborn Functional Components.   There is considerable evidence to support the presence of inborn functional components in all kinds of organisms, that is, functional patterns that develop as a result of genetic influences interacting with properties of the organism's typical environmental niche (Kretchmer & Walcher, 1970). For example, many biological patterns of functioning such as digestion and all metabolism are essentially the same both within and among many species. It is this fact that makes biological research on other animals a source of useful information for understanding human biological functioning. Inborn componentized *behavioral functions* have also been identified. Most organisms appear to have some adaptive, automated behavior patterns "programmed" into them as a result of their evolutionary history, such as breathing; selective sensitivity to certain kinds of stimuli or information. Organisms such as insects and animals display a variety of social behaviors (Allee, 1958). This is what the ordinary person thinks of as "instinctive" behavior. Pavlov (1927) referred to such inborn behavior programs as "unconditioned reflexes."

Newborn human infants display a diversity of inborn behavior patterns; they can breathe, cough, sneeze, suck, swallow, regurgitate, digest, and assimilate certain kinds of food; they can react to heat, cold, pressure, and pain; they can reflexively eliminate urine and feces; they can react to strong light, loud sounds, and some specific stimuli; they can cry, turn their head, move their arms and legs, and perform a variety of reflexes such as grasping (Falkner, 1966; Osofsky, 1979). A limited array of fundamental patterns of emotional arousal may also start as inborn behavior patterns (Plutchik, 1980; Schellenbach, 1987). However, because humans have evolved a protracted, protected period of infancy after birth, many initial inborn behavioral components become operational only as the infant matures biologically. More complex and refined patterns can be elaborated starting from this initial inborn behavioral repertoire.

Self-Constructed Functional Components: Learned Behavior Patterns

Humans are mobile organisms with fairly long life spans. As a result, they face more complicated adaptive problems. In evolutionary terms, environmental variability and organisms' mobility were mutual causal processes. Environmental variability made some amount of mobility adaptive. Mobility functionally increased the diversity and variability of the environment in which the organism lived and functioned. Moreover, the relatively long life span of the human species and its ability to design and construct new social and physical environments has subjected it to increasing amounts of temporal variability and change.

This variability-mobility dynamic probably influenced and was influenced by the evolution of increasingly elaborate neural structures and processes for handling the increasing kinds, amounts, and diversity of information useful to the organism. Thus, primates, such as humans, developed behavioral capabilities for remembering attributes of environments previously experienced, for anticipating events, for constructing new patterns of behavior, and for combining old patterns into new combinations to effectively cope with greater variability. Mayr (1974) used the terms "closed" and "open" behavior programs to refer to these two basic types of evolutionary strategies, the *preprogrammed* and the *self-constructed* behavior patterns.

The capability to construct new behavior patterns is the focus of the study of learning. During the first half of the 20th century, the dominant assumption was that the learning of *all organisms* and of *all behavior* was governed by the same laws (Hilgard, 1948). Two kinds of accumulating evidence has led to a rejection of that premise. First is the evidence that analogous to the distribution of genetic and biological structures among species, some learning processes may be the same in all organisms but others may differ among species. That would be expected if one assumes that new functional principles may appear at different hierarchical levels of organization.

Seligman (1970) describes organisms that learn certain behavior patterns easily as "prepared" for such learning; that is, they appear to have an inborn capability for learning such behavior. Those that find it hard to learn a behavior pattern but can do so with appropriate training are "unprepared." Those that can never learn a particular behavior pattern are "contraprepared." For example, rats run mazes readily because that is part of their behavioral match with the environmental niche for which they evolved. They can learn to press Skinner box levers to get what they want, but using their paws to manipulate objects is less natural for them. They cannot be taught to sing, or to play the guitar, no matter how clever the trainer. Washburn, Jay, and Lancaster (1965) concluded that learning is not a general ability. Each animal can learn some things with ease, others with great difficulty, and others not at all.

Second, it began to appear that different kinds of responses might be learned somewhat differently, such as visceral responses (J. Miller, 1978), movement patterns (Kelso & Clark, 1982), perception (Johansson, vonHofsten, & Jansson, 1980), cognition (Gelman, 1978), and speech (Clark & Hecht, 1983). Even some of those categories have been subdivided. For example, perceptual development is studied by modality (e.g., visual perception; Kolers, 1983). Cognitive learning has been subdivided in many ways, such as memory (Horton & Mills, 1984), concept formation (Medin & Smith, 1984), attitude change (Cialdini, Petty, & Cacioppo, 1981), and instructional psychology (Gagne & Dick, 1983). Learning can produce behavioral components that come to function relatively automatically, analogous to inborn patterns. Such behavioral components are given names like *habits, schemas,* or *personality traits.* The ability to construct one's own behavior patterns and to make them habitual so that they can be run off "automatically" when one is confronted with a frequently encountered environment or task is a very efficient form of adaptation. Structural (biological) evolution involves altering, reorganizing, and elaborating existing structures within particular environmental niches. Functional or behavioral development appears to follow an analogous format. New behavioral components are evolved by combining, reorganizing, or altering existing ones to more effectively deal with particular environmental contingencies and tasks, and to produce particular consequences.

Principles of Learning

Several principles of learning have been proposed.

Classical Conditioning. Pavlov (1927) extensively studied one form of learning that involves adding a new element to an existing behavior-environment pattern; this is called *classical conditioning.* In the presence of particular environmental conditions (called the *unconditioned stimulus* or UCS), an inborn behavior pattern naturally occurs (called the *unconditioned response* or UCR). Salivation at the smell of food is a classical example. If some other kind of response occurs at the same time (e.g., looking in the direction of the food source), it can come to also occur in the presence of the UCS. Such learned response additions to inborn "reflexes" are termed *conditioned responses* or CRs. As Zener (1937) pointed out years ago, UCRs are not simple responses (e.g., salivation) but an organization of responses, a behavior pattern (e.g., orienting, gastric, and skeletal-muscle responses). Adding response components to an existing pattern is a way of constructing more elaborate behaviors from existing behavior-environment patterns.

Classical conditioning can also add a new component stimulus condition, called a conditioned stimulus or CS, to an existing behavior-environment pattern. It then becomes able to elicit the same behavior pattern. This is also sometimes referred to as "sign" or "cue" learning (Mowrer, 1956). For example, if a bell rings when food is presented, it can come to elicit salivation even when food is not presented. This is an important kind of learning because such cues enable people to anticipate and prepare for the occurrence of other important events. In classical conditioning, new behavior and environmental events are assumed to become related to existing patterns because of their spatial-temporal contiguity. Each elaboration opens up new options for potential future elaborations.

Instrumental Learning. Another form of learning is referred to as *instrumental or operant* conditioning (e.g., Skinner, 1953), or *solution learning* (Mowrer, 1956). The basic arrangement is that the occurrence of some event is made contingent upon the performance of some behavior. There are two types of such response-contingent events. In one, the contingent event provides information to guide the flow of behavior; that is, it provides a *cue* (Dollard & Miller, 1950) or a *sign* (Tolman, 1932). In the second type, the contingent event functions as a consequence, often called a *reinforcer* (e.g., reward or punishment), which influences the likelihood of the same behavior occurring in similar circumstances (Skinner, 1953). As in evolution, it is the instrumental utility of response→event relationships that determines which behavior patterns survive and repeat themselves, and which do not.

There are a variety of views about the nature of reinforcement and why it works (Glaser, 1971). Some theorists propose that such reinforcers influence learning by affecting the motivational state of the organism (e.g., "drive reduction": Hull, 1952). Implicit in this position is the notion that equilibrium is a preferred state of organisms. The importance of emotional states in learning, such as fear and hope, has been emphasized by others (Dollard & Miller, 1950; Mowrer, 1956). Kamin (1969) and Rescorla and Wagner (1972) have assembled evidence that the information value of the conditioning contingencies is basic to learning.

Initially, the contingent events considered were environmental and the kinds of responses studied were transactional (i.e., "overt" or "objectively observable" responses). However, it came to be recognized that such contingent events could be other responses (i.e., responses could have cue value or could be self-reinforcing, Bandura, 1976). The pattern of repetition (i.e., the schedule of reinforcement) of such response-contingent event occurrences influences learning (Ferster & Skinner, 1957). For example, if the contingency always occurs under the same circumstances (i.e., reinforcement is continuous), learning is usually more rapid but is easier to extinguish. If the contingency only occurs sometimes (i.e., reinforcement is intermittent), learning is usually slower but harder to extinguish.

There is some question of whether classical and instrumental conditioning represent two different kinds of learning processes (Coleman & Gormezano, 1979). Some have suggested that classical conditioning may influence preparatory responses and in that sense would be similar to the cue-value contingencies of instrumental conditioning. Biofeedback training has demonstrated that UCRs can be influenced by instrumental conditioning (N. Miller, 1978). There is a general operational distinction: In classical conditioning, the contingencies are arranged so that relevant stimulus conditions occur prior to the occurrence of the response (elicited responses). In instrumental conditioning, the response (called emitted responses or operants) must occur so that it can be followed by the relevant contingent event(s). However, it should be noted that the situation arranged for instrumental conditioning represents a set of facilitating and constraining conditions on the kinds of responses that can and are likely to occur. Therefore, the distinction between elicited and emitted responses is relative to one's observational vantage point—that is, to where and when one starts looking at the behavior-environment stream.

Constructing Behavior Patterns. Conditioning procedures have been used to "construct" more complex patterns of behavior. In one form, called *response chaining,* contingencies are arranged so that certain responses will come to occur in a certain sequence. In another form, called *shaping,* one starts with some behavior pattern that occurs (called an *operant)* and, by manipulating event contingencies, progressively alters the nature of the behavior pattern toward some alternate pattern. An example is the training of mentally retarded children to feed themselves by starting with reinforcement of the movement of their hand towards a spoon. Through this process, much like the process of evolution, a new pattern that is very different from the initial pattern may emerge through incremental change.

There are several related phenomena. When a stimulus occurs repetitively, responsiveness to it declines; this is called *habituation.* Familiar events are "taken for granted." Once a behavior pattern has been learned in relationship to a particular stimulus it may also occur in the presence of similar stimuli; this is called *stimulus generalization.* People may be trained to respond to one stimulus but not another; this is known as *stimulus discrimination.* When a learned behavior pattern reoccurs in the absence of the UCS or reinforcing contingencies, the probability of its reoccurrence under similar circumstances declines; this is called *extinction.* However, at a later time it may occasionally reappear, a phenomenon called *spontaneous recovery.* With practice, a behavior pattern changes both in terms of the dropping out of unnecessary components, and the occurrence of finer differentiation of necessary components. Such refined patterns come to occur somewhat automatically, that is, become *habitual.* However, a person does not always behave in exactly the same way in the same circumstances, so people learn somewhat different ways of accomplishing the same result; they develop a *habit family hierarchy* (Hull, 1952).

Cognitive or Information Learning. From the beginning, some theorists argued that what organisms learn is not specific action patterns (e.g., maze-running or key-pecking behavior) but informational representations about their environment and how to interact with it. For example, Tolman (1932, 1959) proposed that animals learned a "cognitive map" of the route through a maze rather than a specific maze-running behavior pattern. They learned "expectancies" (e.g., "if-then" hypotheses) about their environments and their relationships to them. The informational consequences of their behavior served to confirm or disconfirm such cognitions rather than to reinforce transactional behavior patterns.

Gestalt psychologists argued that it was particular patterns of organization of behavior-environment events that were learned (Koffka, 1935). Cognitive reorganization of such information, called *insight,* could lead to sudden (as contrasted to incremental) changes in transactional behavior patterns; this is analogous to the evolutionary notion of *punctuated equilibrium*. Individuals can learn alternate behavior patterns by observing situations without actually performing in them (sometimes called *latent learning*), and can later perform such patterns with little if any practice. Humans appear to learn many social behaviors through such "*social modeling*" (Bandura, 1976). However, only through practice can they develop performance proficiency. Many personality theories emphasize the learning of organizational patterns of behavior-environment events (Lewin, 1935), within which cognitive functions play a key role.

This emphasis on information learning or cognition has become a major force in current psychological research and theorizing. Work in mathematical models of learning and artificial intelligence focus primarily on information learning, and use computer programming analogies to explore cognitive learning and functioning (Cotton, 1976). Perceptual processes provide a flow of information about events (Johansson, von Hofsten, & Jansson, 1980; Kolers, 1983) from which a person constructs *concepts* and *propositions* or *schemas* about the nature of the world and one's relationships to it (Glaser, 1984; Medin & Smith, 1984). These schemas are stored in memory (Horton & Mills, 1984) for later use in guiding future behavior and learning (Gagne & Dick, 1983). In general, people tend to learn and remember what they pay attention to and perceive (Hilgard, 1977a), as well as their self-constructed concepts, the fruits of their successful problem-solving activities, and the consequences of their actions (Estes, 1982).

Learning Complex Behavior Patterns. The dichotomy of whether one learns actions or cognitions is beginning to disappear as a result of research on neurological bases of learning and behavior (Pribram, 1980a), and on motor behavior (Stelmach & Requin, 1980). That research indicates that what is learned is complex patterns of functioning that involve cognitive guidance, control, and regulation of componentized, hierarchically organized patterns of skeletal-muscle functioning shaped during performance by informational feedback, as well as attentional and emotional processes to fit specific biological and situational requirements (Bernstein, 1967; Gallistel, 1980a). Extensive evidence demonstrates that a motor act is never repeated in exactly the same way. Therefore, what is learned cannot be a particular act but must be a set of possibilities for performing that type of act.

Years ago, Hilgard (1948) proposed a concept called "a provisional try." For example, when placed in a maze an animal makes a genuine attempt to discover a route through the maze. Its past experience influences its present performance by being transformed or interpreted to fit present circumstances. (This is analogous to genetic influences on development being channeled by their interaction with current circumstances.) Each "try" aims at producing the same results but is somewhat different from the other tries for several reasons. What is learned is a set of similar optional performances for achieving those results. Principles of learning have been used to try to understand the development of other types of complex behavior patterns, such as attitudes (Burgoon, Burgoon, & Miller, 1981).

The study of development has emphasized *patterns of changes* in the organization of behavior patterns or developmental outcomes (Harris, 1957; Lerner, 1976), rather than processes by which those changes occur. For example, development is characterized as proceeding towards increased differentiation, elaboration, and hierarchical integration (Schneirla, 1957; Werner, 1957), and resulting in qualitatively different patterns often called *stages* (e.g., Piaget, 1983). However, attempts to focus on the "how" of development, such as those by psychoanalysts and by Piaget, emphasize processes for maintaining and elaborating existing organization (e.g., assimilation) and for modifying existing organization when it is disrupted (e.g., accommodation).

Theory, research, and clinical observation concerning the learning influences of various forms of psychotherapy also focus on complexly organized behavior patterns. Earlier theorists focused primarily on the role of thoughts and emotions (Ford & Urban, 1963). A primary assumption for some is that if the way a person thinks is changed, changes in how he or she feels and acts will follow. Thoughts change when existing thought patterns are disrupted by contradictory information (e.g., from a person's own observations and thoughts or from a therapist's statements), and must cope with those disruptions. Some assume that changes in the way people feel will lead to changes in how they think and act. Emotional patterns are changed primarily by having a person actually (e.g., in the therapy relationship) or symbolically (e.g., through imagery or recollections) experience situations in such a way that emotions that normally occur do not (e.g., fear desensitization), or emotions occur that normally do not (e.g., positive feelings about oneself). Psychotherapy is often characterized by the client's defense of existing steady-state patterns, accompanied by small increments of change, and occasionally punctuated by sudden significant changes followed by working through and stabilizing such reorganized steady states (Sahakian, 1969).

More recently, psychotherapy strategies have grown based on the assumption that if there are changes in the way a person acts, different consequences will result, and that in turn will change how they think and feel (Bergin & Garfield, 1971; Goldstein, 1981; Guerney, 1977). Such changes are accomplished primarily by first getting the client committed to the objective, and then demonstrating and/or explaining the behavior pattern to be performed, followed by rehearsal and then practice in relevant circumstances. It is important to note that while different therapy approaches choose different aspects of complex behavior patterns to use as their point of intervention, they all assume that changes in the targeted aspect will result in correlated changes in other parts of the behavior-environment pattern; that is, that the entire pattern will reorganize to accommodate changes in one of its components.

Research and clinical experience with psychopathological states reveal that both gradual and abrupt changes can occur. A person can slowly develop increasingly aberrant ways of functioning and also display relatively sudden major changes in functioning when stresses on and disruptions of current steady state patterns become too severe; these changes are illustrated by terms such as *nervous breakdown, psychotic break, amnesia, fugues,* and *multiple personality* (Hilgard, 1977; Menninger, 1963). Gradual and abrupt changes are also apparent in normal personality, life style, and career development patterns (Ford & Urban, 1966; Osipow, 1968; Sheehy, 1977).

implications from learning for developmental principles

1. Learning functions to create, selectively retain, and repeat functional components and response subcomponents that facilitate effective environmental transactions and steady-state functioning. What can be learned and how are constrained by inborn structural-functional characteristics of the organism.

2. All learning must start from and build upon existing functional components. They may be inborn components (e.g., infants' sucking behavior or UCS-UCR patterns) or previously learned components (e.g., thoughts or motor skills). A person's behavioral repertoire develops through differentiation, elaboration, and recombination of existing functional components. This insures continued, coherent organization of a person's functioning in different kinds of settings for different purposes.

3. All behavior occurs in specific contexts. Therefore, all learning occurs in specific contexts. Learned functional components, then, are organizations of behavior-environment subcomponents, and always include biological, cognitive, arousal, transactional, and environmental elements. Behavior patterns cannot be understood separate from the contexts and consequences for which they are functionally organized, including learned strategies (e.g., learning sets). An organi-

zation of response components learned because of its utility for one purpose in one setting may later turn out to have other uses. However, such "transfer of training" usually does not occur initially without explicit attention and effort.

4. Each functional behavior pattern involves multiple kinds of responses. However, each of those response domains also develops through differentiation and elaboration. Therefore, a diversity of subcomponents exists in each response domain that can be combined in alternate ways with different environmental components to create complex behavior patterns. The greater the number and diversity of response components and functional components in a person's behavioral repertoire, and the greater the flexibility with which they can be organized into different combinations, the greater will be the person's adaptive potential.

5. Learning may involve changes in existing behavior-environment functional components of several types. Previously unrelated response and environmental components may become related. An existing behavior-environment pattern (a) may become elaborated by the inclusion of additional behavioral or environmental components in the pattern; (b) may become attenuated by the exclusion of some behavioral or environmental components; or (c) may become combined with other existing components to create a significantly different pattern.

6. Functional components may evolve through progressive, incremental change (e.g., behavior shaping) or through sudden reorganization or recombination of existing elements (e.g., insight or cognitive restructuring).

7. What is learned is a function of the spatial, temporal, and influential relationships among the kinds and organization of the responses being performed, and relevant environmental contingencies and consequences. In general, one learns what one pays attention to and thinks about and what produces needed, desired, or intended consequences in different kinds of situations.

8. Practice serves to "streamline" functional components by eliminating unnecessary subcomponents; to increase the efficiency and effectiveness of functional components' spatial-temporal organization; and to make them habitual so they can be performed as a unit (or open loop) with little or no conscious direction.

Summary

Principles of change within three different knowledge domains have been identified in this chapter. Systems principles were discussed in previous chapters. The next task is to combine these into one set of principles representing the change and development of living systems.

5

Principles of Human Development and Change

INTRODUCTION

The ideas about development and change abstracted in Chapter 4 from several fields of study are now synthesized to construct a model of individual development and change. First, it is necessary to consider the *what* of development before considering the *how*. The concept of a *behavior episode* provides a way of describing the componentized, hierarchically organized nature of behavior patterns.

BEHAVIOR EPISODES AND FUNCTIONAL COMPONENTS

The living system framework relies heavily on the concept of components. The concept of organization is represented in terms of interrelationships among components that collectively define a living system. Development and change of a living system are represented in terms of changes in components and their relationships. Therefore, a way of thinking about and utilizing the concept of components to understand functional as well as structural development is essential. The issue of components is simply another version of the part-whole and unit of analysis problems discussed earlier.

Different approaches to studying human development have focused on different kinds of components. For example, distinguishing between organisms in terms of physical differences in their *structural components* was a starting point both for biology and for evolutionary theory. The human body has come to be represented physically as a hierarchy of components in which each level of the hierarchy is represented as an organization of structural components defined at lower levels. For example, organelles are one kind of subcellular component. The cell is a complex organization of a variety of smaller components, including organelles. Organs are complex organizations of cells. Organ systems are organizations of organs. The human body is an organization of organ systems.

The task of defining, identifying, and describing *functional components* is much more difficult. Psychologists have proposed various types of components (e.g., reflex arc, conditioned response, habit, trait), but none of these have been generally adequate, and most have not involved the notion of a hierarchy of components. In this living systems framework, the concepts of *behavior episode* and *behavior episode schemata* (BES) will be used to represent a fundamental type of functional component.

A behavior episode is a specific spatial-temporal organization of subcomponents, or kinds of responses (i.e., biological, arousal, governing, transactional) related to an organization of environmental components. Each kind of subcomponent response may itself be understood as an organization of sub-subcomponents of that particular category of behavior (e.g., a hand gesture is composed of a complex organization of muscle enervations). Larger behavior episodes may be represented as an organization of smaller behavior episodes. One may study the development of functional components or behavior patterns at any level in such a hierarchy. However, understanding why a person is doing what he or she is doing in a specific way requires a unit of analysis that encompasses the person as a functional unit. The remainder of this section elaborates on the characteristics of behavior episodes as such a unit.

Behavior is Continuous and Organized as a Control System

All of a person's functions summarized in Fig. 3.3 (p. 78) are all occurring in a context all of the time unless a person is comatose. Behavior patterns vary because the content and parameters of those functions vary. It is impossible to isolate for purposes of study one kind of response (e.g., thoughts), as one can isolate one kind of structural component for study (e.g., cells in vitro). Component responses can be studied by examining their functioning in the context of various types of behavior episode organizations. Understanding a person's motivation involves identifying the determinants of change in the stream of action

(Atkinson & Birch, 1970). The basic question is not *why* a person is behaving (because people are always behaving in some way as long as they are alive), but *why he or she is behaving in one way rather than another in a particular set of circumstances.*

Figure 3.3 in Chapter 3 conveys the idea that all of the basic kinds of functions or behaviors are always occurring in organized fashion, both among themselves and in relationship to an environment. The *pattern* of organization of these functions is always the same (i.e., it is a self-constructing control system), but a person's behavior differs from episode to episode because the *content or kind of behavioral and environmental events* occurring differs from occasion to occasion. Stated in ordinary language, behavior patterns differ because people vary in what they want, how they decide to go about producing the desired consequences, what they actually do, the ways they anticipate and evaluate their progress, the emotions that are aroused in relationship to the activity, the conditions of their biological functioning, the kinds of environments in which they interact, and the attributes of those environments upon which they selectively focus their transactions. If any of those functions are ignored, a person's behavior cannot be fully understood.

If one takes the functional organization of Fig. 3.3 and visualizes it flowing through a space-time matrix, the concept of a behavior episode becomes a dynamic one. A person sets out to produce some consequence(s) through his or her behavior. The person does a variety of things in and to a variety of contextual conditions until the intended consequence occurs, or until his or her attention and behavior are shifted to some other effort. The spatial-temporal content of the flow of the behavior-environment pattern may vary considerably. Yet it has coherence (it "makes sense") if viewed as being organized to produce some consequence(s) in a relevant environment and guided by relevant cues or information; that is, if viewed as a dynamically functioning self-constructing, adaptive control system.

A Behavior Episode Example. Visualize the following. It is the middle of the night. A man gets out of bed. He walks from his bedroom into his living room, kicks an object, utters loud vocalizations, goes to the front door, opens it, peers out, takes a deep breath, closes it, goes to the kitchen, pats the wall several times, moves a wall switch from down to up, opens the refrigerator door, rummages around in the refrigerator, closes the door, moves the wall switch from up to down, goes through the living room, kicks an object, utters loud vocalizations, goes to his bedroom, and gets into bed. That is an objective description of his overt behavior, making no inferences based on those observations. Try to think of an explanation of that pattern before reading the next paragraph.

That evening, for the first time, a 16-year-old son going out on a date had been permitted to take the family car, and the parents had been uneasy about it. The father woke up, realized he hadn't heard his son come in, and became anxious. He got up to see if his son was home. On the way through the living room he stumbled over the briefcase he had left on the floor when he went to bed. He hurt his toe and swore at the briefcase. He opened the front door and looked out to see if the family car was in the driveway. It was, and undamaged. He assumed that meant his son was home so he heaved a sigh of relief and closed the door, his anxiety relieved. He felt hungry and thought of the delicious coconut cream pie they had had for dinner. He decided to see if there was a piece left for a midnight snack. He went to the kitchen, felt around on the wall until he found the light switch, and turned the kitchen light on. He opened the refrigerator and moved its contents around, looking for the pie. He didn't find any so he closed the refrigerator, turned off the lights, and started back to bed. On the way he stumbled over his briefcase again, cursed the pain it caused and his own stupidity, and went back to bed.

How do those two descriptions of the same occurrence differ? The first one includes only information about transactional functions (overt behaviors) and some aspects of the environment, organized in a simple spatial-temporal sequence. The second description adds information about governing, arousal, and biological functions, about additional aspects of the environment, and about past and potential future events; and it provides spatial-temporal organization of that information *in relationship to the consequences towards which the behavior was directed,* that is, in behavior episode form. The first (impoverished) description only provides information about some of *what* happened. The second not only provides more information about *what* happened, but also information about *why* it happened and *when;* it organized the information in a spatial-temporal matrix. What bounds an episode and gives it coherence is the specification of consequences to be produced, that is, the directive function, the context and a person's body state. When a person's intentions change, there is change in the content and organization of that person's behavior patterns and in the contexts towards which his or her actions are directed. Thus, goal transitions mark a shift from one behavior episode to another as illustrated in Figure 5.1.

Hierarchical Organization of Behavior Episodes. Human behavior is multiply determined. Therefore, behavior episodes are organized in nested hierarchies. Large episodes can be represented as organizations

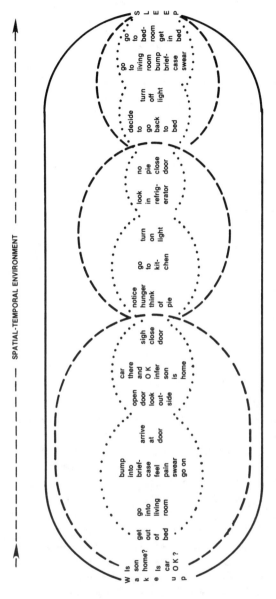

FIG. 5.1 A representation of a hierarchy of behavior episodes. The major episode, which occurs between waking and returning to sleep, is composed of three subepisodes which in turn contain sub-subepisodes.

147

of smaller episodes which can be represented as organizations of different kinds of behavioral and environmental components. For example, the entire sample episode just described, from rising to reentering bed, is composed of three different subepisodes, with sub-subepisodes within each (see Fig. 5.1). The first subepisode was organized by two directive thoughts: "I want to find out if our son is home safely and if the car is ok." All of the behavior between getting out of bed and closing the front door is understandable as part of that subepisode. Within it there are sub-subepisodes (e.g., navigating from the bed to the door, checking the car). The second subepisode began when the father closed the front door, organized by thoughts of his hunger and the pie. It ended when he closed the refrigerator door. Within it there were sub-subepisodes also. The third subepisode was organized by thoughts of returning to bed. It ended when he climbed into bed.

The purpose of this example is to illustrate that behavior "makes sense" only when viewed as a nested or embedded hierarchical set of behavior episodes which are organized to produce desired consequences. Subepisodes have subgoals, and larger episodes and their consequences are organizations of subepisodes. As a successful businessman says, big problems are solved by breaking them up into a set of interrelated smaller problems. The consequences towards which the behavior is directed (i.e., its purpose or goals) and the context in which it occurs convey its organizational coherence.

Behavior patterns are composed of organized hierarchies (or sequentially nested sets) of behavior episodes. Therefore, a behavior pattern can be analyzed at several levels within the hierarchy, depending on which level of components are of interest. Once it is triggered into action, each component functions as a semi-autonomous unit; that is, it has its own internal coherence, while simultaneously serving the larger episode of which it is a part. This is directly analogous to a biologist having the choice of studying the physical organization of the body at the level of the organism, organ system, organ, cell, or subcellular components.

It is characteristic of humans that they are usually trying to accomplish several things simultaneously. A person's functioning is particularly efficient and effective if several desired consequences can be produced with the same behavior pattern. For example, in Fig. 5.1 the same behavior pattern answered two questions: Is son home? Is car OK? Also, there is usually more than one way to produce the same consequence (the principle of *equifinality*). For example, the father could have looked in his son's room rather than the driveway to determine if the son was home.

Conflicts resulting from efforts to simultaneously accomplish multiple objectives are among the basic sources of the kinds of intra- and interpersonal problems with which psychotherapists often deal. For example, if people want two different consequences that seem to them to be mutually contradictory (e.g., family versus career), they often feel distressed because they cannot formulate coherent behavior patterns to accomplish both. Conflict can occur within any other function of a behavioral component; for example, the *control* function (having to choose between alternate courses of action); the *transactional* function (trying to listen to what someone is saying while simultaneously listening to the news); the *arousal* functions (experiencing both anger and fear when unfairly criticized by someone with power over oneself); or the *regulatory* functions (having to choose between contradictory values for deciding how to act in a particular situation).

When there is limited conflict within the hierarchical organization of a person's behavior, and between that person's behavior and environment, he or she is often said to be "well adjusted," or to have an "integrated personality." On the other hand, different kinds of psychopathology are often referred to as representing different kinds and degrees of behavioral conflict or disorganization. If a person readily invents and uses alternate behavior patterns to produce desired consequences, he or she is often referred to as "flexible" or "creative." If a person finds it difficult to invent or to use alternate behavior patterns, he or she is referred to as "rigid" (and "obsessive-compulsive" if the rigidity is extreme).

A behavior episode may be represented, then, as a pattern of behavior which extends over a period of time and has the following attributes: (a) some set of consequences towards which it is directed (the directive function); (b) a variable pattern of activities (i.e., control, arousal, transactional, regulatory, and biological functions) selectively organized with feedforward and feedback to try to produce those consequences; (c) a set of environmental circumstances within which and towards which the behavior is directed; and (d) a termination of the pattern when (1.) the consequences toward which the episode is directed occur, or (2.) some circumstances within or without the person change, preempting an episode because some alternate consequences have become more important, interesting, or possible at that time, or (3.) the evaluation of progress leads to the conclusion that the consequences are unobtainable—at least for the moment. If one imagines Fig. 3.3 flowing through space and time, one has a model of behavior episode.

The pattern of functioning represented in a specific behavior episode occurs only once. Learning increases the probability that the pattern of functioning that "worked" in one episode will be used again in similar future situations, through construction of behavior episode schemata (BES) (see Chapters 9 and 13). When a pattern is sufficiently practiced so that it can be readily performed on future occasions, it has become a functional component or capability. All such functional components of which a person is capable may be called the person's *behavioral repertoire*.

Methodological Implications of Behavior Episode Units. A behavior episode is not really a new unit of analysis. It is implicit in much present and past research. The concept of action cycles has a long history (Young, 1952), and Bruner (1982) describes action cycles in the following way:

> Most of what we speak of in common sense terms as human action is stirred by intentions of the following kind and in the following way. An intention is present when an individual operates persistently toward achieving an end state, chooses among alternative means and/or routes to achieve that end state, persists in deploying means and corrects the deployment of means to get closer to the end state, and finally ceases the line of activity when specifiable features of the end state are achieved. The elements of the cycle, then, comprise aim, option of means, persistence and correction, and a terminal stop order. There are several unspecified features present in this type of cycle. The principal one has to do with the nature of feedback and correction. In the nature of things, feedback in such an action cycle is always context-dependent: It is computed by reference to the feedforward signal inherent in the action aim of the organism....(Moreover) it is not necessary that, in such human action, the actor be able to account for or be conscious of the nature of his intentions. (p. 313–314)

He proceeds to represent adult-infant transactions in terms of such "action cycles."

Forgas (1979) proposed an analogous unit (social episodes) for representing interpersonal interaction patterns. Coutu (1949), a sociologist, proposed a unit called "tensit," meaning tendency-in-situation. Miller, Galanter, and Pribram's (1960) TOTE unit is the same kind of unit, except that it omits the directive function. Tolman (1932, 1959), a learning theorist, called such behavior episodes "acts." Petrinovich (1979) uses the concept of behavioral episode to translate Brunswick's lense model into a probabilistic functionalism approach to understanding humans. Gibbs (1979) uses the concept of transactive or behavioral cycles in his ecological approach.

Much research on learning processes has used the behavioral episode as its unit of analysis. In a frequently used design, a rat was placed in a maze at a starting point. What the rat did between that starting point and its arrival at the end point of the maze (usually a place where food or water was provided) was the behavior studied. Such an event was called a "trial." In effect, it was a clearly prescribed behavior episode. An animal was subjected to many "trials" in the same environment until it could run from the starting to the end point of the maze rapidly and without error (i.e., until it had constructed an habitual behavior episode schemata). The learning process was described in terms of what the rat did between the starting and end points, the time involved, and how that changed across a series of trials or similar behavior episodes.

Much psychological research with humans is implicitly designed in behavior episode form. A task is designed (e.g., memorizing nonsense syllables; solving a problem; performing a motor skill). The tasks may involve a solo performance, or cooperative behavior with others. Subjects are placed in environments organized for the task. They are given information about the task. The environments and instructions are designed to try to standardize (i.e., control) some behavioral episode components (e.g., the directive function—each subject must try to produce the same result), and to permit other components to vary (e.g., the subject's strategy in accomplishing the task). The episode components permitted to vary are the variables measured and studied (e.g., frequency of, or time for, successful task completion; method or strategy of task execution; self-evaluation of performance). Experimental manipulations are typically directed at influencing a particular episode component (e.g., cognitions: self-evaluations or problem-solving strategies; arousal: fear or pleasure; transactions: how task is done). It would be much easier to compare research project results if research designs were clearly represented in behavior episode form.

Identifying behavior episodes as the natural unit of behavior has important methodological implications. For example, when defining variables and deciding how to measure them, the task is to represent either component responses (e.g., goals, values, problem solving-cognitions, emotions) of a behavior episode and relevant aspects of its environment, or the organization of behavior episodes themselves. When selecting a data analysis procedure it is important to distinguish between looking at relationships between components within a behavior episode, relationships between behavior episodes, relationships between different elements or episodes at different levels of a hierarchy of components, or relationships between alternative elements within a particular function (e.g., a person's moral values). Moreover, one should expect that people would differ significantly in both the content and attributes of, and hierarchical organization of, their behavioral components. Therefore, research designs which assume that all people will act alike when subjected to the same circumstances are likely to be limited in the kinds of useful information they will produce. The commonalities detected across a large sample of people may reflect the attributes of the research conditions as much as the attributes of thepeople being studied, except at rather high levels of abstraction. It is necessary to first understand the functioning of the individual (intraindividual consistency and variability) before trying to identify similarities and differences among people (interindividual consistency and variability). The understanding that similar conditions may produce different results in and for people, and that different conditions may produce similar results, suggests a need for research designs that can analyze patterns of individual differences and similarities in spatial-temporal patterns of intraindividual functioning and change. Such replicated, multivariate, single-subject designs merge ideographic and nomothetic concerns, and can produce much more sophisticated and useful group designs (Nesselroade & Ford, 1985, 1987).

Variability and Change in Living Systems

Living systems are open systems that are characterized by patterns of steady state organization. Because they are continuously dissipating and replacing their energy resources through their biological-behavioral functioning, their biological organization is maintained at some distance from equilibrium. Because they are continuously collecting and utilizing information, their behavioral organization—which relies on information—is also continuously varying. Therefore, variability is a natural property of living systems, that is, of steady state functioning. Because they are in continual material, energy, and informational transactions with their environments, the steady state functioning of living systems is continuously subject to additions, deficits, and disruptions that may contribute to changes in steady states. Because they are self-organizing and self-constructing, people design their transactions to maintain or change their steady states. Therefore, it is necessary to distinguish between variability that is characteristic of structural-functional steady states, and variability that represents changes in such steady states. Performance variability is the term typically used to refer to variations that are manifestations of existing steady state capabilities. *Maturation, learning,* and *development* are terms typically used to refer to permanent changes in steady state capabilities.

The following discussion of developmental principles is organized into three categories representing types of variability and change in living systems: (a) performance variability as a function of the maintenance and operation of steady state organization; (b) elaboration of steady state organization through differentiation and elaboration of components; and (c) production of new steady states through disruption-reorganization processes. The proposed principles of development or change synthesize in a living systems framework ideas summarized in Chapter 4 .

A SUMMARY OF PRINCIPLES OF DEVELOPMENT

Three broad principles governing human functioning and development are described in this section along with several subsidiary principles.

Principle I: Self-Organization

I_a Organismic Boundary Conditions
I_b Environmental Boundary Conditions
I_c Selective Action
I_d Individual Differences
I_e Performance Variability
I_f Interdependent Hierarchical Organization

Principle II: Self-Construction

II_a Selection by Consequences
II_b Developmental Flexibility and Sequencing
II_c Environmental Specificity
II_d Performance Change
II_e Capability Change
II_f Habit Formation

Principle III: Self-Reconstruction

III_a Disorganization Flexibility
III_b Stability-Instability Ratio
III_c Transition Protection

Principle I. Self-Organization

Living systems function to establish and maintain patterns of steady state organization in the face of variable, instability-producing influences of either internal or external origin. Such steady state patterns involve both intraindividual equilibration processes among internal components and person-environment equilibration processes. Steady state organization permits considerable functional or performance variability within the boundary conditions defining the steady state(s), but resists major or rapid change of those steady states. These self-organizing processes make it possible for each person to continue to exist and to operate as a coherent structural-functional unit in different and varying environmental contexts. These processes also establish an identity for each person, and since the content of the structural-functional organization may take on many forms they are the basis of individual differences in both biological and behavioral characteristics.

The totality of all possible forms of steady state organization for a type of organism defines a species and the adaptive potential for that species. Self-organization is a stability-producing and maintaining process, produced by negative feedback processes in control systems.

The operation of the self-organization principle is illustrated by the maintenance within necessary boundaries of many biological processes such as body temperature, water balance, and blood pressure; by tissue maintenance activities; by the ability to maintain the coordination and instrumental effectiveness of actions against varying environmental conditions, to maintain and defend personal beliefs against contradictory information.

Temporary deviations beyond the normal boundaries of steady state functioning are illustrated by symptoms of disease such as an elevated body temperature. Given sufficient time, the body's self-organizing processes will usually eliminate or encapsulate the disrupting influence and return functioning to normal boundaries. All that medical treatments can do is to facilitate those self-organizing processes either through strengthening them (e.g., through good nutrition and rest) or by trying to remove the disrupting influence (e.g., through surgery or antibiotic drugs). Temporary changes in psychosocial and motor functioning are illustrated by behavioral changes when one becomes hungry, and the atypical behavior of people when drunk or of some people when away from home in a city where they are unknown (e.g., at a convention). Some deviations from steady states may have drastic consequences in the form of irreversible damage or even death. Therefore, in at least some circumstances, reactive control arrangements are less adaptive than proactive ones. For example, while reactive controls may eventually eliminate an infection, proactive controls such as preventing infections may eliminate the possibility of tissue damage or death.

It is not possible to determine whether there has been either a temporary or permanent change in some steady state unless its normal range of variability is known. Normative data about people in general is typically used to provide such a reference point (e.g., blood pressure). However, individuals differ in their steady state boundary conditions and so judgments about whether current functioning represents temporary or permanent change often require base rate data about the subject's normal steady state boundaries, in addition to group normative information. For example, some individuals' normal blood pressure might be judged to be "low" or "high" when compared to the average for people in general. If attempts are made to alter such a person's normal blood pressure to the group norm, one is actually creating a deviation from his or her normal steady state and may therefore, rather than helping, precipitate other biological problems.

Organismic Boundary Conditions. Humans have a basic matrix of anatomical, physiological, and functional characteristics and capabilities resulting from the evolutionary history of their species. That matrix becomes manifest in a particular structural-functional organization for each person as a result of individual genetic characteristics interacting with the properties of the environment(s) within which development occurs. These organismic boundary conditions constrain, but do not strictly determine, the trajectories of development that may occur. Such boundary conditions create some options but prohibit others (Lennenberg, 1967). Individuals may also have some unique organismic boundary conditions because of their particular sample from the species genetic pool, and because of the way their genetic potentials are shaped during fetal development by their special environment(s).

For example, a child may be born with no arms. Having no arms would eliminate some developmental options potentially available to a normal infant (e.g., becoming a professional basketball player). Similarly, a child may develop with exquisitely sensitive auditory capabilities. That could provide greater potential for developing into a superb musician. Organismic boundary conditions can change following birth and thereby change a person's available developmental options. For example, brain damage resulting from an automobile accident or paralysis resulting from a disease such as polio significantly alter a person's developmental possibilities. Similarly, permanent changes in people's biochemical functioning as they age (e.g., changes in hormonal or neurotransmitter production) may alter both their performance and developmental possibilities.

One socially significant debate about such boundary conditions is whether or to what extent individuals may differ in their potentials for learning and adaptation (e.g., their IQ) because of their organismic boundary conditions. However, *assuming* the existence of organismic boundaries or limits beyond which individuals cannot go because of their genetic-structural-functional history can be dangerous (e.g., assumed limits on the learning ability of some children or of elderly people). The limits may lie not in the individual but in their context (e.g., in the teaching methods used). Therefore, the best social strategy, humanistically speaking, is to assume that there are few organismic limits on learning potentials and to seek to design environments and methods to cultivate the desired functions. Only after strenuous and exhaustive efforts of this kind should the existence of inherent bound aries on developmental and functional possibilities for an individual be accepted.

Structural and functional characteristics evolved in interacting ways, with each development closing some future possibilities while perhaps opening new avenues of development. For example, birds cannot walk very far and people cannot fly, but birds may easily fly south for the winter while people may build fires to keep warm on winter nights. Since humans share some of their evolutionary history with other organisms, comparative study of boundary conditions may be useful. However, new levels of organization may result in new functions and new operating principles. Therefore, it is important to try to identify and understand those species-specific boundaries that may be relatively unique to humans (e.g., the role of cognitive functions in learning). Two species may even share a similar component (e.g., a gene), but because the component is embedded in a different organismic and environmental context, it may function differently, or participate in different functions in different species. Cross species generalization may be quite appropriate for some phenomena but not for others. Demonstrating when it is appropriate is an important responsibility for those who do comparative work. It may be easier to generalize from animals to humans than the reverse (Schwartz, 1974).

Environmental Boundary Conditions. Living systems exist, function, and develop by way of exchanges of *material* (through substances ingested and eliminated), *energy* (through actions and heat dissipation), and *information* (through perception and communication) with their environments. Therefore, developmental and performance possibilities are constrained and facilitated by the kind and organization of the environmental conditions within which a person develops and lives. A person's environment provides and limits options. Different environments provide different possibilities. Therefore, individual differences in performance capabilities (e.g., lower scores of poor and minority group children on scholastic aptitude tests) may be a function of differences in their environmental boundary conditions. Organisms evolved to exist and function in particular environmental niches. Therefore, the basic organismic and environmental boundary conditions must fit together like a hand in a glove for an individual to survive, function, and reproduce. This is sometimes referred to as person-environment fit (e.g., Lerner & Lerner, 1983). For example, humans' respiratory capabilities make it possible for them to extract needed oxygen from a gaseous atmosphere but not from water, while fish have the opposite capability.

Elaborations of inborn functional capabilities through learning also occur as adaptations to particular task-environmental conditions. There-fore, the way individuals function will differ from one set of environ-mental conditions to another. For example, the ways children behave on the playground, in church, or in the dentist's office are quite different. Children born in a city ghetto or in rural isolation will learn to adapt their inborn potentials to their particular environments. The person-environment interaction is a broad avenue through which mutually influential two-way traffic continually flows. Environmental conditions impact upon and influence individual development and functioning, while simultaneously individuals' behavior impacts upon and influences the development and functioning of their environments.

Selective Action.   Conditions within and around persons are continu-ally varying or changing, which means that each person's adaptive conditions change from moment to moment. People cannot deal simul-taneously with all of the conditions within and around them. Biological processes are continuously operative, and selectively and automatically vary in relationship to varying relevant events, both internal and external. However, other behavioral processes (e.g., thoughts, emo-tions, actions) are organized in behavioral episode formats. Therefore, at any moment only some of the existing and varying conditions within and around individuals are relevant to what they are currently trying to do and how they are trying to do it. Moreover, biological processes vary to serve behavioral episode activities (e.g., autonomic nervous system functioning and emotional arousal).

It follows that individuals must be able to selectively organize their behavioral repertoire in relationship to selected, currently relevant aspects of their environments. They selectively respond to events impinging upon them, and they selectively initiate activity to identify and produce desired consequences. Because variability of events is sequentially organized in a space-time matrix, individuals may behave selectively not only in terms of current events but also in terms of event flow. This capability for selective action both in terms of current events (what is happening) and past and potential future events (what has happened or may happen) provides humans with especially powerful adaptive potentials. People may automatically react to some aspects of their current conditions, but complex human behavior results primarily from people making choices or decisions about what to do, when and where, for what purposes (i.e., the directive, regulatory, and control functions). This selective, purposive, or consequence-directed property of human behavior has been one of the most difficult for mechanistically oriented theories of human behavior and development.

Through their selectivity capabilities people may to some extent regulate and control their own development and functioning by emphasizing interactions with some aspects of their environment(s) rather than others, and by the ways they design, organize, and alter their environments. For example, a child in a city ghetto may pursue as primary involvements either school, reading, and youth organizations, or street gangs, petty theft, and drugs. Because of the symbiotic relationship between biological and environmental boundary conditions, humans are both reactive to environmental influences (e.g., through feedback processes) and proactive towards the environment (e.g., through feedforward processes). That is a key reason why children growing up in similar environments can turn out to be so different from each other.

This property of selective action has very important social implications. People make choices and therefore are to an important degree responsible for their own actions and should be held accountable. A strict environmental determinism, illustrated by a famous comedian's line "the devil made me do it," does not operate with humans. On the other hand, individuals' actions should be evaluated within their unique biological and environmental boundary conditions. For example, a severely mentally retarded youth who steals from a store should be judged differently than should a normal child who can be expected to "know better."

Individual Differences. Each human embryo begins its development with a unique combination of genetic potentials drawn from the human genetic pool. Each embryo develops into a human infant in the unique environment of its mother's body. As a result, newborn infants differ from one another in a variety of ways (e.g., size, temperament), and develop in their own unique environments influenced by their own unique products of self-organizing and self-constructing activities. The result is the further cultivation of differences among children. This process continues throughout life. Therefore, patterns of individual differences exist among people from the moment life begins and continue to evolve throughout life.

At any point in time, there are always several possible behavioral or developmental directions open for a person. Two persons with similar possibilities may progressively follow different options, and cumulatively produce divergent developmental trajectories. Individual differences are a natural consequence of evolutionary, genetic, embryological, individual, and social development. On the other hand, two people starting from different developmental conditions may progressively pursue options that converge on similar developmental trajectories;

starting from different conditions individuals may end up at similar destinations. Thus, individual differences exist not as fixed, unchangeable characteristics, but as dynamic patterns which themselves exhibit patterns of variation and change.

This is of great social significance. Just as the diversity of genetic potentials in the genetic pool of a population or species represents its adaptive potential, so too does the diversity of behavioral potentials for an individual or a population represent its functional adaptive potential. The diversity of the population of individual differences in a society is that society's current source of potential creative and adaptive advancement. A society may cherish, cultivate, and protect individual differences because of their social value. The emphasis on individual and civil rights in the United States is a manifestation of that idea. But a society may also choose to deemphasize individual differences by selective breeding, training, and propagandizing. The more a society tries to reduce the individual differences among its citizens, the more it reduces its potential for future adaptation and creative change. Stated in systems terms, the more a living system protects its currently dominant steady state functioning by trying to restrict or eliminate potentially disruptive differences, the more limited become its future developmental possibilities. For centuries, despotic leaders have intuitively recognized this and have both subtly and harshly sought to restrict or eliminate potentially disruptive individual differences among their subjects to protect their power.

Performance Variability. People seldom behave exactly the same way twice, even in the same circumstances. At any moment, all of the performance possibilities of which a person is currently capable is that person's behavioral repertoire. The behavioral repertoire, which results from the developmental-learning history within a person's boundary conditions, may be thought of as a set of functional components that may be performed in a variety of combinations. At birth, a human infant's behavioral repertoire is very limited; that of many less complex organisms never elaborates much beyond such inborn arrangements. Because infants' organismic boundary conditions are still developing and they have only a primitive behavioral repertoire, performance variability is limited. Initially, they react pretty much the same way under similar conditions. They typically do different kinds of things in different circumstances but similar things in similar circumstances. However, it is characteristic of steady state functioning that performances will vary within boundaries, so a baby will not behave exactly the same way on each similar occasion. Therefore, performance variability does not necessarily imply a change in state or learning.

Such variability is valuable because it increases adaptive potential by providing options from which new patterns can be constructed. Three psychological concepts are illustrative: *Habituation* means a person comes to ignore repetitive events and to focus on new or variable events. Repetitive events are subjectively referred to as boring, *Habit formation* means people learn to perform some behavior patterns relatively automatically in repetitive circumstances, to focus their attention and thoughts on novel or variable events, and other actions. *Reactive inhibition* means a particular behavior becomes less likely to occur as a consequence of repetitive performance. For example, people get bored doing the same thing in the same way and tend to vary their approach to a task (e.g., Olympic gymnasts experiment with variations of the "tricks" in their performance routines).

Performance variability capabilities are increased in three ways. First, by elaborating a person's behavioral repertoire (e.g., when a baby becomes able to grasp and manipulate objects). Second, by becoming able to produce the same result with different behavior patterns (the principle of equifinality applied to behavior). For example, a baby may get food either by crying so that someone feeds it or by grasping the food in its hand and stuffing it into its mouth. Third, by becoming able to use the same behavior pattern in different circumstances to produce different results. For example, a child may jump either to get off a chair or to reach an object hanging above its head. Individuals differ in the behavior episode patterns they consistently display, and therefore may be said to have different personalities.

Interdependent Hierarchical Organization. A person is a unit (or system) defined by an organization of structural and functional components (or subsystems). Each component is itself a unit composed of an organization of subcomponents (or sub-subsystems), and so forth. For a person to function as a unit, his or her components must be constrained and coordinated to support and facilitate the maintenance and functioning of the larger system, the person. Similarly, for each component to retain its integrity as a unit, its subcomponents must be constrained and coordinated to facilitate its existence and functioning. The maintenance and functioning of a social system (e.g., a family, a business) also requires that the functioning of the persons who are its components be constrained and coordinated in some ways to serve the interests of the social system. This type of organization is referred to as hierarchical, which means an organization of components composed of mutually influential levels ordered in superordinate-subordinate relationships between levels.

Humans can be represented as very complex hierarchical organizations of structural and functional components. For example, body movement is made possible by a complex skeletal-muscle organization. However, that is composed of muscle groups, which are organizations of individual muscles, which are organizations of muscle fibers, etc. Similarly, the skeletal-muscle organization is one component of a person subject to the influence and coordination of other components, such as the neural-governing organization. In living systems, the hierarchy is developmentally open on both ends. That is, a person can become more complex through the elaboration of the number and organization of components, and also through the differentiation and elaboration of existing components. Similarly, a person's behavioral repertoire may be understood as hierarchically organized; and, as described earlier, behavior episodes are hierarchically organized behavior-environment patterns of activity.

One of the efficiencies of the evolutionary process has been to use the same structure for several functions (e.g., the circulation network for nutrient distribution, waste collection and removal, and thermal regulation). To paraphrase Norman Cameron (1947), the fact that anxiety and blood pressure have but one heart between them, that anger and digestion share the same gut, and that the same chest sighs for air that sighs for love or sympathy, is of fundamental importance in understanding human development and functioning (e.g., symptoms of psychopathology). It follows, then, that attempts to identify specific functions with specific single structures in humans is likely to be a somewhat fruitless quest, except for the narrowest of functions. Hierarchical organization is sometimes interpreted as an autocratic form of organization in which influence flows only from the top down (e.g., from the boss to department heads to the workers). Living systems function through patterns of mutual influence both among components and between hierarchical levels, as well as through feedback and feedforward processes as described in Chapter 3. The phrase *interdependent hierarchy* (sometimes referred to as *heterarchy*) denotes this more "collaborative" or "cooperative" form of hierarchical organization. Because increasing complexity through increasingly specialized componentization requires increased coordination to maintain the system's unity, higher levels in the hierarchy have greater influence in that sense. However, higher levels can accomplish coordinating functions only to the extent that the lower levels are responsive to their influence, and provide them with essential information. The whole facilitates and constrains the existence and functioning of its parts, which in turn facilitate and constrain the existence and functioning of the whole.

The principle of hierarchical organization is of great practical significance since efforts to study, influence, or change a person require explicitness about which components and relationships within and between which hierarchical levels are being targeted. For example, professionals try to alter depressive patterns by influencing biological functioning through chemical intervention (e.g., antidepressants), and by influencing psychological functioning through social intervention (e.g., psychotherapy). Each approach implicitly assumes that there is an interdependent hierarchical organization of biological-behavioral processes and that intervening at one level on some component(s) will also influence other components and levels. Professionals can improve both the efficiency and effectiveness of their services as knowledge increases in regard to the interdependent hierarchical organization of humans.

Principle II. Self-Construction: Elaboration of Existing Organization

As living systems, humans have the capabilities for constructing as well as maintaining new structural and functional organization. One method is through progressive differentiation and elaboration of existing structural-functional organization. This is analogous to the evolutionary doctrine of gradualism, the embryonic process of elaboration within developmental stages, and the notion of behavior shaping through selective reinforcement in learning theory.

People ingest materials, decompose and transform them through their digestive and absorptive functions in the gut and lungs, and transport them to all body structures through the circulatory system. Cells combine those materials with other substances to construct new structures (e.g., the formation of new organs during embryonic development; physical growth and tissue repair). The materials are also used in the generation of energy to fuel all functioning.

Behaviorally, people collect information through their attention-sensory-perceptual processes; and they then combine, decompose, reorganize and transform that information to form general schemata, along with concepts and propositions about themselves, their environments, and their mutually influential relationships and relationship possibilities. These "personal theories" or "schemas" (Glaser, 1984) are used to guide present behavior and are retained for potential future use. The organization and reorganization of patterns of behavior from the existing behavioral repertoire, in order to construct effective behavioral episodes, results from those information based self-construction capabilities. Embryonic development is largely a function of biologically based self-constructing capabilities whereas learning is primarily a function of information based self-constructing capabilities.

The human capability for informational self-construction has fundamental social implications. The theories we use to guide us, and the strategies, methods, and technologies flowing from them, may emphasize or deemphasize the "species-specific" characteristics that make us distinctively human—for example, as in attempts to use conditioning procedures as if their effects were independent of most attentional and cognitive functioning. Which qualities we choose to cultivate are matters of fundamental importance to our personal and social future. Humans are not passive machines, helplessly and blindly shaped by environmental forces and chance events as was implied in the classical mechanistic view. The fact that evolutionary and developmental changes may be initiated from within the organism as well as from environmental influences; that such changes must first be accepted within the organism before facing further tests in the organism's environment; and that organisms may modify the environment which influences them through their own behavior, means that living systems to some extent can influence their own development (Lerner & Busch-Rossnagel, 1981). As the most complex and flexible living system, humans have the greatest self-constructing potential of any species. There are extensive theoretical, scientific, and practical implications in this shift to a view that recognizes that individuals and groups control or influence their own destiny, to some extent. Humanists and modern evolutionists and developmentalists may be on converging roads.

Selection by Consequences. Skinner (1981) used this phrase to represent the powerful causal influence on the construction of behavior patterns of behavior contingent events. The principle of natural selection (by consequences) is fundamental in evolutionary theory. The two words, *selection* and *consequence,* are both important and require further discussion.

Nesselroade (1986) points out that selection and selection effects underlie the fundamental concepts of sampling and generalizability in research design. Analogously, each "provisional try" of an organism to produce some intended consequence may be considered a sampling procedure from a population of possible "tries." If the sampling procedure produces sufficient instances of successful behavior, then a basis for generalization exists (i.e., learning has occurred). Selection involves separating one set of entities from other sets (e.g., separating adults from children; observations from inferences; sound theories from unsound theories; effective actions from ineffective actions). Selection processes are pervasive in both daily life and science. For example, classification is the cornerstone of all knowledge development, and discrimination learning involves distinguishing one class of events from another; in other words, classification and discrimination are selection processes.

Applied to a person's development, selection involves separating and implementing one pattern from a larger set of possible patterns in different types of environments. Selection may be based on one variable or several variables. However, any other characteristics related to those directly selected for will also be indirectly selected. These are called *selection effects*. Such selection effects were illustrated in the earlier discussion of evolutionary theory; that is, correlates of attributes that provided a survival and reproductive advantage were also selected for through evolution, even though they provided no special advantage at the time. Thus, while selection may be focused on only one or a few attributes of a pattern of events, all events in the pattern will be selected for, thereby opening up new selection possibilities.

The question is, how is such selection accomplished in human development? Skinner's (1981) answer is that it happens through consequences. What is a consequence? It is an event whose occurrence is contingent upon the occurrence of some behavior. Behaviors effective in producing certain consequences will be selected for repetition in similar future circumstances, while other behaviors will be "selected out" as possibilities in such circumstances. Survival and reproductive efficiency are the two consequences specified in evolutionary theory as the key selective influences. Species characteristics that produce those consequences are selected for and others are not. Skinner argues that this is a "causal mode" found only in living things.

Behavior-contingent events are of two functional types. One type is an event that signals the probable occurrence of some other event. Skinner called this a *discriminative stimulus*. Others have called it a *signal* or *cue*. Such events may be behavior-contingent only in the sense that they occur in spatial-temporal contiguity to the behavior pattern and its consequence. They may be, but need not necessarily be, produced by the behavior. This type of spatial-temporal contingency is the one upon which classical conditioning theory focused. The second type is an event that is "reinforcing," which describes a behavior-contingent consequence that increases the probability of reoccurrence in similar future circumstances of the behavior pattern just preceding it. A behavior-contingent event is a consequence if, in addition to spatial-temporal contiguity its occurrence is influenced or produced by particular behavior.

The problem with this formulation is that there are always many events occurring at any moment, but only some of them function as cues and consequences. Thus, we have another selection problem. Why are some events selected as cues and consequences from a larger set of simultaneously occurring events? For example, why are some events reinforcing and others not? And why is an event reinforcing in one set of circumstances and not in another? Some of the answers proposed by various learning theorists to these questions were summarized in the earlier discussion of learning theory.

The behavioral episode unit of analysis provides a way of predicting which events will function as cues and consequences and which will not. Only those events to which a person attends can function as cues or consequences. Individuals selectively attend to those events they consider relevant to their current concerns, and ignore the rest. Stated in systems terms, only events that function as feedback signals can serve as cues or consequences. Since the nature of feedback signals varies depending upon what a person is trying to do and upon the intensity or prominence of events, the same kind of event can function as a cue or consequence under one set of circumstances and not another. For example, a bell may function as a cue that food may appear when a person is hungry, but not otherwise. Food may function as a selective consequence when a person is seeking to ease their hunger but not when seeking to win a game.

Stated in ordinary language, something is reinforcing when it is a consequence one is currently intending or desiring; and the next time one wants to produce that kind of consequence one will probably use a similar approach because it "worked." Any other event that is noticed to covary in space and time with the production of the intended consequence can serve as a discriminative stimulus or cue, signaling progress towards, or the probable occurrence of, the intended (and therefore reinforcing) consequence. Not only environmental events, but events occurring within a person may serve as cues and consequences. For example, the occurrence or reduction of the experience of pain or fear may serve as a cue or consequence, as can the taste of food or the sound of beautiful music. It is not the physical event itself (e.g., food) that is "reinforcing," but the consequences provided by interacting with the event (e.g., seeing and eating food). Any behavior that a person evaluates as producing a desired consequence is increasingly likely to be repeated under similar circumstances (i.e., is learned).

Some behavior-environment patterns—such as digestion, nausea, basic emotions—have been selected for in advance by natural selection. The problem is that evolution-based behavioral selection (i.e., the individual's set of inborn patterns) is not effective for dealing with novel circumstances. Therefore, humans evolved with the capability for constructing (i.e., learning) additional behavior-environment patterns, which is what we call learning; and most human behavior is self-constructed.

However, selection by consequence cannot occur until an antecedent behavior-environment pattern occurs. Therefore, there must always be starting points in the existing behavioral repertoire, which Skinner named *operants*, from which behavioral development can evolve through selection by consequence. Because performances will vary somewhat from one occasion to another within similar behavior episodes, what is selected is a *set of alternative performances* for producing the same consequences. Selected out are performances that do not produce those consequences as well or at all. However, people learn a set of *versions* of an effective behavior pattern. People do not need to actually perform the behavior pattern to learn it. Human cognitive capabilities make it possible to learn some behavior-environment contingency patterns "vicariously," or through social modeling by observing others' performances either literally or by reading about them (Bandura, 1977a). Through such a gradual shaping process, an existing behavior pattern can be progressively elaborated and transformed until it ends up being considerably different from that which provided the starting point.

Developmental Flexibility and Sequencing. For a new or different behavior pattern to evolve, it must start with some existing part of the person's behavioral repertoire. Therefore, some capabilities have to develop before others can be learned. For example, people cannot learn calculus or statistics until they first understand fundamental arithmetic operations such as addition and subtraction. Developmental stage theories emphasize this sequencing principle. However, the developmental options available to a person at any point in his or her development are a function of the diversity of possibilities available in their existing behavioral repertoire. The greater the diversity of behavioral capabilities in people's repertoires, the less habitual they are in their performances, and the fewer the prohibitions against alternate, plausible behavioral possibilities, the greater is their developmental flexibility; that is, the more diverse are the future developmental trajectories potentially available to them. For example, a newly retired person with many interests and skills has many more options for using his or her new discretionary time than a person whose interests and skills are limited and have been narrowly tied to his or her job.

Environmental Specificity. All behavior is performed and learned in specific environments in relationship to specific behavior-contingent events. Humans' general representations must be constructed from similar instances. As represented by the behavioral episode unit of analysis, what is learned is not a behavior pattern but a behavior-environment event pattern. As a person's behavioral repertoire evolves, it becomes organized around the classes of behavior settings in which the behavior patterns were learned, as represented in Fig. 5.2. That has been one of the emphases of ecological psychology (Barker, 1968).

These "subrepertoires" may be quite different from each other. For example, the subrepertoires of behavior a person uses in a church, a bar,

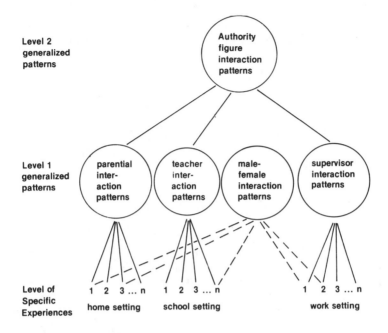

FIG. 5.2 A representation of the hierarchical development and organization of generalized behavior episode schemata learned in relationship to different types of behavior episodes.

and a physician's office will display considerable consistency within each setting, but will differ greatly among settings. Therefore, looking for behavioral consistencies independent of differences in intentions and in performance contexts is likely to produce a very limited representation of the amount and kinds of consistency that are characteristic of a person. "Traits" that are general across all situations for all kinds of behavior episodes are probably few in number, or nonexistent.

However, a person's behavioral repertoire becomes hierarchically organized through learning, so that several subrepertoires for different classes of settings may provide the basis for constructing patterns that are somewhat more transitional. For example, a child may learn a subrepertoire for behaving toward its father in their home. Later, some aspects of that subrepertoire may become combined with some aspects of others (e.g., those used with teachers and supervisors) into a superordinate repertoire used with adult males in general. Aspects of that superordinate repertoire may become combined with other aspects of other repertoire sets into a higher-order repertoire used with all adult authority figures, both male and female. In that way, some aspects of a person's total behavioral repertoire remain specific to particular situations, while others come to be used in a greater diversity of situations.

For example, an adult may have learned to feel, think, and act confidently and competently in work and social settings; and yet continue to think, feel, and act with less confidence and competence in relationships with his or her parents—in effect to remain childlike.

Glaser (1984) summarizes evidence that human problem-solving involves the interactions of a person's "modifiable information structures" or schemas developed from and organized around "domains" of problem-solving "tasks" (i.e., around different types of behavior episodes). In other words, memory is organized around types of situations or behavior settings.

Performance Change. An individual's behavioral repertoire is composed of many components. Each component develops and is used in relationship to particular kinds of intentions, conditions, and consequences. Different behavior patterns develop as part of different kinds of behavior episodes to serve different purposes. One kind of change involves beginning to use an existing behavioral repertoire component in a new context; that is, in a different kind of behavioral episode. One illustration of this is in classical conditioning arrangements in which a new stimulus (the CS) becomes capable of eliciting an old response (the UCR) by being paired with a stimulus condition that already elicits that response (the UCS). A person has not learned a new behavior pattern, but has learned to perform an existing capability in a somewhat different context. One definition of creativity involves the extent to which individuals can invent new possibilities by unique combinations and uses of existing capabilities and circumstances. However, performance changes are subject to selection by consequences. Using an old capability in a new context may be given a "provisional try," but the extent to which that "try" will be repeated and become a behavioral repertoire component will be a function of the relationship between the results produced and what the person was trying to do.

Some behavior patterns developed at one stage of life may no longer be used in later stages of life. However, they may still represent potentials in the person's "library of behavioral programs," although they may have remained "on the shelf" for many years. Thus, another form of performance change is for some dormant component of a person's behavioral repertoire to be reactivated and used. For example, throughout his career a conservative man never traveled more than 200 miles from his home and always drove cautiously. He retired and suddenly began traveling all over the United States and Canada. He bought a little racecar and drove it for awhile. He drove a small motorbike until he had an accident and his wife made him sell it. He seemed to suddenly become an adventuresome spirit. However, other information reveals he had had an adventuresome youth, involving escapades with cars and Navy service during World War I. When he assumed marriage, family, and work roles, he put most of that adventuresome spirit and behavior "on the shelf" because it did not fit with his commitments to his adult roles and responsibilities. With retirement, many of those commitments had been adequately fulfilled and he pulled his adventuresome spirit and behavior "off the shelf" and began using it again.

It is important to emphasize that performance change across situations does not occur automatically. It too is a product of learning. Goldstein and Kanfer (1979) identify three characteristics that research suggests may facilitate generalization or transfer of training, and illustrate how they may be used to enhance the transfer of learning that occurs in psychotherapy settings. One characteristic is *identical elements*. The likelihood of transfer increases with increased similarity between the original learning situation(s) and other situations in which the behavior might be utilized. A second characteristic they label *response availability*. The more frequently a behavior pattern is used, the greater is the likelihood it may be tried in different situations. The third characteristic they call *stimulus variability*. The greater the diversity of situations in which the behavior has been performed, the more likely it is to be tried in a different situation. For example, in the case of the adventuresome retiree, his retirement was similar to his youth in the freedom and opportunity it provided to pursue his personal interests (identical elements). He had had extensive practice in using such behavior patterns during his youth (response availability). He had used those patterns in diverse situations at home and while in the Navy (stimulus variability).

The concept of performance change has important practical implications. For example, a blue collar worker was nearing retirement and dreading it. He could foresee nothing else in his life to give it meaning and pleasure. He found his wife a frequently unpleasant companion and dreaded spending large amounts of time with her. He could not visualize satisfactorily filling his time with house, yard, and garden work. A review of his past brought to light some youthful "dreams" he had filed away because they were impractical at the time. Renewed consideration of those dormant dreams led to plans for reviving them and renewing their pursuit during retirement. Thus, one way to help people alter unsatisfactory life trajectories is to help them identify existing components within their behavioral repertoire that could provide a starting point for new developments.

The performance change principle has important manifestations in the development of psychological distress, behavior disorders, and psychopathology. It involves emotions. A limited number of emotional arousal patterns appear to be a part of humans' inborn behavioral repertoire. However, they are highly learnable in the sense that through learning they can come to be elicited by almost any kind of event. Therefore, through performance change learning, emotions can produce disadvantageous behavior patterns. For example, a military man served at a remote and dangerous post. After a two-week leave to visit home, he returned to the airport to fly back to his post. He panicked and could not board the plane. He had developed a phobia of flying despite the fact that he had a civilian pilot's license and many hours of flying experience. Apparently, the distressing emotions elicited by thoughts of returning to his dreadful post by flying became related to the thoughts and actions of flying themselves, independent of the destination. At that time, the emotional reaction was functional; it prevented his return to his post. However, to this day he will not travel by air and that causes him considerable inconvenience and some embarrassment.

Capability Change. If the only way a person could change was to use existing capabilities in different situations, their behavioral repertoire would be limited to the inborn patterns with which they began life. Capability change involves elaboration of the behavioral repertoire itself. This can be accomplished by creating new components and by combining, reorganizing, or transforming existing components into different patterns. Such changes are invented as *provisional tries* to accomplish something through application of a person's informational self-constructing capabilities. However, whether or not such tries evolve into permanent components of a person's behavioral repertoire will be a function of selection by consequences.

Infants learning to walk provide a good example. They must learn to lift themselves to a standing position; learn to maintain their balance in a standing position; learn to maintain their standing balance while they move one foot ahead of another, and so forth. This is a slow, cumulative process with some efforts ending in failure (which get selected out) and others ending in success (which get selected in) until they can walk smoothly and with confidence.

Capability change learning involves both differentiation within existing components and elaboration into more complex patterns. Differentiation means an increase in the complexity of the internal organization of a component. For example, infants' first efforts to lift themselves to a standing position are awkward, involve some unnecessary movements, and only gross muscle control. With practice, much finer muscle control develops not only in terms of the patterns of muscles involved but also in the timing of their involvement and the sensitivity of their accommodation to varying conditions. Elaboration means creating larger, more complex components by combining existing components in new ways and/or by adding new components. For example, learning to walk involves learning to combine standing with new rhythmic patterns of arm and leg movements in transaction with solid surfaces. This illustrates Werner's (1957) orthogenetic principle that development proceeds from a state of relative globality to a state of increasing differentiation, articulation, and hierarchic integration.

More elaborate *component sets* also evolve. For example, when an infant is learning to lift itself to a standing position it does not always start from the same position. Sometimes it is seated, sometimes kneeling; its arms and legs may be in different configurations, and it may or may not have objects to hold onto which assist it in standing. Different movement patterns are necessary to arrive at a standing position depending upon the starting conditions and upon how those conditions change during the performance of the act. Therefore, over time an infant learns a set of ways for lifting itself to a standing position. The components of the set have certain common properties and some differences. Which component(s) of the set operate in any instance depends upon the initial conditions and how they change during the performance. Behavior patterns that are very complex in both content and coordination can be evolved from very simple beginnings through the combined processes of differentiation and elaboration.

A game of Scrabble provides a useful analogy. In the game, wood squares containing different letters are combined to create words. The creation of a new word must involve some letter(s) of an existing word and a letter may not touch another letter unless it is a part of a word. In the following illustrations, Phase 1 illustrates the beginning of such a game. Phase 2 illustrates a stage of the game in which very few options for creating new words exist (analogous to a limited and habitual behavioral repertoire). Phase 3 illustrates the sudden opening up of many new options as the result of creating a major new word (analogous to a new behavior capability).

```
E A T          E A T          E A T
X              A X    O        A X    O O L O G I C A L
I              N I N O N       N I N O N
T O T          T O T          T O T

Phase 1        Phase 2        Phase 3
```

Phase 4 illustrates that the elaboration of the new options opened up by the new word can create an organization of words much larger and more complex than the dominant network that provided the starting point. Phase 2 might be thought of as analogous to a small child who lives in very impoverished circumstances (e.g., no radio, T.V., newspapers, magazines, books; little conversation in the home, and few toys, objects, or tools with which to learn skills). The child develops a limited and confined behavioral repertoire. However, upon starting to public school the child suddenly has many new available possibilities (e.g., Phase 3). A teacher takes an interest in him or her and provides opportunities and encouragement to learn new competencies in a variety of circumstances. Each new competency opens up new options until the child literally has a new life pattern and a much more promising future (e.g., Phase 4). Starting from the lowest of beginnings the child may evolve into a very competent and successful adult if their biological and environmental boundary conditions permit and facilitate such development.

```
        E A T                    S
        A X   O O L O G I C A L
        N I N O N          A B B R E V I A T I O N
          T O T                 N   A
                                D   C
                                E   E
                                R E A M E R
                                O   I
                                U   C
                                S
                                L
                                Y A R M U L K E
                          Phase 4
```

No matter how constrained one's life becomes there are always some potential starting points for creating new options and new possibilities for oneself, if circumstances permit. In this sense, human development is open-ended throughout life. What a hopeful perspective! Notice that the potential for future development at any point in time is always limited to some set of options, but there is also uncertainty in that it is hard to fully predict which options are to be elaborated, and what new options those elaborations will create.

Habit Formation. During evolutionary transitions, phenotypic variance increases (i.e., there are more different "versions" of the species). As the natural selection process proceeds, phenotypic variance declines (i.e., some of the "versions" are eliminated). Something analogous occurs as a behavior pattern is learned through repetition. Initially, each time a person tries to perform a behavior pattern for similar purposes under similar conditions the "tries" will differ considerably from occasion to occasion (i.e., there will be considerable performance variability).

With repetitive practice, unnecessary elements are eliminated and the organization and timing of the pattern(s) become more "streamlined" (i.e., the performance variability declines). Because the performance conditions are never identical (although they may be quite similar), what a person ends up with is a set of versions of the behavior pattern that match the set of variable conditions under which the pattern was practiced and learned. For example, gymnasts perform their routines over and over again to try to "perfect" them (i.e., to make them as nearly identical as possible to some ideal model). However, during a meet they may make a mistake during the middle of their routine and have to make adjustments. Champion gymnasts do this so smoothly that the ordinary spectator often does not even notice the mistake.

A second consequence of repetitive practice is that the components that make up the behavior pattern come to occur less as separate pieces that have to be coordinated with conscious effort, and more as single larger organizations of components that will occur as a coordinated unit with little conscious effort. In systems terms, the behavior pattern comes to function more like an open loop, with little use of feedback to make alterations during the performance.

This streamlining and automation of a particular kind of behavior episode pattern is called *habit building*. Practice produces functional componentization (i.e., habits). It has great practical significance, enabling people to develop a large number of skilled performance capabilities and to perform them efficiently and effectively without requiring primary attention. This enables people to devote their attention to the less predictable or novel aspects of their environment and performance so that they can make quick accommodations if necessary. It also enables people to do more than one thing at a time. For example, a person can carry out an habitual behavior pattern while thinking about something else or carrying on a conversation. Since it is behavior episode patterns that become habitual, any of the component functions can become habitual. So people form habits of thought, emotional habits, perceptual habits, transactional habits, and even biological habits.

Principle III: Self-Reconstruction: Change Through Disorganization and Reorganization

Change is not always accomplished through the accumulation of small increments of change. Sometimes it occurs more abruptly and sometimes several changes occur simultaneously. Such changes occur in both nonliving and living entities. For example, Fleury (1981) describes transformations in diverse states of matter in which dramatic changes in macroscopic properties result from microscopic interactions among huge numbers of constituent particles. Jantsch (1980) gives many examples of such abrupt transformations in existing entities or organizations. Prigogine (1984) describes how dynamic systems (of which humans are the most complex example) maintain "order through fluctuation" at some distance from equilibrium. Such a system confronted with some disrupting influence (e.g., excessive heat) may be pushed beyond the boundaries defining its current steady state functioning. The system displays a "symmetry break." It can only maintain its integrity as a system by reorganizing into some new steady state pattern. Such reorganization usually produces a more complex form. This kind of change is represented by the concept of punctuated equilibrium in evolutionary theory, of mutations in genetics, of developmental transitions in embryology, of insight in learning theory, and of psychotic break in psychopathology.

A person's existing patterns may be disrupted by intraperson processes (e.g., organ dysfunctions), by transactions with the environment (e.g., being fired from a job, learning one's spouse is having an affair), and by accidents that require emergency measures in some portions of the system to maintain the integrity of the total system (e.g., serious oxygen deprivation, or becoming paralyzed because of an accident). Conflict is a term applied to one frequently occurring type of disruptive influence. Cognitive dissonance refers to disruptions of beliefs by conflicting information.

Through the operation of the self-organizing and self-constructing principles, a person first attempts to assimilate and accommodate disruptions within existing steady state patterns. Under many circumstances that is possible and contributes to differentiation and elaboration of existing patterns (e.g., "cognitive structures," Piaget, 1977).

However, sometimes the existing organization is unable to assimilate or accommodate the disrupting influences. Then it becomes necessary for some reorganization to occur that will enable the body or the person to maintain a sufficient degree of integrity and still cope with the disrupting influence(s). If the disruptions are of biological organization and functioning they will be manifest in biological "symptoms" that represent the body's efforts to cope with the disruption(s) (e.g., elevated body temperature or white blood cell count; changes in blood biochemistry). Selye (1976) spent his career trying to decipher how the body handled such stresses. He proposed three general stages of reorganization that he called the alarm reaction, the resistance stage, and the stage of exhaustion. If the disorganization-reorganization processes involved the entire body (i.e., the total system), he called it the *general adaptation syndrome*. If it involved only some part of the body (i.e., a subsystem) he called it the *local adaptation syndrome*. He assembled evidence to demon strate that if the body is unable to eliminate the stressor and return to its previous normal steady state functioning, it will reorganize its functioning to some different steady state pattern with different boundary conditions as a means of coping with the disrupting influence(s). Such reorganization efforts are subject to selection by consequence; that is, they must "work." The biological consequence of failure to accomplish an adequate reorganization is death, the ultimate selective consequence for living systems.

Psychological or behavioral disorganization also occurs. One signal of disrupting influences is subjective feelings of tension or distress. A second signal is increased variability of behavior or increased deviation from typical steady state functioning (analogous to increased phenotypic variation during evolutionary transitions), as an indication that different ways of coping with the stressor are being tried. For example, as a person sees increasing signs of personal failure on a job or in an important relationship (such as marriage) he or she will feel more and more apprehensive and will make increasingly variable and desperate efforts to succeed. People who function extensively in this "emergency gear" have been termed *type A personalities*, and are more likely than others to develop physical symptoms such as hypertension, ulcers, headaches, or digestive disorders.

A living system cannot continue to exist in perpetual states of disorganization of psychological or behavioral functioning. People's self-organizing, self-constructing capabilities will operate to produce some kind of reorganization that enables them to continue to function at some level. Sometimes those reorganized patterns produce other undesirable consequences as by-products of the coping with the original disrupting influence(s). The terms *psychopathology* and *behavior disorders* represent domains of study of such maladaptive reorganization of behavior patterns (e.g., functional paralyses, neuroses, psychoses). Because the behavior episode is the basic format of behavior patterns, the reorganization may involve environmental and/or behavioral components. For example, one kind of reorganization is to withdraw from and avoid disruptive environmental influences through such things as phobias, running away from home, and divorce. Another kind involves reorganizing thought patterns to protect oneself from thinking disruptive thoughts through, for example, rationalizations and paranoid thought patterns. Another kind involves "forgetting" or "repressing" recollections of disrupting events, as through amnesia. This disorganization-reorganization process produces fairly rapid and significant change in contrast to selection by consequences which is a slower change process and proceeds in relatively small incremental steps. However, the two change processes are interactive. "Revolution" only produces new options. "Evolutionary" processes must follow to select and stabilize some of the new options. For example, new patterns of reorganization are subject to selection by consequence and often several versions are tried before a stable pattern emerges. In psychotherapy, this process of stabilizing a reorganized pattern of functioning is often referred to as "working through."

Not all disorganization-reorganization processes are of the negative kinds illustrated above. In fact, this kind of change process appears to be a significant factor in creative advance and significant personal development. For example, creative scholars often describe how, after struggling to reconcile some seemingly irreconcilable facts or ideas or to solve some seemingly unsolvable problem, they suddenly get a new idea that seems to resolve the dilemma. The term *insight* is commonly used to label such sudden conceptual reorganizations. An interesting corollary (which is discussed more fully in Chapter 13) is that such reorganizations are often accompanied by feelings of excitement or relief. Secure people enrich their lives by exposing themselves to somewhat disruptive new experiences (e.g., through travel, reading, or changing jobs) that force them to continue to change or develop.

Disorganization Flexibility. When some aspect of a person's life is disrupted and disorganized for some reason (e.g., loss of a job, death of a loved one, divorce, moving to a very different environment) that person is likely to consider and try a greater diversity of behavior patterns than when his or her life is flowing smoothly in effective steady state (habitual) patterns. As a result of the disorganization, a person may begin functioning with a behavioral repertoire characteristic of an earlier phase of behavioral development because habitual patterns of behavior are no longer useful or applicable. As a result more behavioral and developmental options may be open. For example, a man was devastated by the discovery that his wife was cheating on him, which led to a separation and plans for a divorce. During that period of disruption he seriously considered and almost implemented a decision to disrupt his entire life by quitting his job, changing his career, and moving to a different part of the country.

During the disorganization stage of this process, it is easier to help people alter their behavior patterns than when they are in habitual steady states, because they are more willing to and/or find it necessary to consider and try alternatives. For example, psychotherapeutic treatment is more effective with a client who is in a transitional period, such as when a psychotic break or neurotic episode has just begun, than after a client has had a long period to reorganize and develop an alternate (albeit maladaptive) functional pattern. That is why crisis intervention techniques are so valuable.

It follows that if people want to change or someone wants them changed (e.g., society's desire to rehabilitate a criminal offender) it may be necessary as a first step to sufficiently disrupt their current functional patterns to increase the probability of occurrence of alternate patterns. For example, in psychotherapy it is often necessary to be patient while clients wander through a variety of defensive talk until they finally begin talking about what bothers them. That kind of serious self-investigation (when effective) leads to both cognitive and emotional disruption, and that is when therapeutic change is most likely. For example, those are the times when the psychotherapist's "interpretations" are likely to have their greatest impact on clients. Similarly, when teaching it is often necessary to disrupt students' existing habits of thinking before they are able to seriously consider alternatives. People who habitually display a willingness to consider alternatives are often termed *open-minded*.

Once again, it should be emphasized that alternative behavior patterns must occur following disorganization and be subject to selection by consequence if they are to become a continuing part of a person's behavioral repertoire. For example, imprisonment is a technique for life-style disruption of criminal offenders. Unfortunately, the skillful cultivation of alternative behavior patterns and their selection by consequence are too seldom practiced (or perhaps practical) in prisons. The more habitual and functional the behavior patterns have become, the more difficult it is to disrupt and change them; and, in effect, the more extreme must be the disrupting influences. Cultural rules often prohibit the use of the most extreme disrupting procedures. It may be that some behavior patterns cannot be altered within the prevailing organismic and environmental (including cultural) boundary conditions.

Stability-Instability Ratio. A person is a dynamic organization of biological and behavioral structural-functional components. In complex organisms (e.g., human adults), change usually takes place through changes in a few specific components at a time while most of the person's functional organization remains relatively stable. The more components that are simultaneously disrupted and the more severe the disruption, the greater will be the disorganization, the more vulnerable will be the person, and the potentially more extensive will be the ensuing reorganization. The greater and more severe the disorganization (or instability), the more likely is the development of dysfunctional behavior patterns (e.g., severe neurotic patterns or psychotic breakdowns). In contrast, the greater a person's stability, and the more habitual a person's behavior, the less likely that person is to display new developmental efforts or to change. The economic concepts of sector and general recession are analogous phenomena at a societal level. In a sector recession, only some economic components are in trouble (e.g., steel industry) while others are doing well (e.g., electronics). In a general recession, many economic components are in trouble and the societal disruption is much greater.

Unless the entire system is seriously dysfunctional, it is desirable to try to maintain the stability in some parts of a person's life while other parts are going through a disorganization-reorganization phase. For example, the man described earlier decided to stay on his job (at which he was very successful) and remain where he was living until he had worked his way through his marital crisis. After that aspect of his life had reached a relatively stable reorganization, he could more adequately consider other changes. Both excessive stability (e.g., "rigid personalities") and excessive instability are usually generally undesirable conditions. Some disruption opens new options while sufficient stability maintains a system's functional effectiveness. It might be noted that organizations, such as governments, businesses, and universities, are also living systems. Periodic changes in organizational leadership are disruptive but characteristically open up new options for organizational development. Therefore, periodic changes in leadership are usually desirable. In democratic governments, the electoral process periodically produces option-increasing disruptions by electing different officials while government bureaucracies maintain operational stability.

Transition Protection. Living systems in transition are more vulnerable to damage, as illustrated by embryonic developmental transitions. When people are going through periods of significant disruption and are struggling to reorganize some facet of their lives, they are less capable of coping with other life demands that ordinarily would not be a problem. Therefore, effective reorganization is facilitated if they are somewhat protected or buffered from some of the usual demands until an effective reorganization of the disrupted aspect of their lives begins to emerge. For example, physically ill people often are put to bed and withdrawn from many daily activities and responsibilities so that their bodies' resources can be focused primarily on recovery from illness. Once the recovery begins, progressive return to normal activity helps facilitate the reorganized pattern following illness. Socially and emotionally troubled people may use their social support network of caring others to help them weather difficult times. The friends of a woman whose husband has recently died rally around her providing food, friendship, and companionship to help her through the grieving period. Seriously disturbed people may be hospitalized and tranquilized temporarily until a disruptive crisis begins to abate. "Self-help" and support groups of many kinds (e.g., Alcoholics Anonymous, groups of divorced people, and people with dying children) function to provide such transition protection and support.

Similarly, when a person is trying to learn a complex, new skill it is helpful to avoid practicing or trying to learn another such skill involving some of the same components until the developing skill has achieved some stability. And a person trying to solve a problem (or write a book) will usually be more effective if able to devote significant blocks of time to the effort, uninterrupted by competing demands or activities.

SUMMARY

From conception to death an individual's functioning and development follow a pattern of organization-variable functioning-habit formation-elaboration governed by the principles of self-organization and self-construction. Periodically this smooth, continuous flow of development is disrupted, producing a pattern of disorganization-option exploration-reorganization guided by principle III, self-reconstruction. This pattern of change or development is a natural part of living. In fact, when organisms stop developing they seem to begin a process of decline.

Next Steps

The basic conceptual framework for trying to understand people as functional units, and how they may develop and change, has now been constructed. In the remaining chapters the utility of the framework is tested by trying to meaningfully organize and interpret within it the existing information about various aspects of human development and functioning. Hopefully, in the process, new perspectives and new hypotheses for empirical testing may emerge.

II

HUMAN PERSONALITY AND THE CONTENT AND ORGANIZATION OF BEHAVIOR

6

Biological Bases of Self-Organization and Self-Construction

INTRODUCTION

Extensive knowledge of the human body, its functions, and how to maintain it existed in ancient Chinese and Egyptian civilizations. However, scientific study of the body's structure and functions began only about 400 years ago, and experimental medicine is less than half that old (Bernard, 1865). Until only a few centuries ago the body was seen more as a home for spirits than as a part of nature. Even today, many of us still implicitly think of our bodies as something "we" live in. How often, for example, have you heard people express irritation that something wrong with their bodies was interfering with what they wanted to do? There is a certain validity to this subjectively sensed truth. The biological structure and functioning of the body do not determine what an individual can or will become. They only put boundaries on the possibilities for psychological and social development and functioning. All other aspects of human functioning are made possible by, and are in part maintainers or destroyers of, this biological base. Biology and behavior are mutually influential aspects of humans, but human behavior cannot be reduced solely to biological causes (Washburn, 1978).

The functioning of primitive organisms is dominated by material and energy exchange processes. When that is the case, biological determinism can explain much of such organisms' behavior. However, as more complex organisms evolved, the growing ability to collect, organize, interpret, transform, and use information to deal with the natural world made organisms decreasingly dependent on the physical-chemical,

183

"here and now" conditions of their environments. This information-based self-construction capability has reached its highest evolutionary form in humans, and is most apparent in human language construction and communicative behavior (Washburn, 1978). The human brain, with its massive capabilities for using information in self-constructing ways, often can override the more primitive components that control behavior in lower organisms. Therefore, generalization from the characteristics of other animals to humans, or vice versa, is risky business; it must be done with great care, particularly if information based processes are involved, as illustrated by generalization to humans from the study of aggression in animals (Lorenz, 1963).

Biological knowledge continues to expand explosively. As McVey (1901) predicted, "the darkness of superstition" is giving way to "the light of biology flooding the world." Therefore, it is difficult for anyone to maintain a full understanding of what is known and emerging. Nevertheless, it is impossible to tell "a coherent story" about human development without considering biological characteristics. Good summaries of different aspects of human biology are available elsewhere (Abramson & Dobrin, 1984; Brown & Stubbs, 1983; Guyton, 1982; Ham & Cormack, 1979; Jacobs, Francone, & Lossow, 1982; J. Miller, 1978; Pike & Brown, 1967; Timiras, 1972). This chapter first summarizes some key aspects of the biological base for material-energy self-organization and self-construction. It then considers biological bases in the nervous system for information-based self-organization and self-construction. Other chapters include some information about the biological bases for each system function.

Yates (1979) has succinctly summarized the characteristics that make biological systems different from all other systems, as follows:

> Biological systems have three striking characteristics: 1) autonomous morphogenesis; 2) invariant reproduction; and 3) teleonomic (purposeful, goal-directed) behavior. They comprise systems that are semiautonomous, yet they may require nonautonomous differential equations for their descriptions: they do not remain invariant with respect to transformations of the time axis. The coefficients are variable; the dynamics are nonlinear; the systems are open to mass, energy and information; the parameters may be distributed; the control is adaptive; and the schematic is lost. (pp. 57–58)

MATERIAL-ENERGY SELF-ORGANIZATION AND SELF-CONSTRUCTION

The Living Cell

Even though it is not the primary level of analysis on which this book is focused, the nature of the living cell is summarized first for four reasons.

First, all living systems are produced from existing germ cells that are small living systems capable of developing into a complete new organism. Second, the componentized organization and functioning of cells illustrates the model of a living system. Third, because individual humans evolve from fertilized cells, and their bodies are complex organization of specialized cells, some general understanding of some of the important properties of cells can contribute to an understanding of normal and deviant individual human development. Fourth, living systems are incredibly complex entities at any level of analysis. To suggest that they are too complex to be understood as entities (as is sometimes implied) is a kind of "cop-out." The same could be said for cells or organelles. It is of basic importance to recognize that humans are organized as an embedded hierarchy, functioning through mutual causal processes within and between levels.

In the 17th century, Robert Hooke examined a slice of cork through a microscope and observed that it was composed of tiny compartments which he called "cells" (i.e., small rooms); this became a basic biological concept. In 1839, Theodore Schwann proposed that cells were the basic building blocks of all life. A person's body contains 75 trillion cells, of about one hundred different types. Cells themselves may be represented as complex organizations of many subcomponents, contained in a membrane, a protoplasm or cytoplasm, and a nucleus (J. Miller, 1978); their molecular basis is increasingly understood (Weinberg, 1985).

Cell Membranes.   Membranes provide the boundary between the cell and its surrounding environment and between subcomponents within the cell. (One fundamental way of distinguishing a system from its context is to identify its boundary.) But, because the cell is itself an open, living system, the membrane must be permeable permitting some transactions with its environment and excluding others (Bretscher, 1985). Within the body, each cell is immersed in a fluid environment called intercellular fluid. The circulatory system empties materials potentially useful to each cell into the intercellular fluid. Like a truckload of raw materials for a factory, a molecule of material floating in the intercellular fluid may attach itself to the cell membrane (as a truck might back up to the factory loading dock). If the molecule, the cell, and the part of the membrane to which the molecule becomes attached collectively provide an appropriate constellation of conditions, the molecule is "received" or "transported" into the cell and its material becomes available for participation in and utilization by the cell's internal biochemical functions.

Membrane surfaces are selective in terms of which molecules will be permitted to enter the cell. Such selective membrane surfaces are often referred to as cell receptors (e.g., opiate receptors), and there are many types that differ among cells (Marx, 1985a). Substances can pass through the membrane in three ways. Some substances diffuse through the membrane "pores" or matrix. Others are picked up by special carrier substances and actively transported through the membrane. Sometimes the membrane actually engulfs substances which touch it, a process called endocytosis. In a similar fashion, "left-over" materials from internal cellular activity are passed out through the cell membrane into the intercellular fluid where they can be transported away through the circulatory system. Cells may utilize materials taken into themselves to produce chemical substances that can be secreted to influence other cells (e.g., neurotransmitters, hormones). The selectivity of membrane permeability to substances can be altered or "tuned" by a variety of chemical substances. At a cellular level, governing functions are accomplished through biochemical processes.

Cell Nuclei. The cell nucleus is also enclosed in a permeable membrane. It contains organizations of basic genetic material called chromosomes where the replication of protein and the key nucleic acids DNA and RNA is controlled. In a sense, the nucleus is the "executive suite" for biological self-organization and self-construction, providing governing functions at the cellular level. For example, Beadle (as quoted in J. Miller, 1978) asserts that there are five billion nucleotide bases in the cell nucleus. They and their organization represent the "library of knowledge" that has accumulated over millions of years of evolution, and which is used to create each human.

Cell Cytoplasm. Between the cell membrane and the nuclear membrane is the cytoplasm which contains thousands of structures called organelles. For example, the Golgi apparatus is responsible for the production and/or packaging of protein; mitochondria are the energy power plants of life; *lysosomes* break down large molecules (e.g., fats) into constituents that can be used by the mitochondria; *ribosomes* are active in protein synthesis; and *centrioles* and *kinetosomes* are important in cell division. Each of these subcellular components "is a closely integrated structure, equipped with self-regulatory devices, and enjoys an advanced form of self-government" (Koestler, 1967).

Permeating the cytoplasm is a complexly organized membranous system that connects the cell and nuclear membranes, providing a means of communication and material exchange between the extracellular and intranuclear environments as well as within the cytoplasm, and also providing structural form and motility (Weber & Osborn, 1985).

Material Distribution and Cell Metabolism. All of the chemical processes inside the cell are referred to as cell metabolism, including catabolic (breaking down) and anabolic (synthesizing) processes. Cell metabolism may be roughly subdivided into three basic types of interrelated self-constructing functions: production of energy; building the physical structures of cells; and decomposing, transforming, and synthesizing materials into forms essential for the other two functions. Energy is essential to accomplish any kind of work or action. It must be liberated from materials obtained from the environment by a complex pattern of chemical transformations involving some 50 different steps.

Proteins compose about three quarters of the body solids (e.g., genes, enzymes, structural proteins, oxygen transporting proteins, proteins related to muscle contractions), and over 50,000 different kinds have been identified so far (*Science*, January, 1981). Each protein participates in different functions (e.g., Marx, 1980).

Amino acids are the principal constituents of proteins. Proteins are ingested in a person's diet, transformed through digestive processes into amino acids, which are then absorbed into the blood stream and transported into cells throughout the body, where they are again transformed into different kinds of proteins. The blood plasma concentration of each type of amino acid is held fairly constant by control system arrangements. If plasma concentrations fall too low, amino acids are released from cells; and if plasma concentrations become too high, amino acids are transported back into cells. One function of the body's circulating hormones is to influence the balance between tissue proteins and circulating amino acids.

Within cells, two basic types of proteins perform different functions. *Enzymes* catalyze different kinds of chemical activity (e.g., the synthesis of lipids, glycogen, and ATP). *Structural proteins*, combined with lipids, form cellular structures (e.g., organelles). The types of proteins a cell can form regulate its functional characteristics. Different kinds of cells have different protein production patterns. Protein synthesis is regulated by genes, and therefore embryonic tissue specialization results from different combinations of genes becoming dormant or remaining active and regulating different kinds of protein production (Gehring, 1985; Wilson, 1985). J. Miller (1978) summarizes much additional information representing cells as living systems.

Cells as Wholes and Parts

Thus, a cell is a complex organization of many components and processes (i.e., a living system in its own right), which requires internal governing processes to insure that it functions as a unit. In addition, its functioning must be coordinated with that of many other cells in order for organs and individuals to function as units. There are two primary methods of intercellular communication: systems of hormones and systems of neurons. Both use chemical messengers. Neurons send discrete messages to specific cells, while hormonal governance influences cells in a more generalized way (Snyder, 1985). Intracellular governance is also accomplished by chemical messengers (Berridge, 1985). Thus, cells and organizations of cells have a mutually influential, hierarchical form of governance to make it possible for the organism to function as a unit.

Koestler (1967) coined the term "holon" to identify components of organization which function both as quasi-independent units and as components of larger units, from cells to societies. The study of holons at one level of analysis may provide helpful but insufficient knowledge for understanding units at another level. A living systems framework makes it apparent that no level of analysis is inherently any better or worse than any other, and a full understanding of living systems, e.g., humans, can only be accomplished within a multilevel, multi-disciplinary framework. Reductionism and emergentism positions can both be understood in terms of levels of organization (Wimsatt, 1972, 1976). What are needed are unifying conceptual frameworks that can synthesize information both within and across levels of analysis.

FROM A CELL TO A PERSON

Development must start from some existing organization. In living systems, it starts with germ cells called *gametes:* ova in females and spermatozoa in males. However, ovum and sperm each only represent half a person. They must merge into one cell, a process called *fertilization,* to create a germ cell from which a person can develop. This budding system embeds itself onto the nutritive wall of the uterus so that it can, like a parasite, live off the woman's body until it is ready to enter the world through the vagina about nine months later. An extensive structure, called the placenta, develops an interface between the maternal and the embryonic circulation to accomplish the exchange of nutrients and waste while protecting the fetus from other potentially damaging materials. Mother and fetus must function as a two-component system.

The Reproductive Transaction. Reproductive physiology is the field that studies the biological aspects of reproduction. Sexual physiology is the study of factors influencing the sexual transaction to produce fertilization. Thus, while reproductive organs are specialized for species reproduction, the entire body is involved in the sexual transaction necessary for reproduction. Because the incentive-consequence information matrix related to the transaction is pleasurable, it may itself be sought as a goal. This behavioral separation of a pleasurable sexual transaction from the species-survival reproductive process (assisted by contraceptive technologies) has become a major theme and issue in human societies. What was, in evolutionary terms, a means to an end has become an end in itself!

Structural-Functional Biological Organization

The process by which a single cell evolves into a complex living system, such as a person, was briefly summarized in Chapter 4. Because special functional capabilities emerge as a result of the organization or interdependence of structural components in living systems, fields such as human biology and medicine find it useful to study and treat the body in terms of subsystems or groups of organs or structures that interact in an organized way to carry out important functions. Therefore, structural (anatomy) and functional (physiology) organization must be understood as two sides of the same coin. However, there is not a one-to-one correspondence between the two. A structural component may be involved in more than one functional system, each functional system involves many structural components, and each organ system is to some extent interdependent with the others so that the entire body can function as a unit.

These structural-functional systems, operating in a self-regulatory fashion, are responsible for biological existence. Cannon (1939) anticipated control system theory by recognizing that such biological processes represent "...a condition which may vary but which is relatively constant." He labeled this dynamic process *homestasis*. Empirical evidence about many biological functions, such as thirst, does not conform to a simple mechanical engineering control system model (e.g., Toates, 1979). However, more complex control systems involving hierarchical control arrangements within which set points may be varied or biased, and within which positive and negative feedback as well as feedforward are operative, do appear adequate to encompass both Cannon's original conception and existing empirical data.

In psychology, manifestations of biological functions have been referred to in terms of concepts such as *drives* (e.g., hunger, thirst), *needs* (e.g., for oxygen or sleep), or *survival motives*. In this psychological sense, any homeostatically controlled biological function could be considered a physiological drive. Attempts have been made to consider all human behavior as directly or indirectly motivated by these biological functions or their derivatives, as in some learning theories. However, evidence suggests that only some aspects of human behavior can be accounted for in these terms (e.g., Cofer & Appley, 1964; Hall, 1961; White, 1959).

A typical biological or medical classification of biological structural-functional components includes the skeletal-muscular system; supportive tissue elements including connective tissue; the cardiovascular and hemopoietic system; the digestive system, liver, and related organs; the respiratory system; the urinary system; the male and female reproductive systems; the integumentary system including the skin and its appendages; the endocrine system; and the nervous system including related sensory mechanisms. Medical specialities are built around such classifications. For example, a gastroenterologist specializes in the digestive system, a neurologist in the nervous system, and an orthopedist in the skeletal-muscular system.

Because these systems are physical components that can to some extent be viewed as semiautonomous parts, the possibility exists for manufacturing replacement components such as artificial limbs, kidneys, hearts, and glands. Man-made imitations of some structures (e.g., arteries, corneas) have not yet been invented, so organ transplantation from one body to another is a growing technology. Surgeons are largely "structural engineers" who focus on repair, replacement, or removal of structural components. Often, instead of structures being removed, new artificial structures are added to improve upon or substitute for the functional limitations of existing natural structures (e.g., eyeglasses, hearing aids, telephones, power steering, wheelchairs).

Subsystem Interrelationships. As was pointed out earlier, it is characteristic of living systems that a structure may participate in more than one function. Therefore, any categorization of biological components cannot be mutually exclusive in terms of the structures involved. For example, the mouth and skin are involved in both material and information-exchange functions. Moreover, a classification system like the one first presented is simply a tool for examining a diverse array of phenomena, and should not obscure the beautifully integrated, hierarchically organized complexity of the human body. Since people are self-constructing, self-organizing living systems, their sense of individuality should emerge as a biological reality.

PROCESSES SERVING BIOLOGICAL SELF-ORGANIZATION AND SELF-CONSTRUCTION

There are extensive sets of biological structures and functions which intervene between the material input (e.g., eating, breathing) and output (e.g., acting, elimination) transactions that might be called "throughput" functions in systems jargon. They involve the transformation, distribution, and utilization of materials within the body for the construction, maintenance or repair, and operation of the structure, and for reproduction. This section briefly summarizes some information about that set of biological processes. First it focuses on the distribution of the materials to the specific cells which are the site for any given activity. However, as in any community, waste products and debris are generated through living system functioning, and invasions of "tourists" and "predators" must be controlled. Therefore the security, sanitation, maintenance, and repair structures and functions of the body are also considered.

Material Distribution: The Cardiovascular Subsystems

The cell is the primary site of biological self-construction activities. The body must deal with two kinds of distribution objectives, one constructive and one protective. The first involves the distribution of useful materials to the cells and the removal of useless materials from the cells. That is the basic purpose of the circulatory system. However, not all of the materials that enter the body are useful. Some are living "invaders" seeking to "loot" the body of materials useful to the invaders. In addition, structures involved in the constructive activities of the body wear out, break down, and become useless. Like old automobiles abandoned on city streets, they become obstructions and potential contaminants to the life of the city (or body). Therefore, a second distribution system called the *lymphatic system*, linked to the first, plays an important role in such protective functions.

The cardiovascular subsystem, composed of "pumps," "pipelines," and "selective filters," distributes nutrients to cells through intercellular fluids, collects waste products from cells to be delivered to sanitation and maintenance components such as the kidneys, and delivers protective forces to various neighborhoods as needed. In addition, there are mechanisms for manufacturing and warehousing the "vehicles" used as transports, and essential materials for maintaining and repairing the components of the system.

The Structure of the Cardiovascular Subsystem. The heart is the "pump"; it has its own built-in power source that can vary its rate of functioning, as required by changes in activity in various parts of the body, to maintain a transportation flow relevant to current needs. Thus, pulse rate, pulse rhythm, and blood pressure are key measures (i.e., vital signs) of the load being placed on the pump, and of its operation. The heart is one of the few components of the body for which there is no back-up system. Materials are circulated through miles of flexible tubes of various sizes. That is the *vascular system* which has three components: The tubes carrying blood *from* the heart *to* the cells are the *arterial* subsystem; those carrying it *to* the heart *from* the cells are the *venous* subsystem; and very small tubes called *capillaries* connect the arterial and venous subsystems, thereby completing the circuit. The walls of the capillaries are very thin, permitting an exchange of substances with intercellular fluid primarily through diffusion. In this way, new materials are delivered to cells and waste materials are collected and returned to the circulatory system via the intercellular fluid. Since each cell is itself a living system, every cell must be close to a continuous supply of needed materials. Therefore, there are approximately 10 billion capillaries in the human body.

Kinds of Materials Circulated. The blood contains diverse materials floated in a stream of straw-colored fluid called *plasma* which is similar to intercellular fluid. It carries (a) many kinds of materials necessary for cell construction, function, and repair, and for energy production called *metabolites;* (b) excretory products released by cells; and (c) synthetic products constructed and exported by cells. Pike and Brown (1967) summarize "some" (over 150) of these plasma constituents in eight categories: minerals, such as iron; carbohydrates, such as glucose; proteins, such as globulins; lipids, such as cholesterol; nonprotein nitrogenous substances, such as amino acids; vitamins, such as ascorbic acid; enzymes, such as lipase; and hormones, such as insulin. In addition, oxygen is necessary for transforming and using these materials. Therefore, the plasma contains red-colored cells called *erythrocytes* which carry oxygen to the cells and carbon dioxide away from them. The plasma also carries "white" or colorless cells called *leukocytes,* and platelets called *thrombocytes* which aid in blood clotting and vascular repair mechanisms. Finally, the plasma carries waste products to disposal sites.

The red cells, or erythrocytes, are designed to absorb and release oxygen and carbon dioxide quickly. They are produced in the bone marrow. Oxygen-absorbing hemoglobin in red cells also binds to carbon monoxide, illustrating the concept of evolution to an environmental niche. Humans evolved in a gaseous atmosphere in which carbon monoxide was not an issue. It is undoubtedly an accidental evolutionary side effect that the same substance that evolved to carry oxygen also combines with and retains carbon monoxide, which if breathed will "suffocate" a person by prohibiting oxygen uptake.

The Circulatory Process. The circulatory system is conveniently represented as composed of three sets of components: the heart, the pulmonary circulation, and the systemic circulation. The heart is divided into two halves, each of which is divided into two parts. Blood from the venous subsystem flows into the right half of the heart which pumps blood through the pulmonary arteries to the lungs, where it gets rid of carbon dioxide and picks up oxygen. This oxygenated blood returns to the left half of the heart which pumps blood into the systemic circulation.

There are three main kinds of arteries in the systemic circulation: elastic arteries (the aorta); muscular (distributing) arteries; and arterioles. They each function somewhat differently.

The heart pumps blood in "spurts" (called pressure pulses) into the aorta, which passively stretches under that systolic pressure. Between spurts, the stretched elastic walls of the aorta slowly contract, producing the diastolic pressure without which the blood pressure would fall to zero between spurts. Systolic pressure is typically slightly over half again as high as diastolic pressure (e.g., 120/80). Sets of muscular arteries branch from different parts of the aorta to serve different parts of the body: the brain, head, neck, lungs, and arms; the thorax (i.e., the chest area); the lower trunk including the abdominal area and gastrointestinal functions; and two main branches serving each leg.

Since parts of the body vary in their need for blood depending on how active they are or whether damage has occurred somewhere, it is often necessary to increase blood flow to some parts and decrease it to others. Therefore, the branching muscular arteries are encased in circularly disposed smooth muscle tissue that can contract to narrow the internal size (i.e., lumen) of those tubes whenever desirable. Narrowing some muscular arteries and relaxing others makes possible a highly variable distribution of blood volume to different parts of the body.

Maintaining an adequate blood flow requires substantial pressure within the system. However, the walls of capillaries are very thin so that materials can be exchanged with intercellular fluid by diffusion through them; the general system pressure would be excessive for the thin capillary walls. Therefore, between the muscular arteries and capillaries there are small connecting arteries called *arterioles* that have a special structure enabling them to function as pressure-reducing "valves," to protect the capillary beds. Blood flows through the capillary beds intermittently. Low oxygen increases the rate of flow and high oxygen decreases it. This is only one of the many feedback control arrangements regulating basic biological processes. Because of pressure differences, materials diffuse out of capillaries into intercellular fluid at their arterial end, and are reabsorbed into capillaries at their venous end.

The capillaries connect with small veins, which feed into larger veins, which feed into still larger veins, which finally return the blood to the right half of the heart. The venous subsystem serves as a blood reservoir, and contains approximately 65% of all blood in the body. Within many veins there are small valves which keep venous blood from flowing "backwards" and permit it to flow in only one direction, namely, towards the heart. Damage to such valves causes blood to collect there, resulting in what are called varicose veins. Whenever a person moves or tenses some muscles, the veins in that area are squeezed and blood is pushed towards the heart (called the venous or muscle pump). Thus, physical activity is an important influence on good blood circulation. The heart has its own private arterial-capillary-venous circuit, called the coronary circulation.

Regulating Material Distribution

Blood flow must pick up materials essential for biological processes from their two input sources: the lungs and the GI tract. The pulmonary circulation carries blood through the lungs, where it picks up new supplies of oxygen and unloads carbon dioxide. A portion of the systemic circulation circulates blood through the gastrointestinal tract where diverse products of the digestive process are absorbed into the blood stream. The body also manufactures and stores additional materials which the blood must collect as it flows through different organs (e.g., liver, spleen, thyroid).

What and how much of these materials is needed where and when is highly variable in different parts of the body as a function of varying kinds and rates of behavior. Therefore, the circulatory system must be able to vary its distribution pattern in terms of rate, amount, kind, and locale, depending upon need. Given the fact that there are hundreds of kinds of substances involved, billions of cells, and complexly and continuously varying operational circumstances, the control and regulatory problems are immense.

There are basically four ways in which the pattern of blood flow can be varied: (a) varying the output of the heart; (b) varying the pressure and volume in various body parts through patterns of vasodilation and vasoconstriction; (c) varying the rate of diffusion and absorption of different kinds of materials between capillaries and intercellular fluid, and (d) varying the functioning of the venous pump.

The heart has a base rate capacity sometimes called its permissive range within which variations in cardiac output are controlled by variations in the functioning of the venous subsystem. There are individual differences in the permissive range, which can be modified by experience. For example, heavy athletic training can raise the ceiling of the permissive range by as much as 50%. In addition, both heart rate and strength of heart contraction can be influenced by both sympathetic and parasympathetic autonomic nervous system (ANS) subsystems, and can approximately double the permissive level. Heart functioning can also potentially be influenced by CNS functioning (e.g., as in self-induced trances or emotional states), because the ANS and CNS are coupled system components.

Vasodilation and vasoconstriction in the arteries and arterioles are regulated by patterns of chemical, humoral, nervous, and local tissue variables. Variations in calcium, potassium, magnesium, hydrogen, and sodium ions and carbon dioxide concentration are illustrative chemical influences. Vasoconstrictors such as epinephrine, norepinephrine, or angiotensin, and vasodilators such as histamines, prostoglandins, and kinins are illustrative humoral influences. ANS influences come primarily from SNS stimulation which can affect both arterial and venous walls. Local tissue states are illustrated by variations in metabolic activity and related deficits and surpluses of different substances (e.g., oxygen and carbon dioxide). Variations in diffusion and absorption rates in capillary beds are influenced by variables such as hydrostatic and osmotic pressure differences between internal and external surfaces of capillary membranes. Variations in venous pumping results from variations in the rate and vigor of muscular activity.

Imagine how overwhelming the task of coordinating all of these methods of influencing the distribution of blood flow would be if it had to be done by some "boss" in the brain, which monitored each relevant variable separately and tried to continuously "make decisions" about which influential variables to manipulate in what patterns. Instead, this complex problem of coordination is efficiently solved in two ways.

The first is to use distributed authority through interdependent hierarchical organization. For example, some adjustments can be made relatively independently by local controls operating at cellular and capillary levels. If circumstances exceed the boundaries within which such local controls can be effective, additional higher level control processes may be triggered into action (e.g., ANS stimulation). Thus, a cascade of influences may spread upward through the control hierarchy. The reverse may also happen. Such complex differential distribution problems can be solved by collaborative orchestration of multiple methods, as illustrated by body temperature control in an earlier chapter.

A second method is to monitor a variable with which the functioning of many other variables is linked. That provides an index of the status of a network of variables; and it might be possible to make adjustments to influence the whole network based on information about the status of one key variable. Oxygen concentration appears to be such a variable. Since metabolic activity requires oxygen, the rate of oxygen usage is a general index of the rate of metabolic activity. By making blood flow adjustments to increase or decrease oxygen availability, one is simultaneously adjusting to some extent the availability of all other nutrients available in the blood and adjusting the capacity to remove waste products.

Sometimes, sudden shifts in blood circulation occur and must be dealt with rapidly (e.g., a wound or hemorrhage). Therefore, some rapid-acting procedures are available for that purpose. Some are mechanical, such as the capillary fluid shift. Some are nervous system mechanisms, such as the baroreceptor reflex and the CNS ischemic response. Fast-acting hormonal influences are also available. For example, sympathetic nervous system arousal will release norepinephrine and epinephrine into the blood where they can trigger vasoconstriction for as long as they circulate. Production of an even more powerful vasoconstrictor, angiotensin II, is an indirect consequence of reduced blood flow in the kidneys. Other compounds, such as bradykinin, produce vasodilation and increased capillary permeability. Since limbic system based emotional arousal triggers SNS arousal and the production of the kinds of chemical compounds just mentioned (among others), anticipatory adjustments of circulatory processes can occur. Thus, a frightened person may experience a racing heart and an angry person an increase in blood pressure.

Longer term (i.e., days, weeks, or months) arterial regulation of blood pressure is accomplished through sensitive renal-body fluid mechanisms. For example, only a small increase in fluid retention can produce hypertension in humans. If frequent or "chronic" SNS arousal occurs over a lengthy period, permanent alterations of the steady state functioning of the kidneys may occur. Chronic human hypertension is typically the result of some structural or functional change in this renal-body fluid regulatory arrangement.

The Lymphatic Subsystem. This is a secondary system of "pipelines," linked to the primary circulatory system, through which fluids and materials can flow from the intercellular spaces into the blood. It is similar in structure and circulatory mechanisms to the venous system. It has three main functions: (a) conservation of plasma proteins and fluid; (b) defense against infection; and (c) lipid absorption through intestinal lymphatics.

Lymph has essentially the same composition as the intercellular fluid in the part of the body from which it comes. More than half the lymph is derived from the liver and intestines, probably because those are major sites for defense against invading organisms and for lipid absorption, two of the three main lymphatic functions.

A key function of the lymphatic system is to collect and carry away from cells substances of high molecular weight which cannot enter capillary beds, such as proteins and large particulate matter. If they accumulate around cells, within a a few hours blood capillary processes would become so abnormal that life could not continue. The lymphatic system also helps to regulate the amount of fluid around cells. Moreover, the lymphatic subsystem functions to collect and help destroy potentially damaging invading entities (as will be described later). The lymphatic subsystem contains lymphatic tissue structures called lymph nodes. They function as part of the body's defensive system, and filter out or destroy potentially damaging organisms or materials before they can enter the blood stream.

This summary illustrates the intricate and yet beautifully orchestrated functioning of a componentized, hierarchically organized set of control systems to maintain essential steady state regulation and to adjust those steady states either temporarily or permanently as circumstances demand. Also, since the cardiovascular system serves the entire body, it illustrates nicely how a person functions as a larger system through the synchronized functioning of many component structures and processes.

Hierarchically Organized Material Production and Storage.   Each cell has "short term" storage of essential materials, enabling it to briefly function independently. This is backed up by "local storage" of materials in the intercellular fluid. "Regional storage" is provided by blood and some tissue (e.g., fat cells) which store and release essential materials as local storage becomes depleted. Finally, "centralized storage" (e.g., the liver) provides reserves for the entire body.

Unlike other nutrients, oxygen cannot be directly stored and transported in the plasma. It is stored in red blood cells which function as "delivery vans." These delivery vans wear out, and are sometimes lost through openings in the body's boundaries (e.g., through bleeding). Therefore, myeloid tissue, or bone marrow, continually manufactures a replacement of red blood cells.

The spleen recycles worn-out red blood cells as blood flows through it. It uses the hemoglobin to manufacture bile pigment (bilirubin) which the liver collects, and extracts iron from the hemoglobin so it can be used to manufacture new red blood cells. In that sense, the spleen functions as a waste-removal filter for the blood. The spleen also functions as a "storage tank" for a reserve supply of red blood cells that can be released quickly into the blood stream when a sudden increase in oxygen demand is placed on the system.

Not all materials absorbed from the gastrointestinal tract are in a form cells can use. Other tissues or organs (e.g., fat cells, endocrine glands, intestinal mucosa) help modify the absorbed substances into useful forms, and store surplus materials until needed. Chief among these "chemical factory" transformation and storage organs is the liver. It constructs several compounds necessary for digestion and cell metabolism, such as bile, plasma proteins, creatine, urea, plasma lipids, and cholesterol; it degrades fatty acids, helps maintain a normal blood glucose level, and can store large amounts of glycogen, a key ingredient for the energy-producing activities of all cells. Additional surplus supplies are stored in other parts of the body (e.g., loose connective tissue, subcutaneous skin tissue), particularly in fat cells.

The adaptive advantage of being able to store surplus nutrients is obvious. During their evolution, animals did not always have adequate food supplies available to provide needed nutrients. Therefore, by overeating when food was available, and by storing surpluses, they could always have essential nutrients available for their functioning even when nothing was available to eat. Some humans develop an "over-storage" problem called obesity. In interesting contrast, oxygen was continuously available in the environmental niche in which mammals evolved. Therefore, no oxygen storage capability evolved because it was not necessary.

Security, Sanitation, Maintenance, and Repair

Biological structures and functions can be disrupted in a variety of ways, including invasion by "foreign" substances, contamination from by-products of cellular construction and operation activities, normal "wear and tear," and structural damage. Therefore, as part of its self-organizing, self-constructing capabilities, the body maintains "security systems" to protect itself, "sanitation departments" to collect and remove waste and debris, and "maintenance departments" to repair and replace parts.

Security Subsystems. The human body is continually exposed to potentially damaging or destructive "foreign invaders" of the body's boundaries; that is, of the skin, the wet epithelium linings of the gastro-intestinal tract, the respiratory passages, and the urinary-sexual passages. Sometimes the biological ability to distinguish "self" from "nonself" breaks down and the security forces may attack their own body's tissues. This is called *autoimmune disease.* Security arrangements and forces must be deployed to try to prevent invasion at any boundary, to quickly oppose invaders that succeed in breaking through a boundary, to be able to bring mobile reserve defenders to any locality as needed, and to provide additional lines of defense if invaders succeed in breaking through the local defenses.

The first line of defense functions to prevent invasion through tissue

boundary barriers, and through their ability to secrete chemical com
pounds that can repel or kill potential invaders. Anything that weakens
these barriers (e.g., starvation, illness) increases the danger of invasion
(infection).

If invaders breach these barriers they are immediately opposed by two
types of local defenses. First, if a virus invades a cell, the damaged cell
produces a small protein called interferon (of which there are several
kinds) which binds to receptors of neighboring cells of the same type.
That triggers the synthesis of enzymes that inhibit viral protein synthesis, thereby preventing damage to neighboring cells. It is analogous to a
neighborhood burglar alarm that signals everyone to lock their doors
and windows when a burglar enters any home in the neighborhood.

The second kind of local defense is accomplished by cells called
leukocytes or "white cells" because they are relatively colorless of which
there are three special types: *granulocytes, lymphoid cells,* and *mononuclear
phagocytes.* Each type has several subtypes which display a variety of
forms at different stages of their maturation. Each type performs
somewhat different functions in an overall defensive strategy.

The cells are deployed throughout the body in an hierarchical defensive strategy. Some are lodged in local tissue (like the neighborhood
cop), and take on a different appearance in each different tissue (e.g.,
Kupffer cells in the liver or alveolar microphages in the lungs). Some are
mobile reserves, continuously circulating in the blood, ready to move to
invasion sites anywhere in the body. Some are lodged in regional
centers (e.g., spleen, lymph nodes) to provide backup forces for the
blood's mobile reserves and to serve as a third line of defense. Some are
located in "police academies" (e.g., the thymus) where they are prepared for specialized defensive roles, and where some of them may
reproduce themselves if necessary. Some are regularly being born in
hemopoietic tissue (bone marrow) from which they can be shipped to
various parts of the body for maturation and defense. Obviously, this is
a very complex security arrangement involving considerable cooperation among different kinds of defenders, and only some of its broad
properties can be mentioned here. Details may be found elsewhere
(Abramson & Dobrin, 1984; Cline, 1975; Ham & Cormack, 1979).

The primary role of *granulocytes* (e.g., neutrophils) and *mononuclear
phagocytes* (e.g., macrophages) is to immobilize and destroy invaders
and to remove damaged or dying cells and cell debris. This is accomplished in a two-stage process of encapsulation and destruction. The
defending cell encapsulates the invader in a container inside itself
(called phagocytosis), and fills the container with enzymes that kill and
digest the invader. To accomplish this phagocytic function, the defending cell must physically contact the invader, often by moving to the
invader through a process called *chemotaxis* (Snyderman & Goetzel,

1981). Chemical compounds on the invader or at the invasion site function like a beacon, attracting white cells located in that neighborhood (like the local cop on the beat). If there is local tissue damage, a complex process called inflammation occurs, in effect "walling off" the damaged area (called *brawny edema*). The result is like putting police barricades around a neighborhood to produce a slowdown in the spread of the invaders, giving local defenses more time to control the invasion.

If the invasion is sizable, chemical products of the battle attract to the invasion site, through chemotaxis, additional mobile reserve defenders to help with the battle; this in turn may trigger release of additional forces from regional centers (e.g., the spleen) and increased production of new defenders (e.g., in the bone marrow). Thus, physicians use an increased white blood cell count as an indicator that a battle is underway against an infection somewhere in the body. This basic defensive strategy of "seek, immobilize, and destroy" is supplemented by an elaborate, special-purpose defensive force called the *immune system* that is an evolutionary emergent in vertebrates. It provides a capability for distinguishing "self" from "nonself," and for "remembering" previous invaders and quickly producing a defensive force, specialized for each specific kind of invader, if they should return on future occasions. Its coordination and operation is accomplished by biochemical feedforward and feedback processes (Tonegawa, 1985).

This specialized family of defenders is called *lymphocytes* of which there are two general types, sometimes called B and T cells, which use different strategies to perform their defensive functions, and concentrate on different kinds of invaders. For example, B cells are most effective against acute bacterial infections while T cells seem to be most effective against chronic bacterial infections, some viruses, and fungi. They are also the primary attackers of transplanted organs and malignant cells (Herberman & Ortaldo, 1981). When they contact an antigen for which they have a specialized sensitivity, the B-cell *defensive strategy* is to rapidly divide to produce many cells which are transformed into a different version called *plasma cells*. These produce a special kind of protein (immunoglobulins) called *antibodies*. Within a week or two this process can flood the system with billions of such specialized antibody molecules.

Antibodies are attracted to and bind to antigens, that is, the molecules on the surface of invaders. They also bind to a family of special enzymes circulating in the blood, called *complement*, which can initiate a sequence of chemical reactions capable of neutralizing and killing the invader. That is why B-cell strategy is called *humoral immunity*.

The T-cell *defensive strategy* is different. Antigen contact also produces rapid T-cell multiplication. However, T cells attach themselves to the invader directly and release chemical compounds that attract phagocytic cells, which can then devour and destroy the invaders. Therefore, T-cell strategy is called *cellular immunity*.

A special thing happens the first time these immune system strategies are used against a specific antigen. Some B or T cells that are produced do not enter into the current battle. They are called "memory cells" because, of the thousands of antigens to which they may be exposed, they will react only to the one for which they became sensitized during the first invasion and can very quickly produce a large number of specialized defenders like themselves to fight that kind of invasion. It is analogous to developing some police who specialize only in housebreakers, some in rapists, some in embezzlers, and so on, and then having their children, grandchildren, and great-grandchildren follow in the same specialization. Cellular immunity is longer lasting than humoral immunity.

The more frequently a person is invaded, the larger, more widely dispersed, and more diversified his or her defensive forces will become. Small invasions are less dangerous but they also result in memory cells, so vaccination procedures can create acquired immunity. Some of the chemical processes associated with immune reactions can produce some discomforting side effects called allergies.

If invaders get past the first two lines of defense, they can enter the lymphatic circulatory system where lymphatic tissue rich in defenders (e.g., lymph nodes) represent a third line of defense. If invaders succeed in penetrating into the blood stream, they face a fourth line of defense in the spleen which stores and produces leukocytes for defensive purposes. It is also a centralized storage area that can respond to sudden bursts of activity (e.g., fight and flight) by rapidly infusing large numbers of both red and white cells into the blood stream.

There is growing evidence that the nervous and immune systems are "inextricably interconnected" (Marx, 1985b). Emotional states such as depression and anger may suppress or facilitate immune functions, and immune system functioning may be trainable. Finally, there is some evidence of a relationship between immune and endocrine functioning (Woloski et al., 1985). Thus, it appears that other functions may regulate immune system functioning and vice versa.

Protein nutrition is particularly important for these defenses because so many of the defensive structures and processes are proteins or protein-dependent (e.g., antibodies and enzymes). Therefore, the best defense against disease is a good offense: Stay in peak health through appropriate nutrition and sanitation, exercise, sleep, and a positive outlook on life, and invaders will find you a very inhospitable host.

Sanitation Subsystems. The body's overall chemical composition remains relatively constant every day although a great variety of solids, liquids, and gases regularly enter and leave the body. Some way of regulating the body's composition by selectively retaining and eliminating materials in the circulatory system is essential. Except for substances such as oxygen and carbon dioxide, the kidneys have the primary responsibility for performing these "sanitation" functions and process about 24% of the total cardiac output per minute (Brenner & Rector, 1981; Jacob, Francone, & Lossow, 1982).

Two duplicate kidneys produce urine which is a complex solution of approximately 96% water in which organic and inorganic substances such as wastes from protein metabolism, salts, toxins, hormones, and pigments are dissolved. Its constituents vary depending upon the body's current excesses and deficits.

Controlling the water volume and concentration of materials in the urine enables the body to regulate the constituents of the blood, and through that the homeostasis of body fluids and other materials. For this reason, urinalysis has long been one method for diagnosing disease. For example, 5000 years ago Egyptian physicians diagnosed diabetes by tasting the patient's urine for sweetness.

The primary functional component of a kidney is called a *nephron*, and each kidney contains about one million nephrons. Each nephron has two subcomponents, a renal corpuscle and tubule extensions, which in turn are composed of subsubcomponents.

Urine is formed in two stages: (a) glomerular filtration and (b) tubular reabsorption and secretion. Nutritionally valuable substances (e.g., glucose, amino acids) are almost completely reabsorbed; while waste products (e.g., urea) are little or not reabsorbed, or are secreted. Other materials (e.g., sodium ions, calcium, phosphate, and sulfate ions) are actively reabsorbed in accord with the body's current needs.

The ability to regulate water retention was an important evolutionary development. When fluid loss exceeds fluid intake, hypothalamic receptors sensitive to the osmotic pressure of blood plasma stimulate the release of the antidiuretic hormone (ADH) from the posterior pituitary gland. ADH functions to increase water reabsorption in the kidneys. In addition, changes in the volume or pressure of blood flowing through the kidneys releases an enzyme (renin) that functions through a series of steps to stimulate the secretion of an adrenal steroid hormone called *aldosterone*. Aldosterone functions to increase sodium and water retention, and therefore to raise blood volume and pressure. The kidneys also function to regulate the blood's acid-base balance. Through the kidney's continuous filtering process, unabsorbed urine gradually collects in the bladder from which it is periodically discharged.

Maintenance and Repair Subsystems. At birth, the human body has only a few final construction processes that remain to be completed.

Between birth and adult maturity, the organization of the body does not change but organizational processes become more efficient and the body gets bigger. Such physical growth results from increasing both the number and/or size of different kinds of cells. However, once constructed the body exists in steady state conditions requiring tissue maintenance, replacement, and repair.

Cells in the embryonic blastula phase are *totipotent*, meaning they can reproduce any kind of cell. Cells become more specialized through embryonic development and can reproduce only cells of their specialization. Mature body cells may be categorized into three types in terms of their ability to reproduce themselves: nonreproducing, regularly reproducing, and infrequently reproducing (Ham & Cormack, 1979).

Nonreproducing cells cannot replace themselves or elaborate their number. Neurons are the prime example. However, they have two compensating features that provide exceptional plasticity throughout life, and particularly during the early phases of development (Lerner, 1984): some ability to regenerate neuronal fibers if the cell body remains healthy, and the ability to increase or decrease their dendritic and axonal interconnections. Organs composed of nonreproducing cells (e.g., the brain) are particularly vulnerable to depreciation from structural damage and aging.

Regularly reproducing cells include body tissue involved in functions in which they wear out, are used up, or are lost from body surfaces. Examples are *epithelial* tissue such as skin and the lining of the GI tract; *connective* tissue such as red and white blood cells; and *muscle* tissue such as striated muscles. Only subsets of such cells called *stem* or *germinative cells*, can reproduce. The cell turnover is quite large and rapid in some tissue, such as red blood cells. Organs composed of regularly reproducing cells are less vulnerable to permanent damage and the difficulties of aging. However, the reproductive capability of the germinative cell population may decline somewhat with poor nutrition, poor health, or increasing age.

Infrequently reproducing cells have a long life span and are less susceptible to destruction or "wearing out" as they perform their functions. Examples include liver cells, secretory cells of the pancreas, and cells of hormone-producing glands. However, if a significant amount of such tissue is damaged, the remaining healthy cells may begin to subdivide again to produce new tissue.

Tissue damage inevitably cuts or damages some blood vessel(s), and sets in motion a complex *repair subsystem* composed of three interacting damage-control processes. One process involves smooth muscle contractions which reduce the diameter of the vessel at the damage point. In a second simultaneous process, blood components called *platelets* begin to collect there. When one contacts a damaged vascular wall, it immediately becomes larger, irregularly shaped and sticky. It also secretes substances that cause other nearby platelets to do the same thing. This positive feedback loop produces a growing number of such transformed platelets which stick or clump together to form a platelet plug. In minute ruptures which occur frequently in all humans, the platelet plug will completely stop blood loss.

For larger holes a third mechanism, *blood coagulation*, is necessary. This mechanism involves many interacting chemical processes too detailed to describe here. It results in production of molecules called fibrin monomers which combine to form a network of long, threadlike fibers at the damage site, a bit like the threads on a loom. That network begins to entrap other materials in the blood, such as platelets, blood cells, and plasma. A substance released in this process (the fibrin-stabilizing factor) functions as an enzyme to bond the network of fibrin threads together. The result is called a *blood clot*, which begins to contract, squeezing out the fluid in it and pulling together the broken edges of the damaged blood vessel. One current interest in this whole repair process is that it may be one of the elements in the origins of atherosclerosis by leaving "rough spots" which may collect deposits from the blood, thereby obstructing blood flow.

Once the blood loss is controlled, a wound can be repaired by constructing a protective layer of new cells. Then, the construction of new tissue can take place under that protective layer until the wound is completely healed.

SUMMARY

Several biological processes have been summarized to illustrate how they are governed by an hierarchically organized, complexly interrelated set of structural-functional components utilizing feedback and feedforward processes, to maintain the total system in an appropriate steady state and to protect and repair it when disrupting influences occur. Moreover, it was illustrated that these processes are guided by a set of internal "rules" relatively independent of direct environmental influences.

However, since humans are open systems they must carry out complex behavioral transactions with variable environments to insure the availability of the necessary ingredients for such biological processes. Such transactions are based on the collection, organization, creation, and use of information. Therefore, key features of the biological base for information-based governing functions are summarized in the following section.

BASES FOR BEHAVIORAL SELF-ORGANIZATION AND SELF-CONSTRUCTION

The complexity of a system can be represented by the number and nature of its components and their interdependencies. As complexity increases, so does the need for increasingly centralized coordination of components if unitary functioning is to be maintained as supplements to coordinating mechanisms and processes within and among components. In humans, functional coordination is accomplished through material (biochemical) and informational (neural) processes. The structures that make these governing functions possible are those which produce and distribute chemical "messengers" (e.g., neurotransmitters and hormones), and those that transform information into bioelectric-biochemical codes and organize, transform, store, and use that information to direct, control, and regulate system functioning.

The earliest form of coordination Mother Nature evolved was biochemical. Information-based coordination is a later evolutionary emergent. However, as in all componentized hierarchically organized evolution, the newer coordinating mechanisms and processes did not replace the old but used them and added to them. Thus, in humans, biochemical and information-coordination arrangements are mutually influential processes.

The Organized Complexity of the Nervous System

The structures supporting the governing functions are enormously complex. For example, Weiss (1978) estimates that shortly after birth the human brain totals about 100 billion nerve cells. Each has branching connections with an average of about 10,000 other cells. Thompson, Berger, and Perry (1980b) estimate that the number of possible interconnections in a human brain exceeds the number of atoms in the universe. The reconstitution of each cell's molecular endowment occurs from one to ten times each week. They estimate that this produces a total, "almost astronomical variance of 10^{26} for each individual brain." To produce systematic functioning from such complexity requires "order in the gross with subordinated freedom in the small" (Weiss, 1978). "Order in the gross" is produced through a complex structural-functional organization of neurons and glands. "Subordinated freedom in the small" is accomplished through componentization and hierarchical organization.

The neuron is the basic structural unit of the nervous system. It is organized into various kinds of structural groupings that are interrelated both vertically and horizontally (Pribram, 1980a).

The nature of these neurological structures (i.e., their morphology) has been examined through dissection, manipulation, and direct observation, and the relationships between structure and function have been explored in different organisms in several ways (Rosenzweig, 1984). Among them have been experimental stimulation; study of natural, surgical, and experimental damage; and electrical and chemical manipulation of neuronal functioning (Dismukes, 1979; John & Schwartz, 1978; Masterton & Berkley, 1974; J. Miller, 1978; Noback & Demarest, 1981; Sokolov, 1977; Thompson, Berger, & Perry, 1980a, 1980b; Uttal, 1978; Wittrock, 1980a; see also *Scientific American*, 1979).

Each of these methods has its weaknesses. For example, Isaacson (1980) says that lesions in any brain structure "will undoubtedly induce secondary effects in all remaining systems directly interconnected with it" and in other systems with indirect connections. Changes resulting from such circumstances must be understood in terms of "aberrant functions of multiple systems." In addition, evolution has produced different organizations of multiple systems. Therefore, caution must be exercised in generalizing from data about one species to another, such as differences in sensory coding operations (Davidson, 1980; Jerison, 1976).

Despite massive and growing amounts of information in this vital and exciting domain, from study of a variety of animals, a clear understanding of the nature of neural structural differences and their functional consequences in humans cannot yet be constructed on the basis of available knowledge (Uttal, 1978; *Scientific American*, 1979). What follows is an attempt to discern the emerging outlines of the nervous system's structural-functional organization; in other words, to try to characterize the "forest" while ignoring much of the interesting details about the "trees" within it.

Neurons: The Basic Structural-Functional Component

The *neuron* is the fundamental structural component for information-based coordination. Several different versions exist. The most common multipolar neuron will be described. Structurally, there are three major subcomponents: (a) the cell body or *soma*; (b) a set of short projections, called *dendrites*, that progressively subdivide into many smaller branches (like tree branches); and (c) a single longer projection, called an *axon*, that may have a few smaller branches called *collaterals*. The dendrites are the information collectors. Because of the many dendritic branches, information may simultaneously be collected by one neuron from many other neurons. Each branch may pick up information from different or multiple sources.

Information Recoding Between Bioelectric and Biochemical Markers. When a dendrite is appropriately stimulated, a bioelectric current is triggered, the size of which is directly proportional to the amplitude of the stimulation (i.e., they are graded electrical potentials). Several kinds may be triggered. One is a positive or excitatory potential (resulting from cell membrane depolarization). Another is a negative or inhibitory potential (resulting from cell membrane hyperpolarization). Others are more complex, and are often called *modulators*. All electrical "currents" flow to the cell body "headquarters." Multiple, simultaneous messages must produce a result a bit like the babble of conversations at a cocktail party. The only way to deal with such a babble is to focus on information of interest and ignore the rest. Neurons apparently do something like that. The multiple messages, in the form of different patterns of electrical potentials, are integrated by the cell in some way more complicated than simple summation (e.g., Bullock, 1959; Dismukes, 1979). Sometimes the integration produces a net electrical "current" that reaches a critical level (called a threshold), and the cell "headquarters" will trigger a sudden surge of "current" (called the action potential) down the axon to its tip. That action potential is always a complete discharge. As a popular song says, it's "all or nothing at all." So, the only way it can vary or code information is in the time-varying frequency patterns of its discharge (the same coding method used in digital computers).

At the tip of the axon there are small containers, called vesicles, containing different chemical compounds, called *neurotransmitters*, manufactured by the neuron. Neurons differ in the kinds of neurotransmitters they produce and respond to (Emson, 1983). These chemicals differ in their functions. Some produce excitatory potentials in nearby neurons (e.g., acetylcholine) and others produce inhibitory potentials (e.g., GABA). There is considerable interest in the possibility that deficiencies or excesses of neurochemicals may influence learning (e.g., McGaugh et al., 1980) and functional disorders (e.g., Whitehouse et al., 1982).

Chemical compounds other than neurotransmitters may affect or be secreted by neurones, such as *neurohormones* and *endogenous opiates*. Imbalances in such chemicals may be involved in some kinds of functional or psychological disorders (e.g., Dismukes, 1979; Marx, 1981b; Olson et al., 1979). Neurons appear to be differentially sensitive to different kinds of chemicals, and "receptors" for various chemical messages may exist at other cell membrane sites besides at the synaptic juncture. Such "autoreceptors" or "regulatory receptors" are responsive to the neurotransmitter(s) emitted by the neuron on which they are located. They probably "form a part of a feedback system regulating neurotransmitter synthesis and neuronal activity" (Spear, 1980). It is "humbling" to consider the "complex tapestry" revealed by modern neuroscience (Panksepp, 1986). Most neurons produce multiple neurochemicals and have multiple receptors, and many synapses exhibit tendencies for homeostatic regulation.

Such differential sensitivities appear to have two kinds of functional correlates. First, they seem to produce a kind of "selective perception" on the part of some neurons, giving special "weighting" to different kinds of information (e.g., Kolata, 1979; Sokolov, 1977; Zeki, 1980). So it appears that neurons, like people, have their own biases, filtering out some kinds of information and emphasizing other kinds. Second, some neurons may be able to emit more than one neurotransmitter, giving them capabilities for differential treatment of messages received, but also they would have capabilities for varying the messages they transmit through biochemical differences as well as through frequency modulation of axonal discharges.

When an action potential reaches the axon tip of a neuron, some of the chemical compound is spilled from its vesicles into the tiny spaces between the axon and the dendrites of any other neuron neighbors, called the synapse, triggering a bioelectrical response in any (receptive) dendrite it touches. Thus, the information is converted from a bioelectrical marker to a chemical marker and back into an electrical marker. A neuron can "fire" many times a second. It is the pattern of those volleys (i.e., the *organization* of the marker) that contains the message.

Neurons' Information Sources and Audience. However, like humans, a neuron passes along information primarily to "friends and neighbors," that is, to those with whom it has contact and who are prepared to receive and respond to the kinds of messages (i.e., neurochemicals) delivered. Different neurons may respond differently to the same biochemical message. Kinsbourne and Hicks (1978) call such neuronal arrangements *functional cerebral space*. Axons can target specific other neurons and since axons may be of different lengths, the "others" don't have to be "next-door neighbors." Axons can simultaneously affect more than one neuron, and have three basic kinds of targets. Some neurons (i.e., interneurons) simply exchange information with other neurons; that is, they are just part of the bureaucracy. Others influence glands to increase or decrease their chemical output or *hormones*. Still others give "reports" and "instructions" to structures involved in environmental transactions (e.g., to muscles or sensory structures).

There is much yet to learn about the functioning of neurons. Their capabilities are more complicated than the summary just completed (Stevens, 1979). For example, there are reciprocal synapses, and synapses between dendrites as well as between axons and dendrites (e.g., Dismukes, 1979; Noback & Demarest, 1981).

Thus, each neuron can receive information from many sources, differentially weight each report, interrelate multiple messages, and, when the integrated information has certain attributes, send out a selective report to others with whom it has contact. Neurons don't just "transmit" information, they "process" it. It is a bit like the newsroom of a local newspaper. Staff reporters are in contact with various news sources around town. The information they collect is given to the editorial staff. They in turn select and organize the relevant information into a news story for the next edition of their paper, combining some reports and discarding others to create a coherent story which is distributed to interested readers.

Can the dendrites (like staff reporters) receive different instructions from time to time, alerting them to be particularly sensitive to certain kinds of information if it occurs? In other words, can individual neurons be "tuned" through feedforward processes to the kinds and amounts of neurotransmitters to which they should respond? There is some evidence that they can neurochemically (Dismukes, 1979; Olson et al., 1979; Watkins & Mayer, 1982). Moreover, "unused" neurons (as in sensory deprivation) tend to become sluggish and less responsive (e.g., Harris, 1981).

Dynamic Neuronal Connections. The body cannot produce new nerve cells. You have all you will ever have when you are born. Therefore, if one of them is destroyed, it cannot be replaced. However, a nerve cell is destroyed only if the cell body (the "headquarters") is destroyed. If the cell body is intact, damaged dendrites and axons may regenerate themselves so that functional capabilities are not lost (just as some lower organisms can regenerate limbs). Axonal sprouting can occur if part of an input to a neuron (or neuron group) is lost (Cotman, 1980). In fact, dendritic and axonal structures appear to be naturally dynamic or changeable depending upon a variety of conditions (Cotman, 1978). For example, during early development in many parts of the nervous system axons sprout an overabundance of connections. However, as development proceeds (and an individual's experience accumulates), some of those extra synapses disappear; in other words, axons "specialize" in selected targets. In general, neuronal interconnections become more organized (Purpura, 1981; Purves & Lichtman, 1980). Moreover, if they are not used (as illustrated by sensory deprivation or muscular immobilization), neurons appear to deteriorate. In contrast, stimulation seems to facilitate dendritic or axonal regeneration and elaboration (e.g., Almli & Finger, 1984; Harris, 1981; Lerner, 1984; Purpura, 1981). Nerve cells require "informational nutriment" as well as "material nutriment" to stay healthy and functional. Functional regeneration following damage is more likely the earlier in life the damage occurs (Kalil & Reh, 1979).

ORGANIZATIONS OF NEURONS: THE NERVOUS SYSTEM

The nervous system is an organization of different kinds of neurons with different functional specializations arranged in hierarchical fashion.

A Government Analogy

Like the United States Government, the nervous system has local offices, regional offices, and national offices, which are functionally interrelated. The local offices are the ones "closest to the action." Within offices, there are sections responsible for somewhat different functions. There are different departments of government, which may have their own hierarchy of local, regional, and national offices, but which must coordinate their functions in certain ways with components of other departments.

All levels and functions of government may be directly or indirectly influenced by the executive office of the president which establishes and revises policy objectives (i.e., the directive functions), and exercises leadership through direct communication with various parts of government and the general public. The president's decisions and actions are also influenced by that two-way communication process. Congress considers alternate ways of achieving social objectives, selects preferred approaches, passes laws, and appropriates resources to implement those approaches (i.e., the control functions). The administrative departments are responsible for implementing and administering programs, and for collecting relevant information which can be used by various governmental units to guide and evaluate the effort and to plans for the future (i.e., the transactional functions). The Office of the President, the Supreme Court, the Attorney General's office, the Office of Management and Budget, the Controller's office, and Congress all monitor the flow of activity to assure that it is legal, is being conducted efficiently, and is achieving the intended results (i.e., the regulatory functions). They may issue policies and guidelines or change laws, from time to time, to try to produce better results; that is, to influence the control and transactional functions. The Congressional Record, Library of Congress, National Archives, national museums, and departmental files organize and store information which may have some future value, and make it available for use when needed (i.e., the memory functions).

The General Pattern of Organization

The structural-functional organization of the nervous system (NS) will be summarized by starting with the local offices and administrative departments, and moving progressively to the executive office. It should be reemphasized, however, that the evolutionary significance of the NS is that it makes possible the coordinated functioning of the individual as a complexly organized unit; therefore the NS must function as one dynamically integrated information system (Granit, 1977; Uttal, 1978).

Coordination of Biological and Transactional Functions. The NS is composed of two coupled systems, one monitoring and influencing internal body functioning (the *autonomic* nervous system—ANS) and the other monitoring and influencing person-environment relationships (the *central* nervous system—CNS). Figure 6.1 represents the parallel coupled ANS, CNS, and brain.

The two coordination tasks are coupled. In a living system, the internal biological functions are dependent upon the energy and material exchanges with the external environment. Similarly, transactions with the external environment depend upon the effective functioning and energy production of the internal processes. A higher level of coordination must accomplish that coordination, and that is the executive function of the brain. However, some coordination takes place in regional offices in the spine, and local offices in various body segments. Some functional differences between left and right brain hemispheres may be related to the internal-external governing problems a person faces (Hecaen, 1969; Luria, 1973).

Lateral and Vertical Organization. Consider the spinal column to represent a vertical axis of the body. In general, for purposes of *functional operation* (i.e., *behavior*), the nervous system is organized *laterally*, radiating from that axis. Sensory nerves enter at the back of the axis and motor nerves exit at the front of the axis. Information collection (input through afferent nerves) and signals for action (output through efferent nerves) are organized in layers, or segments, like a group of bicycle wheels stacked on top of one another. The information collection and the action nerves relevant to the functions of each layer are organized within that layer like the spokes of the bicycle wheel.

The *integration and coordination* among those operational layers or segments is organized *vertically*. For example, the coordination or

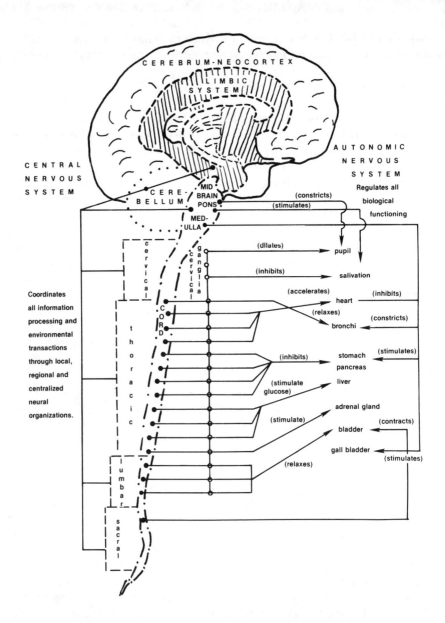

FIG. 6.1. A representation of some aspects of the nervous system's hierarchical organization, illustrating some of the interrelationships and functions of the internally focused autonomic system and the externally focused central system, and the brain's centralized coordinating role.

governing of sensory-motor functions at the "regional" level is accomplished by a network of "connector neurons" (called interneurons) between vertebral segments within the spinal cord.

Recall that the body is composed of many structural components. However, the organization of the functional capabilities of those many components is not totally constrained by their structural organization. Humans start life with a few relatively simple functional patterns and quickly construct more. By combining simpler functional components in a variety of ways, an array of larger, somewhat different functional patterns can be created. The number of combinations possible through this kind of arrangement is enormous. The consequence is an organism capable of flexibly producing a huge diversity of behavior patterns, matched to equally diverse environmental conditions, within structural limitations.

The greater the diversity of functional components that can be constructed, coordinated, and integrated into a single pattern, the more elaborate and detailed are the governing arrangements that are needed. As one ascends the nervous system structure vertically, the potential complexity and diversity of behavioral capabilities is enlarged by the increasingly comprehensive nature of the coordinating and integrating functions that can be performed (MacLean, 1982). For example, more than one brain area and neurobiochemical system participates in each psychobehavioral process, practically every neurochemical system is widely dispersed within the brain, and many neurochemical systems converge upon single brain areas (Panksepp, 1986). Because of its componentized, hierarchical organization, the highest governing levels influence local operating units primarily through intermediate levels rather than directly.

Local and Regional Operations: Peripheral, and Spinal Components

Central Nervous System (CNS) *Components.* The CNS has input (sensory) and output (motor) components. The *sensory neurons* function as reporters. They collect detailed information, filter and organize it a bit, and send reports to branch offices in or near the spinal column or in the brain. Humans are organized in segments identified by the bone components (vertebrae) of the spinal column. The cell bodies of sensory nerves below the head are located in clusters (called *ganglia* or *nuclei*) near the spinal cord. From there, the axons for all sensory neurons in each body segment form a bundle or cable and enter their spinal segment. Sensory neurons originating above the neck (e.g., from the eyes or ears) follow a similar pattern, only they do not pass through a vertebral segment. Consequently, they are called *cranial nerves*. *Motor neurons* which organize skeletal muscle actions exit from the same vertebral segment that their related sensory neurons enter. All body functions and activities below the head are directly controlled by the sensory-motor neurons that enter and leave the spinal column.

The sensory and motor neurons for each segment interface through synapses within their vertebrae segments. In these spinal *"branch offices,"* additional filtering and organizing of information takes place. Moreover, each branch office can take certain actions for the good of its locale without consulting "headquarters." Such local actions appear to be of at least three types, which have been called *spinal reflexes, oscillators,* and *servomechanisms* (Gallistel, 1980a, 1980b). However, these are not simple sensory-motor arcs; rather they are "dynamic, integrative units relating movements to the outside world" (Trevarthen, 1980). There is evidence that some learning can take place at these first-level branch offices.

Next, several spinal segments are linked into networks, forming a kind of *"regional office"* (called a *plexus*) that coordinates the functioning of regions of the body (e.g., the arms and hands). A considerable amount of coordination is accomplished by these spinal arrangements (e.g., Swazey, 1968).

However, the local and regional governing circuits can be influenced by commands from the brain and by external forces such as the resistance encountered when trying to lift an object. Both action and information collection can be "pretuned" by feedforward signals from the brain (Eccles, 1976; Gallistel, 1980a; Miles & Evarts, 1979).

There also appears to be a kind of memory capacity in these spinal networks, because some functional components appear to be automated at these levels and can be triggered into operation in different patterns of organization by feedforward influences descending from the brain (Grillner, 1975). Finally, through sensory and motor neurons within the vertebral column, information is transmitted to and from brain structures.

Autonomic Nervous System (ANS) Components. Parallel to CNS is another set of neurons that control the body's internal biological functioning, such as the glands and the circulatory and respiratory systems. These neurons compose the autonomic nervous system (ANS).

ANS neurons course through the vertebral column connecting with central brain mechanisms and exiting from vertebrae at the same places as the motor neurons. They also interface with other ANS neurons in ganglia (ANS "branch offices") located outside, but near, the spinal column. The ANS ganglia from each segment are linked together in a "chain," making possible a "regional" level of ANS coordination, as for example through cardiac, pulmonary, and pelvic autonomic plexuses. For each ganglia, ANS neurons influence specific internal organs. There are two parallel ANS divisions. The *parasympathetic* (PNS) division emerges from the top and bottom of the spinal column, while the *sympathetic* (SNS) division emerges from middle segments (see Fig. 6.1). They work in complementary or synergistic fashion. With each organ, one division stimulates and the other inhibits activity.

In general, the *SNS* functions to mobilize the body for action. For example, under its stimulation eyes dilate and alertness increases; the spleen may release more red blood cells; epinephrine and norepinephrine are increased; blood pressure and the concentration of blood sugar increase; and blood flow to the skeletal muscles is increased while flow to the skin, viscera, and sexual organs is inhibited. The preparation can vary from mild (as in normal activities) to extreme (as in life-threatening emergencies).

In contrast, the *PNS* functions primarily to organize the internal operation of the body for its self-constructing (autopoietic) functions. For example, it stimulates the various organs and processes involved in digestion, waste removal, and the storage of food supplies; it causes respiration to become slower and more regular, the pupils of the eyes to constrict, and vigilance to decrease (sleep is dominated by the parasympathetic division). It also facilitates the self-constructing activities of reproduction (e.g., coitus). Thus, the PNS prepares the body for recuperation, construction, and reproduction of its parts and itself.

The ANS interfaces with the CNS so that each can influence the other, which provides a basis for biofeedback procedures. The enteric nervous system influencing the gastrointestinal tract is a semiautonomous ANS subsystem that can function relatively independently. Material exchange processes are so fundamental for living systems' existence that they must not be too constrained by other parts of the government (e.g., like the Federal Reserve system).

Centralized Government: The Brain

Evolution of the Brain. The brain is an organization of many different structures for, and methods of, governing which have accumulated slowly over the long evolutionary history of living systems (Dumont & Robertson, 1986). Remnants of "feudal systems" are combined with more "democratic" forms. The evolutionary process can be construed as a kind of positive feedback loop. As functional capabilities elaborated to deal with more variable and social environments, more centralized governmental forms evolved to effectively coordinate them. More centralized coordination increased the capability for and occurrence of functional variability, which in turn stimulated the development of additional centralized governmental forms. Thus, the governmental capabilities provided by the CNS and ANS represent an integrated accumulation of many different governmental structures and methods that emerged to serve evolving forms of life (Armstrong & Falk, 1982).

The resulting government is hierarchical, but not rigidly so in the sense of a "line and staff" organization (e.g., a military command structure). It is a form of collaborative management in which each component has certain authority and responsibilities, which constrains and is constrained by other governmental components. Damage to a single component typically may degrade but not totally obliterate an important function. Gallistel (1980a, 1980b) refers to this as a *lattice hierarchy* and Weimer (1977) as a coalition of hierarchical structures. As a result of these cooperative interactions (i.e., larger organizations), new functional capabilities emerge which are not present in the components themselves. Such distributed systems obviously have significant survival advantages (Mountcastle, 1978).

Structural-Functional Organization of the Brain. MacLean (1970a, 1982) has characterized the brain's elaborate network of governing structures and functions as representing three broad phases of evolutionary development, which he called the *triune brain.* The earliest forms of centralized government are dominant in the brains of reptiles, so he calls that level the *reptilian brain* or *R-Complex.* In Fig. 6.1, it would be approximated by structures below the cerebrum and limbic system. Additional structures evolved from the R-complex as patterns of mobility, feeding, and reproduction in an environment populated with other animals made "social" behaviors of fundamental importance, requiring more complex and variable behavior patterns, and forms of government. MacLean terms this second level the *paleo* (old or primitive) *mammalian brain.* In Fig. 6.1 it is approximated by the area labeled *limbic system.* The *neo* (new) *cortex* evolved to provide a third level of government capable of obtaining, constructing, and using increasingly detailed information; for increased variability and precision of actions; and for communicating with others, necessary for constructing more complex social arrangements. MacLean termed this the *neomammalian brain,* approximated by the cerebrum in Fig. 6.1.

Of course, these three levels evolved from and in interaction with one another, so that it is the relative prominence of each level that is different in the different stages of evolution. MacLean argues that the philosophical view of humans as "rational animals" has led to an overemphasis on, and some misinterpretations of, the structures and functions of the neocortex. He believes that the influence of much of the lower (earlier) levels of government is still powerfully manifested in current human behavior patterns. For example, the behavior of humans in committee meetings reminds him of the preenings, struttings, and status displays observable in a colony of monkeys.

Recall that organization exists when there are constraining and facilitating conditionalities among subcomponents. As the organization of governing structures of the brain elaborated, both kinds of conditionalities probably operated. Some of the governing functions of lower levels probably became constrained or perhaps even eliminated as they were integrated with emerging higher levels (e.g., some increasing capability for "impulse" or emotional control by the neocortex). Also new functions emerged (e.g., language capabilities). Recall also that development in living systems occurs through differentiation, growth, transformation, and reorganization of the existing system. The brain did not evolve by adding completely new parts. New parts were created by differentiation, elaboration, and transformation of existing parts. Therefore, it would be impossible to have new structural-functional capabilities emerge that were not linked to, and influenced by, earlier structural-functional patterns.

This mode of development produces a brain which is truly one finely integrated functional-structural system (Uttal, 1978). While others do not agree with all of MacLean's proposals and speculations, similar broad structural-functional patterns are well recognized and commonly used as a way of describing the brain (e.g., Noback & Demarest, 1981; Wittrock, 1980). Therefore, MacLean's categories will be used to organize the following discussion of the nervous system.

Comprehensive Coordination and Precise Control of Behavior. It is important to emphasize both complexity and detail. The higher governing levels probably evolved to make possible not only the more *comprehensive coordination* of behavior, but *more precise, flexible control over the detail* of those patterns as well. Both are necessary to produce the exquisitely organized skills of a fine musician, athlete, or craftsperson. Much detailed information about the vertical and horizontal organization of neural structures has been developed and summarized for use by medical students and others (e.g., Noback & Demarest, 1981). However, our knowledge of the functional significance of those complex structural arrangements is still very limited, although it is growing rapidly (Mishkin, 1986; Thompson, 1986).

Level 1 Centralized Government: The R-Complex

Structurally, level 1 includes components such as the medulla, pons, midbrain, and cerebellum (see Fig. 6.1). All of the cranial nerves juncture here. The sensory-motor neurons connecting the rest of the body to the brain through the spinal column also connect through these structures. Located here are automated controls for basic life support systems such as blood circulation, respiration, and sleep. Other automated controls help regulate olfaction, vision, hearing, and taste, "providing some selective gating and tuning of input to perception" (Trevarthen, 1980); deal with head movement and acceleration and the body's relation to gravitational force; adjust the operation of the eyes and ears; influence the use of the mouth and nose for breathing and eating (e.g., salivation). Some mechanisms for selective filtering, amplification, and attenuation of information inputs and outputs are here, as are controls for a variety of automated motor patterns. Level 1 also coordinates some "display" motor patterns which convey information to other organisms about motivational or emotional states (e.g., facial expressions, Ekman, 1978; lizards' social head gestures, MacLean, 1982). Visual space is mapped here to some extent and is anchored to the midline of the brain when the body is at rest, providing a stable reference point for "a body-centered map of the behavioral field" (Trevarthen, 1980). The rest of the nervous system is "activated" with signals from the brain stem's reticular activating structures, which is of great importance in the phenomena of consciousness and attention. Some controls and functional components for posture and movement are also located here.

The cerebellum is a key structure in the regulation of motor behavior (Eccles, 1977; Ito, 1984). One portion facilitates extensor muscle tone, and a different portion facilitates flexor muscle tone through the motor-spinal circuits. The cerebellum has extraordinarily intricate refinements of neuronal organization which make possible precise coordination of the flow of motor behavior in a varying spatial-temporal matrix, in cooperation with higher governing levels. Throughout life, but particularly in the early years, one is "engaged" in an incessant teaching program for the cerebellum. Some habituated action program components may be retained at level 1 (Eccles, 1977).

The cerebellum "monitors and makes corrective adjustments" in transactional behaviors initiated by other parts of the brain, and appears to perform a predictive function (Guyton, 1982). It contributes to the construction and retention of motor skills. Its neurological differentiation continues developing into childhood (Bernstein, 1967). Thus, the cerebellum functions as a primary regulatory structure during the course of movements to insure a well timed, coordinated flow of motor behavior in relationship to varying body-environment conditions.

Damage to the cerebellum disrupts this regulatory function, but does not destroy the ability to move. For example, with such damage a person reaching for a glass of water will "overshoot" or "undershoot" the glass, knocking it over or missing it altogether. Visual feedback can substitute for the lost cerebellar control, but only cerebellar regulation can produce the rapid, finely coordinated flow of motor behavior—environment transactions essential for most complex motor-behavior patterns (Ito, 1984).

An Efficient but Rigidly Programmed Bureaucracy. Level 1 government rules primarily by rote, routine, and ritual. It is bound to the here and now, with which it copes through a standard and limited behavioral repertoire. Most of level 1's functional components are automated as a result of evolutionary and maturational history, producing relatively stereotyped behavior patterns, which fit the normative conditions of the relevant environmental niche like a music box that can play only a few songs (MacLean, 1970b).

The semiautonomy of this government level is poignantly illustrated by humans who have had higher brain levels destroyed. They can continue to live as "human vegetables" as long as people around them protect and feed them. Level 1's rigid and narrowly limited bureaucratic procedures and controls are inadequate for more variable circumstances. A more adaptive and flexible form of government is needed.

Level 2 Centralized Government: The Limbic System

Increased mobility, social interactions, and environmental variability produced more complicated governance problems. More flexibility and variability became necessary both in the operation of the organism's internal biological processes and their sensory-motor behavior patterns. Therefore, there occurred over time the elaboration of competencies for retaining and using information to organize and guide instrumental and social behavior, and for more complex orchestration of supporting biological processes.

Evaluative and Anticipatory Functions. But, there is an important difference between information and meaning. Information represents *objects* and *events*. Meaning results from an evaluation of their present and potential influence on individuals and their activities. For example, looking at a plant provides information about it. Tasting and smelling it gives it self-referent meaning. Thus, taste and smell are related to evaluative processes for helping discriminate between edible and inedible materials. Such evaluations are immediate, and largely involuntary.

As the spatial-temporal environmental matrix of organisms' behavior expanded, the task of giving information self-referent meaning became more elaborate. As organisms interacted with their environments, they needed to evaluate the flow of events in terms of their personal significance for current and future operations, including potential social interactions (e.g., predator-prey or mating relationships). It was important that these evaluative processes become anticipatory in nature to enable discrimination between events to be approached because they would produce "positive" consequences, and events to be avoided because they might produce "negative" consequences.

A second level of governing structures evolved then: (a) to make possible greater variability in sensory-motor and internal biological functioning, and increased coordination of the two; (b) to elaborate capacities for information storage and use, with regard to the spatial-temporal attributes of their environment; (c) to elaborate capabilities for behaving in terms of probable future events by utilizing past experience; and (d) to elaborate the capacity for giving self-referent meaning to events through subjective evaluative processes.

In all vertebrates there is a general neural structure, located above (or in front of) the structures of level 1, called the *forebrain*. From it evolved in interacting fashion the cerebral cortex and the limbic system structures (Armstrong & Falk, 1982), until the forebrain came to dominate human life (Sarnat & Netsky, 1974; Trevarthen, 1980).

Limbic system structures evolved that elaborated (a) the governance and learning of sensory-motor patterns, for carrying out transactions with the environment, and anticipatory evaluative capabilities, particularly for social interaction; (b) autonomic-biochemical functions, for producing a more variable internal milieu; and (c) the coordination of the two, so that internal functioning could be more precisely adjusted to meet external demands, and vice versa. Among the structures included are the hypothalamus, pituitary gland, hippocampus, amygdala, septal nuclei and limbic cortex, basal ganglia, and thalamus. These brain components have similar features in all mammals, suggesting that they probably persist in their "animalistic" functioning in humans although functionally modified by mutually influential relationships with the neocortex (MacLean, 1970b). Collectively, they provide a governing structure "...that links plans for actions with evaluation of their consequences for the well being of the organism" (Trevarthen, 1980). The key role of level 2 in coordinating biochemical forms of governance (e.g., endocrine subsystems) is discussed first.

Coordination Through Biochemical Communication. Biochemical communication was the first kind of governing influence that evolved. In ancient forms of life, modified amino acids may have signaled metabolic needs of cells (Tomkins, 1975), functioning as "tissue factors" (Kolata, 1982). Later, they became intercellular communicators, and finally, as neurons evolved, they became linked to neuronal processes. Both bioelectric and biochemical mechanisms cooperate in regulating embryonic development and organismic functioning (Harris, 1981). The number of chemical compounds discovered to influence brain functions, such as hormonal and neurochemical compounds, has been rapidly increasing (e.g., Dismukes, 1979; Kenney, 1980; McGeer & McGeer, 1980; Olson et al., 1979; Panksepp, 1986). Two basic organ systems are in contact with all parts of the body: the nervous system and the circulatory system. The nervous system distributes information and the circulatory system distributes material. Any material that enters the blood stream has the potential to influence any part of the body. Different bodily processes are regulated by different kinds of chemical compounds that circulate in the blood. Only compounds that have a general bodily effect are called *hormones* (meaning "to arouse to activity"). Different hormones are manufactured by different endocrine glands and distributed in the circulating system to regulate different kinds of body processes.

For example, female and male gonads secrete compounds that influence sexual development and functioning, and sexual differentiation of the CNS (MacLusky & Naftolin, 1981). The thyroid secretes hormones that influence the general metabolic processes of the body. The adrenal (or suprarenal) glands manufacture multiple compounds, some of which function to prepare the body for significant actions. The pineal gland secretions appear to have an opposite effect. They seem to exert a synchronizing, stabilizing, and moderating influence on many physiological processes (Romijn, 1978). Many internal biochemical processes function in cyclical fashion (Quabbe, 1977), and pineal secretions help mediate such cyclical biological functioning (Follett & Follett, 1981). Other cells may also secrete hormonal compounds, so the endocrine glands seem to function as "production" and "warehouse" centers to insure a ready supply and to make the compounds quickly available to the entire body (Ham & Cormack, 1979).

Neurons transmit information within themselves through bioelectric processes. However, neurotransmitters and neuromodulators are significantly involved not only in synaptic transmission between neurons, but also in regulating neuronal functioning (e.g., raising or lowering neuronal sensitivity to different kinds of influences). The number of chemical compounds known to influence brain functioning is large and growing (e.g., dopamine, noradrenalin, adrenalin, serotonin, B-endorphins). Many of the drugs taken by humans to influence different brain-related functions are similar to various kinds of neurochemical compounds (e.g., morphine, tranquilizers, antidepressants). The influences of such drugs, such as reducing emotional distress or triggering hallucinations, are accomplished largely through influencing limbic system functioning (McGeer & McGeer, 1980; Sachar & Baron, 1979).

In summary, hormones and neurochemicals perform governing functions that are essential to life. They regulate the general metabolic functioning of cells; physical growth and development, including the development of sexual differences; the mineral and water balances of the body; intermediate metabolism of carbohydrates, proteins, and fats; and generalized preparation for increased activity or rest and restoration. They also influence thought processes, moods, and emotions. While each compound appears to have a specific role, they are mutually influential. Therefore, it is the *pattern* in which different compounds occur, not each compound singly, that exerts the governing influence (Brady, 1970; McGeer & McGeer, 1980). But how is the chemical symphony orchestrated to insure harmonious functioning? Direct neural connections to endocrine glands are limited, except for the adrenals.

Governing Endocrine Processes: Hypothalamus-Pituitary Coordination.
The pituitary gland is the central governing component for the endocrine symphony. It secretes several kinds of tropic (i.e. "to nourish") hormones, each of which stimulates the growth and functioning of one specific endocrine gland. The level of each hormone in the blood influences the pituitary through a negative feedback control system. Since the pituitary is nourished by blood-carrying hormones that it triggers from other glands, the pituitary can be indirectly influenced by feedback from its own activity. A control systems model requires that feedforward and feedback processes be accomplished. These are usually thought of as information functions. However, they can also be accomplished through material exchanges. Hormonal regulation occurs by providing feedfoward and feedback functions primarily through biochemical rather than informational influences. But what regulates the pituitary to serve a person's behavior?

The hypothalamus is the phylogenetically ancient apex of the autonomic nervous system (ANS). Its neural circuits are numerous and complex, linking the CNS to the governance of the the body's internal milieu through the ANS. The influence of the hypothalamus on the pituitary is exercised biochemically. It secretes some neurohormones that regulate the anterior pituitary gland and others that regulate its posterior portion (Guillemin, 1978; Schally, 1978). In return, the hypothalamus and other neural structures can be influenced by blood hormonal balances regulated by the pituitary. The hypothalamus is also extensively connected with the limbic system and the neocortex. That makes it possible for sensory-motor activity as well as emotional and thought processes to directly influence autonomic, hormonal, and neurochemical governing functions and to be influenced by them.

The limbic system is primarily responsible for arousal processes qualitatively reflected in sensory and emotional experience. Therefore it is linked to the evaluative functions, helping to give some kinds of information the self-referent meanings of "good-bad" and "approach-avoid" (e.g., Noback & Demarest, 1981; Trevarthen, 1980). These evaluative-action patterns are essential for survival, since without them the ability to distinguish between what is dangerous and safe, beneficial or harmful, would be lost (Adams, 1979). Such evaluations, to be of any value, must be related to appropriate actions, such as fight, flight, sex, and seeking. The hypothalamus functions as a regulating center linking the three different streams of government—the CNS, the ANS, and the hormonal (through the pituitary)—to provide an integration of the effects of these three governmental subsystems. Thus, the hypothalamus translates limbic system evaluative-emotional responses into patterns of autonomic and pituitary-hormonal activity required for the forms of appropriate action. Obviously, this has to be a very intricate organization of many control processes linked with a diversity of feedforward and feedback arrangements (e.g., Axelrod and Reisine, 1984). Dysfunctions in neural endocrine functioning are being implicated in some brain-anchored diseases such as Alzheimer's syndrome (Coyle, Price, & Delong, 1983), in schizophrenia (Barnes, 1987), and may be related to immunocompetence (Riley, 1981).

Coordinating Transactional Behaviors. At this second governing level, the *thalamus* and *basal ganglia* function primarily to provide for more complex coordination of sensory-motor functioning, including voluntary control of movement (Mishkin, 1986). All sensory pathways and sensory portions of the neocortex have direct projections to thalamic nuclei, except for olfaction. Thus, the thalamus functions as a kind of "network newsroom" in which different reports can be synthesized into one coherent story. It also has extensive two-way interconnections with the motor regions of the neocortex. Within the thalamus, then, it becomes possible to interrelate the flow of diverse incoming messages about "what is going on" with the flow of diverse outgoing messages about "what should be done" to produce high-level governing of all sensory-motor or transactional functions.

The primary role of the basal ganglia appears to be coordination between the neocortex and thalamus to produce sensory-motor integration (Hicks, 1980). They have mutually influential relationships to the cerebellum, the thalamus, and the motor regions of the cerebral cortex (Norback & Demarest, 1981).

Two limbic system structural-functional organizations have now been described. One, the thalamus and basal ganglia, functions primarily to govern activity in relationship to the external environment. The other, the hypothalamus-pituitary (with their linkages to the hormonal and autonomic systems), functions primarily to govern the internal milieu. Some way of regulating the relationships between those two systems is essential.

Regulating Biological and Transactional Processes. In many respects, the *limbic system* parallels the hypothalamic visceral column in functional and anatomic relations (Trevarthen, 1980). Thus, it is closely linked to the structures and processes involved in monitoring and governing the biological processes of the body (Hockman, 1972). It is influenced by all sensory systems including olfaction, which is one of the most primitive sensory regulatory systems (MacLean, 1970b). Therefore, an examination of the regulatory role of olfaction is a useful way of beginning a discussion of limbic system regulatory functions.

The sense of smell was probably the first really effective "distance" receptor. Odors have a qualitative valence, that is, they smell good or bad. Good smells produce approach responses and bad smells produce avoidance responses. Consequently, such evaluations have both material and social "motivational" characteristics. Odors help animals to find appropriate food and to avoid ingesting potentially damaging substances; to distinguish friends from enemies, and to identify potential mates; and odors provide a basis for learning and remembering personally meaningful objects and events.

These, then, appear to be special functions of the limbic system: (a) understanding the potential personal significance or meaning of events through evaluation of the qualitative attributes of experience; (b) regulation of biological functioning to stimulate and support activity directed at producing desired environmental consequences and avoiding negative ones; and (c) facilitation of the selection and storage (or retention in memory) of "successful" or "useful" information and behavior patterns. These are largely the regulatory governing functions in the living systems framework. The limbic system also participates in the information-based self-constructing functions (e.g., learning) (Numan, 1978). MacLean (e.g., Holden, 1979a) argues that we all act in terms of what we believe to be true, real, or right, and that those evaluative, emotionally laden judgments are anchored in limbic system processes rather than in the neocortex.

Limbic system structures are functionally sensitive to circulating hormones (Isaacson, 1980) and a variety of neurochemicals. Pain subduing drugs, hallucinogenic and psychoactive substances, stimulants, and tranquilizers seem to inactivate, block, or substitute for natural neurohormones and neurotransmitters (McGeer, Eccles, & McGeer, 1978). Thus, limbic system structures such as the amygdala and basal ganglia appear capable of monitoring and regulating the qualitative aspects of experience arising from both internal and external sources (Pribram, 1977; 1980a).

Learning and Memory. One limbic system structure, the *hippocampus,* has extremely elaborate and extraordinarily specialized dendritic and synaptic patterns in humans. It appears to be involved in human learning memory-forming processes (Mishkin, 1986; Rosenzweig, 1984). The hippocampus participates in the building and storage of representations of spatial or linguistic configurations ("cognitive maps") that have been functionally related to activity of the organism (O'Keefe & Nadel, 1978) and to temporal processing (Solomon, 1980). Since behavior naturally flows in spatial-temporal episodes, it would seem reasonable that evolution would have produced structures for combining spatial and temporal information. Pribram and McGuinness (1975) propose that the hippocampus coordinates the input arousal activity of the amygdala with the output arousal activity of the basal ganglia, giving rise to the sense of "effort" in coordinating behavior. It functions "as a retaining and retrieval device for integration of experiences with purpose in memory" (Trevarthen, 1980).

It makes sense for limbic system structures to be involved in learning and memory formation because of their evaluative function. The storage of behavior-environment patterns evaluated as producing desirable consequences ("positive reinforcement") and those evaluated as avoiding or terminating undesirable ones ("negative reinforcement") would be the most useful information to retain. Chemical compounds that affect metabolism appear to influence the learning process through the limbic system (e.g., McGaugh et al., 1980). Instrumental learning and autonomic activity appear to be linked, and this is probably accomplished through limbic system functions (e.g., Miller & Dworkin, 1980). Electrical stimulation in various parts of the hypothalamic-limbic system-thalamic network has been demonstrated to have powerful reinforcing effects on behavior (e.g., Olds, 1977; Teitelbaum et al., 1980). Cholinergic imbalances or deficiencies have been linked to some memory dysfunctions in elderly people (Bartus et al., 1982).

Moreover, the most useful information would be of behavioral programs that "worked" and the environmental context(s) in which they "worked" (i.e., information about, or "maps" of, behavioral episodes). The hippocampus seems to function as a part of the brain system that codes and learns "the goal directed or salient aspects of the stimulus world in relation to adaptive behavior" (Thompson et al., 1980a).

In summary, this second level of centralized government plays a leading role in the integration of diverse information and functional patterns into complexly organized behavioral programs; in the coordination of the operation of internal biological and environmentally oriented behavioral processes within themselves and with one another; in the evaluative regulation of the flow of experience; and in the selective retention of those behavior-environment episodes that may have future value.

Level 3 Central Government: The Cerebrum or NeoCortex

Structural Organization. The neocortex is a huge mass of complexly interrelated neurons located above and around the other brain structures (see Fig. 6.1). In general, the neocortex is composed of neurons vertically organized in columnar modules, like pencils standing on their erasers. The columns are formed by non-neural glia support cells, and are filled with six layers of neurons. Each layer is composed of somewhat different kinds of neurons (Eccles, 1977; Ham & Cormack, 1979; Szentagothai & Arbib, 1975). Information processing appears to occur vertically, moving from the bottom layer towards the cortical surface. Each modular component contains many neurons (estimates range from 2,500 to 10,000) so each one has a complicated internal structure for organizing, transforming, and distributing information within it. There are an estimated four million such modules in the neocortex of one human brain.

Szentagothai (1973; Szentagothai & Arbib, 1975) has proposed that the cortical modules are analogous to integrated electronic microunits for handling information computations. Although the modules differ somewhat in different neocortical areas, their organization is fundamentally similar. There are input channels (afferent fibers), complex internal interacting channels, and output channels (primarily pyramidal cell axons). Every module appears to function as an integrated component, so they represent a set of similar parallel processing units providing "a mesh of feedforward and feedback excitatory and inhibitory lines" producing a level of complexity far beyond existing electronic microcircuits (Eccles, 1976). Module outputs are very diverse, ranging from high-frequency discharges from hundreds of pyramidal cells to typical low-level discharges characteristic of the neocortex in the resting state. Modules with similar functional responsibilities are grouped together in cortical areas (e.g., the sensory cortex). However, many of the modules appear to be generalists rather than specialists and are scattered throughout the cortex.

Cortical and subcortical areas are complexly interrelated by a huge number of axons that loop back and forth under the cortical folds,

connecting cortical areas both within and between cerebral hemispheres, and in subcortical structures (Pribram, 1980a; Trevarthen,
1980). The complex processes of perception, memory, thought, and
voluntary action must involve organizations of modules which influence
one another primarily through the axons of their pyramidal cells (Eccles,
1976; Gasanov et al., 1980). But what is the nature of that organization?

Functional Organization. Lashley (1960) made it clear that neither
sensory nor motor functions are stored or controlled in narrowly
specified cortical areas, illustrated by the phenomena of sensory equivalence and motor equivalence. Moreover, huge amounts of cortex (e.g.,
the visual cortex) could be destroyed without obliterating a particular
memory. It is almost as if something learned is stored everywhere at
once, or at least in many places at once (John et al., 1986). How could
that be?

Perhaps learning results in a distributed storage, like having many
copies of the same document filed in many different places. There is a
technical procedure for image processing that can do just that called
holography. Pribram (1971; 1980a) and others have proposed that this is
probably the technique used by the human brain.

There are problems with this formulation. Each cell is tuned to a
limited band width of the spectrum of spatial frequencies. Therefore,
how could the total representation be accomplished? Leith (1976)
developed an approach to optical holograms in which segments of the
total picture are represented in strips. During image reproduction, the
strips are integrated into a three-dimensional whole. Such composite or
multiplex holograms have the additional advantage of being able to
represent three-dimensional movement as well. Pribram (1980b) asserts:

> Many of the receptive fields of the cells of the visual cortex have the shape
> of strips, elongated ovals or rectangles (Spinelli, Pribram, & Bridgeman,
> 1970). The discovery that such cells were tuned to specific orientations
> (Hubel & Weisel, 1962) has ordinarily been interpreted as an indication
> that the cells were "detecting" the orientation of lines as features of input.
> However, the output of each cell is, as we have seen, as sensitive to spatial
> frequency (and often also to movement and direction of movement). It is,
> therefore, more appropriate to view the output of the cell as representing
> an integral part of spatial frequency, orientation of a strip, movement and
> direction—an integral mathematically and functionally similar to that
> produced when a multiplex hologram is illuminated. (p. 58)

What brain process could correspond to the illumination of such a
hologram with light? Pribram suggest that selective attention provides
one possibility.

There are other plausible possibilities. Perhaps the primary role of the neocortex is in current operations (i.e., the organization and coordination of intentional activities), and in abstracting from current activities information that may be valuable in the future (i.e., the learning process). Perhaps permanent retention is the function of some other components of the brain, such as the hippocampus. The cortex would need to be able to tap those "files" at any time to draw upon that information for current operations, but it would not need to own the files (as a computer may activate a file as required by a program it is running). In this kind of hypothetical functional arrangement, the vertical connections among brain structures would be more critical than the horizontal connections among neuronal structures in the neocortex. This would mean that horizontal sectioning procedures separating areas of the cortex from one another would be far less disruptive than vertical sectioning separating cortical structures from subcortical structures. There is experimental evidence supporting that notion (e.g., Guiard, 1980). Penfield (1954) and Denny-Brown (1962) have proposed that neocortex functioning is regulated or controlled by some integrative subcortical structures and functions.

If vertical organization were the basic design, then the distinction between long-term and short-term memory functions might have a neurological basis. Short-term memory could be a function of the neocortex because it would be related to current operations, but long-term memory could be a function of other structures. However, since learning and memory are always inferred from current specific behavior, it is also plausible that learning and memory have not been affected in either instance, but that their relationships to current concerns and performance capabilities have been disrupted.

As with temperature regulation and other functions, the information-storage function probably has a long evolutionary history. Therefore, information storage in humans may involve a combination of hierarchically organized structures and methods. Thompson (1986) asserts that memory and cognitive properties "seem to emerge as collective properties of systems of neurons." For example, in nonhuman primates, vocalization seems to be a function of subcortical (e.g., limbic system) structures. Only in humans does speech come under primary neocortical control. However, that control does not replace the lower-level, more "primitive" components; it only influences their organized functioning. Speech continues to remain dependent on limbic system structures in important respects (Ploog, 1980).

Such an hierarchical arrangement would mean that a person might be quite functional with considerably less than the usual amount of neocortex, as illustrated by the research of John Lorber, a British neurologist. One university student with only a millimeter of neocortical tissue rather than the usual 4.5 centimeters thickness is socially completely normal, has an IQ test score of 126, and has earned a first class honors degree in mathematics. His skull is mostly filled with cerebrospinal fluid (Kolata, 1980). The implication is that the importance and role of the neocortex may have been overemphasized and that of the other brain structures underemphasized in understanding the governing of much of human behavior.

Much knowledge about brain structures and their biophysical functioning exists, but little is known about the relationships of those structures to cognitive functions (Verzeano, 1980). Current ideas about brain-behavior relationships are highly speculative and may be as much a product of implicit philosophical assumptions as of facts, illustrated by current "split brain" theorizing (Corballis, 1980). What follows is presented as one speculative possibility suggested by the living systems framework.

The Neocortex: Informational and Behavioral Self-Construction. The brain is a dynamic system. It carries out complex cognitive functions through the ways in which large numbers of neurons are organized both horizontally within levels (e.g., within the neocortex) and vertically between levels (e.g., between the neocortex and limbic system) (John & Schwartz, 1978; Verzeano, 1980). Limbic system governing structures appear to perform an integrative function, bringing together sensory-motor-autonomic-biochemical factors into complex functional patterns. What then could be the general function of the neocortex? This living systems framework suggests that it may specialize in three types of governing contributions. What is it that particularly distinguishes humans from other organisms? It is their ability to take the information collected through their senses, and to decompose it, reorganize it, abstract it, and transform it in order to (a) create new information (i.e., new ideas); (b) create, and make highly efficient, new behavior-environment patterns; and (c) efficiently store in cross-referenced form massive amounts of perceived and constructed information and behavior programs. The human neocortex must play a leading role in those evolutionarily emergent, information based, self-construction competencies.

The neocortex can use the fruits of experience to "write" new behavioral programs to supplement those written for the organism by its evolutionary history. To do this, humans must be able to abstract from the continuing flow of their experience a diversity of patterns of consistency and variability concerning their environments, their own system functioning, and the self-referent significance of such information. Humans must be able to decompose the flow of specific experiences into invariant themes of recurring behavior-environment patterns, and be able to recombine them into new possibilities. They must be able to retain and reuse that information to free themselves from being bound spatially and temporally to the here and now. Writing new behavioral programs also requires a specification of what they are being written for. Therefore humans must be able to imagine or intend possible futures for themselves in their environments, and then be able to design alternative ways of trying to achieve those futures. This may result in the performance of patterns of behavior somewhat different than any they may have performed before. In short, the special contribution of this highest level of government is to convert humans from primarily "reactive" functioning—in which what they do is controlled primarily by what their living conditions demand—to "active," self-*directing*, self-*controlling*, self-*regulating*, self-*constructive* functioning.

Verzeano (1980) provides relevant neurological evidence. For example, some of the neurons in the neocortex are turned on and off by incoming information. However, many other neuronal ensembles are continually active, producing a "rhythmic barrage of impulses that 'sweep' or 'scan' " through the neuronal networks at lower levels, "selecting" salient information from them and also influencing them (i.e., giving "instructions" to them). Through excitatory and inhibitory activities, a "moving matrix" of neuronal activity circulates through cortical, thalamic, and cortico-thalamic circuits "looking for" useful information in the flow of current activity and "distributing" useful information derived from previous experience (e.g., Bernstein, 1967).

Pribram (1971, 1980a) argues that different parts of the cerebral cortex are designed to abstract different kinds of information. For example, one portion abstracts invariants from the flow of experience. Another portion abstracts "familiarities from episodic variations" of "recurring organism-environment relationships." He also proposes a function of "image" formation, which stores accurate information about environmental attributes (as represented in vision, audition, etc.) through holographic processes. To paraphrase, we collect information about "what's there," "how it works," "how it affects me," and "how I can deal with it."

Kinsbourne (1982) proposes that selective focal attention functions to make finer distinctions in the stimulus patterns "perceived in meager detail in the peripheral sensory field." Moreover, he suggests that different parts of the neocortex specialize somewhat in two different classes of specific information. He suggests that the left brain focuses on specific features (i.e., on item information), and the right brain focuses on configurational features (i.e., relational information). In a similar vein, J. Levy (1980) concludes that the left hemisphere cortical functions focus on "distinctive subordinate features" while the right focuses on "critical form invariants" that identify the whole pattern. O'Keefe and Nadel (1978) report that the hippocampus shows lateral specialization analogous to that of the neocortex. Spatial-temporal maps appear to be stored in the right hippocampus (e.g., people whose right hippocampus is destroyed lose such maps and cannot form new ones). Verbal-semantic maps appear to be stored in the left hippocampus.

The Neocortex: Self-Organization and Self-Direction. Another specialized function of the neocortex appears to be the purposive initiation and control of behavior; that is, the direction, organization, and ongoing coordination of the flow of behavior to serve current concerns (the directive and control functions in the living systems framework). Research on lateralization of function of the neocortex lends credibility to this proposal. Bilateral symmetry of the body and nervous system is typical in mobile animals. In the normal brain, functioning is integrated by extensive connections of the two halves of the cerebrum through the interhemispheric commisural system. This provides "mental unity" for the organism.

Bilateral symmetry is most adaptive for organisms whose primary mode of adaptation to their environment is *reactive* (i.e., organisms that are primarily stimulus controlled). However, with internally generated or purposive behaviors that are not direct reactions to the environment, bilateral symmetry is less important, and asymmetry (i.e., lateral specialization) may have advantages because such behaviors represent operations on rather than reactions to the environment. Therefore hemispheric lateralization of function may have evolved, at least in part, to overcome the potential conflict between the hemispheres in the initiation and control of behavior. Speech and verbal thought are the epitome of intentional behaviors and require very fine, ongoing behavioral coordination. Keeping the task in one hemisphere would make such fine motor and verbal coordination easier.

While one or the other hemisphere may be dominant in initiating and controlling different kinds of behavior patterns, the connections between the two insure cooperation and unity of function. Severing the hemispheric connections disrupts (though it does not destroy) some of this cooperative capability because they are also connected indirectly through lower brain centers. Severing hemispheric connections can alleviate some dysfunctions. For example, in epileptic seizures the brain is flooded with arousal in the limbic system, severely disrupting behavioral organization. Severing hemispheric connections can reduce or eliminate such seizures (Caramazza & Berndt, 1978; Corballis, 1980; Gazzaniga & LeDoux, 1978; Guiard, 1980; Kinsbourne, 1982; Levin, 1980; Prohovnik, 1978; Sperry, 1982). It is worth reemphasizing here, however, that the normal brain is involved as a whole in all behavior. Therefore, the special "leading role" of some structures must be understood as a components functioning as a part of a much larger system (Uttal, 1978).

The Neocortex and Memory. It seems probable that several information retention structures and processes evolved through evolutionary history to fit the structural design and functional demands and capabilities of different species. Such componentized design and development is one of the most pervasive aspects of the evolutionary process. Therefore, it seems reasonable to expect that the evolution of memory functions followed that path. If the structural-functional organization of memory processes is componentized and hierarchical, then can the broad outlines of that organization be identified?

Brain stem-cerebellum structures "store" some behavioral programs (e.g., expressive displays). This primitive information storage capability may have been elaborated in humans. It is a common tactic in evolutionary development to elaborate some of the functional capabilities already available in existing structures rather than to invent new ones. While the neocortex is undoubtedly involved in learning new behavioral programs, when they become automated they may be retained at subcortical levels. That may be one of the reasons that automated behavioral programs (i.e., habits) are so hard to change.

More complex habitual behavioral programs which integrate more elaborate relationships between biological and transactional functional processes may be retained in structures at the second governing level of the brain (e.g., in the hippocampus). Because complex functional patterns are organizations of smaller components, the full pattern probably is not retained at one level. Rather it may be something like a computer program of instructions with a main program and a diversity of subroutines that may be called upon when useful. It is a situationally relevant program, not just a behavioral program. For example, electrical stimulation of limbic system structures can produce full-blown behavior patterns, (e.g., drinking and sexual behaviors); however, which pattern occurs is influenced by the situation in which the stimulation occurs (Pribram, 1976a). These could be thought of as "metabehavior" programs that organize and coordinate the functioning of components stored at lower governing levels.

Behavior programs themselves may not be retained in the neocortex. What may be retained there is information about desirable and undesirable consequences (i.e., potential goals), and the conceptual and propositional information abstracts that can be used to reconstruct or revise existing behavioral programs or to construct new ones relevant to new circumstances. The modular organization of the neocortex would facilitate the discrimination of detail from larger patterns. By organizing information into components that can be combined in a variety of ways to form larger patterns or create new ones, the brain would be using the same fundamental paradigm for organizing information that biological evolution has used so well for organizing biological structures (i.e., componentized, hierarchical arrangements). Moreover, following the principle that the same structural component can participate in more than one complex functional pattern, neocortical (e.g., thinking) processes could occur through shifting combinations of such information modules. The modules in any such functional pattern might be widely dispersed in the cortex, as long as they can physically interact through axonal projections.

The informational store in the neocortex probably also functions to define or anticipate future possible or probable occurrences and to guide the selection and operation of behavioral programs accordingly (i.e., to specify goals and to anticipate contingencies). Bernstein (1967) and Pribram (1976a) have concluded that representations of environmental consequences to be produced by behavior are stored in the neocortex. Pribram terms these "actions." They guide the formulation of movement programs at lower levels that serve to achieve intended consequences.

The operations just described are essentially the directive, control, and regulatory functions of the living systems framework operating at the total organism level. These are essentially the same functions ascribed by Luria (1973) to the third principal component of his model of the brain which "creates *intentions*, forms *plans* and *programs* of his actions," monitors their performance, "regulates his behavior so that it conforms to these plans and programs," compares "the effects of his actions with the original intentions," and corrects any mistakes.

The Neocortex and Learning. It is probable that the neocortex is involved in the learning of such behavioral programs through concentrated effort and attention to details, influenced by the evaluative activity of the limbic system. For example, when a person is learning to play the piano, considerable concentrated attention and thought must be invested in specifying what is to be done, in determining which keys should be struck, when and how to hit them, and in what temporal-spatial pattern. The learner will puzzle over what he or she is doing wrong and how to correct it. However, after a piece is heavily practiced and well learned, the behavior pattern (and the music resulting therefrom) is produced in a smooth and flowing pattern with concentration on the result to be (and being) produced, while ignoring the details of the execution (see Chapter 14).

Studies of electrical patterns of brain functioning during learning and habit formation lend credibility to this view. Initially, the electrical pattern is widely dispersed across the neocortex. As learning and habit formation proceed, the electrical pattern becomes less distributed and more localized. "Irradiation" yields to "consolidation." Habit formation leads to gradual disappearance of the electrical arousal pattern (John, 1976). One of the efficiencies of human governing structures and functions is that they can automate behavioral programs to deal effectively with repetitive conditions, and preserve their most constructive capabilities (i.e., those of the neocortex) for dealing with variable, novel, interesting, and potentially advantageous or disadvantageous conditions.

SUMMARY

The structures of the brain and nervous system are organized hierarchically with distributed authority for coordinating action patterns, through the CNS; for coordinating the functioning of the internal milieu, through the ANS; and for coordinating action pattern demands with internal processes to meet those demands. Limbic system structures anchor arousal-evaluative processes that not only regulate and support current behavior patterns, but also influence what is selectively learned and remembered. The neocortex plays a leading role in the selection and construction of information components, and in flexibly organizing them into different kinds of behavior patterns. However, those information-based self-constructing, self-organizing functions require information-related arousal functions of attention and consciousness. These are examined in Chapter 7.

7

Information-Consciousness-Attention (ICA) Arousal

INTRODUCTION

Overview

The phenomena of consciousness, attention, and perception are examined in some detail in Chapters 7 and 8 because they provide the basic information and organization from which all other psychological-behavioral functions are constructed. Consciousness and attention processes selectively activate the central nervous system to produce selectivity in perception, cognition, and action. From redundancies in the flow of sensory stimulation, perceptual processes abstract consistencies which can be used to accurately guide current behavior in current situations. Those first order representations become the basis for the construction of more elaborate and abstract thought processes.[1] However, before proceeding to examine those functions, it is essential to understand the nature of, and interrelationships of, consciousness, attention, and perception.

Since all behavior is fueled by energy, variable behavior requires variability in the amount, distribution, and use of energy. The selective and variable production, distribution, and use of energy to fuel the organization and execution of varying behavior patterns in varying

---

[1]How such cognitive representations come into existence and how they function are examined in detail in Chapters 9 through 12, so those issues are not considered here. For the time being, the reader is asked to accept their existence and role.

environments is the primary role of the arousal functions. Because arousal functions help regulate behavior through their *selectivity* and their *energizing* functions, they have been identified by many people as part of the concept of *motivation* (Cofer & Appley, 1964).

Recurrent transactional tasks in relatively unvarying environments can be accomplished repetitively with automated behavior patterns which function in a machinelike fashion, illustrated by the functioning of many simpler living systems. However, few of the attributes of human environments have that degree of invariance; they are filled with continually varying, often unpredictable circumstances. Therefore, humans evolved with capabilities for rapidly and flexibly varying the flow of their behavior in timely fashion: varying what they do for different purposes, times and places, and at different rates and intensities.

For example, casually scanning the street as you walk along it at night takes little effort. Intensively scanning the shadows in front of you to see if someone is lurking there requires concentrated and focused attention. A casual game of tennis requires less energy expenditure than performing against stiff competition. Life is not like driving at a steady pace on a four-lane highway with the cruise control on. It is more like driving in a busy city with lots of starts and stops, periods of acceleration and slowing down, sudden maneuvers to meet unexpected circumstances, and perhaps even an occasional "fender bender." Therefore, both cars and people must be able to quickly vary the amount, distribution, and use of energy to meet life's variable conditions. Moreover, driving in busy city streets requires the driver to behave in anticipation of the actions of others. Similarly, a person must be able to anticipate and prepare in advance for changes in effort and activity. Finally, just as automobiles must periodically be serviced and refueled, so too must people stop and periodically renew themselves and their energy supplies through eating, rest, and recuperation.

Two Kinds of Arousal Functions

Arousal functions make these variable energy processes possible. Evolution produced two kinds in humans, one related to information-based transactions and one to material-energy transactions. *Information-consciousness-attention (ICA)* arousal variably energizes the nervous system for the selective collection, transformation, construction, and use of *information* in directing, controlling, and regulating behavior. *Activity-emotional arousal (AE)*, variably energizes material-energy transactional behaviors or *actions* to help selectively produce desired environmental consequences. Information-focused arousal (i.e., some level of consciousness) is a prerequisite for activity-emotional arousal.

Death occurs when these arousal capabilities disappear. For example, as I wrote these words I was called to the funeral of my 90-year-old father who had died suddenly. In death, his appearance was unchanged, except that there was no thought, no activity, no potential for behavior. No longer were his big arms capable of scooping a small child into the air, producing a squeal of delight. No longer could he think wise or loving thoughts and share them with others. No longer could he shed a tear or roar with laughter. The flame of life had died, the energy of which made possible consciousness, thought, and actions. "Brain death" represents the loss of ICA arousal capabilities, and terminates the capability for information nutriment. "Heart death" terminates the capability for material nutriment to the body, and signals the loss of AE arousal capabilities. These losses might more accurately be called "person" death, since death of subcomponents such as cells comes thereafter. Thus, life and death are not distinguished by what a person is, thinks, feels, or does, but by the continuous presence or absence of basic arousal functions. Therefore, to be alive means to always be aroused in some way and to some degree. The question is not whether a person is aroused, but what the nature is of his or her current pattern of arousal.

Since energy production is a consequence of cellular metabolic processes, arousal functions must involve variations in biological functioning. Since variations in arousal functions serve environmental transactions, whose selective nature depends primarily upon information, arousal functions must be influenced by the person's governing functions. Thus, arousal patterns must be understood as a function of mutual causal processes among multiple behavioral functions and varying environmental circumstances. Since the role of arousal functions is to influence the person's behavioral organization they will manifest themselves in all other aspects of behavior. This has presented conceptual or definitional problems in past theorizing, in which emotional patterns have sometimes been defined by their biological manifestations (e.g., galvanic skin response), their transactional manifestations (e.g., facial expressions), or their governing components (e.g., conscious subjective experience).

The living systems representation of arousal functions is based on several assumptions. Humans are conceived of as having evolved structures and processes, the purposes of which are to selectively produce varying patterns of arousal to serve different adaptive purposes (Plutchik, 1980). Through evolutionary development, different patterns of the arousal process have become differentially related to different kinds of behavior patterns. This is because of the survival and reproductive advantage to organisms who evolved "built-in" relationships between energizing processes and vital behavior patterns serving information collection, interpersonal bonding, defense against biological damage, acquisition of food, and development of sexual relationships (Lindsley, 1951; Sheer, 1961).

The term *arousal functions* is used in Chapters 7 and 13 to refer to processes that control and regulate patterns of energy generation and distribution within a person. ICA arousal and AE arousal influence one another through informational and biochemical processes. Within both of these types of arousal, there are general and specialized arousal functions as summarized in Table 7.1. Specific concept labels for each specialized arousal function within the two basic types are discussed later. The word "pattern" will be attached to each concept label representing a specific arousal function when it is intended to refer to the organization of biological, governing, and transactional behaviors typically representing it (e.g., anger pattern, attentional pattern).

The term *affect* is often used as a synonym for the term *emotion*. It is also used to refer to the conscious, subjective aspect of emotions or other body processes (e.g., pain). Such dual usage is confusing. To facilitate clarity, we use the term *affect* only in the second sense.

Some scholars have proposed that there is only one kind of arousal that can vary in intensity, duration, and contextual relationships (e.g., Duffy, 1962; Schachter & Singer, 1962). However, accumulating evidence supports the view that more than one arousal function exists. For

TABLE 7.1

Illustration of the Types of Terms Applied to Generalized and Specialized Arousal Functions within Each Basic Type of Arousal
ICA = Information–Consciousness–Attention Arousal
AE = Activity–Emotional Arousal

	Information Transactions	Material–Energy Transactions
	ICA Arousal	AE Arousal
Generalized Arousal	Vegetative level of neural activation	Basic biological functioning (e.g., cell metabolism)
	Sleep	Relaxed
	Awake-Conscious	General readiness to respond
Specialized Arousal	Alert or vigilant	
	Selectively attentive	Energizing specific behavior patterns (e.g., walking)
	Intention and set: Preparing to perform a specific behavior pattern	Different kinds of emotions
	Information processing	

example, Lacey (1967) distinguishes among behavioral, cortical, and autonomic arousal. Smythies (1970) identifies different reticular activating system (RAS) arousal functions as including the control of sleep and wakefulness; phasic and tonic motor control; modifications of the reception, conduction, and integration of all sensory inputs; and direct influence on many visceral functions. Pribram and McGuinness (1975) describe three specialized but interrelated neural arousal mechanisms. Vanderwolf and Robinson (1981) identify two RAS arousal functions, and Eysenck (1982) concludes that there are at least two kinds. Factor analytic studies comparing subjective feeling terms produce one dimension anchored in attention-cognitive processes (e.g., bored-alert-engaged in thought), and another dimension anchored in physical activity processes (e.g., energetic-calm-exhausted). Other dimensions identified reflect variations in hedonic tone of subjective characteristics of emotional experiences (e.g., elated-irritated-sad-affectionate-regretful) (Purcell, 1982).

The position taken here is similar to these proposals in assuming that there are two general types of arousal serving the two different types of transactional processes; i.e., information processing and action. It differs somewhat, however, in proposing that there are specialized subtypes related to different kinds of behavior patterns. Both types of arousal have been receiving increasingly intensive study during the past two decades. The work of John (1976), Lindsley (1960), Magoun (1958), Orem and Barnes (1980), Pribram (1976a, 1976b), and Wittrock (1980), illustrates the study of ICA arousal. The work of Arnold (1960), Grings and Dawson (1980), Leshner (1977), Lindsley (1970), McGuinness and Pribram (1980), Routtenberg (1968), Plutchik (1980), and Tarpy (1977) illustrates research on AE arousal. ICA arousal is examined in this chapter, and AE arousal is considered in Chapter 13.

HISTORICAL PERSPECTIVE ON ICA AROUSAL

The science of psychology had its beginnings in the late 1800s in attempts to study the phenomena of "mental life," including attention and consciousness, phenomena that have puzzled philosophers and scientists for centuries (Globus, Maxwell, & Savodnik, 1976). During the first half of the 1900s, the dominant definition shifted to the study of behavior (i.e., actions), and the phenomena of attention and consciousness either became ignored or was treated as epiphenomena. Following World War II, interest in attention and consciousness was renewed, stimulated by technical developments (e.g., radar, which required vigilant human monitoring of information) and social developments (e.g., the growing use of mind altering drugs). Theoretical and empirical work in humanistic and cognitive psychology, and neurophysiology, also stimulated renewed interest (Hilgard, 1977a; Sperry, 1976). The phenomena of consciousness and attention have always been important in psychotherapy theory and practice (Ford & Urban, 1963).

Initially, two functional characteristics of attention and consciousness were emphasized. Following Wundt, Titchner (1913) focused on *clarity* or *intensity*. In contrast, James (1890) focused on *selectivity*. In addition to the information-processing functions of attention, Pillsbury (1908) emphasized its influence on the initiation and control of action; the influence of *intention* was considered a function of *attention*. Most current work on ICA arousal explores ideas and methods developed by these pioneers.

Interest in attention and consciousness was never completely dormant in the 1900s. For example, the concept of *unconscious processes*, which Freud gave prominence, was explored. J. Miller (1942) entitled his book Unconsciousness, but much of its substance addressed the phenomena of attention. He identified 16 different uses of the term *unconscious*, and proposed two principles that determine the contents of consciousness. The "economic utility principle" asserts that information becomes part of the contents of consciousness only if it "...is necessary for the business at hand;" information which is of "little interest" or unlikely to be "of future use" is likely to be forgotten. The "pleasure principle" (taken from Freud) means that pleasurable things tend to enter consciousness and painful experiences tend to be repressed. Miller also implied a variability principle by asserting that attention shifts because "consciousness tends to shun monotony." Attention wanders when a task involves little novelty, when the current environment is either relatively changeless or is understood and under control, or when sudden changes occur in the flow of events.

During this same period, Russian scholars studied many of the phenomena of attention and consciousness under Pavlov's concept of the *orienting reflex* (Sokolov, 1963). It is characterized by several physiological functions including pupillary dilation, galvanic skin response, a vasomotor response resulting in an increased blood volume in the brain and decreased blood volume in the limbs, depression of the cortical alpha rhythm, and heart rate deceleration. Current research often uses one or more of these as indicators of attentional functioning. The orienting reflex also involves a directing of sensory receptors toward relevant information sources; it increases or decreases the sensitivity of sensory receptors, and it amplifies and attenuates processes involved in selective information collection and processing.

The reemergence of attention and consciousness as important topics in mainstream psychology began in the 1950s as a correlate of changes in perceptual theory (Broadbent, 1958). Since the 1960s, widespread interest has developed in the nature and influence of consciousness and attention on different aspects of behavior (Bakan, 1966; Davidson & Davidson, 1980; Egeth & Bevan, 1973; Eysenck, 1982; Globus, Maxwell, & Savodnik, 1976; Hale & Lewis, 1979; Hilgard, 1977b; Jantsch & Waddington, 1976; Kahneman, 1973; Kornblum, 1973; Mackworth, 1970; Moray, 1970; Neisser, 1967; Ornstein, 1973; Posner, 1978; Schwartz & Shapiro, 1976, 1978; Underwood & Stevens, 1979).

Related Concepts

Research and theorizing about consciousness and attention occur under other concept labels (Moray, 1970). Studies of *concentration* involve intensity of focus on some task and the extent to which distracting information or stimuli interfere with successful task performance (e.g., solving arithmetic problems). In *vigilance* studies, the speed and accuracy of detecting the occurrence of a particular event in a general flow of events is studied (e.g., watching the "blips" on a radar screen). In *selective* (or *divided) attention* studies, people are exposed to several messages and are required either to select and respond to only one, or to alternate responding to one and then another. Selective *search* tasks involve identifying the presence of particular elements in a larger set of elements (e.g., to find any triangles in a set of diverse geometric figures). Sometimes physiological measures that vary with attentional functioning are used. These four kinds of tasks emphasize ICA arousal influences on the input or information-collection aspects of behavior episodes.

Two other approaches focus on the output or action aspects of such episodes. In *activation* studies, people must be prepared to act, but since they do not know what is going to happen they cannot prepare to act in a specific way. In studies of *set*, individuals prepare to act in a particular way, and perform the appropriate action when the relevant event(s) occur. Measures of brain activity, muscle tension, reaction time, and accuracy of response are often used as indicators of preparatory effectiveness.

THE ORGANIZING FUNCTION OF ATTENTION

In humans, the function of attention is to selectively activate relevant neural circuits to produce selectively targeted, coordinated behavioral functioning. The *content* of a behavior episode results from the governing functions—which specify the target for the behavior, define the nature of the task, and the information that will be relevant, and the evaluative criteria to be applied—and from the current biological and environmental conditions. However, the *organization* of the flow of behavior episodes is a selective energizing function of ICA arousal. Thus, the phenomena of attention and consciousness must be understood as "an essential property of the nervous system" which is related to "the functional unity of our bodies" (Chauchard, 1979). Shallice (1978) refers to this as the *control function* of consciousness and Collier (1956) describes consciousness as a regulatory field. Generalized neural activation produces base rate arousal (i.e., a person is to some degree conscious or awake). Then, brain processes can be selectively energized and organized through attentional functioning. Concepts like Hebb's (1949) cell assemblies or Shallice's (1978) dominant action systems represent biological and behavioral examples of such selectively energized patterns of functioning. The control or regulatory function of attention has been one focus of Russian and Eastern European approaches (Dobrolowicz, 1977; Wojciszke, 1980). It is also in accord with Sperry's (1976) proposal that "brain" and "conscious experience" exert mutual causal influences on each other. Similarly, Carver (1979) has proposed a cybernetics model of self-attention processes.

Human behavior always occurs in episodes that involve all of the behavioral functions (see Chapters 3 and 5). Research on ICA arousal has emphasized different concepts, depending on which aspect of a behavior episode was emphasized. When the focus is on the organization of *information monitoring and collection* functions, the term *attention* and its variants (e.g., vigilance) are typically used. When the focus is on the organization of *information processing* functions, terms such as *thinking* and *remembering* are used. When the focus is on the organization of sensory-motor *patterns*, the terms *intention* and *set* are often used. If the focus is on the *intensity and/or specificity of ICA arousal*, the terms *alertness, concentration,* or *effort* are typically used. No single term is generally used to encompass all of these manifestations of ICA arousal. The terms *concentration, volition* and *will* all carry a connotation of some general organizing force. The old (e.g., psychoanalytic) notion of "psychic energy," which Csikszentmihalyi (1978) has identified with the phenomenon of attention, refers to such an internally generated force. Näätänen (1982) relates selective attention to endogenous electrical brain activity.

Some neuroscientists have focused on the organizing function of neural activation (Levin, 1980). Epileptic seizures dramatically illustrate the deterioration of the organizing function of attention and consciousness. The nervous system cannot function "when excitation is unbridled and lawless." Coherently organized perception, thinking and action require an orderly, carefully timed pattern of neural excitations.

BIOLOGICAL BASES OF CONSCIOUSNESS AND ATTENTION

ICA arousal provides a base rate kind of arousal which must involve several brain structures. People who are in a coma cannot respond to external stimulation or carry out transactions with their environment. They cannot think or experience emotions. They have no consciousness. They are merely vegetables. However, when their nervous systems are aroused above such comatose states, other behavioral functions become possible. Therefore, all other arousal states (e.g., emotions) may be thought of as additions to, or variations on, some base rate state of ICA arousal of the central nervous system.

The Reticular Activating System (RAS)

Direct or indirect stimulation of neurons by external sources of energy (e.g., sights or sounds) is one important source of nervous system stimulation. However, the brain doesn't just sit there waiting for external stimulation. It is self-organizing through internal (endogenous) sources of stimulation. Just as the heart has its own endogenous energy source which produces the rhythmic heartbeat, so too has the brain its own endogenous energy source to produce a base rate of neural arousal. Just as the heart can vary its base rate beat to serve different types of circumstances, so too can the brain produce specialized variations on its endogenously produced base rate arousal.

A minimal level of endogenously produced ICA arousal must exist before the brain will respond to external stimulation. "Instant-on" TV sets provide an analogy. They always have a low level of electrical current being applied to their electronic circuits, even when turned off (i.e., "unconscious"). That way, when the TV set is turned on (i.e., "awakened") the picture and sound appear immediately as an elaboration of an existing arousal state. When the TV set is on, the brightness of the picture and the loudness of the sound can be varied (i.e., the arousal level can be adjusted selectively). Moreover, a TV set can focus on only one program (i.e., one channel) at a time. Analogously, in the human brain there are structures that produce variable levels of base rate arousal, and that also participate in producing specialized, selective neural arousal patterns. The reticular activating system (RAS), anchored in the first ("reptilian") level of the brain, is the structure primarily responsible for this endogenous ICA arousal. It is a primitive structure of mostly short-fibered, many-branched neurons. Its general function is to variably "tune" the bioelectrical and biochemical functioning of the nervous system to produce an alert organism, ready to act when necessary. Variations in neural arousal patterns have been observed in decorticate animals (Vanderwolf & Robinson, 1981), indicating that the RAS can perform arousal functions independent of the neocortex. The RAS provides both a generalized activation of brain structures, and specialized activation of specific areas of the brain (which are related to the contents of consciousness) (Vernon, 1966). Incoming sensory information goes directly to the higher brain structures and simultaneously into the RAS through collateral sensory fibers. The higher brain structures also have connections with the RAS (French, Hernandez-Peon, & Livingston, 1955). Thus, the RAS can be simultaneously influenced directly by incoming information, and indirectly by higher brain structures' transformations of that same information. Some RAS neurons appear to be specialized for certain kinds of sensory information while others function as generalists.

Sources of Generalized ICA Arousal

Within the RAS there exist neural components that vary the general level of "tuning" of the nervous system up and down in regular cycles or natural rhythms (LaVie, 1979). Endogenous oscillators ("biological clocks") of many types exist in most living systems (Takahashi & Zatz, 1982) and vary in terms of the time span involved in each cycle. Circadian rhythms represent oscillators with approximately a 24-hour cycle (Aschoff, 1981).

Mammalian functioning appears to be regulated by at least two basic kinds of "clocks" or "pacemakers" that can be influenced by synchronizing signals from the environment (called *zeitgeber*). One oscillator, influenced by the environmental light-dark cycle, regulates a number of functions, including a basic rest-activity cycle. A second oscillator appears to be influenced by an "eat-fast" zeitgeber, and affects functions like core body temperature (Moore-Ede et al., 1982). Usually, biological functions covary synchronously in such rhythms (e.g., body temperature and electrolyte levels). However, they can become desynchronized and may affect people's health, which appears to happen more often in the elderly (Regestein, 1980) than in other people.

The sleep-wakefulness cycle in humans is an ICA circadian rhythm (Kety et al., 1967). Within it, there is a shorter cycle about 60 minutes long in infants and about 90 minutes long in adults, termed the *basic rest-activity cycle* (BRAC) (Berg & Berg, 1979). The normal lower boundary of generalized ICA arousal is deep sleep. Even during sleep, BRAC cycles are apparent. During deep sleep the eyes are quiet (called NREM sleep). Periodically the arousal level will rise as revealed in rapid eye movement (called REM sleep). During a full night of sleep, a person will cycle back and forth between NREM and REM sleep, and the length of these cycles change with age (Roffwarg et al., 1966). The fact that dreaming occurs during the REM sleep phases illustrates that the brain has become more aroused, an inference supported by changes in electrical brain activity patterns. It is during REM phases that nature's demands or worries may fully awaken one and make it difficult to return to sleep.

During sleep, there occurs a constellation of changes in biological functions, such as cardiovascular and endocrine functions, and cerebral circulation (Orem & Barnes, 1980), which are, in general, characteristic of parasympathetic nervous system dominance. Therefore, the sleep or rest phase of the BRAC appears to facilitate the self-organizing, self-constructing functions of the body by significantly reducing the flow of information within the system and the energy demands upon it (e.g., Horne, 1979; Orem & Barnes, 1980). Basic biological functions covary with different *levels* of arousal, increasing in variability as ICA arousal increases. They also covary with different kinds of arousal. For example, when a person is vigilant for information, heart rate and blood pressure typically decline. The greater the deceleration the more rapid the reaction time when the relevant information appears. In contrast, heart rate and blood pressure increase when a person selectively attends to preparation for or initiation of action (Lacey & Lacey, 1970).

Sleep-wakefulness cycles could result from oscillations in the relative dominance of a "sleep system" in caudal RAS structures and an "arousal or vigilance system" in rostral RAS structures that are "reciprocally connected in dynamic equilibrium" (Hernandez-Peon, 1966). When the sleep cycle is dominant, electrical activity of the brain is characterized by long, slow synchronous rhythms. During relaxed waking states, it is characterized by a more rapid "alpha" rhythm. During focused attention and differential sensory stimulation, the alpha rhythm becomes more differentiated and less regular. The RAS is connected to sensory inputs. Therefore, its activity can be quickly changed by sufficiently strong sensory inputs. The thalamus is the main entryway to the neocortex for almost all efferent sensory information. There is extensive two-way communication between the thalamus and all parts of the cerebral cortex involving two separate but interacting thalamocortical systems. One, the diffuse thalamocortical system, is a direct extension of the brain stem RAS, and is involved in more generalized cortical arousal. The other is highly differentiated, involves specific nuclei of the thalamus, is involved in more specialized patterns of arousal, and is indirectly influenced by RAS functioning.

External and Internal Sources of Specialized ICA Arousal. Specialized neural activation patterns are revealed by neocortical electrical patterns called event-related brain potentials (ERPs). Different ERP patterns are produced by different kinds of events, and appear to represent "subroutines" of information handling within the brain (Donchin, 1981). There are at least two types of specialized arousal eminating from the RAS (Smythies, 1970; Vanderwolf & Robinson, 1981) involving somewhat different reticular-cortical circuits (Pribram & McGuinness, 1975). One type of circuit is related to information collection and processing called the ascending reticular activating system (ARAS). A second type is related to motor activity, called the descending reticular activating system (DRAS).

Pribram and McGuinness (1975) have described three interrelated limbic system structural pathways that participate with the RAS in regulating neural arousal. One is focused on *information inputs,* or "arousal." They believe its control circuit is centered on the amygdala. A second pathway is focused on *behavioral outputs,* or "activitation," which they identify with the basal ganglia. However, information inputs and behavioral outputs must be coordinated. They propose that a third hippocampal component serves this purpose. For example, *attention* may be focused on certain kinds of information, making it more salient in the pattern of brain functioning (i.e., arousal). *Intention* may be focused on potential courses of actions, perhaps producing a preparatory set to perform certain actions (i.e., activation). However, an effective, coordinated behavioral episode can only result if these two processes are coordinated, combining relevant information with relevant potential actions (i.e., effort) through *thoughtful concentration.*

The Ascending Reticular Activating System (ARAS). In the brainstem RAS, norepinephrine-containing neurons lie laterally and serotonin-containing neurons lie largely medially. Their axons project upward into the hypothalamus-limbic system circuits. In addition, the thalamus-neocortical circuit contains an elaborate network of fine norepinephrine- and serontonin-containing fibers. Through these two circuits plus the interactions between them, concentrations of norepinephrine, dopamine, and seratonin neurotransmitters can be delivered to influence synaptic circuits in both the autonomic and sensory-motor nervous systems (Kety, 1970).

The influence of ARAS on nervous system arousal has been demonstrated in a variety of ways. Stimulate it in a sleeping animal and the animal will wake up. Stimulate it in an awake animal, and the animal will become more alert. Damage it, and apathy, coma, or even death will occur. The level of excitation in higher brain structures is varied through the reticulo-thalamo-cortical circuits, as evidenced by changing electrical patterns in the neocortex and hippocampus. There appear to be two primary functions of the ARAS. One is a generalized activation of neural structures. The other appears to be a selective excitation of the nervous system in such a way as to amplify, attenuate, filter, and organize specific incoming and previously stored information relevant to serving the person's current concerns.

There is physiological evidence to support the idea of a "specific attention mechanism" (Gellhorn & Loofbourrow, 1963; Lindsley, 1960). This attention mechanism begins to affect sensory signals at the periphery of the central nervous system and continues to do so throughout the entire system. In a person who is awake, sensory inputs (e.g., visual, auditory) selectively alter brain activity (Harter & Previc, 1978; Matthysse, 1977; Näätänen, 1982; Näätänen & Michie, 1976; Parasuraman, 1978). Selective attention to particular sensory inputs produces different patterns of electrical brain activity (Hillyard et al., 1973; Hillyard & Picton, 1977; Lindsley, 1957; Lukas, 1980).

Neural structures involved in attentional processes appear to be particularly sensitive to novelty. For example, a new (or different) stimulus pattern changes electrical brain activity, but repetition of the same stimulus produces habituation. Attentional processes probably evolved to deal with variable or novel events of potential personal significance (Megela & Teyler, 1979). Generalized seizures, which appear to result from an unorganized flood of neural activation, may involve the reversal of synaptic events involved in habituation, since ERPs are enhanced in them. Such seizures involve an excess of excitation, often producing "unconsciousness." This illustrates that consciousness must result from more than the *amount* of neural arousal. Otherwise "hyperconsciousness" rather than unconsciousness should occur during generalized seizures. Different kinds of drugs can enhance or reduce the amplitude of ERPs (Faingold, 1978; Faingold & Stittsworth, 1980).

Thus, the primary role of the ARAS is "as a sleep-wakefulness controlling arousal mechanism" involved with "the control and regulation of electrocortical rhythms, particularly their synchronized state" which in turn are related to the behavioral states "of arousal, awareness, alertness, vigilance, and attention" (Lindsley, 1970). Because monitoring information is essential for feedback-regulatory functions, it makes sense that attentional capabilities would be related to the monitoring function.

The Descending Reticular Activating System (DRAS). The DRAS functions to selectively arouse those portions of the nervous system that organize and control the transactional functions. Pribram (1971) refers to this as a feedforward function of the brain. It influences both information collection and actions. Selectively focusing attention "tunes" or "biases" sensory receptors and other nervous system components to increase their sensitivity to the selected information and decrease it to other information (John, 1976; Lindsley, 1970; Magoun, 1958; Pribram, 1971; Tarpey, 1977). Functional terms such as *selective attention* and *set* refer to such feedforward tuning. There is evidence that "focusing attention" is a brain function different from those that control bodily orientation of sensory receptors (e.g., Remington, 1980).

When attention is focused on potential actions (often called *intention*), it functions to selectively organize motor behaviors, including speech. The DRAS provides a structural basis for thoughts to influence sensorimotor activity. Studies of voluntary or "willed" action (e.g., Kornhaber, 1974) reveal changes in electrical patterns of brain function after an intent to act is established and before the action actually begins. DRAS functioning can also influence biological processes controlled primarily by the autonomic nervous system (e.g., Sperry, 1976). For example, biofeedback procedures involve focusing a person's attention on some biological function, or correlate thereof, to intentionally try to adjust the value of the variable being monitored (e.g., blood pressure) (White & Tursky, 1982).

The Biological Basis of Consciousness

The RAS does not by itself account for consciousness. Some level and pattern of electrical brain activity is always occurring as long as a person is alive, but a person is not always conscious. Even when awake people are selectively conscious, and perform many habitual acts "automatically" without being aware of them. People are rendered unconscious in preparation for major surgery by the administration of anesthetics that act on neural sites above, or in addition to, the brain stem, which houses the RAS (e.g., Eger, 1974).

Where, then, is the structural basis for the function called *consciousness?* Penfield (1975) concludes that control of consciousness lies between the brain stem and the neocortex; probably in ARAS-limbic system-neocortical circuits. For example, damage or destruction of the ARAS circuit disrupts or destroys attention and consciousness, while disruption of DRAS circuits does not affect consciousness. This implies that consciousness evolved to serve information monitoring (i.e., feedback) and processing (i.e., thinking), rather than control of action (i.e., feedforward functions).

Sperry (1976) proposed that consciousness is an emergent phenomenon resulting from increasingly complex organization of neural structures. He doesn't see anything "separating the conscious from the unconscious neural events—aside from organizational coherence." The phenomena of consciousness have been examined in relationship to the cerebral hemispheres both when they are normally connected and when they are separated by surgery or by a birth anomaly (Guiard, 1980; Prohovnik, 1978; Sperry, 1982). In the normally connected cerebral hemispheres, the two halves work together as a functional unit even though there appears to be considerable lateral hemispheric specialization. However, when the two halves are surgically separated, each half displays some arousal patterns and contents of consciousness not shared by the other half (Corballis, 1980; Sperry, 1976). This implies that the neural arousal processes related to consciousness originate at levels below the cerebral hemispheres. Therefore, behavioral organization and coordination must be a product of vertical as well as horizontal neural arousal patterns (Pribram, 1980a, 1980b).

Kinsbourne (1974a, 1974b) has proposed a theory of interhemispheric interaction and coordination based upon asymmetrical ICA arousal controlled by negative feedback loops between hemispheres, which appears to fit a considerable amount of evidence (Guiard, 1980; Prohovnik, 1978). A primary function of the cerebral commissures appears to be to force the hemispheres to function cooperatively through the maintenance of attentional unity in the brain as a whole (Ellenberg & Sperry, 1980). Such unity is essential so that the individual can function normally as an integrated unit, consciousness being typically a unified and unitary experience. Two "bosses" who may give contradictory interpretations of what's going on and different instructions for action could create confusion.

The Concept of Mutual Entrainment. Dewan (1976) gives examples from engineering control systems to illustrate how functions may emerge as *properties of the organization of an entire system*, rather than being localized in a specific structural component of such a system; this is called the *mutual entrainment of oscillations.* Something is said to oscillate when it occurs in the same repetitive pattern. Biological clocks are a form of such oscillators. When two or more oscillating functions mutually influence one another so that their cyclical functioning is synchronized, mutual entrainment is said to occur. For example, each muscle cell in the heart is an autonomous oscillator. Collectively, as part of a single heart, they synchronize their rhythms and the heart beats as a unit. However, sometimes that synchronization breaks down; this is called *fibrillation.* If mutual entrainment of the individual cells is not restored (e.g., by an electric shock to the heart), a person will die. Mutual entrainment may occur among as well as within organisms. For example, fireflies in southeast Asia may synchronize their flashing as a part of their sexual display activity. Whole bushes of them may flash exactly in unison (Buck & Buck, 1968). Human crowd/conformity behaviors may be a social form of such mutual entrainment (e.g., as at a rock music concert).

N. Wiener (1961) illustrated how mutual entrainment works with a large system of electrical power generators. Each generator functions as an oscillator with feedback controls to produce a steady 60 cycle per second output, but may vary in a range around that 60 cycle output. However, if many such generators are linked together, they mutually entrain one another. If one speeds up, the others slow it down, or if its output slows down, the others speed it up. The stability and accuracy of the whole system of generators is much greater than any single one. They have become self-organizing, not because there is some "governor" controlling the whole system, but because it is an emergent property of the functioning of the entire system. The organization of body temperature regulation mechanisms described in an earlier chapter appears to produce such a "virtual governor."

Moreover, Dewan (1976) explains how sets of mutually entrained units may interact *as sets*, producing further mutual entrainment among sets in hierarchical fashion. He uses mutual entrainment as an analogy for the function of consciousness. Consciousness occurs, he suggests, when the functioning of many similar structures (e.g., Hebb's, 1949, "cell assemblies") become mutually entrained in particular ways. That would explain why it has not been possible to identify the phenomenon of consciousness with a particular part of the brain. Attention and consciousness help organize information and behavior, but do not have a primary role in varying the intensity and amplitude of actions. That requires AE arousal (see Chapter 13).

LEVELS OF ICA AROUSAL

The general level of neural arousal produced by the RAS can vary dramatically. A comatose person is incapable of any behavior except that which is fully automated at brain stem levels, such as breathing. Healthy people approach this state when they fall into a "deep" (NREM) sleep during which (a) they are relatively unresponsive to external stimulation; (b) the electrical activity of the brain displays a slow, regular repetitive form; (c) the eyes are closed and there is very little eye movement; (d) there is no dreaming; and (e) physiological functions (such as breathing and cardiovascular activity) fall into regular patterns characteristic of PNS dominance. This is the *minimal ICA arousal state.*

Being awake or conscious represents the *base rate ICA arousal level* necessary for the effective collection, organization, and use of information to direct, regulate, and control all other behavior in a variable environment. As Luria (1976) put it, this "optimal state of cortical neurodynamics" characterizing the waking state "is maintained by the normal state of the brain stem and reticular formation." Lowering this optimal "cortical tone" removes "the most important condition for selective psychological processes." Base rate ICA arousal must be present before specialized arousal functions (i.e., selective attention and emotions) can occur.

Patterns of ICA Arousal. There are degrees of arousal between the minimal and base rate levels. For example, REM sleep might be thought of as a partial or near wakefulness state. In that state there is considerable eye movement, although the eyes remain closed. There may be some motor activity or vocalizations. The electrical activity of the brain and basic physiological functions are more similar to a waking state. The person may be somewhat responsive to external stimulation. However, REM states are easily distinguishable from base rate arousal states because the behavior patterns are fragmented rather than well organized, and little or no learning can occur. A "twilight" or "reverie" state lies between the partial wakefulness of REM sleep and the fully awake state. It can involve considerable conscious cognitive activity, but it is less "tightly" or logically organized than a fully awake state.

To summarize, marginal states of base rate ICA arousal can and do occur. However, transactional functioning is very limited, and any conscious content is primarily internally rather than externally generated. Resulting behavior patterns are fragmented and disorganized both within themselves as they flow through time (e.g., as in dream scenarios), and between the behavior and environment. Little or no learning can occur in such states of partial wakefulness.

Distinctions Between Consciousness and Its Informational Content

Information is the key to adaptive functioning in an unpredictable environment. To be adaptive, behavior must be selective and targeted. To be *selective*, individuals must be able to identify and monitor primarily that information relevant to their current concerns. In information-processing terms, they must be able to select and "amplify" the relevant signals and to "filter out" the noise or irrelevant information. To be *targeted* they must select and implement, from among the many possible patterns of behavioral organization, one that might successfully produce the intended consequences within current environmental contingencies. The subjective experience of consciousness is a manifestation of the existence of a base rate level of ICA arousal which makes these functions possible.

However, the existence of a *level* of ICA arousal which makes possible information collection, processing, and use is not the same thing as the *kind* of information being processed; just as having a computer "turned on" is not the same as the application of a particular data processing program to a specific information input. Stated behaviorally, *there is a difference between the phenomenon of consciousness and the contents or states of consciousness.* The raw phenomenon of base rate neural arousal, of which consciousness is a manifestation, is content-free.

Two kinds of evidence reveal the existence of a state of consciousness. The first is manifest in a person's ability to collect and use information. For example, when physicians judge whether a patient is still comatose they may ask questions such as "Can you hear me?" or give instructions, such as "Wiggle your toes." The second type of evidence is the person's subjective experience. When consciousness is present, the content and quality of subjective experience can be rich and highly varied, and a person can report that information to others.

When base rate ICA arousal exists, only some portion of the information-processing activities continuously occurring is subjectively experienced as the content of consciousness. Therefore, *unconscious processes* are a normal and necessary part of human functioning. They contribute to the precision and efficiency of human behavior. Both the substance and organization of the informational content of consciousness varies from moment to moment, so the content of consciousness is both a selective and a dynamic flow of events. Periods of consciousness with *different kinds and organization of informational content* are often referred to as *states of consciousness.*

Typically, the informational content of consciousness reflects current environmental as well as bodily and cognitively generated information, and makes possible distinctions between self and environment. However, under certain conditions, the informational content of consciousness can be composed of limited, unusual, or unusually organized information as in dreaming, meditation, trances, or drugged states. These are often referred to as *altered states of consciousness* (Fromm, 1976; McCabe et al., 1978; Rao, 1978; Schuman, 1980; Sugerman & Tarter, 1978; Tart, 1976; Walsh, 1980). Some Eastern religions use practices aimed at producing a state of consciousness devoid of all content, that is, a state of pure consciousness. Also, it appears that the consciousness distinction between self and environment sometimes can be eliminated, producing a sense of unity or "oneness" with the universe, which is referred to as a *transpersonal state of consciousness.*

What determines the content of consciousness? It is selective attention. For example, different meditation methods use different methods of selective attention. Some involve focusing on an external object, some on a particular thought or image, and some try to maintain an unfocused or diffuse attentional state. Procedures that rely on focused attention are sometimes termed *concentration practices* (e.g., yoga) which can produce trancelike states. Hypnotic induction procedures use concentration practices. There is some evidence of a relationship between selective attention capabilities and hypnotizability (Graham & Evans, 1977; Karlin, 1979). In general, meditation procedures appear to produce lowered arousal states, as illustrated by greater synchronization and slowing of EEG brain activity, lowering of respiratory rate and/or volume, heart rate decrease, and a decrease in electrodermal activity and/or reactivity that is typical of PNS dominance (Schuman, 1980). In fact, meditators frequently fall asleep for some period during meditation (Pagano et al., 1976). This lowered arousal level probably accounts for the unusually organized or less organized content of consciousness that occurs in meditation. A closer examination of the relationship of attention to the organization of information collection and processing follows.

INFORMATION MONITORING AND COLLECTION: ATTENTION

Arousal of ICA information monitoring and collection has been examined most extensively. Hilgard (1977b), using hypnosis as an experimental procedure, observed manifestations of the functioning of consciousness processes that he called "monitor" and "hidden observer." He selected these terms because the related subjective experience occurred "as if" people were observing what was happening and what they were doing independent of their participation in the events. The informational contents of consciousness are determined by attentional monitoring of information originating within or without one's body. Therefore, *the phenomenon of consciousness and control of its contents are functions of the attentional processes involved in the feedback-regulatory components of human behavior.* At any moment, humans *are* (and can be) conscious only of that information in the "field" of their attention. Humans can *become* conscious of any information upon which their attention can be focused. Therefore, all attention is selective attention because it monitors only some of all the possible information available at a given time (Johnston & Dark, 1986). Attentional selectivity is a function of directive thoughts and/or the stimulus properties of external or body state information.

It is useful to subdivide into three domains the information that can be monitored. First, people can monitor any information generated outside of their bodies for which they have sensory capability. For example, humans have no sensory receptors for directly monitoring atomic radiation. Second, people can consciously monitor some information generated by their internal biological processes (e.g., heart rate, pain), but not others (e.g., cell metabolism). Third, people can monitor some of the information generated by their governing (thoughts) and arousal (emotions) functions. Remembering or thinking involves inhibiting the transactional functions and focusing attention on internal information-processing activities.

The information source on which attention is focused has physiological correlates. For example, focusing on external information produces cardiac deceleration and increased respiration. Focusing on subjective processes (e.g., affects and thoughts) produces more nonspecific electrodermal responses (Epstein et al., 1978; Kagan & Rosman, 1964). Different patterns of behavioral organization are also relevant to different information sources. A focus on information collection involves inhibition of actions. A focus on information processing (thinking) involves inhibition of actions and perception of environmental events. A focus on action involves restriction of thinking.

Relationships Between Diffuse and Focal Attention

Generalized ICA arousal and selective attentional arousal interact in information monitoring and affect the content of consciousness. Terms sometimes used to identify this distinction include *diffuse* and *focused* attention (Baroni et al., 1980); *global* and *focal* attention (Alwitt, 1981); the phenomenological distinction between *ground* and *figure* (Hoeller, 1977); and *diffuse* or *incidental* and *central* stimuli in the attentional field (Lane, 1979); and the *attentional spotlight* (Johnston & Dark, 1986).

There are important differences, however, in the properties of the information that becomes conscious through selective attention (sometimes called *focal awareness*) and through generalized monitoring. Information organized through selective attentional processes has a conscious clarity of form and detail, and has direct, influential relationships with other aspects of the ongoing behavior pattern (e.g., a person will press a key or verbally label an event when it occurs). Such information is likely to be remembered, at least in the short term. In contrast, general background information is likely to have a vague conscious form with little detail (if noticed at all); it usually has little direct influence on the ongoing behavior pattern, and is unlikely to be remembered (Egeth & Bevan, 1973; Eysenck, 1982; Moray, 1970; Salmaso et al., 1982). Research on selective attention using dichotic listening and shadowing procedures continues to confirm that people remember best what they attend to, and remember only vaguely (if at all) information they do not attend to (Bookbinder & Osman, 1979; Inoue, 1981; Johnston & Dark, 1986). Studies of preschoolers in more natural situations (e.g., TV watching) have produced similar findings. Children at this age tend to focus their attention on the picture and to ignore the sound, and generally remember the visual information much better than the auditory information (Hayes & Birnbaum, 1980).

Base rate ICA arousal, and the conscious content resulting therefrom, is largely influenced and controlled by properties of stimuli. Certain stimulus properties such as intensity (e.g., a sharp pain or loud sound), variability (e.g., the movement of other organisms), and personal relevance (e.g., a sweet taste, one's image in a mirror, or another human) appear to have an inborn evolutionary salience (Moray, 1970). They naturally "attract attention." Advertising and media specialists (Jörg, 1978) make practical use of both stimulus-controlled and meaning controlled selective attention; for example, they increase the sound level for TV commercials and they tell you their products will increase your sex appeal.

Information monitoring guided solely by base rate ICA arousal appears to function a bit like a citizens band radio scanner. All available information is scanned in an unbiased, casual way. Such might be the state of someone lying on a lawn chair on a lazy afternoon with nothing to do and nothing on his or her mind. One may notice a gentle breeze, a butterfly, a distant sound, a sense of bodily relaxation, or a hunger pang. However, a sudden scream nearby, the appearance of a loved one, or a bee lighting on one's nose will produce focused attention. Like a CB scanner, a person can "lock onto" a signal bearing personally important or especially interesting information.

When humans are awake they may be reading, eating, walking, thinking, working, or making love, but they are usually doing something. Therefore, a condition dominated by global, diffuse, stimulus-controlled attention is the exception. When personal objectives are directing behavior, which information "attracts attention" is a function not so much of the properties of the events themselves as of their potential relevance to the person's current concerns (Egeth & Bevan, 1973). Personal goals guiding current BES "prime" selective attention through semantic influences (Johnston & Dark, 1986). Selective attention functions to amplify potentially relevant information and to filter out or ignore potentially irrelevant information.

Both generalized information scanning and selective information collection and monitoring are usually going on at the same time (Csikszentmihalyi, 1978). The selective information that is monitored might be thought of as the "figure" or "focus," with the generalized information considered as the "ground" or "periphery" of the attention-consciousness field. Selective attention typically involves intentional or self-directed information search and perception (see Chapter 8). Cognitive processes make the distinction between what is probably relevant or irrelevant, so that the selectivity of attention is influenced by the governing functions (the "voluntary aspect" of attention as proposed by Broadbent, 1970) which in turn are influenced by the information selectively collected. It is a mutual causal process (Näätänen, 1982). Thus, the selectivity of attention-information collection is a function both of the level of neural arousal and the importance of the information (Deutsch & Deutsch, 1963).

The development of both focal and peripheral information monitoring and collection functions makes considerable evolutionary sense. Adaptive behavior must be selective, which requires that much of what is in the environment, or what is happening, be ignored. However, circumstances change. Therefore, an arrangement in which the organism superficially monitored the flow of "background" events for gross indicators of potentially important new occurrences would be a useful and efficient safeguard against the possibility of ignoring something important. It is like a spotlight in which entities or events in the center of the beam can be seen in clear detail, and those on the beam's fringes can be only dimly discerned. This was Wundt's (1912) position. In focal attention which he called *blickpunkt*, events are clearly and distinctly perceived. In peripheral attention which he called *blickfield*, gross aspects may be perceived, but not details. If some gross signal occurs, then one can temporarily interrupt what one is doing, redirect focal attention to the gross signal, and "check it out" to see if it represents anything important.

This phenomenon can be readily observed in people who are simultaneously engaging in social interaction and watching TV. For example, I sometimes only vaguely listen to my wife while watching a TV football game. If I hear a word or phrase from her that sounds important (like "spend money"), I'll "tune in" her and "tune out" the TV. Bevan (1967) considered such phenomena in the framework of adaptation level theory (Helson, 1964). Moray (1970) referred to monitoring a "running average" or "some kind of adaptation level" in each "channel" to describe the process by which background information is superficially monitored in case something important occurs. Dichotic listening research has demonstrated that if a person monitors information in one ear with focal attention, he or she can monitor only gross aspects of information in the other ear with diffuse or peripheral attention.

Surprise and the Startle Response. The term *startle response* refers to the interruption of ongoing activity to "check out" suddenly or unexpectedly occurring new information. Tomkins (1962) referred to this as a "resetting affect," or a "general interrupter of ongoing activity." It may be accompanied by a subjective experience typically labeled *surprise*. It is analogous to an announcer breaking into a TV show stating, "We interrupt this program for an important news bulletin." The bulletin may or may not be important to you, but the announcement usually gets you to stop what you are doing for a moment to find out what is happening.

A startle reaction may involve both a refocusing and an amplification or concentration of attentional arousal. The refocusing involves "locking onto" specific kinds or sources of information, or information in specific locations. The amplification is manifested in increased sensitivity to potentially relevant information. For example, slight sounds not ordinarily noticed may be clearly heard. There is some evidence that sensitization occurs in one part of the startle neural circuit and habituation in another part (Davis et al., 1982). Ongoing activity is momentarily halted, and while the "checking out" process occurs, no new activity is initiated. So, the startle response not only alters information collection activity but also alters a person's "set" for action. It is a specialized, amplified version of the more common stimulus control of selective attention mentioned earlier. Sokolov (1963) distinguished between phasic (i.e., startle) and tonic (i.e., intentional) orienting reactions, and identified correlates of the phasic orienting response such as vasoconstriction in the extremities (where physical action is reduced); vasodilation in the head (where information search and examination is emphasized); and physical orientation of sensory receptors towards the stimulus source (sometimes called a "what is it?" reflex by Pavlovians).

Scanning and Focusing: Interacting Techniques for Information Collection

At any moment, only a limited portion of the "current news" can be attended to because *focused attention* can encompass only a limited amount of information, called the *attention span* or *channel capacity*. A person can increase the amount of information encompassed by shifting attentional focus sequentially from one domain to another; this is called *scanning*. The techniques of scanning and focusing must interact in effective information collection.

Scanning. Humans continually scan their environments for information, an activity often accompanied by subjective experiences of curiosity or interest. The sequence of scanning may be organized spatially (e.g., examining one object and then another), in terms of sensory modalities (e.g., by looking at something, then feeling it, and then mouthing it as infants often do), or in terms of kinds of information. Scanning behavior overcomes channel capacity limitations identified in both research and clinical work (Rapaport, 1960). Neisser (1967) has proposed that the limitation is not in attentional capacity but in immediate or short-term memory. The current informational capacity of consciousness may be the same thing as one's short-term memory capacity.

In any case, although experimentally separating capacity limitations from other factors has proven difficult, there is general agreement that information input limitations do exist (Duncan, 1980; Egeth & Bevan, 1973). However, attention span limitations are relative to how the information is organized. If information is "chunked" into larger configurations that can be perceived as units (e.g., if one perceives a word rather than individual letters), the amount of information that can be handled can be increased (Miller, 1956b). Thus, information capacity is a function of information organization. This suggests that parts of the environment that readily appear as units, or that have attributes that the perceiver can fit together more readily, should be more easily recognized and remembered than less "chunkable" parts of the environment (Garner, 1978).

Focusing. Focused attention functions to select and/or create, from a stimulus array, an organized pattern of information. If the stimulus array is clearly and simply organized, and/or familiar, the information organization is easily perceived as given. However, if it is more complex, and/or unfamiliar, it takes more attentional time and effort to impose some personally relevant organization upon it (e.g., "What is it?" "What might it do?"). This "feature integration" aspect of attentional functioning has been used as a cornerstone of one theory of attention (Treisman & Gelade, 1980). Different individuals may organize the information array around different features, thereby yielding somewhat different percepts of the same array of information. Scanning and focusing interact.

The Functional Utility of Focusing-Scanning Patterns. People's environments consist of nested sets of attributes, objects, and events. The most salient parts of the natural environment are typically those entities and events that are relatively stable, well-organized, and easily distinguished from their context (e.g., objects, distinctive sounds). Thus, humans evolved to be especially sensitive to such "surface level" information. However, by focusing and scanning different combinations of information, humans can become informed about any set or subset.

Discriminating entities and events from one another and from their contexts is basic to all learning. People have to discriminate things before they can adaptively manipulate them. Research on stimulus generalization (Honig & Urcuioli, 1981) indicates that once a discrimination is learned, behaviors related to that particular discrimination are also likely to occur in regard to similar stimulus arrays. Entities or events with similar properties are responded to "as if" they are alike (i.e., are members of the same set).

Human infants display what appears to be an inborn attentional preference for some configurational complexity and variability (Fantz & Yeh, 1979). For example, 4-month-old babies look longer at faces than at abstract forms. Older children, for whom faces in general are familiar, look longer at a "scrambled" face or body than at undistorted ones (Kagan, 1968). The effort involved in dealing with complex, unfamiliar informational arrays can be observed in an infant's or small child's intent facial expression, which somewhat resembles a scowl, and can be misinterpreted as representing fear. Through synthesis (e.g., *that's a face*) and/or analysis (e.g., *that's an eye*), an informational array can be organized into coherent units. Still, the number of such units that can be handled consciously at any moment is limited.

Psychoanalytically oriented psychologists studying the "cognitive control functions of the ego" formulated similar principles of scanning and focusing (Gardner, 1966; Gardner & Long, 1963; Klein, 1958). Their *scanning* principle refers to the ways in which people scan sources of information to organize and control their behavior. It is related to information variability. Their *field articulation* principle refers to the ways in which people concentrate attention on personally relevant stimuli and inhibit attention to irrelevant stimuli. There are individual differences in the functioning of these two principles. Rapoport (1960) has summarized the psychoanalytic theory of *attention cathexis* in 17 propositions that represent ways in which different conditions influence the development and functioning of these attentional capabilities.

In summary, the current information-handling capacity of the attention-consciousness function is limited. This has been conceptualized in terms of limited channel capacity, process sets (Duncan, 1980) and competence (Pribram, 1980). The limitation is a function of both the kind and organization of information. The kind of information is a function of the various sensory modalities. Typically, humans direct focal attention to only one modality at a time, sometimes termed "modality priming" (Johnston & Dark, 1986). However, other modalities may simultaneously be monitored with peripheral attention. The information perceived appears to be a function both of its organization in the natural world and of organization imposed on the informational array by the person's focusing-scanning pattern. A person cannot attend to everything at once. Scanning compensates for that limitation by shifting attentional focus among available information sources. Orienting one's sensory receptors towards an information source and directing one's attention towards it are related but not identical processes; for example, people can aim their eyes at something without looking at it. This natural information selectivity is adaptive because people cannot and need not carry out transactions with all aspects of their environment simultaneously.

Stimulus Control and Intentional Control of Information Monitoring. The information attended to at any moment is, in part, a function of the properties of the stimulus array to which a person is exposed. *Variability* and *novelty* "attract" attention. Monotony, familiarity, or repetitiveness "repel" attention (Dember & Earl, 1959; Mackworth, 1970). Variability and novelty are terms for characterizing the uncertainty, unfamiliarity, and unpredictability of events which result when the observer cannot organize the information so as to represent and understand current and probable future conditions (i.e., "what's happening now?" and "what may happen next?") in terms of previous experiences.

People cannot behave towards unfamiliar or uncertain events in an anticipatory or predictive way, but must "stay on their toes" so they can act in terms of current conditions and then quickly or appropriately change actions from moment to moment as needed. They can behave only in terms of the present rather than in terms of probable futures. Behaving solely in terms of present conditions is *stimulus-controlled behavior.* Behavior that is guided primarily by predictions of probable future conditions is *intentionally controlled behavior.* Both are valuable capabilities, and humans use both.

Behaviorally, the process of identifying consistency and predictability in novel circumstances is often described as trying to "understand" something. A key role of the sense organs is to "create a measure of predictable invariance" so that "deviations from this norm" can be recognized and explored (Granit, 1980). Once events become predictable (i.e., are understood), it then becomes possible to develop consistent, habitual ways of responding to them. Stated behaviorally, habitual components can function unconsciously, leaving attention and consciousness free to deal with novel or unpredictable events. For example, experienced drivers do not pay attention to or think about the basic act of driving. Instead, they monitor the flow of events through which they are driving, alert to the occurrence of unpredictable events (such as a child running into the street) that may require a sudden alteration of their habitual driving patterns.

Development of Selective Attention Across the Life Span

The focusing and scanning functions of attention are inborn processes that begin functioning during the first few days of life and are inherently selective (Bahrick et al., 1981). They are part of "the great complex of regulatory and adaptive mechanisms" present in normal individuals at birth, which enhance organized information flow from the environment to the person (Stechler et al., 1966). Studies of infant visual attending has provided the most information (Haith, 1980). Alert inactivity may be observed in neonates during the first six hours after delivery. They can and do make visual and auditory pursuit movements toward events around them, but the duration of such pursuit is limited. Newborns appear to be predisposed to use concurrent visual and auditory information to control exploration (Olson & Sherman, 1983). Initially, information monitoring does not occur simultaneously with motor movements. They appear to be uncoupled.

During the first month coupling begins to appear. If the information source is familiar, some motor behavior may occur while the infant is attending to the object of information. However, more complex visual tasks (i.e., those containing more unfamiliar information) continue to require motor inactivity while "deliberate inspection" (i.e., focused scanning) of the information source occurs. Two kinds of what appear to be emotionally based reactions may be observed in such attending behavior. "Pleasure" may be displayed by a panting kind of breathing, rudimentary smiles, occasional soft cooing, and perhaps some rhythmic limb movements. "Nonpleasure" may be shown by looking away from the object, as if the infant is "blocking out" the information for some reason. Thus, newborn infants use both scanning and focusing; the latter increases in duration and frequency, and becomes linked up with different patterns of motoric behavior as the infant matures (Stechler & Latz, 1966).

Initially, attention appears to be primarily under stimulus control, with preference for simple patterns and highly contrasting elements. However, preferences gradually shift towards more subtle variations in contrast and configuration (Fantz & Yeh, 1979). By three to six months of age, attention becomes increasingly influenced by what the infant knows about the objects and events around it, particularly in the social domain (Olson & Sherman, 1983). The human face appears to be especially interesting to infants, particularly faces with shifting, unfamiliar expressions (McCall & Kennedy, 1980; Sherrod, 1979). For example, it doesn't take new parents long to learn that they can get their baby's attention by making "funny faces."

Studies of children across the first decade of life indicate that (a) attentional preferences shift from familiar informational arrays to incongruous, novel event configurations (Lewis, 1978); and (b) children gain more control over informational input by increasing their capabilities for concentrating focal attention on relevant events, ignoring irrelevant events, and inhibiting motor activity while involved in information collection and processing. Their attention becomes less stimulus controlled and more intentionally controlled (Hale & Alderman, 1978; Hale et al., 1978; Lane, 1979; F. Levy, 1980; Zukier & Hogan, 1978). The trend appears to be towards greater flexibility in the use of attentional strategies to control information monitoring and collection (Chapman, 1981; Sexton & Geffen, 1979).

Children's self-control of attentional deployment can be improved with training using procedures such as modeling, verbal instruction, and pointing (Dusek, 1978; Schworm, 1979; Vlietstra, 1978). As their children's selective attention skills improve, parents shift their "training procedures" to further facilitate that skill development (Bridges, 1979; Tyler et al., 1979). Training procedures have been developed to improve self-controlled selective listening in adults, as in military intelligence work (Schendel, 1979). Methods for stimulus control of attentional deployment have become highly developed by media and advertising specialists (Jörg, 1978).

Inadequate self-control of selective attention has been identified as a frequent symptom of psychopathology such as schizophrenia (Chapman, 1956a, 1956b), although the extent to which it contributes to the development of such disturbances is still in doubt (Bush, 1977; Garmezy, 1977; D. Shakow, 1979; Silberschatz, 1978). There is also growing evidence that deficits in selective attention control are characteristic of learning-disabled and hyperactive children (Copeland & Wisniewski, 1981; Hallahan et al., 1978; Loiselle et al., 1980; Pelham, 1981), and that such deficits persist for periods of years during both infant (Waldrop et al., 1978) and child (Butter, 1977) development. Excessively self-focused attention may be influential with regard to the arousal of emotions, such as fear (Brocker & Hutton, 1978). For example, Irwin Sarason (1972) has proposed that test anxiety results primarily from "self-preoccupied" thinking.

Factors Affecting Concentration or Attentional Self-Control. The more complex and variable the total stimulus array, the more difficult it is to concentrate attention on one portion of the array and to ignore the rest. For example, just now I was trying to read an article on attention while my son was loudly playing popular music on his stereo. Keeping track of what I was reading was very difficult because the music kept "demanding" my attention. Loud, suddenly shifting information, like that in much popular music, has an inborn attentional salience. When background information is highly salient, it takes a significant effort, called concentration, to acquire and maintain selective attentional control over information input.

People differ in the extent to which they can concentrate their attention on certain information and ignore the rest. Some appear to be able to almost completely inhibit informational inputs irrelevant to their current concerns. For example, a football quarterback has said that in an exciting game he is unaware of the crowd, the weather, or his aches and pains. "I shut out everything except the players and the play." Superior athletes in all sports often cite a "loss of concentration" as a reason for poor performance. The inability to concentrate one's attention produces symptoms characteristic of severe psychopathology. For example, one person said, "Things are coming in too fast. I lose my grip of it and get lost"; or "I am attending to everything at once and as a result I do not really attend to anything" (McGhie & Chapman, 1961).

As people age, it typically becomes more difficult to shift concentration from one information array to another, and it takes longer to do so. In addition, the elderly are more easily distracted by irrelevant information (Schonfield, 1980). This developmental process appears to be the reverse of that which occurs in infancy and childhood. As children develop, intentional selective-attentional control capabilities increase and stimulus control of attention declines in relative importance. In the aged, the influence of stimulus control of attention increases while intentional selective attention control declines. The reasons for these reversals are not yet clear, but one influence may be a general decline in the efficiency of the arousal functions.

It is hard to sustain focused attention in environments with low levels of variability. Faced with a monotonous environment, people are likely to generate variable information within themselves (e.g., by thinking or daydreaming), often signaled by unfocused visual behavior (Holland & Tarlow, 1975). In dreams, there is little attentional control. One experiences an uncontrollable drift in the contents of consciousness. Attention seems paralyzed, unable to organize or direct mental events (Csikszentmihalyi, 1978); dreams are complex, self-constructed or hallucinatory experiences (Roffwarg et al., 1966).

Changes in biological functioning (e.g., through drug usage) can affect attentional control and therefore skilled performance (Hink, 1978). On the other hand, drugs have been used to try to enhance attentional control in hyperactive children (Thurston et al., 1979). Fatigue makes it more difficult to maintain attentional self-control. Interrupting a pattern of activity that requires close attentional control, and doing something else for awhile, appears to temporarily improve attentional self-control capability for that task (Egeth & Bevan, 1973).

The personal importance of the information being monitored affects attentional control, sometimes termed "semantic" or "schema based" attention (Johnston & Dark, 1986). For example, in a championship tennis match, or when one is trying to locate on radar a submarine that may sink one's ship, attentional control appears easily maintained. The temporal sequence may also influence attentional control. For example, a person's vigilance may decline, but if something occurs that signals that an important event is about to occur, attentional control may suddenly improve. Finally, hypnotic induction procedures function to get an individual to temporarily relinquish "the use of his own native, self-protecting, and alerting mechanisms" and to "place himself and his sense of 'security' in the hands of another" (Kubie, 1961). A hypnotized person's behavior is much more susceptible to stimulus control (i.e., he or she is much more "suggestible").

Summary. Humans have two kinds of inborn, interrelated inform-ation-monitoring functions. Scanning canvases the total array of available information to check on what is there. Focusing zeros in on specific, currently interesting or relevant information in order to understand and use it to predict and control events. In infants, attention is primarily stimulus controlled. As people develop, they gain increasing intentional control over the deployment of their attention through concentration skills. Individuals vary in the efficiency of their concentration skills. Concentration skills can be improved with training; they can be facili-tated or interfered with by drugs, fatigue, other biological states such as illness, and the number and complexity of distractors in the environ-ment; and they may decline in the elderly. Usually, people monitor gross aspects of background information while concentrating focal attention on specific information, and will interrupt ongoing activity if some background information signals events of potential personal significance.

The informational content of consciousness in the waking state is controlled by focal attention. This functional selectivity, and the capacity limitations of consciousness, limit the information that can be con-sciously handled at any moment. The learning of habitual behavioral components frees the attention to deal with variable, novel, unpredict-able events, while the person behaves habitually with regard to familiar, consistent events.

Selective collecting and organizing of information relevant to current concerns and conditions is essential for effectively organized behavior episodes. Effectively organized behavior would be impossible if there were multiple, unorganized, and unrelated kinds of information guid-ing it. It would be analogous to an employee receiving different, unrelated, and perhaps contradictory information and instructions from several supervisors about what is happening, what to do, and how to do it. The result would be confusion, ineffectiveness, and perhaps immobilization. It is now appropriate to turn from examination of the role of ICA arousal in the organization of information collection, to its role in organizing behavioral outputs.

ATTENTIONAL ORGANIZATION OF ACTIONS: INTENTION

For a person to carry out a useful, effective transaction with the environment, one behavior pattern out of many possible ones must be activated. Moreover, since conditions are likely to be changing as the behavior proceeds, it must be possible to progressively revise the behavior pattern while it is in progress. The multiple response capabilities of the skeletal-muscle and biological subsystems must be orchestrated into a single coherent symphony of activity to produce appropriate consequences within current contingencies. It is an enormously complex problem. And yet, humans solve it easily every moment of every day (see Chapter 13).

Information Coordination and Behavioral Coordination. Imagine how impossible life would be if a person was unable to produce just one effectively targeted behavior pattern at a time. For example, try to stand up and sit down simultaneously. Indeed, such confusion has been observed in damaged humans. For example, a patient whose corpus callosum was sectioned displayed conflicting behavior patterns for a period following surgery, such as trying to put on a piece of clothing with one hand and pull it off with another (Smith & Akelaitis, 1942). Attempts to perform conflicting behavior patterns have also been observed in split-brain animals (Trevarthen, 1965). It is impossible to implement two instructions simultaneously if to do so requires contradictory behavior patterns. Yet it is common for humans to be confronted with contradictory behavioral requirements. The contradiction may be in the person's desires or intentions. For example, both the lobster and the roast duck may sound equally good but you can order only one. The contradiction may be the result of conflicting environmental demands. For example, the mother of a child who has been "messing around" with food at the dinner table may tell the child to eat, while the father may tell the child to leave the table. Obviously, the child cannot do both. Or, it may be between one's intentions and environmental demands. For example, a child's parents may say it is time to go to bed but the child may want to stay up and continue playing.

There are three ways humans have of dealing with such contradictions. The easiest way is to ignore one and to organize one's behavior to follow the other. For example, one can choose the duck and forget the lobster this time. A more complicated possibility is to organize a behavior pattern that will serve both. For example, I'll order the duck, you order the lobster, and we'll share. Humans are good at this kind of solution (particularly in Chinese restaurants). Indeed, most behavior patterns simultaneously serve more than one objective. But this solution still involves only one coordinated behavior pattern. It is simply a cleverly constructed one that is designed to produce several desirable results with one set of actions. A third strategy that is sometimes possible is to perform two different behavior patterns simultaneously if (a) they are structurally and functionally not mutually incompatible; and (b) one of them is a heavily practiced habit that can be effectively performed "automatically," while one concentrates on performing a second behavior pattern. For example, in one study a secretary was able to read and type material while simultaneously reciting stories she had previously memorized (Schaeffer, 1975).

Intention, Neural Activation, and Transactional Functions

How is the selective organization of one among many possible behavior patterns accomplished? It is a function of directed attention, guided by the information-processing functions of the brain. Shallice's (1978) "dominant action system" view presumes that consciousness is an evolutionary answer to the problem of ensuring that one set of intentions "has control of all the musculature and mental machinery" required to carry out successful behavior. Similarly, Bruner (1974) concludes that aroused intention is a key factor in organizing skilled action in infants. Carver and Scheier (1981) assume that attentional focus "is an important determinant of people's perceptions and constructions of reality" and "has a major impact on people's actions." To carry out a complex program of action requires concentrated attention. Just as a person may select one informational input rather than another, so too may they select one action output rather than another (Moray, 1970). Broadbent (1970) used the term *stimulus-set* to refer to selective information monitoring and *response-set* to refer to selective responding as a function of selective attention processes.

Interaction of Governing and ICA Arousal Functions in Organizing Behavior. ICA arousal in the form of selective attention can selectively activate an organized pattern of neural circuits, but it must be "told" which circuits to activate. That guidance is provided by the information-based governing functions of the brain. This idea is not new. For example, William James (1910) used the phrase "an anticipatory image of a movement's sensible effects" in discussing what guides voluntary actions. Chapter 14 reviews versions of James' view in the work of Bernstein (1967), Kohout (1976, 1981), Turvey (1977), Granit (1980), Gallistel (1980), and others. Pribram (1976) concluded that the guiding representation in the motor cortex "was neither of individual muscles nor of movements, but of actions" defined as a cognitive representation of the environmental consequences of movements. This is essentially the meaning of the term *intention*, or in other words, the aim of an action. One definition of the word *intent* makes the link to ICA arousal, i.e., directed with "strained" or "eager" attention.

Intentions Selectively Influence Both Sensory and Motor Patterns. As discussed in Chapters 8 and 14, transactional behaviors have two interrelated aspects. One is the pattern of skeletal-muscle action which Anokhin (1969) refers to as a "program of action." The other aspect is the pattern of selective information monitoring essential for effectively guiding the program of action. Anokhin (1969) refers to this feedback function as the "acceptor of effect." It involves neural processes in afferent (i.e., information input) portions of the nervous system that reflect "...all the essential attributes of future results" which includes not only the final intended result(s), but also all of "...the intermediary stages in the performance of the behavioral act" representing subresults that must be obtained on the way to producing the intended final result. Underlying such patterns of sensory-perceptual-motor behaviors is a correlated adjustment of relevant biological processes to insure that energy production and distribution (and removal of waste by-products) is appropriate in amount and distribution to support the action program being performed. A simple example of this abstract idea is reaching for a glass of water to have a drink. It is the integrated interaction of the motor actions and relevant information monitoring that produces a smoothly flowing, successful reaching, grasping, and drinking episode.

Attentional processes are the only functions presently known to directly influence (through the ARAS and DRAS) selective neural activation under the influence of both thought and sensory-perceptual inputs. Since information collection and actions must occur in coupled patterns if behavior episodes are to be effectively organized and completed, it makes sense that the structural-functional arrangements to produce both types of activation would be linked. As Pribram (1980) put it, "intentionality is to perception" as "intention is to action." The existence of interrelated ascending and descending pathways in the reticular activating system gives additional plausibility to such a theory. Moreover, it has been demonstrated that some parts of the brain (e.g., the basal ganglia) influence both sensory input and motor functioning by changing the "set points" of receptors in sense organs and circuits and in muscles and neuromuscular circuits; that is, they can function as "intentionality mechanisms" (Pribram, 1971, 1976). In Fig. 3.3 (see p. 78), the arrows extending from the control functions forward to the transactional functions represent the feedforward activating signals that produce coordinated sensory-motor functioning.

The basic premise of this position, then, is that a cognitive representation of the consequences to be produced by the action (called an intention) somehow triggers selective activation of neural circuits through ICA arousal functions to produce both a relevant, well-organized motor act and selective information collection to help organize and guide that action to produce the targeted consequence. Which behavior pattern is activated in any particular instance is a function of the person's intent, the person's relevant behavior repertoire, and existing facilitating and constraining conditionalities within the person and the environment; but the coordinating neural activation pattern results from selective, directed attention.

Research on the influence of ICA arousal on motor behavior is skimpy. There is considerable anecdotal evidence concerning the influence of attentional processes such as concentration in producing skilled performances by athletes and musicians. Sports psychologists have begun to examine the function of attention and concentration in organizing motor behavior (Silva, 1979; VanSchoyck & Grasha, 1981). The targeting of most transactional behavior is more a function of intentional than of stimulus control because most human behavior functions in a predictive, targeted way. The transition from acting solely in terms of present events to acting in terms of probable future events is a major developmental landmark that occurs relatively early in infancy. One can observe it in a game of peek-a-boo with an infant. In young children, it is apparent in their ability to search for a toy that has been hidden from them. Four-month-old infants display such predictive, targeted actions (von Hofsten, 1980). Improvements in its use come through practice and learning. Congenital anomalies may affect the development of the use of controlled attention to facilitate motor coordination (O'Donnell et al., 1979).

Intentional practice of a behavior pattern may function a bit like "debugging" a new computer program. It progressively eliminates unnecessary informational considerations and unnecessary action components, and improves timing. The result is improved functional efficiency in organization and speed of the behavior pattern. Habitual behavior patterns become functional units in their own right. Each such "behavior program" is learned and developed in relationship to specific "targets" and target contexts. Clusters or families of behavioral programs are learned relevant to clusters or families of similar target - target context combinations. Thus, mature people have *sets of behavioral programs* relevant to *sets of intentions and contexts* (see Chapter 14). When confronted with a particular intention and context, attentional processes activate one behavioral program from the relevant set. Earlier it was pointed out that the contents of consciousness are a function of feedback (i.e., efferent or incoming circuits) rather than feedforward (i.e., afferent outgoing neural circuits). As Pribram (1976) pointed out, this idea is also not new. A turn-of-the-century scholar named Ferrier attempted to produce evidence to refute Wundt's view that efferent rather than afferent neural circuits were the basis of perceptions about motor activity. William James (1910) believed that Ferrier demonstrated "conclusively" that one could only be conscious of "a consequence, and not an antecedent, of the movement itself." The content of consciousness is related to the regulation of intent and the consequences of actions, rather than to the process of acting (Pribram, 1980).

Expectancy, Anticipation, and Set

Feedforward activation processes couple relevant action and information collection processes into a coordinated behavior episode. The nature of this coupling can be examined by manipulating it in some way. For example, a person may be instructed to perform certain actions when specific signals occur. The information collection component is active and the person is prepared to act. However, the action is inhibited until the relevant signal is recognized by the person. Then, the inhibition is released and the action performed. The terms *expectancy* and *set* are typically used to describe such circumstances. The nature of expectancies or sets has been examined across a wide range of issues including their normal construction, maintenance, and functioning (McLean & Shulman, 1978); their role in psychopathology (Shakow, 1979); and their involvement in psychotherapy (Goldstein, 1962). McLean and Shulman (1978) concluded that an expectancy "shares the properties of activated memory representations." Learning an expectancy or set requires the involvement of attention, but once it is acquired it can function somewhat automatically, like any habitual pattern. Therefore, an expectancy or set is a behavior pattern activated by an intention and ICA arousal, in which action components are temporarily inhibited.

The utility of expectancies or "mental" sets is that they can improve the speed, efficiency, and accuracy of both information collection and motor behavior. Knowing *where* an event is likely to occur improves accuracy of detecting such events (e.g., Sekuler & Ball, 1977). Similarly, knowing *when* a significant event is likely to occur affects both vigilance and accuracy of detection (e.g., Colquhoun & Baddeley, 1964). Speed of detecting the occurrence of a specified event—that is, reaction time—is increased if warning signals alert the observer that the event is impending, and/or if the observer's history of experience enables him or her to anticipate when it will occur (Niemi & Näätänen, 1981). This occurs whether the relevance of the event is defined in terms of its meaning or in terms of physical attributes (Foster, 1962). Knowing *what* to look for also facilitates responding. For example, if people know in advance the general topic of a prose passage that they will hear, they will remember more of the passage after they hear it than if they are unaware of the topic. The advance knowledge appears to activate some relevant information schema to which the new prose passage can be related. Such a "memory set" appears to facilitate learning and recall (Leahey & Holtzman, 1979).

Expectation of successfully performing an act facilitates actual motor performance (Bandura, 1982a, 1982b). For example, when confronted with a fear-inducing task (i.e., picking up a live boa constrictor), people who were confident that they could do it despite their fear were more likely to complete the task than those who held a doubtful expectation, although both groups reported experiencing about the same amount of fear while attempting to perform the task. Confident subjects tended to keep their attention focused on the task, while doubtful people withdrew from attempting the task earlier if they increased their focus on themselves rather than the task (Carver, Blaney, & Scheier, 1979). Shakow (1979) has proposed that normal people develop many functional expectancies that help make their behavior more efficient and effective by facilitating "attention to the relevant, and inhibition of response to the irrelevant." In schizophrenics, this ability to maintain a "generalized set" breaks down, and the schizophrenic tries to adapt using "segmental sets" which are directed to partial, minor, and sometimes unrelated aspects of the total stimulus-response configuration. As a result, the organization of their behavior episodes is often fragmented and ineffective.

Information collection and action are interrelated aspects of coherent behavior episodes. Sometimes an effort is made to uncouple the information collection function from the motor action function so the former can be studied separately. Strictly speaking, this is not possible since a person always functions as an organized unit. A way of approximating such a decoupling, however, is to ask the subject for an information output that will reveal what has been attended to rather than asking the subject to perform a motor act (i.e., to *say* something rather than *do* something). Strictly speaking, this too is a motor act.

However, such verbal communications are often assumed to more directly reflect the influence of attention on information collection and thought processes rather than attention's influence on the organization of overt programs of action. This leads to consideration of thought processes as a third kind of behavioral organization influenced by attentional functioning.

Remembering and Thinking: Attentional Organization of Thought Processes

Much is assumed in the following discussion of cognitive functioning that will be examined in more detail in Chapters 9 through 12.

Bartlett (1958) proposed that one might assume that thinking is "a complex and high-level kind of skill" that has basic properties in common with "lower" motor skills, such as direction, and timing or organization. However, he also noted that it probably had "its own peculiar characteristics" since any process built upon simpler functions is likely to develop properties of its own. Sherrington (1941) suggested that mind "seems to have arisen in connection with the motor act." Granit (1980) notes that the human mind appears to be "the ultimate designer of programs" which the motor apparatus carries out.

According to Bartlett, thinking is not simply the description of something which is there, but is the use of information about something "to get somewhere else." Moreover, he argued that thinking behavior cannot be accounted for primarily in terms of responses to "an immediate external environment." Getting from "here" to "there" requires a succession of interconnected steps that fill information gaps until some "terminus" is reached or completeness achieved. From any starting point, there is usually more than one succession of steps that can be used to arrive at essentially the same terminus, and the process itself may lead to a somewhat different terminus than originally intended. Similarly, Luria (1976) concluded that cognitive processes are "active and selective forms of reflection of reality," which are "controlled by appropriate motives," and involve "a hierarchical system of self-regulatory acts."

Thinking as a Simulated Behavioral Episode. These descriptions sound very much like descriptions of behavior episodes, except that the actual performance of a motor act is inhibited or omitted, and the information inputs to the behavior episode come primarily from internally stored information rather than from external "current news." Therefore, it may be useful to try to understand thinking (including remembering) as a *simulated behavior episode.* The term simulation means to represent a system by a device that imitates the behavior of the system. In Bartlett's presentation, thinking involves all the functions represented in the basic living systems model. Thinking is targeted toward a terminus (the directive function). It involves organizing an effort in a succession of steps (the control function). It involves monitoring progress towards the terminus and using that feedback to alter the operating plan (the regulatory function). It is influenced by the state of the equipment used (the biological functions). Instead of actually performing the actions and monitoring their consequences, however, they are imagined (i.e., transactional functions and their probable consequences are simulated). It is the inhibition of action, and the substitution of symbolic representations of potential actions and consequences for real ones, that converts an actual behavioral episode to a simulated one; that is, into a thinking episode.

As Bartlett suggested, thinking has properties that behavioral episode action patterns do not have. The behavioral episodes that can be simulated are not limited by the boundaries of the person's actual transactional capabilities or existing environmental conditions. For example, crippled persons can imagine themselves playing football. Fiction writers can imagine unseen or nonexistent worlds. Scientists can imagine entities, events, and relationships they (and others) have never observed, and may never be able to observe. They can then construct or perform simulated behavior episodes using such symbolic representations "as if" they represented real events. In other words, humans can mentally simulate behavior episodes which they have never performed and might never be able to perform. Such simulated behavior episodes have had a powerful effect on the history of human existence, from the world's religion, to formal scientific theories. It has frequently occurred in the history of science that imagining unobserved phenomena (e.g., "germs") helped stimulate the development of observational tools (e.g., microscopes) which converted an imagined event into an observable one, a simulated episode into an actual one.

Simulated behavior episodes, like regular ones, are organized through directed information-attention arousal. Remembering is "...a complex process of active searching" (Luria, 1976). Like all behavior episodes, it is directed by some consequence to be produced. For example, "Who was the third President of the United States?" is a thought that initiates a simulated behavior episode directed toward the consequence of producing the correct answer: "John Adams? No, he was from New England and the third president was from the South." As in regular behavior episodes, the behavior pattern begins and its consequences are monitored to help guide it towards the desired consequence. The informational feedback serves the regulatory function: "Adams wasn't from the South. It has to be someone else." Additional constraints on the behavior pattern are introduced to further control the search. "He was an author of the Declaration of Independence. Benjamin Franklin? No, he was never president. Madison? He was from the South but he didn't author the Declaration of Independence. The Louisiana Purchase was made during the third presidency, and he lived at Monticello, a place which reflects his architectural interests and skills. Thomas Jefferson? That's it! Check the search constraints to be sure. They all fit: Washington, Adams, *Jefferson*, Madison, Monroe." As with all behavior episodes, there is a subjective sense of completeness and accomplishment when the consequence sought is produced. Problem-solving thinking is a more complicated version of the same kind of simulated behavior episode. It starts with a direction, such as "What causes child abuse?" "How can I resolve the conflict with my child?" "Why is she mad at me?" "How can our operating costs be reduced?"[2]

Such initiating thoughts direct attention towards producing a consequence which will answer the question (i.e., complete the behavior episode). That results in selective activation of some neural circuits relevant to the appropriate behavior pattern and the inhibition of others which are irrelevant. Luria (1976) refers to this as the neurodynamic conditions for mnemonic activity. "Strong stimuli" dominate neural organization and produce "strong responses" while "weak" ones are easily inhibited or produce "weak responses." This Pavlov called the "law of strength." Such dominant "systems of excitation" give such psychological processes their necessary selectivity (Luria, 1976).

As in all behavior episodes, the principle of *equifinality* operates. More than one behavior pattern may lead to essentially the same consequence; e.g., more than one line of thinking may lead to the same conclusion. Moreover, once a behavior episode is initiated, it may also produce alterations of intentions and unanticipated consequences. In Luria's (1976) terms this requires "optimal mobility of nervous processes" to switch from "one system of connections to another." Thus, feedforward and feedback processes operate in simulated behavior episodes just as they do in regular behavior episodes. Attentional

---

[2]These examples are presented in terms of conscious verbal symbols. That is not intended to imply that all thought occurs in that form. As is discussed in Chapters 9 through 12 that is probably not the case. Not all thought is conscious, and as Freud's distinction between primary and secondary process thought indicates, not all thought content is verbal and organized according to logical or linguistic rules. The functions involved in a simulated behavior episode are *probably* not restricted to rational, conscious verbal thought processes.

274 INFORMATION-CONSCIOUSNESS-ATTENTION (ICA) AROUSAL

processes influence selective activation of conceptual possibilities through selective influence on information feedback and feedforward.

Simulated behavior episodes can become habitual, just as can regular behavior episodes (e.g., stereotyping). Like any other type of habitual skilled response, once the behavior episode is well under way, any additional information will either be ignored or will produce an attempt to incorporate it into the ongoing episode without disrupting it (Bartlett, 1958). For example, a person may not have been invited to a friend's party and wonder why. If that person habitually thinks of him- or herself as uninteresting and unattractive, they are likely to construct an explanation which supports that habitual self-evaluation. Moreover, they are unlikely to consider alternative possibilities. Habits are efficient, but constraining. Like well-worn ruts on a dirt road, it's hard to get out of them until you get to the end, regardless of what occurs.

Attention Serves One Master at a Time

Three types of behavior episodes towards which attention can be directed have been considered. First, there are episodes focused primarily on information collection, organization, and retention. Second, there are episodes focused primarily on producing some consequence(s) as a result of targeted motor activity. Third, some episodes focus primarily on remembering and thinking. The *content* of each type of episode is determined by the specification of the consequence(s) to be produced (the directive function) and the conditions prevailing at the time; but the *organization* of the behavior pattern is actually accomplished by selective ICA arousal of relevant neural circuits.

ICA arousal can be focused on only one type of behavior episode at a time. Moray (1970) emphasizes that attentional selectivity applies not just to "the control of inflow of information" but applies generally to the "allocation of processing capacity to input, output, transformations and calculations." Moreover, he says, if we attend to "input space" (information-collection episodes), the person's capacity to handle "output space" (action-oriented episodes) suffers, or vice versa. Attention can be focused primarily upon organizing either input (information-collection tasks), throughput (remembering and thinking tasks), or output (implementation of action plans), but not more than one at a time.

For example, have you ever had the experience of trying to read and understand something (an information-collection episode), and found your thoughts wandering off to some unsolved problem or concern (a simulated episode)? Suddenly you realized that you "read" a page or more and did not recall anything you read. Or, in reverse, have you ever been trying to think through an idea or concern and had someone keep interrupting your flow of thought by talking to you? You cannot focus your attention upon organizing your behavior towards an external and an internal information source and consequence simultaneously. It has to be one or the other. If you try to do both, or alternate back and forth between them, neither behavior pattern will be very well organized, efficient, or effective. Similarly, have you ever tried to concentrate your effort on making something or on playing a good game of tennis—an action episode—and found your effort disrupted because some worry or an intrusion by others distracted you? Skilled action results from concentrated effort and attention, and deteriorates when attention "wanders elsewhere."

Attention, Consciousness, and Learning Without Awareness

At the peak of influence of a mechanistic behaviorism perspective, Greenspoon (1955) reported an experiment which seemed to demonstrate the automatic, unconscious effects of reinforcement on verbal behavior. He used the typical therapist's "um-hmm" response to selectively reinforce subject utterances, thereby altering their frequency of occurrence. The fact that the reinforcing effects apparently were independent of the subjects' awareness, and that the behavior was the kind that people assumed to be subject to conscious control created quite a stir. It seemed a clear demonstration that humans were indeed machines whose behavior was shaped by external events; and that their subjective impression that they exerted intentional control over their own behavior was simply an epiphenomenon. It triggered considerable interest in the question of whether there was learning without awareness.

Following Greenspoon's publication, a flow of studies addressing the learning-without-awareness issue produced contradictory results (Salzinger, 1959). However, evidence began to accumulate that, in the operant conditioning paradigm, learning occurred only for those people who were able to verbalize an approximately correct recognition of the conditioning contingencies. Finally, two direct replications of the Greenspoon study (Dean & Hiesinger, 1964; Spielberger & DeNike, 1962) failed to confirm his findings. People who were aware of the contingencies learned and those who were unaware did not. As the research designs became more rigorous and controlled, the results consistently supported the view that awareness was an essential condition for learning to occur (Benish & Grant, 1980; Cohen, 1964; Erickson, 1962; Eriksen & Doroz, 1963; Goodstein et al., 1964; Lanyon, 1964; Mercier & Ladouceur, 1977). The use of more thorough and effective methods of assessing subjects' awareness helped clarify the issue (Chatterjee & Eriksen, 1960; Davis & Hess, 1962; Matarazzo et al., 1960).

Eriksen's (1960) reinterpretation of this stream of research demonstrated that subjects were aware of much of what was going on but were often giving primary attention to factors different from those the experimenter had preselected as important. Displaying little awareness of the experimenter's choice was interpreted to mean that learning without awareness had occurred, when, in fact, awareness of other correlated factors was present. The learning-without-awareness issue was also addressed within a classical conditioning paradigm, which also supported the conclusion that awareness of the relationships between the conditioned and unconditioned stimulus was a necessary but not sufficient condition for human autonomic conditioning to occur (Dawson & Furedy, 1976; Dawson et al., 1979; Perruchet, 1980).

Recently, this issue has been addressed in another way with dual task, dichotic listening, or shadowing research designs. In general, the results support the same conclusion. People remember what they attend to and remember little of what they do not attend to. There is some evidence that under such conditions limited remembering of gross features of the unattended information may occur (Kellogg, 1980). Moreover, when a person is operating under a particular attentional-action set, information relevant to that set, but of which the person appears to be unaware, can influence behavior (Davis, 1964). This is probably analogous to the triggering of habitual behavior patterns by "unnoticed" events. Such an interpretation would be coordinate with the view presented earlier that focal attention monitors information of primary interest, while peripheral attention monitors gross aspects of the rest of the concurrent information field for cues of potentially important occurrences. Moreover, the "scan and focus" patterns of attentional-perceptual processes, both within and between sensory modalities, helps insure that information relevant to the current behavior episode is likely to become represented.

Research results support two general conclusions. If information inputs are to be consciously remembered, they must be "attended to, recognized, and coded" (Hilgard, 1977a). Only those aspects of current information flow "to which attention is directed" enter short-term or working memory. Only those "receiving rehearsal" will have "the processing necessary to establish a basis" for long-term memory or recall (Estes, 1976). The *level* of arousal associated with the experience appears to influence learning. Attention appears to perform a "signal amplification" kind of function for purposes of learning and remembering, analogous to a recording level control on a tape recorder. Too low a setting produces vague or nondetectable storage; too high a setting produces distortion and unclear recordings; optimal levels produce clear, easily reproducible recordings. Intention to learn something (i.e., pre-tuning relevant neural circuits) probably facilitates learning.

Simply noticing information can affect short-term memory. However, once learning has occurred and habitual patterns have been developed, events to which people respond with only peripheral attention (and therefore which they may not be able to later report having noticed) can trigger automated patterns into operation. For example, experienced car drivers often report realizing they have driven several miles and have no recollection of the environment through which they have driven.

"Priming" neural circuits with prior cues influences the probability of related responses occurring when the person is exposed to relevant information below recognition levels (Krasner & Ulmann, 1963; Spence & Holland, 1962). While the neurophysiology of learning is still a largely unsolved puzzle, it is reasonably clear that the limbic system, and particularly the hippocampus, plays an important role (Wickelgren, 1979). For example, bilateral resection of the hippocampus disrupts short-term memory but does not affect long-term memory (Luria, 1976). The hippocampus appears to be a key bridge between the neocortex and other limbic structures (Routtenberg, 1968; Vanderwolf & Robinson, 1981). Since the RAS and the limbic system appear to be the primary neural structures for the arousal functions, there appears to be a neurological basis for arousal processes to be influential in learning.

The psychoanalytic notion of attention cathexis may be another way of talking about attention's amplification function. Attention is not the only factor influencing learning. As Miller suggested in 1942, an experience's potential future utility, or the "economic utility principle," is another factor (e.g., George, 1980). Such other factors are considered in later chapters.

If attention and awareness are necessary conditions for learning, then what will be learned will be a function of whichever one of the three types of behavior episodes described earlier is the focus of attention. Different types of episodes probably involve somewhat different types of neural circuits (Luria, 1976). Episodes focused on information collection, organization, and retention will increase information stores but not the instrumental or transactional behavior repertoire. Episodes focused on behaviorally influencing the environment will produce learning which elaborates one's transactional behavior repertoire. Episodes focused on remembering and thinking will produce reorganization and transformation of existing information stores.

However, it should be reemphasized that not everything learned is accessible to consciousness. Current conditions and one's current intentions activate a behavior episode schemata which organizes and guides functioning in that specific episode. Only portions of that schemata are available to consciousness but through those portions the entire schemata may be influenced because it functions as a unit. An analogy may help understand this idea. Imagine shining a flashlight on the surface of a pond on a dark night. Throw a stone into the center of the circle of light. A cascade of ripples will move outward from the point of impact. When the ripples reach the edge of the circle of light, they will disappear from sight. However, they continue to affect the water surface in the darkness beyond. Similarly a conscious thought can trigger feedforward influences that organize aspects of the behavior pattern outside awareness.

As Tomkins (1961) proposed, attentional and emotional arousal processes appear to perform an amplification—attenuation function. Excessive amplification (or arousal) can produce distortions in the information and therefore in its use. It appears that emotional arousal can augment information-attention arousal in the amplification and storage of information. Excessive emotional arousal may produce so much augmentation of neural excitation that finely coordinated behavior patterns cannot be maintained.

SUMMARY

ICA arousal organizes selective perception, thought, and action. There are different levels of ICA arousal ranging from deep sleep through base rate arousal to concentrated attention. The contents of consciousness represent information in feedback circuits which results from perception or cognition; such awareness is necessary for learning to occur. Attention represents the selective channeling of ICA arousal, guided by properties of events and intentions. Chapter 8 examines information monitoring or perceptual processes as the starting point for understanding the basis for information self-construction.

How such cognitive representations come into existence and how they function are examined in detail in Chapters 9 through 12, so those issues are not considered here. For the time being, the reader is asked to accept their existence and role.

These examples are presented in terms of conscious verbal symbols. That is not intended to imply that all thought occurs in that form. As is discussed in Chapters 9 through 12 that is probably not the case. Not all thought is conscious, and as Freud's distinction between primary and secondary process thought indicates, not all thought content is verbal and organized according to logical or linguistic rules. The functions involved in a simulated behavior episode are *probably* not restricted to rational, conscious verbal thought processes.

8

Information Transactions and Perception

INTRODUCTION

Information exchanges between people and their environments provide the basis for behavioral self-construction and self-organization, just as material and energy transactions provide the basis for biological self-construction and self-organization. Information makes coordination of behavior-environment transactions possible. This coordination is accomplished through the use of information which, like food, is collected in many forms but, like food, must be transformed and combined into other forms to be useful for behavioral self-organization and self-construction.

It is useful to subdivide discussion of human information exchanges with their environments into information collection and information conveying functions. *Perception* will be discussed in this chapter, and information conveying, or communication, will be discussed in a later chapter. Information transactions function to enable humans to tolerate, create, and manage complexity and variability, and to protect them from the unfamiliar or from uncertainty (DeLong, 1972).

THE NATURE OF INFORMATION AND HUMAN INFORMATIONAL CAPABILITIES

The concepts of information and informational processes are critical for understanding living systems (J. Miller, 1978). What is information? A description or measure of an entity's organization is a description or measure of the pattern of relationships or conditionalities among its components. That is what is meant by information. Information is not a physical entity, therefore, but represents the properties termed *organization* or *pattern*. The more complex the pattern, the more information it contains. To illustrate this, a measure of information quantity (organization) was discovered to be the converse of a measure of entropy (disorganization) (e.g., Ashby, 1962; Weiner, 1948). The explosive growth of communication technologies and servomechanisms during this century led to the first efforts to rigorously deal with information in theoretical and mathematical terms (e.g., Shannon, 1948). Information technologies such as libraries, media, and computers, and energy, such as food and fuel, are the twin pillars of modern societies.

Zeman (1962; as translated in J. Miller, 1978) relates information to basic physical concepts, as follows:

> If mass is the measure of the effects of gravitation, and of the force of inertia, and energy the measure of movement, information is in the quantitative sense the measure of the organization of the material object.... Matter, space, time, movement, and organization are in mutual connection. (p. 42)

It follows that the process of producing and maintaining increasingly complex organizations of material entities (e.g., of person-environment relations) involves information, as well as materials and energy. Indeed, the very word *process* means change in condition over time. Monitoring and using information about change, therefore, becomes essential for the existence, development, and functioning of living systems.

To accomplish continual steady state maintenance and change, living systems have evolved a variety of structures and functional arrangements for collecting, transforming, constructing, using, and sending out information in spatial-temporal patterns. Since information represents the *organization of phenomena*, it follows that biological structures specialized to collect and use information must be sensitive to the spatial and sequential-temporal organizational properties of physical stimulation rather than just to their elements. Patterned sensation and perception must be the foundation of information collection.

Markers and Messages

The physical nature of the events stimulating human senses (e.g., light waves, chemical compounds) does not provide information, but serves as the *carrier for the information*, sometimes called the *marker*. For example, the carrier or marker that delivers a spoken message to one's telephone receiver is electricity. However, the message or information is contained in the *pattern* of electrical impulses, not in the electricity itself. Therefore, the same information can be delivered with more than one type of marker. For example, the message "Good luck" can be coded into a pattern of air pressure for hearing, onto a pattern of ink on a page for reading, or onto a pattern of ridges or holes on paper for reading with touch. The same message can be initiated on one marker (e.g., air pressure waves), converted onto another marker for transmission (e.g., electrical pulses), and onto another marker for reception (e.g., a pattern on an oscilloscope). *The information remains the same,* because although the physical nature of the marker changes, the *organizational properties are invariant.*

Engineers call mechanisms that convert information from one marker system to another *transducers.* Many types may be found in living systems (J. Miller, 1978). Other organisms have developed some receptor and transducer organs sensitive to physical markers that are different from humans (e.g., magnetic fields in pigeons, electrical fields in torpedo fish). To broaden their information-collecting capabilities, humans have invented structures that can collect information on markers which the human cannot innately sense (e.g., radar) and transduce it onto a marker humans can sense (e.g., the visual image on a radar screen).

This capability to code the same information on different markers is significant for human information transactions in two ways. First, it means that different sensory modalities may substitute for one another in collecting information (e.g., braille reading by touch can substitute for visual reading), and different motor patterns may substitute for one another in delivering information (e.g., writing can substitute for speaking). Second, neurons convert all information collected on different markers (e.g., light, sound) to the same kind of bioelectrical and biochemical markers. Information coded onto one kind of marker is easier to compare and integrate than information coded onto different markers, even though the codes may be different. For example, it is easier to understand and integrate several messages (e.g., some written, some spoken) in the same language than if each message is in a different language. Thus, human sensory structures are both information collectors and transducers.

However, even though neurons carry information on the same kinds of markers, the information may be represented in different codes by organizing the marker differently. J. Miller (1978) calls structures that perform this function "decoders" on the input side and "encoders" on the output side, and describes various kinds of coding possibilities. Moreover, each sensory organ codes multiple variables (i.e., kinds and attributes of events), and multiple parameters. Such transducer and decoder-coder structures exist throughout the nervous system. This marker-coding distinction is very important for understanding the biological-behavioral characteristics of human information transactions. For example, different patterns of stimulus coding can be transduced into a similar pattern of sensoriperceptual coding, e.g., the perception of yellow can result from different patterns of light waves (Hochberg, 1968).

Information and Variability. Defining information as pattern or organization has another important implication. The more complex the organization of phenomena, that is, the more different components and relationships there are, the greater the amount of information available. Organization may be temporal or sequential as well as spatial, and the complexity of sequential organization is manifest in the changes or variability of components and relationships. Therefore, although sense organs may be physically affected by a marker which does not vary, there is little information in invariant stimulation. For example, place a person inside a completely white sphere and their eyes would be stimulated, but there would be little information. It is the differences or *variability* in the material marker stimulating the sense organ that provides information.

Therefore, human information mechanisms (e.g., sense organs, neurons, the brain) had to evolve to detect and deal with differences, or changes within and around them; that is, with variability. For example, people automatically come to cease noticing unvarying or repetitive (i.e., uninformative) stimulation through a process called *habituation.* Through their own actions people also produce variability in the stimulation of their sense organs; they seek or construct information. For example, the human eye is continually doing a small dance (called *saccadic eye movements)* which produces variability in visual stimulation, and without which the visual image fades, e.g., Ditchburn & Ginsberg, 1952). Moreover, the basic nature of some markers is a kind of "vibrating" or intrinsically variable material, such as light.

If something never changes, if it is always exactly the same, then it is perfectly predictable and easily adapted to; and complex nervous systems would not then be necessary. But humans evolved and exist in highly variable environments and create additional variability through their own actions. Therefore, the human sensory and neural structures evolved as *variability* or *uncertainty analyzers,* identifying and abstracting consistencies and differences in spatial-temporal patterns of variability in kinds and attributes of events; and as *variability* or *uncertainty controllers* to organize people's functioning to produce patterns of consistency and variability within themselves and in their environmental relationships.

There is increasing evidence that human perceptual systems are tuned especially "to abstracting information from stimulus change over time" (Johansson et al., 1980). Moreover, the evolution of our information-collecting capabilities was selective. In physics, quantum mechanics is used to represent a world "far beyond our common experience" of the everyday world (Rohrlich, 1983). The world our senses reveal directly to us is only a portion of the total reality of our universe. The rest we can only imagine through our creative thought; we can then look for evidence of those imagined worlds on markers our senses can detect. For example, the human concepts of time and space rest upon the experiencing of events as occurring sequentially. Perhaps, just as our visual apparatus is sensitive to only some wavelengths of light, so too we may experience only a limited portion of a multidimensional space and time (Nesselroade, 1983).

It is exceedingly difficult to create a nonvariable environment for humans because of their self-stimulating capabilities, as researchers on stimulus deprivation and political practitioners of "brainwashing" have discovered. An environment of continuous severely limited variability (i.e., informational impoverishment) is restrictive or disruptive of behavioral organization and development; it attenuates relevant neural development (e.g., Brown, 1973; R. Lerner, 1984), and is psychologically distressing if prolonged (e.g., Fisk & Maddi, 1961). A temporary reduction of information, such as during quiet rest, is essential and often pleasurable, but prolonged monotony becomes dissatisfying or boring. Rapaport (1958) argued that stable behavior patterns require a regular diet of "stimulus nutriment." Humans must be nourished with information as well as food if they are to survive and flourish both structurally and functionally.

PERCEPTION

Sensory or information-collecting structures, then, evolved to select — from the elaborate, variable flow of information that continually bathes a person — that portion most relevant to the person's current needs and intentions. The word *select* must be emphasized. It would be impossible to deal simultaneously with all the different kinds of variability to which a person is continually exposed. Therefore, human perceptual processes evolved not only for information collection, but also for information organization and reduction through a selectivity that involves not only "editing" but also some "thematic organization" processes.

How humans come to know the nature of their environment has fascinated philosophers for centuries (Boring, 1929), and three basic ideas have long histories (Urban, 1983).

Representationism (proposed at least as long ago as Plato) maintains that the world and our perceptions of it are different but related. The human mind constructs ideas of what the world is like through contacts with the world by way of the senses. *Realism,* or *presentationism* (illustrated by John Locke's ideas), assumes that objects can directly affect other objects, including humans. Therefore, humans perceive objects directly as they exist. *Phenomenalists* (e.g., David Hume) believe that all that humans can know is sense experience itself. Reality is whatever the perceiver construes it to be.

The following summary of two currently influential approaches illustrates how different basic assumptions have led perceptual theorists and researchers in different directions. The phenomenal and representationism views are often mixed together in what is sometimes termed cue theories (Haber, 1978). Because that combined view has been dominant for a century, it will be called the *traditional* view. Realism is currently manifest in perceptual theory and research based upon the *ecological* approach.

The Traditional View of Perception

The basic question with which perceptual theorists have struggled is that of the relationship between the physical stimulation of sense organs and the psychological experience called *perception* (Johansson et al., 1980).

The preferred answer since the 1800s was built upon mechanistic and associationistic assumptions. For example, Titchener (1913) asserted that sensations were "of course" the basic elements from which perceptions and other "complicated phases of the mind" were constructed. It followed that the study of perception should involve the study of the origin and nature of sensations and the way the brain combined them into perceptions. Helmholtz (1925) brought this view to full flower in the study of vision.

Hockberg (1974) summarized the essence of this associationistic view. Humans do not directly perceive events. Rather they construct their perceptions from discrete physical sensations triggered by physical stimuli related to the object of perception (e.g., by rods and cones in the eye). These elementary sensations are transmitted to the brain where they are subject to some kind(s) of cognitive processing through which they are integrated with one another and with memories to produce a conscious perception (i.e., idea) of the object and its meaning. The idea of "computations" used in information processing theories is an attempt to represent combinatorial rules and processes guiding perceptual and cognitive construction. Things are not *directly* perceived; humans *construct* representations of things by combining current sensations and past experiences. Thus, perception is an information processing act of cognition.

Most of the perceptual research guided by this view has tried to explain how the assumed processes worked, rather than to examine the validity of the basic assumptions. For example, because perceptions are constructed, they may be accurate or inaccurate. Therefore, some research sought to identify variables that influenced the construction of accurate perceptions or misperceptions. In a ten-volume Handbook of Perception (Carterette & Friedman, 1973 to 1978), much though not all of the work summarized was guided primarily by this traditional view.

The Ecological View of Perception

There were always alternatives to that traditional view. For example, gestalt psychologists (Koffka, 1935; Kohler, 1964) argued that configurational factors were fundamental to perception, and that the meaning or value of a thing is perceived as immediately as other aspects (e.g., an apple says "eat me").

The current major challenger to the traditional view is called ecological perception, formulated primarily by Gibson (1950, 1966, 1979) who was heavily influenced by Koffka (Reed & Jones, 1982). It has been criticized and the traditional view defended (e.g., Fodor & Pylyshyn, 1981); defended and the assumptions and explanations of the "establishment" position criticized (Turvey, Shaw, Reed, & Mace, 1981); and elaborated (Michaels & Carello, 1981).

It starts with different assumptions. The function of perception is to make organisms' everyday behavior practical and successful. Therefore, the proper "objects" of perceiving are the same as those of activity. Human sensoriperceptual systems evolved to match humans' terrestrial environmental niche, the way a key fits its lock. Perceptual capabilities evolved to provide information not about the environment, but about the environment-in-relationship-to-the-person. Gibson invented the term *affordances* as a label for such perceptions (i.e., the environment plus the behavioral possibilities it affords the person).

Gibson argues that most of the research support for the traditional view was built upon data obtained from an immobile perceiver in a static environment. Therefore, those research findings—which represent a very narrow portion of the more general case of an active perceiver in a dynamic, continually varying environment—are largely irrelevant for understanding natural perceptual functioning. Moreover, the environment is organized hierarchically in natural "nested sets" of objects and events, providing active perceivers with options for the focus of their perceptual activity; for example, you may look at a person, or at that person's eyes (Gibson, 1979).

Gibsonians propose that perceptions are direct, conscious manifestations of the information collected by the sense organs, rather than inferences or representations cognitively constructed by the person from sensory elements. The neural inputs from sensory organs are already organized and do not have to have organization imposed upon them by the brain.

In the tradition of Brentano's 19th-century *act psychology*, perception is considered an intentional activity rather than a reaction to stimulation. Selective perception results from an active seeking for information and a direct awareness of the affordances of the environment. Perception is related to, but is not the same as, cognition.

A Merger is Needed

The dialectic triggered by the competition of these alternate views appears to be producing progressive movement towards a view which preserves some basic ideas of each while modifying others (Carterette & Friedman, 1978; Cutting, 1981; Haber, 1978; Johansson, von Hofsten, & Jansson, 1980; Noble, 1981; Weintraub, 1975). A movement towards merger is perhaps best represented by a shift towards research designs focusing on perceptual activity in dynamic and more natural settings, termed *event* perception (Johansson et al., 1980).

Perceptual and cognitive processes do appear to be different, though related. *Information pickup* differs from *information processing*. Ecologists are demonstrating the importance of clearly differentiating between the physical stimulus or carrier and the invariant properties in the organization of the stimulus flow. Inconsistency about that distinction has been one source of confusion. The evolutionary value of perception is that it provides immediate, accurate information about current, potentially behaviorally relevant circumstances.

However, there may be a tendency for perceptual ecologists to throw the baby out with the bathwater. While perception and cognition may be different processes, they are mutually influential. Feedback processes, the source of perceptions, are a function not only of what is happening "out there" but also of the current state of the rest of the system, as "pretuned" through feedforward processes for actively selective behavior to serve the individual's current concerns. What follows attempts a merger of the traditional and ecological streams of ideas in a form appropriate to a living systems perspective.

The Relationship Between Perception and Cognition. The term *perception* has been used with different meanings, resulting in confusion and miscommunication. In the traditional view, perceptions are considered to be ideas about the world manufactured by mental processes; that is, perception is "indirect." That position confuses perceptions with cognitions and therefore with the *meaning* of experiences. An alternate definition appears sounder in a living systems framework. Perceptions are direct, conscious, accurate manifestations of information contained in the spatial-temporal pattern of sense organ stimulation; in other words, as coded onto some marker. Perception is "direct." By selectively directing attention to certain aspects of an information array, one may perceive subsets of information some of which have historically been labeled *sensory qualities* such as brightness and color. However, such discriminable components of percepts are no more basic than any other percept. The world exists in nested sets of phenomena, and one may perceive information at different levels in such hierarchies.

Thus, perceptions are conscious representations of a particular spatial-temporal instance of a phenomenon. They are always "here and now." But cognitive capabilities enable humans to transform perceptions into conceptions, and through their use to transcend the immediate spatial-temporal moment with their behavior. Conceptions are generalized informational forms, or ideas, abstracted or constructed from the redundant (or invariant) aspects of *sets* of perceptions. Shepard (1984) relates an ecological view of perception to concept formation and thought processes. Through concept formation, the redundant aspects of perceptions can be used in a predictive or anticipatory fashion to make behavior more effective.[1]

For example, if one perceived a situation that was completely new, one could only act on the basis of the perceived information. However, human habitats are complex and variable, and identical perceptions

---

[1]The rationale for scientific methods as an approach to knowledge development rests upon distinctions between percepts and concepts. In science, the ultimate test of the soundness of ideas (concepts) rests upon their relationships to observations (percepts). Perception represents a noninferential source of evidence for the formulation and testing of human beliefs (Turvey et al., 1981). Careful observations (i.e., perceptions) are "facts." Using sets of perceptions and careful reasoning, it is possible to construct generalized representation about some aspect of the universe or oneself. That is inductive science. Starting with a generalized idea (concept) about the nature of some phenomena, it is possible to predict what one should observe (perceive) in an appropriate specific instance. If the actual observations coincide with the prediction, then the generalized explanation gains a degree of credibility. That is deductive science. Notice that both inductive and deductive science start with the assumption that perceptions of specific instances provide direct, accurate information about things and events. Both make a careful distinction between observation (perception) and inference (conception).

seldom reoccur. By comparing a current perception with conceptual representations of similar past perceptions, one can convert the unfamiliar to the familiar. One can attribute to a particular perception the properties of the conceptual representation to which it is recognized as being similar. Such attributions add meaning to perceptions. One can then behave both in terms of both *perceived* and *conceived meaning*. This distinction makes it clear that there are no "perceptual illusions," but only conceptual ones. For example, if one immerses part of a straight stick in water it will be accurately perceived as a bent stick because that is the information conveyed from the reflected light through the eyes to the brain. To conclude that the stick was really crooked would be an interpretive or conceptual error (Turvey et al., 1981).

Viewed this way, both the ecological and traditional perceptual theorists are partly right. Perception is always direct, and may sometimes contain sufficient information to adequately guide behavior, as the ecologists propose. However, conceptual constructions from past experience combine with perception's "current news" to construct meanings that more effectively guide behavior, as the traditionalists propose. Moreover, conceptions can be used to imagine future possibilities which guide selective perceptual behavior; that is, to specify what the viewer should look for or try to perceive that would be relevant to current concerns. *Conceptions* (cognitions) are a source of *feedforward processes* while *perceptions* represent *feedback processes*.

By carefully distinguishing between perception and cognition, some of the apparent contradictions between the traditional and ecological views can be resolved. Therefore, to avoid miscommunication here, definitions of several key terms are provided.

> Perception: a direct, conscious apprehension of a specific current instance of a particular object or event, its context, and its relationship to the perceiver, resulting from the interaction of sense organs with material-energy markers carrying information which represents the properties of the phenomena observed.[2]

---

[2]These definitions are anchored here to perceptions. So defined, they might be referred to as first-order abstractions. Through cognitive processes, higher-order abstractions can be formed which represent sets of first order concepts and propositions. The cognitive processes involved in concept and proposition formation, recognition, and meaning attribution may be the same whether they are applied to constructing ideas from sets of perceptions or from sets of other ideas. The section on governing functions explores this idea more fully.

Concept: an abstract idea or belief constructed from a set of
            perceptions that represents some shared or invari-
            ant properties of the members of the set.

Proposi-   an abstract idea representing some redundant or
tion: invariant functional relationship between con-
            cepts. It is constructed from a set of perceptions of
            a kind of functional relationship repetitively oc-
            curring between instances of concepts.

Recognize: to be aware of a current perception being an
            instance of a previously formed concept, proposi-
            tion, or combination thereof.

Meaning: an interpretation or inference that attributes to a
            perception properties of the concept and/or prop-
            ositional classes of which the perception is recog-
            nized as an instance.[3]

The Integration of Perception, Conception, and Action. A continual flow
of selective material-energy transactions with the environment is essential for the existence, functioning, and development of living systems. In
limited variability environments, the essential transactions can be mechanically automated. For example, a plant in fertile soil, regularly
exposed to appropriate amounts of sun and moisture, can live and grow
without benefit of elaborate information-collecting capabilities. However, in complex, highly variable, and relatively unpredictable environmental niches, adaptive actions pose a much more difficult problem.
Under those circumstances, the ability to collect (perceive), organize,
construct and retain (conceive), and use information to guide environmental transactions would be essential for survival, growth, and reproduction.

Human sensory-perceptual capabilities evolved to provide information at the level of practical action (e.g., spatial mobility, feeding,
reproducing) under conditions called by Gibson the *terrestrial environment* (1966). The terrestrial environment is physically structured and

---

[3]These definitional distinctions have great practical significance. For example, it is
commonplace in counseling and psychotherapy for clients to talk about events in their
lives in conceptual rather than perceptual terms. Skillful counselors and therapists often
help clients learn to distinguish between and compare their perceptions of *what actually
happened* and their *interpretations* of such perceptions. Such distinctions help clients alter
faulty habits of thinking, feeling, and acting by contrasting the "facts" of perception with
the potentially faulty attributed meanings resulting from cognitive interpretations. Unfortunately, many professionals are conceptually careless about these distinctions and refer to
client conceptualizations as perceptions; saying, for example, a client *perceived* herself as
inadequate.

organized. It is composed of objects, materials, and energy forms with different properties (e.g., color, texture, chemical composition). Its components exist in configurations of spatial relationships. Moreover, it is dynamically organized. Some objects move or are movable and some are stable. The component objects, materials, and energy forms are related in sequential patterns of covariation and mutual influence. As a result, the nature of the environmental components and their spatial configurations may vary or change from one time to another. Sequential (time-related) changes occur in organized patterns. Therefore, effective action requires dealing with variable spatial-temporal configurations of different kinds of objects, materials, and energy forms, or what Gibson (1979) calls *environmental layouts.* Surrounding the terrestrial surface is a gaseous atmosphere through which objects, materials, and energy forms can readily move. The environment is organized in nested hierarchies. Any object or event can be considered to be composed of parts which are also composed of parts. Or, any object or event may be considered a part of a larger whole. Human sensoriperceptual capabilities evolved to collect information under such conditions.

This terrestrial environment provides two basic possible methods for information collection by humans. The first is by physical contact with solid, liquid, or gaseous surfaces or substances (e.g., touch, pain). The second is by physical contact with some material-energy form carried to them by the gaseous atmosphere in which they are immersed (e.g., sounds, odors). Humans evolved sensory-perceptual capabilities to use both "contact" senses and "distance" receptors. Contact senses provide information about the "here and now." Distance receptors provide information about future-contact possibilities. The ability to collect and use future-oriented information frees humans from the immediacy of their contact environments and therefore has special adaptive value.

Stimulus Flow Fields and Sensory-Perceptual Dynamics

The environment in which a person is embedded is continuous, highly organized, and variable both in its own properties and organization and in relationship to the person. Therefore, a person is continuously impacted by a complex, variable flow of physical stimulation from the current environment carrying multiple kinds of information. Moreover, through their intentional actions people selectively influence the nature and rate of the stimulus-information flow impinging upon them.

The metaphor of the eye as a camera and the retinal image as a static snapshot is unsound for dealing with stimulus (informational) flow fields, and has misguided many efforts to understand perception (Braunstein, 1976). The shift from an image model to a flow model

(Johansson et al., 1980) eliminates some issues and raises others. Humans' perceptual capabilities surely evolved to be adaptive in dealing with information flows rather than with static scenes. Perception of static images must be considered a special case of the more general form of dynamic perception (Haber, 1978).

Invariance Across Transformations. The alternative to the "snapshot" image model is to assume that if the environmental information flow is continuous, the perceptual activity related to that flow must also be continuous. But how can the stability in the world be perceived if the stimulus information flow is continually changing? If environmental stability is to be directly perceived through a flow model, there would have to be invariant information inherent in the variable flow.

Braunstein (1976), Gibson (1979), Johansson (1978), and others have demonstrated that such invariant information is manifest in the flow of visual information on the retina through a process called *perspective transformation.* Shaw, McIntyre, and Mace (1974) have related the concept of invariance to the concept of symmetry which has played an important explanatory role in the natural sciences, and they have demonstrated its utility. An entity is symmetrical if there is something that can be done to it so that after it is done the entity remains the same as before. Such changes are sometimes referred to as transformations. For example, the information in the statement "I love you" can be coded onto writing movements, transformed into a written statement on a valentine, and transformed again into a visual perception when read. The information is invariant through all transformations. A form of mathematics called *group theory* has been used to describe such invariant or symmetrical properties (Cassirer, 1944).

Taking Snapshots vs. Watching Movies vs. Participating. If one could stop the flow and look at a cross-sectional "slice" or "snapshot" of an instant in time, it would appear as an organization of motionless, unchanging components as they appear from a stationary observational vantage point. For example, a table top would seldom appear to be a rectangle in static observation. However, the flow itself has characteristics of organization that contains useful information (like a movie rather than a snapshot). It is the dynamic information about change trajectories that is often most important for adaptive behavior. Things that are static or unchanging are perfectly predictable, and therefore are easy to deal with. Many types of environmental changes are possible (e.g., components coming into and out of existence in one's current perceptions). Since people are also a component in the perceptual process in the form of participant observers, changes in their attributes that can influence perception are also occurring. Variables like duration and rate of flow (or change) themselves have properties of stability and variability (Gibson, 1966, 1979; Turvey et al., 1981; Cutting, 1981).

Events and Perception of Invariants. However, perceptual-motor functioning occurs in "real time," or in the present. Therefore, people's actual perceptual-motor behavior cannot be organized in terms of a continuous, unending flow of information. It has to be subdivided into "chunks" that are behaviorally useful and have some internal coherence. In perceptual theory and research, those "chunks" are called events and perception of them is called *event perception* (Johansson et al., 1980). Cutting (1981) argues that such events are the basic unit of perception. The terms event and experience are two sides of the same coin. *Event* refers to the phenomena viewed from the point of view of the environment (i.e., the objective observer), and *experience* to the same phenomena from the perceiver's point of view (i.e., the subjective observer) (Shaw et al., 1974).

It becomes necessary, then, to define events, and a variety of suggestions have been made (Cutting, 1981; Gibson, 1979, 1982; Heider, 1959; Johansson et al., 1980). Webster defines an event as that which occupies a restricted portion of four-dimensional space-time. Gibson (1979) suggests the general criterion that events have "a beginning and an end," as a step towards identifying such "restricted portions." Cutting (1981) proposes that the variable surface organization of events manifests an underlying organization (i.e., a "deep structure") containing variant and invariant components. It is the underlying invariant components that give a restricted portion of the spatial-temporal flow an internal coherence, that defines it as an event. Moreover, it is changes in some of those invariant components that identify the "beginning" and "end" of an event, i.e., the flow transition from one pattern of organization to a somewhat different one.

Cutting (1981) proposes two kinds of invariants: topographic and dynamic. *Topographic invariants* are the physical objects and their spatial organization that remain essentially the same during the event. An example is the horizon ratio for perceptually determining the size of terrestrial objects. The relative ratios of an object's top, bottom, and horizon line scaled to the height of the observer give accurate information about the height of any object. Relative position of an object in a layout is another topographic invariant. *Dynamic invariants* are regularities in the pattern of change that occurs during the event. For example, a golfer watches the line of flight of his ball to estimate where it will land. The location of the ball is continuously changing, but its trajectory displays invariance.

All human perceptual systems probably evolved for monitoring a continuous information flow to detect both topographical and dynamic invariants (Horridge, 1978).

Event Perception and Behavior Episodes. However, if the objective is to understand people's behavior-environment transactions, then variant and invariant properties of a person and of her/his environment must be considered together in defining an event. Over 25 years ago, a "new look" began in perception with recognition that what people perceive is a function of their dynamic state, or, in other words, their current preparation for perception and action (Bruner, 1957; Neisser, 1967). What is perceived at any moment results from the interaction of the pattern of stimulation-information at the sensory receptors and the "expectancies," "states of motivation," and "attention" of the perceiver (Cooper & Shepard, 1978). This does not contradict the notion of direct perception. It only modifies it to say that (a) what people perceive, out of all that is presently available to perceive, is what they pay attention to; (b) they typically pay attention to what they are looking for; and (c) what they are looking for is a function of what they are trying to do and what they expect to happen. Human perception is usually intentional perception rather than reactive or stimulus-controlled perception.

Stated in living systems terms, the governing functions "tune" sensory-perceptual-motor functions, through feedforward processes, to focus on information and actions relevant to the current intentions and action plans of the person. Cognitive activity significantly influences what is perceived and how that information will be used, but it does not construct the perceptions. Stimulus conditions (e.g., sudden, unexpected events) can influence the perceptual focus, but feedforward from the governing functions is increasingly the dominant influence as humans mature. It should now be apparent that event perception is an aspect of a behavior episode, which was described in Chapter 5 as the basic unit of analysis for understanding humans' behavior in their natural contexts. As Cutting (1981) put it, events are not only the units of perception but they are "our very units of existence."

Perception, Time, and Causality. Events occur in nested sets. They may be considered as components of larger events, and as composed of subevents. Humans perceive attributes of the flow of events, such as succession, duration, and rhythm, in addition to perceiving their content. And this capability is probably inborn since it appears very early in life. Perceptions of such flow characteristics provide the basis for humans' conception of time (Fraisse, 1978, 1984).

Perception of succession or sequence can be distinguished from perception of simultaneous occurrences. For both, there must be an observable difference between two or more events. However, to perceive sequence, there must be a noticeable transition of state, spatial location, or appearance and disappearance of events. Such transitions are represented in alternating periods of stability (i.e., event duration) and change (i.e., transition duration). Perception of the flow properties of duration and transition yield the sense of time passing as well as of movement. Perception of one event influencing a succeeding event provides the basis for the human concept of causality. Perception of a repetitive pattern of event durations and transitions is what is meant by a rhythm (e.g., the swinging pendulum; the beat in music). Perception of rhythms and rhythmic actions appear to be coupled in humans.

All human perception is anchored to the *observational vantage point of a perceiver*. Therefore, all information will be perceived in a *self-referent form* (e.g., near or far; in front or behind). Self-referent perceptions simultaneously provide information about the perceiver and the perceived environment. For example, touching an object simultaneously provides information about the surface touched and about the act of touching. Individuals are mobile and manipulative. Therefore, by their own actions they can influence their environment and themselves in perceptible ways. This provides the basis for perceptions of themselves as "causes" or as being influenced by other events.

Perceptual Codes. The form or code in which perceptual information is cognitively represented or stored has been an issue of continuing debate (Haber, 1978). Paivio (1978) describes four views: (a) verbal coding; (b) imagistic coding by perceptual modality; (c) dual coding, which combines imagistic and verbal coding; and (d) common coding which proposes that all information is transformed into a single, higher order code at the cognitive representational level. Both verbal and imagistic coding appear to occur. For example, hallucinations have been reported representing most sensory modalities. Dreams are primarily imagistic. Some information supports the dual and common coding views (Paivio, 1978). Since at a neurological level all information is coded on the same kind of neuronal marker, a physical basis exists for a common code.

An *hierarchical view of coding* may be useful. Imagistic coding related to each modality and kind of marker (e.g., sights, odors, sounds) probably occurs. However, cognitive processes appear to involve higher order abstractions derived from imagistic perceptions. Therefore, thinking may utilize some common informational code that can represent and combine modality specific imagistic codes. It is possible that abstract thought occurs in both verbal and nonverbal codes, as suggested by anecdotal evidence of creative thinking.

In summary, information collection in humans is specialized in terms of different kinds of sense organs sensitive to different markers which code different kinds of information. Each sensory-perceptual modality can provide some information unique to itself and some information redundant of that provided by other modalities. Information is perceived in terms of specialized modalities, and the modalities can be differentially tuned by cognitive processes for selectively monitoring information to serve current concerns and actions. In natural settings, the specialized information from different modalities is correlated and provides an integrated view of the current situation.

Sense Organs as Dynamic Information Collectors

Until relatively recently, theorizing about sensory structures has been dominated by the classical machine model of humans. Sense organs were assumed to be passive receptors that passed along to the brain each element of stimulation where it was organized to guide selective responding (Morgan & Stellar, 1950). This view is "no longer tenable" (Leibowitz & Harvey, 1973). The passive, mechanical receiver view is being replaced by a more dynamic one, emphasizing perceptual activity as a form of "intentional search for useful information" resulting in "a systematic change in the stimulus flow" (Johansson et al., 1980).

Sensory receptors appear to combine "selective reporting," "editing," and perhaps even some "creative writing." Some information is ignored, some discarded, and some progressively reorganized, beginning with the receptors and proceeding through the neural pathways to the brain. Information inputs are organized both by amplifying (enhancing) some signals and by adapting to (diminishing) other signals (Koshland, Goldbeter, & Stock, 1982). This occurs both within and among neurons. Low levels of stimulation which may interfere with effective information collection must be diminished; currently irrelevant information must be filtered out.

There are two interacting forms of amplification and several ways of accomplishing each. *Magnitude amplification* takes a weak signal (e.g., the signal your radio antenna picks up) and enhances it into a stronger signal (e.g., as you do when you turn up the volume on your radio). Notice that this process amplifies everything in the signal, including the "static." The dim figure you see in the shadows as you walk down a lonely street at dusk, or a faint sound in the dark, illustrate weak signals that a person might amplify in the attempt to recognize them and to discern their significance. *Sensitivity amplification* selectively amplifies changes in the intensity of one stimulus pattern in the context of a much larger pattern of stimulation. The level of amplification must be controlled, however, because amplification and improvements in performance are not linearly related. A third process, *adaptation*, helps make this possible. It functions to desensitize the sensing apparatus to the background stimuli.

These three processes function cooperatively to produce exquisitely sensitive "selective tuning" possibilities. In engineering terms, the ratio of *signal* (the information of current concern) to *noise* (the irrelevant and/or random information) is a way of representing the clarity of information. Amplifying the relevant information (i.e., increasing the signal) and filtering out or attenuating the irrelevant information (i.e., decreasing the noise) selectively organizes information in whatever ways are most useful to the person at that moment. The larger the sensitivity amplification the narrower the range of stimuli or information emphasized. Stated in less technical language, by concentrating on trying to see or hear what is going on (magnitude amplification), a person can pick up more and clearer information. By concentrating on specific aspects of what is going on and ignoring everything else (sensitivity amplification and adaptation), a person can be particularly sensitive to information or events he or she considers important.

Hierarchic Organization of Information-Collecting Functions

These information-handling processes are organized hierarchically, although probably not serially, as some approaches have assumed (e.g., Lindsay & Norman, 1972). What the brain finally receives is a bit like a finished movie that is composed of a selective combination of actual scenes that were shot, although much (perhaps most) of the film was left on the cutting-room floor and never included in the movie. Moreover, movies are not constructed from film that becomes accidentally available. Of all of the scenes that might have been shot, only some are included in the final script; of the flow of objects, events, and actions within a scene which might have been captured, the camera focuses directly on only a few. The film's director specifies in advance what is wanted as defined by the script outlining the plot and action. That is what the camera operators try to capture, and only that.

Similarly, the brain sends feedforward signals to receptor organs selectively biasing them for and against certain kinds of information. Expectancy, anticipation, and intention are examples of psychological terms referring to these selectively biasing processes. Weber's law indicates that the subjective experience of stimulus intensity is but some reduced or amplified version of it (e.g., Stevens, 1961), and some of this selective amplification and attenuation occurs at the receptor level (e.g., Eccles, 1966; Jernigan & Wardell, 1981). Sensory thresholds vary, altering the range of physical stimuli that will be effective, and sensory components filter out some information (e.g., the yellow lens of the eye filters out much of the ultraviolet spectrum). Selective organization also occurs. For example, in both animal and human vision, adjacent cells in the retina interact directly with one another, producing a kind of "editing" or "synthesis" of the stimulus field impacting upon the retina (e.g., McColloch, 1965). Considerable "information processing" occurs before information gets to the "main" brain.

A physical basis exists for neuronal-level information processing. Most neurons transmit information from one to another using chemical messengers. The dendrites of each neuron are selectively sensitive to different neurotransmitters, and this sensitivity can be "tuned" by other neurochemicals. Some neurochemicals activate and others inhibit the information-transmission functions of neurons. The temporal pattern of these activating and inhibiting influences shape neurons' information-processing activities. Therefore, selective editing and synthesis of multiple "messages" can occur at the neuronal level.

Structurally, the neuronal pathways from the sensory receptor surfaces to the brain are connected horizontally at various levels by specialized types of "connecting" neurons (e.g., amacrine cells in the retina of the eye) which function through graded local potential changes (like an analogue computer), rather than as transmitting sensory neurons do through action potentials (like a digital computer) (Freeman, 1975; Shepherd, 1974). Wherever such horizontal connecting networks exist, there is a structural basis for organizing the information collected by many individual neurons into patterns, and the first level of connecting networks exists at the sensory receptor level. This also provides a structural basis for the concept of information "chunking" (i.e., grouping bits of information into larger units) which was proposed as a way of overcoming the structural limitations on the capacity of any sensory channel (Miller, 1956a). It also provides a structural basis for patterned perception. Thus, the structural arrangement of sensory receptors and their pathways to the brain provides for several hierarchically related levels at which information can be progressively organized.

The basic form of the question now appears to be what kinds of information processing occur in what structures and in what patterns and sequences. Considerable evidence indicates that processing is hierarchical, beginning with the sensory organs (J. Miller, 1978). It appears that some fundamental format is being followed for feature detection in all sensory modalities. Cooperative efforts among sensory specialists to identify multimodal commonalities have been urged (e.g., von Bekesy, 1967).

A summary of some of the structural-functional attributes of each sensory-perceptual modality follows to examine their correspondence to this living systems framework. Their structures and four interrelated functional issues will be considered. These include (a) whether the primary function is to collect information about what is occurring inside (interoceptors) or outside (exteroceptors) the body; (b) the nature of the physical marker(s) to which they are sensitive (e.g., mechanical, chemical, thermal, or photic); (c) whether the information results from direct contact with the information source (as in taste) or from indirect contact (as in vision); and (d) what useful kinds of information are provided. Far more is known about the biological structure and functioning of sense organs than about their informational functioning. Here again, it is necessary to combine facts with speculation to try to tell a coherent story. These are active fields of study (e.g., Held et al., 1978), and knowledge in them is rapidly changing and expanding.

Perception of Body Contact and Context: Collecting Information from Pressure, Texture, Temperature, and Tissues

This category of information collection has historically been called the *cutaneous* or skin senses (Titchener, 1913; Woodworth, 1938). *Somaesthesis* (Boring, 1942) has become the standard term in psychology (e.g., Hahn, 1974; Sherrick, 1966). It includes touch, temperature, pressure, pain, and vibration, among other sensations. Sometimes information collection with regard to body position and posture (frequently called *kinesthesis)* is included in this same category. Gibson (1966) and Kennedy (1978) have introduced the functionally oriented term, *haptic system* (i.e., to lay hold of), to subsume this set of components. Biologists frequently contrast them with the "organs of special sense" (e.g., vision and hearing), implying both that they defy neat classification and that they provide general or diversified information. They can be stimulated by mechanical, chemical, thermal, and perhaps even photic markers. They provide information about many properties of the environment that are in immediate contact with the body (and therefore of potential immediate value or harm), as well as information about how the body is affected by its context. In addition, they provide information about the condition of body tissues.

The Classical Special Receptor Approach. Through much of its history, psychology has been dominated by thinking that is atomistic (i.e., experience is composed of basic elements), associationistic (i.e., complex patterns are created by linking or associating basic elements), and mechanistic (i.e., functional patterns are invariant under exactly the same structural and environmental conditions). These assumptions, and they are only that, are nowhere more apparent than in the history of the study of human information collection; this is especially so in the sensory domain (e.g., Titchener, 1913). The basic informational elements were termed *sensations,* and differences in kind were indicated by qualitative differences in subjective experience. Various lists of basic sensory elements were proposed, of which the modern list of human senses is a philosophical and empirical descendant. Presuming these to be basic elements, the old view assumed that there should be sensory structures specialized for each type of subjectively identified sensation. Each type of sensation was believed to be produced by, as Titchener (1913) put it, "a definite, specially developed bodily organ." Therefore, for nearly a century scientists have sought to locate the specialized physical receptors for each introspectively identified basic sensory quality. Darian-Smith (1982) identifies eight structurally different receptors (i.e., Pacinian corpuscles, Meissner's corpuscles, Merkel's disks, naked nerve endings, the corpuscles of Ruffini, and the Krause endbulb).

Sensory Patterning as an Emerging Alternative. Despite extensive research by many scientists, there is still no real agreement about which somaesthetic receptors give rise to which sensory qualities, and the number of possible types of suggested receptors grows. Commenting upon this proliferation, just in the domain of tactile sensitivity, Hahn (1974) wondered if researchers were making the same kind of mistakes they had made in efforts to classify areas of the cerebral cortex; there, they had finally decided, "...not every observable difference among cells meant that they belonged to different populations." Somaesthetic receptors do not seem to be fully specialized in specific sensory qualities (e.g., the same receptor may be stimulated with different kinds of stimuli). The functionally determined maps of the distribution of receptors on the body differ somewhat among individuals and may differs within an individual across observational occasions.

The findings have become so complex that some scholars have questioned the notion that there are receptors specialized only for each specific quality (e.g., Nafe & Kenshalo, 1962; Rose & Mountcastle, 1959), and have tried to construct nonphenomenologically based categories (Melzak & Wall, 1962). What is being questioned in alternate formulations is not whether people experience things like "warmth," "cold," "smoothness," "roughness," or "pain," but whether the premise is sound that these are basic sensory elements for each of which there must be a specialized sensory receptor.

Accumulating evidence is pushing scientists to search for alternate explanations. A person is continually bathed in a changing flow of organized patterns of stimulations that contain accurate information about the environment and ways in which it is changing. Gibson's (1969, 1979) alternative proposes that human sensory structures, and their related central nervous system components, evolved as "...ways of seeking and extracting information about the environment from the flowing array of ambient energy," that is, from the stabilities or invariants in the changing patterns which provide reliable information about the person and his or her environment. For example, a chair is "sensed" as a single object, even though the pattern of light reflected from it is quite different as a person walks around it, because there are stabilities or invariants in that changing pattern of light. Gibson believes that adaptive functioning "depends on the ability of the individual to detect the invariants" in the environment, that this is what the human sensory apparatus is designed to do, and that a person "ordinarily pays no attention whatever to the flux of changing sensations." It follows that the neural signals transmitted to the central nervous system represent a *pattern* of consistencies and spatial-temporal changes of such patterns.

This perspective makes it unnecessary to postulate the existence of different sensory elements and specialized receptors for each. *The percept lies in the pattern of stimulation* as actively collected by the organizations of sensory neurons. The "organs of perception" are governed by the brain "so that the whole system of input and output resonates to the external information." Moreover, the information provided by different sensory neurons/receptors is overlapping—the same form may be detected by sight and touch—providing both richer detail and internal confirmation of percept accuracy.

Agreement with this position does not require one to "throw the baby out with the bathwater." It now appears probable that the associationists were partly right, but that they had things backwards. Information at the receptor and lower brain levels is organized and reflects "reality" as it exists. The evolution of the neocortex, however, has produced the capability of "analyzing" or "decomposing" such wholes into their elements or components. Thus, the parts are perceptually and conceptually differentiated from the whole (as in embryonic development) rather than the whole being constructed from the parts (as proposed by associationistic psychology). In fact, early research on sensation required extensive training to teach subjects how to decompose perceptions into the researcher's basic sensory units. This proved difficult because subjects kept "doing what comes naturally," that is, reporting their perceptions of objects. Since this was not what interested the researcher, it was called the "object error." It is possible, and for some purposes useful, to decompose a perception into smaller components that compose its organization. It is misleading, however, to treat the smaller components as a more basic unit than the perception itself. Information is hierarchically organized, and can be examined at different levels.

Such a shift in basic assumptions eliminates some puzzles, but raises others. For example, the search for sensation-specific receptor cells in the skin and body tissue becomes less important, but it becomes necessary to try to understand how a changing flow of stimulation across a network of receptor cells produces an organized pattern of neuronal stimulation, which accurately represents certain features of the environment and consistently yields certain kinds of subjective experiences. The environment must be accurately perceived to insure species survival, and direct perception is a far less risky solution than one that requires each person to learn to associate basic sensory elements into accurate perceptions.

The concept of direct, patterned perception has been examined at this point, even though it applies to all sensoriperceptual structures, because the issues are more obvious in the sensory functioning of the body surfaces and tissues. It is known that there are many sensory elements distributed throughout the surface of the skin and in the connective tissue beneath it. Many of them are simply bare nerve endings, while some show identifiable differences in structure as described by Ham and Cormack (1979). This arrangement permits multiple sensory structures to be simultaneously stimulated when an object or a flow of air touches some body surface.

The movement of the body surface across an object produces changing gradients in the pattern of excitation of the multiple receptors in that body surface. Just as the eye is designed to dance back and forth across objects during looking activity to facilitate accurate abstraction of the invariants in the light pattern, so too is the skin designed so that movement across it makes possible the abstraction of consistencies from cutaneous information flow. Just as the rods and cones in the eye cooperate to produce multiattribute results, so too the sensory structures of the skin probably cooperate in ways not yet recognized to produce all the multifaceted sensations of touch from a baby's soft, warm, smooth skin to an alligator's hard, cold, rough skin. For example, when a person passively touches something, neurons in the somatosensory part of the cortex are aroused. However, when a person actively manipulates and "feels" an object with his or her hand(s), many other parts of the cortex become active as well (Darian-Smith, 1982). Information can be simultaneously collected about both patterns and subpatterns or detail.

The nerve endings and sensory structures buried deeper in the body, wrapped around the tubes of the circulatory system and embedded in the smooth muscles of visceral organs, probably serve two functions. One is to provide internal information feedback loops to facilitate the automated operation of these body components (e.g., vasodilation and constriction). The other is to provide an alarm signal (i.e., pain), when some tissue is being stressed or damaged.

Finally, the body contact and condition information domain provides a primary basis for a sense of self, of distinguishing between "me" and "not me." When a person touches an object, or an object touches a person, information is simultaneously provided both about the "touchee" and the "touched." For example, a boy recovering from an automobile accident may touch a gift given him to explore its surface, or he may touch the gift to determine if "feeling" is returning to his fingers.

Information about body posture and motion are related to information about body contact and condition. Vestibular information provides a pervasive spatial frame, and as body parts move, muscle and joint information are an integral part of the pattern. The probable evolutionary relationship of somaesthetic sensations and movement is hinted at by three interesting cutaneous sensations. If several equidistant (but relatively close together) points on the skin surface are stimulated in sequence, about a second apart, they will be experienced as being equidistant; but they will be experienced as being separated by different-sized spaces if the time intervals between stimulation of each point are unequal. This has been termed the *tau effect*. Conversely, the subjectively experienced time interval between stimulation of points on the skin will covary with the size of the spatial interval between the points, called the *kappa effect*. Both effects also appear in other sensory modalities (Fraisse, 1984). A related phenomenon has been termed *sensory saltation* (Geldard, 1982). If several points on the skin surface are repetitively stimulated in sequence with mechanical, electrical, or thermal stimuli, at appropriate time intervals, the stimulation will be experienced as "jumping" from one point to another. Sensory saltation also occurs in other sensory modalities (e.g., the perceived "motion" of still photographs resulting from their sequential presentation). All three of these phenomena illustrate the relativity of time and space in cutaneous experience (Jones & Huang, 1982). Gellard (1982) infers that there must be some general neural structures and functions that produce this perception of motion from the spatial-temporal flow of stimulation in many sensory modalities.

What could be the evolutionary significance of such an arrangement? Primitive organisms utilized information provided by movement, either of objects or events flowing past them, or from their own actions. In the absence of sensitive "distance" receptors, patterns of stimulation distributed spatially and temporally across body surfaces could provide some motion-relevant information. Moreover, if some qualitative differentiation of components of the information flow were added (e.g., smooth-rough; hot-cold), fairly complex adaptive environmental transactions would become possible. To work effectively, however, the information collecting structures would have to be dispersed rather than concentrated (as are the eyes). That is exactly what exists in this haptic domain.

Taste and Smell Perception: Chemically Coded Information

Living systems must ingest useful materials from their environment to live and function, and must avoid contact with materials that might be harmful. Therefore, material ingestion and interaction must be selective. Many of the salient properties of materials by which such selections can be made are represented in their chemical composition, so sampling their composition provides valuable information. That is accomplished through processes of taste and olfaction. There is still considerable uncertainty about the structural basis for chemoreception of flavors and odors (Beets, 1978), but there appear to be both chemospecific and more patterned processes (Pfaff, 1985).

Structural-Functional Components for Taste. The neuronal receptors for taste are mostly located on the upper surfaces of the tongue ranging from front to back. Individual receptor cells are organized into groups of up to 25; because of their shape, these cells are called *taste buds*. A small passage, the inner taste pore, extends from the surface of each bud into a small cavity or pit in its center. Each of the taste cells in that bud have microvilli (small hairlike extensions) projected into the pit. Substances taken into the mouth become dissolved in saliva, which can then enter the pit of taste buds, bathing the microvilli, and triggering neuronal impulses (Ham & Cormack, 1979). A baby has about 10,000 taste buds. Receptor taste cells are regularly dying and being replaced. However, the total number of taste cells declines by middle age, producing a reduction in taste sensitivity in older people (Noback & Demarest, 1981).

It used to be thought that each receptor was specialized for one basic taste sensation such as sweet, sour, salty, bitter, and possibly alkaline and metallic, and that all tastes were produced by combinations of these (Ham, 1969). Recent evidence indicates that each receptor has a wide sensitivity to a spectrum of chemicals, with a larger response to a particular type of chemical, called the "best stimulus." "Best stimulus" types are unevenly distributed along the tongue (e.g., sweet toward the front, bitter towards the back) (Pfaffmann et al., 1979).

Pfaffmann (1969) formulated a pattern theory of taste-quality discrimination. Pfaffmann et al. (1979) assert that within each modality, there are "...specific clusters of afferent nerves specific for the different qualities of sensation..." and that interaction occurs at the receptor level through "...gating or inhibitory lateral interactions among receptors and similar integrative processes." It is also probable that there are "...multiple receptor sites on the taste cell membrane," and that each receptor cell is "...affected by activity of the cells in their immediate environment," both of which would contribute to patterning of informationcollection at the receptor level. Moreover, activation thresholds for different neurons may vary through time, contributing to the spatial-temporal patterning of taste sensations. Through this design, the number of taste qualities that could be sensed is very large (Erickson, 1968). But taste buds are not the only source of information resulting from eating and drinking. The mouth has all of the same kinds of information-collecting capabilities as the external skin (after all, its lining is also a form of skin). Tactile and pressure sensations yield information about the size, shape, texture, and hardness of material; small children often reject food because of its "feel" rather than its taste. Thermal receptors yield temperature information, and other receptors may produce the experience of pain. Proprioceptive feedback from chewing, swallowing, and possibly stomach activity are also part of the pattern. The interaction of all of this information results in an additional experience called "flavor" (Pfaffmann et al., 1979). Thus, taste-flavor perceptions are the foundation of an important *evaluative function* regulating material transactions (Pfaffmann et al., 1977). Its "positive-negative" experiential quality of this function called its "hedonic value," is related to the complex pattern of taste information, and not simply to sensory magnitude (Pfaffmann et al., 1979). This hedonic valuing capability is present even in newborn infants. Taste, therefore, provides the primary mechanism for the regulation of most material transactions, identifying the palatability or noxiousness of diverse materials.

This hedonic valuing characteristic is an important factor in learning, producing individual preferences and aversions for the taste-flavor patterns of different materials. Clinical evidence suggesting that food preferences are also influenced by emotional experiences implies a possible relationship between emotional and perceptual valuing (regulatory) processes.

Structural-Functional Components for Olfaction. The neural receptors for *smell* or *odor* are in the nose, located near the mucous membrane surfaces of the nose. From birth onward individuals lose olfactory neurons and the sensitivity of their sense of smell progressively declines (Ham, 1969). It should not be surprising, then, that children "turn up their noses" at foods that adults may enjoy. Through disease, it is possible to lose all olfactory sensitivity.

The dendrite of each olfactory cell ends in a tiny knob from which six to eight long cilia (i.e., hairlike streamers) extend, which are enmeshed with the cilia of other olfactory cells nearby, and with the microvilli of the supporting sustentacular cells. A fluid secreted by cells in the nose bathes all of these hairlike projections, and functions as a solvent for inhaled chemical compounds. These dissolved compounds can trigger reactions in olfactory neurons (Noback & Demarest, 1981).

The physical basis of neurophysiological coding of qualitatively different odors is still unknown. The actual receptor sites are probably located on the olfactory cilia (Engen, 1973; Noback & Demarest, 1981). As with taste, olfactory receptors are probably each reactive to a range of volatile substances, but each probably reacts most strongly to a particular type.

There is a fairly rapid and significant adaptation to an odor if one is exposed to it for a period of time. Moreover, mixtures of odors may eliminate, mask, amplify, or produce other odors (Engen, 1973). Olfactory sensations can be triggered by minute traces of excitants (Noback & Demarest, 1981). Individual differences in olfactory sensitivity do not appear to be genetically based (Hubert et al., 1980). Newborn infants do not display discriminating olfactory sensitivity (Guillory et al., 1979), although differential response to odors appears by one month of age (Guillory et al., 1980). Olfaction interacts with taste in producing flavor sensitivity. Smelling a substance can evoke other preparatory biological functions such as salivation, hydrochloric acid secretion, and motor activity. The ability to identify common food substances declines dramatically when the sense of smell is eliminated from the process (e.g., Mozell, 1971).

Smell also has important hedonic value which can influence learning. The intensity and the pleasantness or unpleasantness of odors influences approach-avoidance behavior (Moncrieff, 1966). In odor similarity studies, a hedonic (pleasantness-unpleasantness) factor usually accounts for most of the variance in similarity judgments (Engen, 1973).

The sense of smell is the most primitive form of information collection "at a distance." It is the first kind of information collection that evolved upon which anticipatory action could be based. Many animals live largely in a world of odors. The sense of smell does more than enable animals to find food. Because different animals generate different odors, and because the same animal may generate distinctly different odors at different times (e.g., a female in "heat"), odors help animals avoid enemies and find friends and mates.

Because the sense of smell is of evolutionary significance in many patterns of social behavior, it does more than just pick up information about odors. It sensitizes and activates other neural systems, particularly "...those which are substrates for emotional behavior patterns" (Noback & Demarest, 1981). For example, in many animals, odors can produce aggressive behaviors and sexual stimulation. While the sense of smell is less dominant in humans, remnants of its evolutionary importance remain (Engen, 1973). For example, along the lateral wall of each nasal cavity are patches of erectile tissue which, when engorged with blood, can partially block the nasal passageway and produce sneezing. Erotic or sexual stimulation may produce that effect. One youth was reported to sneeze every time he saw a pretty girl (so control your sneezing in mixed company) (Ham, 1969). Olfaction connections in the primitive limbic system were probably the precursors of the evolution of humans' much more complex evaluative capabilities such as their patterns of emotional arousal.

Visual Perception: Collecting Information from Light Waves

Vision is the dominant information collector in humans. Of all nerve fibers entering and leaving the central nervous system, an estimated 38 percent are associated with vision (Case, 1966). Vision can collect a greater diversity of information about what is going on in the "outside world," and a person's relationship to it, than any other sense organs. It can collect information about form, size, color, distance, movement, and relationships among objects, as well as changes and rates of change in any of those factors, and information about oneself. The eyes are sensitive to a limited range of frequencies of electromagnetic phenomena.

Structure of the Eye. Cornsweet (1970) provides extensive information about anatomical and physiological factors in vision. The *retina*, which collects the information, is a part of the brain that has "migrated" to the body surface and differentiated in a special way. The other components of the eye simply protect and nourish the retina and help get the information to it. The eye approximates a sphere formed by a layer of fibrous sclerotic tissue that is open to the world on one side. The opening to the world is covered by a "window pane" called the *cornea*.

Behind the cornea is a clear liquid, called the *aqueous humor*, which nourishes the living tissues in the front part of the eye and functions as a pressure-maintaining mechanism that helps to maintain the precise geometrical configuration of the eye. Behind it are two input control devices. The iris can control the amount of light admitted to the eye by making the pupil larger or smaller. The lens organizes the light so it will form clear images on the retina. The lens is flexible, and muscles attached to it can make it thicker or thinner by relaxing or contracting. This variable focusing arrangement provides one of the first "editorial" possibilities of the eye itself.

Between the fibrous shell of the sphere and the retina is a middle layer called the *choroid*, which is pigmented so that it provides a dark background for the light-sensitive cells of the retina to prevent light infiltration and reflection that would interfere with clear vision. The retina has ten layers composed of five different kinds of neurons, and light must pass through those layers before it can stimulate the bottom layer of photoreceptive cells (Ham & Cormack, 1979). It will simplify matters to think of the retina as composed of two functionally different layers of cells. The outer layer (i.e., the layer nearest to the back wall of the eye) collects the information. The inner layer (i.e., the layer closest to the center of the eye) organizes that information and carries it from the eye into the central nervous system.

Humans have both day and night vision. This is accomplished by retinal cells containing different kinds of pigment which perform the same function as the pigments on the inner surface of a television tube. One kind of pigment, rhodopsin, is very sensitive to light but, like the first TV sets, produces only "black and white pictures." It makes night vision possible. A second type of pigment, photopsin, is affected by brighter light and produces "colored pictures" like modern TV sets. Each pigmented epithelium cell has related to it a dendritic connection shaped either like a cylinder or rod (the cells containing rhodopsin), or a cone (the cells containing photopsin). Photopsin is comprised of three somewhat different pigments that are differentially sensitive to light in different wavelengths representing three primary colors: blue, green, and red, or short, middle, and long wavelengths (Jacobs, 1976; Mollon, 1982). All other colors can be created through combinations of these three (Nathans, Thomas, & Hogness, 1986).

These photoreceptor cells are linked to bipolar cells in the inner (information-organizing) layer of the retina, which are in turn linked to another kind of connecting neuron, ganglion cells, which carry the information from the eye into the central nervous system.

However, the structure is more complicated than that. Where the photoreceptor cells synapse with the bipolar connectors, there are other horizontal connector cells that provide direct connections between rods and cones. Where the bipolar cells synapse with the transmitting ganglion cells, there are additional horizontal connections accomplished by amacrine cells. There are also axons that come from cell bodies within the brain and connect up at this same point, and are therefore potentially capable of affecting retinal operation through feedforward functions.

It is estimated that the retina contains 70 to 140 million rods, 7 million cones, and one half to 1 million ganglia fibers leading to the brain. This means that each ganglion cell usually carries information to the brain from more than one photoreceptor cell, an arrangement called *conver gence*. This convergence is particularly important for low-light or "night" vision.

Cones are much more densely packed in the fovea than in other parts of the retina, and there are no rods in the fovea. There is little convergence among foveal cells, which means that each transmits its signals on a relatively direct "through channel" to the brain. For these reasons, the clearest, sharpest "pictures" are produced at the fovea. Saccadic eye movements and eye and head rotation bring different portions of a scene to the fovea. A newborn infant's vision is probably somewhat "fuzzy" since this specialized retinal region is not fully developed at birth (Abramov et al., 1982).

Information Organization in the Eyes. Several kinds of "information processing" appear to occur at the retinal level (Jacobs, 1976), involving feedforward, feedback, and organizing processes. Emerging theoretical (e.g., Gibson, 1966, 1979) and empirical (e.g., DeValois & DeValois, 1980; Foley, 1978; Haber, 1978) perspectives concerning spatial perception illustrate the complexity of these processes. The light that impinges upon the retina is highly organized, as a result of the multiple ways in which it "bounces off" everything. This reflected light contains information about properties of the environment such as texture, linear perspective, motion, and relative position. The pattern of reflected light produces gradients of stimulation across the entire retina that will vary over time as the person and/or the environment moves. These stimulus gradients will also vary slightly between the two eyes. What is transmitted to the brain is an abstract of the consistencies resident in the flow of stimulation across the surfaces of the two retinas.

There appear to be cells differentially tuned to depth perception in front of, behind, and at the point on which the eye focuses (DeValois & DeValois, 1980). The visual system appears to spatially filter the image, with low frequencies identifying objects and high frequencies identifying details within objects (Ginsburg, 1971). Selective attention probably provides the feedforward mechanism for identifying and synthesizing features of a complex visual field (Treisman & Gelade, 1980).

Looking and Seeing. The pattern of visual stimulation is shaped by the person's looking behaviors and attentional focus, and appears to be filtered and transformed in the coding process in order to amplify those portions of most immediate interest and deemphasize those of less immediate interest to the person. Visual images fade and disappear perceptually in seconds if variability of retinal stimulation is not present (Arend, 1973); therefore the visual system is in continual motion, producing variable stimulation as it actively searches for and abstracts relevant information from the flow of stimulation (Gibson, 1979).

Variable Stimulation and Perceptual Stability. There are two related issues of perceptual stability: (a) how humans perceive the stability of the physical world despite varying visual stimulation; and (b) how the visual world is perceived as stable as the perceiver moves through it (Haber, 1978). Perceptual stability is probably a function of visual masking in which the perception of one visual pattern interferes with the perception of another. Humans' purposive search for information results in visual persistence of certain parts of the information flow across the retina and suppression of other parts (Breitmeyer, 1980), so that some aspects of the information "accumulate" in the visual system and progressively and differentially primes responses (Eriksen & Schultz, 1979). Shape constancy is a good illustration of perception as an invariance over specific sensory data (Lappin & Preble, 1975).

Turvey (1977a, 1977b) proposes the following explanation for visual perceptual stability in a flow field of information. Imagine that you could stop the stimulus flow for a moment and examine a single retinal image. The relationships among the components of that image can be represented in two spatial coordinate systems: (a) Where the image lies on the retina, called the *retinal coordinates;* and (b) relationships among the components of the image independent of their location on the retina, called *ordinal coordinates.*

Now, start the stimulus flow again and watch what happens to the components in relationship to those two sets of coordinates. Components' relationships to their retinal coordinates vary, but the relationships among the components remain the same within the ordinal coordinate system. As a result, retinal coordinate information is suppressed while ordinal coordinate information is not. Thus, perception of environmental stabilities appears to result from ordinal coordinate information which accurately represents relationships among components of the perceiver's four-dimensional space-time environment.

Retinal Functioning and Perceptual Stability. Through feedfoward and feedback processes, the visual system is primed to amplify sensitivity to some aspects of the flow and to inhibit others. For example, to clearly perceive something people adjust their eyes so that the object(s) or phenomena of interest are represented in the foveal stimulation pattern, the region of the highest visual acuity. Such intentional adjustments result from feedforward processes provided by individuals' intentions and expectations.

However, the fovea occupies only a small portion of the total retinal surface. The peripheral retina has somewhat different but related functions, such as perception of sudden environmental changes, or distinguishing between object motion and self-locomotion (Johansson et al., 1980); this indicates there may be two visual systems, one "focal"and one "ambient" (Dichgans & Brandt, 1978; Trevarthen, 1978). This representation of retinal functioning fits well with the nature of attentional functioning discussed in Chapter 7, to the effect that events of primary concern are the center of attention while peripheral attention monitors the context for gross signals of potential relevance.

The Nature of Visual Percepts. It appears probable that human evolutionary history produced a visual system designed to readily perceive certain kinds of invariance adaptively useful in the earth's terrestrial environment. For example, three month old infants perceive substance, shape, and elasticity as invariant properties of objects (Gibson, Owsley, Walker, & Megaw-Nyce, 1979; Walker, Owsley, Megaw-Nyce, Gibson, & Bahrick, 1980). Perception of topological properties such as connectedness or closedness of shapes may be another example (Chen, 1982). Infants appear able to perceive many properties of their environments by 6 months of age (e.g., color, texture), and display competence in abstracting invariant features from visual displays (e.g., grandpa's big nose) (Cohen, DeLoache, & Strauss, 1979).

Gibson (1979) argues that the visual perceptual system evolved to pick up information about configurations of places, objects, and substances with multiple attributes (e.g., texture, color, rigidity, viscosity, vaporizability) useful in humans' natural habitats such as places to sleep, drink, or eat. Events are changes that occur in such configurations and their properties with or without the influence of the perceiver's actions. Events have properties. They may be slow or fast, reversible or nonreversible, repeating or nonrepeating. While infants appear to enter the world with capabilities for perceiving many (though not all) of the properties of places, objects, and substances, the use of those capabilities is greatly influenced by perceptual learning (Gibson, 1969). For example, when children are confronted with an object-sorting task, the ability to use multiple attributes of the objects to sort them into classes increases with age (Firth, 1978).

Hierarchical Organization and Selective Perception. Phenomena are organized in nested hierarchies. A place (e.g., one's home) is a component of a larger place (e.g., a neighborhood), and is composed of components (e.g., rooms and objects) which themselves are organizations of subcomponents (e.g., doors and windows). Events are also organized in nested hierarchies. Any perception is of a particular phenomenon at a particular level in a hierarchy.

Since multiple levels are always available for potential perception, which level is perceived at any moment is at least partly a matter of choice. A perceptual focus on one level prohibits a simultaneous focus on another. Therefore, natural visual perception is necessarily directed and selective. One aspect of visual functioning that develops is the ability to focus perception on different hierarchical levels. By 3 to 4 years of age, children readily differentiate parts and wholes, and perceive components in relationship to wholes of which they are a part. This facilitates rapid recognition with only cursory visual exploration. Things can be seen in their entirety with a glance, and one distinctive cue is sufficient for recognition. One consequence of impaired vision is restriction of this capability, and consequent restrictions on learning (Barraga, Collins, & Hollis, 1977).

Since the environment is seldom static, and the perceiver and his or her sense organs are usually in motion, the informational bases for the formation of both concepts and propositions are simultaneously present; this makes possible the construction of personal theories or schemata. Therefore, event perception is the natural information source for constructing the substance of the governing functions.

Movement is perhaps the most important kind of event to be perceived (Braunstein, 1978; Johansson, 1978), particularly movement by other humans and animals (Johansson, 1973). There are three important types: object motion; locomotion of the perceiver; and object manipulation by the perceiver. Perception of motion is a function of the viewer's observational vantage point, sometimes called the *station point* (Haber, 1978), and of three interrelated sets of spatial coordinates: environment-centered, object-centered, and viewer-centered. Different kinds of motion are perceived in terms of different sets of spatial coordinates (Cutting & Proffitt, 1982).

Object Motion. Objects exist in environmental layouts. Their location and relationships to other parts of the layout may be represented by environment-centered spatial coordinates. Objects are composed of components. The relationships of an object's components may be represented by its object-centered coordinates independent of the environmental coordinates. Visual perception of object motion uses both object- and environment-centered coordinates anchored to the viewer-centered spatial coordinates. A variety of kinds of object motion have been studied (Braunstein, 1976, 1978).

The movement of any object can be represented as a trajectory within environmental spatial coordinates (sometimes called *absolute motion*).

However, in the natural world space is populated by objects and substances configured in environmental layouts. Therefore, humans perceive the motion of an object in terms of (a) changes in the relationships of its components within its object-centered coordinates relative to its environment-centered coordinates (sometimes called relative motion); and (b) changes in its position in its environment-centered coordinates relative to the viewer's body-centered coordinates (sometimes called common motion). The result is a combination of information which accurately predicts the trajectory of a moving object in relationship both to the environment and to the viewer's observational vantage point (Cutting & Proffitt, 1982; Johansson, 1973).

Cutting (1981) proposes that every object has two centers: one about which all mass is distributed, called the *center of gravity*; the second, the point within the object around which all movement occurs, called the center of moment (Cutting, Proffitt, & Kozlowski, 1978). For example, for each moving body component during walking, an invariant point can be identified around which that component moves. Viewers can use such center of moment information to identify the nature of objects; as, for example, whether a walker is a female or male or a friend (Barclay, Cutting, & Kozlowski, 1978; Cutting, Proffitt, & Kozlowski, 1978; Kozlowski & Cutting, 1977); wheels or bushes (Cutting, 1982; Cutting & Proffitt, 1982); or an aging head (Cutting, 1978).

Such center of moment information nicely illustrates the value of relevant feedback reference signals. It is unnecessary to use all of the available information. It is more efficient to monitor some variable (e.g., centers of moment) sufficient for the purpose of recognizing and tracking moving objects.

The viewer's perception of object motion can specify impending contact or increasing separation. If one focuses on an object moving towards or away from one's observational vantage point, the resulting stable perception of the object represents a fixed point in the visual flow field. As the object moves toward or away from the person, the visual flow field radiates in exponential fashion around that fixed point producing three types of feedback signals. The changes in the radiation of that visual flow field are subjectively perceived as growing larger as it approaches or smaller as it retreats. Rate of movement is reflected in an index of change of the radiation of the visual flow field. Another index is an increase or decrease in the perceived detail of surface texture or components of the moving object (Gibson, 1979).

Perception of Locomotion. Much human perception occurs from a moving rather than a stationary observational vantage point. As a result, it is necessary for humans to distinguish between visual flow field changes produced by object motion and that produced by their own locomotion. Visuomotor coordination in space-time is a function of the optic flow field (Lee, 1980; Lee & Reddish, 1981). Something more is needed, however, for humans to perceptually distinguish object motion and locomotion. That something appears to be peripheral vision. The peripheral retina responds to global changes in the optic array producing the perception of self-motion (in interaction with the vestibular system), while the fovea responds to detailed information about the fixated object producing perception of object motion (Johansson et al., 1980).

A commonly experienced illusion is illustrative. Imagine sitting in an immobile car. Beside you another car slowly begins to move. Because you are looking straight ahead, you see the motion through your peripheral vision. As a result, you seem to be moving. However, it is experienced as somehow abnormal because other relevant information is absent (e.g., changes in the foveal optic flow field around the fixated object). If you turn your head and look directly at the car beside you, the perception changes and you see it moving rather than yourself because the foveal flow field now says "object motion" and the peripheral flow field says "no personal motion."

Object Manipulation. The ability to simultaneously see one's arms and hands and the objects being manipulated provides the basis for visal feedback information necessary for guiding precise and precisely timed manipulative activities (Lee, 1978). Arm movements appear to be organized at the brain stem level while hand and finger movements appear to involve cortical mechanisms (Johansson et al., 1980). Gross arm and hand reaching appears shortly after birth. Infants look at the target object rather than at their hands. Their vision functions to define the target location of the movement and to anchor the movement to that target (Whiting & Cockerill, 1974). At about 6 months, infants begin to use visual feedback to correct reaching errors and to control the act (Lasky, 1977), and they become able to reach for and grasp moving as well as stationary objects (von Hofsten & Lindhagen, 1979). Such predictive reaching demonstrates the operation of fairly complicated directive function capabilities in early infancy.

Visual Perception and Reading. Reading involves visual perception of written material, and both structural and functional variables influence this capability (Dalby, 1979; Rayner, 1978). Haber (1978) argues that perceptual behavior must produce an integration of successive glances into a continuous, stable panoramic view of a flow of events, whether the flow represents an environmental scene or a page of written material.

The distinction between perceptual and cognitive processes is especially apparent in reading. Symbolic visual perception involves two kinds of information coding. The first coding is the imagistic perception of the words themselves. However, unlike direct perception of events, the direct perception of words does not contain the relevant information. Therefore, understanding what one reads is an act of *cognition* which translates one's imagistic *perception* of the words into meanings represented by previously learned abstractions (see Chapter 9 for further consideration of the relationship of words to concepts).

In reading, as in other visual perception, it is the redundancies in the stimulus flow that anchor both perception and meaning. Those redundancies are hierarchically organized, and the reader may focus at any level (e.g., letters, words, sentences). Therefore, written text has a variety of consistencies helpful in reading: (a) the visual features of letters; (b) possible letter sequences in words, which are constrained by spelling rules; (c) the rules of grammar, which impose severe restrictions on the permissible sequence of words in sentences and to some extent on sequences of sentences; (d) cultural or stylistic restrictions such as scientific vs. news writing; (e) printing conventions such as starting proper names with a capital letter. Thus, reading is influenced by the characteristics of the text's organization, the reader's ability to recognize and use the relevant organizational rules, and the interaction of the reader's knowledge with the content of the text.

Reading skill progresses from a focus on small perceptual chunks (e.g., letters or words) to larger perceptual chunks (e.g., phrases or sentences). Readers learn to recognize and understand phrases and sentences in a single glance utilizing familiar cues (i.e., redundancies), just as a person may be recognized by a distinguishing feature. As with all other perception, reading involves abstracting meaning from a continuous flow of perceived events captured with a succession of glances. That abstracting process is guided by the reader's intentions or expectations with regard to the text, interacting with the text and the reader's prior knowledge. Reading involves perception of symbolic events rather than the actual events.

Auditory Perception: Collecting Information from Air Pressure Variations

There must be invariant properties in the information coded onto air pressure waves if sounds are to be directly perceived.

Acoustical Physics: Sound Generation and Transmission. Any event that mechanically disturbs a gaseous or liquid medium creates a wave motion in that medium which may vary in kind and intensity. For example, a substance may move, vibrate, and bump into or rub against another substance. Such wave patterns move outward in the medium in all directions from the point of origin, much like the ripples in a pond when one throws a pebble into it. How far the "ripples" will go before they end is a function of the nature and intensity of the originating disturbance, and the properties of the medium.

The first wave is called the *wave front*. It precisely specifies the direction of a sound-producing event for any observational vantage point. The sequence of waves that follow are called the *wave train*. The organization of the wave train provides information about the nature of the originating event, and its termination: (a) the mixture of frequencies in the wave train duplicates the movement or vibrating frequencies of the originating event(s) (e.g., rubbing vs. pounding); (b) the temporal course of the event is mirrored by the sequence of transients in the wave train (e.g., change from rapid to slow pounding); and (c) the intensity of the event is represented in the amplitude of the wave form (e.g., hard vs. gentle pounding). Attributes (a) and (b) are invariant across distance from the origin, but amplitude varies with distance, slowly declining to zero. This spatial-temporal organization of the wave pattern contains the information that humans can perceive as sounds.

Any complex wave form can be represented by selectively combining simple curves called *sine waves* that differ in frequency, amplitude, and phasing in relationship to one another; this is called *Fourier analysis*. Therefore, the fundamental variables in physical acoustics—frequency (pitch), amplitude (loudness), and phasing (duration)—are attributes of sine waves.

Acoustical physics has provided the primary model for understanding auditory physiology and perception. Since combinations of frequency, amplitude, and temporal sequence can be used to characterize sound waves, it seemed sensible (a) to try to determine how the ear codes those physical variables for transmission to the brain; (b) to study perception of the corresponding component sensations of pitch, loudness, and duration; and (c) to assess hearing deficiencies in terms of those basic properties (Dallos, 1981; Eisenberg, 1976; Lass, McReynolds, Northern, & Yoder, 1982; Moore, 1982; Trahiotis & Robinson, 1979).

Perception of Auditory Events. However, there has been growing dissatisfaction with accoustical physics as the model for understanding audition. Just because the physics of sound is conveniently represented by a few physical elements, it does not follow that human auditory perceptual capabilities evolved to perceive and combine those elements. For example, a song can be readily recognized whether it is played fast or slow, loud or soft, or in a different octave. There is invariance of information across a variety of transformations of pitch, loudness, and duration. An alternate possibility is that human audition evolved to perceive complex, flowing patterns of sounds typical of their natural environment; that is, adaptively meaningful sound events (Gibson, 1966; Jones, 1978). Such an alternate view has great practical implications. Accurate evaluation of a person's hearing depends on the kinds of signals used in the assessment. For example, evidence from research on infants and children suggests that the routinely used pure tones and band noises are of limited utility because they are abstract and lack personal significance (Eisenberg, 1976). Currently, there are over 200 kinds of hearing aids designed around the principles of acoustical physics, and hearing aid prescription is often a function of "inspired guesswork" (Moore, 1982). The design and prescription of hearing aids might be quite different if tested against their utility for perceiving natural auditory events of importance to a person, such as listening to one person speak in a noisy environment. Elderly people often turn off their hearing aids in social contexts because they amplify everything equally.

Hearing involves time-related, configurational invariants of auditory events. Meaningful sounds contain important information not represented by simple pitch, loudness, and duration (Gibson, 1966). Such variables can occur in multiple patterns producing many higher order variables. A device called a sound spectrograph provides a configurational representation or "picture" of an auditory event (Gibson, 1966; Moore, 1982). Like a fingerprint, each auditory event spectrogram has its unique configuration. For example, "voice prints" can be used to identify people, as can fingerprints.

Human auditory perceptual capabilities (including the ear and its functions) probably evolved to provide representations of auditory events as illustrated by sound spectrograms. Infants display extensive auditory competence during the first few weeks of life (Eisenberg, 1976), and differential responding to different sounds (Berg & Berg, 1979; Eimas, 1975; Spears & Hohle, 1967). Moreover, complex, variable sound patterns attract infants' interest, while continuous, unvarying sounds are quickly habituated to or ignored, resulting in reductions in arousal and sometimes ending in sleep (Spears & Hohle, 1967). Auditory perception requires selective variable stimulation of the ear, some of which humans produce by their own actions.

The Biological Basis of Audition. The human ear contains structures for collecting two kinds of information: (a) sound; and (b) the body's relationship to earth or gravity. Early in evolutionary history, organisms had a generalized "force detector." Through the evolutionary processes of componentization and specialization, the generalized structure evolved into two related but functionally autonomous structures, each specializing in a different kind of force detection, sound and gravity (Gibson, 1966). Only sound-detecting structures are considered here.

The ear collects information primarily from outside the body, although some body sounds can also be heard. For example, auditory feedback regulating one's vocalizations appears to involve both external and internal sources. The information is coded on air pressure waves. Information, about the nature of events, their location relative to the person's body, and changes in these two classes of information (e.g., movement) can be coded and perceived. Vision can only provide information about surface appearances. Hearing can sometimes provide information about what is within those surfaces, as when a child shakes a Christmas package to get clues about its contents.

The gross structural characteristics of audition have been known for some time. However, knowledge of how those structures transduce and decode the sound wave information continues to be elusive. Understanding of cochlear structure and function "...is in a state of revolution," and the validity of fundamental concepts concerning the basis of hearing "...is now questioned" (Dallos, 1981). Following is a summary of the gross structural-functional characteristics of audition, and then a consideration of some of the new functional possibilities.

The auricle or ear helps channel air pressure waves into a small tube (the external *auditory meatus*), which connects with a flexible, fibrous tympanic membrane or eardrum designed to permit multidirectional flexibility. Tiny muscles control the tension on the eardrum. They relax the eardrum when one sleeps, making it more responsive to even very small sounds. When one is awake and alert, the muscles tighten the eardrum, making it less sensitive to minor sounds that might be distractions from important tasks (Hugelin, Dumont, & Paillas, 1960).

On the other side of this membrane is an epithelial-lined chamber of bone called the *tympanic* cavity, connected to the back of the mouth (i.e., the nasopharynx) by an open tube called the *eustachan tube* which maintains an appropriate air pressure on each side of the membrane. In this middle ear chamber are three small, interconnected bones called the *ossicles*, one of which is fastened to the inner surface of the eardrum. The bony chamber wall opposite the eardrum contains upper and lower holes, or "windows." The lower, round window is covered by a flexible membrane. The upper, oval window has no covering, but is filled by a tightly fitted movable bone (the stirrup) attached through the two other small bones to the eardrum. It fits and moves in the oval window hole a bit like a piston in an engine.

On the other side of this wall of bone is a maze of interconnected spaces in the skull, called the *bony labyrinth*, filled with a similarly shaped maze of interconnected membranous sacs and tubes, analogously called the *membranous labyrinth*. The bony labyrinth is filled with an extension of cerebral-spinal fluid, called *perilymph*, which surrounds the sacs and tubes of the membranous labyrinth that are filled with another fluid called *endolymph*. One sac (the saccule) interconnected with one flattened tube are involved in the hearing process. The tube is in a portion of the bony chamber that is coiled in a spiral of decreasing radius, like a snail's shell, so it is called the *cochlea*. The tube divides the bony chamber into an upper part which connects with the oval window and through it with the bony chain and the eardrum; and a lower part which connects to the lower round window. The inner floor of the coiled tube (cochlear duct) is covered by a strip of flexible material called the *basilar membrane*, on which rests a strip of cells called the *organ of corti* containing sensory cells called *hair cells*. They synapse in complex ways with the neurons whose cell bodies lie in the spiral ganglia. Each hair cell has tiny, fan-shaped projections called microvilli. There are thousands of hair cells organized in a column four or five cells wide throughout the tube. There is one row of inner hair cells and three to five rows of outer hair cells. Each hair cell base has a rounded form and contains nerve endings. Therefore, if some force causes the hair to bend and "rock" on its rounded base, neuronal signals will be triggered. Different patterns of movement will produce different patterns of neuronal signals (Ham & Cormack, 1979).

Functionally, variable waves of air pressure are captured by the external ear and channeled into a tube, causing a vibration of the eardrum, producing a pattern of movement in the chain of bones connected to it. One of the little bones moving in the oval window sets up vibrations in the perilymph liquid, propagating a traveling wave pattern throughout the tube and its endolymph fluid. This motion produces patterns of movement in the hair cells, producing patterns of neuronal signals that are transmitted to the brain. There are many fewer neuronal fibers than hair cells. Therefore many fibers converge in each neuron, providing a structural basis for some information organization and summarization at the sensory receptor level.

Information Organization in the Ears. Newly emerging evidence indicates that nature may have developed several solutions to coding the various aspects of information carried on sound waves, and that "...a heterogeneity of auditory mechanisms...may have to be entertained" (Dallos, 1981) that are hierarchically organized (Cazals et al., 1979; Gernandt, 1959). An analogy may help convey the potential value of information organization at this sensory level. Imagine each hair cell to be a differently tuned string on a single musical instrument. By plucking patterns of strings different songs can be played. Listeners do not separately hear the vibration pattern of each string. Rather, they hear the musical theme and its variations. Analogously, what is transmitted to the brain from the ear is probably not the information from the vibration of each hair cell, but the information represented by the pattern of interrelated vibrations of many hair cells.

Evidence is accumulating that reveals "...striking differences in morphology and innervation between inner hair cells and outer hair cells," clearly implying that they probably perform different but interacting functions. Inner hair cells transmit information to the central nervous system while outer cells may not. Outer hair cells appear to receive information from the central nervous system (i.e., the autonomic branch) while inner hair cells do not (Dallos, 1981). This suggests that processes of "selective listening" may be influenced by feedforward processes through the autonomic nervous system to the outer hair cells. In more human terms, it may provide a structural base for phenomena such as much more sensitive hearing of strange noises in the dark when one is apprehensive or frightened; or the precise, selective hearing that results from concentrated auditory attention. Evidence of a biological basis for selective hearing is accumulating (Lukas, 1980).

When you stop to consider it, the hearing structures are a kind of "Rube Goldberg" set of mechanisms. Air vibrations have to enter a little tube, where they vibrate a piece of skin, which jiggles some strangely shaped little bones, which poke through a hole and pound on a pool of liquid, making waves that shake a coiled-up tube and everything in it, which wiggles some little cells with hairs on them, which trigger neuronal signals and from all that a person hears a lover's sigh, a baby's cry, or Tchaikowsky's *Pathetique*. The results are tremendous, but the method is weird. No engineer in his right mind would design such a contraption, with so many marker changes and possible points of inefficiency or breakdown. They would do so only if their options were severely limited by the constraint that advances had to be integrated with available components; such is the process of evolution through a componentized, successive approximation design.

Localizing Sound Sources. Humans listen to a sound to obtain three kinds of information about its sources: (a) where it is; (b) what it is; (c) and what it is doing. There are two parts to the *where it is?* decision: whether it comes from within (e.g., one's voice) or outside one's body; and where it is if it is outside. The two decisions are related.

When wave fronts and wave trains impinge upon a person, they will enter one ear slightly before the other unless the person is facing exactly perpendicular to the wave front. That disparity provides a basis for auditory perception of the direction of the sound source. Accurate localization of sound sources requires active information seeking. For example, if a person has his or her head immobilized, and is asked to identify the direction of a sound source, that person will frequently err. However, if free rotation of the head is allowed as in natural, active perception, the confusion disappears (Wallach, 1940).

Perceiving the Nature of the Sound Producing Event. How people perceive the basic elements of pitch, loudness, and duration has been extensively studied. Relatively little research has focused on how people perceive meaningful sounds in natural contexts, such as mothers' perceptions of different infant crys (Wolff, 1971). As a result, little is known about the perception of natural auditory events—of "what is it" and "what is it doing"—except that humans accurately perceive many kinds of complex sounds. Experimental research on variables influencing the perception of sound patterns appears to be growing (Jones, 1978).

Selective Listening and Multiple Streams of Sound. Only in the laboratory under specially controlled conditions can people be exposed to single sound sources and pure tones. In daily life, people are typically exposed to multiple sounds from different directions and at different distances. How do people clearly hear one sound event stream among many, rather than a confusing babble of sounds? Moore (1982) concludes that perception of auditory event streams corresponds well to general gestalt principles: (a) content and location similarity; (b) smooth continuation of sound changes; (c) common fate of parts of a sound; (d) belongingness; and (e) closure.

There are at least four kinds of factors that influence which among multiple, simultaneous sound streams is listened to and heard (Gibson, 1966; Jones, 1976, 1978): (a) attributes of the sounds themselves (e.g., loudness, shrillness); (b) the physical relationships between the sound sources and the listener (e.g., near or far, approaching or receding); (c) selective attention focused on one sound source, leaving others as background sounds; and (d) personal relevance (e.g., the human voice) (Eimas, 1975; Eimas & Tartter, 1979). Other sounds can acquire special significance through learning; for example, the screeching of car brakes.

The Auditory Perception of Human Speech. Speech sounds can be described with the same principles of acoustical physics as any other sounds, and can be directly perceived. However, in natural sounds, the useful information is that coded directly in the acoustical wave train pattern as in one's hearing the wind blowing. In contrast, the informa tion of primary importance in speech sounds lies in the conceptual rather than the perceptual meaning of the words themselves. For example, one may be able to recognize and pronounce a word but not have the foggiest idea of what it means.

Therefore, perception of the meaning of human speech sounds involves dealing with two interacting levels of coding. The first level is the coding of the speech sounds sometimes referred to as *phonetics*. That level of coding and the auditory perception of it has been extensively studied (Carterette & Friedman, 1976; MacNeilage, 1983; Moore, 1982). It is subject to direct perception. The second level is the symbolic coding of information with speech sounds, sometimes called *semantics*. That level of information cannot be directly *perceived*. One listens to and hears phonetic codes, but thinks in terms of semantic and prosodic codes (Darwin, 1976).

Human speech combines expressive vocalization with speech sounds and that is particularly important in social interactions (Darwin, 1976; Fry, 1970). The organization of words provides the information about the events referred to, and the expressive vocalizations provide information about the state and intent of the speaker. When the two kinds of information agree, the message conveyed is clear and unambiguous. In ordinary social interaction, people tend to concentrate on conveying the linguistic message and the expressive message tends to covary relatively automatically. Therefore, the perceived expressive components of speech sounds are typically interpreted as conveying how a person "really feels," if the two messages are in contradiction.

Efforts to understand speech perception have been influenced by the study of the structure of human languages. Therefore, attempts have been made to relate acoustical patterns of speech and their perception to elements of language structure: phonemes, syllables, words, and sentences (Carroll & Bever, 1976; Darwin, 1976; Liberman, Cooper, Shankweiler, & Studdert-Kennedy, 1967). An alternate approach has been to try to identify components of speech perception by observing speech perception disruptions produced by brain lesions (Luria, 1981). Different aspects of speech perception are disrupted by damage in different parts of the brain.

Language organization may be thought of as structured hierarchically (e.g., letters compose words which compose sentences). It may also be understood in functional terms. Words that function as subject, verb, object, and so on are combined according to the grammatical rules of a language to describe an event or convey an idea. Much of the research on speech perception has been anchored to the structural components of speech and their acoustical forms. However, one of the striking characteristics of speech perception is its relationship to the speaker's "seman tic intention"—whether for example it is a command or a question—

rather than to the speech's structural components such as phonemes (Darwin, 1976). Speech is a rapidly flowing, continuously changing, rhythmically organized pattern of sounds (Jones, 1978), and human speech perception capabilities must have evolved to relate dynamic patterns of speech sounds (i.e., speech events) to culturally defined and learned meanings.

There appear to be important structural and functional links between speech perception and speech production (Luria, 1981; Moore, 1982). The most obvious is that one's own speaking is regulated by feedback perception of the sounds being made. Since infants typically first babble (i.e., speak phonemes), then speak words and then phrases and finally sentences, it has sometimes been assumed that speech perception develops in the same sequence. However, that does not necessarily follow. From birth, infants are exposed to the flowing speech sounds typical of adult conversation. Only infrequently are they exposed to single words and almost never to single phonemes. Therefore, it seems more likely that *speech perception* is organized in terms of functional speech events from the beginning, while *speech production* as a complex motor act may develop more haltingly (see Chapter 15).

Ideas discussed earlier when considering visual perception and reading probably also apply here. There are many redundancies in normal speech that can guide speech perception. For example, a single English word may have many meanings (e.g., "can"), but placed with other words in a particular sentence organization governed by the rules of grammar, its possible meanings are constrained into a single one (e.g., "You can do it" vs. "He went to the can"). Stated in ordinary language, people listen to someone talking to try to understand the idea they are trying to express or the event they are trying to describe. The same idea or event can be represented with different combinations of letters and words, (a form of linguistic equifinality), as illustrated by work on sentence comprehension (Carroll & Bever, 1976).

Speech events may be understood as behavioral episodes. The organization of motor behavior provides an analogy (see Chapter 14). Motor acts are organized by an idea of the consequence(s) to be produced by them. The same consequences can be produced by a variety of combinations of muscle actions. Similarly, a person speaks to communicate an idea or describe an event. Different combinations of sounds, words, and gestures may be used to communicate the same information. It is not the particular sounds involved that are important, but the message or information they carry. The function of speech perception is to accurately pick up that information. Warren (1982) has made an initial attempt to relate psychoacoustical phenomena to auditory perception of naturally occurring events.

Body Position: Collecting Information from Gravity and Movement

Behaving is simplified considerably by one's ability to conduct and control it relative to gravity as a stable reference point. Think how much more difficult it would be to maintain postural equilibrium or smooth, coordinated movement if the force of gravity were continually changing. (Everyone would look like as much of a "klutz" as my wife says I am.)

By a combination of information about (a) the body's relation to the gravitational field from the vestibular structures; (b) its relationship to the earth from skin surface contact with the earth and other solid objects; and (c) the relationships of the component bones to each other from sensors in their connecting joints, tendons, and muscles, an accurate and detailed representation of the body's position in its spatial environment is provided. Vectors of change in this complex pattern of information provide accurate information about movement. When this is supplemented by information from the distance senses of vision and hearing, movements can be made in anticipation of potential spatial-temporal configurations that may be confronted (i.e., through feedforward information functions).

Balance and Motion Structures in the Ear.   The vestibular structures in the inner ear are sometimes called *equilibrium receptors* or the basic orienting system. It will be recalled that the inner ear contains two interconnected fluid-filled sacs and several fluid-filled tubes, all embedded in a bony labyrinth. The small sac and one tube are related to hearing. Both sacs and the other tubes are related to posture and motion. The two sacs, called the *utricle* and the *saccule,* are filled with a liquid called *endolymph.* They are lined with epithelial cells resting on connective tissue. Each sac contains a flat disc with sensory endings (the macula). There are two kinds of neuroephithelial cells in this disc. Extending from the ends of each cell are tufts of long, fine hairs (80 or more) of two different kinds. These cells do not float freely in the liquid but are embedded in a gelatinous substance called the *otolithic membrane* that also contains many small granules of calcium carbonate and protein. This makes the substance considerably heavier than the fluid around it. It rests upon the macula like a muffin on a flat plate.

The spatial gravitational field has vertical and horizontal axes. The body, independent of its position in space, has similar coordinates: head-foot (vertical); front-back and left-right (horizontal). When the body coordinates and the spatial axes coincide, then body equilibrium is experienced. The "muffin" or otolithic membrane lies immobile on the "plate" or macula. However, if the head is tilted in any direction, the body's vertical axis will be at an angle to the vertical axis of the gravitational field. Then the muffin will slide down the plate towards its edge in the direction of the tilt. As the otolithic membrane slides across the macula in each sac, the hairs embedded in the macula will be bent in the direction it moves. This provides accurate information concerning the head's position vis-a-vis the gravitational field. If the head accelerates in a straight line, the muffin will slide towards the edge of the plate opposite the direction of acceleration. A quick stop will produce an effect opposite to that. (Both are frequently experienced in a taxi ride through New York City). Thus, this mechanism can provide information about both the body's position in the gravitational field and its linear acceleration. If the rate of movement is constant, the muffin will not slide. That is why people can be flying at a steady 600 miles an hour and feel as if they are not moving.

Connected to the utricle are three tubes that are called the *semicircular canals* because each is shaped approximately like a ring that begins and ends at the utricle. Each ring lies in a plane at approximately right angles to the other two. Therefore, together they represent the three axes of three-dimensional space. The inside of each tube has a lining similar to that of the sacs. Each ring has an enlarged area or swelling called the *ampulla*, within which there is a structure (the *crista*) containing two kinds of information-collecting neuroepithelial cells much like those found on the macula in the sacs. The hairs on these transducer cells extend into the inner cavity of the ring or canal where they are covered by a light, gelatinous, noncellular structure called the *cupula*. The crista functions like the swinging door of a bar in a Western movie, swinging in whatever direction it is pushed by the movement of the liquid in the semicircular canal, bending hairs that trigger neuronal signals in the process. The direction and amount of bending conveys information about the direction and rate of change in rotation.

The same thing can happen in each of the three canals, thereby providing information about angular or rotational acceleration of movement in any of the three dimensions of space. With this combination of information about body position relative to gravity, and about linear and angular acceleration of movement, the basic data concerning position and motion in three-dimensional gravity-filled space is available.

Additional information collectors evolved inside muscles and joints to facilitate finely coordinated skeletal-muscular control. Distributed in various places throughout muscle tissue are special structures called *stretch receptors* since they are stimulated by the mechanical process of stretching. Because these are distributed through all striated muscle groups in the body, they can provide detailed information about the motion of all parts of the skeletal-muscular structure.

In addition, there are nerve endings in the connections between muscles and tendons and in most joints and their ligaments that are stimulated by mechanical pressure, or rubbing, from the movement of the associated muscles and joints. This provides still a third source of movement information. The information provided is related but different. Muscles vary in tension (or pull) and length. Joints vary in rotation and angle. The latter may be more important in basic perception of space and movement (e.g., Rose & Mountcastle, 1959), while the former provides for fine tuning as the body exerts force against another object (e.g., as in sensing weight).

Information Collection and Consciousness

This is an appropriate point to clarify another related issue. Since the beginning of the science of psychology, introspective methods have been basic tools in the study of sensation. As a result, the phenomena of consciousness and those of sensation became linked; that is, sensations were expected to have conscious qualities. That legacy needs to be discarded. Information coded into neuronal, electrical patterns can perform its organizing function without necessarily having attributes that enter consciousness.

As Gibson (1966) has emphasized, *the information lies in the variable pattern of stimulus events and their covarying pattern of sensory arousal. The information is not created by conscious perception of it, although it may be modified or transformed by such perception.* This is generally true of most of the different kinds of information discussed in this chapter. For example, Titchener (1913) found it relatively easy to have subjects identify sensory attributes of auditory and visual information, but vestibular information was inaccessible to them.

The issue of what kinds of information can enter consciousness, and when, is of basic importance and practical significance; but it is important to avoid making the implicit assumption that information that can enter consciousness is somehow basically different from that which does not or cannot, and that the two do not interact. In fact, most information collected by a person at any point in time is "unconscious" in that sense. What one is aware of is only a fragment of the total flow of "current news." It represents one or two "news stories" of current interest to the "editor" from among many being generated by multiple "reporters" in a very busy "newsroom" in the process of producing the "daily paper." Available evidence supports the view that most daily information processing goes on outside awareness; that information surfaces in consciousness primarily on a "need-to-know" or "alarm" basis; and that consciousness is a phenomenon in its own right, separate from the information it may encompass.

Specialized Multimodal Perceptual Capabilities

Bower (1974a) has proposed that in the early stages of evolution, a single perceptual system developed, probably responding to pressure variations on body surfaces. Further evolution produced sensory capabilities for collecting other useful kinds of information (e.g., temperature), but information collected from additional sensory capabilities flowed into the same internal perceptual apparatus.

Bower argues that the high levels of evolutionary complexity represented by humans, and the resulting differences in growth rates of sense and effector organs, made the maintenance of such perceptual unity impossible. The result in humans is multiple sensory-perceptual modalities specialized by the kind of marker on which the information is coded (e.g., light-vision). Each mode can encode some kinds of information and not others. However, some kinds of information can be redundant across perceptual modalities (e.g., size, shape, and number).

The extent and nature of relationships and interactions that can occur among different perceptual modalities in humans is still unclear (Marks, 1978). For example, there is a curious phenomenon called *synthesia* in which percepts in one modality take on qualities appropriate to another modality (e.g., music or voices take on colors or tastes). Perhaps remnants of the primitive, unitary perceptual system proposed by Bower still exist in humans. Patterns of modality-related neuronal structures may eventually provide clues about modality interrelationships (Westheimer, 1984).

Cooperation and Conflict Among Perceptual Modalities. These multiple perceptual systems each appear to have formal arrangements for handling their specialized kinds of information (Mishkin, 1986). They might be thought of as inborn operating rules. Some cross-modal flexibility appears to exist in human infants that is not apparent in adults (Bower, 1978).

For example, a 16-week-old blind baby was fitted with a device that put out ultrasound and that converted reflections from objects of the ultrasound waves into audible sounds. Different aspects of the sound coded information that is typically provided by vision (e.g., pitch coded distance; amplitude coded size). The very first time the ultrasound device was used the baby displayed typical visually guided behaviors, although information about the location and movement of objects was sound-coded. For example, when an object was moved toward its face the baby's eyes converged, and they diverged as the object was moved away again. An object was moved from right to left in his field of vision and he tracked it with his head and eyes and swiped at it with his hand. During the first year, the baby learned a variety of skills typical of sighted babies (e.g., searching for and finding an object hidden behind something). Normally, congenitally blind babies will display none of the kinds of visually guided behaviors just described. Moreover, such perceptual plasticity disappears with maturity.

Information filtering by modality has been demonstrated to exist as early as the sixteenth week of life (Anthony & Graham, 1983). However, in the typical natural situation, the information acquired through multiple sensory modalities manifests spatial-temporal covariation, and that provides the basis for a person to use information in different modalities as representing aspects of the same object or event (e.g., one can see a person's mouth move while hearing the spoken words). Infants use such covariation information. For example, when two movie films were shown superimposed on the same screen with a soundtrack appropriate to only one, four-month old infants attended to the film whose soundtrack was being played (Bahrick, Walker, & Neisser, 1981). In another study, 6 to 8-month-old infants preferred to look at an array of objects that corresponded in number to a sequence of sounds simultaneously presented (Starkey, Spelke, & Gelman, 1983).

Misinterpretation of accurately perceived modality covariation is one source of human errors in judgment and action. For example, my sister received a fine cane as a gift. She was demonstrating its versatility to my mother by showing how the handle could be adjusted. Just as she adjusted the handle, the smoke alarm on the wall above her head began to buzz because of smoke from pork chops frying on the kitchen stove. She thought the noise was coming from her cane, and tried twisting the handle and shaking the cane to stop the noise. Some people use covariation information to make difficult judgments, such as the baseball umpire who watches for the base runner's foot to touch the base while simultaneously listening for the sound of the ball hitting the defender's glove.

What happens if perceptions in different modalities conflict? It is difficult, if not impossible, to simultaneously attend equally to information in two different modalities, or to two different messages in the same modality. Perceptual primacy is determined by the person's current intentions and particularly salient stimulus properties.

Such difficulties are not surprising within a living systems framework. Information collection capabilities evolved as handmaidens to effective action. To serve that function, information feedback (i.e., perceptions) relevant to current behavioral concerns must be selected and monitored and other information ignored. Thus, perceptual conflict is resolved primarily by specification through feedforward processes of the information that will be most useful in serving the person's current objectives. Such primary feedback signals are usually in one modality. All other information in all other modalities is monitored with peripheral attention or not at all (see Chapter 7). In general, when there is a multimodal information conflict unresolved by feedforward processes, information in one modality is relied upon and other information is ignored or transformed to fit (Marks, 1978).[4] Visual perception usually dominates.

Summary

Human information collection capabilities evolved so that information may be collected in many different codes (e.g., sights, sounds, odors) carried on a variety of physical markers (e.g., air pressure waves, mechanical pressure), and transduced from one code (e.g., sights) carried on one marker (e.g., light) into another (e.g., patterns of neuronal firing). Humans are continually bathed in a flow of information, and they selectively perceive invariant aspects of that flow that are relevant to their current concerns and ignore the rest. This is accomplished through informational-attentional feedforward processes. Perceptual information accurately represents the information source and provides the raw data from which cognitive processes can construct, recall, and use generalized information patterns. Those processes are considered in Chapter 9.

---

[4]Frontiers of research in sensory physiology are producing the outline of a biological organization of sensory neurology even more complex than that outlined here (Neff, 1982). From sensory neurons to cortical fields, sensory physiology appears to be designed to provide multiple representations of the external world. The major sensory pathways are no longer viewed as relatively homogeneous. Rather, they appear to be composed of some number of parallel pathways, each carrying information representing some aspect(s) of the external world. As a corollary, there are multiple cortical fields for each sensory modality including at least six for vision. One cannot help but view such highly organized complexity with awe, and wonder how it is orchestrated to produce a symphony rather than a cacophony of information flow.

9

Cognition, Information Processing, and Remembering

INTRODUCTION

This chapter is organized into five parts. First, a brief rationale for the relationship of the physical brain to its information-processing capabilities is provided. The brain is described as a variability analyzer and controller, and a tentative list of inborn capabilities for constructing and using information units is presented. Second, a view is presented that the brain symbolizes information using three types of codes, imagistic, abstract, and linguistic; and a summary is made of the relationships among them. To be represented in consciousness, abstract codes must be transformed into imagistic or symbolic codes.

Third, it is proposed that the brain uses multiple types of codes to construct three different types of information organizations that function as cognitive units. *Schemata,* which function to organize and guide behavior, are constructed from three types of behavior episodes: *instrumental* episodes, *observational* episodes, and *thinking* episodes, differentiated by the extent to which transactional functions are involved. Concepts and propositions are components of schemata that are differentiated from schemata, can become functionally autonomous, and therefore can be used to construct new informational forms independent of particular experiences or contexts from which they originated.

Fourth, these ideas are applied to the beginning stages of cognitive development in infancy to illustrate their operation; the nature of the remembering process is examined, and its role in the revision and elaboration of cognitive units is considered. The developmental principles described in Chapter 4 are applied. The chapter ends with a brief consideration of "metacognitive" or "executive" control processes in governing behavior. This provides a transition to the main topics of Chapters 10, 11, and 12.

INFORMATION AND COGNITIVE FUNCTIONING

Humans' most distinctive characteristic is their information-based self-constructing capabilities. Knowledge is power! It frees humans from being completely dominated by present events. It enables them to transcend space and time by remembering events that have occurred at other times and places, and by conceiving places that they have never been and potential future events. They can then seek ways to travel to the imagined places, and prepare for or act to influence the occurrence of anticipated future events. It enables them to transcend the boundaries of their sensory-perceptual capabilities by imagining things their senses have not and cannot reveal to them, and then creating methods and tools with which to transform information about those imagined events into forms perceptible through their senses.

Knowledge enables humans to transcend their natural environments. Humans can conceive of objects, entities, and environments that have never existed and then invent ways of transforming existing materials and environments into such imagined forms. They can use information to influence one another and to construct and maintain social organizations. It enables humans to transcend the limitations placed upon them by their own bodies by creating ways of altering bodily processes (e.g., drugs, biofeedback), by creating substitutes for faulty body parts (e.g, artificial limbs and organs), and by elaborating their structural-functional capabilities by inventing tools (e.g., airplanes).

Historical Perspective

These are godlike capabilities which philosophers throughout the centuries have tried to understand. Efforts to understand human "mental processes" were the starting point for the discipline of psychology. Early psychologists assumed they were really manifestations of natural processes, and therefore should be understandable through the methods of other natural sciences (Marshall, 1982; Murphy, 1929).

Aristotle (384–322 BC) proposed four primary mental faculties that have influenced ways of categorizing mental phenomena ever since: the common sense; imagination and fantasy; thinking and reasoning; and memory. He also proposed that memory was organized like a library, storing information in different categories, and including a reference or index system for efficiently locating stored information. Modern counterparts appear in distinctions between memory and metamemory, and spatial metaphors for memory.

A mechanistic orientation suggested that if there were different mental faculties, they should be localized indifferent brain structures; therefore, whichever mental faculties were disrupted should reveal which part of the brain was damaged. This localization of function idea turned out to be of limited validity.

An alternate view emerged (see Chapter 6). It held that the brain should be understood as a highly organized organ displaying functional unity, requiring study "of the spatiotemporal and configurational characteristics" of neuroanatomy and neural activity (John & Schwartz, 1978). Instead of looking for a one to one correspondence between damaged brain structures and behavior, neuropathologists began to use a less mechanistic orientation (Ellis, 1982; Goldstein, 1948). A current guiding assumption is that "multipotential and dynamic functional landscapes" may be changed by brain damage and reordered by subsequent behavioral experience (John & Schwartz, 1978). Much modern physical rehabilitation is based on that view. The assumptions and evidence of evolutionary and cellular biology have been applied to the evolution of cognitive functioning (Jerison, 1982), legitimizing the study of animal intelligence (Premack, 1983), and the cellular basis of mental processes (Farley & Alkon, 1985).

As attempts to measure mental functioning developed, the concept of intelligence emerged (Carroll, 1982; Galton, 1883). Binet (Binet & Simon, 1908) created useful measures that gave the concept powerful influence. The study of intelligence and that of cognitive functioning have merged into one broad stream of effort (Sternberg, 1982). Initially, memory and problem solving were studied (Woodworth, 1938). Behaviorism became dominant, research on "mental" processes fell into some disrepute and was later reincarnated in the study of verbal behavior (Skinner, 1957). However, that approach became "the study of esoterica" (Lachman, Lachman, & Butterfield, 1979) and was replaced by the currently dominant information-processing view.

Bartlett (1932), influenced by Lotze's idea (Northway, 1940) that what people remember is a kind of "scheme" or a "plan of action," argued for a view of cognition as a constructive process; advances in information theory, communication engineering, and computer science gave this view credibility. Miller, Galanter, and Pribram (1960) used a cybernetics analogy to represent cognitive functioning in terms of images (similar to Lotze's schemes) and plans for action. Neisser (1967) assumed an active, constructive, symbol-manipulating mind, and Newell and Simon (1972) presented an influential information-processing model based upon systems and computer analogies.

Information processing approaches now dominate the study of human cognition and influence many other human sciences. Humans are considered active information seekers and users. They can change and amplify information, create new symbol structures, and use information to direct, construct, and evaluate actions "by internal processes" (Lachman et al., 1979); that is, they are informationally self-organizing and self-constructing. Viewing humans as symbol-manipulating entities stimulated attempts to use linguistics theory to explain human mental functioning (Chomsky, 1972; Davidson & Harman, 1972). Thus, current cognitive science has a multidisciplinary base.

Format for Summarizing Information About Governing Functions

The range of relevant literature is enormous and growing explosively. Therefore, no one "can seriously claim expert knowledge" about all the available information relevant to cognitive functioning (Lachman et al., 1979). Philosophy (Fodor, 1981), psychology (Anderson, 1983), psycholinguistics (Clark & Clark, 1977), artificial intelligence (Newell, 1980a, 1980b; Simon, 1979) computer science (Schank & Colby, 1973), automata theory and neural sciences (Colby, 1978), and clinical and psychoanalytic psychology (Santostefano, 1978) illustrate the many fields contributing to cognitive science.

Cognitive functioning is studied under rubrics such as concept formation (Medin & Smith, 1984), intelligence (Resnick, 1976; Sternberg, 1982), learning and memory (Tulving, 1983; Wickelgren, 1981), imagistic thinking (Kosslyn, 1980), mathematical thinking (Ginsburg, 1983), creative thinking (Tyler, 1983), cognitive strategies (Pressley & Levin, 1983), developmental psychology (Fischer & Silvern, 1985), attitudes (Cooper & Croyle, 1984), expectancies (Feather, 1982), decision making (Pitz & Sachs, 1984), social cognition (Showers & Cantor, 1985), social inference (Hastie, 1983), moral reasoning (Turiel, 1983), language comprehension and acquisition (Clarke & Hecht, 1983), and instructional psychology (Gagne & Dick, 1983); to say nothing of the large clinical literature in neurology, psychiatry, and psychology concerning dysfunctions in cognitive functioning.

Moreover, people in these diverse fields often do not cite (and therefore perhaps do not read) the same materials. For example, in eight books on human memory, 80% of 3200 publications were cited in only one book. Similar results were found when the bibliographies of seven books on cognition were examined (White, 1985). Moreover, concept labels proliferate producing conceptual confusion (Tulving, 1979). White (1985) gives several examples (e.g., iconic memory = perceptual visual store; symbolic distance effect = semantic congruity effect). This results, in part, from the vitality and creativity within the field. But it poses real difficulties for someone trying to identify conceptual and empirical commonalities and differences.

What follows is an attempt to present a plausible representation of human cognitive development and functioning by relating existing theory and information to the living systems framework. It is necessarily based on a selective review of relevant literature, but it intentionally represents the diverse domains listed above, and considers cognitive phenomena described in the literature on clinical and counseling applications. It is divided into four chapters. Chapter 9 considers ideas and information about how people construct, organize, revise, store, and remember knowledge of themselves and the world. Chapters 10, 11, and 12 consider how that information is used to accomplish the three basic control systems governing functions of direction, regulation, and control. *Metacognition* is one currently popular term for these executive functions.

The study of any phenomenon begins with classification, therefore, Chapters 9 through 12 are designed around a set of five classes derived from the living systems framework and available literature, constructed to encompass the full range of human cognition, and defined to facilitate understanding of the relationships among these five types of cognitive phenomena. They are:

1. Information processing: the operations by which humans mentally manipulate information from perceptions and previously constructed conceptions to construct, organize, revise, combine, and elaborate cognitive representations.

2. Remembering: the process of reactivating organizations of information previously constructed from perceptions and conceptions.

3. Direction: the process of using thoughts about potential future events to organize current behavior.

4. Control: the process of using knowledge about the world and oneself to select, coordinate, and organize courses of action to produce intended consequences.

5. Regulation: the process of using evaluative thought to guide adjustments in the flow of behavior to make behavior more effective and to maintain psychological stability.

A brief summary of some key ideas developed in *earlier* chapters, and clarification of certain terms will provide a useful context for developing the ideas in Chapter 9.

1. Only presently occurring events can influence one another. Only by having surrogates for past and future events active in the present can their influence occur.

2. Both the content and organization of event flows maybe influenced and be influential.

3. The prototypical organization of human functioning is represented in the living systems model described in Chapters 3 through 5. However, to represent the functioning of any particular person in a particular episode, the specific content of each functional component must be specified, e.g., which intentions or goals are performing the directive function; which values and evaluative thoughts are performing the regulatory function.

4. Therefore, it is necessary to ask where that content comes from. There are three sources: (1) "current news" comes from perceptual processes described in Chapter 8; (b) conceptions constructed from sets of similar perceptions; and (c) abstractions constructed from sets of perceptually-based conceptions.

5. Actual behavior episodes are organized and coordinated through a merger of these three types of information.

6. The process of constructing conceptions and abstractions, and of selectively using information to organize and coordinate a behavior episode is called *information processing*.

7. The process of activating specific content in any system as a part of a current behavior episode is called *remembering*.

8. The content activated is called a *memory*, e.g., episode memory; motor memory; semantic memory; script; concept.

The remainder of this chapter examines these information based processes.

Basic Issues

Six basic questions represent key issues toward which cognitive science has been and is currently directed.

1. How and why is information selectively collected, organized, and retained?

2. What kinds of symbolic codes or forms are used in cognitive functioning, and how are they related?

3. In what forms is information organized and retained?

4. How and in what forms is retained information remembered and revised or elaborated?

5. How is information used to organize behavior and execute actions?

6. How are other behavioral functions related to cognition?

This chapter focuses primarily on the first four questions which deal mainly with memory and information processing functions. Later chapters focus on questions 5 and 6, which deal mainly with executive functions.

BASES FOR INFORMATION SELECTION, ORGANIZATION, AND USE

Information, in the dual forms of current perceptions and cognitive representations, organizes a person's behavior. Therefore, if the guiding information is contradictory and not coherently organized, the behavior it organizes will similarly be contradictory and somewhat disorganized. Terms like *confused, ambivalent, uncoordinated,* and *conflicted* illustrate the kinds of subjective feelings people have when their current behavior is being influenced by poorly organized or contradictory information. Disorganization is a threat to the existence of living systems and cannot be tolerated; therefore, cognition is self-organizing to be internally coherent so that the behavior it guides will be coherently organized.

Any kind of human development must have some starting point from which it can begin (see Chapter 5). Just as there are inborn arrangements such as digestion and mentabolism for processing, transforming, distributing, and using *material,* so too are there inborn arrangements for collecting, processing, transforming, distributing, and using *information* (Lachman et al., 1979). What might be the nature of these inborn properties?

Physical Symbol Systems

Brain structures and their information-processing functions evolved to facilitate effective environmental transactions. Therefore, "manipulating symbols" must involve the same brain "architecture" as the "construction of acts" (Pribram, 1971). The relationship between the physical brain and thought is a centuries-old puzzle. The concepts of information and physical symbol systems provide one plausible answer. Turing (1936) formulated an abstract symbolic system whose states and changes of states could be described by a few basic operations. A diversity of physical structures (e.g., computers) can be designed to perform such operations through the manipulation of physical symbol systems (Newell, 1980a; Newell & Simon, 1976). Symbols representing information can be given a physical expression by altering (coding) the organization of some physical carrier (see Chapter 8). Information can then be manipulated by processes that organize and reorganize—code and recode—its physical expression, such as altering the patterns of electrical signals in a telephone to code speech. Sensory and neural structures and processes provide the physical carriers for human symbolic functioning.

Such symbol systems must be capable of three basic types of functions (Newell, 1980a): (a) a memory: an information or data base and storage capability; (b) operators: strategies and processes for selectively collecting, organizing, and reorganizing information, and for using it to organize "outputs" or actions; and (c) controls: special superordinate or "executive" operations for organizing the selective interaction of different kinds of information with different operators. All symbol systems distinguish between operators (i.e., processes for organizing information) and the information operated on (i.e., data, memories, thoughts). To construct their own operations as well as their memories, however, information-processing entities must be able to treat some expressions as data at one time and as operators at another. Systems (like humans) that can revise and elaborate their memory, operator, and control functions can be self-organizing and self-constructing.

Newell (1980a) presents the following three interrelated reasons why physical symbol systems are necessary for general intelligent action:

1. A general intelligent system must somehow embody aspects of what is to be attained prior to attainment of it, i.e., it must have goals. Symbols that designate the situation to be attained...appear to be the only candidate for doing this." Fixed goals built into the system are not adequate "for a general intelligence facing an indefinite sequence of novel and sufficiently diverse goal situations.

2. A general intelligent system must somehow consider candidate states of affairs (and partial states) for the solutions of these goals....Symbols in a symbol system appear to be the only way to designate these, especially as the diversity and novelty of the states and partial states increase without bound.

3. An intelligent system must fashion its responses to the demands of the task environment. As the diversity of tasks expand, there would seem to be no way to avoid a flexibility sufficient to imply universality and hence symbols. (p. 172)

Note that (a) encompasses the directive function, (b) the control function and (c) the regulatory function of this living systems framework. An indefinitely wide variety of such symbol systems can be created, but the human brain is currently the most complex physical structure known capable of physical symbol system functioning. The study of human perception and cognition is the study of the "memory," "operator," and "control" functions by which humans process, construct, and use information. Only "blurred boundaries" separate the "traditional domains" of sensation, perception, and cognition (Simon, 1979). Cognitive scientists refer to operator functions with terms like *thinking, problem solving, concept formation, and information processing*. Control functions, subdivided into directive, regulatory, and control functions in this framework, are frequently termed *metacognitive* or *executive functions*. While these capabilities may be modified through learning, there must be some inborn capabilities that provide the developmental starting points. The evolution of neural structures provided "innate biological constraints" or "epigenetic rules" that "guide the mind along appropriate pathways of choice and development" (Lumsden, 1983). (see also Chapters 5 & 6, and Edelman, 1978.)

Views About Inborn Information Processes

Cognitive Science. Many scholars of human cognition explicitly or implicitly assume inborn memory bases for "primitive" information-processing functions, such as encoding, recognizing, storing, decoding, comparing, and combining information (Lachman et al., 1979; Lachman & Lachman, 1979); generating, differentiating, and elaborating information structures (Erlich, 1979); abstracting and classifying (G. Mandler, 1979); "neural schemata" for organizing information collection (Neisser, 1976); basic information-processing operations (Bower, 1974a); "categorization" of objects or events (Mervis & Rosch, 1981); and representing spatial sequential organization (Byrne, 1982). Bruner et al. (1966) assume that "acculturation," interacting with "primitive and innate symbolic activity," creates development of specialized "cognitive systems," through three systems for processing information, i.e., through action, imagery, and language (Bruner, 1964). Simon (1979) argues that humans have "a basic repertory of mechanisms and processes," that all cognitive developments must be "assembled from this same basic repertory," and that "common principles of architecture" must guide such development. The "concantenation" of "elementary mental processes or operations" produces complex behaviors (Posner & McLeod, 1982). The "fixed capacities of the mind" or its "functional architecture" must be empirically separated from particular "representations and algorithms" (Pylyshyn, 1980). Mental processes are "causal sequences" (controls) of "mental operations" on "mental representations" (Fodor, 1981). "Schematizing" and "categorizing" functions are "primitive, innate human abilities" that help to create "order and structure out of the welter of stimulation." The mind "seeks for and finds regularities, and comes to expect them in the future" (J. Mandler, 1979). New information is organized in terms of "existing memory organization" (Voss, 1979), or "personal experiences or episodes" (Schank & Abelson, 1977).

Intelligence. Scholars studying human intelligence also assume inborn information processing capabilities (Cooper & Regan, 1982; Diamond & Royce, 1980; Meadows, 1983; Scarr & Carter-Saltzman, 1982; Siegler & Richards, 1982; Voss, 1976;). For example, Sternberg (1980) proposes three "elementary" processes: (a) some that "translate" sensory inputs into symbolic representations; (b) some that "transform" one symbolic representation into another; and (c) some that "translate" a symbolic representation into a motor output. Hunt (1983) proposes: (a) choice of an "internal representation for a problem" (memory); (b) strategies for "manipulating the representation" (operators); and (c) ability to execute the information-processing steps required by the strategy (controls). Sternberg and Powell (1982) provide a more elaborate taxonomy.

Personality and Psychotherapy Theory. Scholars focused on persons rather than response processes have also proposed inborn information processes (Ford & Urban, 1963). For example, Freud proposed the pleasure, reality, and repetition compulsion principles, and two kinds of thought processes: *Primary process thought* is imagistic and guided by processes of fusion and condensation different from the controlled, logical format of *secondary process thought*. Carl Rogers proposed two basic self-organizing and self-constructing processes: (a) an inborn tendency to resolve discrepancies or incongruities in experience; and (b) a tendency to maintain and enhance themselves. Sullivan considered *referential processes* to be innate capabilities.

Learning. Learning theories have also assumed inborn processes; examples are classical conditioning and instrumental conditioning (which may be different aspects of one process according to Locurto Terrace, & Gibbon, 1981). At the height of conditioning theory's dominance, Hilgard (1948) commented that it was "strange" that the possibility that humans have evolved "capacities for retaining, reorganizing, and foreseeing experiences" not present in other animals was given so little attention. His speculations anticipated current ideas in cognitive learning. Some behaviors appear to be "intrinsically organized" while others are organized "on the basis of experience" (Schwartz, 1974). Organisms appear to differ in what they can learn, as well as the ease with, and the conditions under which they can learn different kinds of things. For example, rats learn taste and odor-taste aversions more readily than many other animals (Palmerino, Rusiniak, & Garcia, 1980). Some species-specific processes appear to have evolved in more complex organisms (Bitterman, 1975; Schwartz, 1974; Seligman, 1970; Seligman & Hager, 1972).

Humans start life with a set of inborn capabilities for learning and development which regulate their initial developmental trajectory, constrained and facilitated by the environmental context (Scarr-Salapatek, 1976; McCall, 1981). Alternate inborn processes underlying learning have been proposed (Katona, 1940). Human learning results from events' information properties rather than through some "prewired" contiguity or "reinforcement" effects (Garcia, Clarke, & Hankins, 1973; Glaser, 1984). It results in "the acquisition of knowledge" through the modification and combination of "cognitive structure" (Greeno, 1980), which must include knowledge for organizing and guiding the performance of effective actions (Sacerdoti, 1977). In systems terms, learning research has shifted from a primary emphasis on behavioral "output" to an emphasis on "input" and "throughput," or how symbolic representations are formed, altered, and used in problem solving. Merging all three is necessary because all are learned in integrated patterns.

Basic Environmental Properties and Cognitive Evolution. Another source of clues about the nature of basic cognitive functions, is the kind of information they evolved to apprehend and use to enable humans to function effectively in their terrestrial environment. This includes hierarchically and spatially organized objects, and substances and their physical-chemical and functional properties. Moreover, it is a dynamic environment, which varies according to natural laws within which some things are moveable, moving, and tend to change states. Additional dynamic qualities of information flow result from humans' manipulative capabilities and mobility.

The dynamic organization of events provides information about three basic types of relationships: randomness; covariation, which makes it possible to predict future events; and influence or contingency, which makes it possible to control events. Humans' long evolutionary history probably produced different kinds of cognitive capabilities hierarchically related at different levels of neural organization (Pribram, 1984; Oakley, 1983; Tulving, 1985).

A Summary of Probable Inborn Information-Processing Functions

Humans' superior adaptiveness results from their ability to transcend the flux and flow of the here and now, which gives them "one kind of inner freedom" (Deutsch, 1951). They accomplish that by (a) selecting some aspects from the variable flow of current events and ignoring others; (b) organizing the resulting information in ways useful to their current concerns; and (c) combining that "current news" with representations constructed from past experiences and imagined future conditions to organize and guide their current behavior. Therefore, the human brain evolved as a variability analyzer and controller. The "sense of sameness" is the backbone of thinking (James, 1910). Cognitive

processes function to exercise "operant control" over sources of variation in a person's own behavior (Catania, 1978; Fischer, 1980). "Cognitive apprehension" is an abstraction of information that "most generally
characterizes a type of phenomena" (Fowler, 1977). Brain processes
conduct a "dynamic search for invariances" in the flow of experience
(Platt, 1970a). People know and respond to "recurrent regularities" in
their environments by "skilled and patterned acts," "selective perceptual organization," "conventionalized spatioqualitative imagery," and
"linguistic encoding" (Bruner, et al., 1966). It is important to recognize
that regularities of both content (item information) and spatial-temporal
organization (relational information) may be abstracted and represented.

The complexity of human cognitive activity requires "an inherited
organization to execute, control and dynamically pattern" complex
behavior. These cognitive abilities "emerge of their own accord" in a
healthy person and appropriate environment, rather than being taught
to children (Blackmore, 1981). The following basic processes function
within the context of the developmental principles described in Chapter
5.

1. The capability for selectively monitoring multiple kinds of information arising from three basic sources: (a) information about the environment; (b) information arising within the body representing biological,
motoric, affective, and cognitive functioning; and (c) information about
the relationships and interactions among variables from (a) and (b).

2. The ability to distinguish similarities and differences among kinds
and sources of information. Two important consequences of this ability
are the discrimination of self from nonself, and the discrimination of
current from remembered (past) or imagined (future) events.

3. The ability to selectively abstract from sensory-perceptual information flows, and symbolically represent patterns of consistency in content
and flow.

4. The ability to merge information from multiple sensory sources into
multivariate representations, thereby creating informational units of
different size and scope.

5. The ability to construct new symbolizations from previously constructed symbolizations and from combinations of symbolizations and
perceptions, as well as from perceptions.

6. The ability to retain and recall (or reconstruct) previously constructed symbolizations in the absence of the objects and event(s)
symbolized.

7. The ability to use symbolizations and perceptions to organize and
execute behavior patterns in anticipation of events' occurrence.

These inborn capabilities provide the starting points for future cognitive development.

KINDS OF CODES OR SYMBOLIZATIONS USED

Humans' evolutionary history probably produced three interrelated coding or symbolizing capabilities which create the units or chunks of "mental data" manipulated by cognition (Anderson, 1980; Grossberg, 1980; Shepard, 1984); these are *imagistic, abstract,* and *linguistic* coding (Bruner et al., 1966; Paivio, 1975; Yuille & Catchpole, 1977). Diamond and Royce (1980) interpret factor analytic data to support three analogous basic "ways of knowing." Characteristics of each kind of coding and their relationships are reviewed next to provide a basis for proposals about types of information organization.

Imagistic Representations

Imagistic representation was probably the first to evolve. Many species appear to form imagistic representations (Marler & Terrace, 1984; Roitblat, Bever, & Terrace, 1984). For example, bees appear to create "low-resolution eidetic images" of flower patterns (Gould, 1985). Therefore, the construction, retention, and reuse of images is probably the most basic form of coding and thinking of which humans are capable. Its evolution made possible humans' anticipatory or purposive behavior towards "remote objects and events" (Shepard, 1984). All perceptions are imagistic representations (Long, 1980) selectively representing information that is available at sensory surfaces, and coded by sensory modality. Since consciousness evolved as a part of the monitoring process for using information in feedback (sensory-perceptual) circuits to regulate the flow of behavior, only symbolizations coded in perceptible forms can become part of the contents of consciousness. Humans display imagistic representation in memory and thinking, dreaming, and hallucinating.

Imagistic Memory and Thinking. Study of imagistic cognitive capabilities has a long history (Galton, 1883; Holt, 1964). Much anecdotal evidence exists about the role of visual and auditory imagery in scientific discovery and artistic creativity (Ghiselin, 1955; Shepard, 1978). Imagery appears to be more prominent in the thought of children than of adults (Bruner et al., 1966; Piaget, 1962). The ability to create vivid, percept-like, conscious images is called eidetic imagery (Haber, 1979). There is convincing evidence for imaging that is both static (e.g., remembering a scene or picture) and dynamic, for example, visualizing an object from different angles (Ernst, 1977; Haber, 1979; Kauffmann, 1980; Kosslyn, 1980; Sheikk, 1983; Shepard & Cooper, 1982).

Good summaries exist of relevant theories and research (Kosslyn, 1985; Kosslyn, Pinker, Smith, & Shwartz, 1979). Imagistic representations may be by sensory-perceptual modality (vision dominates in humans), but may also combine information from several modalities. For children, the covariation of what they see, hear, and feel with regard to an object or event provides a coherent image, and they may display surprise or apprehension when the modality information does not fit together in familiar ways. Imaging is a "dynamic process" like "an inner perceptual-motor system" (Paivio, 1975).

Perceiving and imaging appear to be similar brain events. For example, visual or auditory imagining interferes with simultaneous visual or auditory perception. Brain damage that affects perception may also affect imagistic functioning. Images appear to function as three-dimensional models. For example, people take more time for scanning or manipulations of more complicated images (e.g., "rotate" or "fold" an image) than of simpler ones. One may imagine a part or all of an object, through processes analogous to selectively focused attention in perception. It is more difficult for people to report details of smaller than larger images of objects. Imagining oneself performing a skilled action can improve later performance.

Imagistic and linguistic thinking are parallel but interacting modes of thought (Paivio, 1971). For example, people profoundly deaf from earliest childhood who have not learned their native language can perform complex thought processes; this indicates that language may be useful for, but is not required for, thought (Furth, 1966). Excessive reliance on imagery may constrain the development and use of other types of coding and vice versa (Sheehan, 1972). Exceptional imagistic abilities appear in some infants with cognitive defects; an example is autistic savants (Rimland, 1978). People with extensive training and practice in imaging often have richer imagistic experience and abilities. For example, I'm envious of an artist daughter-in-law whose dream life is in vivid technicolor; my wife who can look at the color and form of something when shopping, and accurately imagine how it will fit with other colors and forms in one of her artistic creations; a colleague who can close his eyes and imagistically listen to a symphony; and an architect-builder who can visualize his designs taking shape in three-dimensional form as a means of verifying their construction feasibility.

Imagistic representation of spatial configurations is of special adaptive value, and mobile animals, from rats to humans, have a marked ability to remember and use spatial information in a flexible, adaptive way

(Evans, 1980; Herman, 1980; Olton, 1979; Waddell & Rogoff, 1981). The formation of accurate "cognitive maps" is facilitated by physical movement through the environment, and their detail and accuracy can become more elaborate with experience. Visual coding of spatial information is supplemented by kinesthetic and auditory coding of spatial information (Battacchi, Franza, & Pani, 1981). Initially, children conceive of space with reference to body centered coordinates, that is, *egocentrically* (Piaget & Inhelder, 1969). Later, their spatial conceptions elaborate to include object- and context-centered coordinates (see Chapter 8). By adulthood, abstract and linguistic coding forms have come to play an important role in spatial conceptions (Kosslyn & Pomerantz, 1977). Infants' ability to image spatial configurations may provide the precursor for development of numerical abilities (Cooper, 1980).

Dreams and Hallucinations.   Dreams and hallucinations are imagistic representations that occur independently of typical conscious controls and are temporarily mistaken by a person for direct perceptions of real events (Hilgard, 1977). Dreams are hallucinations of the normal, and are imagistic constructions influenced by recent life experiences and concerns (Freud, 1955a). Therefore, psychotherapists sometimes find them useful as sources of information about thoughts and experiences disrupting the functioning of troubled people.

Dreams probably illustrate the most basic form of thought, called by Freud, *primary process thought,* in which the organizing rules of language and logic are replaced with processes similar to perceptual synthesis. Dreams are less constrained by spatial, temporal, and sequential attributes that organize waking perceptions and thought. Dreaming consists of "formulating conceptions and ideas" while asleep which become represented in consciousness in images that are the most efficient and elegant way of expressing them (Hall, 1966). For example, in one dream a "snooty" "academic" colleague from a "southern country" who was having an "uphill struggle" with his career, and who "opposed" some ideas for a "new course," was symbolized as a llama (a snooty looking South American ruminant) walking uphill towards the dreamer who was heading downhill on a bicycle built for two with a colleague who was collaborating on the new course (Blackmore, 1981). Children with limited language capabilities probably still use primary process thought more frequently than adults. Children's dreams tend to realistically reflect aspects of their daily life; disturbing life experiences are often reflected in dreams (Foulkes, 1971; Foulkes & Fleisher, 1975).

Dreaming is a frequently occurring cognitive activity with distinctive properties and with variations associated with biological and psychological states and personality dynamics. More reality-oriented or controlled dreams occur in the first half of the night, while more perceptual, nonreality-tested dreams occur during the second half (Cohen, 1970; Webb & Cartwright, 1978).

Hallucinations are percept-like imagistic constructions that may be induced by hypnotic procedures, or precipitated by biological disruptions and stresses such as disease, fatigue, and drugs, and by psychological disturbances such as psychoses (Hilgard, 1977; Siegel & West, 1975; West, 1962). They may be represented in any sensory-perceptual modality (e.g., sounds, odors, feelings of bugs crawling on the skin), but are most frequently visual or auditory (Cameron & Magaret, 1951). Like dreams, they may be pleasant experiences ("good trips") or unpleasant ones ("bad trips"). Hallucinations of behavior episodes may occur. For example, an 87-year-old woman recovering from a brain disruption spent considerable time threading an imaginary needle and sewing on an imaginary project.

Abstract Representations

Percepts are first-order *information abstractions* representing consistencies in information flows across sensory receptors. Imagistic representations are abstracts of consistencies among similar percepts. They are second-order *information transformations*. Abstracts of consistencies from imagistic representations, and abstracts from such abstracts, are information constructions (e.g., concepts and propositions) with generalized meaning that are *third- and higher order information transformations*. They *cannot become a part of consciousness* because of their generalized nature, but can be represented in consciousness with imaged examples or perceptible symbolic representations such as words. For example, one can have images about particular kinds of dogs, but not about dogs in general; about a specific round object or the word "round," but not about the concept "round." Such generalized concept formation must be "abstract, generative, and nonperceptual" (Weimer, 1977). A diversity of proposals have been made about the nature and formation of abstract representations (Craik, 1979; Medin & Smith, 1984; Wickelgren, 1981).

Since abstract representations are independent of specific objects and events, they free people from the constraints of experiences both of the past and of the here and now. They can be combined and transformed to construct representations of objects, events, or methods not previously perceived, that may not yet exist, or that may not be perceivable. It is what humans can *conceive*, facilitated and constrained by information of what they have perceived or can perceive, that gives them their unique adaptive potentials. That is why such conceptual capabilities have been a cornerstone of definitions of intelligence (Sternberg & Powell, 1983). Abstraction involves building up "relations among relations" and is critical to "fluid intelligence" (Cattell, 1971); it is part of a hierarchy of learning processes (Gagne, 1968). Younger children tend to think in terms of the perceptible or concrete properties of situations; older children tend to focus on and think in terms of abstractions representing dimensions, principles, or rules (Osler & Kofsky, 1966), which Piaget (1976) termed *formal operational thought.*

Abstractions and Intentional, Nonconscious Thought. Historically, thinking with abstract representations was referred to as "imageless thought," and classical introspective methods were used to demonstrate the existence of experiences which are not sensory in character (Holt, 1964; Moore, 1919; Murphy, 1929; Woodworth, 1938). "Imageless" thought represented "meanings" which could be directly expressed in consciousness only through images or words. While the label "imageless" dropped from use, the idea persisted. For example, Piaget (1960, 1962) represents thinking as an activity outside awareness whose symbolic products in the form of images or words are the conscious manifestations of thought. Based on the study of profoundly deaf people with no verbal language capability, Furth (1966) concluded that (a) "intelligent thinking" is an "internal system" involving "hierarchical ordering" of "representations" of experience; and (b) it does not depend upon linguistic symbolization, but rather language use depends on the "structure of intelligence." People can think without words. J. Evans (1980) concludes that people do not reason logically, and that reasoning is neither introspectible nor sequential in organization. Verbal reports about one's reasoning are "rationalizations" of, rather than descriptions of, one's own reasoning processes. Analogies, models, and language are useful tools for giving abstract ideas a consciously perceptible and therefore communicable form.

Semantic memory is one currently popular label for abstract representations (Tulving, 1972). Their construction and use need not involve "actual experience" with the information symbolized. Stored information is generally not a "replica" of some experience, but involves "various levels of recoding" of the information (Estes, 1976). It is one of several kinds of memory codes (Horton & Mills, 1984). Linguistic symbols are normally linked to such abstractions, and therefore are often considered a part of, and sometimes the primary form of, semantic memory.

Linguistic Representation

The construction and use of linguistic symbols is a late evolutionary product. Many animals use gestures and sounds to influence other organisms, but only humans use complex languages (see Chapter 15).

Linguistic communication is an inborn potential that manifests itself in a normal, human communicative environment, but language is not necessary for the having or processing of ideas (Lennenberg, 1967).

A language is composed of symbols, its *lexicon*, which can be organized through the use of a set of rules, its *syntax*, and coded on some physical carrier, its *articulation*, to convey information and meanings, its *semantics*. Language may take many forms (e.g.,mathematics, sign languages), but verbal language is the form that is most pervasive, flexible, and powerful. Because linguistic communication is the primary means for creating and operating human organizations, and is the "glue" for societies and cultures, its social significance is often emphasized (DeLong, 1972). Vygotsky (1962, 1978) proposed that language is initially social; a means through which others can regulate the child's behavior. Only later does a child come to use it to regulate his or her own behavior. Beginning with infancy, social interaction functions to influence and synchronize participants' behavior, and language is a powerful tool for that purpose (Papousek & Papousek, 1975), because words and sentences can elicit similar BES in the communicants.

Languages are perceptible phenomena. People can hear, see, and sometimes feel (e.g., braille) words and sentences. Therefore, like any perceptible phenomena, imagistic representations of language symbols can be formed. Moreover, verbal communication is a motor act, so linguistic representation has both cognitive and motoric components (see Chapter 15). However, unlike other kinds of perceptions and imagistic representations, *linguistic ones have no intrinsic meaning.* For example, children (and students) can learn to recognize and speak words and not have the foggiest idea of what they mean. They become useful (meaningful) when they can function as surrogates for the real thing; that is, for imagistic and abstract representations. Just as the handle on a cup provides a means of manipulating the cup for drinking, so too are linguistic representations "handles" for manipulating and conveying the information and ideas or meanings to which they are linked. Adults typically think with abstract representations, which they give conscious and communicable form with language. The relation of thought to word is a continual movement "from thought to word and from word to thought" (Vygotsky, 1962).

Braine and Rumain (1983) summarize research on the relationships between people's linguistic and conceptual capabilities. They assert that many conclusions about the development of children's reasoning capabilities are erroneous because of failure to distinguish between conceptual capabilities and a person's understanding of linguistic representations of conceptual abstractions. Linguistic organization and the organization of thought are different but related phenomena. The following analogy may be useful: Sentences are related to thoughts as coherent movements are to intended action consequences; and words are related to sentences as muscle contractions are to coherent movements (see Chapter 14).

Because linguistic representations have no intrinsic meanings, their imagistic representations cannot provide a basis for the construction of abstract representations. Recognition of that limitation helps make sense of some research on human memory and cognition based on verbal stimuli. For example, nonsense syllables were constructed as research tools specifically to eliminate any surrogate meanings. Remembering nonsense syllables requires people to rely solely on imagistic properties of the symbols and their organization (e.g., serial position in the list; similar spelling). Only "rote" memorization is possible under these circumstances.

However, if linguistic representations are used as surrogates for other imagistic and abstract representations (e.g., meaningful prose passages), then what is remembered will be influenced primarily by those meanings rather than by the imagistic properties of the words themselves. The same word may represent many possible meanings. The particular meaning intended is identified by the facilitating and constraining conditionalities (i.e., organization) of the linguistic context in which the word is used. "Concepts, not words" are the "atoms" of semantic memory (Wickelgren, 1979). For example, what people remember from prose passages is the "gist," or the general meanings elicited by it from their repertoire of imagistic and abstract representations (Anderson & Bower, 1973; Craik, 1979; Freedle, 1977; Voss, 1979). Remembering can be improved by linking relatively meaningless symbols (e.g., names of strangers) to some meaningful imagistic representation. For example, a list of numbers is more easily remembered if one visualizes oneself walking through a familiar space and associates each number to an object in that space; this is called the *method of loci* (Baltes & Reinhold, 1985).

Verbal psychotherapy is built upon this powerful link between language, memories, and behavior. As people talk about their thoughts, feelings, actions, and memories, the actual troublesome imagistic and abstract representations may become reconstructed, operational, and therefore potentially modifiable. Part of the psychotherapist's skill is to distinguish when that has occurred. Verbal therapeutic interventions (e.g., interpretations) may facilitate change only if the relevant imagistic and abstract representations are also occurring. Otherwise, a therapist may only teach clients to talk differently about their problems without producing more significant changes; this is a not uncommon occurrence (Ford & Urban, 1963, 1967).

In summary, humans are capable of three interrelated types of symbolic representation: (a) imagistic coding retains the properties of information yielded by sensory-perceptual processes; (b) abstract representations are constructed from imagistic codes or from other abstractions and are the most flexible because they represent generalized versions of the particular objects, events, experiences or ideas from which they were constructed; (c) linguistic representations are a special kind of imagistic code which have no intrinsic meanings. Only (a) and (c) can become part of the contents of consciousness because only they have been and can be perceptible in feedback circuits. Linguistic images have special utility because they can transform the great diversity of abstract and imagistic representations humans can create into flexibly communicable (i.e., perceptible) form. That is the basis for the assertion, "To be sure of what you are thinking, you must say it or write it down." Language can be used to talk about imaginary, hypothetical, or real phenomena. Mathematics is a kind of linguistic code designed to be content-neutral and to emphasize propositional information about *relationships* For example, in the symbolic expression $A^2 \times B^2 - C = D$, the letters can stand for any phenomena; it is the symbols "$\times$," "$-$" and "$=$" that carry the important information in this statement.

The sequential nature of language organization makes it impossible to linguistically represent *simultaneously* the organization of, or relationships among, multiple objects, ideas, or components. However, nonlinguistic imagistic and abstract representations can do so. For example, visual and multimedia models are of particular value in conveying complex patterns of information in one "chunk." Johnson-Laird (1981, 1983) proposes that at least some thinking probably occurs using mental models because they can simultaneously represent diverse conceptual and propositional information.

FORMS IN WHICH INFORMATION IS ORGANIZED AND REMEMBERED

Humans organize information using combinations of imagistic, abstract, and linguistic codes so that it can be efficiently retained and used. There appear to be limitations on how many units a person can process at one time ("channel" capacity), but each unit can contain varying kinds and amounts of information. Therefore, the more information represented by each unit, the more complex can be the thought processes which utilize those units. The special value of highly abstract conceptualizations is that they are units representing a great deal of information.

A variety of such units have been proposed (Lachman et al., 1979; Medin & Smith, 1984; Puff, 1979; Tulving & Donaldson, 1972;

Wickelgren, 1981). Each proposal can be supported by some empiricial and/or anecdotal/clinical evidence. Yet it seems unlikely that each represents a unique and different aspect of human cognition. There must be some underlying commonalities in that pile of proposals.

Some proposals emphasize the content of the information. There is declarative and procedural knowledge (Anderson, 1983); sensorimotor, representational, abstract, and intellectual skills (Gagne & White, 1978; Fischer, 1980); episodic and semantic memory (Black & Bower, 1979; Tulving, 1972); autobiographical memories (Robinson, 1976; Rubin, 1985); and in social psychology there are stereotypes, attitudes, opinions, and attributions (Eagly & Himmelfarb, 1978; Fiske & Linville, 1980; Grant & Holmes, 1981; Kelley, 1967). Tulving (1985) proposes that there are at least three structurally and functionally different, but interrelated memory systems. *Procedural memory* is nonconscious action-organizing information learned only through overt responding. *Semantic memory*, a subsystem of procedural memory, represents states of the world not perceptually present that may enter consciousness. *Episodic memory*, a subsystem of semantic memory, represents personally experienced events and their temporal relations in subjective time, which may be consciously remembered.

Other proposals focus primarily on organizational form. There are taxonomies, tree structures, networks, and embedded hierarchies (Friendly, 1979); symbol structures and categories (Halford & Wilson, 1980; J. Mandler, 1979; Newell & Simon, 1972; Rosch & Lloyd, 1978); fuzzy sets (McCloskey & Gluksberg, 1978; Wagner, 1981); concepts and propositions (Anderson, 1980); prototypes (Reed, 1972); personal theories (Carey, 1982); mental models (Johnson-Laird, 1983); images and plans (Miller, Galanter, & Pribram, 1960); frames (Minsky, 1975; Winograd, 1981); schemata of various kinds (Goodman, 1980; Rumelhart & Orton, 1977; Yekovich & Thorndyke, 1981); scripts and plans (Abelson, 1981; Bower, Black, & Turner, 1979; Schank & Abelson, 1977); and nuclear scripts (Carlson, 1981; Tomkins, 1980).

A living systems framework implies three types of information-memory units: Units representing behavior episodes as functional units, for which the label *behavior episode schemata* (BES) appears appropriate; Two types of units representing basic components of behavior episodes, typically called *concepts* and *propositions*.

Representations of Behavior Episodes as Cognitive Units

Since the living systems framework proposes that each person's stream of behavior is organized in terms of episodes, cognition must provide directive, regulatory, control, feedforward, feedback, and information-processing functions in the service of behavior episodes.

Similar ideas have a long history in academic psychology (see the discussion of event perception in Chapter 8). Bain (1855) proposed that constructive intellectual activity requires (a) a feeling of the end to be served; (b) command of the elements to be used; and (c) good judgment of when the end is satisfactorily attained. In all voluntary action, the "essential thing" is "to know what one intends to do" (Moore, 1924). Lewin (1936) emphasized cognitive structures that incorporate a coherent set of events interconnected across space and time. Tolman's goal-directed view (1948, 1955) used an expectancy-value model. Bartlett (1958) describes thinking as using information about "something present" to "get somewhere else." Miller, Galanter, and Pribram (1960) proposed that humans solve problems by using a combination of goal-directed cognitive strategies they called *plans*, guided by knowledge structures called *images*, to link knowledge, action, and evaluation. Peoples "control processes," combined with their "goals" determine the information they will process and what they will do in any situation (Newell, 1973). Behavior functions to "control perceptions" or feedback, against a "reference signal" (i.e., a cognitively represented goal) (Powers, 1973a, 1973b).

Problem solving occurs in an unfamiliar context when a motivated person is trying to achieve some goal (Johnson, 1972) . Jenkins (1974) concluded that what is remembered in any situation depends on "the physical and psychological context" in which the remembered event was experienced, the knowledge and skills brought to the context, and the circumstances under which remembering occurs. The contextualist approach asserts that experience consists of "events" having "quality or meaning as a whole," which result from "transactions" between people and their context (Hultsch & Pentz, 1980). Neisser (1976) views cognition as an active, schema-organized process serving actions that are "hierarchically embedded in more extensive actions," are "motivated by anticipated consequences" organized "at various levels of schematic organization." Intelligence involves "problem-detection strategies," "feature scanning strategies," and "goal analysis strategies" as generalized cognitive competencies (Resnick & Glaser, 1976). Cognitive orientation clusters are organizations of beliefs about goals, means, values, and self (Kreitler & Kreitler, 1976). Human behavior occurs "as a continual stream" involving "periodic changes" (Atkinson, 1977). Schank and Abelson (1977) state that memory is organized around "personal experiences" or "episodes." Klinger (1977) describes the stream of thought as being organized in "segments" defined by different incentive-goal patterns. "Cognitive structures" are "cognitive maps or schema" representing the "environmental regularities and means-ends organization of problem-solving demands" within which "rule competencies" are used "to accomplish goals" (Fowler, 1977).

Colby (1978) concludes that cognition consists of "computational behavior of internal representations" of data, and programs "utilized by an organism to achieve its purposes" and involving "flexible conditional computations" and evaluations of "success or failure in achievement." Erickson and Jones (1978) assert that a "real world problem" presents "initial conditions," specifies a "desired state of affairs" and constraints for "transforming initial conditions into the final (goal) state." Voss (1979) states that verbal learning research has neglected the role of "goal or purpose" in acquiring information. "The knowledge structure" relating to "the individual's construction of the so-called problem space" must be considered.

Simon (1979) characterizes humans as "creatures of bounded rationality" whose behavior is characterized by "highly selective serial search" within complex contexts, guided by their "motivational system," and regulated by "dynamically adjusting multidimensional levels of aspiration." The duration of such a behavior pattern is controlled by "a goal terminating mechanism" enabling people to "satisfice" in relation to their objectives, and an "interrupting mechanism" to make it possible to deal with "urgent needs" in "real time." Cognitive schemas emphasize "the necessary interrelation" among perception, attention, comprehension, memory, and action (Craik, 1979). Affective states such as emotions influence learning, remembering, social judgments and actions (Bower, Gilligan, & Monteiro, 1981; Nisbet & Ross, 1980). Norman (1980) argues that cognitive science must broaden its focus to include all human response processes.

Adaptive behavior depends on information "concerning relationships between actions and outcomes" (Estes, 1982). Sternberg and Salter (1982) define intelligence as "goal-directed adaptive behavior." Feather (1982) speaks of "actions and their potential consequences" as "embedded in a complex means-end structure." In his (A)daptive (C)ontrol of (T)hought theory, Anderson (1983) describes thinking in terms of the activation of a goal in working memory which then activates "a relevant production system" which organizes actions. Human problem solving involves the interaction of a person's "modifiable information structures" developed from and organized around "domains" of problem solving "tasks" (Glaser, 1984). Memory organization packets are representations of previously encountered events useful in predicting what will happen in future, structurally similar events (Sternberg, 1982). James et al. (1978) interpret the concept of "psychological climate" used in industrial psychology and organizational behavior as analogous to higher-order schemata.

In psychoanalytic psychology, the "mental structures" of id, ego, and superego represent interrelated cognitive processes which direct, control and regulate patterns of action (Freud, 1923, 1926). Ego analytic extensions make the behavior episode format more explicit (Holt, 1976). For example, Klein (1970) describes a behavioral unit which combines "ideation, affect and action" involving a "train of thought" beginning with an initial "wish or desire" and ending with "gratification." The conditioning "trial" used by behavior modifers is a carefully designed behavior episode.

This sampling of 36 theorists reveals consensus that (a) cognitive functioning must be understood as a goal-directed behavior pattern involving thoughts defining what to do (the directive function), how to do it (the control function), and evaluating consequences (the regulatory function); (b) cognitive functioning is influenced by the content and organization of relevant stored knowledge, the information provided by the current context and actions, and current arousal and bodily states; and (c) the basic role of cognition is to organize and guide adaptive physical and informational environmental transactions. These are the properties of *behavior episodes*. Representations of behavior episodes, analogous to episodic memory, provide a starting point and basis for constructing other units of different kinds and sizes (Anderson, 1980).

Behavior Episode Schemata (BES)

A person always functions as a unit in a context, so all component functions are always occurring in some form in a variable but organized flow of different kinds of behavior-environment events. Therefore, the information base for constructing representations of behavior episodes potentially includes: (a) relevant thoughts, feelings, actions and body states; (b) current environmental events; and (c) relationships of covariation and influence within and among those behavior and environmental events. Such cognitive units are typically called *schemata*. Other labels may be understood as synonyms (e.g., personal theories, frames, prototypes, episodic memories) or as subtypes of schemata (e.g., scripts, autobiographical memories).

BES are formed from event or behavior episode perceptions (see Chapter 5 & 8 and Fig. 3.3 on pg. 78). They are prototypes in memory of frequently experienced or recurrent types of situations used to interpret new instances of similar situations, including filling in information gaps, to guide problem-solving, and to organize actions (Glaser, 1984; Rumelhart, 1980). Events or episodes provide both item and relational information (Friendly, 1979). A special subset of relational information is its personal relevance, such as methods by which the perceiver can manipulate, organize, or influence events, frequently called *procedural knowledge* (Anderson, 1983). Behavior episodes flow through time while cognitive representations of them must be timeless.

However, the properties of flow may be represented by sequence information as is done in scripts (which are discussed further on). Not all of the item and relational information is of equal salience or importance in a particular event/episode (Ortony, 1979). A "complex of stimuli" produces an "organization of nervous activity" in which some components become "dominant for reaction" while others become "ineffective" (Lashley, 1942). Salience is a function of *item and relational properties, personal objectives* in that situation, and *attentional focus*. Some item properties have more natural, salience for humans than others; for example, the size of an object, the severity of pain, the loudness of sound. Of greater influence is the relationship of the information to the goal(s) or intentions(s) guiding the episode, and its organization. Information irrelevant to that episode is less salient. Information in focal attention is most perceptually and conceptually salient while that in peripheral attention is less salient. This is analogous to the gestalt figure ground distinction.

A BES formed from an event/episode perception contains the information most salient to the organization of the episode and one's participation in it with regard to what happened, when, where, how (including one's actions), with whom or what, and why. Different kinds of episodes yield different kinds of BES (Anderson, 1980; Rumelhart, 1980; Rumelhart & Ortony, 1977).

Three Types of Behavior Episodes.   Figure 9.1 summarizes three basic types of episodes which differ in the extent of involvement of transactional functions. *Instrumental episodes* are prototypical closed loop units in which feedforward and feedback processes are occurring in interrelated fashion. They function to produce through transactional functioning an intended environmental consequence of value to the person. In them, a person carries out motoric and perceptual transactions with the environment under the direction, control, and regulation of governing functions, selectively energized by arousal functions, and facilitated and constrained by current biological structural and functional states. *Observational episodes* inhibit motoric feedforward so that environmental transactions are limited primarily to information collection (e.g., watching television). *Thinking episodes* interrupt transactional feedforward and feedback circuits so that both actions and perceptions are inhibited and replaced by imagined actions and perceptions. For that reason, they might be called *simulated behavior episodes*, an idea supported by evidence reviewed by McGuigan (1978). A diversity of "covert, nonoral" skeletal-muscle responses occur when individuals silently engage in a variety of cognitive or thinking activities. Three types of BES are constructed from these three types of behavior episodes.

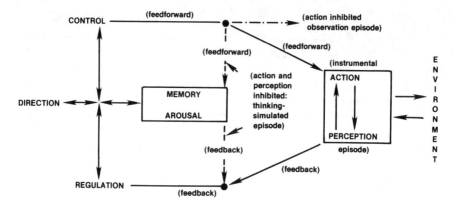

FIG. 9.1 A representation of three types of behavior episodes. In instrumental episodes, a closed loop exists and both action and perceptual transactions with the environment occur. In observational episodes, the feedforward circuit to action is inhibited and only perceptual environmental transactions are occurring. In thinking episodes, both the feedforward and feedback circuits for both action and perceptual transactions are inhibited, while remembering provides *symbolic* action and perceptual components, producing a simulated behavior episode.

Scripts: BES Representing Instrumental Episodes. Scripts, a type of schema that emphasizes transactional components (Wrisberg & Mead, 1981; Prinz & Sanders, 1984), are "conceptual representations of stereotyped event sequences" (Abelson, 1981). Script-schemata are "not only the plan but also the executor of the plan," representing "a pattern of action as well as a pattern for action" (Neisser, 1976). Schank and Abelson (1977) propose that much of memory is organized around repetitive, similar episodes of daily life that involve goals, relevant contexts, actions in relevant contexts, outcomes, and episode endings (e.g., starting a car, shopping for groceries). Such instrumental BES are "skeleton" representations of what to expect and how to behave for some type of purpose in certain kinds of contexts. Several smaller scripts can be combined to function as components of a larger BES.

Cultures define prototypical scripts for action and event sequences directed towards common goals in culturally typical contexts. Culturally shared scripts are easier to learn and make the behavior of members of that culture more predictable and understandable to one another (Bower, Black, & Turner, 1979). Much of socialization involves teaching children culturally sanctioned scripts for different kinds of contexts (e.g., how to behave in church). Like a script for a theatrical performance, an instrumental BES outlines what should be done, where and when, and with what intent; but it permits somewhat different implementations by the performer because it can have action options built into it. Action options represent different kinds of behavior patterns that can produce similar results in somewhat different contexts. The concept of production systems in computer programs (i.e., sets of "if-then" instructions) illustrate a scripted arrangement with built-in action options or subroutines. Repetitive experiences with similar goals in similar contexts are never identical. Therefore, the bases for building optional performances into an instrumental BES exist in variable experience. For example, one's "restaurant script" may provide variations appropriate to a "fancy" restaurant or a "fast-food" diner. Neisser (1976) compared schema-scripts to the genetic concept of genotype rather than phenotype. They provide a framework for possible courses of action, but they must be translated into an appropriate behavior episode through interaction with the current environment (see Chapter 14).

Studies of performance errors by brain-damaged people suggest that the action components of instrumental BES are separable into knowledge about how to do things, or the control function, and mechanisms for actual use of the knowledge, or the transactional functions. Brain damage may disrupt either kind of BES component, resulting in the occurrence of unplanned action options or requiring the use of an action component quite different from the preinjury ones used to achieve the same goal (Roy, 1982).

Higher level abstractions, sometimes called *plans,* can be constructed from sets of BES that share similar properties (e.g., goals). They involve broad, inferential knowledge of large categories of actions and goals relevant to broad classes of contexts, and provide a flexible frame for the revision or construction of specific instrumental BES. Thus, BES can be organized in embedded hierarchies, with context and goal-specific scripts serving as components of, or providing options for, more generalized or complex BES. Very highly generalized BES have been called nuclear scripts (Carlson, 1981; Tomkins, 1980). Individuals may develop several highly encompassing, hierarchically organized BES, some of which may function relatively independently from one another. The clinical phenomena of dissociation and multiple personalities may be manifestations of the dominance of different highly generalized BES on different occasions (Hilgard, 1977).

Some definitions of attitude appear analogous to an instrumental BES, often as a subtype representing interpersonal situations and emphasizing evaluative components. For example, Sherif (1979) defines an attitude as "a cognitive-affective-motivational structure or schema" that is formed by and changed through interaction with the environment. Attitudes have an "affective directionality," or are "selectively biased—positively or negatively" towards the specified domain. Kelman (1979) views an attitude as a "dynamic process" rather than a "static entity," that results from action experiences. Attitudes are "an integral part of action," in which attitudes and actions "are linked in a continuing reciprocal process." Attitudes are grounded in the "functional signifi-cance" a particular situation has for a person, including one's goals (direction), values (regulation), and coping processes (control and transaction) in particular kinds of environments. Once established, attitudes shape the experiences one has with relevant objects and events, affecting information collection, organization, evaluation, and actions. Therefore, they tend to "create conditions for (their) own confirmations" and "minimize the opportunities for (their) disconfirmation." A synthesis of ideas and methods from the attitude literature within a BES framework might prove provocative and useful.

Scene and Event Schemata: Representations of Observational Episodes. Information is power, and humans have an inborn propensity to collect information whenever they can, (often called curiosity) just as people save objects, materials, and mechanical parts because they might be useful someday, humans evolved to collect and retain not only currently useful information but also *potentially* useful information. There are many kinds of circumstances in which people simply observe a scene or event without acting in it or on it (see Fig. 9.1); an example is the act of reading (Graesser, 1981; Yekovich & Thorndyke, 1981). Years ago, Heidbreder (1924) distinguished between "participant" and "spec-tator" behavior.

Observational learning has been referred to as latent learning, vicar-ious or empathic learning, modeling, imitation, and social learning; it occurs in both animals and humans (Bandura, 1977; Bandura & Walters, 1963; Lashley, 1942; Mowrer, 1960; Rosenthal & Zim-merman, 1978; Tolman, 1932). Much infant learning is observational learning (Parton, 1976). Infants spend many of their waking hours in activities whose primary function is to gain information (White, Kaban, Shapiro, & Attanucci, 1977). They will watch and listen to others, and later try to do what they have observed. (Most parents occasionally wish that their children would do what they say rather than imitate what they do.) Observational BES differ from instrumental BES through inhibition of action components. However, emotional compo-nents can sometimes be salient and powerful. For example, one version of the clinical notion of "psychic trauma" involves observation of some event while experiencing intense fear or guilt. The resulting event BES, with a strong emotional component, can significantly influence future perceptions, thoughts and actions in circumstances that activate that BES.

Observational episodes may be symbolic. For example, a person may hear or read a description of an episode. People can form BES from such "second hand" observational episodes by linking the words to their existing cognitive repertoire. Formal education uses this kind of observational episode extensively, and supports it with illustrative instrumental episodes (e.g., laboratory exercises). Nisbett and Ross (1980) believe that many stereotypes and prejudices are initially acquired this way, and are then used to selectively guide future observations which produce confirming evidence, becoming self-fulfilling theories.

Thought Schemata: BES Representating Thinking Episodes. In thinking episodes, such as problem solving, reasoning, decision making, or planning both perceptual and motor transactional behaviors are inhibited (see Fig. 9.1). They "simulate" perceptual-motor transactional components with symbolic substitutes.

For example, Dewey (1933) defined reflective thinking as an intentional activity that tries to resolve a state of doubt or reach a goal. Inhelder and Piaget (1958) assert that in thinking "reality" takes second place to "possibility." Problem solving involves a task environment, the problem solver's representation of the task environment, the task, relevant knowledge, and the "program" used to find a solution (Neimark & Santa, 1975). Reasoning and problem solving involve initial conditions, a desired state of affairs, and a search for information and procedures to transform the initial conditions into the alternative desired state (Erickson & Jones, 1978; Sternberg, 1982). Thinking is a matter of finding one's way through a "problem space" with "allowable moves" and "a well defined goal" (Newell, 1980b). Baron (1982) proposes five phases to reflective thinking: (a) problem recognition; (b) identification of possible solutions or answers; (c) reasoning or search for and recognition of relevant evidence; (d) revision or use of evidence; and (e) evaluation of possibilities.

Just as instrumental BES contain action options, so too do thought schemata contain optional information-processing strategies or heuristics, such as guessing or means-ends analysis. A diversity of heuristics for making decisions with limited information (i.e., under uncertainty), have been identified and studied (Kahneman, Slovic, & Tversky, 1982). People may develop habitual or preferred strategies, sometimes termed *cognitive styles* (Kogan, 1973). Different kinds of thought schemata develop to serve different kinds of objectives in different kinds of contexts. For example, I have sometimes counseled with scholars who had interpersonal or family relationship problems in part because they did not apply the same careful objectivity about information to their personal lives as they did to their scholarly work.

Combinations. Complex adult behavior is often organized across lengthy temporal and spatial domains. Different kinds of schemata may function as components within such complex behavior patterns. For example, an art student walks around an old Victorian-style home she plans to paint, looking at it from several perspectives (an observational episode). She then thinks about which perspective she prefers (a thinking episode). She makes her decisions, sets up her easel and materials, and goes to work (an instrumental episode). Periodically, she may interrupt her efforts with further observational and thinking episodes. Even complex BES may be components of a larger pattern. For example, to complete her painting the student may have to return to the home on several days, and each occasion functions as a component of the larger episode directed towards satisfactory completion of the painting. Through such hierarchically organized sets of BES components people construct behavior patterns that have coherence over many years (e.g., writing a book).

Concepts and Propositions: Components Constructed from BES

Symbolic representations used in thought must be general enough to be applicable to situations not previously experienced (Halford & Wilson, 1980). One of the adapative values of BES is their degree of transituational applicability. However, they are also constrained in their generality because their utility lies primarily in efficiently serving certain kinds of objectives in certain types of contexts. Through operation of the self-construction principle, existing functional components may develop through differentiation and elaboration. Concepts and propositions are flexible components constructed through differentiation from BES.

Concepts. Humans achieve additional behavioral flexibility by constructing representations of components of BES, typically called *concepts* or *constructs*. J. Mandler (1979) suggests that "taxonomic knowledge" is a secondary kind of knowledge built onto a "basically schematically organized memory system," and that taxonomic organization is a function of Western schooling.

Humans' experiences "can be partitioned in a limitless variety of ways" (Medin & Smith, 1984), so why do humans form some concepts and not others? Several possible influences, such as personal goals or relevance, frequency of experience, cultural influences, interpersonal relationships and naturally occurring categories have been identified (Mervis & Rosch, 1981; Rosch & Lloyd, 1978). Keil (1981) proposes that there are evolution-based constraints in the structural-functional design of the human nervous system that make some kinds of abstractions more likely and easier to form than other kinds. The construction of concepts is a continuing process. Each instance of experience may contribute both redundant and new information to concept elaboration. For example, to a small child a duck may have the defining properties of a bird. To a teenager, it may also be represented as something to hunt and to eat. Concepts are also contextually anchored. For example, the concept of duck may have one set of defining properties for a visitor to a zoo and another when the same person visits a Chinese restaurant.

Selective attention influences selective concept formation. Historically, objects and their features have been considered related but different potential targets of attention. More recently, relational information has been added as a third source. In many species, individuals will concentrate on different constellations of cues in different behavioral contexts, and may focus on simple features rather than configurations when that works (Marler & Terrace, 1984) When attention is focused on any component of an episode, imagistic representations can be formed of that component or any of its aspects (e.g., an orange, a sphere, the color orange, an orange's peel, peeling an orange, the edibility or taste of an orange). Abstract representations of consistencies in a set of similar imagistic representations can similarly be constructed, based on "distinguishing features of a stimulus array," or "invariant relations and the higher-order structures that grow out of them" (Keil, 1981). Some attributes may be represented in terms of context-independent feature-object relationships (e.g., a ball is round), but others are context-dependent (e.g., a ball bounces, or floats on water) (Barsalou, 1982). Through attentional and action exploration, people construct an increasing diversity of conceptual components.

For example, my grandchildren play with our beagle-terrier dog named Scooter, and with a big sheep dog named Winston; they see other dogs in their neighborhood, on TV, and in their books. They form imagistic representations of each dog and retain those of dogs with whom they have salient interactions. From those imagistic representations, they also form an idea or concept representing dogs in general. Because adults verbally label these animals both with personal names (e.g., Scooter) and with category names (e.g., dog), those words become related to the imagistic or abstract representations which they signify.

Exemplars of the same concept may occur in many different behavior episodes. Recall of a concept, then, involves retrieval or reconstruction of such exemplar information. Therefore, the meaning of a concept for a person will be as rich as the diversity of behavior episodes which provided exemplar information for its construction. Such an arrangement is flexible and adaptive because no instance need display all attributes of all the concept's exemplars to be recognized as an instance of the concept (Medin & Schaffer, 1979). The term *polythetic class*, is sometimes applied to such concepts.

Propositions. Symbolizations representing objects (e.g., apple, dog) or their attributes (e.g., shape, color) are typically called concepts. Sets of concepts organized into larger units by representations of relationships among them are often called *propositions* and sometimes theories (e.g., "Scooter will chase a ball if I throw it," or "Communists are bad"). Propositions specifying procedures or actions to be performed under certain circumstances are sometimes called *rules* (e.g., do unto others as you would have them do unto you). Information-processing "production systems" are sets of "if-then" rules.

Other kinds of proposition called *procedural knowledge* (Tulving, 1985) or *motor schema*, are those which represent and orchestrate actual sensorimotor (i.e., transactional) functioning (see Chapter 14). Some of this kind of propositional knowledge is manifest in feedforward information which cannot enter consciousness, and might be thought of as a special kind of proposition which can sometimes be consciously represented by verbally stated rules, such as, "in your golf backswing, take the club back low and slow" (Squire, 1982).

Functional Autonomy of Concepts and Propositions. In one sense, concepts and propositions might be thought of as minischema, and the term *concept* is sometimes used encompassing the properties of schemata (A. Miller, 1978). However, they have the special capability of functioning relatively independently from the contexts, events, or episodes from which they are derived (e.g., the concept of gravity). That *functional autonomy* frees them from the constraints of particular kinds of contexts, purposes, and actions, making possible much greater flexibility and generality in their use (Ehrlich, 1979). As functionally autonomous components, they can be combined in many different ways to reconstruct schemata, or to construct new concepts, propositions, and schemata at varying levels of abstraction, just as letters and words can be combined in many ways to construct a diversity of sentences and meanings. Like nuclear scripts, highly abstract concepts and propositions can represent a large realm of item and relational information (e.g., $E = MC^2$).

It is this property of functional autonomy, combined with linguistic labeling, that enables cultures to progressively accumulate and transmit knowledge. One of the tasks of teaching is to make such culturally shared abstractions personally meaningful by linking their verbal labels to individuals' personal schemata.

Concepts About Concepts. Scholars have made diverse proposals about the nature of concepts and propositions. For example, there are classical, probabilistic, polymorphous, correlated attributes, exemplar and prototype definitions of concepts. There are ontological, action, goal-derived, person and event concepts. Each type was developed either to try to account for data incompatible with others, or to designate differences in conceptual content. Despite centuries of consideration, the nature of human concept formation remains a puzzle (Carey, 1982; Medin & Smith, 1984; Mervis & Rosch, 1981; Neimark & Santa, 1975; Smith & Medin, 1981). Since humans can partition information in many ways, perhaps all the types of concepts proposed are valid. Following is an attempt to formulate a plausible rationale for the existence of multiple types of concepts.

One implicit source of disagreement is a version of the part-whole issue of hierarchical organization discussed in Chapter 1 of this book. A concept exists when two or more distinguishable instances of a phenomenon are treated equivalently (Mervis & Rosch, 1981). Some concept definitions emphasize *parts*, such as defining attributes, features, components, or properties of objects or events. Defining attributes could include *static* attributes (e.g., feathers, wings); *dynamic* attributes (e.g., it flys, it makes sounds); *relational* attributes (e.g., it flies in formations, it migrates seasonally); and attributes *personally salient* to the observer (e.g., it's fun to hunt, its edible, it taste good). For example, all instances of a concept should share a set of such necessary and sufficient defining properties in one definition. Polymorphous concepts are probabilistically defined, requiring an instance to have a "sufficient" number of the total set of defining features, but not necessarily all of them; for example, a three-legged cow or a cow that gives no milk would still fit the concept cow (Hampton, 1979, 1981; Medin & Smith, 1984). Equivalence of instances is presumed to result from a weighted, additive combination of component information.

However, objects and events are defined not just in terms of their attributes, but how those attributes are organized. Therefore, other concept definitions emphasize *wholes*; that is, organizations or configurations of attributes (Hayes-Roth & Walker, 1979). For example, in the correlated attributes view, concepts are defined by a set of attributes that consistently occur as a configuration (Mervis & Rosch, 1981). Exemplar concept definitions rely upon typical individual examples of such feature configurations. Prototypes are constructed from concept exemplars to represent their typical feature and relational properties (Medin & Smith, 1984).

These are not mutually exclusive definitions. Theoretically, humans can focus their attention on one or more of a set of attributes and/or their organization. Remember that perception is multimodal, so that perceptions of multiple attributes and their relationships typically occur in spatial-temporal patterns. Some of those patterns are more readily perceived and conceived as units than others, forming "natural" or "basic" categories in the terrestrial environment level of reality within which human cognitive capabilities evolved (e.g., apple versus atom).

Such initial basic concepts can be further differentiated, elaborated, and transformed (Rosch, Mervis, Gray, Johnson, & Boyes-Braen, 1976). This "natural" basic conceptual level appears to be one in which the information value of the abstraction is greatest because, within a category, similarity of content and organization is maximized relative to that between categories (e.g., chair is a more basic concept than furniture). This is analogous to the distinction made in Chapter 2 that within-unit dynamics are more complex than between unit interactions.

However, from infancy to adulthood, there is a major developmental shift from treating perceptions in a holistic manner to considering them component by component (Kemler, 1983). This progressive differentiation of defining attributes is a function of frequency and diversity of experience with varying examples of concepts, and of variability in personal goals and attentional focus (e.g., distinguishing a delicious apple from a crabapple). Such differentiation is useful because it facilitates learning to discriminate among basically similar entities that differ in significant ways, like a pussycat and a polecat. Thus, definition by exemplars and prototypes is given increased precision by supplementing it with probabilistic definition through an increasingly discriminated set of defining attributes. Remember, living systems develop both through increasing *differentiation* (e.g., more detailed specification of defining attributes of concepts) and *elaboration* (e.g., more broadly representative concepts).

As increasingly abstract concepts are formed, exemplar and prototypical definitions become less feasible and functional; examples are concepts like *solid, gravity,* and *ego*. However, defining abstract concepts with configurations of attributes is feasible and useful. Precise distinctions among abstract concepts, such as those scientists seek, may require the "necessary and sufficient features" definition of a concept. Some high-level abstractions are sometimes called *ontological concepts* because they purport to represent "basic categories of existence" (Medin & Smith, 1984).

It is useful to remember the notion of embedded hierarchies at this point. What is a part (or feature) at one level of analysis may be a whole or configuration at another. For example, to a materials scientist a silicon chip may be a complex organization of molecules or atoms, while to an electrical engineer it may be a component in a computer. Therefore, any concept at any level of analysis probably has potentially both configurational (holistic) and attribute (parts) properties. There is some evidence that remembering typically involves global (i.e., configurational) retrieval cues, and then detailed (feature inspection) cues to prime remembering if necessary (Glucksberg & McCloskey, 1981); and may involve moving across levels of abstraction. Peel (1971) distinguishes between the process of *generalization*—broadening a concept to encompass more kinds of instances—and *abstraction*—constructing a broader concept through specification of a set of more broadly encompassing attributes.

Individual Differences in Concept Formation. People differ in their daily living contexts, personal objectives, emotional lability, habits of thinking and acting; they differ, that is, in both the component processes of behavior episodes (including contexts) and the BES formed therefrom. Broadly speaking, three interrelated sources of information provide the basis for concept construction.

1. Attributes of entities and their organization (e.g., "it is a green square with orange holes").
2. Attributes of entities' relationships with their contexts (e.g., "it climbs").
3. Attributes of entities' relationships to the experiencing person (e.g., "it hurts"; "I can influence it").

It follows that the judgment of similarity among instances of the same entity involves both intrinsic similarities (e.g., number 1.) and cognitively imposed similarities (e.g., number 3.) (Eich, 1985). Stated another way, concepts are constructed from salient information. Salience is a function of centrality of features in the organization and the functioning of the entity, frequency of occurrence (Hasher & Zacks, 1984), and personal relevance. Personal relevance is a function of the governing and arousal functions of behavior episodes during which the entity is experienced. Therefore, *object feature salience* is likely to be more similar across individuals than is *personal relevance salience*.

Individuals differ in the intensity and frequency with which they experience and selectively perceive the three different kinds of information. As a result, they may form somewhat different concepts representing the same entity. For example, to one child a rabbit may be a cuddly pet for whom the child feels affection. For another it may be a potential source of food. Such differences can be a source of human misunderstanding. For example, the rabbit lover may be shocked by the rabbit-eater's concept of rabbits.

People also differ in the habits they form in regard to information collection and use they form and that may influence their concept formation. For example, Bruner, Goodnow and Austin (1956) identified some children (called "focusers") who tended to focus on stimulus attributes and others (called "scanners") who tended to test hypotheses by focusing on configurations of features. Words are labels for concepts and their linguistic function reflects different information: *nouns* are concepts for things, and *adjectives* represent their attributes; *verbs* are concepts representing actions; configural information is added with *connectives, adverbs, sentence structure,* and *punctuation.* People usually assume that a concept label has the same meaning for everyone. That is not always the case, and can result in miscommunication. For example, stereotyping involves attributing to another person all features of a concept based on only some observed feature(s) such as black skin.

MEMORY AND SCHEMA, CONCEPT AND PROPOSITION FORMATION

The initial formation of cognitive units is a result of the brain's variability-analyzing and controlling functions operating on current perceptions. Infant cognitive development is the clearest place to see that process. Once formed, cognitive units cannot function to organize behavior or be subject to modification and elaboration unless they can be reactivated. Therefore, the remembering process is examined in this section and its role in cognitive development is briefly considered. The basic change processes underlying cognitive development are then summarized.

Newborns' Observational and Instrumental Behavior Episodes

Infants enter the world prepared for both material and informational transactions with their environment. During their first two years the rate and scope of their cognitive development is remarkable (Bornstein & Kessen, 1979; Osofsky, 1979; Moscovitch, 1984; Mussen, 1983), with important developmental elaborations of their capabilities appearing at transition periods of 2 to 3 months and 7 to 9 months (Emde, Gaensbauer, & Harmon, 1976). Initially, infants' attention and behavior is controlled primarily by the physical aspects of stimuli (Kagan, 1979). However, they show differential responding (or preferences) for different kinds of stimuli. They seem prepared to notice some kinds of environmental contingencies and not others (Sameroff & Cavanaugh, 1979). For example, visually they prefer patterns; they like the sweet taste of sugar and the odor of bananas, and dislike the sour taste of lemon juice and the odor of rotten eggs.

However, nervous system maturation constrains their transactional capabilities. For example, infants from birth to three months of age have some voluntary control only over eye movements, sucking, and gross limb movements such as untargeted kicking. Under appropriate conditions, infants can use those responses to preferentially conduct observational or instrumental behavior episodes.

Observational Episodes. Newborns visually scan the world in a controlled and systematic fashion, and there is a gradual shift from highly constrained scanning to more global scanning. They tend to look longer at stimuli with curved lines; patterns that are irregular, have high contour density, or are more complex; and concentric or symmetrical stimuli. Moreover, they can pick up correlated information from different modalities (e.g., sight and hearing). Maturational influences contribute to dramatic increases in their skill and use of such observational episodes, since the average length of alert periods for newborns is only 5 minutes, but it is 90 minutes for three-month-olds (Fagan, 1984; Haith, 1980; Harris, 1983; Olson & Sherman, 1983).

Instrumental Episodes. Newborns are very good at self-controlled sucking. By fastening a nipple to electronic gadgetry, they can be given the power to intentionally influence their world through sucking—and they will do it. During the first four weeks they will selectively suck to display a preference for their mother's voice. During the first three months, they will suck to select a preferred visual display or to focus one (Mehler, Bertoncini, Barriere, & Jassik-Gerschenfeld, 1978; DeCasper & Fifer, 1980). Similarly, if an infant's leg is mechanically linked to a crib mobile, the infant can learn to manipulate the mobile through untargeted kicking (Olson & Sherman, 1983; Rovee-Collier et al., 1980; Ruff, 1984). This demonstrates that an infant is capable of functioning as a self-directing living system during the first few weeks of life. Instrumental episodes are the key way people initially come to know the world and how to deal with it. Doing and knowing are joined together in intelligent action (Hunt, 1961).

From 3 to 6 months, infants' motor behavior is increasingly under intentional rather than primarily stimulus control (Bruner, 1973). For example, efforts at visually guided reaching and grasping begin around 4 months; the infant will stare at the target object, pump its arms up and down, open and close its hands, and perhaps its mouth. By 6 months, intentional reaching, grasping, mouthing, and manipulating objects has become a well-organized pattern. These infants can maintain controlled and exploratory attention for extended periods of time. That development is of fundamental importance since selective attention controls the information in the feedback circuits from which cognitive components can be constructed, and organizes coordinated action. Because infants can now manipulate as well as look at objects, they are experiencing objects and events in terms of multisensory-perceptual, covarying patterns of information; they can look at, feel, mouth, shake, and manipulate an object. They also are more active in initiating and maintaining social interactions through smiling, vocalizations and object play (Olson & Sherman, 1983). As Piaget (1952b) put it, they seem to be trying to make "interesting spectacles last."

Episode Combinations: Imitation and Expectations. Infants display imitative behavior shortly after birth by observing and then modeling facial gestures (Field & Walden, 1982; Field, Woodson, Greenberg, & Cohen, 1982; Meltzoff & Moore, 1977). Although studies disagree about neonate imitation in the first few days of life (Olson & Sherman, 1983), imitation clearly undergoes considerable development during early infancy (Kagan, Kearsley, & Zelazo, 1978).

Events have sequential properties. Infants display expectations when they behave in preparation for the end of an event while the event is in progress. The mechanisms underlying expectancy formation are present at birth, so the learning of expectancies can begin immediately, and 4- to 5-month-olds clearly display expectancies (J. Mandler, 1984). Expectations are based on the predictability of the order in which events occur in particular contexts (Ruff, 1984). Expectancy formation is of fundamental importance because it provides the starting point for construction of directive thoughts; that is, for the representation of possibilities not yet occurring, which can exert an organizing influence on the rest of behavior. Newborns are also capable of experiencing and of conveying in facial, body, and vocal gestures a variety of affective states (e.g., pain, interest, distress) as a function of behavior episodes; the diversities of affective states displayed elaborates during the first year of life (Schellenbach, 1987).

Infants' Construction of Cognitive Units

Imitation, learning, expectancies, and intentional behavior imply remembering, and therefore cognitive functioning, in early infancy. For example, imitative action follows an observation period; expectancies involve preparation for objects or events not yet present or occurring. Therefore, formation and retention of cognitive representations must begin in the first few weeks of life (Moscovitch, 1984).

Initially, infants' behavior appears to be organized and guided by "current news;" it is *stimulus* controlled. Governing functions (except for inborn processes) do not intervene between perception and action. This is the functional mode Piaget (1952) termed *sensorimotor*, which he thought lasted a year or more. He was wrong. It is much briefer than that (Harris, 1983; J. Mandler, 1984; Olson & Strauss, 1984). Within the first 6 months, more elaborate cognitive functions and memory begin to develop. Schacter and Moscovitch (1984) postulate that infants start life with an *early memory system*. Roughly, this corresponds to the concept of *procedural memory,* i.e., nonconscious memory for where and how to act. They infer that at 8 to 10 months, a significant change occurs in infant memory capability; and they postulate the emergence then of a *late memory system* which corresponds to conscious *episodic memory.* Others believe both processes begin at birth, although they may not develop at the same rate. That is probably the case. The later development of verbal capabilities enables infants to report memories and they do so beginning in the second year of life. Some of their reports are of memories developed between 6 and 12 months of age, before they learned to talk (Asmead & Perlmutter, 1980; Nelson, 1984; Nelson & Ross, 1980).

Instrumental BES Construction. Try to imagine subjective experience from an infant's perspective. There are bodily sensations and multimodal perceptual experiences of the environment occurring in a flow of item and relational information that varies in content, spatial pattern, temporal sequence, and rate. Most of it is new and unfamiliar. That flow is periodically interrupted by sleep, but those interruptions become progressively less frequent and of longer duration.

Newborns initially impose no organization on the flow, other than that which results from inborn structural-functional properties of their nervous system (e.g., sensory-perceptual and selective attention processes). However, the infant's world is organized, and the infant must relate to that organization in minimal self-organizing ways in order to survive (e.g., eat, eliminate, breath, complain when uncomfortable). Therefore, the infant organizes its flow of experience primarily to reflect the environmental event organization of which it is a part, within biologically and genetically based constraints.

There is a high degree of repetitiveness in the newborn's daily experience. Typically, the infant is involved with the same people in the same places participating in the same routines and experiencing the same affects (e.g., distress when hungry). These events have all the properties of behavior episodes except that learned directive, regulatory and control cognitions are not yet guiding them. They provide the starting point for infants' cognitive development.

Infants progressively abstract and create representations of the repetitive and the most salient aspects of that flow of perceptual-affective-motoric information. They begin to form BES that retain the relations among the components of the experience, "be it object, sound, smell, or dynamic sequence" (Kagan, 1979). Retaining the dynamic sequential information is important, because that is a key distinction between schemata (particularly scripts) and concepts as cognitive units. Neonates' maturationally limited sensory-perceptual-motor attentional capabilities probably produce fragmented event experience during the first month or two. Even so, their experience is probably a relatively undifferentiated whole. Therefore, schemata formation probably begins before concept formation or "taxonomic classification" (J. Mandler, 1983, 1984), although both are probably occurring in interactive fashion by the second 6 months of life (Olson & Strauss, 1984). Between 3 and 6 months, infants become able to extract and store information relatively quickly, and longer term retention emerges. From 6 to 12 months, there is extensive growth of infants' knowledge base and remembering capabilities, and the first appearance of the rudiments of language and abstract thought (Olson & Sherman, 1983).

As BES are constructed, they begin to exert a self-organizing influence on infants' behavior. They guide skilled action (Bruner, 1973). What we perceive is affected by what we know from the earliest stages of perceptual processing (Klatzky & Stoy, 1978). One early manifestation of BES's influence is in attentional distribution. For example, infants' attention perseveres longer for events that are "a little different" (e.g., a face with crooked eyes), but not "extremely different" (a face with no eyes), than the event from which the original schema was created (Kagan, 1979). Infants seem to be trying to reconcile similar but not identical representations. But BES cannot exert an influence on current functioning unless they become a part of current "working" memory.

Remembering Cognitive Units

BES are valuable because they guide behavior for selected purposes in specific contexts. Each person develops many BES, concepts, and propositions. Therefore, remembering must selectively activate specific schemata and concepts or propositions under circumstances where they are relevant and useful. Historically, remembering implies consciousness of the remembered. Here, remembering is used in the broader sense of *functional activation of representations* with or without their appearance in consciousness.

Memory Metaphors. Scientists often use analogies or metaphors to provide understanding of something whose qualities are unknown by substituting an explanation of demonstrated utility from some other domain of knowledge. Such metaphors can both guide and misdirect scientific efforts. Roediger (1980) identifies several metaphors underlying proposals about memory and cognition. Memory for immediate events and long-term retention are often differentiated. What follows focuses primarily on long-term memory.

A *spatial storage and search metaphor* makes an analogy between the mind and a physical space. Memories are assumed to be discrete entities that are stored, following learning, in different locations in brain or "mind" space. Remembering requires searching the "storage area" to locate and retrieve the desired or relevant information. Concepts like associative networks, lexicon or dictionary, library, and information file or data set are illustrative of this metaphor. A spatial storage metaphor does not fit evidence of the brain's structural-functional organization very well since, when there is brain damage, there appears to be little correlation between the amount and kind of damaged tissue and the kind of memories "destroyed."

A *construction or reconstruction metaphor*, emphasized by Bartlett (1932), is replacing the previously dominant spatial metaphor. Given a current situation and objective, a person can reconstruct informational representations appropriate to the task. Just as motor acts appear to be constructed or reconstructed when needed, guided by some objective(s) and construction guidelines (see Chapter 14), so too memories may be reconstructed, guided by some purpose and general thematic guidelines. Many versions of schemata proposals are illustrative of this metaphor.

Another is a *resonance metaphor* (Shepard, 1984). Resonance is defined as a pattern of vibration from one source inducing a similar pattern of vibration in another source. For example, a tuning fork tuned for one frequency will resonate to a sound of the same frequency. Analogously, current information or *retrievial cues* may produce a resonant response in neural circuits tuned for different information patterns, thereby yielding a memory; this is called *synergistic ecphory* by Tulving (1983). Just as a great diversity of music can be played on a small number of piano keys, only a few informational components able to resonate in different organizations could produce a diversity of cognitive representations. The phenomena of mutual entrainment discussed earlier may be a manifestation of a resonance process. Resonance is an important phenomenon in electronic circuits.

The *holographic metaphor*, proposed by Pribram (1976b, 1977), combines information and ideas from physics, neurophysiology, and neuropsychology (see Gabor, 1972, and Pribram and Goleman, 1979, for a discussion of holography). It can encompass the resonance and reconstruction metaphors. It attempts to account for several unsolved mysteries of brain functioning: (a) memory storage does not appear to be in particular brain locations, since there is no correspondence between which brain tissue is damaged and which memories are lost; (b) objects can be recognized as the same regardless of the distance or perspective from which they are viewed; and (c) learned skills, such as eating with the right hand, can be transferred without practice to a different brain-body pattern (e.g., eating with the left hand). The following simplified summary is based primarily on Pribram's work.

Optical holograms produce three-dimensional images from a photographic film record of interference patterns of light waves reflected from an object. For example, two rocks thrown into water each form ripples. When those ripples bump into one another, the combined pattern created is an interference pattern formed by the intersection of two wave fronts. Neuronal signal transmission creates such wave fronts. If several wave fronts (i.e., neuronal transmissions) intersect, interference patterns can be created. A third of a century ago, Lashley (1951) concluded that "organizations of neurons" produced "temporally spaced waves" of excitation which overlap and conflict, "creating interference patterns of unimaginable complexity" which must be the basis for memory rather than "anatomically fixed engrams." It is such interference patterns that provide the basis for perception and remembering, Pribram also proposes, just as they are the basis for three-dimensional optical holograms.

A form of mathematics called *Fourier analysis* can represent any complex wave form, such as an interference pattern, as a combination of simple wave forms that can vary in frequency and amplitude. Conversely, any complex wave form can be created by selectively combining a few appropriate simple wave forms. Auditory and visual functioning and human movement (see Chapter 14) have been represented by Fourier analysis. This implies that the brain functions as a frequency analyzer for patterns. If so, it would mean that the brain decomposes (i.e., abstracts) information provided by the senses into simple wave forms that provide the basis for information storage. To reactivate that information pattern in "working memory" or current consciousness, the appropriate set of simple wave forms must be activated and combined (perhaps through a resonance process) to reconstruct a particular complex interference pattern representing the particular schema, concept, procedure, or idea to be remembered. This leads to a view of remembering as a process of information reconstruction through the priming of such interference patterns with current information, or *retrieval cues*.

All proposals about memory must be considered highly speculative, but some physical evidence makes something like a holographic view plausible. For example, all senses produce frequency-coded neuronal signals when stimulated by variable, wavelike physical stimuli such as light or air pressure waves. At least some neurons are selectively responsive to particular frequencies. For example, single cells in the visual system are receptive to a five degree "patch" of a visual field. A complete image is created by the simultaneous arousal (organization) of an appropriate set of neurons representing different patches or frequencies. Images are similarly created by insect eyes that are composed of hundreds of little lenses (a compound lense) instead of one large lense as in the human eye. Compound lenses and patch holograms have a special advantage because they are particularly sensitive ways for representing movement information. Holographic storage is also very efficient, so storage capacity is huge and flexible in its potential use.

The mainstream of work on human memory and cognition has produced ideas that seem to mesh with something like a resonant, reconstructive holographic model. For example, there is extensive evidence that memories are not precise replicas of previous perceptions but are reconstructions of information organizations or "structures" (Puff, 1979). Some cognitive representations are more "basic" than others (e.g., Rosch & Lloyd, 1978), implying that brain evolution made some resonant patterns easier to form than others; one such kind of pattern might be the *terrestrial* order of reality. Moreover, analogous to proposals about "imageless" or "unconscious" thought, only the products (e.g., wave front interference patterns) rather than the process of recombining ideas (e.g., simple wave forms) can become represented in the contents of consciousness; and new combinations can be constructed by individuals, as proposed in the literature on creative thought.

Since the reconstruction, resonance, and holograph metaphors seem closer than other metaphors to the nature of the learning and performance of motor acts and the apparent configurational functioning of the brain (Kesner, 1973; see also Chapters 8 and 14), their potential utility deserves further consideration.

Remembering as Reactivation and Reconstruction. A British philosopher, William Hamilton, proposed in 1858 the concept of *redintegrative* (i.e., reintegrative) mechanisms; it holds that learning results in neural changes such that a complex pattern of cognitive-brain activity can be reactivated by less extensive stimulation than may be present during initial learning (e.g., you can "re-cognize" a person by his or her walk). That idea has renewed credibility today. Cognitive components appear to be "habitual structures that are contacted automatically by input" (Posner & Warren, 1972). *Retrieval cues* is the current favored term for the "less extensive stimulation" necessary to reactivate a particular memory pattern. Ehrlich (1979) defines memory as a set of potential or possible and optional organizations, "a system capable of generating organized structures," rather than an information file. Cofer (1977) called this the *constructive theory of memory.*

It becomes necessary, then, to formulate a way of identifying the kinds of retrieval cues likely to trigger reconstruction of a particular schema. The concept of behavior episode provides a rationale. Remembering capabilities evolved in humans to facilitate identification of information useful for successful performance of "particular tasks in specific contexts" (Cavanaugh & Perlmutter, 1982). BES function to organize and guide specific behavior episodes. Their utility results from their symbolic representation of the redundant and salient content and organizational properties of the behavior episodes from which they were created. Components of a current behavior episode (both behavioral and environmental) that are similar to salient components of a schema will tend to reactivate that schema. People initially respond to a particular situation in terms of a few key, particularly relevant prototypical features (Mischel, 1984).

What are the most salient components of a BES as related to remembering? Current evidence suggests they are the objectives it is designed to serve (the directive function), the context within which the objectives are to be achieved (environment), and related emotional states (arousal functions). The importance of objectives is implicit in memory research designs, but they have not been studied as a retrieval cue because they are typically a part of the independent variable through instructions given to subjects such as "I'm going to show you a set of figures. Push the button each time you recognize one"; or "Write down everything you can recall about the story you just read." Instructions establish the goal for that behavior episode for the subject, and function to organize his or her behavior in that task environment. Implicitly, such instructions are designed to elicit a BES appropriate for that episode.

What is remembered is a function of the similarity between the context in which the BES was learned, called the *encoding context* in memory research, and the *context of recall* (Abelson, 1981; Baker & Santa, 1977; Horton & Mills, 1984; Jenkins, 1974; Tulving & Osler, 1968). While the social context is often minimized in research on memory and cognitive development (e.g., Piaget's research), it is often a significant aspect of real-life behavior episodes. Similarity does not mean just *literal* (e.g., object) similarity. It includes relational or *functional* similarity. For example, a BES of how to relate to one's parents, learned early in life, may be reactivated in adults in any behavior episode requiring them to interact with any adult authority (e.g., a boss or a domineering spouse).

G. Mandler (1980) proposes that remembering is influenced by frequency of repeated exposure to the same information, and a "retrieval component" that involves a search for relevant contextual information such as when and where the item was experienced in the past. For example, 3-month-old infants learned to activate a crib mobile by kicking. Forgetting that capability was usually complete after 8 days. However, if 24 hours before testing the infant again experienced the identical situation including the mobile moving, except that the researcher moved the mobile instead of the infant, the memory of that capability was reactivated as reflected in improved performance the next day (Rovee-Collier, Sullivan, Enright, Lucas, & Fagen, 1980). Repeated experience with the same episode, in the same context with the same objective, facilitates remembering.

Some kind of emotional arousal is often a component of a behavior episode. Remembering is often particularly vivid and detailed in the case of events of high emotional impact, called "flashbulb" memories by Brown and Kulick (1977). The amplifying function of emotional arousal is discussed in Chapter 13. More generally, there is growing evidence that recall is improved when recall-state mood is congruous with mood during learning and therefore presumably with the affective components of the relevant schema (Bower, 1981; Bower, Gilligan, & Monteiro, 1981); however, some emotional states such as depression may interfere with recall (Leight & Ellis, 1981).

Behavior episodes that induce strong fear tend to be avoided in the future. BES that have strong fear as a component also tend to be avoided. That is an important factor in some human psychopathology, illustrated by a phenomenon Freud called *repression*, which involves active avoidance of remembering certain information (Ford & Urban, 1963). Some functional amnesias appear to represent the same phenomenon on a grand scale, in which avoidance of remembering major portions of the person's life occurs. Research on autobiographical personal memories indicates that in the first memories retrieved, affect is a component, implying that affective content influences selective recall. Moreover, when the memory is cued with an affect cue word rather than an object or activity cue word, reaction time is longer and the memory is of more recent vintage (Robinson, 1976).

Schemata differentially facilitate remembering schema-consistent information (Hastie, 1981; Taylor & Crocker, 1981). For example, information that was unrecallable with one schema was remembered when a different schema was activated (Anderson & Pichert, 1978). Greenwald (1980) reviews evidence that people tend to reconstruct memories to maintain existing cognitive organization, including revising memories to be consistent with current beliefs and attitudes. People use schemata as guides in remembering prose or stories. For example, people tend to fill in unstated actions in script-based stories when recalling them. They break long stories into subepisodes to facilitate remembering (Black & Bower, 1979; Bower, Black, & Turner, 1979; Spiro, 1980). Unfamiliar material is understood and remembered better after reading if it is preceded with information designed to elicit an existing schema, called an *advance organizer*, which can help in organizing and understanding the material (Mayer & Bromage, 1980). In fact, instructions given to subjects in most cognitive research are designed to activate a schema to organize and guide the subject's behavior in certain ways. Remembering may be automatic or intentional. Automatic detection results from habitual information-processing routines. Controlled remembering require conscious use of memory priming strategies (Schneider & Shiffrin, 1977a, 1977b).

All behavior episodes occur in a specific context, and information is encoded in relationship to its context; this is called *encoding specificity* (Tulving & Thompson, 1973). Therefore, all schemata are initially situation specific, and might be termed *event* or *episode schemata*. Situation specific schemata are not very useful because identical situations will not occur in the future. Information and procedures learned in one context may not be readily available for use in a different context, unless schema elaboration or generalization occurs through repeated experience with similar behavior episodes. This is the classical problem of transfer of training, or generalization of psychotherapy effects. In general, such transfer or generalization must be trained for if one wants to be sure it will occur (Goldstein & Kanfer, 1979).

Modification of Cognitive Units

Once schemata, concepts, or propositions exist, through processes described in Chapter 5, they can be elaborated in four ways: (a) the detail within them can be elaborated; (b) they can become elaborated in generality and scope; (c) they can be significantly revised; and (d) they can come to function as components of more inclusive units.

It is the organizational properties of cognitive representations that enable them to function as a unit. Imagistically coded cognitions represent the organization of the perceptions from which they were constructed. Abstractly coded units contain organizational properties of their imagistic sources and perhaps others imposed by the constructing process. Linguistically coded representations have a manifest and a latent organization. The *manifest* organization results from the syntax, semantic, and articulation aspects of language. The *latent* organization is that of the imagistic and/or abstract representations the linguistic organization represents and is intended to activate, usually referred to as its *meaning*.

BES have the prototypical organization of the behavior episodes from which they were constructed. Concepts represent a configuration of features defining them and distinguishing them from one another. A list of features is the simplest configuration but usually not the most useful one. The organization of those features is what distinguishes one entity from another. Propositions are organizations of concepts linked by relational information. Any of these types of units can also function as components of larger units. For example, a cow is a component of the concept *mammal* and of a daily script-schema on a dairy farm. They may also be represented as organizations of subcomponents. For example, a face is an organization of eyes, nose, mouth, and ears, separated by areas of skin and hair.

At any moment, some subset of all potential cognitive components in a person's repertoire will be activated as a part of working memory. Of those, a sub-subset will be manifest in the contents of consciousness. Only activated cognitive components can be modified by current information flows.

Current intentions and perceptions of relevant environmental factors are the most influential factors in determining which cognitive components will be activated. You have to name the game before you can figure out how to play it. Together, these directive thoughts and environmental perceptions "map the problem space" and provide constraining and facilitating design conditions within which the behavior episode can be constructed and implemented.

The Basic Change Process. Once schemata, concepts, and propositions exist, they can be reconstructed to organize and guide current behavior episodes. The result is that, in any behavior episode, two patterns of information are simultaneously operative. One is perceptual and provides current news. The other is conceptual and provides information about what has been and what might be. Behavior episodes may be similar to each other but they are never identical. Therefore, some discrepancies in both content and organization will exist between the two information patterns. Such discrepancies can produce behavioral confusion.

It is like the teenager who assumes (based on past experience) that his date will not let him kiss her goodnight, but interprets her current statements and actions as encouraging. Humans usually do something to resolve informational discrepancies. Piaget (1977) utilized the concepts of *assimilation, accommodation,* and *equilibration* to explain how different ways of resolving such discrepancies influenced the development of thought. Block (1982) modified Piaget's rationale somewhat and applied it to personality development.

Assimilation means the use of existing schamata to make sense of new experience. Stability-maintaining processes like assimilation have first priority in living systems. The influence of this process is illustrated by people who manufacture unusual interpretations to make new, seemingly discrepant information fit their current beliefs. *Accommodation* means the revision of schemata to resolve information discrepancies. It fosters change and innovation. *Equilibration* refers to the process by which coherent organization is produced and assimilation and accommodation processes are balanced. Block (1982) proposed the slogan,"Assimilate if you can; accommodate if you must" to represent what he considers an evolutionarily based adaptive imperative.

Discrepancies may be of different kinds and magnitude, and precipitate one of three basic kinds of discrepancy-resolving strategies reflecting one of the three basic processes of development:

1. The discrepancies may simply represent new detail or options within the same basic schema. Perceptual information, particularly about humans, requires interpretation to identify its significance. Such interpretations (often called rationalizations) are influenced by the stability-maintaining, self-organizing processes to try to make them fit existing cognitive organization, often by differentiating that organization to include more detail. Where maintaining the existing organization is very important to a person, highly discrepant information may be rationalized to fit (e.g., maintaining one's pet theory, or self-referent beliefs), because to accept such information as discrepant would require significant and perhaps discomfiting cognitive change. To counteract the potentially self-deluding dangers of assimilative processes, careful scientists intentionally search for evidence to refute their beliefs.

Example: Imagine a person with a BES for driving a car with a three speed manual transmission, whose new car has a five speed transmission. The BES is fundamentally the same, but must be differentiated to include additional gear shift positions.

2. Some of the discrepancies may represent significant differences for some part(s) of the existing BES. Self-constructing processes may operate to revise the existing schema to accommodate the discrepant information by integrating both the old and the new information. Science promotes such accommodative processes to advance human knowledge.

Example: A worker considers his boss an unfeeling, uncaring tightwad. Then he learns that the boss is financially supporting a home for orphaned children and works there as a volunteer once a week. To accommodate that information his conception will have to be revised.

3. The discrepancies may be so disruptive of existing cognitive organization that they cannot be assimilated or accommodated in existing schemata. Two outcomes may follow. Disorganization-reorganization processes may produce a new cognitive organization that weds the previously discrepant information in a new way. Or, self-organizing processes may maintain the existing cognitive organization while self-constructing processes create a new cognitive unit to represent the new information. Keeping organizations of information

cognitively separate that would be seriously disrupting if permitted to combine has been labeled *logic-tight compartments* (like keeping two chemicals separate because combining them would produce an explosion).

Example: A 14-year-old girl thinks of her father as a caring father and a loving husband. One day she comes home early from school and discovers her father having intercourse with her best friend. That shatters her schemata of both her father and her friend, and leaves her confused, frightened, and angry. Eventually, she creates the explanation that her father was drunk and did not know what he was doing (thus salvaging her schema of her father) and that her friend seduced him (thus reorganizing her schema of her friend).

In summary, living systems operate to remain functionally organized. If current organization is perturbed, they will function to maintain the current organization against the perturbation (e.g., assimilation); or revise existing organization to incorporate (and thus eliminate) the perturbation (e.g., accommodation); or create new organization. To an objective observer, the results may not make sense and may seem maladaptive, but from the person's perspective it was the best that could be done under the circumstances and enabled them to retain some degree of functional coherence.

Elaboration of Cognitive Units

The change process just described is continuous. Which types of changes are prominent at any time is a function of the cognitive repertoire one has developed, of personal objectives, of life circumstances, and of biological functioning. Because those are age-correlated variables, the nature of cognitive development may be said to vary across the life span. Space limitations prohibit examination of cognitive development throughout life. However, a few significant issues are briefly considered in the following pages.

Developmental Sequences. Human capabilities typically elaborate in sequential fashion. Babies learn to crawl and later walk. They learn to babble before they speak words. Children typically can learn to solve some kinds of conceptual problems before others. Using the analogy of biological development, some scholars have chosen to emphasize such normative developmental sequences and to argue that human functional capabilities develop through a universal sequence of stages (Reese

& Overton, 1970). The concept of *stages of cognitive development* has been influential, particularly because of Piaget's work (1970). It is important to distinguish between performance potential or competence and actual performance (Stone & Day, 1980). For example, by designing age-appropriate tasks, it has been demonstrated that small children can display capabilities at significantly younger ages than appropriate for Piaget's stage model (Gelman, 1978). Vygotsky (1978) demonstrated that a "zone of proximal development" exists for each child at each age for each capability. Children can perform at one level by themselves but at a higher level with a little help.

There are extensive individual differences in developmental patterns; an invariant cognitive developmental sequence does not seem to exist, and Piaget's stages appear to represent a description of some normative age-related changes in cognitive functioning in relationship to certain kinds of tasks and environments (Brainerd, 1978; Fischer & Silvern, 1985). Gelman (1978) concludes that development in cognitive skill domains follows a kind of componentized elaboration model. The development of some simpler skills provides preconditions for the development of other more elaborate skills (Tomlinson-Keasey et al., 1979). It has become clear that cognitive development is not just the province of childhood, but continues throughout adulthood.

Extensive and growing evidence supports the conclusion that the kind of "hard" stage theory proposed by Piaget and his followers is inadequate and should be abandoned, because adherence to it constrains and obstructs the creation of better alternatives (see Fischer & Silvern, 1985; Overton & Newman, 1982, for good reviews and for alternatives).

Chapter 5 of this book provides a more adequate and inclusive way of understanding developmental sequences than the oversimplified notion of invariant stages. Functional (e.g., cognitive) development is facilitated and constrained by the structural boundaries of the body's current state and by current environmental conditions. The human body develops through a typical sequence of elaboration (i.e., stages) under species-typical environmental conditions. However, in atypical environments bodily developmental patterns can deviate significantly from that norm (Gould & Lewontin, 1974; see also Chapter 4). Specific kinds of functional development cannot occur until the structural development occurs which makes those functions possible. Therefore, certain kinds of functional development may display stagelike properties, as is particularly evident in infancy and early childhood. However, physical structure bounds but does not strictly determine functional development. Therefore, once structure is in place, sequential patterns of functional development will be primarily a function of two other kinds of interacting variables.

First, one often must learn to do some things as a prerequisite to learning to do others. For example, before one can learn to play a Chopin prelude on the piano one must first learn to understand the concepts of notes, chords, rhythm and timing; to read music, to strike the piano keys appropriately, and so on. Therefore, functional development will display sequential properties if one categorizes different kinds of functioning in terms of levels of organizational complexity, which is a sound alternative to the concept of stages (Fischer & Silvern, 1985). Moreover, much functional development manifests equifinality: different persons may arrive at the same level of complexity through different developmental pathways. Therefore, if several individuals display the same complex functional capabilities at the same age it does not follow that their developmental process or sequence was the same.

Second, living systems' functional development can only occur through transactions with their environment(s). Therefore, the nature of the environment can influence the sequence in which human capabilities develop or whether they develop at all. For example, environments may be organized in age-graded ways, facilitating certain kinds of functioning only at certain ages. Certain kinds of human functional capabilities would then be likely to reflect such age-graded properties in their developmental sequence, producing patterns that might appear stagelike in character. Rather than assuming stages and trying to identify them, a more fruitful approach is to focus on how new system states can develop from different kinds of existing states, through different kinds of behavior episodes in different kinds of environments.

At first, everything is new for very young children, so that constructive and accommodative processes abound. Most of their waking hours are spent in activities that enable them to create, elaborate, and revise schemata, concepts, and propositions and to use them in guiding action. For example, in one study of 1- to 3-year-olds (White et al., 1977), about 90% of their waking time was spent in nonsocial, self-initiated tasks. About half of all their time was spent in activities classified as gaining information, exploring, or gaining mastery.

One-year-old children have developed a limited cognitive repertoire of event, spatial and script schemata, and basic concepts, and are beginning to link words to their cognitions. Comprehension of words precedes their use. For example, by the time a sample of children between 9 and 20 months old could speak ten words, they had an average comprehension vocabulary of 60 words, with a high of 182 words (Benedict, 1979). The most essential information for dealing with the world is identity (What is it?) and function (What does it do?). Therefore it is not surprising that a child's vocabulary is initially mostly nouns and verbs. As linguistic comprehension and production evolves it has a powerful interpersonal significance because parents and children can influence what one another are thinking and doing by using words, in addition to actions, to activate relevant concepts, propositions, and schemata.

Environmental Knowledge. Knowledge of the world and how it works is the first and probably always the major domain for which cognitive representations develop, because coping with the environment is the fundamental basis of life. Therefore, a major portion of children's cognitive development involves information about the environment, including the social and cultural environment. Much of formal schooling is focused on this socialization objective. Since the only way of communicating abstractly coded concepts is through their symbolic (usually verbal) surrogates, language competence is critical for the transmission of culturally defined knowledge.

Adults' ability to conceptualize situations, spatial configurations, objects, people, features and relationships among objects, general principles, and so on, all at various levels of abstraction and in various codes is astonishing. Attempts to develop computer programs to simulate human intelligence have reached only a primitive stage because no one knows how to include the typical human broad base of knowledge and its complex organization. There is much tacit knowledge behind human problem solving and action that influences the process, but not as a part of consciousness. For computer simulation to approximate human thinking, it will be necessary to learn how to program them to approximate dynamic organizations of complex BES. Since the social environment is of basic importance for humans, study of social cognition is of increasing interest.

Self-Knowledge. The experiencing person always has his or her body, subjective feelings, and conscious perceptions and cognitions present in *every experience.* Therefore, in every behavior episode, regardless of purpose or context, there is a flow of information about the self as an object with attributes (e.g., tall, clumsy, smart), as an agency of influence on oneself and their environment, and about one's reactions to environmental influences. There are consistencies in that flow of self-referent information that can be abstracted and cognitively represented. Therefore, the self as a physical and functional object becomes the center of a more elaborate array of concepts and propositions than any other object, and self-conceptions are present in every BES. As with any other cognitions, self-organizing processes function to keep them coherently organized. The development of self-referent concepts begins with self-recognition in infancy and continues throughout life (Bertenthal &

Fischer, 1978; Harter, 1983; Markus, 1977). Individuals' beliefs about their characteristics and capabilities are collectively referred to as the *self*, *self-concept*, or *self-system* (Epstein, 1973; Smith, 1978). Evaluative thoughts about ones self exert a powerful influence on both emotions and actions, and may even influence one's health (Antonovsky, 1979). The self-system is considered again in Chapter 11.

the use of information to organize behavior

In the beginning of this chapter, physical symbol systems were described as capable of three kinds of functions: *memory, operators*, and *controls*. Much of this chapter has been about the first function, the construction and remembering of information organizations of various kinds. A brief discussion of operators and controls provides a transition to the next three chapters. Mountcastle (1978) describes the organization of information processing activities of the brain as a *distributed system*, a form of organization in which "the complex function controlled and executed by the system" is not localized in any single part. "Information flows through such a system may follow a number of different pathways, and the dominance of one pathway or another is a dynamic, changing property of the system." (P. 40)

Operators: Strategies for Processing Information

Humans develop procedural as well as substantive knowledge. Some procedural knowledge represents ways of influencing the environment or oneself (e.g., meditation procedures). Some procedural knowledge represents information processing strategies. Such strategies have been given different names at different times. Learning theorists called them *learning sets* (Harlow, 1949), or "learning how to learn." They observed that, after solving a number of similar problems, people develop an efficient approach to dealing with that class of problems. Different approaches may be developed for different classes of problems. Personality theorists called them *cognitive styles* (Baron, 1982; Gardner, 1953; Kagan, Moss, & Sigel, 1963; Witkin, 1978). These were defined as stable individual preferences in the mode of perceptual organization and conceptual categorization of the external environment.

An algorithm is defined as a set of steps that, if performed, will inevitably lead to the solution of a problem (Lachman et al., 1979). Production systems are sets of condition(if)-action(then) procedures organized sequentially (Simon, 1979). Heuristics are general "rules of thumb," inductively arrived at, for guiding decision making (Einhorn, 1982; Simon, 1978).

One reason for trying to identify and study different information-processing strategies is the suspicion that at least some differences in learning and performance may result from inadequate strategies rather than low abilities or lack of knowledge (Cooper & Regan, 1982). Knowledge of strategies (operators) would make it possible to teach people strategies as well as knowledge, as illustrated by teaching people to use memory mnemonics (Higbee, 1979). Differences in cognitive strategies may underlie some performance differences between younger and older adults. Although this "production deficiency" hypothesis has not generally been supported by research on aging, some types of procedural deficiencies do seem to account for some memory differences between older and younger adults, such as difficulty in retaining contextual information and using contextual information in recall (Burke & Light, 1981).

On the other hand, data from amnesic and brain-damaged people do indicate different kinds of memory impairment under different kinds of conditions; an example is *knowing how* versus *knowing that* (Cohen & Squire, 1980; Hirst, 1982; Squire & Slater, 1978; Weingartner & Grafman et al., 1983). Moreover, changes in patterns of neurochemistry in different parts of the brain appears related to different kinds of processing deficiencies (Bartus, Dean, Beer, & Lippa, 1982; Kral, 1979). Further knowledge might contribute to improvements in cognitive functioning of the elderly through appropriate training or biochemical intervention (Boswell, 1979; Schaie, 1980).

Controls: The Organization and Regulation of Thought and Action

A good bit of theorizing about cognition focuses on its organization or structure (Puff, 1979). However, there is no generally accepted definition of either organization or structure. A typical definition might be "patterned relationships among elements in a specified set" (Puff, 1979). This living systems framework suggests that information storage must be in some form of componentized, embedded hierarchies anchored in purposive and contextual information, but with elaborate and flexible linkages among the hierarchies and their constituent components.

The term *memory* is used in two ways: (a) a long lasting record of experience; and (b) a current conscious representation of a past experience. Atkinson and Shiffrin (1968) proposed three kinds of memory: (a) a brief sensory register; (b) a short-term (temporary) memory for current information representations; and (c) a long-term (permanent) memory. The latter appears to occur after a period of "consolidation" which is facilitated by rehearsal and repeated experience, and seems to require a bilaterally intact limbic system (Kral, 1979).

However, inferences about the organization of information that can be remembered or reactivated are based primarily on data produced under the second definition, memory performances. That means that distinguishing between any organization imposed by the control processes involved in memory activation and report on the one hand, and retention organization on the other, is essentially impossible. A one-to-one correspondence between previous experience and current memories appears not to exist. For example, Loftus and Loftus (1980) demonstrate that memories induced by hypnosis and by electrical stimulation of the brain are not really memories, but are information constructions in the same sense that dreams are constructions and not memories.

Remembering probably implies several control processes that can vary and change. For example, elderly people display a longer time lag and increasing difficulty in switching concentration, and are more easily distracted by details, implying a decline in self-control and an increase in stimulus control of behavior organization (Schonfield, 1980). Analogously, one explanation for attentional difficulties in schizophrenics is a decline in "control and maintenance of a selective processing strategy" (Baribeau-Braun, Pictou, & Gosselin, 1983).

This arrangement would make control of processes for differential neural activation crucial in cognitive functioning; that is the arousal functions anchored in the reticular activating system and the limbic system. For example, an 87-year-old woman unable to sleep for 5 days because of emotional distress began to hallucinate and to lose control of her cognitive functioning. Once her nonsleep pattern was interrupted with drugs and she slept and became rested, her cognitive functioning became more typical again. Those very brain structures are the ones that have been identified as critical in "memory formation" and control of the contents of consciousness. Thus, remembering and thinking are probably organized and regulated by flowing patterns of neural activation, orchestrated by information inputs through the senses and by control processes built into the brain by evolution and experience.

It is control processes defined as performing exactly these functions that have been drawing increasing theoretical and empirical attention from scholars. Sternberg (1979, 1982) labels them *metacomponents* which are higher order control processes used for "planning a course of action" (the directive function), "making decision regarding alternate courses of action" during problem solving (the control function), and "monitoring the success of the chosen course of action" (the regulatory function). Flavell (1979) uses the term *metacognition* defined as a person's "awareness and consideration of her or his cognitive processes and strategies." *Metamemory* has been used to refer both to knowledge about memory and executive processes organizing remembering (Cavanaugh & Perlmutter, 1982). Campione, Brown, and Ferrara (1982) distinguish between metacognition, which is knowledge about one's cognition, and *executive control*, one's overseeing, monitoring, and management functions. They argue that the latter is more central to intelligence.

Hilgard (1976, 1977a) concluded that *executive functions* are essential for maintaining order in a person's cognitive functioning. He proposes that there are many "subordinate" cognitive units "each with a degree of unity, persistence, and autonomy of functioning." Moreover, there is some kind of "hierarchical control that manages the competition between these structures." In addition, there must be some kind of "central monitoring and controlling structure" that can control or regulate the priorities expressed in the hierarchical organization.

While the existence and roles of these metacognitive or executive functions is not tied to any particular view of memory and cognitive organization, or of neural structure, they are essential in any model of humans that recognizes their self-organizing, self-constructing, self-directing properties. Therefore, the next three chapters focus on the governing functions of direction, control, and regulation.

10

The Directive Function: Intentions and Personal Goals

INTRODUCTION

Chapter 9 examined how cognitive content is constructed, organized, retained, and remembered. However, that is only part of the story. Individuals' development produces an increasingly elaborate behavior repertoire. That creates a dilemma. In any situation, a particular, relevant action pattern must be selected and effectively implemented from among many possibilities. For half a century, mechanistically inclined scholars tried to prove that situational properties alone produced that selective effect. They failed. The massive data base they generated demonstrated that situational properties constrain and facilitate, but typically do not strictly determine, which action pattern will occur. Other causes are also present. This resulted in the resurgence of interest in *cognition*. Behaviorists never denied that the phenomena of memory and cognition existed, but they did deny that thoughts could function as causes. The cognitive science revolution has reinstated that idea, and much current research aims at demonstrating the causal influence of cognitive processes on action.

Metacognition and Executive Functions

However, the issue of selection remains. It has been shifted from action to cognition. Effective action in any situation requires the selection of particular guiding cognitions from among a person's repertoire of diverse concepts, propositions, and schemata. Therefore, selective processes have become a focus of cognitive science. Two kinds of processes have been identified. One kind involves being able to identify, monitor, and be aware of one's own cognitive functioning and capabilities. It has been called *ego functions* (Hartman, 1958), *reflective access* (Pylyshyn, 1978), *metamemory* (Flavell & Wellman, 1977), and *cognitive monitoring* (Flavell, 1981; Hilgard, 1977b). The (sometimes explicit) assumption with regard to this kind of process is that awareness of alternatives is prerequisite to their selective use. The second kind of process involves the flexible, selective use of one's cognitive capabilities and behavior repertoire to fit a wide range of (often unfamiliar) conditions. It has been called *multiple access* (Pylyshyn, 1978), *controls* (Newell, 1980b), *metacomponents* (Sternberg, 1982), the *self* (Kagan, 1978), and *executive functions* (Campione, Brown, & Ferrara, 1982; Hilgard, 1977a, 1977b).

This living systems model labels the selective, organizing, evaluative cognitive processes *the governing functions*. Three types are derived from a control system model: *direction* (What state or results do I want to produce?) discussed in this chapter; *control* (How can I best produce them?) discussed in Chapter 11; and *regulation* (How can I choose from among alternatives? How can I know if my efforts are succeeding?) discussed in Chapter 12. Regulation includes the monitoring functions emphasized in metamemory and metacognition concepts.

Binet and Simon (1916) characterized "intelligent thought" with the same three functions: (a) a tendency to take and maintain a distinct direction; (b) ability to make "adaptations" to obtain a desired outcome; and (c) powers of self-criticism. Similarly, Flavell (1976) subdivides metacognition into "the active monitoring and consequent regulation and orchestration" of information processing, in relation to "the cognitive objects or data on which they bear", and usually "in the service of some concrete object or goal." Freud's concepts of ego and superego encompass the same three functions. Sometimes metacognition refers more narrowly to the capability for monitoring and influencing one's own cognitive processes.

Governing functions at the person level of organization are accomplished through the use of cognitive components (e.g., ideas, thoughts) constructed from the flow of personal behavior and experience in diverse contexts. Figure 10.1 illustrates that process and summarizes ideas discussed in Chapters 10, 11, and 12. It reflects Deutsch's (1951) argument that any person or society that is to "steer itself" must continually receive a flow of three kinds of information: (a) information about "the world outside"; (b) information about the past "with a wide range of recall and recombination"; and (c) information "about itself and its own parts." If any one of these three streams "be long interrupted," e.g., "by oppression or secrecy," the living system will "lose control over its own behavior" at first for some of its parts, "but eventually also at its very top."

It is important to distinguish between governing functions as processes and the content of cognitive activity. Individuals are born with perceptual, information processing, and governing-function capabilities which provide "a wired-in base upon which to build a large repertory"

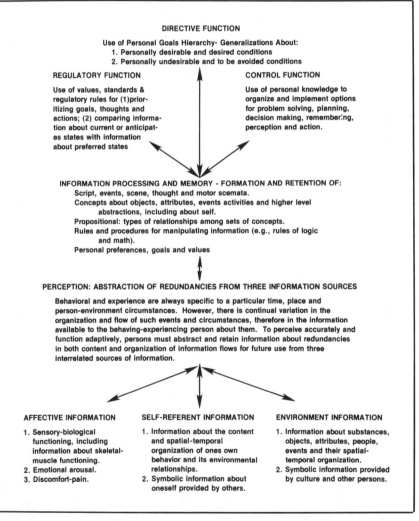

FIG. 10.1 A representation of the origins, nature, and organization of governing functions in relationship to perception, information processing, and memory functions.

(Klinger, 1977); but they are born without cognitive content. Using these inborn capabilities, a person constructs and uses previously constructed cognitive components to create, implement, evaluate, and modify ongoing patterns of behavior.

Although the three governing functions are discussed separately in Chapters 10, 11, and 12 for conceptual purposes, it should be emphasized that they always operate as a team. It is not possible to have one without the others. That is why researchers consistently find there is not a high correspondence between fragmentary representations of intentions, values, plans, and actions (Locke, Shaw, Saari, & Latham, 1981). As McClelland (1985a) emphasizes, "motives, skills, and values" are "independent determinants of action." His research demonstrates that "if taken together" they can account for a much larger portion of action variance than if taken separately.

Motivation as an Explanatory Concept

The concept of *motivation* has traditionally been used to represent the properties of initiation, direction, persistence, and vigor of behavior (Atkinson, 1964). However, it has acquired multiple meanings (McClelland, 1985a) and has become such an inclusive concept that it has lost utility (Cofer & Appley, 1964). The problem is that the concept of motivation has tended to become reified in to a "thing" (e.g., "What is their motive?"), and that is an oversimplified and misleading way to think. The word "motivation" is a shorthand way of talking about different complex, multifaceted patterns of behavior. Therefore, the concept of motivation is not used in this living systems framework because of the imprecision that results from its all-inclusive nature. Rather, the role of each system function motivating human behavior will be emphasized. This chapter emphasizes the selective-directive aspect of the traditional concept of motivation.

If one wants to try to understand (and influence) what a person does and the commitment with which he or she does it, one has to consider that person's body state (e.g., sickness or health); personal goals and aspirations (the directive function); values, standards, and habits of self-evaluation (the regulatory function); understanding of the characteristics and conditions affecting the task and ability to construct an effective behavior pattern (the control function); relevant competencies and skills (the transactional functions); as all those components occur in different kinds of contexts. Figure 10.2 summarizes people's responses to the question, "What are the key characteristics of a motivated person?" People's implicit theories of motivation typically emphasize an organized pattern of particular kinds of directive, regulatory, and arousal functions.

Four types of motivational explanations have emphasized different aspects of the organization of behavior, based on assumptions about types and sources of influences, as summarized in Table 10.1.

Type 1 views assume that humans are complex machines whose every thought or action is determined by powerful events and forces, and that any appearance of self-direction or personal causality is illusory. The controlling events, according to these views, may be contextual. For example, Skinner (1974) states that his form of *behaviorism* moved purpose, "which seemed to be displayed by human action" from a subjective intention or plan "to subsequent selection by contingencies of

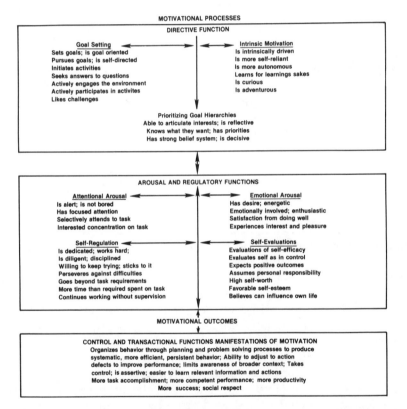

FIG. 10.2 A summary, in living systems terms, of the indicators of a motivated person provided by a group of people and manifesting the implicit theory that the term *motivation* represents a complex, organized pattern of directive, regulatory, and arousal functions. (From M. E. Ford, *Motivation from a Living System Perspective*, manuscript in preparation).

TABLE 10.1
Types of Explanations for the Apparent Purposive or
Goal-Directed Properties of Human Behavior

	Types of Influences	
Sources of Influences	Event-Controlled	Self-Controlled
Situation Properties	1. Environmental contingencies; reinforcers; gods	4. Cognitions learned from and cued by environment
Person Properties	2. Vital force; instincts; needs; drives	3. Will; volition

reinforcement." Day (1978) believes that almost anything is better "than to intentionalize human behavior." In many belief systems, gods or spirits determine human action. In Type 2 views the controlling events may be inside the person. The *drive psychologies* of Freud (1955) and Hull (1943), McDougall's (1908) *instinct theory*, and Maslow's (1954) *need theory* are illustrative. An alternate view is that humans have a significant degree of freedom or autonomy from event control, that they are self controlled. This Type 3 view, illustrated by theologically based ideas of free will and legal doctrines of personal responsibility (Cofer, 1972; Furlong, 1981), assumes that the gift of reason and freedom to choose are innate or God-given attributes.

A Type 4 self-control view considers event control to be mediated by cognitions that function as surrogates for those events in influencing present behavior (e.g., cognitive behaviorism). Some views merge Types 2 and 4 (e.g., Deci, 1980; Rogers, 1946, 1951). One typical hidden assumption is materialistic, holding that motivation involves different kinds of material-energy interactions, such as tension reduction or reinforcement. But, that represents only half the story. Humans are informationally as well as materially self-constructing. That distinction can be linked to the distinction between "reasons" and "causes" for action (Buss, 1978). Reasons represent the purposes directing behavior; causes represent the necessary and sufficient conditions for behavior to occur. Analogously, ego analysts define motives as nonbiological directives and causes as physical conditions (Ford & Urban, 1963).

Cofer and Appley (1964) concluded that the properties of selection and persistence were better characterized by concepts of *anticipation*, a kind of cognition, and *sensitization*, by biochemical or stimulus conditions. They proposed reserving the concept of motivation to represent the invigoration or energizing of a behavior patters (see Chapter 13). Zimbardo (1969) argues that the cognitive control of behavior is particularly human. When humans are "motivated by appetite" and have no choice about enduring "a state of deprivation or noxious stimulation," they reveal their "oneness with the beasts." However, with cognitive capabilities, a human transforms himself "from the object of actuarial determinism to the creator of his own existence." Cognitive influences often take precedence over material ones; for example, people keep working at things important to them despite hunger or pain.

This living systems framework merges situation and person properties, resulting in a synthesis of situational and self-control. Remember that in hierarchically organized systems, a frame of reference useful at one level will often not be useful at another (J. Miller, 1978; Sicinski, 1978). For example, in cells the governing functions are accomplished biochemically; in persons they are accomplished informationally. This discussion of governing functions focuses primarily on the person level of organization, and therefore on information-based governing functions. Scholars who have given the most emphasis to the self-governing characteristics of humans are those whose focus is on the person functioning in significant life contexts (e.g., personality, social, clinical, counseling, educational, and industrial psychologists). It is impossible to ignore humans' self-governing capabilities when dealing with people facing the opportunities, problems, and tasks of life.

Origins of Concepts About the Directive Function

Interest in a "dynamic principle" that gives direction and organization to behavior has been historically persistent and widespread, but has been obscured by the diversity of concept labels used to represent it (Boring, 1957); among those labels are will, volition, purpose, intention, values, hopes, wishes, aspirations, choices, personal causation, self-control, self-determination, anticipation, expectation, motivation, internal locus of control, attitudes, preparation, and set; or instinct, need, drive, determining tendency, incentive, reward, contingency, and reinforcement. Virtually all early investigators of development explored the development of "volition and intentionality" (Cairns, 1983). One of the purposes of this chapter is to try to identify underlying similarities in these different ways of talking about similar phenomena.

Instinct and *will* are two of the oldest concepts (Cofer & Appley, 1964). Instincts could impel action in animals without positing a mind or soul. Modified versions may be found in some current doctrines, such as *need theories, sociobiology,* and *behavior genetics.* Freud (1957b) translated the concept of instinct into a mental representation of some biologically based energy condition. The concepts of will and volition involve using reason and knowledge to rule one's bodily passions, make conscious choices, and control one's actions.

Voluntary action was a descendent of the concept of will. Woodworth (1906) proposed that a "naked thought," or idea of what is to be done, might be the immediate causal antecedent of voluntary movements. Moore (1924) elaborated that into a theory of "conceptual control" of voluntary action that anticipated modern views (see Chapter 14). The concept of *set* produced a productive stream of research that demonstrated the influence of selective preparation for specific perceptions and actions (Gibson, 1941).

Anticipation and *expectation* are concepts that also represent selective preparation for future action that are extensively studied in psychology (Tolman & Brunswick, 1935) and applied in psychotherapy (Goldstein, 1962). For example, if a banana is hidden under one of two cups in view of a monkey and then lettuce is secretly substituted, when the monkey removes the correct cup it will reject the lettuce (usually an acceptable food) and keep looking for the expected banana (Tinklepaugh, 1928). Five-month-old human infants display anticipatory behavior by visually following an object as it passes behind a screen and emerges on the other side, and by looking back at the screen if a different object emerges (Gratch, 1979).

Wants, intentions, and *purposes* are cognitions designating desired potential future states or conditions. Combinations of intentions can organize more complex behavior patterns (e.g., see F. Allport's 1939 concept of telic continuum). *Attitude* also has a long history (G. Allport, 1966; DeFleur & Westie, 1963; Ostrom, 1968). At first it referred to physical postural "attitudes" or sets, but evolved to represent cognitive organizations with two properties: a directive function (e.g., G. Allport, 1935) and a regulatory or evaluative function (e.g., Osgood, 1965). The directive function is a prominent aspect of many psychotherapy theories (Ford & Urban, 1963), and increased self-direction for clients is psychotherapy's most basic goal (Strupp, 1975).

The relation of intentions to actions, thoughts, and feelings "is one of the messiest tangles of puzzles in contemporary philosophy" (Searle, 1981), and in psychology. Increased understanding of human cognition holds the potential for untangling that puzzle. Chomsky (1972) argues that the mind is as real as the sounds we make, that the selective organization of words to convey meanings is evidence of an "organizing principle" in the mind, and that understanding language requires understanding the "surface structure" of words and the underlying "deep structure" processes which produce them.

Scholars such as Ackoff and Emery (1971), Boden (1972), Bruner (1968), deCharms (1968, 1976), Hunt (1965), and Ryan (1970) helped renew the momentum and legitimacy of the study of human purposiveness. Particularly relevant is the work of Carver and Scheier (1981), Deci

(1980), Heckhausen (1973, 1980), Heckhausen and Weiner (1972), Hilgard (1976, 1977b), Klinger (1977), Klinger, Barta, and Maxeiner (1980), Locke (1969a, 1969b, 1978, 1983), Locke, Cartledge, and Knerr (1970), Locke, Shaw, Saari, and Latham (1981), McClelland (1980, 1985a, 1985b), McClelland et al. (1953); of European scholars interested in action theory (Kuhl & Beckman, 1985; von Cranach et al., 1982); of the diversity of people studying achievement motivation (Dweck & Elliott, 1983) and expectancy-value motivation theory (Campbell & Pritchard, 1983), along with that of scholars of motor behavior cited in Chapter 14. Brent (1984), Churchman and Ackoff (1968), Moore and Lewis (1968), Powers (1978), Rosenbluth and Weiner (1968), and Rosenbluth, Weiner, and Bigelow (1968) have applied a systems perspective to understanding purposive functioning. Soviet psychologists such as Leont'ev view people and their development as embedded in a flow of planful action, guided by a hierarchy of agendas, goals, and subgoals, and by changes in them as a situation evolves (Wertsch, 1980).

Bandura, starting from a reinforcement-behavior modification position (1969), has moved progressively through the concept of self-reinforcement (1976) to an emphasis on self-evaluation in the regulation of behavior, which he calls self-efficacy (1977a, 1977b, 1978a, 1978b, 1981), and then to the causal influence of directive thought (mechanisms of agency) interacting with regulatory thoughts to organize behavior (1982a, 1982b, 1986). His perspective, as described in Bandura and Cervone (1983), is becoming increasingly like that of this living systems model:

> The capability for intentional and purposive human action is rooted in cognitive activity. Social learning theory postulates two cognitively based mechanisms of motivation that serve such telec purposes. One mechanism operates anticipatorily through the exercise of forethought. By representing foreseeable outcomes symbolically, future consequences can be converted into current motivators and regulators of behavior. The second major source of cognitive motivation derives from internal standards and self-evaluative reactions to one's performances. (Bandura & Cervone, 1983, p. 1017)

This author is greatly indebted, for the following section, to the collective work and wisdom of these scholars.

Cognitively Orienting Behavior Toward Potential Future Conditions

Two basic assumptions underlie the following discussion of the directive function: (a) people can and do construct cognitive representations of potential future conditions within themselves, in their environment, or in their environmental relationships; and (b) those cognitive representations (frequently called goals, purposes, intentions, or desired consequences) are used to target and organize their functioning and environmental transactions to try to produce the imagined conditions.

This is not a new idea. William James (1890) defined *will* as "a state of mind or image," and *willing* as desiring a potentially available outcome. Mowrer (1960b) argued that symbolic responses are the key to "response initiation and selection." Ego analysts propose that unless *instinctual drives* are cognitively represented as a "wish," they will not have motivating effects (Holt, 1976; Klein, 1970; Rapaport, 1960). *Purpose* is the idea of a goal (Boden, 1972). Kagan (1972) defines *motive* as a cognitive representation of a future state, and Deci (1980) defines them as "cognitive representations of some future satisfied state." It is the person's "current representation of the goal" combined with awareness of "the needs to be satisfied" that exert a causal influence on his or her behavior (Bullinger & Chatillon, 1983). Motor behavior is targeted and organized by a cognition of its intended result (see Chapter 14).

Human Purposes and Meaning in Life

When people describe their lives as meaningful, they usually mean that they are committed to, and pursuing with some reasonable success, valued goals or incentives (Klinger, 1977). When cognitive representations of such (a) potential future, (b) desirable, and (c) believed-to-be-possible states are absent, people experience the devastating conditions called loneliness, depression, helplessness, and hopelessness, and health and life are jeopardized (Antonovsky, 1979).

The drama of real life reveal the importance of human purpose in ways sterile laboratory conditions cannot. For example, in a Nazi concentration camp during World War II, people who saw "no aim, no purpose, and therefore no point in carrying on" were soon lost (Frankl, 1963). Frank (1968) cites accounts of hopelessness hastening the deaths of inmates of prisons and concentration camps, and delaying recovery from some kinds of illnesses. During the siege of Leningrad, individuals held themselves together "by the consciousness of being needed," and without that they began to die (Salisbury, 1969). The most frequent reason given for suicide is helplessness; the person has no purpose for which to continue living (Farber, 1968). Those of us who have experienced intensive psychotherapy with other troubled humans have seen at first hand the devastation of purposelessness and the joy of renewed life direction and accomplishment. The very "tenor and tempo" of people's thoughts and feelings depend on their success in achieving and enjoying goals they value (Klinger, 1977).

Without the direction which purposes give to life, there can be no coherent organization and no reference against which to evaluate one's activities and experiences. Without direction, life is meaningless. Like a ship on a stormy sea without someone steering it, one gets pushed around by the winds and waves of life until one capsizes and sinks to oblivion. Given the fundamental importance of the directive function in human life, it is sad that science has for so long treated it as an epiphenomenon.

DEVELOPMENT OF COGNITIVE
REPRESENTATIONS TO DIRECT BEHAVIOR

Inborn Starting Points

Directive functioning is an inborn human capability whose operation is apparent soon after birth. The view that such capabilities do not emerge until late infancy or early childhood is, in part, an artifact of the research methods and tasks used. As researchers become more innovative about designing tasks to fit infant transactional capabilities, evidence about many functions pushes their starting points closer and closer to birth (or before) (Mussen, Vols. 2 and 3, 1983; Osofsky, 1979). Self-directed functioning can only be displayed through behaviors which a person can control. Newborns have two such behaviors, sucking and visual attending, and others mature during the first few months of life. From the beginning, infants' organized motor activity is under the control of intentions (Bruner, 1973).

Sucking has been observed as early as the third gestational month and, by birth, is an efficient, self-controlled behavior pattern (Bruner, 1968). Three-day-old infants readily learn to suck in order to turn on a recording of someone singing. Moreover, after they learn to do that, they become upset if the singing occurs noncontingent upon their sucking (DeCasper & Carstens, 1981). Six- to 12-week-old infants can learn to selectively suck in order to listen to their mother's voice rather than some other woman's (DeCasper & Fifer, 1980), or to increase the illumination or focus of a picture projected on a screen (Bruner, 1968; Siqueland, 1968).

Newborn infants display distinct and stable visual preferences (Banks & Salapatek, 1983; Olson & Sherman, 1983). By 3 months, they selectively scan and focus, and discriminate among colors, features of figures or objects, and different organizations of features (Cohen, DeLoache, & Strauss, 1979). Voluntary head movements begin by 3 months, and can be used to make a crib mobile move. Infants may smile and coo when they have learned to do that (Watson & Ramey, 1972). Reaching behavior is another early indicator of self-directed infant functioning. Between 6 and 12 weeks of age, if an object to which the infant is visually attending is brought close, its gaze may be fixated on the object with mouthing movements, accompanied by active movement of head, shoulders, and arms. By 3 to 4 months, the object may be grasped and brought to the mouth for "mouthing." Reaching behavior becomes progressively more efficient, even with reference to a moving target, and may become a component of more complex intentional patterns (Bruner, 1968, 1973; Uzgiris & Hunt, 1975; White, 1971).

Infants' initial self-directed functioning must be guided by perceptions, so they are sometimes referred to as stimulus controlled. However, infants quickly begin to construct conceptions or BES which can then function to organize and direct their behavior (Harris, 1983). The development of self-direction cognitions probably occurs in the following pattern in repetitive cycles of different behavior episodes:

1. Perceiving and representing ("I experience X").
2. Recognizing ("X is a familiar experience").
3. Remembering ("I recall experiencing X").
4. Anticipating and expecting ("I remember or imagine X and it can and may occur again").
5. Desiring or preferring ("I know X exists, can reoccur, and I want [or don't want] it to").
6. Intending ("I want [or don't want] X to occur, I believe I can influence X and will try to produce that consequence").

These functions are organized in embedded hierarchies. Each encompasses all those below it. For example, anticipating involves perceiving and representing, recognizing, and remembering. Phases 1 through 5 facilitate selective reacting to events. It is not until Phase 6 that cognitive self-direction becomes proactive. Following is a brief discussion of the relationships among these phases.

Perceiving and Representing

Neonates are capable of multimodal perception, and their perceptual acuity matures rapidly (Olson & Sherman, 1983). Their perceptual representations are imagistic, including the sounds of language, and can function as representations or targets towards which they selectively direct their behavior. From a flow of similar perceptions, infants abstract consistencies, construct prototypical representations (including optional components), retain such representations, which they can reconstruct on future relevant occasions, and revise with future experience. All perceptions are components of a behavior episode. Therefore, the construction of a prototypical representation occurs in the context of an organized flow of behavior episode information (see Fig. 10.1). Those aspects of the episode in focal attention will be most fully represented and retained in a recallable form.

However, feedforward information to senses, muscles, glands, and viscera are also always part of the integrated behavior episode pattern that is organized and learned (see Fig. 10.3), but cannot enter consciousness. Even in observational or thinking episodes in which motor behavior is inhibited, some motor behavior is necessary (e.g., to maintain body posture or to read). Therefore, what is learned or constructed from experience is an organized pattern of total system functioning in particular contexts; that is, a behavior episode schemata (BES). The contents of consciousness (the inner circle of Fig. 10.3) represent the "tip of the iceberg" of ongoing behavior patterns through which the total pattern can be influenced. Selectively directed attention controls the contents of consciousness, and therefore cognitive learning, remembering, and the organization of behavior episode patterns (see Chapters 8 and 9).

Recognizing and Remembering

These initial crude BES are specific to particular people, places, intentions, and consequences (see Schank, 1979, for a similar concept called memory organization packets or MOPs). Once formed, they will tend to be reconstructed and used under similar conditions. If some perceived component of the current episode is sufficiently similar to a conceptual component of the activated BES, it will be "re-cognized" as familiar, in other words, the conception and perception will be merged, creating one coherently organized, currently active information organization that organizes and governs the flow of the current behavior episode.

Since the activated BES and perceptions of the current episode are unlikely to be identical, discrepancies between currently active perceptions and prototype conceptions must somehow be resolved. The prototype may dominate and the perception may be "assimilated" into it by the person's ignoring certain aspects of the current perception, if necessary. The perception may dominate and the prototype "accommodate" by being changed to include the discrepant information within the perception. Or some of both may occur. If the perception of a current episode does not include some component of the guiding BES, the person may perceptually search for the missing component. This is a way of eliminating the discrepancy by trying to add information to the

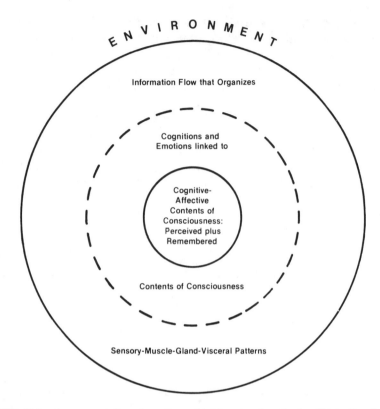

FIG. 10.3   A representation of a pattern of total system functioning illustrating that only a portion of all the information organizing the flow of system activity is part of the contents of consciousness. It is that portion that provides the basis for constructing cognitions that may later be reconstructed and used to intentionally govern all aspects of behavior episode patterns. Since behavior is hierarchically organized, imagining Fig. 10.3 as a cross-section of a cone may more fully represent the nature of the organization.

perception. The game of "peek-a-boo" is illustrative. After the face that an infant has been watching disappears from his or her current perception, the infant remembers it and looks for it.

In familiar, frequently repeated episodes, the processes just described become habitual and occur automatically without conscious effort. However, in less familiar episodes, or when the current episode perceptions and the reconstructed BES differ markedly, conscious effort may be required to recognize perceptions as familiar or to remember components missing from current perceptions. For example, seeing a casual acquaintance when visiting a strange city may require some effort to remember who he or she is because they are "out of context."

Sometimes a fragment of a current episode perception can trigger the reconstruction of a BES quite different from the current one, particularly if the BES has strong emotional components, or/and represents a concern or goal of strong current significance to the person. When that happens, current perceptions may be temporarily ignored and the activated BES turn into a thought episode unrelated to the behavioral or observational episode currently under way (e.g., a person's thoughts may "wander"). For example, a woman was talking to a friend on the phone and the friend asked about a recipe requiring "vitamize margarine." That phrase triggered a childhood memory of sitting and kneading a plastic bag of white margarine with a yellow capsule in it while being subjected to an emotionally distressing experience. For a while, she lost track of her friend's conversation. Hallucinations are probably extreme examples of this process. Memories of past perceptions provide a basis for expectations because they can also function as representations of potential future events.

Anticipating and Expecting

Social learning theory (Kelley, 1955; Rotter, 1954) builds on the assumption that human behavior is basically anticipatory; that people learn expectations through observation, instrumental activity, and social modeling; that their behavior is organized and "channeled" by such expectations; and that their expectations are typically revised to progressively accommodate information from new experiences. Humans construct representations not only about the content of their flowing stream of experience, but also about the organizational properties of the flow itself. Spatial-temporal contiguity and sequence is one such organizational property of great adaptive importance. Consistencies in information about "what occurs with what" or "what follows what" make prediction of events possible. Learning theorists have called events that signal the occurrence of other events *cues* (Dollard & Miller, 1950), *signals* (Mowrer, 1960), or *discriminative stimuli* (Staats & Staats, 1963).

Infants quickly begin to construct propositions with contiguity-sequential properties. For example, a hungry infant may wiggle, wave its arms, kick its legs, and make mouthing movements as it sees its bottle being held out towards it. Anticipatory functioning is essential for transactional functioning because mobile humans must function in a variable, moving environment. For example, reaching and grasping objects involves expectations (predictions) about the continuity and transitions of objects' states in relationship to the reacher and other objects during the act. Such anticipatory behavior is so pervasive that it is often overlooked and understudied by behavioral scientists.

A second organizational property of event flow is relationships of influence of causation. Propositional knowledge about causal relationships enables people not only to predict but also potentially to influence events of interest, and provides the basis for *causal expectations* (Kelley & Michela, 1980). *Attribution theory* (Harvey, Ickes, & Kidd, 1976; Harvey & Weary, 1984) involves the study of causal expectations. An attribution is an application of one's propositional knowledge to try to explain one's observations (Kelley, 1972). Many "attribution errors" involve making causal attributions based on covariation information (e.g., "I resented my brother, wished him dead, he died and I am responsible and guilty").

Infants begin constructing causal representations during the first few weeks of life. For example, Mast et al. (1980) demonstrated with 30 infants 10-to-16 weeks old that they could (a) learn to manipulate the movement of a crib mobile with their foot kicks; (b) display expectations of continuation of that contingency relationship over several hours and days; and (c) display distressed behavior if their efforts to move the mobile no longer succeeded. Some causal expectations represent one's personal capabilities for functioning as a cause. Rotter (1966) proposed that people formulate generalized expectancies about internal or external locus of control for the consequences of their behavior. deCharms (1968, 1976) suggested that people have a basic motivation for experiencing themselves as causal agents in their interactions and that their desire for "personal causation," to function as "origins" rather than "pawns," contributes to all other motives.

Sometimes, expectancy is narrowly defined to include only personal causality expectations. For example, Vroom (1964) defined expectancy as the subjective probability that one's efforts will lead to a given level of a valued outcome. Weiner (1982) argued that causal factors can be viewed as varying on dimensions of (a) internality: whether inside or outside the person; (b) stability: degree of variability in causal factors; (c) globality: generality or specificity of factors; and (d) controllability: degree to which the person can produce variations in causal factors. Different combinations of these dimensions can influence the causal expectancies formed. Bandura's (1977a) concept of *self-efficacy* emphasizes the basic organizing influence of people's expectations about their ability to behave effectively in order to produce desired consequences.

Expectations, then, are cognitions with two key properties essential for self-direction: (a) they are representations of potential future events; and (b) they include propositional knowledge about the flow of events, of which causal relations are of key importance.

Desiring or Preferring

People come not only to expect but to want certain things to happen or not happen. Such preferences for some expectations are products of

regulatory functioning that may be cognitive or affective. Concepts such
as *desiring, wanting,* or *preferring* have evaluative, self-referent content.
Good-bad or positive-negative is the most important dimension used by
people in all known cultures when they judge the characteristics of their
experience and their world (Osgood, May, & Miron, 1975). People come
to desire or prefer the occurrence of events or experiences that are
positively evaluated and the nonoccurrence or termination of those that
are negatively evaluated. Therefore, desires or preferences are cognitive
representations of potential, personally desirable or undesirable events;
they are expectations to which have been added an evaluative component. Incentives are objects, events, or experiences that have become
"emotionally compelling" or desirable for a person (Klinger, 1977). This
kind of "selective biasing for or against" or "affective directionality" is a
(perhaps the) key feature differentiating attitudes from other types of
schemata (Sherif, 1979).

Affective Evaluations. In evolutionary terms, the most basic form of
evaluative experience is affective. As a part of infants' perceiving and
representing ("I experience"), there are often "I like" or "I dislike"
components: "I'm wet, and I dislike it"; "I can move my mobile, and I
enjoy that"; "that smells bad"; "I like being held, but I dislike being
restrained." Carl Rogers (1951) referred to this as "direct organismic
valuing."

Affects are all perceptible subjective, noncognitive evaluative experiences including manifestations of bodily states (see Chapter 12). Emotional arousal represents one very important subtype of affect (see
Chapter 13). Sensory experiences are another subtype. In addition,
there are subjectively perceptible feeling states that are manifestations of
biological-muscular-glandular functioning; examples are feeling energetic, fatigued, or in pain. Affective processes vary in sign (positive-
negative), intensity, and duration, and are of prime importance in
organizing approach and avoidance behavior patterns (Mowrer, 1960).
Some bodily feeling states are of neutral valence (e.g., perceiving one's
heart beat).

Affective evaluations are frequently cited as crucial aspects of goal-
directed functioning, but empirical study of how that influence occurs is
sparse. For example, Young (1955) demonstrates the important role of
affective sensory experience (e.g., taste) in learning and behavior.
Mischel (1973) emphasizes the "subjective desirability" of expected
outcomes in self-regulation. In his reconceptualization of the psychoanalytic theory of motivation, Holt (1976) views a "wish" as initiated by "a
cognitive-affective state." Klinger (1977) proposes that the "relative
value assigned to an incentive" results from an "implicit calculation"

based on "the affects aroused by the incentive in question." Deci (1980) defines motives as "awareness of potential satisfactions." Different kinds of sensory sensitivity and emotional arousal occur in neonates, and the kinds observed elaborate during the first two years of life. Moreover, their occurrence appears to be a function of infants' environments (Campos et al., 1983; Schellenbach, 1987). Therefore, affective/organismic valuing is present from birth.

Cognitive Evaluations. Cognitive regulation is uniquely human, and of special value in the maintenance of social organization. During the first year of life, infants begin to learn cognitive evaluations from those around them, e.g., "That's a *good* girl" or "Don't do that, that's *bad!*" Social groups and cultures develop and maintain value systems, norms, and standards which individuals readily learn. Some of these cognitive evaluations may also be related to affective evaluations (e.g., cognitive evaluations adopted to earn parental love), but others may be relatively free of affect. Sometimes, the cognitive and affective evaluations conflict, and that is one source of dysfunction. For example, sexual activity may be affectively pleasurable, but cognitively it may be evaluated as wrong.

Thus, some expectations or propositional knowledge may be learned with affective and/or cognitive evaluative components. Such desires or preferences involve the cognition: (a) that something not currently present can potentially exist or occur; (b) that it may occur; and (c) that its occurrence is personally desirable or undesirable.

Intending

Deutsch (1951), Ackoff and Emery (1972), Boden (1972), Buckley (1968), and Searle (1979, 1981) provide helpful philosophical and theoretical discussions and resolutions of issues surrounding the concept and nature of purposive functioning. What follows is significantly influenced by their ideas.

An *intention* is a cognition that (a) specifies a desired or preferred state or set of conditions within or around the intending person, (b) that does not presently exist, but (c) that they believe has the potential to exist (an expectation), (d) as a result of the person's efforts to make it exist (a causal attribution), and (e) that the person makes a commitment to try to produce. Desires are transformed into intentions by addition of such productive commitments (Klinger, 1977). Such a commitment rests on a causal attribution that one may be able to influence the relevant circumstances. Triandis (1980) defines a "behavioral intention" as a "self-instruction" to act in a certain way. However, such instructions are not always self-generated. For example, if I had waited for my sons to "instruct themselves" to mow our lawn, I'd have grown old while waiting. However, they would mow it if asked to; that is, they accepted as a guiding intention a goal that someone else defined. It is important to recognize that for such instructions by others to function as a personal goal the person must make a *commitment* to it. For my sons, mowing the lawn did not in itself have a positive value and a personal commitment. But as a subgoal to the broader goals of family life, mowing the grass acquired value and commitment. One of the great skills of parenting and leadership is being able to get children, employees, or associates to commit themselves to goals that are not initially self-generated. For example, every researcher works hard to create conditions to "motivate" subjects to commit themselves to the terms and tasks of the researcher's study.

The words *goal, purpose,* and *motive* (as in "What was the motive for the crime?") are often used to represent such intended states. For example, Deutsch (1951) defines a *goal* as "a final condition" in which the behaving person "reaches a definite correlation in time or in space with another object or event." Such final conditions may be within the person (e.g., an emotional state or cognitive resolution of a problem), in the environment (e.g., to complete the construction of a home), or in the person's relationship to his or her context (e.g., to earn the love of another). They may be short-term (e.g., to buy new shoes), medium-term (e.g., to complete a college degree), long-term (e.g., to give birth to and rear happy, healthy children), or continuous (e.g., to be happy or to serve God).

An intentional state specifies its own *conditions of satisfaction* (Searle, 1981), the desired set of conditions to be produced or maintained by one's intentional behavior. These might be called *intended consequences.* Not all consequences of one's behavior are intended. For example, one may hate and have a desire to "get even with" a person. At the same time, one may have an intention to get to work by driving one's car. While driving to work, one may hit and kill a pedestrian who coincidentally turns out to be the hated person. While killing the hated person was a consequence of one's intentional car-driving behavior, the killing itself was not an intended consequence of that behavior (Searle, 1981). The distinction between intended and unintended consequences of people's behavior permeates humans' evaluations of, and expectations about, social interactions. It is codified in many laws (e.g., the distinction between premeditated murder and unintended manslaughter; the insanity defense). The ability to infer and use information about intentionality appears in early childhood and grows rapidly (Whiteman, Brook, & Gordon, 1977).

An intention defines a discrepancy to exist between conditions that are current or expected and others that are intended and desired. This is the prototypical problem that control system models are designed to handle (Carver & Scheier, 1981). The function of intentional behavior is to reduce, remove, or prevent the occurrence of a particular discrepancy, that is, to produce or maintain a desired set of conditions. Such discrepancies may take three basic forms. In one form, the person imagines not currently existing, but desirable, conditions. Then intentional behavior functions to remove the discrepancy by transforming the current into the desired conditions, which is often called *approach behavior*. For example, one may intend to buy an ice cream sundae because of a desire to enjoy its good taste.

In the second form, the person imagines future conditions in which some undesirable current conditions no longer exist. Then intentional behavior functions to remove the discrepancy by transforming the current conditions to eliminate the undesirable components. For example, one may take aspirin to get rid of a headache. In the third form, one imagines the potential future existence of undesirable conditions and behaves to remove the discrepancy by preventing the transformation of the current conditions into the potential undesirable conditions. For example, one may lie to avoid parental disapproval and discipline, or prolong a social encounter which one does not want to end. Forms 2 and 3 are frequently called *avoidance behavior*. Some personality concepts represent different intentional "styles." For example, an "optimist" is one who emphasizes seeking and creating desirable conditions; a hypochondriac emphasizes the avoidant forms.

In summary, expectations are cognitions based on propositional knowledge that enables a person to anticipate or predict potential events based on current conditions. Desires are expectations that have acquired a positive or negative evaluative component as a result of affective and/or cognitive evaluative experiences. Intentions are desires to which are added both the causal attribution that one may be able to produce the desired consequence through one's behavior, and a personal commitment to try to do so.

ORGANIZATIONS OF INTENTIONS: PERSONAL GOAL HIERARCHIES

Personal goal hierarchies appear in two forms: (a) a set of goals or intentions organizing each behavior episode; and (b) all of a person's repertoire of both currently and potentially active personal goals.

Behavior Episode Goal Hierarchies

All propositional knowledge, including expectations, can be used to guide behavior; any expectation, therefore, can potentially become an intention by adding appropriate evaluations and commitment to it. An old clich says that one solves big problems by breaking them down into small problems and solving them one by one. Information-processing approaches to problem solving use that subgoal approach (Farley, 1980, Siegler, 1983).

Establishing subgoals requires using propositional knowledge to componentize the larger problem or behavior episode into "chunks" which can be performed relatively independently. Each component or subepisode has consequences which it is responsible for producing (i.e., serving as an end in itself), and those subconsequences are also a necessary part of the total "conditions of satisfaction" required for the larger goal (Searle, 1981). Expectations that have not themselves been learned with desirable or undesirable evaluations, and which therefore do not ordinarily function as desires and intentions, may acquire temporary value and function as intentions by virtue of their utility in producing some of the "conditions of satisfaction" for some desired goal. When intentions serve both as ends in themselves, *endogenous behavior*, and as means to other ends, *exogenous behavior* (Kruglanski, 1975), they are typically called *subgoals*. Human behavior occurs in behavior episodes that are organized by an embedded hierarchy of goals and subgoals, that is, a personal goal hierarchy (see Fig. 10.1). Proximal subgoals (a) provide immediate incentives and guides for behavior and (b) sustain efforts towards the larger goals by providing signs of progress and by producing some *conditions of satisfaction* and increased *self-efficacy* (Bandura, 1982b; Bandura & Schunk, 1981).

The process by which a person becomes set to pursue a goal Klinger (1977) labels commitment, and the resulting state one of "current concern." Kiesler (1971) emphasizes that commitment is not an either-or phenomenon but occurs in degrees, from being committed to a goal to either attaining it, or disengaging from it. The boundaries or conditions of satisfaction for an intention are defined by the range of alternative outcomes the person would find acceptable. Sherif (1979) demonstrates that the degree of "involvement" (analogous to commitment) significantly influences the kind of behavior that may result and the likelihood of changing relevant beliefs.

Because people typically function under the simultaneous influence of multiple goals, multiple states of current concern usually must be reconciled with one another to produce effective behavior. They must be assigned relative priorities through evaluative (regulatory) processes, and organized functionally and temporally. Otherwise, one's behavior will be directed by contradictory messages and will become erratic, and perhaps disorganized. Humans display several goal-integration strategies.

One of the efficiencies of human behavior is that a single pattern of behavior may simultaneously fulfill combinations of intentions or goals. One kind of combination involves multiple, relatively independent goals. For example, one may carefully plan what one eats to simultaneously (a) avoid gaining weight; (b) prevent cancer; (c) provide a nutritionally sound diet; and (d) enjoy eating. While they are not hierarchically organized, each goal introduces constraining conditions of satisfaction which limit alternatives (i.e., restricting one's degree of freedom), so the resulting behavior pattern must honor the collective conditionalities. For example, eating french fries, fatty hamburgers, and rich desserts might serve objective (d) but not the others. Another combination involves an embedded hierarchy of goals that may be simultaneously accomplished with a single behavior pattern. For example, scoring the goal may simultaneously win the game, win the championship, elicit respect, produce personal satisfaction, and earn a salary bonus.

A third goal combination involves a temporally embedded hierarchy in which at least some goals must be sequentially accomplished, and accomplishing later goals is contingent upon accomplishing some subgoals first. Such contingent relationships among goals is often referred to as their "instrumentality" in expectancy-value theories of motivation (Campbell & Pritchard, 1983). For example, to become a physician, one must complete medical school. That requires completing a baccalaureate degree, which requires completing a set of courses, which requires meeting each course's requirements.

The mutual interdependence of temporally embedded goal hierarchies provides two important types of flexibility. First, constructing a behavior pattern to meet subgoals' conditions of satisfaction is constrained somewhat less because they are pursued sequentially. Second, if commitment to the larger goal is abandoned, there may still be utility in the subgoal accomplishment. For example, a student may complete requirements for admission to medical school, and then abandon his or her goal of being a physician. The baccalaureate degree, initially completed as a subgoal, can be used in other ways (e.g., as preparation for a management role in a health related industry). Such embedded hierarchy goal organizations enable people to keep their future options open, because accomplishing the subgoal fulfills some of the conditions of satisfaction for several alternate larger goals.

Goal Priorities and Values. A person is usually committed to more intentions or goals than can be integrated into a single behavior episode. Therefore, typically, it is necessary to organize each behavior episode to reflect only some current concerns while inhibiting others. Failure to do so results in inefficient and perhaps ineffective behavior. For example, this morning I set out to accomplish three goals: (a) to arrange for repairs on my car; (b) to make some final decisions on a house we are having built; and (c) to complete this chapter. As I tried to work on (c), thoughts about (a) and (b) kept intruding. I tried to concentrate my attention on the writing to eliminate those "distracting concerns," that is, competing or conflicting intentions, but with limited success. Finally, I interrupted my writing, accomplished (a) and (b) and then returned to (c) with greater concentration and efficiency.

It is characteristic of life, particularly social life, that people often cannot do what they want, when they want to, to get something they want. Some goals have to be delayed to pursue others or because conditions are not yet appropriate. Therefore, it becomes essential for people to learn ways of inhibiting goal-directed or consummatory behavior until appropriate conditions for pursuing those goals exist. Mischel (1981) has studied behavioral strategies small children invent to accomplish such *delay of gratification.*

The multiple goals directing a behavior episode typically differ in their degree of personal importance at that moment. Therefore, intentions or goals are hierarchically organized not only in terms of subgoal relationships but also in terms of relative value and commitment. Much of the research on adult behavior and work motivation or job satisfaction focuses on the influence of differences in value and commitment for different kinds of goals, such as promotion, pay, supervisor or coworker approval, or meeting personal standards (Kopelman, 1979; Locke et al., 1981; Raynor & Entin, 1981; White, Mitchell, & Bell, 1977).

Klinger (1977) and colleagues (Klinger, Barta, & Maxeiner, 1980) report that the intensity of goal commitment, the goal's attractiveness or incentive value, the subjective probability of successful pursuit, the instrumentality for reaching the goal, and the time left before something must be done all combine to influence when, how, and how much one thinks about the goal. Moreover, affective responses appear to be prominent features of the "leading edges" of new thought segments. The intensity and nature of the affect related to obstructions to and accomplishment of the goal(s) are indicators of the goal's importance; and there are outcome-related (evaluation of performance feedback) and attribution-related (evaluation of anticipated consequences) affects (Weiner, Russell, & Lerman, 1979; see also Chapter 13).

When a set of current concerns cannot all be served with one behavior episode, they must be organized as separate sets and each accomplished through different behavior episodes. Therefore, at any moment, one must "give up something to get something else." However, each set of concerns need not be completely satisfied in one episode.

For example, after writing three pages of this chapter, I stopped and took my car to the garage for repairs. I then met with a vendor to provide information so he could prepare a bid on some construction activity for our later consideration. With those subgoals accomplished for those two sets of concerns, I returned to my writing. Notice that none of the three sets of concerns were completely accomplished. I made progress on one, then another, and returned to make further progress on the first, that is, I accomplished subgoals in each domain.

That is the typical organization of the flow of a person's behavior. Behavior is organized in behavior episodes around sets of personal goal hierarchies or intentions. Alternation among episodes occurs for three basic types of reasons. First, as in the examples above, one accomplishes some subgoals in one episode, which provides a convenient stopping point so that some other concerns can be pursued. Second, one may run into obstacles that at least temporarily prohibit continued pursuit of that goal hierarchy (e.g., the vacuum cleaner breaks down on "cleaning day"). Third, current events unrelated to the current behavior episode may require interruption of it. For example, Mother Nature may demand a visit to the bathroom, or a visitor may arrive. Social organizations often structure work or other activities to synchronize the beginning and end of individuals' behavior episodes; examples are regularly scheduled meetings and standard closing times.

Dynamics of the Directive Function

Humans are self-organizing and self-constructing. Committing oneself to goals not yet accomplished creates incomplete organization. Incomplete organization or disorganization elicits efforts to transform it into some coherent organizational form. When progress towards, or accomplishment of, a set of current concerns is not occurring, an incomplete behavior episode (i.e., incomplete organization) exists. A person will try to create organizational coherence, either by increased striving to accomplish current goals or by abandonment of them (at least temporarily). This was a key idea in Lewin's (1935) dynamic psychology. His students demonstrated that incompleted tasks continue to influence behavior (Ovsiankina, 1928; Zeigarnik, 1927).

Cognitive dissonance theory (Festinger, 1957) proposes, and research indicates, that inconsistent perceptions and cognitions create unpleasant or discomforting affect which people are likely to try to resolve through their behavior (Eagly & Himmelfarb, 1978; Higgins, Rhodewalt, & Zanna, 1979; Zanna, Higgins, & Taves, 1976). This dissonance effect is most apparent when the current information conflicts with important beliefs about oneself (Allport, 1943; Rogers, 1951); or as a result of actions for which a person feels responsible, such as discrepancies between goals, values, and current feedback (Greenwald & Ronis, 1978;

Wicklund & Brehm, 1976). The idea that response-response conflict (e.g., anger-fear or ought-want evaluative thoughts) is a factor in personality disorders, is a broader version of dissonance theory, sometimes called *conflict theory* (Ford & Urban, 1963).

This helps explain one of the benefits of componentizing complex behavior episodes by establishing subgoals. Achieving a subgoal creates a sense of completeness or accomplishment for two reasons: (a) a component behavior episode (i.e., a subepisode) has been completed; and (b) by completing a subepisode, some of the "conditions of satisfaction" for the larger episode are also met. That "sense of" or evaluation of accomplishment has two benefits. First, it provides a comfortable and efficient point at which to interrupt a complex behavior episode. Second, it is a manifestation of evaluations by the regulatory process that the discrepancy between desired and existing states has been reduced, which produces positive affect and facilitates continued effort (see Chapter 13).

The Goal Hierarchy Repertoire

As people go through life, they develop a diversity of personal goals and ways of behaving to try to achieve them. The process begins in infancy, as manifest in infants' efforts to manipulate and control their relationships with their environment. For example, last night I watched a video tape of our eighth grandchild covering his life from 3 to 9 months. At 3 months, he exerted great effort to control his hands and arms sufficiently to reach, grasp, and mouth a toy, and displayed joy when he succeeded or distress when he failed. By 6 months, he could carry out such targeted reaching more readily, but was struggling to control his body sufficiently to move it from one place to another. By 8 months, he could crawl rapidly across the floor to reach a desired object or person, and use his legs to maneuver his walker to pursue the vacuum cleaner. At 9 months, he stood up one morning and walked unaided across the room, clearly pleased with himself.

Initially, each of those goal-directed behavior episodes required concentrated effort and attention. With practice, each became efficient, relatively effortless, and automatic performances (i.e., habits), when a current behavior episode required them. More complex behavior patterns in older children are organizations of such simpler ones that infants have struggled to learn. For example, to obtain a desired toy (the primary goal), this 9-month-old can now roll over (subgoal 1), stand (subgoal 2), walk to a coffee table (subgoal 3), reach and grasp the toy (subgoal 4), and play with it (conditions of satisfaction for the primary goal).

As described in Chapters 8, 9, and 14, transactional and cognitive capabilities become more complex and flexible because they become componentized, automated, and elaborated in this way, requiring little attentional effort to the subgoal episodes themselves, that is, they become *habits*. In adults, many such subgoal-directed behavior episode components are so automated and occur so frequently to serve so many other types of goals that one does not recognize their existence until they are lost. For example, an adult who loses his or her legs must develop alternate mobility methods to achieve goals that were previously automatic and easy.

As children mature into adults, accomplishments that were once primary goals come to function largely as subgoals in the service of other kinds of personal-social goals. For example, people come to want to "fix their car," "dance," "avoid pain," "get a job," "get married," "be happy," and "serve God." Such goals become organized in hierarchies related to broad domains or contexts of life (e.g., work, family, friendships). These personal-social goal hierarchies typically become organized around relatively long-term, enduring goals, such as to have a network of close friends; served by intermediate goals, such as to plan a vacation with friends for next summer; and by short-term goals, such as to call a friend tomorrow to see how she is.

Wadsworth-Winell (Wadsworth, 1983; Wadsworth & Ford, 1983; Winell, 1987) has been conducting a program of basic and applied research aimed at developing methods for assessing personal-social goal hierarchies; understanding how they are organized, change, and influence other aspects of behavior; and developing methods for helping people become more effectively self-directing. She has found considerable stability in intermediate and long-term goals, and much variability in short-term goals since they represent day-to-day subgoals in the service of larger goals.

She has also found extensive individual differences in the content and organization of personal goal hierarchies. For example, some people function mostly in terms of short-term goals, with little thought about how they may relate to tomorrow or to the longer term future. In contrast, others are deeply committed to some long-term goal(s) and try to orchestrate their intermediate and short-term goals to serve such enduring concerns. Some people have most of their lives organized around one domain of life, such as their work or their family, while others have elaborate goals for many domains. She has also found that the very process of making their personal goal hierarchies explicit is usually interesting to them, often enlightening, and sometimes produces changes in people's day-to-day strategies of living. Vocational interest measurement is a tool for trying to identify individual's personal goals and values that might guide their choice of and planning for a career trajectory.

Individual's goal hierarchy repertoires change throughout life in two basic ways. First, goals may be added (e.g., becoming a "born-again" Christian), subtracted (e.g., giving up a previously held career objective), or reorganized (e.g., making money may cease to be an end in itself and become a means of helping others). Second, those portions of the goal hierarchy repertoire to which one has made a commitment may change. For example, a talented young artist married and devoted her efforts to facilitating her husband's career, and to her home, children, and friends. Her artistic goals were deactivated by withdrawing commitment, but not personal value. When her husband retired, she reactivated her commitment to her artistic goals and became a successful, admired artist. Desires may be latent for many decades of life, yet still represent potential goals. Skillful career counselors often bring such "latent" desires to their clients' consciousness so they can be considered as potential current goals.

The Organizing Influence of Personal Goals

Intentions are cognitions that specify the consequences one wants to produce, but not how to produce them. They provide selective "design constraints" (i.e., facilitating and constraining conditionalities) on the content and organization of the behavior aimed at producing those consequences. As Henry Murray (1938) put it years ago, a *need* is a construct which "stands for a force . . . in the brain region" which "organizes perception, apperception, intellection, conation, and action" to transform "in a certain direction" "existing, unsatisfying situation." Because there are usually several ways to produce the same consequences (the principle of *equifinality*), knowledge of the guiding goal(s) is usually not sufficient to predict a person's actions. Several important distinctions must be made (Searle, 1981), as summarized in Fig. 10.4, to link intentions to actions.

An example will clarify Fig. 10.4. My wife decides she wants to go shopping for groceries (primary goal). She could go alone or arrange to go with a friend; she and her friend must decide who will drive; she can go to one or several stores; she can decide to buy some products at one store and different ones at another (establishing subgoals). She picks up her friend, drives to the first store and shops (intentions in action-movements-transactional pattern). While there, she meets and visits with an old friend. When she leaves the store, she discovers someone has hit her car and files an accident report with the police (unintended consequences). She finishes her shopping and returns home with all the groceries on her list (primary intended consequence).

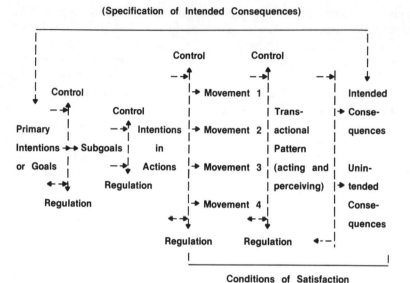

FIG. 10.4 A representation of the relationship between governing functions, actions, and consequences in a behavior episode. Primary goals specify intended consequences. Subgoals componentize the effort to produce those consequences, and guide organization of transactional patterns composed of movement components specified by action intentions, that implement the subgoals. The transactional pattern produces intended and unintended consequences. The relationships between the movements, the transactional pattern, and the intended consequences produce the conditions of satisfaction for the goals.

Each behavior episode in a person's life is guided by some subset of that person's goal hierarchy repertoire, including goals adopted as a result of suggestions by or demands from the environment. Understanding a person's behavior on a particular occasion requires knowledge of the subset of their goals or intentions guiding that behavior episode. Many efforts to predict behavior from intentions have been unsuccessful because they have dealt with generalized goals and categories of behavior. However, specific intentions can predict specific actions in specific situations (Fishbein, 1980). Identifying broader patterns of functioning across time and multiple occasions requires knowledge of a person's goal hierarchy repertoire and its coupling to other system functions. Identifying such functional consistencies has been a primary objective of personality and social psychology (see Chapter 16).

Intentions Influence Performance. The beneficial effects of goal-setting on task performance "is one of the most robust and replicable findings in the psychological literature," and goals demonstrably influence transactional functions or performance by directing attention, mobilizing effort, increasing persistence, and motivating strategy development (Locke, Shaw, Saari, & Latham, 1981). For example, goal-setting in an industrial environment increased employee performance by an average of more than 40% and saved one company $250,000 on just one job (Locke et al., 1980). When the goal and circumstances severely constrain behavioral options, as when there are specific intentions in specific situations, the intentions strongly predict actions (Azjen & Fishbein, 1974). Goals selectively activate beliefs and action. For example, if parole board members or judges believe the primary goal of imprisonment is incapacitation of criminals, their sentencing strategies and attributions for crime are different than if they consider the goal of imprisonment to be rehabilitation (Carroll & Weiner, 1982).

Intentions Influence Selective Attention and Perception. Goals influence selective attention processes (Atkinson & Shiffrin, 1968; Carver & Scheier, 1981). For example, people were asked to selectively listen for a particular word in a list of words. When they heard the word, they displayed classical physiological signs of the orienting reaction. However, they also produced orienting reactions to words that *meant* the same thing, but not to words that *sounded like* the key word (Luria & Vinogradova, 1959). Treisman (1969) cites evidence that people can attend to only one "target" at a time, but can attend to more than one attribute or dimension of that target. Subjects observing with different goals attend to different behavioral features (Cohen & Ebbesen, 1979).

Intentions Influence Information-Processing and Remembering. Observers' purposes not only influence selective attention, but also guide how they categorize, process, and recall information (Jeffrey & Mischel, 1979). Current concerns influence the content of people's thoughts, including influencing their dreams (Klinger, 1971). People interpret and remember one another's behavior in terms of assumptions about their intentions (Newtson, 1976; Pressey & Kuhlen, 1957). People understand and recall events according to a hierarchical, goal-directed schema applied to a behavior episode. For example, Lichtenstein and Brewer (1980) found that people recall best actions that are most directly related to the actor's assumed goals, and recall least those events that were not goal-related. Moreover, during recall, people tend to distort irrelevant or unconnected events to make them goal-relevant (Owens & Bower, 1979). Accurate social cognition about the meaning and predictability of others' behavior requires distinguishing between acts that are intended and those that are accidental (Shantz, 1983). In group interactions, children tend to assume a goal structure for the interaction and then to behave accordingly (Hartup, 1983).

In any behavior episode, once desired consequences are specified, there still remains the task of figuring out how to achieve the intended consequences within current environmental, body, and behavioral constraints and opportunities, and within the constraints of the regulatory criteria that have been activated. That is the governing role of the control functions which will be examined in Chapter 11.

11

Control Functions: Problem Solving and Behavior Organization

INTRODUCTION

After providing some historical perspective, Chapter 11 is divided into two parts. First, the nature and operation of control function cognitions are reviewed, including problem formulation, reasoning, problem solving, and plan formulation and execution, along with the concept of environment and its relationships to control functions. Then, ideas about the organization and development of control functions are summarized. The chapter ends with consideration of the relationship of language development and emotions to the development of control functions.

Directive function cognitions specify a desired and intended state or set of consequences. Regulatory function cognitions are evaluative thoughts used to set priorities, to select from among behavioral options, and to evaluate progress towards intended states. Within these "design criteria" and the facilitating and constraining conditions of current body and environment states, the control function combines current perceptual information with one's knowledge base about oneself and the world, and one's behavioral repertoire, to formulate and guide the execution of a behavior pattern likely to produce the intended consequences. The brain evolved to organize and guide actions, so cognition is "intrinsically motoric" and the "mind" is a "motor system" (Weimer, 1977). The cognitive component of "prospective intentions" is a "plan" which includes representations of "similar past actions," the "current situation," and "the course of future actions" (Brand, 1984).

Goals and values are only dreams unless a person can formulate and successfully execute behavior patterns that turn such dreams into reality. And many dreams die on the lips of the dreamer from lack of these competencies. Intelligence tests are primarily measures of information-processing and control functions which are limited by mental retardation (Campione, Brown, & Ferrara, 1982). The concept of control is sometimes used much more narrowly, as in the beliefs that one can behave in ways "that can influence the aversiveness of an event" (Thompson, 1981).

HISTORICAL PERSPECTIVE

There were two early streams of research about how humans use information to guide their adaptive efforts and solve problems. One focused on problem solving behavior in animals and humans. The second focused on human thinking "of the verbal sort" (Woodworth, 1938). A later stream involved attempts to study and measure human intelligence. Reasoning, problem solving, and intelligence are such interrelated concepts that "it is often difficult to tell them apart" (Sternberg, 1982a).

Ackoff (1957) presents a framework for understanding the organization of "behavioral elements" within which individuals deal with "decision problems" in a "purposeful state." The elements include objectives (the directive function), valuation of each objective (the regulatory function), and possible courses of action, the efficiency of each potential course of action in achieving each objective, and the probability of choice for each course of action (the control function). Information-processing approaches (Reitman, 1964) represent decision making as a three-component process: (a) specifying an initial or existing state; (b) specifying a desired or terminal state; and (c) transformations that will get from (a) to (b). Harvey (1966) characterized components of the control function in similar terms: Attaining goals or solving problems requires (a) "the analysis of the situation into its necessary parts"; (b) "organizing them into appropriate means-ends relationships"; and (c) "employing them in ways consonant with the end sought." This requires flexibility and creativity to "generate alternative means to a valued end," and to "assimilate diversity and contradicting events" without giving up the goal.

The nature and operation of these control functions have been studied under multiple concept labels. *Reasoning* (Revlyn & Mager, 1978) is the study of thinking which involves organizing information and drawing conclusions in a rule-governed way, and formal logic is only one kind of rule-governed thinking (Braine & Rumain, 1983). *Inference* (Nisbett &

Ross, 1980) involves reasoning from available information to a representation of other implications and possibilities. *Attribution theory* (Harvey & Weary, 1984) focuses on one type of inference called *causal attributions*, and how they influence people's behavior. *Beliefs* are propositions that particular objects, circumstances, or actions exist (e.g., "I believe she loves me") or will produce a particular state of affairs (e.g., "she'll marry me if I ask") (Audi, 1979; Fishbein & Azjen, 1975; Goldman, 1970).

Problem solving (Kleinmuntz, 1966) is perhaps the broadest concept, and computer information-processing analogies have stimulated new and more detailed study of problem-solving processes (Newell & Simon, 1972; Simon, 1978). The study of *creative thinking* (Ray, 1967) focuses on how people create new ideas and solutions to problems. For example, one method is to simultaneously think of two or more contradictory images or ideas with the objective of removing the contradiction (Rothenberg, 1978, 1979).

Choice, judgment, and *decision making* (Janis & Mann, 1977; Kahneman, Slovic, & Tversky, 1982) label thought processes targeted to produce outcomes (e.g., decisions) which can then organize and guide action. The interface between thought and action, and increasing system complexity and automation, has led the fields of engineering, and industrial and organizational psychology to emphasize planning and decision-making cognitive processes (MacCrimmon & Taylor, 1983; Wickens & Kramer, 1985). Decision making may involve *simulated behavior episodes* in which potential alternative courses of action are imagined and evaluated to provide a basis for choosing and implementing one alternative. The organization of the flow of individuals' transactional behaviors is a manifestation of control function operation.

Control functions include strategies of perceiving and thinking. Some ego analysts and psychologists have studied the different kinds of cognitive strategies or "styles" people develop and use, such as field dependence-independence (Back et al., 1979; Gardner & Long, 1960). Santostefano (1978) reviews cognitive control styles and describes a child diagnostic and therapeutic approach that focuses on control functions.

Mowrer (1947) used a tripartite-process classification to represent control function phenomena: (a) a "problem posing" process and (b) a "problem solving" process which (c) yield and guide "directed action." The labels under which control functions have been studied emphasize one or more of these three processes. For example, research on choice, judgment, and decision making has focused on (a) and (b), while research on reasoning and cognitive styles focuses primarily on (b). Research on creative thinking has tended to emphasize the option-generation aspects of (b), but not its option-selection aspect. Problem-solving research tends to focus on all three, while the study of skills tends to focus primarily on (c). Historically, research on intelligence has been largely the study of control functions (Sternberg, 1982a).

THE OPERATION OF CONTROL FUNCTIONS

Mowrer's three-process classification has modern counterparts. For example, Baron (1982) proposes that reflective thought occurs in a five-phase iterative or recursive process: (a) problem recognition; (b) enumeration of possibilities; (c) reasoning; (d) revision of possibilities; and (e) evaluation. Sternberg's (1980) "componential subtheory" of human intelligence has five component processes which function at three hierarchically related levels (Sternberg, 1982a): (a) metacomponents (involved in planning courses of action, making decisions about changes during reasoning or problem solving, and monitoring processes); (b) performance components (involved in the execution of a reasoning or problem solving strategy); (c) acquisition components (processes involved in learning strategies for reasoning or problem solving); (d) retention components (processes used in remembering knowledge or strategies); and (e) transfer components (processes involved in generalizing strategies and solutions from one task to another).

Information-processing models (e.g., Simon, 1978) utilize a similar sequential, component-process approach in computer simulations of problem-solving activities. Carefully designed algorithms will lead to the best possible answer (if there is one) and will be error-free. However, efforts to design computer programs that mimic human thinking, called *artificial intelligence*, have run into difficulty because humans often do not seem to think in such orderly, sequential ways, and they use knowledge generation and remembering processes that computers cannot yet mimic (Dehn & Schank, 1982).

For example, people typically do not canvas all aspects of a problem situation, nor do they formulate and evaluate all alternatives before selecting one. Rather, they typically focus on a few seemingly important or interesting aspects, and ignore many others. They often settle for the first adequate solution they construct rather than continuing to look for a best solution, that is, they *satisfice* rather than *optimize*. Instead of using precise rules, or *algorithms*, people invent short-cut rules called *heuristics* that specify general operations (sometimes called "test-action" pairs). While not as precise as algorithms, heuristics work efficiently in producing reasonably adequate solutions much of the time. It is a kind of operation by analogy; in effect saying, "this worked before in similar situations, so I'll try it again."

Therefore, although it is useful for conceptual purposes to subdivide control processes into sequentially related categories, it is important to recognize that such subdivisions are artificial constructions to serve as tools for understanding an integrated process. Scholars too often talk as if the conceptual categories they have invented to organize and interpret their data actually exist inside their subjects' heads; examples are Piaget and Kohlberg (Stone & Day, 1980). Some general issues about the reasoning process are considered next to provide a context for considering problem formulation, problem solving and plan formulation, and plan execution.

The Reasoning Process

Historically, the study of reasoning has typically assumed that it corresponds to the rules of some humanly constructed formal system of logic, such as syllogistic reasoning, and probabilistic statistical models of reasoning. But neither children nor adults typically reason in terms of such formal models (Braine & Rumain, 1983; Kahneman, Slovic, & Tversky, 1982), although they can be taught to do so. Therefore, what have typically been characterized as "errors" in reasoning are better understood as differences in the ways people actually reason from special purpose formal models humans have constructed.

For example, humans ordinarily comprehend a communication (e.g., a sentence) not only in terms of its construction, but also in terms of what they know about the communicator and his/her intentions, as well as knowledge of the specific subject matter, general knowledge of the world, and general communication conventions. Accurate conclusions are frequent though much of the information used in the process is unstated. In contrast, some kinds of formal logic focus solely on the content and organization of the communication (e.g., sentence) itself. Natural reasoning (e.g., the representative heuristic, Kahneman, Slovic, & Tversky, 1982) appears to involve (a) comprehension processes, (b) logical reasoning processes, and (c) nonlogical strategies (Braine & Rumain, 1983). Farley (1980) provides a useful theoretical discussion of some issues in knowledge-based problem solving.

In addition, because many of the kinds of research tasks given subjects are in verbal form, and because people are often asked to represent the processes and results of their reasoning in verbal form, it is frequently assumed (sometimes explicitly) that reasoning is a verbal process. That is probably not the case. For example, children's conceptual capabilities develop in advance of their language capabilities; poor performance of young children on at least some kinds of reasoning tasks is more the result of their language comprehension processes than the nature of their conceptual functioning. In fact, there are extensive language comprehensive errors at all ages (Braine & Rumain, 1983).

Sentences are composed of words linked sequentially according to rules. Speaking or writing requires constructing chains of words. Yet, the meaning cannot be inferred from the words alone, but depends on their organization and the larger context of the communication. Unfortunately, the componentized, sequential organization of verbal communication fits nicely with an associationistic model of human behavior, and implies that thought involves the association of concepts and words.

That is probably a misguiding metaphor. Reasoning processes are probably more analogous to the merging of magnetic fields or to the phenomena of resonance. Thinking probably occurs through the merger and differentiation of information organizations (cognitions and perceptions) tested against criteria (conditions of satisfaction). If a particular merger meets most of its conditions of satisfaction, a problem may be said to be solved. If it does not, subjective uncertainty and discomfort occur, and an alternate fusion of information may be tried or a person may abandon the effort. One may be able to represent in linguistic form the parts of the process of which one can become conscious, but the representation should not be mistaken for the process itself. For example, just because we can represent our thinking in logical form does not mean it occurs that way. On the other hand, logical rules may constrain the kinds of information constructions manipulated.

In general, it appears to be the *products* of reasoning processes—the output from one phase which served as the input to another—of which people can become aware, rather than the processes involved (Braine & Rumain, 1983). It is information in feedback circuits of which people can become conscious. Therefore, all thought processes (as contrasted to products) are probably unconscious in that sense. So the following discussion of component processes does not necessarily imply that people are aware of them while they are thinking.

Problem Formulation

Behavior episodes are organized to produce *conditions of satisfaction* for some intention(s) and regulatory criteria. The goals may be personal constructions or may be adopted from the social or natural environment. Goals are embedded in situational contexts (Showers & Cantor, 1985), and so the organization of behavior episodes begins when people commit themselves to realize some intention(s) in some context(s).

Schemata as Problem Defining Cognitions. The activated intentions, in combination with perceptions of the context in which their conditions of satisfaction are to be sought, trigger or "prime" (Klinger, 1971; Showers & Cantor, 1985) the reconstruction of a schema relevant to that goal-context combination. Therefore, differences in the ways people represent problems may be largely a function of differences in their BES repertoire, as illustrated by differences between socioeconomic classes (Houtz, Montgomery, & Kirkpatrick, 1979). Information retrieval is a function of the similarity between the organization of previously constructed cognitions and current perceptions (Medin & Schaffer, 1979).

The balance of influence can vary between intentions and situational factors in determining what kind of BES will be reconstructed. When "pressing goals," "cherished beliefs," and "strong emotions" are involved, people may "fly in the face of" obvious situational factors and construct a schema to more closely fit relevant goals, beliefs, and emotions (Showers & Cantor, 1985). On the other hand, whenever some aspect of the situation is made disproportionately salient (e.g., through its distinctiveness or emotion-eliciting properties), it will exert a stronger influence on the nature of the schema constructed. What is absent as well as what is present in the situation may be influential (Nisbett, Borgida, Crandall, & Reed, 1982; Ross & Anderson, 1982). Subgoals anchor subepisodes which serve as means to larger goals. Therefore, activation of a relevant schema may also be a function of subcomponent "operators" (Farley, 1980). Since behavior episodes are dynamic, internally consistent, spatial-temporal event flows, the schemata which guide them must also be understood as dynamic information organizations which may undergo changes as an episode unfolds and new perceptual information primes other conceptual information.

An activated BES is a prototypical knowledge-procedural format (i.e., goal specifications, regulatory criteria, affective qualities, and information about environmental contingencies) which provides "design criteria" for the formulation of an appropriate solution or plan of action to produce the conditions of satisfaction for certain kinds of intentions in certain types of context. Therefore, it guides the construction and implementation of a relevant behavior episode within current environmental and interpersonal conditions (Snyder, 1978); that is, functions as a "mental model" representing the relevant variables and their relationships (Johnson-Laird, 1981, 1983).

The selective influences of such BES are illustrated in studies of attitudes, expectancies, beliefs, and sets. For example, consistent bias in the way people answer questionnaire items has been called *response sets* (Cronback, 1946; Siller & Chipman, 1963). Selective approaches to learning tasks have been called instructional or *learning sets* (Howell & Kreidler, 1964; Siegel & Siegel, 1965). Attitudes' and expectancies' selective influence have been a particular interest in the study of social issues and interpersonal relations. Stereotypes, social prejudices, and beliefs about others and oneself are maintained by selectively attending to information consistent with them, and either ignoring disconfirming information or reinterpreting it to fit (Cooper & Fazio, 1979; Rotter, 1978). Moreover, BES may lead one to selectively behave in ways which elicit consequences confirming one's guiding beliefs; and scholarly research is not immune from such biasing influences (Darley & Fazio, 1980; Rosenthal, 1976). However, although the selective influence of BES may sometimes produce undesirable consequences, it is usually highly efficient and adaptive.

Constructing effective ways of transforming the current state of a system to an alternate preferred state, or preventing its transformation to an unpreferred state, requires beginning with an accurate representation of the current state and the preferred or nonpreferred alternative(s). Therefore, a key aspect of problem formulation involves identifying the present and intended states of the system (Connolly & Miklausich, 1978). BES can vary in the extent to which the information contained therein adequately represents these states, and therefore can vary in the effectiveness of behavior episodes constructed from them. Some intention(s)/context combinations have been experienced so frequently by a person that the relevant BES have become very efficient in producing effective behavior episodes without further problem-solving thought (i.e., they are habits). At the other extreme, the intention(s)/context combination may be so unfamiliar that the person has no relevant BES in his or her repertoire. Under those conditions, the person must start from "scratch," and try to piece together conceptual and propositional knowledge borrowed from multiple schemata into a relevant BES.

BES also vary in their elaborateness. Some may encompass only limited information and narrowly defined "scripts," that is, they are inflexible. Others may encompass extensive amounts of information and contain a diversity of optional scripts for alternate courses of action to serve the same objectives; they are flexible. Such differences are apparent in comparisons between novices and experts in a problem domain (Showers & Cantor, 1985).

Obviously, the effectiveness of a behavior episode will be heavily influenced by the extent to which the guiding BES adequately encompasses the full range of relevant knowledge and information about the current context. Therefore, it is not surprising that one robust finding in problem-solving research is that better problem solvers spend relatively more time understanding the nature of the problem, while poorer problem-solvers tend to jump to solution formulation with whatever schema is initially activated (Sternberg, 1982a). Kagan (1966) studied individual differences in such "reflective-impulsive" cognitive styles.

Creating an effective behavior episode is difficult when the current intention(s)/context combination is a "deviant member" of a set "of earlier situations of the same sort" (Raaheim, 1974). Such "problem spaces" may range from being "ill-defined" to "well-defined" (Newell & Simon, 1972). Stated in common sense terms, the way you think about a problem and what you know about it will influence how successful you can be in solving it. The "framing" or structuring of a problem will influence how people try to solve it, the kinds of solution options generated, and evaluations of the relative attractiveness of the options (Griggs & Newstead, 1982; Kahneman & Tversky, 1984). For example, labeling the price difference between cash and credit card purchases "cash discounts" rather than "credit card surcharges" influences people's attitudes about using credit cards.

Many "errors" in problem solution are the result of inaccurate or insufficient problem formulation. For example, incorrect encoding of the premises of a problem is responsible for many reasoning errors (Revlin & Mayer, 1978). When faced with complex, unfamiliar issues (e.g., risk assessment of exposure to hazardous substances), people may not have enough knowledge to formulate a useful schema, and may behave "irrationally" (Sage & White, 1980). The problem formulation may not prime an appropriate schema. For example, if a problem formulation is changed in irrelevant ways, people may not recognize it as an example of a familiar problem for which they have familiar and successful solutions. Or if the problem formulation changes are not perceived as actually producing a different kind of problem, people may utilize an inappropriate schema (Sweller & Gee, 1978). Intelligence is sometimes thought of as an ability to flexibly transfer problem-solving skills from one situation to another, and mentally retarded people are particularly weak at making such a transfer (Campione, Brown, & Ferrara, 1982).

Problem formulation is dynamic and continues throughout the problem solving process. For example, one may be guided initially by a particular schema, but revise components of it as new contingencies are identified, difficulties lead to problem reformulation, new evaluative criteria are included, the context for problem solution changes, or the guiding intentions become altered or divided into subgoals. Focusing on subproblem solutions involves creating "child schemas" within the "parent schema" to guide each subproblem solution, as illustrated by Norman (1981) in an interesting study of action slips.

Problem Solving and Plan Formulation

Once a problem has been formulated within a BES, people try to formulate a solution within the constraints of the situation. The BES primes or makes more salient some aspects of a person's knowledge base and the problem-solving environment, so that much information is ignored and only potentially relevant information is considered through selective attention to current and stored information. People tend to focus on covariation between their current schema and current situation, and to ignore "nonmatch" or "negative" covariation information (Crocker, 1981).

Cognitive Styles.   People develop and use different methods for selectively controlling the content and organization of information they use in problem solving, often termed *cognitive styles* or *controls* (Santostefano, 1969). Some scholars (e.g., Witkin et al., 1977) argue that such information selection styles become methods of thinking or information processing as well. Underlying most of the styles studied are "attentional behaviors" which are "truly a key to adaptive coordination" with one's environment and within oneself (Gardner et al., 1961).

For example, people differ in the extent to which they deploy their attention narrowly or broadly, called *scanning style* (Kogan, 1971); in the extent to which they rely on contextual cues versus internally generated information in making judgments about the relative spatial positioning of objects or themselves, or in perceiving components of an organized visual array as separate or separable from the array, labeled *field dependence-independence* (Witkin et al., 1977); in the extent to which they rely on visual (e.g., imaging) versus haptic (e.g., feeling) information, called a *visual-haptic style* (Lowenfeld & Brittain, 1970); in the extent to which they can control their reactions to contradictory or intrusive cues, called distractability, or a *constricted-flexible style* (Gardner et al., 1959); in the extent to which they focus on similarities in their perceptions and minimize differences, called *leveling,* or tend to maximize differences, called *sharpening* (Holtzman & Klein, 1959); and in their preferred approach to categorizing perceived similarities and differences in a smaller number of broadly defined or a larger number of more narrowly defined categories, called *categorizing style* (Kogan, 1971) or *equivalence range* (Gardner, 1953).

Other dimensions could have been examined, and one suspects individual differences (or cognitive styles) could have been identified there also. While individuals display some cross-task consistency in their selective attention-perceptual functioning, there is also considerable intraindividual variability from task to task. Moreover, some proposed measures of cognitive styles may actually be indicators of other variables, for example, the embedded figure test of field dependence-independence may be primarily a measure of spatial abilities (Widiger, Knudson, & Rorer, 1980).

Simulating Behavior Episodes During Problem Solving. Making sound decisions or selecting effective courses of action often involves withholding a commitment to, and action on, a particular decision, or withholding action until relevant variables and multiple options are adequately considered. This is particularly important the more ambiguous or complex the situation and the more elaborate the set of intentions whose conditions of satisfaction must be met (Cosier, 1978). Such simulated episodes involve imagining or "playing through," rather than acting out, optional solutions or action patterns and their potential consequences (Nuttin, 1984) (see Chapter 9). The "simulation heuristic" is a strategy of cognitively constructing and evaluating alternative scenarios (Kahneman & Tversky, 1982).

Conceiving of Options. Constructing alternatives and evaluating them to select the correct or most appropriate alternative are separable processes. The typical approach (at least early in life) is to generate an alternative, evaluate it, implement it if it passes the test(s), or create another alternative if it does not. A more complex approach is to withhold evaluation of any option until many options have been generated. Measures of creative thinking often focus on people's option-generating capabilities. Option generation may be thought of as a subepisode within a larger problem-solving episode (Houtz et al., 1979). The psychoanalytic distinction between primary and secondary process thought is somewhat similar. Primary process thought is not constrained by reality testing, but is organized around subjective criteria of "drive, need, and affect." Secondary process thought is a logic-determined process focused on "mastering reality," and requires conscious reality testing of actual or potential courses of action (Suler, 1980).

A problem-solving technique called "brainstorming" permits no evaluation during the option-generating phase of discussion. If evaluation comes too early in the process, many potentially useful ideas may be inhibited. Another technique in promoting option generation is to identify apparently contradictory ideas or information and to try to construct a formulation that will remove the contradiction (Rothenberg, 1978, 1979). Challenging an option proposed by one expert with a critique of it or a different option proposed by another expert also helps prevent too early foreclosure of option-generation activity (Cosier, 1978).

Evaluating Options and Making Decisions. Much problem-solving research is focused on how people evaluate and choose from among options, and on the kinds of errors they make in that process (Janis & Mann, 1977; Kahneman et al., 1982; Pitz & Sachs, 1984; Slovic, Fischoff,

& Lichtenstein, 1977; Wickens & Kramer, 1985). MacCrimmon and Taylor (1983) summarize strategies that have been identified.

Options may be considered as hypotheses, and option evaluation as hypothesis testing (Gettys & Fisher, 1979; Tumblin & Gholson, 1981). Small children tend to act on the basis of their initial hypotheses and to continue such action in the face of disconfirming feedback, called *response set hypotheses*. However, most older children and adults learn to evaluate hypotheses against probable or actual consequence information, called *prediction hypotheses* (Tumblin & Gholson, 1981). Hypothesis generation and evaluation is a recursive process. People develop one or more hypotheses (or options) that seem plausible, and then select from among that set of possibilities. Properties of the set (e.g., set size and diversity) influence the decision (Duncan, 1978). Through simulation or actual tryout, people obtain and use feedback information to evaluate their plausible hypotheses.

Such tests involve multiple criteria, such as: (a) the extent to which it is likely to produce the desired consequences; (b) whether it is within the constraints of the relevant environment; (c) whether it is within the limits of one's physical capabilities and resources; (d) whether it has dangerous, frightening, or undesirable consequences; (e) the extent to which the person considers (her)himself capable of effectively performing the required actions. Thus, the evaluation process involves people drawing upon their conceptual and propositional knowledge about events (e.g., What is it? How does it work?) in relationship to themselves (e.g., How will it affect me? How might I influence it? Am I capable of influencing it?). Cast in this form, the essential relationship between knowledge of the world and of oneself in problem solving activity becomes apparent in the evaluative-regulatory processes.

If the evaluation is not sufficiently supportive, a person may try another hypothesis in the original set, or may generate additional ones. The larger the original set, the less likely new hypotheses will be added to it (Gettys & Fisher, 1979). The quality of decisions or problem solutions are usually improved when people think carefully about (i.e., evaluate) advantages and disadvantages of alternatives before choosing one. An old adage says, "Look before you leap." That appears to have another benefit. People who have thought through the possible shortcomings of the course of action they adopt appear better able to withstand the stress that is produced when things go wrong (Janis & Mann, 1977). Anticipated difficulties are less disconcerting than unanticipated ones.

Most problems are multicriteria, involving multiple goals, values, and environmental-behavioral contingencies (Eshragh, 1980). People often have to problem-solve under *uncertainty* when they (a) do not know which events may affect their efforts and outcomes; (b) have inadequate propositional knowledge about potential causal factors; (c) have little control over at least some relevant variables; and (d) are in a changing or unstable context. People also problem-solve under *complexity* when the potentially relevant factors are large in number, very heterogeneous, abstract, and highly interrelated; and under *conflict* when there are conflicting goals, values, and environmental conditions (MacCrimmon & Taylor, 1983). Life is full of trade-offs.

Conceptions of Cause-Effect Relations. Tversky and Kahneman (1982) assert that it is "a psychological commonplace" that people try to create a coherent interpretation of the events that they observe and experience, despite such uncertainty, complexity, and conflict. Moreover, they argue, schemas of cause-effect relations serve to produce such coherence. People look for and find organization, even in random events; they look for certainty rather than probability (Sojberg, 1979). In addition, people's intentions usually focus on influencing or controlling the flow of events. Therefore, people usually seek and retain propositional knowledge about cause-effect relations among objects, action, and events ("Baconian" probability theory) rather than relative event frequency information ("Pascalian calculus" probability theory) (Cohen, 1979).

Research has compared the accuracy of human decision making with a model based on a theory of chance events; that is, on probability theory. Humans seem to make many more errors than statistical models on the kinds of problems studied (Kahneman, Slovic, & Tversky, 1982; Slovic, Fischoff, & Lichtenstein, 1977). People violate "the logic of statistical prediction" by disregarding factors such as prior base rates, information reliability, sample characteristics, and prior outcome probabilities (Kahneman & Tversky, 1973), using instead generalized heuristics based on conceptions of cause-effect relations.

But the ability to construct and use cause-effect heuristics probably evolved as an adaptive mechanisms for coping with a complex, dynamic environment (Hogarth, 1981; Pitz & Sachs, 1984), in which knowledge about how to influence and control events is far more powerful than knowledge limited to predicting occurrences. Other event characteristics (e.g., salience for one's current goals) are more important than frequency when influence rather than prediction is the objective (Ross & Anderson, 1982). For example, a behavior pattern is likely to be repeated if it demonstrates on a single occasion a powerful way of producing desired results. This illustrates the commonly used *representative heuristic* which not only guides actions, but also enables people to create hypotheses about probable cause-effect relations never observed before by anyone. Scientists often reason by analogy.

Causal attributions represent people's understanding of the "causal structure of the world" including their own ability to function as a cause; it is, therefore, an "important determinant" of what people will try to do or not do, and of their self-evaluations (Kelley & Michela, 1980). One basic distinction is under what conditions causality is attributed primarily to the person, *internal locus of control*, or to events, *external locus of control*. A diversity of factors influence causal attributions and their consequences (Harvey, Itkes, & Kidd, 1976; Harvey & Weary, 1984; Jones et al., 1972). These include current information about events, the attributor's beliefs and expectations about probable causes in that kind of situation, current goals, and emotions (i.e., motivation).

As the living systems framework proposes, these factors are mutually influential, and causal attributions may be modified during the flow of a behavior episode (Kelley & Michela, 1980). For example, causal beliefs exert a selective influence on the collection and interpretation of information, but the information collected may modify the causal belief through feedback processes. Moreover, people tend to maintain their causal beliefs by rejecting or ignoring contradictory information (e.g., people tend to attribute success to their efforts, and failure to situational factors). Relationships also exist between causal attributions and emotions (Weiner, Russell, & Lerman, 1979). Finally, since humans consistently experience themselves as intentional actors, it is not surprising that they overemphasize the causal influence of people's intentions and actions and underemphasize situational influences. This has been called the *fundamental attribution error*.

Learning Decision Making Strategies. Humans can construct and use many kinds of rules, guidelines, heuristics, and schemas. Describing the way people currently learn to think is different from studying how they can be taught to think more effectively. Therefore, research might focus on designing improved heuristics and decision making rules, on ways of improving the use of existing ones, and on how to train people to use them. Braine and Rumain (1983) propose that this should include both comprehension processes (performance components) and inference schemas (reasoning programs). Such comprehension and reasoning processes involve not only knowledge, but also values and emotions; in other words, hypothesis testing involves an interplay between regulatory and control processes. Kahneman and Tversky (1984) point to a principle clinicians regularly observe: "experience value" (affective experiences) and "decision value" (based on imagined or observed contingencies and consequences) are not identical and may conflict. "Stimulus" information and "emotional" information may serve different functions (Leventhal, 1982). Through their evaluative-regulatory function, different kinds of emotional arousal can alter the weight a person gives to different factors in a decision.

Different models of decision-making processes have been formulated and studied. For example, *preference* or *decision trees* organize options so that, through choices between pairs of options, people methodically converge on a decision (Pearle, Kim, & Fiske, 1981; Tversky & Sattath, 1979). *Fault trees* are a version in which things that could go wrong are hierarchically organized in categories to facilitate diagnosing difficulties. Psychological *cost-benefit methods* (Ekehammar, 1978a; 1978b), and *nonprobabilistic diagnostic approaches* (Fox, 1980) also exist. Rather than asking which of these and others humans use, it may be more valuable to ask which ones can they learn to use and which ones are most useful under different circumstances (e.g., the contrast between a novice and an expert dealing with the same kind of decision) (Showers & Cantor, 1985).

Plan Execution

Plan execution is extensively examined in Chapters 14 and 15. However, one other issue deserves comment here. People sometimes continue with a decision and course of action despite its relative ineffectiveness, and generate a diversity of cognitive maneuvers (e.g., defense mechanisms) to justify the maintenance of continuation of such seemingly self-defeating patterns (Janis & Mann, 1977). Research on how people control their reactions to anticipated or actual noxious events may shed light on this issue (Thompson, 1981). Increased knowledge of how to help people relinquish self-defeating patterns and to consider and try potentially better alternatives would be of great practical value in clinical work and in dealing with interpersonal conflict. This will involve more knowledge about the relationships between the stability-maintaining self-organizing functions and the flexibility-enhancing self-constructing functions.

The Environment and Control Functions

Behavior always occurs in an environment, which is a primary source of the conditions of satisfaction for most behavior. The environment must be considered during the formation, evaluation, and execution of potential behavioral options. Therefore, understanding the nature of environments in relationship to, or as a component of, human functioning is of fundamental importance, as emphasized by operant psychologists. Unfortunately, a thorough examination of this important and very large domain of issues is not possible here. A brief consideration will point out some directions.

A human environment can only be defined relative to some specified human(s). For example, your environment could be defined as all phenomena external to you, including other people. Some have limited the definition to only those phenomena in immediate spatial-temporal proximity to the person(s) of interest, while others conceive of hierarchically organized environments which include both proximal and distal phenomena (Bronfenbrenner, 1979).

Historically, the discipline of psychology has been somewhat schizophrenic about the environment. On the one hand, its importance has always been emphasized. On the other, serious efforts to develop theories about its nature, and methods of classifying and measuring environments and their attributes, are fairly recent. The dominant concept has been the *stimulus*. Gibson (1960) described eight basic areas of disagreement about its meaning and concluded that it was not a useful environmental concept.

Active organism models require a different view. The person-situation relationship must be seen as a continuous "dynamic interaction" process in which people "actively seek or avoid" some situations, "influence and transform" environments to serve their purposes through their behavior, and are influenced by environments at "different levels of generality" (Magnusson & Endler, 1977b). People can plan their own behavior, and then go to, or create, a setting in which to carry it out (Russell & Ward, 1982). People do not primarily react to situations; they act upon them to try to produce intended and desired consequences.

Trait psychology approaches have foundered on data which indicates that "global, situation-free" personality or behavioral consistencies do not exist. Even small children can conceptually transform identical situations in ways that may even reverse their impact (Mischel, 1984). An unsatisfactory alternative idea is the extreme phenomenological view that it is the way people conceive of their environment that is critical, and, therefore, one can ignore the actual environment and focus on people's cognitive representation of it. In this living systems framework, both are important. The potential actions and consequences any situation affords a person are a function both of the properties of the situation and of how a person perceives and conceives of those properties.

Building a scientific approach to the study of environments requires assuming that there is a reality separate from humans' conception of it, that human perceptual capabilities evolved to provide accurate representations about "what's out there," and that people construct conceptions from their perceptions. Unfortunately, psychologists and counselors often confuse the two. For example, a psychotherapist may say "She perceived he was angry." Anger cannot be perceived. What can be perceived are behaviors like voice volume and quality, language content, and facial gestures. One may infer from those perceptions that the person is angry. Therefore, a more precise statement would be that "She formed the conception that he was angry from her perceptions of his behavior." One basic psychotherapeutic tactic is to get people to compare their actual perceptions with their erroneous conceptions.

If the actual nature of the environment and people's perception of it significantly correspond, then developing ways of representing environments can provide a basis for identifying and influencing how people of different ages and conditions will probably perceive them and give guidance to environmental designs. For example, changes in lighting may accommodate visual changes with aging (Fozard, 1981). Moreover, since conceptions are constructed from perceptions, one should be able to infer the conceptions people are likely to form based on knowledge of the kinds of environments they typically experience. One may even influence the conceptions formed by manipulating environmental variables. That is what formal schooling is all about. Finally, since environments provide the constraining and facilitating conditions and intended consequences for behavior, understanding how certain kinds of behavior patterns and environments become "packaged" together in humanly useful ways should be valuable.

Every study of humans occurs in a specific context and involves manipulating or controlling some aspect of that context (e.g., task requirements, reinforcers, measurement procedures). However, researchers seldom directly consider the implications of the theory of environment that is implicit in their procedures. Too often there is an implied mechanistic assumption of transsituational generality of behavior in the methods used and interpretations made.

Efforts to forge explicit ways of conceiving of and measuring environmental variables have been growing, often under the banner of environmental psychology (Creids, 1973; Ittelson, 1978; Magmusson, 1980; Russell & Ward, 1982; Sells, 1963; Stokols, 1979; Wicker, 1979; Winterholder, 1980). Developmental researchers are giving increased emphasis to the importance of environmental factors (Altman & Wohlmill, 1978; Bronfenbrenner & Crouter, 1983), with most attention given to the influence of the social environment on the development of cognitive and transactional capabilities of infants and small children. However, since they spend 80 to 90% of their waking hours with nonsocial stimulation (Parke, 1978), the impact on development of other environmental variables deserves increased attention (e.g., development of propositional knowledge, particularly of themselves as causal agents).

Certain key ideas are emerging that are compatible with this living systems framework. One is that the environment is organized and that what people perceive is patterns of environmental organization rather than stimulus elements (Gibson, 1960; Ittelson, 1978). Few people continue to think that behavior-environment relationships can be "reasonably dealt with" through an S→R approach (Russell & Ward, 1982). Stokols (1979) focuses on patterns of environmental variables in relationship to a person's prior plans and goals. A person's representation of the "situation state" within which a problem is to be solved influences the general solution plan he or she formulates (Farley, 1980). Moreover, spatial, temporal, dynamic, and historical properties of environments must be considered, such as ranges, magnitudes, distributions, rates, and durations (Winterhalder, 1980). An environment is experienced as a whole through multimodal perception of dynamic spatial-temporal environmental configurations (Ittelson, 1978). And it is experienced transactionally, that is, in relationship to what one is trying to do and in terms of one's personal impact (Magnusson, 1980).

Generalized knowledge starts with classification. The same domain of phenomena can be represented with different kinds and orders of classification to serve different purposes. Therefore, with a domain as large and diverse as the environment, multiple classification systems to serve different purposes would probably be useful, and several different kinds have been proposed. Some are based on qualitative differences in kinds of phenomena, such as Sells' (1963) scheme for describing environments in physical-geographic terms. It is useful to distinguish between what something is and where it is; research has focused on the nature of, and how people construct, *spatial schemata*, or *cognitive maps* (Downs & Stea, 1977).

A more elaborate classification in terms of kinds of phenomena subdivides physical phenomena into natural and designed environments, and human phenomena into social-interpersonal and cultural environments. The natural environment includes all natural phenomena such as sun, clouds, trees, and animals. The designed environment includes all humanly constructed physical objects and processes such as houses, clothes, cars, processed foods, and eyeglasses. (In this era of genetic engineering, however, the boundary between natural and designed environments is being blurred.)

Humans also construct interpersonal-social and cultural environments. Even natural and designed environments are experienced in large part in terms of their social and symbolic meaning (Ittelson, 1978). People's physical, social, and cognitive development and functioning occurs in and is influenced by different kinds of social units that are hierarchically organized in nested sets, such as families and communities (Altman & Wohlwill, 1978; Walberg, 1976). Close interpersonal relationships, such as with friends and relatives, influence individuals' social-emotional functioning (Hartup, 1983; Longino & Lipmann, 1981). *Proxemics* focuses on both physical and interpersonal closeness, examining, for example, crowding, privacy, and intimacy (Russell & Ward, 1982). Neighborhoods may provide more or less favorable environments for individual and family functioning (Garbarino & Sherman, 1980). Work settings are particularly important in adult life (Bronfenbrenner & Crouter, 1982; Kohn & Schooler, 1978). Cultural environments are illustrated by languages, laws, institutional forms such as governments, and beliefs systems such as racial and gender prejudice or religious beliefs.

Some classification schemes combine environmental and behavioral variables (Magnusson, 1980). The best known is called *behavior settings* (Wicker, 1979). A behavior setting is (a) a particular arrangement of physical objects in a specific physical location; within which (b) particular kinds of behavioral programs are expected to occur. Therefore, the behaviors of people and the physical arrangements within the boundaries of the setting are highly coordinated. For example, when people go to church, they expect a particular physical environment and the behaviors of all those present are "choreographed" in ways all understand. The dentist's office, a school room, and an athletic arena illustrate different kinds of behavior settings. The participants are usually upset if someone performs an inappropriate behavioral program for a particular setting (e.g., "mooning" the teacher or dancing on the table during a committee meeting).

Barker (1968) proposed that behavior settings function as self-regulating social systems. If some essential component is missing or malfunctioning (e.g., the chairperson is absent, or a committee member tries to divert the committee from its usual process), the participants will take the necessary steps to preserve or restore the behavior setting pattern. Behavior settings may be more or less rigidly organized and programmed.

Another kind of classification scheme uses spatial-temporal proximity and complexity criteria. Perhaps the best known of these is Bronfenbrenner's (1977) ecological model which builds upon the concept of behavior setting. He classified environments into four subclasses which he proposes are interrelated as a nested hierarchy. Each level represents an organization of both physical and social phenomena. A *microsystem* is a particular behavior setting. A *mesosystem* is all those microsystems in which a person participates at any particular time in his or her life. An *exosystem* extends mesosystems to include social institutions (e.g., one's church) that impinge upon and influence the immediate behavior settings represented by one's micro- and mesosystems. *Macrosystems* are the overarching institutional patterns of the culture or subculture (e.g., the legal system) of which the previous three categories are manifestations. It is like a child on the bottom of the pile of a group of children on the school ground. Those immediately above him are the only ones in direct physical contact, but those on top and the size of the pile also affect the bottom person's welfare.

The realization is growing that human life is influenced for both good and ill by environments that humans have created. It follows that if humans have the power to shape their lives by their environmental creations, a much more sophisticated view about the design and management of environment-behavior systems is essential. Studer (1969, 1971, 1978, 1980) is the most articulate and visionary spokesman for this perspective. He starts with the premise that a problem exists when there is a disparity "between the way things are and ought to be." He argues that the design of physical, social, and cultural environments is an act of intervention to change a human setting or system "via (re)organization of its supporting environment." He considers many important issues, not the least of which is the value question of how and by whom should decisions be made about the "ought to be" issues, that is, about the human results desired from the environments to be created. Designing such behavior-contingent environments is a complicated technical problem, but establishing the goals and criteria which such designed environments should meet is a value question. The two are often confused.

The power of Studer's ideas is illustrated by the influence and utility of *operant psychology*, which has resulted primarily from its sophisticated programming of environments (i.e., of environmental contingencies and reinforcers) to produce specific, desired behavior patterns. In fact, all professional methodologies represent manipulations of selected environmental factors to alter selected personal characteristics; examples are the surgeon's tools, the physicians' drugs, the interpersonal and language behaviors used by counselors, teachers' audiovisual displays, advertisers' media messages, and the welfare benefits provided to influence the quality of life for poor families. One powerful way to influence a person's behavior is through its immediate environmental consequences. For example, Studer suggests that to reduce horn honking on city streets one need only make the horn sound more loudly inside the car than out.

In summary, every facet of human life is shaped by environments. Phenomena of such fundamental importance require more intensive and sophisticated theoretical and empirical study than has yet been mounted. The starting point is clear formulation of shared classification systems for specifying environmental variables as units of analysis. This would make it possible to compare results across studies, and environments' influence on human development could be more systematically studied and better understood.

THE DEVELOPMENT OF CONTROL FUNCTIONS

The primary body of data on which theories of cognitive development are based comes from research on reasoning, problem-solving behavior, and the development of intelligence, with samples composed of children and adolescents. The types of tasks and measures used in such research emphasize control functions. Therefore, theories designed to explain these data may be considered primarily theories of the development and operation of control functions.

State Models and Piaget's View of Cognitive Development

The most comprehensive and influential such theory during the middle third of the 20th century was constructed by Piaget (1928, 1952b, 1954, 1955, 1970; Piaget & Inhelder, 1969). Using the intensive study of individual children and different kinds of problem solving tasks, he sought to reveal how understanding and skill in using basic categories of knowledge developed, such as causality (Piaget, 1930), quantities (Piaget, 1952a), and space (Piaget & Inhelder, 1956). He proposed that cognition developed through stages of cognitive organization defined by the use of different methods of thinking termed operations: infants use a primitive set, called sensorimotor operations; older children encompass that set in a more elaborate approach called *concrete operations*; and adults use sophisticated logic called *formal operations*. Piaget's theory stimulated the production of a massive, varied, and valuable body of relevant information.

The function of a scientific theory, as with any schema, is to guide problem solving and action. If a theory is unsound but popular, it misguides efforts and constrains people's thinking. Piaget's stage theory of cognitive development is considered unsound on several grounds and should be discarded (Braine & Rumain, 1983; Brown & Desforges, 1979; Gardner, 1979; Gelman & Baillargeon, 1983; Keating, 1979; Siegel & Brainerd, 1978; Siegler, 1978; Stone & Day, 1980). Braine and Rumain (1983) describe his proposed stages of reasoning as originally derived

from a system of logic Piaget constructed. His data were then interpreted within that framework. However, they demonstrate that his
system of logic is "badly paradoxical" and, therefore, is problematic to
serve as a "psychological model of anything." Moreover, they conclude
that his formulae are not mental operations at all. They are "a way of
coding data, not of manipulating it."

It is not the data that are being questioned, but their interpretation.
There is "little evidence" supporting the idea of major stages in cognitive
development as proposed by Piaget (Gelman & Baillargeon, 1983), even
when restricted to his relatively narrow range of problem-solving tasks.
When tasks representing a much broader range of symbolic functioning
are considered (e.g., visual or musical symbolism), his stage model is
even less relevant. The kind of thinking people construct and display
may be a function not only of the information perceived, but of the code
and carrier on which it is represented (Gardner, 1979). Piaget's model of
formal operations "bears little or no resemblance" to the actual cognitive
processes and skills which "generate the end products" produced by
subjects across various tasks and contexts (Stone & Day, 1980). After a
careful critique of Piaget's epistimology, Brown and Desforges, (1979)
conclude that there is a strong case for abandoning Piaget's model and
reinterpreting the data. The data suggest that cognitive development is
a process of gradual increase in, and integration of, a growing diversity
of knowledge and skill mastery; and that cognitive performance appears
to vary with the nature of the task and the person's experience with it
(Siegler, 1978).

Representing human's functional development in terms of a few
universal stages has been a popular and influential approach, as in
Freud's *psychosexual stages*, Piaget's *cognitive stages*, and Erikson's (1963)
psychosocial stages. They are seductive in their seeming simplicity and
they have a surface plausibility. However, describing a classification
system useful in distinguishing among different patterns of functioning
is one thing. Arranging those classes in a temporal sequence and
arguing that such arbitrarily defined groupings of content and sequence
represent a universal and irreversible human developmental pattern is
quite another. The inadequacies of stage theories lie (a) in their oversimplification by trying to encompass the functional diversity of humans
in a few broadly defined classes; and (b) in the rigidity of the sequential
and organizational arrangements that are proposed.

Two Faulty Assumptions.   Two assumptions that may be valid in other
domains but invalid for representing functional development in humans
seem to implicitly undergird stage model proposals. First, since biological development displays some irreversible stagelike structural development, stagelike functional development is plausible since structure

makes function possible, and a few functional developments have stagelike properties (e.g., puberty, menopause). However, such biologically linked functional specializations are an inadequate mode of adaptation for the special nature of humans. Cognitive capabilities evolved in humans precisely to overcome the rigidity of inborn functional patterns, by constructing their own patterns to fit their variable and changing environments (Rozin, 1976).

Some inborn cognitive capabilities emerge from the interaction of genetic and environmental influences. These become available very early as a function of CNS maturation. Since all human environments share certain properties (e.g., spatial configurations, movement, variations in size and quantity, modifiability through actions), it is not surprising that neurologically undamaged humans construct some common knowledge about those properties, perhaps facilitated by inborn sensitivities to such important pervasive conditions.

However, humans construct physical and social environments to serve their purposes, and different sets of humans may construct somewhat different environments, illustrated by cultures and languages. Therefore, many of the cognitions individuals construct result from their interactions with "the partly objectivated (crystallized) structures" of their society and culture (Aebli, 1978). Since cultures differ, some of the cognitions people construct from such interactions will differ. These involve not only content, but also humanly constructed procedures and rules, such as formal logic, or calculus.

The second implicit assumption is that humans are all the same kind of machine, and like all machines should function the same way within a broad range of conditions. If that were the case, then humans should display patterns of functional development universal across diverse societies, cultures, and environments. Part I of this book argues against such a mechanistic model and for a view of humans as self-constructing entities.

It is important not to throw the baby out with the bath water, however. To conclude that Piaget's stage model of cognitive development should be abandoned does not mean that data generated by his view or other theoretical contributions he made should also be rejected. For example, one may regard his sensory-motor, concrete, and formal categories of operations not as developmental stages, but as classes of different types of cognitive functioning people display. Viewed that way, one may consider whether those three classes adequately encompass the data, or whether additional classes are necessary. Moreover, even though his stage model appears unsound, there is convincing support for his general idea that human thinking typically develops from a loosely organized, perceptually dominated, relatively inflexible pattern towards an increasingly organized, intentional, conceptually dominated, increasingly flexible, rule guided pattern in adulthood; with increasing use of mental representations of reality, but also of "possibility" to guide behavior (Piaget, 1976). It is time to use the empirical and conceptual base constructed by Piaget and the "Genevan school" to build a more adequate view of cognitive development, rather than continuing to guide theory and research with Piaget's stage model.

Other Views About Development

Alternative conceptualizations exist. For example, in embryology Waddington (1956) introduced the notions of *epigenetic landscape* and *canalization* as metaphors for understanding development. Both biological and behavioral development are dynamic processes which occur within broad organismic and environmental constraints, and which may pursue somewhat different channels for individuals depending on the nature of the experiential "landscape" through which their lives flow; they are processes which may change channels under some conditions. Modern *developmental behavioral genetics* (Plomin, 1986) supports such a view.

Heinz Werner (1961) proposed that development proceeds from simple to more complex hierarchical organization, called the *orthogenetic principle*. For example, he proposed the more elaborate the hierarchical organization the more developed is a system of thought. Cognition proceeds from perceptual groupings through primitive abstractions to broader conceptualizations. Cognitive development progressively frees a person from the domination of the current situation, self-generated cues compete with environmental cues, and actions can be delayed while thought proceeds.

Humans are not born with innate ideas. They are born with certain information-collection and processing capabilities which they use to construct ideas and additional information-processing methods. These inborn capabilities may be particularly sensitive to certain kinds of information, just as some biological propensities are differentially sensitive to certain kinds of material transactions. The ability to construct abstractions which refer to things and events one or more symbolic steps removed from direct perception is a "hallmark of human cognition," and the processes involved and constructions that result may differ somewhat with the form of symbol system that is used; this may be, for example, pictorial, tactual, verbal, or musical (Gardner, 1979). Different symbol systems may represent the same things, so commonalities across symbol systems may be represented by higher-order abstractions. Higher-order abstractions involve "a building up of relations among relations" (Cattell, 1971).

What Develops? What is it that develops, then? One group of scholars (Siegler, 1978) suggests at least the following: metacognition or the control or evaluation of one's thoughts; an increase in working memory as cognitive operations become automated; problem solving rules; more complete encoding of information relevant to current problem solving efforts; the generation and testing of subgoals as means towards larger goals; and the use of numerical concepts and procedures. Kendler (1979) presents a "dual component" view that encompasses development of both the information organization and action coordination control functions. An "encoding" component "analyzes, integrates, and stores" information, and a "behavior regulation" component "initiates, monitors, and evaluates" behavioral outputs. Similarly, the "Genevan School" (Bullinger & Chatillon, 1983) is increasingly focused on understanding complex relationships between actions and representations, with an emphasis on the role of goals. They suggest that cognitive development is thought to have two objectives: understanding and producing solutions. Children appear to develop three kinds of "schemes": (a) *presentative schemes*—concepts representing "the permanent and simultaneous characteristics of common objects"; (b) *procedural schemes*—action sequences as means to accomplish specific goals; and (c) *operatory schemes*—combining presentative and procedural schemes into more generalized and flexible schemes.

James et al. (1978) suggest that "cognitive construction competencies," "encoding strategies," and "self-regulatory systems" may have developmental trajectories. Using the concept of states of system change (Hall & Fagan, 1956), Kearsley, Buss, and Royce (1977) suggest three types of change: (a) differentiation of ways in which information can be organized, reorganized, and used (system segregation); (b) organization and coordination of differentiated factors (system consolidation); (c) combining into fewer generalized factors (consolidation systematization).

Sternberg and Powell (1983) identify several important "loci" of intellectual development: (a) knowledge-base elaboration; (b) processes (e.g., young children have difficulty dealing with order relations); (c) memory; (d) strategies (e.g., an increased use of more of the information given in a problem situation in a more integrative way); (e) ways of representing information (e.g., increased use of larger "chunks," and inclusion of more detail); and (f) process latencies (e.g., timing and duration of mental processes). They also propose four "transparadigmatic" principles of development on which they believe there is wide agreement.

1. More sophisticated control strategies develop with age, such as the strategies of planning ahead, simultaneous and successive synthesis, and monitoring.

2. Information processing becomes more nearly exhaustive as a correlate of age, illustrated by using more of the available information in

problem solving, an increased likelihood of looking for and testing alternative explanations or possibilities, and increased consideration of multiple causation.

3. Comprehension of successively higher order relations develops as people grow older, such as development of higher order principles and abstractions.

4. Flexibility in the use of strategies or information increases, such as knowing when to change strategies or when to transfer or transform information.

Another way to gain an understanding of normal cognitive development is to examine dysfunctions in development. Based on research on mental retardation, Campione, Brown, and Ferrara (1982) identify four interdependent "determinants of performance" on intellectual tasks that may change as parts of an interactive system: speed or efficiency of information processing; the content and organization of the person's knowledge base, including procedural knowledge; task-appropriate strategies; and executive control, including the choice, timing, sequencing, and monitoring of cognitive activities.

What follows is an attempt to sketch a view of control function development within a living systems framework that captures the main currents of these and other existing theory and data. It is similar to Sternberg's "government" model of intelligence, and uses the four categories of Campione et al.

Control Function Development from a Living Systems Perspective

First There is Perceptually Guided Behavior. Initially, infants' behavior is organized and guided by perceptual information which is multimodal and relatively undifferentiated, representing both body-affective and environmental states. Directive function content organizing infant behavior episodes is provided by current perceptions. From the beginning, infants' self-organizing properties precipitate efforts to create coherent episodes of perception-action-environment patterns (e.g., Piaget's sensorimotor operations). They fairly quickly begin to develop more selective and sophisticated attention-deployment strategies to produce more efficient and effective encoding of information relevant to current concerns (Baron, 1978). Response contingent stimulation, which enhances infants later learning performances, facilitates development of such attentional strategies (Finkelstein & Ramey, 1977).

The initial home environment has a significant influence on infants' later social and cognitive functioning (Parke, 1978). The intensity, consistency, and regularity of the environment, the extent to which the child has access to the home for play and exploration, the responsiveness of the materials such as toys which the child can manipulate, the complexity of the environment with which the child can interact, and the diversity of inanimate objects to interact with all influence cognitive development (McCall, 1974). Infants' social interactions have an important impact on cognitive development; an example is when and how maternal language is used. Infants behave selectively as a function of linguistic-prosodic communication from parents long before they are able to speak, implying that the meaning of the communication is recognized (Ramey et al., 1978).

However, too much stimulation (i.e., too intense or complex) can have a detrimental effect on a child (Parke, 1978). For example, high noise levels in the home adversely affect the ability to attend to relevant stimulus features. Too little or too much complexity or intensity of stimulation appears to influence development adversely (Wohlwill & Heft, 1977). Infants may also be exposed to nonhome environments (e.g., daycare and preschool). However, evaluation of infant stimulation programs aimed at improving early cognitive development reveals that home-based programs seem to have greater impact than institution-based programs, although both have impact (Haskins et al., 1978).

Constructs Representing Perceptions. As soon as infants begin functioning perceptually, their informational self-constructing properties begin to construct and retain representations of perceptions. Such representations are specific to particular behavior episodes. Therefore, *episode memories* are the first level of abstractions from perceptions, termed *preoperations* by Piaget. They are probably crude schemata since perception is multimodal and the ability to restrict attention to specific elements in a perceptual field is a skill that grows with experience (and perhaps maturation). These initial schemata contain information about objects, actions, and their relations (Case, 1985).

Infants function purposively shortly after birth (see Chapter 10). Evidence that children delight in making things happen, in influencing events, has been around for a long time (Groos, 1901). Therefore, causal relationships between actions and objects or events are salient components of infants' initial schemata. Moreover, experience in functioning as a causal agent, called *contingent stimulation* in behaviorist terms, facilitates later learning and cognitive development (Gunnar, 1980).

Shultz (1982) contrasts two theories of causality humans have constructed. The philosopher, Hume, argued that causality is inferred from conditions of regular succession, and temporal and spatial contiguity. An alternate view, called generative causality, is that causes are directly perceived to produce (generate) effects. His research indicates that people from at least 2 years old to adults in both Western and non-Western primitive cultures rely primarily on generative causality in their interpretation of events. Thinking of causality in terms of Hume's definition does occur, but is a later cognitive development. Infants' causality information comes from two sources (Shultz, 1982): (a) their perceptions are experienced as effects or consequences of environmental events; and (b) their actions produce perceptible direct effects, and others' actions directly affect them. Therefore, behavior episode information from which causal attributions can be constructed is available and used from birth onward.

Conceptions Constructed From Perceptual Schemata. An arrangement in which people only had conceptions of each behavior episode to guide their future behavior would be very inflexible since no episode is twice the same. Therefore, people's informational self-constructing capabilities operate to abstract consistency from sets of perceptually based schemata, creating prototypical BES which represent such sets. These might be called *second-order abstractions*, e.g., Piaget's *concrete operations*. Once constructed, they can function as units of thought providing infants with two simultaneous sources of information with which to guide their actions; perceptions of the current episode and conceptions representing previous experiences with that type of episode. The use of such conceptions in problem solving begins at least by the second year of life, and perhaps before (Case, 1985). There is virtually "universal agreement" among developmental psychologists that this major transition to conceptual guidance of behavior occurs during the 2nd to 4th year of life for most children (Gardner, 1979).

It is the flexible merging of conceptions with perceptions in guiding behavior that distinguishes human intelligence from that of other organisms. The ability to form and use conceptions enables people to transcend the here and now in their problem-solving activities. They can combine knowledge of the past and thoughts of potential futures with knowledge of current circumstances in order to guide current actions. Conceptually guided behavior enables infants to become much more proactive in engaging their world, and parents often say their baby "is becoming a real person" when that begins to occur. Humans' development of conceptualizations requires no tutelage (though it is facilitating), but appears to be the natural, universal consequence of the operation of humans' self-organizing and self-constructing capabilities in their typical environmental niche (Berzonsky, 1978).

However, the initial second-order schemata abstractions are still relatively situation-specific because they are prototypical BES representing narrowly defined sets of behavior episodes. However, they are also more differentiated. Concepts and propositional knowledge, including procedural knowledge, are formed through this second order abstracting process. For example, a ball is a round object which will roll if pushed or bounce if thrown. Thus, initial prototypical BES become more clearly componentized through this differentiation process, laying the groundwork for those components to become functionally autonomous so they can be used in the construction of new schemata and behavior episodes.

The initial construction of propositional and procedural knowledge provides the base from which more abstract causality attributions can be constructed later. Both *conditionality* (if) and *causality* (because) concepts appear at 2 to 3 years of age, with causality appearing first. Such young children display understanding of both meanings of "because," that is (a) physical or generative causation; and (b) reasons or motives. The most frequent meaning of "because" for young children seems to be psychological motivation (Braine & Rumain, 1983; Shultz, 1982). Perhaps that should not be surprising, since the experiences with causality that have the greatest affect associated with them are infants' own intentional efforts to function as a cause. That would lead naturally to the construction of the proposition that people cause things by acting intentionally. The elaboration of a child's knowledge base through this construction process manifest itself in improved memory and problem-solving performances (Case, 1985; Chi, 1981). Awareness of the truth or falsity of statements also begins to appear around 2 years of age (Braine & Rumain, 1983).

In addition, task-appropriate strategies and executive control procedures begin to develop from this base of episode experiences. There are two intertwined aspects of problem solving: strategies and representations. Initially, the representations are perceptual and strategies are guided by perceptions. For example, by 12 months of age most infants will set aside an obstacle in order to reach a desired object if it is visible. By 18 months they can use an object as a means to an end, such as pulling the pillow towards them to reach a toy upon it. However, the ability to implement strategies guided by conceptions rather than solely by perceptions (e.g., of their goals) emerges later after some conceptual construction has been accomplished. Concepts and strategies regarding numbers and their use are illustrative. Many 3-year-olds can perform rudimentary counting tasks that involve several properties of number systems (Gelman & Gallistel, 1978).

Preschool age children (4- to 6-years-old) appear to have rudimentary forms of many of the problem-solving processes previously identified in adults, but these will not be apparent if the context and presentation of the problem is too different from their BES repertoire, or if the encoding-representation aspects of the task are beyond their current conceptual capabilities (Klahr & Robinson, 1981). In general, the construction of strategic and self-control processes proceeds from a perceptual to a more abstract and detailed representation. For example, in search behavior tasks, children first use a "concrete" systematic strategy in which they compare the global configuration of pictures. By second grade, they have constructed an array of "distinctive features" concepts, and they then begin to develop a strategy of trying to match pictures in terms of their distinctive features (Rothman & Potts, 1977).

Search in spatial environments displays similar developmental features in 2- to 6-year-olds. Three types of search strategies appear to develop in the following sequence: (a) associative procedures (e.g., Look where it was last or where it usually is); (b) simple but general comprehensive search (e.g., If you do not know where it is, look everywhere); and (c) logical search (e.g., Think of all the places it might be, select those that seem most likely, and look there first). Development of such search strategies appears to depend on (at least) spatial representations (e.g., memory for locations associated with missing objects or events); knowledge of generally applicable search procedures; and processes of reasoning that permit modification of search strategies to fit a particular situation (Wellman, Sommerville, & Haacke, 1979). For example, there is an age-related increase in proficiency in constructing and using cognitive maps of spatial environments. This appears to result, at least partially, from increased accuracy in the construction of linear spatial representations in which environmental landmarks serve as organizers (Siegel, Allen, & Kirasic, 1979).

The contexts in which children are constructing their initial BES are dynamic spatial configurations of physical objects within which events, the children's observations, and their goal-directed efforts occur. Therefore, the initial procedural and strategic knowledge constructed will be anchored to the contexts which it represents and the kinds of objectives and tasks carried out in those contexts. For example, search strategies learned later do not supersede those learned earlier. They all continue to be available to the child. Even at the earliest ages studied, search strategies differ from task to task and context to context, and such task-induced strategy differences themselves change during the preschool years (Wellman, Sommerville, & Haacke, 1979).

Therefore, very young children typically have developed "relatively rich and complex" cognitive capabilities and "reasoning structures" and a diversity of BES, but they are typically domain (e.g., situation/problem) specific. The range of circumstances in which each kind of BES is applied by very young children is remarkably narrower than with older children. It follows that to discover the cognitive capabilities of very young children requires the construction of tasks that will elicit their relatively situation-specific BES (e.g., Vygotsky's zones of proximal development). This has led to considerable underestimation of young children's cognitive capabilities since they tend to fail researchers' tasks, because the latter do not call forth the child's relevant BES (Gelman & Baillargeon, 1983). As researchers have invented a greater diversity of age-appropriate tasks, the capabilities of the very young have been made increasingly apparent.

The elaboration and use of BES during the first few years of life is explosive and produces rapid increases in small children's problem-solving capabilities. Much of their cognitive construction results from their unaided observations and efforts to explore and influence their environment. However, demonstration and instruction by older children or adults has a significant impact. Children are attracted to people who present interesting and rewarding behavior models, possibilities of action, and the knowledge, tools, and materials that make actions possible (Aebli, 1978). Encouragement of 2- to 5-year-olds to take an analytic attitude toward tasks helps them to adopt and continue to use more systematic strategies (Richards & Siegler, 1981). This may result, in part, from teaching them how to control information flow and processing through attention-deployment skills. For example, more proficient performers are more likely to attend to relevant dimensions of a problem than are poorer performers. Experts and novices as well as nonretarded and retarded children differ in their selective attention practices and in the encoding of information (Campione et al., 1982).

Rules and procedures for organizing the content, timing, and sequencing of problem-solving cognitions and actions (executive functions) are constructed along with the other capabilities just discussed. Much of this occurs through the child's own self-constructing activities which involve practice in self-control functioning. Adults can facilitate development of self-control procedures, but simply telling a child what to do is not sufficient. Also essential is overt use of the skills, reinforcement for that use, fading of external checking, and training in covert implementation (O'Leary & Dubey, 1979). Methods of monitoring, self-instruction, questioning, relatedness-seeking, reasoning by analogy, restructuring a problem, or defining and evaluating options before acting are powerful control procedures that facilitate effective problem solving. Differences in such control capabilities distinguish between retarded and nonretarded children (Campione et al., 1982). For example, retarded children fail to acquire and produce strategies to meet demands of a variety of problems and fail to transfer instructed strategies beyond the original training context. Children diagnosed as inefficient learners have particularly severe problems with control processes.

Differentiation and Elaboration. One important aspect of cognitive development involves going from a specific, context-bound behavior repertoire to a more general use of one's repertoire. Cognitive functioning is never completely context-free, but the degree of generalization and flexibility in the applicability of knowledge, procedures, and strategies across different kinds of situations can vary greatly. Less experienced, less intelligent, less mature people suffer from a greater degree of contextual binding. Similarly, the functioning of novices tends to be more context bound than that of experts in the same situation (Brown, 1982). Another aspect involves the process of gradually elaborating and connecting together components of knowledge, strategy, and skill into larger integrated patterns. The ultimate degree of such flexibility results when a person can consciously represent the components and consciously and intentionally organize and reorganize them into different combinations to serve different purposes in different situations (Rozin, 1976).

For example, in the past I played several games on my pool table with my nine grandchildren. One game simply involved rolling balls up and down the table; another involved trying to hit one ball with another; sometimes I asked them to tell me the number on the ball before rolling it, and if they did not know it I would whisper it to them so they could say it. Sometimes more than one child played, so rules of "taking turns" and "sharing the balls" had been practiced. On this occasion, five grandchildren ages 2 1/2 to 6 wanted to play at the same time, creating considerable conflict and noise. The 5-year-old announced he was making up a game in which all could play, and enunciated the following: The white ball would be placed in the middle of the table, and the person who hit it the most times would win; each person would receive three balls and would take turns trying to hit the white ball; before they rolled their ball, they had to give its number, but because the younger children could not read their numbers, he announced it was OK to whisper the number to them so they could say it. Clearly, he constructed a larger new BES, "the game," by combining several smaller BES he had earlier learned separately in the same context. This example also illustrates that children guide their behavior with concepts and procedures before they are able to cognitively represent them and consciously manipulate them. For example, while the 2-, 3- and 4-year-olds could not have created the game, they understood it and could play it "according to the rules."

About the time children typically enter public school (6-7 years of age), they have developed a sizeable repertoire of reasoning procedures. Strategies for using them involve activating a reasoning procedure relevant to the current problem and then applying it until the problem is solved, or activating a different one if the first one fails (Braine & Rumain, 1983). By this age, normal children can abstract "underlying dimensions" and rules from specific perceptions and schemata, and use those abstractions in their problem solving activities (Case, 1985). Children beyond kindergarten age manifest truly planful behavior that is strategically suited to task demands (Kemler, 1978).

Control Functions and Language Development. Auditory functioning begins during fetal life, and infants discriminate a "vast array" of speech sounds. Moreover, infants discriminate speech sounds in much the same manner regardless of language and cultural differences (Aslin, Pisoni, & Jusczyk, 1983). Therefore, from birth children have the capability to perceive and use information coded on speech sounds (see also Chapter 15).

Perception is multimodal. Perceptually based schemata are constructed from a flow of interrelated information resulting from vision, audition, touch, movement, and affect. Speech sounds are a part of that flow. Both mothers and fathers regularly talk to their babies while bathing, dressing, feeding, and playing with them, and may read to them at bedtime. Moreover, even very young infants will vocalize back to their parents and thereby try to influence them (Osofsky & Connors, 1979; Parke, 1979; Shatz, 1983). Therefore, language is experienced as an instrumental part of behavior episodes from the very beginning, and growing evidence of the importance of contextual factors in understanding communications should not be surprising (Danks & Glucksberg, 1980).

It follows that as infants construct BES from their perceptions, those schemata may include relevant speech sounds. For example, the taste of the milk, the feel of the nipple in the mouth, the pleasant feeling of being full and warm, the smiling face, the feel of a gentle caress, and the softly spoken words "I love you" are all part of one kind of episode from which a BES can be constructed. Therefore, many of the second-order abstractions infants and small children construct have a language component which functions as a symbolic representative of some or all of that abstraction. Once such BES are constructed, hearing or seeing the linguistic components of them can trigger reconstruction of some version of the BES. The conceptual abstractions which words activate, and the BES in which those words are embedded, represent their meanings.

Language is experienced in the context of actions, but it is relatively meaningless until it becomes an integral part of the perceptions it is to represent. For example, 2-year-olds will put objects in containers and on surfaces regardless of whether the preposition "in" or "on" is used in the instructions about the task to be performed (Clark, 1983). Once language components are integrated into the child's abstractions, they can function as a "handle" for manipulating that abstraction and combining it with others. Because the abstractions that children construct are initially episode-specific, it should not be surprising that linguistic components of these abstractions would also be used initially in domain specific ways. For example, young children may comprehend the same communication in one task but not another. As experience diversifies, children progressively revise their abstractions to be both more elaborate and more detailed. Therefore, learning a language looks like the "accretion of instances to small paradigms" (Clark & Hecht, 1983).

Understanding of verbal communications develops in small children before they can produce such communications, and development of communicative skills continue to lag behind verbal comprehension during the early years. Communication requires coordinating comprehension and production skills, and that is a complicated advance in behavioral organization (Clark & Hecht, 1983). Linguistic representations have no inherent meaning. They are arbitrary symbols for other information organizations and are functional among people who have adopted the same linguistic codes for representing them. Words are not knowledge; they are arbitrary representatives of knowledge whose power comes from their shared meanings. One of the functions of formal education is to construct such shared meanings and to teach a shared linguistic code for them. People can construct private meanings and codes for themselves, but this will have no social utility and others may consider them "crazy" (e.g., the private language of some psychotics). Clark (1983) describes a diversity of ways in which small children misuse words in the process of learning shared codes. For example, "fly" may be used to refer to a fly, dirt, or toes.

The source of the power of language to help organize and control one's own and others' behavior is now apparent. One can use words to manipulate complexes of meanings (i.e., previously constructed abstractions and BES) and to help construct different combinations of meanings. Language is a tool for reasoning, planning, problem solving, and influencing the environment, but the tool is not the meaning any more than the cup is the coffee. Miller and Johnson-Laird (1976) emphasize the tool-like qualities of language when they argue that a word's meaning consists of a set of "decision procedures" that govern its use and application, and a set of "relations" that can be constructed between its meanings and the meanings of other words. Thus, it is a uniquely human characteristic that the information components used to accomplish the control functions are indexed with language symbols which provides a very efficient way to manipulate and communicate information in order to formulate problems, define options, evaluate and select alternatives, organize actions, and influence others. Words communicate information only to the extent that they stimulate reconstruction of relevant abstractions in the mind of the person receiving the communication.

Constructing Abstractions From Abstractions. Once a person has a repertoire of abstractions, he or she can operate on those in the same way as on perceptions, and can construct new abstractions to represent them (see Chapter 9). This may occur with BES, concepts, propositions, procedures, and strategies, as well as with goals and values (see Chapters 10 and 12). One value of these higher order abstractions is that they make it possible to represent larger "chunks" of information or more "meanings" in a single unit. The larger the chunks and the more automated their use, the more efficient and rapid communication, information processing and problem solving activities can be. The only way such higher order abstractions can be made perceptible is through perceptible representations, and language is the most efficient means of achieving this. Therefore, the construction and use of higher order abstractions is closely linked to elaboration of one's linguistic capabilities.

Evidence suggests that the adolescent developmental period is a time of rapid elaboration of such higher order knowledge and process components (Berzonsky, 1978; Case, 1985). Older adolescents typically use more abstract reasoning processes with both physical and social tasks than do younger adolescents (Keating & Clark, 1980). However, the extent to which this occurs and the nature of the elaborations constructed appear to be highly variable between individuals and within persons across their life domains. It also seems to depend not only on their basic cognitive potentials (Campione et al., 1983) and their previously constructed repertoire of second order abstractions, but also on the nature of their life tasks and the training they have received. It may well be that in many aspects of their lives people can function adequately without resort to higher order cognitive functioning. For example, efforts to document the existence of Piaget's proposed stage of formal operations revealed that many adolescents and adults do not display that more elaborate and controlled form of cognitive functioning, at least on the tasks used in such studies. Similarly, Tversky and Kahneman (1981) report that adults often act in terms of the most readily available framing of a problem and do not bother trying to generate or consider alternative possible framings.

Simon (1979) argues that "problem solving with awareness" should be the aim of education. He believes that skills are transferable from one task to another when the principles underlying them are understood, and that many problem strategies such as means-ends analysis and hypothesis and test methods can and should be taught. However, one important efficiency in control function operation is that not all regulation and control of behavior need be accomplished consciously. Self-correction and control of well-practiced behavior patterns can occur outside of conscious effort (Anderson, 1982; Brown et al., 1983).

Development of control functions has been studied far less in adults than in children. However, it appears that the general pattern is for knowledge, procedures, and strategies to become both more generalized as a person learns new relevance for them and more differentiated as finer discriminations are added to make them more selective (Anderson, 1982). Schaie (1980) concludes that most abilities (as measured by formal intelligence and ability tests) peak when people are around 31 to 35 years of age, and remain relatively stable on the average into their 60s.

Schaie (1978) argues that many adult roles and responsibilities require development of cognitive strategies which are efficient at integrating more complex information at higher levels of hierarchical relationships. Therefore, the development of more elaborately organized and integrated knowledge components, procedures and strategies, and BES may be an important characteristic of the adult years. For example, Boswell (1979) demonstrated that adults manifested a more integrative, organizing, synthesizing pattern of cognition whereas adolescents displayed a more analytic style when making interpretations of linguistic metaphors. Similarly, Showers and Cantor (1985) ascribe the following properties to the cognitive functioning of experts: (a) they have a great deal of well-organized knowledge and efficient schematic organization in their preferred domains; (b) they have sufficient knowledge to make unusually fine discriminations, and their efficient organization frees cognitive capacity to elaborate their knowledge or to process schema-inconsistent information that might be otherwise ignored; and (c) they have more flexibility to choose a more effortful or more automatic cognitive strategy, and may choose controlled or systematic processing or less precise heuristic processing.

However, recall that BES are prototypes of different sets of behavior episodes. Therefore, a person may develop the kind of expert cognitive functioning described above in one domain of life but not in others. Moreover, these are not irreversible cognitive "stages." People retain in their repertoire all the BES knowledge, procedures, and strategies they have developed, although earlier ones may be embedded in larger, later developing hierarchies. However, under certain circumstances, the less elaborate components may reemerge and be used. For example, old "bad habits" may reoccur for an athlete, or a fatigued scientist may make an error in reasoning or procedure typical of his graduate school days.

Although most elderly people are capable of quite impressive problem solving and decision making (Schaie, 1980), on the average there does seem to be some modest decline in memory and problem-solving capabilities in the elderly (Arenberg, 1982, 1983; Poon, 1985; Reese & Rodeheaver, 1985). Like people at every other age, the elderly are quite different from one another in this regard, but there is some evidence that their abilities may become more interdependent as they become older (Cunningham, 1980). One developmental possibility is that there may be a general slowing of all processes including information processing (Birren, Woods, & Williams, 1980). A second suggestion (perhaps related to the first) is that there may be a decline in the kinds of higher order "executive and control operations" that make possible "powerful integration and transfer of information" (Labouvie-Vief, 1985).

However, Reese and Rodeheaver (1985) suggest that many elderly do not use their available competence to solve experimental problems more efficiently. There may be several potential reasons for this. If their life style progressively reduces their self-directed functioning and social contacts, the loss of that "stimulus nutriment" may produce a performance decline (Rodin & Langer, 1980). If they no longer have personal goals toward which they want to strive and through which they can experience some satisfaction, then they may not make the effort to function at a higher cognitive level.

Emotions and Control Function Development

The idea of mutual causal relationships between emotions and cognitions has been prominent in psychotherapy theory for a century (Ford & Urban, 1963). Rapaport (1961) summarized several views about emotional valence and memory and studied the role of the quality and intensity of emotional arousal in remembering. Recently a revival has occurred of empirical study of emotion-cognition relationships (Fiske & Clarke, 1982; Izard, Kagan, & Zajonc, 1984). Emotions and their development are extensively considered in Chapter 13, so only a few comments are relevant here.

Two extensive and influential programs of research on these issues are being conducted on infants and young children by Sroufe and colleagues (Sroufe, 1979; Sroufe, et al., 1984), and on adults by Bower and colleagues (Bower & Cohen, 1982; Gilligan & Bower, 1984). Their results indicate that emotions can have a strong influence on how people perceive, think, and act with regard to themselves, both in their problem-solving activities and socially; and that reciprocal influence between emotions and cognitions is to be expected.

For example, Bower concludes that (a) emotional arousal influences selective perception, with information congruent with the perceiver's current mood being more salient, standing out more, arousing more interest, and causing "deeper" processing; (b) there is greater learning of material congruent with current mood; (c) current emotions influence what people can retrieve from memory, and events learned in a particular mood or emotion are best retrieved by somehow reinstating that mood or emotion; (d) emotions influence thinking and judgment; for example, happy people increase their estimates of the possibility of positive future events, whereas depressed subjects increase their estimates of the probability of catastrophes; and (e) current emotions influence social judgments; for example, happy people tend to be charitable, loving, and positive in their evaluations of others, whereas depressed people are quick to notice signs of flagging friendships, to overinterpret remarks as personally denigrating, and to exaggerate the slightest criticism; and angry people tend to be ready to find fault, to take offense, and may vent their anger on innocent bystanders.

Moreover, Sroufe and others (Cohn & Tronick, 1982) find that from infancy onward emotional expressions (e.g., facial, vocal) regulate interpersonal transactions. It appears that emotional communication between adults and infants can mediate the learning process (Campos & Barrett, 1984). For example, positive facial gestures encourage interaction; angry ones do the reverse. Such findings make sense if emotions are understood as performing regulatory-evaluative and amplifying functions (see Chapter 13).

There appear to be two inborn ways in which emotions may be aroused within a behavior episode. The first may be a form of resonance phenomena, often referred to as *empathy* (Hoffman, 1984). Emotional expressions in one person may arouse similar emotions in an observer. The second way is a function of the dynamics of behavior episodes as described in Chapters 5 and 13. Depending upon the progress made towards accomplishing one's intentions, and obstructions or other events that occur during the episode, different kinds of emotional arousal may occur. That means that since one's BES are constructed from behavior episodes, such schemata may have an emotional component if emotion was significantly present during the episode(s) which it represents. Then when such a BES is reconstructed, it is likely to trigger some degree of its original emotional component. Fiske (1982) calls this *schema triggered affect*. On the other hand, since the reconstruction of a BES may be triggered by components of current episodes, the arousal of a particular emotion may trigger reconstruction of a generalized BES of which that kind of emotion is a component. The schema then exerts an organizing influence on current behavior. That is probably the basis for many of Bower's findings. Thus, thoughts may influence emotions and emotions may influence thoughts.

Qualitatively different kinds of emotions facilitate different developmental patterns. For example, some (such as fear) facilitate *avoidance* of the relevant circumstances; whereas others (such as interest or pleasure) facilitate *approach* to the relevant circumstances. This is true for cognition as well as action. For example, people tend to mentally rehearse memories of happy or successful episodes, and to avoid thinking about or remembering episodes that frighten or upset them. Freud hypothesized that the reason many of his patients were unable to remember certain events was because they were unable to overcome some inhibiting force, a phenomenon he called *repression*. He was probably describing cognitive fear-avoidance patterns. Many of Freud's therapeutic techniques were aimed at getting past this "censoring" process.

Emotional intensity also influences learning and performance. Emotional arousal appears to function as an amplifier or attenuator of learning and action. Moderate intensities of most emotions appear to facilitate learning and performance. Thus, teachers try to "interest" and "motivate" students, and coaches try to get athletes "up" for a contest. However, too great intensity disrupts smooth and effective performance (Campos & Barrett, 1979). Experiences that have intense emotion as a component appear to be more deeply impressed in one's memory system (e.g., "flashbulb" memories).

It appears that this can provide a starting point for the later development of personality disturbances, particularly if such intense emotional experiences occur before a child's cognitive development has progressed to where he or she have some reasonable capacity for abstract thought and can use words as handles for organizing, controlling, and manipulating meanings. The flexibility and diversity of control strategies may become seriously limited or significantly facilitated by the emotional components of BES. For example, a person may come to avoid whole problem-solving domains, strategies, and procedures, because of negative early experiences; or may build whole career trajectories from early experiences full of positive affect.

Because emotions play an important regulatory role in interpersonal relationships, the development of adult social cognitions and interpersonal styles are probably significantly influenced by learned emotional components of interpersonal BES. For example, a girl's fear of her father's disapproval or rejection may become elaborated into a more generalized BES which creates discomfort as an adult in many other kinds of relationships with adult males. Generalized behavior strategies may be developed as a function of the quality and intensity of emotional experience. For example, "mastery-oriented" children tend to persist longer in the face of failure and to remember their successes and use them in support of their self-efficacy beliefs. On the other hand, children with a "helpless orientation" tend to give up faster in the face of failure, and to forget or ignore the relevance of their successes (Mineka & Henderson, 1985).

The construction of personal goals, the selection of specific goals on specific occasions, and the selection of means to achieve goals are all influenced by evaluative processes. Therefore, the regulatory function is examined in the next chapter.

12

Regulatory Functions: Biochemical, Affective, and Cognitive

INTRODUCTION

This chapter begins with an historical perspective on regulatory functioning. Next, the basic objectives and methods of living system regulation are identified. The two most primitive regulatory methods, biochemical and affective, are then discussed. The remainder of the chapter examines the particularly human method of cognitive regulation, focusing on three types: self-evaluation; regulation of performance; and regulation of social relations with a special focus on moral reasoning.

ORIGINS AND CHARACTERISTICS OF REGULATION IN COMPLEX SYSTEMS

Deutsch (1951) concludes that any complex, goal-seeking system must have "stable operating rules" it uses "to decide the relative preferences and priorities" in organizing "the reception, screening and routing of all signals" if it is to function as a unified system. Moreover, these "operating rules" must themselves be subject to and modifiable by feedback processes. Pugh (1977) proposes that humans evolved biologically as "a value-driven decision system" to facilitate species survival as the "ultimate goal" in the "game of life." However, this goal is "too far distant" for current actions to be weighed against it. Therefore, humans evolved with capabilities for "assigning" shorter term "values" to immediate actions which indirectly serve the fundamental evolutionary goals of survival and reproduction. Similarly, Hoffman (1981) argues that evolutionary processes probably did not directly select for social altruism, but for some "mediating mechanism," such as empathic emotional responding, that could produce altruistic behavior "under appropriate conditions."

Humans instead of appear to have an inborn valuing process that matures under appropriate conditions (Rogers, 1951; Swanson, 1980) which enables them to regulate their functioning, to construct personal and social values from their own experience, and to adopt values constructed and provided by other humans. These constructed values are evaluative cognitions that function as standards instead of criteria by which people can judge or evaluate their behavior (Smith, 1969) and regulate interpersonal relations (Kim & Rosenberg, 1980).

The operation of this valuing process results in "a learned organization of rules" or a "value system" which a person uses "for making choices and resolving conflicts" between two or more desirable "modes of behavior," that is, *instrumental values* or between two or more "terminal states to strive for," that is *terminal values*. In addition, these values are used as "standards for evaluating ourselves and others," "justifications for thoughts and actions," and as "guides for maintaining or enhancing self-esteem" (Rokeach, 1968, 1973, 1979). Thus, this valuing or regulatory process functions to establish priorities among goals and means, and to influence transactional behaviors so they produce consequences that conform to those priorities. Historically, several views of this valuing process have been proposed.

Hedonism is an ancient concept about behavior regulation (Windelband, 1901). It assumes that "pleasurable" behavior will be pursued while "unpleasurable" behavior will be avoided. *Pleasure* is broadly defined to encompass pleasures of the body, of social interactions, of the mind or the spirit. Proposals that "reward" and "punishment" influence learning are modern relatives. Garcia, Clarke, and Hankins (1973) summarize evidence demonstrating that consequences function as rewards only in relationship to what the organism is trying to do.

Conscience is another old and influential regulatory concept (Bier, 1971). Ancient Greeks viewed conscience as a god-given facet of human nature, functioning as one of the checks and balances in a carefully regulated universe, in relationship to individuals' specific acts. Early Christians viewed humans as having a god-given essence, and believed that if their actions went beyond the moral limits of their nature they would experience the "pain of conscience." Moral regulation proposes that humans develop standards of right and wrong and are motivated to abide by those standards (Sears, 1960).

Social organization requires that individual and social interests be balanced. *Moral thinking* and *judgment* function to regulate the distribution of the benefits and burdens of social collaboration (Rawls, 1971); that is, to coordinate the person's functioning as a living system with his or her functioning as a component of a larger living system. Culture transmits *moral principles* and *social regulatory rules, standards,* or *norms.* Psychological study of social regulatory rules and processes includes social conventions, norms, and moral reasoning and behavior (Kohlberg, Levine, & Hewer, 1983; Kurtines & Gewitz, 1984; Piaget, 1932; Rest, 1979; Turiel, 1983). Absence of moral regulation was once considered an illness, called *moral insanity.*

However, moral reasoning represents only one category of regulatory cognitions. There are others. For example, Freud's concept of *superego* included not only self-reproach for forbidden activities (conscience or morality), but more generally involved setting standards and establishing values including values about oneself, termed the *ego ideal.* Rogers (1951) considered conflict between self-constructed and socially imposed evaluative thoughts to be a major source of psychological disturbance. Moreover, all thinking and action requires using values to establish priorities and make choices among options.

There are several definitions of *value* (Baier, 1969; Howard, 1985; Kilmann, 1981). One resulting point of confusion should be clarified. Sometimes, value is defined as something one wants (e.g., Locke, 1983). The term *valence* typically represents something's value from a person's subjective view, and *incentives* are consequences that are valued (Campbell & Pritchard, 1983). Used in that sense, it represents a desired consequence or goal, that is, the directive function. At other times, value represents principles or criteria for evaluating and choosing among alternative ideas and actions. In the latter usage, values refer to regulatory functions. Such evaluative criteria may be applied to choices among goals, among means for achieving goals, or even among alternate evaluative criteria; and to evaluations of relative personal effectiveness, relative personal preference, or of relative social desirability or acceptability.

Attitudes are most often defined as regulatory cognitions, for example, they represent a favorable or unfavorable evaluation of, or action tendency towards, the attitude object (Page, 1980). The evaluative role of affect as a component of attitudes is often emphasized (Kiesler, 1982; Zajonc, 1980). Attitudes are believed to influence behavior, but research has often revealed only weak or occasional relationships between attitudes and actions (Wicker, 1969). However, that research is flawed (Page, 1980); and recent research suggests that attitudes based on direct experience or at the same level of specificity as the behavior being predicted can predict relevant behavior (Cooper & Croyle, 1984; Eagly &

Himmelfarb, 1978; Fazio & Zanna, 1978). Some attitude definitions are analogous to the concept of schema (Lingle & Ostrom, 1981). Using the concept of attitude in so many different ways is confusing and reduces its utility. Its evaluative function appears to be its most emphasized and distinguishing characteristic (Page, 1980).

Unfortunately, in this as in other domains (e.g., Ford & Urban, 1967), scholars studying human regulatory functioning or values develop conceptual framework and then appear to get encapsulated in them, neglecting exploration of other related approaches. For example, three orientations that emphasize values are *achievement motivation* which is popular in educational settings (Dweck & Elliott, 1983), *expectancy-value theory*, emphasized in industrial psychology and organization behavior (Campbell & Pritchard, 1983), and *moral reasoning* and *behavior*, emphasized in social-personality research (Rest, 1983). The three review chapters just cited collectively contain 542 references. None were cited in all three books, and only seven were cited in two of the three.

Three Interrelated Regulatory Objectives

To maintain functional unity and carry out successful transactions with the environment, humans continually set priorities among competing desires and demands and evaluate their functioning and its consequences by dealing with three types of regulatory problems.

1. They must regulate their internal biological, affective, and cognitive functioning to maintain internal coherence and functional unity. The literature on biological homeostasis, cognitive dissonance, psychological conflict, and self-concept illustrates this type of regulatory problem.

2. They must regulate their relationships with their environment to maintain desirable physical and social steady states, and to effectively produce intended consequences. The literature on achievement motivation, setting personal priorities, performance regulation, and skill development illustrates this type of regulatory problem. A special subtype of behavior-environment regulation involves regulating interpersonal or social relationships, illustrated by the literature on morality, social norms or conventions, and impression management.

3. They must regulate the relations between their internal states and their behavior-environment relationships so that there is behavioral coherence and they function as a unit, a person; that is illustrated by relationships between perception-cognition-emotion and action patterns as discussed in the literature on counseling and psychotherapy.

Three Regulatory Methods: Biochemical, Affective, Cognitive

In a living systems framework, the way regulation is accomplished depends primarily on three types of variables: (a) the nature of the consequences or preferred states towards which system behavior is currently directed; (b) the nature of the feedback signals monitored to represent current states in the comparison; and (c) the kind of comparison rules, values, or standards used to make the comparison and evaluation (see Chapter 3). Since (a) represents the directive function, (b) and (c) are the primary issues to be examined under the regulatory function.

Living systems evolved three basic kinds of interrelated regulatory methods, probably in the following order. The first simple organisms regulated themselves through *biochemical feedback* from their own functioning and from their environments. *Affective regulation* came next, and is apparent in many other organism besides humans. Sensory-perceptual information processes probably evolved from biochemical regulators, with some sensory qualities subjectively experienced as attractive or aversive (e.g., tastes, odors, pain). Emotional processes are a more advanced form of affective regulation. They probably evolved to facilitate the more complex environmental interactions characteristic of mobile and social organisms by merging informational and biochemical methods. They help regulate person-environment relations and internal biological processes to support such transactions. The third method is *cognitive regulation,* manifest in evaluative forms of thought, and used to deal with all three types of regulatory problems mentioned earlier.

REGULATION BY BIOCHEMICAL METHODS

The human body is organized to maintain an enormous number of biological variables within certain boundaries. Cannon (1932) named this dynamic process homeostasis. If something (e.g., activity, injury, or infection) pushes some variable(s) beyond the steady state boundaries, the body functions to reduce that discrepancy until the relevant biological functions return to a steady state range. Biochemically based regulation was discussed in Chapter 6, so only a brief discussion is provided here. An entire issue of Scientific American (Weinberg, 1985) describes current knowledge about the elaborate patterns of biochemical regulation at the cellular and molecular levels.

Hippocrates called this process the healing force of nature that cures from within. Selye (1976) recognized that the biological patterns labeled as disease were really manifestations of the body's "fight for health," its efforts to restore an appropriate biochemical homeostasis. The biological response of the body to any demand that perturbs its normal steady states he called *stress.* Defined that way, stress is a normal, natural, and necessary part of living, and not just a "bad" thing.

The feedback signals monitored to regulate biological functions are primarily biochemical in nature. Inborn values typically function to keep biological deviations within some "normal" steady state boundaries. When normal biological processes are insufficient to accomplish this "self-righting" objective, other "agents" (e.g., drugs) may be used to establish a new defensive steady state, which Selye called *heterostasis*. Or, if the system is subject to chronic perturbations, functional reorganization may occur to revise "hemeostatic settings" and establish new steady states. *Biofeedback* is a training procedure designed to help individuals use cognition to help regulate biological processes (Stern & Ray, 1977).

Individuals may differ in their normal biological steady states either because of inborn constitutional differences or because their life styles have produced steady state changes. This has important practical implications. For example, a single measure of a patient's blood pressure may be compared to the average blood pressure of people in general. Excessive deviation from the group norm is often considered a pathological symptom, and remedial procedures may be prescribed (e.g., hypertension medication). There are two important potential sources of error in that procedure from a living systems perspective. First, a single measure of a biological function may (a) accurately represent the person's normal steady state, (b) be a temporary "normal" deviation from that steady state, or (c) be a more persistent deviation from the person's normal steady state. With only one measure, there is no sure way to distinguish between the three possibilities.

Second, since individuals may differ in their steady state settings for biological processes, a measure of some biological process in a person may be significantly different from the group norm but still fall within his or her personal normal steady state. The only way to accurately identify a person's normal biological steady state is to take multiple measures on multiple occasions. Significant, persistent deviations from personal norms have potentially important implications health. Deviations from group norms may or may not have important health implications.

Because the body functions as a unit, biological processes equilibrate their steady states to one another since they are linked in complex, mutually influential regulatory patterns. Therefore, treatment to bring a biological process closer to the group norm may actually disrupt a person's normal steady state and precipitate adjustments in other biological steady states, perhaps with serious consequences. For example, my elderly father's biological functioning was seriously disrupted when a young physician changed the medication pattern successfully used for years to regulate his diabetic condition, in an effort to bring his biological status closer to a "preferred" group norm. Moreover, different steady state boundaries may be "normal" for different groups of people (e.g., different ages or genetic histories).

One way of observing regulatory functioning is to disrupt a system and observe its efforts to recover from the disruption (Hofstadter, 1941), as for example through a glucose tolerance test. Biological structural-functional organization makes all other functions possible. Therefore, disruptions of other functions (e.g., memory) may be a manifestation of biological disruptions (e.g., a brain tumor). Psychotherapists sometimes use a "disrupting" technique to observe clients' psychological regulatory processes, as, by focusing client attention on distressing topics or memories. *Defense mechanism* is the psychoanalytic label for psychological regulatory processes used to deal with psychologically disrupting influences.

AFFECTIVE REGULATORY METHODS

There are two kinds of affects: those that provide feedback about sensory and bodily functioning; and those that reflect different kinds of emotional arousal (See Chapter 13). Emotional affective regulation is more learnable than sensory and bodily affective regulation.

Affective experience has a sense of immediacy about it, and its regulatory influence an apparent automaticity, leading Zajonc (1980) to argue that affective experience and its regulatory influence does not require prior cognitive evaluation for its occurrence. He distinguishes "cognitive judgments" as dealing with "qualities that reside in the stimulus," from "affective judgments" that identify the state of the "judge" in relation to "the object of judgment." He proposes that affective regulation derives from "a parallel, separate, and partly independent (from cognition) system" It follows that affect can be aroused "without the participation of cognitive processes," where he means by *cognition* "something more than pure sensory input," some kind of "mental work" that "transforms pure sensory input" into some other form (Zajonc, 1984). His argument rests primarily on the proposal that affects can be triggered by "minimal sensory input that need not be transformed into meaningful information" by cognitive processes.

Evidence about the relationships among sensations, perceptions, affects, and cognitions (see Chapters 8, 9, and 13) makes such a proposal implausible if he truly means *sensations*. However, if by "pure sensory input" he means something like Gibson's concept of direct perception of objects, events, and affordances, then his proposals have some substance. Many kinds of affects can be triggered in infants by direct perceptions as yet unaffected by cognitive learning (see Chapter 13). For example, they react with avoidance to some tastes and odors and with approach to others. They display different kinds of emotions depending on the characteristics of ongoing behavior episodes. Thus, for infants "preferences need no inferences" as Zajonc argues. This living systems position proposes that there is an inborn set of evaluative (do not read that to mean *conceptual)* responses to certain kinds of information which provide the starting point for construction of a regulatory repertoire. Moreover, those inborn bases can continue to function throughout life, so that some affective reactions may continue to be primarily the result of direct perception (e.g., sulfuric acid "stinks" for both infants and adults).

However, cognitions are constructed from direct perceptions and from other cognitions (see Chapter 9). Once a person has developed a cognitive repertoire, then direct perceptions merge with reconstructed cognitions or memories in governing ongoing behavior episodes. Therefore, in older children and adults there is seldom if ever direct perception unaffected by learned conceptions and evaluations. They combine the "current news" of perceptions with their history of experience represented in conceptions to regulate their behavior episodes.

Moreover, those perception-conception mergers can become habitual, and can function automatically (without conscious representation). Affects elicited by cognitive habits are as rapid and automatic as those elicited by direct perceptions. They represent cognitive-affective behavioral components, triggered as a unit by perceptions. In fact, a key adaptive value of habits is that a person can behave as quickly and efficiently as if the behavior pattern were "hard wired"; learned habits and inborn "habits" are functionally similar. Animals and humans both display affective preferences (habits) for objects to which they are repeatedly exposed, even when awareness of the triggering information is precluded (Kunst-Wilson & Zajonc, 1980). Therefore, in adults it is impossible to distinguishing perceptually from perceptually-cognitively triggered affective reactions.

This provides a solid basis for Lazarus's (1982, 1984) disagreement with Zajonc about the subtype of affects called emotions. Lazarus maintains that "cognition (of meaning) is a necessary precondition for emotion," but that mutual causality exists. Emotions are elicited by cognitive evaluations (Campos & Barrett, 1984), but they can also be "powerful influences on how we think and interpret events."

These two positions can be combined. Zajonc's description accurately represents the inborn affective regulatory "starting points" for development, while Lazarus's description accurately represents the typical affective regulatory pattern of emotions after learning and cognitive development have begun to occur. Moreover, some affective regulation appears less learnable than others (e.g., olfaction vs emotion), so that even in adults Zajonc's representation may still apply to some affective regulatory processes.

Sensory Affective Regulation

Sensory-based affects reflect direct perceptual "affordances" as proposed by Gibson. For example, odors and flavors vary in their valence from tasting and smelling "good" to "bad." Touch, sounds, sights, and food textures vary from being pleasing through neutral to unpleasant. And these basic sensory evaluative affects are apparent in infants. They provide immediate and direct evaluative regulatory information. For example, things that taste or smell bad are more likely to be biologically disrupting than things that taste or smell good; lights, sounds, or movements that are too bright, too loud, or too abrupt are more likely than others to signal dangers to be avoided.

The valence of sensory affects automatically regulates approach or avoidant behavior without requiring learning. They represent an inborn regulatory capability. For example, the "most pleasant" sound typically selected by people falls in a narrow band centered around 399 Hz (Patchett, 1979). Some sensory-based affects are learnable. For example, as a child I was given castor oil in grape juice. It took decades for me to extinguish the resulting habitual nauseous response to the sight or smell of grape juice. Such learned taste aversions are commonplace (Logue, Ophir, & Strauss, 1981). Similarly, some events that initially elicit negative sensory affects (e.g., the taste of martinis or spicy foods) can, through learning come to elicit positive affects.

Body State Affective Regulation

Some kinds of variations in body tissue states are accompanied by affective feedback signals. Factor analytic and clustering methods used to study nonemotional activation terms have identified at least four kinds (Purcell, 1982).

Relaxed-Contented-Drowsy. This affective state represents the experience of general biological homeostasis. The conditions under which it occurs include: being well fed, physically relaxed, warm, and comfortable; having no concentration of attention in any direction and no intentionally organized pattern of thought; and having no physical discomfort or pain. It represents a base rate arousal-affective state between sleep, selectively attentive alertness, and directed action. Anyone who has observed and held a well rested, healthy, dry, warm, comfortable baby who has just been fed has observed this condition. Adults also experience this condition, for example after intercourse, or when awakening from or going to sleep. Behaviorally, it usually leads to inactivity.

Alert-Restless-Energetic. This is a deviation from base rate biological homeostasis in which a person is intentionally, selectively reactive and proactive to stimulation, and ready for action. It typically occurs when one is physically health and rested, and/or as a manifestation of anticipatory sets preparing one to carry out environmental transactions. Such feelings can be observed in a child "looking for something to do." Adults sometimes feel this way in the morning after a good night's sleep, a good breakfast, a brisk shower, and an interesting day to look forward to; or when they are ready to do something but have nothing to do (like a teenager with nothing to do on a Saturday night). Sometimes, it may be colored by a sense of muscular tenseness. Behaviorally, it typically leads to exploratory or instrumental environmental transactions.

Physical Discomfort. Any significant deviation in any biological variable (e.g., body water balance) will produce compensating shifts in other variables to protect the welfare of the person until the troublesome deviation can be corrected. Such deviations (which might be thought of as tissue biochemical deficits or excesses), and the related compensating shifts in other variables, may be manifest in affective feedback (e.g., hunger pangs, dry mouth and throat, itchy skin).

The concepts of *need* or *drive* typically represent such biological deviations. For example, hunger is induced by depriving a person of food; the greater the deprivation, the greater the steady state deviation, and the greater the physical discomfort. Reduction in such deficits and their related affects through instrumental behavior episodes facilitates relevant learning.

Disruptions in biological steady state patterns trigger corrective self-organizing functions, some of which are manifest in affective experience. For example, oxygen deprivation quickly shifts the nervous system into a "red alert" condition, and the sympathetic nervous system goes into "high gear"; motor behavior becomes powerful and extensive to obtain more oxygen for breathing. The resulting affective experience is similar to that of other emergency reactions such as fear. Similarly, disruption of brain tissue functioning with drugs or through deprivation of essential nutrients produces affective feedback (e.g., diabetic episodes, feelings of anxiety or euphoria from drugs).

Many biological deviations do not have direct affective manifestations, but have correlates that produce affective states. For example, a drop in blood pressure may be experienced as a cold, clammy feeling. Certain changes in blood chemistry may be experienced as headaches and some tissue deficits and excesses as muscle cramps. In general, such biological deviations lead to behavior patterns that function to reduce or terminate the resulting physical discomfort by restoring an acceptable steady state. Not all biological deviations from steady states lead to negative affect. For example, some addictive drugs exert their seductive influence through eliciting positive affects or alleviating negative ones.

The principle of *equifinality* operates here in two ways. First, there is usually more than one kind of behavior that will ease such discomfort. For example, thirst may be quenched by a drink of water, pop, or a beer. Different behavioral solutions have different correlated consequences, so evaluation of alternatives in terms of their correlated consequences may be desirable (e.g., each of two drugs may relieve pain, but one may produce addiction). Second, a particular kind of biological deviation may result from a variety of antecedents. For example, gastrointestinal affects similar to hunger may result from some kinds of emotional arousal or illness (e.g., heart dysfunctions). The action people take to relieve or terminate the discomfort will be influenced by their evaluation of its cause. Accurate interpretation of evaluative feedback is essential for constructing sound regulatory behaviors. For example, tense or anxious people frequently experience gut sensations similar to hunger pangs, sometimes eat to reduce this gut discomfort, and may produce other problems. An illustrative case is that of a University executive who was often tired and tense, and ate and drank a lot to ease his discomfort. The eventual result was a serious weight problem and a heart attack.

Other deprivations (e.g., in trace minerals and vitamins) may be slow and progressive, taking a long time to produce compensating reactions with affective manifestations. In general, the task of medical diagnosis is to identify the pattern of deviations from steady-state functioning, called *symptom syndromes*, and to infer which deviations are compensatory and which ones represent the precipitating biological deviations. Since many components of such syndromes are only observable by the person in whom they occur, through their affective feedback manifestations, medical diagnosis still must rely heavily on patients' subjective observations of affective experience, that is, on the patient telling the doctor "where it hurts."

Pain: A Special Kind of Body State Affective Regulation

Steady state deviations that involve tissue damage (e.g., a wound) or a major deviation from normal tissue functioning that may produce damage (e.g., a severe muscle cramp), produce an aversive affective feedback called *pain*. Pain has an imperative quality, and usually leads immediately to behavior aimed at reducing or terminating it. Pain is not an emotion, but it may help elicit emotions (e.g., in conditions evaluated as dangerous: "I may die").

Pain has long been a topic of human concern (e.g., Livingston, 1943), but there has been a major expansion of interest in its scientific study during the past 20 years (Bonica & Albe-Fessard, 1976; Liebeskind & Paul, 1977; Melzak & Wall, 1965; Sternbach, 1978; Weisenberg, 1977). The title of one book, *The Puzzle of Pain* (Melzak, 1973) is still apt. An early theory, called *specificity theory*, postulated specific pain receptors in body tissue projecting to a pain center in the brain. Contradictory evidence led to alternate explanations, sometimes termed *pattern theories*. There appears to be both "central summation" of tissue-generated signals and some control by the brain over the input of pain signals to it. Pain typically has a physical origin, but it is a psychological phenomenon, as is the experience of all other sensory inputs (Melzak & Wall, 1965).

Pain is Hierarchically Organized. Like the experiences of taste and odor, pain involves both sensory and affective-evaluative dimensions (Melzak & Torgerson, 1971). The sensory attributes are illustrated by terms such as throbbing, stabbing, burning, tingling, soreness, and aching. The affective-evaluative attributes are illustrated by terms such as annoying, agonizing, unbearable, sickening, and nagging. The aversive quality of pain appears to be a function of the affective-evaluative attributes. The sensory attributes led theorists to think of pain as "the end product of a linear sensory transmission system," but the affective-evaluative attributes reveal that pain is a dynamic, hierarchical neural process "which involves continuous interactions among complex ascending and descending systems" (Melzak & Dennis, 1978).

Pain's hierarchical control system has at least four levels: the spinal cord, the brainstem reticular activating system, the thalamus-limbic system circuits, and the cortex. At the first level, the dorsal horns of the spinal cord, control mechanisms subject to influences by feedforward signals from the brain can serve as a "gate," increasing or decreasing the flow of peripheral sensations into the spinal cord and to the brain, providing the basis for Melzak and Wall's (1965) *gate control theory* of pain. However, evidence indicates that the brainstem reticular formation and the limbic system play an important affective-evaluative role in pain experience. Thus, the brain structures that are involved in the affective-evaluative attributes of taste, smell, and emotions are also involved in the affective aspects of pain experience. For example, people who are congenitally insensitive to pain or who have had a frontal lobotomy still report experiencing the sensory components of pain, but the affective-aversive quality is greatly diminished or eliminated (Melzak & Dennis, 1978).

What could be the evolutionary value of such an hierarchical arrangement? The evaluative experience of pain leads to behavior that protects the damaged or stressed tissue until it can heal. In addition, as with noxious odors and tastes, it provides a basis for learning avoidance of circumstances that might produce physical damage. However, protection of damaged tissue might not always be adaptive. For example, when in danger, it would be adaptive if an animal or human were temporarily unaware of the tissue damage (i.e., of pain), so that it would continue to energetically protect itself either through fight or flight.

Bolles and Fanselow (1980) propose that the pain system activates recuperative behaviors such as resting and body care responses. The fear system activates defensive behaviors of freezing or flight. Each may inhibit the other. It appears that the aversive-affective qualities of pain can be interrupted at several levels in a hierarchical arrangement of multiple ascending and descending neural circuits (Melzak & Dennis, 1978). Moreover, portions of these circuits manufacture chemical compounds (e.g., endorphins) that function as anesthetics, temporarily attenuating the experience of pain (Bolles & Fanselow, 1982; Hosobuchi & Li, 1978). For example, at a behavioral level, men wounded in battle appear to experience much less pain than men with similar surgically produced wounds (Beecher, 1956). The typical pain experience is called *acute pain*. A more complex and enduring experience is called *chronic pain*.

Acute Pain.   An acute pain experience usually results from some organic cause (e.g., a burned hand). It has an initial phasic component in which pain is quickly experienced, followed by a tonic component during which pain may be experienced for a more extended period of time. Like other sensory information, affective signals experienced as pain may be filtered out or modified at several levels of the nervous system.

Several circumstances can alter information about tissue damage or stress or prevent it from becoming conscious (Bolles & Fanselow, 1982; Liebeskind & Paul, 1977; Melzak & Dennis, 1978). One way is to physically or chemically block the incoming pain signals, as for example through surgery or local anesthesia. Such strategies are most effective at the lower levels of the pain control hierarchy (e.g., at the spinal level), because at higher levels the ascending pain signals become more dispersed to more areas of the nervous system. In addition, cognitive processes can exert feedforward control from higher brain centers on pain feedback. There probably exist within the brainstem "powerful and endogenous centrifugal mechanisms of pain control" that function relatively automatically in lower animals. However, human cognitive capacities "to think, to believe, and to hope" enable people "under the appropriate conditions, to find and employ our pain inhibitory resources" (Liebeskind & Paul, 1977).

People usually actively select that information relevant to their current concerns and generally ignore the rest, or vaguely monitor it with peripheral attention; this is true of pain information. Such "gating" appears to occur both at the periphery and brainstem levels (Melzak & Dennis, 1978). People injured while intensely preoccupied with what they are doing may not notice any pain (Beecher, 1959). Their first realization that they are injured may come from the sight of their own blood. Hypnotic analgesias are another example (Hilgard & Hilgard, 1975; Orne, 1974), although they often allow awareness of some less severe pain.

Peoples attitudes about, expectations of, and sense of control over their pain can influence the nature and severity of the pain experienced, and even the effectiveness of drugs administered to reduce pain (Weisenberg, 1980). The brain's manufacturing sites for opiate-like compounds appear to be linked to pain pathways, and to provide for temporary analgesias (i.e., interruption of regulatory feedback) and the inhibition of pain-motivated behavior at times when self-defense and escape may be critical. Fear may be the primary trigger for their production (Bolles & Fanselow, 1982). Methods for self-control of pain experience appear to be learnable. One of the oldest methods is counter-irritation, sometimes termed hyperstimulation or stimulation-produced analgesia (Liebeskind & Paul, 1977; Melzak, 1973). For example, some people dig their fingernails into their hands when in the dental chair to reduce pain sensations. Needle and electrical acupuncture, and transcutaneous electrical nerve stimulation appear to be more sophisticated methods for producing pain-inhibiting neural stimulation. Since such stimulation does not need to be at the site of origin of the pain signals, the inhibiting effects appear to occur at higher neural levels. However, these methods are only effective sometimes, with some people. For example, even in China only 15–20% of surgical patients receive acupuncture as the only anesthetic, and it is combined with psychological procedures (Liebeskind & Paul, 1977; Melzak & Dennis, 1978).

Some control of pain experience may be possible by concentration procedures. For example, one man has experienced several severe accidents (e.g., the severing of his toes) and much pain. He reports that as soon as he realizes he is injured, he concentrates his attention on the injured part of his body, eliminating most pain, and producing voluntary reduction of blood flow from the injury. The central processes which help control acute pain experiences are probably critical for the experience of chronic pain.

Chronic Pain. The phenomenon of chronic pain is puzzling, and forces recognition of the importance of central brain processes in the regulatory experience of pain. Much chronic pain has a genuine organic antecedent (e.g., cancer patients) and clinical management of such pain is well advanced (Holden, 1979b). However, there are chronic pain syndromes for which organic causes seem not to be present, such as phantom limb pain (Sunderland, 1968). After a limb has been removed and the remaining stump has completely healed, individuals may experience pain as if coming from the limb that is no longer there. Similarly, paraplegics with total spinal cord lesions may experience chronic body pain. Patients continue to suffer severe pain in the abdomen, groin, or legs after receiving total spinal cord sections at thoracic or lumbar levels, or even after removal of an entire section of the spinal cord. Under those circumstances, it is impossible for peripherally arising pain signals in the "disconnected" parts of the body to reach the brain, and yet people report "burning," "crushing," or "cramping" kinds of pains felt "as if" they were in the disconnected body parts.

Hallucinations in other sensory modalities are assumed to be mentally manufactured, because a percept-like image is experienced in the absence of sensory inputs appropriate to that image. That seems to be precisely the nature of phantom pain. Low back pain and the neuralgias are other frequent types of chronic pain that are often difficult to alleviate. Here, too, surgical interruption of neuronal pain pathways is often ineffective, suggesting significant brain influences on the regulatory experience (Liebeskind & Paul, 1977; Melzak & Dennis, 1978).

Since phantom pain cannot be resulting from damaged or stressed tissue, the brain must be able to generate pain experiences. Brain-generated pain is just as real to the person as is organically based acute pain. This may result from memory-like processes (Melzak, 1973) or neuronal "pattern generating mechanisms" (Melzak & Loeser, 1978). Since other sources of sensation (e.g., visual, auditory) give rise to memories that can later function to influence behavior in new circumstances, it does not seem unreasonable to expect that all kinds of sensory inputs, including pain, could function in that way. It may be useful to look for similarities (e.g., memory formation, hallucinatory dynamics) and differences (e.g., habituation processes) between pain and other kinds of sensory experience. Cases of congenital indifference to pain also implies high-level brain influences on pain experience (Boyd & Nie, 1949).

Emotional Affective Regulation

Two types of emotions appear to have evolved as primitive regulatory (i.e., evaluative-selective activation) processes to facilitate two kinds of adaptive functioning (see Chapter 13). Different kinds of emotions help regulate behavior in relationship to different kinds of behavior episode conditions, including interpersonal conditions. *Instrumental emotions* help regulate ongoing behavior episodes to produce intended consequences. *Social emotions* regulate interpersonal relationships to produce and maintain cohesive social organization.

Emotions are the most flexible and therefore the most influential form of affective regulation because of their learnability. Basic emotions are inborn, perceptually triggered behavior patterns, but their occurrence may be modified through learning in two ways: (a) they can become linked to many different kinds of eliciting conditions, and (b) their patterns can become combined or abbreviated (see Chapter 13). Emotions can become elicited not only by percepts but also by the evolutionarily most recent regulatory method, *evaluative thoughts*. Evaluative thoughts or cognitive "appraisal processes" are the primary elicitor of emotional arousal in adults (Bower & Cohen, 1982; Cohn & Tronick, 1982). Klinger (1977) proposes that objects and events become *incentives* (valued objectives) by virtue of their capacity to arouse emotions; "value" is an "affect dimension" (Klinger, Barta, & Maxeiner, 1980). Therefore, cognitive regulation is considered in the next section.

COGNITIVE REGULATORY METHODS

Evaluative thoughts, particularly anticipatory ones, are an especially powerful regulatory method that is probably unique to humans; self-control results from cognitive regulatory processes. For example, Bandura (1977a, 1980) asserts that people are self-motivated when they make "self-satisfaction" or "tangible gratifications" "contingent upon certain accomplishments." The phrase "contingent upon" implies a regulatory process. His key concept is *self-efficacy* (Bandura, 1977b), which represents self-evaluative thoughts about how well one can execute different courses of action to accomplish one's objectives. Russian scholars emphasize the regulatory role of language (Harris, 1979; Vygotsky, 1962). Verbal regulation is said to monitor, control, plan, and organize behavior arising in some nonverbal functioning

(Zivin, 1979). Even more broadly, every decision or choice involves selection from among options through a "judgment process" (Sherif, 1979). There must be criteria for such selection; that is, for regulating competition among alternative goals and means for control of behavior. The concepts of value, valence, and utility are used by scholars of choice and decision making to represent such criteria; for example, in fields such as in economics, cultural anthropology, political science, history, management science, and philosophy (Kahneman & Tversky, 1984). Pascal (1941), a 15th-century mathematician, proposed a way of calculating what has since come to be called the "expected utility" of an action. Modern versions of Pascal's idea are called *expectancy-value theories* of motivation (see Campbell & Pritchard, 1983).

The Distinction Between Directive and Regulatory Functions. Such regulatory-evaluative criteria function as constraining and facilitating conditionalities on the organization of behavior, and therefore, modify the influences of the directing intentions or goals. Because of this coupling of directive and regulatory functions in shaping problem-solving thought and actions, the two are often "lumped together" or treated interchangeable in some discussion. For example, a person is described as having as a goal "being honest." However, honesty is not an end in itself, but a criterion for selecting among alternative means to desired ends; that is, honest people typically regulate their behavior with certain kinds of social rules, regardless of their goals.

The directive and regulatory functions are related in another way. Intentions or goals are the product of previous learning. Expectations become intentions when personal value and commitment are added (see Chapter 10). Therefore, current goals reflect prior evaluative (i.e., regulatory) processes. Confusion will be reduced if differences in the functional roles of goals and regulatory criteria are recognized, and their patterns of interaction and influence studied.

Subtypes of Evaluative Thoughts. There is far more empirical and clinical literature concerning the nature and role of evaluative thoughts in human functioning than can be summarized here; for example, the extensive research on attitudes, beliefs, and values (Howe, 1980). One useful way to organize that diversity is in terms of differences in the content of the regulatory process. In recent years, people have begun to make important functional distinctions among subtypes of evaluative thoughts (Bowerman, 1978; Harter, 1983; White, 1963). There are evaluations of the relationships between events and their consequences, and between actions and their influence on events; evaluations of the desirability of consequences of actions and events, and of ones own characteristics; and evaluations of one's competence to perform certain actions. Three major categories will be used here that can encompass much of the relevant literature: *self-regulation, performance regulation,* and *social regulation.* The regulatory process itself is the same in all three types. What differs is the nature of the goals involved in the regulatory comparison, the nature of the relevant feedback information and its sources, and the nature of the comparison criteria or rules used. Moreover, the three are probably interrelated.

Cognitive regulation of one's organization of ideas about oneself, often called the *self-concept* or self-system, and its relationship to one's actions uses self- or other-generated evaluative feedback about one's qualities, competencies, beliefs, and actions. *Self-efficacy, self-esteem,* and *self-evaluation* are typical regulatory concepts. Cognitive regulation of performance effectiveness uses feedback information often termed *knowledge of results* (e.g., job performance), and regulatory criteria termed *standards* or *values.* Cognitive regulation of one's social relationships uses feedback about the influence of one's actions (and indirectly one's beliefs) on other persons and social groups, using regulatory criteria often called *moral principles,* and *social values* or *social conventions.*

Self-Regulation Through Self-Evaluative Thoughts

People construct different kinds of behavior episode schemata (BES) to represent the characteristics of different kinds of behavior episodes, so BES differ in the kinds of behaviors, environmental objects, conditions, and organization they encompass.

However, the person doing the behaving is continuously present, both as a physical object and a functional system in all episodes. Since one's physical existence and self-referent experience provide the only source of uninterrupted experiential continuity throughout one's life, they provide the information base for construction of one's personal identity and sense of continuous existence. Clinically, disruption of that sense of continuity is a devastating experience. The organization of cognitions constructed from self-referent experience have been called the *self-concept, self-system,* or *self,* and their omnipresence helps produce coherence among multiple BES.

The self was of significant scholarly interest before behaviorism's dominance of psychology in the middle half of the 20th century (Cooley, 1902; James, 1890; Mead, 1934). People's self-conceptions have been prominent issues in theorizing by humanistic psychologists and psychotherapists (Lecky, 1945; Rogers, 1951; Snygg & Combs, 1949; psychoanalytic ego psychology). The cognitive revolution has brought a resurgence of interest in theory and research about the nature, functioning, and development of people's self-referent thoughts (Buss, 1980;

Lewis & Brooks-Gunn, 1979; Smith, 1978; Suls, 1982; Suls & Greenwald, 1980; Wegner & Vallacher, 1980; Wylie, 1979). There is renewed interest in self-conceptions in personality theory (Greenwald, 1980; Loevinger & Knoll, 1983). Harter (1983) provides a good summary of evidence about the development of individuals' self-system. The self-regulatory function of "private speech" is receiving attention (Zivin, 1979).

The Development of Self-Conceptions. People's flow of experience includes *self-referent information,* that is, information about their properties as they function in behavior episodes, in every behavior episode, and they construct cognitions representing such self-referent consistencies as part of each BES. Those organized sets of self-referent cognitions or self-schemata are probably initially situation-and BES-specific because they are constructed from particular behavior episodes; that is, they are contextually linked (Mancuso & Ceely, 1980). However, as with other cognitions, higher order abstractions can be progressively constructed from initial self-cognitions until they become highly generalized self-conceptions.

Because self-referent experience pervades all behavior episodes, it is probably easier for such highly generalized conceptions to develop about one's self than about any other object or aspect of experience. There is general empirical support for gradual differentiation and hierarchical elaboration of self-conceptions from "self-description based on concrete observable characteristics" (e.g., physical attributes, material possessions, actions) to "trait-like constructs" and later to "more abstract self-definitions" based on subjective processes such as "inner thoughts, emotions and attitudes" (Harter, 1983). Moreover, individuals function to conserve the consistency and coherence of their organization of self-referent ideas (Epstein, 1981; Greenwald, 1980), and use them to guide their behavior. One's organization of self-referent thoughts functions as a set of personal theories about ones self and relationships with the world (Brim, 1976; Epstein, 1973).

Self-conceptions have properties unique to them, properties that cannot be present in nonself conceptions. People experience other entities in their world as objects with certain properties, functional characteristics, and potentialities for affecting them. However, people experience themselves not only as objects ("me") but also as a causal agent ("I") (Dickstein, 1977). People can simultaneously view themselves from both objective and subjective observational vantage points. For example, they can not only observe their emotional actions, they can also feel their emotional arousal; they can simultaneously touch themselves and feel touched; they can compare their thoughts about the consequences they seek with the actions they perform and with their perceptions of the consequences their actions seem to produce. The perceived contingencies between infants' self-directed actions and outcomes are immediate and consistent and provide the basis for constructing schemata-expectancies about themselves in relationship to their world (Lewis & Brooks-Gunn, 1979).

Two kinds of self-referent information that can only be directly observed subjectively are one's thoughts and affects. One can observe indicators of thoughts and affect in others, but can only experience them directly in one's self. This fact has led some to distinguish between the private and the public self, a distinction providing a cornerstone of self-identity. One can know things about oneself that others cannot know (except through self-disclosure), and one can "hide" one's feelings and thoughts from others.

Self-conceptions can be both descriptive (e.g., female, black, employed, married), and evaluative (e.g., admired, rejected, helpless, competent). It is important to distinguish between the two (Beane & Lipka, 1980; Germain, 1978). Selective attention to, and perception of, self-referent information can lead to constructing ideas about some aspects of oneself and not others. One can construct goals about one's self (e.g., to lose weight, to learn a new skill), options for influencing one's self (e.g., self-instructions, exercise), and self-evaluative thoughts and criteria (e.g., self-esteem, self-efficacy). Such selectively constructed self-conceptions may be relatively accurate in the eyes of others, or they may be inaccurate, such as the slender ballerina who considers herself fat or the accomplished person who evaluates himself or herself as incompetent.

Self-Evaluative Self-Conceptions. Because one's structural and functional characteristics provide ones only means for producing desired consequences, one's beliefs about one's capabilities for influencing ones environment play a particularly important role in organizing ones behavior. Because one's welfare and opportunities are significantly a function of one's social environment, evaluative thoughts about one's social acceptability are also of basic significance. Self-evaluative thoughts powerfully influence one's subjective states of satisfaction and dissatisfaction. As Harter (1983) put it, self-evaluative thoughts are not "merely cold cognitive appraisals," but they also "provoke an affective reaction, which in turn may mediate behavior." The regulatory functioning of emotions and thoughts become linked (see Chapter 13).

Albert Bandura (1976, 1977a, 1977b, 1978a, 1978b, 1982a, 1982b, 1986; Bandura & Cervone, 1983) has conducted the most extensive, continuous research program focused on understanding the role of evaluative thoughts in influencing actions (see Bandura, 1981, 1986 for good summaries). He has convincingly demonstrated that different kinds of evaluative thoughts play different roles in an individual's functioning. For example, one may evaluate certain events as desirable, and certain behaviors as likely to produce those events, but still not try to perform the behaviors because one evaluates oneself as incapable of adequately performing the necessary behaviors. Thoughts about one's capabilities for functioning as a causal agent are termed by Bandura, *self-efficacy;* others use terms such as *self-confidence, subjective competence,* or *causal attributions* about locus of control (Bowerman, 1978; Harter, 1983). Self-efficacy thoughts are anticipatory or *simulated performance evaluations,* as contrasted to actual performance evaluations while behavior is in progress.

The impact of self-efficacy thoughts on behavior is a function of one's current goals, one's standards for achieving those goals, one's level of dissatisfaction with their performance or current state, and of environmental circumstances. People don't much care how they perform on tasks that are not personally significant. Task performance evaluated as inadequate does not necessarily produce performance deficits. It is those performance evaluations that lead people to believe they are unlikely to be able to produce the desired consequences—that produce lower self-efficacy—that lead to reduced effort or giving up. If one has a high level of self-efficacy for a task, then the greater the discrepancy between actual performance and one's performance standard, the greater one's self-dissatisfaction and the greater the effort to improve. However, under the same conditions, a person with low self-efficacy for that task will be more likely to give up. The greater the situational aids, supports, and inducements, the less likely that the performance will be evaluated as the result of one's own competence; the locus of control will be evaluated as being elsewhere.

As with other cognitive constructions, hierarchical levels of self-efficacy evaluations can be constructed. One may evaluate one's self as competent in one kind of task and incompetent in another; as competent in a family of similar tasks and incompetent in others; as generally competent or incompetent in most tasks. People function to maintain their organizations of self-evaluative thoughts (Rogers, 1951) through their self-organizing properties. For example, when outcomes are important to people, they tend to take credit for successful performance and deny responsibility for failure; that is, to maintain favorable self-evaluations and to avoid unfavorable ones (Greenwald, 1980; Heider, 1944). However, if their self-evaluative habits are negative, people may selectively perceive information that confirms their incompetence; this is a problem psychotherapists often find in patients. Langer (1979) documents the harmful effects of erroneous self-evaluations of incompetence.

Self-esteem refers to evaluations of one's personal and social worth, rather than to evaluations of one's competence. It may be constructed, in part, from evaluations of performance feedback. For example, while people are in school, their self-esteem and educational accomplishment appear to be significantly related; but later in life, self-esteem and occupational status are related while the impact of educational attainment fades (Bachman & O'Malley, 1977). However, self-esteem appears to be significantly influenced by the actual or anticipated social evaluative feedback provided by others. For example, people with high communication apprehension tend to have low self-esteem (McCrosky, Paley, Richmond, & Falcione, 1977).

In many tasks, people are socially interdependent for producing desired outcomes. This requires knowledge about and acceptance of the goals and behaviors of others and meshing one's interests and actions with theirs (e.g., in computer programming teams, Weinberg, 1971). Thus, there is feedback not only about task accomplishment, but also about social relationships as instrumentalities for task accomplishment (McClintock, 1978). Moreover, social acceptance appears to be of inborn importance to humans (see Chapter 13), so evaluative feedback from others has a basic significance of its own. This has led some to propose that one's self-concept is largely a social product (Porter & Washington, 1979). Self-evaluative thoughts interact with evaluations of transactional functioning. Therefore, cognitive regulation of performance is considered next.

Performance Regulation

To be effective, environmental transactions must be guided by relevant information. Therefore, cognitive regulation of such performances is of fundamental importance. Performance regulation that has been most thoroughly studied in regard to work performance-job satisfaction (see Campbell & Pritchard, 1983; Locke, 1983, for recent reviews), and achievement motivation (See Dweck & Elliott, 1983; Fyans, 1980, for recent reviews). Early studies of performance regulation grossly oversimplified the process, often implicitly assuming one goal and regulatory rule or value combination. However, further empirical work revealed that people guide their job performance with a personal goal hierarchy. Therefore, multiple values (i.e., regulatory criteria) of varying influence relative to multiple goals must be simultaneously operative.

For example, factor analytic studies of *job dimensions* or sources of *job satisfaction* have produced from 4 to 20 categories of job consequences against which job satisfaction may be evaluated (Dawis, Lofquist, & Weiss, 1968; Quinn & Cobb, 1971; Vroom, 1964). Ilgen, Fisher, and

Taylor (1979) consolidate them into three sources of feedback that people can use to evaluate their performance: (a) the task environment including feedback inherent in the task (e.g., task accomplishment), and feedback contingent on task accomplishment (e.g., pay); (b) other people, and (c) self-judgments. Locke (1973) developed two broad categories, each of which contains subcategories: (a) events (e.g., task activity, task success, pay, promotion, responsibility, physical working conditions); and (b) agents (e.g., self, supervisor, subordinate(s), co-workers, customers). Dweck and Elliott (1983) divide achievement motivation goals into two broad categories: (a) learning goals (e.g., to increase competence); and (b) performance goals (e.g., obtain favorable and avoid unfavorable judgments of personal competence). Parsons and Goff (1980) suggest dividing achievement into process and accomplishment goals and argue that in any achievement situation *incentive value* is composed of multiple process and accomplishment values. However, these and similar studies primarily represent descriptions of kinds of performance consequences (i.e., goals) towards which people frequently direct their actions. They provide little information about the kinds of regulatory criteria people use. For example, by what criteria do people decide when their task accomplishment on a job is satisfactory? When their pay is adequate? When their work meets with the approval of their supervisor? Of their coworkers? What kind of feedback information do they look for, and what criteria do they use to evaluate it? On the same job, different people may use different criteria.

Moreover, since typically people are simultaneously seeking combinations of consequences, they will often have to place priorities on them, giving some more importance than others. What kinds of evaluative criteria do people use to establish priorities, and how are they hierarchically organized? For example, how do employees determine the trade-off between the objective of excelling in task accomplishment and the possibility of coworker rejection because of competitive comparisons? Do they change their regulatory criterion from "excellent" to "adequate" task accomplishment? To do so would implicitly lower the goal priority of supervisor approval. Or do they give coworker approval a lower priority?

These examples illustrate that the discrepancies between goals and relevant feedback information can be reduced by (a) altering the nature or priority of goals against which the performance is compared; (b) altering the comparison or regulatory criteria used; or (c) altering the feedback information used. In the typical behavior episode, guided by multiple goals and regulatory criteria, it is probable that all three are used in combination to create a coherently organized, personal goal and regulatory criteria hierarchy. Moreover, that hierarchical organization is probably dynamic and may change during an episode. For example, an employee may have excellence in task accomplishment and supervisor approval higher in his or her goal hierarchy than coworker approval. However, at work, coworker disapproval of their "eager beaver" approach may be so strong or embarrassing that they shift coworker approval to a higher priority before the day is over. Similarly, the person's regulatory criteria may change. For example, their initial evaluative criteria for performance excellence may be substandard compared with similar employees, requiring a shift to higher personal standards if they hope to keep their job.

Difficulty in establishing a goal and evaluative criteria hierarchy that leads to adequate simultaneous satisfaction for all of one's objectives is a common source of intra- and interpersonal conflict and of affective discomfort. For example, in job or school situations there are typically direct task goals (e.g., successful task accomplishment); consequences contingent on task accomplishment (e.g., pay, grades); social consequences (e.g., approval of teachers or coworkers); and self-efficacy consequences (e.g., maintenance of self-respect). Creating behavior patterns that simultaneously produce all of these conditions of satisfaction within current environmental and personal competence constraints is not a simple task, and skill in doing so is one major product of effective child socialization.

Some evidence suggests that developmental changes occur in goal priorities and regulatory criteria. For example, there appears to be a dramatic decline over the grade school years in children's intrinsic interest in learning (i.e., direct task accomplishment goals) compared to their desire to obtain teacher approval and good grades through their performance (Harter, 1981). However, task accomplishment goals and criteria appear to regain some priority in post grade school years (Heckhausen, 1981).

These data may illustrate a process of differentiation and elaboration of personal goal hierarchies and regulatory criteria. For example, when children first enter grade school, they have a whole new social milieu with which to cope. To some extent they are in competition with other children, perhaps for the first time, for attention and approval of significant adults (e.g., their teachers) and their peers. Moreover, social approval is a contingency used by some teachers to influence and control a classroom of energetic and diverse youngsters. Therefore, it should not be surprising that social approval goals and regulatory criteria might assume increased priority for many grade school children.

However, as they proceed through school, the classroom and peer group conditions they experience vary and they find different organizations of governing functions effective in different settings. Increased skill in organizing personal goal and regulatory criteria hierarchies to meet different behavior episode conditions may result, such as combining task accomplishment and social approval goals in more integrated ways.

More research needs to be directed at how people construct, organize, use, and revise performance regulatory criteria. Questions that might be addressed include: 1. What kinds of regulatory-evaluative criteria do people use (a) to establish priorities among their personal goals both in general and within particular behavior episodes? (b) to evaluate alternate potential behavior patterns for accomplishing their objectives? (c) to select and evaluate feedback information about progress towards their objectives? and (d) to evaluate alternate potential regulatory criteria? 2. How and when do people construct or learn such criteria? 3. How do the criteria they use influence attention-perceptual processes? 4. How do they become organized both in general and in specific behavior episodes?

There are some clues in existing scientific and clinical literature. For example, Ilgen, Fisher, and Taylor (1979) argue that people approach task with a "set" for feedback consistent with their history of experience in similar tasks. They must first accurately perceive the relevant feedback information, and then they must evaluate it as *relevant* and *credible*. For example, if your mother or father criticizes your artistic creation, you may ignore that feedback as irrelevant and not credible because they have no expertise or talent in art. However, you may become irritated or discouraged because you implicitly interpret that feedback as relevant, credible information about their regard for your general competence.

A diversity of regulatory criteria besides (reduce the discrepancy to zero) were illustrated in Chapters 2 and 3; for example, (reduce the discrepancy to a certain level). People can achieve many goals at different levels rather than simply failing or succeeding. For example, one student may use a C grade as a satisfactory standard for school performance (reduce the discrepancy to a certain level), while another accustomed to always earning an A (reduce the discrepancy to zero) might consider a C a failure. People appear to adjust their performance standard with experience (regulate the discrepancy around a floating average) (Campbell & Pritchard, 1983; Locke, 1983). This process of progressively adjusting performance standards, or the evaluative criteria, is a source of continued effort towards improvements in human endeavors. Achieving excellence in any endeavor is impossible without critical self-appraisal "which apprehends the norm and holds it before us as a basis for judgment" (J. E. Smith, 1980).

Research on levels of aspiration (Frank, 1941; Lewin, Dembo, Festinger, & Sears, 1944) addressed people's development and use of performance standard criteria. Research on that general idea is reincarnate as "subjective estimates of probability of task success" or "expectancy confidence" in current expectancy-value models (Klitzner & Anderson, 1977; Wollert, 1979). People develop different habitual criteria about the performance standards they set for themselves, and many people prefer a "more challenging" to an "easier" task (Locke, 1983). But clinicians describe clients who have a habit of setting lower performance standards in order to avoid the misery of evaluating themselves as failures.

Equity theory (Adams, 1965) examines how people develop and use social comparison criteria to evaluate the adequacy of their performance and the related consequences (e.g., salary). Identifying consistent patterns of goal-evaluative criteria selection could be one significant focus of personality research. Humans are social organisms living in complexly organized, mutually interdependent groups. They require regulation of social relations among their components or group members. That kind of regulation will be examined next.

Cognitive Regulation of Social Relations

Individuals function as components of social groups, which are themselves living systems. As such, social groups also require social-regulatory processes to coordinate the functioning of their human components. Organization is present when constraining and facilitating conditionalities exist (see Chapter 3). In human terms, this means that the continued existence and functioning of social organizations requires regulatory rules and processes (a) which constrain the functioning of each person in certain ways (e.g., you shall not steal another's property); (b) which facilitate their functioning in other ways (e.g., you will be cared for when you can not care for yourself); and (c) which subordinate some individual interests to the welfare of the social organization (e.g., you will serve and perhaps die for your country in times of war).

Social organizations differ in the relative emphasis placed on these three kinds of conditionalities, and the kinds of regulatory rules constructed for each. For example, totalitarian states place heavy emphasis on category (c), while democracies give more emphasis to categories (a) and (b). Parenting practices can be characterized in terms of different emphases on different types of regulatory rules (Maccoby & Martin, 1983). However, all three types of regulation must exist to some extent for social organization to be maintained. Anarchy exists when these regulatory arrangements break down, and when each component of the social group or society functions solely in its self-interest. Conditions in Lebanon in the 1980s are illustrative, where government is ineffective and different political factions continue to slaughter one another.

Social organizations are living systems. Therefore, when their continued existence and functioning is threatened, self-organizing regulatory processes will operate to try to maintain or restore the organization. For example, during the Vietnam war protests on American university campuses, the universities' functioning was disrupted. Public and legislative reactions threatened further disruption through reduction of financial and public support. A diversity of regulatory methods were tried, ranging from negotiation with, through discipline or expulsion of the disrupters, to calling in police or military force.

Humans have developed two interrelated social-regulatory methods: (a) to impose and enforce regulatory rules on social components through power and physical arrangements external to the organization's components, whether social groups or individuals (e.g., through laws and punishment, police action, imprisonment); (b) to make the regulatory rules and processes properties of the components themselves so that they become self-regulating in relationship to the social organizations of which they are a part.

When person-based self-regulation begins to break down, societies typically increase external regulation as stability-maintaining processes. For example, public discouragement with the growth of violent crime and with seemingly ineffective rehabilitative programs produced pressure in the United States for increased external regulation (e.g., enlarged emphasis on imprisonment, reinstatement and use of the death penalty). Similarly, when Polish labor organizations threatened existing political and social arrangements in Poland, military force was called in to maintain the status quo while steps were taken to neutralize the influence of the disrupting components. Efforts to control racial strife in South Africa in the 1980s are also illustrative.

Because humans are self-constructing living systems, social regulation cannot be permanently accomplished by external regulation alone, or even primarily. There must be shared commitments among the social components and generally agreed upon regulatory rules by which each component abides (even if that agreement results from the threat of external coercion). Even in totalitarian societies, extensive efforts are focused on cultivating shared beliefs and establishing laws that will regulate individuals' behavior to help maintain the existing social organization. Externally imposed social regulation can only supplement, but cannot permanently replace individual self-regulation. That principle has fundamental practical implications for all kinds of social groups from families to societies.

After a flurry of work on personal social or moral regulation early in this century (Hartshorne et al., 1928, 1929, 1930; Piaget, 1932/1965), the topic was relativly dormant for a quarter of a century. It continued to receive some attention in personality theory (Sears, 1960), but it was the

Piaget based research program of Kohlberg, beginning with his doctoral dissertation (Kohlberg, 1958), that breathed new vitality into this domain (see Kohlberg, 1969, for a good summary of his ideas; see Rest, 1983, for a recent relevant review).

Regulation of social relationships is considered here under four topics: (a) the types of social-moral regulatory criteria humans construct and use; (b) sources of such regulatory rules; (c) the development and organization of social-moral evaluative thoughts; and (d) the relationship of moral reasoning to moral behavior.

Types of Social-Moral Evaluative Criteria.   Some social regulatory concepts refer to properties of social groups and some to individuals' beliefs. Table 12.1 illustrates how such concepts parallel one another and facilitates synthesis across some discipline boundaries. For example, psychologists use person-attribute concepts for phenomena similar to that anthropologists and sociologists discuss with group-attribute concepts. People studying moral reasoning recognize "that not all human values are . . . moral values" (Rest, 1983), but they do not clearly specify the distinctions. Rest (1979, 1983) asserts that morality criteria are limited to justice and fairness in social relations. Rawls (1971) proposes that moral reasoning regulates the benefits and burdens of social collaboration. Turiel (1978, 1983) reports evidence that, from early childhood onward, people think quite differently about morality criteria and other social regulatory criteria. Rest (1983) criticizes Turiel's distinction on grounds that both morality and social convention relate to social organization. That is true because they are both subtypes of social regulatory criteria. However, the subdivision is useful because one primarily promotes group identity and cohesion, while the other protects individual or subgroup welfare.

For example, many customs and social conventions promote intragroup cohesion and identity by eliminating individual differences (e.g., Do you wear your school colors to athletic contests?). Moral values also promote synchronization of group components, but add requirements that the methods of synchronization do not damage or exploit some of the group's components in the interest of others (e.g., protection of life and possessions). Laws primarily represent codified application of shared ethical-moral principles. Most efforts to identify and classify different types of social regulatory criteria have focused on the subtype called morality, and several different classification systems have been proposed (Damon, 1980; Eisenberg-Berg, 1979; Kohlberg, 1976; Rest, 1979, 1983). In general, they all seem to encompass principles of *self-interest, social responsibility, equity,* and *reciprocity.*

Sources of Social Regulatory Criteria.   Social regulatory thoughts are constructed from two primary information sources: subjectively experi-

TABLE 12.1

An Illustrative Summary of Different Classes of Regulatory Rules or Principles, Relevant Concept Labels for Each Class when Referred to as a Property of a Social Group or a Person, and Their Hierarchical Relationships to one Another

Social Regulatory Function	Concept Labels	
	Group Attributes	Person Attributes
Authoritative standards for typical or expected forms of behavior representing long-established practices within a group, which function to regulate and coordinate functioning in the group Examples: marital fidelity; property rights	Social customs, mores, and norms	Values and ideals for evaluating behavior as correct, useful, or good
Arbitrary standards for social behavior in particular kinds of situations based on accepted usage Example: dress codes	Social conventions	Conventional values
Principles or rules that function as guidelines for evaluating actions in terms of their impact on the welfare, rights, and responsibilities of others Example: protection of life	Ethics	Moral values
Formally established rules of conduct recognized as binding on all group members, and enforced with sanctions by some controlling authority within the group Example: laws about murder	Laws	Values about legally defined rules of conduct

enced affective information and social perceptions. Such cognitive constructions can then function as a third source of information for the construction of additional regulatory thoughts. Rogers (1951) proposes that it is conflict between values constructed from affective (organismic) versus social bases that is at the core of many psychological problems. In recent years, more empirical attention has been given to the social and cognitive than to the affective sources.

The role of emotions in regulating social relations has received considerable attention in psychotherapy theory and practice, and in personality and social psychology. In Chapter 13, one subtype of basic emotions is called *social emotions*. It is argued that they evolved in humans to help regulate social relations since humans' survival and reproductive advantages were a function of social organization. Different kinds of social interactions trigger different kinds of emotions (e.g., affection, loneliness, guilt, or shame). For example, Ausubel (1955) concluded that shame and guilt are among "the most important psychological mechanism" for the socialization of individuals to conform to social standards, and that their occurrence is a function of particular kinds of social perceptions and social cognitions. Scholars have coined the word, *socioemotional* to designate the close link between emotions and social phenomena (Campos, Barrett, Lamb, Goldsmith, & Steinberg, 1983). For example, some emotions provide the initial basis for infant-adult bonding so essential for infant survival. Behavioral indicators of emotions, such as facial gestures or voice intonations and volume, powerfully influence infant-adult social interactions before extensive infant learning has occurred.

Dienstbier (1984) concludes that emotions and thoughts function as different but related regulatory processes in moral socialization. Current thoughts or circumstances in a behavior episode involving morality issues trigger the activation of a relevant schema composed of "a complex of values, attitudes, cognitions, and emotional responses." Emotions may be triggered both by schema-related thoughts and by perceptions of the current social episode. The kind and intensity of the emotions aroused are both important, and people's behavior appears to be affected differently by attributions of the cause of an emotional experience to internal or external sources.

Perceptions of social interactions of oneself and others is the second information source for social regulatory criteria. To function as components of social organizations such as families and villages, infants must learn, and learn to live by, regulatory criteria and processes which govern those social organizations: they must become socialized. The rules may differ within the same type of organization (e.g., between families), between types of situations for the same organization (e.g., the family at home versus in a public place), and from one social organization to another (e.g., family versus school versus peer groups); and the rules may be contradictory (e.g., what is OK with peers may not be OK at home). Therefore, children must learn both the existing regulatory rules, and organizations and settings in which each is appropriate. Adults may have to learn new regulatory criteria in an unfamiliar culture.

The first two groups to which children must become socialized are their families (Maccoby & Martin, 1983) and their peers (Hartup, 1983). Therefore, children's first social regulatory beliefs reflect family and peer values. The ways in which people come to conceptualize and reason about their social world and social relations has spawned a new field of study called *social cognition* (Shantz, 1983), of which social-regulatory conceptions are a subset. Socialization is efficient because children need only to learn, rather than construct, the nature and operation of existing social regulatory rules.

The development and use of personal rules of moral behavior happens in the broader context of "progressive understanding of the purpose, function, and nature of social arrangements" (Rest, 1983), as a component of general social learning (Perry & Perry, 1984). For example, psychoanalytic theory views moral development as a function of the child's active efforts to internalize societal rules through family interactions which function as representatives of the culture (Hoffman, 1963). Rest (1983) subdivides the knowledge-information processing base for moral functioning into four interrelated components analogous to aspects of behavior episodes: (a) perceiving and interpreting the situation in terms of potential impact on people's welfare; (b) evaluating potential courses of action against moral criteria; (c) selection of a moral course of action to achieve moral outcomes; and (d) executing the selected course of action in a moral way.

However, not all social relationships are regulated by established rules which can be learned. Individuals also construct their own interaction rules through the evaluative feedback they provide one another during the interaction. The influence of such interpersonal evaluations is a function of the BES within which the information is interpreted (Meyer et al., 1979; Shrauger & Schoeneman, 1979). Frequent interaction with the same persons can result in the construction of shared regulatory rules specific to their relationship, and may differ from one relationship to another. For example, during the first few months of life, infant-parent interactions become regulated by qualitatively different facial gestures and vocalization that occur contingently with different behavior patterns. Only later does verbal language become linked to the regulatory criteria constructed (Maccoby & Martin, 1983; Shantz, 1983).

Earlier in this century, Mead (1934) and Vygotsky (1962) argued that language and cognition have their origins in social interactions: recent research gives that view increasing empirical credibility (Lamb & Sherrod, 1981). For example, infants explore other humans with integrated, multimodal sensory-perceptual activities, and appear to be more sensitive to their dynamic (e.g., actions and emotional expressions) than to their static features. After the second month of life, infants' memories of their associations with others' behaviors become relatively stable. They learn how they are influenced by and can influence the behavior of others. Such early knowledge appears to be organized in, and progressively differentiated within, schema-scripts (Nelson, 1981).

Moreover, as Vygotsky proposed, children's cognitive development appears to be accelerated by social interactions that require them to mesh their thoughts and actions with those of others (Doise & Mackie, 1981). In addition, infants begin early to recognize that they and others have "psychological selves," or internal states of affect, intention, and thought, and this knowledge importantly influences their actions and social interactions. By their third year, the ability to recognize or infer the intentions and feelings of others and to recognize their own as they interrelate is fairly well developed (Bretherton, McNew, & Beeghly-Smith, 1981). This growing empathic capacity facilitates the performance of prosocial behaviors, the formation of friendships through reciprocal behaviors, and cognitive constructions to regulate social interactions (Marcus, 1980).

Individuals come to social interactions with "qualitative differences" in the ways their conceptions of "social reality" are organized. Therefore, effective interpersonal relations require "perspective coordination" among the participants (Selman, 1980). Perspective coordination skill is learned through practice in inferring others' perspectives and then acting accordingly. Infants cannot do that (so Piaget called them egocentric), but that skill develops rapidly thereafter. Children learn to guide their behavior (a) through knowledge of what people typically think, feel, or do in particular situations (called normative, consensus, or social-category information); (b) through knowledge of what the particular person typically thinks, feels, or does in that kind of situation (called consistency information); and (c) through using self-knowledge to estimate others' perspectives (often called situational or individual role taking) (Higgins, 1981; Shantz, 1983).

Perspective coordination or interpersonal synchronization can be significantly influenced by an affectively based process called empathy (Goldstein & Michaels, 1985; Hoffman, 1982). Empathy appears to be analogous to a resonance process. Its primitive version involves a personal emotional experience triggered by perceptions of another and related to the kind of emotion the other appears to be experiencing. Such "affective matching" occurs in parent-child interactions during the child's first 2 years (Maccoby & Martin, 1983). In adults, social cognitive learning combines affective matching with cognitively trying to take the other's perspective and communicating to the other person a feeling of caring and of trying to understand in a nonjudgmental way (Goldstein & Michaels, 1985). Most psychotherapists rely heavily on this adult form of empathic responding in their efforts to help troubled people.

Maccoby and Martin (1983) suggest that during childhood socialization (a) the emotions children experience during episodes of interpersonal interactions with parents may be at least as important in develop ing regulatory habits as the cognitive lessons they are learning; and (b) that parents' affective displays may have greater impact on their children's affective responses than the cognitive content of their communications. As expected within this living systems perspective, perceptual-affective regulation occurs first. Cognitive social regulation evolves through social learning. The two interact, but each can function relatively independently of the other.

Kohlberg's Theory: An Inadequate Example. The most extensive effort to create a developmental theory of cognitive social regulation is Kohlberg's theory of moral development, based upon Piaget's stage model of general cognitive development. Kohlberg proposed that everyone progresses through a sequence of different types of moral reasoning in the same order (although not necessarily at the same rate); that such development is irreversible, so people do not regress to "lower" stages once they have reached a "higher" one; that individuals' moral reasoning will be dominated by the type of reasoning characteristic of their current developmental stage; and that moral reasoning in later stages is "better" or "higher" than in earlier stages.

The concepts of *stages* and *moral reasoning typologies* are related but different. Kohlberg devised a set of classificatory rules (which he called scoring criteria) to classify peoples reasons for choosing one course of action over another in a moral dilemma. His content analysis focused on thematic and logical similarity of sets of reasons which he called *form of reasoning* rather than focusing on specific kinds of moral rules, which he called *moral content*. As others have pointed out (Levine, 1979; Simpson, 1974; Sullivan, 1977), it is methodologically impossible to separate "form" from "content." Therefore, Kohlberg's typology represents higher-order abstractions or general classes of moral criteria; that is, their "underlying organization and assumptive base" (Rest, 1983), defined by multiple content and form criteria.

In all polythetic classification schemes, of which Kohlberg's types of moral reasoning is an example, the defining attributes of each category (or type of moral reasoning) overlap somewhat, and no instance must meet all defining attributes to be considered an example of that type. Therefore, such classification decisions are often complicated, because classification decision rules reflect which and how many attributes must be present for an instance to be considered a member of a class. To some extent, classification schemes are arbitrary; they are designed to serve the designer's purposes. All publicly shared knowledge is anchored to agreed-upon classification schemes, and alternative schemes are possible. For example, Kohlberg and Wasserman (1980) present a 10-category classification scheme of universal moral values. Therefore, the first step in examining a theoretical proposal is to examine its classification scheme; that is, its basic concepts.

Kohlberg also arranged his classes of moral criteria into an age-graded sequence which he called *stages of development*. Much research has assumed the validity of his classification scheme and has focused upon the validity of his proposed developmental sequence. It is important to recognize these as separate but related issues. If the classification scheme is unsound for its purpose, then theories about development built upon it will be inadequate. Or, the researcher may shape the classification scheme to fit theoretical presuppositions.

The extensive body of empirical evidence generated by Kohlberg and others over a quarter of a century supports the conclusion that the kinds of moral reasoning and the criteria people use do elaborate as a correlate of age. However, this evidence does not support Kohlberg's stage model of development despite claims to the contrary (see Rest, 1983). A diversity of inadequacies have been identified in both his theories and his methods (Alston, 1971; Braun & Baribeau, 1978; Damon, 1980; Eisenberg-Berg & Neal, 1979; Garbarino & Bronfenbrenner, 1976; Gardner, 1979; Haan, 1978; Henry, 1980; Hoffman, 1980; Karniol, 1978; Kurtines & Grief, 1974; Levine, 1979; Moran & Joniak, 1979; Page & Bode, 1980; Peters, 1971; Rest, 1983; Simpson, 1974; Sullivan, 1977; Trainer, 1977; Turiel, 1983).

Kohlberg's classification of types of moral reasoning appears to reflect a particular philosophical position and a particular methodology. His proposed stages reflect a particular set of (Western) values (e.g., high levels of logical reasoning are best); this introduces biases into his methods for collecting and interpreting data. His model is vulnerable to most of the criticisms directed at Piaget's rationalistic approach from which it is descended (see Chapter 9). It represents a narrow segment of the kinds of evaluation processes people use to regulate their social behavior. For example, he largely ignores affective regulation and affective-cognitive interactions. Diverse evidence raises serious doubts that the sequence in which he has arranged his categories of moral reasoning reflect a universal, irreversible developmental sequence for every person in every context; it even raises doubts his classification scheme adequately represents both the consistency and diversity of moral reasoning.

At any but perhaps the earliest ages, the type of moral reasoning people use is not typically composed of more than 50% of one type of moral reasoning as asserted by Kohlberg and Wasserman (1980). For example, Trainer (1977) examined Kohlberg's doctoral dissertation data for his 86 subjects and found that 70 had less than 45% of their responses of one type. Of these, 27 had less than 35% and only 11 had more than 50% of their responses of a particular type. As Kohlberg's dissertation sample matured, they typically continued to use at least three of Kohlberg's types of moral reasoning (Kramer, 1968); and in the latest scoring system follow-up approximately 80% received "minor" as well as "major" moral "maturity" scores (Colby, 1979).

Kohlberg's primary research tactic has involved the questionable procedure of generalizing from *interindividual consistencies in groups* of people measured on a single occasion, to support his theory of *intraindividual* moral development. Little empirical evidence about actual patterns of individual development has been produced, but available data displays extensive intraindividual variability. For example, of two individual profiles presented in his thesis, one is bimodal and the other used four of Kohlberg's six categories of moral reasoning with about equal frequency. Other data indicates that (a) adults typically use multiple types of moral reasoning; (b) variability is particularly high in the adolescent years; and (c) even when people begin using one of the more abstract types (reach a "higher stage") they continue to use other types (e.g., show "stage reversals") (Haan, Smith, & Block, 1968; Kohlberg & Kramer, 1969; Page & Bode, 1980; Rest, 1983; Turiel, 1969; White, Bushnell, & Regenemer, 1978).

The pervasiveness of discrepant findings led to revisions of Kohlberg's classification (scoring) rules to reduce unwanted variability, on the assumption that it was the measurement procedures rather than the classification scheme or the theory that was at fault (Colby et al., 1980). The changes are not trivial. For example, the same protocols scored with the 1958 rules and a revised set of scoring rules correlated only .39 (Rest, 1983). Greater consistency appears to be obtained primarily by classification rules which involve discarding discrepant data through a successive approximation method of classification (Page & Bode, 1980; Rest, 1979, 1983). The measurement procedures have been reshaped to support the theory. Moreover, measurement methods others have tailored to small children reveal that they are capable of using a greater diversity of moral reasoning and criteria than Kohlberg's theory acknowledges (Darley, Klosson, & Zanna, 1978; Eisenberg-Berg & Neal, 1979; Eisenberg-Berg & Roth, 1980; Karniol, 1978; Schleiffer & Douglas, 1973; Wellman, Larkey, & Sommervile, 1979). The kinds of moral reasoning elicited from 4-year-olds through adults varies with the level of sophistication of the language or the media used in the measures, with their informational content, and with whether the circumstances evaluated are hypothetical or real.

Classifying people as manifesting a "higher" or "lower" kind of morality is itself a value judgment with potentially significant social implications. Kohlberg's designation of some approaches to morality as better than others seems to reflect his personal philosophy, and others are possible. As Urban (1980) put it, "by adopting the rationalist posture, he faces the dilemma of moral relativism, from which he tries to escape by postulating a developmental norm, but winds up in a cultural and historical relativism instead."

Kohlberg's rationale and methods have stimulated an enormous amount of research aimed at documenting and refining it. Its influence has been good because of the massive amount of useful information it has generated. However, its influence has become negative because its theoretical and methodological dominance, despite serious inadequacies, now constrains the interpretation of relevant data and the development of alternate, broader views. Koestler (1967) noted that despite extensive evidence concerning the inadequacy of a particular theoretical framework for understanding humans, it often continues to be influential in misdirecting scholarly efforts in its domain. In my opinion, that has occurred with Kohlberg's approach. Its limitations are sufficiently extensive so that study of moral development in particular, and social regulatory processes in general, would profit from new, more broadly conceived efforts and a relegation if Kohlberg's model and measurement methods to psychology's history.

Moral, Affective, Cognitive, and System Development.   It is time to build upon the results of, rather than within, Kohlberg's framework. If cognitive and affective regulation are linked, then one should expect some correspondence between classification schemes for the two kinds of regulation. For example, one common functional classification of affect is approach-avoidance. Analogously, Tisak and M. Ford (1982) examine active and inhibitive morality. Eisenberg-Berg (1979) argues for the study of prosocial-cooperative moral criteria to supplement study of criteria aimed at avoiding negative social consequences. In living systems terms, social organization requires both facilitating and constraining regulation, and both affective and cognitive regulation should manifest subtypes within those two broad classes.

As Rest (1983) points out, Piaget's proposals about cognitive organization (which Kohlberg adopted) predated the more recent explosion of knowledge about cognition. Proposals about the organization of moral reasoning should be compatible with general knowledge about cognition. For example, Rest (1983) assumes that the basic organizations of moral thinking are best represented as "different schemes of (social) cooperation" rather than rigid, irreversible stages. Reformulating the concept of stages of development in terms of the concept of system states (Dubin, 1978; Urban, 1987) may be useful. A system is an organization of components each of which may take on different values.

A system is said to be dynamic (a) when it maintains stability in the face of variability in component values, called a system steady state; and (b) when it can change to a new state as a function of changes in component values. In living systems, many steady states are reoccurring (e.g., sleep-wakefulness, habitual performances). Some do not reoccur (e.g., an adult cannot physically become a child again). The concept of stages promulgated by Piaget and Kohlberg asserts that cognitive functioning develops through a series of such nonreoccurring system states.

A living systems framework proposes a clear alternative. What happens during functional (i.e., psychological-behavioral) development is that the states in which the system may function become both more diverse and more elaborate. Which potential system state is operative at any moment will be a function of the facilitating and constraining properties both of the current system and its context. Most such states can, therefore, be reoccurring. For example, an adult may at times use childlike reasoning or become incontinent like an infant. *Probabilistic epigenesis* is one name given to a similar alternative view (Gottlieb, 1983).

Within this view, research should focus on (a) the diversity of states of which the system is or can become capable (e.g., Vygotsky's *"zone of proximal development"*); (b) the conditions under which such state capabilities can develop; and (c) the conditions under which different system states become operative. To demonstrate the existence of irreversible cognitive stages, it is necessary to demonstrate that under no conditions can certain previously operative system states become operative. If one discards the "blinders" imposed on interpreting the data by Kohlberg's classification scheme, measurement procedures, and stage theory, the data seem to be better represented by a probabilistic epigenetic or living systems framework.

Most of the research on moral reasoning has used a limited range of controlled contexts, as in studies of "moral dilemmas," usually using verbally simulated rather than actual situations; and it has assumed a normatively expected developmental environment for the persons studied. Little attention has been given to variability across different kinds of contexts, a deficiency which Shantz (1983) notes is typical of the general field of social cognition. Study is needed of relationships between the development of social regulatory cognitions and changes in individuals' social context.

Examples include studies of covariation of different parenting styles with the development of different patterns of thought, emotions, and actions among children (Maccoby & Martin, 1983); and studies of relationships between individuals' behavior patterns and patterns of peer group functioning (Hartup, 1983). Moreover, the impact of different contexts on the values and behavior patterns different children develop must be understood as interactive, which would make inappro priate the continued use of simplistic additive or elaborative models of social development (Hartup, 1980). For example, a strong shift to dependence on peers for value orientation during adolescence typically does not occur unless the parents are uninvolved, inattentive, and unsympathetic towards their children (Elder, 1980). Moreover, where the child adopts the values regulating social relationships within the family along with their consequences, it is probable that they will tend to selectively involve themselves with peer groups whose values are compatible with their own.

Methodologically, erroneous inferences about cognitive development will result when based solely on interindividual, single measurement occasion data (Nesselroade & Ford, 1985, 1987). Research using designs that will provide data about intraperson social cognitive development is seriously needed (Shantz, 1983).

Values are Hierarchically Organized.   The developmental principles in Chapter 5 predict that social regulatory cognitions will develop from low-level abstractions representing perceptions of particular social situations, to progressively more abstract representations organized in componentized and embedded hierarchies. The research on moral development generally supports that prediction. In that sense, people move from lower to higher levels of abstraction in their moral reasoning.

However, those principles also predict (a) that regulatory cognitions will be learned initially in relationship to sets of similar situations; (b) that regulatory cognitions may differ for different kinds of situations; (c) that since participation in different kinds of social situations is to some extent age-graded within a particular culture, there will be some covariation between age and social regulatory criteria used; (d) that individuals will differ in the sequence in which they learn different kinds of regulatory strategies because of differences in their social contexts; (e) that they may differ in the organization of their regulatory conceptions (e.g., some may have all such cognitions organized in a tight hierarchy, while others may have several relatively unrelated hierarchies); (f) that the kinds and levels of abstraction of regulatory principles that individuals develop will differ as a function of their social experiences; and (g) that regulatory functioning may become highly habitual and individuals may not find it easy to consciously represent the evaluative reasoning guiding their behavior.

Relationships Between Cognitive Social Regulation and Action.   Blasi (1980) reviewed 75 relevant studies and concluded that existing evidence documents a relationship between values and actions. Other research also supports that conclusion (Rest, 1983). However, these are generally correlational studies using group designs and the correlations are typically modest at best. Efforts to influence moral functioning using Kohlberg's and other conceptions (Berkowitz & Oser, 1985) have not produced impressive or consistent results. This may be at least partly because the evaluation research designs used have frequently been flawed (Sebes & Ford, 1984). Cognitive regulatory processes can be used not only to justify socially desirable behaviors, but also to justify the most henious actions against others, as history demonstrates (Haan, Aerts, & Cooper, 1985). Thus, understanding the relationship between moral reasoning and moral action is much more complicated than the simple linear relationships assumed in the data analytic models used in most studies.

One problem has been an oversimplification of the expected relationships. This living systems framework makes it clear that the relationships between social regulatory cognitions and actions are indirect. What one does in a particular instance will usually be a function of multiple and simultaneously operating goals and regulatory criteria, one's perception and interpretation of the constraining and facilitating conditions of the current situation, one's behavioral repertoire, one's self-perceptions relevant to that situation, one's estimates of the intents and probable actions of others, and the affects one is experiencing at the time. The relative influence of each of these components will vary with the nature of the behavior episode and the extent to which habitual functioning can prevail. Stated in systems terms, when a system is composed of multiple components, system states cannot be adequately predicted solely on the basis of knowledge of the value of only one component. It is the pattern of values for all the components comprising the system that defines its states (Dubin, 1978).

The findings of the extensive studies of moral behavior by Hartshorne and colleagues (1928, 1929, 1930) illustrate the necessity for understanding moral functioning not as as general trait, but as a product of situational-perceptual-cognitive-affective interactive processes. For example, they found that there was no high degree of consistency in the moral behavior of children. They might cheat, lie, or steal in one situation but not another. High cheaters were no more likely to steal than low cheaters. In living systems terms, how one acts (including moral actions) must be understood as a component of a BES guided behavior episode. People develop a repertoire of BES, and the components of each (including the regulatory components) may differ depending on the purposes and contexts for which the BES was constructed. System states change as a function of changes in the values of their components and of components of their contexts.

Emotional arousal evolved before cognitive regulation to regulate the relations among internal states action patterns, and interactions with contexts. Therefore, emotions are examined in the next chapter.

13

Energizing Selective Action and Emotional Arousal

INTRODUCTION

For effective functioning within their highly variable environments, the intensity and rate of humans' behavior varies dramatically, therefore requiring the production and use of varying amounts of energy. Humans are functionally organized to "fine tune" their production and distribution of energy to match their energy-using demands. That matching process is exquisitely automated and occurs without conscious planning or intentional regulation through a coordinated symphony of the central nervous (CNS), the autonomic nervous system (ANS), the endocrine system, the circulatory system, and local tissue and muscle conditions. Components in the "energy-transducing system" are closely interrelated through "a series of complicated feedback loops" that involve "chemical messengers," an "omnipresent nerve network," and "mechanical and hydraulic linkages" (Shepard, 1982). Multiple variables are involved such as the availability of nutrients, fluids, and minerals; oxygen for "burning" those fuels, appropriate temperatures for efficient "combustion," and a variety of chemical compounds to influence the process. Different circumstances require different patterns of "tuning" in different parts of the body, so it is more complicated than just turning the "volume" up or down.

Cells function as energy transducers, combining materials in chemical processes that transform stored energy to perform "work" (e.g., muscle contractions). The necessary materials are provided in a varying flow by the circulatory system, which obtains oxygen through respiration and other materials from many body organs and tissues. Therefore, significant variations in energy production and utilization involve coordinated variability in most aspects of biological functioning. There is a general pattern for accomplishing that, herein called *activity arousal*. It is considered in the next section. Following that, specialized variations on that general pattern, called *emotional arousal*, are examined.

ACTIVITY AROUSAL

Energy production and utilization vary in amount and body location as a function of the vigor and kind of activity being performed. For example, contrast dozing on the beach on a summer afternoon with fighting the waves to save a drowning child. In deep sleep, there is little motor activity, electrical brain waves and breathing are slow and regular, pulse rate and blood pressure are lowered, and there is little eye movement. At this low level of parasympathetic nervous system (PNS) dominated activity, a person uses only approximately 65 calories per hour. As ICA arousal and activity increase, the CNS and the sympathetic nervous system (SNS) of the ANS mobilize appropriate amounts of energy when and where needed to support variable activity levels. For example, heart rate increases to pump blood more rapidly; blood pressure rises; the rate of blood flow to the skeletal muscles and brain increases; blood vessels of the abdominal-pelvic viscera constrict to reduce energy usage there; contraction of the smooth muscles of the stomach, intestine, and other viscera is inhibited; coagulation time of the blood is decreased; breathing rate and volume increase; the spleen releases stored red blood cells into the bloodstream to provide more oxygen transport capacity; sweat glands excrete faster to help dissipate the increased heat being generated and to remove wastes; and fatigue is inhibited (Tarpy, 1977).

Quantitative Variations

The *amount* of energy needed can vary extensively. For example, dressing in the morning uses about 118 calories per hour, jogging five miles in an hour about 600 calories, and walking upstairs about 1,100 calories per hour. Such variations require coordinated alteration of energy-producing biological processes. For example, strenuous exercise can increase blood flow in the muscles more than twentyfold, cardiac output 5 to 7 times normal rates, the removal of fat and other fuels from storage, and the blood concentration of free fatty acid as much as tenfold. Strenuous exercise may increase metabolic rate up to 2,000% of normal in trained athletes (Guyton, 1982).

Biochemical Influences. Local muscle tissue conditions and the CNS regulate short-term energy usage. Under longer term or emergency energy demands, the ANS and endocrine system regulate hormonal secretions into the blood stream which have profound and prolonged effects upon body tissues. The hypothalamus, "boss" of the ANS, "tunes" biological processes by linking CNS functioning to ANS and to endocrine methods for regulating energy production. In addition, it produces compounds that regulate hormone secretions from the pituitary gland, which in turn regulate secretions from many other glands and tissues. Moreover, neurons secrete a diversity of neurohormonal substances. Presently there are over forty such chemical compounds that are known to directly or indirectly alter cell and tissue functioning and energy production and utilization (Shepard, 1982).

Such chemical influences are orchestrated in complex patterns because they interact in their biological effects. Equifinality is apparent, since the same specific biological consequence can be produced with different patterns of neural-biochemical functioning (e.g., increases in heart rate can be produced in different ways). Multivariate mutual causality is nowhere more evident than in these neural-biochemical patterns (Brady, 1970) which involve a complex network of feedforward and feedback regulatory and control arrangements. Moreover, individual differences in neural-biochemical patterning influenced by genetic factors affect other behavior patterns such as differences in temperament (Grings & Dawson, 1978). For example, all members of a species display the same kinds of arousal patterns, but some individuals "react faster, with greater vigor, or more frequently than others" (Bruell, 1970).

Distributional Variations

Deviations from minimal levels of energy needs occur when a person does "work" through the operation of different living system functions. Variable governing functions use varying amounts of energy through the nervous system activity. Transactional functions represent another kind of work. For example, while the skeletal muscles constitute about 40% of a person's body weight, they receive only about 15% of the blood flow when they are at rest. However, that ratio changes drastically when the muscles become active. Biological self-organizing and self-construction functions, such as physical growth and tissue repair, represent a third kind of work.

The *location* of energy needs can vary extensively, depending on the nature of the activity. For example, sometimes the digestive system uses more energy and the legs do not need much (e.g., after a big dinner). Selective energy production requires selective resource distributions, so that parts that need more energy get more raw materials and parts that are not as active get less. For example, vasodilation occurs in active muscles to increase their blood supply, while vasoconstriction continues in inactive muscles. Blood flow increases in active parts of the neocortex. Information processing involves a somewhat different pattern than information collection; for example, heart rate accelerates rather than decelerates and skin resistance decreases. The greater the mental effort, the greater the magnitude of the changes (Grings & Dawson, 1978).

The Influence of Voluntary Action.　The regulation of energy production is hierarchical. Minor adjustments can be handled at local governing levels, but more extensive adjustments require coordination at higher governing levels. Voluntary action is controlled by CNS functioning: biological processes are coordinated by ANS and endocrine system adjustments. Centralized coordination of action demands with biological processes is accomplished through interactions of the neocortex, limbic system, and hypothalamus. Energy production through cell metabolism is controlled by general properties of cells and their extracellular fluids under base rate, self-maintenance conditions. However, increased energy demands such as the contraction of muscle fibers must be supported by surrounding tissue and the circulatory system, which draw upon other organs.

Voluntary action is initiated by a "directive" from the brain. That produces increased neural activity, efferent discharge from areas of the motor cortex, and preparatory alteration of the ANS pattern that generally increases SNS and decreases PNS activity. Heart rate and cardiac output begin to increase. Throughout the body, the arterioles (small blood vessels) of the skeletal muscles temporarily dilate. Reduction of blood flow to abdominal organs and the skin begins. At this point, the changes provide general support for initiating action anywhere in the body.

The motor cortex signals travel down the pyramidal fibers through the spinal cord to innervate the contraction of the relevant muscles, and to the cardioregulatory centers of the medulla where the heart rate can be directly influenced by them. The neural signals trigger processes that convert the stored chemical energy in the activated muscle cells into a tension that can perform external work. That disturbs the steady state of the muscle cells, and triggers compensatory mechanisms through positive and negative feedback loops which draw upon materials stored nearby to replace those used so that energy conversion can continue. The movement and temperature increase resulting from the muscle fiber contractions, along with metabolic products and local chemical factors, stimulate further dilation of the arterioles in the active muscles, thereby increasing their blood flow.

Meanwhile, arterioles in other muscles that receive no further SNS or local stimulation return to their normal constricted state. The result is selective distribution of the blood supply to actively contracting muscles where it is most needed. If the activity is sufficiently extensive and long-lasting, local adjustments will be insufficient and higher level regulation will become operative (e.g., respiration increases to increase the oxygen supply, and the SNS stimulates further dilation of the blood vessels in the active muscles). If the degree of physical exercise and its duration increase markedly, then biochemical changes (e.g., hormonal secretions) may occur to facilitate the higher rate of energy generation and utilization. There is a continuous flow of feedforward-feedback influences within and between governing levels that regulates the energy production and utilization functions (Winegrad, 1965). As prolonged voluntary effort produces severe fatigue, the muscle contractions may shift towards a more rhythmic, synchronized pattern, sometimes termed "phase of overcoming fatigue," and the action can then continue effectively a while longer (Morehouse & Miller, 1976). Thus, evolution has produced hierarchically organized energizing arrangements, with local regulation supplemented by regional and system-wide governance as needed.

Other Influences on Activity Arousal.   When biochemical and metabolic processes in the body go awry, activity level may be affected. In addition, the cognitive system controls activity level. The degree of arousal is determined by "the degree of *effort* required by the situation as *interpreted* by the *individual*" (Duffy, 1951). This is humorously illustrated by the person who tries to lift an apparently heavy box and nearly falls over backward because the effort exerted far exceeds the weight of the empty box. Different causes may produce similar changes in activity level, but require different treatment. For example, the treatment for a person with retarded activity levels resulting from a hypothyroid condition would be quite different from that for a person who is deeply discouraged or depressed.

Activity arousal is so pervasive and fundamental a part of everyday life that it often escapes notice. We stroll casually on a beautiful day. We go from immobility to a dead run in a second when playing tennis. We sit quietly reading. Our activity level and energy requirements vary continually throughout each day. A great deal is known about nutrition, metabolism, and their behavioral influences (Galler, 1984), and about perceptual and motor development in children (Cratty, 1970). However, how humans organize their energy production to support shifting patterns of activity arousal seems less well understood.

Activity Arousal and Nonemotional Feeling or Affective States

Some aspects of the biological functioning of the body can be attended to and enter consciousness. The ability to monitor internal states makes possible some voluntary control over biological processes through intentional selection of behavior patterns to influence such states (e.g., in response to abdominal pain one could stop eating, rest, take medication, or have surgery). Biofeedback procedures are based on this monitoring capability. Some monitored biological information is quite specific, such as the rate's of one's heartbeat or dryness of one's mouth. In addition, people can become aware of more generalized biological states, leading to some theoretical confusion since some of those states have been mistakenly classified as different kinds of emotional arousal (Ekman, 1984). It is true that different kinds of emotional arousal produce subjectively recognizable differences in feeling states. However, it does not follow that all types of feeling states reflect emotional arousal. Here the terms *feelings* or *affects* are used to encompass all subjectively recognizable body states, and the term *emotional arousal* to represent one subset of such affects.

Five Types of Nonemotional Affects. There are at least five subjectively recognizable types of feeling states that are manifestations of different biological-muscular patterns: relaxed-contented-drowsy; alert-restless-energetic; sluggish-tired-fatigued; physical discomfort; pain. Such affects may have a positive/negative valence, as do sensory affects (e.g., "that's delicious" or "that stinks"). Other affects may have a neutral valence (e.g., heartbeat). It is because experiences with positive valence are sought after and those with negative valence avoided that such biological states are said to have motivational qualities. It is the consequence that the behavior should produce that the affective valence helps identify, not the particular behaviors by which the consequence might be produced. These five types of affect represent different kinds of feedback signals reflecting activity arousal. Their regulatory roles are discussed more fully in Chapter 12.

In summary, bodily activity both affects and is affected by carefully orchestrated, hierarchically organized, variable energy producing an distributing processes. Most of these are highly automated and occur outside of awareness. However, manifestations of some body processes are monitored as feedback signals with positive or negative valences through attention-perceptual functions to guide self-organizing and self-constructive processes. Activity arousal emerges as the activity pattern unfolds. However, regulatory arousal in preparation for antici pated future conditions has special adaptive value. That is one of the primary functions of emotional arousal.

EMOTIONAL AROUSAL

Emotions represent complex patterns of preparation for different kinds of behavior demands that augment and amplify or attenuate activity arousal patterns. One component of emotional patterns provides informational feedback which people can consciously monitor and use to regulate their behavior. Therefore, emotions wed arousal and regulatory functions (see Chapter 12).

Historical Perspective

Interest in human emotions has a long history. Philosophers such as Aristotle and Nietsche as well as many scientists have sought to understand the role of emotions in behavior. Spinoza (Elwes, 1951) soundly characterized emotions as body modifications "whereby the active power of the said body is increased or diminished, ordered or constrained." Animals display emotions (Darwin, 1872), suggesting a long evolutionary history. For a century, the nature of emotions (James, 1884; Reymert, 1928, 1950), their development (Bridges, 1932), and their functioning in normal and disordered behavior (Freud, 1938; McDougall, 1933) has interested psychologists.

During the decade of the 1960s, theoretical and empirical examination of emotions mushroomed (Arnold, 1960; Buck, 1984; Duffy, 1962; Gellhorn & Loofbourrow, 1963; Greenberg & Safran, 1987; Knapp, 1963; Plutchik, 1962; Tomkins, 1962, 1963) and have continued unabated ever since (e.g., Candland et al., 1977; DeRivera, 1977; Ekman, 1973; Izard, 1977; Kemper, 1978; Lewis & Michalson, 1983; Lyons, 1980; Plutchik & Kellerman, 1980; Royce & Diamond, 1980; Russell, 1980). At least two major streams of scientific work have stimulated scholarly study of emotions. Advances in biology, particularly in neurology and neuroendocrinology, have brought much new, relevant information to light (Dunbar, 1954; Gasanov, 1974; Grings & Dawson, 1978, 1980; McGeer & McGeer, 1980; Pribram, 1967, 1971), and have fueled an explosion of pharmacological methods for influencing emotions (Tallman et al., 1980). In addition, emotional arousal has been extensively manipulated and studied with regard to its motivational properties (Cofer & Appley, 1964; Mowrer, 1960b; Young, 1961) and development, particularly in infants and young children (Izard, 1982; Lewis & Rosenblum, 1978).

Despite all this work, there is still no generally shared theoretical perspective concerning the nature and functioning of emotions, nor any

consistent terminology for describing and representing emotional phenomena. Emotions, feelings, affects, moods, arousal, activation, and
other terms are used with specific (though different) definitions by
some, and as if they were synonyms by others (Ekman, 1984). What
follows is an attempt to weave together threads of agreement to try to
tell a coherent story about the arousal and regulatory functioning of
human emotions within a living systems framework.

The Regulatory and Preparatory Functions of Emotions

As evolutionary products, emotions must have (or have had) some
adaptive utility. What might that be?

Evolutionary Origins of Different Emotions. Human behavior is a dynamic process flowing through space and time to selectively interact
with the individual's contexts to produce desired consequences and to
avoid or prevent undesirable ones. Therefore, effective behavior must
function not only in terms of "what's here" (the present), but also in
terms of "what's coming" (probable futures). Effectively targeted behavior requires both accurate observations and meaningful predictions. At
any point in time, the kinds of observations and predictions that are
needed are a function of the person's current behavioral episode.
Therefore, the utility of observations and predictions must be based on
an evaluation of their potential relevance to the individual's current
well- being and objectives; that is, based on upon their personal
meaning.

The most ancient form of this evaluative capability is the sense of
smell (see Chapter 8). Odors enable animals to "decide" in advance
whether a particular object of action is likely to produce "good" or "bad"
consequences in material exchange activities. The evaluative process
itself requires *investigatory activity* (e.g., orienting the body and head,
sniffing, licking the material). Then, *preparatory-consummatory activity*
could be initiated based on the resulting evaluative prediction (e.g.,
salivation; body movements to obtain the food). Thus, evaluative-
predictive processes are the trigger for organizing cognitive, autonomic,
endocrine, and sensory-motor components to support personally meaningful actions (e.g., eating, sexual encounters).

This model supports Plutchik's (1980) proposals that emotions
evolved and continue to function as primitive regulatory (i.e.,
evaluative-selective activation) processes. Emotional arousal patterns
probably evolved from the precursor evaluative-preparatory structural-
functional arrangements for smell and taste. For example, different
species and individuals emit different odors, so they smell different.
This discrimination could be linked to predictions or evaluations of their

potential personal relevance, and used to guide actions. So the evaluative capabilities of olfaction became linked to preparatory behavior patterns for social interaction with other animals. For example, when olfaction made it possible to predict which animals might be potential mates, that prediction could become linked to arousal patterns that served sexual behavior.

Thus, through an evolutionary process, animals evolved a set of differential arousal-behavior patterns, each of which was triggered into action by odor-based evaluative predictions (do not read that as cognitive predictions) meaningful for their current behavior episodes. Some were related to feeding and drinking activity, others to sexual activity, others to capturing prey, and others to escaping from predators. The animal has only one body, so the same biological processes are involved in all arousal patterns. A mechanistic tradition has encouraged a search for particular kinds of processes that distinguish one arousal pattern from another. Seen in this light, that is a fruitless search. It is primarily the organization of biological processes and their parameters, rather than the presence or absence of particular ones, that distinguishes many arousal patterns from one another.

Once this basic evaluative-preparation-for-action capability was constructed, it could evolve further modifications and elaborations. Three of importance to humans have occurred. The limbic system-hypothalamus axis coordinates these functions. (The limbic system was once called the rhinencephalon or "nose brain.") First, recall that all senses (e.g., vision, audition) evolved inputs into the limbic-hypothalamus circuit, diversifying the information sources upon which evaluative predictions and preparations for action could be based. Therefore, not only odors, but also sights, sounds, and other information could come to trigger differential patterns of arousal. Second, because limbic system structures are extensively linked to the neocortex in two-way communication, self-generated information (i.e., thoughts) could also trigger anticipatory and preparatory arousal patterns. Third, the attention-consciousness (ICA) arousal functions influence the brain structures involved in activity-emotional arousal functions. Therefore, some manifestations of arousal patterns could "enter" consciousness. This made it possible for people to distinguish between different arousal patterns and to give them different labels (e.g., pleasure, anger). Such affective information could then become part of the process itself. For example, awareness of a particular arousal pattern (e.g., anger) could trigger evaluative predictions (e.g., "I'll get punished") that could trigger other arousal patterns (e.g., fear).

These evaluative-predictive-preparatory patterns function as inborn action patterns. In humans, the evolution of cognitive governing capabilities not tied solely to the "here and now" of perceptions has introduced a greater degree of flexibility to emotional functioning. Thoughts could represent events not perceptually present, and expand humans' anticipatory capabilities, both by inhibiting and by triggering differential patterns of activity and emotional arousal.

Activity arousal varies with current conditions, but emotional arousal varies as a function of anticipated conditions. Emotions "help us know what to expect" and as a result they help us "to prepare for appropriate action" (Mowrer, 1960b); they result from "a change in the sets, expectations, and anticipations" produced by perceived events (Pribram, 1976a); they "depend on meanings" (Gellhorn & Loofbourrow, 1963); the emotion of stress "is in the eyes of the perceiver" (Cofer & Appley, 1964). When something is "intuitively appraised" as desirable, "we feel an attraction towards it"; and when "intuitively appraised" as threatening "we feel repelled from it" or "we feel urged to avoid it" (Arnold, 1960). Emotions function to prepare bodily processes to support approach or avoidant behavior (Grinker et al., 1956).

Chevalier-Skolmikoff (1973) suggests that many primate facial expressions are "intention movements," representing "the incomplete and preparatory phases of initially noncommunicative activities" (e.g., threat stares and posture as the first part of attack behavior). Therefore, certain kinds of facial expressions evolved as components of emotional patterns (Ekman, 1984). Young (1968) proposed that emotions function to "sustain" or "terminate" behavior episodes.

There is considerable evidence to support this scenario (Black, 1970). Electrical and mechanical stimulation of hypothalamic-limbic system circuits in diverse organisms produces emotional patterns of different types (e.g., rage, fear, affection) whereas stimulation of other brain structures typically does not trigger emotions (Leshner, 1977; Tarpey, 1977). Animals will behave to stimulate areas that produce "positive" emotional responses, and to terminate stimulation that produces "negative" emotions. Damage to limbic system circuits alters emotional functioning in humans and other mammals. Moreover, the limbic system has extensive interrelationships with the brain stem reticular activating system, and can add variations to (and be influenced by) ICA arousal.

Papez (1937) first proposed that the limbic system provides a neural mechanism for emotions. MacLean (1970b) describes three major limbic system subdivisions, two of which are linked to the primitive olfactory apparatus, and the third which largely bypasses it. One subdivision, fed by the amygdala, appears to be focused primarily on self-preservation emotions and behaviors (e.g., feeding, fighting, self-protection). The second, connected to the septal pathway, appears to be focused primarily on arousal patterns related to survival of the species (e.g., pleasure, cooperative social interactions such as grooming, and sexual behaviors). These two subdivisions are closely related and "presumably attributable to the olfactory sense," which has a long evolutionary history of "playing an important role in both feeding and mating" (MacLean, 1970b). The third subdivision (the largest in humans) is essentially nonexistent in reptiles, probably reflecting a shift from olfactory to visual influences on arousal functions. It is connected with the evolutionarily newer prefrontal cortex which seems to be involved in insight and foresight, providing capability for triggering emotions independent of external events (e.g., through dreams). Epileptic hippocampal seizure discharges tend to stay within the limbic system, and seizure experiences are filled with evaluative and emotional content (MacLean, 1970a). These structural arrangements support viewing emotional arousal as being represented by a central state (e.g., Bindra, 1970), coupled with differing patterns of ANS controlled biological functioning (Delgado, 1970), and expressive behaviors (Ekman, 1984), with some genetically based individual differences (Bruell, 1970).

Neuroregulators appear to be significantly involved in the occurrence and experience of emotions (Ax, 1953; Barchas et al., 1978; Marx, 1985c; Shildkraut & Kety, 1967;). So far, over 40 such compounds have been identified that may influence neuronal transmission, called *neurotransmitters*, or that may amplify or damper neuronal activity, called *neuromodulators*. Limbic system structures differ in their concentration of neuroregulators (e.g., norepinephrine—hypothalamus; dopamine—basal ganglia), and mood-altering drugs appear to act through their influence on neuroregulatory chemical functions in such structures. Like olfactory-related arousal patterns, emotional arousal is episodic, occurring only when relevant conditions exist rather than continuously as is ICA arousal. Therefore, emotional arousal adds variations to ICA arousal and to ongoing patterns of activity, either amplifying or attenuating them.

Emotional Arousal and Learning. These "good" or "bad," "successful" and "nonsuccessful" kinds of evaluations play a critical role in learning (Berlyne, 1964). Spatial-temporal contiguity of events plus some evaluative reaction to them both appear to be necessary for the learning of most behaviors. People tend to learn behaviors that help produce desired consequences or that prevent or terminate undesirable ones. Since the limbic system regulates emotional arousal, it appears probable that it plays a fundamental role in learning. The hippocampus may be a likely point of interface between the neocortex and the limbic system for this learning process (e.g., MacLean, 1970b; Routtenberg, 1968). Differential ICA and AE arousal appear to perform an information amplifying and attenuating function within the learning process through limbic system activity. Moreover, one of the adaptive characteristics of basic emotional arousal patterns is that they are highly "learnable"; that means that through learning almost any kind of event can come to trigger any emotion.

In summary, emotional patterns function to provide information *about the potential positive or negative personal value of current and probable future conditions or consequences; to alter the body's current biological arousal pattern; and to prepare for relevant actions.* Although excesses or deficits of emotional arousal can be disruptive and maladaptive, emotions evolved to facilitate effective adaptation.

The Number of Emotional Arousal Patterns

Is there one kind of emotional arousal that individuals may interpret differently, or are there different kinds?

Only One Kind. Research by Schachter and Singer (1962) was interpreted to support the first view. Two groups of students were injected with epinephrine (a neurohormone), and two with a saline solution. No group knew which they received. One epinephrine and one saline group took an examination in a hostile social environment and the others took the same exam in a friendly context. The epinephrine students reported feeling more hostile or more friendly than the saline groups in both exam conditions, implying that what people call the "arousal" they are experiencing is determined by the setting rather than by the nature of the arousal process itself. Based on such research, Schachter (1964) presented a "two factor" theory which asserted that arousal is undifferentiated except in attributes such as intensity and duration. The cognitive label given each experience is the result of the current circumstances and the individual's experiential history.

This view continues to be presented as credible (e.g., in general psychology texts) despite the fact that the design and interpretation of the original study was seriously flawed (Marshall & Zimbardo, 1979; Maslach, 1979); and that it is not supported by other research (Cotton, 1981; Kemper, 1978; Manstead & Wagner, 1981). Recent reviews of Schachter's theory and related evidence (Leventhal & Tomarken, 1986; Reisenzein, 1983) conclude that there is no convincing evidence that physiological arousal is a necessary condition for an emotional state, nor that emotional states may result from cognitive labeling of subjective experiences.

This living systems framework suggests an alternate interpretation of the Schachter and Singer (and related) data. If some biological change is triggered (as would occur with injections of epinephrine) which is a component of some emotional arousal patterns, a person's subjective experience might reflect that change. However, since it is only a fragment of a natural emotional arousal pattern (and may be a component of more than one kind of pattern), it is "out of context." With only a fragment of a pattern, a person would rely more heavily on contextual cues if asked to label a subjective experience. The logical fallacy in this whole stream of research is the assumption that manipulating one variable (e.g., epinephrine) will produce a full, natural emotional arousal pattern. The evidence is conclusive that it is the *patterning* of neuroendocrine functioning that varies in emotional arousal and that neuroendocrine components are only one part of emotional arousal behavior patterns (Ekman, 1984).

Several Kinds. Four types of evidence support the view that there are several different patterns of emotional arousal; this is the *differential emotions theory* (Ekman, 1984; Izard, 1977; Plutchik, 1980).

First, there is extensive and replicated evidence that electrical stimulation of specific areas of the brain, or lesioning of those areas, can trigger different emotional behavior displays. For example, Olds (1955, 1962) reported that electrical stimulation of the septal region of a rat's brain facilitated learning and performance, while stimulation of other areas produced neutral effects and still others produced avoidance learning. Others observed that electrical stimulation of areas in a cat's brain produced fear-like reactions and avoidance behavior that could be conditioned and could function as punishment in learning situations (Delgado, Roberts & Miller, 1954; Delgado, Rosvold, & Looney, 1956). Brown and Cohen (1959) reported that electrical stimulation of the lateral hypothalamic area in cats' brains often produced "rage" and related locomotor reactions. Lesions in appropriate brain regions of typically ferocious wild rats and cats can make them tame and calm (Ursin & Kaada, 1960), or can release controls in ordinarily tame animals so they become ferocious and unmanageable (Spiegel et al., 1940). Studies on monkeys (Bursten & Delgado, 1958), cats (Sidman, Brady, Boren, Conrad & Schulman, 1955), and bottlenose dolphins (Lilly & Miller, 1962) all demonstrate that stimulation of selected brain areas is positively reinforcing (rewarding).

Electrical stimulation of humans' septal region produces reports of pleasurable feelings (Heath, 1954; Sem-Jacobsen, 1958). Lesions in the "emotive brain" may affect emotion related behavior patterns such as aggressiveness, fearfulness, sexual behavior, and social relations (Konorski, 1967; MacLean, 1970a). While similar emotional patterns may be triggered by stimulation of more than one brain structure, the evidence firmly supports the "remarkable finding" that different "negative" patterns (e.g., fear, rage) and "positive" patterns (e.g., pleasure, sociability) are functionally related to different anatomical sites (e.g., amygdala, septum) (MacLean, 1963; Tarpy, 1977). The influence of a variety of neurochemicals and psychotropic drugs on different kinds of emotional experiences lends further plausibility to differential emotion theory.

Second, differences in action patterns related to different arousal conditions display commonalities cross-species and cross-culturally including facial expressions, motor patterns, and skin appearance (Darwin, 1872; Ekman, 1973; Izard, 1977). Some of these differences are apparent in newborn humans (Schellenbach, 1987). Different species display similarities in basic arousal patterns (Konorski, 1967), and species-specific differences in the ways in which each kind of emotion is displayed.[1] For example, the fierce posture of a cat with its accompanying growl, the bared fangs of the dog with its snarl, the combative stance of a monkey when cornered; or the flashing eyes, set mouth, scowling eyebrows, and harsh invective of the human are all consistent manifestations of anger but not fear. In anger, the limbs are used for striking (apes); striking, scratching, and kicking (humans); clawing (cats); and trampling (elephants); while in fear those same limbs are used for running away, climbing trees, or hiding the eyes. In anger, the human face may become flushed because of dilated blood vessels, while in fear it may become pale because the same vessels are constricted. In animals, the hair may stand erect in anger, but not in fear. In summary, there appear to be prototypical instrumental behavior patterns linked to different kinds of emotional situations that have both communicative and action-oriented significance.

Third, efforts to identify emotion-specific hormonal or blood chemistry attributes have produced some possibilities, such as the catecholamine hypothesis of rewards (Wise, 1978), and an increase in hormones that help increase energy availability through their glycolytic, gluconeogenic, or lipolytic actions (Leshner, 1977). Some studies report a relationship of epinephrine to fear, anxiety, or depression, and of norepinephrine to anger or aggression. However, some studies do not. In general, attempts to link specific biological variables to specific emotions have been unsuccessful.

From a living systems perspective, that is not surprising. Biological processes always occur in complexly organized patterns, and shifts in steady states are shifts in patterns. For example, heart rate can be elevated in many kinds of arousal, such as physical activity, sexual

---

[1] The existence of arousal patterns in other species similar to those which humans report experiencing is an inference based on observations of overt behaviors. The use of terms such as anger and fear in discussing the behavior patterns of other species does not necessarily imply that they have a subjective consciousness of such emotions similar to humans; it only implies that the patterns appear to be functionally similar.

excitement, anger, or fear. Changes in absolute levels of hormones are probably relatively undifferentiated consequences of emotional arousal. A more meaningful approach would be to examine "the broader patterning or balance of secretory and visceral change" in relationship to "historical and situational aspects of behavioral events" to identify patterns "associated with both episodic and persistent emotional interactions" (Brady, 1970). Just as the same components of the body (e.g., mouth, arms) may be involved in different action patterns but organized in different functional configurations, so too may the same biochemical and physiological components be involved in different patterns related to emotional arousal (Berlyne, 1967). Ekman (1984) and Ekman, Levenson, and Friesen (1983) report evidence supporting such a pattern analysis approach. For example, they found that the patterning of heart rate, left- and right-hand temperatures, skin resistance, and forearm flex or muscle tension differed for happiness, sadness, anger, and fear.

Fourth, subjective experience differentiates people's experiences of emotions such as love, anger, or depression as qualitatively different. Many words are used to represent emotional experiences, but people typically cluster them into groups representing a limited number of types of emotions (Plutchik, 1980).

The Utility of Emotions

Tropisms are inflexible reflexive reactions to specific kinds of stimulus patterns with specific kinds of movements. They are common in primitive organisms. Departures from tropistically shaped behavior patterns to a more plastic nervous system is a distinguishing feature of humans (Dubos, 1973). Alland (1967) asserts that evolution has produced two broad types of adaptations; innate responses (e.g., tropisms), and learning. After studying over 60 animal species, Breland and Breland (1966) concluded that most organisms deal with their environment with inborn "fixed action patterns" that occur under species-specific conditions, a view similar to that developed by ethologists (Lorenz, 1981).

Plutchik (1980) proposes that basic emotional arousal patterns evolved as one type of inborn pattern. Each kind emerged to deal with one of eight types of pervasive adaptation problems commonly faced by most organisms; these are incorporation, rejection, destruction, protection, reproduction, reintegration, orientation, and exploration. Each prototypical adaptation pattern has related to it a particular kind of emotional arousal in humans and other species. In addition, he suggests that emotional patterns are related to four basic types of "existential" problems that are social in nature: social hierarchy; territoriality (or what aspects of the environment "belong" to an organism); identity (including group membership); and temporality (or the limited duration of life and interpersonal relationships). Izard (1977) proposes that evolution produced eight to ten fundamental emotions that "are subserved in innate neural programs."

In summary, the weight of neurological, biological, psychological, and behavioral evidence supports the conclusion that humans have a limited number of basic emotional arousal patterns that are products of a long evolutionary history and that are elicited by different types of conditions. However, because learning has become a dominant process in humans, their inborn emotional patterns are modifiable through learning in two ways: (a) almost anything can become an eliciting condition for an emotional arousal pattern; and (b) the organization of the pattern itself may become modified.

Emotions enable people to behave more *selectively* to more *effectively cope with varying environmental conditions* in three ways: (a) by providing informational evaluations useful in guiding one's own activities (e.g., positive or negative feeling states); (b) by adjusting biological functioning to prepare for and to execute different kinds of activity demands; and (c) by adjusting the relationship between themselves and some salient aspect(s) of their environment through actions (e.g., approach or avoidance action patterns) or through communications (e.g., facial expressions and vocalizations). It is important to emphasize that emotional arousal patterns function in a context and in order to facilitate behavioral episodes.

The Nature of Emotional Arousal Behavior Patterns

Knapp (1981), using a psychoanalytic framework, identifies three interrelated components of emotional arousal: (a) hedonic evaluation (a brain process); (b) activation-deactivation (a biological process with psychological manifestations); and (c) expressive mobilization (motor-expressive displays). The "core" is hedonic evaluation, which "automatically activates urges for expression and action." Through learning, components (b) and particularly (c) can be uncoupled from component (a), or modified.

Lewis and Michalson's (1983) structural model of emotional arousal involves five components:

1. Elicitors—environmental or internal events which can trigger emotions,
2. Receptors—neurophysiological structures which react to elicitors,

3. Emotional states—a particular constellation of changes in somatic and/or neurophysiological activity,
4. Emotional expressions—motoric and vocal gestures or expressions, and
5. Emotional experience—the interpretation and evaluation of the perceived emotional state and expression.

Their components (2) and (5) correspond to Knapp's hedonic evaluation component; their component (3) to his biological component; and their component (4) to his expressive mobilization component.

Ekman (1984) proposes three similar interrelated "emotion systems": cognition; specific autonomic nervous system activity; and facial and vocal expressiveness. He believes that emotions are "a set of characteristics...organized...into a coherent pattern." Empirical and clinical evidence supports Knapp's three component model as summarized in Fig. 13.1. Collectively, particular organizations of the three components will be referred to as an *emotional pattern*.

Emotional Arousal. This hedonic evaluation component is a CNS evaluative process, analogous to the olfactory evaluation process, and probably anchored in the limbic system-hypothalamic circuits. Kety (1970) concludes that there is anatomical, physiological, pharmacological, and behavioral evidence suggesting "the existence of an important neural system, parallel and complimentary to the sensorimotor systems" related to more primitive brain components, "which evaluates experience and the outcome of action in terms of built-in or acquired survival value," and which "integrates adaptive, vegetative, and endocrine behavior," and "which reinforces learning and colors recall." Similarly, Arnold (1970) proposes that "emotion proper" results from an "appraisal" mediated by the limbic system. Hedonic evaluation is probably the primary source of the conscious experience of emotions. Her proposal is supported by experiments in which the viscera are disconnected from the brain (e.g., by surgical or drug sympathectomy of the ANS), revealing that SNS activity is not "the sole substrate of emotion" and that "ANS feedback per se (is not) a necessary condition for aversive learning or emotion" (Tarpy, 1977). Thus, people can experience emotional arousal, behave emotionally, and display emotionally based learning even when their ANS and brain are disconnected.

This limbic system based, evaluative-appraisal process is very rapid, and does not have to involve prior *conscious* cognitive processing of the information triggering it. Thus, Zajonc's (1980) argument that such "affective judgments" may precede in time, and be fairly independent of, cognitive processing has some validity. However, that would be true only for the perceptually anchored conditions associated with the inborn

FIG. 13.1 A representation of the three interrelated components of an emotional arousal behavior pattern. The pattern is initiated by a CNS evaluation which triggers a limbic system pattern experienced as emotional arousal. That triggers biological adjustments through the ANS and endocrine systems to prepare the body for appropriate action. It also triggers expressive and motoric actions instrumental in dealing with the emotion-eliciting situation.

emotional fixed action patterns. As Mowrer (1960a; 1960b) made evident, emotional responding is highly learnable, and almost anything can become a triggering event under appropriate learning conditions. Such learning is information based.

Stated in living systems terms, while direct perceptions elicit emotions in infants, evaluative thoughts are the primary elicitor of emotional patterns in adult humans. *Evaluative thoughts* —interpretations of the personal meaning of events—are learned and may occur in relationship to current perceptions or independent of external events (e.g., "Just thinking about it makes me mad," or emotions during dreams). However, Lazarus (1982) points out that cognitive evaluation does not have to be "deliberate, rational, and conscious." As with any other habit, once an habitual pattern of emotional responding to any set of events is formed, it can function in an automated way appearing similar to inborn, perceptually triggered patterns; and it can also approximate Zajonc's description. Regulatory thought is considered more fully in Chapter 12.

The limbic system emotional arousal component augments the pattern of ICA arousal in the CNS, sometimes becoming excessive so that the nervous system becomes "flooded" with arousal, producing disruption of behavioral organization. For example, Patrick (1934a, 1934b) placed individuals in a room with several exit doors. People rapidly learned how to find the unlocked door and leave. Then, on experimental trials, individuals were unexpectedly and continuously subjected to emotionally arousing stimuli (e.g., a shower of cold water). The effects on their efforts to find the unlocked door were profound. In place of the orderly, rational attempts displayed earlier, people would typically show perseverative reactions such as repeatedly tugging at the door that was unlocked on the previous trial, or would run randomly around the experimental room. In extreme, disorganizing emotional states people sometimes do things they would never consider doing otherwise (e.g., beat their child or spouse).

As every fine musical or athletic performer knows, a moderate degree of emotional arousal helps increase the precision and effectiveness of behavior patterns (e.g., it helps to "play with" emotion), but excessive emotional arousal disrupts carefully organized behavior patterns and produces "errors." Efficient learning occurs at optimal levels of arousal (Hebb, 1955). Emotional arousal appears to function as a kind of amplifier increasing the effective strength and organization of other responses. For example, persons with paresis resulting from known organic lesions have performed acts when under severe emotional stress that were considered beyond their capacity (Kennard, 1947). Thoughts may also be amplified. For example, a psychotherapy client who admired other women's dresses spoke of wanting to "tear them off their backs" rather than the less amplified "I would like to have one too." It is not yet clear whether differences in level of arousal are primarily a function of the intensity of arousal or neural excitation (Hebb, 1955; Lindsley, 1961), or of some change in the synchronization or equilibration of neural functioning as suggested by Pribram (1971). Another possibility is that it may be a function of the extent to which different neural circuits are aroused, and the amount of neurochemicals secreted.

Biological Activation-Deactivation. The second component of emotional patterns adjusts biological processes to prepare for different kinds of activity demands. The hypothalamus links the limbic system to the ANS and to the endocrine system by way of the pituitary. Through it, the emotional arousal component becomes translated into supporting biological activation patterns. Making these biological functions the primary way of characterizing emotions has been one of the barriers to a fuller understanding of emotional patterns. While there is a natural coupling of the limbic system emotional arousal component and the biological activation component,they can become partially or totally uncoupled through development, learning, or physical damage. Therefore, the biological activation-deactivation pattern for a particular emotion may not be identical for each person. Moreover, no single response can serve as a reliable indicator of a particular emotion (e.g., palmar sweating) since each can occur under nonemotional conditions.

Emotional arousal changes biological processes primarily through the increased excitation of SNS circuits, corresponding changes in PNS functioning, and alterations in patterns of hormonal secretion. The more extreme the level of emotional arousal, the greater will be the shift in biological functioning. Some patterns of emotional arousal appear to function primarily to "shut down" the fueling of behavioral activity (e.g., discouragement-depression). Sometimes reductions in activity may have survival advantage. For example, animals can protect themselves from a potential predator either by running away or by becoming immobile.

Muscles, organs, and glands in the human body respond to antagonistic stimulation (e.g., one signal increases the stomach's motility while another decreases it). It is the controlled balance among these antagonistic signals that produces organized behavior. The many possible combinations of activation and inhibition of all parts of the body produce a tremendous variety in the responses to be found in emotional arousal behavior patterns (Gellhorn & Loofbourrow, 1963). In one instance, there may be vasodilatation in the stomach, and in another there may be vasoconstriction. One may have increased or decreased heart rate, increased or decreased adrenaline secretion, and so forth. Similarly, the *amount* of increase or decrease may be slight or relatively great. Moreover, the same pattern of response may be triggered by perceptions of, and thoughts about, quite different situations, such as the critical comments of one's parent or the affectionate actions of one's sweetheart towards someone else.

Neonates display significant individual differences in base rate "tuning" of these biological energy-producing and energy-utilizing functions (Fries, 1961), manifest in behavioral differences that are frequently referred to as differences in *temperament*. Temperamental differences between parent and child may influence the kind and quality of relationship that develops between them, and therefore the child's development. Imagine the poor mother who is "largo and legato" in her behavior with a child who is "prestissimo and staccato" in her actions. Each would find it difficult to understand or share activities with the other (e.g., one's preference for contemplative reading versus the other's for participation in sports). Lewis and Michalson (1983) propose that temperamental differences, such as those identified by Thomas, Chess, Birch, Hertzig, and Korn (1963), influence the emotional life of children by "intensifying particular emotional states and affecting their sequential flow." Since emotional arousal patterns represent specialized variations on base rate ICA and activity arousal, initial individual differences in those base rates are likely to contribute to individual differences in emotional arousal behavior patterns.

Transactional Behavior Mobilization. The third component is expressive and instrumental behaviors which translate emotional arousal and biological activation into relevant environmental transactions. These include both actions and communicative behaviors which provide cues about a person's emotional state.

In infants, there are inborn transactional behavior patterns associated with different kinds of emotional arousal (Schellenbach, 1987). For example, an infant thwarted in its attempts to obtain and retain a desired object is likely to emit an "angry" facial expression, display harsh, shout-like crying, produce slashing movements of arms and legs, stiffen its torso, arch its spine, and get red in the face. In contrast, an alert baby interested and involved in some activity will display a different facial expression, may emit soft, cooing-like vocalizations, will produce some body tension with reaching movements of the arms and perhaps some coordinated leg kicking, and have normal color in its face.

Facial gestures have been extensively studied, beginning with Darwin. Ekman's (1972, 1984) reviews of research on animals, infants, children, and members of different cultures converge on the conclusion that there is a "major genetic contribution in the morphology of facial expression" and that there are "particular patterns of facial-muscular movement associated with particular emotions" and their subjective qualities. There are species-specific differences in the expressive format of different emotions, but closely related species tend to have similar facial expressions (Chevalier-Skolnikoff, 1973). While the form of the facial expression is relatively invariant within species, their eliciting conditions are subject to experiential elaboration. Izard (1977) concluded on the basis of "robust cross-cultural evidence" that emotions are innate, universal, intraindividual processes that have "innately stored neural programs, universally understood expressions, and common experiential qualities."

There has been considerable recent interest in the expressive significance of other body movements or postures (e.g., "body language"). The study of infant emotional development has examined vocalizations such as laughing and crying and motor patterns reflecting approach towards, withdrawal from, or avoidance of different conditions (Lewis & Rosenblum, 1978). However, if the form rather than the content of the motor pattern is examined, certain consistencies are apparent. For example, positive emotions such as affection or pleasure are expressed through seeking involvement with the eliciting circumstances and manipulating objects in an exploratory or instrumental manner. Negative emotions such as fear or discouragement take the form of getting away from or avoiding the eliciting circumstances. For example, Sroufe and Wunsch (1972) observed that when an infant cries it "pulls back...and turns from the stimulus," but when it laughs it "maintains an orientation towards," "reaches for," and "seeks to reproduce" the eliciting event.

The principle of equifinality applies to transactional behaviors. There are many different ways of producing the same result. Through learning, adults acquire a diversity of transactional patterns by which the same kind of emotional arousal may be manifest. Therefore, the correspondence between particular transactional responses and types of emotional arousal is quite variable.

The Development of Emotions

Emotions have great adaptive value because they quickly and automatically make it possible to: (a) evaluate the potential personal significance of current or probable events, objects, or organisms; (b) organize biological processes to support an appropriate pattern of action; and (c) produce communicative and instrumental actions relevant to the evaluations. Each function is anchored in different body components: Component (a) is anchored in the brain, primarily limbic-system-hypothalamic circuits; component (b) is anchored in the ANS and the glands and organs it controls; component (c) is anchored in the CNS and the sensory-motor functions it controls. There are multiple feedforward and feedback processes within and among these three components so that, as an emotional arousal behavior pattern unfolds, each influences the others in a network of mutual causal processes.

Humans' evolutionary history has produced a limited number of qualitatively different inborn emotional patterns that can be elicited by particular kinds of conditions. In humans, the neurological-psychological component is the initial and primary source of the subjective experience of emotional arousal. However, that conscious, subjective experience is elaborated and perhaps amplified as feedback from the functioning of biological and transactional components of the patterns arrives at appropriate brain centers.

It is a part of their utility that all components of emotional patterns become operative quickly. However, they are not simultaneous. The neural component typically occurs first and the pattern spreads out from there, like the circles that spread from the point of impact when one throws a rock into a pond of water (see Fig 13.1). However, emotional patterns can be elicited by activation of biological or transactional components (Ekman, 1984; Ekman, Levenson, & Friesen, 1983;). Once an emotion's biological components are activated, the effects within the body will continue for some time after the eliciting conditions terminate, just as the ripples in a pond continue outward for some time after the rock has sunk to the bottom. However, if eliciting circumstances keep reoccurring before the pattern has subsided (analogous to continuing to drop rocks in the pond before the ripples from the last one have disappeared), the scope and amplitude of the pattern can be increased. In that way, persistent moods or "chronic" emotions can occur. In normal circumstances, an emotional pattern is an episodic, situation specific, and relatively short-lived variation on base rate arousal patterns (Rapaport, 1971). Minor arousal may trigger neural but not biological or transactional components, much as a grain of sand may create a local disturbance in a pond, but not generate spreading "ripples." Berscheid (1983) calls these minor arousals "feelings" or "little emotions" because of the absence of the biological components. For an emotional pattern to persist, it must be continually "retriggered" by some kinds of relevant events (e.g., thoughts).

Sources of Individual Differences in Emotional Patterns. The configuration of an individual's emotional patterns can be altered in several ways. First, through learning, each pattern can become associated with many different kinds of events, objects, or organisms as elicitors. For example, sexual excitement can become triggered by nonhuman objects (e.g., a shoe); this is called a *fetish*. Even a person's own responses (e.g., biological sensations; thoughts) can become learned emotional pattern elicitors, and one of the important ways humans can make themselves happy, mad, or miserable is through cognitively self-generated emotional patterns. One important source of individual differences in personality development lies in the diversity of events that can elicit each kind of emotional pattern. For example, a person who has learned to be afraid of many things will develop an avoidant, withdrawing, highly restricted life style. In contrast, a person who has learned to find pleasure in many different kinds of activities is usually more exploratory and adventuresome in his or her activities. With repeated experience, emotional habits can be constructed. Lacey et al. 1963) describe phenomena of situational stereotypy in the expression of emotions. When such habits become formed, a person may experience an emotional pattern and not be aware of what elicited it. Mandler (1975) refers to these as *organized action sequences.*

A second way in which emotional patterns can be altered involves "streamlining" the initial pattern by eliminating some elements. For example, the transactional components of an anger pattern may be inhibited when it occurs on the job, but the biological components (e.g., gastric and circulatory changes) may still occur. Sometimes such partial patterns become mislabeled by people (e.g., as "feeling tense," or experiencing "indigestion") and they act in terms of those labels (e.g., take medications) rather than deal with the anger or other emotion directly. The transactional components are most easily modified because they are under CNS voluntary control. For example, people can learn to inhibit their impulse to run away or to strike someone. Children learn such tactics at an early age, although skill and subtlety in doing so increase with experience; children with difficulty in inhibiting transactional components are said to have inadequate "impulse control" or to be "acting out."

Individual differences also develop in the biological components. For example, in one person, galvanic skin response may go up when he is anxious, but in another it will not; one person's palms may sweat, another's not. Nevertheless, there appears to be some interindividual commonality. For example, Ax (1953) has reported some consistent average differences among emotional patterns on 14 physiological measures. However, people like Wenger (1948; Wenger et al., 1961), Lacey (1950; Lacey & Van Lehn, 1952; Lacey, Bateman, & Van Lehn, 1953), and Malmo (1959) report evidence suggesting that each person develops, through learning, his or her own somewhat idiosyncratic patterns of biological emotional responding, which interact with somewhat different genetic and biological bases.

Consequences of Persistent or Excessive Emotional Arousals. Excessive or chronic emotional arousal may produce temporary or permanent changes in a person's biological functioning. The term *stress* is sometimes used to refer to consequences of persistent or excessive emotional arousal. Proctor et al. (1957) have suggested that increased arousal may produce a switch from sympathetic to parasympathetic functioning, just as the temperature sensors in the skin may produce perceptions of cold when the temperature gets too hot. Thus, some biological responses that occur during intense emotional states may seem incongruous in terms of their functional utility. For example, of what utility is it for a terror-stricken person to have his or her muscles become flaccid? In some conditions, such as panic states, it is almost as if all the person's response systems had been flooded with arousal, "spilling over" into systems not normally affected, so that coordinated behavior is overwhelmed, biological functioning disrupted, and exaggerated responses occur in an incoherent or disorganized way.

Normally, emotional arousal is only a temporary occurrence, and subsides after a particular episode ends. However, people sometimes keep stimulating the emotional pattern so that it persists. If high emotional arousal is maintained over an extended period of time, biological functions involved in the arousal pattern may well go through an adaptive process that results in a permanent "returning" of the processes involved, so that some kind of reorganization is created that avoids continuous, excessive, and potentially damaging disruption of all the response systems. A system far from equilibrium is more vulnerable to disruption and reorganization.

Several behavioral strategies may serve this end. The person's responsiveness to situational events in general and to disturbing ones in particular may be reduced or eliminated by staying out of such situations, ignoring crucial events, or evaluating them in a less upsetting manner. Restricting or localizing the disturbance resulting from the excessive arousal by learning to inhibit the occurrence of some parts of the emotional pattern is another strategy. Persistent emotional arousal may produce physiological damage (as in some types of hypertensive or ulcer patients), which can then set up another cycle of biological and behavioral accommodation. Moreover, a person may evaluate some amplified biological response (e.g., a "racing" heart) so that it functions as an emotional elicitor (e.g., "I'm having a heart attack"). That can function as a positive feedback loop, producing further arousal deviations from normal base rate levels.

The paradoxical nature of some ANS responses of mental patients supports the notion that reorganization of components of arousal patterns has occurred to preserve some degree of functional unity. When the "integrative determinants" or "essential variables" of a system are strained to a critical point, "emergency" adaptive processes are activated, "often with a sacrifice of some functions of the original system"; this results in sudden system reorganization through a "step-function" or a "jump-state," which increases the system's chances of maintaining functional coherence and survival (Grinker et al., 1956). (See Toman, 1956, for a similar view.) For example, although emotional excitement typically produces a sharp rise in blood sugar in normal people it may not do so in some schizophrenics (Whitehorn, 1934); the facial skin temperature of some neurotics may increase during fright rather than decrease as it typically does in normal people (Jacobsen Kehlet, Larsen, Munkuad, & Shinhoj, 1955). In some chronic schizophrenics, body temperature rises rather than falls in a cold bath (Buck et al., 1950); and blood pressure falls rather than rises in the cold pressor test (Igersheimer, 1953).

Selye (1976) spent much of his life trying to understand the functioning of these kinds of processes, and developed the notion of a three-phase *general adaptation syndrome* representing how the body copes with stress. The first phase involves alarm reactions. If the stress is prolonged, the second phase of resistance or adaptation occurs, revealed in immune system changes and a decline in ANS symptoms. This adaptation is at some sacrifice of the system, however, and if the adaptation is at too great an expense it cannot be maintained for any extensive period. Then, the third stage of exhaustion may occur.

Elaboration of Emotional Patterns. A third way in which basic emotional patterns may change is that they may elaborate. To account for the apparent diversity of emotions, Plutchik (1980) proposed an analogy to a color wheel. There are a limited number of primary colors (and emotions). By mixing primary colors (emotions) in different combinations, many different shades of a variety of colors (emotions) can be produced. The fusion of compatible emotional arousal pattern could be a mechanism for this. Humans often function in complex circumstances. They are frequently pursuing several kinds of consequences at the same time. Therefore, people sometimes have several kinds of emotional patterns elicited simultaneously or in rapid succession. Some elements of the patterns may be mutually contradictory and unable to occur at the same time (e.g., heart rate cannot simultaneously increase and decrease; one cannot smile and frown at the same time). Therefore, only one of two competing elements could occur. However, other elements may not be contradictory and so both could occur at the same time, even though they are parts of different emotional patterns. Thus, one might get a partial fusion of two different emotional patterns, creating a somewhat different composite pattern. Obviously, the pattern would have to be coherently organized, and that would exert a design constraint on the kinds of fusions that could occur. For example, a child who was severely punished whenever he or she displayed anger might learn to respond with fear to his own anger pattern. The result could be a partial fusion of the anger and fear patterns. For example, the child might inhibit his overt expression of anger and instead fearfully try to withdraw from the situation before something bad happens, but might still think angry thoughts and get a "knot" in his stomach.

In summary, humans' multiple labels for different kinds of emotions could represent (a) the occurrence of essentially the same emotional pattern, but in different BES contexts; (b) a modified pattern in which some elements have been eliminated; and (c) an elaborated pattern through fusion of different emotional patterns. The labeling itself can influence the configuration's transactional components. For example, a person may label what is primarily a fear pattern as illness, and seek medication or surgery for it rather than dealing with the fear producing circumstances.

The Basic Human Emotional Arousal Behavior Patterns

Both empirical and theoretical approaches have been used to identify the number and kind of basic human emotional patterns. One of the most influential approaches is that of Ekman (1972, 1973, 1984) and Izard (1977, 1979). Using facial expressions as indicators of different emotional patterns, they have studied infants and adults in both descriptive and experimental designs, and have sought to identify biological, psychological, and behavioral variables that covary with facial expressions in many of the world's cultures. Izard proposes that ten different emotional patterns are empirically justified: interest/excitement, joy, surprise, distress/anguish, anger, disgust, contempt, fear, shame, and guilt. Most of these have been replicated in several factor analytic studies (Fuenzalida , Emde, & Pannabecker, 1981). Comparative data from animals' facial expressions provide additional support. It is curious that this approach has yielded mostly "negative" emotions. Where, for example, is affection? Ekman concludes that there is reasonably strong evidence for fear, surprise, anger, disgust, distress and happiness, and weaker evidence for interest, contempt, and shame.

Cattell (1957) identified ten types of emotions from factor analyses of descriptive items related to the objective expression of emotions and motivations. He proposed that each basic emotion has a particular function identified as a goal or aim. They are: Sex or lust→mating; fear→escape; loneliness→gregariousness; pity or succorance→protectiveness; curiosity→exploration; pride→self-assertion; sensuous comfort→narcissism; despair→appeal; sleepiness→rest seeking; and anger→pugnacity. To some extent his categories mix body affective states (e.g., sleepiness) with emotional affective states. Nowlis (1970) identified 11 "mood" factors which included both emotional and other affective categories: aggression; anxiety; surgency; elation; concentration; fatigue; social affection; sadness; skepticism; egotism; and vigor. Osgood et al. (1975) identified three basic connotative dimensions from cross-cultural data: evaluation (good-bad); potency (strong-weak); and activity (active-passive). Differences in factors among scholars is partly a function of the kind of information covered by the measures (e.g., no fatigue factor will emerge unless fatigue measures are included), the method of measurement (e.g., paired comparison; degree of presence or absence), and the nature of emotional patterns (e.g., interest and boredom may load on the same factor because they cannot occur together, but that doesn't mean they are part of the same emotional arousal pattern. See C. Ford, 1987).

Research on infants (Emde, Gaensbauer, & Harman, 1976; Lewis & Rosenblum, 1978) identifies commonly observed emotional patterns, including: *distress*—crying, grimacing; *delight*—smiling, kicking legs, flailing arms; *anger*—flushed face, shouting cry, body stiffening, slashing movements of arms and hands; *affection*—fixing gaze on another person, smiling, patting or caressing another person; *fear*—crying, a sober look, ceasing activities, tensing muscles, averting head, opened eyes, face pallor; *jealousy*—display of distress or anger when attention or affection is given to someone towards whom the infant might feel rivalry, such as parent or sibling; *shyness, coyness, embarrassment, shame*—averting eyes, blushing, moving body in awkward nervous fashion; *sympathy*—displaying a sensing or understanding of another's distress; *disgust*—pulling back of lips, lifting nose, averting face from stimulus source. Infants and very small children appear to be more expressive than older children and adults (Charlesworth & Kreutzer, 1973). Experimental and clinical studies of brain functioning in humans and other animals provide additional evidence of different emotions, but have not been used as a primary empirical base for identifying a human basic human set of emotions.

Theoretically based typologies have been constructed by philosophers and psychologists. For example, McDougall (1921, 1933) proposed that many animals, including humans, have "instincts" or "propensities" for behavior. He argued that, when activated, each instinct had associated with it a distinct emotional pattern such as flight—fear; repulsion—disgust; curiosity—wonder; pugnacity—anger; self-abasement—subjection; self-assertion—elation; and parental—tender. He suggested three criteria for identifying primary emotions: They may occur in exaggerated intensity, implying some freedom from voluntary control; similar patterns occur in animals phylogenetically close to humans; and complex emotions result from mixtures of primary emotions. The Wittenberg symposia (Reymert, 1928, 1950) provide additional examples of typologies.

Plutchik's (1980) typology is grounded in evolutionary theory. He argues that emotional patterns evolved as a kind of behavior pattern that functions as a general solution for each fundamental type of adaptive-problem situation animals and humans face, analogous to DNA as a biological solution to assuring basic types of adaptive capabilities throughout nature. Their utility is demonstrated by their presence and continuation in many different species. He considers emotions as "adaptive devices in the struggle for individual survival at all evolutionary levels."

Plutchik proposes five criteria for distinguishing a primary from a derived emotional pattern: (a) it should be related to some basic, adaptive, biological processes; (b) it should appear in some form at all evolutionary levels; (c) its definition should be independent of particular neural structures or body parts; (d) its definition should be independent of introspection, although introspection may be used to help identify such a pattern in humans; (e) it should be defined primarily in relationship to "goal-directed behavioral data," or "response-as-affecting-stimulus" as Tolman put it.

Plutchik has identified 8 basic emotional patterns summarized in Table 13.1, each of which can be referred to with "functional" language (e.g., protection), "subjective" language (e.g., fear), or "behavioral" language (e.g., escaping). He also briefly mentions an alternative, "more speculative" view that emotional patterns evolved to deal with four basic types of existential (social), problems that he labels *hierarchy, territoriality, identity,* and *temporality,* implying that at least some emotions evolved to deal with social relationships.

TABLE 13.1
Plutchik's Eight Basic Emotional Patterns

Function	Subjective Experience	Behavior
Protection	Fear, Terror	Withdrawing, Escaping
Destruction	Anger, Rage	Attacking, Biting
Reproduction	Joy, Ecstasy	Mating, Possessing
Reintegration	Sadness, Grief	Crying for help
Incorporation or Affiliation	Acceptance, Trust	Pair Bonding, Grooming
Rejection	Disgust, Loathing	Vomiting, Defecating
Exploration	Expectancy, Anticipation	Examining, Mapping
Orientation	Surprise, Astonishment	Stopping, Freezing

The social function of emotions is a basic premise of proposals made by Kemper (1978) and DeRivera (1977). Kemper assumes that "events in the social environment instigate emotions," as a result of "real, imagined, or anticipated outcomes in social relationships." Human interdependence means that much of what they accomplish is the result of "coaction." Control of social relations through "status" and "power" behaviors provides the primary context for the occurrence of emotions. He subclassifies emotions into three types based on their eliciting conditions rather than their behavioral properties: *structural,* resulting from the "relatively stable structure of the relationship" examples are security, guilt, megalomania, fear/anxiety, happiness, shame, embarrassment/humiliation, and depression; *anticipatory,* resulting from the person's view of the future state of the relationship; examples are satisfaction, disappointment, resignation, consternation, astonishment; and *consequent,* resulting from *relational outcomes of interaction episodes.* In Kemper's model, 170 different kinds could occur.

DeRivera assumes that emotions govern people's "object relations," particularly with their social environment. He focuses on the nature of the "movement" or function of each type of emotion, since each reflects a particular kind of "transformation" of the person's relation to theirworld. Emotional arousal is a set or system of "transformations." For that reason he calls his theory a *structural* one. According to DeRivera, there are essentially two types of "movement": towards and away; and two types of action objects: self and others. This provides a limited number of types of object relations. Different kinds of transformation rules may guide each of those relationships (e.g., "give up"). The emotion experienced is a function of the type of object relationship and type of transformation rule involved.

These examples illustrate the diversity of classifications of emotions that have been developed. There is considerable consistency within that diversity, however. The following generalizations are suggested as a starting point:

1. Emotional patterns evolved because of their utility in regulating environmental interactions to produce valued consequences. A limited number of different kinds of patterns evolved because of their utility in dealing with different kinds of pervasive, prototypical adaptive tasks. The appearance that there are many different kinds results from the capability of basic emotions to occur in combinations and in different contexts.

2. Some emotions regulate environmental relationships in general (including human relationships), while others evolved specifically to regulate social relationships because cooperative group living has a survival and reproductive advantage.

3. Emotional patterns are organizations of neural, psychological, biological, and transactional response components. The neural-psychological components are the core of emotional arousal; the biological and transactional components represent elaborations of the core to prepare the person for, and enable the person to execute, actions that regulate environmental interactions to produced valued consequences.

4. Emotional patterns are modifiable through learning. They can come to be elicited by diverse events both around and within a person, and may be labeled differently depending on the context. Components may be added or eliminated, thereby producing different versions of each pattern or fusions of different patterns.

Two Functional Categories of Emotion: Instrumental and Social

Human behavior is organized in behavior episodes. Within this living system framework, emotions influence the direction and content of behavior episodes through their regulatory functions and the "positive-negative" valences they give experience and through the physiological and transactional manifestations they trigger. They also influence information organization and storage, thereby indirectly influencing the directive function.

A behavior episode is a pattern of behavior occurring in a specific context, which extends or persists over time, directed toward producing intended consequence(s) (see Chapters 3 and 5). An episode terminates and another begins when (a) the consequence is obtained; (b) it appears unattainable, at least at that time in that context; or (c) some circumstance within or outside the person preempts the behavior episode because something else has become more interesting or important. One set of basic emotions functions to help regulate the operation of all behavior episodes. These will be termed *instrumental emotions*. They were probably the first to evolve.

Humans evolved as social beings. Individuals function as components within their group(s). As with any living system, there must be a pattern of functional relationships among the components (i.e., the individuals) that makes possible some degree of autonomous functioning of each person, while simultaneously ensuring that they all work together sufficiently to maintain the functional effectiveness and existence of the larger system (i.e., the group). *Social emotions* evolved to help perform these social regulatory functions. They can begin performing their regulatory function in infancy because children learn to make inferences about others' intentions and feelings during the first two years of life (Dunn, 1986). Instrumental and/or social emotions can occur in combination, producing a fusion of the characteristics of two (or perhaps more) basic patterns that may become habitual through learning.

Particular kinds of emotion occur as a function of different aspects of behavior episodes. Berscheid (1983), Cattell (1957), DeRivera (1977), Ekman (1984), Kemper (1978), Mandler (1975), Plutchik (1980), and Rogers (1951), take analogous positions. The occurrence of emotions is less a function of "discrete properties of stimulation," and more the result of "how the individual relates past, present and future to his or her goals and strivings." Evaluative thoughts which "monitor the relationship between events and the organisms goals" represent the key to understanding both "the elicitation of emotion and its specific quality" (Campos & Barrett, 1984). Eight instrumental emotions and six social ones are proposed as the basic human emotions in the following pages.

Instrumental Emotions

Four kinds of emotions regulate the initiation, continuation, and termination of behavior episodes. Four others regulate behavior when potentially disruptive or damaging circumstances occur during the course of a behavior episode. These eight kinds of emotional patterns appear in one form or another on most theorists' lists. Each performs a different kind of regulatory function in behavior episodes.

Curiosity — Interest — Excitement. Information is power for a living system. The more information it has about its environmental niche and how it functions, the more flexibly and effectively the individual can behave. Therefore, encouraging and facilitating the collection and organization of new information produces results of great adaptive value. Curiosity — interest — excitement serves that function. It triggers and maintains information-collection behaviors, and cognition construction. It is the emotion of exploration and investigation. Variability and novelty that is not too extreme are conditions which activate it (Wohlwill, 1981).

Disinterest — Boredom — Apathy. There is little utility in collecting information that is already familiar. Some regulatory mechanism for discouraging or terminating exploration of familiar environments would have adaptive utility. That appears to be the function of disinterest - boredom — apathy. It tends to terminate unnecessary exploration and to trigger a search for novelty. It also tends to be activated in contexts evaluated as familiar, repetitive, or relatively unvarying.

Satisfaction — Pleasure — Joy. When a behavior episode is initiated, the consequence toward which it is directed will often not be readily available. Therefore, some regulatory mechanism to encourage continued effort towards producing the consequence or repeating previously successful behaviors would be valuable. That is the function of satisfaction — pleasure — joy. It is the emotion of accomplishment and mastery. It is activated by evaluations indicating progress towards desired/intended consequences.

Downhearted — Discouraged — Depressed. However, sometimes the consequence sought seems not available or unable to be produced at that time and place. It would be maladaptive to perseverate in unsuccessful efforts in an unending fashion. As the saying goes, "What's the point of beating your head against a stone wall?" Regulating the termination of unsuccessful behavior patterns is the function of this pattern. It is the emotion of incompetence, failure, helplessness, and hopelessness. It is activated by evaluations indicating actual or probable lack of progress towards desired consequences.

The first two and last two might be considered as functional pairs. The opposite members of each of these pairs cannot occur simultaneously (e.g., one cannot simultaneously be interested and bored, or satisfied and discouraged). Moreover, as the three-word labels convey, each can vary in intensity. Therefore, they might be represented as two rather than four emotional patterns that can range from positive to negative. Current evidence supports considering them to be different patterns. The next four emotions regulate coping with disruptve or potentially damaging circumstances that can occur during behavior episodes.

Startle—Surprise—Astonishment. During a behavior episode, the individual selectively attends to relevant conditions and ignores or vaguely monitors other concurrent conditions. Although that is very efficient, it can also be potentially self-defeating. One could miss an important opportunity, or be hurt or killed if unusual new circumstances are ignored. The function of startle—surprise—astonishment is to interrupt ongoing behavior so the individual can "check out" new events for their potential personal significance. It is a bridge between ICA and AE arousal, reorienting and intensifying focal attention. It is activated by unexpected, sudden, or intense events.

Annoyance—Anger—Rage. While pursuing intended consequences, one may find one's efforts interfered with by other conditions. Successful completion of the behavior may require overcoming those thwarting conditions, and that may require an intensification of behavior. That is the function of annoyance—anger—rage. It is the emotion of attacking and overcoming. It is elicited by conditions evaluated as interfering with progress toward desired or intended consequences.

Dislike—Disgust—Loathing. During a behavior episode, a person may confront potentially contaminating conditions or material which, if contacted or ingested, could produce sickness and possible death. Dislike—disgust—loathing is the emotion of revulsion and rejection, and nausea is a biological response to such conditions. It regulates avoidance behavior toward environmental conditions evaluated as foul or noxious.

Wariness-Fear-Terror. Other types of conditions (such as other animals) could hurt, injure, or kill the individual. Therefore, caution when confronted with excessively novel, unfamiliar, and unpredictable circumstances and preparation to "get the hell out of there" if they should turn out to be dangerous would have great adaptive utility. That is the regulatory function of wariness—fear—terror. It is the emotion of avoidance and escape from circumstances evaluated as uncontrollable, unpredictable, or potentially hurtful.

Social Emotions

Three emotional patterns regulate interpersonal bonding, which is essential for successful reproduction and the formation and continuity of new social groups. Three others regulate conformity to, or cooperation with, social organizations (e.g., status and power functions) and the beliefs and expectations of the group. Hopefully, further empirical work will clarify whether these are different basic emotions or social manifestations of instrumental emotions. Comparative research with other animals supports the concept of social emotions (Harlow, 1971; Harlow & Mears, 1979). For example, two "strong cohesive forces" in many troops of lemurs are "attraction to infants" and "friendly behavior" (Jolly, 1966). What follows tentatively assumes that they are evolutionary emergents and basic emotions.

Sexual Arousal — Pleasure — Excitement. The "bottom line" in evolution theory is survival and reproductive effectiveness. Reproduction of humans requires a sexual encounter between a male and a female. Therefore, arousal patterns that facilitate, encourage, and reinforce sexual encounters would be of basic evolutionary utility. Sexual arousal — pleasure — excitement is the emotion of courtship and mating. It is aroused by cues (e.g., sounds, sights, odors) evaluated as suggesting a potentially sexually receptive member of the opposite sex.

Acceptance — Affection — Love. However, reproduction involves more than copulation and conception. The pregnant female and fetus must survive pregnancy. The helpless infant must be sheltered, nourished, and socialized if it is to survive and become behaviorally effective. A mechanism for the cultivation of interpersonal bonding, continuing mutual commitment, and trust would facilitate such social relationships. That is the function of acceptance — affection — love. It is the emotion of caring and sharing; of interpersonal commitment, succorance, and sacrifice.

Loneliness — Sorrow — Grief. It follows that separation from those with whom one has such a relationship is potentially dangerous and damaging. A person emotionally bonded to others functions as a semi-autonomous, semi-dependent component of that larger social system. If that system of mutually advantageous relationships is disrupted or destroyed (e.g., by abandonment or death of a loved one), the loss threatens the person's welfare and requires a major reorganization of his or her daily pattern of living. Therefore, some regulatory process that functions to restore or replace broken significant social bonds would be of considerable utility. That is the function of loneliness—sorrow—grief. It is the emotion of separation from others with whom one has an affectionate relationship. It encourages and seeks union or reunion with others to alleviate the misery.

Embarrassment—Shame (Guilt)—Humiliation. For any social system to function effectively as a unit, its individual components must be constrained and must cooperate in certain ways. In social groups, those relationships are regulated by shared social norms or values and rules of conduct. There are two basic ways in which such constraining values and rules of conduct can be maintained in a group. One way is for the regulating process to be a part of each person. Then, if that person should begin to violate, or consider violating, such a social value or conduct code, feedback processes within them would bring their behavior back within, or keep it within, acceptable boundaries. That is the function of embarrassment—shame (guilt)—humiliation. It is the emotion of interpersonal wrongdoing, conformity, submission, and subjugation. It results from a realization (or anticipation) of the violation of social values and conduct codes, and an expectation of rejection by others.

The other way of accomplishing social regulation is by action of the system upon the deviating component in a form that the deviator is likely to find noxious, leading him or her to avoid or discontinue deviant behaviors unacceptable to the group. Two other social emotions perform that regulatory function.

Resentment—Jealousy—Hostility. One kind of deviation that is disruptive of group cohesion is for one person to seek the status, power, possessions, or interpersonal relationships (e.g., mate) currently associated with another. Actual or potential coercive, punishing actions towards that competing person may be necessary and useful for terminating, or preventing the occurrence of, such disruptive behavior. The function of resentment—jealousy—hostility is to signal a situation of rivalry and to facilitate overcoming the rival.

Scorn—Contempt—Disdain. The behavior of some individuals may violate group norms of cleanliness, social manners, or the competence with which tasks are carried out, and/or may threaten its welfare. Regulatory processes for getting the individual to "either shape up or ship out" could be useful under those circumstances. That is the function of scorn —contempt—disdain. It is the emotion of rejection of others evaluated as having behaved in an unacceptable, disgusting, or incompetent way. It functions behaviorally to influence others to submit or conform to social norms, and to accept a subordinate role in the group; or it may function to reject them from the group.

Other kinds of emotional labels probably refer to these same basic patterns, or combinations of them. For example, sympathy, tenderness, and pity probably represent the affection pattern manifested toward someone who is somehow helpless, vulnerable, or suffering. Anguish is similar to grief. Pride is probably a version of the pleasure of mastery, perhaps with a little self-love thrown in. One could play this game of inventing possible combinations at great length. Hopefully, the issues will eventually be empirically resolved. However, the extensive modifiability of emotional arousal patterns, and the individual differences that result, make it a very complicated problem to investigate.

The list of proposed instrumental and social emotions includes all of Plutchik's and Izard's categories. One additional instrumental pattern is proposed, that of disinterest—boredom—apathy. Izard believes that social emotions are simply combinations of the others. He considers sexual arousal a "drive" rather than an emotional pattern. He may be correct. However, there is support for considering social emotions as evolutionary emergents. For example, love is usually considered different from pleasure by ordinary folks (e.g., Fuenzalida et al., 1981).

Emotional patterns are more primitive regulatory processes than thoughts. However, in humans, thought processes have evolved regulatory and control functions. Therefore, emotions can be elicited and inhibited by evaluative thoughts, and vice versa.

Defining Attributes of the Basic Emotions

This section has two purposes. First, to facilitate identification and study of different emotional patterns, indicators that have been or could be used to identify the occurrence of each kind of pattern are summarized. Indicators of the subjective, biological, and transactional components and of typical eliciting conditions will be summarized. Second, to support proposing these as basic emotions, evidence of the extent to which each meets the criteria for basic emotions are examined: (a) Can some form of it be observed in at least one other species? (b) Can it be observed in human infants during the first two years of life? (c) Do components of the pattern appear to be universally present in intact humans?; and (d) Does it appear to have some utility or function? It is important to reemphasize that the biological and transactional components of emotional patterns are trainable. Therefore, their manifestations in infancy should show more interindividual and intersituational consistency than in experienced older children and adults. The patterns summarized should be considered prototypical descriptions.

The Instrumental Emotions

Curiosity — Interest — Excitement. This pattern helps regulate collection, construction and retention of useful information about (a) the environment; (b) the individual's own capabilities; and (c) interrelationships among and within (a) and (b) (Wong, 1979).

The *transactional components* represent the approach behavior tendencies of "to explore or search," and secondarily "to welcome or be with" (Plutchik, 1980). They include selectively orienting sensory receptors towards aspects of the environment; focused attention (e.g., eyebrows down; gaze fixed or tracking a stimulus) and perhaps facial expressions of pleasure (e.g., smiling; eyes wide open with eyebrows lifted) as the exploration produces new nonthreatening information; motor movements involving manipulation and pursuit of objects of interest (Fiske & Maddi, 1961; Hunt, 1965; Izard, 1977; Spitz, 1946; Sroufe & Waters, 1976).

Information about the *biological components* of this pattern is sparse. The transactional components are more elaborate and varied than the simple orienting reaction. Therefore, the biological components are probably different from those of the orienting reaction. Zukerman (1979) proposes that "sensation seeking" is a function of the levels of neurochemicals in the limbic system reward areas. Under some conditions, factors such as diet, drugs, nervous system lesions, and endocrine functioning can affect exploratory activity. Pronounced individual differences in restless (e.g., exploratory) activity exist, implying some temperamental differences (Cofer & Appley, 1964; Wong, 1979).

The *subjective components* are experienced as heightened and focused attention; attraction towards the objects, events, or activities involved; and often a sense of animation, invigoration, or excitement. The uncertainty of novel circumstances may provoke both curiosity and slight apprehension (Izard, 1977).

The *eliciting conditions* involve variability, novelty, surprisingness, incongruity, complexity, uncertainty, or conflict that is not too extreme (Berlyne, 1960; Izard, 1977; Plutchik, 1980). Any discrepant experience which produces some "cognitive dissonance" elicits interest and activity to reduce the uncertainty (Berlyne, 1960). However, excesses of those conditions are likely to elicit fear and avoidance rather than interest, particularly in young organisms (Welker, 1961). Being able to control the occurrence or activity of novel events tends to make them interesting rather than frightening (Gunnar-Vongnechten, 1978). When predictable circumstances become less predictable, exploratory behavior increases. It is as if the individual is trying to renew the familiar as well as to reduce the uncertainty of the new circumstances (Wong, 1979).

Other species such as rats and monkeys display this pattern (Harlow & Mears, 1979; Lester, 1969; Mowrer, 1960; Redican, 1982; Wong, 1979). For example, monkeys will spend hours manipulating a little door to get a 10-second glimpse of something interesting on the other side (Butler, 1957). *Human infants* display exploratory behavior within days after birth in visual-facial displays. As motor coordination capabilities mature, mouthing, reaching, touching, and other more elaborate exploratory patterns become apparent (Emde, Kligman, Reich, & Wade, 1978; Hunt, 1965; Schellenbach, 1987; Sroufe, 1979; Stone, Smith, & Murphy, 1973; White, 1975). Vocalizations (e.g., cooing) and smiling during such activity imply positive valence of the experience (Sroufe & Waters, 1976; White, 1975).

All humans appear to experience and display this pattern. The literature of every culture refers to it, and prototypical facial expressions are the same in both primitive and advanced cultures (Hass, 1970; Izard, 1977). G. Allport (1955) concluded that exploration of novel circumstances and possibilities is a cornerstone of personal growth and creativity. White (1959) called this *competence motivation*.

Interested exploration of the environment (and later of ideas) functions to *regulate person-environment transactions* in several ways. Exploration facilitates both observational and instrumental learning (Wong, 1979), promoting the elaboration of concepts, propositions, competencies, skills, and intelligence. Moreover, displays of interest (e.g., attentiveness and smiling) exert a regulatory influence on interpersonal relationships (Fiske & Maddi, 1961; Spitz, 1946; Sroufe & Waters, 1976; Tomkins, 1962; Zukerman, 1974;).

The regulatory function of this pattern is bounded by two other regulatory processes. At one extreme, fear limits exploratory behavior (Mowrer, 1960a, 1960b). Excessive uncertainty is potentially dangerous because it leaves the individual with no basis for anticipating what may happen or for deciding what to do. "Approach with caution" is its message. For example, baby monkeys rush back and temporarily cling to their mothers when confronted with too much novelty. After visual exploration from their safe perch reassures then, they will continue their exploration (Harlow & Mears, 1979). At the other extreme, excessive habitual behavior reduces variability in experience and restricts elaboration of personal knowledge, capabilities, and opportunities. This, too, can be maladaptive.

Disinterest—Boredom—Apathy. This emotional pattern limits the restrictive influence of habitual behavior by encouraging withdrawal from or avoidance of repetitive, highly familiar circumstances which the person has mastered. It has received surprisingly little scholarly attention. About 40 papers on the subject were published from 1926 to 1979

(Smith, 1981). Research on stimulus deprivation and vigilance tasks provides some relevant information. Its status as a pattern is supported by factor analytic studies which separate curiosity and boredom into orthogonal scales (Naylor, 1981); "bored" clusters with terms like "blue" and "sad," and is close to terms like "sluggish," "tired," and "drowsy" (Purcell, 1982).

The *transactional* components represent avoidance behaviors, characterized by tendencies "to stop activity," "to reject or get rid of," or "to withdraw or get away" (Plutchik, 1980). For example, children will discard one toy after a while and look for something else to do. People may impose variability on repetitive tasks. For example, long distance truck drivers may read signs or listen to their radio to remain alert (McBain, 1970). A second form of avoidance is to withdraw into oneself (e.g., "daydreaming"). This is manifest in slower response times, increased variability in kind and accuracy of responses and increased "undirected" motor activity. Drowsiness and actual sleep may occur (Fiske & Maddi, 1961; Smith, 1981).

Information about *biological* components is almost nonexistent. Boredom may be accompanied by decreases in attentiveness, heart rate, blood pressure, oral temperature, and skin conductance (Smith, 1981). The *subjective* components have a negative valence. People report increased feelings of lethargy or fatigue, irritation, sleepiness, increased difficulty in maintaining focused attention, increased daydreaming or thinking; and they tend to be more aware of body sensations such as pain or hunger. In repetitive tasks, people report that increased effort is required to maintain focused attention and adequate performance. Subjective ratings of boredom and objective ratings of performance adequacy do not correlate well because such increased effort can prevent performance decrements (Cofer & Appley, 1964; Fiske & Maddi, 1961; Smith, 1981). Environments which involve extreme and continuous stimulation deprivation first produce relaxation and sleep. Following that, people may begin to experience hallucinations and delusions, feel as if their behavior is "falling apart," and feel frightened (Bexton et al., 1954). Information "nutriment" is essential to maintain and elaborate behavioral organization.

The *eliciting conditions* include an unvarying or predictable environment, or stereotyped, repetitive tasks. Habitual acts are not very interesting. Elements of unfamiliarity, things still to be learned, or levels of skill yet to be achieved are essential for avoiding boredom. Once a novel environment becomes familiar and its challenges have been mastered, the same environment may be perceived as monotonous and elicit boredom. The learning theory concept of reactive inhibition dealt with analogous phenomena (Cofer & Appley, 1964; Fiske & Maddi, 1961; McClelland, Atkinson, Clark, & Lowell, 1953; Smith, 1981; White,

1959). Monotony lies not just in the environment, but also in the "eyes of the beholder."

Little information exists about this emotional pattern in *other species* or *human infants*. Both rats and monkeys, when isolated in impoverished environments, increase their self-stimulation behaviors, or become apathetic and perhaps fall asleep (Harlow & Mears, 1979; Issac, 1952; Mowrer, 1960b). Emde et al. (1978) report observing a "bored-sleepy" appearance in 3- to 4-month-old infants. Infants who live in impoverished environments display apathetic behavior (Hunt, 1965; Spitz, 1945). Cross-cultural evidence that boredom occurs in *all humans* is sparse. Studies of vigilance, and of monotony in work settings in a variety of industrialized countries, have revealed patterns of disinterest and boredom.

Avoidance of repetitive and monotonous environments *regulates person-environment transactions* to facilitate exploration and learning new information and behaviors. Information is "a measure of one's freedom of choice"; so "a greater freedom of choice, greater uncertainty, greater information go hand in hand" (Weaver, 1953). Humans respond habitually to redundancy so that their limited information-processing capacity can be focused on novel and variable information which could expand their possibilities.

Satisfaction—Pleasure—Joy. A behavior episode is an incomplete behavior-environment organization until its intended consequence is produced. The regulatory function of a system compares its present state with an intended future state to adjust the system's functioning to produce a closer match between the two. The experience of satisfaction, pleasure or joy signals progress toward a closer match, or the completion of a coherent organization of behavior-environment events (i.e., a successful behavior episode). For example, football fans increasingly display pleasure as their team successfully moves the ball towards a touchdown.

The *transactional components* are approach behaviors, displaying tendencies "to welcome or be with" or "to embrace or mate" (Plutchik, 1980). In contrast, to interest-instigated exploratory behavior, transactional behaviors regulated by satisfaction—pleasure—joy are more selectively and persistently targeted onto specific objects/people or events related to the behavior episode's guiding intentions. For example, children may curiously explore an area out of interest, but if they are playing hide-and-seek they will methodically explore the area to find someone. The persistence and intensity of actions and of the display of pleasure is a function of the value placed on the consequence sought, the initial level of uncertainty about achieving it, the complexity of the task requirements, and the degree of competence required to produce the desired results (Harter, 1978; Izard, 1977; Jennings et al., 1979; Locke et al., 1970: Plutchik, 1980; Stotland, 1969). Little information is available about the *biological components* of pleasure. There is some anecdotal evidence that positively toned emotions may contribute to good health (Antonovsky, 1979; Cousins, 1979). Little empirical study of the biology of hope, happiness, and joy has been accomplished (Hebb, 1949; Izard, 1977; Tiger, 1979; Tomkins, 1962).

The *subjective* components represent positive affect different from sensory (e.g., taste) pleasure (Chapman et al., 1976). There is an anticipation of the occurrence of the desired consequence, and a willingness to expend effort to try to produce it, sometimes labeled *optimism* or *hope*. There is a zestful and energetic feeling related to successful completion of the episode. There is often retrospective mental rehearsal of the episode with pleassurable feelings, as illustrated by sports fans who "replay" aspects of a game won by their team. Positive evaluative thoughts of aspects of the episode are present. The greater the goal attainment expectations, the more important the goal, and the more challenging the task, the more intense will be the positive subjective experience when the goal is achieved (Harter, 1978; Izard, 1977; Locke et al., 1970; Stotland, 1969; White, 1959;).

The *eliciting conditions* lie in subjective evaluations of the progressive effectiveness of the current behavior episode (Schachtel, 1959), such as, progress toward a creative accomplishment, formulating the solution to a problem, or reunion with a valued person or object (Izard, 1977; Harlow & Mears, 1979). Pleasure results from "the object achieved" (Yampey, 1980). *Other species*, such as monkeys and apes, display a similar pattern when solving puzzles or problems, or when involved in play activities (Harlow & Mears, 1979; Mowrer, 1960; Plutchik, 1980; Van Hooff, 1973). *Infants* display pleasure when expectations are confirmed (as in peek-a-boo games) and when they successfully manipulate their environment (Hiatt et al., 1979; Sroufe, 1979). Laughter upon making a discovery, resolving some uncertainty (e.g., removing a mask revealing a parent's face), or successfully completing actions occurs during the first year of life (Bridges, 1932; Izard, 1977; Lewis & Rosenblum, 1978; Sroufe, 1979; Sroufe & Waters, 1976;). Cross-cultural evidence of facial expressions indicates that *all humans* probably experience this emotion (Boucher & Ekman, 1975; Ekman, 1982), and some attributes of pleasure-related vocalizations are recognizable in different spoken languages (Kramer, 1964). Anecdotal evidence from the literature of different cultures supports the generality of this pattern.

Pleasure's positive valence regulates *person-environment transactions* to facilitate the continuation and repetition of successful behavior episode schemata. It facilitates learning, and attachment or commitment to objects or persons who share in successful accomplishments. It facilitates increased levels of skill development, as well as establishment and attempted achievement of higher performance goals, because successfully accomplishing "difficult" tasks yields more pleasure than accomplishing "easy" ones (Izard, 1977; Lewis & Rosenblum, 1978; Locke et al., 1970; Stotland, 1969; Tiger, 1979). Anticipation of a desired result is often accompanied by subjective excitement and movement, sometimes characterized as a build-up of "tension." Successful completion of the effort is often evidenced by some energetic display (e.g., laughter, hand-clapping, jumping up and down), characterized as "tension release." This has led some theorists to erroneously conclude that tension reduction is the cause of pleasure.

Downhearted—Discouraged—Depressed. This emotion facilitates "giving up" on efforts evaluated as ineffective. Typically, it may vary from mild downheartedness to temporary severe discouragement. A more persistent and disabling form, termed melancholia or depression, has been extensively studied. Akiskal and McKinney (1975) note that discouragement is "a ubiquitous, universal emotional response" to everyday experiences of loss or frustrated efforts. Although they pose the question of where normal discouragement ends and depressive illness begins, all of the theories and research they reviewed deal with depressive illness. Similarly, Zung (1973) reviewed methods for clinically distinguishing between normal discouragement and signs of depressive illness. Normal discouragement results from specific failure experiences. Little theoretical or empirical attention has been devoted to its adaptive value (Dorpat, 1977). Serious depression involves anticipating future failures or losses in an array of circumstances that are expected to continue (Dorpat, 1977).

The *transactional components* represent avoidant behaviors, with tendencies "to stop activity," "to withdraw or get away," or "to cry or mourn" (Plutchik, 1980). People "give up" on activities which they assume to be ineffective in producing intended results, and they do one of two types of things. Typically, there will be a shift to a different kind of behavior episode; that is, they will "try something else." More intense discouragement may be followed by a time-limited period of inactivity or restless, untargeted behavior; in this case, the "giving up" is more generalized. In depressive illness; there is a generalized withdrawal. Psychomotor retardation (sometimes alternating with psychomotor agitation) is one manifestation of a general "slowing down" of most response processes (Akiskal & McKinney, 1975; Dorpat, 1977; Radloff, 1977). There may be some withdrawal from social interaction, manifested in such behaviors as a reduction in talking or gaze aversion (Natale, 1977), crying, a reduction in eating, disruption of sleep patterns, and constipation (Akiskal & McKinney, 1975; Cooke, 1980; Giambra, 1977; Radloff, 1977). The prototypical facial expression is characterized by a pulling down of the eyebrows, wrinkles across the bridge of the nose, partially closed eyes with wrinkles at the corners, and mouth closed or slightly open with corners turned down. In monkeys and small children it is similar to a pouting expression (Ekman, 1982; Izard, 1977).

The biological *components* of depression but not of discouragement have been extensively studied. There may be a genetic vulnerability for developing depressive illness (Akiskal & McKinney, 1975; Cadoret, 1974). Three kinds of depression-related biochemical processes interact in a complex network of positive and negative feedback loops to regulate this pattern (Akiskal & McKinney, 1975): (a) the role of ions and their exchanges during nerve transmission, which is influenced by body sodium balance; (b) hormonal variations (e.g., pituitary, hypothalamic, adrenal, thyroid) influenced by the limbic ANS circuits; and (c) imbalances of neurotransmitters at important synaptic junctions in the brain. The utility of lithium in treating depression maybe related to such deficiencies (Akiskal & McKinney, 1975; Daly, 1978; Sourkes, 1977). The well-documented greater frequency of depression in women and older people may, in part, be a function of changing patterns of biochemical functioning normatively characteristic of them (McGeer & McGeer, 1980; Sourkes, 1977). The physiology of depression and that of physical fatigue appear somewhat similar, perhaps because both function to facilitate a cessation of ongoing behavior.

Subjective components have a negative valence which can vary from mild to extreme, and manifest a slowing down and decline in organization of response processes. These include loss of energy and appetite; feelings of fatigue; feeling sad, helpless and hopeless; decreased ability to experience pleasure (including diminished sexual interest); poor concentration, slow thinking, or mixed-up thoughts; lowered self-esteem and increased self-reproach; and perhaps suicidal thoughts (Akiskal & McKinney, 1975; Dorpat, 1977; Giambra, 1977; Shapiro, 1979). Evidence does not support Freud's contention that depression is anger turned inward (Akiskal & McKinney, 1975; Shapiro, 1979), but feelings of guilt are frequently present.

The typical *eliciting* conditions involve actual or anticipated failure to obtain, retain, or recover something a person values. Because intimate relationships (e.g., marriage) are such important sources of many satisfactions, their disruption is a frequent trigger of discouragement or depression (Heins, 1978; Schwarz & Zuroff, 1979). Depression eliciting thoughts often appraise something desired as unattainable because the person evaluates him- or herself as incompetent or unable to control events. Once learned, such anticipatory evaluative thoughts can elicit discouragement and/or depression without validation by actual events because withdrawal patterns prevent testing the assumptions. The learning and functioning of such evaluative attributions is a cornerstone of some influential theories of depression (Beck, 1967; Garber &Seligman, 1980; Seligman, 1975). However, they are mutually influential. Thoughts can elicit depressive reactions, and moods of discouragement and depression can elicit negative thoughts (Garber & Hollon, 1980; Harvey, 1981; Lewinsohn, Steinmetz, Larson, & Franklin, 1981; Miller & Norman, 1979; Wortman & Dintzer, 1978). Events which alter normal patterns of biochemical-neurotransmitter-limbic system functioning (e.g., viral infections; hypothyrodism; chronic discouragement) can also trigger depressive emotional patterns. Chemical or anatomical lesioning of limbic system "reward centers" disrupts the occurrence of depressive reactions (Akiskal & McKinney, 1975).

Similar "giving up" patterns have been experimentally produced in *other species*, such as dogs (Seligman, 1975), monkeys (Kaufman & Rosenblum, 1967), and chimpanzees (Dorpat, 1977). Depressive patterns have also been observed in *human infants* and young children (Blumberg, 1978; Bowlby, 1973; Cytryn, McNew, & Bunney, 1980; Dorpat, 1977; Welner, 1978). "Giving up" behaviors can be observed in the play of infants when confronted with activities beyond their capabilities. *All humans* appear to be vulnerable to depressions, since they have been mentioned throughout recorded human history (Menninger, 1963). For example, the second century physician, Galen, spoke of melancholic dispositions, and "black bile" was considered a determinant of depressive reactions. Epidemiological studies reveal that depression occurs in most countries and cultures (Turns, 1978).

This emotion regulates *person-environment transactions* to terminate unsuccessful efforts. Its noxious qualities encourage the reorganization of thoughts and actions towards other means and/or ends (Arieti, 1978; Dorpat, 1977; Wortman & Dintzer, 1978). Freud's "reality principle" represents a similar view. The ego functions to test reality so that hopeless efforts can be replaced by effective ones, and irrevocable losses can be avoided or substituted for (Ford & Urban, 1963). Behavior theory assumes that removal of relevant discriminative and reinforcing stimuli will reduce the occurrence of related behavior patterns, and depressed people behave as if they were on an extinction trail (Mathews, 1977). To control the disrupting impact of undesirable circumstances, infants may reduce activity, withdraw, and heighten their perceptual barriers against environmental stimulation; this is called *conservation-withdrawal:* (Schmale & Engel, 1975).

Developmentally, empirical evidence supports the following view (Wortman & Dintzer, 1978). Normal discouragement results when a person's efforts in a particular behavior episode are not succeeding. The person typically develops causal attributions about why they are not. If he or she assumes that the desired result cannot be produced, or that the goal is worth no further effort, the normal response is give up and do something else. If the person assumes success may still be possible, he or she is likely to invent and try alternate means, sometimes termed the *facilitation effect*. Individuals may develop generalized habits of evaluative or attributional thoughts leading them to anticipate future loss of, or failure at, most things they value; such thoughts can continually elicit discouragement and/or depression and "giving up" behaviors, through rumination about how terrible the future is likely to be. Such chronic emotional arousal can produce a reorganization of underlying biochemical-neurochemical processes, and those neurochemical inbalances may then contribute to maintaining the depressive pattern. Thus, adaptive discouragement can become maladaptive depressive illness. Viewed that way, the suicidal tendencies of some depressives who anticipate such a miserable future is understandable.

Remedying an extreme depressive pattern requires disrupting it (e.g., through biochemical interventions), and then trying to help the person alter his or her overgeneralized habits of evaluative thought. Interruption of normal discouragement can be accomplished by (a) doing things which produce positive emotions (e.g., going to a funny movie); (b) engaging in tasks which produce a sense of purpose and accomplishment, and self-evaluations of competence; and (3) involving oneself in pleasant and satisfying interactions with other people (Lewinsohn et al., 1978). These methods "work" because they represent the kinds of alternative behaviors which should naturally follow from discouragement. Reevaluating and altering one's own evaluative thoughts may also sometimes be useful.

Annoyance–Anger–Rage. This emotion functions to help overcome circumstances evaluated as actually or potentially interfering with obtaining, retaining, or reobtaining something a person wants or values. Until recently, aggression received more study than anger; for example, study of the "frustration-aggression hypothesis" (Averill, 1978; Biaggio, 1980). For example, only about 2% of 1,800 citations on aggression were cross listed under anger (Crabtree & Moyer, 1977). While frustrating conditions are likely to produce anger, and anger is likely to be followed by aggression, the occurrence of aggressive behavior does not require anger as an antecedent (Cofer & Appley, 1964).

Aggressive action against frustrating circumstances is an inborn transactional component of the anger pattern. However, people can (and usually do) learn to inhibit socially tabooed aggressive acts, and to substitute alternative, socially acceptable transactional behaviors (e.g., verbal persuasion). It is "the predominating combination of factors" (Goodenough, 1931), rather than particular behaviors that identifies the presence of a particular emotion, such as anger (Averill, 1978).

The prototypical *transactional components* represent approach behaviors since they involve attempts to influence the "object of our anger" (DeRivera, 1977), and to promote action tendencies like "to attack or hurt," and "to reject or get rid of," along with learned avoidance tendencies "to withdraw or get away" (Plutchik, 1980). An angry infant stiffens its body and arches its back; draws its feet and legs up and down in jerky, vigorous motions; and may display fairly well-coordinated slashing or striking movements with hands and arms. Its face may become flushed and there maybe rapid breathing and perhaps breath-holding; vocalizations may include a loud, sharp, usually sustained crying pattern, or sometimes snarling, growling, or grunting sounds; the lower lip may be drawn down with teeth bared, the muscles of the eyebrows move inward and downward creating a frown, and the eyes may be directed at the instigating object or squinted if crying occurs.

Beyond infancy, children display three types of expressive anger patterns (Goodenough 1931). The pattern of *undirected energy* (often termed a "temper tantrum") includes jumping up and down, screaming, throwing themselves on the floor, etc. *Resistance* includes efforts to get around or remove the frustrating circumstance, or to refuse to conform to unacceptable demands (e.g., pulling hard on a toy stuck under a chair or sulking). *Retaliation* or *aggression* involves an attack upon the offending conditions through behaviors such as biting, hitting, kicking, and name calling. Averill (1978), Ekman (1982), and Izard (1977) provide additional information about similar manifestations in adults.

The *biological components* reflect a temporary increase in SNS excitation (Zillmann, 1979) which prepares the person for more vigorous physical action (Izard, 1977); symptoms include increased heart rate, flushed skin; rapid breathing, and tensed muscles, accompanied by an increase in blood supply (Mayes, 1979). Under prolonged or repetitive anger arousal, other biological functions such as menstruation and the production of breast milk may be disrupted (Goodenough, 1931). Constipation may increase. Energy and biological mobilization occurs suddenly, but will gradually subside if no further provocation occurs, or will be reduced by motoric action. Actions directed towards something other than the frustrating agent are less effective in reducing the arousal. Further provocation occurring during anger arousal can further intensify it (Zillmann, 1979). Intense levels of anger arousal increase muscular power but decrease coordination. Fatigue and illness increase irritability and vulnerability to anger episodes. In children, anger outbursts are more frequent shortly before meal times (Goodenough, 1931; Izard, 1977; Stratton, 1926).

The valence of the *subjective components* has both positive (e.g., similar to excitement) and negative qualities. One is likely when angry to feel tense and jittery; to have a feeling of increased energy or strength and an impulse to act or strike out at the interfering circumstances; and the face and skin may feel warm. One may notice increased respiration and heart rate. These reactions feel automatic and somewhat beyond one's control (e.g., feeling "gripped by anger") (Averill, 1978). There are likely to be hostile thoughts. With intense arousal, thought patterns may become irrational and/or disorganized. Persistent or reoccurring levels of anger arousal may be accompanied by occasional feelings of dizziness, gastric discomfort, and/or headaches (Zillmann, 1979).

The eliciting *conditions* involve evaluation of events as interfering with successful completion of a behavioral episode. In behavioristic terminology, anger results from nonreinforcement of an anticipation or expectation (Spence, 1960). A common definition of frustration is that it is the state of a motivated organism when its goal behavior is thwarted (Cofer & Appley, 1964). Physical or psychological restraints or obstructions which keep a young child from doing what it "intensely desires to do" will elicit anger (Izard, 1977). As children mature, difficulty in completing self-directed activity may provoke anger (e.g., failure to construct a tower with blocks). Conditions which pose a threat to an adult's physical, psychological, or social well-being may elicit anger; such conditions may involve the threat of physical assault, insults, criticism (particularly if undeserved) (Berkowitz 1969; Olweus, 1972; Zillmann, 1979). For adults, many goals are symbolic (e.g., to maintain self-esteem, solve a conceptual problem), or social (e.g., to obtain or retain status and power). Therefore, the potentially obstructing conditions may be symbolic or social (Averill, 1978). Some environments may be more obstructing than others. For example, Goodenough (1931) found that child displays of anger were more frequent the more adults there were in the household. The intensity and duration of the anger pattern is a function of the degree of fatigue, the importance of the obstructed goal, the strength of the instigator (e.g., a mild criticism versus a harsh insult), the degree of interference, and the number of behavior patterns frustrated (Cofer & Appley, 1964). Anger patterns occur more frequently if they usually produce what the child wants (Goodenough, 1931).

Pigeons, rats, cats, lions, monkeys, gorillas, and turtles illustrate *other species* which display aggressive and expressive behavior patterns analogous to the human anger pattern under similar eliciting conditions (Berkowitz, 1969; Bigelow, 1972; Calhoun, 1972; Hutchinson, 1972; Melges & Poppen, 1976; Plutchik, 1980). *Human infants* display anger patterns early in the first year of life (Goodenough, 1931; Izard, 1977; Sroufe, 1979; Watson & Watson, 1921). In children, the duration of an anger episode seldom lasts more than 5 minutes, and peak in frequency at around 2 years of age. Expressions of anger are quite similar in *all human* cultures studied. The basic pattern is essentially the same in blind and sighted children (Averill, 1978; Ekman, 1982; Leff, 1977; Plutchik, 1980; Shimoda et al., 1978). References to anger appears throughout human history, and is present in most religions. The first major treatise on anger was written by Seneca (50 A.D.) (reprinted in Basore, 1963) The primitive automaticity of the anger pattern has been recognized in law. Thus, crimes of "passion" are punished less severely than crimes of "intent" in most cultures (Averill, 1978).

The anger pattern functions to regulate *person-environment transactions* to remove or overcome conditions which interfere with accomplishing or obtaining one's objectives. When one's goals, possessions, or physical and psychological integrity is threatened, anger mobilizes one's energy to defend and overcome with vigor and strength (Izard, 1977). Expressive components of the pattern also help to regulate interpersonal relationships by upholding or enforcing personal and social norms, and power and status relationships (Averill, 1978; Kemper, 1978).

Anger and fear patterns are frequently linked for at least two reasons. First, some dangerous, interfering conditions may also instigate fear (e.g., the danger of physical assault). Second, punishment and rejection elicit fear, which inhibits anger expressions. As a result of such training, the experience of anger can become an elicitor of fear.

Startle—Surprise—Astonishment. Startle interrupts ongoing behavior and is probably not an emotion (Ekman, 1984), but surprise has emotional properties (see Chapter 7). This pattern is triggered by sudden, unexpected events producing action tendencies "to stop activity" and "to explore or search" (Plutchik, 1980). In evolutionary terms, "freezing" and "checking out" sudden events probably had significant adaptive value. If unexpected motion or sound signaled a predator, the potential prey was less likely to be noticed or attacked immediately if it were motionless. In the prototypical pattern, the person is immobile and alert, and muscles tense, eyes wide open, as if preparing for locomotion (Izard, 1977). Unexpected events may bring good or bad news. Therefore, subjectively the experience may have some of the qualities of excitement, curiosity, or interest if the information is evaluated as "good news," or fear if evaluated as "bad news."

Wariness—Fear—Terror. This emotion facilitates actions to avoid being damaged or killed. Damage may involve disruption of biological or psychological organization. This emotion has been extensively studied in animals, children, and adults (Bowlby, 1973; Hinde, 1970; Lader, 1969); in learning (Cofer & Appley, 1964; Mowrer, 1960b); in stress and illness (Basowitz et al., 1955); and in disastrous situations (Bahnson, 1964). The results generally support a three-component model of emotions (Izard, 1977; Rachman, 1978; Sluckin, 1979).

As with other emotional patterns, some individual differences in its occurrence may be related to genetic predispositions (Koranyi, 1977; Slater & Shields, 1969), and individual differences in biological and transactional components can and do develop through learning (Koranyi, 1977; Lacey, 1967; Slukin, 1979; Spielberger, 1972). Therefore, it should not be surprising that multivariate studies of fear patterns in adults typically find modest intercorrelations among indicators of subjective, biological, and transactional components (Archer, 1979; Cattell, 1972). This does not mean there is no basic pattern; rather it means that individuals may develop different versions of it and a person's pattern may vary from occasion to occasion. Rather than considering it a synonym for fear, anxiety is best considered a mixture of negative emotions such as fear, guilt, shame, and depression (Izard, 1972), and sometimes even excitement (e.g., "The children are anxious for Christmas to come").

The *transactional components* are typically avoidant behaviors, reflecting action tendencies "to withdraw or get away"; "to stop activity"; and sometimes "to reject or get rid of" and "to cry or mourn" (Plutchik, 1980). Humans have evolved several interrelated mechanisms for preventing harm to themselves (Archer, 1979). The most primitive pattern is *physical withdrawal* or *escape*, typical of infants (Smith, 1979). However, it is more adaptive to withdraw before being hurt, so *avoidance* or "anticipatory withdrawal" is a second pattern. A third pattern involves *becoming immobile*, or "freezing." In animals, *feigning death* (e.g., "playing possum") is a special form of tonic immobility. Predators will often lose interest in a prey when it appears dead or helpless. Ghastly stories of human massacres reveal that some humans have escaped death in precisely this way. "Fainting from fear" may be a form of these two primitive patterns. Finally, *threatening behavior* or *attack* may be used when the various forms of avoidant behavior are not possible or appear likely to be ineffective (Izard, 1977). There is a prototypical facial expression of fear (Izard, 1977). Some alarm calls may occur, usually involving higher frequency sounds, as in an infant's crying or a call for protection ("Help!").

The pattern of *biological components* is prototypically somewhat different in normal fear, intense fear, and chronic fear responses (Archer, 1979; Cattell, 1972; Gellhorn, 1965; Koranyi, 1977; Mayes, 1979). In normal fear, the function is to prepare the body for quick, emergency action to avoid or escape potential harm. Therefore, the prototypical pattern is one primarily of increased SNS activity: The rate and strength of the heartbeat increase; the blood supply is redistributed; blood sugar and red blood cells increase; deeper respiration and bronchial dilation occur; rate of blood coagulation and lymphocites increase, preparing the body to fight invasions.

This pattern optimizes short-term benefits for immediate action to the potential detriment of long-term growth, reproduction, and disease resistance if the pattern persists over extended periods of time. Escape from, avoidance or control of the eliciting conditions will terminate the fear pattern (Gunnar, 1980; N. Miller, 1978). However, for adults in modern societies, fear elicitors are usually psychological and social, and vigorous physical action is not an appropriate terminator. Therefore, fear arousal patterns may occur frequently or be maintained for more extended periods. Such "chronic" fear arousal may result in some retuning of the basic patterns and perhaps some biological damage (Grinker et al., 1956; Selye, 1976).

Sometimes a fear episode may be very intense, as during wartime combat (Koranyi, 1977). Extreme fear appears to arouse the entire ANS, and a variety of PNS responses get mixed in with the SNS pattern (e.g., urination, defecation, nausea). Such "flooding" of the autonomic nervous system with excitation disrupts the organization and flexibility of all behavioral functions, producing irrational and maladaptive functioning (Gellhorn, 1965).

The *subjective components* have a negative affective quality. There are feelings of muscular tension, apprehension, and uncertainty about what may happen, and thoughts about wanting to get away from the troublesome circumstances, or to be as inconspicuous as possible (analogous to "freezing"). This may involve a form of response inhibition (Izard, 1977; Spielberger, 1972). In extreme fear there may be an experience of dread or panic. The perceptual and behavioral field shrinks to the "here and now" of a few centrally important factors, reducing behavioral flexibility. Mental "turbulence" and disorganization may occur. Thoughts of the fearful circumstances may be avoided or repressed; purposeful mentation may be slowed or disorganized; there may be a temporary block to the processing and assimilation of information; and there may be a feeling of loss of control of mental and physical behavior (Bahnson, 1964; Koranyi, 1977). When there is no apparent cause for fear, the affect may be called anxiety. When fear patterns are frequent or persistent, dream content is likely to be influenced. Experienced psychotherapists often note that dream emotions are "honest," accurately reflecting the dream's thematic significance no matter how obscure the dream symbolism (Lesse, 1959).

The prototypical *eliciting conditions* involve events evaluated as of real or potential danger, including the presence of possible attackers (Russell, 1979). Epstein (1972) identified three basic types of eliciting conditions each of which has evolutionary significance (Russell, 1979):

(a) primary overstimulation (e.g., loud sounds); (b) cognitive incongruity (e.g., unfamiliar objects or events); and (c) response unavailability (e.g., having no behaviors with which to control or avoid the noxious circumstances).

In infants, for example, inborn elicitors include sudden loud noises, loss of physical support, visual cliffs, looming of figures over the infant, and strange/discrepant persons or objects. They are more powerful in combination than separately (Jersild & Holmes, 1935; Russell, 1979; Smith, 1979; Sroufe, 1979). These decline in influence and other elicitors develop as infants grow older. The most important development is that the child's imagistic and evaluative thoughts become increasingly important elicitors of fear; common examples are imagining dangerous animals, being afraid of the dark, and anticipating loss of parents (Jersild & Holmes, 1935; Sroufe, 1979). Wolman (1978) describes over 50 kinds of circumstances which frequently produce fear in children.

In older children and adults, self-referrent schemata and social relationships become behavioral organizations to be defended as much as the physical body. For example, paratrooper trainees experience fear as much because of their anticipation of possible rejection by their buddies and superiors if they fail as because of their anticipation of possible bodily harm (Basowitz et al., 1955; Izard, 1972; Lader, 1969). The developmental shift is generally away from immediate environmental threats to anticipated, cognitively represented threats which increasingly relate toward social relationships. Some biological components of a fear pattern may be triggered by organic dysfunctions and be interpreted as "feeling anxious" (e.g., a gall bladder "attack").

Protection responses to noxious stimuli occur in many *different species* "from the amoeba to humans" (Plutchik, 1980), including rodents, dogs, monkeys, and baboons (Archer, 1979; Cofer & Appley, 1964; Darwin, 1872; Hinde, 1970; Salzen, 1979; Seligman, 1975). There are some species differences in the nature of the pattern, and some species-specific eliciting stimuli. *Human infants* display precursors of the fear pattern during the first 6 months; prototypical fear patterns begin to occur fully during the second six months of life (Bowlby, 1973; Jersild & Holmes, 1935; Lewis & Rosenblum, 1974; Schellenbach, 1987; Smith, 1979; Sroufe, 1979).

Humans throughout history and diverse cultures have struggled with fear. Ancient writings such as Egyptian hieroglyphics mention it, as do Oriental and Western philosophers, and most religions (Osofsky, 1979; Reymert, 1928; Spielberger, 1972). It has been prominent in the theory and practice of psychopathology and psychotherapy (Ford & Urban, 1963). Prototypical facial expressions of fear are similar in different cultures, unless modified by special culture-specific display rules (Ekman, 1972, 1973, 1982).

Fear helps regulate *person-environment* transactions to protect the individual against harm. It may have evolved from primitive protective contact responses (Salzen, 1979) under predation pressure (Archer, 1979). By influencing avoidance of, or protection from, other species and conspecifics invading the individual's territory, inclusive fitness processes may have been facilitated (Smith, 1979).

In modern human societies, where avoidance of harm tends to depend upon nonphysical behaviors (e.g., verbal negotiation, police protection) the prototypical transactional components of fear may have less adaptive value. However, fear-avoidance socialization is still effective in promoting caution in children about potentially dangerous conditions. Moreover, moderate amounts of fear help regulate social systems by facilitating avoidance of interpersonal conflict over possession, status, and roles (Kemper, 1978). In that sense, anger and fear may interact in social regulation. Threat gestures by one person may elicit fear in another and cause them both to be wary about how they interact. Since new elicitors are readily learned, fear-avoidance patterns can be quickly linked to any new dangers that society might invent (e.g., environmental pollution).

Dislike—Disgust—Loathing. This pattern functions to produce rejection or avoidance of potentially contaminating conditions (Izard, 1977; Plutchik, 1980). It has been subjected to relatively little empirical study. It is more than a sensory reaction (e.g., a bitter taste is considered "bad" but not necessarily disgusting by humans). In studies involving Americans, terms and facial expressions representing disgust and those representing contempt are rated as similar. Sanitation habits and public health practices protect most Americans from frequent exposure to physically putrid environments, but people often apply the term *disgust* to certain types of repugnant behaviors or habits (Kemper, 1978).

The *transactional components* represent avoidant behaviors, involving action tendencies of "to reject or get rid of" or "to withdraw or get away" (Plutchik, 1980). There is a characteristic facial expression (Ekman & Friesen, 1975), which is often accompanied by turning the head and moving away from the repugnant source. It may also be accompanied by retching and/or vomiting. No information about *biological components* has been found, except that the senses of taste and smell and the oral rejection of injested materials seems to be related to this emotion. The *subjective components* have a negative valence. There is a feeling of closing up of the throat, and people may say "it makes me feel sick to my stomach." They feel "repelled" by the appearance, odor, or taste of the object, material, or behavior. Their thoughts are usually about getting away from the repugnant circumstances or person. The initial *elicitors* appear to be noxious tastes and smells (Ekman, 1982; Izard, 1977). With learning, people also experience the sight of rotten, putrid material as an elicitor (e.g., seeing another person's vomit). With further learning, people may experience thoughts or memories as elicitors. *Other species* retch and vomit, and disgustlike reactions have been observed in rats (Young, 1949).

Adultlike facial expressions of disgust have been observed in *infants*, particularly when confronted with some bad odor or something which tastes unpleasant (Bridges, 1932; Ekman, 1982; Izard, 1978; Young & Decarie, 1977). Essentially the same facial expression is recognized as signaling disgust in all *humans* in a variety of the world's cultures. Avoidance of putrid conditions helps regulate *person-environment* transactions to reject or avoid conditions that might produce illness or death or degrade one in the eyes of others. It may also perform a social regulation function, by producing rejection or avoidance of people whose poor personal hygiene or behavior is noxious and unacceptable (Izard, 1977; Plutchik, 1980).

The Social Emotions

Instrumental emotions help regulate all behavior episodes, including those involving other people. For example, one can experience joy in collaborative accomplishments, or anger when someone obstructs one's efforts. However, social emotions function primarily to regulate: (a) intimate interpersonal interactions; and (b) the construction and maintenance of social organization, for example, *hierarchy* and *territoriality*. Social group living is an evolutionary product that requires commitment and attachment to other individuals and a balancing of self-interest and allegiance to the group. Social emotions not only guarantee that individuals will have a propensity for group affiliation, but also that such affiliations will be innately pleasurable and their disruption innately unpleasurable (DeLong, 1972). Research on social emotions is limited, but growing interest in understanding "close" relationships (e.g., marriage) is producing increased attention to social emotions (Berscheid, 1983).

Sexual Arousal—Pleasure—Excitement. The sexual arousal pattern functions to promote and regulate reproduction. It is the emotion of courtship and mating. The initial scientific studies of sexuality were predominantly anthropological (Mantegazza, 1932) and medical (Sulloway, 1983). Knowledge of sexual physiology developed early in human history, and practical knowledge of sexual arousal was systematically taught in preparation for sexual relations in many early human cultures (Symons, 1979). Empirical study of sexuality in biology was a natural consequence of evolutionary theory's premise of reproductive advantage (Hutchinson, 1978). It became an issue of major clinical interest as a result of Sigmund Freud's work (Ford & Urban, 1963). Empirical investigation of human sexuality by psychologists and sociologists is fairly recent (Kinsey et al., 1948, 1953; Masters & Johnson, 1966). Sexual arousal was initially conceived of as a biological drive analogous to hunger and thirst, a view still held by some (Izard, 1977). The female estrous cycle lends credibility to that view, but it ignores evidence that male animals' sexual arousal seems to be more stimulus-controlled than biologically precipitated.

Lust and *love* are different emotional arousal patterns. In literature, the arts, and the social sciences affection and love have often been interpreted to be a function of sexual drives. Love is not listed in the indices of Kinsey's (1948, 1953) studies of human sexuality. However, Symons' (1979) synthesis of diverse evidence supports the existence of a sexual emotion which is related to sexual behavior, and different from the feelings and behaviors involved in caring for children, and from affectionate relationships in general. There is empirical evidence that romantic or affectionate relationships are not preconditions for sexual arousal, and vice versa (Fisher & Byrne, 1978). Harlow's views concerning multiple affectional systems in monkeys supports this view (Harlow, 1971; Harlow & Mears, 1982).

The *transactional components* represent approach behaviors. They are composed of two parts: an attraction-seduction phase, and intercourse. The attraction-seduction pattern takes many forms as a function of social-cultural variables and personal history and capabilities (Juhasz, 1973; Kinsey et al., 1948, 1953; Masters & Johnson, 1966; Symons, 1979). Attraction and seduction perform three functions: to signal interest (e.g., flirting); to indicate availability (e.g., "your place or mine"); and to physically arouse (e.g., kissing and petting). The intercourse phase involves a union of the male and female genitals, along with synchronous, rhythmic body movements until orgasm. During intercourse the face may take on an expression similar to that of severe pain, with expanded nostrils, open mouth, pursed lips, and furrowed brow. Vocalizations may occur. The acuity of all senses decreases. It is a whole-body response which tends to shut out the external world.

The *biological components* are essentially the same for men and women. The pulse rate, respiration rate and depth, and blood pressure increase markedly; the peripheral blood flow increases; bleeding from wounds may be reduced; tumescence of distensible tissue occurs (e.g., penis, nipples); special vaginal, cervical, and penis secretions occur; nasal and salivary secretions increase; pupils dilate, narrowing the range of vision;

the entire nervous system is involved and rhythmic neuromuscular contractions occur throughout the body. The biological components are similar, though not identical, both to those of an anger arousal pattern and to a pattern of very vigorous physical exercise (Kinsey et al., 1953; Masters & Johnson, 1966). While hormonal patterns vary in sexual functioning, they do not appear to cause sexual arousal in humans (Hutchinson, 1978; Symons, 1979).

The *subjective components* have a positive valence. People feel warm (probably because of the increased peripheral blood flow). They experience a sense of growing excitement and of muscle tension. They may notice some of the biological changes. Their attention narrows, and their thoughts tend to focus on the other person, on their own feelings, and on anticipations of what may ensue. As intercourse proceeds, pleasurable sensations are produced and the level of subjective excitement increases. Orgasm produces a sudden release of tension, followed by a period of relaxation (Kinsey et al., 1948, 1953; Masters & Johnson, 1966; Symons, 1979).

The typical *eliciting conditions* are somewhat different for men and women. Negative tissue states such as illness, fatigue, or pain decrease susceptibility for both. Physical attractiveness and sight of the naked body are usually more stimulating for males than for females. Appearance is correlated with potential reproductive success in women (e.g., health and youth), and therefore may have some evolutionary potency for males. The market for pornography has been largely a male market throughout history. The interpersonal component appears more important for women than for men, although flirtation and seductive interpersonal behavior have potency for both. While both sexes can arouse themselves with thoughts or fantasy, this appears more frequent and effective in men than in women. Sexual arousal may be more easily conditioned to a variety of stimuli for men; for example, sexual fetishes are more prevalent among men (Cook, 1981; Gebhard, 1965; Kinsey et al., 1948, 1953; Masters & Johnson, 1966; Symons, 1979;).

The sexual behavior of many *other species* has been studied (Beach, 1965, 1976; Ford & Beach, 1951; Harlow, 1971; Hutchinson, 1978; Symons, 1979). There are many similarities, but humans differ in some important ways. A key one is that in most mammals, male and female sexual activity occurs only during extrous cycles. In contrast, the pleasurable aspect of sexual emotional arousal may facilitate human sexual activity at any time. Freud's proposals concerning *infant sexuality* shocked people, but sexual behavior (including what looks like orgasms without ejaculation) has been observed in both male (Kinsey et al., 1948) and female (Kinsey et al., 1953) infants during the first year of life. Small children masturbate and speak of the good feelings it produces

(Broderick, 1973; Rothchild, 1973). *All humans* display similar sexual patterns in all cultures, modified somewhat by cultural differences (Mantegazza, 1932; Symons, 1979; Van Gulik, 1961).

Sexual arousal *regulates person-environment transactions* by functioning to bring potentially appropriate mates together, and to produce coordination of both mood and behavior to facilitate successful intercourse. Through its positive subjective qualities it encourages repeated sexual activity, thereby increasing the likelihood of successful fertilization of the female. Through their learnability in humans, the cues that elicit and maintain sexual arousal can proliferate (Adler, 1978; Beach, 1965; Symons, 1979).

Acceptance—Affection—Love. This emotion functions to regulate more permanent social bonding and to facilitate the interpersonal sharing and caring behaviors celebrated in story and song throughout human history. It is a cornerstone of great religions (e.g., Christianity) (Mellen, 1981). It is considered important in most forms of psychotherapy (Ford & Urban, 1963). Some theorists consider it nearly as basic as physiological and safety needs (Maslow, 1954). Despite all this, it has received less attention from scholars than most other emotions (Izard, 1977). Social systems (e.g., families) must insure both the welfare of their members and their cooperative production and sharing of resources and mutual security. This often requires personal sacrifice in the interest of others. Affection provides such a regulatory influence, supplemented in humans by thought processes.

Although Freud initially emphasized sexuality, psychoanalytic theory has evolved so that the "life instinct" and "procreative instinct" are not considered identical (Menninger, 1963). The world's greatest lovers have not been the Don Juans but people like Jesus and Albert Schweitzer. Based on anthropological and comparative animal studies, Eibl-Eibesfeldt (1971) and Symons (1979) conclude that sexual and affectionate emotional patterns are different and do not serve the same functions. Ainsworth (1974) and Sroufe (1979) view infant-mother attachment as an affectional rather than sexual bond. Bowlby (1980) believes that intimate attachment to others provides the "hub" around which a person's life revolves at every age. It anchors their enjoyment of life, and is the base for giving support and enjoyment to others. Evidence about affection comes largely from the study of other animals (Eibl-Eibesfeldt, 1971; Harlow & Mears, 1982), anthropological studies (Eibl-Eibesfeldt, 1971; Symons, 1979), or clinical-anecdotal data (Ford & Urban, 1963; Menninger, 1963). The infant attachment research (Osofsky, 1979) and the increasing study of close relationships among adults (Kelley et al., 1983) provides a growing base of empirical evidence.

The *transactional components* represent approach behaviors. It is a bilateral approach pattern called the "dual mode" by existential psychotherapists (Ford & Urban, 1963). It is manifest in a pattern of positive reciprocity, of "mutual effectance" (Ainsworth, Bell & Stayton, 1974); of "synchrony" or "mutual adaptation" (Osofsky & Connors, 1979); of "mutual engagement" or "role complementarity" (Mueller & Vandell, 1979); with action tendencies "to embrace or mate" and "to welcome or be with" (Plutchik, 1980). This pattern involves cooperative and shared activity, including the giving and receiving of attention, objects, comfort, and concern. It frequently involves body contact, such as caressing, cuddling, and kissing. Facial gestures typically include eye contact, raised eyebrows, open eyes, and smiling (Eibl-Eibesfeldt, 1971; Noller, 1978). Vocalizations may include comfort sounds such as sighing and cooing, and statements of welcome or caring, usually presented softly. The pattern also involve undefensive sharing of private thoughts and feelings that would not be shared in ordinary relationships.

Little information exists about the *biological components*; most available information deals with the *subjective components*. Five interrelated attributes may be present in varying degrees depending upon the occasion and the intensity and duration with which affection occurs: (a) admiration and respect for the loved one, emphasizing positive attributes and ignoring or deemphasizing negative ones; (b) trust and confidence that the other will not be hurtful or deceptive; a sense of being one or of belonging together; a desire to share; (c) feelings of tenderness; a desire to help, comfort, and shelter the other; a willingness to sacrifice self-interest for the other's interest, when he or she is hurt or in danger; (d) a desire to be with the other person; to touch, and to display affection; and (e) an absorption in the loved person, which may reduce consideration for and involvement with others, and may involve a desire to possess the loved one to the exclusion of others (Anant, 1967; Frost, Stimpson, & Maughan, 1978; Plutchik, 1980; Rosenman, 1978; Rubin, 1970; Tesser & Paulhus, 1976).

Information about *eliciting conditions* is sparse except in infant attachment research. Sackett (1979) found that mothers' affectionate displays towards their infants (e.g., looking, vocalizing, touching or caressing) were followed by infant affectionate responses several seconds later, which continued briefly after mothers stopped but were then followed by unhappy facial gestures and vocalizations. Renewal of their mothers' affectionate displays restored infants' affectionate responding. Mothers report affectionate feelings when their infants' behavior implies affection. Among adults in most cultures, friendly, affectionate displays by one person tend to elicit reciprocating displays from the other. Berscheid (1983) concludes that while positive emotions, like affection and shared joy, facilitate initial "close" relationship formation, it is the nature andext of the "meshing" of the two individuals' lives into one social system that helps maintain close relationships over extended periods. Periodically experienced affection can be sufficient to maintain close relationships.

Other species display similar patterns (Eibl-Eibesfeldt, 1971; Symons, 1979), and monkey love has been extensively studied (Harlow, 1971; Harlow & Mears, 1982). Monkey infant-mother affectional interaction and comforting body contact is developmentally important, and such bonding mechanisms probably evolved to insure infant survival (Mellen, 1981). Paternal care of infants is also common among mammals, but is often obscured by female dominance of child care (Snowdon, 1983). Without affectionate peer interactions during childhood, adult monkeys do not display normal adult sexual behaviors or affectionate behaviors towards the young. Harlow proposed that different "affectional systems" involving parents, peers, and others emerge in a particular developmental sequence. Lasting adult "friendships" occur among male chimpanzees (Mellen, 1981).

Infants display affectionate behaviors during the first year of life (Osofsky, 1979; Waters et al., 1979; Wenar, 1978). Patterns of affection have been observed in *diverse humans* in many cultures of the world (Eibl-Eibesfeldt, 1971; Symons, 1979). There may be a genetic component in sociability (Buss & Plomin, 1975). Cultural records exist of love relationships between men and women in all the great literate societies (Mellen, 1981). In studies about what gives meaning to Americans' lives, feeling loved and wanted, friends and family, and helping and sharing or loving others typically top the list (Klinger, 1977). Psychotherapists observe that disruptions in, or loss or absence of, affectionate relationships causes much human distress, and that acquiring or restoring such relationships has great "healing" influence (Hartog et al., 1980). Affectionate relationships enable individuals to weather the storms of life more readily and with less personal damage.

Affection helps regulate *person-environment transactions* to facilitate the continuing mutual commitment essential for individual survival and for creating and maintaining cohesive social groups. The nearly universal patterns of nuclear family, extended kinship, and incest taboo may have roots in affectional bonding (Eibl-Eibesfeldt, 1971; Stephens, 1963; Symons, 1979). There are other survival advantages of cooperative social relationships, such as increased productivity and security through the division of labor. Species with a capacity for cooperation and altruism, such as the social vertebrates and social insects, have achieved a much higher degree of social organization (Eibl-Eibesfeldt, 1971; Symons, 1979).

Loneliness—Sorrow—Grief. This emotion helps regulate group cohesion by making separation from others, particularly from affectionate relationships, a distressing experience, thereby promoting efforts to restore such relationships (Averill, 1968; Plutchik, 1980). Interest in parent-infant attachment, in bereavement through death of a loved one, divorce, and in aging has increased research on loneliness and grief (Birren & Sloane, 1980; Bowlby, 1980; Peplau & Perlman, 1982).

The *transactional components* of grief over the death of a loved one have been most extensively described. The prototypical pattern in less drastic separations appears to be basically the same, but of less amplitude and duration. The pattern may be described as one of avoidance behaviors (i.e., trying to terminate the unhappy experience of separation or loss) or of approach behaviors (i.e., trying to restore the interrupted affectionate relationship), characterized by action tendencies "to cry or mourn" and "to withdraw or get away" (Plutchik, 1980). Its transactional expression varies among cultures and as a function of the person's previous experiences and present circumstances (Izard, 1977; Jacobs & Douglas, 1979; Peplau & Caldwell, 1978; Warren, 1981).

The typical facial expression is like a "cry face." Crying and wailing may occur. Talk about the interrupted relationship and efforts to restore the relationship are likely to occur, such as seeking contact with the other person, and/or with things and places which are reminders of that person. Involvement with others and typical daily activities may be somewhat disrupted and there may be restless, somewhat aimless activity. Alternatively, the grieving or lonely person may immerse him or herself in work or daily activities, or turn to other close, affectionate relationships (Hass-Hawkings, 1978).

Little empirical information exists about the *biological components* (Birren & Sloane, 1980; Jacobs & Douglas, 1979). Study of *subjective components* is more extensive, beginning with Freud's (1957a) classic work. When an affectionate relationship is interrupted, people may initially not realize or believe the loss. In extreme grief, they may feel dazed or numb; this may be followed by feelings of distress, sadness, and wanting to cry. There may be a shortness of breath, a choking feeling in the throat, and other somatic symptoms, such as gastric distress. There will be two types of thoughts: thoughts of social disconnectedness and longing (e.g., an anxious painful yearning for someone) (Hartog, Audy, & Cohen, 1980); and thoughts about the lost person and ways the relationship might be renewed. Loss of interest in other people or activities, and a decline in the ability to experience positive emotions may occur.

Interpersonal loss may also trigger other emotions. For example, interruption of a desired relationship can function as any other goal obstruction and elicit anger. Guilt may ensue from self-blame for theloss. The loss's threat to a person's security may produce feelings of disorganization and fright. Hopelessness about renewing the relationship may produce depression. Thoughts about the lost relationship may keep reinvigorating the unhappy feelings—sometimes for months or years. A loneliness pattern may occur even in anticipation of a loss. Successful renewal of the relationship (e.g., as in finding a lost child) may produce joy as with achieving any valued objective. The normal pattern is for people to "work through" their reaction to a loss, reorganize their thinking, activities, and affectional relationships, and proceed with a future orientation (Birren & Sloane, 1980; Bowlby, 1980; Izard, 1977; Jacobs & Douglas, 1979; Lindemann, 1944; Peplau & Caldwell, 1978; Warren, 1981). People may experience this emotion not only because of recent loss of an affectionate relationship but also because of a continuing perceived deficit in such relationships (Peplau & Caldwell, 1978).

The *eliciting conditions* are real or anticipated deprivation of affection-ate relationships. Small children may interpret being temporarily left by the parent (e.g., at a day care center) as such a loss. Death or divorce may leave a child with only one parent, and elicit loneliness. A loved one going away temporarily, a geographical move, the loss of a close friend or lover, or the leaving a job illustrate some of the many disruptions of affectionate relationships that may precipitate loneliness, sadness, or grief. Berscheid (1983) characterizes a close relationship as the mutual interdependence of experience and daily behavior; that is, they come to function as a larger system. Separation of individuals with such a relationship tears apart such interdependencies, disrupting each person's habitual interpersonal and affectionate patterns.

Social isolation may precipitate loneliness in a social person but not in a solitary person. Loneliness is learnable. Therefore, a person can develop an affectionate attachment to anything, such as a pet, posses-sion, or idea, and can experience sorrow over its loss. Like all emotional arousal, it will dissipate with time unless continually reinvigorated by thoughts about or exposure to things and situations that serve as reminders (Birren & Sloane, 1980; Bowlby, 1980; Hass-Hawkings, 1978; Peplau & Caldwell, 1978; Sermat, 1978; Warren, 1981; Wood, 1978).

Some *other species* display similar patterns, and the closer phylo-genetically the organism is to humans the more similar the pattern; for example, chimpanzees (Darwin, 1872; Ekman, 1982; Jacobs & Douglas, 1979; Van Hooff, 1973;). The "hell of loneliness" has been experimen-tally produced in monkeys, and some animals may suffer greatly when isolated (Audy, 1980). Loneliness/grief patterns have been observed in *infants* deprived of affectionate and attentive parental or human care, particularly for an extended period of time (Ainsworth, et al., 1974; Bowlby, 1973, 1980; Spitz, 1945). Ancient writings refer to sadness and grief patterns among *other humans* and were included in early attempts to develop diagnostic categories (e.g., "melancholia" and "lovesick-ness") (Menninger, 1963). Bereavement patterns and practices have been observed in a variety of cultures (Jacobs & Douglas, 1979; Warren, 1981). A prototypical facial expression of sadness appears to be universal (Ekman & Friesen, 1975).

This emotion helps regulate *person-environment transactions* to retain or restore a person's affectionate social relationships. The interruption of an affectionate relationship disorganizes habitual social patterns (e.g., a widow soon learns that her social life changes because she is no longer a "couple"), and the organizational dynamics of thoughts and feelings. The extent and duration of the disorganization is a function of the severity of the loss. As in the case of a physical wound which must heal, time is required for psychosocial reorganization to occur before people can adapt to such a loss. The greater the disorganization, and the more frequent the invigoration of the loneliness or grief pattern, the longer the reorganization will take. Much of the clinical literature on grief focuses on this "working through" process, which is facilitated in several ways. The transactional behaviors signal distress to others and tend to elicit their attention and caring behaviors. A person tends to seek solace from other interpersonal relationships, thereby encouraging the cultivation of other affectionate relationships (Birren & Sloane, 1980; Hass-Hawkings, 1978; Peplau & Caldwell, 1978; Warren, 1981; Wood, 1981). There is some evidence that the downhearted/depressed and lonely/grieving patterns are related, but different, constructs (Weeks, Michela, Peplau, & Bragg, 1980).

Shyness (Embarrassment) — Shame (Guilt) — Humiliation. To maintain a cohesive social group, all component persons must function to perform their allocated role(s) and must constrain their individual functioning in conformity to the rules governing the larger social group. Social groups differ in the range and kind of deviations they permit. Conformity to group dynamics can be accomplished by regulatory processes internal or external to each component person. This emotional pattern produces feelings of discomfort which can be reduced by closer conformity to requirements of the group.

Some theorists (Tomkins, 1963) consider shame and guilt manifesta-tions of the same basic pattern, while others (Izard, 1977) consider them to be two different patterns. Still others (Plutchik, 1980) consider them to be combinations of basic patterns. Some empirical evidence supports the view presented here that they are one basic pattern, and that the different terms reflect primarily differences in eliciting conditions and related thought patterns (Fehr & Stamps, 1976; Mosher & White, 1981). Self-report data suggest that shame, guilt, and humiliation are much more negatively experienced than shyness and embarrassment (which have some positive qualities).

The *transactional components* represent avoidant behaviors which function to prevent or to alter the shame- or guilt-producing conditions and/or convey renewed conformity to the group's dynamics. Guilty people tend to avoid behaving in ways which are socially tabooed (Mosher, 1966; Schill & Althoff, 1975). Prototypically, there is gaze aversion in the presence of another. The head may be turned sideways and tilted downwards as if in subordination. The face may be covered with the hands. The person may slouch, making the body look smaller. Overt behavior may generally be inhibited and there may be some incoordination and an increase in speech disturbances. The person's statements are likely to divert attention from him or herself (e.g., a shy person may ask questions of a more social companion). People may apologize for their "bad" behavior to seek forgiveness and renewed acceptance. They tend to present themselves in a subordinate position, physically and socially, with action tendencies "to withdraw or get away," "to stop activity," and "to cry or mourn" (Darwin, 1872; Edelmann & Hampson, 1979; Izard, 1977; Pilkonis, 1977a; Pines & Zimbardo, 1978; Plutchik, 1980; Tomkins, 1963).

Biological components have been given little study. People frequently report blushing, increased pulse, pounding heart, perspiration, and gastric uneasiness (Darwin, 1982; Izard, 1977; Pines & Zimbardo, 1978; Tomkins, 1963). Lie detectors are presumed to measure biological manifestations of guilt. The *subjective components* often manifest ambivalence. On the one hand, the person may feel tense, apprehensive, and nervous, as in shyness. On the other hand, in embarrassment there may also be some pleasurable feelings, since the tabooed thoughts or behaviors may themselves have been pleasurable (Izard, 1977). There is a heightened self-consciousness, a feeling that matters intended to be private and personal have been publicly exposed. There are typically self-critical and remorseful thoughts about one's behavior and about having ones norm-violating behavior or incompetence exposed. There is worry about or fear of the criticism and rejection of others. There is a sense of having been reduced in status and stature in the eyes of others.

There may be uncertainty about what to do or say (e.g., confess, deny, or hide), since group acceptance can be restored in several ways: (a) by acknowledging responsibility and seeking forgiveness; (b) by convincing the group one is not responsible for what occurred (i.e., that one did not transgress); or (c) by withdrawing and becoming inconspicuous in the hope that people may forget one and one's transgression. When the emotion is anticipatory (e.g., shyness), there is ambivalence about whether to behave and suffer the risk of being revealed as foolish or incompetent, or to do nothing, remain inconspicuous and suffer the risk of being isolated and ignored (Buss, 1980; Cheek & Buss, 1981; Crozier, 1979; Izard, 1977; Mosher, 1966; Pilkonis, 1977b; Pines & Zimbardo, 1978; Zimbardo, 1977).

The prototypical *eliciting conditions* involve public exposure (or anticipated public exposure) of thoughts and/or acts not socially appropriate or acceptable. The thoughts or acts themselves often produce pleasure; otherwise they would not be performed (e.g., stealing a desired object; having illicit sexual relationships). Rather it is the actual or anticipated negative evaluation by others who may discover the transgression that elicits shame or guilt. Learned self-evaluative thoughts can function as surrogates for censorship by others; this is sometimes called *moral guilt*, and was the role assigned to the superego by Freud. Blushing in embarrassment is similar to the skin flush observed during sexual arousal, implying that the embarrassment/shame pattern may have evolved in relationship to sexual privacy (Eibl-Eibesfeldt, 1971). Patterns of flirtation exist in most human cultures, and some of the nonverbal responses are similar to components of the embarrassment pattern (Edelmann & Hampson, 1979; Eibl-Eibesfeldt, 1971; Tomkins, 1963). The terms shyness, embarrassment, shame, and guilt are often used as synonyms, supporting the view that the emotional pattern is fundamentally the same under all of these conditions. In extreme circumstances, when a person's transgressions are severely and publicly censored, a person is said to be humiliated; this is characterized as an intensely miserable state. Social rejection and termination of valued social relationships through separation are different forms of becoming isolated from desired social relationships (Buss, 1980; Cheek & Busch, 1981; Colby, 1977; Crozier, 1979; Friesen, 1979; Izard, 1977; Pilkonis, 1977b; Pines & Zimbardo, 1978; Tomkins, 1963; Zimbardo, 1977).

Little information exists about this emotion in *other species*. Study of social hierarchies and territorial arrangements indicate that they are constructed and maintained through mutual causal patterns of aggressive dominance and submission (Mellen, 1981). Conformity to such controls is displayed by submission and subordination (e.g., accepting a lower priority for access to food, territory, and mates). These social patterns appear functionally analogous to this human emotional pattern (Beach, 1965; Eibl-Eibesfeldt, 1971; Plutchik, 1980; Symons, 1979).

Human *infants* do not appear to display this pattern. It first appears in most children between 3 and 5 years of age. It depends on the development of certain cognitive functions (e.g., discrimination of familiar people from strangers; ability to understand simple rules of conduct) which are not fully functional in infants, and upon the prior emergence of the valuing of the acceptance and affection of others (Buss,

Iscoe, & Buss, 1979; Izard, 1977). *Other humans* from Samoans to Eskimos, from Orientals to Western Europeans, and in many subcultures in the United States display this pattern. The form in which people describe it has been frequently replicated in factor analytic studies. However, the conditions which elicit it and the frequency of its occurrence in individuals differs with cultural norms and socialization patterns (Crozier, 1979; Eibl-Eibesfeldt, 1971; Friesen, 1979; Fuenzalida et al., 1981; Izard, 1977; Pilkonis, 1977b; Pines & Zimbardo, 1980).

This emotion helps regulate *person-environment transactions* to facilitate cooperative group living, which involves four basic social issues: social hierarchy; territoriality; personal identity; and temporality (Plutchik, 1980). In other words, the rules governing social interactions within such groups serve to define and protect status, role, property, personal rights and responsibilities, and mutual obligations for the health and welfare of the group and the individuals within it. Social organization requires a compromise between the satisfactions of personal accomplishment and those of group acceptance and rejection. This emotional pattern helps to forge that compromise by inhibiting the performance of behaviors which might be intrinsically pleasurable and satisfying but are socially unacceptable or prohibited. The taboos may involve the person, rights, or property of others (producing "guilt"), or the accepted patterns and processes of social and sexual relationships (producing "embarrassment or shame"). Inhibiting one's social behaviors in anticipation of possible criticism, rejection, or affectionate gestures by others is termed shyness (Buss, 1980; Crozier, 1979; Friesen, 1979; Izard, 1977; Kemper, 1978; Mosher, 1966; Zimbardo, 1977). Ineffective compromises are manifest in self-defeating behavior patterns. Thus, shyness, shame, and guilt appear in many descriptions of psychopathology and of psychotherapeutic efforts (Colby, 1976, 1977; Ford & Urban, 1963).

Others in a social group can impose aversive consequences to unacceptable deviations in order to encourage the deviator to "get back in line." The final two social emotions serve that function, and are discussed next.

Resentment—Jealousy—Hostility. This emotion regulates competition for affectionate and sexual relationships, and for preferred roles, resources, and status. Limited information is available about this pattern, but it occurs in close relationships (Berscheid, 1983). However, it has manifested itself throughout human history. It appears in the Christian bible story of Cain and Abel. Shakespeare used it in his plots. Freud considered unresolved infantile jealous rivalries to be the core of most, if not all, psychopathology, as in the *Oedipal* and *Electra complexes* (Ford & Urban, 1963). Adler (Ford & Urban, 1963) proposed that birth order was psychologically important because it influenced children's competitive position for parental love and attention, making sibling rivalry an important issue in child development. Rivalry and jealousy begin occurring in the early preschool years, and may be somewhat more frequent with girls than with boys (Brooks, 1937). Problems of jealousy are manifest in some forms of psychopathology; an example is delusional paranoid jealousy (Cameron, 1963). "Mastery" motivaes have been proposed, with envy and jealousy said to result from social rivalry for dominance (Woodworth, 1940).

The *eliciting conditions* for jealousy involve rivalry with another: (a) for a desired affectionate and/or sexual relationship; or (b) for preferred roles, resources, and status. One results from the desire to *be loved* best; the other from the desire to *do* best. The prototypical *transactional components* are characterized by the action tendencies "to attack or hurt" and "to reject or get rid of" (Plutchik, 1980). These, along with the *biological and subjective components*, are similar to those of the anger pattern. However, the behaviors are focused upon particular, personally relevant interpersonal relationships, and the person's resentful thoughts are focused both upon the rival and upon the cherished role or person. The subjective quality is negative.

Symons (1979) reports that sexual jealousy appears to be universal among *all humans*, particularly among males. In many *other species* males compete with rivals for status and for mates in the social "pecking order." This is accomplished through threatening postures, facial expressions, and vocalizations, followed by physical combat if necessary. However, the function of the combat if it occurs is not to kill the rival but to get him or her to submit to one's possession of territory, social position, or mates. Females compete with other females (at least sexually) to attract competent mates (Eibl-Eibesfeldt, 1971; Hebb, 1972; Symons, 1979). The extension of this pattern to rivalry for all kinds of desired human roles and relationships may have been an evolutionary or cultural development. Once *children* learn to distinguish self from others, and to give others identities, it becomes possible to elicit jealous reactions in them.

This may be a social version of the anger pattern, or a mixture of other emotions such as anger, fear, and disgust (Izard, 1977; Kemper, 1978; Plutchik, 1980). The tentative assumption here is that this emotion evolved (probably through differentiation from the anger pattern) to regulate affectionate/sexual and hierarchical relationships in human groups.

Scorn—Contempt—Disdain. This emotion also functions to produce conformity to social group requirements. If an individual behaves in an unacceptable way (e.g., in terms of personal uncleanliness, crude social manners, incompetence in tasks, or striving for hierarchical position for which they are not considered qualified), others in the group can protect the group's organization and norms in one of two ways. They may influence the deviator to submit and conform to the group norms, or they may make the violator an outcast. The Amish pattern of "shunning" illustrates the systematic use of scorn and rejection as a social regulatory mechanism.

There appears to have been little theoretical or empirical interest in this pattern. The *transactional components* may be characterized as avoidant behaviors, with action tendencies "to attack or hurt," "to reject or get rid of," or "to withdraw or get away" (Plutchik, 1980). Contempt and disgust are similar, but studies of facial expressions and other evidence suggests that they are different basic patterns (Ekman, 1982; Izard, 1971, 1977). Factor analytic studies of human ratings of emotion words sometimes produce both a disgust and a contempt factor, and other times a single disgust/contempt factor (Fuenzalida et al., 1981; Izard, 1977).

In the typical facial expression of contempt, the eyebrow is "cocked"; the face is elongated and the head tilted slightly upward. That, and body posture, may give the impression that one is withdrawing from the contemptible person. The other person may be described as inferior and unworthy. The *subjective components* involve thoughts of personal superiority to, and thoughts critical or rejecting of, the contemptible person. There is an impulse to get away from that person or to "put him in his place." In contempt, there is less hostility, distress, and fear reported than there is in anger and disgust; there is more positive emotion, producing the characteristics of "cold" anger (Izard, 1977). Feeling and/or being superior to others in some way represents a kind of success, and success breeds positive emotion. Moreover, inferiors are not usually to be feared because they rarely pose any threat to one's well-being.

The *eliciting conditions* seem to involve unacceptable or disgusting appearance and/or behavior, or claims to status equal to or superior to one's own without the credentials and characteristics to support the claim (Kemper, 1978). In *other species*, social animals use threat gestures and aggressive behaviors to get a conspecific to retain or accept its lower ranking. The coercive behaviors, which usually stop short of actual aggressive behavior, usually end as soon as the other acknowledges in some way its subordinate position (Eibl-Eibesfeldt, 1971; Mellen, 1981). Analogous status-protecting behaviors have been observed among *other humans* in more primitive societies, particularly with regard to the ability to attract and keep sexual partners (Symons, 1979). There is little information about this pattern in children, except that it appears to provide a basis for social prejudice observed in them (Izard, 1977).

OVERVIEW

There is far more information about the instrumental emotions than about the social emotions, particularly the positive social emotions. Given the fundamental importance of cooperative group living in all human societies, a fuller understanding of the role of emotions in regulating social organization and interaction would have great potential value.

The concept of motivation was discussed in Chapter 10. It will be recalled that expectations become desires with the addition of value, and desires become intentions with the addition of commitment. As desires and intentions are learned, affective experiences, particularly emotions, produce evaluative information that provides one primary base for learned values and commitment. In addition, in any behavior episode, emotions influence the intensity and persistence with which the episode is pursued. Thoughts and emotions interact in complex patterns. Emotions have a positive-negative subjective valence, and therefore a regulatory influence. People learn to seek consequences or set goals for themselves that produce satisfying, interesting, exciting consequences, and to avoid consequences that produce negative emotions. On the other hand, the kind of emotion that people experience is triggered by their evaluative thoughts about how well they are doing or about the personal relevance of the consequences.

Governing and Arousal Functions and Actions

The value of humans' capacities to construct informational abstracts and to vary their arousal states lies in their use in directing, controlling, and regulating behavior episodes to produce desired and intended consequences. This usually involves environmental transactions. Therefore, the organization of actions is examined in the next two chapters.

14

Transactional Functions: Organization
of Actions

INTRODUCTION

As living systems, people exist, develop, and function through three types of environmental transactions: material, energy, and informational. The construction of body structures and the production of energy to fuel all human behavior require obtaining relevant materials from the environment, transforming them into useful forms that can be absorbed into the body, and discharging back into the environment those materials that cannot be or have not been used by the body. They also involve preventing entrance into the body of potentially disruptive materials. The skin, the ingestion- digestion-elimination system, and the respiratory structures and functions make such material transactions possible.

Energy transactions occur when people act to physically influence their relationships with the environment through motor behaviors such as walking, swimming, and manipulating objects. The skeletal-muscle structures and functions provide the basis for such energy transactions. Material and informational transactions (e.g., eating, looking, talking) also utilize energy transactions.

Effective energy and material transactions must be selective. Behavior is effectively selective when it is organized and guided by relevant information. Information collection was examined in Chapter 8. People also communicate information as a means of influencing one another. Structures which make vocalization and writing possible provide the primary basis for such communications. Skeletal-muscle structures also make gestural, nonvocal communication possible.

It will be recalled that one of the efficiencies in the design of the human body is that the same structure can participate in more than one function. For example, the mouth participates in energy, material, and informational transactions. Therefore, the biological structural-functional basis for the three basic types of transactions are not mutually exclusive. However, when the same structure participates in different functions, the structural-functional pattern of which it is a part differs (Gallistel, 1980b). Different structures are discussed in relationship to the functions for which they seem to be primary.

Chapter 14 first considers material transactions, represented by the import of food, liquids, and gases, and the export of wastes. Motor behavior, the primary form of energy transactions, is considered next. A brief review of the structural basis for motor behavior is followed by examination of its hierarchical componentized functional organization. Then, the dynamics and development of movement patterns are examined. Communication is considered in Chapter 15.

MATERIAL EXCHANGES

The human body opposes the eroding effects of the second law of thermodynamics: that is, it maintains itself, grows, becomes more complexly organized; it fuels its activities by accomplishing useful solid, liquid, and gaseous material transactions while prohibiting harmful ones. Therefore, several components of the body evolved to serve these transactional functions.

The Covering Boundary: Skin, Hair, and Nails

Its boundaries define a system in relationship to its context. A person's skin is the physical boundary through which anything entering or leaving the body must pass, and its characteristics give each person a physical identity.

The Skin. The skin has an outer layer, or epidermis composed of epithelial cells, and a second layer, or dermis composed of soft connective tissue. These two layers, which are tightly bonded together, provide four other kinds of structures: sweat and sebaceous glands; hair and hair follicles; and nail grooves and nails. The skin is anchored to an extensive layer of soft connective tissue, the *subcutaneous tissue* with irregularly spaced bundles of collagen fibers. This structural arrangement provides considerable flexibility of movement and function.

The skin performs several important functions: The outer layer provides a protective coating of dead epithelial cells covered with keratin which provides a barrier to disease organisms. It is nearly waterproof, so it keeps the body from dehydrating or from becoming bloated from excessive absorption of water. Sebaceous glands at the base of the hair follicles secrete a fatty material, called sebum, which provides protective lubrication to the skin. It also protects the body from excessive ultraviolet light.

Its sweat glands eliminate wastes by excreting water containing unnecessary salts and some urea. The skin helps regulate body temperature by adjusting the amount of internal heat radiated from the body or the amount of external heat absorbed. Skin also manufactures vitamin D when exposed to ultraviolet light.

Appearance differences contribute to a person's physical identity through such things as skin and hair colors and skin texture; fingerprints, for example, are personally unique. Variations in skin appearance provide diagnostic clues to physicians. Skin color can be red in hypertension, bronze in some glandular conditions, blue with cyanosis, yellow in jaundice; skin texture may be dry and cracked, wet and moist, sandpaper rough, or have various skin rashes; hair can look lifeless, or be falling out; skin odor can be affected by changes in excretions with illness; and nails can display altered growth, color, or pitting.

Liquid and Solid Material Transactions

Understanding material exchange processes requires a distinction between what is "inside" and what is "outside" a person's body. Imagine a stack of doughnuts. The holes would form a tube. Is the air in the doughnut-hole tube inside or outside the doughnuts? It is outside, of course. Like that stack of doughnuts, the human body has a tube running through it from top to bottom, the *gastrointestinal* (GI) *tract*, and the contents of that "food tube" are outside the human body in the same sense that the air inside the doughnut holes is outside the doughnuts. The contents of the GI tract have to get through the wall of the tube to get inside the body. Similarly, the air inside one's lungs is outside the body and must be filtered through lung surfaces to get inside the body. Therefore, ingestion, digestion, respiration, and elimination involve getting the appropriate substances inside the GI tract and lungs, altering those substances into forms that can be absorbed into the blood stream, and getting rid of the substances that are not absorbed. The inside surfaces of the GI tract and lungs are covered with epithelial tissue analogous to skin. It provides a permeable boundary between the body and its environment.

The "Food Tube" or GI Tract. Structurally, the GI tract consists of a muscular tube about 25 feet long which has several segments beginning with the mouth, which is the entrance, and including the pharynx, esophagus, stomach, small and large intestines, rectum, and ending with the anus which is the exit. It is encased in smooth muscle tissue that, through patterns of contraction, can move material around and through the tube.

Fastened to this tube are several other structures that produce chemicals necessary to help transform materials in the tube into absorbable forms. These include the salivary glands; the liver, gall bladder, and pancreas; and tiny glands in the lining of the stomach. Other cells produce mucus to keep the lining moist, facilitate its activity, and provide a barrier to undesirable materials.

The mouth prepares material for swallowing and collects chemically coded information through taste. This material enters the stomach through the pharynx and esophagus. The stomach is a muscular elastic bag, with a valve at the bottom to keep things in it. It can expand to hold approximately $1\frac{1}{2}$ quarts. It adds chemicals and mixes ingredients within it through rhythmic muscular movements. After 3 to 4 hours of processing, the material is transformed into a milky-appearing, semiliquid called *chyme*, and passed on to the small intestine. Some materials may be absorbed from the stomach (e.g., alcohol, water), providing quick availability of certain substances (as when a diabetic quickly needs blood sugar).

Most of the digestive and absorptive process takes place in the small intestine or duodenum where material is decomposed, through addition of digestive chemicals from the liver and pancreas, into basic molecules of glucose, fatty acids, and amino acids necessary for cell metabolism. Those molecules are small enough to be absorbed through the epithelial lining of the intestine. After this process is completed, the remaining material, still in essentially a liquid form, is passed on into the large intestine. There the small amount of nutritive material still remaining is absorbed, along with water; leaving the residual materials, along with bacteria and cellular debris, as a soft solid called *feces*. This is deposited in the lower end of the tube, or rectum, and expelled through the anus at a convenient time.

Gaseous Transactions: Respiratory Structures

Cell metabolism requires a continuous supply of oxygen, and elimination of carbon dioxide, a dangerous by-product. That is the primary function of the respiratory structures and functions, including the *nose, sinuses, pharynx, glottis, larynx, trachea, bronchial tubes,* and the *lungs*. The lungs are located in a skeletal-muscular "cage" formed primarily by the ribs, vertebral column, and sternum. At the bottom of the cage is a sheet of muscular tissue called the diaphragm. Air is inhaled and exhaled by rhythmic contraction and relaxation of the muscles in the walls and floor of the cage. The muscles of the diaphragm, sometimes assisted by those in the gut, can be used to force air out in a controlled flow. That makes speaking and singing possible.

As the air passes through the nose, it is moistened, warmed, and filtered. Particulate contaminates are filtered out by the hairs, where they then stick in thick mucous liquid produced by nasal tissue and sinuses, drain into the back of the mouth, and down through the "food tube." The air then moves through the nasopharynx, larynx, and into two bronchial tubes, each of which serves one lung. Just as blood-carrying arteries progressively subdivide into smaller and smaller tubes ending in an extensive network of capillaries, so too bronchial tubes subdivide into smaller and smaller tubes, called the *bronchial tree*. The lung is permeated with very small tubes, called *bronchioles*, each of which is surrounded by small chambers, called *air chambers*, which in turn are surrounded by even smaller circular chambers, called *alveoli*, filled with capillaries. This provides a huge number of surfaces through which oxygen can be absorbed and the waste gases eliminated. Respiration serves a minor water excretion function as well.

Under some conditions the smooth muscles encasing the bronchial tubes will increase their tonus, and their mucus lining will swell, reducing the inner size of the tubes and thereby reducing air flow. That produces a miserable and dangerous condition called *asthma*. The bronchial tree is connected to both divisions of the autonomic nervous system, so breathing can potentially be affected by anything that produces autonomic activity, such as exercise and emotional arousal.

MOTOR BEHAVIOR

Prologue

Scholars of motor behavior have converged upon a representation of human action that is surprisingly similar to this living systems framework. There is near unanimity that most motor behavior is purposive or goal directed (i.e., voluntary). They agree that it is self-constructing. They recognize that motor programs and schemata cannot be detailed specifications for action because the specifics of a behavior pattern have to be constructed as it is occurring. They describe a diversity of hierarchically organized, mutually influential control and regulatory processes starting with monosynaptic spinal circuits and ending with complex cerebral processes. They emphasize componentization as a mechanism for elaborating behavioral capabilities and for making possible a high degree of behavioral flexibility; and they agree that the organization and execution of motor behavior can only be understood as a function of the system as a whole.

Introduction

Through motor behaviors, people obtain and ingest the essential materials and information, find and relate to other humans, create and use tools, explore unfamiliar circumstances, play, protect themselves from danger, and shape their environments to serve their purposes. Entertainment industries (e.g., dance, music, and athletics) have made the cultivation of high levels of motor skills a road to fame and fortune. The essence of the concept of skill is "an ability to achieve defined goals with an efficiency beyond that of the experienced person" (Elliott & Connolly, 1974).

The growing research on motor behavior (Bernstein, 1967; Bruner, 1973; Gallistel, 1980a; Granit, 1970; Kelso & Clark, 1982; Kohout, 1981; Lashley, 1929; McMahon, 1984; Miles & Evarts, 1979; Schmidt, 1975; Shaw & Bransford, 1977; Sherrington, 1906; Stelmach, 1976; von Holst, 1973; Weiss, 1941) has been significantly influenced by Bernstein, a brilliant Russian physiologist. A volume resulting from a NATO advanced study institute (Stelmach & Requin, 1980) and Volume 39 of *Advances in Neurology* (Desmedt, 1983) provide an excellent perspective on the range of ideas and work currently being pursued. Grillner (1985) summarizes evidence of the hierarchical, componentized organization of actions.

Some scholars, primarily in Europe and Russia, have developed significant work around "action theory," or the study of goal-directed action (Harre & von Cranach, 1982). Many different kinds of motor behavior have been studied ranging from single muscle fiber contractions to complex behaviors such as running and piano playing. Changes in motor performance competence with age, learning, and damage have been studied. Emphasis on athletics and on the relationship of physical activity to health, has led to increasingly sophisticated efforts to develop applied approaches to motor behavior in health, physical education, and athletics (Cratty, 1967; Lawther, 1977; Kelso & Clark, 1982; Singer, 1975).

Attempts to develop a symbolic language with which to describe movement are centuries old. One recent system of analyzing and recording dance movement called *Labanotation* (Hutchinson, 1970), uses basic variables similar to those used by scholars of motor behavior.

The central objective of the study of motor behavior is to understand how people produce coordinated movements, "at will," in an appropriate and desired relationship to their current environment in order to produce desired consequences (Whiting, 1980). The following examination of relevant theory and knowledge is organized into four parts. First, the structural basis for performing movements summarized. Next, the different kinds of motor components are considered. Then, the kinds of factors involved in the construction and operation of movement patterns will be summarized. Finally, the development of movement patterns from infancy through adulthood is discussed.

The Structural Basis for Actions

Motor behavior is made possible by the skeletal-muscle subsystems, along with the loose connective tissue, which give the body both structural rigidity and strength, and flexibility of movement capabilities.

The Skeleton. The skeleton is a rigid yet flexible structure of 206 bones upon which the rest of the body is hung and encased, protected and moved around. As a structural material, bone is an engineer's dream, being light but exceptionally strong and durable. Like other tissue, bones exist in a dynamic yet steady state (Urist, DeLange, & Finerman, 1983). They develop and are maintained through a combination of bone construction and resorption. If these two processes get out of balance, problems develop, the most widely known of which is *osteoporosis* or porous bones. Bones function, in part, as a kind of calcium "bank." Like any bank account, if withdrawals exceed deposits over an extended period of time, deficits will occur and the bank will be in trouble. Calcium is fundamental to many cell activities of which normal muscle contraction and bone growth are two.

The skeleton's central pillar, called the *axial skeleton*, includes the skull, vertebrae, ribs, and sternum. The shoulder girdle, the bones of the arms and hands, the pelvic girdle, and the legs and feet—called the *appendicular skeleton—connect* with this central pillar. The skeletal design is the key to much of the body's postural flexibility. The spine, composed of 33 flexibly joined vertebrae, has extraordinary strength but is also amazingly flexible.

The spinal column is hollow, providing a protected conduit through which nerve fibers run connecting every part of the body to the central headquarters of the brain. In general, the hierarchical control centers of the body and their branch offices are organized along the axis of this structural column, with the main control centers sitting on top of the column inside the "headbone" (the boss usually gets the penthouse office).

Bones are connected by three types of joints: immovable, slightly movable, and freely movable or *synovial* joints. Synovial joints make possible humans' diversity of locomotor and manipulative movements, and include most of the joints in the body. A synovial joint is encased in a flexible tissue capsule. The joint cavity is cushioned and lubricated by other tissues and may contain pressure sensors. The capsule encasing the joint is further strengthened by bands of collagen fibers called *ligaments,* a kind of "cable" with very high tensile strength that can withstand strong pulls in the direction in which the fibers run, without stretching. The result is a very flexible, yet strongly connected and durable joint. Different types of synovial joints make possible different kinds of motion. Ball-and-socket joints permit movement in all planes as well as rotation (e.g., the hip joint). Hinge joints permit flexion and extension in one plane (e.g., the elbow). Ellipsoid joints permit motion in two planes at right angles to one another (e.g., the wrist). Saddle joints permit similar motion (e.g., the thumb), while pivot joints permit rotation only.

Skeletal Muscles. Without muscles, bones would just hang there, like a skeleton in a closet. There are three types of muscle tissue. Smooth muscle is typically distributed in sheets of fibers in the walls of body "tubes" (e.g., in the digestive, circulatory, and respiratory components) and is controlled by the autonomous nervous system (ANS). Cardiac muscle is located only in the heart, and is innervated by the ANS. Skeletal muscles are generally attached to the skeleton, and are responsible for moving the bones. They are controlled by the central nerous system, which converts a persons intentions into action, and are often termed *voluntary muscle* as a result. Skeletal muscle can also provide tonus, but its distinguishing characteristic is its ability to provide episodic, rapid, powerful contractions. Collectively, skeletal muscles can lift and move hundreds of pounds. Skeletal muscles are composed of large elongated muscle cells interspersed with connective tissue that carries nerves and blood supplies and provides a "frame" or "harness" to help support the action of muscles. Skeletal muscles are fastened to bones with "cables" called *tendons* that are similar in composition to ligaments. By contracting and uncontracting in elaborate patterns, sometimes in cooperation and sometimes in opposition to one another, muscles function as a system of elastic "ropes" controlling the skeletal "levers" to produce an immense array of activity from jogging to chewing to playing a violin.

The structure of muscles illustrates again Mother Nature's use of hierarchical organization. Each muscle is composed of many *muscle fibers.* Each fiber is composed of several hundred to several thousand smaller units called *myofibrils*. Each myofibril contains approximately 1,500 myosin and 3,000 *actin filaments*. Moving upward in the hierarchy, one finds that each motor nerve fiber innervates many muscle fibers. Thus, muscular action can vary through summation of the number or rate of fibers innervated. These arrangements also manifest the principle of componentization. Each bone with its associated muscles, tendons, ligaments, and joint(s) can move in only limited ways. However, multiple components working together make possible a great diversity of movements. This feature, along with CNS componentization, makes possible functional organization of motor activity that is componentized in *coordinative structures* and is hierarchically organized (Bernstein, 1967; Gallistel, 1980a; Kohout, 1981).

Loose Connective Tissue. The skeletal-muscular structures and all other body organs are surrounded and permeated by connective tissue composed of several kinds of cells and intercellular substances. Unlike the substances forming the ligaments and tendons, the fibrous material in the connective tissue will stretch because the collagen fibers, while nonstretchable themselves, are woven into sheets with fibers running in different directions. That permits some "give" or "stretch" when such sheets are pulled in one direction or another, something like a two-way stretch girdle. A layer of this kind of material under the skin permits the flexibility necessary to accommodate skeletal-muscular motion. This pervasive loose connecting tissue, along with the skeletal-muscular system, gives the body its structural strength, stability of form, and protection as well as providing a stable frame for its mobility. In addition, it provides an energy storage capability and a defense against invaders.

Types of Motor Coordination Components

Motor behaviors must be coordinated dynamically with a flow of environmental events. This requires both response-response coordination and behavior-environment coordination.

Coordination of motor behavior means the selective activation and inhibition of specific components of motor behavior in an organized combination so that they function as a unit to produce a specifiable consequence within the varying constraints and opportunities of the action environment. The process of evolution has produced a diversity of neural mechanisms for accomplishing such coordination. They range in complexity from coordination performed within a single cell to coordination provided by the brain. Knowledge about CNS structures is far greater than about their functioning as the coordinator of those elemental activities in the service of the organism (Weiss, 1941). This section attempts to tell a coherent story about the coordination of motor behavior by piecing together information about how hierarchically organized coordinating arrangements probably evolved and function (Bernstein, 1967; Brown, 1975; Desmedt, 1983; Gallistel, 1980a; Grillner, 1985; Hinde, 1966; Kohout, 1981; Stelmach & Requin, 1980; Weiss, 1941).

It appears that the behavioral potentials of every species of animal, including humans, has been profoundly influenced by its evolutionary history; this includes social behaviors (Brown, 1975; Hinde, 1966; Lewontin, 1984). Dogs provide an example. Terriers were bred to go into burrows after other animals; a barkless dog was bred to aid game poachers who wanted to avoid detection; and other dogs were bred for other charactistics.

Evolution of Types of Behavior Coordination Components.   Human behavior coordination capabilities are a product of componentized evolution. It is the functional differences made possible by structural differences that are the vehicle of evolution. Simple coordinating arrangements that "worked" in simple organisms were retained, elaborated, and added to as humans evolved. *Behavior genetics* tries to identify the nature and mechanisms of genetic influences on behavior development; those developmental pathways are diverse, complicated, and the consequence of interacting polygenic and environmental influences (McClearn & DeFries, 1973; Plomin, 1986; Schneirla, 1957).

The first coordinating components to evolve were highly stereotyped and controlled by specific types of stimuli, mediated by simple neural and/or biochemical circuits, and appear in essentially the same form in all members of a species (Brown, 1975). Central nervous systems evolved because they make possible more flexible coordination and therefore more diverse behavior, but early CNS components were also very simple, spinal reflexes (Sherrington, 1947). Illustrative are stretch reflexes, which help maintain body posture, and may be found in organisms all the way from crayfish and cats to humans. In the simplest circuit, there is only one synapse in the spinal cord (i.e., it is a monosynaptic reflex). Building upon these simple reflex circuits, more centralized CNS components evolved to produce more flexibly coordinated behavior patterns. While still species-typical stereotyped motor patterns, which become functional with minimal learning, they can be elicited by a greater diversity of stimuli and the pattern may vary somewhat in form to fit current circumstances, as illustrated by the flight and songs of insects (Eibl-Eibesfeldt, 1970; Hinde, 1966; Lorenz, 1970; Tinbergen, 1951).

Weiss (1941) dramatically demonstrated the unmodifiability of such inborn programs. He surgically reversed the limbs of an infant salamander. He found that when the salamander tried to walk its back legs walked forward and its front legs pushed its in reverse. Moreover, it did not relearn how to walk with its new "hookup." There seemed to be a central "score" for walking that was muscle specific. He concludes that this level of neural centers contains "a definite repertoire of such fixed and discrete scores" (e.g., for ambulation and turning), each of which can be displayed as a whole or not at all. Their form is influenced very little by sensory inputs or opportunities for motor activity.

These inborn motor programs are the basic units of coordinated behavior inherent in neural organization (Gallistel, 1980a; Grillner, 1985). Put in Skinnerian terms, each species starts life with the capability for a set of operants, each of which is most likely to occur under particular circumstances characteristic of the environmental niche within which that species evolved. Evolution organized spinal reflexes into larger units, and in humans there are spinal organizations that can generate locomotion movements when stimulated, even if separated from the brain (Grillner, 1985). Weiss (1941) refers to these as an "existential minimum of vital performances" upon which varying degrees of improvements are called for and can occur.

As environments elaborated, the narrow flexibility of such inborn "motor scores" (analogous to musical scores) was supplemented by brain-level coordinating components. Like the spinal cord, the cerebral motor cortex and cerebellum appear to be a summing point for the interactions of central programs and peripheral feedback in the coordination of behavior, but at a much more complex level of coordination (Grillner, 1985; Miles & Evarts, 1979).

Thus, hierarchically organized coordinating mechanisms and processes evolved. It should be emphasized that elaboration of neural coordinating arrangements accompanied changes in the sensoriskeletal-muscle structures and organization, which made possible different action capabilities. For example, as bipedal walking evolved, the entire system—not just a component—became reorganized and changed (Washburn, 1959, 1978). Moreover, synchronization with other biological functions had to occur. For example, rate of locomotion and rate of breathing had to be synchronized (Bramble & Carrier, 1983). In addition, different methods of locomotion became more biologically efficient, depending on the rate of movement (Hoyt & Taylor, 1981).

As more centralized coordination evolved, more flexible connections with the musculature also evolved. There is a network for detailed coordination of muscles in the spinal segments. However, some alpha and gamma motoneurons have independent pathways from the cortex lacking a compulsory spinal link (Granit, 1970). Thus, instructions can sometimes be sent directly to the "workers" at various "work sites" without having to deal with a bunch of "middle level bureaucrats." Weiss (1941) referred to such self-constructing centralized coordination as coordination "by individual design and discovery," rather than "by predesign and evolutionary tradition." Through such learning, "non-preformed, 'invented,' coordination patterns" become dominant and "obscure the more ancient stereotyped patterns with which they coexist and overlap." Learning a new movement probably involves learning to "combine and sequence" specific neural components used "to control the innate movement patterns in a novel way" (Grillner, 1985).

Voluntary control of facial expressions illustrates this idea. Some "automated" facial expressions manifesting emotional arousal are controlled at brain stem levels in many animals (Ekman, 1977, 1979). Although that primitive system is still present in humans, they can learn to override such primitive, automated "muscle scores," and intentionally present any desired facial expression to influence events (e.g., smile to hide their anger) (Myers, 1968).

Thus, cognitive coordinating components evolved as a preformation of dynamics for building behavior patterns utilizing (at least in part) more primitive components rather than preformation of the patterns themselves (Kugler, Kelso, & Turvey, 1980). Behavioral self-constructing capabilities were added to biological self-constructing processes. A summary follows of kinds of coordinating components and processes present in humans as a result of this evolutionary process.

Person Characteristics Influencing Movement Patterns

Any movement pattern must be understood as involving interrelationships among characteristics of the actor and characteristics of the action context. Person characteristics will be considered first.

Body Coordinates. A person cannot interact with objects and events unless and until his or her body is positioned in space to do so. Russell (1976), Stelmach and Larish (1980), and others have suggested that movement or motor memory may be coded in spatial rather than, or in addition to, skeletal-muscle terms. However, two sets of spatial coordinates are involved. In spatial coordinate systems, a limited number of referents maintain invariant relationships with one another providing a predictable framework for behavior. One set exists in a person's environment; another within the person's own body, sometimes called the *body schema* or *egocentric spatial reference system*. The parts of the body are permanently configured in invariant relationships to one another (e.g., "the headbone's connected to the neckbone"), which can be represented in terms of spatial coordinates anchored to the midline of a person's body (e.g., head-feet, right-left, and front-back) independent of the body's location in the environmental spatial system. Some motor behaviors only involve relating one body component to another (e.g., scratching one's head). However, because most motor behavior includes relating one's body to environmental configurations, some form of appropriate matching of the two sets of spatial coordinates must occur. There is some evidence that body-centered spatial information can be coded in memory independently of environmental information. However, since the natural state is for the body to function as a unit in a context, some kind of integration of information from both body centered and environmental spatial coordinate systems would be of most value (Lashley, 1951; Russell, 1976; Stelmach & Larish, 1980).

Skeletal-Muscle Components. The hard work is always accomplished by the honest laborers in the work force. All else simply organizes and targets their efforts. The skeletal-muscle components are the body's honest laborers. In the final analysis, all movement is accomplished by having bones connected by joints assume a smoothly varying configuration of angular relationships with one another and in relationship to environmental factors. Sets of muscles spanning each joint provide the means for flexibly adjusting the angle of the bones connected at each joint and the amount of power devoted to the effort. This arrangement has been usefully represented theoretically as pairs of springs acting across joints (Bizzi, 1980; Kugler et al., 1980). Therefore, each pair of bones connected at a joint and the muscles, ligaments, and tendons spanning each joint must function as a unit, and such units have been termed *coordinative structures* (Glencross, 1980; Hays & Marteniuk, 1976; Kugler et al., 1980).

Complex action patterns are produced by the organization of component coordinative structures. Such organizations will vary depending on (a) the starting point of the muscle-bone-joint configuration (e.g., standing from a prone or sitting position); (b) the current environmental forces affecting each skeletal-muscle component; and (c) the state of tension, biochemical condition, length, and energy production and utilization of each muscle fiber involved. Moreover, as the performance is in progress the status of those three sets of variables and their interrelationships are continually changing.

Kugler et al. (1980) suggest that it is useful to think of actions as resulting from two "fluxes of force": (a) "reactive, frictional, gravitational, and contact forces" resulting from skeletal and environmental factors, and (b) "muscular forces" resulting from internal neurological and biochemical factors. Because (a) varies during the flow of action (and sometimes unpredictably so), the specifics of muscular forces cannot be prescribed in advance by the brain. This means that a motor performance cannot be represented solely as the "running off" of a behavioral program designed in advance by the brain.

The basic problem for producing coordinated motor behavior is to overcome the "peripheral indeterminacy" resulting from the "extreme abundance of degrees of freedom" characterizing the functional task, since the effective form of any action is decided "at the last spinal and myoneural synapse, at the muscle," and "in the mechanical and anatomical changes of force in the limb being moved". (Bernstein, 1967). Motor output is ultimately determined by the mechanical properties of the motor units and specific hierarchies of activation (Granit, 1970). The brain can specify in advance what is to be done, but it must function cooperatively with many other functional components to produce a coordinated act. Complex movements are normally carried out "subconsciously and with consummate skill"; one is voluntarily conscious only of a "general directive" concerning the direction and nature of the movement pattern (Eccles, 1977).

Neurological Coordinating Components. There appears to be wide agreement that the neocortex alone cannot accomplish all the coordination and that there must be some kind of multiple component, multilevel arrangement governing motor behavior (Kelso & Stelmach, 1976; Stelmach & Requin, 1980). Thus, while there is a network for detailed cooperation of muscles in the spinal segments, some alpha and gamma motoneurons have independent pathways from the cortex lacking a compulsory spinal link (Granit, 1970). Motor control is organized in a modular fashion (Bizzi, 1980) and complex motor acts appear to be controlled by "the system as a whole" (Schmidt, 1980). The result is distributed motor control arrangement, alleviating any one part of the nervous system of excessive coordinating demands (Arbib, 1972; Kugler et al., 1980).

How many different kinds of neurological coordinating components for motor behavior exist in humans, and how do they interact? No clear consensus has emerged but many different proposals have been made (Bernstein, 1967; Desmedt, 1983; Gallistel, 1980; Miles & Evarts, 1979; Schmidt, 1975; Stelmach & Requin, 1980; von Holst, 1973). Some theorists subsume all components under one broad type, such as movement structures (Tyldesley, 1980) or coordinative structures (Glencross, 1980; Kugler et al., 1980), which are any combination of bones and muscles constrained to function as a unit whether a finger or the entire body. Other theorists have proposed multiple components. Although they use different concept labels, their proposals converge on four different types of components. For discussion purposes here, they are called *automated execution components, timing components, servo components,* and *cognitive components.*

Automated Execution Components. These are units of motor behavior that run off automatically when triggered into action, without significant modification by feedback while in progress. Sherrington's (1947) concept of reflex, which Gallistel (1980a) has broadened, is probably the most familiar such unit. Smith (1980) summarizes evidence concerning the programming of stereotyped limb movements by "spinal generators" that are capable "of recruiting motor units to adjust for kinetic demands" without supraspinal coordination. Each limb appears to have "a collection of generator networks," each of which can function independently. By combining multiple independent components in different patterns, great action flexibility can occur. Hinde (1966) provides evidence from lower organisms of motor behaviors controlled at the spinal level. Other terms such as muscle length/tension ratios (Marteniuk & MacKenzie, 1980) may represent more specific versions of such local government components.

The concept of "open loop" in control system theory is another type of automated execution component (Kelso & Stelmach, 1976; Miles & Evarts, 1979). A control system involves a feedforward side in which information triggers action, and a feedback side in which information about the action is made available to modify the action. The two together form a closed loop. If the feedback side is omitted, an open loop exists. Open loop behavior, sometimes referred to as ballistic (i.e., following a given trajectory), has been identified in a variety of organisms (Hinde, 1966; Hinde & Stevenson, 1969). Ballistic movements have also been studied at the level of single muscles (Desmedt & Godaux, 1977, 1978). Some skilled motor behaviors must be performed so rapidly that there is not time to utilize error-correcting feedback (e.g., a *prestissimo* passage on the piano). Open loop patterns can be constructed through habit-forming practice. In fact, attempting to use feedback disrupts the smooth flow of habitual behaviors. Reflexive and open loop components illustrate the reactive side of human behavior. They both represent "chunks" of behavior that will occur as a unit whenever appropriate internal or external circumstances trigger them into action, and do not require preplanning and organizing the behavior before it can be executed.

Timing Components. Motor behavior represents a flux of behavioral events related to a flux of environmental events. This presents two problems of timing: elements of the behavior patterns must be timed in relationship to (a) one another; and (b) environmental events. Muscles must receive "the necessary impulse at the necessary moment" (Bernstein, 1967). Timing involves control and regulation of the rate at which a sequence of behaviors is performed, and of the phasing (or relative timing) of behaviors with one another and with the occurrence of environmental events. The cerebellum "appears crucial for the perfection of the (coordination of) movements" (Grillner, 1985). Shaffer (1980) and Rosenbaum and Patashnik (1980) postulate "mental clocks" by which timing can be regulated. Shaffer, who studied concert pianists, suggests that learning produces an "abstract timing schedule" for movements that can be realized against an "internal clock."

Many kinds of behavior (e.g., walking) involve repetitive, rhythmic performances. Some rhythmic behaviors appear to be organized in spinal neural structures for which the concepts of *central pattern generators* (Brown, 1975), *spinal generators* (Smith, 1980), and *oscillators* (von Holst, 1973) have been formulated. Two or more simple oscillating patterns can be combined into a more complex oscillation by adding their patterns together. If they cycle in different phases (i.e., one starts and ends before another) their combination will produce a different cyclic pattern than either has by itself. A form of mathematics called *Fourier analysis* was developed for representing complex oscillating patterns as a combination of simple oscillations (e.g., sine waves). Bernstein (1967) demonstrated that many types of motor behaviors could be represented by Fourier analysis (e.g., running). The rhythmic patterns of two different oscillators can influence one another so that they cycle in a fixed phase relationship with one another; that is, they become coupled. Such coupling or mutual entrainment is discussed in Chapter 9. Some biophysical scientists have proposed that many aspects of the organization and functioning of living systems can be appropriately conceptualized as ensembles of coupled and mutually entrained nonlinear oscillators, sometimes called *limit-cycles* (Yates, Iberall, & Marsh, 1972; Yates & Iberall, 1973; Nicolis & Prigogine, 1978).

Many kinds of complex rhythmic behavior patterns have been identified (e.g., insect songs, bird flight; swimming, walking, respiration, and heartbeat) (Gallistel, 1980a), and many rhythmic behaviors can be centrally generated rather than regulated by feedback (Brown, 1975; Roberts & Roberts, 1983). Walking or running behaviors illustrate the phenomena. Each leg and arm must swing in phasic synchrony with one another, and the amplitude (i.e., power of each step) and frequency (i.e., rate of steps taken) can vary within the same pattern of coupled oscillations. Kelso, Holt, Kugler, and Turvey (1980) point out that an advantage of oscillatory systems is that they do not require ongoing feedback and "executive" control to guide their functioning as does a typical servomechanism.

Servo Components. The basic model of servo components is the control system unit described in Chapter 3. They exist at various levels, all the way from small servo components, such as the four neuron muscle stretch reflex (Brown, 1975) to the person functioning as a servo component (Bernstein, 1967). Larger servo components may be viewed as organizations of sets of smaller servo components, (Miller, Galanter, & Pribram , 1960). For example, myotatic (i.e., muscular) feedback in motor control is a complex servomechanism in which the myotatic feedback can be parameterized in terms of a negative feedback of position, velocity, and acceleration; each of which is involved in a different feedback loop (i.e., a smaller servo) which are all independently regulated but which have to function in a coordinated fashion (Terquolo, Dufresne, & Soechting, 1980). McFarland (1971) and Gallistel (1980a) describe servomechanism controls in other organisms, such as *chemotaxis,* and *phototaxis.* Alpha and gamma motoneuron functioning might be represented in servomechanism terms (Granit, 1970).

The oculomotor smooth pursuit system (i.e., the eyes following an object) is an example of a smaller servo component (Wertheim, 1980). It is conceptualized as a closed loop feedback system that acts as a velocity servo using visual feedback signals that are velocity coded. Arbib (1980) summarizes evidence of how cerebellar damage may affect some aspects of complex motor performance but not others, as an example of an even more complex servo component. Feedforward signals based upon information about the characteristics of future action can modulate sensorimotor functioning by pretuning processes (Requin, 1980). Visual feedback facilitates preparatory muscular activity related to walking and running (Lee, 1980).

Efforts to understand motor behavior at the person level have emphasized three types of feedback representing three types of servomechanisms that must be coupled to produce effective motor behavior (Glenncross, 1980; Kelso & Stelmach, 1976; Klein, 1976;): (a) response or direct sensory feedback resulting from the action itself (e.g., from the pattern of muscular contractions); (b) internal feedback generated from structures within the nervous system (e.g., from cortically based motor commands); and (c) external feedback or knowledge of results based upon environmental events related to the behaviors performed. Complex behavior patterns in most, if not all, organisms appear to involve some feedback control. Vocal behavior is an example. Singing or talking behavior can be disorganized by inserting time delays between the emitting of the sound and the individual's hearing it.

Person level feedback is important in the initial performance of, and the learning of, a motor pattern, but is too slow to facilitate rapid, skilled behavior. Therefore, through repetitive practice, people construct auto-mated execution components. In technical jargon, habit formation converts a closed loop to open loop functioning (e.g., Hays & Marteniuk, 1976). That is a key reason why skilled behavior is so much more efficient.

Cognitive Components. There appear to be two types of cognitive coordinating components. One specifies the objective(s) of the behavior (the directive function); the other deals with the means by which the objective(s) will be pursued (the control and regulatory functions). Brain motor commands appear to be patterned in terms of movements rather than in terms of muscles; the brain does not "choose" which muscle fibers will be activated (Desmedt & Godaux, 1981; Phillips & Porter, 1977;).

The role of the *directive function* was first clearly stated by Bernstein (1967). He concluded that action is directed by an "image or represen-tation of the result of the action." Similarly, Pribram (1976) defined a cognitive component that he called actions as representations of envi-ronmental consequences to be produced by behavior. A variety of other terms refer to this directive function. Bruner (1974), Bizzi (1980), and Glenncross (1980) use the term *intention*. Whiting (1980) refers to *strategic intentions* and to the image of an act; Shaffer (1980) to a *plan;* Requin (1980) to *action project definition;* Glenncross (1980) to *desired outcomes;* and Hutchinson (1970) to *directional destination* when referring to the programming of a dance. Terms like *centralized motor programs* or *commands* have been used by several theorists (Gallistel, 1980a; Hayes & Marteniuk, 1976; Kelso et al., 1980; Requin, 1980; Russell, 1976; and Schmidt, 1980). Thus, there appears to be wide agreement that one type of cognitive component specifies the intended results of behavior, which sets in motion regulatory and control processes aimed at those results. These specified consequences might be termed *personal goals,* which may be "final or intermediate" (Bernstein, 1967).

For example, when people throw darts at a dart board, they typically concentrate on the part of the dart board target they want to hit. That anchors the whole act. However, in preparing to throw, they may first think of how to stand and how to hold the dart (i.e., subgoals). When the act is a well-practiced habit (an open loop), concentrating on a subgoal can anchor the entire act. As another example, a golfer may concentrate on where he or she wants the ball to go, or on some component of the total act such as the backswing (e.g., "take the club back low and slow"). Deficits resulting from certain types of cortical lesions in humans can disrupt this directive function (Teuber, 1964). For example, a patient with frontal cortical lesions could still anticipate the course of events to some extent, but could not picture himself as a "potential agent" in relationship to events.

The *control and regulatory* cognitive components have also been referred to with a variety of terms. For example, Schmidt's (1975) "recall schema" is responsible for the generation of impulses to the musculature to carry out actions (i.e., the control function). It involves the relationships between actual outcomes and response specifications built up through experience. His "recognition schema" is responsible for evaluation of response-produced feedback that makes possible the generation of error information that can be used to modify the operation of the recall schema (i.e., the regulatory function). Other terms used include *plan* (Shaffer, 1980), *motor programs* or motor programming (Gallistel, 1980a; Glenncross, 1980; Hayes & Marteniuk, 1976; Ostry, 1980; Requin, 1980), *action systems* (Shallice, 1978), and *image of achievement* (Whiting, 1980). Kelso et al. (1980) propose a simulations component that derives the sensory consequences of the motor command before it is executed. Such arrangements are sometimes referred to as a *model referenced control system*.

There is wide agreement that detailed specifications of muscular actions by cognitive components would work only if the environment and the state of the organisms remained stable; that the organization of any act cannot be complete before the start of a movement; and that further organization must occur in "real time" as the movement is being executed (Ostry, 1980; Shallice, 1978). The central program establishes a framework and general direction for behavior "by selectively potentiating coherent sets of behavioral options." Which of the potentiated options is actually performed is a function of "decisions" made at local levels based on local information (Gallistel, 1980a). For example, suppose a person is told to write his or her name. The consequence to be produced is the name in writing. Presumably, the person has a generalized motor schema for writing that name. With pen and paper, seated at a desk, the person will execute that schema largely by moving fingers and hands. With chalk, he or she stands and writes the name on a wall blackboard, using primarily the elbow and shoulder while the fingers remain relatively fixed (Schmidt, 1980). The consequences to be produced and the generalized motor schema are essentially the same, but the implementing conditions are quite different. These kinds of phenomena have led some theorists to propose that motor programs must represent rules for designing action programs rather than action blueprints (Glenncross, 1980).

Ostry (1980) compares levels of motor processing to a *corporate hierarchy* in which the flow of control is achieved by instructions of a very general sort and where each level of the hierarchy maintains virtually independent control over the details of its internal operations and the means by which its goals are achieved. Such a multilevel, componentized organization addresses similar problems in different ways and communicates by passing on only that information which is necessary for incorporation in another level's autonomous functioning. Gallistel (1980a) uses the concept of a *lattice hierarchy* to indicate that, in addition, each component may receive and send general instructions from and to several other components simultaneously; and must resolve conflicts among, and must synthesize, the instructions in some way.

Environmental Factors Influencing Movement Patterns

All motor behavior functions to relate a person to properties of the space-time world in ways that serve that person's needs and intentions (Lee, 1980). Therefore, environmental factors represent limiting and facilitating conditions for the development and functioning of individuals' motor behavior.

Gravity. The human body evolved to function in the earth's invariant gravity field. Whether a person is lying down, walking, or climbing, there is a constant line of gravity which provides a stable anchor to which all body postures and movements must conform.

Spatial Coordinates. Three dimensional space is also another invariant property of people's environment. All actions can be mapped in terms of those coordinates (e.g., east-west, north-south, and up-down) (Russell, 1976; Stelmach & Larish, 1980). The three dimensions may be represented by attributes of a particular space, and that is the way New Yorkers often give strangers directions (e.g., "go to Park Avenue and turn right to 51st Street"). Since two objects cannot occupy the same spatial location at the same time, the physical relationships between objects can be represented by their spatial coordinates.

Objects and Their Attributes. The spaces in which humans live are filled with a diversity of objects, including other humans. A person's actions are usually selectively directed towards some object(s) as a means of producing some intended consequence(s) (e.g., a kiss from a loved one). The presence or absence of different kinds of objects in a person's environment is one way in which his or her role, status, and opportunities are defined (e.g., poverty-stricken vs. wealthy). Objects vary in their stability, location, and existence. The greater the *objects' permanence* (to use Piaget's term), the easier it is for people to behave effectively in relationship to them even when they cannot perceive the objects (e.g., as in blindness). The attributes of objects (e.g., shape, color, movement) provide discriminable cues that people can use to guide their actions in relationship to objects.

Spatial Configuration. The organization of objects in the environment facilitates and constrains a person's motor behavior. Imagine a completely flat surface with no objects upon it (e.g., an empty room). One may walk in any direction with equal ease. In contrast, imagine hiking through a mountainous countryside with thickets, streams, slopes, animals, and holes in the ground. One may not walk in any direction with equal ease, and cannot walk in some directions at all. The nature of environmental organization tends to channel behavior in some directions rather than others.

Time. Events often occur in irreversible sequences. Just as some chemicals can never "unmix" once they have been mixed together, so too once biological and behavioral organizations have developed they cannot be "undeveloped" (although they may be altered by further development in different directions). Humans invented the concept of time to represent their perception of the irreversible, sequential flow of events. Movement of a person through an environment, or of an environment past a person, creates a sequential flow of events. Therefore, the concept of time and movement are intertwined. The term *phasing* means relative timing and is used to label the temporal relationships between the occurrence of two or more events. Behavior is organized in "real time" (i.e., what is happening right now). The phasing of various components of behavior with one another and with environmental events in "real time" is a hallmark of effectively coordinated behavior (Bernstein, 1967; Kugler et al., 1980; Lee, 1980; Ostry, 1980; Schmidt, 1980).

The Hierarchical Organization of Coordinating Components

Coordinating components are organized to produce a movement that has "the homogeneity, integration, and structural unity" essential for effective environmental transactions (Bernstein, 1967). The result is an hierarchical organization in which higher order components can flexibly combine those lower in the hierarchy to construct a diversity of complex patterns of motor behavior (Bernstein, 1967; Elliott & Connolly, 1974; Gallistel, 1980; Kelso & Stelmach, 1976; Kohout, 1981; Turvey, 1977; Shallice, 1978; Stelmach & Requin, 1980; von Cranach & Kalbermatten, 1982). Weiss (1941) proposed use of at least six levels of coordination:

Level 1: the neuron; Level 2: the muscle; Level 3: the muscle group; Level 4: the organ; Level 5: the organ system; Level 6: the organism as a whole. Additional levels could be considered. Therefore, if one's purpose is to understand a person as a functional unit (i.e., at Level 6), that person's transactional behaviors must be understood as a multilevel organization of components. Bernstein (1967) used a musical analogy. He noted that the road to understanding the coordinated functioning of a symphony orchestra does not lie in the analysis of the tonal and expressive resources of each instrument, but in the technical construction of the score and its execution by the conductor. Human knowledge about the nature of coordinating components is greatest at the lower levels of the hierarchy, but level 6 is the one that excites many current scholarly interests and efforts (Stelmach & Requin, 1980).

Hierarchical Organization and Motor Behavior Pathology. Some evidence comes from the study of motor behavior pathology. Kohout (1981) has summarized Bernstein's (1947) proposals for a structural-functional hierarchy; and kinds of motor behavior pathology relate to disruptions at each level (see Table 14.1).

Kohout suggests the following four questions about hierarchical levels to guide examination of a movement act:

1. What is the leading functional level determining the aim and strategy of the act?
2. What are the other levels that participate in the execution of the act?
3. Given a detail, or component of movement, which subordinate level is bound by it?
4. Given a subordinate level, what parts or components of a task are determined by that level?

To illustrate the point, he summarizes Bernstein's report of a patient with a certain brain lesion. First, the patient was asked to raise his hand as high as possible. He succeeded in raising his hand just above the waist. This represents control of the mutual position of body segments (Level B). Next, he was asked to touch a dot on the wall placed 10–12 centimeters higher than he was able to raise his hand in the first task. He was able to touch that dot, but not another point 10 centimeters higher. In this task, Level C is the leading functional level; that is, the spatial field controlling the position of the limb in the space. Finally, he was asked to take down an object hanging on a hook placed as high as the second point he could not touch in the second task. Here, the leading functional level is D; that is, the level of object-oriented actions. In other

TABLE 14.1
The Levels of Bernstein's Motor Hierarchy and Their Functional Characteristics
(from Kohut, 1981, as modified by Ford)

Functional Level of	Substratum Level	Main Characteristics and Functions	Typical Pathology
A Paleo-kinetic regulations	Rubro-spinal	Tonic regulations	Dystonia (lack of muscle tonus)
B Synergies	Thalmo-pallidary	Controls synergies, control parameters-coordinates of the mutual position of body segments, relative mutual positions and velocities	Asynergia (faulty coordination of muscles)
C Spatial field	Pyramido-strial	Pseudometrical, projectively geometric level; control framed in terms of position of body segments with respect to the external (environmental) coordinates	Ataxia (incoordination of actions)
D Object-directed	Pre-motor	Nonmetrical, topological level; topological relations in the space, representation of abstract percepts corresponding to objects in the environment	Apraxia (disruption of purposeful movement)
E Symbolic coordinations	Higher cortical levels	Representation and manipulation of symbolic concepts; names, semiotic aspects of writing, aspects of speech, etc.	

words, the nature of the functional deficits that will be manifest as a result of damage to some neural structure may appear in only some of the levels of coordination, or appear differently in different levels. Moreover, different kinds of feedback play a primary role at different levels; for example, proprioceptive feedback at Level B and visual feedback at level C.

Weiss (1941) concluded that CNS behavioral integration represents "self-regulatory systemic action." It is "a system of systems, each of which consists of subsystems"; that is, "a functional hierarchy." Koestler (1967) concurs.

The Dynamics of the Organization of Actions

Actions are movements composed of organizations of motor components coordinated with environmental components to produce some targeted consequence. Therefore, a reflexive reaction to stimulation is a movement but not an action, although action patterns include reflexive reacting components.

The representation that is described here draws upon what appear to be similar views (though represented with somewhat different concept labels) by Bernstein (1967) Elliott and Connolly (1974), Gallistel (1980a), Glenncross (1980), Ostry (1980), Requin (1980), Shaffer (1980), Turvey (1977), and Whiting (1980). It might be briefly represented as a cascading pattern of "decisions" concerning what to do, in which components at each level in the hierarchy function semi-autonomously, constrained (but not fully determined) in how they can function by the current state of other components with which they are linked above, below, and beside them. Moreover, it must be a dynamic process since conditions within the actor's body, within the environment, and in the relationships between the two are in a continual, somewhat unpredictable flux.

General Design. The hierarchically organized, dynamic cascading pattern of mutually influential components (what Gallistel calls a lattice hierarchy) appears to combine the types of motor control mechanisms just discussed (Stelmach & Diggles, 1982). At the upper levels of the hierarchy there appears to be generalized motor program control (e.g., Keele, 1981; Schmidt, 1975) which may specify certain kinds of rules, parameters, or perhaps sets of motor units to guide construction of an action, without specifying the details of the action pattern. The phenomena of motor equivalence make it evident that more than one combination of muscular actions can achieve the same result. Therefore, it appears that some form of distributed control must be operative at lower levels of the hierarchy (Arbib, 1981; Stelmach & Diggles, 1982). In distributed control arrangements, the components involved "rule by consensus" or dynamic interaction with no single component serving as "commander" (Kugler et al., 1980). Psychological and neurological conceptions and evidence appear to be converging toward a three-stage model of motor organization: (a) action project definition or response determination; (b) motor program specification or building; and (c) movement execution (Requin, 1980).

A Living System Representation of the Dynamics of an Action. The following description of the organization and execution of an action can be interpreted as a BES in action. It represents a kind of decision tree with multiple influences flowing up and down its branches so that "decisions" at any level by any component are facilitated and constrained by its own current state and by multilevel influences upon it.

A directive cognitive component specifies some consequences to be produced, in some kind of context. This is a form of "modeling of the future" (Bernstein, 1967). Cognitive components involved in actions are predictive or anticipatory (Requin, 1980). Directive cognitions selectively configure the nervous system through attentional (ICA activation) processes in ways appropriate to the action task as defined by the directive cognitions, i.e., they trigger the activation of a relevant BES.

The BES includes control and regulatory cognitive components relevant to the directives that have been issued. Several possible control and regulatory components are "potentiated" (Gallistel, 1980a), becoming potentially available to control and regulate the action. They in turn potentiate a set of possibly relevant motor programs. The current state of the body and its immediate environment influences which of the set of potentiated motor programs becomes operational. That program triggers a particular organization of automated execution components, timing components, and servo components which directly control the muscular activities. The particular organization of basic components that occurs is a product of (a) previous "practice" of various behavior patterns in similar contexts with similar consequence targets; and (b) current operating conditions such as the attributes and spatial configuration of surrounding objects, the body's spatial positioning, the configuration of the body parts, conditions of the senses and musculature, and pain (Singer, 1975).

Once the action begins, each of the basic components in the pattern may alter its activity within the constraints of the general action plan, according to its own component rules of operation, as a function of the flow of changing circumstances within and around that component. Further instructions from higher authorities are not necessary for adjustments as long as the range of variability in the operating conditions remains appropriate for the operating program. If conditions change sufficiently, changes in the controlling motor program may occur, either by triggering a different member of the set of potentiated motor programs or by modifying the existing motor program. If none of the potentiated motor programs produce the intended consequences, or if, in the course of performing the action, conditions change so that the potentiated motor programs become ineffective, changes may occur in the control and regulatory components which in turn will potentiate new behavioral options. This dynamic process of adjusting the functioning of components within themselves, between components at the same hierarchical level, and between hierarchical levels, continues until the specified consequence is achieved or conditions change sufficiently that some other directive cognition and BES become dominant. In a sense, the behavior pattern is being constructed while it is being performed. However, it can be constructed only with existing components and within existing design constraints provided by the activated BES and current body-environment conditions and configurations. The greater the number of optional components in the BES and motor program, and the greater the diversity of component combinations with which people have experience, the more flexible can their behavior be. And, of course, the converse is true.

The organization of behavior at any moment represents a cross-sectional "slice" of an action pattern that is flowing through a four-dimensional space-time matrix. If a different "slice" were taken at a different moment, the configuration of behavioral components and environmental conditions composing the action pattern would still be coherent but somewhat different. An understanding of the meaning of the action pattern rests upon understanding the relationships between the guiding intentions, the current body and environmental conditions and states (i.e., the potential sources of intended consequences), and the trajectories of change in those conditions and states. To avoid misunderstanding, it should again be emphasized that the functioning of the components may not be a part of the contents of consciousness, particularly if the action patterns are highly practiced and habitual.

The Development of Motor Behavior Capabilities

In this section, information is reviewed about neonatal motor behavior, the maturation of motor behavior capabilities during the early years of life, and the development of skilled action patterns. The study of children's motor development was very active during the 1930s (Bayley, 1935; Gesell and Thompson, 1934; Halverson, 1937; McGraw, 1935; Shirley, 1931; Wild, 1938). The fruits of that pioneering work found its way into pediatrics practice (Osofsky, 1979). Since 1960 there has been a resurgence of interest in understanding motor development in adults as well as children (e.g., biomechanics; exercise physiology; human performance; and perceptual-motor development). Sports medicine and physical rehabilitation illustrate important applied fields. Books by Barrow (1977), Cratty (1970), Gallahue (1982a, 1982b), and Singer (1975) illustrate current efforts and summarize information about the development of motor behavior based upon both maturational and learning processes. What follows is an attempt to tell a coherent story about human motor development from infancy into adulthood from a living systems perspective. All those who study motor behavior recognize that other attributes of people, such as their cognitive and emotional functioning, influence motor behavior development. However, since the primary purpose of this chapter is to concentrate on motor behavior, those other aspects have been examined in other chapters.

Motor Development Phases and Functional Categories. It is useful to organize information about motor development into four somewhat overlapping, phases (Gallahue, 1982a). The *reflexive phase* begins with the fetus in utero and extends through about one year of age. During the first months of life, infant movement is primarily under stimulus control and is coordinated primarily at spinal and primitive brain levels. As brain maturation proceeds, reflexes begin to be replaced by a *rudimentary movement phase* in which the beginnings of voluntary motor control appear. That begins shortly after birth and extends through the first 2 years of life. Myelination of the brain is typically completed by 1 year of age, and by 2 the brain structurally appears to be very similar to the adult brain (Espenschade & Eckert, 1980). From about 2 to 7 years of age, having mastered rudimentary movements, children begin to elaborate their basic motor skills in a *fundamental movement phase.* By 7 years of age, most children have developed a large repertoire of smoothly functioning motor habits that provide the base from which *complex skill development* can be evolved throughout the rest of their lives.

The discussion of each phase will be organized around four basic movement categories. *Postural movements* function to establish and maintain the relationship of the body to the force of gravity. *Locomotor movements* make it possible to move the body through the environment. *Manipulative movements* involve reaching, touching, grasping, moving, and manipulating objects. *Expressive movements* convey information about the internal states or intentions of a person. It is curious that this fourth category seldom appears on scholars' lists of reflexes or motor behaviors. Expressive behaviors are the first communicative action patterns of which infants are capable that are effective in influencing their environment to produce desirable consequences. They are discussed in Chapter 15.

Neonatal Motor Behavior: Infant Reflexes. Every pregnant woman knows that motor behavior begins while the fetus is still in her womb. The duration and intensity of fetal movements are correlated with measures of motor development for several years after birth (Walters, 1965). Newborn infants have a sizeable repertoire of inborn motor behaviors. Some are reactions involving the total body and its orientation to gravity while others involve head, limb, mouth, and torso movements not primarily directed to gravitational orientation. Development always starts with what exists and elaborates upon it; therefore, inborn reflexes appear to represent a starting point for the development of more complex motor patterns (Cratty, 1970; Gallahue, 1982a).

Postural related reflexes function to maintain the upright position of the head and body in relationship to the line of gravity affecting the body. The labyrinthine righting reflex is elicited when a baby is held in an upright body position and then tilted forward, backward, or to the side. When a baby, held by one or both hands, attempts to remain upright by flexing its arms, it displays the pull-up reflex. Parachute reflexes are an extension and tensing of the arms or legs if the baby is rapidly lowered towards the ground. It has the appearance of an attempt to cushion an anticipated fall. Propping reflexes occur when a seated infant is pushed off balance. Arms extend in an apparent effort to prop the body against a complete fall.

Locomotor reflexes are motor pattern components related to moving the body through space. In the Babinski reflex, the toes of the foot extend or spread when the sole of the foot is stroked. It is replaced by the plantar reflex, in which the toes contract rather than extend, as the neuromuscular system matures. Tonic neck reflexes adjust arm and leg extension and flexion in relationship to head position. Neck and body righting reflexes function to produce an alignment of head, trunk, and legs.

Manipulative reflexes are illustrated by the Moro reflex in which there is a sudden extension and bowing of the arms and extension of the fingers accompanied by a similar, though less vigorous action of the legs and toes. It may be a remnant of the clinging reflex by which infants of some lower animals hang on to the mother as she moves. The startle reflex is elicited by abrupt, sharp changes in stimulation. In the palmar-mental reflex, the chin muscles contract which lifts the chin up when the base of the palm is scratched. The palmar-mandibular or Babkin reflex is produced by applying pressure to the palms of both hands and includes mouth opening, closing of eyes, and flexing the head forward. In the search reflex, the infant will turn its head toward the source of stimulation when its cheek is stimulated. Nursing mothers sometimes refer to this as "rooting" behavior. Similarly, if the area above or below the lips is stimulated the sucking reflex will be elicited. The grasping reflex appears if the infant's palm is stimulated with an object.

Expressive reflexes are motor patterns that signal something about infants' subjective states. The distress pattern is the most obvious. In it there are slashing movements of the arms, a jerky flexion and extension of the legs, a cry-face expression, and loud, abrasive crying vocalizations. It can be elicited by hunger or physical discomfort. Object interest is displayed by a fixation of the eyes on an object, immobilization of most of the body, and perhaps minor arm and hand movement. Similarly, social interest is displayed by eye fixation on a person but is more frequently accompanied by arm, hand and perhaps some leg movement. Other infant expressive patterns include smiling, wariness-fear withdrawal reactions when confronted with strange and unfamiliar circumstances, and anger-rage patterns when motor behavior is physically constrained or obstructed. While expressive reflexes have been ignored by most scholars studying motor behavior, information about their nature, eliciting conditions, and developmental patterns has become extensive through research on emotions (Bridges, 1932; Izard et al., 1980; Sroufe, 1979; Schellenbach, 1984). Expressive reflexes appear to represent the first and most primitive methods by which infants regulate their environmental interactions (see Chapters 13 & 15).

Physiological reflexes and body characteristics are well developed in young infants. Examples include heartbeat, the pupillary reflex, swallowing, the anal reflex, and orientation responses. Factors such as body size, proportions, and composition are important influences on infants' behavioral capabilities. For example, newborn infants' muscles are small, watery, and possess fewer nuclei than those of adults. Their skeleton is primarily cartilaginous and much lower in mineral content. As a consequence, infants lack both the strength and the leverage to support themselves or objects and to direct their limbs and fingers precisely, until such body characteristics mature. Infants' information-collecting and nervous systems are more advanced at birth than is their skeletal-muscle system. As a result, it is sometimes difficult to determine whether an infant's inability to perform certain motor acts is primarily the result of neurological or skeletal-motor inadequacies (Eichorn, 1979).

Diagnostic Implications. Many prenatal factors may affect an infant's development, such as the mother's nutritional status, drugs she takes, heredity factors, other medical problems of the mother, and stresses related to the birth process (Brackbill, 1979; Gallahue, 1982a; Kopp & Parmelee, 1979). One major approach to diagnosing such developmental dysfunctions is based on comparing the infant's reflex or behavioral functioning with what is normatively expected. Neurological dysfunction is implied when (a) a reflex continues beyond the age at which it is typically inhibited by the maturing nervous system; (b) a reflex that is typically there is absent; (c) reflex responses are bilaterally unequal; and (d) a response is considerably stronger or weaker than is typical. A variety of methods have been developed for accomplishing such diagnostic evaluations (Brazelton, Als, Tronick, & Lester, 1979; Rosenblith, 1979; Self & Horowitz, 1979; Yang, 1979).

Rudimentary Movements. In the first few weeks of life, infants display some capability for voluntary control over some aspects of their behavior. For example, infants can and will use their sucking capabilities to select recordings of their own mothers' voices, or to select or focus pictures projected before them. The capacity for voluntary control over movement accelerates rapidly during the first 2 years of life as infants' skeletal-muscle and nervous systems mature. This growing capacity for voluntary control of behavior is manifest in the increasing inhibition of reflexive responding, in increased control over the use of what were initially reflexive patterns, and in the progressive elaboration of the kinds and complexity of motor behaviors that they can perform (Wyke, 1975; Zelazo, 1976). Rudimentary movements represent complex new tasks for an infant. The rapidity with which rudimentary movement competence develops is a function of the extent to which the movement is practiced if the biological basis for the movement has matured. In general, mastering rudimentary movements appears to involve the use of visual feedback (e.g., as in walking) which becomes less important once control of the movement has developed.

Establishing voluntary control over *postural stability* in opposition to gravity is a task that occupies most of the first year of life. It proceeds from head to toe. The ability to lift the head develops between 2–5 months of age. At 6–8 months infants typically have discovered how to roll from their stomachs to their backs and vice versa, and have learned to sit alone. By 6 months they can typically stand with support, and by 11–12 months they can pull themselves to a standing position and stand alone. They display obvious pleasure in having mastered gravity's influence on them. And well they might, because this requires control over a complex configuration of interacting body and environmental variables.

Manipulation by arm and hand movements is controlled by the upper portions of the spinal cord as well as the brain. Voluntary arm and hand movement control tends to emerge somewhat ahead of control of the lower limbs. Three basic aspects of manual manipulation come under voluntary control first. Reaching for an object typically begins during the first 3 months, and by 6 months it is usually efficiently accurate. Reflexive grasping of an object is present in newborns. By 3–5 months infants can intentionally (although crudely) grasp an object with one or both hands, and can successfully reach for and grasp moving objects. This suggests that predictive reaching capabilities are "prewired" to some extent (von Hofsten, 1980; von Hofsten & Lindhagen, 1979). At first, the movements are slow and awkward, but by 7–10 months reaching and grasping occur in one smooth continuous movement, with palm and finger coordination. By 14 months a child's grasping behavior is similar to an adult's.

By 8 months of age, they not only grasp objects but manipulate them in other ways (e.g., bang them on something, or visually examine them). Males are typically more vigorous than females in such manipulations (Kopp, 1976). Such object manipulations are usually accompanied by expressive behaviors of pleasure. By about 12 months, infants have discovered how to release objects as well as how to grasp them, and they begin to have fun dropping objects into containers. By 18 months, the basics of reaching, grasping, manipulating, and releasing have been combined into one smooth action and the base has been established for learning more complex manipulative skills.

Locomotion first requires postural stability. Therefore, the mode of locomotion used by infants must be a function of the kinds of postural as well as limb control they have developed. For example, the first locomotion method developed by many infants results from their combined ability to lift their head and chest off the floor and to reach with their arms while on their stomach. The result is a kind of sliding movement sometimes called "scooting" which may occur at 3–6 months. As some voluntary control of legs develops, crawling becomes possible, followed by creeping as more voluntary control of arms, hands, knees, and legs develop.

Walking can begin to develop as soon as an infant has learned to stand when supported. Walking requires rhythmic, controlled shifts in upright, stable posture. The term *toddler* is nicely descriptive of the first walking movements, which are hesitant and irregular, with the arms not used reciprocally as a way of controlling postural stability and motion. Infants' first attempts at independent walking usually occur between 10 and 15 months. Around 18 months, the gait smooths out, the length of step declines slightly and becomes regular and the arms-legs-torso-head movements become synchronous and fluid in relationship to one another and to the environment. The basis is then available for elaboration of upright locomotion into the diversity of forms that make childhood games so much fun.

Self-produced locomotion significantly influences infants' cognitive, emotional, and social development. It provides a basis for distinguishing between self and non-self; for learning to extract the invariant forms of solid objects; for the onset of wariness of heights, and for spatial mapping, as of environmental landmarks, in order to understand relationships among objects (Campos, Svejda, Campos, & Bertenthal, 1981).

Fundamental Movement Development. By the time infants are 2 years old they have typically mastered the rudimentary postural, manipulative, and locomotor movement capabilities. From that base of competence, they can explore and elaborate the movement potentials of their bodies and experiment with the impact they can have on their environment. All movement is governed by basic principles of physics such as relationships among mass, force, and acceleration of an object's movement. Therefore, refinements in movement control require increased precision in estimating the force to be exerted or absorbed in relationship to the masses of the entities involved to produce the intended consequences (e.g., climbing on a chair, catching a ball). This requires an increase in predictive or anticipatory capabilities. Stated differently, movement can be thought of as a sequence of states in which the configuration of related components in each state is a function both of current and probable future conditions. Amazingly, most children by the age of 2 have become fairly proficient at this very complex "computational" process.

As people (including infants) practice movements, they never perform them exactly the same way twice. There is *repetition without repetition* (Bernstein, 1967; Whiting, 1980). Therefore, BES and habit formation must involve the trying out (accidentally or intentionally) of optional performance schemes. So, the nervous system must have capabilities for abstracting and retaining information about both the invariant properties of similar movement patterns and the types of variability possible around such basic "themes." From a large set of similar but different actual performances, a prototypical BES with options for different possible performances is constructed.

Development results from *maturation, learning, and performance*. Structural changes resulting from further biological maturation between 2 and 6 years of age facilitate further motor proficiency development (Walker, 1952). Trunk, leg, and arm length increase. Longer and stronger legs along with increased ability to lock the knee make it possible to carry more body weight and to be more precise and forceful in locomotor patterns. Broader shoulders and longer arms facilitate manipulative capabilities. Changes in head and body proportion make postural stability easier. Muscular and nervous system maturation makes possible finer and more complex skeletal-muscular coordination.

These maturational developments are manifest in changes in physical and motor fitness. Physical fitness factors include improvements in muscular strength and endurance, circulatory-respiratory endurance, and muscular flexibility. Motor fitness factors include improvements in agility, coordination, balance, speed, and power (Gallahue, 1982a). Temporary (e.g., maturational delays, illness) or permanent (e.g., genetic anomalies; tissue destruction) disruptions or dysfunctions of biological components will be manifest in deviations of physical and motor fitness factors. Children usually overcome temporary disruptions naturally with little long-term behavioral consequences. Children can often be helped to overcome or effectively compensate for permanent disruptions if they are recognized and attended to early enough. Methods have been developed for assessing the developmental pattern of fundamental motor skills in children to facilitate development (Haubenstricker, 1978; McClenaghan & Gallahue, 1978a).

Special training is of little value in the development of movement skill until the necessary biological base has adequately matured. Then, training appears to have greater impact on more complex movements (e.g., throwing a ball) than on more fundamental movements (e.g., jumping) (Cratty, 1970). There are sizeable individual differences in motor maturational rates and patterns and in environmental influences (Malina, 1980) which produce individual differences in the development of different kinds of fundamental movement control (McClenaghan & Gallahue, 1978a). However, there does appear to be a normative sequence of phases through which children develop control over fundamental movement patterns (McClenaghan & Gallahue, 1978b).

Motor skills develop through the reciprocal influences of differentiation and integration (self-organization and self-construction) (Cratty, 1970). Differentiation is manifest in the progressive refinement of an initially gross and awkward movement pattern into a well-coordinated, efficient action. Integration is manifest in bringing various response components into coordinated interaction in larger, more complex motor patterns. The first clumsy attempts at a movement pattern (e.g., jumping) do not include some components of the final, skilled performance such as preparatory actions and follow-through. With practice, the child includes more of the necessary components but they typically are not performed correctly at the outset. Finally, all of the necessary components become integrated into a well-coordinated, purposeful act and unnecessary components become eliminated.

To work, a motor program must not only activate the appropriate muscular patterns but also activate them in a carefully sequenced and timed way. A pattern may be altered by feedback, representing important aspects of the flow of action. Hay (1979) reports evidence suggesting a developmental pattern in the use of feedback.

Feedforward and Feedback Influence Learning. A novel movement pattern starts with three basic ingredients: (a) an intention to perform and learn the movement; (b) the current environmental and body conditions and positions which facilitate and constrain how the movement can begin to occur and how it can be executed to produce the intended consequences; and (c) the existing response repertoire from which components can be selected and organized into a relevant movement pattern. The intention activates, through feedforward processes, a BES relevant to the present context and potentiates a hierarchy of movement components (Schmidt, 1975). Information about body-centered and environmental spatial coordinates is involved (Russell, 1976). As movement execution begins, coordination among components must occur both within and between governing levels. That requires a diversity of types of feedback and feedforward influences among components and between governing levels. For example, information conveyed by spindle and tendon afferents about the state of a muscle may influence motor control at the spinal level, or through relatively short loops through the cerebellum and motor cortex. This feedback may be directed at the same muscle, or different muscles that function as antagonists or synergists. Its effects may be inhibitory or facilitatory (Klein, 1976).

Feedforward functions to produce preparatory adjustments for response determination, motor program selection, and movement execution (Requin, 1980). *Feedback* produces changes in the spatial-temporal configuration of the components involved and in their parameters (e.g., timing and force) as the performance is under way to improve its effectiveness and efficiency. Feedforward and feedback processes function to influence and change which components will participate in the performance; the sequencing of their occurrence; their relative timing or phasing in relationship to one another and to relevant environmental variables such as synchronizzation of the body and environmental spatial coordinates; and their relative force, or the relationships among the various muscular and environmental forces involved (Schmidt, 1980). Glenncross (1980) suggests that it is useful to subdivide feedforward and feedback influences into four functional categories: (a) sensory guidance and control; (b) advance planning and programming; (c) presetting and tuning; and (d) amendment procedures during behavior execution.

At least three types of amendment-producing feedback appear to be involved (Kelso & Stelmach, 1976): (a) *kinesthetic feedback* resulting from movement of muscle fibers and joints, often termed *response produced feedback;* (b) internal feedback of information generated by various neural components, such as between the motor cortex and the cerebellum, sometimes termed *corollary discharge* or *efference copy;* and (c) relevant information collected from the environment through various senses, such as vision, typically called *knowledge of results.* Moreover, the organization of the feedback information is also important in its utility (Stelmach & Szendrovits, 1981).

Feedback and feedforward processes also make learning possible. The first performance of a novel movement is typically hesitant, slow, and clumsy; it includes some unnecessary components, and excludes other useful ones. The function of practice is to shape the clumsy "first try" into a smooth, efficient, and effective performance. Initial performances require concentrated attention and effort. Through multiple performance "tries," a person abstracts from feedback and feedforward information representations about what consistently "works," and creates a BES for use in regulating and controlling similar future efforts.

Since different combinations of components will produce similar results depending upon variations in environment-body configurations and conditions, what is abstracted and stored is a *set of possible performance combinations* rather than just one "best way."

As fundamental movement capabilities develop, they are used and practiced by children. The days of small children are filled with sitting, climbing, running, gesturing, manipulating objects, and many other fundamental movement patterns. Therefore, they are continually learning to move and are updating, refining, and elaborating their repertoire of fundamental movement plans or programs. Such heavily practiced movement programs come to function as units or components in their own right. This might be thought of as a motor equivalent to information "chunking" (Miller, 1956). By organizing smaller pieces into a coherent unit (or "chunk") through extensive practice, the person can manipulate the larger unit rather than dealing with all the smaller pieces. That is the efficiency of componentization.

Such componentization has several important consequences. The movement requires less energy expenditure because it has become more efficient. Such habitual performances do not require the concentrated attention necessary during the early learning process (Klein, 1976). That means that the kind of feedback that is useful and necessary will vary with the phase of acquisition of the movement skill (Arbib, 1980; Singer, 1975). For example, visual feedback may be very helpful while learning a novel movement, but may not be necessary or may even be disruptive after the movement has become habitual (Smyth, 1978). However, if neural damage disrupts other feedback control processes, visual feedback can sometimes be used as a replacement to restore good coordination (e.g., in reaching for an object) since the visual and motor systems are functionally closely related (Lee, 1980).

Sometimes portions of the feedback can be omitted at various governing levels after the movement pattern is well learned. Stated more technically, portions or all of the movement can come to function as an *open loop* kind of automated component. That is of great benefit, since the time required for transmission of certain kinds of feedback is so great that smooth, rapid movements (e.g., playing a fast passage on a piano) would be impossible if each movement component (e.g., finger) required centralized feedback control (Schmidt, 1980; Schmidt, Zelaznik, Hawkins, Frank, & Quinn, 1979). This efficiency consequence of learning is apparent in many species. For example, in bird song auditory feedback is critical during learning but not essential once the movement pattern is well established (Keele & Summers, 1976). A primary function of childhood play is to develop a wide array of efficient, habitual fundamental movement capabilities that can function as open loops.

Once rudimentary *postural stability* tasks are mastered (i.e., standing), more demanding postural problems can be attempted and solved. Static postural problems are those in which the body remains in one location, but the body's center of gravity, line of gravity, and base of support may vary. Examples include bending or squatting to pick up something, twisting or turning, reaching for or catching an object, and sitting while manipulating objects as in the act of eating. Typically children have mastered these by 5–6 years of age (Gallahue, 1982a). Dynamic postural problems are those in which the body is moving through space, requiring a continuous adjustment of postural stability.

Fundamental *locomotion movements* involve the ability to (a) selectively use diverse movements to accomplish the movement's purpose; (b) to shift movements quickly and smoothly as needed; and (c) to synchronize the movement with changing environmental conditions (Gallahue, 1982a). Examples include vertical and horizontal jumping, running, hopping or skipping, climbing, walking on a line or a beam, and body rolling as in a somersault. Often, such behaviors require synchronization with those of other people as in games of tag or wrestling, or with rhythms such as marching to music. Many children's games are designed around the exercise of various locomotion movements.

Manipulating objects involves control of the force given to or received from the objects involved, and more complicated manipulations involve using objects to influence one another in a controlled way. Accurate manipulations involve estimates of the mass, trajectory, rate of movement, and distance between relevant objects. Such estimates are confirmed or disconfirmed by the consequences produced. Therefore, each attempted manipulation by children may be thought of as a little experiment in influencing their world. As they discover how to successfully perform a particular manipulation, they may do it over and over again, and display excitement and pleasure as their competence increases and they repeatedly confirm that it "works."

Fundamental manipulative movements involve propulsive and/or absorptive actions (Gallahue, 1982a). Propulsive movements are illustrated by throwing, kicking, or striking a ball. Such actions involve not only manipulating the ball with the arms and hands or legs and feet but also a combination of stepping, swinging, turning, and stretching postural and locomotor movements. Thus, movement components previously developed separately must become coordinated into a more complex and targeted dynamic pattern. Absorptive movements involve positioning the body or limbs in the path of an approaching object to stop or deflect its movement. Learning to catch a ball is an example. Many manipulations involve both propulsive and absorptive movements (e.g., playing catch with a ball). Manual dexterity is an important kind of manipulative movement, but it has been subject to less empirical study (Cratty, 1970). Examples include dropping objects into small holes, threading beads on a string, dressing a doll, playing cars, and drawing or coloring. Parents struggle with the consequences of children exercising their newly developing skills, consequences requiring parental activity such as cleaning the lipstick pictures off the bedroom walls, or preventing the shocking experience of sticking a metal object into a wall socket.

Other Developmental Implications. The excitement and pleasure small children display as their locomotive and manipulative competencies evolve is a joy to behold. There is no more exhilarating experience for children than to discover they can manipulate and control aspects of their environment to their own ends. Interference with successful manipulations typically produces an outburst of anger. Children can learn to "give up" quickly or to persist in their efforts at accomplishment despite temporary failure, depending on the feedback they get from the consequences of their own efforts and the encouragement or criticism from those around them. The child's development and recognition of such growing competence is probably the initial foundation on which both self-confidence and successful interpersonal relationships are built. For example, many adults can remember that one of their most embarrassing and disappointing experiences during childhood was to be chosen last (or not at all) by their peers for some game, because their locomotive and manipulative skills were inadequate. Young children are more physical than conceptual in what they do and value in one another. Therefore, parents do well to make an early investment in cultivating reasonable levels of competence in diverse fundamental movement skills, and to permit small children to take risks of minor physical hurts in the interest of developing their motor competence and personal confidence in dealing with their world.

Complex Skill Development. By the time children are 6 to 8 years old they typically have developed a base of competence in the use of fundamental movement capabilities from which more complex, skilled movements can be developed. Individual differences in fundamental movement competence facilitate and/or constrain the kinds of complex skills they may proceed to try to learn. For example, a child with high levels of diverse locomotion skills can easily learn to dance or to play various kinds of ball games well. In contrast, a child with less fluent, graceful, and flexible locomotor competence will face difficulty, embarrassment, and perhaps social rejection in attempting to learn the same things. What is remarkable about skilled movement, such as in athletic or musical performance, is (a) the diverse combinations of skeletal-muscle patterns that are used to achieve the same general result; (b) the fluency, rate, economy, and accuracy of the sequential actions; (c) the expressiveness that is manifest in the carefully phased rhythms of timing and intensity; and (d) the generative flexibility through which the flow of action is rapidly altered to produce a performance appropriate to a dynamically changing context (Shaffer, 1980). Moreover, as the concept of tacit knowledge suggests, skilled performance is accomplished through the operation of a set of rules generally unknown to the person following them. Such beautiful execution of a complex motor behavior score can only result from lengthy, repetitive practice.

Skill development is not a matter primarily of trial and error learning. Trial and error learning is a fall-back expedient humans use when they are in an unpredictable environment, cannot understand the conditions they face, and either have no applicable cognitive components available to guide their movements, or cannot decide which ones to use (Ricocur, 1966). With mature children and adults, potentially relevant functional components of many types and levels have already been developed and can be performed with a reasonable degree of skill. Therefore, when a person decides to try to develop a particular complex skill he or she is able to immediately organize existing components of the available behavior repertoire into a relevant "first try." Elliott and Connolly (1974) refer to functional components which have become a part of a larger movement pattern as *operational subroutines*. To develop a complex skill, an appropriate set of such functional components must be coordinated in advance of their execution to form a single, more complex action unit. Moreover, several such complex components can be organized into a coordinated sequence to produce a large-scale performance, as in playing a piano concerto (Gallistel, 1980a; Shaffer, 1980). In other words, complex, skilled movement patterns are hierarchically organized and composed of interrelated nested sets of functional movement components.

Practice helps develop highly skilled performance capabilities in three ways. First, it can increase the fluency of complex performances. That is, the movement sequence unfolds smoothly at precisely the right rate, with no wasted motion, and with a high degree of precision or accuracy. Second, practice can increase the expressiveness of the movement sequence. That is, the sequence acquires a definite rhythm of timing and of varying intensity, giving it a quality of gracefulness. The importance of precise timing is particularly evident in musical, dance, and athletic performances in which the rhythm of the movement is fundamental to success. Third, it increases generative flexibility. That is, the performance can be smoothly altered in a variety of ways so that it is appropriate to its context for a large diversity of contexts (Shaffer, 1980). At a more general level, practice produces generalized spatial-temporal conceptual frameworks, or "cognitive maps," which provide a frame of reference for the skilled performance of movement sequences (Gallistel, 1980a). Human development of such spatial location codes appears to occur, at least in part, in reference to body-centered spatial coordinates (Larish & Stelmach, 1982).

Physical educators, sports specialists, dancers, and musicians have given much attention to *training procedures* for producing complex skills. Singer (1975) provides a good summary and demonstrates the use of a systems analysis approach to designing such training programs. First, he emphasizes that meaningful practice depends on the learner's state of *readiness to learn*. In addition to maturational or physical readiness, he refers to the learner's psychological state of preparedness to "heed relevant cues," to "concentrate on task demands," and to "practice conscientiously," that is, a relevant BES must be activated to organize and regulate the learning activity. Such learners are said to be motivated. Next, it is important for the learner to *understand what he is trying to learn;* that is, what the finished performance should look like. The learner must be able to specify (intend) desired outcomes. Third, the training pattern must be designed to *start with the learner's current level of skill*, that is, a relevant BES. That determines what kinds of feedback may be most useful in what sequence in the training program, and the sequence in which aspects of the skill will be practiced. Usually, although not always, skill in the simpler components of complex acts must be developed first.

Since the purpose of the training is to prepare the trainee to perform with skill in some kind of natural situation (e.g., under "game conditions"), *training for transfer of training* to such natural settings is important. A key way of doing that is to design the training situation to be as similar to the natural performance situation as possible; for example, having varsity football players practice against other players who run the offensive and defensive formations of the next opponent. Training in variable circumstances tends to produce better performance in novel tasks and better retention of the skill level (Carson & Wiegand, 1979; Kelso & Norman, 1978; Moxley, 1979). The impact of variable training may be lessened in simpler tasks and short training periods (Moore, Reeve, & Pissanos, 1981).

Various issues about training formats have been studied, such as the length, frequency, and work-rest ratio of practice sessions; massed versus distributed practice; and initial training for speed versus for accuracy. In general, no particular pattern of such variables appears to have a clear superiority over others. Which pattern of training procedures is desirable in a particular instance is a function of the trainees' current level of skill and the goals of training, that is, the operative BES organizing the practice. Whether to first practice components (the parts) or entire performance (the whole) appears to be a function of task complexity and organization. If the task is high in complexity (i.e., has many components) but low in organization (i.e., has relatively low interdependence of its components), practicing the parts may produce better results. Skills involving high organization—that is, which function more as a coherent unit—may be learned more efficiently by focusing on the whole performance (Singer, 1975).

One interesting variable that has generated renewed interest is the usefulness of *covert* as contrasted to *overt* practice. Overt practice involves physically practicing the skill. Covert practice involves mental rehearsal of the skill performance without physical practice, that is, it is a *simulated behavior episode.* Singer (1975) asserts that all athletes subject themselves to some form of mental rehearsal before, during, and even after a performance. There is considerable evidence that mental rehearsal, including the vividness of the mental imagery used, can improve performance on a variety of skills (Corbin, 1975; Ryan & Simmons, 1981, 1982; Singer, 1975). In general, it appears that physical practice produces more skill development than mental rehearsal alone and that each does better than no rehearsal at all. A combination of the two can be useful.

Skilled performance requires *concentration.* In the judgment of expert performers, concentration appears to play a key role in the organization and execution of complex motor skills. For example, if a golfer hits a bad shot or a musician makes a mistake they may speak of a "break" in their concentration. Yet scholars and professionals studying motor behavior seem to ignore the critical role of concentrated attention on effective performance. For example, the word *concentration* did not appear in any of the subject indexes of 11 books on motor behavior that were examined. The word *attention* appeared in only three, but was discussed solely in terms of information collection and not in terms of the organization its role in action.

The function of concentrated attention in the organization and execution of behavior was discussed at some length in Chapter 7. Concentrated attention appears to perform three types of functions in the organization and execution of complex motor skills. First, it appears to prevent potentially disruptive information from having any effect on skilled actions. Second, it appears to be necessary to maintain the careful timing and sequencing of the execution of the behavioral components involved, and of precise variations in the intensity of effort necessary for a skillful performance. Third, it makes possible precise, selective monitoring and control of a few feedback and feedforward variables crucial for the effective control and regulation of the skill execution, in an environment that may vary unexpectedly. It would be a contribution of both theoretical and practical significance if scholars of motor behavior could discover how individuals learn to use controlled, concentrated attention to produce complex patterns of skilled action.

Motor Skills and Communication.   Humans have two ways of influencing their environments. The first is by physical manipulation of, action on, or movement through it. That has been the focus of this chapter. The second way is by emitting information, coded on different types of markers, designed to influence other organism capable of collecting and processing information from those markers. That is the focus of Chapter 15.

15

Transactional Functions: Communication

INTRODUCTION

Physical action is the fundamental way that all organisms influence and relate to their environment. Humans have added potent information-based methods to their physical actions. Through communicative acts people can powerfully influence their social environments. After defining the nature and functions of communication, this chapter describes three kinds of communication: behavior-correlated information emission, gestural communication, and symbolic communication.

Communication and Social Organization

Social organization is made possible through the exchange of information among component members. Many organisms have information-collecting capabilities. As a result, their behavior can be influenced by the information as well as the actions impinging upon them, for example, emitting odors, making sounds, or performing expressive movements (Brown, 1975). Organisms from insects to humans display two complementary types of interactions: (a) "self-centered, egoistic drives" functioning to promote personal advancement and self-preservation; and (b) "group centered, more or less altruistic drives" functioning to preserve the group and at least some of its members (Allee, 1958). The creation of social organization requires combining and compromising among these "self-assertive" and "integrative" tendencies (Koestler, 1967). To serve their adaptive purpose, organisms create

diverse social organizations that are regulated by communication capabilities (Lewis, 1983). Nonhuman organisms use primarily nonvocal
means of communication such as emitting odors and making expressive
gestures, although vocalization plays an increasing role in more advanced primates (Snowdon, Brown, & Peterson, 1983).

Humans appear to have evolved in the context of small social groups
(Coon, 1963; Hamburg, 1963), and so development of communicative
capabilities was essential. Stated in systems terms, each person is
simultaneously a living system functioning as a quasi-independent unit,
and a subsystem of larger living systems (e.g., a family); this requires
people to balance their individuality against the constraints and benefits
provided by social group membership. Similarly, groups must balance
their constraints on their human components that are in the group's
interest, with some acceptance and facilitation of the individual's
existence and functioning. No group or society, even the most tyranni-
cal and oppressive, can continue to exist and function if it does not keep
a sufficient number of its members alive, functional, and reasonably
cooperative. Conversely, if individuals will not give up some of their
own freedom in the interest of the larger group, anarchy will reign and
the group will be destroyed. Since both individuals and groups are
dynamic systems, both may change with time.

Therefore, communication is a fundamental method of social regulation. Physical means (e.g., flogging, imprisonment) are of far less
general regulatory utility. Different groups may use different communication patterns, and such differences are probably one important basis
of intergroup misunderstanding and conflict (DeLong, 1972). The dynamics, continuity, and change of human cultures are products of
human communication capabilities. That is why education (e.g.,
schools) and information media (e.g., TV) are so fundamentally important in complex modern societies. Children must internalize and behave
in terms of the conventional understandings of their social group so that
their behavior becomes predictable and acceptable to others in the
group. Children quickly internalize and function smoothly within the
communication system of their society. Those that cannot are treated
differently, for example, being institutionalized or allowed to die
(Birdwhistell, 1970).

Communication as a Special Form of Information Conveying

Anything about people may convey information about them (e.g., blood
pressure, body posture, clothing). Recall that information is represented

in the organization of material and energy carriers or "markers." Therefore, since human behavior is organized both within itself and in relationship to environments, every behavior pattern automatically conveys information.

However, it is useful to distinguish between two types of information conveying: (a) attributes and information about a person conveyed as *correlates* of their actions; and (b) behaviors that have intentional communication as their primary function (Shatz, 1983). The same body structures may be used. The distinction lies in the way the information is coded with the behavior. In (a) the information is an unintended by-product of the organization of the act. In contrast, intentional communication involves (1) an arbitrary, socially shared signal system or code; (2) a communicator (or encoder) who organizes and conveys information using that code; and (3) a communicatee (or decoder) who understands and responds systematically to that code (Dittman, 1972; Wiener, Devoe, Rubinow, & Geller, 1972).

Humans' primary means of intentional communication is with symbol systems such as language, mathematics, and art forms. Some kinds of non-verbal behaviors such as head, face, and hand gestures, or voice intonations, may also be formally coded for intentional communication; examples are a smile of greeting, or a wave goodbye (Ekman, 1977; LaFrance & Mayo, 1978). However, other nonverbal behaviors (such as reaching for a pencil, blushing, the growling of one's stomach) provide unintended clues to a person's current physical state, mood, or intent. They convey information but are not communications.

Communicative acts have three interrelated properties: the kinds of actions, carriers, or markers used, such as hand gestures or vocalizations (Harper, Wiens, & Matarazzo, 1978); the types of codes used, such as emblems or emotional expressions; and the communicative intent or function, for example, interpersonal regulators (Ekman, 1977; H. Smith, 1979).

Three interacting kinds of information conveying behaviors will be examined: behavior-correlated information emission, gestural communication, and symbolic communication. Information is simultaneously conveyed through multiple "channels" (Weitz, 1974), and cannot be understood by interpreting "isolated bits of behavior"; it is the "configurations, the patterns" of elements that make accurate interpretation possible (Scheflen, 1968). The information provided by different channels usually fits together and is confirmatory, but sometimes different channels provide different messages and confuse the receiver. Understanding channel differences and relationships is theoretically and professionally useful.

Nonverbal, Behavior-Correlated Information Emission

Four types of factors influence the selective organization of transactional behaviors: (a) the intent; (b) the person's repertoire of possible behaviors; (c) the current state and dynamics of the body and of regulatory and controlling thoughts; and (d) current states and dynamics of the behavioral context. Therefore, as a correlate of every pattern of behavior, information is emitted that an observer can use to make inferences about those four sets of conditions. The same organization of skeletal-muscle components simultaneously creates actions and conveys information (Birdwhistell, 1970), but any other observable biological function also conveys information (e.g., changes in skin color resulting from circulatory changes).

Clues About Governing Functions. Spatial orientation of sensory structures, body postures, arm-hand movements, locomotion, and the related contextual variables provide clues about a person's current intentions.

Clues About Behavioral Repertoire. Behavior patterns performed with a high degree of skill imply a history of practice and a repertoire of similar or related potential performances. My oldest son capitalized on that assumption by learning to play one piano piece. He declined requests for encores (because he knew nothing else), but others inferred that he knew more. Conversely, if a person performs an act awkwardly, does not perform an expected act in an appropriate circumstance, or declines to attempt an act, the inference of lack of an appropriate repertoire is likely to be drawn (e.g., a child who avoids joining in a game, or plays clumsily with many mistakes).

Clues About Biological and Arousal States. Inferences about health status, nature of consciousness states, and emotional arousal may be based on biological and motor cues. For example, a child's hot, red face while sitting quietly in a room of normal temperature, combined with lethargic movements, difficulty maintaining an attentional focus, coughing, and avoiding pleasurable activities all imply a possible illness. Inferences about states or contents of consciousness use motoric cues about attention. For example, if students' eyes are closed during one of my lectures, I might infer they are asleep. (However, they assure me it only enables them to concentrate harder.) Inferences about emotional states use muscular and biological cues. Facial expressions are a prime example (Ekman & Oster, 1979). Muscular tension, changes in respiration, sweating, excessively vigorous actions, and inappropriate urination or defecation also imply emotional arousal or illness.

Environmental States and Dynamics. People organize their contexts (when possible) to facilitate their functioning, thereby providing useful clues about themselves. For example, a home decorated with antiques implies a different set of interests and values than one decorated with chrome, vinyl, and abstract art. An office's decor may imply a person of high or low power and status.

The Organization *of* Communicative Acts

Communication is defined as intentional information conveying, but "intentional" does not necessarily mean "consciously intended" (see Chapters 7 and 10). Communication uses motor behavior as the carrier of information. As described in Chapter 14, the organization of actions begins with an idea of the results or consequences to be produced. That potentiates a set of alternative action patterns that might "work." The person initiates the performance of one of them. Such preparation and initiation of action involves a hierarchical cascade of "decisions" at various levels, progressively committing the muscular configuration to a relevant organization. The specifics of the act are finalized in the process of performing it, and may be altered as unexpected conditions occur or as information feedback indicates the current behavior trajectory is less effective than desired. The revision may involve discarding the original action plan and initiating an alternative one. Since complex behavior often simultaneously serves multiple intentions, alterations in the pattern during its performance may reflect changes in some, but not necessarily all, of the guiding ideas.

Communicative Acts: A Type of Motor Behavior. Since communicative acts are symbolically coded motor patterns, they must be organized in the same fashion (Kelso, Tuller, & Harris, 1983; MacNeilage, 1970). Communication starts with an intention to communicate some information or idea and/or an intended impact on the receivers of the communication. That is why students are taught to first specify the audience and the message before preparing a speech. Infants display evidence of an "intention to communicate" during their first 6 to 9 months (Harding, 1981, 1982).

Communicative acts differ from other actions in that a crucial phase must intervene between the intention and the action. That is the selection and use of a motoric carrier (e.g., speech or writing actions), and of the symbolic code(s) to be used in conveying the message (e.g., English or German). Thus, the performance of a communicative act might be thought of as involving four phases: (a) a decision to communicate certain information, the *communicative intent*; (b) the selection of a mode of communication; (c) the selection of the symbolic code(s) to be used; and (4) the organization and execution of the motor pattern used as the communicative mode, that is, the carrier or marker on which the information is coded.

The *symbolic coding phase* involves three interrelated subcomponents: (1.) the selection of a schema for organizing the information to be conveyed, called the *semantic component* (i.e., the meaning of the message); (2.) the selection of the symbols (e.g., words) to be used, called the *lexical component;* and (3.) the organization of the selected symbols in appropriate patterns of sequence, rate, and amplitude to convey the intended meaning, called the *syntactic component.* The rules for organizing the lexical components to express the semantic component are called the *grammar* for the coding system used (Marin & Gordon, 1980; MacNeilage, 1980). Shepard (1984) conjectures that syntax or grammatical rules function to map between "complex multi-dimensional structures in the representational system" and "one-dimensional strings of discrete communicative gestures." In living systems terminology, abstract thought can only be communicated to others by transforming it into perceptible symbolic codes. Communicative disorders resulting from different kinds of brain damage suggest some componentization of brain structures to give different portions of the brain a leading role in each coding function (Berndt & Caramazza, 1980; Zurif, 1980).

The symbolic coding or lexical phase produces a general symbolic plan and potentiates a set of possible words (i.e., a relevant lexicon) and a set of organizational (or syntactic) options. However, the details of the gestures, words, and sentences are not planned in advance. As in all actions, the details of the communicative act are constructed and revised during the performance. Once a communicative act is initiated, in some (as yet unknown) hierarchical manner a pattern of muscular action is organized and performed which codes and conveys the information or idea to produce intended consequences. Evolution produced a hierarchically organized set of neural controls for vocalization (Jürgens & Ploog, 1981). It is a collaborative hierarchy, or "coalitional" organization (Kelso & Tuller, 1981; Turvey, Shaw, & Mace, 1978) involving patterns of mutual influence.

As the communication is being performed, the person monitors feedback signals of two types: (a) information about the coding accuracy; and (b) information about the impact of the communication on the target audience. If there are multiple objectives, multiple feedback signals will be monitored. For example, the communicator may simultaneously be trying to convey information and to elicit approval from the audience, and may therefore look for signs of both understanding and approval. Either kind of feedback may lead to midstream modifications of the communicative action. For example, a person may realize his or her sentence structure is confusing, stop in midsentence, and start over. Or the person may notice audience inattention and make verbal or gestural changes to try to attract its attention.

As with other kinds of intention-action combinations, there are always multiple ways of conveying the same ideas and producing the same impact. Even very young children will rephrase their communications to elicit understanding of their message (Greenfield, 1980). The same information can be coded onto different carriers, such as written or spoken words, or gestures. To convey (encode) or receive (decode) a communication, then, depends primarily on understanding and being competent in the use of the relevant coding system(s) rather than upon the particular motor patterns used to carry the communication. The same motor components can be organized the same and yet convey quite different information depending on the interpretation of that code. For example, a forefinger held in the air could mean "We are #1"; "may I go to the bathroom?", or "I wish to speak."

The fact that different motor patterns can code the same information has great adaptive importance. If for some reason a person loses the ability to control certain kinds of muscles, the same information can be communicated (i.e., coded on) some other, undamaged motor capability (Cicone, Wapner, Foldi, Zurif, & Gardner, 1979; Stokoe, 1978). Moreover, if in the middle of a communicative act one modality is inadequate (e.g., one "cannot find the words"), an alternate modality can supplement it (e.g., conveying an object's shape with hand gestures). The two sections that follow are broadly defined by the kinds of actions or "motor markers" used to code the information.

Nonvocal or Gestural Communication

All animals communicate in some way. While many use vocalizations to some extent (e.g., a dog's bark or a bird's song), nonvocal or gestural communication is the most primitive form of animal communication (Mehrabian, 1972), utilizing patterns that are both simple (e.g., bared teeth) or complex (e.g., a courtship dance) (Hinde, 1972).

Ploog and Jurgens (1981) propose that any organism's communicative capabilities must have a minimum of four parts: (a) structural and functional motor capabilities for generating the species-specific signals; (b) neural system arrangements for organizing and controlling the coding and performance of the signaling acts; (c) sense organs that are sensitive to the species-specific signaling carriers and codes; and (d) neural arrangements for decoding the signals into a potentially useful message. In humans, neural arrangements in the newer parts of the brain dominate and coordinate more primitive neural controls that are more influential in lower organisms.

Only humans have the neural and motor arrangements in the mouth, jaw, and face to organize and produce speech sounds and elaborate brain capabilities for symbolic coding and decoding of messages. Therefore, while humans share nonvocal communication capabilities with their more primitive ancestors, they have integrated those capabilities with their speech and language capabilities. However, nonvocal communicative behaviors develop first, and long before they understand language, human infants can communicate nonverbally (Mayo & LaFrance, 1978). Once speech communication skills are acquired, they are typically accompanied by supportive or elaborative gestural communication. The study of nonverbal communication has been growing rapidly since the mid-1950s (Buck, 1984; Duncan, 1969; Ekman & Friesen, 1969a; Feldman, 1982; Mehrabian, 1972; Raffler-Engel, 1980), with practical interest in its role in deception and in psychotherapy transactions (Blondis & Jackson, 1977; Ekman, 1981; Ekman & Friesen, 1982).

Kinds of Nonverbal Behaviors Used for Communication. Nonverbal communication is often subdivided by the kinds of behaviors and body parts involved. *Proxemics* (Hall, 1963) focuses on spatial variables such as the distance maintained between people while interacting. *Kinesics* (Birdwhistell, 1970; Dittman, 1972; Knapp, 1972) studies body gestures, like those used in posture and locomotion, as well as hand and facial gestures.

Hand gestures code many types of information, from a caress to a threat, from applause to rejection, from specifying shapes or amounts to specifying direction; and methods of classifying them have been developed (Friesen, Ekman, & Wallbott, 1979; Wiener et al., 1972). Hand gestures are also commonly used as adjuncts to verbal communication (Jancovic, Devoe, & Wiener, 1975). Parents use hand gestures to communicate with children, and the pattern of use changes with the age of the child (Guttmann & Turnure, 1979). Here, as in other domains, one structure can substitute functionally for another; for example, one can "talk" with a deaf person using culturally coded, standardized hand gestures rather than speech.

Facial gestures have a powerful interpersonal influence (Tomkins, 1962), are extensively used (Ekman, 1978; Harper et al., 1978), and are particularly important in conveying information about affect (Ekman, Friesen, & Ellsworth, 1972; Ekman & Oster, 1979; Izard, 1971). People tend to monitor and control (or disguise) those behaviors that are most informative and for which they have been held most accountable, which include the things they say and their facial gestures (Ekman & Friesen, 1969b). There are approximately 30 facial muscles, and a system has been developed for classifying expressions as organizations of different facial muscle action patterns (Ekman & Friesen, 1976).

The communicative use of facial gesture subcomponents has been studied. For example, gaze behaviors influence interpersonal interactions (Argyle & Cook, 1976; Ellsworth & Ludwig, 1972). Looking into another person's eyes, which has been termed *interocular intimacy* by Tomkins (1963), conveys interest, concern, or affection, and sometimes aggression as in "staring someone down." Eyebrow gestures are used as adjuncts to speech, or to communicate conversational signals and emotional states (Ekman, 1978, 1979; Keating, Mazur, & Segall, 1977).

Different kinds of brain damage can affect facial gestures differently. For example, left hemisphere damage tends to result in amplified facial expressions, while right hemisphere damage appears to reduce facial expressiveness (Blurton Jones, 1972; Buck & Duffy, 1980; Ekman & Oster, 1979; Nyström, 1977; Trevarthen, 1980). Facial gestures are usually combined with speech, hand gestures, body position, and contextual factors in communicative episodes, and may convey different meanings depending on the communicative context (Spignesi & Shor, 1981).

Vocalization and speech communication are tightly linked, but not the same. Speech involves words. Vocalization is sometimes called *paralanguage* (Trager, 1958), or the prosodic aspects of speech, and involves sounds but not words. Vocalization characteristics include variations in pitch, loudness, rate, timing, hesitations, and silences, in addition to vocal gestures such as crying, cheering, and laughing. Without such vocal variations, speech seems monotonous and unexpressive (e.g., computer-generated speech).

Functional Classification of Communicative Acts. Representing non-verbal communication in terms of the kinds of movements used is analogous to representing verbal communication as spoken or written. Both are classifications of carriers. Some other approach is required to classify codes and meanings.

One alternative is to use functional classifications, such as the sharing of interpersonal attitudes, particularly of intimacy and status; the display and recognition of emotion; and the regulation of social interaction (Argyle, 1975); or the conveyence of affect, regulation of interactions, and performance of referential functions (Raffler-Engel, 1980). Ekman (1977) proposed five functional categories: *emblems* (movements that are substitutes for words); *illustrators* (movements that accent, modify, or punctuate speech); *regulators* (movements that influence listener-speaker roles during conversation); *adaptors* (self- or object-manipulations related to subjective states); and *affect displays* (gestures conveying information about subjective states) (Harper, Wiens, & Matarazzo, 1978).

Communicative acts can also be related to three broad types of communication objectives: (a) to share with others one's subjective experiences, such as perceptions, memories, thoughts, ideas, emotions, and sensations; (b) to exchange information and ideas with others; and (c) to influence, control, and regulate the behavior of other organisms (Benelli, D'Odorico, Levorato, & Simion, 1977; LaFrance & Mayo, 1978).

Different Types of Nonverbal Codes. Codes are systematic ways of organizing a carrier to convey information. When knowledge of a code is shared among a group of people it becomes a basis for communication. Each code can represent some but not all kinds of information. The more diverse and precise the information a code can represent, the more communicatively useful it is. Verbal languages are the most flexible codes invented so far. For nonverbal gestures to function as communicative acts, some shared gestural code must be used and both sender and receiver must understand it. As with languages, different cultures may develop different nonverbal coding systems. Attempts at cross-cultural communication lead to misunderstandings when people are not familiar with one another's nonverbal codes. For example, in some cultures shaking the head from side to side may mean "yes" or "I agree" while in other cultures it may mean "no" or "I disagree."

Gestural codes that convey information about subjective or affective states, called *expressive displays*, are present in many species, and human facial expressive displays have been extensively studied (Ekman & Oster, 1979; see Chapter 13). It appears that these affective facial codes are an evolutionary product (Jürgens & Ploog, 1981). For example, the facial musculature of infants is fully formed and functional at birth; several different emotional expressions occur by 4 weeks of age (Schellenbach, 1987); and babies respond differentially to "happy," "sad," and "angry" faces (Ekman & Oster, 1979). People in different cultures label certain facial expressions of emotion with the same emotional terms, and display the same basic facial expressions when experiencing the same emotions; but the display may be modified by culture-specific display rules since facial gestures are subject to voluntary control. Expressive facial gestures are typically components of, and signal the possible occurrence of, larger action patterns (e.g., anger-attack; fear-escape). Therefore, they can function not only to convey information about subjective states but also to regulate social interactions. Because of their social-regulatory function, humans may intentionally use facial gestures to influence the behaviors of others (Ekman & Friesen, 1982). Cultures have different "display rules" in regard to when certain kinds of expressive gestures are considered appropriate.

Other gestural codes convey other states such as pain or nausea. Hand gestures used as adjuncts to speech may also code subjective states. For example, pounding the table with one's fist while speaking signals anger, whereas clapping hands together in applause may signal pleasure. Some vocal codes signal subjectives states. Examples include screaming (in fear); laughing (in joy); moaning (in pain); and snarling (in anger). Animals and humans generally produce sounds representing their "motivational states" that function to influence the "motivational states" of their hearers (Brown, 1975). This link has led to proposals that human speech is closely linked to emotions (DeLong, 1972). Certainly, the vocal or prosodic aspects of speech (and singing) are used extensively to stir human emotions and their related types of actions.

Another type of gestural code symbolically represents the information to be conveyed. Ekman (1977) calls such codes *emblems*. They may be either pictoral (i.e., iconic) or symbolic (i.e., arbitrary). In pictoral coding, the movement in some way resembles what it signifies. That is the primary basis of primitive "sign" languages. Such pictoral codes are often culture-specific. For example, the gesture symbolizing suicide is, in New Guinea, pretended strangling; in the U.S., a hand pointed towards the head as if it were a gun; and, in Japan, a pantomime of stabbing oneself in the belly with a sword. In symbolic coding the movements have specific meanings, analogous to words. "Sign" languages used to communicate with deaf people are a good example (Stokoe, 1978). Some of them such as "finger spelling" are simply substitute codings for the language being used.

However, it is not necessary to use an existing symbol system as the basis for gestural coding rules. Symbol systems are human constructions, and many versions can be invented. For example, American Sign Language (ASL) is an invented gestural language with a grammar distinct from English. Very young deaf children have developed gestural vocabularies and grammars of their own (Goldin-Meadow & Feldman, 1975, 1977). Of course, people who invent their own symbol systems, such as deaf children and psychotic adults, cannot communicate through them with others unless the others can "crack the code."

Some gestural codes function to supplement the information conveyed in speech. Ekman (1977) refers to such codes as *illustrators*, usually involving hand and arm movements. For example, *batons* are movements that accent a particular word; *underliners* emphasize a phrase, clause, sentence or idea; *kinetographs* depict a bodily or nonhuman action; *rhythmics* depict the pacing or rhythm of an event;

and *diectics* are movements that point to the referent. No one code is necessarily better than another, but shared codes are important in producing group identity and cohesion, and identifying group membership (DeLong, 1972). This is true of other organisms too. For example, female cricket frogs from Georgia respond only to males whose mating calls have a Georgia dialect, and those from Texas only to males with a Texas dialect (Ploog & Melnechuk, 1969).

Finally, some codes function to regulate interpersonal interaction. For example, most cultures have some kinds of gestures signaling greeting and farewell. Some gestures regulate interpersonal intimacy. For example, raising one's eyebrows and gazing into another person's eyes, beckoning someone to come closer, opening one's arms and extending them towards another, and caressing another, all convey liking and encourage more intimate interactions. In contrast, averting one's gaze, holding the palm outward towards a person, maintaining considerable space between oneself and another, and avoiding physical contact all imply caution or dislike and discourage intimate interactions (Harper et al., 1978).

Some gestural codes influence perceptions of status and role. For example, lowered eyebrows may convey dominance (Keating, Mazur, & Segall, 1977). Other codes influence conversational transactions, and children learn such conversational rules (Ekman, 1979; Greenfield, 1980; Mayo & LaFrance, 1978). For example, certain gaze behaviors and eye brow gestures help signal conversational turn-taking and there are subcultural differences in their use. A raised or lowered voice at the end of a sentence or phrase, and a pause in conversation, may be combined with gaze behavior to signal turn-taking. Nonverbal cues play an important role in regulating the exchange of listener-speaker roles in adults (Duncan & Fiske, 1977), and nursery-school children already use some turn-yielding cues (DeLong, 1977). People often use their social behavior to communicate information about themselves to others. Such self-presentations are conveyed for the purpose of influencing what others think of them or of establishing, maintaining, or refining the general image of or attitudes about them that others hold (Baumeister, 1982). Psychotherapists make extensive, intentional use of nonverbal behaviors to influence client behaviors. Counselor persuasiveness is correlated with gesticulation rate, facial activity including eye contact, and speech volume and rate. Affiliative gestures such as positive head nods and head gestures, eye contact, smiles, and forward body lean appear to be particularly influential (Edinger & Patterson, 1983). Actors become very skillful in the use of nonverbal forms of communication to convey qualities such as the personality, intent, mood, and status of the character they are portraying.

Coding systems are sometimes combined, and sometimes used as alternatives for conveying the same information. Research on the relationships between gestural and verbal language in aphasic communication has led to the hypothesis of a "central organizer" that controls important features of the encoding process for all motor system modalities or carriers of information (Cicone, Wapner, Foldi, Zurif, & Gardner, 1979). This would make possible the use of alternate combinations of motor modalities to express the same idea and/or the modification of the communication pattern during its execution if feedback suggested that was desirable. Humans typically use nonverbal gestural codes in conjunction with speech and language; therefore, that is examined next.

Verbal and Symbolic Communication

Humans have developed a variety of symbolic codes for communication using different carriers, such as numbers, music, drawing, and other art forms; but verbal codes are the most versatile, and speech and writing are their primary carriers.

Origins of Speech Capabilities. Speech is a powerful form of social action. In animals, the influence of learning on species- or population-typical vocalizations is limited to a few kinds of mammals and birds. Even there, genetic factors significantly influence vocal development (Brown, 1975). In contrast, learning has a more fundamental influence on speech development in humans, within their genetic and structural constraints (Lennenberg, 1967; Lindblom, 1983; Ohala, 1983).

Human language and speech capabilities are a function of "species-specific cognitive propensities," which consist of a process of "categorization and extraction of similarities" (Lennenberg, 1967). The biological properties of the brain that enable humans to construct and use languages also apparently limits the range of natural language possibilities. In addition, certain specializations of anatomy and physiology limit possible variations in speech and account for some of the universal features of natural languages. However, within those structural-functional boundaries much potential for diversity still exists, as manifest in the many different languages humans have developed (Ohala, 1983).

Historical Perspective on the Study of Verbal Communication. The power of speech is so impressive that humans once considered it a gift of the gods. Research on human speech began as early as the 7th century B.C. Despite various theoretical formulations and much study over the ensuing centuries, it still remains a fascinating puzzle (Critchley, 1967; Harnad, Steklis, & Lancaster, 1976; Marx, 1967). A massive amount of information has accumulated about its anatomical and physiological bases (Dickson & Maue-Dickson, 1982); its perception and production (Bouhuys, 1968; Cole, 1980; Eimas & Miller, 1981; MacNeilage, 1983; Sebeok, 1974); how children acquire language and speech capabilities (Peng & von Raffler-Engel, 1979; Shatz, 1983; Yeni-Komshian, Kavanagh, & Ferguson, 1980); how to diagnose and treat language and speech disorders in both children (Costello, 1984) and adults (Holland, 1983); and how to improve singing performances (Proctor, 1980).

The assumptions guiding efforts to understand verbal communication and speech have changed from time to time (Cooper, 1983). Interest initially focused on the structure of language and produced a discipline called *linguistics*. As people began to focus on speech itself, linguistics led to viewing speech as a string of symbols composed of basic units called *phonemes*. The revolution in communications technology beginning in the 1920s (e.g., the telephone and radio) led to an engineering interest in speech and the acoustics of speech. Static units of analysis were used at first (e.g., steady-state frequency components of speech sounds), but there was soon a shift to the study of dynamically changing sound spectrums. Study of *speech acoustics* was linked to sound perception because the two had to fit together, like a baseball and a catcher's mitt.

The phonetic and acoustic views of speech began to merge into *acoustic phonetics* following World War II. It was assumed that the acoustic patterns of speech sounds were composed of phonetic elements, leading to the study of articulatory processes by which people produced the acoustic patterns representing different phonemes. That led to a problem termed *coarticulation* (Fowler, 1978). The phonemes do not appear separately in the acoustic stream of speech sounds. Rather, they are merged into more complex patterns; that is, they are coarticulated. Much effort and elaborate logical argument has gone into trying to explain how the articulation of each phoneme is influenced by those that precede and follow it.

This is a nice example of how basic assumptions force scientists into investigating certain kinds of questions rather than others. If the associationistic assumption that speech sounds are constructed from phonemes is discarded, the problem of coarticulation disappears and become instead redefined. The linkage to be understood is not between basic articulatory elements (phonemes) and basic verbal symbols, but rather between the dynamic organization of articulatory patterns and the sound patterns they produce. Understanding that linkage would provide a basis for studying how meaning is coded onto sound patterns, the auditory perception of those patterns, and decoding or comprehending their meaning (Liberman, 1983; Stevens & Blumstein, 1981).

Thus, a shift is occurring from a linguistic approach to a speech production and comprehension approach; a shift from the linguistic product or codes used to the processes of language production and comprehension (Clark & Hecht, 1983). Knowledge about speech communication can therefore be summarized into four interrelated functional components and their respective biological bases: (a) the sensorimotor capabilities for producing speech sounds; (b) the brain structures and processes for creating and applying linguistic codes to the organization of motor patterns; (c) the auditory capabilities for perceiving speech; and (d) the brain structures and processes for comprehending verbal communication. Auditory capabilities are considered in Chapter 8 and comprehension in Chapter 9, so only (a) and (b) are considered here.

The Production of Speech Sounds. A major portion of research on speech production has focused on how communication acts are produced; that is, how the information is coded upon the act rather than upon what is communicated. There are a diversity of structural-functional motor components that must function as a coordinated whole to produce speech (Dickson & Maue-Dickson, 1982; Ohala, 1983; Proctor, 1980), usefully considered as three interrelated functions: (a) the production of a controlled air flow which provides the energy source and carrier for sound production; (b) the production of sounds; and (c) the shaping of sounds into verbal codes. The structures involved can be represented as a system of air pressure chambers connected by valves that can be adjusted to control air flow among the chambers, and pistons for producing variations in air pressure within the chambers (Ohala, 1983).

Speech and singing require a delicate and precise control of pressure, volume, and rate of air flow through the various chambers. The lungs and the muscles of the neck, stomach, rib cage, and diaphragm that control the inhaling-exhaling respiratory cycle provide the primary means of air flow control. The lungs connect to the upper part of the throat through a tube called the trachea. At the top of that tube is the larynx whose initial evolutionary value was to serve as a valve. When closed, it prevents solids and liquids from entering the lungs, forcing them into the esophagus where they can be swallowed into the stomach. When open, the valve permits air to flow into and out of the lungs. By the muscular variation of pressure on the lungs, the air pressure within the lungs can be varied. By the opening and closing of the larynx "valve," the volume and rate of air flow can be varied.

Sound production is possible because evolutionary processes produced a modification of the larynx called the vocal folds (or "cords"). These two pieces of elastic, fibrous tissue can be adjusted by muscles attaching them to the walls of the larynx. Because they must remain flexible and are subjected to a lot of use, they are covered by special kinds of epithelial tissue that are kept wet by glandular secretions. By configuring the vocal folds in varying patterns and forcing air past them with different pressures and at different rates, they will vibrate in different patterns producing varying patterns of air turbulence. Air flow variations in combination with vocal fold control of the pattern of air turbulence can produce sounds that vary in frequency, amplitude, sequencing, and timing. The action of the larynx in producing sounds is called *phonation* or *voicing*.

Individuals differ in both their air flow control and their vocal fold characteristics and control, and therefore in their sound-voicing capabilities. These variables may change with age and result in changes in voicing. For example, to prevent such maturational changes, young boys were once castrated to preserve their beautiful singing voices (Proctor, 1980). With an adult's lung capacity and a child's small larynx, they had unique vocal characteristics; one could, for example, maintain a high C for two minutes.

Sound shaping into verbal codes, or word formation, requires the additional involvement of supralaryngeal structures including pharynx, soft palate, oral cavity, tongue, lips, jaw, and nasal cavity. By appropriate muscular action in the cheeks, jaw, and throat, the configuration of the oral and nasal resonance chambers can be varied. Through adjustment of the positioning and movement of the soft palate, tongue, and lips, the air pressure and rate and volume of flow can be varied. Finely coordinated variations in the configuration of these variables to produce speech sounds is called articulation, the final phase of speech production.

The human speech apparatus places *structural limitations* on the kinds and organization of speech sounds that are possible (Lindblom, 1983; Ohala, 1983; Stevens, 1983; Stevens & Blumstein, 1981). Moreover, the limitations are dynamic; that is, a function of the flow of speech. As an analogy, you can reach for a drink while seated or standing, but the form of behavior will be quite different because of the different starting positions of your body. Similarly, when the vocal folds and supralaryngeal structures are configured to produce a certain sound at a specific point in the speech flow, only some of all possible sounds can be voiced next because of the spatial configuration from which the next movement must begin.

Stevens (1983) asserts that there are a limited number of basic features of speech which have unique acoustic properties to which the auditory system responds in a distinctive way. The production of a speech segment is organized to achieve a desired acoustic goal, and articulatory structures are programmed to produce an appropriate sequence of target configurations or states. He says that there are only 15-20 such basic features that describe the phonetic contrasts in all languages, but each language uses only some of them. Ostwald (1975) argues that the human auditory system evolved to recognize speech sounds as uniquely different from all other sounds.

Liberman (1982) takes a similar position. His work on speech processes began with efforts in the 1940s to design a "talking machine" to read printed material to blind people. He assumed that the machine needed to produce a distinctive sound for each letter. By combining these sounds, human talking could be imitated. (Letter sounds are approximately the basic phonemes of a language.) That associationistic approach failed, and led him to try to understand how human speech is really formulated. He decided that speech transmission and reception had evolved to fit together like a hand and glove; that is, its biological base provides "a coherent system, like echolocation in the bat"; and that it composes "distinctive processes adapted to a distinctive function" which is to make feasible the communication of very diverse messages with limited capabilities. He argues that the structures that function to produce speech sounds can produce only a limited number of sounds, such as frequency sweeps, fricatives (frictionless passages of voiceless breath against a narrowing in the vocal tract);,and silences between sounds. Each of these is identified with a somewhat different organization of the speech-producing structures.

Liberman argues that speech is produced by constructing varying organizations of this limited set of component sounds flowing through time at varying rates, termed a *phonetic process*. It is the pattern of organization of the basic component sounds of speech that produces the speech code. Several such components (phonetic segments) "...are conveyed simultaneously by a single segment of sound." Different acoustic cues can be combined to produce the same phonetic percept (a form of equifinality). They are "perceptually equivalent for that purpose" because they are "common products of the same linguistically significant gesture."

For example, when people have their jaw movement frozen by clamping a "bite block" between their teeth, they can still speak in an intelligible way by making compensatory articulatory movements. They find an alternative way of coding the same information on their remaining articulatory capabilities (Oller & MacNeilage, 1983). Hebb (1949) referred to this as *motor equivalence*. It is the organized pattern of auditory cues that is the functional unit of speech, and the separate contributions of the components of the pattern "are not sensed as separate." It is "a matter of apprehending a structure," rather than apprehending elements and associating them in the brain. Sounds not utilizing such a phonetic organization are heard as sounds but not as speech.

Just as the coordinates of visual cues relative to one another remain invariant while their coordinates on the retina may vary, so too the relationships among speech-relevant phonetic cues may remain invariant even though the pattern of auditory stimulation they produce may vary. Liberman argues that the invariant patterns in speech are products of the articulatory capabilities of the speech structure, and that the speech perception centers in the human brain evolved to abstract such patterns of invariance from the variable flow of auditory stimulation. Thus, a biological base for speech perception evolved to fit speech articulation capabilities (Jürgens & Ploog, 1981; Zurif, 1980). The organization of human languages, then, must reflect this basic structural-functional arrangement.

Keenan (1976) proposes that there may exist a set of language universals, obscured by the heterogeneity of human languages, that provide a pool of possibilities from which the pattern of different languages may be built. There may be no universal feature common to all languages, but all languages may be constructed of features from the same universal set. Perhaps Keenan's set of language universals may be defined by Liberman's set of articulatory (phonetic) capabilities. For example, infant vocalizations during the first 15 weeks of life display many features of adult speech, though not coordinated in speech forms. They can produce all possible adult speech sounds, including "French vowels and trills," and "German umlaut and gutteral sounds" (Osgood, 1955). Moreover, infants can discriminate the major acoustic properties underlying phonemic contrasts at least in English (Shatz, 1983; Yeni-Komshian, Kavanagh, & Ferguson, 1980). Liberman's and Keenan's proposals may be applications of the concept of componentization discussed in chapters 2 and 3 of this book.

Motor coordination, in general, is organized in componentized, hierarchical fashion using components termed *coordinative structures* (see Chapter 14). The idea of componentization has been used to represent patterns of locomotion (Easton, 1972) and other patterns of motor behavior (Greene, 1972; Turvey, 1977a). A coordinative structure "generates an equivalence class of movements'" organizationally it is "nested," and frequently it is "cyclic in nature" (as in running). Several smaller coordinative structures (components) may be hierarchically combined to create a larger coordinative structure.

Fowler (1978) proposes that this is the way speech is organized and functions, since it, too, is a form of motor behavior. The organized functioning of the speech structures differs for vowels and consonants, although many of the same structures are involved in both. For example, although the tongue is involved in articulating both, the tongue tip is particularly involved in articulating consonants (Perkell, 1969). The articulatory gestures involved in producing consonants and vowels "are products of different (coordinated) neuromuscular systems" (Fowler, 1978). Producing consonant sounds appears to represent a more complex motor coordination task. For example, specialists in our local speech and hearing clinic say that "half our business is dealing with S, R, and L."

Fluent speech is produced by coordinated interactions among the respiratory, laryngeal, and supralaryngeal structures within certain ranges of velocity, displacement, positioning, and timing. It appears that such finely tuned coordinated interactions can be disrupted by physiological and psychological factors, producing movement patterns characteristic of stutterers (Zimmerman, 1980). Developmentally, newborn infants can produce a variety of vocalizations, and vocal play begins in the second 6 months of life (Starke, 1981). Prior to the age of 3, children recognize important temporal parameters of the language they are learning, and use them. However, because of their less mature neuromotor capabilities, children speak more slowly and have longer phonetic segments (B. Smith, 1978). Gestural and verbal communication capabilities probably develop in simultaneous and interacting ways, although gestural communication capabilities are the first to become functional.

Information Coding of Motor Behavior. Thought processes (or governing functions) specify the coding patterns to be represented in the motor patterns, and control the articulatory expression (Marin & Gordon, 1980). As mentioned earlier, the coding process has three aspects. First, the person must decide on the consequence(s) to be produced by the communication, and there are two types. The *semantic aspect* involves specifying the meaning or message to be conveyed. The *pragmatic aspect* involves identifying the desired impact of the message on the receiver(s) of the communication. For example, speech acts may take forms such as informing, ordering, warning, disapproving, challenging, questioning, and thinking (Bruner, 1982; Searle, 1969). Establishing communication objectives is a directive function analogous to establishing the target for other kinds of motor behaviors.

These semantic and pragmatic decisions provide design specifications for the communicative act. To fulfill those specifications, a coding pattern must be formulated appropriate for the motor modality to be used (e.g., hand gestures, speech), and which the receiver of the communication will understand. For speech, this involves selecting an appropriate combination of content words (e.g., nouns, verbs, adjectives) called the *lexical component*. There is always more than one combination of content words that can convey the same meaning and impact, just as there is always more than one combination of muscle actions to produce the same motor behavior consequence (Kreckel, 1982).

However, the content words must be organized into an appropriate pattern if they are to convey the intended meaning. Such organizing processes are called the *syntactic* cqomponent and reflect the grammatical rules of the language being used. Syntactic processes involve the sequencing of the content words and the selection and placement of function words or grammatical morphemes (e.g., pronouns, articles, prepositions, conjunctions) to appropriately connect and sequence the content words into relevant meaningful segments or phrases. The lexical and syntactic components of the coding process are manifestations of the control functions of thought in designing and executing behavior patterns.

Computer-based efforts to simulate human language functions have dispelled some oversimplified ideas about human communication (Waldrop, 1984). At first, researchers assumed that the mind could be modeled as a processor of symbols, like a computer program. That approach succeeded in simulating only relatively simple language functions. It has led to the recognition that language is more than words. The meaning of a communication depends on its context and involves an extensive body of knowledge. For example, speakers shape their communications to fit their assumptions about the knowledge of their listener(s). Communications to nonknowledgable listeners include different content than for knowledgable listeners (Goodwin, 1981). Communication functions to influence the environment as do other kinds of motor acts.

In Chapter 9, it was proposed that words are simply "handles" for manipulating abstract concepts. Artificial intelligence (AI) research is beginning to emphasize the distinction between the symbolic representation of information to communicate it, and the mental manipulation of ideas or meanings. This is based on the fact that human information processing and communication is embedded in a very large personal (and often shared) knowledge reservoire. AI research is now trying to include things such as goals, plans, scripts, and themes (i.e., knowledge frames that provide an inferential base, such as knowledge of a person's occupation related to general properties of that occupation). In other words, a shift has occurred from a primary focus on the lexical and syntactic aspects of the coding process to the relationship between those and the semantic aspects. People "hear" words and sentences but they "think" with abstractions or meanings. Just as different combinations of muscle actions can produce the same consequences, so too can different combinations of words and gestures convey the same meaning and have the same influence. The information coding with which people think is not the same as the symbolic coding with which they communicate (see Chapter 9). Oden (1987) suggests that one reason some promising approaches to understanding cognition were abandoned is because they "made the complexity of human cognition apparent."

The actual motor performance, or *articulatory expression*, of a message is controlled and regulated by the selective, facilitating and constraining influences of the semantic, lexical, and syntactic processes. As with other motor behaviors, the organization of the flow of speech appears to be constructed as a part of the process of performing the act. One may "mentally" rehearse a sentence or speech before actually speaking it to be sure it "comes out right," but in ordinary conversation that is not typical. People listen to themselves speak and use that auditory feedback to regulate the articulatory flow of their speech, to insure that it meets the message or semantic requirements guiding it. The importance of regulatory auditory feedback is demonstrated by the difficulty people have in maintaining a coherent flow of speech when they cannot hear themselves talk, or when the auditory feedback is experimentally delayed so that it is out of phase with what is being spoken. People also visually monitor listeners' reactions and may modify their speech flow to better regulate those reactions.

Vocal and nonverbal coding is correlated with the lexical and syntactic organization of speech. For example, variations in intonation, loudness or pacing (i.e., the expressive or prosodic vocalizations), and hand and facial gestures all add information, emphases, and "punctuation" which contribute to producing the intended consequences.

Children construct, from their flow of percepts, meanings associated with different kinds of events relevant to types of situations and in a cultural context, that is, percepts are interpreted within currently operative BES. One aspect of those contextual variables is the verbal code(s) used to represent different meanings in their culture (Halliday, 1978). Therefore, children typically develop concepts and learn verbal codes representing them as consistently related aspects within sets of percepts. Moreover, because concepts are constructed in relationship to one another, the relevant codes are also learned in relationship to one another, such as "illness" and "cold" (de Saussure, 1974). Learning a language seems like the "accretion of instances to small paradigms" (Clark & Hecht, 1983). Initially, both verbal and nonverbal codes are learned in interpersonal situations.

Children learn to comprehend language before they learn to produce it (Clark & Hecht, 1983), as illustrated by the much larger size of their recognition vocabulary compared to their speaking vocabulary, that is, language can activate relevant BES in children before they can construct meaningful sentences. Their initial language learning comes from hearing others speak. Since people usually speak in sentences as well as words, children learn not only vocabulary but also phrases and grammatical rules governing the organization of phrases. For example, one patient who was unable to produce speech was given a typewriter at the age of 30. Within a few days, that patient began to typewrite in fluent, syntactically good English (Fourcin, 1975). Children learning to speak correct errors in their own speech, progressively moving toward greater similarity to adult pronunciation forms. They appear to match perception of their own speech with recollections of the speech of others, and correct their speech to reduce the discrepancy (Clark & Hecht, 1983).

Through hearing others speak, then, children develop a listening or comprehension repertoire of lexical (i.e., vocabulary) and syntactic (i.e., rules of language organization) behaviors that can be used to communicate semantic meanings (i.e., concepts and propositions), and to organize and guide their speaking behavior or articulation. As they learn to speak, they draw upon that repertoire of words and language rules to convey their meanings. They develop habits of speaking through practice, just as they develop other kinds of motor habits. Such habits involve both content and style. Familiar words and phrases are more frequently used to convey content. In addition, certain types of sentence structure, emphases, intonations, and speaking rates become habitual (e.g., a Southern accent vs. a New England accent). The concept of coordinative structures as applied to speech (Kelso & Tuller, 1981) is another way of talking about such motor-speech habits and their possible combination into larger units of expression.

Speech Communication and Language Disorders.   Language comprehension is often represented by four interrelated types of functions (Clark & Clark, 1977; Clark & Hecht, 1983): (a) a phonological (or speech sound) analyzer; (b) a syntactic parser (or organizer of grammatical speech); (c) a lexicon (or vocabulary file); and (d) a semantic interpreter (or meaning abstracter). To account for speech behavior, an articulation or speech motor control function must be added. Different parts of the brain appear to play a leading role (though not the sole role) in each function. Speech comprehension and production involves the simultaneous functioning of a number of areas of the brain, each of which has a special role in the speech process. Damage in different areas usually produces different symptom patterns of language disruption (Jürgens & Ploog, 1981; Luria, 1981; Marin & Gordon, 1980; Zurif, 1980).

For example, one kind of lesion which occurs in a specific area of the frontal lobe of the neocortex produces a pattern of speech disruption symptoms called *Broca's aphasia*. This involves (a) slow, very effortful, and sometimes distorted articulation, accompanied by prosodic limitations such as reduced voice inflections and rhythms; (b) agrammatism, or speech without good grammatical organization and omitting function words, or grammatical morphemes, such as of, and, or, but, which help to meaningfully organize content words; and (c) comprehension difficulties in listening and reading because of primary reliance on content words (e.g., nouns, verbs) and their sequencing, rather than upon syntactical characteristics, to understanding the meaning.

Berndt and Caramazza (1980) propose that Broca's area plays a key role in the syntactic parsing function, and that damage to that area disrupts people's ability to grammatically organize their speech. They argue that the language disruption symptoms of Broca's aphasia are either direct manifestations of disruption of the syntactic parser, or are compensatory behaviors resulting from such disruption. Moreover, Broca's area is located near a part of the neocortex heavily involved in motor control in general, and facial motor control in particular, and damage to it apparently also disrupts articulatory motor control. Thus, speech is slow and requires great effort, and its prosodic aspects (e.g., rhythm and inflections) are severely limited. The speech of patients with Broca's area damage, then, represents their best effort to communicate their messages in the face of disturbed articulatory abilities and an impaired syntactic parser.

Wernicke's aphasia is associated with lesions in the posterior third of the left superior temporal gyrus. Such patients can still speak fluently (in contrast to those with Broca's aphasia), but have difficulty finding content words for intended referents. The result is speech that seems syntactically adequate but of unclear meaning. For example, a patient might say, "Let's get the shopping center. Oh good, and there he's dead." Thus, Wernicke's aphasics suffer from semantic and lexical function disruptions (Caramazza & Berndt, 1978; Marin & Gordon, 1980). Wernicke's area is relatively near sensory areas of the cortex and more distant from the motor areas. Disruptions of meaning construction in Wernicke's aphasia, in contrast to disruptions of speech organization and performance in Broca's aphasia may be a function of one's closer relationship to the sensory areas and the other's closer relationship to the motor areas of the neocortex.

There can be speech disruptions without neural damage. For example, if a person has conflicting ideas about the message they intend to communicate, or if the person is in conflict about whether to speak or not, the feedforward processes may potentiate contradictory response tendencies that may be manifest in speech disruptions such as stuttering. Similarly, high levels of emotional arousal may amplify preparatory and performance functions to the point where smooth performance is disrupted, or shifts in attention away from the task of speaking may disrupt speech patterns (Zimmerman, 1980; Zimmerman, Smith, & Hanley, 1981). Natural speech often includes a diversity of defects, such as fragments, blocking on a word, restarts, pauses, hesitations, and grammatical omissions (Goodwin, 1981). Norman (1981) describes action slips including speech errors occurring for three reasons: errors in formation of the guiding intention; faulty activation of schemas; and failure in satisfying conditions for triggering the action. Fromkin (1980) provides many examples of such communicative slips.

Writing. The production of writing is similar to speech, although writing involves issues of spelling while speech involves issues of pronunciation. Therefore, it seems likely that the semantic, lexical, and syntactic coding processes would be the same for both, although the motor pattern (i.e., articulation) through which the code is expressed is different. There is some evidence in support of that view in studies of language disruptions resulting from brain damage. For example, in Broca's aphasia writing ability is often as impaired as speech (Goodglass & Kaplan, 1972).

Concluding Comments. Human information capabilities are arranged so that information may be collected in many different codes carried on a variety of markers which can be recoded onto one marker (e.g., patterns of neuronal firing when viewed biologically, speech when delivered vocally, or writing when delivered nonvocally). The potential efficiency and effectiveness of such an arrangement is obvious. Vocalization, especially in its most refined form of speech, is a capability which makes possible patterns of complex social interactions and their transmission from one generation to another. Speech transformed into a written marker produces a permanent record of the conveyed information; that is, it "time binds" information. Therefore, symbolic communication (e.g., speech, writing, music, art, theater) is the cornerstone of human culture, and the primary mechanism of humanly generated social (and biological) evolution. This capability probably evolved in correlation with others valuable for group living (e.g., social bonding and selective behavior towards kin) as a survival and adaptive strategy.

Components and Persons. Chapters 1 through 5 developed a general conceptual framework for understanding individuals as structural-functional units, i.e., as a particular kind of organization of structural and functional components. Chapters 6 through 15 focused on component structures and processes. The final chapter returns to consideration of a person as an organization of these components.

16

The Person and Personality Development

INTRODUCTION

The objective of this book has been to create a conceptual framework for understanding individuals as structural-functional units in continual transaction with their contexts. One key assumption of the effort was explicitly stated recently by Singer and Kolligian (1987) who suggested that it is "time that we begin building our personality models out of the available knowledge in psychology itself" (p. 563). The first five chapters construct such a framework. Chapters 6 through 15 describe how existing information and ideas about different aspects of humans can be related to, and their relationships understood, within that framework. This chapter returns to the central objective of understanding persons, which has been the mission of personality and psychotherapy theory. Personality theory asks "What is the nature of the consistencies across time and situations that give individuals their personal identity? How do those patterns change? How are people alike and different in their patterns of consistency and change?"

First, the relationship of this living systems framework to personality theorizing and research is considered in this chapter. Then, a living systems representation of persons and their personalities is sketched. A limited number of citations are included to support the basic ideas. Support for the various components of the sketch can be found in previous chapters.

THE STATE OF PERSONALITY THEORY AND RESEARCH

The Nature of Personality

Historically, the study of human personality has focused on the same objectives and issues to which this book is directed, using many of the same assumptions. For example, nearly half a century ago, Murray (1938) said:

> The prevailing custom in psychology is to study one function or one aspect of an episode at a time—perception, emotion, intellection or behavior—and this is as it must be ... But, the psychologist who does this should recognize that he is observing merely a part of an operating totality, and that this totality, in turn, is but a small temporal segment of a personality. Psychology must construct a scheme of concepts for portraying the entire course of individual development and thus provide a framework into which any single episode—natural or experimental—must be fitted. (p. 4). The organism is from the beginning a whole, from which the parts are derived by self-differentiation. The whole and its parts are mutually related; the whole being as essential to an understanding of the parts as the parts are to an understanding of the whole. (p. 39)

Others proposed similar views. For example, a person is a dynamic "totality of systems" which can differ in both content and process (Lewin, 1935). G. Allport (1937, 1955) defined personality as a "dynamic organization" within a person of "psychophysical systems" that determine the person's "unique adjustment to the world." Some theorists (Freud, 1933; Murphy, 1947) emphasize intraperson dynamics, and characterize personality development as "the gradual transformation from biological organism to biosocial person" (Cameron, 1963). Others emphasize the interpersonal (Sullivan, 1953) and social (Young, 1952) origins of personality. Starting with Freud, most theorists of personality have characterized persons as dynamic organizations of different kinds of responses or functions (Hall & Lindzey, 1978; Janis, Mahl, Kagan, & Holt, 1969) that have continuity in time and across contexts, and that are not solely the result "of the social and biological pressures of the moment" (Maddi, 1976).

Problems and Issues

Reviewers of theories and evidence resulting from the pursuit of these grand objectives paint a discouraging picture. There is little agreement about the basic "elements" of personality, the nature of their organization, the "boundaries" of personality, and how it interacts with other phenomena (Sanford, 1968). Personality theory "is in sad shape" and the "vast proportion" of personality research "is inconsequential, trivial, and pointless" even though well done (Sechrest, 1976). Some suggest there may be no such thing as personality (Helson & Mitchell, 1978), and others (Pervin, 1985) assert that they learn more about human personality from their professional practice than from the empirical literature. The problem is one "of aggregating diverse and often contradictory data" into a "coherent picture" (Achenbach & Edelbrock, 1984), and the lack of such aggregation gives one "little feeling of a cumulative body of knowledge" (Hoffman, 1977).

However, despite such difficulties and criticisms, Loevinger and Knoll (1983) observe that "age does not wither nor custom stale" interest in understanding personality consistency. There is continued emphasis on the need to understand humans as complex organizations of multiple, continuously interacting person and situation variables (Magnusson & Endler, 1977), whether the focus is on component processes such as memory (Jenkins, 1974) or the person as a unit (Mischel, 1977).

One of the most persistent debates has been over the extent to which behavior and personality characteristics tend to be situation-specific or to display generality across occasions and situations. Thorndike (1906) viewed personality as composed of organizations of discrete habits and, therefore, relatively situation-specific. In contrast, G. Allport (1937) viewed behavior as centrally organized and purposive, and believed therefore that personality traits should display cross-situation, cross-occasion generality. Mischel's (1968) influential book marshalled evidence and arguments for situational variability and against generalized personality traits. While acknowledging that people do behave differently in different situations, Cattell (1957), Block (1977), Epstein (1979, 1982), and others present evidence and arguments that some cross-occasion, cross-situation generality also exists.

Needed: Integrative Theory and Research

What is needed is more generally integrating theory and research (Hoffman, 1977; Sechrist, 1976) which can reveal the nature of "the complex, integrated, organized, and patterned behavior of individuals over time" (Pervin, 1985). Without such integrative theories, it is "easy to overemphasize" the importance of particular personality constructs and processes, such as causal attribution (Phares & Lamiell, 1977). Many existing personality theories emphasize different aspects of humans, viewed "through the glasses of their promulgators" (Corsini & Marsella, 1983). Cattell (1979, 1980) and Royce (Royce & Powell, 1983) have recently tried to create more integrative conceptual frameworks using a systems orientation.

One barrier to progress toward an integrated view has been the use of research designs and data analytic models that can produce only fragmented pictures of persons, and whose assumptions may not fit the nature of humans.[1] One alternative has been to use case study methods to identify a variety of individual patterns, and then to look for commonalities and differences across many individuals (Murray, 1938; White, 1966). A life-span orientation towards development has used this approach for comparisons across both individuals and generations (Lowenthal, Thurnher, & Chiriboga, 1976).

The intensive study of individual lives is a sound strategy because knowledge about people in general can only be derived from accurate knowledge of individuals. However, some theoretical framework is needed both to guide the selection of variables and to help organize the mass of information collected. In addition, data analytic methods are needed that can represent organizations of mutually influential variables to identify consistencies and differences in those *patterns* across contexts and occasions. Health and human services professionals must make such selective and integrative interpretations daily because their efforts to facilitate the lives of others require it. To the extent that they can guide such professional decisions with sound theories and supporting evidence, they can be more precise and effective in their intervention efforts (Alexander & Malouf, 1983; Ford & Urban, 1967).

There are other research design alternatives. For example, Soviet researchers use the "transforming experiment" in which efforts to change phenomena occur while they are being studied. Nesselroade and Ford (1985, 1987) suggest ways of combining features of single-subject, group, and longitudinal designs to yield clear pictures of both individuals (idiographic knowledge) and of similarities and differences across individuals (nomothetic knowledge).

What follows attempts to illustrate the potential of this living systems framework for these purposes. Urban (1987) illustrates how psychopathology can be understood within a living systems framework; therefore, this topic is excluded here, although information about dysfunctional development does shed important light on normal functioning.

THE DEVELOPMENT AND FUNCTIONING
OF A PERSON

First, patterns of intraindividual development and functioning are considered. Following that, a brief discussion focuses the framework upon an understanding of interindividual differences and similarities in such patterns.

---

[1]However, Epstein and O'Brien (1985) have demonstrated that even these methods can reveal more about personality consistencies than they have in the past if they are used in a more careful and sophisticated way.

From the Beginning There is Organization

From the moment of conception until birth, a living system goes through multiple transformations and elaborations of structural-functional organization. This embryonic phase of individual development is dominated by material-energy transactional and self-constructing processes, regulated by genetic structures and processes, within the uterine environment. However, there is functional development as well. As soon as a structure is fully formed, it begins operating even though that function is not yet essential for life. For example, the fetal heart begins to beat before blood and blood vessels are available to it; peristaltic movements and digestive secretions begin to occur in a well-developed gastrointestinal tract before it has food to process; the fetus within the uterus moves its legs and arms and makes grasping movements with its hands.

Such *in utero* functioning produces self-generated information flows across sensory receptors and through the developing nervous system, facilitating integrated structural-functional development. Some flows of information from within and outside the mother's body (e.g., heart beat, music) may contribute to integrative functional development.

Change Must Always Start with Existing Components

Unlike a machine that can be constructed by assembling previously constructed parts, a person can only develop through differentiation, elaboration, and transformation of existing components through self-construction processes. That is true for functional as well as structural development. New organs develop from existing tissue organization; new conceptions develop from existing perceptual, conceptual, and information-processing capabilities; new motor skills evolve from in-born and previously constructed motor capabilities.

This method of constructing increasingly complex organization from existing organization insures that the person will always maintain organizational unity, since the new organization is an elaboration of the old, rather than being grafted onto it. Moreover, this strategy makes it possible to combine the high degree of functional *efficiency* that comes with specialization of components, with the superior *adaptability* that can result from the well coordinated efforts of many component specialists. It produces a form of organization called an *embedded, nested,* or *lattice hierarchy* which maintains unity of functioning through a complex web of mutual influences, but within which some components have more influence on larger portions of the organization than others (e.g., contrast neocortical coordination with that of spinal ganglia), and each component is functionally semiautonomous.

Biological Self-Construction and Temperament. The basic biological structural-functional organization is essentially complete in the normal newborn, although some maturational "finishing up" must be completed during infancy. Subsequent to birth, most biological self-construction is focused on elaboration of the physical size of existing components; improving the efficiency of physiological functioning; and on operating, maintaining, and repairing the existing structures. Since that biological organization on which behavioral development depends is largely complete and functional relatively soon after birth, information based self-construction can begin almost immediately, and it does.

However, newborns differ in their physiological "tuning", due to the interaction of genetic and uterine environmental influences during fetal development. There are differences in metabolism, feeding cycles, vital functions, autonomic functioning, sensory-perceptual reactiveness, and the quality, intensity, and tempo of motoric and vocalization patterns (Buss & Plomin, 1975; Fries, 1961; Sears, Maccoby, & Levin, 1957). For example, some infants when held are relaxed and cuddly while others are tense and stiff; some cry softly while others have an irritating yowl. While such temperamental differences may change through childhood (Bates, 1980), they influence the nature of early informational transactions with the environment, and therefore the initial information-behavior constructions infants may build. For example, energetic, active, noisy infants are likely to elicit different reactions from phlegmatic, unresponsive mothers than from active, sensitive ones. Thus, people's initial biological patterns not only provide facilitating and constraining conditions for their development, but also exert selective influences on their environments' responses to them.

BEHAVIOR EPISODE SCHEMATA: UNITS OF PERSONALITY ORGANIZATION

Traits, Dispositions, Attitudes, and Personality Organization

Personality development involves "processes of internalization" through which infants and children develop an "inner life" and construct their own "world of reality," which they rapidly learn to distinguish from their experiences with their bodies and their environments (Cameron, 1963). This psychoanalytic emphasis on information- and affect-based representations anticipated the major themes in modern cognitive-personality psychology. However, cognition and affect represent only two of several kinds of components composing personality/behavior patterns. Four terms—*traits, dispositions, attitudes,* and *personality variables*—are most frequently used to identify such consistent patterns.

Technically, a *trait* is a summary description of some kind of human functioning that is "temporally stable and cross-situationally broad" (Epstein & O'Brien, 1985). A specific act is always "the product of many determinants." It is only by observing the repeated occurrence of acts "having the same significance" in contexts "having the same significance" that one can identify personality consistencies or traits (G. Allport, 1955). People often reify trait names into having an actual existence "in a person," rather than using them as convenient ways of discussing patterns of consistency. Allport initially distinguished between consistencies typical of a specific person, termed *individual traits* or *dispositions,* and those typical of people in general, termed *common traits.* He distinguished traits from attitudes because the latter involve evaluative reactions to specific types of objects.

Cattell (1950) used factor analysis to identify different kinds of consistencies or traits. *Surface* traits are clusters of manifest variables; *source* traits are underlying variables manifest in surface traits; *dynamic* traits represent motivational consistencies; *temperamental* traits represent stylistic and affective consistencies; *ability* traits represent different kinds of cognitive and competence consistencies; *constitutional* traits have strong genetic determinants; and *environmental mold* traits are primarily learned consistencies. Obviously, these are different types of categories: some refer to differences in kind (e.g., temperamental and ability traits); some refer to determinants of consistency (e.g., constitutional and environmental mold traits); some refer to levels of analysis (e.g., surface and source traits).

Both Allport and Cattell conceived of traits as being hierarchically organized, and of personality as a complex and differentiated organization of traits that provides functional consistency but that undergoes developmental change (G. Allport, 1955, 1961; Cattell, 1979, 1980). What they did not provide was a theoretical framework for explaining the kinds and organizations of consistency that might develop. This chapter attempts to fill that gap.

Clearly, one could focus on many kinds of consistencies, such as in biological structure or processes; in physical appearance; in patterns of actions; in attentional and sensory-perceptual functioning; in affective-emotional functioning; in personal goals; in values and regulatory functioning; in problem-solving and control functions; in contexts utilized; and in consistent patterns of flow and change in such organizations.

Different kinds of consistency are apparent at different levels of analysis, and each level is useful for some purposes. For example, a focus on behavior in a *particular type of situation* may reveal some types of consistencies, while a focus on a *diverse set of situations* may reveal other types (Mischel, 1979). Similarly, intraindividual consistencies reflect different information than interindividual similarities, although they may be related. There may be variability at one level of analysis and consistency at another. Unnecessary confusion results when scholars are not explicit about such differences in levels of analysis (Epstein & O'Brien, 1985).

Most personality research examines component-level interindividual consistencies, so most personality traits studied represent consistencies in component functions (e.g., cognition, causal attributions and self-efficacy evaluations, actions, affect) among groups of people measured on one or two occasions. However, if a primary objective is identification of consistencies in complex patterns of functioning, then some other unit of analysis is necessary that can represent patterns of organization of multiple components. The concept of *behavior episode schemata* is proposed as such a unit. Cattell's attitude paradigm, "In this (situation) I want (so much) to do (this) with (that)," has many similar attributes.

Behavior Episode Schemata (BES)

Chapter 5 described the concept of behavior episodes as manifestations of the organized functioning of the self-organized, self-constructing control system described in Chapter 3. The flow of a person's behavior may be understood as a temporal organization of behavior episodes. In effect, a behavior episode can be visualized as Fig. 16.1 (an abbreviated version of Fig. 3.3, p. 18) flowing through contexts and time, displaying variable content within patterned consistency. Figure 16.1 represents the basic functional organization of any behavior episode. To represent a particular behavior episode, the specific content of each function for that episode must be specified, for example, the specific goals or intentions organizing that episode; the particular values and evaluative thoughts regulating it; the particular environmental factors influencing it.

Three factors constrain the content and organization of each behavior episode: (a) what the person is trying to do (the directive function); (b) the nature of the context(s) in which the episode is occurring; and (c) the biological boundaries provided by the body and its current state. Other functions are selectively organized to produce the intended consequences within those constraints.

Each behavior episode is a temporary occurrence. At a particular place and time, a person selectively directs his or her behavior towards certain consequences and towards using or dealing with certain environmental contingencies, while in certain bodily states. At another place and time, the combination of the person's objectives, behaviors, bodily states, and

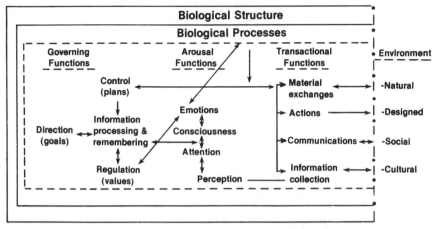

FIG. 16.1   A schematic summary of the basic structural–functional organization of a person represented as a living system; that is, a self-organizing, self-constructing control system, functioning as an open system or dissipative structure.

environmental contingencies will be different. Even when the objectives are the same, the implementing conditions will be different, or in the same environment the person may pursue different objectives. Moreover, the principle of equifinality states that the same final state of an open system may be arrived at from different initial conditions and in different ways. Since no two behavior episodes will ever be identical, learning the behavior pattern used in each episode would be ineffective and probably impossible. Something more general must be learned to guide future behavior.

Behavior episodes provide the basis for the construction, through learning, of prototypical representations of sets of similar episodes. The term *behavior episode schemata* (BES) is proposed for such generalized patterns because they transcend particular instances, and yet function as a unit to organize specific behavior episodes. BES are functional components composed of an organization of subcomponent functions. Somewhat different BES are constructed from different kinds of sets of actual behavior episodes. Traditional personality traits typically represent consistencies in BES components (e.g., causal attributions used in control functions).

BES construction is discussed in Chapters 9 through 12 on the governing functions. Briefly, episodes with similar goals in similarly perceived contexts define a similar set of episodes from which a useful BES can be constructed. It is what people attend to, and therefore perceive, that is the primary determinant of contextual similarity. By selectively attending to similar features of different contexts, a person can make objectively dissimilar contexts into functionally similar ones.

However, not all aspects of BES must be conscious. Since a behavior episode pattern functions as a unit, all aspects that are related to those that are part of consciousness can become part of a BES (e.g., motor patterns). *Selection* of some variables has *selection effects* on related variables (Nesselroade, 1986; Nesselroade & Ford, 1987).

When beginning a new episode with similar goals and similar perceived environmental characteristics, the person activates a relevant BES which guides that behavior episode. The concept of *schema* is often used to refer to the cognitive aspects of such guiding patterns, and *motor schema* to represent transactional components of the patterns. However, such cognitive and motor schemata are subcomponents of a more inclusive BES that encompasses all the aspects summarized in Fig. 16.1.

Affective Components in BES Construction

In both evolutionary and ontogenetic terms, affective experiences precede the development of evaluative thought as regulatory processes. Affective components are present in every behavior episode from infancy onward, providing subjective valences that vary from positive through neutral to negative valence; for example, things hurt or feel good; they elicit interest, affection, or anger. In general, people lead their lives to "accentuate the positive and eliminate the negative" as much as possible through the learning of approach and avoidance behavior patterns. Some of these may become highly generalized. For infants, what is positive and what is negative is defined solely by the valence of their affective states during behavior episodes. Affective regulation continues to play an important role throughout life for everyone, but learned evaluative thoughts—including those regulating the occurrence of emotions—play an increasingly important regulatory role as children grow up.

Affects influence BES construction in two important ways. The first is their impact on the directive function and the construction of personal goals. People construct cognitive representations of objects and events which have produced positive or negative affect (e.g., a cookie, a hot stove). Such representations can then operate through the directive function as intentions to organize a behavior episode, either to produce another positive experience, or to avoid the occurrence of a negative one. Thus, the affective components of behavior episodes add to concepts and expectations the values necessary to convert them to intentions or personal goals. The second impact is on the learning and performance process itself. Emotional arousal patterns can vary in degree as well as kind. As levels of emotional arousal increase, they appear to perform an amplifying function in terms of impact both on current performance and on learning. Behavior episodes in which strong emotional arousal is one component appear to influence the characteristics of the BES more than do similar episodes involving little emotional arousal.

The learning of *phobias* is illustrative. For example, an adult may have experienced thousands of behavior episodes which occurred in enclosed spaces such as elevators. However, if as a component of *one* episode (e.g., being trapped in an elevator with a dangerous person), that adult experiences intense fear, he or she may thereafter always experience fear when in small enclosed spaces, or even when thinking about being in them. The impact of that one behavior episode can be more powerful than thousands of others in shaping the relevant BES. At a less intense scale, memory for events that occur in conjunction with strong emotion seem more readily remembered (e.g., "flashbulb" memories); and reactivating the original emotional state facilitates remembering the related events. Emotional arousal can also facilitate or interfere with the smooth coordination of cognitive and motoric aspects of behavior episodes, depending on the intensity of the emotion.

BES and Observational and Simulated Behavior Episodes

Chapter 9 subdivided behavior episodes into three types: instrumental, observational, and thinking. The preceding discussion has focused primarily on instrumental episodes (which include action components) as the basis for BES construction. However, BES may also be constructed from observational and thinking episodes.

Learning through observational episodes—imitation or social modeling ("monkey see, monkey do")—is a pervasive influence on development throughout life. By inhibiting one's own actions and observing the behavior of others in specific contexts, individuals can construct BES which they can later use to guide the construction of instrumental behavior episodes. For example, concern over the effects of television on the aggressive or prosocial behavior of children assumes the influence of observational episodes upon viewers' construction of BES. Observational episodes are a primary means by which cultural characteristics are transmitted from generation to generation. They are extensively used in formal education. Personal goals and values can be adopted from social observation as well as being self-constructed, and may produce conflicting values. Psychotherapy theorists often emphasize the intrapsychic conflicts produced when socially learned and self-constructed values conflict (Ford & Urban, 1963).

"Think before you act" is a phrase reflecting the value of thinking episodes as a basis for constructing BES. By inhibiting transactional functions and using previously constructed cognitive components, a person can simulate behavior episodes. They can imagine different behavior patterns and their probable consequences, compare alternatives, and activate a BES that appears most likely to guide the construction of a successful instrumental episode in relevant contexts. People's abilities to run internal simulations undergird a number of ideas in cognitive science (Oden, 1987). The development of effective strategies and skills for "impulse control" or "delay of gratification" is a cornerstone of capabilities for constructing situationally and temporally more complex BES through thinking episodes. Most children develop such strategies during the first few years of life (Mischel, 1979).

BES are Dynamic, Flexible, and Hierarchically Organized

BES are dynamic in two senses: they may change with additional learning; and their content may vary within limits, depending on the context. Since each actual behavior episode in a set of similar episodes involves somewhat different operating conditions, the behavior that "works" in one episode will not be identical with that which works in another episode. Remember the principle of equifinality: there is usually more than one means to the same end. Therefore, different patterns of control and transactional functions (i.e., of "how to do it") are learned to serve the same goals and values (i.e., directive and regulatory conditions); and the affect may vary among episodes.

People characteristically combine instrumental, observational, and thinking episodes in constructing BES. For example, children may watch someone perform a task (observational episode). They may then try to perform it themselves (instrumental episode). When they do not succeed, they may stop and rethink what they did to identify where they went wrong and to identify alternatives (thinking episode). They may then try again, or ask for another demonstration before making another effort. As a result, BES are progressively differentiated and elaborated through self-organizing (assimilative) and self-constructing (accommodative) processes to include optional means to serve essentially the same ends and values in variable contexts. These optional means are analogous to subroutines or algorithms ("if-then" choices) in computer programs. Such flexibly organized BES are highly adaptive, because they provide variability of actions in a framework of thematic consistency.

For example, a 5-year-old may yearn for a cookie. He or she may ask mom for one. If rebuffed there, s/he may try to "sweet talk" grandpa into providing a cookie. If that tactic fails, s/he may try to "con" a younger sibling or a playmate into getting the cookie. If all else fails, he or she may "swipe" one, and hope not to get caught. The consistency in such a pattern lies not in the actions performed, but in the guiding directive and regulatory thoughts and persistent environmental and bodily constraints.

Moreover, just as different means may serve the same ends, so too may the same means simultaneously serve multiple ends. Being able to produce several desired consequences with one action pattern is highly efficient and adaptive. For example, suppose the 5-year-old wants a cookie, wants to avoid mother's disapproval, and wants to show love for his or her grandmother. The child might try to produce all three results simultaneously by asking mother for a cookie to be shared with grandma. Similarly, a professional person might simultaneously enjoy a good meal, seal an important business deal, and impress the boss, by giving a successful dinner party for a wealthy client.

By combining such multipurpose means with optional means, more complex and flexible BES can be constructed. It is another example of the advantages to be derived by combining componentized specialization with coordination in hierarchical organization. Given a goal and a context, a relevant BES is reconstructed or "potentiated." Based on the directing goal(s), regulatory criteria, and interpretations of perceptions of current bodily and environmental conditions, specific action plans and transactional subcomponents are activated and implemented from among the options within the BES. Relevant features of the flow of the behavior episode are monitored and, through regulatory processes, the control function action plan and/or the transactional subcomponents are altered if necessary to increase behavior episode effectiveness. Such alterations can be accomplished smoothly by drawing upon other optional subcomponents within the BES. If the BES does not include other relevant options, the person will either persist in the original approach, or interrupt the effort permanently or temporarily until they can construct new options through observation and thinking episodes.

Automating BES Through Repetition

Frequently repeated episodes result in the construction of BES that can function fairly automatically to guide the execution of behavior episodes of the same type. As described in Chapter 14, practice produces functional components that operate as open loops. Recall that one of the advantages of componentization is that a relatively simple signal (or stimulus) can trigger the operation of a component and its complicated pattern of activity. BES are complex functional components and can become somewhat automated in that way. For example, old married couples have developed habitual interaction routines that occur regularly in certain circumstances. Sometimes those can be troublesome to, and misinterpreted by, others. For instance, the adult children of an elderly couple convinced their parents to a see a marriage counselor to try to reduce the frequent and sometimes angry arguments between them during their "golden years." The counselor convinced the parents to try the rule, "don't say anything if you can't say something nice." The parents became increasingly unhappy under that regimen. Finally, the counselor realized that their argumentative pattern was their primary way of relating to one another, and that without it they felt isolated and estranged from one another. He encouraged them to return to their own ways. It was primarily those around them, rather than the parents, who were unhappy with that habitual pattern.

Components of BES can also become automated. For example, based on his research on self-regulation in children, Mischel (1979) reports that the construction and operation of complex plans (the control function) may become "more automatic, abbreviated, and rapid," organized in an "increasingly complex hierarchy," and not requiring "extensive or explicit self-instructions" for their implementation.

Constructing Hierarchical Organizations of BES

The original BES constructed by small children have few optional components and are related to a narrowly defined set of behavior episodes and contexts; they tend to be situation-, goal-, task-, and behavior-specific. This has caused some confusion in interpreting results of research on small children. When they are unable to do the tasks provided by the researcher, it is often inferred that they do not have the relevant capabilities. However, if tasks or behavior episodes are defined that match the kinds of BES small children have constructed (i.e., if the goals, procedures, and context are presented in familiar and understandable terms), children often display capabilities other tasks did not reveal. Moreover, different task definitions may be necessary to elicit the same demonstration of competence from different children because their BES differ. Defining relevant tasks for the study of prelinguistic children involves considerable guesswork about the nature of their BES, but observational knowledge about the contexts within which children have constructed potentially relevant BES can provide solid clues (e.g., kinds of games they have played; their favorite toys).

The next developmental step involves constructing more broadly applicable BES by organizing several of the initial, narrow BES into broader patterns. One BES may participate as a subcomponent in several more inclusive BES. For example, once children have learned to stand (a simple BES), they can combine that with other somewhat different sets of BES into the more complex BES of walking, jumping, or climbing. Similarly, once a child has constructed a simple idea, that idea can be combined with other ideas to construct more complex ideas. This process of constructing more generalized BES as organizations of component BES accelerates rapidly during the early grade school years. Specialization through componentization and elaboration by coordinating components is the key to the rapid elaboration of children's competencies.

As described particularly in Chapters 9 and 14, even more abstract BES can be constructed as organizations of a set of generalized BES. Moreover, each generalized BES could function as a member of several more abstract BES. Theoretically, this process could continue by progressively building increasingly more generalized BES as organizations of less inclusive BES, until every behavior episode in a person's life might be guided by a very highly generalized BES. Albert Schweitzer's life may be an illustration. It is said that he constructed a life style anchored in the belief that life in all of its forms is the most fundamental value, and therefore all life should be preserved and protected. The organization of each act of each day was guided by that overriding conviction. Such a highly integrative BES could only function through orchestrating the patterns of lower order BES which serve as functional components of particular behavior episodes.

Few people integrate everything into one highly generalized BES. Some people's BES remain relatively narrow throughout their lives, while others construct more elaborate BES of differing scope and complexity. One of the defining attributes of differences in intelligence is differences in the ability to generalize principles and practices across increasingly diverse contexts and tasks. Stated differently, more intelligent people construct more complex and flexible BES with which to organize their behavior episodes. The capacity to link words to these more abstract BES and their components increases the ability both to more flexibly construct and use BES, and to control their reconstruction and operation.

Self-Referent and Social BES Components

The greater the number and diversity of behavior episodes in which specific objects and events occur, the more frequently and prominently will those objects and events appear as aspects of BES. Since one's physical and psychological self is present in every episode, it should not be surprising that similar self-referent components may appear in many types of BES (e.g., self-efficacy cognitions). Since one's own capabilities are the means by which one influences one's world, thoughts about one's capabilities powerfully influence what one does. Harter (1983) summarizes evidence about different kinds of self-referent cognitions. Markus and Wolff (1987) characterize the "self-concept" as dynamic and changeable, and "providing the incentives, standards, plans, rules, and scripts" for behavior. They link it to a cybernetics model in a way that make self-concept similar to the model in Fig. 16.1. It is probably more accurate to think of self-referent thoughts as only one type (but a very important type) of cognition.

Since babies are typically sheltered, nourished, and socialized in families, and since humans live in social contexts, other humans are present in many behavior episodes. Not surprisingly, therefore, many BES contain similar components regarding relationships with significant other people. Moreover, interpersonal relationships in behavior episodes are frequently related to the occurrence of different kinds of emotions (e.g., affection, anger, fear), and the interpersonal-affective aspects of BES are key sources of both enduring satisfactions and distress.

Construction and Functioning of Superordinate BES

Tomkins (1980; Carlson, 1981) describes a form of highly generalized BES which he calls a *nuclear script*. Some sets of behavior episodes may have a very positive or negative salience because of their emotional components. For example, a child may experience interactions with some person as very frightening or very pleasurable, and construct a BES that includes those emotional components. That BES can form a nucleus from which is constructed — through differentiation and elaboration, across thousands of behavior episodes — a BES that guides a wide range of adult behavior episodes. Components representing strong emotions are more readily generalized across situations than cognitive components (e.g., Mowrer, 1960).

For example, a childhood BES that includes strong anticipation and fear of father's disapproval or hurtful actions may become elaborated so that, as an adult, the person has a BES in which those evaluative thoughts and emotions are important components guiding behavior episode involving any adult male. To alter such a pervasive BES requires altering the nuclear BES at its core. That is particularly difficult if the nuclear BES was constructed when the child was prelinguistic and therefore unable to label and describe the components of the nuclear BES. Imagistic representations (e.g., dreams) may be a means of access to such highly generalized BES components.

Freud proposed that it is *repressed memories* of original episodes that form the core of such as problem. In contrast, this living systems view asserts that the *components of currently operative BES* are at fault. The Freudian view requires remembering and working through repressed memories. This view requires finding some way of activating and then modifying currently functioning BES. Recalling old memories may be a useful procedure for activating troublesome BES so they become available for potential modification, because behavior must occur to be modified. The psychoanalytic emphasis on "working through" transference phenomena illustrates a process of activating and modifying troublesome BES, as does the "empty chair" technique of gestalt psychotherapy.

The concept of *life-style* connotes an elaborately organized constellation of BES which display some highly generalized internal consistency. For example, a person may be a big spender, a risk-taker, a cautious and unassertive follower, or a bold leader. The search for personality traits has typically been a search for such component consistency across many BES. Unfortunately, most trait concepts are inferences about *intraindividual consistencies* based upon data representing *interindividual consistencies*. That strategy should be reversed (Nesselroade & Ford, 1987). Usually, a person's entire repertoire of BES is generally coherent; that is, he or she has an integrated personality.

However, through extended experience a person may construct distinctly different BES constellations to guide behavior episodes. For example, when guiding her behavior with one constellation, a woman may appear to be one kind of person (e.g., a kind, responsible mother and wife), and a different kind when guided by a different constellation (e.g., a party girl). The phenomena of multiple personalities probably reflects personality organizations in which radically different complex BES constellations may alternate in organizing a person's behavior.

Similarly, in amnesia some of a person's BES are rendered nonfunctional. For example, a man with a severe early history of emotionally distressing interpersonal relationships and losses was trying to care for his father who was slowly dying. Simultaneously, he was struggling with a very demanding and emotionally distressing work situation. One day he suddenly didn't recognize any of his family or friends, didn't remember he had a father who was dying, and was unable to remember how to perform skills required on his job. By rendering that large constellation of BES inoperative, he succeeded in eliminating the emotional distress that had become unbearable, and in restoring some behavioral organization with which he could live. In more theoretical terms, the frequency and pervasiveness of noxious emotional arousal made it impossible for the system to maintain its existing steady states. It went through a disorganization-reorganization cycle which provided a new steady state not disrupted by noxious emotions.

Persistence as an Aspect of BES

This living systems framework proposes that once a behavior episode is initiated, it will continue, with adjustments of activity, until the regulatory comparison between the current and intended state is satisfied. Then that behavior episode ends and another begins. However, a behavior episode may also terminate because it is preempted by another, situational conditions may change, or because of discouragement about the possibility of producing the intended state. It is typically the case that a behavior episode is not immediately nor always successful. What is it that influences a person to persist, give up, or try again later?

Research on learning indicates that behavior patterns that always succeed, and are therefore learned under *continuous reinforcement* are more readily extinguished (people quit trying more quickly) than are behavior patterns that succeed only part of the time, that is, are acquired under *intermittent* or *partial reinforcement.* For example, partial reinforcement is not only as effective as continuous reinforcement in reversing learned helplessness deficits, but also produces more persistent effort in extinction circumstances (Mineka & Henderson, 1985). The important human implication of this is that experiencing some failure is useful because people must learn to weather difficulties and temporary failures in the process of striving for desired consequences. They must learn that if they do not persist in the face of failure, or give up too soon, they will not get what they want, and that reasonable persistence often pays off.

Criteria for persisting or giving up are constructed as regulatory components of BES. It cannot be overemphasized that behavior must be understood as a contextual-temporal event flow. Both the content and flow properties of behavior episodes provide important information. In constructing their BES from a set of behavior episodes, people construct criteria for monitoring not only the relationship of the current to the desired status of the intended consequence(s), but also for monitoring its flow properties to estimate the likelihood that progress may be made in the future towards reducing that discrepancy.

For example, a highly successful college football coach teaches his players to believe that if they just keep executing each play well, something good will eventually happen. Frequently (although not always) they come from behind to win, sometimes in the last few minutes or seconds of a game, because the players interpret the discrepancy in the score as something they can still overcome and they intensify their efforts. Momentary failure is not interpreted as permanent failure. In contrast, "chronic losers" may interpret momentary failure as a sure signal that they will eventually fail again and so they begin to give up, thereby helping that evaluation to become a self-fulfilling prophecy.

Typically, people learn to be more persistent in some kinds of behavior episodes than in others; that is, the regulatory criteria constructed may be somewhat different from one BES to another. Parenting practices and peer social modeling influence the kinds of persistence criteria children construct in their BES. For example, when my sons were small I would sometimes secretly create minor difficulties and temporary failures in their play activities, and then encourage and help them to persist in their efforts to succeed so they would learn not to give up too soon. In a ping pong game, for instance, I would take the lead and in the end let them catch me and beat me, but not every time (partial reinforcement). On the other hand, parents who resolve difficulties for a child at the first sign of failure may be teaching "giving up" rather than persistence regulatory rules. Giving up too soon, or refusing to give up when a situation has become hopeless, are both maladaptive. Therefore, learning to identify and monitor cues (feedback) with which to regulate persisting or giving up is an important part of constructing effective BES and of self-regulation.

PERSONALITY: ORGANIZATIONS OF BEHAVIOR EPISODE SCHEMATA

BES of various kinds and scope, and their shared components, provide the basis for the cross-situational and temporal consistency that represents each person's identity, or *personality*. However, it is important to be clear about the kinds of consistency that can reasonably be expected. There continues to be extensive debate about this issue among scholars of personality (Page, 1983; Pervin, 1985). Some argue for considerable cross-situational (Block, 1977; Epstein, 1979, 1982) and temporal (Mischel, 1979) stability. Others argue that cross-situational (Mischel & Peake, 1982) and temporal (Brim & Kagan, 1980) consistency is severely limited. Fifty years ago Allport and Odbert (1936) identified 1,800 personality terms and 4,500 trait names in a standard English language dictionary. There are undoubtedly more now. Some way of reducing this diversity to some more coherent form is needed. Cattell (1957) used factor analysis to construct empirically derived categories. An alternative approach is to use a theoretical framework to identify types of consistency. This living systems framework can be used for that purpose.

The kinds of consistency that can characterize a person are predictable from the nature and organization of the types of BES the person has constructed. One can look for consistencies in the behavior episode action patterns generated by different BES; for characteristics of BES components that are common to many types of BES as manifest in a diversity of behavior episodes; for consistencies in organizational properties of the BES; and in strategies for constructing and maintaining those organizations. It should be noted that BES (and their components) may differ in the extent of their generality across situations and occasions. This transforms the question of *whether* such consistency exists, into the question of *what kinds* of consistency exist under *what kinds of conditions* for each person. First, consistencies in BES component functions are considered in the following pages. Broader consistencies are discussed after that.

Situational and Temporal Consistency in Transactional Patterns

Behaving in exactly the same way in all kinds of situations would be rigid and maladaptive. The human brain evolved precisely to overcome such machinelike rigidity typical of more primitive organisms. Therefore, it is inappropriate to expect cross-situational and temporal consistency in an individual's actions. However, habit formation is one of the efficiencies of human behavioral self-construction. Therefore, some cross-situational and cross-occasion consistency in transactional patterns should develop. Transactional patterns will usually display some stability, but typically will not be highly generalized across situations (Mischel, 1968). Under what circumstances should such consistency be expected?

Woodworth (1937), nearly half a century ago, proposed an answer that modern personality theorists are moving towards (Lord, 1982; Mischel, 1979). People behave similarly in situations they perceive to be similar with respect to what they are trying to do and the consequences they are trying to produce in that situation. There are three conditions specified in that statement. The first is behavior, by which he meant *actions*. The second is *goals*. Behavior episodes are similar to the extent that they are directed towards similar consequences, or display consistency in "teleonomic trends" (F. Allport, 1937). The third is *perceived similarity of the situation*. Since perception evolved to provide information about what is "really there," perceived and actual situations are usually similar (except in pathological conditions), although selective perception and conceptual interpretation make some aspects of a situation more salient than others.

Behavior episodes function to produce selected consequences at specific times and places. Therefore, they are always situation-specific. BES are constructed from sets of similar behavior episodes, so they too are specific to particular kinds of personal goal/situation constellations. Even more generalized BES, within which more narrowly defined ones may function as components, simply represent more inclusive personal goal/situation constellations. Therefore, the degree of transactional consistency should typically be greater within such constellations than between them.

However, even within BES goal/situation constellations, considerable behavioral variability should be expected. The special adaptive value of self-constructed BES is their flexibility, which results from (a) constructing multiple action options to produce the conditions of satisfaction for any set of goals in varying situations, and (b) constructing coherent action patterns to simultaneously serve different goal combinations in the same situation. Therefore, one should not generally expect to find a high degree of cross-situation consistency in action patterns, even within BES constellations, except where strong habits are functional and the context remains stable from episode to episode (e.g., a gymnast's high bar routine may be quite similar from meet to meet).

Two kinds of conditions will increase situational and temporal consistency of actions. First, highly structured, norm-regulated situations prescribe how people must act, leaving little room for action variability. BES constructed from such episodes will reflect such restrictions. Both intra- and interindividual action variability will be restricted in such contexts. A Sunday morning church service is illustrative. People's behavior will show a high degree of consistency during their church's service from week to week, and all of the people in the congregation will behave in similar ways (intra- and interpersonal cross-occasion consistency). However, if a friend takes a person to worship at a church with a drastically different ritual, they will have no relevant BES and will be uncertain about how to act. Similarly, some jobs are so highly structured that there is little opportunity for behavioral variability. In contrast, situations that are ambiguous or weak in normative pressures provide greater latitude for individuals to construct BES that provide for alternate ways of behaving (Pervin, 1985).

Second, habit formation increases both situational and temporal consistency of actions. For example, a business person who does the same job in the same office at the same desk for many years develops routines. One executive I knew, for instance, had the following daily routine: First he read the pile of correspondence and reports on his desk labeled "immediate action" by his secretary; then she came in and he dictated memos and letters; then he had a cup of coffee; then he made phone calls to implement decisions, consult, and so on; then he worked on the less urgent reports. He scheduled all of his meetings in the afternoon, and put the most controversial ones near the end of the day knowing that "quitting time" pressures would help regulate the length of the meeting. Occasionally, this routine would be altered by demands from his boss, or unexpected and urgent events, but not often.

Habit formation can also produce stylistic consistencies. For example, one executive always carried on extensive monologues in every meeting, not knowing when to stop talking. Colleagues dreaded and avoided such meetings because of that executive's "verbal diarrhea." That pattern also occurred at cocktail parties and in other interpersonal situations (he never had any children). In summary, one may find some consistency in transactional patterns in situations and with BES that significantly constrain and facilitate particular action options. In addition, situations that remain relatively stable permit the construction and use of habitual BES and therefore produce greater transactional consistency in such situations. However, since BES are constructed to represent different types of goal-situation combinations, with componentized construction to provide considerable action flexibility to meet varying circumstances, general transactional pattern consistency across diverse goal-situation combinations is likely to be quite low.

Consistencies in Other BES Components

While each BES is constructed to represent a particular set of behavior episodes, some kinds of components may be common to many BES. For example, Buss and Craik (1983) distinguish between behavioral consistency and dispositional consistency. Mischel (1973) proposes that consistency may be found in a person's competencies, encodings, expectancies, values, goals/plans, and self-regulating systems. Singer and Kolligian (1987) similarly focus on "private experience" as a locus of personality consistency. In living systems terms, consistency may be found in each of the biological, governing, and arousal functions as components of a diversity of BES.

Personal goals (the directive function) provide one kind of "dispositional" consistency. For example, if one knows a person is studying to become a physician, a great diversity of actions in a diversity of situations over an extended period of time all become understandable as coherent parts of a general but highly variable behavior pattern organized to serve that broad goal. Moreover, BES and the behavior episodes they organize can be differentiated from one another in terms of the kinds of personal goal hierarchies they serve. For example, if one knows that today a woman is trying to (a) prepare for a visit to her grandchildren, (b) complete some orders for her art work, and (c) care for certain needs of an elderly parent, her diverse actions during the day can be meaningfully organized into three different patterns. The consistency within each of the three sets of behavior episodes is represented not in the similarity of the actions themselves, but in their shared function of contributing towards the same objective(s). Stated simply, if you know what a person is trying to do, his or her actions usually make sense.

Personal values and self-evaluations (the regulatory function) are another type of component that can provide considerable temporal and cross-situational consistency. For example, if you know that a person deeply values human life, such diverse activities as petitioning against the execution of a condemned person, contributing money for research on cancer, volunteering as a home health aide for the elderly, requesting that his or her organs be donated after death for transplant to others, and participating in a demonstration against abortion may all be understood as different expressions of the same basic values.

A person's self-evaluation of personal worth or competencies is another kind of regulatory cognition that provides consistency. For example, people who evaluate themselves as uninteresting, poor conversationalists, and socially inept will have a tendency to avoid social situations, and to be quiet and unobtrusive when they have to participate in them. A man who evaluates others with certain qualities (e.g., old, female, black) as less competent or of less worth than himself is likely to treat them differently than others with qualities he admires. Much of the personality consistency to which attitude research is addressed is consistency in evaluative-regulatory functioning.

Problem-solving strategies (the control function) provide another kind of consistency. For example, one person may typically "jump to a conclusion" and try to act upon the first solution that comes to mind. In contrast, another person may characteristically delay action while consciously generating and evaluating alternative potential solutions, and carefully plan implementation of the solution chosen. Propositional knowledge and other beliefs may provide consistency in the formulation and execution of plans. For example, people with different habits of causal attribution are likely to behave differently. People who believe that what happens to them is usually caused by events beyond their control are likely to display different patterns than people who believe they are master or mistress of their own destiny.

Attentional strategies (arousal and perceptual functions) may also provide consistency. For example, some people may be able to maintain concentrated attention for extended periods of time while others may find maintaining concentrated attention difficult. People develop different habits of selective attention. For example, a status conscious woman at social occasions consistently "looks over the shoulder" of the person she is talking with to keep track of what the "important people" are doing and with whom. An artist takes note of the form and color of objects, while a money-conscious person takes note of their cost.

Emotional patterns (arousal functions) can become generalized across diverse situations. For example, one person may consistently confront new experiences with interest and excitement, while another may do so with apprehension or fear. One person may openly and frequently display affection, while another may seldom experience affectionate feelings or may find it difficult to express them.

Consistencies in BES Organization

People may differ in the organizational properties of their BES. For example, some people may have a BES repertoire composed of relatively narrowly defined, situation-specific BES. They may be said to be "rigid" because they find it difficult to vary their behavior appropriately as situations vary. Others may have elaborately organized BES in their repertoires, with diverse optional components that can be activated depending upon situational and goal variations. They may be said to be "flexible" because of their ability to vary their behaviors as circumstances vary. Some may have BES dominated by short-term goals (i.e., they "live for today"), while others may organize their daily lives around important long-term goals (Winell, 1987).

The components of one person's BES repertoire may seldom conflict and may be easily combined in various ways to serve various circumstances. Such a person may be said to have an "integrated" personality. In contrast, another person's BES repertoire may have many contradictory or conflicting components. For example, some of this person's BES may organize the behavior patterns typical of a kind, considerate, supportive person, while other BES may produce the patterns of a thoughtless, self-centered, exploitive person. The only way such contradictory BES can exist and function within the same personality is to be organized so that they never interact. This might be termed a "segregated" personality.

Temporal organization of change patterns may also be observed. For example, one person's BES repertoire may be differentiating and elaborating as the person is continually exposed to new experiences and tries to develop new competencies. Such a person might be said to have a "developing" personality. Another person's BES repertoire may display signs of breakdown or progressive fragmentation of BES organization. This might be termed a "regressing" or "deteriorating" personality.

Strategies for Maintaining/Constructing BES Organization

One way to gain an understanding of how a system functions is to disrupt it and see what it does to deal with the disruption. People differ in their strategies for maintaining or restoring BES organization in the face of disrupting information. Some strategies focus on defending the status quo organization (self-organizing processes). Others use disrupting information to differentiate and elaborate BES organization (self-constructing processes). Block (1982) applies his version of Piaget's assimilation and accommodation processes to personality maintenance and development.

Psychoanalytic theory calls strategies focused in maintaining organizational status quo *defense mechanisms*. The disrupting information may be self-generated (e.g., conflicting self-evaluative thoughts), or may be information provided by the environment (e.g., evaluations by others). A diversity of such "defensive" strategies have been described. For example, *rationalization* eliminates the disrupting influence of information by reinterpreting it to fit some existing BES organization. The first defensive strategy Freud described was *conversion*, through which the disruption is transformed into something else. If one cannot reinterpret the disrupting information to fit, other strategies are required.

One can ignore the information, a strategy called *denial*, as did the mother who continued to try to nurse her baby after it died. If it is self-generated disrupting information, ignoring or denying its existence is often called *repression* or *suppression*. If the disrupting information cannot be ignored, it may be segregated from, or made irrelevant to, existing BES in some way. One way is to interpret it as irrelevant; that is, to disown it or disavow responsibility for it, or to attribute it to others, a process called *projection*. For example, a child confronted with a broken dish may disown responsibility ("I didn't do it"), or blame a sibling ("Ryan did it"). Casting one's personal devils out onto others is an ancient, self-protective ritual. Substituting a socially accepted action component in a BES for one that might be disruptive or unacceptable is called *sublimation* or *substitution*. For example, an academic dean I knew would occasionally become furious with the behavior of some of his faculty. Instead of "blowing his top" he would forcefully drive his little red sports car around isolated mountain roads until he had calmed down and could behave more rationally.

Such BES organization-maintaining strategies should not be considered abnormal. Humans' self-organizing properties must be implemented somehow, so everyone uses some kinds of organization-maintaining strategies at all levels. Since the person is present as actor and perceiver in all behavior episodes, self-referent thoughts are pervasive components of BES and become coherently organized. The "self-concept" literature gives considerable attention to strategies for "protecting" one's organization(s) of self-referent thoughts. The excessive or extreme use of any self-organizing strategy may produce BES that are dysfunctional, so the consequences may be "pathological." For example, one defining attribute of paranoia is excessive and habitual use of the defensive strategy of projection.

The use of BES-maintaining strategies may become habitual, and people may differ in the strategies they adopt. Denial and projection may be used extensively by one person, rationalization may be the preferred mode of another, and repression and sublimation may habitually be used by another. Thus, the kinds of organization-maintaining strategies habitually used provide another kind of personality consistency.

However, if all that people did was to protect the status quo there would be no development. Therefore, people also develop strategies for using new (and therefore potentially disruptive) information to differentiate and elaborate their BES repertoire. For example, some people develop regulatory criteria which explicitly evaluate their current beliefs as tentative and potentially subject to change rather than as "right." Such regulatory criteria predispose a person to revise current BES to accommodate new information. They are often characterized as "enjoying learning," "having an open mind," or as "undefensive."

Some people develop strategies that place constraints on this openness, by segregating groups of BES into different patterns and performing accommodation within but not across such groups. For example, a person may keep his generalized prejudices about females or blacks segregated from BES about women or blacks in specific roles (e.g., as entertainers; sports figures). Such people have been characterized as having "logic-tight compartments" or cultural stereotypes. Some people develop strategies of inhibiting action components of BES, or of "delaying gratification," while they consider and try to accommodate to divergent information, or cognitively simulate alternative plans to construct one that can encompass the relevant information. "Perspective taking" labels a strategy of trying to interpret information within what one thinks may be the BES of another.

These and other self-constructing strategies can also result in dysfunctional patterns if used excessively. For example, a person who continuously modifies personal views to accommodate the discrepant views of others ends up with unstable BES with which to construct behavior episodes. A person who tries to accommodate all kinds of conflicting information within a single BES may end up with such an overgeneralized BES that it has little functional utility in organizing specific behavior episodes. Just as with self-organizing strategies, people develop habitual strategies of self-construction. The habitual use of particular strategies provides another form of personality consistency. More research on the kinds of self-organizing and self-constructing strategies people develop, how they are developed, and their effects, would be valuable. Some traditionally important personality constructs represent combinations of BES components (e.g., see the discussion of motivation in Chapter 10).

A PERSON'S PERSONALITY AND PERSONALITY TYPES

It should now be apparent that no individual's personality can be characterized by any one of the types of consistency described above. Efforts to do so will produce grossly oversimplified, fragmented, often misleading, and relatively useless characterizations. Rather, it is the organization of the different types of consistency a person has developed that gives him or her some enduring identity across situations and time, and makes predictions about and interpretations of that person's functioning possible.

It follows that while the study of interindividual differences (the primary source of personality traits in the past) may help identify the different types of consistency people *may develop*, it cannot provide a base for describing the nature or coherent organizations of such traits or component consistencies a person *has* developed; that is, a person's *personality*. That can only be accomplished by the study of intra-individual variability across situations and occasions so as to identify which of the many possible kinds of consistency the person has constructed, and how those different kinds of consistency are organized into BES patterns for that person. This seems to be the kind of strategy Buss and Craik (1983) have characterized as *multiple act analysis* based on dispositional categories. The BES unit provides an organizational framework within which the various types of consistency can be integrated to represent a person. The following example illustrates this idea.

One can start constructing such a personality "picture" by characterizing a person's major personal goal hierarchies and primary life contexts within which he or she pursues those goals. For example, "X" has four major personal goal hierarchies in life: to become wealthy; to excel in his or her work; to be respected and admired by colleagues; and to have a happy family life. Note that certain kinds of goals are not present, such as to be a responsible, contributing citizen, or to fulfill a religious faith. Both what is consistently present and what is absent are essential parts of an adequate personality description. "X" is a junior partner in a major law firm specializing in corporate law; lives on a three-acre estate in a wealthy suburb of a metropolitan area, with a spouse who has an independent career, a 13-year-old son and a 4-year-old daughter. This brief sketch of *key life contexts* defines behavior-setting boundaries and probabilities for the kinds of BES likely to be present, and the patterns of behavior episodes likely to be observable. For example, one can make some general predictions about the behavior patterns likely to occur in the work context, the kinds of social involvements likely to be present, and even the kinds of family issues and interaction patterns likely to occur.

One then can begin to elaborate that picture by identifying consistencies in BES components. For example, "X" is a paraplegic as a result of an automobile accident during high school and uses a motorized wheelchair for mobility (a biological structural-functional consistency). "X" considers that physical disability a weakness, resents it, and watches for signs of rejection and negative evaluations by others (regulatory and control functions consistencies). "X" habitually uses projection as a defense mechanism. For example, when "X" loses a court case "X" tends to explain the loss as resulting from the opinions of the judge and jury being colored by their evaluations of "X" being a cripple. Moreover, not being promoted to senior partner in the law firm is also assumed to be influenced by the handicap. To compensate for this handicap, "X" studies intensively to become THE expert on corporate law in the firm, and seeks the toughest cases to try to demonstrate this superior expertise (self-organizing and self-constructing strategy consistencies).

This sketchy personality description demonstrates that by identifying consistencies in different types of BES components, and then by organizing those in BES patterns, a picture of a person emerges. The generalized representation can then be used both to predict probable patterns of behavior and to interpret the meaning of and reasons for particular behavior episodes.

Finally, once such "personality pictures" have been constructed and verified for a sizable number of individuals, it then becomes possible to make interindividual comparisons of patterns to try to identify clusters of individuals who have similar patterns. The construction of such cross-person typologies then begins to build a sound nomothetic knowledge base (see Urban, 1987, for applications of this view to psychopathology). Nesselroade and Ford (1985, 1987) discuss some of the issues and possible research methods relevant to such an approach; but new developments in research design and in data analytic techniques, as well as attitudinal changes in funding and publication sources, will be necessary to effectively pursue this strategy on a larger scale for understanding and representing human personality.

Epilogue: Social Implications of the Living Systems Framework

The assumptions about the nature of humans and their world that we use to guide our lives have a powerful influence upon what we do, how we live, how we deal with and try to influence one another, and therefore upon the evolution of the future in which we will have to live. Therefore, it is important to consider the broader import of these assumptions. The philosophical, social, and personal implications of the emerging perspective about the nature of both the natural world and ourselves, briefly described in Chapter 2, and manifested in this living systems framework, are profound. One way of assessing any conceptualization about the nature of humans is to consider its potential social applications. Therefore, a brief consideration of some implications of this living systems framework follow.

No longer are things and human life to be ultimately understood as the products of random accidents. The universe is composed of dynamic, evolving, componentized patterns of organization, and these patterns are themselves related to one another in different ways and to different degrees. "Nature" appears to abhor disorganization, and functions through transforming processes to continually maintain and evolve organization. Energy is conserved, though its manifestations in structures and processes go through continual transformations. To understand the material world, humans must understand those energy/material structures and processes. But that is only part of the story. Materialism is an inadequate base for understanding humans. The properties of organization must also be understood. They are manifest as information. The concepts of information and energy/material must be combined to enable us to understand humans.

Recognizing information as being equally important but different from energy/material as basic phenomena of the universe has vast implications. Information makes social organization possible. Therefore, free access to communication media, libraries, and other information sources from which accurate information can be obtained is essential for modern societies. Without essential information, individuals cannot effectively regulate their personal behavior and pursue their personal goals in a way that meshes with the larger social environment of which they are a component. Moreover, since effective behavioral development is a product of humans' information-based self-constructing capabilities, an adequate flow of information nutriment is as essential as food for sound and healthy human development.

Like all other entities in the universe, an individual is a temporary organization of patterns of energy embedded in a context which in turn is embedded in a larger context. As living systems, humans function during their existence to maintain and elaborate their structural and functional organization within the facilitating and constraining conditions of their contexts. At any moment, their potential future developmental directions are defined by their current structural-functional organization and that of their contexts. Their future is determined by the flow of events in the present, not by the past. The properties of that present flow are a product both of the past (as manifest in material and informational patterns and trajectories previously constructed) and of the current energy/material and organizational dynamics. Therefore, there are always several alternate developmental trajectories possible for living systems at any point in time. Moreover, developmental change is likely to produce additional and unforeseeable possibilities, as has been demonstrated by biological evolution. Therefore, development is an open-ended process progressively closing off some old options and simultaneously opening up new ones.

What a hopeful view! No matter how bad things get for people, they are only constrained, rather than completely trapped, by their status quo. Starting from the lowest and most impoverished conditions, people may evolve to a higher and more fulfilling station and style of life. Moreover, as asserted by the principle of equifinality, there are multiple trajectories that may lead to the same state. Therefore, permanent personal and contextual constraints such as one's genetic heritage or physical handicaps (called *fixed rules* by Arthur Koestler) may block some trajectories but leave open, or open up, others (termed *flexible strategies* by Koestler). Conversely, a person may start life in an advantaged position, but can end up "at the bottom of the barrel."

In a larger sense, an individual's temporary existence ends, but the evolution of societies as living systems continues as new individuals develop. Societies also have multiple developmental trajectories open to them at any point in time. Societal stability is maintained by self-organizing processes (e.g., shared belief systems, bureaucracies). Societal change results from self-constructing processes which usually involve questioning or disrupting current trajectories and considering alternatives (e.g., Is the national security of Russia and the U.S. really dependent upon huge military establishments?). If self-organizing processes are too inflexible and operate to prevent any kind of change, system imbalances may become so severe that disorganization-reorganization processes, such as revolution come into play to produce change. Once an organizational transformation occurs (a *bifurcation* in Prigogene's terms), new and unforeseen possibilities are likely to be a by-product, and may lead to better or worse conditions.

Since multiple (and to some extent unknowable) futures are possible, and since living systems have attributes of self-organization and self-construction, which future occurs can be influenced by humans within the boundaries and constraints of the larger systems of our globe and universe (i.e., within nature's "fixed rules"). We are not totally helpless in the hands of fate. We are partly responsible as individuals and societies for what occurs in our future. Moreover, future possibilities not available to us now will surely emerge as a part of the dynamics of living system functioning. What will they be? How can we use them? What new dangers might we face? Like a good mystery story or a TV drama series, the current plot is clear, but how it will evolve is uncertain. We have choices we can pursue, however. And that fact has profound implications for individuals' and societies' approaches to life.

Individuals are simultaneously living systems in their own right and subsystems of larger living systems, such as families and communities. They function in mutual causal relationships in which the welfare of individuals and the social organizations of which they are components are dependent upon the effective functioning of one other. This creates an essential dynamic tension between individual freedom and social responsibility. Governments that too severely constrain the functioning of too many of their citizens become increasingly inflexible and unadaptive within their larger context, because their constraints restrict the effective functioning of their subsystems, thereby inhibiting the creation of new and potentially advantageous social options by their human components. An example is South Africa today. On the other hand, excessive emphasis on individual rights and freedom from societal constraints create an ineffective society (in the extreme, anarchy) and ultimately jeopardize both the society and the welfare and existence of its individual members. An example is Lebanon today. Because the development of living systems is dynamic and open-ended, the nature of the balance between individual freedom and social responsibility must also be dynamic and evolving. Stable yet adaptive societies must have processes for maintaining and adjusting that balance.

Elaboration of the complexity and efficiency of living system functioning through componentization (e.g., specialization) provides not only advantages but also dangers. For example, if the entire system's functioning is crucially dependent upon a single component, then dysfunctions of, or coercive demands by, that component can jeopardize the entire system (e.g., the human heart at the person level or economic monopolies at societal levels). Therefore, the most adaptive living systems will evolve within them alternate modes for accomplishing crucial functions. For example, when an oil cartel jeopardized other countries' economies, these countries sought to meet their energy needs in alternative ways. Societies and persons become vulnerable when their functioning becomes too dependent upon single subsystems within them or on single components of their contexts.

The recognition of individuals as intentional, valuing self-constructing organisms, rather than solely reactive entities, has many implications for a diversity of social processes and practices. A few illustrations follow.

If employees are viewed as self-governing components of a larger living system, rather than as mechanical components of a machine, then the challenge is to create work situations in which (a) the employee's personal goals and the organization's goals are linked in mutually beneficial ways, and (b) employees evaluate what they do as important to both their personal goals and those of the organization, and believe their efforts are valued by their supervisors. In this way, people's self-organization and self-construction can be accomplished in significant part through directing their efforts toward facilitating the success of the larger organization. In turn, the long-term success of the larger organization rests in part upon creating conditions that facilitate employees' accomplishment of important non-work related personal goals (e.g., through fringe benefits; flexible work schedules; day care for children of working mothers). Moreover, as living systems, each employee has some potential for constructing new ideas about how to improve organizational functioning, and finds interest and satisfaction in life through making progress towards personally constructed or chosen goals. Therefore, work arrangements in which employees can help to create their own tasks and/or methods of task accomplishment have the potential to increase both productivity and job interest and satisfaction. Finally, activities that have become habitual tend to elicit boredom. Arrangements which enable employees to generate variability and new challenges in their task environment are likely to result in higher morale and lower employee absenteeism and turnover.

Understanding that humans are self-organizing and self-constructing makes it clear that professionals in health and human services fields cannot change people's functioning by doing things to them. People are not reactive objects that can be molded by others. Rather, such professionals should interpret their interventions as methods of collaborating with clients to facilitate their self-organizing, self-constructing capabilities. They must do things WITH people, not TO them. For example, physicians cannot cure people. Rather, through the use of drugs, surgery, advice, and encouragement they can assist a person's biological self-organizing and self-constructing processes to restore a healthier steady state. Carl Rogers approach to counseling and psychotherapy is based on this alternate view, although he unnecessarily limited his intervention methods in implementing it. Even coercive methods of change work only if people at least minimally cooperate with them.

The view of regulatory processes proposed herein has important implications. Individuals are self-regulating. Therefore, social groups and societies cannot control the behavior of their members solely through external regulatory processes (e.g., laws, police, courts, punishment). At a psychological and social level, self-regulation results from the interaction of emotions and evaluative cognitions. To cultivate individuals who regulate their own behavior with values or rules that mesh with those of the social organizations of which they are a part requires socialization processes which facilitate individuals' self-construction of such regulatory habits. Moreover, these socialization processes must impact upon both emotions and cognitions.

This is a domain in which the dynamic tension between individual freedom and social responsibility has been manifest in public schools. In the interest of individual freedom, American public schools have been increasingly prohibited from (or have avoided for political and legal reasons) including systematic values socialization within their processes. This was not always the case, as examination of an old McGuffy's reader will reveal. Other institutions, such as family and church, continue to have such a responsibility. However, the role of public education in values socialization has been taken over by the mass media whose choice of messages about values is guided primarily by profit rather than by decisions about how to help create a healthy society. Thoughtful consideration of how our society can accomplish appropriate self-regulating socialization would be timely.

As intentional, valuing, self-organizing, self-constructing entities, individuals are responsible for their own behavior within the constraints of their bodies and contexts. Conceived of as living systems, people are not appropriately excused from responsibility for their actions because they "come from a bad environment," for example. Many exemplary citizens began in "bad environments." "The devil made me do it" (a metaphor popularized by an American comedian) is an inappropriate explanation for socially unacceptable behavior. However, unavoidable major constraints on intentional and regulatory capabilities, such as severe mental retardation or psychotic conditions, are appropriate bases for treating irresponsible behaviors differently because such constraints make people truly incapable of governing their own behavior effectively. Similarly, individuals and organizations are appropriately held accountable for consequences of their actions that they might have reasonably anticipated (e.g., contaminating ground water with toxic wastes), but not for consequences they could not have reasonably anticipated (e.g., the death of people shot by an employee just dismissed).

Recognizing that words are only "handles" by which people manipulate concepts represented as images or abstractions is of significance for many professionals. For example, teachers rely heavily on language as a teaching tool. Their challenge is to invent ways of linking language symbols to the learner's abstract and imagistic representations and their BES repertoires in accurate and useful ways. For example, a student may learn to emit the "right" string of words on a test, but not to use the concepts those words represent for later decision-making and action. Moreover, recognizing that life is a flowing stream of behavior episodes in which humans strive to achieve valued goals is critical for helping people learn. Skillful teachers activate within students relevant behavior episode schemata which the students then use to guide their learning activity, and differentiate and elaborate them through learning for future use. However, as the old adage goes, you can lead a horse to water but you can't make him drink. It is the learner who must make a commitment to pursue meaningful goals through his or her own effortful activities, and who must take the responsibility for learning.

This framework makes it clear that there are three fundamental ways in which human life may be influenced. First, the constraining and facilitating biological conditions of a person's body may be altered, either directly through procedures correcting deviant biological growth, development, and functioning, or through prostheses. The medical professions emphasize this approach. Second, the constraining and facilitating conditions of people's environments may be altered. For example, designing buildings, communities, and transportation systems specifically to serve physically handicapped people has facilitated new possibilities for them. Anti-discrimination laws illustrate changing constraining conditions through social environment alterations. The design professions and political and legal institutions emphasize this approach. Third, helping people elaborate their own governing (cognitive) and transactional (skills) capabilities creates new options and potential outcomes for them, that is, new potential developmental trajectories, sometimes called opportunities. Education, counseling, and psychotherapy emphasize this approach. The family is unique among social institutions in that it has the capability to use all three types of methods.

A family is a living system of which family members are components. For the family to function as a coherent unit or system, it must have governing processes to which family members conform and that identify objectives and regulatory rules which family members understand and live by. Since social governing processes occur through information exchanges, there must be clear and sufficient communication among family members if the family is to function effectively. In addition, there must be a shared environment within which family functions can be performed. These provide constraining and facilitating conditions (or boundary conditions) for the functioning of individual family members.

But the family unit must also serve individual development and functioning. Therefore, to enable individual family members to lead productive and satisfying lives, family boundary conditions should provide opportunities for each person to make choices, develop competencies, and carry out activities that serve their own purposes as well as the family's. Moreover, the family organization must be dynamic. Individual family members change through growth, development, learning, aging, marriage, divorce, and death; and the larger context within which the family functions also changes. Therefore, family governing processes, boundary conditions, and activity patterns should undergo progressive transformations to maintain the coherence of intrafamily functioning and of interactions with the larger context.

The implications for parenting are clear. Children need to be provided with clear, stable boundary conditions (e.g., regulatory rules, firm but fair discipline, a healthy and affectionate environment) within which they can function and develop. They need to be provided with a stable and secure social frame within which they can construct and operate their own governing functions. They need bounded freedom. Moreover, they need to be provided with a diversity of behavior episode opportunities through which they can experience the satisfaction of successful accomplishment of personal goals; of persistence in the face of initial failure; of the elaboration of skills and favorable self-evaluative thoughts (e.g., of self-efficacy); and through which they can develop regulatory rules and strategies for governing interpersonal relationships. Such experiences result in children's construction of behavior episode schemata that provide a starting point for elaborating their lives in other social contexts (e.g., school).

Creating these system properties to promote child development requires parents to be firm in enforcing boundaries (providing necessary constraining conditions), and flexible in encouraging the child's initiative and activities (providing facilitating conditions). Balancing the two is not an easy task because the child's desires and the adult's need to maintain the boundary conditions sometimes conflict; and because performing the governing role of a parent may conflict with other parental goals. Finally, as children develop, the system boundaries and governing processes must evolve to accommodate the changes.

Hopefully, this book will stimulate the reader to consider implications of their own assumptions about humans, or to explore other implications of this living systems framework. If so, this effort will have fulfilled one of its objectives.

Final Comment

The primary objective of this lengthy book has been to encourage scholars and professionals in many diverse fields to renew their efforts to understand and represent individuals as self-organizing, self-constructing, structural-functional unities embedded in environments which they both influence and are influenced by. This effort honors both the strategies and fruits of analytic science, which necessarily focuses on parts of persons. No study can study everything. However, if the only result of science is to produce a "catalogue of parts" with no way of organizing them to represent a person, then its social utility will be severely limited. Frameworks for integrating that "part" knowledge will help reveal the meaning of being human. This book proposes and seeks to demonstrate the heuristic utility of one such view, as does the array of empirical and theoretical applications in a companion edited volume (Ford & Ford, 1987).

It is hoped that this effort will stimulate others, particularly young professionals in training, both to explore the heuristic utility of this framework in their own work, and to formulate alternate and better frameworks to serve these same purposes. I have no doubt that there are many deficiencies in these proposals. I hope others will help identify them, correct them, and replace this framework with a more adequate one. Of one thing I am convinced: Without some such integrative framework, we will never be able to fully understand ourselves or one another, and are likely to be increasingly engulfed with mountains of data and empirical generalizations which can only lie in a heap, like pebbles on a shore. I believe we can make progress towards constructing useful integrative frameworks if we discard the belief that such a goal is not presently possible, and take the risk of trying. Hopefully, a more human, less mechanistic view of ourselves will help us to construct more humane societies.

References

Abelson, J. (1980). A revolution in biology. *Science, 209,* 1319–1321.

Abelson, R. P. (1981). Psychological status of the script concept. *American Psychologist, 36,* 715–727.

Abramson, D. L., & Dobrin, P. B. (Eds.). (1984). *Blood vessels and lymphatics in organ systems.* New York: Academic Press.

Abramov, I., Gordon, J., Hendrickson, A., Hainline, L., Dobson, V., & Labossiere, E. (1982). The retina of the newborn human infant. *Science, 217,* 265–267.

Achenbach, T. M., & Edelbrock, C. S. (1984). Psychopathology of childhood. *Annual Review of Psychology, 35,* 227–256.

Ackoff, R. L. (1957). Towards a behavioral theory of communication. *Management Science, 4,* 218–234.

Ackoff, R. L., & Emery, F. E. (1971). *On purposeful systems.* Chicago: Aldine.

Ackoff, R. L., & Emery, F. E. (1972). On ideal-seeking systems. In L. von Bertalanffy & A. Rapoport (Eds.), *General systems yearbook* (Vol. 17, pp. 17–24). Washington, DC: Society for General Systems Research.

Adams, D. B. (1979). Brain mechanisms for offense, defense, and submission. *The Behavioral and Brain Sciences, 2,* 201–241.

Adams, J. S. (1965). Inequity in social exchange. In L. Berkowitz (Ed.), *Advances in experimental social psychology* (Vol. 2, pp. 267–299). New York: Academic Press.

Adler, N. T. (1978). On the mechanisms of sexual behaviour and their evolutionary constraints. In J. B. Hutchison (Ed.), *Biological determinants of sexual behavior* (pp. 657–695).

Aebli, H. (1978). A dual model of cognitive development: Structure in cultural stimulation: Construction by the child. *International Journal of Behavioral Development, 1,* 221–228.

Ainsworth, M. D. S., Bell, S. M., & Stayton, D. J. (1974). Infant-mother attachment and social development: "Socialization" as a product of reciprocal responsiveness to signals. In M. P. M. Richards (Ed.), *The integration of a child into a social world* (pp. 128–156). Cambridge: Cambridge University Press.

Akiskal, H. S., & McKinney, W. T., Jr. (1975). Overview of recent research in depression.

Archives of General Psychiatry, 32, 285–300.

Alexander, J. F., & Malouf, R. E. (1983). Intervention with children experiencing problems in personality and social development. In P. H. Mussen (Ed.), *Handbook of child psychology: Vol. 4. Socialization, personality, and social development* (pp. 913–981). New York: Wiley.

Alland, A. J. (1967). *Evaluation and human behavior.* Garden City, NY: Natural History Press.

Allee, W. C. (1958). *The social life of animals* (rev. ed.). Boston: Beacon Press.

Allport, F. H. (1934). The J curve hypothesis of conforming behavior. *Journal of Social Psychology, 5,* 145–183.

Allport, F. H. (1937). Teleonomic description in the study of personality. *Character and Personality, 50,* 202–214.

Allport, F. H. (1939). Rule and custom as individual variations of behavior distributed upon a continuum of conformity. *American Journal of Sociology, 44,* 897–921.

Allport, F. H. (1954). The structuring of events: Outline of a general theory with applications to psychology. *Psychological Review, 61,* 281–303.

Allport, G. H. (1935). Attitudes. In C. Murchison (Ed.), *Handbook of social psychology* (pp. 798–844). Worcester, MA: Clark University Press.

Allport, G. W. (1937). *Personality: A psychological interpretation.* New York: Henry Holt.

Allport, G. W. (1943). The ego in contemporary psychology. *Psychological Review, 50,* 451–478.

Allport, G. W. (1955). *Becoming: Basic considerations for a psychology of personality.* New Haven: Yale University Press.

Allport, G. W. (1961). *Pattern and growth in personality.* New York: Holt, Rinehart & Winston.

Allport, G. W. (1966). Attitudes in the history of social psychology. In M. Jahoda & N. Warren (Eds.), *Attitudes* (pp. 19–25). Hammondsworth, Middlesex: Penguin Books.

Allport, G. W. (1967). The open system in personality theory. *Journal of Abnormal and Social Psychology, 61,* 301–311.

Allport, G. W., & Odbert, H. S. (1936). Trait names: A psycho-lexical study. *Psychological Monographs, 47(1,* Whole No. 211).

Almli, C. R., & Finger, S. (Eds.). (1984). *The behavioral biology of early brain damage.* New York: Academic Press.

Alston, W. P. (1971). Comments on Kohlberg's from its to ought. In W. Mischel (Ed.), *Cognitive development and epistimology* (pp. 130–150). New York: Academic Press.

Altman, I., & Wohlwill, J. F. (1978). *Children and the environment.* New York: Plenum Press.

Alwitt, L. F. (1981). Two neural mechanisms related to modes of selective attention. *Journal of Experimental Psychology, 7,* 324–332.

Amosov, N. (1968). Simulation of thinking processes. In H. Von Foerster, H. White, B. J. Peterson, & J. K. Russell (Eds.), *Purposive systems* (pp. 34–66). New York: Spartan Books.

Anant, S. S. (1967). Belongingness, anxiety and self-sufficiency: Pilot study. *Psychological Reports, 20,* 1137–1138.

Anderson, J. R. (1980). Concepts, propositions and schemata: What are the cognitive units? In H. E. Home, Jr. (Ed.), *Nebraska Symposium on Motivation* (Vol. 28, pp. 121–162). Lincoln: University of Nebraska Press.

Anderson, J. R. (1982). Acquisition of cognitive skill. *Psychological Review, 89,* 369–406.

Anderson, J. R. (1983). *The architecture of cognition.* Cambridge, MA: Harvard University Press.

Anderson, J. R., & Bower, G. H. (1973). *Human associative memory.* Washington, DC: Winston.

Anderson, P. W. (1978). Local moments and localized states. *Science, 201,* 307–316.

Anderson, R. C., & Pichert, J. W. (1978). Recall of previously unrecallable information following a shift in perspective. *Journal of Verbal Learning and Verbal Behavior, 17*, 1–12.

Ando, A., Fisher, F., & Simon, H. A. (1963). *Essays on the structure of social science models.* Cambridge, MA: MIT Press.

Angyal, A. (1965). *Neurosis and treatment.* New York: Wiley.

Anokhin, P. K. (1969). Cybernetics and the integrative activity of the brain. In M. Cole & I. Maltzman (Eds.), *A handbook of contemporary Soviet psychology (pp. 830–856).* New York: Basic Books.

Anthony, B. J., & Graham, F. K. (1983). Evidence for sensory-selective set in young infants. *Science, 220*, 742–743.

Antonovsky, A. (1979). *Health, stress, and coping.* San Francisco: Jossey-Bass.

Arbib, M. A. (1972). *The metaphorical brain.* New York: Wiley Interscience.

Arbib, M. A. (1980). Interacting schemas for motor control. In G. E. Stelmach & J. Requin (Eds.), *Tutorials in motor behavior* (pp. 71–81). Amsterdam: North-Holland.

Arbib, M. A. (1981). Perceptual structures and distributed motor control. In V. B. Brooks (Ed.), *Handbook of physiology: Vol. 3. Motor control.* American Physiological Society.

Archer, J. (1979). Behavioural aspects of fear. In W. Sluckin (Ed.), *Fear in animals and man* (pp. 56–85). New York: Van Nostrand Reinhold.

Arenberg, D. (1982). Changes with age in problem solving. In F. I. M. Craik & S. Trehub (Eds.), *Aging and cognitive processes* (pp. 221–236). New York: Plenum Press.

Arenberg, D. (1983). Memory and learning do decline late in life. In J. E. Birren, J. M. A. Munnichs, H. Thormae, & M. Marois (Eds.), *Aging: A challenge to science and society: Vol. 3. Behavioral sciences and conclusions* (pp. 164–179). Oxford: Oxford University Press.

Arend, L. E., Jr. (1973). Spatial differential and integral operations in human vision: Implications of stabilized retinal image fading. *Psychological Review, 80*, 374–395.

Argyle, M. (1975). *Bodily communication.* New York: International Universities Press.

Argyle, M., & Cook, M. (1976). *Gaze and mutual gaze.* London: Cambridge University Press.

Arieti, S. (1978). A psychotherapeutic approach to severely depressed patients. *American Journal of Psychotherapy, 32*, 33–47.

Armstrong, E. (1983). Relative brain size and metabolism in animals. *Science, 220*, 1302–1304.

Armstrong, E., & Falk, D. (Eds.). (1982). *Primate brain evolution.* New York: Plenum Press.

Arnold, M. B. (1960). *Emotion and personality* (Vols. 1–2). New York: Columbia University Press.

Arnold, M. B. (1970). Brain function in emotion: A phenomenological analysis. In P. Black (Ed.), *Physiological correlates of emotion* (pp. 261–286). New York: Academic Press.

Aschoff, J. (Ed.). (1981). *Handbook of behavioral neurobiology: Vol. 4. Biological rhythms.* New York: Plenum Press.

Aschoff, J., Daan, S., & Groos, G. A. (Eds.). (1982). *Vertebrate circulation.* New York: Springer-Verlag.

Ashby, W. R. (1956). *An introduction to cybernetics.* New York: Wiley.

Ashby, W. R. (1962). Principles of the self-organizing system. In H. Von Foerster & G. W. Zopf (Eds.), *Principles of self-organization* (pp. 108–118). New York: Pergamon Press.

Ashmead, D. H., & Perlmutter, M. (1980). Infant memory in everyday life. In M. Perlmutter (Ed.), *New directions for child development: Children's memory* (Vol. 10, pp. 1–16). San Francisco: Jossey-Bass.

Aslin, R. N., Pisoni, D. B., & Jusczyk, P. W. (1983). Auditory development and speech perception in infancy. In P. H. Mussen (Ed.), *Handbook of child psychology: Vol. 2. Infancy and developmental psychobiology* (pp. 573–688). New York: Wiley.

Atkinson, J. W. (1964). *An introduction to motivation.* Princeton, NJ: Van Nostrand.

Atkinson, J. W. (1977). Motivation for achievement. In T. Blass (Ed.), *Personality variables in social behavior* (pp. 25–108). Hillsdale, NJ: Lawrence Erlbaum Associates.

668 REFERENCES

Atkinson, J. W., & Birch, D. (1970). *The dynamics of action*. New York: Wiley.
Atkinson, R. C., & Shiffrin, R. M. (1968). Human memory: A proposed system and its control processes. In K. W. Spence & J. T. Spence (Eds.), *The psychology of learning and motivation: Advances in research theory* (Vol. 2, pp. 89–195). New York: Academic Press.
Audi, R. (1979). Wants and intentions in the explanation of action. *Journal of the Theory of Social Behavior, 9,* 227–249.
Audy, J. (1980). Man, the lonely animal. In J. Hartog, J. R. Audy, & Y. A. Cohen (Eds.), *The anatomy of loneliness*. New York: International Universities Press.
Auger, P. (1980). Coupling between N levels of observations of a system (biological or physical) resulting in creation of structures. *International Journal of General Systems, 6,* 83–100.
Ausubel, D. P. (1955). Relationship between shame and guilt in the socialization process. *Psychological Review, 62,* 378–380.
Averill, J. R. (1968). Grief: Its nature and significance. *Psychological Bulletin, 70,* 721–748.
Averill, J. R. (1978). Anger. In H. H. Howe, Jr. & R. A. Dienstbier (Eds.), *Nebraska Symposium on Motivation* (Vol. 26, pp. 1–80). Lincoln: University of Nebraska Press.
Ax, A. F. (1953). The physiological differentiation between fear and anger in humans. *Psychosomatic Medicine, 15,* 433–442.
Axelrod, J., & Reisine, T. D. (1984). Stress hormones: Their interaction and regulation. *Science, 224,* 452–459.
Axelrod, R., & Hamilton, W. D. (1981). The evolution of cooperation. *Science, 211,* 1390–1396.
Azjen, I., & Fishbein, M. (1974). Factors influencing intentions and the intention-behavior relation. *Human Relations, 27,* 1–15.
Bachman, J. G., & O'Malley, P. M. (1977). Self-esteem in young men: A longitudinal analyis of the impact of educational and occupational attainment. *Journal of Personality and Social Psychology, 35,* 365–380.
Back, K. T., Stansell, J., Ragan, T. J., Ausburn, L. J., Ausburn, F. B., & Huckabay, K. (1972). Cognitive styles: A bibliography and selected annotations. *USAFHRL Technical Report*, pp. 78–90.
Bahnson, C. B. (1964). Emotional reactions to internally and externally derived threat of annihilation. In G. H. Grosser, H. Wechsler, & L. Greenblatt (Eds.), *The threat of impending disaster* (pp. 251–280). Cambridge, MA: MIT.
Bahrick, L. E., Walker, A. S., & Neisser, U. (1981). Selective looking by infants. *Cognitive Psychology, 13,* 377–390.
Baier, K. (1969). What is value. In K. Baier & N. Rescher (Eds.), *Values and the future* (pp. 33–67). New York: Free Press.
Bain, A. (1855). *The senses and the intellect*. London: Parker.
Bakan, P. (Ed.). (1966). *Attention: An enduring problem in psychology*. Princeton, NJ: Van Nostrand.
Baker, L., & Santa, J. L. (1977). Semantic integration and context. *Memory and Cognition, 5,* 151–154.
Baltes, P. B., Cornelius, S. W., & Nesselroade, J. R. (1978). Cohort effects in behavioral development: Theoretical and methodological perspectives. In W. A. Collins (Ed.), *Minnesota Symposium on Child Psychology* (Vol. 11, pp. 1–63). Hillsdale, NJ: Lawrence Erlbaum Associates.
Baltes, P. B., Reese, H. W., & Lipsitt, L. P. (1980). Life span developmental psychology. *Annual Review of Psychology, 31,* 65–110.
Baltes, P. B., & Reinhold, K. (1985). *Testing-the-limits and the study of intellectual reserve capacity (plasticity) in old age*. Unpublished manuscript, Max Planck Institute for Human Development and Education, Berlin, West Germany.
Baltes, P. B., & Willis, S. L. (1977). Toward psychological theories of aging and

development. In J. E. Birren & K. W. Schaie (Eds.), *Handbook of the psychology of aging* (pp. 128–154). New York: Van Nostrand Reinhold.

Baltes, P. B., & Willis, S. L. (1979). Life-span developmental psychology, cognition, and social policy. In M. W. Riley (Ed.), *Aging from birth to death* (Vol. 1, pp. 15–46). Boulder: Westview Press.

Bandura, A. (1969). *Principles of behavior modification.* New York: Holt, Rinehart & Winston.

Bandura, A. (1976). Self-reinforcement: Theoretical and methodological considerations. *Behaviorism, 4,* 135–155.

Bandura, A. (1977a). *Social learning theory.* Englewood Cliffs, NJ: Prentice-Hall.

Bandura, A. (1977b). Self-efficacy: Toward a unifying theory of behavioral change. *Psychological Review, 84,* 191–215.

Bandura, A. (1978a). The self-esteem in reciprocal determinism. *American Psychologist, 33,* 344–358.

Bandura, A. (1978b). Reflections on self-efficacy. In S. Rachman (Ed.), *Advances in behavior research and therapy* (Vol. 1, pp. 237–269). Oxford, UK: Pergamon Press.

Bandura, A. (1981). Self-referent thought: A developmental analysis of self-efficacy. In J. H. Flavell & L. Ross (Eds.), *Social cognitive development: Frontiers and possible futures* (pp. 200–239). Cambridge, UK: Cambridge University Press.

Bandura, A. (1982a). Self-efficacy mechanism in human agency. *American Psychologist, 37,* 122–147.

Bandura, A. (1982b). The self and mechanisms of agency. In J. Suls (Ed.), *Social psychological perspectives on the self* (Vol. 1, pp. 3–39). Hillsdale, NJ: Lawrence Erlbaum Associates.

Bandura, A. (1986). *Social foundations of thought and action.* Englewood Cliffs, NJ: Prentice-Hall.

Bandura, A., & Cervone, D. (1983). Self-evaluative and self-efficacy mechanisms governing the motivational effects of goal systems. *Journal of Personality and Social Psychology, 45,* 1017–1028.

Bandura, A., & Schunk, D. H. (1981). Cultivating competence, self-efficacy and intrinsic interest through proximal self-motivation. *Journal of Personality and Social Psychology, 41,* 586–598.

Bandura, A., & Walters, R. H. (1963). *Social learning and personality development.* New York: Holt, Rinehart & Winston.

Banks, M. S., & Salapatek, P. (1983). Infant visual perception. In P. H. Mussen (Ed.), *Handbook of child psychology* (Vol. 2, 4th ed., pp. 435–572). New York: Wiley.

Barclay, C. D., Cutting, J. E., & Kozlowski, L. T. (1978). Temporal and spatial factors in gait perception that influence gender recognition. *Perception and Psychophysics, 23,* 145–152.

Barchas, J. D., Akil, H., Elliott, G. R., Holman, R. B., & Watson, S. J. (1978). Behavioral neurochemistry: Neuroregulators and behavioral states. *Science, 200,* 964–973.

Baribeau-Braun, J., Picton, D. W., & Gosselin, J. Y. (1983). Schizophrenia: A neurological evaluation of abnormal information processing. *Science, 219,* 874–876.

Barker, R. G. (1963). *The stream of behavior.* New York: Appleton-Century-Crofts.

Barker, R. G. (1968). *Ecological psychology: Concepts and methods for studying the environment of human behavior.* Stanford, CA: Stanford University Press.

Barnes, D. M. (1987). Biological issues in schizophrenia. *Science, 235,* 430–433.

Barnes, R. H. (1967). Experimental animal approaches to the study of early malnutrition and mental development. *Proceedings of American Societies for Experimental Biology.*

Baron, J. (1978). Intelligence and general strategies. In G. Underwood (Ed.), *Strategies of information processing* (pp. 403–450). New York: Academic Press.

Baron, J. (1982). Personality and intelligence. In R. J. Sternberg (Ed.), *Handbook of human intelligence* (pp. 308–350). Cambridge: Cambridge University Press.

Baroni, M. R., Job, R., Peron, E. M., & Salmaso, P. (1980). Memory for natural settings: Role of diffuse and focused attention. *Perceptual and Motor Skills, 51,* 883–889.

Barraga, N. C., Collins, M., & Hollis, J. (1977). Development of efficiency in visual functioning: A literature analysis. *Journal of Visual Impairment and Blindness, 10,* 387–391.

Barrow, H. M. (1977). *Man and movement: Principles of physical education* (2nd ed.). Philadelphia: Lea & Felinger.

Barsalou, L. W. (1982). Context-independent and context-dependent information in concepts. *Memory and Cognition, 10,* 82–93.

Bartlett, F. C. (1958). *Thinking: An experimental and social study.* New York: Basic Books.

Bartlett, F. C. (1932). *Remembering: An experimental and social study.* Cambridge: Cambridge University Press.

Bartus, R. T., Dean, R. L., III, Beer, B., & Lippa, A. S. (1982). The cholinergic hypothesis of geriatric memory dysfunction. *Science, 217,* 408–417.

Basowitz, H., Persky, H., Korchin, S. J., & Grinker, R. R. (1955). *Anxiety and stress.* New York: McGraw-Hill.

Bates, J. E. (1980). The concept of difficult temperament. *Merrill-Palmer Quarterly, 26,* 299–319.

Battacchi, M. W., Franza, A., & Pani, R. (1981). Memory processing of spatial order as transmitted by auditory information in the absence of visual cues. *Memory and Cognition, 9,* 301–307.

Baumeister, R. F. (1982). A self-presentational view of social phenomena. *Psychological Bulletin, 9,* 3–26.

Bayley, N. (1935). The development of motor abilities during the first three years. *Monograph of the Society for Research on Child Development, 1,* 1–26.

Beach, F. A. (Ed.). (1965). *Sex and behavior.* New York: Wiley.

Beach, F. A. (1976). Sexual attractivity, proceptivity, and receptivity in female mammals. *Hormones and Behavior, 7,* 104–138.

Beane, J., & Lipka, R. (1980). Self-concept and self-esteem: A construct differentiation. *Child Study Journal, 10,* 1–6.

Beck, A. (1967). *Depression: Clinical, experimental and theoretical aspects.* New York: Harper & Row.

Beecher, N. K. (1956). Relationship of significance of wound to the pain experienced. *Journal of the American Medical Association, 161,* 1609–1613.

Beecher, H. K. (1959). *Measurement of subjective responses.* New York: Oxford University Press.

Beer, S. (1964). *Cybernetics and management.* New York: Wiley.

Beets, M. G. J. (1978). *Structure-activity relationships in human chemoreception.* London: Applied Science.

Benedict, H. (1979). Early lexical development: Comprehension and production. *Journal of Child Language, 6,* 183–200.

Benelli, B., D'Odorico, L., Levorato, C., & Simion, F. (1977). La nascita dello scopo conoscitivo nelle prime forme communicative infantili. *Archivio d. Psicologia Neurologia e Psichiatria, 3,* 365–384.

Benish, W. A., & Grant, D. A. (1980). Subject awareness in differential classical eyelid conditioning. *Bulletin of the Psychonomic Society, 15,* 431–432.

Bennett, A. F., & Ruben, J. A. (1979). Endothermy and activity in vertebrates. *Science, 206,* 649–654.

Bensinger, T. H. (1961). The human thermostat. *Scientific American, 204,* 134–147.

Berg, W. K., & Berg, K. M. (1979). Psychophysiological development in infancy: State, sensory function, and attention. In J. Osofsky (Ed.), *Handbook of infant development* (pp. 283–343). New York: Wiley.

Bergin, A. E., & Garfield, S. L. (Eds.). (1971). *Handbook of psychotherapy and behavior change.*

New York: Wiley.

Berkowitz, L. (Ed.). (1969). *Roots of aggression*. New York: Atherton Press.

Berkowitz, M. W., & Oser, F. (Eds.). (1985). *Moral education: Theory and application*. Hillsdale, NJ: Lawrence Erlbaum Associates.

Berlyne, D. E. (1960). *Conflict, arousal and curiosity*. New York: McGraw-Hill.

Berlyne, D. E. (1964). Emotional aspects of learning. *Annual Review of Psychology, 15*, 115–142.

Berlyne, D. E. (1971). Arousal and reinforcement. *Nebraska Symposium on Motivation* (Vol.15, 1–110). Lincoln: University of Nebraska Press.

Bernard, C. (1957). *An introduction to the study of experimental medicine*. New York: Dover Publications. (Originally published 1865)

Berndt, R. S., & Caramazza, A. (1980). A redefinition of the syndrome of Broca's aphasia: Implications for a neuropsychological model of language. *Applied Psycholinguistics, 1*, 225–278.

Bernstein, N. A. (1967). *The coordination and regulation of movements*. London: Pergamon Press.

Bernstein, N. A. (1947). *O postroenii Dvzenij*. Moscow.

Berridge, M. J. (1985). The molecular basis of communication within the cell. *Scientific American, 253*, 110–121.

Berscheid, E. (1983). Emotion. In H. H. Kelley, E. Berscheid, A. Christensen, J. Harney, T. Huston, G. Levinger, G. McClintock, A. Peplau, & D. Peterson, (Eds.), *The psychology of close relationships* (pp. 110–168). San Francisco: Freeman.

Bertenthal. B. I., & Fischer, K. W. (1978). Development of self-recognition in the infant. *Developmental Psychology, 14*, 44–50.

Berzonsky, M. D. (1978). Formal reasoning in adolescence: An alternative view. *Adolescence, 13*, 279–290.

Bevan, W. (1967). Behavior in unusual environments. In H. Helson & W. Bevan (Eds.), *Contemporary approaches to psychology* (pp. 409–411). Princeton, NJ: Van Nostrand.

Bexton, W. H., Heron, W., & Scott, T. H. (1954). Effects of decreased variation in the sensory environment. *Canadian Journal of Psychology, 8*, 70–76.

Bhaskar, R. (1978). *A realist theory of science* (2nd ed.). Atlantic Highlands, NJ: Humanities Press.

Biaggio, M. K. (1980). Assessment of anger arousal. *Journal of Personality Assessment, 44*, 289–298.

Bickhard, M. H. (1979). On necessary and specific capabilities in evolution and development. *Human Development, 22*, 217–224.

Bier, W. C., Jr. (1971). *Conscience: Its freedom and limitations*. New York: Fordham University Press.

Bigelow, R. (1972). The evolution of cooperation, aggression, and self-control. In J. K. Cole & D. D. Jensen (Eds.), *Nebraska Symposium on Motivation* (Vol. 20, pp. 1–57). Lincoln: University of Nebraska Press.

Bijou, S. W., & Ruiz, R. (Eds.). (1981). *Behavior modification: Contributions to education*. Hillsdale, NJ: Lawrence Erlbaum Associates.

Bindra, B. (1970). Emotion and behavior theory: Current research in historical perspective. In P. Black (Ed.), *Physiological correlates of emotion* (pp. 3–22). New York: Academic Press.

Binet, A., & Simon, T. (1908). Le dveloppement de l'intelligence chez les enfants. *L'Anne Psychologique, 14*, 1–94.

Binet, A., & Simon, T. (1916). *The development of intelligence in children* (E. S. Kite, Trans.). Baltimore: Williams & Wilkins.

Birdwhistell, R. L. (1970). *Kinesics and context*. Philadelphia: University of Pennsylvania Press.

Birren, J. E., & Sloane, R. B. (1980). *Handbook of mental health and aging*. Englewood Cliffs,

NJ: Prentice-Hall.

Birren, J. E., Woods, A. M., & Williams, M. V. (1980). Behavioral slowing with age: Courses, organization and consequences. In L. W. Poon (Ed.), *Aging in the 1980s: Psychological issues* (pp. 281–292). Washington, DC: American Psychological Association.

Bitterman, M. E. (1975). The comparative analysis of learning. *Science, 188,* 699–709.

Bizzi, E. (1980). Central and peripheral mechanisms in motor control. In G. E. Stelmach & J. Requin (Eds.), *Tutorials in motor behavior* (pp. 131–143). Amsterdam: North-Holland.

Black, I. B. (1982). Stages of neurotransmitter development in autonomic neurons. *Science, 215,* 1198–1203.

Black, J. B., & Bower, G. H. (1979). Episodes as chunks in narrative memory. *Journal of Verbal Learning and Verbal Behavior, 18,* 187–198.

Black, P. (Ed.). (1970). *Physiological correlates of emotion.* New York: Academic Press.

Blackmore, W. R. (1981). Human software. *Behavior Research Methods and Instrumentation, 13,* 553–570.

Blasi, A. (1980). Bridging moral cognition and moral action: A critical review of the literature. *Psychological Bulletin, 88,* 1–45.

Blatt, M., & Kohlberg, L. (1975). The effects of classroom moral discussion upon children's level of moral judgment. *Journal of Moral Education, 4,* 129–161.

Block, J. (1977). Recognizing the coherence of personality. In D. Magnusson & N. S. Endler (Eds.), *Personality at the crossroads: Current issues in interactional psychology* (pp. 37–63). Hillsdale, NJ: Lawrence Erlbaum Associates.

Block, J. (1982). Assimilation, accommodation, and the dynamics of personality development. *Child Development, 53,* 281–295.

Blondis, M. N., & Jackson, B. E. (1977). *Nonverbal communication with patients.* New York: Wiley.

Blumberg, M. L. (1978). Depression in children on a general pediatric service. *American Journal of Psychotherapy, 32,* 20–32.

Blurton-Jones, N. G. (Ed.). (1972). *Ethological studies of child behavior.* Cambridge, UK: Cambridge University Press.

Boden, M. A. (1972). *Purposive explanation in psychology.* Cambridge, MA: Harvard University Press.

Bohm, D. (1973). *Fragmentation and wholeness* (The Van Leer Jerusalem Foundation Series). New York: Humanities Press.

Bolles, R. C., & Fanselow, M. S. (1980). A perceptual-defensive- recuperative model of fear and pain. *Behavioral and Brain Sciences, 3,* 291–323.

Bolles, R. C., & Fanselow, M. S. (1982). Endorphins and behavior. *Annual Review of Psychology, 33,* 87–101.

Bondareff, W. (1980). Neurobiology of aging. In J. E. Birren & R. B. Sloane (Eds.), *Handbook of mental health and aging* (pp. 75–99). Englewood Cliffs, NJ: Prentice-Hall.

Bonica, J. J., & Albe-Fessard, D. (Eds.). (1976). *Advances in pain research and therapy* (Vol. 1). New York: Raven Press.

Bookbinder, J., & Osman, E. (1979). Attentional strategies in dichotic listening. *Memory and Cognition, 7,* 511–520.

Boring, E. G. (1929). *A history of experimental psychology.* New York: Appleton-Century.

Boring, E. G. (1942). *Sensation and perception in the history of experimental psychology.* New York: Appleton-Century.

Boring, E. G. (1957). *A history of experimental psychology.* New York: Appleton-Century-Crofts.

Boring, E. G. (1960). The psychologist's concept of mind. *Journal of Psychological Researches, 4*(3).

Bornstein, M. H., & Kessen, W. (Eds.). (1979). *Psychological development from infancy: Image to intention*. Hillsdale, NJ: Lawrence Erlbaum Associates.

Boswell, D. A. (1979). Metaphoric processing in the mature years. *Human Development, 22*, 373–384.

Boucher, J. D., & Ekman, P. (1975). Facial areas and emotional information. *Journal of Communication, 25*, 21–29.

Bouhuys, A. (Ed.). (1968). Sound production in man. *Annals of New York Academy of Sciences, 155*, 1–39.

Boulding, K. (1980). Science: Our common heritage. *Science, 207*, 831–836.

Bower, G. H. (1981). Mood and memory. *American Psychologist, 36*, 129–148.

Bower, G. H., Black, J. B., & Turner, T. J. (1979). Scripts in memory for text. *Cognitive Psychology, 11*, 177–220.

Bower, G. H. & Cohen, P. R. (1982). Emotional influences in memory and thinking: Data and theory. In M. S. Clark & S. T. Fiske (Eds.), *Cognition and emotion: The 17th Carnegie-Mellon Symposium* (pp. 291–332). Hillsdale, NJ: Lawrence Erlbaum Associates.

Bower, G. H., Gilligan, S. G., & Monteiro, K. P. (1981). Selective learning caused by affective states. *Journal of Experimental Psychology: General, 110*, 451–473.

Bower, G. H., & Hilgard, E. R. (1981). *Theories of learning* (5th ed.). Engelwood Cliffs, NJ: Prentice-Hall.

Bower, T. G. R. (1974a). The evolution of sensory systems. In R. B. MacLeod & H. L. Pick, Jr. (Eds), *Perception: Essays in honor of J. J. Gibson* (pp. 141–152). Ithaca, NY: Cornell University Press.

Bower, T. G. R. (1974b). *Development in infancy*. San Francisco: W. H. Freeman.

Bower, T. G. R. (1978). Perceptual development: Object and space. In E. C. Carterette & M. P. Friedman (Eds.), *Handbook of perception: Vol. 8. Perceptual coding*. New York: Academic Press.

Bowerman, W. R. (1978). Subjective competence: The structure, process and function of self-referent causal attributions. *Journal for the Theory of Social Behavior, 8*, 45–75.

Bowlby, J. (1973). *Attachment and loss: Vol. 2. Separation, anxiety and anger*. New York: Basic Books.

Bowlby, J. (1980). *Attachment and loss: Vol. 3. Sadness and depression*. New York: Basic Books.

Boyd, D. A., Jr., & Nie, L. W. (1949). Congenital universal indifference to pain. *Archives of Neurology and Psychiatry, 61*, 402–412.

Brackbill, Y. (Ed.). (1967). *Infancy and early childhood*. New York: The Free Press.

Brackbill, Y. (1979). Obstetrical medication and infant behavior. In J. Osofsky (Ed.), *The handbook of infant development* (pp. 76–125). New York: Wiley.

Brady, J. V. (1970). Endocrine and autonomic correlates of emotion. In P. Black (Ed.), *Physiological correlates of emotion* (pp. 95–129). New York: Academic Press.

Braine, M. D. S., & Rumain, B. (1983). Logical reasoning. In P. H. Mussen (Ed.), *Handbook of child psychology: Vol. 3. Cognitive development* (pp. 263–340). New York: Wiley.

Brainerd, C. J. (1978). The stage question in cognitive-development theory. *The Behavioral and Brain Sciences, 2*, 173–213.

Bramble, D. M., & Carrier, D. R. (1983). Running and breathing in mammals. *Science, 219*, 251–256.

Brand, M. (1976). *The nature of causation*. Urbana, IL: University of Illinois Press.

Brand, M. (1984). *Intending and acting: Toward a naturalized action theory*. Cambridge, MA: MIT Press.

Braun, C. M. J., & Baribeau, J. M. C. (1978). Subjective idealism in Kohlberg's theory of moral development. *Human Development, 21*, 298–301.

Braumstein, D. R. (1976). *Depth perception through motion*. New York: Academic Press.

Braumstein, M. L. (1978). Perception of motion. In E. C. Carterette & M. P. Friedman (Eds.), *Handbook of perception* (Vol. 8, pp. 147–172). New York: Academic Press.

Brazelton, T. B., Als, H., Tronick, E., & Lester, B. M. (1979). Specific neonatal measures:

The Brazelton Neonatal Behavior Assessment Scale. In J. Osofsky (Ed.), *The handbook of infant development* (pp. 185–215). New York: Wiley.

Breitmeyer, B. G. (1980). Unmasking visual masking: A look at the "why" behind the veil of "how." *Psychological Review, 87,* 52–69.

Breland, K., & Breland, M. (1966). *Animal behavior.* New York: Macmillan.

Brenner, B. M., & Rector, F. C. (Eds.). (1981). *The kidney* (Vols. 1–2, 2nd ed.). Philadelphia: W. B. Saunders.

Brent, S. B. (1978a). Motivation, steady-state, and structural development. *Motivation and Emotion, 2,* 299–332.

Brent, S. B. (1978b). Prigogine's model for self-organization in nonequilibrium systems. *Human Development, 21,* 374–387.

Brent, S. B. (1984). *Psychological and social structures.* Hillsdale, NJ: Lawrence Erlbaum Associates.

Bretherton, I., McNew, S., & Beeghly-Smith, M. (1981). Early person knowledge as expressed in gestural and verbal communication: When do infants acquire a "theory of mind"? In M. E. Lamb & L. R. Sherrod (Eds.), *Infant social cognition* (pp. 333–374). Hillsdale, NJ: Lawrence Erlbaum Associates.

Bretscher, M. S. (1985). The molecules of the cell membrane. *Scientific American, 253,* 100–108.

Bridges, A. (1979). Directing two-year-olds' attention: Some clues to understanding. *Journal of Child Language, 62,* 211–226.

Bridges, K. M. B. (1932). Emotional development in early infancy. *Child Development, 3,* 324–341.

Brigham, T. A. (1980). Self-control revisited: Or why doesn't anyone actually read Skinner anymore. *The Behavioral Analyst, 3,* 25–35.

Brim, O. G. (1976). Life-span development of the theory of oneself: Implications for child development. In H. W. Reese (Ed.), *Advances in child development and behavior* (Vol. 2, pp. 242–253). New York: Academic Press.

Brim, O. G., Jr., & Kagan, J. (Eds.). (1980). *Constancy and change in human development.* Cambridge: Harvard University Press.

Broadbent, D. E. (1958). *Perception and communication.* London: Pergamon Press.

Broadbent, D. E. (1970). Stimulus set and response set: Two kinds of selective attention. In D. I. Mostofsky (Ed.), *Attention: Contemporary theory and analysis.* New York: Appleton-Century-Crofts.

Brocker, J., & Hulton, A. B. (1978). How to reverse the vicious cycle of low self-esteem: The importance of attentional focus. *Journal of Experimental Social Psychology, 14,* 564–578.

Broderick, C. B. (1973). Sexual behavior among preadolescents. In A. M. Juhosz (Ed.), *Sexual development and behavior* (pp. 20–35). Homewood, IL: Dorsey Press.

Bronfenbrenner, U. (1977a). Toward an experimental ecology of human development. *American Psychologist, 32,* 513–530.

Bronfenbrenner, U. (1977b). Lewinian space and ecological substance. *Journal of Social Issues, 33,* 199–212.

Bronfenbrenner, U. (1979). *The ecology of human development.* Cambridge, MA: Harvard University Press.

Bronfenbrenner, U., & Crouter, A. C. (1982). Work and family through time and space. In S. Kamermann & C. D. Hayes (Eds.), *Families that work* (pp. 39–83). Washington, DC: National Academic Press.

Bronfenbrenner, U., & Crouter, A. C. (1983). The evolution of environmental models in developmental research. In P. H. Mussen (Ed.), *Handbook of child psychology* (4th ed.): *Vol. 1. History, theory and methods* (pp. 357–414). New York: Wiley.

Brooks, F. D. (1937). *Child psychology.* Boston: Houghton Mifflin.

Brown, A., Bransford, J., Ferrara, R., & Campione, J. (1983). Learning, remembering, and understanding. In P. H. Mussen (Ed.), *Handbook of child psychology (4th ed.): Vol. 3. Cognitive development* (pp. 77–166). New York: Wiley.

Brown, A. L. (1982). Learning and development: The problem of compatibility access and induction. *Human Development, 25*, 89–115.

Brown, A. M., & Stubbs, D. W. (Eds.). (1983). *Medical physiology.* New York: Wiley.

Brown, G., & Desforges, C. (1979). *Piaget's theory: A psychological critique.* Boston: Routledge & Kegan Paul.

Brown, G. W., & Cohen, B. D. (1959). Avoidance and approach learning motivated by stimulation of identical hypothalamic loci. *American Journal of Physiology, 197*, 153–1157.

Brown, J. L. (1973). Visual sensitivity. In P. H. Mussen & M. R. Rosenzweig (Eds.), *Annual review of psychology* (Vol. 24, pp. 151–186). Palo Alto, CA: Annual Review.

Brown, J. L. (1975). *The evolution of behavior.* New York: W. W. Norton.

Brown, R., & Kulick, J. (1977). Flashbulb memories. *Cognition, 5*, 73–99.

Brozek, J. (1978). Nutrition, malnutrition, and behavior. *Annual Review of Psychology, 29*, 157–177.

Bruell, J. H. (1970). Heritability of emotional behavior. In P. Black (Ed.), *Physiological correlates of emotion* (pp. 23–26). New York: Academic Press.

Bruner, J. (1957). Perceptual readiness. *Psychological Review, 64*, 123–152.

Bruner, J. S. (1964). The course of cognitive growth. *American Psychology, 19*, 1–15.

Bruner, J. S. (1968). *Processes of cognitive growth: Infancy.* Worcester, MA: Clark University Press.

Bruner, J. S. (1973). Organization of early skilled action. *Child Development, 44*, 1–11.

Bruner, J. S. (1974). The organization of early skilled action. In M. P. M. Richards (Ed.), *The integration of a child into a social world.* London: Cambridge University Press.

Bruner, J. S. (1982). The nature of adult-infant transaction. In M. von Cranach & R. Harré (Eds.), *The analysis of action* (pp. 313–327). Cambridge: Cambridge University Press.

Bruner, J. S., Goodnow, J. J., & Austin, G. A. (1956). *A study of thinking.* New York: Wiley.

Bruner, J. S., Olver, R. R., Greenfield, P. M., Hornsby, J. R., Kenney, H. J., Maccoby, M., Modiano, N., Mosher, F. A., Olson, D. R., Potter, M. C., Reich, L. C., & Sonstroem, A. M. (1966). *Studies in cognitive growth.* New York: Wiley.

Bryant, S. V., French, V., & Bryant, P. J. (1981). Distal regeneration and symmetry. *Science, 212*, 993–1002.

Buck, J., & Buck, E. (1968). Mechanism of rhythmic synchronous flashing of fireflies. *Science, 159*, 1319–1327.

Buck, C. W., Carscallen, H. B., & Hobbs, G. E. (1950). Temperature regulation in schiophrenia. *Archives of Neurology and Psychiatry, 64*, 828–842.

Buck, R. (1984). *The communication of emotion.* New York: Guilford.

Buck, R., & Duffy, R. J. (1980). Nonverbal communication of affect in brain-damaged patients. *Cortex, 16*, 351–362.

Buckley, W. (1967). *Sociology and modern systems theory.* Englewood Cliffs: NJ: Prentice-Hall.

Buckley, W. (Ed.). (1968). *Modern systems research for the behavioral scientist.* Chicago: Aldine.

Bullinger, A., & Chatillon, J-F. (1983). Recent theory and research of the Genevan School. In P. H. Mussen (Ed.), *Handbook of child psychology (4th ed.): Vol. 3. Cognitive development* (pp. 231–262). New York: Wiley.

Bullock, T. H. O. (1959). Neuron doctrine and electrophysiology. *Science, 129*, 997–1002.

Burgess, R. L., & Garbarino, J. (1982). Doing what comes naturally? An evolutionary perspective on child abuse. In D. Finkelhor, R. J. Gelles, G. T. Hotaling, & M. A. Straus (Eds.), *Issues and controversies in the study of family violence* (pp. 88–101). Beverly Hills, CA: Sage.

Burgoon, J. K., Burgoon, M., & Miller, G. R. (1981). Learning theory approaches to persuasion. *Human Communications Research, 7,* 161–179.

Burke, D. M., & Light, L. L. (1981). Memory and aging: The role of retrieval processes. *Psychological Bulletin, 90,* 513–546.

Bursten, B., & Delgado, J. M. R. (1958). Positive reinforcement induced by intracerebral stimulation in the monkey. *Journal of Comparative and Physiological Psychology, 51,* 6–10.

Burt, C. (1962). The concept of consciousness. *British Journal of Psychology, 53,* 229–242.

Bush, M. (1977). The relationship between impaired selective attention and severity of psychopathology in acute psychiatric patients. *British Journal of Medical Psychology, 50,* 251–265.

Buss, A. H. (1980). *Self-consciousness and social anxiety.* San Francisco: Freeman.

Buss, A. H., Iscoe, I., & Buss, E. H. (1979). The development of embarrassment. *Journal of Psychology, 103,* 227–230.

Buss, A. H., & Plomin, R. (1975). *A temperament theory of personality development.* New York: Wiley.

Buss, A. H., & Plomin, R. (1984). *Temperament: Early developing personality traits.* Hillsdale, NJ: Lawrence Erlbaum Associates.

Buss, A. R. (1978). Causes and reasons in attribution theory: A conceptual critique. *Journal of Personality and Social Psychology, 36,* 1311–1321.

Buss, D. M., & Craik, K. H. (1983). The act frequency approach to personality. *Psychological Review, 90,* 104–126.

Butler, R. A. (1957). The effect of deprivation of visual incentives on visual-exploration motivation in monkeys. *Journal of Comparative and Physiological Psychology, 50,* 177–179.

Butter, H. J. (1977). Attention, sensory reception, and autonomic reactivity of hyperkinetic adolescents: A follow-up study. *Psychiatric Journal of the University of Ottawa, 2,* 106–111.

Byrne, R. W. (1982). Geographical knowledge and orientation. In A. W. Ellis (Ed.), *Normality and pathology in cognitive functions* (pp. 239–264). New York: Academic Press.

Cadoret, R. J. (1973). The genetics of affective disorder and genetic counseling. *Social Biology, 23*(2), 116–122.

Cairns, R. B. (1983). The emergence of developmental psychology. In P. H. Mussen (Ed.), *Handbook of child psychology (4th ed.): Vol. 1. History, theory, and methods* (pp. 41–102). New York: Wiley.

Calhoun, J. B. (1972). Disruption of behavioral states as a cause of aggression. In J. K. Cole & D. D. Jensen (Eds.), *Nebraska Symposium on Motivation* (Vol. 20, pp. 183–260). Lincoln: University of Nebraska Press.

Cameron, N. (1947). *The psychology of behavior disorders.* Boston: Houghton-Mifflin.

Cameron, N. (1963). *Personality development and psychopathology: A psychodynamic approach.* Boston: Houghton-Mifflin.

Cameron, N., & Magaret, A. (1951). *Behavior pathology.* New York: Houghton-Mifflin.

Campbell, J. P., & Pritchard, R. D. (1983). Motivation theory in industrial and organizational psychology. In M. D. Dunnette (Ed.), *Handbook of industrial and organizational psychology* (pp. 63–130). New York: Wiley.

Campione, J. C., Brown, A. L., & Ferrara, R. A. (1982). Mental retardation and intelligence. In R. J. Sternberg (Ed.), *Handbook of human intelligence* (pp. 392–492). Cambridge, UK: Cambridge University Press.

Campos, J. J., & Barrett, K. C. (1984). Toward a new understanding of emotions and their development. In C. E. Izard, J. Kagan, & R. B. Zajonc (Eds.), *Emotion, cognition, and behaviors* (pp. 230–252). Cambridge, UK: Cambridge University Press.

Campos, J. J., Barrett, K. C., Lamb, M. E., Goldsmith, H. H., & Steinberg, C. (1983). Socioemotional development. In P. H. Mussen (Ed.), *Handbook of child development: Vol. 2. Infancy and developmental psychobiology* (pp. 783–916). New York: Wiley.

Campos, J. J., Svejda, M. J., Campos, R. G., & Bertenthal, B. (1981). The emergence of self-produced locomotion: Its importance for psychological development in infancy. In D. Bricker (Ed.), *Intervention with at-risk and handicapped infants: From research to application* (pp. 145–216). Baltimore, MD: University Park Press.

Candland, D. K., Fell, J. P., Deen, E., Leshner, A.I., Tarpy, R. M., & Plutchik, R. (1977). *Emotion*. Monterey, CA: Brooks/Cole.

Cannon, W. B. (1939). *The wisdom of the body* (rev. ed.). New York: W. W. Norton.

Capra, F. (1977). *The tao of physics*. New York: Bantam Books.

Caramazza, A., & Berndt, R. S. (1978). Semantic and syntatic processes in aphasia: A review of the literature. *Psychological Bulletin, 85,* 898–918.

Carey, S. (1982). Semantic development: The state of the art. In W. Wanner & L. R. Gleitman (Eds.), *Language acquisition: The state of the art* (pp. 347–389). New York: Cambridge University Press.

Carlson, R. (1981). Studies in script theory: I. Adult analogues of a childhood nuclear scene. *Journal of Personality and Social Psychology, 40,* 501–510.

Carroll, J. B. (1982). The measurement of intelligence. In R. J. Sternberg (Ed.), *Handbook of human intelligence* (pp. 29–122). Cambridge, UK: Cambridge University Press.

Carroll, J. M., & Bever, T. G. (1976). Sentence comprehension: A case study in the relation of knowledge and perception. In E. E. Carterette & M. P. Friedman (Eds.), *Handbook of perception: Vol. 3. Language and speech* (pp. 299–339). New York: Academic Press.

Carroll, J. S., & Wiener, R. L. (1982). Cognitive social psychology in court and beyond. In A. Hastorf & A. Isen (Eds.), *Cognitive social psychology*. New York: Elsevier.

Carson, H. L. (1975). The genetics of speciation at the diploid level. *American Naturalist, 109,* 83.

Carson, L. M., & Wiegand, K. L. (1979). Motor schema formation and retention in young children: A test of Schmidt's schema theory. *Journal of Motor Behavior, 11,* 247–251.

Carterette, E. C., & Friedman, M. P. (Eds.). (1973–1978). *Handbook of perception* (Vols. 1–10). New York: Academic Press.

Carterette, E. C., & Friedman, M. P. (Eds.). (1976). *Handbook of perception: Vol. 7. Language and speech*. New York: Academic Press.

Carterette, E. C., & Friedman, M. P. (Eds.). (1978). *Handbook of perception: Vol. 8. Perceptual coding*. New York: Academic Press.

Carver, C. S. (1979). A cybernetic model of self-attention processes. *Journal of Personality and Social Psychology, 37,* 1251–1281.

Carver, C. S., Blaney, P. H., & Scheier, M. F. (1979). Focus of attention, chronic expectancy, and responses to a feared stimulus. *Journal of Personality and Social Psychology, 37,* 1186–1195.

Carver, C. S., & Scheier, M. F. (1981). *Attention and self-regulation: A control theory approach to human behavior*. New York: Springer-Verlag.

Case, J. (1966). *Sensory mechanisms*. New York: Macmillan.

Case, R. (1985). *Intellectual development: Birth to adulthood*. Orlando, FL: Academic Press.

Cassirer, E. (1944). The concept of group and the theory of perception. *Philosophy and Phenomenological Research, 5,* 1–35.

Catania, A. C. (1978). The psychology of learning: Some lessons from the Darwinian revolution. *Annals of the New York Academy of Sciences, 309o,* 18–29.

Cattell, R. B. (1950). *Personality: A systematic, theoretical and factual study*. New York: McGraw-Hill.

Cattell, R. B. (1957). *Personality and motivation: Structure and measurement*. New York: Harcourt, Brace & World.

Cattell, R. B. (1971). *Abilities: Their structure, growth and action*. Boston: Houghton-Mifflin.

Cattell, R. B. (1972). The nature and genesis of mood states: A theoretical model with experimental measurements concerning anxiety, depression, arousal, and other mood states. In C. D. Spielberger (Ed.), *Anxiety: Current trends in theory and research* (Vol. 1, pp. 115–178). New York: Academic Press.

Cattell, R. B. (1979). *Personality and learning theory* (Vol. 1). New York: Springer.

Cattell, R. B. (1980). *Personality and learning theory* (Vol. 2). New York: Springer.

Cautela, J. R. (1970). Covert reinforcement. *Behavior Therapy, 1,* 33–50.

Cavanaugh, J. C., & Perlmutter, M. (1982). Metamemory: A critical examination. *Child Development, 53,* 11–28.

Cazals, Y., Aran, J. M., Erre, J. P., Guillaume, A., & Hawkins, J. E., Jr. (1979). "Neural" responses to acoustic stimulation after destruction of cochlear hair cells. *Archives of Otorhinolaryngology, 224,* 61–70.

Chapman, L. J., Chapman, J. P., & Raulin, M. L. (1976). Scales for physical and social anhedonia. *Journal of Abnormal Psychology, 85,* 374–382.

Chapman, L. J. (1956a). Distractibility in the conceptual performance of schizophrenics. *Journal of Abnormal Social Psychology, 53,* 286–291.

Chapman, L. J. (1956b). The role of distracter in the "concrete" performance of schizophrenics. *Journal of Personality, 25,* 130–141.

Chapman, M. (1981). Dimensional separability or flexibility of attention? Age trends in perceiving configural stimuli. *Journal of Experimental Child Psychology7, 3,* 332–349.

Charlesworth, W. R., & Kreutzer, M. A. (1973). Facial expressions of infants and children. In P. Ekman (Ed.), *Darwin and facial expression* (pp. 91–168). New York: Academic Press.

Chatterjee, B. B., & Eriksen, C. W. (1960). Conditioning and generalization of GSR as a function of awareness. *Journal of Abnormal and Social Psychology, 60,* 396–403.

Chauchard, P. (1979). Cerebral control and attention. *Psychotherapy and Psychosomatics, 31,* 334–343.

Cheek, J. M., & Busch, C. M. (1981). The influence of shyness on loneliness in a new situation. *Personality and Social Psychology Bulletin, 7,* 572–577.

Cheek, J. M., & Buss, A. H. (1981). Shyness and sociability. *Journal of Personality and Social Psychology, 41,* 330–339.

Chen, L. (1982). Topological structure in visual analysis. *Science, 218,* 699–700.

Chevalier-Skolnikoff, S. (1973). Facial expression in human primates. In P. Ekman (Ed.), *Darwin and facial expression.* New York: Academic Press.

Chi, M. T. H. (1981). Knowledge development and memory performance. In M. Friedman, J. P. Das, & N. O'Connor (Eds.), *Intelligence and learning* (pp. 73–96). New York: Plenum Press.

Chomsky, N. (1972). *Language and mind.* New York: Harcourt, Brace, Jovanovich.

Churchman, C. W. (1979). *The systems approach and its enemies.* New York: Basic Books.

Churchman, C. W., & Ackoff, R. L. (1950). Purposive behavior and cybernetics. *Social Forces, 29,* 32–39.

Churchman, C. W., & Ackoff, R. L. (1968). Purposive behavior in cybernetics. In W. Buckley (Ed.), *Modern systems research for the behavioral scientist.* Chicago: Aldine.

Cialdini, R. B., Petty, R. E., & Cacioppo, J. T. (1981). Attitude and attitude change. *Annual Review of Psychology, 32,* 357–404.

Cicone, M., Wapner, W., Foldi, N., Zurif, E., & Gardner, H. (1979). The relation between gesture and language in aphasics communication. *Brain and Language, 8,* 324–349.

Clark, E. V. (1983). Meanings and concepts. In P. H. Mussen (Ed.), *Handbook of child psychology: Vol. 3. Cognitive development* (pp. 787–840). New York: Wiley.

Clark, E. V., & Hecht, B. F. (1983). Comprehension, production, and language acquisition. *Annual Review of Psychology, 34,* 325–349.

Clark, H. H., & Clark, E. V. (1977). *Psychology and language.* New York: Harcourt, Brace, Jovanovich.

Clark, M. S., & Fiske, S. T. (Eds.). (1982). *Cognition and emotion: The 17th Carnegie-Mellon Symposium.* Hillsdale, NJ: Lawrence Erlbaum Associates.

Cline, M. J. (1975). *The white cell.* Cambridge, MA: Harvard University Press.

Cofer, C. N. (1972). *Motivation and emotion*. Glenview, IL: Scott Foresman.

Cofer, C. N. (1977). On the constructive theory of memory. In I. C. Uzgiris & F. Weizmann (Eds.), *The structure of experience* (pp. 319–342). New York: Plenum Press.

Cofer, C. N., & Appley, M. H. (1964). *Motivation: Theory and research*. New York: Wiley.

Cohen, B. H. (1964). The role of awareness in meaning established by classical conditioning. *Journal of Experimental Psychology, 67*, 373–378.

Cohen, C. E., & Ebbesen, E. B. (1979). Observational goals and schema activation: A theoretical framework for behavior perception. *Journal of Experimental Social Psychology, 15*, 305–329.

Cohen, D. B. (1970). Current research on the frequency of dream recall. *Psychological Bulletin, 73*, 433–440.

Cohen, L. B., DeLoache, J. S., & Strauss, M. S. (1979). Infant visual perception. In J. D. Osofsky (Ed.), *Handbook of infant development* (pp. 393–438). New York: Wiley.

Cohen, L. J. (1979). On the psychology of prediction: Whose is the fallacy? *Cognition, 7*, 385–407.

Cohen, N. J., & Squire, L. R. (1980). Preserved learning and retention of pattern-analyzing skills in amnesia: Dissociation of knowing how and knowing that. *Science, 210*, 207–210.

Cohn, J., & Tronick, E. (1982). Communicative rules and the sequential structure of infant behavior during normal and depressed interaction. In E. Tronick (Ed.), *The development of human communication and the joint regulation of behavior*. Baltimore: University Park Press.

Colby, A. (1979). Paper presented to summer institute on morality and moral development. *Center for Advanced Study in the Behavioral Sciences*. Stanford, CA.

Colby, A., Gibbs, J., Kohlberg, L., Speicher-Dubin, B., Power, C., & Candel, D. (1980). *Standard form scoring manual*. Cambridge, MA: Harvard Graduate School of Education, Center for Moral Education.

Colby, K. M. (1976). Clinical implications of a simulation model of paranoid processes. *Archives of General Psychiatry, 33*, 854–857.

Colby, K. M. (1977). Appraisal of four psychological theories of paranoid phenomena. *Journal of Abnormal Psychology, 86*, 54–59.

Colby, K. M. (1978). Mind models: An overview of current work. *Mathematical BioSciences, 39*, 159–185.

Cole, R. A. (Ed.). (1980). *Perception and production of fluent speech*. Hillsdale, NJ: Lawrence Erlbaum Associates.

Coleman, S. R., & Gormezano, I. (1979). Classical conditioning and the "Law of Effect": Historical and empirical assessment. *Behaviorism, 7(2)*, 1–33.

Collier, R. R. (1956). Consciousness as a regulatory field: A theory of psychopathology. *Psychological Review, 63*, 360–369.

Colquhoun, W. P., & Baddeley, A. D. (1964). Role of pretest expectancy in vigilance decrement. *Journal of Experimental Psychology, 68*, 156–160.

Connolly, T., & Miklausich, V. M. (1978). Some effects of feedback error in diagnostic decision tasks. *Academy of Management Journal, 21*, 301–307.

Cook, M. (Ed.). (1981). *The bases of human sexual attraction*. New York: Academic Press.

Cook, T. D., & Campbell, D. T. (1979). *Quasi-experimentation: Design and analysis issues for field settings*. Chicago: Rand McNally.

Cooke, D. J. (1980). The structure of depression found in the general population. *Psychological Medicine, 10*, 455–463.

Cooley, C. H. (1902). *Human nature and the social order*. New York: Charles Scribner's Sons.

Coon, C. (1963). *The origin of races*. New York: A. Knopf.

Cooper, F. S. (1983). Some reflections on speech research. In P. F. MacNeilage (Ed.), *The production of speech* (pp. 275–290). New York: Springer-Verlag.

Cooper, J., & Croyle, R. T. (1984). Attitudes and attitude change. *Annual Review of*

Psychology, 35, 394–426.

Cooper, J., & Fazio, R. H. (1979). The formation and persistence of attitudes that support intergroup conflict. In W. G. Austin & S. Worchel (Eds.), *The psychology of intergroup relations.* Monterey, CA: Brooks/Cole.

Cooper, L. A., & Regan, D. T. (1982). Attention, perception and intelligence. In R. J. Sternberg (Ed.), *Handbook of human intelligence* (pp. 123–169). Cambridge, UK: Cambridge University Press.

Cooper, L. A., & Shepard, R. N. (1978). Transformation on representations of objects in space. In E. C. Carterette & M. P. Friedman (Eds.), *Handbook of perception: Vol. 8. Perceptual coding* (pp. 104–146). New York: Academic Press.

Cooper, R. G., Jr. (1980). Perception of numbers by infants. *Science, 210,* 1033–1034.

Copeland, A. P., & Wisniewski, N. M. (1981). Learning disability and hyperactivity: Deficits in selective attention. *Journal of Experimental Child Psychology, 32,* 88–101.

Corballis, M. C. (1980). Laterality and myth. *American Psychologist, 35,* 284–295.

Corbin, C. B. (1982). Mental practice. In W. Morgan (Ed.), *Ergogenic aids and muscular performance.* New York: Academic Press.

Cornsweet, T. N. (1970). *Visual perception.* New York: Academic Press.

Corsini, R. J., & Marsella, A. J. (Eds.). (1983). *Personality theories, research and assessment.* Ithaca, IL: Peacock.

Cosier, R. A. (1978). The effects of three potential aids for making strategic decisions on prediction accuracy. *Organizational Behavior and Human Performance, 22,* 295–306.

Costello, J. M. (Ed.). (1984). *Speech disorders in children: Recent advances.* San Diego, CA: College-Hill Press.

Cotman, C. W. (Ed.). (1978). *Neuronal plasticity.* New York: Raven Press.

Cotman, C. W. (1980). Synaptic growth as a plasticity mechanism in the brain. In K. F. Thompson, L. H. Hicks, & V. B. Shvyrkov (Eds.), *Neural mechanisms of goal-directed behavior and learning* (pp. 145–166). New York: Academic Press.

Cotton, J. L. (1981). A review of research on Schachter's theory of emotion and the misattribution of arousal. *European Journal of Social Psychology, 11,* 365–397.

Cotton, J. W. (1976). Models of learning. *Annual Review of Psychology, 27,* 155–187.

Coursin, D. B. (1967). Overview: Relation of nutrition to central nervous system development and function. *Proceedings of the American Societies for Experimental Biology,* January-February.

Cousins, N. (1979). *Anatomy of an illness.* New York: W. W. Norton.

Coutu, W. (1949). *Emergent human nature.* New York: Alfred A. Knopf.

Cowles, R. B. (1958). Possible origin of dermal temperature regulation. *Evolution, 12,* 347.

Coyle, J. T., Price, D. L., & Delong, M. R. (1983). Alzheimer's disease: A disorder of cortical cholinergic innervation. *Science, 219,* 1184–1190.

Crabtree, J. M., & Moyer, K. E. (1977). *Bibliography of aggressive behavior.* New York: Alan R. Liss.

Craig, K. D., Best, H., & Best, J. A. (1978). Self-regulatory effects of monitoring sensory and affective dimensions of pain. *Journal of Consulting and Clinical Psychology, 46,* 573–574.

Craik, F. I. M. (1979). Human memory. *Annual Review of Psychology, 30,* 63–102.

Craik, K. H. (1973). Environmental psychology. *Annual Review of Psychology, 24,* 403–422.

Cratty, B. J. (1967). *Movement behavior and motor learning.* Philadelphia: Lea & Felinger.

Cratty, B. J. (1970). *Perceptual and motor development in infants and children.* New York: Macmillan.

Critchley, E. (1967). *Speech origins and development.* Springfield, IL: Charles C. Thomas.

Crocker, J. (1981). Judgment of covariation by social perceivers. *Psychological Bulletin, 90,* 272–292.

Cronbach, L. J. (1946). Response sets and test validity. *Educational and Psychological*

Measurement, 6, 475–494.

Crozier, W. R. (1979). Shyness as a dimension of personality. *British Journal of Social and Clinical Psychology, 18,* 121–128.

Csikszentmihalyi, M. (1978). Attention and the holistic approach to behavior. In K. S. Pope & J. L. Singer (Eds.), *The stream of consciousness.* New York: Plenum Press.

Cunningham, W. R. (1980). Age comparative factor analysis of ability variables in adulthood and old age. *Intelligence, 4,* 133–149.

Cutting, J. E. (1978). Perceiving the geometry of age in a human face. *Perception and Psychophysics, 24,* 566–568.

Cutting, J. E. (1981). Six tenents for event perception. *Cognition, 10,* 71–78.

Cutting, J. E. (1982). Blowing in the wind: Perceiving structure in trees and bushes. *Cognition, 12,* 25–44.

Cutting, J. E., & Proffitt, D. R. (1982). Minimum principle and the perception of absolute, common, and relative motions. *Cognitive Psychology, 14,* 211–246.

Cutting, J. E., Proffitt, D., & Kozlowski, L. (1978). A biomechanical invariant for gait perception. *Journal of Experimental Psychology, 4,* 357–372.

Cytryn, L., McKnew, D. H., Jr., & Bunney, W. E., Jr. (1980). Diagnosis of depression in children: A reassessment. *American Journal of Psychiatry, 137,* 22–25.

Dagenais, J. J. (1972). *Models of man.* The Hague: Martinus Nijhoff.

Dalby, J. T. (1979). Deficit or delay: Neuropyschological models of developmental dyslexia. *Journal of Special Education, 13,* 239–264.

Dallos, P. (1981). Cochlear physiology. *Annual Review of Psychology, 32,* 153–190.

Daly, R. M. (1978). Lithium-responsive affective disorder. *New York State Journal of Medicine, 78,* 594–601.

Damon, W. (1980). Structural-developmental theory and the study of moral development. In M. Windmiller, N. Lambert, & E. Turiel (Eds.), *Moral development and socialization* (pp. 35–68). Boston: Allyn & Bacon.

Danks, J. H., & Glucksberg, S. (1980). Experimental psycholinguistics. *Annual Review of Psychology, 31,* 391–417.

Darian-Smith, I. (1982). Touch in primates. *Annual Review of Psychology, 33,* 155–194.

Darley, J. M., & Fazio, R. H. (1980). Expectancy confirmation processes arising in the social interaction sequence. *American Psychologist, 35,* 867–881.

Darley, J. M., Klosson, E. C., & Zanna, M. P. (1978). Intentions and their contexts in the moral judgments of children and adults. *Child Development, 49,* 66–74.

Darwin, C. J. (1976). The perception of speech. In E. C. Carterette & M. P. Friedman (Eds.), *Handbook of perception: Vol. 7. Language and speech* (pp. 175–218). New York: Academic Press.

Darwin, C. R. (1872/1955). *The expression of emotions in man and animals.* New York: Philosophical Library.

Darwin, C. R. (1859/1964). *On the origin of the species by means of natural selection, or the preservation of favored races in the struggle for life.* Cambridge, MA: Harvard University Press.

Davidson, D., & Harman, G. (Eds.). (1972). *Semantics of natural language.* New York: Humanities.

Davidson, R. J. (1980). Consciousness and information processing. In J. M. Davidson & R. J. Davidson (Eds.), *The psychobiology of consciousness* (pp. 11–46). New York: Plenum Press.

Davidson, J. M., & Davidson, R. J. (1980). *The psychobiology of consciousness.* New York: Plenum Press.

Davis, K. G., & Hess, H. F. (1962). The effectiveness of concepts at various levels of awareness. *Journal of Experimental Psychology, 63,* 62–67.

Davis, M., Parisi, F., Gendelman, D. S., Tischer, M., & Kehne, J. H. (1982). Habituation and sensitization of startle reflexes elicited electrically from the brainstem. *Science, 218,* 688–689.

Davis, P. (1964). Discrimination without awareness in a psychophysical task. *Perceptual and Motor Skills, 18,* 87–90.

Dawis, R. V., Lofquist, L. H., & Weiss, D. J. (1968). A theory of work adjustment (a revision). *Minnesota Studies in Vocational Rehabilitation XXIII.* Minneapolis: University of Minnesota Press.

Dawson, M. E., Catania, J. J., Schell, A. M., & Grings, W. W. (1979). Autonomic classical conditioning as a function of awareness of stimulus contingencies. *Biological Psychology, 9,* 23–40.

Dawson, M. E., & Furedy, J. J. (1976). The role of awareness of human differential autonomic classical conditioning: The necessary-gate hypothesis. *Psychophysiology, 13,* 50–53.

Day, W. (1978). Contemporary behaviorism and the concept of intention. In J. K. Cole & W. J. Arnold (Eds.), *Nebraska Symposium on Motivation* (Vol. 23, pp. 100–127). Lincoln: University of Nebraska Press.

Dean, S. J., & Hiesinger, L. (1964). Operant level, awareness and the Greenspoon effect. *Psychological Reports, 15,* 931–938.

De Beer, G. R. (1940). *Embryos and ancestors.* Oxford: Clarendon Press.

DeCasper, A. J., & Carstens, A. A. (1981). Contingencies of stimulation: Effects on learning and emotion in neonates. *Infant Behavior and Development, 4,* 18–36.

DeCasper, A. J., & Fifer, W. P. (1980). Of human bonding: Newborns prefer their mothers' voices. *Science, 208,* 1174–1176.

DeCharms, R. (1968). *Personal causation: The internal affective determinants of behavior.* New York: Academic Press.

DeCharms, R. (1976). *Enhancing motivation: Change in the classroom.* New York: Irvington.

Deci, E. L. (1980). *The psychology of self-determination.* Lexington, MA: Lexington Books.

DeFleur, M. L., & Westie, F. R. (1963). Attitude as a scientific concept. *Social Forces, 42,* 17–31.

DeGreene, K. B. (1970). Systems and psychology. In K. B. DeGreene (Ed.), *Systems psychology* (pp. 92–127). New York: McGraw-Hill.

DeGreene, K. B. (1978). Force fields and emergent phenomena in sociotechnical macrosystems: Theories and models. *Behavioral Sciences, 23,* 1–14.

Dehn, N., & Schank, R. (1982). Artificial and human intelligence. In R. J. Sternberg (Ed.), *Handbook of human intelligence* (pp. 352–391). Cambridge: Cambridge University Press.

Delgado, J. M. R. (1970). Modulation of emotions by cerebral radio stimulation. In P. Black (Ed.), *Physiological correlates of emotion* (pp. 189–204). New York: Academic Press.

Delgado, J. M. R., Roberts, W. W., & Miller, N. E. (1954). Learning motivated by electrical stimulation of the brain. *American Journal of Physiology, 179,* 587–593.

Delgado, J. M. R., Rosvold, H. E., & Looney, E. (1956). Evoking conditioned fear by electrical stimulation of subcortical structures in the monkey brain. *Journal of Comparative and Physiological Psychology, 49,* 373–380.

DeLong, A. J. (1972). The communication process: A generic model for man-environment systems. *Man-Environment Systems, 2,* 263–313.

DeLong, A. (1977). Yielding the floor: The Kinesic signals. *Journal of Communication, 27,* 98–103.

Dember, W. N., & Earl, R. W. (1959). Analysis of exploratory, manipulative, and curiosity behaviors. *Psychological Review, 64,* 91–96.

Denny-Brown, D. (1962). The midbrain and motor organization. *Procedures of the Royal Society of Medicine, 55,* 527–538.

DeRivera, J. (1977). A structural theory of emotions. *Psychological Issues Monograph, 10*(4, Whole No. 40). New York: International Universities Press.

Desmedt, J. E. (Ed.). (1983). Motor control mechanisms in health and disease. *Advances in neurology* (Vol. 39). New York: Raven Press.

Desmedt, J. E., & Godaux, E. (1977). Ballistic contractions in man: Characteristic recruitment pattern of single motor units of the tibialis anterior muscle. *Journal of Physiology, 264,* 673–693.

Desmedt, J. E., & Godaux, E. (1978). Ballistic contractions in fast or slow human muscles: Discharge patterns of single motor units. *Journal of Physiology, 285,* 185–196.

Desmedt, J. E., & Godaux, E. (1981). Spinal motoneuron recruitment in man: Rank deordering with direction but not with speed of voluntary movement. *Science, 214,* 933–936.

Deutsch, J. A., & Deutsch, D. (1963). Attention: Some theoretical considerations. *Psychological Review, 70,* 80–90.

Deutsch, K. W. (1950). Mechanism, teleology and mind. *Philosophy and Phenomenological Research, 12,* 185–223.

Deutsch, K. W. (1951). Mechanism, organism and society. *Philosophy of Science, 18,* 230–252.

DeValois, R. L., & DeValois, K. K. (1980). Spatial vision. *Annual Review of Psychology, 31,* 309–341.

Dewan, E. M. (1976). Consciousness as an emergent causal agent in the context of control system theory. In G. G. Globes, G. Maxwell, & I. Savodnik (Eds.), *Consciousness and the brain: A scientific and philosophical inquiry* (pp. 181–199). New York: Plenum Press.

Dewey, J. (1933). *How we think: A restatement of the relation of reflective thinking to the education process.* Boston: Heath.

Diamond, S. R., & Royce, J. R. (1980). Cognitive abilities as expressions of three "ways of knowing." *Multivariate Behavioral Research, 15,* 31–56.

Dichgans, J., & Brandt, T. (1978). Visual-vestibular interaction: Effect on self-motion perception and posture control. In R. Held, H. W. Leibowitz, & H. L. Teuber (Eds.), *Handbook of sensory physiology* (pp. 755–804). New York: Springer.

Dickson, D. R., & Maue-Dickson, W. (1982). *Anatomical and physiological bases of speech.* Boston: Little Brown.

Dickstein, E. (1977). Self and self-esteem: Theoretical foundations and their implications for research. *Human Development, 20,* 129–140.

Dienstbier, R. A. (1984). Role of emotion in moral socialization. In C. E. Izard, J. Kaplan, & R. B. Zajonc (Eds.), *Emotions, cognition and behavior* (pp. 480–505). New York: Cambridge University Press.

Dismukes, R. K. (1979). New concepts of molecular communication among neurons. *The Behavioral and Brain Sciences, 2,* 409–448.

Ditchburn, R. W., & Ginsborg, B. L. (1952). Vision with a stabilized retinal image. *Nature, 170,* 36–37.

Dittman, A. T. (1972). *Interpersonal messages of emotion.* New York: Springer.

Dobrolowicz, W. (1977). On conceptions concerning attention. *Przeglad Psychologiczny, 20,* 315–335.

Dobzhansky, T., Ayala, F. J., Stebbins, G. L., & Valentine, J. W. (1977). *Evolution.* San Francisco: Freeman.

Doise, W., & Mackie, D. (1981). On the nature of social cognition. In J. Forgas (Ed.), *Social cognition.* London: Academic Press.

Dollard, J., & Miller, N. E. (1950). *Personality and psychotherapy.* New York: McGraw-Hill.

Donchin, E. (1981). Surprise! ... Surprise? *Psychophysiology, 18,* 493–513.

Dorpat, T. L. (1977). Depressive affect. *The Psychoanalytic Study of the Child, 32,* 3–227.

Downs, R. M., & Stea, D. (1977). *Maps in minds: Reflections on cognitive mapping.* New York: Harper & Row.

Dubin, R. (1978). *Theory building* (rev. ed.). New York: The Free Press.

Dubos, R. J. (1973). *A god within*. London: Angus & Robertson.

Duffy, E. (1951). The concept of energy mobilization. *Psychological Review, 58,* 30–40.

Duffy, E. (1962). *Activation and behavior*. New York: Wiley.

Dumont, J. P. C., & Robertson, R. M. (1986). Neural circuits: An evolutionary perspective. *Science, 233,* 849–852.

Dunbar, H. F. (1954). *Emotions and bodily changes* (4th ed.). New York: Columbia University Press.

Duncan, J. (1978). Response selection in spatial choice reaction: Further evidence against associative models. *Quarterly Journal of Experimental Psychology, 30,* 429–440.

Duncan, J. (1980). The demonstration of capacity limitation. *Cognitive Psychology, 12,* 75–96.

Duncan, S., Jr., & Fiske, D. W. (1977). *Face-to-face interaction: Research, methods and theory*. Hillsdale, NJ: Lawrence Erlbaum Associates.

Duncan, S. D., Jr. (1969). Nonverbal communication. *Psychological Bulletin, 72,* 118–137.

Dunn, J. (In press). Understanding feelings: The early stages. In J. Bruner & H. Weinreich-Haste (Eds.), *Making sense: The child's construction of the world*. London: Methuen.

Dusek, J. B. (1978). The effects of labeling and pointing on children's selective attention. *Developmental Psychology, 14,* 115–116.

Dweck, C. S., & Elliott, E. S. (1983). Achievement motivation. In P. H. Mussen (Ed.), *Handbook of child psychology (4th ed.): Vol. 4. Socialization, personality, and social development* (pp. 643–691). New York: Wiley.

Eagly, A. H., & Himmelfarb, S. (1978). Attitudes and opinions. *Annual Review of Psychology, 29,* 517–554.

Easton, T. (1972). On the normal use of reflexes. *American Scientist, 60,* 591–599.

Eccles, J. C. (Ed.). (1966). *Brain and conscious experience*. New York: Springer-Verlag.

Eccles, J. C. (1976). Brain and free will. In G. G. Globus, G. Maxwell, & I. Savodnik (Eds.), *Consciousness and the brain: A scientific and philosophical inquiry* (pp. 101–122). New York: Plenum Press.

Eccles, J. C. (1977). *The understanding of the brain* (2nd ed.). New York: McGraw-Hill.

Edelman, G. M. (1978). Group selection and phasic reentrant signaling: A theory of higher brain function. In G. M. Edelman & V. B. Mountcastle (Eds.), *The mindful brain* (pp. 51–95). Cambridge, MA: MIT Press.

Edelmann, R. J., & Hampson, S. E. (1979). Changes in non-verbal behaviour during embarrassment. *British Journal of Social and Clinical Psychology, 18,* 385–390.

Edinger, J. A., & Patterson, M. L. (1983). Nonverbal involvement and social control. *Psychological Bulletin, 93,* 30–56.

Edmunds, L. N., & Adams, K. J. (1981). Clocked cell cycle clocks. *Science, 211,* 1002–1013.

Eger, E. I., II. (1974). *Anesthetic uptake and action*. Baltimore: Williams & Wilkins.

Egeth, H., & Bevan, W. (1973). Attention. In B. B. Wolman (Ed.), *Handbook of general psychology* (pp. 395–418). Englewood Cliffs, NJ: Prentice-Hall.

Ehrlich, S. (1979). Semantic memory: A free elements system. In C. R. Ruff (Ed.), *Memory organization and structure* (pp. 195–218). New York: Academic Press.

Ehrman, L., & Parsons, P. A. (1981). *Behavior genetics and evolution*. New York: McGraw-Hill.

Eibl-Eibesfeldt, I. (1970). *Ethology, the biology of behavior*. New York: Holt, Rinehart & Winston.

Eibl-Eibesfeldt, I. (1971). *Love and hate*. New York: Holt, Rinehart & Winston.

Eich, J. M. (1985). Levels of processing, encoding specificity, elaboration and charm. *Psychological Review, 92,* 1–38.

Eichorn, D. H. (1979). Physical development: Current foci of research. In J. Osofsky (Ed.), *The handbook of infant development* (pp. 253–282). New York: Wiley.

Eimas, P. D. (1975). Speech perception in early infancy. In L. B. Cohen & P. Salapetak (Eds.), *Infant perception from sensation to cognition: II: Perception of space, speech and sound* (pp. 193–232). New York: Academic Press.

Eimas, P. D., & Miller, J. L. (Eds.). (1981). *Perspectives on the study of speech.* Hillsdale, NJ: Lawrence Erlbaum Associates.

Eimas, P. D., & Tartter, S. (1979). On the development of speech perception: Mechanisms and analogies. In H. W. Reese & L. P. Lipsitt (Eds.), *Advances in child development and behavior* (Vol. 13, pp. 155–194). New York: Academic Press.

Einhorn, H. J. (1982). Learning from experience and suboptimal rules in decision making. In D. Kahneman, P. Slovic, & A. Tversky (Eds.), *Judgment under uncertainty: Heuristics and biases* (pp. 268–286). Cambridge, UK: Cambridge University Press.

Eisenberg, R. B. (1976). *Auditory competence in early life.* Baltimore: University Park Press.

Eisenberg-Berg, N. (1979). Development of children's prosocial moral judgment. *Developmental Psychology, 15,* 128–137.

Eisenberg-Berg, N., & Neal, C. (1979). Children's moral reasoning about their own spontaneous pro-social behavior. *Developmental Psychology, 15,* 228–229.

Eisenberg-Berg, N., & Roth, K. (1980). Development of young children's prosocial moral judgment: A longitudinal follow-up. *Developmental Psychology, 16,* 375–376.

Ekehammar, B. (1978a). Toward a psychological cost-benefit model for educational vocational choice. *Scandinavian Journal of Psychology, 19,* 15–27.

Ekehammar, B. (1978b). Psychological cost-benefit as an intervening construct in career choice models. *Journal of Vocational Behavior, 12,* 279–283.

Ekman, P. (1972). Universal and cultural differences in facial expressions of emotion. In J. K. Cole (Ed.), *Nebraska Symposium on Motivation* (Vol. 9, pp. 207–284). Lincoln: University of Nebraska Press.

Ekman, P. (Ed.). (1973). *Darwin and facial expression.* New York: Academic Press.

Ekman, P. (1977). Biological and cultural contributions to body and facial movement. In J. Blacking (Ed.), *The anthropology of the body* (A.S.A. Monograph No. 15, pp. 39–84). New York: Academic Press.

Ekman, P. (1978). Facial signs: Facts, fantasies, and possibilities. In T. Sebeok (Ed.), *Sight, sound and sense* (pp. 124–156). Bloomington: Indiana University Press.

Ekman, P. (1979). About brows: Emotional and conversational signals. In M. von Cranach, K. Foppa, W. Lepenies, & D. Ploog (Eds.), *Human ethology* (169–249). New York: Academic Press.

Ekman, P. (1981). Mistakes when deceiving. *Annals of the New York Academy of Sciences, 364,* 269–278.

Ekman, P. (Ed.). (1982). *Emotion in the human face* (2nd ed.). Cambridge, UK: Cambridge University Press.

Ekman, P. (1984). Expression and the nature of emotion. In K. Scherer & P. Ekman (Eds.), *Approaches to emotion.* Hillsdale, NJ: Lawrence Erlbaum Associates.

Ekman, P., & Friesen, W. V. (1969a). The repertoire of nonverbal behavior: Categories, origins, usage, and coding. *Semiotica, 1,* 49–58.

Ekman, P., & Friesen, W. V. (1969b). Nonverbal leakage and clues to deception. *Psychiatry, 1,* 88–105.

Ekman, P., & Friesen, W. V. (1975). *Unmasking the face.* Englewood Cliffs, NJ: Prentice-Hall.

Ekman, P., & Friesen, W. V. (1976). Measuring facial movement. *Environmental Psychology and Nonverbal Behavior, 1,* 56–75.

Ekman, P., & Friesen, W. V. (1982). Felt, false, and miserable smiles. *Journal of Nonverbal Behavior, 6,* 238–252.

Ekman, P. W., Friesen, W. V., & Ellsworth, P. (1972). *Emotions in the human face.* New York: Pergamon Press.

Ekman, P., Levenson, R. W., & Friesen, W. V. (1983). Autonomic nervous system activity distinguishes among emotions. *Science, 221,* 1208–1210.

Ekman, P., & Oster, H. (1979). Facial expression of emotions. *Annual Review of Psychology, 30,* 527–554.

Elder, G. (1980). *Family structure and socialization.* New York: Arno Press.

Eldredge, N., & Gould, S. J. (1972). Punctuated equilibria: An alternative to phyletic gradualism. In T. J. M. Schoof (Ed.), *Models in paleobiology* (pp. 82–115). San Francisco: Freeman, Cooper.

Ellenberg, L., & Sperry, R. W. (1980). Lateralized division of attention in the commissurotomized and intact brain. *Neuropsychologia, 18,* 411–418.

Elliott, J., & Connolly, K. (1974). Hierarchical structure in skill development. In K. Connolly & J. Bruner (Eds.), *Growth of competence* (pp. 135–168). New York: Academic Press.

Ellis, A. W. (Ed.). (1982). *Normality and pathology in cognitive functions.* New York: Academic Press.

Ellsworth, P. C., & Ludwig, L. M. (1972). Visual behavior in social interaction. *Journal of Communication, 22,* 375–403.

Elwes, R. H. (Ed.). (1951). *The chief works of Benedict de Spinoza* (Vol. 2). New York: Dover.

Emde, R. N., Gaensbauer, T., & Harmon, R. J. (1976). *Emotional expression in infancy: A biobehavioral study.* New York: International Universities Press.

Emde, R. N., Kligman, D. H., Reich, J. H., & Wade, T. D. (1978). Emotional expression in infancy: I. Initial studies of social signaling and an emergent model. In M. Lewis & L. A. Rosenblum (Ed.), *The development of affect* (pp. 125–148). New York: Plenum Press.

Emson, P. C. (Ed.). (1983). *Chemical neuroanatomy.* New York: Raven.

Endler, N. S., & Magnusson, D. (1976). Toward an interactional psychology of personality. *Psychological Bulletin, 33,* 956–974.

Eng, E. (1978). Looking back on Kurt Lewin: From field theory to action research. *Journal of the History of the Behavioral Sciences, 14,* 228–232.

Engen, T. (1973). The sense of smell. *Annual Review of Psychology, 24,* 187–206.

Epstein, S. (1972). The nature of anxiety with emphasis upon its relationship to expectancy. In C. D. Spielberger (Ed.), *Anxiety: current trends in theory and research* (Vol. 2, pp. 52–96). New York: Academic Press.

Epstein, S. (1973). The self-concept revisited or a theory of a theory. *American Psychologist, 28,* 404–416.

Epstein, S. (1979). The stability of behavior: I. On predicting most of the people much of the time. *Journal of Personality and Social Psychology, 37,* 1097–1126.

Epstein, S. (1981). The unity principle versus the reality and pleasure principles, or the tale of the scorpion and the frog. In M. D. Lynch, A. A. Norem-Hebeisen, & K. Gergen (Eds.), *Self-concept: Advances in theory and research* (pp. 27–37). Cambridge, MA: Ballinger.

Epstein, S. (1982). The stability of behavior across time and situations. In I. Robin, A. M. Aronoff, A. M. Barclay, & R. Zucker (Eds.), *Further explorations in personality* (Vol. 2). New York: Wiley.

Epstein, S., & O'Brien, E. J. (1985). The person-situation debate in historical and current perspective. *Psychological Bulletin, 98,* 513–537.

Epstein, S., Rosenthal, S., & Szpiler, J. (1978). The influence of attention upon anticipatory arousal, habituation, and reactivity to a noxious stimulus. *Journal of Research in Personality, 12,* 30–46.

Erickson, E. H. (1963). *Childhood and society.* New York: W. W. Norton.

Erickson, J. R., & Jones, M. R. (1978). Thinking. *Annual Review of Psychology, 29,* 61–90.

Erickson, R. P. (1968). Stimulus coding in topographic and nontopographic afferentmodalities: On the significance of the activity of individual sensory neurons.

Psycho logical Review, 75, 447–465.

Eriksen, C. W. (Ed.). (1962). *Behavior and awareness.* Durham, NC: Duke University.

Eriksen, C. W., & Doroz, L. (1963). Role of awareness in learning and use of correlated extraneous cues on perceptual tasks. *Journal of Experimental Psychology, 66,* 601–108.

Eriksen, C. W., & Schultz, D. W. (1979). Information processing in visual search: A continuous flow conception and experimental results. *Perception and Pschophysics, 25,* 249–263.

Erlich, S. (1979). Semantic memory: A free elements system. In C. R. Puff (Ed.), *Memory organization and structure* (pp. 195–218). New York: Academic Press.

Ernest, C. H. (1977). Imagery ability and cognition: A critical review. *Journal of Mental Imagery, 2,* 181–216.

Eshragh, F. (1980). Subjective multi-criteria decision making. *International Journal of Man-Machine Studies, 13,* 117–141.

Espenschade, A. S., & Eckert, H. M. (1980). *Motor development.* Columbus, OH: Merrill.

Esser, A. H. (Ed.). (1971). *Behavior and environment.* New York: Plenum Press.

Estes, W. K. (1959). The statistical approach to learning theory. In S. Koch (Ed.), *Psychology: A study of a science II* (pp. 380–491). New York: McGraw-Hill.

Estes, W. K. (Ed.). (1976). *Handbook of learning and cognitive processes: Vol. 4. Attention and memory.* Hillsdale, NJ: Lawrence Erlbaum Associates.

Estes, W. K. (1982). Learning memory and intelligence. In R. J. Sternberg (Ed.), *Handbook of human intelligence* (pp. 170–224). Cambridge, UK: Cambridge University Press.

Evans, G. W. (1980). Environmental cognition. *Psychological Bulletin, 88,* 259–287.

Evans, J. St. B. T. (1980). Current issues in the psychology of reasoning. *British Journal of Psychology, 71,* 227–239.

Everitt, A. V., & Huang, C. Y. (1980). The hypothalamus, neuroendocrine, and autonomic nervous systems in aging. In J. E. Birren & R. B. Sloane (Eds.), *Handbook of mental health and aging* (pp. 100–133). Englewood Cliffs, NJ: Prentice-Hall.

Eysenck, M. W. (1982). *Attention and arousal.* Berlin: Springer-Verlag.

Fagan, J. F., III. (1984). Infant memory: History, current trends, relations to cognitive psychology. In M. Moscowitch (Ed.), *Infant memory* (pp. 1–28). New York: Plenum Press.

Faingold, C. L. (1978). Brainstem reticular formation mechanisms subserving generalized seizures: Effects of convulsants and anticonvulsants on sensory-evoked potential. *Progress in Neuro-Psychopharmacology, 2,* 401–422.

Faingold, C. L., & Stittsworth, J. D., Jr. (1980). Comparative effects of pentylenetetragol on the sensory responsiveness of lateral geniculate and reticular formation neurons. *Electroencephalography and Clinical Neurophysiology, 49,* 168–172.

Falkner, F. (Ed.). (1966). *Human development.* Philadelphia: W. B. Saunders.

Fantz, R. L., & Yeh, J. (1979). Configurational selectivities critical for development of visual perception and attention. *Canadian Journal of Psychology, 33,* 277–287.

Farber, M. L. (1968). *Theory of suicide.* New York: Funk & Wagnalls.

Farley, A. M. (1980). Issues in knowledge-based problem solving. *IEEE Transactions on Systems, Man, and Cybernetics* (SMC), *10,* 446–459.

Farley, J., & Alkon, D. L. (1985). Cellular mechanisms of learning, memory and information storage. *Annual Review of Psychology, 36,* 419–494.

Fazio, R. H., & Zanna, M. P. (1978). On the predictive validity of attitudes: The roles of direct experience and confidence. *Journal of Personality, 46,* 228–243.

Fazio, R. H., & Zanna, M. P. (1981). Direct experience and attitude-behavior consistency. *Advances in Experimental Social Psychology, 14,* 161–202.

Feather, N. T. (Ed.). (1982). *Expectations and actions: Expectancy-value models in psychology.* Hillsdale, NJ: Lawrence Erlbaum Associates.

Fehr, L. A., & Stamps, L. E. (1976). Guilt and shyness: A profile of social discomfort.

Journal of Personality Assessment, 4, 481–484.

Feldman, R. S. (Ed.). (1982). *Development of nonverbal behavior in children.* New York: Springer-Verlag.

Ferster, C., & Skinner, B. F. (1957). *Schedules of reinforcement.* New York: Appleton-Century-Crofts.

Festinger, L. (1957). *A theory of cognitive dissonance.* Stanford, CA: Stanford University Press.

Field, T. M., & Walden, T. (1982). Perception and production of facial expressions in infancy and early childhood. In H. W. Reese & L. P. Lipsitt (Eds.), *Advances in child development and behavior* (Vol. 16, pp. 171–212). New York: Academic Press.

Field, T. M., Woodson, R., Greenberg, R., & Cohen, D. (1982). Discrimination and imitation of facial expressions by neonates. *Science, 218,* 179–181.

Finch, C. E., & Hayflick, L. (1977). *Handbook of the biology of aging.* New York: Van Nostrand Reinhold.

Finkelstein, N. W., & Ramey, C. T. (1977). Learning to control the environment in infancy. *Child Development, 48,* 809–819.

Firth, C. D. (1978). Feature selection and classification: A developmental study. *Journal of Experimental Child Psychology, 25,* 413–428.

Fischer, K. W. (1980). A theory of cognitive development: The control and construction of hierarchies of skills. *Psychological Review, 8,* 477–531.

Fischer, K. W., & Silvern, L. (1985). Stages and individual differences in cognitive development. *Annual Review of Psychology, 36,* 613–648.

Fishbein, M. (1979). A theory of reasoned action: Some applications and implications. In M. M. Page (Ed.), Beliefs, attitudes and values. *Nebraska Symposium on Motivation* (Vol. 27, pp. 65–116). Lincoln: University of Nebraska Press.

Fishbein, M., & Ajzen, I. (1975). *Beliefs attitude, intention and behavior: An introduction to theory and research.* Reading, MA: Addison-Wesley.

Fisher, W. A., & Byrne, D. (1978). Sex differences in response to erotica? Love versus lust. *Journal of Personality and Social Psychology, 36,* 117–125.

Fiske, D. W., & Maddi, S. R. (1961). *Functions of varied experience.* Homewood, IL: Dorsey Press.

Fiske, S. T. (1982). Schema-triggered affect: applications to social perception. In M. S. Clarke & S. T. Fiske (Eds.), *Cognition and emotion: The Carnegie-Mellon Symposium* (pp. 57–78). Hillsdale, NJ: Lawrence Erlbaum Associates.

Fiske, S. T., & Linville, P. W. (1980). What does the schema concept buy us? *Personality and Social Psychology Bulletin, 6,* 543–557.

Flavell, J. H. (1976). Metacognitive aspects. In L. B. Resnick (Ed.), *The nature of intelligence* (pp. 231–236). Hillsdale, NJ: Lawrence Erlbaum Associates.

Flavell, J. H. (1979). Meta cognition and cognitive monitoring. *American Psychologist, 34,* 906–911.

Flavell, J. H. (1981). Cognitive monitoring. In W. P. Dickson (Ed.), *Children's oral communication skills* (pp. 35–60). New York: Academic Press.

Flavell, J. H., & Wellman, H. M. (1977). Metamemory. In V. Kail, Jr., & J. W. Hogen (Eds.), *Perspectives on the development of memory and cognition.* Hillsdale, NJ: Lawrence Erlbaum Associates.

Fleury, P. A. (1981). Phase transitions, critical phenomena, and instabilities. *Science, 211,* 125–131.

Fodor, J. A. (1981). *Representations: Philosophical essays on the foundations of cognitive science.* Cambridge, MA: MIT Press.

Fodor, J. A., & Pylyshyn, Z. (1981). How direct is visual perception? Some reflections on Gibson's "ecological approach." *Cognition, 9,* 139–196.

Foley, J. M. (1978). Primary distance perception. In R. Held, H. W. Leibowitz, & H. L.

Tauber (Ed.), *Handbook of sensory physiology: Vol. 8. Perception* (pp. 181–213). Berlin: Springer.

Follett, B. K., & Follett, D. E. (Eds.). (1981). *Biological clocks in seasonal reproductive cycles.* New York: Halstead (Wiley).

Ford, C. M. (1987). *Emotional patterns as personality components of behavior episodes.* Work in progress, College of Business Administration, The Pennsylvania State University.

Ford, C. S., & Beach, F. A. (1951). *Patterns of sexual behavior.* New York: Harper & Row.

Ford, D. H., & Urban, H. B. (1963). *Systems of psychotherapy.* New York: Wiley.

Ford, D. H., & Urban, H. B. (1966). College dropouts: Successes or failures. In L. A. Pervin, L. E. Reik, & W. Dalrymple (Eds.), *The college dropout and the utilization of talent.* Princeton, NJ: Princeton University Press.

Ford, D. H., & Urban, H. B. (1967). Psychotherapy. *Annual Review of Psychology, 18,* 333–372.

Ford, M. E., & Ford, D. H. (Eds.) (1987). *Humans as self-constructing living systems: Putting the framework to work.* Hillsdale, NJ: Lawrence Erlbaum Associates.

Forgas, J. (1979). Social episodes: The study of interaction routines. *European Monographs in Social Psychology, 17.* London: Academic Press.

Foster, H. (1962). The operation of set in a visual search task. *Journal of Experimental Psychology, 63,* 74–83.

Foulkes, D. (1971). Longitudinal studies of dreams in children. In J. Mosserman (Ed.), *Science and psychoanalysis.* New York: Grune & Stratton.

Foulkes, D., & Fleisher, S. (1975). Mental activity in relaxed wakefulness. *Journal of Abnormal Psychology, 84,* 66–75.

Fourcin, A. J. (1975). Language development in the absence of expressive speech. In E. H. Lennenberg (Ed.), *Foundations of language development* (pp. 263–268). New York: Academic Press.

Fowler, C. A. (1978). Coarticulation and theories of extrinsic timing. *Journal of Phonetics, 6,* 37–67.

Fowler, W. (1977). Sequence and styles in cognitive development. In I. C. Uzgiris & F. Weizmann (Eds.), *The structuring of experience* (pp. 265–296). New York: Plenum Press.

Fox, J. (1980). Making decisions under the influence of memory. *Psychological Review, 87,* 190–211.

Fozard, J. L. (1981). Person-environment relationships in adulthood: Implications for human factors engineering. *Human Factors, 23,* 7–27.

Fraisse, P. (1978). Time and rhythm perception. In E. C. Carterette & M. P. Friedman (Eds.), *Handbook of perception: Vol. 3. Perceptual coding* (pp. 203–247). New York: Academic Press.

Fraisse, P. (1984). Perception and estimation of time. *Annual Review of Psychology, 35,* 1–36.

Frank, J. D. (1941). Recent studies of the level of aspiration. *Psychological Bulletin, 38,* 218–226.

Frank, J. D. (1968). The role of hope in psychotherapy. *International Journal of Psychiatry, 15,* 383–395.

Frank, J. D. (1978). Kurt Lewin in retrospect: A psychiatrist's view. *Journal of the History of the Behavioral Sciences, 14,* 223–227.

Frankl, V. E. (1963). *Man's search for meaning: An introduction to logotherapy.* New York: Washington Square.

Frederick, J. F. (Ed.). (1981). Origins and evolution of eukaroytic intracellular organelles. *Annals of the New York Academy of Sciences* (Vol. 361). New York: New York Academy of Sciences.

Fredericksen, G. H. (1975). Representing logical and semantic structure of knowledge acquired from discourse. *Cognitive Psychology, 7,* 371–378.

Freed, W. J., deMedinaceli, L., & Wyatt, R. J. (1985). Promoting functional plasticity in the damaged nervous system. *Science, 227,* 1544–1552.

Freedle, R. O. (Ed.). (1977). *Discourse production and comprehension.* Norwood, NJ: Ablex.

Freeman, W. (1975). *Mass action in the nervous system.* New York: Academic Press.

French, J. D. Herna'ndes-Peo'n, R., & Livingston, R. B. (1955). Projections from cortex to cephalic brain stem (reticular formation) in monkey. *Journal of Neurophysiology, 18,* 44–55.

Freud, S. (1933). *New introductory lectures in psychoanalysis.* New York: W. W. Norton.

Freud, S. (1938). *The basic writings of Sigmund Freud* (A. A. Brill, Trans.). New York: Random House.

Freud, S. (1955a). *The interpretation of dreams.* New York: Basic Books.

Freud, S. (1955b). *The standard edition of the complete psychological works of Sigmund Freud* (J. Strachey, Ed.). London: Hogarth Press.

Freud, S. (1957a). Mourning and melancholia. In J. Strachey (Ed. and Trans.), *Standard edition of the complete psychological works of Sigmund Freud* (Vol. 14). London: Hogarth Press. (Original work published 1915)

Freud, S. (1957b). Instincts and their vicissitudes. In J. Strachey (Ed. and Trans.), *Standard edition of the complete psychological works of Sigmund Freud* (Vol. 14). London: Hogarth Press. (Originally published 1915)

Freud, S. (1961). The ego and the id. In J. Strachey (Ed. and Trans.), *Standard edition of the complete psychological works of Sigmund Freud* (Vol. 19). London: Hogarth Press. (Originally published 1923)

Freud, S. (1961). Inhibition, symptoms, and anxiety. In J. Strachey (Ed. and Trans.), *Standard edition of the complete psychological works of Sigmund Freud* (Vol. 20). London: Hogarth Press. (Originally published 1926)

Friendly, M. (1979). Methods for finding graphic representations of associative memory structures. In C. R. Puff (Ed.), *Memory organization and structure* (pp. 85–125). New York: Academic Press.

Fries, M. E. (1961). Some factors in the development and significance of early object relationships. *Journal of American Psychoanalytic Association, 9,* 669–683.

Friesen, V. I. (1979). On shame and the family. *Family Therapy, 6,* 39–58.

Friesen, W. V., Ekman, P. & Wallbott, H. (1979). Measuring hand movements. *Journal of Nonverbal Behavior, 4,* 97–112.

Fromkin, V. (Ed.). (1980). *Errors of linguistic performance: Slips of the tongue, ear, pen, and hands.* New York: Academic Press.

Fromm, E. (1976). Altered states of consciousness and ego psychology. *Social Service Review, 50,* 557–569.

Frost, T., Stimpson, D. V., & Maughan, M. R. C. (1978). Some correlates of trust. *Journal of Psychology, 99,* 103–108.

Fry, D. B. (1970). Prosodic phenomena. In B. Malmberg (Ed.), *Manual of phonetics* (pp. 365–410). Amsterdam: North-Holland.

Fuenzalida, C., Emde, R. N., & Pannabecker, B. J. (1981). Validation of the differential emotions scale in 613 mothers. *Motivation and Emotion, 5,* 37–45.

Furlong, F. W. (1981). Determinism and free will: Review of the literature. *American Journal of Psychiatry, 138,* 435–346.

Furth, H. G. (1966). *Thinking without language.* New York: The Free Press.

Fyans, L. (Ed.). (1980). *Recent trends in achievement motivation theory and research.* New York: Plenum Press.

Gabor, D. (1972). Holography, 1948–1971. *Science, 177,* 299–313.

Gagné, R. M. (1968). Contributions of learning to human development. *Psychological Review, 75,* 177–191.

Gagné, R. M., & Dick, W. (1983). Instructional psychology. *Annual Review of Psychology, 34,* 261–295.

Gagné, R. M., & White, R. T. (1978). Memory structures and learning outcomes. *Review of Educational Research, 48,* 187–222.

Gallahue, D. L. (1982a). *Understanding motor development in children.* New York: Wiley.

Gallahue, D. L. (1982b). *Developmental movement experiences for children.* New York: Wiley.

Galler, J. R. (Ed.). (1984). *Nutrition and behavior: Human nutrition: A comprehensive treatis* (Vol. 15). New York: Plenum Press.

Gallistel, C. R. (1980a). *The organization of action: A new synthesis.* Hillsdale, NJ: Lawrence Erlbaum Associates.

Gallistel, C. R. (1980b). From muscles to motivation. *American Scientist, 68,* 398–409.

Galton, F. (1883). *Inquiries into human faculty and its development.* London: Macmillan.

Garbarino, J., & Bronfenbrenner, U. (1976). The socialization of moral judgment and behavior in cross-cultural perspective. In L. Likona (Ed.), *Moral development and behavior.* New York: Holt, Rinehart & Winston.

Garbarino, J., & Sherman, D. (1980). High-risk neighborhoods and high-risk families: The human ecology of child maltreatment. *Child Development, 51,* 188–198.

Garber, J., & Hollon, S. D. (1980). Universal versus personal helplessness in depression: Belief in uncontrollability or incompetence? *Journal of Abnormal Psychology, 189,* 56–66.

Garber, J., & Seligman, M. E. P. (Eds.). (1980). *Human helplessness: Theory and applications.* New York: Academic Press.

Garcia, J., Clarke, J. C., & Harkins, W. G. (1973). Natural responses to scheduled rewards. In P. P. Bateson & P. H. Klopfer (Eds.), *Perspectives in ethology* (Vol. 1, pp. 1–41). New York: Plenum Press.

Gardner, H. (1979). Developmental psychology after Piaget: An approach in terms of symbolization. *Human Development, 22,* 73–88.

Gardner, R. W. (1953). Cognitive styles in categorizing behavior. *Journal of Personality, 22,* 214–233.

Gardner, R. W. (1966). Cognitive controls of attention development as determinants of visual illusions. In P. Bakan (Ed.), *Attention* (pp. 58–75). Princeton, NJ: Van Nostrand.

Gardner, R. W., Holtzman, P. S., Klein, G. S., Linton, H., & Spence, D. P. (1959). Cognitive control: A study of individual consistencies in cognitive behavior. *Psychological Issues, 1(Whole No. 4).*

Gardner, R. W., & Long, R. I. (1960). Cognitive controls as determinants of learning and remembering. *Psychologia, 3,* 165–171.

Gardner, R. W., & Long, R. I. (1962). Cognitive controls of attention and inhibition: A study of individual consistencies. *British Journal of Psychology, 53,* 381–388.

Gardner, R. W., Long, R. I., Lohrenz, L., Schoen, R., & Riggin, G. (1961). The stability and generality of cognitive attitudes. *Final Progress Report on Research Grant* (No. M-2454). Rockville, MD: National Institute of Mental Health.

Garmezy, N. (1977). The psychology and psychopathology of attention. *Schizophrenia Bulletin, 3,* 360–369.

Garner, W. R. (1978). Selective attention to attributes and to stimuli. *Journal of Experimental Psychology: General, 107,* 287–308.

Gasanov, G. G. (Ed.). (1974). *Emotions and visceral functions.* Moscow: Elm Press.

Gasanov, U. G., Galoshina, A. G., & Bogdanov, A. V. (1980). A study of neuron systems activity in learning. In R. F. Thompson, L. H. Hicks, & V. B. Shvyrkov (Eds.), *Neural mechanisms of goal-directed behavior and learning* (pp. 341–352). New York: Academic Press.

Gazzaniga, M. S., & LeDoux, E. (1978). *The integrated mind.* New York: Plenum Press.

Gebhard, P. H. (1965). Situational factors affecting human sexual behavior. In F. A. Beach (Ed.), *Sex and behavior* (pp. 483–495). New York: Wiley.

Gehring, W. J. (1985). The molecular basis of development. *Scientific American, 253,* 153–162.

Geldard, F. A. (1982). Saltation in somesthesis. *Psychological Bulletin, 92,* 136–175.

Gellhorn, E. (1965). The Neurophysiological basis of anxiety: A hypothesis. *Perspectives in Biology and Medicine, 8,* 488–515.

Gellhorn, E., & Loofbourrow, G. N. (1963). *Emotions and emotional disorders: Hoeber Medical Division.* New York: Harper & Row.

Gelman, R. (1978). Cognitive development. *Annual Review of Psychology, 29,* 297–332.

Gelman, R., & Baillargeon, R. (1983). A review of some Piagetian concepts. In P. H. Mussen (Ed.), *Handbook of child psychology: Vol. 3. Cognitive development* (pp. 167–230). New York: Wiley.

Gelman, R., & Gallistel, C. R. (1978). *The child's understanding of number.* Cambridge, MA: Harvard University Press.

George, C. (1980). Attention and information processing in human instrumental learning. *Anne'e Psychologique, 80,* 481–500.

George, F. H. (1977). *The foundations of cybernetics.* New York: Gordon & Breach Science Publishers, Inc.

Gerard, R. W. (1968). The neurophysiology of purposive behavior. In von Foerster, J. D. White, L. J. Peterson, & J. K. Russell (Eds.), *Purposive systems* (pp. 25–34). New York: Spartan Books.

Gerard, R. W. (1969). Hierarchy, entitation, and levels. In L. L. Whyte, A. G. Wilson, & D. Wilson (Eds.) *Hierarchical Structures* (pp. 87–109). New York: American Elsevier.

Germain, R. B. (1978). Self-concept and self-esteem reexamined. *Psychology in the Schools, 15,* 386–390.

Gernandt, B. E. (1959). Vestibular mechanisms. In J. Fields (Ed.), *Handbook of physiology: Sec. 1. Neurophysiology* (Vol. 1, pp. 549–564). Bethesda, MD: American Physiological Society.

Gesell, A., & Thompson, H. (1934). *Infant behavior: Its genesis and growth.* New York: McGraw-Hill.

Gettys, C. F., & Fisher, S. D. (1979). Hypothesis plausibility and hypothesis generation. *Organizational Behavior and Human Performance, 24,* 93–110.

Ghiselin, B. (Ed.). (1955). *The creative process.* New York: Mentos Books.

Ghiselin, M. T. (1969). *The triumph of the Darwinian method.* Berkeley: University of California Press.

Giambra, L. M. (1977). Independent dimensions of depression: A factor analysis of three self-report depression measures. *Journal of Clinical Psychology, 33,* 928–935.

Gibbs, J. C. (1979). The meaning of ecologically oriented inquiry in contemporary psychology. *American Psychologist, 34,* 127–140.

Gibson, E. J. (1969). *Principles of perceptual learning and development.* New York: Appleton-Century-Crofts.

Gibson, E. J., Owsley, C. J., Walker, A., & Megaw-Nyce, J. (1979). Development of the perception of invariants: Substance and shape. *Perception, 8,* 609–619.

Gibson, J. J. (1941). A critical review of the concept of set in contemporary experimental psychology. *Psychological Bulletin, 38,* 781–817.

Gibson, J. J. (1950). *The perception of the visual world.* Boston: Houghton-Mifflin.

Gibson, J. J. (1960). The concept of stimulus in psychology. *American Psychologist, 15,* 694–703.

Gibson, J. J. (1966). *The senses as perceptual systems.* Boston: Houghton-Mifflin.

Gibson, J. J. (1979). *The ecological approach to visual perception.* Boston: Houghton-Mifflin.

Gibson, J. J. (1982). The problem of event perception. In E. Reed & R. Jones (Eds.), *Reasons for realism: Selected essays of James J. Gibson.* Hillsdale, NJ: Lawrence Erlbaum Associates.

Gilbert, W. (1981). DNA sequencing and gene structure. *Science, 214,* 1305–1312.

Gilligan, S. G., & Bower, G. H. (1984). Cognitive consequences of emotional arousal. In C. E. Izard, J. Kagan, & R. B. Zajonc (Eds.), *Emotions, cognitions, and behavior* (pp.

547–588). Cambridge, UK: Cambridge University Press.

Ginsburg, A. P. (1971). *Psychological correlates of a model of the human visual system*. Master's thesis GE/EE 715-2 Wright-Patterson AFB, OH: Air Force Institute of Technology.

Ginsburg, H. P. (Ed.). (1983). *The development of mathematical thinking*. New York: Academic Press.

Glaser, R. (Ed.). (1971). *The nature of reinforcement*. New York: Academic Press.

Glaser, R. (1984). Education and thinking: The role of knowledge. *American Psychologist, 39*, 93–104.

Glencross, D. J. (1980). Levels and strategies of response organization. In G. E. Stelmach & J. Requin (Eds.), *Tutorials in motor behavior* (pp. 551–566). Amsterdam: North-Holland.

Globus, G. G., Maxwell, G., & Savodnik, I. (Eds.). (1976). *Consciousness and the brain: Scientific and philosophical inquiry*. New York: Plenum Press.

Glucksberg, S., & McCloskey, M. (1981). Decisions about ignorance: Knowing that you don't know. *Journal of Experimental Psychology: Human Learning and Memory, 7*, 311–325.

Goldin-Meadow, S., & Feldman, H. (1975). The creation of a communication system: A study of deaf children of hearing parents. *Sign Language Studies, 8*, 225–234.

Goldin-Meadow, S., & Feldman, H. (1977). The development of language-like communication without a language model. *Science, 197*, 401–403.

Goldman, A. I. (1970). *A theory of human action*. Englewood Cliffs, NJ: Prentice-Hall.

Goldschmidt, R. (1940). *The material basis of evolution*. New Haven, CT: Yale University Press.

Goldstein, A. P. (1962). *Therapist-patient expectancies in psychotherapy*. New York: Macmillan.

Goldstein, A. P. (1981). *Psychological skill training*. New York: Pergamon Press.

Goldstein, A. P., & Kanfer, F. H. (Eds.). (1979). *Maximizing treatment gains, transfer enhancement in psychotherapy*. New York: Academic Press.

Goldstein, A. P., & Michaels, G. Y. (1985). *Empathy: Development, training, and consequences*. Hillsdale, NJ: Lawrence Erlbaum Associates.

Goldstein, K. (1939). *The organism*. New York: American Book Co.

Goldstein, K. (1948). *Language and language disturbance*. New York: Grune & Stratton.

Goodenough, F. L. (1931). *Anger in young children*. Minneapolis: University of Minnesota Press.

Goodglass, M., & Kaplan, E. (1972). *The assessment of aphasia and related disorders*. Philadelphia: Lea & Felinger.

Goodman, G. S. (1980). Picture memory: How the action schemata affects retention. *Cognitive Psychology, 12*, 473–495.

Goodstein, L. D., Lanyon, R. I., Radtke, R. C., Olson, S. P., & Lowe, C. A. (1964). Verbal conditioning in a new sentence construction task: A further study. *Psychological Reports, 15*, 97–98.

Goodwin, C. (1981). *Conversational organization*. New York: Academic Press.

Gottlieb, G. (1976). Conceptions of prenatal development: Behavioral embryology. *Psychological Review, 83*, 215–234.

Gottlieb, G. (1983). The psychological approach to developmental issues. In P. H. Mussen (Ed.), *Handbook of child psychology: Vol. 2. Biology and infancy* (pp. 1–26). New York: Wiley.

Gould, J. L. (1985). How bees remember flower shapes. *Science, 227*, 1492–1494.

Gould, S. J. (1977). *Ontogeny and phylogeny*. Cambridge, MA: Belknap Press of Harvard University Press.

Gould, S. J. (1980). Is a new and general theory of evolution emerging? *Paleobiology, 6*, 119–130.

Gould, S. J. (1982). Darwinism and the expansion of evolutionary theory. *Science, 216*, 380–387.

Gould, S. J. , & Lewontin, R. C. (1974). The Spandrels of San Marco and the Panglossian paradigm: A critique of the adaptationist program. In J. M. Smith & R. Halliday (Eds.), *The evolution of adaptation by natural selection*. London: The Royal Society of London.

Graesser, A. C. (1981). *Prose comprehension beyond the word*. New York: Springer-Verlag.

Graham, C., & Evans, F. J. (1977). Hypnotizability and the deployment of waking attention. *Journal of Abnormal Psychology, 86*, 631–638.

Granit, R. (1970). *The basis of motor control*. New York: Academic Press.

Granit, R. (1977). *The purposive brain*. Cambridge, MA: MIT Press.

Granit, R. (1980). Reflections on motoricity. *Perspectives in Biology and Medicine, 23*, 171–178.

Grant, P. R., & Holmes, J. G. (1981). The integration of implicit personality theory schemas and stereotype images. *Social Psychological Quarterly, 44*, 107–115.

Gratch, G. (1979). The development of thought and language in infancy. In J. D. Osofsky (Ed.), *Handbook of infant development* (pp. 439–461). New York: Wiley.

Greenberg, L. S., & Safran, J. D. (1987). *Emotion in psychotherapy*. New York: Guilford Press.

Greene, P. H. (1972). Problems of organization of motor systems. In R. Rosen & F. Snell (Eds.), *Progress in theoretical biology* (pp. 304–335). New York: Academic Press.

Greenfield, P. M. (1980). Towards an operational and logical analysis of intentionality: The use of discourse in early child language. In D. Olson (Ed.), *The social foundations of language and thought*. New York: W. W. Norton.

Greeno, J. G. (1980). Psychology of learning, 1960–1980: One participant's observations. *American Psychologist, 35*, 713–728.

Greenspoon, J. (1955). The reinforcing effect of two spoken sounds on the frequency of two responses. *American Journal of Psychology, 68*, 409–416.

Greenwald, A. G. (1980). The totalitarian ego: Fabrication and revision of personal history. *American Psychologist, 35*, 603–618.

Greenwald, A. G., & Ronis, D. L. (1978). Twenty years of cognitive dissonance: Case study of the evolution of a theory. *Psychological Review, 85*, 53–57.

Griggs, R. A., & Newstead, S. E. (1982). The role of problem structure in a deductive reasoning task. *Journal of Experimental Psychology: Learning, Memory and Cognition, 8*, 297–307.

Grillner, S. (1975). Locomotion in vertebrates: Central mechanisms and reflex interaction. *Physiological Review, 55*, 247–304.

Grillner, S. (1985). Neurobiological bases of rhythmic motor acts in vertebrates. *Science, 228*, 143–149.

Grings, W. W., & Dawson, M. E. (1978). *Emotions and bodily responses*. New York: Academic Press.

Grings, W. W., & Dawson, M. E. (1980). *Emotions and bodily responses: A psychophysiological approach*. New York: Academic Press.

Grinker, R. R. (Ed.). (1956). *Toward a unified theory of human behavior*. New York: Basic Books.

Grinker, R. R., Korchin, S. J., Basowitz, H., Hamburg, D. A., Sabshin, M., Persky, H., Chevalier, J. A., & Borad, F. A. (1956). A theoretical and experimental approach to problems of anxiety. *A.M.A. Archives of Neurology and Psychiatry, 76*, 420–431.

Groos, K. (1901). *The play of man* (E. L. Baldwin, Trans.). New York: Appleton.

Grossberg, S. (1980). How does a brain build a cognitive code? *Psychological Review, 87*, 1–51.

Gubernick, D. J., & Klopfer, P. H. (1981). *Parental care in mammals*. New York: Plenum Press.

Guerney, B. G., Jr. (1977). *Relationship enhancement*. San Francisco: Jossey-Bass.

Guiard, Y. (1980). Cerebral hemispheres and selective attention. *Acta Psychologica, 46*,

41–61.

Guillemin, R. (1978). Peptides in the brain: The new endocrinology of the neuron. *Science, 202*, 390–402.

Guillory, A. W., Self, P. A., Francis, P., & Paden, L. L. (1979). *Odor perception in newborns*. Paper presented at the annual meeting of the Southwestern Psychological Association, San Antonio, TX.

Guillory, A. W., Self, P. A., & Paden, L. L. (1980). *Odor sensitivity in one month infants*. Paper presented at the International Conference on Infant Studies, New Haven, CT.

Gunnar-Vongnechten, M. R. (1978). Changing a frightening toy into a pleasant toy by allowing the infant to control its actions. *Developmental Psychology, 14*, 157–162.

Gunnar, M. R. (1980). Control, warning signals, and distress in infancy. *Developmental Psychology, 16*, 281–289.

Gunnar, M. (1980). Contingent stimulation: A review of its role in early development. In S. Levine & H. Ursin (Eds.), *Coping and health* (pp. 101–119). New York: Plenum Press.

Guthrie, R. D. (1970). Evolution of human threat display organs. *Evolutionary Biology, 4*, 257–307.

Guttmann, A. J., & Turnure, J. E. (1979). Mothers' production of hand gestures while communicating with their preschool children under various task conditions. *Developmental Psychology, 15*, 197–203.

Guyton, A. C. (1982). *Human physiology and mechanisms of disease* (3rd ed.). Philadelphia: W. B. Saunders.

Haan, N. (1978). Two moralities in action contexts: Relationships to thought, ego regulation, and development. *Journal of Personality and Social Psychology, 36*, 286–305.

Haan, N., Aerts, E., & Cooler, B. (1985). *On moral grounds: The search for practical morality*. New York: University Press.

Haan, N., Smith, M. B., & Block, J. (1968). The moral reasoning of young adults. *Journal of Abnormal and Social Psychology, 10*, 182–201.

Haber, R. N. (1978). Visual perception. *Annual Review of Psychology, 29*, 31–59.

Haber, R. N. (1979). Twenty years of haunting eidetic imagery: Where's the ghost. *The Behavioral and Brain Sciences, 2*, 583–629.

Hahn, J. F. (1974). Somesthesis. *Annual Review of Psychology, 25*, 216–246.

Haith, M. M. (1980). *Rules that babies look by: The organization of newborn visual activity*. Hillsdale, NJ: Lawrence Erlbaum Associates.

Hale, G. A., & Alderman, L. B. (1978). Children's selective attention with variation in amount of stimulus exposure. *Journal of Experimental Child Psychology, 26*, 320–327.

Hale, G. A., & Lewis, M. (Eds.). (1979). *Attention and cognitive development*. New York: Plenum Press.

Hale, G. A., Tameel, S. S., Green, R. W., & Flaugher, J. (1978). Effects of instructions on children's attention to stimulus components. *Developmental Psychology, 14*, 499–506.

Halford, G. S., & Wilson, W. H. (1980). A category theory approach to cognitive development. *Cognitive Psychology, 12*, 356–411.

Hall, A. D., & Fagan, R. E. (1956). Definition of a system. *General Systems Yearbook, 1*, 18–28.

Hall, C. (1966). *The meaning of dreams*. New York: McGraw-Hill.

Hall, C. S., & Lindzey, G. (1978). *Theories of personality* (3rd ed.). New York: Wiley.

Hall, E. T. (1963). A system for the notation of proxemic behavior. *American Anthropologist, 65*, 1003–1026.

Hall, J. F. (1961). *Psychology of motivation*. New York: Lippincott.

Hallahan, D. P., Cajar, A. H., Cohen, S. B., & Tarver, S. G. (1978). Selective attention and locus of control in learning disabled and normal children. *Journal of Learning Disabilities, 11*, 231–236.

Halliday, M. A. K. (1978). *Language as a social semiotic*. London: Edward Arnold.

Halverson, H. M. (1937). Studies of the grasping responses in early infancy. *Journal of Genetic Psychology, 51,* 437–449.

Ham, A. W. (1969). *Histology* (6th ed.). Philadelphia: Lippincott.

Ham, A. W., & Cormack, D. H. (1979). *Histology* (8th ed.). Philadelphia: J. P. Lippincott.

Hamburg, D. A. (1963). Emotions in the perspective of human evolution. In P. Knapp (Ed.), *Expressions of the emotions in man* (pp. 300–317). New York: International Universities Press.

Hampton, J. A. (1978). Polymorphous concepts in semantic memory. *Journal of Verbal Learning and Verbal Behavior, 18,* 441–461.

Hampton, J. A. (1981). An investigation of the nature of abstract concepts. *Memory and Cognition, 9,* 149–156.

Harding, C. G. (1981). *A longitudinal study of the development of the intention to communicate.* Paper presented at the biennial meeting of the Society for Research on Child Development, Boston, MA.

Harding, C. G. (1982). Development of the intention to communicate. *Human Development, 25,* 140–151.

Harlow, H. (1949). Learning sets. *Psychological Review, 56,* 51–65.

Harlow, H. F. (1971). *Learning to love.* New York: Ballantine Books.

Harlow, H. F., & Mears, C. (1979). *The human model: Primate perspectives.* Washington, DC: W. H. Winston & Sons.

Harnad, S. R., Steklis, H. D., & Lancaster, J. (1976). Origins and evolution of language and speech. *Annals of the New York Academy of Sciences.* New York: New York Academy of Sciences.

Harper, R. G., Wiens, A. N., & Matarazzo, J. D. (1978). *Nonverbal communication: The state of the art.* New York: Wiley.

Harris, A. (1979). Historical development of the Soviet theory of self-regulation. In G. Zivin (Ed.), *The development of self-regulation through private speech* (pp. 51–78). New York: Wiley.

Harris, D. B. (Ed.). (1957). *The concept of development.* Minneapolis: University of Minnesota Press.

Harris, P. L. (1983). Infant cognition. In P. H. Mussen (Ed.), *Handbook of child psychology* (4th ed): Vol. 2. Infancy and developmental psychology (pp. 689–782). New York: Wiley.

Harris, W. A. (1981). Neural activity and development. *Annual Review of Physiology, 43,* 687–710.

Harter, M. R., & Previc, F. H. (1978). Size-specific information channels and selective attention: Visual evoked potential and behavioral measures. *Electroencephalography and Clinical Neurophysiology, 45,* 628–640.

Harter, S. (1978). Effectance motivation reconsidered. *Human Development, 21,* 34–64.

Harter, S. (1981). A model of intrinsic mastery motivation in children: Individual differences in developmental change. In W. A. Collins (Ed.), *Minnesota Symposium on Child Psychology* (Vol. 14, pp. 215–255). Hillsdale, NJ: Lawrence Erlbaum Associates.

Harter, S. (1983). Developmental perspectives on the self-system. In P. H. Mussen (Ed.), *Handbook of child psychology* (4th ed., pp. 275–385). New York: Wiley.

Hartman, H. (1958). *Ego psychology and the problem of adaptation.* New York: International Universities Press.

Hartog, J., Audy, J. R., & Cohen, Y. A. (Eds.). (1980). *The anatomy of loneliness.* New York: International Universities Press.

Hartshorne, H., & May, M. A. (1928). *Studies in the nature of character: Vol. 1. Studies in deceit.* New York: Macmillan.

Hartshorne, H., May, M. A., & Moller, J. B. (1929). *Studies in the nature of character: Vol. 2. Studies in self-control.* New York: Macmillan.

Hartshorne, H., May, M. A., & Shuttleworth, F. K. (1930). *Studies in the nature of character:*

Vol. 3. Studies in the organization of character. New York: Macmillan.

Hartup, W. W. (1980). Two social worlds: Family relations and peer relations. In M. Rutter (Ed.), *Scientific foundations of developmental psychiatry.* London: Heinemann.

Hartup, W. W. (1983). Peer relations. In P. H. Mussen (Ed.), *Handbook of child psychology (4th ed.): Vol. 4. Socialization, personality and social development* (pp. 103–196). New York: Wiley.

Harvey, D. M. (1981). Depression and attributional style: Interpretations of important personal events. *Journal of Abnormal Psychology, 90,* 134–142.

Harvey, J. H., Ickes, W. J., & Kidd, R. F. (Eds.). (1976). *New directions in attribution research* (Vol. 1). Hillsdale, NJ: Lawrence Erlbaum Associates.

Harvey, J. H., & Weary, G. (1984). Current issues in attribution theory and research. *Annual Review of Psychology, 35,* 427–459.

Harvey, O. J. (Ed.). (1966). *Experience, structure and adaptability.* New York: Springer.

Hasher, L., & Zacks, R. T. (1984). Automatic processing of fundamental information: The case of frequency of occurrence. *American Psychologist, 39*(12), 1372–1388.

Haskins, R., Finkelstein, N. W., & Stedman, D. J. (1978). Infant-stimulation programs and their effects. *Pediatric Annals, 7,* 99–128.

Hass, H. (1970). *The human animal.* New York: Putnams Sons.

Hass-Hawkings, G. (1978). Intimacy as a moderating influence on the stress of loneliness in widowhood. *Essence, 2,* 249–258.

Hastie, R. (1981). Schematic principles in human memory. In E. T. Higgins, C. P. Herman, & M. P. Zanna (Eds.), *Social cognition: The Ontario Symposium* (Vol. 1). Hillsdale, NJ: Lawrence Erlbaum Associates.

Hastie, R. (1983). Social inference. *Annual Review of Psychology, 34,* 511–542.

Haubenstricker, J. (1978). A critical review of selected perceptual-motor tests and scales currently used in the assessment of motor behavior. In D. M. Landers & R. W. Christine (Eds.), *Psychology in motor behavior and sport* (pp. 536–543). Champaign, IL: Human Kinetics.

Hawkins, D. (1968). The nature of purpose. In A. von Foerster, J. B. White, L. J. Peterson, & J. K. Russell (Eds.), *Purposive systems* (pp. 163–179). New York: Spartan Books.

Hay, L. (1979). Spatial-temporal analysis of movements in children: Motor programs versus feedback in the development of reaching. *Journal of Motor Behavior, 11,* 189–200.

Hayek, F. A. (1952). *The sensory order.* Chicago: University of Chicago Press.

Hayes, D. S., & Birnbaum, D. W. (1980). Preschoolers' retention of televised events: Is a picture worth a thousand words? *Developmental Psychology, 16,* 410–416.

Hayes, K. C., & Marteniuk, R. G. (1976). Dimensions of motor task complexity. In G. E. Stelmach (Ed.), *Motor control: Issues and trends* (pp. 201–228). New York: Academic Press.

Hayes-Roth, B., & Walker, C. (1979). Configural effects on human memory: The superiority of memory over external information sources as a basis for inference verification. *Cognitive Science, 3,* 119–140.

Heath, R. G. (1954). Behavioral changes following destructive lesions in the subcortical structure of the forebrain in cats. In R. G. Heath (Ed.), *Studies in schizophrenia: A multidisciplinary approach to mid-brain relationships* (pp. 83–84). Cambridge, MA: Harvard University Press.

Hebb, D. O. (1949). *The organization of behavior.* New York: Wiley.

Hebb, D. O. (1955). Drives and C.N.S. (Conceptual nervous system). *Psychological Review, 62,* 243–254.

Hebb, D. O. (1972). *Textbook of psychology.* Philadelphia: Saunders.

Hécaen, J. (1969). Aphasic, apraxic and agnostic syndromes in right and left hemisphere lesions. In P. J. Winken & G. W. Bruyn (Eds.), *Handbook of clinical neurology* (Vol. 4, pp. 291–371). Amsterdam: North-Holland.

Heckhausen, H. (1973). Intervening cognitions in motivation. In D. E. Berlyn & K. B. Madsen (Eds.), *Pleasure, reward, preference* (pp. 217–242). New York: Academic Press.

Heckhausen, H. (1980). *Motivation und Handeln: Lehrleuch der Motivationpsychologie.* Berlin: Springer-Verlag.

Heckhausen, H. (1981). The development of achievement motivation. In W. W. Hartup (Ed.), *Review of child development research* (Vol. 6). Chicago: University of Chicago Press.

Heckhausen, H., & Weiner, B. (1972). The emergence of a cognitive psychology of motivation. In P. C. Dodwell (Ed.), *New horizons in psychology* (Vol. 2). London: Penguin.

Heidbreder, E. (1924). An experimental study of thinking. *Archives of Psychology,* (Whole No. 73).

Heidbreder, E. (1933). *Seven psychologies.* New York: Appleton-Century.

Heider, F. (1944). Social perception and phenomenal causality. *Psychological Review, 51,* 358–374.

Heider, F. (1959). On perception, event structure, and psychological environment. *Psychological Issues, 1,* 1–123.

Heins, T. (1978). Marital interaction in depression. *Australian and New Zealand Journal of Psychiatry, 12,* 269–275.

Held, R. (1965). Plasticity in sensory motor systems. *Scientific American, 213,* 84–94.

Held, R., Leibowitz, H. W., & Teuber, H. L. (Eds.). (1978). *The handbook of sensory physiology: Vol. 8. Perception.* Berlin: Springer.

Helmholtz, H. L. F. von (1924–25). *Helmholtz's treaty on physiological optics* (1–3 Vols). J. P. C. Southal (Ed., & Trans.) Rochester, NY: Optical Society of America. (Originally published 1909–1911; translated from 3rd ed.)

Helson, H. (1964). *Adaptation-level theory.* New York: Harter & Row.

Helson, R., & Mitchell, V. (1978). Personality. *Annual Review of Psychology, 29,* 555–585.

Henderson, N. D. (1982). Human behavior genetics. *Annual Review of Psychology, 33,* 403–440.

Henry, R. M. (1980). A theoretical and empirical analysis of "reasoning" in the socialization of young children. *Human Development, 23,* 105–125.

Henshel, R. L. (1971). Sociology and prediction. *American Sociologist, 6,* 213–220.

Herberman, R. B., & Ortaldo, J. R. (1981). Natural killer cells: Their role in defenses against disease. *Science, 214,* 24–30.

Herman, J. F. (1980). Children's cognitive maps of large-scale spaces: Effects of exploration, direction and repeated experience. *Journal of Experimental Child Psychology, 29,* 126–143.

Hernandez-Peon, R. (1966). The neural substrate of attention. In P. Bakan (Ed.), *Attention* (pp. 181–206). Princeton, NJ: Van Nostrand.

Herrick, C. J. (1956). *The evolution of human nature.* Austin: University of Texas Press.

Hiatt, S. W., Campos, J. J., & Emde, R. M. (1979). Facial patterning and infant emotional expression: Happiness, surprise, and fear. *Child Development, 50,* 1020–1035.

Hicks, L. H. (1980). The basal ganglia and psychomotor behavior. In R. F. Thompson, L. H. Hicks, & V. B. Shvyrkov (Eds.), *Neural mechanisms of goal-directed behavior and learning* (pp. 153–166). New York: Academic Press.

Higbee, K. L. (1979). Recent research on visual mnemonics: Historical roots and educational fruits. *Review of Educational Research, 49,* 611–629.

Higgins, E. T. (1981). Role-taking and social judgment: Alternative developmental perspectives and processes. In J. H. Flavell & L. Ross (Eds.), *Social cognitive development: Frontiers and possible futures* (pp. 119–153). New York: Cambridge University Press.

Higgins, E. T., Rhodewalt, F., & Zanna, M. P. (1979). Dissonance motivation: Its nature, persistence, and reinstatement. *Journal of Experimental Social Psychology, 15,* 16–34.

Hilgard, E. R. (1948). *Theories of learning.* New York: Appleton-Century-Crofts.

Hilgard, E. R. (1976). Neodissociation theory of multiple cognitive control systems. In G. E. Schwartz & D. Shapiro (Eds.), *Consciousness and self-regulation: Advances in research* (Vol. 1, pp. 137–169). New York: Plenum Press.

Hilgard, E. R. (1977a). Controversies over consciousness and the rise of cognitive psychology. *Australian Psychologist, 12,* 7–26.

Hilgard, E. R. (1977b). *Divided consciousness; Multiple controls in human thought and action.* New York: Wiley.

Hilgard, E. R. (1980). Consciousness in contemporary psychology. *Annual Review of Psychology, 31,* 1–26.

Hilgard, R., & Bower, G. H. (1966). *Theories of learning.* New York: Appleton-Century-Crofts.

Hilgard, E. R., & Bower, G. H. (1975). *Theories of learning* (4th ed.). Englewood Cliffs, NJ: Prentice-Hall.

Hilgard, E. R., & Hilgard, J. R. (1975). *Hypnosis in the relief of pain.* Los Altos, CA: Kaufmann.

Hillyard, S. A., Hink, R. F., Schwent, V. Z., & Picton, T. W. (1973). Electrical signs of selective attention in the human brain. *Science, 182,* 177–180.

Hillyard, S. A., & Picton, T. W. (1977). Event related brain potentials and selective information-processing in man. In J.E. Desmedt (Ed.), *Cerebral evoked potentials in man.* Basel: Karger.

Hinde, R. A. (1966). *Animal behavior.* New York: McGraw-Hill.

Hinde, R. A. (1970). *Animal behavior: A synthesis of ethology and comparative psychology* (2nd ed.). New York: McGraw-Hill.

Hinde, R. A. (Ed.). (1972). *Nonverbal communication.* Cambridge, UK: Cambridge University Press.

Hinde, R. A., & Stevenson, J. G. (1969). Goals and response control. In L. R. Aronson, E. Tobach, J., Rosenblatt, & D. S. Lehrman (Eds.), *Development and evaluation of behavior* (Vol. 1, pp. 216–237). San Francisco: Freeman.

Hink, R. F. (1978). Vigilance and human attention under conditions of methylphenidate and secobarbital intoxication: An assessment using brain potentials. *Psychophysiology, 15,* 116–125.

Hirst, W. (1982). The amnesic syndrome: Descriptions and explanations. *Psychological Bulletin, 9,* 435–460.

Hochberg, J. (1968). In the minds eye. In R. N. Haber (Ed.), *Contemporary theory and research in visual perception* (pp. 303–331). New York: Holt, Rinehart & Winston.

Hochberg, J. (1974). The perceptual world. In R. B. MacLeod & H. L. Pick, Jr. (Eds.), *Perception* (pp. 141–152). Ithaca, NY: Cornell University.

Hockman,C. H. (Ed.). (1972). *Limbic system mechanisms and autonomic function.* Springfield, IL: Charles Thomas.

Hoeller, K. (1977). Attention: Traditional versus phenomenological approaches. *Review of Existential Psychology and Psychiatry, 15,* 227–240.

Hoffman, L. (1981). *Foundations of family therapy: A conceptual framework for systems change.* New York: Basic Books.

Hoffman, M. L. (1963). Child rearing practices and moral development: Generalizations from empirical research. *Child Development, 34,* 295–318.

Hoffman, M. L. (1977). Personality and social development. *Annual Review of Psychology, 28,* 295–321.

Hoffman, M. L. (1980). Moral development in adolescence. In J. Adelson (Ed.), *Handbook of adolescent psychology.* New York: Wiley-Interscience.

Hoffman, M. L. (1981). Is altruism part of human nature? *Journal of Personality and Social Psychology, 40,* 121–137.

Hoffman, M. L. (1982). Affective and cognitive processes in moral internalization. In E. T.

Higgins, D. N. Ruble, & W. W. Hartup (Eds.), *Social cognition and social behavior: Developmental perspectives*. Cambridge, UK: Cambridge University Press.

Hoffman, M. L. (1984). Interaction of affect and cognition on empathy. In C. E. Izard, J. Kagan, & R. B. Zajonc (Eds.), *Emotion, cognition and behavior*. Cambridge: Cambridge University Press.

Hofstadter, A. (1941). Objective teleology. *Journal of Philosophy, 38,* 29–39.

Hofsten, C. von, & Lindhagen, K. (1979). Observations on the development of reaching for moving objects. *Journal of Experimental Child Psychology, 28,* 158–173.

Hogarth, R. M. (1981). Beyond discrete biases: Functional and dysfunctional aspects of judgmental heuristics. *Psychological Bulletin, 90,* 197–217.

Holden, C. (1979a). Paul McLean and the triune brain. *Science, 204,* 1066–1068.

Holden, C. (1979b). Dying, and the health care systems. *Science, 203,* 984–985.

Holland, A. L. (Ed.). (1983). *Language disorders in adults*. San Diego, CA: College-Hill Press.

Holland, M. K., & Tarlow, G. (1975). Blinking and thinking. *Perceptual Motor Skills, 41,* 403–406.

Holt, R. R. (1964). Imagery: The return of the ostracized. *American Psychologist, 19,* 252–257.

Holt, R. R. (1976). Drive or wish? A reconsideration of the psychoanalytic theory motivation. *Psychological Issues, 9,* 158–198.

Holtzman, P. S., & Klein, G. S. (1959). The "schematizing process": Attitudes in sensitivity to change. *American Psychologist, 5,* 312.

Honig, W. K., & Urcuioli, P. J. (1981). The legacy of Guttman and Kalish (1956): Twenty-five years of research on stimulus generalization. *Journal of the Experimental Analysis of Behavior, 36,* 405–445.

Horridge, G. A. (1978). A different kind of vision: The compound eye. In E. C. Carterette & M. P. Friedman (Eds.), *Handbook of perception: Vol. 8. Perceptual coding* (pp. 3–82). New York: Academic Press.

Horne, J. A. (1979). Restitution and human sleep: A critical review. *Physiological Psychology, 7,* 115–125.

Horton, D. L., & Mills, C. B. (1984). Human learning and memory. *Annual Review of Psychology, 35,* 361–394.

Hosobuchi, Y., & Li, C. H. (1978). The analgesic activity of human B-endorphin in man. *Communications in Psychopharmacology, 2,* 33–37.

Houtz, J. C., Montgomery, C., & Kirkpatrick, L. (1979). Relationships among measures of evaluation ability (problem solving), creative thinking, and intelligence. *Contemporary Educational Psychology, 4,* 47–54.

Howard, G. S. (1985). The role of values in the science of psychology. *American Psychologist, 40,* 255–265.

Howe, H. E., Jr. (Ed.). (1980). Beliefs, attitudes and values. *Nebraska Symposium on Motivation* (Vol. 27). Lincoln: University of Nebraska Press.

Howell, W. C., & Kreidler, D. L. (1964). Instructional sets and subjective criteria levels in a complex information-processing task. *Journal of Experimental Psychology, 6W8,* 612–614.

Hoyt, D. F., & Taylor, C. R. (1981). Gait and the energetics of locomotion in horses. *Nature, 292,* 239–240.

Hubert, H. B., Fabsitz, R. R., Feinleib, M., & Brown, K. S. (1980). Olfactory sensitivity in humans: Genetic versus environmental control. *Science, 208,* 607–608.

Hugelin, A., Dumont, S., & Paillas, N. (1960). Tympanic muscles and control of auditory input during arousal. *Science, 13,* 1371–1372.

Hull, C. L. (1943). *Principles of behavior*. New York: Appleton-Century-Crofts.

Hull, C. L. (1952). *A behavior system: An introduction to behavior theory concerning the individual organism*. New Haven: Yale University Press.

Hultsch, D. F., & Pentz, C. A. (1980). Research on adult learning and memory: Retrospect and prospect. *Contemporary Educational Psychology, 5,* 298–320.

Hunt, E. (1983). On the nature of intelligence. *Science, 219,* 141–146.

Hunt, J. McV. (1961). *Intelligence and experience.* New York: Ronald Press.

Hunt, J. McV. (1965). Intrinsic motivation and its role in psychological development. In D. Levine (Ed.), *Nebraska Symposium on Motivation* (Vol. 3, pp. 189–282). Lincoln: University of Nebraska Press.

Hutchinson, A. (1970). *Labanotation.* New York: Theatre Arts Books.

Hutchinson, J. B. (Ed.). (1978). *Biological determinants of sexual behavior.* New York: Wiley.

Hutchinson, R. R. (1972). The environmental causes of aggression. In J. K. Cole & D. D. Jensen (Eds.), *Nebraska Symposium on Motivation* (Vol. 20, pp. 155–181). Lincoln: University of Nebraska Press.

Igersheimer, W. W. (1953). Cold pressor test in functional psychiatric syndromes. *Archives of Neurology and Psychiatry, 70,* 794–801.

Ilgen, D. R., Fisher, C. D., & Taylor, M. S. (1979). Consequences of individual feedback on behavior in organizations. *Journal of Applied Psychology, 64,* 349–371.

Inhelder, B., & Piaget, J. (1958). *The growth of logical thinking from childhood to adolescence.* New York: Basic Books.

Inoue, T. (1981). Effects of shadowing and selective attention in dichotic listening. *Psychologia: An International Journal of Psychology in the Orient, 24,* 21–31.

Isaacson, R. L. (1980). Limbic system contributions to goal-directed behavior. In R. F. Thompson, L. H. Hicks, & V. B. Shvyrkov (Eds.), *Neural mechanisms of goal-directed behavior and learning* (pp. 409–423). New York: Academic Press.

Issac, W. (1962). Evidence for a sensory drive in monkeys. *Psychological Reports, 11,* 175–181.

Ittelson, W. H. (1978). Environmental perception and the urban experience. *Environment and Behavior, 10,* 193–213.

Ito, M. (1984). *The cerebellum and neural control.* New York: Raven.

Izard, C. E. (1971). *The force of emotion.* New York: Appleton-Century-Crofts.

Izard, C. E. (1972). Anxiety: A variable combination of emotions. In C. D. Spielberger (Ed.), *Anxiety: Current trends in theory and research* (Vol. 1, 51–114). New York: Academic Press.

Izard, C. E. (1977). *Human emotions.* New York: Plenum Press.

Izard, C. E. (1978). On the ontogenesis of emotions and emotion-cognition relationships in infancy. In M. Lewis & L. A. Rosenblum (Eds.), *The development of affect* (pp. 389–413). New York: Plenum Press.

Izard, C. E. (1979). Emotions as motivations: An evolutionary-developmental perspective. In R. Diensthier (Ed.), *Nebraska Symposium on Motivation* (Vol. 26, pp. 163–200). Lincoln: University of Nebraska Press.

Izard, C. E. (Ed.). (1982). *Measuring emotions in infants and children.* Cambridge, UK: Cambridge University Press.

Izard, C. E., Huebner, R. R., Risser, D., McGinnes, G. C., & Dougherty, L. M. (1980). The young infant's ability to produce discrete emotion expressions. *Developmental Psychology, 16,* 132–140.

Izard, C. E., Kagan, J., & Zajonc, R. B. (Eds.). (1984). *Emotions, cognition and behavior.* Cambridge: Cambridge University Press.

Jacob, S. W., Francone, C. W., & Lossow, W. J. (1982). *Structure and function in man.* Philadelphia: W. B. Saunders.

Jacobs, G. H. (1976). Color vision. *Annual Review of Psychology, 27,* 63–90.

Jacobs, S., & Douglas, L. (1979). Grief: A mediating process between a loss and illness. *Comprehensive Psychiatry, 20,* 165–176.

Jacobsen, E., Kehlet, H., Larsen, V., Munkuiad, I., & Shinhoj, K. (1955). Investigations into autonomic responses during emotion. *Acta Psychiatry and Neurology Scandinavia, 30,*

607–625.

Jacobson, C. B., & Magyar, V. L. (1968). Genetic evolution of LSD. *Clinical Proceedings of the Children's Hospital, 24,* 153–161.

Jacobson, H. (1955). Information, reproduction, and the origin of life. *American Scientist, 43,* 119–127.

James, L. R., Hater, J. J., Gent, M. J., & Bruni, J. R. (1978). Psychological climate: Implications from cognitive social learning theory and interactional psychology. *Personnel Psychology, 31,* 783–813.

James, W. (1884). What is emotion? *Mind, 9,* 188–204.

James, W. (1890). *Principles of psychology, Vol. 1.* New York: Henry Holt.

James, W. (1910). *Principles of psychology.* New York: Holt.

Jancovic, M. A., Devoe, S., & Wiener, M. (1975). Age-related changes in hand and arm movements as nonverbal communication: Some conceptualizations and an empirical exploration. *Child Development, 46,* 922–928.

Janis, I. L., Mahl, G. F., Kagan, J., & Holt, R. R. (1969). *Personality, dynamics, development, and assessment.* New York: Harcourt, Brace, and World.

Janis, I. L., & Mann, L. (1977). *Decision making: A psychological analysis of conflict, choice and commitment.* New York: The Free Press.

Jantsch, E. (1980). *The self-organizing universe.* Oxford: Pergamon Press.

Jantsch, E. (1981). Autopoiesis: A central aspect of dissipative self-organization. In M. Zeleny (Ed.), *Autopoiesis: A theory of living organization.* New York: Elsevier North Holland, Inc.

Jantsch, E., & Waddington, C. H. (1976). *Evolution and consciousness.* Reading, MA: Addison-Wesley.

Jeffrey, K. J., & Mischel, W. (1979). Effects of purpose on the organization and recall of information in person perception. *Journal of Personality, 47,* 397–419.

Jenkins, J. J. (1974). Remember that old theory of memory? Well forget it! *American Psychologist, 29,* 785–795.

Jennings, K. D., Harmon, R. J., Morgan, G. A., Gaiter, J. L., & Yarrow, L. J. (1979). Exploratory play as an index of mastery motivation: Relationships to persistence, cognitive functioning, and environmental measures. *Developmental Psychology, 15,* 386–394.

Jerison, H. J. (1976). Paleoneurology and the evolution of mind. *Scientific American, 234,* 90–101.

Jerison, H. J. (1982). The evolution of biological intelligence. In R. J. Sternberg (Ed.), *Handbook of human intelligence* (pp. 723–791). Cambridge, UK: Cambridge University Press.

Jernigan, M. E., & Wardell, R. W. (1981). Does the eye contain optimal edge detection mechanisms? *ICEE Transactions on Systems, Man, and Cybernetics, SMC-11(6),* 441–444.

Jersild, A. T., & Holmes, F. B. (1935). Children's fears. *Child Development Monograph, 20.* New York: Teachers College, Columbia University.

Johansson, G. (1973). Visual perception of biological motion and a model for its analysis. *Perception and Psychophysics, 14,* 201–211.

Johansson, G. (1978). Visual event perception. In R. Held, H. W. Leibowitz, & H. L. Teubier (Eds.), *Handbook of sensory physiology* (pp. 675–711). New York: Springer.

Johansson, G., von Hofsten, C., & Jansson, G. (1980). Event perception. *Annual Review of Psychology, 31,* 27–63.

John, E. R. (1976). Model of consciousness. In G. E. Schwartz & D. Shapiro (Eds.), *Consciousness and self-regulation* (Vol. 1, pp. 1–50). New York: Plenum.

John, E. R., & Schwartz, E. L. (1978). The neurophysiology of information processing and cognition. *Annual Review of Psychology, 29,* 1–29.

John, E. R., Tang, Y., Brill, A. B., Young, R., & Ono, K. (1986). Double-labeled metabolic maps of memory. *Science, 233,* 1167–1175.

Johnson, D. M. (1972). *Systematic introduction to the psychology of thinking.* New York: Harper.

Johnson-Laird, P. N. (1981). Mental models in cognitive science. In D. A. Norman (Ed.), *Perspectives on cognitive science* (pp. 147–191). Hillsdale, NJ: Lawrence Erlbaum Associates.

Johnson-Laird, P. N. (1983). *Mental models: Towards a cognitive science of language, inference, and consciousness.* Cambridge, MA: Harvard University Press.

Johnston, W. A., & Dark, V. J. (1986). Selective attention. *Annual Review of Psychology, 37,* 43–75.

Jolly, H. (1966). Lemur social behavior and primate intelligence. *Science, 153,* 502–506.

Jones, B., & Huang, Y. L. (1982). Space-time dependencies in psychophysical judgment of extent and duration: Algebraic models of the tau and kappa effects. *Psychological Bulletin, 91,* 129–142.

Jones, E. E., Kanouse, D. E., Kelley, H. H., Nisbett, R. E., Valins, S., & Weiner, B. (Eds.). (1972). *Attribution: Perceiving the causes of behavior.* Morristown, NJ: General Learning Press.

Jones, M. R. (1976). Time, our lost dimension: Towards a new theory of perception, attention, and memory. *Psychological Review, 3,* 323–355.

Jones, M. R. (1978). Auditory patterns: Studies in the perception of structure. In E. C. Carterette & M. P. Friedman (Eds.), *Handbook of perception: Vol. VIII. Perceptual coding* (pp. 255–285). New York: Academic Press.

Jörg, S. (1978). Aspects of attention. In Ferusehen U. Biladung, *Perception, development, and communication* (pp. 57–74). Munchen: Saur. (Special English Issue).

Juhasz, A. M. (Ed.). (1973). *Sexual development and behavior.* Homewood, IL: Dorsey Press.

Jürgens, U., & Ploog, D. (1981). On the neural control of mammalian vocalization. *Trends in Neurosciences, 1,* 135–137.

Kagan, J. (1966). Reflectivity-impulsivity: The generality and dynamics of conceptual tempo. *Journal of Abnormal Psychology, 71,* 17–24.

Kagan, J. (1967). On the need for relativism. *American Psychologist, 22,* 131–142.

Kagan, J. (1968). On cultural deprivation. In D. G. Glass (Ed.), *Environmental influences* (pp. 211–250). New York: Rockefeller University Press.

Kagan, J. (1972). Motives and development. *Journal of Personality and Social Psychology, 22,* 51–66.

Kagan, J. (1978). On emotion and its development: A working paper. In M. Lewis & L. A. Rosenblum (Eds.), *The development of affect.* New York: Plenum Press.

Kagan, J. (1979). Structure and process in the human infant: The ontogeny of mental representation. In M. H. Bornstein & W. Kessen (Eds.), *Psychological development from infancy: Image to intention* (pp. 162–184). Hillsdale, NJ: Lawrence Erlbaum Associates.

Kagan, J., Kearsley, R. B., & Zelazo, P. R. (1978). *Infancy: Its place in human development.* Cambridge, MA: Harvard University Press.

Kagan, J., Moss, H., & Sigel, I. E. (1963). Psychological significance of styles of conceptualization. In J. Wright & J. Kagan (Eds.), *Monographs of the Society for Research in Child Development, 23*(2).

Kagan, J., & Rosman, B. L. (1964). Cardiac and respiratory correlates of attention and an analytic attitude. *Journal of Experimental Child Psychology, 1,* 50–63.

Kahneman, D. (1973). *Attention and effort.* Englewood Cliffs, NJ: Prentice-Hall.

Kahneman, D., Slovic, P., & Tversky, A. (Eds.). (1982). *Judgment under uncertainty: Heuristics and biases.* Cambridge, UK: Cambridge University Press.

Kahneman, D., & Tversky, A. (1973). On the psychology of prediction. *Psychological Review, 80,* 237–251.

Kahneman, D., & Tversky, A. (1982). The simulation heuristic. In D. Kahneman, P. Slovic,

& A. Tversky (Eds.), *Judgment under uncertainty: Heuristics and biases* (pp. 201–210). New York: Cambridge University Press.

Kahneman, D., & Tversky, A. (1984). Choices, values, and frames. *American Psychologist, 39,* 341–350.

Kalil, K., & Reh, T. (1979). Regrowth of severed axons in the neonatal central nervous system: Establishment of normal connections. *Science, 205,* 1158–1160.

Kamin, L. J. (1969). Selective association and conditioning. In N. J. MacKintosh & W. K. Honig (Eds.), *Fundamental issues in associative learning* (pp. 42–64). Halifax: Dalhousie University Press.

Karlin, R. A. (1979). Hypnotizability and attention. *Journal of Abnormal Psychology, 88,* 92–95.

Karniol, R. (1978). Children's use of intention cues in evaluating behavior. *Psychological Bulletin, 85,* 76–85.

Kart, C. S., Metress, E. S., & Metress, J. F. (1978). *Aging and health.* Menlo Park, CA: Addison-Wesley.

Katona, G. (1940). *Organizing and memorizing: Studies in the psychology of learning and teaching.* New York: Hafner.

Kaufman, I., & Rosenblum, L. (1967). Depression in infant monkeys separated from their mothers. *Science, 155,* 1030–1031.

Kaufmann, G. (1980). *Imagery, language, and cognition: Toward a theory of symbolic activity in human problem-solving.* Bergen, Norway: Universitatsforlaget.

Kearsley, G. P., Buss, A. R., & Royce, J. R. (1977). Developmental changes and the multidimensional cognitive system. *Intelligence, 1,* 257–273.

Keating, C. F., Mazur, A., & Segall, M. H. (1977). Facial gestures which influence the perception of status. *Sociometry, 40,* 374–378.

Keating, D. F., & Clark, L. V. (1980). Development of physical and social reasoning in adolescence. *Developmental Psychology, 16,* 23–30.

Keating, D. P. (1979). Thinking processes in adolescence. In J. Adelson (Ed.), *Handbook of adolescent psychology.* New York: Wiley.

Keele, S. W. (1981). Behavioral analysis of motor control. In V. B. Brooks (Ed.), *Handbook of physiology: Vol. III. Motor control.* American Physiological Society.

Keele, S. W., & Summers, J. J. (1976). The structure of motor programs. In G. E. Stelmach (Ed.), *Motor control: Issues and trends* (pp. 86–142). New York: Academic Press.

Keenan, E. D. (1976). Language universals. In S. R. Harvard, H. D. Steklis, & J. Lancaster (Eds.), *Origins and evolution of language and speech.* Annals of the New York Academy of Sciences, Vol. 200. New York: New York Academy of Sciences.

Keil, F. C. (1981). Constraints on knowledge and cognitive development. *Psychological Review, 88,* 197–227.

Kelley, G. A. (1955). *The psychology of personal constructs.* New York: W. W. Norton.

Kelley, H. H. (1967). Attribution theory in social psychology. In D. Levine (Ed.), *Nebraska Symposium on Motivation* (Vol. 15, pp. 192–238). Lincoln: University of Nebraska Press.

Kelley, H. H. (1972). Causal schemata and the attribution process. In E. E. Jones, D. E. Kanouse, H. H. Kelley, R. E. Nisbett, & Valins (Eds.), *Attribution: Perceiving the causes of behavior* (pp. 151–174). Morristown, NJ: General Learning Press.

Kelley, H. H., Berscheid, E., Christensen, A., Harvey, J., Huston, T., Levinger, G., McClintock, E., Peplau, A., & Peterson, D. (1983). *The psychology of close relationships.* San Francisco: W. H. Freeman.

Kelley, H. H., & Michela, J. L. (1980). Attribution theory and research. *Annual Review of Psychology, 31,* 457–501.

Kellogg, R. T. (1980). Is conscious attention necessary for long-term storage? *Journal of Experimental Psychology: Human Learning and Memory, 6,* 379–390.

Kelman, H. C. (1979). The role of action in attitude change. In M. M. Page (Ed.), *Beliefs, attitudes, values: Nebraska Symposium on Motivation* (Vol. 27, pp. 117–194). Lincoln, NE: University of Nebraska Press.

Kelso, J. A. S., & Clark, J. E. (Eds.). (1982). *The development of movement control and coordination.* new York: Wiley.

Kelso, J. A. S., Holt, K. G., Kugler, P. N., & Turvey, M. T. (1980). On the concept of coordinative structures as dissipative structures: II. Empirical lines of convergence. In G. E. Stelmach & J. Requin (Eds.), *Tutorials in motor behavior* (pp. 49–70). Amsterdam: North-Holland.

Kelso, J. A. S., & Norman, P. E. (1978). Motor schema formation in children. *Developmental Psychology, 14,* 153–156.

Kelso, J. A. S., & Stelmach, G. E. (1976). Control and peripheral mechanisms in motor control. In G. E. Stelmach (Ed.), *Motor control: Issues and trends* (pp. 1–40). New York: Academic Press.

Kelso, J. A. S., & Tuller, B. (1981). Toward a theory of apractic syndromes. *Brain and Language, 12,* 224–245.

Kelso, J. A. S., Tuller, B., & Harris, K. S. (1983). A "dynamic pattern" perspective on the control and coordination of movement. In P. F. MacNeilage (Ed.), *The production of speech* (pp. 137–174). New York: Springer-Verlag.

Kemler, D. G. (1978). Patterns of hypothesis testing in children's discriminative learning: A study of the development of problem-solving strategies. *Developmental Psychology, 14,* 653–673.

Kemler, D. G. (1983). Holistic and analytic modes in perceptual and cognitive development. In T. Tighe & B. E. Shepp (Eds.), *Perception, cognition, and development: Interactional analyses* (pp. 77–102). Hillsdale, NJ: Lawrence Erlbaum Associates.

Kemper, T. D. (1978). *A social interactional theory of emotions.* New York: Wiley.

Kendler, T. S. (1979). The development of discrimination learning: A level of functioning explanation. In H. W. Reese & L. P. Lipsett (Eds.), *Advances in child development and behavior* (Vol. 13, pp. 83–118). New York: Academic Press.

Kennard, M. A. (1947). Autonomic interrelations with the somatic nervous system. *Psychosomatic Medicine, 9,* 29–36.

Kennedy, J. M. (1978). Haptics. In E. C. Carterette & M. P. Friedman (Eds.), *Handbook of perception: Vol. VIV. Perceptual coding* (pp. 289–314). New York: Academic Press.

Kenney, N. J. (1980). A case study of neuroendocrine control of goal-directed behavior: The interaction between angiotensin II and prostaglandin E: in the control of water intake. In R. F. Thompson, L. H. Hickes, V. B. Shvyrkov (Eds.), *Neural mechanisms of goal directed behavior and learning* (pp. 437–446). New York: Academic Press.

Kesner, R. (1973). A neural system analysis of memory storage and retrieval. *Psychological Bulletin, 80,* 177–203.

Kety, S. S. (1970). Neurochemical aspects of emotional behavior. In P. Black (Ed.), *Physiological correlates of emotion* (pp. 61–72). New York: Academic Press.

Kety, S. S., Evarts, E. V., & Williams, H. L. (Eds.). (1967). *Sleep and altered states of consciousness.* Baltimore: Williams & Wilkins.

Kiesler, C. A. (1971). *The psychology of commitment: Experiments linking behavior to belief.* New York: Academic Press.

Kiesler, C. A. (1982). Comments on E. Berscheid's attraction and emotion in interpersonal relations. In M. S. Clark & S. T. Fiske (Eds.), *Affect and cognition: The 17th annual Carnegie Symposium on Cognition.* Hillsdale, NJ: Lawrence Erlbaum Associates.

Kilmann, R. H. (1981). Toward a unique/useful concept of values for interpersonal behavior: A critical review of the literature on value. *Psychological Reports, 48,* 939–959.

Kim, M. P., & Rosenberg, S. (1980). Comparison of two structural models of implicit personality theory. *Journal of Personality and Social Psychology, 38,* 375–389.

Kinsbourne, M. (1974a). Lateral interactions in the brain. In M. Kinsbourne & W. L. Smith

(Eds.), *Hemispheric disconnection and cerebral function* (pp. 239–259). Springfield, IL: Charles Thomas.

Kinsbourne, M. (1974b). Mechanisms of hemispheric interactions in man. In M. Kinsbourne & W. L. Smith (Eds.), *Hemispheric disconnection and cerebral function* (pp. 260–285). Springfield, IL: Charles Thomas.

Kinsbourne, M. (1982). Hemispheric specialization and the growth of human understanding. *American Psychologist, 37,* 411–420.

Kinsbourne, M., & Hicks, R. (1978). Functional cerebral space: A model for overflow, transfer, and inference effects in human performance. In J. Pequin (Ed.), *Attention and performance* (Vol. II, pp. 345–362). Hillsdale, NJ: Lawrence Erlbaum Associates.

Kinsey, A. C., Pomeroy, W. B., & Martin, C. E. (1948). *Sexual behavior in the human male.* Philadelphia: W. B. Saunders.

Kinsey, A. C., Pomeroy, W. B., & Martin, C. E. (1953). *Sexual behavior in the human female.* Philadelphia: W. B. Saunders.

Kirsch, I. (1977). Psychology's first paradigm. *Journal of the History of the Behavioral Sciences, 13,* 317–325.

Kitchener, R. F. (1978). Epigenesis: The role of biological models in developmental psychology. *Human Development, 21,* 141–160.

Klahr, D., & Robinson, M. (1981). Formal assessment of problem-solving and planning processes in preschool children. *Cognitive Psychology, 13,* 113–148.

Klatzky, R. L., & Stoy, A. M. (1978). Semantic information and visual information processing. In J. W. Cotton & R. L. Klatzky (Eds.), *Semantic factors in cognition* (pp. 71–102). Hillsdale, NJ: Lawrence Erlbaum Associates.

Klein, G. S. (1958). Cognitive control and motivation. In G. Lindzey (Ed.), *Assessment of human motives* (pp. 87–118). New York: Rinehart.

Klein, G. S. (1970). *Perception, motives, and personality.* New York: Alfred A. Knopf.

Klein, R. M. (1976). Attention and movement. In G. E. Stelmach (Ed.), *Motor control: Issues and trends* (pp. 143–173). New York: Academic Press.

Kleinmuntz, B. (Ed.). (1966). *Problem solving: Research method and theory.* New York: Wiley.

Klinger, E. (1971). *Structure and functions of fantasy.* New York: Wiley.

Klinger, E. (1977). *Meaning and void: Inner experience and the incentives in people's lives.* Minneapolis: University of Minnesota Press.

Klinger, E., Barta, S. G., Maxeiner, M. E. (1980). Motivational correlates of thought content: Frequency and commitment. *Journal of Personality and Social Psychology, 39,* 1222–1237.

Klitzner, M. D., & Anderson, N. H. (1977). Motivation and expectancy x value: A functional measurement approach. *Motivation and Emotion, 1,* 347–365.

Knapp, M. L. (1972). *Nonverbal communication in human interaction.* New York: Holt, Rinehart & Winston.

Knapp, P. (Ed.). (1963). *Expression of the emotions in man.* New York: International Universities Press.

Knapp, P. (1981). Core processes in the organization of emotions. *Journal of the American Academy of Psychoanalysis, 9,* 415–434.

Koestler, A. (1967). *The ghost in the machine.* New York: Macmillan.

Koestler, A. (1978). *Janus.* New York: Random House.

Koffka, K. (1924). *The growth of the mind.* New York: Harcourt, Brace.

Koffka, K. (1935). *Principles of gestalt psychology.* New York: Harcourt, Brace, & World.

Kogan, N. (1971). Educational implications of cognitive styles. In G. S. Lesser (Ed.), *Psychology and educational practice.* Glenview, IL: Scott, Foresman.

Kogan, N. (1973). Creativity and cognitive style: A life-span perspective. In B. B. Baltes & K. W. Schaie (Eds.), *Life-span developmental psychology: Personality and socialization* (pp. 146–178). New York: Academic Press.

Kohlberg, L. (1958). *The development of modes in moral thinking and choice in the years ten to sixteen.* Unpublished doctoral dissertation, University of Chicago.

Kohlberg, L. (1969). Stage and sequence: The cognitive-developmental approach to socialization. In D. Goslin (Ed.), *Handbook of socialization theory and research* (pp. 347–480). Chicago: Rand McNally.

Kohlberg, L. (1976). Moral stages and moralization. In T. Likona (Ed.), *Moral development: Current theory and research.* New York: Holt, Rinehart & Winston.

Kohlberg, L., & Kramer, R. B. (1969). Continuities and discontinuities in childhood and adult moral development. *Human Development, 12,* 93–120.

Kohlberg, L., Levine, C., & Hewer, A. (1983). *Moral stages: A current formulation and a response to critics.* Basel/New York: Karger.

Kohlberg, L., & Wasserman, E. R. (1980). The cognitive-developmental approach and the practicing counselor: An opportunity for counselors to rethink their roles. *The Personnel and Guidance Journal, 58,* 599–567.

Kohler, I. (1929). *Gestalt psychology.* New York: H. Liveright.

Kohler, I. (1964). The formation and transformation of the perceptual world. *Psychological Issues, 3,* Monograph #12.

Kohn, M. L., & Schooler, C. (1978). The reciprocal effects of the substantive complexity of work and intellectual flexibility: A longitudinal assessment. *American Journal of Sociology, 84,* 24–52.

Kohout, L. J. (1976). Representation of functional hierarchies of movement in the brain. *International Journal of Man-Machine Studies, 8,* 699–709.

Kohout, L. J. (1981). Control of movement and protection structures. *International Journal of Man-Machine Studies, 14,* 397–422.

Kolata, G. B. (1979). Mental disorders: A new approach to treatment. *Science, 203,* 36–38.

Kolata, G. B. (1980). Is your brain really necessary? *Science, 210,* 1232–1235.

Kolata, G. B. (1981). Genes regulated through chromatin structure. *Science, 214,* 775–776.

Kolata, G. B. (1982). New theory of hormones proposed. *Science, 215,* 1383–1384.

Kolers, P. A. (1983). Perception and representation. *Annual Review of Psychology, 34,* 129–166.

Konorski, J. (1967). *Integrative activity of the brain.* Chicago: University of Chicago Press.

Kopelman, R. E. (1979). Directionally different expectancy theory predictions of work motivation and job satisfaction. *Motivation and Emotion, 3,* 299–317.

Kopp, C. B. (1976). Action-schemes of 8 month-old infants. *Developmental Psychology, 12,* 361–362.

Kopp, C. B., & Parmelee, A. H. (1979). Prenatal and perinatal influences on infant behavior. In J. Osofsky (Ed.), *The handbook of infant development* (pp. 29–75). New York: Wiley.

Koranyi, E. K. (1977). Psychobiological correlates of battlefield psychiatry. *The Psychiatric Journal of the University of Ottawa, 2,* 3–19.

Kornblum, S. (Ed.). (1973). *Attention and performance* (Vol. IV). London: Academic Press.

Kornhuber, H. H. (1974). Cerebral cortex, cerebellum, and basal ganglia: An introduction to their motor functions. In F. O. Schmitt & F. G. Worden (Eds.), *The neurosciences: Third stage program* (pp. 267–280). Cambridge, MA: MIT Press.

Koshland, D. E., Goldbeter, A., & Stock, J. B. (1982). Amplification and adaptation in regulatory and sensory systems. *Science, 217,* 220–225.

Kossakowski, A. (1980). Psychology in the German Democratic Republic. *American Psychologist, 35,* 450–460.

Kosslyn, S. M. (1980). *Image and mind.* Cambridge, MA: Harvard University Press.

Kosslyn, S. M. (1985). Mental imagery ability. In R. J. Sternberg (Ed.), *Human abilities.* San Francisco: W. H. Freeman.

Kosslyn, S. M., Pinker, S., Smith, G. E., & Shwartz, S. P. (1979). On the demystification of mental imagery. *The Behavioral and Brain Sciences, 2,* 535–581.

Kosslyn, S. M., & Pomerantz, J. P. (1977). Imagery, propositions, and the form of internal representations. *Cognitive Psychology, 9,* 52–76.

Kozlowski, L. T., Cutting, J. E. (1977). Recognizing the sex of a walker from a dynamic point-light display. *Perception and Psychophysics, 21,* 575–580.

Kral, V. A. (1979). Memories and engrams: A clinical viewpoint. *Canadian Journal of Psychiatry, 24,* 423–430.

Kramer, E. (1964). Elimination of verbal cues in judgments of emotion from voice. *Journal of Abnormal and Social Psychology, 68,* 390–396.

Kramer, R. (1968). *Moral development in young adulthood.* Unpublished doctoral dissertation, University of Chicago.

Krasner, L., & Ullmann, L. P. (1963). Variables affecting report of awareness in verbal conditioning. *Journal of Psychology, 56,* 193–202.

Kreckel, M. (1982). Communicative acts and extralinguistic knowledge. In M. von Cranach & R. Harre (Eds.), *The analysis of action* (pp. 267–312). Cambridge, UK: Cambridge University Press.

Kreitler, H., & Krietler, S. (1976). *Cognitive orientation and behavior.* New York: Springer.

Kretchmer, N., & Walcher, D. N. (1970). Environmental influences on genetic expression. *Fogarty International Center Proceedings,* No. 2, Washington, DC: U.S. Government Printing Office.

Kruglanski, A. W. (1975). The endogenous-exogenous partition in attribution theory. *Psychological Review, 82,* 387–406.

Kubie, L. S. (1961). Hypnotism. *Archives of General Psychiatry, 4,* 40–54.

Kugler, P. N., Kelso, J. A., & Turvey, M. T. (1980). On the concept of coordinative structures as dissipative structures: I. Theoretical lines of convergence. In G. E. Stelmach & J. Requin (Eds.), *Tutorials in motor behavior* (pp. 3–47). Amsterdam: North-Holland.

Kuhl, J., & Beckman, J. (1985). *Action control: From cognition to behavior.* Berlin: Springer-Verlag.

Kuhn, T. S. (1978). *The essential tension: Selected studies in scientific tradition and change.* Chicago: University of Chicago Press.

Kunst-Wilson, W. R., & Zajonc, R. B. (1980). Affective discrimination of stimuli that cannot be recognized. *Science, 301,* 557–558.

Kurtines, W., & Grief, E. (1974). The development of moral thought: Review and evaluation of Kohlberg's approach. *Psychological Bulletin, 81,* 453–470.

Kurtines, W., & Gewitz, J. L. (1984). *Morality, moral behavior, and moral development.* New York: Wiley.

Labouvie-Vief, B. (1985). Intelligence and cognition. In J. E. Birren & K. W. Schaie (Eds.), *Handbook of the psychology of aging* (Vol. 2, pp. 500–530). New York: Van Nostrand Reinhold.

Lacey, J. I. (1950). Individual differences in somatic response patterns. *Journal of Comparative and Physiological Psychology, 43,* 338–350.

Lacey, J. I. (1967). Somatic response patterning and stress: Some revisions of activation theory. In M. H. Appley & R. Trumball (Eds.), *Psychological stress* (pp. 69–83). New York: Appleton-Century-Crofts.

Lacey, J. I., Bateman, D. E., & Van Lehn, R. (1953). Autonomic response specificity: An experimental study. *Psychosomatic Medicine, 15,* 8–21.

Lacey, J. I., Kagan, J., Lacey, B., & Moss, H. A. (1963). The visceral level: Situational determinants and behavioral correlates of autonomic response patterns. In P. H. Knapp (Ed.), *Expression of the emotions in man* (pp. 161–196). New York: International Universities Press

Lacey, J. I., & Lacey, B. C. (1970). Some autonomic-central nervous system interrelationships. In P. Black (Ed.), *Physiological correlates of emotion* (pp. 205–228). New York: Academic Press.

Lacey, J. I., & Van Lehn, R. (1952). Differential emphasis in somatic response to stress. *Psychosomatic Medicine, 14,* 71–81.

Lachman, J. L., & Lachman, R. (1979). Theories of memory organization and human evolution. In C. R. Puff (Ed.), *Memory organization and structure* (pp. 133–190). New York: Academic Press.

Lachman, R., Lachman, J. L., & Butterfield, E. C. (1979). *Cognitive psychology and information processing: An introduction.* Hillsdale, NJ: Lawrence Erlbaum Associates.

Lader, M. H. (Ed.). (1969). Studies of anxiety. *British Journal of Psychiatry* (Special Publication No. 3).

Ladouceur, R. (1974). An experimental test of the learning paradigm of covert positive reinforcement in deconditioning anxiety. *Journal of Behavior Therapy and Experimental Psychiatry, 5,* 3–6.

LaFrance, M., & Mayo, C. (1978). Cultural aspects of nonverbal communication. *International Journal of Intercultural Relations, 2,* 71–89.

Lamb, M. E., & Sherrod, L. R. (Eds.). (1981). *Infant social cognition: Empirical and theoretical considerations.* Hillsdale, NJ: Lawrence Erlbaum Associates.

Lane, D. M. (1979). Developmental changes in attention-deployment skills. *Journal of Experimental Child Psychology, 28,* 16–29.

Langer, E. J. (1979). The illusion of incompetence. In L. C. Perlmuter & R. A. Monty (Eds.), *Choice and perceived control* (pp. 301–313). Hillsdale, NJ: Lawrence Erlbaum Associates.

Lanyon, R. I. (1964). Verbal conditioning and awareness in a sentence construction task. *The American Journal of Psychology, 77,* 472–475.

Lappin, J. S., & Preble, L. D. (1975). A demonstration of shape constancy. *Perception and Psychophysics, 17,* 439–444.

Larish, D. D., & Stelmach, G. E. (1982). Spatial orientation of a limb using egocentric reference points. *Perception and Psychophysics, 32,* 19–26.

Lass, N. J. McReynolds, L. V., Northern, J. L., & Yoder, D. E. (Eds.). (1982). *Speech, language, and hearing: Vol. 3. Hearing Disorders.* Philadelphia: W. B. Saunders.

Lashley, K. S. (1929). *Brain mechanisms and intelligence.* Chicago: University of Chicago Press.

Lashley, K. S. (1942). An examination of the "continuity theory" as applied to discriminative learning. *Journal of General Psychology, 26,* 241–265.

Lashley, K. S. (1951). The problem of serial order in behavior. In L. A. Jeffries (Ed.), *Cerebral mechanisms in behavior* (pp. 112–146). New York: Wiley.

Lashley, K. S. (1960). Continuity theory of discriminative learning. In F. A. Beach, D. O. Hebb, C. T. Morgan, & H. W. Nissen (Eds.), *The neuropsychology of Lashley* (pp. 421–431). New York: McGraw-Hill.

Lasky, R. E. (1977). The effect of visual feedback of the hand on the reaching and retrieval behavior of young infants. *Child Development, 48,* 112–117.

Laszlo, E. (1972). *The systems view of the world.* New York: George Braziller.

Lawther, J. D. (1977). *The learning and performance of physical skills* (2nd ed.). Englewood Cliffs, NJ: Prentice-Hall.

Lavie, P. (1979). Ultradian rhythms in alertness: A pupillometric study. *Biological Psychology, 9,* 49–62.

Lazarus, R. S. (1982). Thoughts on the relations between emotions and cognitions. *American Psychologist, 37,* 1019–1024.

Lazarus, R. S. (1984). On the primacy of cognition. *American Psychologist, 39,* 124–129.

Leahey, T. H., & Holtzman, R. R. (1979). Intention and attention in the recall of prose.

Journal of General Psychology, 101, 189–197.

Leake, C. D. (1969). Historical aspects of the concept of organizational levels of living material. In L. L. Whyte, A. G. Wilson, & D. Wilson (Eds.), *Hierarchical structures* (pp. 147–160). New York: American Elsevier.

Lecky, P. (1945). *Self-consistency: A theory of personality:* New York: Island Press.

Lee, D. N. (1978). The function of vision. In H. Pick & F. Saltzman (Eds.), *Modes of perceiving and processing information* (pp. 159–170). Hillsdale, NJ: Lawrence Erlbaum Associates.

Lee, D. N. (1980). Visuo-motor coordination in space-time. In G. E. Stelmach & J. Requin (Eds.), *Tutorials in motor behavior* (pp. 281–295). Amsterdam: North-Holland.

Lee, D. N., & Reddish, P. E. (1981). Plummeting gannets: A paradigm of ecological optics. *Nature, 293,* 293–294.

Leff, J. (1977). The cross-cultural study of emotions. *Culture, Medicine, and Psychiatry, 1,* 317–350.

LeGare, M. (1980). Overlapping functional systems: A theory for vertebrate central nervous system function in terms of informal systems analysis. *Behavioral Science, 25,* 89–106.

Leibowitz, H. W., & Harvey, L. O., Jr. (1973). Perception. *Annual Review of Psychology, 24,* 207–240.

Leight, K. A., & Ellis, H. C. (1981). Emotional mood states, strategies, and stage-dependability in memory. *Journal of Verbal Learning and Verbal Behavior, 20,* 251–275.

Leith, E. N. (1976). White light holograms. *Scientific American, 235,* 80.

Lennenberg, E. H. (1967). *Biological foundations of language.* New York: Wiley.

Lerner, J. V., & Lerner, R. M. (1983). Temperament and adaptation across life: Theoretical and empirical issues. In P. B. Baltes & O. G. Brim, Jr. (Eds.), *Life-span development and behavior* (Vol. 5, pp. 198–233). New York: Academic Press.

Lerner, R. M. (1976). *Concepts and theories of human development.* Reading, MA: Addison-Wesley.

Lerner, R. M. (1978). Nature, nurture, and dynamic interactionism. *Human Development. 21,* 1–20.

Lerner, R. M. (1980). Concepts of epigenesis: Descriptive and explanatory issues. *Human Development, 23,* 63–72.

Lerner, R. M. (Ed.). (1983). *Developmental psychology: Historical and philosophical perspectives.* Hillsdale, NJ: Lawrence Erlbaum Associates.

Lerner, R. M. (1984). *On the nature of human plasticity.* Cambridge, UK: Cambridge University Press.

Lerner, R. M., & Busch-Rossnagel, N. (Eds.). (1981). *Individuals as producers of their own development: A life-span perspective.* New York: Academic Press.

Leshner, A. I. (1977). Hormones and emotions. In D. K. Candlan, J. P. Fell, E. Keen, A. I. Leshner, R. Plutchik, & R. M. Tarpy (Eds.), *Emotion* (pp. 85–148). Belmont, CA: Brooks/Cole (Wadsworth).

Lesse, S. (1959). Experimental studies on the relationship between anxiety, dreams and dream-like states. *American Journal of Psychotherapy, 13,* 440–455.

Lester, D. (1969). *Explorations in exploration.* New York: Van Nostrand-Reinhold.

Levenson, E. H. (1975). *A holographic model of psychoanalytic change. Contemporary Psychoanalysis, 12*(1). New York: Academic Press.

Leventhal, H. (1982). The integration of emotion and cognition: A view from the perceptual-motor theory of emotion. In M. S. Clark, & S. T. Fiske (Eds.), *Affect and cognition: The 17th Annual Carnegie Symposium on Cognition.* Hillsdale, NJ: Lawrence Erlbaum Associates.

Leventhal, H., & Tomarken, A. J. (1986). Emotion: Today's problems. *Annual Review of Psychology, 37,* 565–610.

Levin, D. A. (1970). Developmental instability and evolution in peripheral isolates. *American Naturalist, 104,* 343.

Levin, M. (1980). Consciousness and the highest cerebral centres, with remarks on the Penfield-Walshe controversy. *The Journal of Mental Science, 106,* 1398–1404.

Levine, G. C. (1979). The form-content distinction in moral development research. *Human Development, 22,* 225–234.

Levine, S. (1966). Sex differences in the brain. *Scientific American, 214,* 84–90.

Levy, F. (1980). The development of sustained attention (vigilance) in children: Some normative data. *Journal of Child Psychology and Psychiatry and Allied Disciplines, 21,* 77–84.

Levy, J. (1980). Cerebral asymmetry and the psychology of man. In M. C. Wittrock (Ed.), *The brain and psychology* (pp. 245–321). New York: Academic Press.

Lewin, K. (1935). *A dynamic theory of personality: Selected papers.* New York: McGraw-Hill.

Lewin, K. (1936). *Principles of topological psychology.* New York: McGraw-Hill.

Lewin, K., Dembo, T., Festinger, L., & Sears, P. S. (1944). Level of aspiration. In J. McV. Hunt (Ed.), *Personality and the behavior disorders* (Vol. 1, pp. 333–398). New York: Ronald Press.

Lewin, R. (1980). Evolutionary theory under fire. *Science, 210,* 883–886.

Lewin, R. (1981a). Do jumping genes make evolutionary leaps? *Science, 213,* 634–636.

Lewin, R. (1981b). Seeds of change in embryonic development. *Science, 214,* 42–44.

Lewin, R. (1981c). Do chromosomes cross talk? *Science, 214,* 134–135.

Lewin, R. (1982). Biology is not postage stamp collecting. *Science, 216,* 718–720.

Lewin, R. (1984). Why is development so illogical? *Science, 224,* 1327–1329.

Lewin, R. (1985). Pattern and process in life's history. *Science, 229,* 151–153.

Lewinsohn, P. M., Munoz, R. F., Youngden, M. A., & Zeiss, A. M. (Eds.). (1978). *Control your depression.* Englewood Cliffs, NJ: Prentice-Hall.

Lewinsohn, P. M., Steinmetz, J. L., Larson, D. W., & Franklin, J. (1981). Depression-related cognitions: Antecedent or consequence? *Journal of Abnormal Psychology, 90,* 213–219.

Lewis, M. (1978). Attention and verbal labeling behavior in preschool children: A study in the measurement of internal representations. *Journal of Genetic Psychology, 133,* 191–202.

Lewis, M., & Brooks-Gunn, J. (1979). *Social cognition and the acquisition of self.* New York: Plenum Press.

Lewis, M., & Michalson, L. (1983). *Children's emotions and moods.* New York: Plenum Press.

Lewis, M., & Rosenblum, L. A. (Eds.). (1974). *The origins of fear.* New York: Wiley.

Lewis, M., & Rosenblum, L. A. (Eds.). (1978). *The development of affect.* New York: Plenum Press.

Lewis, T. (Ed.). (1983). *Insect communication.* Orlando, FL: Academic Press.

Lewontin, R. C. (1981). On constraints and adaptation. *Behavioral and Brain Sciences, 4,* 244–245.

Lewontin, R. (1984). *Human diversity.* New York: Freeman.

Liberman, A. M. (1982). On finding that speech is special. *American Psychologist, 37,* 148–167.

Liberman, A. M., Cooper, F. S., Shankweiler, D. P., & Studdert-Kennedy, M. (1967). Perception of the speech code. *Psychological Review, 74,* 431–461.

Liberman, M. Y. (1983). Uncommon approaches to the study of speech. In P. F. MacNeilage (Ed.), *The production of speech* (pp. 265–274). New York: Springer-Verlag.

Lichtenstein, E. H., & Brewer, W. F. (1980). Memory for goal directed events. *Cognitive Psychology, 12,* 412–445.

Liebeskind, J. C., & Paul, L. A. (1977). Psychological and physiological mechanisms of pain. *Annual Review of Psychology, 28,* 41–60

Lilly, J. C. (1956). Mental effects of reduction of ordinary levels of physical stimuli on intact healthy persons. *Psychiatric Research Reports, 5,* 1–9.

Lilly, J. C. (1962). The effect of sensory deprivation on consciousness. In K. E. Schaefer (Ed.), *International symposium on submarine and space medicine: Vol. 2. Environmental effects on consciousness* (pp. 93–95). New York: Macmillan.

Lilly, J. C., & Miller, A. M. (1962). Operant conditioning of the bottlenose dolphin with electrical stimulation of the brain. *Journal of Comparative and Physiological Psychology, 55*, 73–79.

Lindblom, B. (1983). Economy of speech gestures. In P. F. MacNeilage (Ed.), *The production of speech*. New York: Springer Verlag.

Lindemann, E. (1944). Symptomatology and management of acute grief. *American Journal of Psychiatry, 101*, 141–148.

Lindsay, P. H., & Norman, D. A. (1972). *Human information processing*. New York: Academic Press.

Lindsley, D. B. (1951). Emotion. In S. S. Stevens (Ed.), *Handbook of experimental psychology* (pp. 473–516). New York: Wiley.

Lindsley, D. B. (1957). Psychophysiology and motivation. In R. M. Jones (Ed.), *Nebraska Symposium on Motivation* (pp. 44–104). Lincoln: University of Nebraska Press.

Lindsley, D. B. (1960). Attention, consciousness, sleep and wakefulness. In J. Field (Ed.), *Handbook of physiology-neurophysiology* (Vol. 3, pp. 1553–1593). Washington, DC: Amerian Physiological Society.

Lindsley, D. B. (1961). The reticular activating system and perceptual integration. In D. E. Sheer (Ed.), *Electrical stimulation of the brain* (pp. 513–534). Austin: University of Texas Press.

Lindsley, D. B. (1970). The role of nonspecific reticulo-thalamo-cortical systems in emotion. In P. Black (Ed.), *Physiological correlates of emotion* (pp. 147–189). New York: Academic Press.

Lingle, J. H., & Ostrom, T. M. (1981). Principles of memory and cognition in attitude formation. In R. E. Petty, T. M. Ostrom, & T. C. Brock (Eds.), *Cognitive responses to persuasion* (pp. 399–420). Hillsdale, NJ: Lawrence Erlbaum Associates.

Livingston, W. K. (1943). *Pain mechanisms*, New York: Macmillan.

Locke, E. A. (1969a). Purpose without consciousness: A contradiction. *Psychological Reports, 25*, 991–1009.

Locke, E. A. (1969b). What is job satisfaction? *Organizational Behavior and Human Performance, 4*, 303–336.

Locke, E. A. (1973). Satisfiers and dissatisfiers among white collar and blue collar employees. *Journal of Applied Psychology, 58*, 67–76.

Locke, E. A. (1978). The ubiquity of the technique of goal setting in theories and approaches to employee motivation. *Academy of Management Review, 3*, 594–601.

Locke, E. A. (1983). Nature and causes of job satisfaction. In M. D. Dunnette (Ed.), *Handbook of industrial and organizational psychology* (pp. 1297–1350). New York: Wiley.

Locke, E. A., Cartledge, N., & Knerr, C. S. (1970). Studies of the relationship between satisfaction, goal-setting, and performance. *Organizational Behavior and Human Performance, 5*, 135–158.

Locke, E. A., Feren, D. B., McCaleb, D. M., Shaw, K. N., & Denny, A. T. (1980). The relative effectiveness of four methods of motivating employee performance. In K. Duncan, M. Gruneberg, & D. Wallis (Eds.), *Changes in working life*. New York: Wiley.

Locke, E. A., Shaw, K. N., Saari, L. M., & Latham, G. P. (1981). Goal setting and task performance 1969-1980. *Psychological Bulletin, 90*, 125–152.

Locurto, C. M., Terrace, H. S., & Gibbon (Eds.). (1981). *Autoshaping and conditioning theory*. New York: Academic Press.

Loevinger, J., & Knoll, E. (1983). Personality: Stages, traits, and the self. *Annual Review of Psychology, 34*, 195–222.

Loftus, E. F., & Loftus, G. R. (1980). On the permanence of stored information in the brain. *American Psychologist, 35,* 409–420.

Logue, A. W., Ophir, I., & Strauss, K. E. (1981). The acquisition of taste aversions in humans. *Beahviors Research and Therapy, 19,* 319–333.

Loiselle, D. L., Stamm, J. S., Maitinsky, S., & Whipple, S. C. (1980). Evoked potential and behavioral signs of attentive dysfunctions in hyperactive boys. *Psychophysiology, 17,* 193–201.

Lomov, B. F. (1980). Introductory remarks to the Soviet-American Symposium on Neurophysiological Mechanisms of Goal-Directed Behavior. In F. Thompson, L. H. Hicks, & V. B. Shvyrkov (Eds.), *Neural mechanisms of goal-directed behavior and learning* (pp. 3–10). New York: Academic Press.

Long, G. M. (1980). Iconic memory: A review and critique of the study of short-term visual storage. *Psychological Bulletin, 88,* 785–820.

Longino, C. F., Jr., Lipmann, A. (1981). Married and spouseless men and women in planned retirement communities: Support network differentials. *Journal of Marriage and the Family, 43,* 169–177.

Lord, C. G. (1982). Predicting behavioral consistency from an individual's perception of situational similarities. *Journal of Abnormal and Social Psychology, 42,* 1076–1088.

Lorenz, K. (1963). *On aggression.* New York: Harcourt, Brace & World.

Lorenz, K. (1970). *Studies in animal and human behavior* (Vol. 1). (R. Martin, Trans.). Cambridge, MA: Harvard University Press.

Lorenz, K. Z. (1981). *The foundations of ethology.* New York: Springer-Verlag.

Lovejoy, C. O. (1981). The origin of man. *Science, 211,* 341–350.

Lowenthal, M. F., Thurnher, M., Chivriboga, D. (Eds.). (1976). *Four stages of life.* San Francisco: Jossey-Bass.

Lowenfeld, V., & Brittain, W. L. (1970). *Creative and mental growth* (5th ed.). New York: Macmillan.

Lukas, J. H. (1980). Human auditory attention: The olivochochlear bundle may function as a peripheral filter. *Psychophysiology, 17,* 444–452.

Lumsden, C. J. (1983). Neuronal group selection and the evolution of hominid cranial capacity. *Journal of Human Evolution, 12,* 169–184.

Lumsden, C. J., & Wilson, E. O. (1981). *Genes, mind and culture.* Cambridge, MA: Harvard University Press.

Luria, A. R. (1973). *The working brain.* New York: Basic Books.

Luria, A. R. (1976). *The neuropsychology of memory.* Washington, DC: V. H. Winston & Sons.

Luria, A. R. (1981). *Language and cognition.* New York: Wiley.

Luria, A. R., & Vinogradova, O. S. (1959). An objective investigation of the dynamics of semantic systems. *British Journal of Psychology 50,* 89–105.

Lyons, W. (1980). *Emotion.* Cambridge, UK: Cambridge University Press.

Maccoby, E. E., & Martin, J. A. (1983). Socialization in the context of the family: Parent-child interaction. In P. H. Mussen (Ed.), *Handbook of child development (4th ed.): Vol. 4. Socialization, personality and social development* (pp. 1–102). New York: Wiley.

MacCrimmon, K. R., & Taylor, R. N. (1983). Decision making and problem solving. In M. D. Dunnette (Ed.), *Handbook of industrial and organizational psychology* (pp. 1397–1454). New York: Wiley.

MacKenzie, B. D. (1977). *Behaviourism and the limits of scientific method.* Atlantic Highlands, NJ: Humanities Press.

Mackworth, J. F. (1970). *Vigilance and attention.* Baltimore: Penguin Books.

MacLean, P. (1963). Phylogenesis. In P. H. Knapp (Ed.), *Expression of the emotions in man* (pp. 16–35). New York: International Universities Press.

MacLean, P. D. (1970a). The triune brain, emotion and scientific bias. In F. O. Schmitt (Ed.), *The neurosciences second study program* (pp. 336–348). New York: The Rockfeller

University Press.

MacLean, P. D. (1970b). The limbic brain in relation to the psychoses. In P. Black (Ed.), *Physiological correlates of emotion* (pp. 130–147). New York: Academic Press.

MacLean, P. D. (1982). On the origin and progressive evolution of the triune brain. In E. Armstrong & D. Falk (Eds.), *Primate brain evolution* (pp. 291–316). New York: Plenum Press.

MacLusky, N. J., & Naftolin, F. (1981). Sexual differentiation of the central nervous system. *Science, 211,* 1294–1324.

MacNeilage, P. F. (1970). Motor control of serial ordering of speech. *Psychological Review, 77,* 182–196.

MacNeilage, P. F. (1980). Distinctive properties of speech motor control. In G. E. Stelmach & J. Requin (Eds.), *Tutorials in motor behavior* (pp. 607–621). Amsterdam: North-Holland.

MacNeilage, P. F. (Ed.). (1983). *The production of speech.* New York: Springer-Verlag.

Maddi, S. R. (1976). *Personality theories: A comparative analysis* (3rd ed.). Homewood, IL: Dorsey Press.

Magnusson, D. (Ed.). (1980). *Toward a psychology of situations: An interactional perspective.* Hillsdale, NJ: Lawrence Erlbaum Associates.

Magnusson, D., & Endler, N. S. (Eds.). (1977a). *Personality at the crossroads: current issues in interactional psychology.* Hillsdale, NJ: Lawrence Erlbaum Associates.

Magnusson, E., & Endler, N. S. (1977b). Interactional psychology: Present status and future prospects. In D. Magnusson & N. S. Endler (Eds.), *Personality at the crossroads: Current issues in interactional psychology.* Hillsdale, NJ: Lawrence Erlbaum Associates.

Magoun, H.W. (1958). *The waking brain.* Springfield, IL: Charles C. Thomas.

Malacinski, G. M.,. & Bryant, S. V. (Eds.). (1984). *Pattern formation.* New York: Macmillan.

Malina, R. M. (1980). Environmentally related correlates of motor development and performance during infancy and childhood. In C. Corbin (Ed.), *A textbook of motor development* (pp. 31–53). Dubuque, IA: W. C. Brown.

Malmo, R. B. (1959). Activation: A neurophysiological dimension. *Psychological Review, 66,* 367–386.

Mancuso, J. C., & Ceely, S. G. (1980). The self as memory processing. *Cognitive Therapy and Research, 4,* 1–25.

Mandler, G. (1975). *Mind and emotion.* New York: Wiley.

Mandler, G. (1979). Organization, memory, and mental structure. In C. R. Puff (Ed.), *Memory organization and structure* (pp. 304–320). New York: Academic Press.

Mandler, G. (1980). Recognizing: The judgment of previous occurrence. *Psychological Review, 87,* 252–271.

Mandler, J. M. (1979). Categorical and schematic organization in memory. In C. R. Puff (Ed.), *Memory organization and structure* (pp. 255–302). New York: Academic Press.

Mandler, J. M. (1983). Representation. In J. H. Flavell & E. M. Markman (Eds.), *Cognitive development: Vol. 3. Manual of child psychology* (pp. 420–494). New York: Wiley.

Mandler, J. H. (1984). Representation and recall in infancy. In M. Moscovitch (Ed.), *Infant memory* (pp. 75–102). New York: Plenum Press.

Manicas, P. T., & Secord, P. F. (1983). Implications for psychology of the new philosophy of science. *American Psychologist, 38,* 399–413.

Manicas, P. T., & Secord, P. F. (1984). Implications for psychology: Reply to comments. *American Psychologist, 39,* 922–926.

Manoccho, A. J., & Dunn, J. (1970). *The time game: Two views of a prison.* Beverly Hills, CA: Sage.

Manstead, A. S., & Wagner, H. L. (1981). Arousal, cognition and emotion: An appraisal of two-factor theory. *Current Psychological Reviews, 1,* 35–54. 4.

Mantegazza, P. (1932). *Sexual relations of mankind.* New York: Falstaff Press.

Marcus, R. F. (1980). Empathy and popularity of preschool children. *Child Study Journal,*

10, 133–145.

Margolis, R., & Popkin, N. (1980). Marijuana: A review of medical research with implications for adolescents. *The Personnel and Guidance Journal, 59,* 7–14.

Marin, O. S. M., & Gordon, B. (1980). Language and speech production from a neuropsychological perspective. In G. E. Stelmach & J. Requin (Eds.), *Tutorials in motor behavior* (pp. 524–536). Amsterdam: North-Holland.

Marks, L. E. (1978). Multimodal perception. In E. C. Carterette & M. P. Friedman (Eds.), *Handbook of perception: Vol. 8. Perceptual coding* (pp. 321–343). New York: Academic Press.

Markus, H. (1977). Self-schemata and information processing about the self. *Journal of Personality and Social Psychology, 35,* 63–78.

Markus, H. & Wurf, E. (1987). The dynamic self-concept: A social psychological perspective. *Annual Review of Psychology, 38,* 299–337.

Marler, P., & Terrace, H. (Eds.). (1984). *The biology of learning.* Berlin: Springer-Verlag.

Marshall, G. D., & Zimbardo, P. G. (1979). Affective consequences of inadequately explained physiological arousal. *Journal of Personality and Social psychology, 37,* 970–988.

Marshall, J. C. (1982). Models of the mind in health and diseases. In A. W. Ellis (Ed.), *Normality and pathology in cognitive functions* (pp. 1–18). New York: Academic Press.

Martenuik, R. G., & MacKenzie, C. L. (1980). A preliminary theory of two-handed coordinated control. In G. E. Stelmach & J. Requin (Eds.), *Tutorials in motor behavior* (pp. 185–197). Amsterdam: North-Holland.

Maruyama, M. (1963). The second cybernetics: Deviation-amplifying mutual causal processes. *American Scientist, 51,* 164–179.

Marx, J. L. (1980). Calmodulin: A protein for all seasons. *Science, 203,* 274–176.

Marx, J. L. (1981a). Gene control puzzle begins to yield. *Science, 212,* 653–655.

Marx, J. L. (1981b). Brain opiates in mental illness. *Science, 214,* 1013–1015.

Marx, J. L. (1981c). Electric currents may guide development *Science, 211,* 1147–1149.

Marx, J. L. (1984). New clues to developmental timing. *Science, 226,* 425–426.

Marx, J. L. (1985a). A potpourri of membrane receptors. *Science, 230,* 649–651.

Marx, J. L. (1985b). The immune system "belongs in the body." *Science, 227,* 1190–1192.

Marx, J. L. (1985c). "Anxiety peptide" found in brain, *Science, 227,* 984.

Marx, O. (1967). The history of the biological basis of language. In E. H. Lennenberg (Ed.), *Biological foundations of language* (pp. 443–469). New York: Wiley.

Maslach, C. (1979). Negative emotional biasing of unexplained arousal. *Journal of Personality and Social Psychology, 37,* 953–969.

Maslow, A. H. (1954). *Motivation and personality.* New York: Harper & Row.

Mast, V. K., Fagen, J. W., Rovee-Collier, C. K., & Sullivan, M. W. (1980). Immediate and long-term memory or reinforcement context: The development of learned expectancies in early infancy. *Child Development, 51,* 700–707.

Masters, W. H., & Johnson, V. E. (1966). *Human sexual response.* Boston: Little, Brown.

Masterton, R. B., & Berkeley, M. A. (1974). Brain function: Changing ideas on the role of sensory, motor, and association cortex in behavior. *Annual Review of Psychology, 25,* 277–310.

Matarazzo, J. D., Saslow, G., & Pareis, E. N. (1960). Verbal conditioning of two response classes. *Journal of Abnormal and Social Psychology, 61,* 190–206.

Mathews, C. O. (1977). A review of behavioral theories of depression and a self-regulation model for depression. *Psychotherapy: Theory, Research and Practice, 14,* 79–86.

Matthysse, S. (1977). The biology of attention. *Schizophrenia Bulletin, 3,* 370–372.

Maturana, H. R. (1975). The organization of the living: A theory of the living organization. *International Journal of Man-Machine Studies, 7,* 313–332.

Maugh, T. H., II. (1981). A new understanding of Sickle Cell emerges. *Science, 211,* 266.

Mayer, R. E., & Bromage, B. K. (1980). Different recall protocols for technical texts due to advance organizers. *Journal of Educational Psychology, 72,* 209–225.

Mayes, A. (1979). The physiology of fear and anxiety. In W. Sluckin (Ed.), *Fear in animals and man* (pp. 24–55). New York: Van Nostrand-Reinhold.

Mayo, C., & LaFrance, M. (1978). On the acquisition of nonverbal communication: A review. *Merrill-Palmer Quarterly, 24,* 213–228.

Mayr, E. (1954). Change of genetic environment and evolution. In J. Huxley, A. C. Hardy, & E. B. Ford (Eds.), *Evolution as a process* (pp. 157–180). London: George Allen & Unwin.

Mayr, E. (1963). *Animal species and evolution.* Cambridge, MA: Harvard University Press.

Mayr, E. (1974). Behavior programs and evolutionary strategies. *American Scientist, 62,* 650–659.

Mayr, E. (1982). *The growth of biological thought.* Cambridge, MA: Harvard University Press.

McBain, W. N. (1970). Arousal, monotony, and accidents in line driving. *Journal of Applied Psychology, 54,* 509–519.

McCabe, M. P., Collins, J. K., & Burns, A. M. (1978). Hypnosis as an altered state of consciousness: I. A review of traditional theories. *Australian Journal of Clinical and Experimental Hypnosis, 6,* 39–54.

McCall, R. B. (1974). Exploratory manipulation and play in the human infant. *Monographs of the Society for Research in Child Development, 39,* (1550).

McCall, R. B. (1981). Nature-nurture and the two realms of development: A proposed integration with respect to mental development. *Child Development, 52,* 1–12.

McCall, R. B., & Kennedy, C. B. (1980). Attention of 4-month old infants to discrepancy and babyishness. *Journal of Experimental Child Psychology, 29,* 189–201.

McClearn, G. E. (1981). Animal models of genetic factors in alcoholics. *Advances in Substance Abuse, 2,* 185–217.

McClearn, G. E., & De Fries, J. C. (1973). *Introduction to behavioral genetics.* San Francisco: Freeman.

McClelland, D. C. (1980). Motive dispositions: The merits of operant and respondent measures. In L. Wheeler (Ed.), *Review of personality and social psychology* (Vol. 1). Beverly Hills, CA: Sage.

McClelland, D. C. (1985a). How motives, skills and values determine what people do. *American Psychologist, 40,* 812–825.

McClelland, D. C. (1985b). *Human motivation.* Glenview, IL: Scott Foresman.

McClelland, D. C., Atkinson, J. W., Clark, R. A., & Lowell, E. L. (1953). *The achievement motive.* New York: Appleton-Century-Crofts.

McClenaghan, B. A., & Gallahue, D. L. (1978a). *Fundamental movement: A developmental and remedial approach.* Philadelphia: W. B. Saunders.

McClenaghan, B. A., & Gallahue, D. L. (1978b). *Fundamental movement: Observation and assessment.* Philadelphia: W. B. Saunders.

McClintock, C. G. (1978). Social values: Their definition, measurement and development. *Journal of Research and Development in Education, 12,* 121–137.

McCloskey, M. E., & Gluksberg, S. (1978). Natural categories: Well defined or fuzzy sets. *Memory and Cognition, 6,* 462–472.

McColloch, W. S. (Ed.). (1965). *Embodiments of mind.* Cambridge, MA: MIT Press.

McCrosky, J. C., Daly, J. A., Richmond, V. P., & Falcione, R. L. (1977). Studies of the relationship between communication apprehension and self-esteem. *Human Communications Research, 3,* 269–277.

McDougall, W. (1908). *An introduction to social psychology.* London: Methuen.

McDougall, W. (1921). *An introduction to social psychology.* Boston: Luce.

McDougall, W. (1933). *The energies of men.* New York: Scribners.

McFarland, D. J. (1971). *Feedback mechanisms in animal behavior.* London: Academic Press.

McGaugh, J. L., Martenez, J. L., Jr., Jensen, R. A., Messiny, R. B., & Vasquez, B. J. (1980).

Central and peripheral cathecholomine function in learning and memory processes. In R. F. Thompson, L. H. Hicks, & V. B. Shvyrkov (Eds.), *Neural mechanisms of goal-directed behavior and learning* (pp. 75–91). New York: Academic Press.

McGeer, P. L., Eccles, J.C., & McGeer, E. G. (1978). *Molecular neurobiology of the mammalian brain*. New York: Plenum Press.

McGeer, P. L., & McGeer, E. G. (1980). Chemistry of mood and emotion. *Annual Review of Psychology, 31,* 273–307.

McGhie, A., & Chapman, J. (1961). Disorders of attention and perception in early schizophrenia. *British Journal of Medical Psychology, 34,* 103–116.

McGraw, M. (1935). *Growth: A study of Johnny and Jimmy*. New York: Appleton-Century-Crofts.

McGuigan, F. J. (1978). Imagery and thinking: Covert functioning of the motor system. In G. E. Schwartz & D. Shapiro (Eds.), *Consciousness and self-regulation: Advances in research and theory* (Vol. 2, pp. 37–100). New York: Plenum Press.

McGuiness, D., & Pribram, K. (1980). Emotion and motivation in attention. In M. C. Wittrock (Ed.), *The brain and psychology* (pp. 95–139). New York: Academic Press.

McLean, J. P., & Shulman, G. L. (1978). On the construction and maintenance of expectancies. *Quarterly Journal of Experimental Psychology, 30,* 441–454.

McMahon, T. A. (1984). *Muscles, reflexes and locomotion*. Princeton: Princeton University Press.

McMullen, E. (1983). Values in science. In P. D. Asquith & T. Mickles (Eds.), *Proceedings of the 1982 Philosophy of Science Asociation* (Vol. 2, pp. 3–23). East Lansing, MI: Philosophy of Science Association.

McVey, W. E. (Ed.). (1901). *The human machine: Its care and repair*. Topeka, KS: Herbert S. Reed.

Mead, G. (1934). *Mind, self, and society*. Chicago: University of Chicago Press.

Meadows, P. (1957). Models, systems, and science. *American Sociology Review, 22,* 3–9.

Meadows, S. (Ed.). (1983). *Developing thinking: Approaches to children's cognitive development: Psychology in progress*. London: Methuen.

Medin, D. L., & Schaffer, M. M. (1979). Context theory of classification learning. *Psychological Review, 85,* 207–238.

Medin, D. L., & Smith, E. E. (1984). Concepts and concept formation. *Annual Review of Psychology, 35,* 113–138.

Meehl, P. E. (1977). Specific etiology and other forms of strong influence: Some quantitative meanings. *Journal of Medical Philosophy, 2,* 33–53.

Meehl, P. E. (1978). Theoretical risks and tabular asterisks: Sir Karl, Sir Ronald, and the slow progress in soft psychology. *Journal of Consulting Clinical Psychology, 46,* 806–834.

Meethan, A. R. (1969). *Encyclopedia of linguistics, information and control*. London: Pergamon Press.

Megela, A. L., & Teyler, T. J. (1979). Habituation and the human evoked potential. *Journal of Comparative and Physiological Psychology, 93,* 1154–1170.

Mehler, J., Bertoncini, J., Barriere, M., & Jassik-Gerschenfeld, D. (1978). Infant recognition of mother's voice. *Perception, 7,* 491–497.

Mehrabian, A. (1972). *Nonverbal communication*. Chicago: Aldine-Atherton.

Melges, F. T., & Poppen, R. L. (1976). Expectation of rewards and emotional behavior in monkeys. *Journal of Psychiatric Research, 13,* 11–21.

Mellen, S. L. W. (1981). *The evolution of love*. Oxford: Freeman.

Meltzoff, A. N., & Moore, M. K. (1977). Imitation of facial and manual gestures by human neonates. *Science, 198,* 75–78.

Melzak, R. (1973). *The puzzle of pain*. New York: Basic Books.

Melzak, R., & Dennis, S. G. (1978). Neurophysiological foundations of pain. In R. A. Sternbach (Ed.), *The psychology of pain* (pp. 1–26). New York: Raven Press.

Melzak, R., & Loeser, J. D. (1978). Phantom body pain in paraplegics: Evidence for a central "pattern generating mechanism" for pain. *Pain, 4,* 195–210.

Melzak, R., & Torgerson, W. W. (1971). On the language of pain. *Anesthesiology, 34,* 54.

Melzak, R., & Wall, P. D. (1962). On the nature of cutaneous sensory mechanisms. *Brain, 85,* 331–356.

Melzak, R., & Wall, P. D. (1965). Pain mechanisms: A new theory. *Science, 150,* 971–979.

Menninger, K. A. (1954). Psychological aspects of the organism under stress. *Journal of the American Psychoanalytic Association, 2,* 67–106, 280–310.

Menninger, K. (1963). The vital balance. *New York: Viking Press.*

Mercier, P., & Ladouceur, R. (1977). Attention in awareness and performance in verbal conditioning. *Psychological Reports, 41,* 863–873.

Mervis, C. B., & Rosch, E. (1981). Categorization of natural objects. Annual Review of Psychology, 32, 89–115.

Mesarovic, M. D., & Macke, D. (1969). Foundations for a scientific theory of hierarchical systems. In L. L. Whyte, A. G. Wilson, & D. Wilson (Eds.), Hierarchical structures *(pp. 29–50). New York: American Elsevier.*

Meyer, W-U., Bachmann, M., Biermann, U., Hempelmann, M., Plöger, F. O., & Spiller, H. (1979). The informational value of evaluative behavior: Influences of praise and blame on perceptions of ability. *Journal of Educational Psychology, 71,* 259–268.

Michaels, C. F., & Carello, C. (1981). *Direct perception.* Englewood, NJ: Prentice-Hall.

Miles, F. A., & Evarts, E. V. (1979). Concepts of motor organization. *Annual Review of Psychology, 30,* 327–362.

Miller, A. (1978). Conceptual systems theory: A critical review. *Genetic Psychology Monographs,* 97–126.

Miller, G. A. (1956a). Psychology's block of marble. *Contemporary Psychology, 1,* 252.

Miller, G. A. (1956b). The magical number seven, plus or minus two, or some limits in our capacity for processing information. *Psychological Review, 63,* 81–97.

Miller, G. A., Galanter, E., & Pribram, K. H. (1960). *Plans and the structure of behavior.* New York: Holt, Rinehart & Winston.

Miller, G. A., & Johnson-Laird, P. N. (1976). *Language and perception.* Cambridge, MA: Belknap/Harvard University Press.

Miller, I. W., III., & Norman, W. H. (1979). Learned helplessness in humans: A review and attribution theory model. *Psychological Bulletin, 86,* 93–118.

Miller, J. G. (1942). *Unconsciousness.* New York: Wiley.

Miller, J. G. (1978). *Living systems.* New York: McGraw-Hill.

Miller, J. H., & Reznikoff, W. S. (Eds.). (1978). *The operon.* Cold Spring Harbor NY: Cold Spring Harbor Monograph Series.

Miller, N. E. (1978). Biofeedback and visceral learning. *Annual Review of Psychology, 29,* 373–404.

Miller, N. E., & Dworkin, B. R. (1980). Different ways in which learning is involved in homeostesis. In R. F. Thompson, L. H. Hicks, & V. B. Shvyrkov (Eds.), *Neural mechanisms of goal-directed behavior and learning* (pp. 57–73) New York: Academic Press.

Miller, S. M. (1979). Controllability and human stress: Method, evidence and theory. *Behavior Research and Therapy, 17,* 287–304.

Milsum, J. H. (Ed.). (1968). *Positive feedback.* Oxford: Pergamon Press.

Mineka, S., & Henderson, R. W. (1985). Controllability and predictability in acquired motivation. *Annual Review of Psychology, 36,* 495–529.

Minsky M. A. (1975). A framework for representing knowledge. In P. Winston (Ed.), *The psychology of computer vision.* New York: McGraw-Hill.

Mischel, W. (1968). *Personality and assessment.* New York: Wiley.

Mischel, W. (1973). Towards a cognitive social learning reconceptualization of personality. *Psychological Review, 80,* 252–283.

Mischel, W. (1977). On the future of personality measurement. *American Psychologist, 32,* 246–254.

Mischel, W. (1979). On the interface of cognition and personality: Beyond the person-situation debate. *American Psychologist, 34,* 740–754.

Mischel, W. (1981). Metacognition and the rules of delay. In J. H. Flavell & L. D. Ross (Ed.), *Social cognitive development: Frontiers and possible futures* (pp. 240–271). New York: Cambridge University Press.

Mischel, W. (1983). Alternatives in the pursuit of predictability and consistency of persons: Stable data that yield unstable interpretation. *Journal of Personality, 51,* 578–604.

Mischel, W. (1984). Convergences and challenges in the search for consistency. *American Psychologist, 39,* 351–364.

Mischel, W., & Peake, P. K. (1982). Beyond deja vu in the search of cross-situational consistency. *Psychological Review, 89,* 730–755.

Mishkin, M. (1986). Behaviorism, cognitivism, and the brain. *Distinguished Scientific Contribution Award Address,* American Psychological Association, Washington, DC.

Mollon, J. D. (1982). Color vision. *Annual Review of Psychology, 33,* 41–85.

Moncrieff, R. W. (1966). *Odour preferences.* New York: Wiley.

Moore, B. C. J. (1982). *An introduction to the psychology of hearing* (2nd ed.). New York: Academic Press.

Moore, J. B., Reeve, T. G., & Pissanos, B. (1981). Effects of variability of practice in a movement education program on motor skill performance. *Perceptual and Motor Skills, 52,* 779–784.

Moore, O. K., & Lewis, D. J. (1968). Purpose and learning theory. In W. Buckley (Ed.), *Modern systems research for the behavioral scientist* (pp. 250–255). Chicago: Aldine.

Moore, T. V. (1919). Image and meaning in memory and perception. *Psychological Monographs, 27,* 2–242.

Moore, T. V. (1924). *Dynamic psychology.* Philadelphia: Lippincott.

Moore-Ede, M. C., Sulzman, F. M., & Fuller, C. A. (1982). *The clocks that time us: Physiology of the circadian timing system.* Cambridge, MA: Harvard University Press.

Moran, J. J., & Joniak, A. J. (1979). Effect of language on preference for responses to a moral dilemma. *Developmental Psychology, 15,* 337–338.

Moray, N. (1970). *Attention: Selective processes in vision and hearing.* New York: Academic Press.

Morehouse, L. E., & Miller, A. T., Jr. (1976). *Physiology of exercise* (7th ed.). St. Louis: C. V. Mosby.

Morgan, C. T., & Stellar, E. (1950). *Physiological psychology.* New York: McGraw-Hill.

Moscovitch, M. (1984). *Infant memory.* New York: Plenum Press.

Mosher, D. L. (1966). The development and multitrait-multimethod matrix analysis of three measures of three aspects of guilt. *Journal of Consulting Psychology, 30,* 25–29.

Mosher, D. L., & White, B. B. (1981). On differentiating shame and shyness. *Motivation and Emotion, 5.*

Mountcastle, V. B. (1978). An organizing principle for cerebral function: The unit module and the distributed system. In G. M. Edelman & V. B. Mountcastle (Eds.), *The mindful brain* (pp. 7–50). Cambridge, MA: MIT Press.

Mowrer, O. H. (1947). On the dual nature of learning: A reinterpretation of "conditioning" and "problem-solving." *Harvard Educational Review, 17,* 102–148.

Mowrer, O. H. (1956). Two factor learning theory reconsidered, with special references to secondary reinforcement and the concept of habit. *Psychological Review, 63,* 114–128.

Mowrer, O. H. (1960a). *Learning theory and behavior.* New York: Wiley.

Mowrer, O. H. (1960b). *Learning theory and the symbolic processes.* New York: Wiley.

Moxely, S. E. (1979). Schema: The variability of practice hypothesis. *Journal of Motor Behavior, 11,* 65–70.

Mozell, M. M. (1971). The chemical senses: II. Olfaction. In J. W. Kling & L. A. Riggs (Eds.), *Experimental psychology* (3rd ed., pp. 193–222). New York: Holt, Rinehart & Winston.

Mueller, E. C., & Vandell, D. (1979). Infant-infant interaction. In J. O. Osofsky (Ed.), *Handbook of infant development* (pp. 591–622). New York: Wiley.

Murphy, G. (1929). *An historical introduction to modern psychology.* New York: Harcourt Brace.

Murphy, G. (1947). *Personality: A biosocial approach to origins and structure.* New York: Harper & Brothers.

Murphy, G. (1949). *An historical introduction to modern psychology* (rev. ed.). New York: Harcourt Brace.

Murray, H. A. (1938). *Explorations in personality.* New York: Oxford University Press.

Mussen, P. H. (Ed.). (1983). *Handbook of child psychology* (4th ed., Vols. 1–4). New York: Wiley.

Myers, R. E. (1968). Neurology of social communication in primates. In H. Hofer (Ed.), *Neurology, physiology, and infectious diseases. Proceedings of the Second International Congress of Primatology* (Vol. 3). Basel, Switzerland: Kareyer.

Näätänen, R. (1982). Processing negativity: An evoked-potential reflection of selective attention. *Psychological Bulletin, 92,* 605–640.

Näätänen, R., & Michie, P. T. (1976). Early selective-attention effects on the evoked potential: A critical review and reinterpretation. *Biological Psychology, 8,* 81–136.

Nafe, J. P., & Kenshalo, D. R. (1962). Somesthetic senses. *Annual Review of Psychology, 13,* 201–2224.

Natale, M. (1977). Induction of mood states and their effect on gaze behaviors. *Journal of Consulting and Clinical Psychology, 45,* 960.

Nathans, J., Thomas, D., & Hogness, D. S. (1986). Molecular genetics of human color vision: The genes encoding blue, green, and red pigments. *Science, 232,* 193–202.

Naylor, F. D. (1981). A state-trait curiosity inventory. *Australian Psychologist, 16,* 172–183.

Neff, W. D. (Ed.). (1982). *Contributions to sensory physiology* (Vol. 7). New York: Academic Press.

Neimark, E. D., & Santa, J. L. (1975). Thinking and concept attainment. *Annual Review of Psychology, 26,* 173–205.

Neisser, V. (1967). *Cognitive psychology.* Englewood Cliffs, NJ: Prentice-Hall.

Neisser, V. (1976). *Cognition and reality: Principles and implications of cognitive psychology.* San Francisco: Freeman.

Nelson, K. (1981). Social cognition in a script framework. In J. H. Flavell & L. Ross (Eds.), *Social cognitive development: Frontiers and possible futures* (pp. 77–118). New York: Cambridge University Press.

Nelson, K. (1984). The transition from infant to child memory. In M. Moscovitch (Ed.), *Infant memory* (pp. 103–130). New York: Plenum Press.

Nelson, K., & Ross, G. (1980). The generalities and specifics of long-term memory in infants and young children. In M. Perlmutter (Ed.), *Children's memory: New directions for child development* (Vol. 10, pp. 87–102). San Francisco: Jossey-Bass.

Nesselroade, J. R. (1983). Temporal selection and factor invariance in the study of development and change. In P. B. Baltes & O. G. Brim, Jr. (Eds.), *Life-span development and behavior* (Vol. 5, pp. 60–89). New York: Academic Press.

Nesselroade, J. R. (in press). Sampling and generalizability: Adult development and aging research issues examined within the general methodological framework of selection. In K. W. Schaie, R. T. Campbell, W. M. Meredith, & S. C. Rawlings (Eds.), *Methodological issues in aging research.* New York: Springer.

Nesselroade, J. R., & Ford, D. H. (1985). P-technique comes of age: Multivariate, replicated, single-subject designs for research on older adults. *Research on Aging, 7,*

46-80.

Nesselroade, J. R., & Ford, D. H. (1987). Methodological considerations in modeling living systems. In M. E. Ford & D. H. Ford (Eds.), *Humans as self-constructing living systems: Putting the framework to work*. Hillsdale, NJ: Lawrence Erlbaum Associates.

Newell, A. (1973). You can't play 20 questions with nature and win: Projective comments on the papers of this symposium. In W. G. Chase (Ed.), *Visual information processing*. New York: Academic Press.

Newell, A. (1980a). Physical symbol systems. *Cognitive Science, 4,* 135-183.

Newell, A. (1980b). Reasoning, problem solving, and decision processes: The problem space as a fundamental category. In R. Nickerson (Ed.), *Attention and performance* (Vol. 8). Hillsdale, NJ: Lawrence Erlbaum Associates.

Newell, A., & Simon, H. A. (1972). *Human problem solving*. Englewood Cliffs, NJ: Prentice-Hall.

Newell, A., & Simon, H. A. (1976). Computer science as empirical inquiry: Symbols and search. *Communications of the ACM, 19,* 113-126.

Newtson, D. (1976). Foundations of attributions: The perception of ongoing behavior. In J. Harvey, W. Ickes, R. Kidd (Eds.), *New directions in attribution research* (pp. 223-247). Hillsdale, NJ: Lawrence Erlbaum Associates.

Niemi, P., & Näätänen, R. (1981). Foreperiod and sample reaction time. *Psychological Bulletin, 89,* 133-162.

Nicolis, G., & Prigogine, I. (1978). *Self-organization in non-equilibrium systems: From dissipative structures to order through fluctuations*. New York: Wiley (Interscience).

Nisbett, R. E., Borgida, E., Crandall, R., & Reed, H. (1982). Popular induction: Information is not necessarily informative. In D. Kahneman, P. Slovic, & A. Tversky (Eds.), *Judgment under uncertainty: Heuristics and biases* (pp. 101-116). Cambridge, UK: Cambridge University Press.

Nisbett, R. E., & Ross, L. D. (1980). *Human inference: Strategies and shortcomings of social judgment*. Englewood Cliffs, NJ: Prentice-Hall.

Noback, C. R., & Demarest, R. J. (1981). *The human nervous system* (3rd ed.). New York: McGraw-Hill.

Noble, W. G. (1981). Gibsonian theory and the pragmatist perspective. *Journal of Theory of Social Behavior, 11,* 65-85.

Noller, P. (1978). Sex differences in the socialization of affectionate expression. *Developmental Psychology, 14,* 317-319.

Norman, D. A. (1980). Twelve issues for cognitive science. *Cognitive Science, 4,* 1-32.

Norman, D. A. (1981). Categorization of action slips. *Psychological Review, 88,* 1-15.

Northway, M. L. (1940). The concept of the "schema." Part I. *British Journal of Psychology, 30,* 316-325.

Novikoff, A. B. (1945). The concept of integrative levels if biology. *Science, 101,* 209-215.

Nowlis, V. (1970). Mood: Behavior and experience. In M. B. Arnold (Ed.), *Feelings and emotions* (pp. 261-278). New York: Academic Press.

Numan, R. (1978). Cortical-limbic mechanisms and response control: A theoretical review. *Physiological Psychology, 6,* 445-470.

Nuttin, J. R. (1984). *Motivation, planning, and action: A relational theory of behavioral dynamics*. Hillsdale, NJ: Lawrence Erlbaum Associates.

Nyström, M. (1977). Neonatal facial-postural patterning during sleep. *Psychological Research Bulletin, 17,* 1-20. (Lund University, Sweden).

Oakley, D. A. (1983). The varieties of memory: A phylogenetic approach. In A. Mayes (Ed.), *Memory in animals and humans* (pp. 20-82). Workingham, UK: Van Nostrand Reinhold.

O'Brien, S. J., & Nash, W. G. (1982). Genetic mapping in mammals: Chromosome map of domestic cat. *Science, 216,* 257-265.

Oden, G. C. (1987). Concept, knowledge and thought. *Annual Review of Psychology, 38,* 203–27.

O'Donnell, J. P., O'Neill, S., & Staley, A. (1979). Congenital correlates of distractibility. *Journal of Abnormal Child Psychology, 7,* 465–470.

Ohala, J. J. (1983). The origin of sound patterns in vocal tract constraints. In P. F. MacNeilage (Ed.), *The production of speech* (pp. 189–214). New York: Springer-Verlag.

O'Keefe, J., & Nadel, L. (1978). *The hippocampus as a cognitive map.* Clarendon, NY: Oxford University Press.

Olds, J. (1955). Physiological mechanisms of reward. In M. R. Jones (Ed.), *Nebraska Symposium on Motivation* (pp. 73–139). Lincoln: University of Nebraska Press.

Olds, J. (1962). Hypothalamic substrates of reward. *Physiological Review, 42,* 554–604.

Olds, J. (1977). *Drives and reinforcements: Behavioral studies of hypothalamic functions.* New York: Raven Press.

O'Leary, S. G., & Dubey, D. R. (1979). Applications of self-control procedures by children: A review. *Journal of Applied Behavior Analysis, 12,* 449–465.

Oller, D. K., & MacNeilage, P. F. (1983). Development of speech production: Perspectives from natural and perturbed speech. In P. F. MacNeilage (Ed.), *The production of speech* (pp. 91–108). New York: Springer-Verlag.

Olson, G. A., Olson, R. D., Kastin, A. J., & Cog, D. H. (1979). Endogenous opiates: Through 1978. *Neuroscience and Biobehavioral Reviews, 3,* 285–299.

Olson, G. M., & Sherman, T. (1983). Attention, learning and memory in infants. In P. H. Mussen (Ed.), *Handbook of child psychology* (4th ed., Vol. 2, pp. 1001–1080). New York: Wiley.

Olson, G. M., & Strauss, M. S. (1984). The development of infant memory. In M. Moscovitch (Ed.), *Infant memory* (pp. 29–48). New York: Plenum Press.

Olton, D. S. (1979). Mazes, maps, and memory. *American Psychologist, 34,* 583–596.

Olweus, D. (1972). Personality and Aggression. In J. K. Cole & D. D. Jensen (Eds.), *Nebraska Symposium on Motivation* (Vol. 20, pp. 261–321). Lincoln: University of Nebraska Press.

Orem, J., & Barnes, C. D. (Eds.). (1980). *Physiology in sleep.* New York: Academic Press.

Orne, M. T. (1974). Pain suppression by hypnosis and related phenomena. In J. J. Bonica (Ed.), *Advances in neurology* (Vol. 4). New York: Raven Press.

Ornstein, R. E. (Ed.). (1973). *The nature of human consciousness.* San Francisco: Freeman.

Ortony, A. (1979). Beyond literal similarity. *Psychological Review, 86,* 161–180.

Osgood, C. E. (1953). *Method and theory in experimental psychology.* New York: Oxford University Press.

Osgood, C. E. (1965). Cross cultural comparability in attitude research via multilingual semantic differentials. In I. Steiner & M. Fishbein (Eds.), *Current studies in social psychology* (pp. 95–106). New York: Holt, Rinehart & Winston.

Osgood, C. E., May, W. H., & Miron, M. S. (1975). *Cross-cultural universals of affective meaning.* Urbana: University of Illinois Press.

Osipow, S. H. (1968). *Theories of career development.* New York: Appleton-Century-Crofts.

Osler, S. F., & Kofsky, E. (1966). Structure and strategy in concept learning. *Journal of Experimental Child Psychology, 4,* 198–209.

Osofsky, J. D. (Ed.). (1979). *Handbook of infant development.* New York: Wiley.

Osofsky, J. D., & Connors, K. (1979). Mother-infant interaction: An integrative view of a complex system. In J. D. Osofsky (Ed.), *Handbook of infant development* (pp. 519–548). New York: Wiley.

Ostrom, T. M. (1968). The emergence of attitude theory 1930–1950. In T. M. Ostrom, A. G. Greenwald, & T. C. Brock (Eds.), *Psychological foundations of attitude* (pp. 1–32). New York: Academic Press.

Ostry, D. J. (1980). Execution-time movement control. In G. E. Stelmach & J. Requin

(Eds.), *Tutorials in motor behavior* (pp. 457–468). Amsterdam: North-Holland.

Ostwald, P. (1975). The sound system of man. *Communication, 2,* 31–50.

Overton, W. F., & Newman, J. L. (1982). Cognitive development: A competence-activation/utilization approach. In T. M. Field, A. Huston, J. C. Quay, L. Troll, & G. E. Finley (Eds.), *Review of human development* (pp. 217–241). New York: Wiley.

Ovsiankina, M. (1928). Die Wiederaufnahme unterbrochene Handlunger. *Psychologische Forschung, 2,* 302–379.

Owens, J., & Bower, G. H. (1979). The "soap opera" effect in story recall. *Memory and Cognition, 7,* 185–191.

Pagano, R. R., Rose, R. M., Stivers, R. M., & Warrenburg, S. (1978). Sleep during transcendental meditation. *Science, 191,* 308–309.

Page, M. M. (Ed.). (1980). Beliefs, attitudes and values. *Nebraska Symposium Motivation Vol. 27.* Lincoln: University of Nebraska Press.

Page, M. M. (Ed.). (1983). *Personality: Current theory and research.* Lincoln: University of Nebraska Press.

Page, R., & Bode, J. (1980). Comparison of measures of moral reasoning and development of a new objective measure. *Educational and Psychological Measurement, 40,* 317–329.

Paivio, A. (1971). *Imagery and verbal processes.* New York: Holt, Rinehart & Winston.

Paivio, A. (1975). Imagery and synchronic thinking. *Canadian Psychological Review, 16,* 147–173.

Paivio, A. (1978). The relationship between verbal and perceptual codes. In E. C. Carterette & M. P. Friedman (Eds.), *Handbook of perception* (Vol. 8, pp. 375–395). New York: Academic Press.

Palmerino, C. C., Rusiniak, K. W., & Garcia, J. (1980). Flavor-illness aversions: The peculiar roles of odor and taste in memory for poison. *Science, 208,* 753–755.

Panksepp, J. (1986). The neurochemistry of behavior. *Annual Review of Psychology, 37,* 77–107.

Papez, J. W. (1937). A proposed mechanism of emotion. *Archives of Neurology and Psychiatry, 38,* 725–743.

Papousek, H., & Papousek, M. 1975. Cognitive aspects of preverbal social interactions between human infants and adults. In *Proceedings of the CIBA Foundation Symposium: Parent-infant interaction.* New York: Associated Scientific Publishers.

Parasuraman, R. (1978). Auditory evoked potentials and divided attention. *Psychophysiology, 15,* 460–465.

Parke, R. D. (1978). Children's home environments; Social and cognitive effects. In I. Altman & J. F. Wohlwill (Eds.), *Children and the environment* (pp. 33–82). New York: Plenum Press.

Parke, R. D. (1979). Perspectives on father-infant interaction. In J. Osofsky (Ed.), *Handbook of infant development* (pp. 549–590). New York: Wiley.

Parke, R. D., & Asher, S. R. (1983). Social and personality development. *Annual Review of Psychology, 34,* 465–510.

Parsons, J. E., & Goff, S. B. (1980). Achievement motivation and values: An alternate perspective. In L. Fyans (Ed.), *Recent trends in achievement motivation theory and research.* New York: Plenum Press.

Parton, D. A. (1976). Learning to imitate in infancy. *Child Development, 47,* 14–31.

Pascal, B. (1941). *Penses: The provincial letters* (W. F. Trotter & T. M'Crie, Trans.) New York: Modern Library.

Patchett, R. F. (1979). Human sound frequency preferences. *Perceptual and Motor Skills, 49,* 324–326.

Patrick, J. R. (1934a). Studies in rational behavior and emotional excitement: I. Rational behavior in human subjects. *Journal of Comparative Psychology, 18,* 1–22.

Patrick, J. R. (1934b). Studies in rational behavior and emotional excitement: II. The effect of emotional excitement on rational behavior in human subjects. *Journal of Comparative Psychology, 18,* 153–195

Pattee, H. H. (Ed.). (1973). *Hierarchy theory: The challenge of complex systems.* New York: George Braziller.

Pavlov, I. P. (1927). *Conditioned reflexes* (G. V. Anrep, Trans.). London: Oxford University Press.

Pearl, J., Kim, J., & Fiske, R. (1981). Goal directed decision structuring systems. *Cognitive Systems Laboratory* (Tech. Rep. No. CLA-ENG-81-21). Los Angeles: University of California.

Peel, E. A. (1971). Generalizing and abstracting. *Nature, 230,* 600.

Pelham, W. E. (1981). Attention deficits in hyperactive and learning-disabled children. *Exceptional Education Quarterly, 2,* 13–23.

Pene, J. (1982). Can linguistics contribute to the study of verbal behavior? *The Behavioral Analyst, 1,* 9–21.

Penfield, W. (1954). Studies of the cerebral cortex of man: A review and an interpretation. In J. F. Delafresnaye (Ed.), *Brain mechanisms and learning* (pp. 284–309). Oxford: Blackwell.

Penfield, W. (1975), *The mystery of the mind; A critical study of consciousness and the human brain.* Princeton, NJ: Princeton University Press.

Peng, F. C. C., & von Raffler-Engel, W. (Eds.). (1979). *Language acquisition and developmental kinesics.* Hiroshima, Japan: Bunka Hyoron (U.S. Distributor: ISBS).

Peplau, L. A., & Caldwell, M. A. (1978). Loneliness: A cognitive analysis. *Essence, 2,* 207–220.

Peplau, L. A., & Perlman, D. (Eds.). (1982). *Loneliness: A sourcebook of current theory, research, and therapy.* New York: Wiley.

Pepper, S. (1942). *World hypotheses.* Berkeley: University of California Press.

Perkell, J. (1969). *Physiology of speech production: Results and implications of a quantitative cineradiographic study.* Cambridge, MA: MIT Press.

Perruchet, P. (1980). Conditionnement classique chez l'homme et facteurs cognitifs: II. Le conditionnement moteur. *L'Anne Psychologique, 80,* 193–219.

Perry, D. G., & Perry, L. C. (1984). Social learning, causal attribution and moral internalization. In J. Bisanz, G. L. Bisanz, & P. Kail (Eds). *Learning in children: Progress in cognitive development research,* (pp. 105–136). New York: Springer-Verlag.

Pervin, L. A. (1985). Personality: Current controversies, issues and directions. *Annual Review of Psychology, 36,* 83–114.

Peters, J. M., Preston-Martin, S., & Yu, M. C. (1981). Brain tumors in children and occupational exposure of parents. *Science, 213,* 235–236.

Peters, R. S. (1971). Moral development: A plea for pluralism. In W. Mischel (Ed.), *Cognitive development and epistemology* (pp. 237–267). New York: Academic Press.

Petrinovich, L. (1979). Probabilistic functionalism: A conception of research method. *American Psychologist, 34,* 373–390.

Pfaff, D. W. (Ed.). (1985). *Taste, olfaction and the central nervous system.* New York: Rockfeller University Press.

Pfaffmann, C. (Ed.). (1969). *Olfaction and taste* (Vol. 3). New York: Rockefeller University Press.

Pfaffmann, C., Frank, M., & Norgren, R. (1979). Neural mechanisms and behavioral aspects of taste. *Annual Review of Psychology, 30,* 283–325.

Pfaffmann, C., Norgren, R., & Grill, H. J. (1977). Sensory affect and motivation. *Annals of the New York Academy of Science, 290,* 18–34.

Phares, E. J., & Lamiell, J. T. (1977). Personality. *Annual Review of Psychology, 28,* 113–140.

Phillips, C. G., & Porter, R. (1977). *Corticospinal neurones: Their role in movement.* New York:

Academic Press.

Piaget, J. (1928). *Judgment and reasoning in the child*. London: Routledge & Kegan Paul.

Piaget, J. (1930). *The child's conception of physical causality*. London: Routledge & Kegan Paul.

Piaget, J. (1965). *The moral judgment of the child*. (M. Gabain, Trans.). New York: Free Press. (Originally published 1932)

Piaget, J. (1952a). *The child's conception of number*. London: Routledge & Kegan Paul.

Piaget, J. (1952b). *The origins of intelligence in children*. New York: Routledge & Kegan Paul.

Piaget, J. (1954). *The construction of reality in the child*. New York: Basic Books.

Piaget, J. (1955). *The language and thought of the child*. New York: New American Library.

Piaget, J. (1960). *Psychology of intelligence*. Totowa, NJ: Littlefield, Adams.

Piaget, J. (1962). *Play, dreams and imitation in childhood*. New York: W. W. Norton.

Piaget, J. (1970). Piaget's theory. In P. H. Mussen (Ed.), *Carmichael's manual of child psychology* (Vol. 1, pp. 703–732). New York: Wiley.

Piaget, J. (1976). *The psychology of intelligence*. Totowa, NJ: Littlefield, Adams.

Piaget, J. (1977). *The development of thought: Equilibrium of cognitive structures*. New York: Viking.

Piaget, J. (1983). Piaget's theory. In P. H. Mussen (Ed.), *Handbook of child psychology (4th ed.): Vol. 1. History, theory, and methods* (pp. 103–128). New York: Wiley.

Piaget, J., & Inhelder, B. (1956). *The child's conception of space*. London: Routledge & Kegan Paul.

Piaget, J., & Inhelder, B. (1969). *The psychology of the child*. New York: Basic Books.

Piaget, J., & Inhelder, B. (1973). *Memory and intelligence*. New York: Basic Books.

Pike, R. L., & Brown, M. L. (1967). *Nutrition: An integrated approach*. New York: Wiley.

Pilkonis, P. A. (1977a). Shyness, public and private, and its relationship to other measures of social behavior. *Journal of Personality, 45*, 585–595.

Pilkonis, P. A. (1977b). The behavioral consequences of shyness. *Journal of Personality, 45*, 596–611.

Pillsbury, W. (1980). *Attention*. New York: Macmillan. (Originally published 1908)

Pines, A., & Zimbardo, P. G. (1978). The personal and cultural dynamics of shyness: A comparison between Israelis, American Jews and Americans. *Journal of Psychology and Judaism, 3*, 81–101.

Pitz, G. F., & Sachs, N. J. (1984). Judgment and decision: Theory and application. *Annual Review of Psychology, 35*, 139–163.

Platt, J. (1970a). *Perception and change*. Ann Arbor: University of Michigan Press.

Platt, J. (1970b). Hierarchical restructuring. In L. von Bertalanffy & A. Rapoport (Eds.), *Systems yearbook* (Vol. 15, pp. 49–54). Washington, DC: Society for General Systems Research.

Plemons, K., Willis, S. L., & Baltes, P. B. (1978). Modifiability of fluid intelligence in aging: A short-term longitudinal training approach. *Journal of Gerontology, 33*, 224–231.

Plomin, R. & Thompson, L. (in press). Life-span developmental behavioral genetics. In P. B. Baltes, D. L. Featherman, & R. M. Lerner (Eds.), *Life span development and behavior* (Vol. 8), (pp. 1–31). Hillsdale, NJ: Lawrence Erlbaum Associates.

Plomin, R. (1986). *Genetics, development and psychology*. Hillsdale, NJ: Lawrence Erlbaum Associates.

Ploog, D. (1980). Emotions as products of the limbic system. *Medizinische Psychologie, 6*, 7–19.

Ploog, D., & Jürgens, V. (1981). Vocal behavior of nonhuman primates and man. *Brain Research Review, 3*, 35–61.

Ploog, D., & Melnechuk, T. (1969). Primate communication. *Neurosciences Research Program Bulletin, 7*.

Plutchik, R. (1962). *The emotions: Facts, theories, and a new model*. New York: Random

House.

Plutchik, R. (1980). *Emotion: A psychoevolutionary synthesis.* New York: Harper & Row.

Plutchik, R., & Kellerman, H. (Ed.). (1980). *Emotion: Theory, research, and experience: Vol. 1. Theories of emotion.* New York: Academic Press.

Poon, L.W. (Ed.). (1980). *Aging in the 1980s.* Washington, DC: American Psychological Association.

Poon, L. W. (1985). Differences in human memory with aging: Nature, causes, and clinical implications. In J. E. Birren & K. W. Schaie (Eds.), *Handbook of the psychology of aging* (3rd ed., pp. 427–462). New York: Van Nostrand Reinhold.

Popper, K. R. (1963). *Conjectures and refutations.* New York: Harper and Row.

Porter, J. R., & Washington, R. E. (1979). Black identity and self-esteem: A review of studies of black self-concepts. *Annual Review of Sociology, 5,* 53–74.

Posner, M. I. (1978). *Chronometric explorations of mind.* Hillsdale, NJ: Lawrence Erlbaum Associates.

Posner, M. I., & McLeod, P. (1982). Information processing models in search of elementary operations. *Annual Review of Psychology, 33,* 477–514.

Posner, M. I., & Warren, R. E. (1972). Traces, concepts, and conscious constructions. In A. W. Melton & E. Martin (Eds.), *Cording processes in human memory* (pp. 25–44). Washington, DC: Winston & Sons.

Powers, W. T. (1973a). *Behavior: The control of perception.* Chicago: Aldine.

Powers, W. T. (1973b). Feedback: Beyond behaviorism. *Science, 179,* 351–356.

Powers, W. T. (1978). Quantitative analysis of purposive systems: Some spadework at the foundations of scientific psychology. *Psychological Review, 85,* 417–435.

Premack, D. (1983). Animal cognition. *Annual Review of Psychology, 34,* 351–362.

Pressey, S. L., & Kuhlen, R. G. (1957). *Psychological development through the life span.* New York: Harper Brothers.

Pressley, M., & Levin, J. R. (Eds.). (1983). *Cognitive strategy research: psychological foundations.* New York: Springer-Verlag.

Pribram, K. H. (1967). The new neurology and the biology of emotion: A structural approach. *American Psychologist, 12,* 830–838.

Pribram, K. H. (1971). *Languages of the brain: Experimental paradoxes and principles in neuropsychology.* Englewood Cliffs, NJ: Prentice-Hall.

Pribram, K. H. (1976a). Self-consciousness and intentionality. In G. E. Schwartz & D. Shapiro (Eds.), *Consciousness and self-regulation* (Vol. 1, pp. 51–100). New York: Plenum Press.

Pribram, K. H. (1976b). Problems concerning the structure of consciousness. In G. Globus, G. Maxwell, & I. Sawodnik (Eds.), *Consciousness and the brain* (pp. 51–100). New York: Plenum Press.

Pribram, K. H. (1977). Peptides and protocritic processes. In L. H. Miller, C. A. Sandman, & A. J. Kastin (Eds.), *Neuropeptide influences on the brain and behavior* (pp. 213–232). New York: Raven Press.

Pribram, K. H. (1980a). Image, information, and episodic models of central processing. In R. F. Thompson, L. H. Hicks, & V. B. Shvyrkov (Eds.), *Neural mechanisms of goal-directed behavior and learning* (pp. 319–346). New York: Academic Press.

Pribram, K. H. (1980b). Mind, brain, and consciousness: The organization of competence and conduct. In J. M. Davidson & R. J. Davidson (Eds.), *The psychobiology of consciousness* (pp. 47–64). New York: Plenum Press.

Pribram, K. H. (1984). Brain systems and cognitive learning processes. In H. L. Roitblat, T. G. Bever, & H. S. Terrace (Eds.), *Animal cognition* (pp. 627–656). Hillsdale, NJ: Lawrence Erlbaum Associates.

Pribram, K. H. (1986). The cognitive revolution and mind/brain issues. *American Psychologist, 41,* 507–520.

Pribram, K. & Goleman, D. (1979, February). Holographic memory. *Psychology Today* (pp. 71–84).

Pribram, K. H., & McGuinness, D. (1975). Arousal, activation, and effort in the control of attention. *Psychological Review, 82,* 116–149.

Prigogine, I (1976). Order through fluctuation: Self-organization and social system. In E. Jantsch & C. H. Waddington (Eds.), *Evolution and consciousness* (pp. 99–123). Reading, MA: Addison-Wesley.

Prigogine, I. (1978). Time, structure and fluctuations. *Science, 201,* 777–785.

Prigogine, I., & Stengers, I. (1984). *Order out of chaos.* New York: Bantam Books.

Prinz, W., & Sanders, A. F. (Eds.). (1984). *Cognition and motor processes.* Berlin: Springer-Verlag.

Proctor, D. F. (1980). *Breathing, speech, and song.* New York: Springer-Verlag.

Proctor, L D., Knighton, R. S., & Churchill, J. A. (1957). Variations in consciousness produced by stimulating reticular formation of the monkey. *Neurology, 7,* 193–203.

Prohovnik, I. (1978). Cerebral lateralization of psychological processes: A literature review. *Archiv für Psychologie, 130,* 161–211.

Puff, C. R. (Ed.). (1979). *Memory organization and structure.* New York: Academic Press.

Pugh, G. E. (1977). *The biological origin of human values.* New York: Basic Books.

Purcell, A. T. (1982). The structure of activation and emotion. *Multivariate Behavioral Research, 17,* 221–251.

Purpura, E. (1981). *Plasticity of the central nervous system.* Invited address, Society for Research in Child Development, Boston.

Purves, D., & Lichtman, J. W. (1980). Elimination of synapses in the developing nervous system. *Science, 210,* 153–157.

Pylyshyn, Z. W. (1978). When is attribution of beliefs justified? *Behavioral and Brain Sciences, 1,* 592–593.

Pylyshyn, Z. W. (1980). Computation and cognition: Issues in the foundations of cognitive science. *The Behavioral and Brain Sciences, 3,* 111–169.

Quabbe, H. J. (1977). Chronobiology of growth hormone secretion. *Chronobiologia, 4,* 217–246.

Quinn, R., & Cobb, W. (1971). *What workers want: Factor analysis of importance ratings of job facets.* Ann Arbor, MI: Institute for Social Research.

Raaheim, K. (1974). *Problem solving and intelligence.* Oslo: Universitetsferlaget.

Rachman, S. (1978). Human fears: A three systems analysis. *Scandinavian Journal of Behaviour Therapy, 7,* 237–245.

Rachman, S. (1981). The primacy of affect: Some theoretical implications. *Behavior Research & Therapy, 19,* 279–290.

Radloff, L. S. (1977). The CES-D Scale: A self-report depression scale for research in the general population. *Applied Psychological Measurement, 1,* 385–401.

Raff, R. A., & Kaufman, T. C. (1983). *Embryos, genes, and evolution.* New York: Macmillan.

Raffler-Engel, W. von (1980). *Aspects of nonverbal communication.* The Netherlands; SWETS Publishing Service.

Raisbeck, G. (1964). *Information theory.* Cambridge, MA: MIT Press.

Ramey, C. T., Farran, D. C., Campbell, F. A., & Finkelstein, N. W. (1978). Observations of mother-infant interactions: Implications for development. In F. D. Minifie & L. L. Loyd (Eds.), *Communicative and cognitive abilities: Early behavioral assessment* (pp. 397–441). Baltimore: University Park Press.

Ramey, C. T., & Finkelstein, N. W. (1978). Contingent stimulation and infant competence. *Journal of Pediatric Psychology, 3,* 89–96.

Rank, A. W. (1961). *Behavioral concepts: Frequency of usage and relative modifiability in experienced and inexperienced judges.* Unpublished master's thesis, The Pennsylvania State University.

Rao, K. (1978). Psychology of transcendence: A study of early Buddhistic psychology. *Journal of Indian Psychology, 1,* 1–21.

Rapaport, D. (1958). The theory of ego autonomy: A generalization. *Bulletin Menninger Clinic, 22,* 13–35.

Rapaport, D. (1960). On the psychoanalytic theory of motivation. In M R. Jones (Ed.), *Nebraska Symposium on Motivation* (Vol. 8, 173–247). Lincoln: University of Nebraska Press.

Rapaport, D. (1961). *Emotion and memory.* New York: Science Editions.

Rapaport, D. (1971). *Emotions and memory* (5th ed.). New York: International Universities Press.

Rapoport, A. (1968). A Philosophical view. In J. H. Milsum (Ed.), *Positive feedback.* Oxford: Pergamon Press.

Rapoport, A. (1970). Modern systems theory: An outlook for coping with change. In L. von Bertalanffy & A. Rapoport (Eds.), *General systems* (Vol. 15, pp. 15–26). Washington, DC: Society for General Systems Research.

Rapoport, A., & Horvath, W. J. (1959). Thoughts on organization theory and a review of two conferences. *General Systems, 4,* 89–93.

Raup, D. M. (1981). Evolution and the fossil record. *Science, 23,* 289.

Rawls, J. A. (1971). *A theory of justice.* Cambridge, MA: Harvard University Press.

Ray, W. S. (1967). *The experimental psychology of original thinking.* New York: Macmillan.

Rayner, K. (1978). Eye movements in reading and information processing. *Psychological Bulletin, 85,* 618–660.

Raynor, J. O., & Entin, E. E. (Eds.). (1981). *Motivation, career, striving, and aging.* Washington, DC: Hemisphere Publishing Corp.

Redican, W. K. (1982). An evolutionary perspective on human facial displays. In P. Ekman (Ed.), *Emotion in the human face* (2nd ed., pp. 212–280). Cambridge, UK: Cambridge University Press.

Reed, E., & Jones, R. (1982). *Reasons for realism. Selected essays of James J. Gibson.* Hillsdale, NJ: Lawrence Erlbaum Associates.

Reed, S. K. (1972). Pattern recognition and categorization. *Cognitive Psychology, 3,* 382–407.

Reese, H. W., & Overton, W. F. (1970). Models of development and theories of development. In L. R. Goulet & P. B. Baltes (Eds.), *Life-span developmental psychology: Research and theory* (pp. 116–145). New York: Academic Press.

Reese, H. W., & Rodeheaver, D. (1985). Problem solving and complex decision making. In J. E. Birren & K. W. Schaie (Eds.), *Handbook of the psychology of aging* (2nd ed., pp. 474–499). New York: Van Nostrand Reinhold.

Regestein, Q. R. (1980). Insomnia and sleep disturbances in the aged. *Journal of Geriatric Psychiatry, 13,* 153–171.

Reisenzein, R. (1983). The Schachter theory of emotions: Two decades later. *Psychological Bulletin, 94,* 239–264.

Reitman, W. R. (1964). Heuristic decision procedures, open constraints, and the structure of ill-defined problems. In M. Shelley & G. Bryan (Eds.), *Human judgments and optimality.* New York: Wiley.

Remington, R. W. (1980). Attention and saccadic eye movements. *Journal of Experimental Psychology: Human Perception and Performance, 6,* 726–744.

Requin, J. (1980). Toward a psychobiology of preparation for action. In G. E. Stelmach & J. Requin (Eds.), *Tutorials in motor behavior* (pp. 373–398). Amsterdam: North-Holland.

Rescorla, R. A., & Wagner, A. R. (1972). A theory of Pavlovian conditioning: Variations in the effectiveness of reinforcement and nonreinforcement. In A. H. Black & W. F. Prokasy (Eds.), *Classical conditioning II: Current research and theory* (pp. 64–99). New York: Appleton-Century-Crofts.

Resnick, L. B. (1976). *The nature of intelligence.* Hillsdale, NJ: Lawrence Erlbaum Associates.

Resnick, L. B., & Glaser, R. (1976). Problem solving and intelligence. In L. B. Resnick (Ed.), *The nature of intelligence* (pp. 205–230). Hillsdale, NJ: Lawrence Erlbaum Associates.

Rest, J. R. (1979). *Development in judging moral issues*. Minneapolis: University of Minnesota Press.

Rest, J. R. (1983). Morality. In P. H. Mussen (Ed.), *Handbook of child psychology (4th ed.): Vol. 3. Cognitive development* (pp. 556–629). New York: Wiley.

Revlin, R., & Mayer, R. E. (Eds.). (1978). *Human reasoning*. Washington, DC: Winston.

Reymert, M. L. (Ed.). (1928). *Feelings and emotions*. Worcester, MA: Clark University Press.

Reymert, M. L. (Ed.) (1950). *Feelings and emotions*. New York: McGraw-Hill.

Richards, D. D., & Siegler, R. S. (1981). Very young children's acquisition of systematic problem-solving strategies. *Child Development, 52*, 1318–1321.

Ricoeur, P. (1966). *Freedom and nature: The voluntary and the involuntary*. Chicago: Northwestern University Press.

Riegel, K. F. (1976). The dialectics of human development. *American Psychologist, 31*, 689–700.

Riesen, A. H. (1966). Sensory deprivation. In E. Stellar, & J. M. Spragne (Eds.), *Progress in physiological psychology* (pp. 117–148). New York: Academic Press.

Riesen, A. H. (1975). *The developmental neuropsychology of sensory deprivation*. New York: Academic Press.

Riley, V. (1981). Psychoneuroendocrine influences in immunocompetence and neoplasia. *Science, 212*, 1100–1109.

Rimland, B. (1978). Savant capabilities of autistic children and their cognitive implications. In G. Serban (Ed.), *Cognitive defects in the development of mental illness*. New York: Brunner-Mazel.

Roberts, A., & Roberts, B. (Eds.). (1983). *Neural origin of rhythmic movements*. Cambridge, UK: Cambridge University Press.

Robinson, J. A. (1976). Sampling autobiographical memory. *Cognitive Psychology, 8*, 578–595.

Rodin, J., & Langer, E. J. (1980). The effects of labeling and control on self-concept in the aged. *Journal of Social Issues, 36*, 12–29.

Roediger, H. L., III (1980). Memory metaphors in cognitive psychology. *Memory and Cognition, 8*, 231–246.

Roffwarg, H. P., Muzio, J. N., & Dement, W. C. (1966). Ontogenetic development of the human sleep-dream cycle. *Science, 152*, 604–619.

Rogers, C. R. (1946). Significant aspects of client-centered therapy. *American Psychologist, 1*, 415–422.

Rogers, C. R. (1951). *Client-centered therapy*. New York: Houghton-Mifflin.

Rohrlich, F. (1983). Facing quantum mechanical reality. *Science, 221*, 1251–1255.

Roitblat, H. L., Bever, T. G., & Terrace, H. S. (1984). *Animal cognition*. Hillsdale, NJ: Lawrence Erlbaum Associates.

Rokeach, M. A. (1968). A theory of organization and change within value-attitude systems. *Journal of Social Issues, 24*, 13–33.

Rokeach, M. (1973). *The nature of human values*. Riverside, NY: The Free Press.

Rokeach, M. (Ed.). (1979). *Understanding human values: Individual and societal*. New York: Free Press.

Romijn, H. J. (1978). The pineal, a tranquilizing organ? *Life Sciences, 23*, 2257–2274.

Rorer, L. G., & Widiger, T. A. (1983). Personality structure and assessment. *Annual Review of Psychology, 34*, 431–464.

Rosch, E., & Lloyd, B. B. (Eds.). (1978). *Cognition and categorization*. Hillsdale, NJ: Lawrence Erlbaum Associates.

Rosch, E., Mervis, C. B., Gray, W. D., Johnson, D. M., & Boyes-Braem, P. (1976). Basic objects in natural categories. *Cognitive Psychology, 8,* 382–439.

Rose, J. (Ed.). (1978). Current topics in cybernetics and systems. *Proceedings of the Fourth International Congress of Cybernetics and Systems, Amsterdam, Netherlands.* Berlin: Springer-Verlag.

Rose, J., & Bilciu, C. (1977). *Modern trends in cybernetics and systems* (Vols. 1–3). Berlin: Springer-Verlag.

Rose, J. E. & Mountcastle, V. B. (1959). Touch and kinesthesis. In J. Field, H. W. Magoun, & V. E. Hall (Eds.), *Handbook of physiology: Sec. 1. Neurophysiology: Vol. 1* (pp. 387–430). Bethesda, MD: American Physiological Society.

Rosenbaum, D. A., & Patashnik, O. (1980). A mental clock setting process revealed by reaction times. In G. E. Stelmach & J. Requin (Eds.), *Tutorials in motor behavior* (pp. 487–499). Amsterdam: North-Holland.

Rosenbleuth, A., & Wiener, N. (1950). Purposeful and nonpurposeful behavior. *Philosophy of Science, 17,* 318–326.

Rosenbleuth, A., & Wiener, N. (1968). Purposeful and non-purposeful behavior. In W. Buckley (Ed.), *Modern systems research for the behavioral scientist* (pp. 232–237). Chicago: Aldine.

Rosenbleuth, A., Wiener, N., & Bigelow, J. (1968). Behavior, purpose and teleology. In W. Buckley (Ed.), *Modern systems research for the behavioral scientist* (pp. 221–225). Chicago: Aldine.

Rosenblith, J. F. (1979). The Graham Rosenblith behavioral examination for newborns: Prognostic value and procedural issues. In J. Osofsky (Ed.), *The handbook of infant development* (pp. 216–252). New York: Wiley.

Rosenman, M. F. (1978). Liking, loving, and styles of loving. *Psychological Reports, 42,* 1243–1246.

Rosenthal, R. (1976). *Experimenter effects in behavioral research.* New York: Irvington.

Rosenthal, T. L., & Zimmerman, B. J. (1978). *Social learning and cognition.* New York: Academic Press.

Rosenzweig, M. R. (1984). Experience, memory and the brain. *American Psychologist, 39,* 365–376.

Ross, L., & Anderson, C. A. (1982). Shortcomings in the attribution process: On the origins and maintenance of erroneous social assessments. In D. Kahneman, R. Slovic, & A. Tversky (Eds.), *Judgement under uncertainty: Heuristics and biases* (pp. 129–152). Cambridge, UK: Cambridge University Press.

Rothchild, E. (1973). Emotional aspects of sexual development. In A. M. Juhosz (Ed.), *Sexual development and behavior* (pp. 5–19). Homewood, IL: Dorsey Press.

Rothenberg, A. (1978). Translogical secondary process cognition in creativity. *Journal of Altered States of Consciousness, 4,* 171–187.

Rothenberg, A. (1979). Einstein's creative thinking and the general theory of relativity: A documented report. *American Journal of Psychiatry, 136,* 38–43.

Rothman, B. S., & Potts, M. (1977). Children's search behaviors and strategy choices in problem solving. *Child Development, 48,* 1058–1061.

Rotter, J. B. (1954). *Social learning and clinical psychology.* New York: Prentice-Hall.

Rotter, J. B. (1966). Generalized expectancies for internal versus external control of reinforcement. *Psychological Monographs, 80,* 1–28.

Rotter, J. B. (1978). Generalized expectancies for problem solving and psychotherapy. *Cognitive Therapy and Research, 2,* 1–10.

Routtenberg, A. (1968). The two arousal hypothesis: Reticular formation and limbic system. *Psychological Review, 75,* 51–80.

Rovee-Collier, C. K., Sullivan, M. W., Enright, M., Lucas, D., & Fagen, J. (1980). Reactivation of infant memory. *Science, 208,* 1159–1161.

Roy, E. A. (1982). Action and performance. In A. W. Ellis (Ed.), *Normality and pathology in cognitive functions* (pp. 265–298). New York: Academic Press.

Royce, J. E. (1961). *Man and his nature.* New York: McGraw-Hill.

Royce, J. R., & Buss, A. R. (1976). The role of general systems and information theory in multi-factor individuality theory. *Canadian Psychological Review, 17,* 1–21.

Royce, J. R., & Diamond, S. R. (1980). A multifactor-system dynamics theory of emotion. *Motivation and Emotion, 4,* 263–298.

Royce, J. R., & Powell, A. (1983). *Theory of personality and individual differences.* Englewood Cliffs, NJ: Prentice-Hall.

Rozin, P. (1976). The evolution of intelligence and access to the cognitive unconscious. *Progression in Psychology and Physiological Psychology, 6,* 245–280.

Rubin, D. C. (Ed.). (1985). *Autobiographical memory.* Cambridge, UK: Cambridge University Press.

Rubin, M. D. (1968). History of technological feedback. In J. H. Milsum (Ed.), *Positive feedback.* Oxford: Pergamon Press.

Rubin, Z. (1970). Measurement of romantic love. *Journal of Personality and Social Psychology, 16,* 265–273.

Ruff, H. A. (1984). An ecological approach to memory. In M. Moscovitch (Ed.), *Infant memory (pp. 49–74). New York: Plenum Press.*

Rumelhart, D. E. (1980). Schemata: The building blocks of cognition. In R. Spiro, B. Bruce, & W. Brewer (Eds.), *Theoretical issues in reading comprehension.* Hillsdale, NJ: Lawrence Erlbaum Associates.

Rumelhart, D. E., & Ortony, A. (1977). The representation of knowledge in memory. In R. E. Anderson, R. J. Spiro, & W. E. Montague (Eds.), *Schooling and the acquisition of knowledge.* Hillsdale, NJ: Lawrence Erlbaum Associates.

Russell, D. G. (1976). Spatial location cues and movement production. In G. E. Stelmach (Ed.), *Motor control: Issues and trends* (pp. 67–85). New York: Academic Press.

Russell, J. A. (1980). A circumplex model of affect. *Journal of Personality and Social Psychology, 39,* 1161–1178.

Russell, J. A., & Ward, L. M. (1982). Environmental psychology. *Annual Review of Psychology, 33,* 651–688.

Russell, P. A. (1979). Fear-evoking stimuli. In W. Sluckin (Ed.), *Fear in animals and man* (pp. 86–124). New York: Van Nostrand Reinhold.

Ryan, E. D., & Simons, J. (1981). Cognitive demand, imagery, and frequency of mental rehearsal as factors influencing acquisition of motor skills. *Journal of Sport Psychology, 3,* 35–45.

Ryan, E. D., & Simons, J. (1982). Efficacy of mental imagery in enhancing mental rehearsal of motor skills. *Journal of Sport Psychology, 4,* 41–51.

Ryan, T. A. (1970). *Intentional behavior: An approach to human motivation.* New York: Ronald Press.

Sacerdoti, E. D. (1977). *A structure for plans and behavior.* New York: Elsevier/North-Holland.

Sachar, E. J., & Baron, M. (1979). The biology of affective disorders. *Annual Review of Neurosciences, 2,* 505–518.

Sackett, G. P. (1979). The lag sequential analysis of contingency and cyclicity in behavioral interaction research. In J. Osofsky (Ed.), *Handbook of infant development* (pp. 623–649). New York: Wiley.

Sage, A. P., & White, E. B. (1980). Methodologies for risk and hazard assessment: A survey and status report. *IEEE Transactions on Systems, Man, and Cybernetics, SMC-10,* 425–446.

Sahakian, W. S. (Ed.). (1969). *Psychotherapy and counseling.* Chicago: Rand McNally.

Salisbury, H. E. (1969). *The 900 days: The siege of Leningrad.* New York: Harper & Row.

Salmaso, P., Baroni, M.R., Job, R., & Peron, E. M. (1982). Aims, attention and natural settings: An investigation into memory for places. *Italian Journal of Psychology, 8,* 219–233.

Salzen, E. A. (1979). The ontogeny of fear in animals. In W. Sluckin (Ed.), *Fear in animals and man* (pp. 125–163). New York: Van Nostrand Reinhold.

Salzinger, K. (1959). Experimental manipulation of verbal behavior: A review. *Journal of General Psychology, 61,* 65–94.

Sameroff, A. J., & Cavanaugh, P. J. (1979). Learning in infancy: A developmental perspective. In J. D. Osofsky (Ed.), *Handbook of infant development* (pp. 344–392). New York: Wiley.

Sanford, N. (1968). Personality: The field. In D. L. Sills (Ed.), *International encyclopedia of the social sciences* (Vol. 2, pp. 587–606). New York: The Free Press.

Santostefano, S. G. (1969). Cognitive controls versus cognitive styles: Diagnosing and treating cognitive disabilities in children. *Seminars in Psychiatry, 1,* 291–317.

Santostefano, S. (1978). *A biodevelopmental approach to clinical child psychology: Cognitive controls and cognitive control therapy.* New York: Wiley.

Santostefano, S. (1980). Clinical child psychology: The need for developmental principles. In R. L. Selman & R. Yando (Eds.), *New directions for child development: Clinical developmental psychology* (Vol. 7). San Francisco: Jossey-Bass.

Sarason, I. G. (1972). Experimental approaches to test anxiety: Attention and the uses of information. In C. D. Spielberger (Ed.), *Anxiety: Current trends in theory and research* (Vol. 2, pp. 195–222). New York: Academic Press.

Sarnat, H. B., & Netsky, M. G. (1974). *Evolution of the nervous system.* Oxford: Tavistock.

Satinoff, E. (1978). Neural organization and evolution of thermal regulation in mammals. *Science, 201,* 16–21.

de Saussure, F. (1974). *Course in general linguistics.* Glasgow: Collins.

Scarr, S., & Carter-Saltzman, L. (1982). Genetics and intelligence. In R. J. Sternberg (Ed.), *Handbook of human intelligence* (pp. 792–896). Cambridge, UK: Cambridge University Press.

Scarr-Salapatek. (1976). An evolutionary perspective on infant intelligence: Species patterns and individual variations. In M. Lewis (Ed.), *Origins of intelligence* (pp. 163–198). New York: Plenum Press.

Schachtel, E. G. (1959). *Metamorphosis.* New York: Basic Books.

Schachter, S. (1964). The interactions of cognitive and physiological determinants of emotional state. *Advanced Experimental Social Psychology, 1,* 49–80.

Schachter, S., & Singer, J. (1962). Cognitive, social and physiological determinants of emotional state. *Psychological Review, 69,* 379–399.

Schacter, D. L., & Moscovitch, M. (1984). Infants, amnesics, and dissociable memory systems. In M. Moscovitch (Ed.), *Infant memory* (pp. 173–216). New York: Plenum Press.

Schaeffer, L. H. (1975). Multiple attention in continuous verbal tasks. In P. M. A. Rabbitt & S. Dornic (Eds.), *Attention and performance.* London: Academic Press.

Schaie, K. W. (1978). Toward a stage theory of adult cognitive development. *Journal of Aging and Human Development, 8,* 129–1138.

Schaie, K. W. (1979). The primary mental abilities in adulthood: An exploration in the development of psychometric intelligence. In P. B. Baltes & O. G. Brim, Jr. (Eds.), *Life-span development and behavior* (Vol. 2, pp. 67–115). New York: Academic Press.

Schaie, K. W. (1980). Intelligence and problem solving. In J. E. Birren & R. B. Sloane (Eds.), *Handbook of mental health and aging* (pp. 262–284). Englewood Cliffs, NJ: Prentice-Hall.

Schally, A. V. (1978). Aspects of hypothalamic regulation of the pituitary gland. *Science, 202,* 18–28.

Schank, R. C. (1979). *Reminding and memory organization. An introduction to MOPs.* ARPA Technical Report No. 170. New Haven: Yale University Department of Computer

Science.

Schank, R. C., & Abelson, R. P. (1977). *Scripts, plans, goals and understanding: An inquiry into human knowledge structures.* Hillsdale, NJ: Lawrence Erlbaum Associates.

Schank, R. C., & Colby, K. M. (1973). *Computer models of thought and language.* San Francisco: Freeman.

Scheflen, A. E. (1968). Human communication: Behavioral programs and their integration in interaction. *Behavioral Science, 13,* 44–55.

Schellenbach, C. J. (1984). *A multivariate systems approach to infant emotional development.* Unpublished doctoral dissertation, The Pennsylvania State University.

Schellenbach, C. (1987). A systems approach to the ontogenesis of emotions. In M. Ford & D. Ford (Eds.), Humans as self-constructing living systems: Putting the framework to work. *Hillsdale, NJ: Lawrence Erlbaum Associates.*

Schendel, J.D. (1979). *Guidelines for effective selective listening.* U.S. Army Research Institute for the Behavioral and Social Sciences *(RR 1215).*

Schildkraut, J. J., & Kety, S. S. (1967). Biogenic amines and emotion. *Science, 156,* 21–30.

Schill, T., & Althoff, M. (1975). Drug experiences, knowledge and attitude of high and low guilt individuals. *Journal of Consulting and Clinical Psychology, 43,* 106–107.

Schleiffer, M., & Douglas, V. I. (1973). Effects of training on the moral judgment of young children. *Journal of Personality and Social Psychology, 28,* 62–68.

Schmale, A. H., & Engel, G. L. (1975). The role of conversation withdrawal in depressive reactions. In E. J. Anthony & T. Beneded (Eds.), *Depression and human existence* (pp. 183–198). Boston: Little, Brown.

Schmidt, R. A. (1975). A schema theory of discrete motor skill learning. *Psychological Review, 82,* 225–260.

Schmidt, R.A. (1980). On the theoretical status of time in motor program representation. In G. E. Stelmach & J. Requin (Eds.), *Tutorials in motor behavior* (pp. 145–166). Amsterdam: North-Holland.

Schmidt, R. A., Zelanik, H., Hawkins, B., Frank, J. S. & Quinn, J. T., Jr. (1979). Motor-output variability: A theory for the accuracy of rapid motor acts. *Psychological Review, 86,* 415–451.

Schneider, W., & Shiffrin, R. (1977a). Controlled and automatic information processing: I. Detection, search and attention. *Psychological Review, 84,* 1–66.

Schneider, W., & Shiffrin, R. (1977b). Controlled and automatic human information processing: II. Perceptual learning, automatic attending, and a general theory. *Psychological Review, 84,* 127–190.

Schneirla, T. C. (1957). The concept of development in comparative psychology. In D. B. Harris (Ed.), *The concept of development* (pp. 78–108). Minneapolis: University of Minnesota Press.

Schonfield, A. E. D. (1980). Learning, memory, and aging. In J. E. Birren & R. B. Sloane (Eds.), *Handbook of mental health and aging* (pp. 214–244). Englewood Cliffs, NJ: Prentice-Hall.

Schuman, J. (1980). The psychophysiological model of meditation and altered states of consciousness: A critical review. In J. M. Davidson & R. J. Davidson (Eds.), *The psychobiology of consciousness* (pp. 333–378). New York: Plenum Press.

Schwartz, B. (1974). On going back to nature: A review of Seligman and Hoger's biological boundaries of learning. *Journal of the Experimental Analysis of Behavior, 21,* 183–198.

Schwartz, G. E., & Shapiro, D. (Eds.). (1976). *Consciousness and self-regulation* (Vol. 1). New York: Plenum Press.

Schwartz, G. E., & Shapiro, D. (Eds.). (1978). *Consciousness and self-regulation* (Vol. 2). New York: Plenum Press.

Schwartz, J. C., & Zuroff, D. C. (1979). Family structure and depression in female college students: Effects of parental conflict, decision-making power, and inconsistency of love.

Journal of Abnormal Psychology, 88, 398–406.

Schworm, R. W. (1979). The effects of selective attention on the decoding skills for children with learning disabilities. *Journal of Learning Disabilities, 12, 639–644.*

Science. (1980). A complete issue of Science devoted to research on genetics and DNA. *Science, 209,* 1319–1438.

Science. (1981). The complete index to man. *Science, 211, 33–36.*

Science. (1982). Computers: A survey of trends and limitations. *Science, 215,* 760–765.

Scientific American. (1979). *The brain.* New York: Freeman.

Searle, J. R. (1969). *Speech acts.* Cambridge, UK: Cambridge University Press.

Searle, J. R. (1979). What is an intentional state? *Mind, 88,* 74–92.

Searle, J. R. (1981). The intentionality of intention and action. *Separata de Manuscrito,* 4(2), 77–101. (Campinas, Brazil)

Sears, R. R. (1960). The growth of conscience. In I. Iscoe & H. Stevenson (Eds.), *Personality development in children* (pp. 92–111). Austin: University Texas Press.

Sears, R. R., Maccoby, E. E., & Levin, H. (1957). *Patterns of child rearing.* Evanston, IL: Row, Peterson.

Sebeok, T. A. (Ed.). (1974). *Current trends in linguistics* (Vol. 12, Part 4). The Hague: Mouton.

Sebes, J. M., & Ford, D. H. (1984). Moral development and self-regulation: Research and intervention planning. *The Personnel and Guidance Journal, 62,* 379–382.

Sechrest, L. (1976). Personalities. *Annual Review of Psychology, 27,* 1–27.

Sekuler, R., & Ball, K. (1977). Mental set alters visibility of moving targets. *Science, 198,* 60–62.

Self, P. A., & Horowitz, F. D. (1979). The behavioral assessment of the neonate: An overview. In J. Osofsky (Ed.), *The handbook of infant development* (pp. 126–164). New York: Wiley.

Seligman, M. E. P. (1970). On the generality of the laws of learning. *Psychological Review, 77,* 406–418.

Seligman, M. E. P. (1975). *Helplessness.* San Francisco: Freeman.

Seligman, M. E. P., & Hager, J. L. (Eds.). (1972). *Biological boundaries of learning.* New York: Appleton-Century-Crofts.

Sells, S. B. (1963). An interactionist look at the environment. *American Psychologist, 18,* 696–702.

Selman, R. L. (1980). *The growth of interpersonal understanding.* New York: Academic Press.

Selye, H. (1946). The general adaptation syndrome and the diseases of adaptation. *Journal of Clinical Endocrinological Metabolism, 2,* 117–130.

Selye, H. (1976). *The stress of life* (rev. ed.). New York: McGraw-Hill.

Sem-Jacobsen, C. W. (1958). Comment. In H. H. Jasper, L. D. Proctor, R. S. Knighton, W. C. Noshay, & R. T. Costello (Eds.), *Reticular formation of the brain* (pp. 725–726). Boston: Little, Brown.

Seneca, L. A. M. (50 AD). On anger. Reprinted in J. W. Basore (Trans.), *Moral essays* (1963). Cambridge, MA: Harvard University Press.

Sermat, V. (1978). Sources of loneliness. *Essence, 2,* 271–276.

Sexton, M.A., & Geffen, G. (1979). Development of three strategies of attention in dichotic monitoring. *Developmental Psychology, 15,* 299–310.

Shaffer, L. H. (1980). Analyzing piano performance: A study of concert pianists. In G. E. Stelmach & J. Requin (Eds.), *Tutorials in motor behavior* (pp. 443–455). Amsterdam: North-Holland.

Shakow, D. (1979). *Adaptation in schizophrenia: The theory of segmental set.* New York: Wiley-Interscience.

Shallice, T. (1978). The dominant action system: An information-processing approach to consciousness. In K. S. Pope & J. L. Singer (Eds.), *The stream of consciousness* (pp.

117–157). New York: Plenum Press.

Shannon, C. E. (1948). A mathematical theory of information. *Bell System Technical Journal, 27,* 379–423, 623–656.

Shannon, C. E., & Weaver, W. (1949). *The mathematical theory of communication.* Urbana: University of Illinois Press.

Shantz, C. V. (1983). Social cognition. In P. H. Mussen (Ed.), *Handbook of child psychology (4th ed.): Vol. 3. Cognitive development* (pp. 495–555). New York: Wiley.

Shapiro, M. B. (1979). The relation of guilt and other feelings to the diagnosis of depression. *British Journal of Medical Psychology, 52,* 123–132.

Shapiro, J. A. (1983). *Mobile genetic elements.* New York: Academic Press.

Shatz, M. (1983). Communication. In P. H. Mussen (Ed.), *Handbook of child psychology: Vol. 3. Cognitive development* (pp. 841–890). New York: Wiley.

Shaw, R., McIntyre, M., & Mace, W. (1974). The role of symmetry in event perception. In R. B. MacLeod & H. L. Pick, Jr., (Eds.), *Perception: Essays in honor of James J. Gibson* (pp. 276–310). Ithica, NY: Cornell University.

Shaw, R., & Bransford, J. (Eds.). (1977). *Perceiving, acting, and knowing.* Hillsdale, NJ: Lawrence Erlbaum Associates.

Sheehan, P. (Ed.). (1972). *The function and nature of mental imagery.* New York: Academic Press.

Sheehy, G. (1977). *Passages.* New York: Bantam Books.

Sheer, D. E. (Ed.). (1961). *Electrical stimulation of the brain.* Austin: University of Texas Press.

Sheikk, A. A. (Ed.). (1983). *Imagery: Current theory, research, and application.* New York: Wiley.

Shepard, R. N. (1978). Externalization of mental images and the act of creation. In B. S. Randhawa & W. E. Coffman (Eds.), *Visual learning, thinking, and communication* (pp. 133–190). New York: Academic Press.

Shepard, R. N. (1984). Ecological constraints on internal representation: Resonant kinematics of perceiving, imagining, thinking, and dreaming. *Psychological Review, 91,* 417–447.

Shepard, R. N., & Cooper, L. A. (1982). *Mental images and their transformations.* Cambridge, MA: MIT Press/Bradford Books.

Shephard, R. J. (1982). *Physiology and biochemistry of exercise.* New York: Praeger.

Shepherd, G. M. (1974). *The synaptic organization of the brain: An introduction.* New York: Oxford University Press.

Sherif, C. W. (1979). Social values, attitudes, and the involvement of the self. In M. M. Page (Ed.), *Beliefs, attitudes and values. Nebraska Symposium on Motivation* (Vol. 27, pp. 1–64). Lincoln: University of Nebraska Press.

Sherrick, C. E. (1966). Somesthetic senses. *Annual Review of Psychology, 17,* 309–336.

Sherrington, C. (1906). *Integrative action of the nervous system.* Cambridge, UK: Cambridge University Press.

Sherrington, C. S. (1941). *Man on his nature.* Cambridge, UK: Cambridge University Press.

Sherrington, C. S. (1947). *The integrative action of the nervous system* (1st ed.). New Haven: Yale University Press.

Sherrod, L. R. (1979). Social cognition in infants; Attention to the human face. *Infant Behavior and Development, 2,* 279–294.

Shimoda, K. Argyle, M., & RicciBitti, P. (1978). The intercultural recognition of emotional expressions by three national racial groups: English, Italian, and Japanese. *European Journal of Social Psychology, 8, 169–179.*

Shirley, M. (1931). *The first two years: A study of twenty-five babies: I. Postural and locomotor development. Minneapolis: University of Minnesota Press.*

Showers, C., & Cantor, N. (1985). Social cognition: A look at motivated strategies. *Annual*

Review of Psychology, 36, 275–305.

Shrauger, J. S., & Schoeneman, T. J. (1979). Symbolic interactionist view of self-concept: Through the looking glass darkly. *Psychological Bulletin, 86,* 549–573.

Shultz, T. R. (1982). Rules of causal attribution. *Monographs of the Society for Research in Child Development, 47*(1, Serial No. 194).

Sicinski, A. (1978). The concepts of "need" and "value" in the light of the systems approach. *Social Science Information, 17,* 71–91.

Sidman, M., Brady, J. V., Boren, J. J., Conrad, D. G., & Schulman, A. (1955). Reward schedules and behavior maintained by intracranial self-stimulation. *Science, 122,* 830–831.

Siegel, A. W., Allen, G. L., & Kirasic, K. C. (1979). Children's ability to make bidirectional distance comparisons: The advantage of thinking ahead. *Developmental Psychology, 15,* 656–657.

Siegel, L., & Siegel, L. C. (1965). Educational set: A determinant of acquisition. *Journal of Educational Psychology, 56,* 1–12.

Siegel, L. S., & Brainerd, C. J. (Eds.). (1978). *Alternatives to Piaget: Critical essays on the theory.* New York: Academic Press.

Siegel, R. K., & West, L. J. (Eds.). (1975). *Hallucinations: Behavior, experience, and theory.* New York: Wiley.

Siegler, R. S. (Ed.). (1978). *Children's thinking: What develops?* Hillsdale, NJ: Lawrence Erlbaum Associates.

Siegler, R. S. (1983). Information processing approaches to development. In P. H. Mussen (Ed.), *Handbook of child psychology (4th ed.): Vol. 1. History, theory and methods* (pp. 129–212). New York: Wiley.

Siegler, R. S., & Richards, D. D. (1982). The development of intelligence. In R. J. Sternberg (Ed.), *Handbook of human intelligence* (pp. 897–974). Cambridge, UK: Cambridge University Press.

Silberschatz, G. (1978). Selective attention and changes in clinical state. *Journal of Research in Personality, 12,* 197–204.

Siller, J., & Chipman, A. (1963). Response set paralysis: Implications for measurement and control. *Journal of Consulting Psychology, 27,* 432–438.

Silva, J. M. (1979). Behavioral and situational factors affecting concentration and skill performance. *Journal of Sport's Psychology, 1,* 221–227.

Simon, H. A. (1969). *The sciences of the artificial.* Cambridge, MA: MIT Press.

Simon, H. A. (1978). Information-processing theory of human problem solving. In W. K. Estes (Ed.), *Handbook of learning and cognitive processes* (Vol. 5, pp. 271–296). Hillsdale, NJ: Lawrence Erlbaum Associates.

Simon, H. A. (1979). Problem solving and education. In D. T. Tuma & F. Reiff (Eds.), *Problem solving and education: Issues in teaching and research.* Hillsdale, NJ: Lawrence Erlbaum Associates.

Simon, H. A. (1979). *Models of thought.* New Haven: Yale University Press.

Simpson, E. L. (1974). Moral development research: A case study of scientific cultural bias. *Human Development, 17,* 81–106.

Simpson, G. G., Pittendrigh, C. S., & Tiffany, L. H. (1957). *Life: An introduction to biology.* New York: Harcourt, Brace.

Singer, J. L. & Kolligan, J. Jr. (1987). Personality: Developments in the study of private experience. *Annual Review of Psychology, 38,* 533–74.

Singer, M. (1980). Recombinant DNA revisited. *Science, 209,* 1317.

Singer, R. N. (1975). *Motor learning and human performance.* New York: Macmillan.

Siqueland, E. R. (1968). *Conditioned sucking and visual reinforcers with human infants.* Paper presented at Eastern Regional Meeting, Society for Research in Child Development, Worcester, MA.

Sjöberg, L. (1979). Strength of belief and risk. *Policy Sciences, 11,* 39–57.

Skinner, B. F. (1938). *The behavior of organisms: An experimental analysis.* New York: Appleton-Century-Crofts.

Skinner, B. F. (1953). *Science and human behavior.* New York: Macmillan.

Skinner, B. F. (1957). *Verbal behavior.* New York: Appleton-Century-Crofts.

Skinner, B. F. (1959). *Cumulative record.* New York: Appleton-Century-Crofts.

Skinner, B. F. (1966). The phylogeny and ontogeny of behavior. *Science, 153,* 1205–1213.

Skinner, B. F. (1974). *About behaviorism.* New York: Knopf.

Skinner, B. F. (1981). Selection by consequences. *Science, 213,* 501–504.

Slater, E., & Shields, J. (1969). Genetical aspects of anxiety. In M. H. Lader (Ed.), *Studies of anxiety. British Journal of Psychiatry* (Special Publication No. 3). Ashford, Kent: Headley Brothers, Ltd.

Slovic, P., Fischoff, B., & Lichtenstein, S. (1977). Behavioral decision theory. *Annual Review of Psychology, 29,* 1–39.

Sluckin, W. (Ed.). (1979). *Fear in animals and man.* New York: Van Nostrand Reinhold.

Smart, M. S., & Smart, R. C. (1967). *Children: Development and relationships.* New York: Macmillan.

Smith, B. (1978). Temporal aspects of English speech production: A developmental perspective. *Journal of Phonetics, 6,* 37–67.

Smith, C. S. (1969). Structural hierarchy in inorganic systems. In L. L. White, A. G. Wilson, & D. Wilson (Eds.), *Hierarchical structures* (pp. 61–86). New York: American Elsevier.

Smith, E. E., & Medin, D. L. (1981). *Categories and concepts.* Cambridge, MA: Harvard University Press.

Smith, H. A. (1979). Nonverbal communication in teaching. *Review of Educational Research, 49,* 631–672.

Smith, J. E. (1980). Science and conscience. *American Scientist, 68,* 554–558.

Smith, J. L. (1980). Programming of stereotyped limb movements by spinal generators. In G. E. Stelmach & J. Requin (Eds.), *Tutorials in motor behavior* (pp. 95–115). Amsterdam: North-Holland.

Smith, K. U., & Akelaitis, A. J. (1942). Studies on the corpus callosum. *Archives of Neurology and psychiatry, 47,* 519–543.

Smith, M. B. (1969). *Social psychology and human values.* Chicago: Aldine.

Smith, M. B. (1978). Perspectives on selfhood. *American Psychologist, 33,* 1053–1063.

Smith, P. K. (1979). The ontogeny of fear in children. In W. Sluckin (Ed.), *Fear in animals and man* (pp. 164–198). New York: Van Nostrand Reinhold.

Smith, R. P. (1981). Boredom: A review. *Human Factors, 23,* 329–340.

Smyth, M. M. (1978). Attention to visual feedback in motor learning. *Journal of Motor Behavior, 10,* 185–190.

Smythies, J. R. (1970). *Brain mechanisms and behavior* (2nd ed.). New York: Academic Press.

Snowdon, C. T. (1983). Ethology, comparative psychology, and animal behavior. *Annual Review of Psychology, 34,* 63–94.

Snowdon, C. T., Brown, C. H., & Peterson, M. R. (Eds.). (1983). *Primate communication.* New York: Cambridge University Press.

Snyder, M. (1978). *On the nature of social knowledge.* Invited contribution at Midwestern Psychological Association, Chicago.

Snyder, S. H. (1985). The molecular basis of communication between cells. *Scientific American, 253,* 132–141.

Snyderman, R., & Goetzel, E. J. (1981). Molecular and cellular mechanisms of leukocyte chemotaxis. *Science, 213,* 830–837.

Snygg, D., & Combs, A. W. (1949). *Individual behavior: A new frame of reference for psychology.* New York: Harper.

Sokolov, E. N. (1963). *Perception and the conditioned reflex.* New York: Macmillan.

Sokolov, E. N. (1977). Brain functions: Neuronal mechanisms of learning and memory. *Annual Review of Psychology, 28,* 85–112.

Soll, D. R. (1979). Timers in developing systems. *Science, 203,* 841–849.

Solomon, P. R. (1980). A time and place for everything? Temporal processing views of hippocampal function with special reference to attention. *Physiological Psychology, 8,* 254–261.

Somorjai, G. A. (1978). Surface science. *Science, 201,* 489–495.

Sourkes, T. L. (1977). Biochemistry of mental depression. *Canadian Psychiatric Association Journal, 22,* 467–481.

Spear, L. P. (1980). Psychopharmacological approach to memory processing. In R. F. Thompson, L. H. Hicks, & V. B. Shvyrkov (Eds.), *Neural mechanisms of goal directed behavior and learning* (pp. 425–435). New York: Academic Press.

Spears, W. C., & Hohle, R. H. (1967). Sensory and perceptual processes in infants. In Y. Brackbill (Ed.), *Infancy and early childhood* (pp. 51–121). New York: The Free Press.

Spence, D. P., & Holland, B. (1962). The restricting effects of awareness: A paradox and an explanation. *Journal of Abnormal and Social Psychology, 64,* 163–174.

Spence, K. W. (1960). *Behavior theory and learning: Selected papers.* Englewood Cliffs, NJ: Prentice-Hall.

Sperry, R. W. (1976). Changing concepts of consciousness and free will. *Perspectives in Biology and Medicine, 20,* 9–19.

Sperry, R. (1982). Some effects of disconnecting the cerebral hemispheres. *Science, 217,* 1223–1226.

Spiegel, E. A., Miller, H. R., & Oppenheimer, M. J. (1940). Forebrain and rage reactions. *Journal of Neurophysiology, 3,* 538–548.

Spielberger, C. D. (Ed.). (1972). *Anxiety: current trends in theory and research* (Vol. 1). New York: Academic Press.

Spielberger, C. D., & DeNike, L. D. (1962). Operant conditioning of plural nouns: A failure to replicate the Greenspoon effect. *Psychological Reports, 11,* 355–366.

Spignesi, A., & Shor, R. E. (1981). The judgement of emotion from facial expressions, contexts, and their combinations. *The Journal of General Psychology, 104,* 41–58.

Spiro, R. J. (1980). Accommodative reconstruction in prose recall. *Journal of Verbal Learning and Verbal Behavior, 19,* 84–95.

Spitz, R. A. (1945). Hospitalism, an inquiry into the genesis of psychiatric conditions in early childhood. In *The psychoanalytic study of the child: A yearbook* (pp. 53–75). New York: International Universities Press.

Spitz, R. A. (1946). The smiling response: A contribution to the ontogenesis of social relations. *Genetic Psychology Monographs, 34,* 57–125.

Squire, L. R. (1982). The neuropsychology of human memory. *Annual Review of Neuroscience, 5,* 241–273.

Squire, L. R., & Slater, P. C. (1978). Anterograde and retrograde memory impairment in chronic amnesia. *Neuropsychologia, 16,* 313–322.

Sroufe, L. A. (1979). Socioemotional development. In J. D. Osofsky (Ed.), *Handbook of infant development* (pp. 462–516). New York: Wiley.

Sroufe, L. A., Schork, E., Motti, F., Lawroski, N., & Lafreniere, P. (1984). The role of affect in social competence. In C. E. Izard, J. Kagan, & R. B. Zajonc (Eds.), *Emotions, cognitions and behavior.* Cambridge, UK: Cambridge University Press..

Sroufe, L. A., & Waters, E. (1976). The ontogenesis of smiling and laughter: A perspective on the organization of development in infancy. *Psychological Review, 83, 173–189.*

Sroufe, L. A., & Wunsch, J. P. (1972). The development of laughter in the first year of life. *Child Development, 43, 1326–1344.*

Staats, A. W., & Staats, C. K. (1963). *Complex human behavior.* New York: Holt, Rinehart

& Winston.

Stacey, B. G. (1975). Men and machines. Bulletin of British Psychological Society, *28*, 270–276.

Stanley, S. M. (1979). *Macroevolution: Pattern and process.* San Francisco: Freeman.

Stark, R. E. (1981). Infant vocalization: A comprehensive view. *Infant Mental Health Journal, 2*, 118–128.

Starkey, P., Spelke, E. S., & Gelman, R. (1983). Detection of intermodal numerical correspondence by human infants. *Science, 222*, 179–181.

Stebbins, G. L., & Ayala, F. J. (1981). Is a new evolutionary synthesis necessary? *Science, 23*, 967–971.

Stebbins, G. L., & Ayala, F. J. (1985). The evolution of Darwinism. *Scientific American, 253*, 72–85.

Stechler, G., Bradford, S., & Levy, H. (1966). Attention in the Newborn: Effect on motility and skin potential. *Science, 151*, 1246–1248.

Stechler, G., & Latz, E. (1966). Some observations on attention and arousal in the human infant. *Journal of the American Academy of Child Psychiatry, 5*, 517–525.

Stelmach, G. E. (Ed.). (1976). *Motor control: Issues and trends.* New York: Academic Press.

Stelmach, G. E., & Diggles, V. A. (1982). Control theories in motor behavior. *Acta Psychologica, 50*, 83–105.

Stelmach, G. E., & Larish, D. D. (1980). Egocentric referents in human limb orientation. In G. E. Stelmach & J. Requin (Eds.), *Tutorials in motor behavior* (pp. 167–184). Amsterdam: North-Holland.

Stelmach, G. E., & J. Requin (Eds.). (1980). Tutorials in motor behavior. Amsterdam: North-Holland.

Stelmach, G. E., & Szendrovits, L. D. (1981). Error detecting and correction in a structured movement task. *Journal of Motor Behavior, 13*, 132–143.

Stephens, W. N. (1963). *The family in cross-cultural perspective.* New York: Holt, Rinehart & Winston.

Stern, R. M., & Ray, W. J. (1977). *Biofeedback potential and limits.* Lincoln: University of Nebraska Press.

Sternbach, R. A. (1978). *The psychology of pain.* New York: Raven Press,

Sternberg, R. J. (1979). The nature of mental abilities. *American Psychologist, 34*, 214–230.

Sternberg, R. J. (1980). Sketch of a componential subtheory of human intelligence. *Behavioral and Brain Sciences, 3*, 573–584.

Sternberg, R. J. (Ed.). (1982b). *Handbook of human intelligence.* Cambridge, UK: Cambridge University Press.

Sternberg, R. J. (1982a). Reasoning, problem solving, and intelligence. In R. J. Sternberg (Ed.), *Handbook of human intelligence* (pp. 225–307). Cambridge, UK: Cambridge University Press.

Sternberg, R. J. (1985). Human intelligence: The model is the message. *Science, 230*, 1111–1118.

Sternberg, R. J., & Powell, J. S. (1982). Theories of intelligence. In R. J. Sternberg (Ed.), *Handbook of human intelligence* (pp. 975–1000). Cambridge, UK: Cambridge University Press.

Sternberg, R. J., & Powell, J. S. (1983). The development of intelligence. In P. H. Mussen (Ed.), *Handbook of child development: Vol. 3. Cognitive development* (pp. 341–419). New York: Wiley.

Sternberg, R. J., & Salter, W. (1982). Conceptions of intelligence. In R. J. Sternberg (Ed.), *Handbook of human intelligence* (pp. 3–28). Cambridge, UK: Cambridge University Press.

Stechler, G., Bradford, S., & Levy, H. (1966). Attention in the newborn: Effect on motility and skin potential. *Science, 151*, 1246–1248.

Stevens, C. F. (1979). The neuron. In *The brain: A scientific American book.* New York: W. H.

Freeman.

Stevens, K. N. (1983). Design features of speech sound systems. In P. F. MacNeilage (Ed.), *The production of speech* (pp. 247–261). New York: Springer-Verlag.

Stevens, K. N., & Blumstein, S. E. (1981). The search for invariant accoustic correlates of phonetic features. In P. D. Eimas & J. L. Miller (Eds.). *Perspectives on the study of speech* (pp. 1–38). Hillsdale, NJ: Lawrence Erlbaum Associates.

Stevens, S. S. (1961). The psychophysics of sensory function. In W. A. Rosenblith (Ed.), *Sensory communication* (pp. 1–34). New York: Wiley.

Stokoe, W. C. (1978). Sign codes and sign language: Two orders of communication. *Journal of Communication Disorders, 11,* 187–192.

Stokols, D. (1979). A congruence analysis of human stress. In I. G. Sarason & C. D. Spielberger (Eds.), *Stress and anxiety.* Washington, DC: Hemisphere.

Stone, C. A., & Day, M. C. (1980). Competence and performance models and the characterization of formal operational skills. *Human Development, 23* 323–353.

Stone, L. J., & Church, J. (1957). *Childhood and adolescence.* New York: Random House.

Stone, L. J., Smith, H. T., & Murphy, L. B. (Eds.). (1973). *The competent infant.* New York: Basic Books.

Stotland, E. (1969). *The psychology of hope.* San Francisco: Jossey-Bass.

Stratton, G. M. (1926). Emotion and the incidence of disease. *Journal of Abnormal and Social Psychology, 21,* 19–23.

Strupp, H. H. (1975). Psychoanalysis, "focal therapy" and the nature of the therapeutic influence. *Archives of General Psychiatry, 32,* 127–135.

Studer, R. G. (1969). The dynamics of behavior-contingent physical systems. In G. Broadbent (Ed.), *Design methods in architecture.* London: Lund Humphries.

Studer, R. G. (1970). The dynamics of behavior-contingent physical systems. In H. Proshansky, W. H. Ittelson, & L. G. Rivlin (Eds.), *Environmental psychology: Man and his physical setting* (pp. 56–75). New York: Holt, Rinehart & Winston.

Studer, R. G. (1971). Human systems design and the management of change. *General Systems, 16,* 131–143.

Studer, R. G. (1978). the design and management of environment-behavior systems. In H. Hanloff (Ed.), *Bedingunden des Lebens in des Zukunft und die Folgen fu;r die Erzlehung* (pp. 20–32). Berlin: Technische Universitat Berlin.

Studer, R. G. (1980). Environmental design and management as evolutionary experimentation. *Design Studies, 1,* 365–371.

Studer, R. G., & Barton, E. M. (1974). *Aggregate effects of incremental changes in the social environment of the older person.* Paper presented at the 82nd Annual American Psychological Association Convention, New Orleans.

Sugerman, A. A., & Tarter, R. E. (1978). *Expanding dimensions of consciousness.* New York: Springer.

Suler, J. R. (1980). Primary process thinking and creativity. *Psychological Bulletin, 88,* 144–165.

Sullivan, E. V. (1977). A study of Kohlberg's structural theory of moral development: A critique of liberal social science ideology. *Human Development, 20,* 352–376.

Sullivan, H. S. (1953). *The interpersonal theory of psychiatry.* New York: W. W. Norton.

Sulloway, F. J. (1983). *Freud, Biologist of the mind.* New York: Basic Books.

Suls, J. (Ed.). (1982). *Psychological perspectives on the self* (Vol. 1). Hillsdale, NJ: Lawrence Erlbaum Associates.

Suls, J., & Greenwald, A. G. (1983). *Psychological perspectives on the self* (Vol. 2). Hillsdale, NJ: Lawrence Erlbaum Associates.

Sunderland, S. (1968). *Nerves and nerve injuries.* Edinburgh: Livingston.

Swanson, J. L. (1980). The morality of conscience and the morality of the organism: Valuing from the Gestalt point of view. *The Gestalt Journal, 3,* 71–85.

Swazey, J. P. (1968). Sherrington's concept of integrative action. *Journal of the History of Biology, 1,* 57–89.

Sweller, J., & Gee, W. (1978). Einstellung, the sequence effect, and hypothesis theory. *Journal of Experimental psychology: Human Learning and Memory, 4,* 513–526.

Symons, D. (1979). *The evolution of human sexuality.* New York: Oxford University Press.

Szentágothai, J. (1973). Synaptology of the visual cortex. In R. Jung (Ed.), *Handbook of sensory physiology* (Vol. 7, Part 3, pp. 269–324). Berlin-New York: Springer-Verlag.

Szentágothai, M. J., & Arbib, M. A. (1975). The module concept in cerebral cortex architecture. *Brain Research, 95,* 475–496.

Takahashi, J. S., & Zatz, M. (1982). Regulation of circadian rhythmicity. *Science, 217,* 1104–1111.

Tallman, J. F., Paul, S. M., Skolnick, P., & Gallager, D. W. (1980). Receptors for the age of anxiety: Pharmacology of the Benzodiazepines. *Science, 207,* 274–282.

Tarpy, R. M. (1977). The nervous system and emotion. In D. K. Candland, J. P. Fell, E. Keen, A. I. Leshner, R. M. Tarpy, & R. Plutchik (Eds.), *Emotion* (pp. 150–188). Monterey, CA: Brooks/Cole (Wadsworth).

Tart, C. T. (1975). *States of consciousness.* New York: Dutton.

Taylor, S. E., & Crocker, J. (1981). Schematic bases of social information processing. In E. T. Higgins, C. A. Herman, & M. P. Zanna (Eds.), *Social cognition: The Ontario Symposium* (Vol. 1, pp. 89–134). Hillsdale, NJ: Lawrence Erlbaum Associates.

Teitelbaum, P., Schallert, T., DeRyck, M., Whishaw, I., & Golani, I. (1980). Motor subsystems in motivated behavior. In R. F. Thompson, L. H. Hicks, & V. B. Shvyrkov (Eds.), *Neural mechanisms of goal-directed behavior and learning* (pp. 127–143). New York: Academic Press.

Terquolo, C. A., Dufresne, J. R., & Soechting, J. F. (1980). The utilization of myotic feedback in motor control. In G. E. Stelmach & J. Requin (Eds.), *Tutorials in motor behavior* (pp. 231–240). Amsterdam: North-Holland.

Tesser, A., & Paulhus, D. L. (1976). Toward a causal model of love. *Journal of Personality and Social Psychology, 34,* 1095–1105.

Teuber, H. L. (1964). The riddle of frontal lobe function in man. In J. M. Warren & K. Akert (Eds.), *The frontal granular cortex and behavior* (pp. 410–444). New York: McGraw Hill.

Thom, T. (1970). Topological models in biology. In C. H. Waddington (Ed.), *Towards a theoretical biology* (pp. 152–179). Chicago: Aldine.

Thomas, A., Chess, S., Birch, H. G., Hertzig, M., & Korn, S. (1963). *Behavioral individuality in early childhood.* New York: New York University Press.

Thompson, D. W. (1942). *On growth and form.* New York: The Macmillan Company. (Originally published 1917)

Thompson, R. F. (1986). The neurobiology of learning and memory. *Science, 233,* 941–947.

Thompson, R. F., Berger, T. W., & Perry, S. D. (1980a). Brain mechanisms of learning. In R. F. Thompson, L. H. Hicks, & V. B. Shvyrkov (Eds.), *Neural mechanisms of goal-directed behavior and learning* (pp. 221–240). New York: Academic Press.

Thompson, R. F., Berger, T. W., & Perry, S. D. (1980b). Brain anatomy and function. In M. C. Wittrock (Ed.), *The brain and psychology* (pp. 3–32). New York: Academic Press.

Thompson, R. J., Jr. (1979). Effects of maternal alcohol consumption on offspring: Preview, critical assessment, and future directions. *Journal of Pediatric Psychology, 4,* 265–276.

Thompson, S. C. (1981). Will it hurt less if I can control it? A complex answer to a simple question. *Psychological Bulletin, 90,* 89–101.

Thorndike, E. L. (1906). *Principles of teaching.* New York: Sieber.

Thurston, C. M., Sobol, M. P., Swanson, J., & Kinsbourne, M. (1979). Effects of methylphenidate (ritalin) on selective attention in hyperactive children. *Journal of Abnormal Child Psychology, 7,* 471–481.

Tiger, L. (1979). *Optimism: The biology of hope*. New York: Simon & Schuster.

Timiras, P. S. (1972). *Developmental physiology and aging*. New York: MacMillan.

Tinbergen, N. (1951). *The study of instinct*. Oxford: Clarendon Press.

Tinklepaugh, O. L. (1928). An experimental study of representative factors in monkeys. *Journal of Comparative Psychology, 8*, 197–236.

Tisak, M. S., & Ford, M. E. (1982). *Active and inhibitive morality: Conceptual distinctions and reasoning development*. Paper presented at the American Psychological Association, Washington, DC.

Titchner, E. B. (1913). *A textbook of psychology*. New York: The MacMillan.

Toates, F. M. (1975). *Control theory in biology and experimental psychology*. London: Hutchinson Educational.

Toates, F. M. (1979). Homeostasis and drinking. *Behavioral and Brain Sciences, 2*, 95–139.

Tolman, E. C. (1932). *Purposive behavior in animals and men*. New York: Appleton-Century.

Tolman, E. C. (1948). Cognitive maps in rats and men. *Psychological Review, 55*, 189–208.

Tolman, E. C. (1955). Principles of performance. *Psychological Review, 62*, 315–326.

Tolman, E. C. (1959). Principles of purposive behavior. In S. Koch (Ed.), *Psychology: A study of a science* (Vol. 2, pp. 92–157). New York: McGraw-Hill.

Tolman, E. C., & Brunswik, E. (1935). The organism and the causal texture of the environment. *Psychological Review, 42*, 43–77.

Toman, J. E. P. (1956). Stability vs. adaptation. In R. R. Grinker (Ed.), *Toward a unified theory of human behavior*. New York: Basic Books.

Tomkins, G. M. (1975). The metabolic code. *Science, 189*, 760–763.

Tomkins, S. S. (1962). *Affect, imagery, and consciousness, Vol. I: The positive affects*. New York: Springer.

Tomkins, S. S. (1963). *Affect, imagery, and consciousness, Vol. II: The negative affects*. New York: Springer.

Tomkins, S. S. (1980). Script theory: Differential magnification of affects. In H. E. Howe, Jr., & R. A. Diensthier (Eds.), *Nebraska Symposium on Motivation* (Vol. 26, pp. 201–236). Lincoln: University of Nebraska Press.

Tomlinson-Keasey, C., Eisert, D. C., Kahle, L. R., Hardy-Brown, K., & Keasey, B. (1979). The structure of concrete operational thought. *Child Development, 50*, 1153–1163.

Tonegawa, S. (1985). The molecules of the immune system. *Scientific American, 253*, 122–131.

Toulmin, S., & Goodfield, J. (1962). *The architecture of matter*. New York: Harper & Row.

Trager, G. L. (1958). Paralanguage: A first approximation. *Studies in Linguistics, 13*, 1–12.

Trahiotis, C., & Robinson, D. E. (1979). Auditory psychophysics. *Annual Review of Psychology, 30*, 31–61.

Trainer, F. E. (1977). A critical analysis of Kohlberg's contributions to the study of moral thought. *Journal for the Theory of Social Behavior, 71*, 41–63.

Treisman, A. M. (1969). Strategies and models of selective attention. *Psychological Review, 76*, 282–299.

Treisman, A. M., & Gelade, G. (1980). A feature integration theory of attention. *Cognitive Psychology, 12*, 97–136.

Trevarthen, C. B. (1965). Functional interactions between the cerebral hemispheres of the split-brain monkey. In G. C. Ettlinger (Ed.), *Functions of the corpus callosum*. London: Churchill.

Trevarthen, C. B. (1978). Modes of perceiving and modes of action. In H. L. Pick & E. Saltzman (Eds.), *Modes of perceiving and processing information* (pp. 99–136). Hillsdale, NJ: Lawrence Erlbaum Associates.

Trevarthen, C. B. (1980). Functional organization of the human brain. In M. C. Wittrock (Ed.), *The brain and psychology* (pp. 33–91). New York: Academic Press.

Triandis, H. C. (1980). Values, attitudes, and interpersonal behaviors. In M. M. Page (Ed.),

Beliefs, attitudes, and values: Nebraska Symposium on Motivation (Vol. 27, 195–260). Lincoln, NE: University of Nebraska Press.

Tulving, E. (1972). Episodic and semantic memory. In E. Tulving, & W. Donaldson (Eds.), *Organization of memory* (pp. 381–403). New York: Academic Press.

Tulving, E. (1979). Memory research: What kind of program? In L. G. Nilsson (Ed.), *Perspectives on memory research* (pp. 19–34). Hillsdale, NJ: Lawrence Erlbaum Associates.

Tulving, E. (1983). *Elements of episodic memory*. Oxford: Oxford University Press.

Tulving, E. (1985). How many memory systems are there? *American Psychologist, 40,* 385–398.

Tulving, E., & Donaldson, W. (Eds.). (1972). *Organization of memory*. New York: Academic Press.

Tulving, E., & Osler, S. (1968). Effectiveness of retrieval cues in memory for words. *Journal of Experimental Psychology, 77,* 593–601.

Tulving, E., & Thompson, D. M. (1973). Encoding, specificity, and retrieval processes in episodic memory. *Psychological Review, 80,* 352–373.

Tumblin, A., & Gholson, B. (1981). Hypothesis theory and the development of conceptual learning. *Psychological Bulletin, 90,* 102–124.

Turiel, E. (1969). Developmental processes in the child's moral thinking. In P. Mussen, J. Langer, & M. Covington (Eds.), *Trends and issues in developmental psychology* (pp. 92–133). New York: Holt, Rinehart & Winston.

Turiel, E. (1977). Distinct conceptual and developmental domains: Social convention and morality. In C. B. Keasey (Ed.), *Nebraska Symposium on Motivation* (Vol. 25). Lincoln, NE: University of Nebraska Press.

Turiel, E. (1983). *The development of social knowledge: Morality and convention*. Cambridge, UK: Cambridge University Press.

Turing, A. M. (1936). On computable numbers, with an application to the Entscheidungs problem. *Proceedings of the London Mathematics Society* (Series 2), *41,* 230–265.

Turns, D. (1978). The epidemiology of major affective disorders. *American Journal of Psychotherapy, 32,* 5–19.

Turvey, M. T. (1977a). Preliminaries to a theory of action with reference to vision. In R. Shaw & J. Bansford (Eds.), *Perceiving, acting, and knowing: Towards an ecological psychology* (pp. 211–265). Hillsdale, NJ: Lawrence Erlbaum Associates.

Turvey, M. T. (1977b). Contrasting orientations to a theory of visual information processing. *Psychological Review, 84,* 67–88.

Turvey, M. T., Shaw, R. E., & Mace, W. (1978). Issues in the theory of action. In J. Requin (Ed.), *Attention and performance* (Vol. VII). Hillsdale, NJ: Lawrence Erlbaum Associates.

Turvey, M. T., Shaw, R. E., Reed, E. S., & Mace, W. M. (1981). Ecological laws of perceiving and acting: In reply to Fodor and Pylyshyn. *Cognition, 9,* 237–304.

Tversky, A., & Kahneman, D. (1981). The framing of decisions and the psychology of choice. *Science, 211,* 453–458.

Tversky, A., & Kahneman, D. (1982). Causal schemas in judgements under uncertainty. In D. Kahneman, P. Slovic, & A. Tversky (Eds.), *Judgment under uncertainty: Heuristics and biases*. Cambridge, UK: Cambridge University Press.

Tversky, A., & Sattath, S. (1979). Preference trees. *Psychological Review, 86,* 542–573.

Tyldesley, D. A. (1980). The role of the movement structure in anticipatory timing. In G. E. Stelmach & J. Requin (Eds.), *Tutorials in motor behavior* (pp. 511–523). Amsterdam: North-Holland.

Tyler, L. E. (1978). *Individuality*. San Francisco: Jossey-Bass.

Tyler, L. E. (1983). *Thinking creatively*. San Francisco: Jossey-Bass.

Tyler, S., Foy, H., & Hutt, C. (1979). Attention and activity in the young child. *Journal of Educational Psychology, 49,* 196–197.

Ullman, P., & Krasner, L. (Eds.). (1965). *Case studies in behavior modification*. New York:

Holt, Rinehart, & Winston.

Underwood, G., & Stevens, R. (Eds.). (1979). *Aspects of consciousness, Vol. I: Psychological Issues*. London: Academic Press.

Urban, H. B. (1978). The concept of development from a systems perspective. In P. B. Baltes (Ed.), *Life-span Development and Behavior* (Vol. 1). New York: Academic Press.

Urban, H. B. (1983). Phenomenological-humanistic approaches. In M. Hersen, A. E. Kazdin, & A. S. Bellack (Eds.), *The clinical psychology handbook, Part II: Personality theories and models* (pp. 155-175). New York: Pergamon Press.

Urban, H. B. (1987). Dysfunctional systems: Understanding pathology. In M. E. Ford & D. H. Ford (Eds.), *Humans as self-constructing living systems: Putting the framework to work*. Hillsdale, NJ: Lawrence Erlbaum Associates.

Urban, H. B., & Ford, D. H. (1962). Man: Robot or pilot? In A. A. Schneiders & P. J. Conti (Eds.), *Selected papers from the ACPA meetings of 1960, 1961* (pp. 149-156). New York: American Catholic Psychological Association.

Uribe, R. B. (1981). Modeling autopoiesis. In M. Zeleny (Ed.), *Autopoiesis: A theory of living organization*. New York: Elsevier North Holland.

Urist, M. R., DeLange, R. J., & Finerman, G. A. M. (1983). Bone cell differentiation and growth factors. *Science, 20*, 680-686.

Ursin, H., & Kaada, B. R. (1960). Functional localization within the amygdaloid complex in the cat. *Electroencephelographic. Clinical Neurophysiology, 12*, 1-20.

Uttal, W. (1978). *The psychobiology of mind*. Hillsdale, NJ: Lawrence Erlbaum Associates.

Uzgiris, I. C., & Hunt, McV. (1975). *Assessment in infancy*. Urbana, IL: University of Illinois Press.

Vanderwolf, C. H., & Robinson, T. E. (1981). Reticulo-cortical activity and behavior: A critique of arousal theory and a new synthesis. *Behavioral and Brain Sciences, 4*, 459-514.

VanGulik, R. H. (1961). *Sexual life in ancient China*. Leiden: E. J. Brill.

Van Hooff, J. A. R. A. M. (1973). A structural analysis of the social behaviour of a semicaptive group of chimpanzees. In M. von Cranach & I. Vine (Eds.), *Social communication and movement* (pp. 75-162). New York: Academic Press.

Van Schoyck, S. R., & Grasha, A. F. (1981). Attentional style variations and athletic ability: The advantages of a sports-specific test. *Journal of Sport Psychology, 3*, 149-165.

Vernon, M. D. (1966). Perception, attention, and consciousness. In P. Bakan (Ed.), *Attention* (pp. 35-57). Princeton, NJ: D. Van Nostrand.

Verzeano, M. (1980). The activity of neuronal networks in cognitive functioning. In R. F. Thompson, L. H. Hicks, & V. B. Shvyrkov (Eds.), *Neural mechanisms of goal-directed behavior and learning* (pp. 353-373). New York: Academic Press.

Vlietstra, A. G. (1978). The effect of strategy training and stimulus saliency on attention and recognition in preschoolers. *Journal of Experimental Child Psychology, 25*, 17-32.

von Bekesy, G. (1967). *Sensory inhibition*. Princeton, NJ: Princeton University Press.

von Bertalanffy, L. (1940). Der organismus als physikalisches system betrachtet. *Die Naturwissenschaften, 28*, 521-531.

von Bertalanffy, L. (1968). *General system theory*. New York: George Braziller.

von Bertalanffy, L. (1975). *Perspectives on general systems theory*. New York: George Braziller.

von Cranach, M., & Harre, R. (Eds.). (1982). *The analysis of action*. Cambridge: Cambridge University Press.

von Cranach, M., & Kalbermatten, U. (1982). Ordinary interactive action: Theory, methods, and some empirical findings. In M. von Cranach & R. Harre (Eds.), *The analysis of action* (pp. 115-161). Cambridge: Cambridge University Press.

von Cranach, M., Kalbermatten, U., Indermuhle, K., & Gugler, B. (1982). *Goal-directed action* (M. Turton, Trans.). New York: Academic Press.

von Eye, A. (1984). Konfigurationsanalytische typisierung multivariates verlaufskuruen.

Psychologische Beitrage, 26, 37–51.

von Foerster, H. (1962). Communication amongst automata. *American Journal of Psychiatry, 118,* 866–867.

von Foerster, H., White, J. D., Peterson, L. J., & Russell, J. K. (Eds.). (1968). *Purposive systems.* New York: Spartan Books.

von Foerster, H., & Zopf, G. W. (Eds.). (1962). *Principles of self-organization.* New York: Pergamon Press.

von Hofsten, C. (1980). Predictive reaching for moving objects by human infants. *Experimental Child Psychology, 30,* 369–382.

von Hofsten, C., & Lindhagen, K. (1979). Observations on the development of reaching for moving objects. *Journal of Experimental Child Psychology, 28,* 158–173.

von Holst, E. (1973). *The behavioral physiology of animals and man: Selected papers of Eric von Holst.* Coral Gables, FL: University of Miami Press.

Voss, J. F. (1976). The nature of "the nature of intelligence." In L. B. Resnick (Ed.), *The nature of intelligence* (pp. 307–316). Hillsdale, NJ: Lawrence Erlbaum Associates.

Voss, J. F. (1979). Organization, structure, and memory: Three perspectives. In C. R. Puff (Ed.), *Memory organization and structure* (pp. 376–398). New York: Academic Press.

Vroom, V. (1964). *Work and motivation.* New York: Wiley.

Vygotsky, L. S. (1962). *Thought and language.* Cambridge, MA: The MIT Press.

Vygotsky, L. S. (1978). *Mind in society: The development of higher psychological processes.* Cambridge, MA: Harvard University Press.

Waddell, K. J., & Rogoff, B. (1981). Effect of contextual organization on spatial memory of middle-aged and older women. *Developmental Psychology, 17,* 878–885.

Waddington, C. H. (1956). *Principles of embryology.* London: Allen & Unwin.

Waddington, C. H. (1976). Evolution in the subhuman world. In E. Jamtch & C. H. Waddington (Eds.), *Evolution and consciousness: Human systems in transition.* New York: Addison-Wesley.

Wadsworth, M. W. (1983). *Patterns of personal goal hierarchies.* Unpublished doctoral dissertation, The Pennsylvania State University.

Wadsworth, M. W., & Ford, D. H. (1983). The assessment of personal goal hierarchies. *Journal of Counseling Psychology, 30,* 514–526.

Wagner, W. (1981). A fuzzy model of concept representation in memory. *Fuzzy Sets and Systems, 6,* 11–26.

Walberg, H. J. (1976). Family environment and cognitive development: Twelve analytic models. *Review of Educational Research, 46,* 527–551.

Waldrop, M. F., Bell, R. Q., McLaughlin, B., & Halverson, C. F. (1978). Newborn minor physical anomalies predict short attention span, peer aggression, and impulsivity at age 3. *Science, 199,* 563–565.

Waldrop, M. M. (1984). Natural language understanding. *Science, 224,* 372–374.

Walker, A. S., Owsley, C. J., Megaw-Nyce, J., Gibson, E. J., & Bahrick, L. E. (1980). Detection of elasticity as an invariant property of objects by young infants. *Perception, 9,* 713–718.

Walker, R. H. (1952). Body-build and behavior in young children: Body-build and nursery school teacher's ratings. *Monograph of the Society for Research in Child Development, 3,* 27–84.

Wallach, H. (1940). The role of head movements and vestibular and visual cues in sound localization. *Journal of Experimental Psychology, 27,* 339–368.

Walsh, D. A. (1975). Age differences in learning and memory. In D. S. Woodruff & J. E. Birren (Eds.), *Aging: Scientific perspectives and social issues.* New York: D. Van Nostrand.

Walsh, R. (1980). The consciousness disciplines and the behavioral sciences: Questions of comparison and assessment. *American Journal of Psychiatry, 137,* 663–673.

Walters, C. E. (1965). Prediction of post-natal development from fetal activity. *Child*

Development, 33, 801–808.

Warren, R. M. (1982). *Auditory perception: A new synthesis.* New York: Pergamon Press.

Warren, W. G. (1981). Bereavement: A brief review. *Australian Psychologist, 16*, 77–92.

Washburn, S. L. (1959). Speculations on the interrelations of the history of tools and biological evolution. In J. N. Spuhler (Ed.), *The evolution of man's capacity for culture* (pp. 21–31). Detroit, MI: Wayne State University Press.

Washburn, S. L. (1978). Human behavior and the behavior of other animals. *American Psychologist, 33*, 405–417.

Washburn, S. L., Jay, P. C., & Lancaster, J. B. (1965). *Science, 150*, 1541.

Waters, E., Wippman, J., & Sroufe, L. A. (1979). Attachment, positive affect, and competence in the peer group: Two studies in construct validation. *Child Development, 50*, 821–829.

Watkins, L. R., & Mayer, D. J. (1982). Organization of endogenous opiate and nonopiate pain control systems. *Science, 216*, 1185–1192.

Watson, J. B. (1924). *Behaviorism.* New York: W. W. Norton.

Watson, J. B., & Watson, R. R. (1921). Studies in infant psychology. *Scientific Monthly, 7*, 493–515.

Watson, J. S., & Ramey, C. T. (1972). Reactions to response contingent stimulation in early infancy. *Merrill-Palmer Quarterly, 18*, 217–227.

Weaver, W. (1948). Science and complexity. *American Scientist, 36*, 536–644.

Weaver, W. (1953). Recent contributions to the mathematical theory of communication. *Etc: A Review of General Semantics, 10*, 273.

Webb, W. B., & Cartwright, R. D. (1978). Sleep and dreams. *Annual Review of Psychology, 29*, 223–252.

Weber, K., & Osborn, M. (1985). The molecules of the cell matrix. *Scientific American, 253*, 110–121.

Weeks, D. G., Michela, J. L., Peplau, L. A., & Bragg, M. E. (1980). Relation between loneliness and depression: A structural equations analysis. *Journal of Personality and Social Psychology, 39*, 1238–1244.

Wegner, D. M., & Vallacher, R. R. (Eds.). (1980). *The self in social psychology.* New York: Oxford University Press.

Weimer, W. B. (1977). A conceptual framework for cognitive psychology: Motor theories of the mind. In R. Shaw & J. Bransford (Eds.), *Perceiving, acting, and knowing* (pp. 267–311). Hillsdale, NJ: Lawrence Erlbaum Associates.

Weinberg, G. M. (1971). *The psychology of computer programming.* New York: Van Nostrand Reinhold.

Weinberg, R. A. (1985). The molecules of life. *Scientific American, 253*, 48–57.

Weiner, B. (1982). An attribution theory of motivation and emotion: Focus, range, and issues. In N. T. Feather (Ed.), *Expectations and actions: Expectancy value models in psychology* (pp. 163–204). Hillsdale, NJ: Lawrence Erlbaum Associates.

Weiner, B., Russell, D., & Lerman, D. (1979). The cognition-emotion process in achievement-related contexts. *Journal of Personality and Social Psychology, 37*, 1211–1220.

Weingartner, H., Grafman, J., Boutelle, W., Kay, W., & Martin, P. (1983). Forms of memory failure. *Science, 221*, 380–382.

Weintraub, D. J. (1975). Perception. *Annual Review of Psychology, 26*, 234–289.

Weisenberg, M. (1977). Pain and pain control. *Psychological Bulletin, 84*, 1008–1044.

Weisenberg, M. (1980). The regulation of pain. *Annals of the New York Academy of Sciences, 340*, 102–114.

Weiss, P. (1939). *Principles of development.* New York: Henry Holt.

Weiss, P. (1941). Self-differentiation of the basic patterns of coordination. *Comparative Psychology Monographs, 17*, 96.

Weiss, P. (1966). Aging, a corollary of development. In N. W. Shock (Ed.), *Perspectives in experimental gerontology* (pp. 311–322). Springfield, IL: Charles C. Thomas.

Weiss, P. A. (1971). *Hierarchically organized systems in theory and practice*. New York: Hafner.

Weiss, P. A. (1978). Analytic research has proved the systems character of all nature. In J. Rose (Ed.), *Current topics in cybernetics and systems* (pp. 303–304). Berlin-Heidelberg/New York: Springer-Verlag.

Weisskopf, V. (1961). Quality and quantity in quantum physics. In D. Lerner (Ed.), *Quantity and quality*. New York: Glencoe Free Press.

Weisskopf, V. (1980). Address at the Einstein session of the Pontifical Academy of Sciences. *Science, 207*, 1163–1165.

Weitz, S. (Ed.). (1974). *Nonverbal communication: Readings with commentary*. New York: Oxford University Press.

Welker, W. I. (1961). An analysis of exploratory and play behavior in animals. In D. W. Fiske & S. R. Maddi (Eds.), *Functions of varied experience* (pp. 175–226). Homewood, IL: The Dorsey Press.

Wellman, H., Larkey, C., & Sommerville, S. C. (1979). The early development of moral criteria. *Child Development, 50*, 869–873.

Wellman, H., Sommerville, S. C., & Haake, R. J. (1979). Development of search procedures in real-life spatial environments. *Developmental Psychology, 15*, 530–542.

Welner, Z. (1978). Childhood depression: An overview. *Journal of Nervous and Mental Disease, 166*, 588–593.

Wenar, C. (1978). Social initiative in toddlers. *Journal of Genetic Psychology, 132*, 231–246.

Wenger, M. A. (1948). Studies of autonomic balance in army air force personnel. *Comparative Psychology Monographs, 19*, 1–110.

Wenger, M. A., Clemens, J. L., Coleman, D. R., Cullen, T. B., & Engel, B. T. (1961). Autonomic response specificity. *Psychosomatic Medicine, 23*, 185.

Werner, H. (1957). The concept of development from a comparative and organismic point of view. In D. G. Harris (Ed.), *The concept of development* (pp. 125–148). Minneapolis, MN: University of Minnesota Press.

Werner, H. (1961). *Comparative psychology of mental development*. New York: Science Editions.

Wertheim, A. H. (1980). Information processing mechanisms involved in ocular pursuit. In G. E. Stelmach & J. Requin (Eds.), *Tutorials in motor behavior* (pp. 433–440). Amsterdam: North-Holland.

Wertsch, J. V. (1980). *The concept of activity in Soviet psychology*. White Plains, NY: Sharpe.

West, L. J. (Ed.). (1962). *Hallucinations*. New York: Grune & Stratton.

Westheimer, G. (1984). Spatial vision. *Annual Review of Psychology, 35*, 201–226.

White, B. L. (1971). *Human infants: Experience and psychological development*. Englewood Cliffs, NJ: Prentice-Hall.

White, B. L. (1975). *The first three years of life*. Englewood Cliffs, NJ: Prentice-Hall.

White, B. L., Kaban, B., Shapiro, B., & Attanucci, J. (1977). Competence and experience. In I. C. Uzgiris & F. Weizmann (Eds.), *The structuring of experience* (pp. 115–152). New York: Plenum Press.

White, C. B., Bushnell, N., & Regenemer, J. L. (1978). Moral development in Bahamian school children: A 3-year examination of Kohlberg's stages of moral development. *Developmental Psychology, 14*, 58–65.

White, L. & Tursky, B. (Eds.) (1984). *Clinical biofeedback: efficacy and mechanisms*. New York: Guilford.

White, M. J. (1985). On the status of cognitive psychology. *American Psychologist, 40*, 117–119.

White, R. W. (1959). Motivation reconsidered: The concept of competence. *Psychological Review, 66*, 297–333.

White, R. W. (1963). Ego and reality in psychoanalytic theory. *Psychological Issues,*

Monograph No. 3.

White, R. W. (1966). *Lives in progress* (2nd ed.). New York: Holt, Rinehart & Winston.

White, S. E., Mitchell, T. R., & Bell, C. H., Jr. (1977). Goal setting, evaluation apprehension, and social cues as determinants of job performance and job satisfaction in a simulated organization. *Journal of Applied Psychology, 62,* 665–673.

Whitehead, A. N. (1925). *Science and the modern world.* New York: Macmillan.

Whitehorn, J. C. (1934). The blood sugar in relation to emotional reactions. *American Journal of Psychiatry, 13,* 987–1005.

Whitehouse, P. J., Price, D. L., Struble, R. G., Clark, A. W., Coyle, J. T., & DeLong, M. R. (1982). Alzheimer's disease and senile dementia: Loss of neurons in the basal forebrain. *Science, 215,* 1237–1239.

Whiting, H. T. A. (1980). Dimensions of control in motor learning. In G. E. Stelmach & J. Requin (Eds.), *Tutorials in motor behavior* (pp. 537–550). Amsterdam: North-Holland.

Whiting, H. T. A., & Cockerill, I. M. (1974). Eyes on hand--eyes on target? *Journal of Motor Behavior, 6,* 27–32.

Whiteman, M., Brook, J. S., & Gordon, A. S. (1977). Perceived intention and behavioral incongruity. *Child Development, 48,* 113–116.

Whyte, L. (1969). Organic structural hierarchies. In R. G. Jones & Brandt (Eds.), *Unity and diversity in systems.* New York: George Braziller.

Whyte, L., Wilson, G., & Wilson, D. (Eds.). (1969). *Hierarchical structures.* New York: American Elsevier.

Wickelgren, W. A. (1979). Chunking and consolidation: A theoretical synthesis of semantic networks, configuring in conditioning, S-R versus cognitive learning, normal forgetting, the Amnesic syndrome, and the hippocampal arousal system. *Psychological Review, 86,* 44–60.

Wickelgren, W. A. (1981). Human learning and memory. *Annual Review of Psychology, 32,* 21–52.

Wickens, C. D., & Kramer, A. (1985). Engineering psychology. *Annual Review of Psychology, 36,* 307–348.

Wicker, A. W. (1969). Attitudes vs. actions: The relationship of verbal and overt behavioral responses to attitude objects. *Journal of Social Issues, 25,* 41–78.

Wicker, A. W. (1979). Ecological psychology: Some research and prospective developments. *American Psychologist, 34,* 755–765.

Wicklund, R. A., & Brehm, J. W. (1976). *Perspectives on cognitive dissonance.* Hillsdale, NJ: Lawrence Erlbaum Associates.

Widiger, T. A., Knudson, R. M., & Rorer, L. G. (1980). Convergent and discriminant validity of measures of cognitive styles and abilities. *Journal of Personality and Social Psychology, 39,* 116–129.

Wiener, M., Devoe, S., Rubinow, S., & Geller, J. (1972). Nonverbal behavior and nonverbal communication. *Psychological Review, 79,* 185–214.

Weiner, N. (1948). *Cybernetics: Control and communication in the animal and the machine.* New York: Wiley.

Wiener, N. (1961). *Cybernetics.* Cambridge, MA: MIT Press.

Wild, M. (1938). The behavioral pattern of throwing and some observations concerning its course of development in children. *Research Quarterly, 3,* 20.

Wilder, J. (1967). *Stimulus and response: The law of initial value.* Bristol, UK: John Wrights.

Williams, C. D. (1959). The elimination of tantrum behavior by extinction procedures. *Journal of Abnormal and Social Psychology, 59,* 269.

Williamson, P. G. (1981a). Palaeontological documentation of speciation in cenozoic molluscs from Turkana Basin. *Nature, 293,* 437–443.

Williamson, P. G. (1981b). Morphological stasis and developmental constraint: Real problems for neo-Darwinism. *Nature, 294,* 214–215.

Wilson, A. (1985). The molecular basis of evolution. *Scientific American, 253,* 110–121.

Wilson, E. O. (1975). *Sociobiology: The new synthesis.* Cambridge, MA: Harvard University Press.

Wilson, J., Erwin, V. G., McClearn, G. E., & Plomin, R. (1982). Acute metabolic and behavioral tolerance to ethanol. *Alcoholism: Clinical and Experimental Research, 6,* 318.

Wimsatt, W. C. (1972). Teleology and the logical structure of function statements. *Studies in History and Philosophy of Science, 3,* 1–80.

Wimsatt, W. C. (1976). Reductionism and levels of organization. In G. C. Globus, G. Maxwell, & I. Savodnik (Eds.), *Consciousness and the brain: A scientific and philosophical inquiry* (pp. 199–266). New York: Plenum Press.

Windelband, W. (1901/1958). *A history of philosophy* (Vol. 1). (J. H. Tufts, Trans.) New York: Harper & Row.

Winegrad, S. (1965). Energy exchange in striated muscle cells. In W. S. Yamamoto & J. R. Brobeck (Eds.), *Physiological controls and regulations.* Philadelphia: W. B. Saunders.

Winell, M. W. (1987). Personal goals: The key to self direction in adulthood. In M. E. Ford & D. H. Ford (Eds.), *Humans as self-constructing living systems: Putting the framework to work.* Hillsdale, NJ: Lawrence Erlbaum Associates.

Winograd, T. (1981). What does it mean to understand language? In D. Norman (Ed.), *Perspectives on cognitive science* (pp. 231–264). Norwood, NJ: Ablex.

Winterhalder, B. (1980). Environmental analysis in human evolution and adaptation research. *Human Ecology, 8,* 135–170.

Wise, R. A. (1978). Catecholamine theories of reward: A critical review. *Brain Research, 152,* 215–247.

Wishell, R. A. (1980). Relaxation, exercise, and aging. In J. E. Birren & R. B. Sloane (Eds.), *Handbook of mental health and aging* (pp. 943–958). Englewood Cliffs, NJ: Prentice-Hall.

Witkin, H. A. (1978). Cognitive styles in personal and cultural adaptation. *The 1977 Heinz Werner Lectures.* Worcester, MA: Clark University Press.

Witkin, H. A., Moore, C. A., Goodenough, D. R., & Cox, P. W. (1977). Field-dependent and field-independent cognitive styles and their educational implications. *Review of Educational Research, 47,* 1–64.

Witkop, C. J., Jr. (1967). Genetics and nutrition. *Proceedings of the American Societies for Experimental Biology.*

Wittrock, M. C. (Ed.). (1980). *The brain and psychology.* New York: Academic Press.

Wittrock, M. C. (1980a). Learning and the brain. In M. C. Wittrock (Ed.), *The brain and psychology* (pp. 371–403). New York: Academic Press.

Wohlwill, J. F. (1981). A conceptual analysis of exploratory behavior. In H. Day (Ed.), *Advances in intrinsic motivation and aesthetics* (pp. 341–364). New York: Plenum.

Wohlwill, J. F., & Heft, H. (1977). Environments fit for the developing child. In H. McGurk (Ed.), *Ecological factors in human development* (pp. 125–138). Amsterdam: North Holland.

Wojciszke, B. (1980). The cognitive shift in social psychology and the problem of consciousness. *Polish Psychological Bulletin, 11,* 3–12.

Wolff, P. H. (1971). Mother-infant relations at birth. In J. G. Howels (Ed.), *Modern perspectives in international child psychiatry* (pp. 20–97). New York: Brunner/Mazel.

Wollert, R. W. (1979). Expectancy shifts and the expectancy confidence hypothesis. *Journal of Personality and Social Psychology, 37,* 1888–1901.

Wolman, B. B. (1978). *Children's fears.* New York: Grosset & Dunlap.

Woloski, B. M. R. N. J., Smith, E. M., Meyer, W. J., III, Fuller, G. M., & Blaloch, J. E. (1985). Corticotrophin-releasing activity of monokines. *Science, 230,* 1035–1036.

Wong, P. T. P. (1979). Frustration, exploration, and learning. *Canadian Psychological Review, 20,* 133–144.

Wood, L. A. (1978). Loneliness, social identity, and social structure. *Essence, 2,* 259–270.

Woodworth, R. S. (1906). The cause of a voluntary movement. *Studies in Philosophy and*

Psychology by Former Students of Charles Edward Garman (pp. 351–392). Boston and New York.

Woodworth, R. S. (1937). *Psychology*. New York: Henry Holt.

Woodworth, R. S. (1938). *Experimental psychology*. New York: Henry Holt.

Woodworth, R. A. (1940). *Psychology* (4th ed.). New York: Henry Holt.

Wortman, C. B., & Dintzer, L. (1978). Is an attributional analysis of the learned helplessness phenomenon viable? A critique of the Abramson-Seligman-Teasdale reformulation. *Journal of Abnormal Psychology, 87*, 75–90.

Wright, B. E. (1966). Multiple causes and controls in differentiation. *Science, 153*, 30–37.

Wrisberg, C. A., & Mead, B. A. (1981). Anticipation of coincidence in children: A test of schema theory. *Perceptual and Motor Skills, 52*, 599–606.

Wundt, W. (1912/1973). *An introduction to psychology*. New York: Arno.

Wyke, B. (1975). The neurological basis of movement: A developmental review. In K. S. Holt (Ed.), *Movement and child development*. London: William Heinemann Medical Books.

Wylie, R. C. (Ed.). (1979). *The self-concept. Vol. 2: Theory and research on selected topics* (rev. ed.). Lincoln: University of Nebraska Press.

Yamamoto, W. S., & Brobeck, J. R. (1965). *Physiological controls and regulation*. Philadelphia: W. B. Saunders.

Yampey, N. (1980). About the concept of happiness. *Acta Psyquiatrica y Psicologica de America Latina, 26*, 308–317.

Yang, R. K. (1979). Early infant assessment: An overview. In J. Osofsky (Ed.), *The handbook of infant development* (pp. 165–184). New York: Wiley.

Yates, F. E. (1979). Physical biology: A basis for modeling living systems. *Journal of Cybernetics and Information Science, 2*, 57–70.

Yates, F. E., & Iberall, A. S. (1973). Temporal and hierarchical organization in biosystems. In J. Urquhart & F. E. Yates (Eds.), *Temporal aspects of therapeutics* (pp. 17–34). New York: Plenum Press.

Yates, F. E., Iberall, A. S., & March, D. J. (1972). Integration of the whole organism: A foundation for theoretical biology. In J. A. Behnke (Ed.), *Changing biological problems: Directions toward their solution* (pp. 110–132). New York: Oxford University Press.

Yekovich, F. R., & Thorndyke, P. W. (1981). An evaluation of alternative functional models of narrative schemata. *Journal of Verbal Learning and Verbal Behavior, 20*, 454–469.

Yeni-Komshian, G. H., Kavanagh, J. F., & Ferguson, C. A. (Eds.). (1980). *Child phonology, Vol. 1: Production. Child phonology, Vol. 2: Perception*. New York: Academic Press.

Young, G., & Decarie, T. G. (1977). An ethology-based catalogue of facial vocal behavior in infants. *Animal Behaviour, 25*, 95–107.

Young, K. (1952). *Personality and problems of adjustment*. New York: Appleton-Century-Crofts.

Young, P. T. (1949). Food seeking drive, affective process, and learning. *Psychological Review, 56*, 98–121.

Young, P. T. (1955). The role of hedonic processes in motivation. In M. R. Jones (Ed.) *Nebraska Symposium on Motivation* (Vol. 3, 50–89). Lincoln, NE: University of Nebraska Press.

Young, P. T. (1961). *Motivation and emotion*. New York: Wiley.

Young, P. T. (1968). Affective processes. In M. B. Arnold (Ed.), *The nature of emotion* (pp. 222–237). Baltimore: Penguin Books.

Yuille, J. C., & Catchpole, M. J. (1977). The role of imagery in models of cognition. *Journal of Mental Imagery, 1*, 171–180.

Yunis, J. J. (1983). The chromosomal basis of human neoplasia. *Science, 221*, 227–236.

Yunis, J. J., & Prahash, O. (1982). The origin of man: A chromosomal pictorial legacy.

Science, 215, 1525–1529.

Zajonc, R. B. (1980). Feeling and thinking: Preferences need no inferences. *American Psychologist, 35*, 151–175.

Zajonc, R. B. (1984). The primacy of affect. *American Psychologist, 39*, 117–123.

Zanna, M. P., Higgins, E. T., & Taves, P. A. (1976). Is dissonance phenomenologically aversive? *Journal of Experimental Social Psychology, 12*, 530–538.

Zeigarnik, B. (1927). Ueberdas Behalten von erledigten und unerledigten Handlungen. *Psychologische Forschung, 9*, 1–85.

Zeki, S. (1980). The representation of colors in the cerebral cortex. *Nature, 284*, 412–419.

Zelazo, P. (1976). From reflexive to instrumental behavior. In L. P. Lipsett (Ed.), *Developmental psychobiology: The significance of infancy.* Hillsdale, NJ: Lawrence Erlbaum Associates.

Zeleny, M. (Ed.). (1981). *Autopoiesis: A theory of organization.* New York: Elsevier North Holland.

Zener, K. (1937). The significance of behavior accompanying conditioned salivary secretion for theories of the conditioned response. *American Journal of Psychology, 50*, 384–403.

Zillmann, D. (1979). *Hostility and aggression.* Hillsdale, NJ: Lawrence Erlbaum Associates.

Zimbardo, P. G. (Ed.). (1969). *The cognitive control of motivation: The consequences of choice and dissonance.* Glenview, IL: Scott Foresman.

Zimbardo, P. G. (1977). *Shyness.* Reading, MA: Addison-Wesley.

Zimmerman, G. (1980). Stuttering: A disorder of movement. *Journal of Speech and Hearing Research, 23*, 122–136.

Zimmerman, G., Smith, A., & Hanley, J. M. (1981). Stuttering: In need of a unifying conceptual framework. *Journal of Speech and Hearing Research, 24*, 25–31.

Zivin, G. (Ed.). (1979). *The development of self-regulation through speech.* New York: Wiley.

Zukav, G. (1979). *The dancing Wu Li masters.* New York: Bantam Books.

Zukerman, M. (1974). The sensation seeking motive. *Progress in Experimental Personality Research, 7*, 79–148.

Zukerman, M. (1979). *Sensation seeking: Beyond the optimal level of arousal.* Hillsdale, NJ: Lawrence Erlbaum Associates.

Zukier, H., & Hogan, J. W. (1978). The development of selective attention under distracting conditions. *Child Development, 49*, 870–873.

Zung, W. (1973). From art to science: The diagnosis and treatment of depression. *Archives of General Psychiatry, 29*, 328–337.

Zurif, E. B. (1980). Language mechanisms: A neuropsychological perspective. *American Scientist, 68*, 305–311.

Author Index

Subject Index

Dr. George E. Clark

School of Business & Industry
One SBI Plaza
Florida A&M University
Tallahassee Florida 32307

Dear Dr. Clark: This book lists for $69 95.
I'm selling it to you at my cost of
$49 95 plus mailing costs. You can pay by
check to Donald H. Ford, 130 S245 Cabin Lane,
State College, PA 16801